I0605134

PROPER OF THE MASS

PROPER OF THE MASS

Entrance, Offertory
and
Communion Antiphons
for
Sundays and Solemnities

by

Fr. Samuel F. Weber, O.S.B.

BENEDICT XVI INSTITUTE
Archdiocese of San Francisco

IGNATIUS PRESS SAN FRANCISCO

With Ecclesiastical Approbation
Most Reverend Salvatore Joseph Cordileone
Archbishop of San Francisco
March 19, 2014

Cover design by Roxanne Mei Lum

ISBN 978-1-62164-011-0

Library of Congress Control Number 2014957339

Published by Ignatius Press, San Francisco

Printed in the United States of America

In Dedication

Marie Bernadette Weber

August 5, 1958 — March 16, 2014

May the Lord bless you and keep you.
May the Lord make his face to shine upon you,
and be gracious to you.
May the Lord lift up his countenance upon you,
and give you peace.

— Numbers 4:24-26

CONTENTS

PROPER OF TIME

PROPER OF SAINTS

RITUAL MASSES

VARIA

Foreword

by

Archbishop Salvatore Joseph Cordileone

Soon after his conversion, Saint Augustine described how moved he was by psalms chanted in the churches of Milan:

> I wept at the beauty of your hymns and canticles, and was powerfully moved at the sweet sound of Your Church's singing. Those sounds flowed into my ears, and the truth streamed into my heart: so that my feelings of devotion overflowed, and the tears ran from my eyes, and I was happy in them. [1]

"Those sounds flowed into my ears, and the truth streamed into my heart." What a noble description of liturgical song! The marriage of melody and psalmody inspired Augustine to write both an extremely influential work on music and the most complete patristic commentary on the psalms to come down to us.

Father Samuel F. Weber has provided the Church in the English-speaking world a most valuable resource in this book, which offers musical settings of the psalm verses and other texts provided by the Church for the celebration of the Eucharist. In doing so, he has filled a lacuna in the recent translation of the Roman Missal. That is to say, while the Missal *generally* provides musical settings for the Ordinary and Propers of the Mass, it does not do so for the Entrance Antiphon, Offertory, and Communion Antiphon. Now, thanks to the efforts of Father Weber, a recognized expert in the field of chant, it is possible for us to sing the entire Eucharistic liturgy.

It is often said, and rightly so, that we should aim at singing the Mass, not just singing at Mass, but old habits die hard, and in many places the "four hymn sandwich" is still being served, a relic from the days before the Second Vatican Council when provision was made to allow vernacular hymns to be sung at Mass. There is a rich tradition of hymn-singing in English, and the choice of the best of that repertoire can certainly enhance our liturgical celebrations. However, in the Church's liturgical rites hymns are tradi-

[1] *Confessions, IX. 6*. Tr. by Frank Sheed.

tionally prescribed for the Divine Office. Historically speaking, the use of hymns in the Mass is actually a very recent innovation, as the preference has always been to use texts directly drawn from the Scriptures. The Second Vatican Ecumenical Council emphasized the centrality of the Scriptures to our worship, and taught: "Hence in order to achieve the restoration, progress, and adaptation of the sacred liturgy it is essential to promote that sweet and living love for Sacred Scripture to which the venerable tradition of Eastern and Western rites gives testimony."[2]

This vision of the restoration and promotion of the sacred liturgy in the life of the Church was certainly one of the fundamental themes of Vatican II. Indeed, the terms "restoration" and "restoration and promotion of the sacred liturgy" are repeated frequently all throughout its Constitution on the Sacred Liturgy, *Sacrosanctum Concilium*. From our perspective of fifty years historical distance from the Council, though, one might ask just what, exactly, was it that needed to be "restored"?

The answer can be found in another, closely related, theme repeated throughout the Constitution on the Sacred Liturgy, a principle which had been gaining momentum for many decades prior to the Council and which the Council sought to advance for the effectiveness of the Church's proclamation of the Gospel moving into the future: the principle of active participation of the faithful in the liturgical celebration. This phrase, originally coined by Pope Saint Pius X in his motu proprio *Tra le Sollecitudini* of 1903, has become the defining principle of the Church's efforts toward liturgical renewal in this last half-century since the Council.

Unfortunately, it seems there has been a good deal of misunderstanding of what this principle really stands for, given that it is commonly confused for the idea that everyone present must be "doing something." A needed clarification of this point was made by the Congregation for Divine Worship and the Discipline of the Sacraments in 2004:

> ... from the fact that the liturgical celebration obviously entails activity, it does not follow that everyone must necessarily have something

[2] Constitution on the Sacred Liturgy of the Second Vatican Ecumenical Council, *Sacrosanctum Concilium*, n. 24.

> concrete to do beyond the actions and gestures, as if a certain specific liturgical ministry must necessarily be given to the individuals to be carried out by them. Instead, catechetical instruction should strive diligently to correct those widespread superficial notions and practices often seen in recent years in this regard, and ever to instill anew in all of Christ's faithful that sense of deep wonder before the greatness of the mystery of faith that is the Eucharist, in whose celebration the Church is forever passing from what is obsolete into newness of life.[3]

Rather than such "superficial notions and practices," the principle of active participation can best be understood in the context of Saint Paul's teaching about the Church as the Body of Christ (cf. 1 Cor 12): the various liturgical roles should be exercised in a way that expresses the corporate unity of the worshipping community. Not all the members are the same; their roles are different, but all, in their diversity, are integral to the body and necessary for its good health and effective functioning. For example, when the reader is proclaiming a lesson or the choir is singing a piece, everyone else present participates by actively listening. Perhaps a better word to express this teaching of the Council ("*actuosa*" in the original Latin) is "engaged": we are present to the liturgical action, allowing it to seep down into the depths of our consciousness. Thus, in speaking of the "restoration" of the sacred liturgy, the Council fathers articulated their vision of restoring the liturgy to what it was always meant to be: Catholics at Mass engaged in understanding and praying the liturgy with heart and mind, and this active engagement expressed in their reciting and singing the parts of the Mass proper to them, rather than sitting (or kneeling, as the case may be) as passive observers, saying their own private prayers. That is, personal devotion is to enhance one's full, active and conscious participation at Mass, not substitute for it.

At the same time, in the reform of the Order of Mass since the Council, the lay faithful now commonly exercise certain roles

[3] Congregation for Divine Worship and the Discipline of the Sacraments, Instruction *Redemptionis Sacramentum: On certain matters to be observed or to be avoided regarding the Most Holy Eucharist.*

in the liturgical action that previously they had not: lectors, extraordinary ministers of Holy Communion, cantors, and so forth. It is most appropriate, then, that this present work is being offered under the auspices of the Benedict XVI Institute for Sacred Music and Divine Worship, of which Father Weber is the founding director. It is the mission of the Institute to provide, not simply training, but *formation* for the lay faithful in exercising these ministries. It is critical that those who lead their brothers and sisters in the worship of the one, true God be themselves the most engaged – in the fullest sense of the word – in the Church's liturgy not just during the liturgical action, but in their very spirituality: lectors should have a special love for the Word of God and understanding of biblical history and theology, *lectio divina* should be a regular part of their prayer; extraordinary ministers of Holy Communion should cultivate a healthy Eucharistic piety and have a particular appreciation for the Church's profound theology of the Eucharist and the rites and practices she has developed over the centuries to express and strengthen this belief among the faithful; all of the Church's liturgical ministers must constantly seek to appropriate to themselves the true spirit of Catholic worship and an affection for her liturgical rites.

This having been said, at the heart of liturgical renewal – and therefore of the Benedict XVI Institute – is the restoration of the Church's repertoire of sacred music as the patrimony of *all* of the members of the Body of Christ. Active participation finds an especially eloquent expression in the voices of the faithful united in singing the praises of God in communion with their ancestors in the faith. As the Council says: "Religious singing by the people is to be intelligently fostered so that in devotions and sacred exercises, as also during liturgical services, the voices of the faithful may ring out according to the norms and requirements of the rubrics."[4] In urging that the "treasure of sacred music … be preserved and fostered with great care," it specifically called upon bishops and "other pastors of souls" to "be at pains to ensure that, whenever the sacred action is to be celebrated with song, the whole body of the faithful may be able to contribute that active participation which is rightly theirs."[5]

---

[4] *Sacrosanctum Concilium*, n. 118.

[5] *Sacrosanctum Concilium*, n. 114.

In order to translate these directives into reality, though, practical and concrete means of assistance must be put into place. This is where this present work of Father Weber is invaluable: it provides a resource to enable our people and musicians to sing the biblical texts assigned by the Church to the various moments of the liturgy. Moreover, to assist as many as possible in this endeavor, Father Weber provides four options for each text, to take into account the relative expertise of choirs and congregations. In doing so, he has responded to the vision set forth by the Second Vatican Ecumenical Council of the true vocation of composers of Church music:

> Composers, filled with the Christian spirit, should feel that their vocation is to cultivate sacred music and increase its store of treasures.
>
> Let them produce compositions which have the qualities proper to genuine sacred music, not confining themselves to works which can be sung only by large choirs, but providing also for the needs of small choirs and for the active participation of the entire assembly of the faithful.[6]

It is my hope that many will take advantage of this superb resource, so that the sounds of the psalms may flow into our ears and their truth reach our hearts. It was precisely this experience that was so pivotal in Saint Augustine's pilgrimage to sainthood. May it be so for us, for this, ultimately, is the true end not only of the Church's worship but, indeed, of all that she does: the glory of God and the sanctification of His people.

Most Reverend Salvatore Joseph Cordileone
Archbishop of San Francisco
Chairman of the Board of the Benedict XVI Institute
for Sacred Music and Divine Worship

[6] *Sacrosanctum Concilium*, n. 121.

Introduction concerning Chant Technique

I) Notation

The notes and groups of notes (neums) used in the chant appear on a four-line staff. Two CLEF SIGNS are used to indicate the relative pitch of the notes:

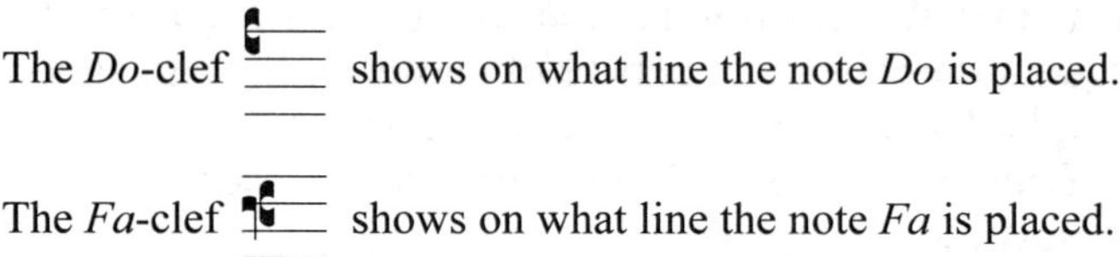

The *Do*-clef shows on what line the note *Do* is placed.

The *Fa*-clef shows on what line the note *Fa* is placed.

These clefs may appear on any line depending on the range of the melody to be sung, so that the notes of the piece may be placed on the staff lines and spaces, thus avoiding, as far as possible, the use of leger lines above or below the staff.

The GUIDE is a sign placed at the end of each line of Gregorian music to indicate in advance the first note of the following line. It is also employed in the course of a line when the extension of the melody demands a change in the place of the clef, to show the relative pitch of the first note after the change.

Three kinds of BAR-LINES are used:

The DOUBLE BAR which indicates the end of a piece or a change of choir. The FULL BAR which indicates the end of a phrase and a full pause in the singing. The HALF BAR indicates divisions known as clauses or members, hence the half bar is also called the member bar. It cuts the two middle lines of the staff. The QUARTER BAR indicates divisions known as sections or incises. It cuts only the top line of the staff. The part played by each of these signs has to do with the pronunciation of the musical phrase in respect to the greater rhythm of the piece. If BREATH must be taken at either the half bar or the quarter bar, it must be taken off the value of the the note before. The same holds true of the COMMA or VIRGULA.

The only place for a stop or full pause in the singing is at the full bar or the double bar.

The only accidental permitted in the chant is the FLAT, which may only be used on the note *si (ti)*. The flat is effective only a) as long as the word lasts, b) until the next bar line of any kind, c) until revoked by the NATURAL SIGN . Since at the present time there is confusion about the duration of the flat, the present volume employs the repetition of the flat and natural sign beyond the scope of these rules to aid in correct interpretation.

When only a single note is to be sung on a syllable of a word, the PUNCTUM is used. Its value or duration may be modified in two ways: *a)* by the addition of a dot , which doubles its length; *b)* by the HORIZONTAL EPISEMA , which prolongs the note without necessarily doubling it. The terms "doubles its length" and "prolongs the note" are approximate. These terms are always to be understood in the wider context of the requirements of the natural speech rhythm of the text and the artistic interpretation of the melodic line. Any mechanical or staccato rendering of the chant is to be avoided.

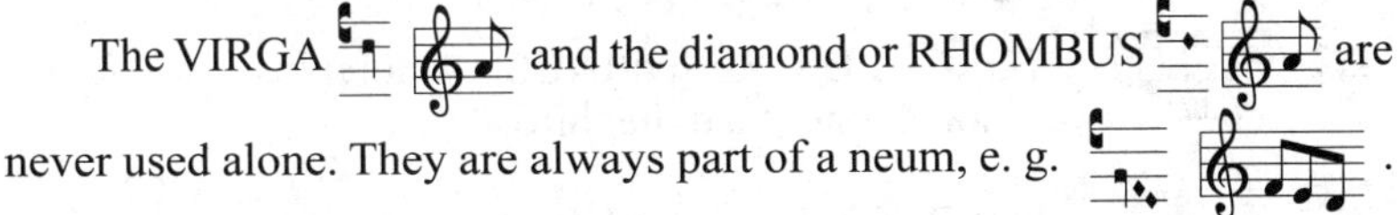

The VIRGA and the diamond or RHOMBUS are never used alone. They are always part of a neum, e. g. .

When more than a single note is to be sung on a syllable of a word, the derived NEUM is used. The derived neum is, therefore, a group of notes sung over the same syllable. Sometimes more than a single neum is required to indicate all the notes to be sung on the same syllable.

a) Neums of two notes:

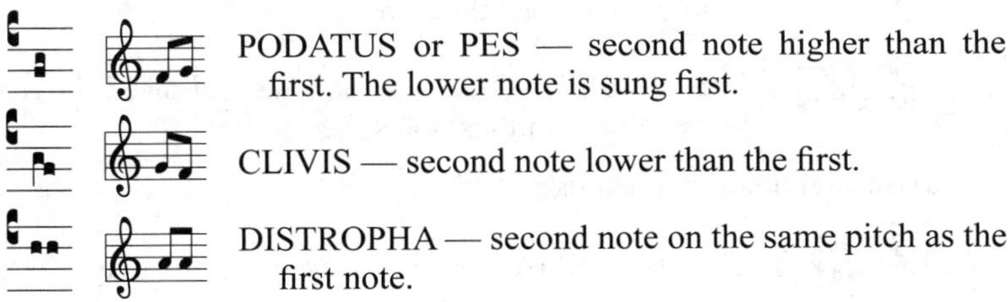

PODATUS or PES — second note higher than the first. The lower note is sung first.

CLIVIS — second note lower than the first.

DISTROPHA — second note on the same pitch as the first note.

BIVIGA — doubles the note but with an expression of force firmness, whereas the distropha designates lightness.

b) Neums of three notes:

TORCULUS — second note higher than first and third.

PORRECTUS — second note lower than first and third.

CLIMACUS — each successive note lower than the preceeding.

It may have more than three notes:

SCANDICUS — each successive not higher than the preceeding.

It may have more than three notes:

SALICUS — each successive note higher than the preceeding, with a slight prolongation and the rhythmic support on the second last note.

TRISTROPHA — all three notes on the same pitch.

c) Neums of four notes:

TORCULUS RESUPINUS — torculus with fourth note higher than the third.

PORRECTUS FLEXUS — porrectus with fourth note lower than the third.

CLIMACUS RESUPINUS — climacus with fourth note higher than the third.

SCANDICUS FLEXUS — scandicus with fourth note lower than the third.

PES SUBIPUNCTIS — podatus followed by descending rhombus notes.

d) Special notes and neums:

The QUILISMA is found in ascending passages. The note immediately preceding this jagged note must be distinctly prolonged and emphasized.

2) The Modes

At the beginning of each chant melody will be found a number (from one to eight) which indicates the mode in which the piece ends.

When psalm verses are sung with a chant melody, the singers use the psalm tone formula with the ending that matches the return to the beginning of the chant melody. When the chant melody is marked 7. c, use the psalm tone marked 7. c. When the chant melody is marked 7. d, us the psalm tone marked 7. d. For example, the chant melody

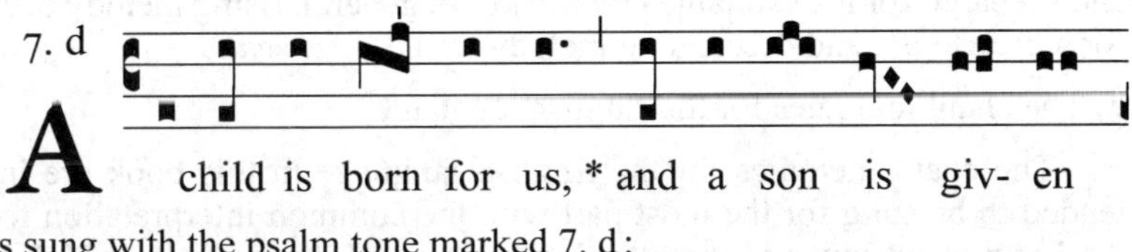
7. d
A child is born for us, * and a son is giv- en

is sung with the psalm tone marked 7. d:

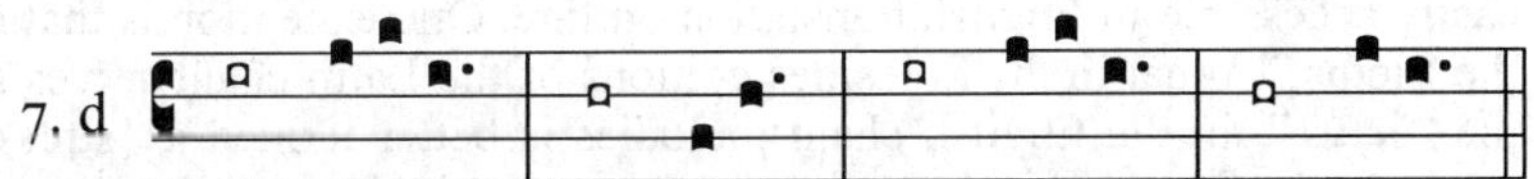
7. d

The chant melody

7. c
A child is born for us, * and a son is giv- en

is sung with psalm tones marked 7. c:

7. c

3) Expression

The singing of the chant must be characterized by the three virtues of sobriety, simplicity and restraint. This requires on the part of the singer a mind disciplined in the art of prayer as well as in the art of music. But this does by no means imply that the chant is to be sung heavily or slowly. There must never be a sensation of dragging in the rendition of the chant. It must be sung *lightly* and it must *move*. The rhythm, the melody and the text all contribute to this lightness and movement which makes the chant by nature so capable of lifting our minds and hearts to God in liturgical prayer.

To sing the chant beautifully and in a manner worthy of its high purpose, more is necessary than a mere understanding of the fundamental theory of the chant. The proper use of the voice is of equal importance. Any choir attempting to sing chant successfully must also give some very definite and disciplined attention to the following: 1) proper breathing; 2) tone production; 3) ear training; 4) voice blending; 5) development of a rhythmic sense; 6) rendering the melodies with a smooth, legato, sustained tone. As to dynamics, there must never be any sudden or exaggerated changes in volume. Regarding the speed or tempo, a good norm is this: the notes should follow each other in the same pace as syllables of the text would follow each other in a sensible reading and phrasing of the words. At all endings the choir should make it a rule to slow down and quiet down. That is to say, cadences should be softened and prepared for by a suitable *ritardando*. In general, rising melody calls for a *crescendo*, and descending melody for a *decrescendo*.

4) The chant melodies for the English language

The chant melodies for the English language in this book are intended to be sung for the most part with the common interpretation for the Latin chant given in the introduction to the *Liber Usualis*, which is easily accessible in English translation on line. One exception is that of the "ictus." What in the Solesmes editions of the Latin chant serves as the "ictus", in the English chant melodies is better termed a "stress" mark. In the first place this mark is used to assist in the proper presentation of the sacred text in English. In the second place, when the melody departs from the text, the "stress" mark is used to indicate the first and most important note of a group of notes. Example:

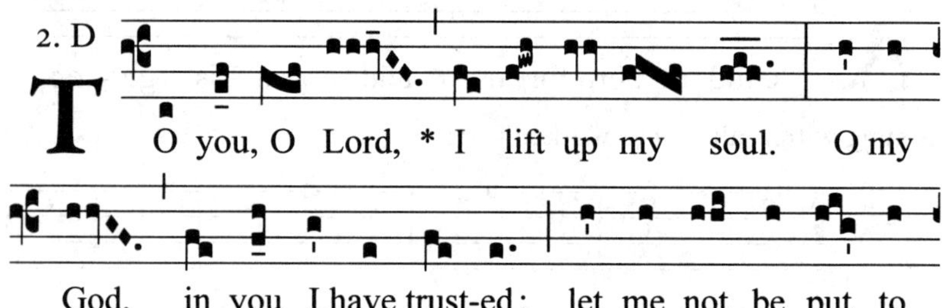
2. D
T
O you, O Lord, * I lift up my soul. O my
God, in you I have trust-ed; let me not be put to

1) To aid with the proper chanting of the English text, a "stress" mark occurs above these syllables:

O my God, in you **I** have trusted; let me not ...

2) On the word "put" the chant melody moves beyond the accent of the text. Here the "stress" mark is used to help the singer know which note of the chant carries the stress:

... let me not be put _ to ...

The "stress" mark also reminds the singers to take the time necessary to pronounce the letter "t" on the end of the word "put", and then also to pronounce clearly the letter "t" on "to," the word that follows:

God, in you I have trust-ed; let me not be put to

When preparing to chant the melodies, it will be helpful first to read the text aloud in a speaking voice. Once the sense of the text with its accent patterns, the special needs of its vowels, consonants, consonant clusters, etc., has been established, then proceed to wedding the melody to the sacred text in chanting.

5) The arrangement of the pages

This volume contains settings for the Entrance and Communion antiphons of the *Roman Missal, Third Edition,* 2010. In addition, Offertory antiphons, for the most part translations made by the editor of the texts given in the *Graduale Romanum* (1974), are also provided *ad libitum.*

In general, four settings are provided for each antipon: (i) through-composed, elaborate; (ii) through-composed, medium; (iii) using a Gregorian (Latin) psalm tone pattern; (iv) using an English psalm tone pattern. In some cases, based on the possibilities of the English text, one or more of the four settings is not provided.

These four levels of settings, moving from complex to very simple, are provided in order to encourage the chanting of the Antiphons proper to each Mass. It is the hope of the editor that one of the four settings will be suitable to any pastoral situation.

A word on the arrangement of the pages of this book. Settings (i) and (ii) are given first. These are followed by optional proper psalm verses using the appropriate psalm tone. These psalm verses are based on the Latin Vulgate and are the arrangement of the editor. They are intentionally arranged to fit the needs of the Gregorian psalm tone patterns sung with English words.

Settings (iii) (Gregorian psalm tone) and (iv) (English psalm tone) then follow.

6) Chanting the appointed psalms

As time allows, it is praiseworthy — though not required — to chant selected verses of the appointed psalm. The use of these psalm verses, however, is always *optional.*

There are a number of possibilities for using verses of the appointed psalm:

1. The antiphon may be sung *alone* without any psalm verses.

2. The Antiphon may be *repeated* after each psalm verse, or group of verses.

3. The Antiphon may be sung *at the beginning and conclusion* of the selected psalm verses, without any intervening repetition.

4. The *Glory be to the Father* may be included before the final repetition of the Antiphon. Settings of the *Glory be to the Father* in the various modes may be found on pp. 976-984. The use of the doxology is optional.

At the Entrance, care should be taken to end the chanting when the Celebrant arrives at the chair. In the same way, the Mass should not be delayed at the Offertory or Communion. The chanting may cover the sacred action, but should not prolong it unduly.

5. Psalm verses are provided set to both Latin and English psalm tones. These psalm settings may be used with any of the four possible settings of the Antiphons, as may be determined best for any given situation.

7) The asterisk (*)

The asterisk may indicate:

a) The intonation of an antiphon. The cantor may intone an antiphon to the *. The whole choir may then join in.

b) In a psalm tone, the * indicates the mediant of the tone. A pause appropriate to the accoustics follows the *, roughly equivalent to a quarter rest in modern notation. It is important that the singers not rush through the * at the mediant. For the sacred chant, the silence is as important as the sound.

c) The return of the second half of a responsory.

8) Chants of the Lectionary

The intervening chants of the Lectionary (Responsorial Psalms, Gospel Acclamations, Sequences) are not provided in this volume.

PROPER OF TIME

PROPER OF TIME

ADVENT

FIRST SUNDAY OF ADVENT

Entrance Antiphon *Ad te levavi. Cf. Ps 24:1-3*

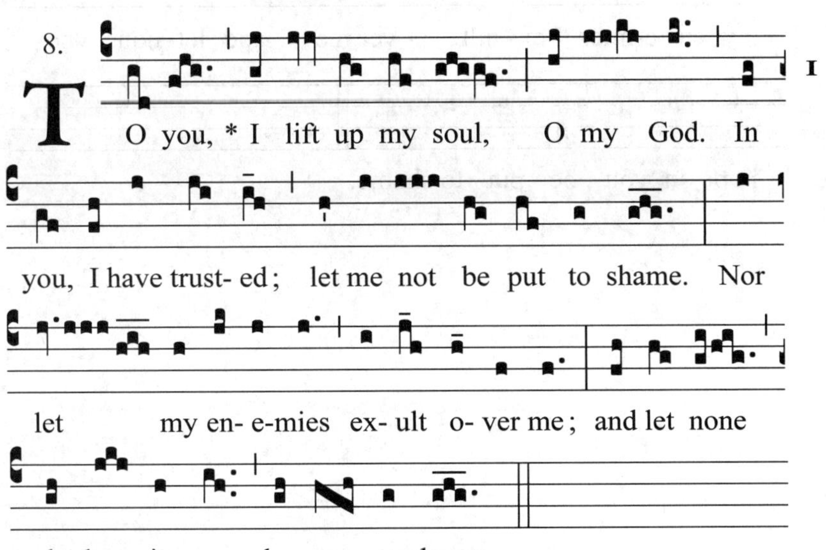
- i -
8.
To you, * I lift up my soul, O my God. In
you, I have trust- ed; let me not be put to shame. Nor
let my en- e-mies ex- ult o- ver me; and let none
who hope in you be put to shame.

- ii -

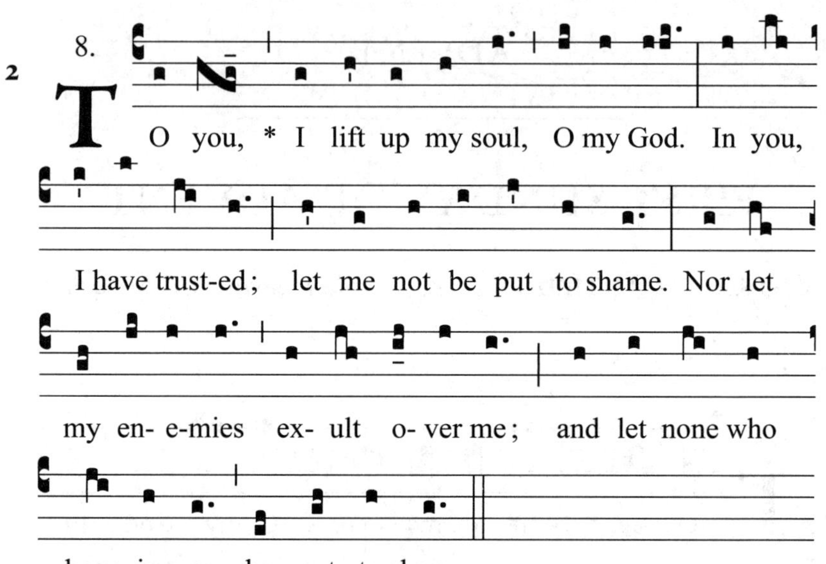
2
8.
TO you, * I lift up my soul, O my God. In you,
I have trust-ed; let me not be put to shame. Nor let
my en- e-mies ex- ult o- ver me; and let none who
hope in you be put to shame.

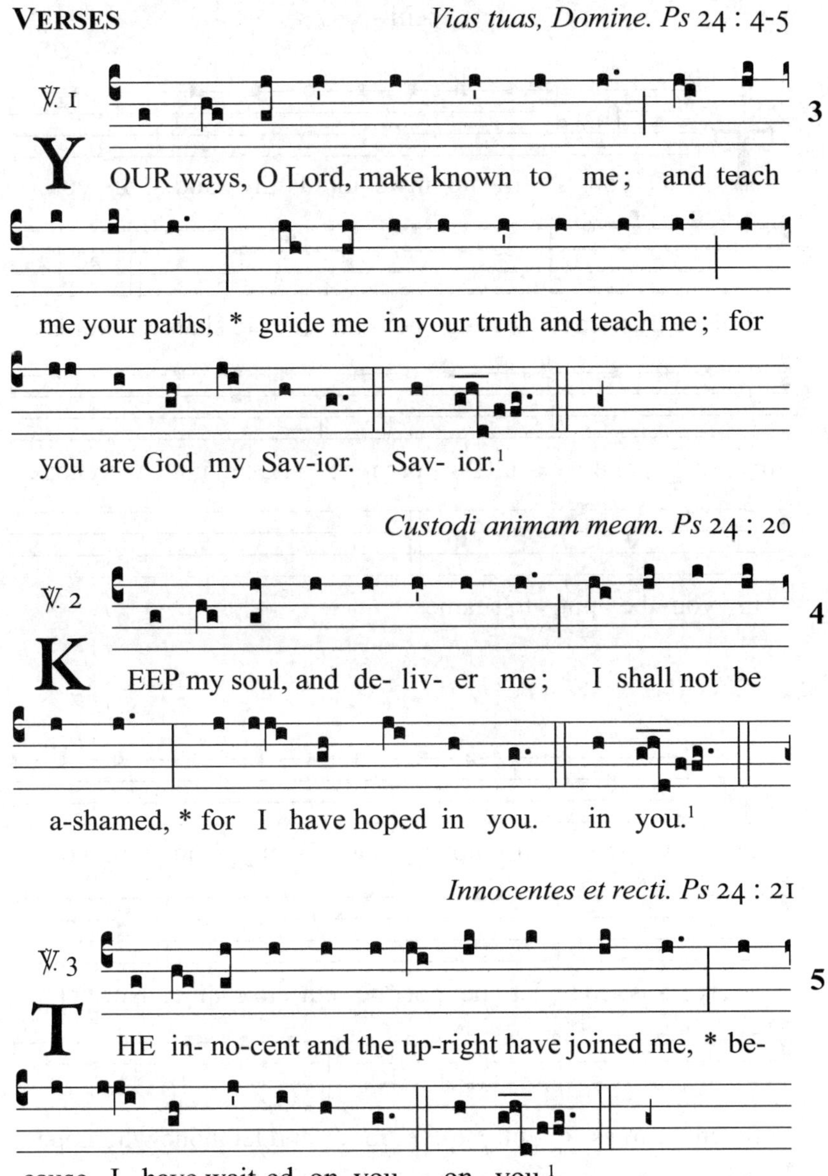
VERSES
Vias tuas, Domine. Ps 24 : 4-5
℣. 1
3
YOUR ways, O Lord, make known to me; and teach
me your paths, * guide me in your truth and teach me; for
you are God my Sav-ior. Sav- ior.[1]
Custodi animam meam. Ps 24 : 20
℣. 2
4
KEEP my soul, and de- liv- er me; I shall not be
a-shamed, * for I have hoped in you. in you.[1]
Innocentes et recti. Ps 24 : 21
℣. 3
5
THE in- no-cent and the up-right have joined me, * because I have wait-ed on you. on you.[1]

[1] The second ending is used when antiphon - i - follows the verse. When other antiphon settings or verses follow immediately, the first ending is used.

- iii -

6

8.
TO you, I lift up my soul, O my God. * In you,
I have trust-ed; let me not be put to shame. Nor let
my en- e- mies ex- ult o- ver me; and let none who hope
in you be put to shame.

Or:

7

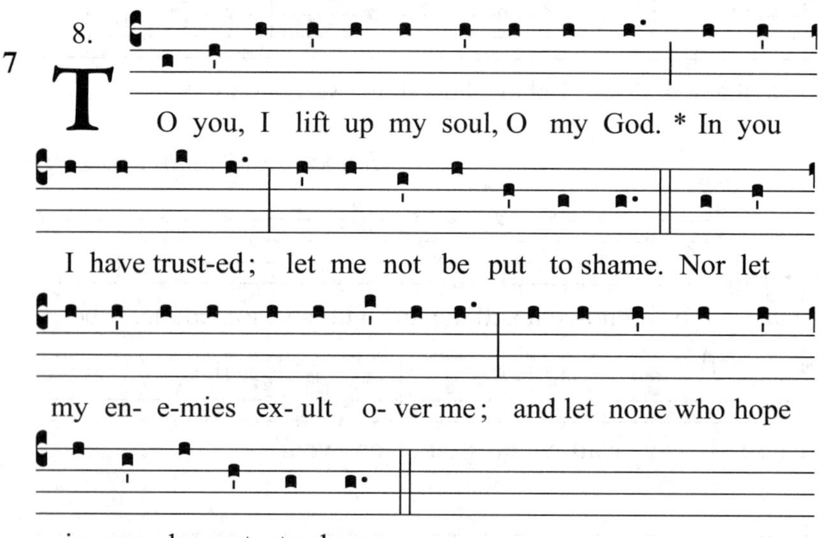
8.
TO you, I lift up my soul, O my God. * In you
I have trust-ed; let me not be put to shame. Nor let
my en- e-mies ex- ult o- ver me; and let none who hope
in you be put to shame.

- iv -

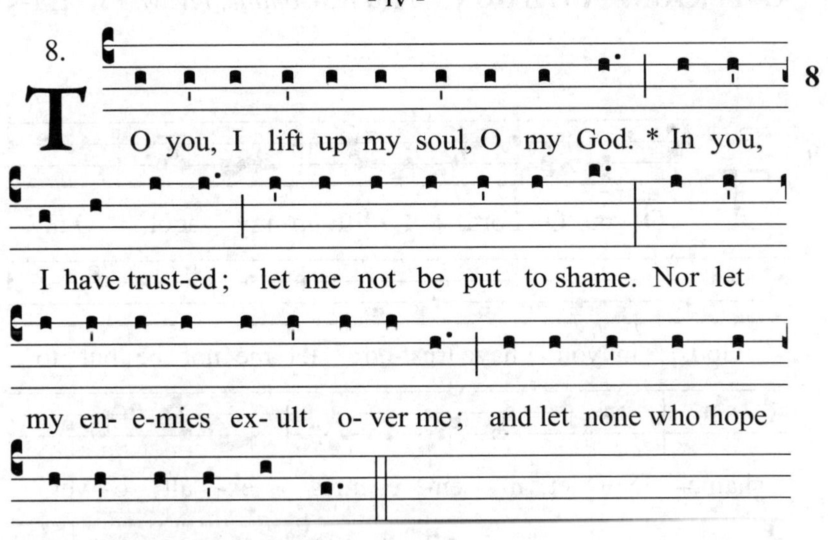
8.
TO you, I lift up my soul, O my God. * In you,
8
I have trust-ed; let me not be put to shame. Nor let
my en- e-mies ex- ult o- ver me; and let none who hope
in you be put to shame.

OFFERTORY ANTIPHON *Ad te, Domine, levavi. Ps* 24:1-3

- i -

9

2.
TO you, O Lord, * I lift up my soul. O my God, in you I have trust-ed; let me not be put to shame. Nor let my en- e- mies ex- ult o- ver me; and let none who hope in you be put to shame.

- ii -

10

2.
TO you, O Lord, * I lift up my soul. O my God, in you I have trust- ed; let me not be put to shame. Nor let my en- e-mies ex- ult o-ver me; and let none who hope in you be put to shame.

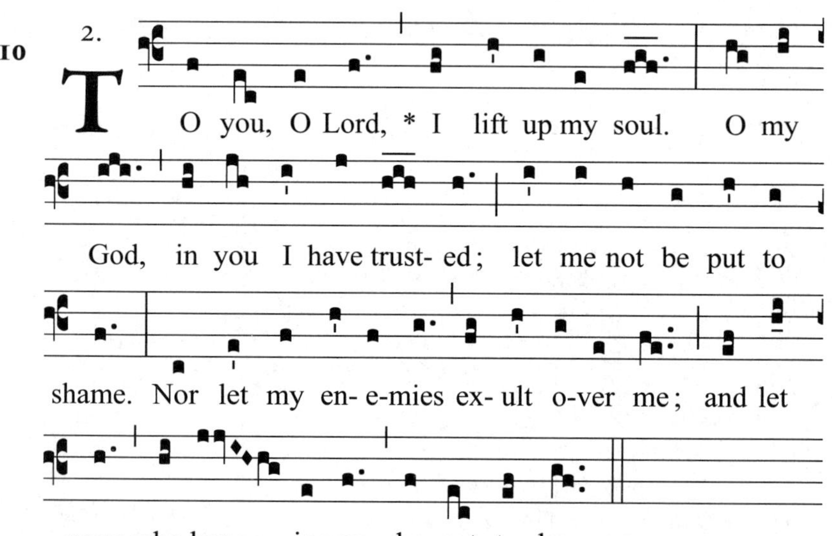

VERSES *Reminiscere miserationum tuarum. Ps* 24 : 6-7

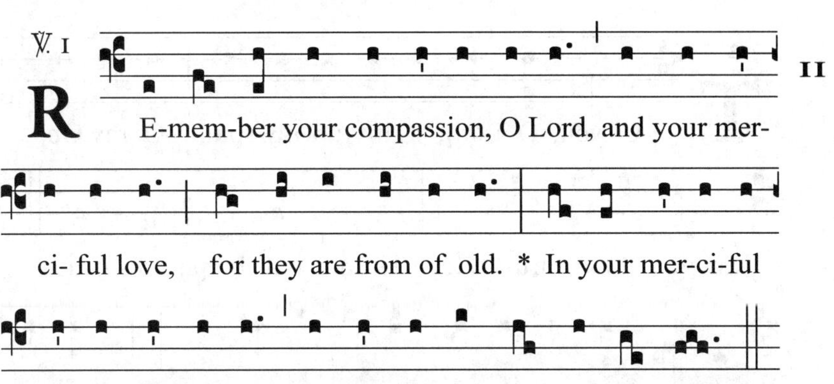
℣. 1
11
R E-mem-ber your compassion, O Lord, and your mer-
ci- ful love, for they are from of old. * In your mer-ci-ful
love re-member me because of your goodness, O Lord.

De necessitatibus meis. Ps 24 : 17-18

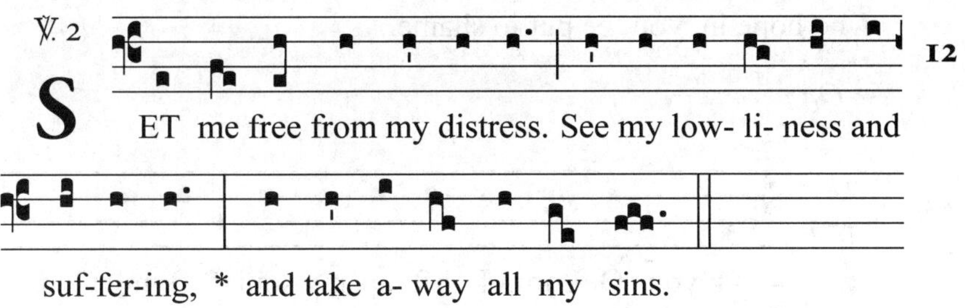
℣. 2
12
S ET me free from my distress. See my low- li- ness and
suf-fer-ing, * and take a- way all my sins.

Custodi animam meam. Ps 24 : 20

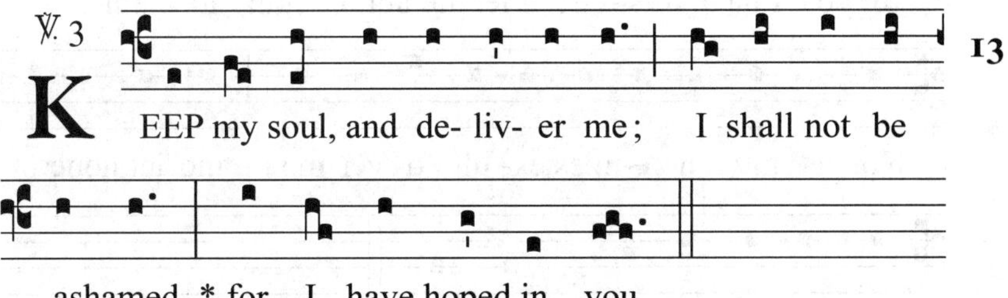
℣. 3
13
K EEP my soul, and de- liv- er me; I shall not be
ashamed, * for I have hoped in you.

- iii -

14 
2.
T O you, O Lord, I lift up my soul. * O my God,
in you I have trust-ed; let me not be put to shame.
Nor let my en- e-mies ex- ult o- ver me; and let none
who hope in you be put to shame.

Or:

15 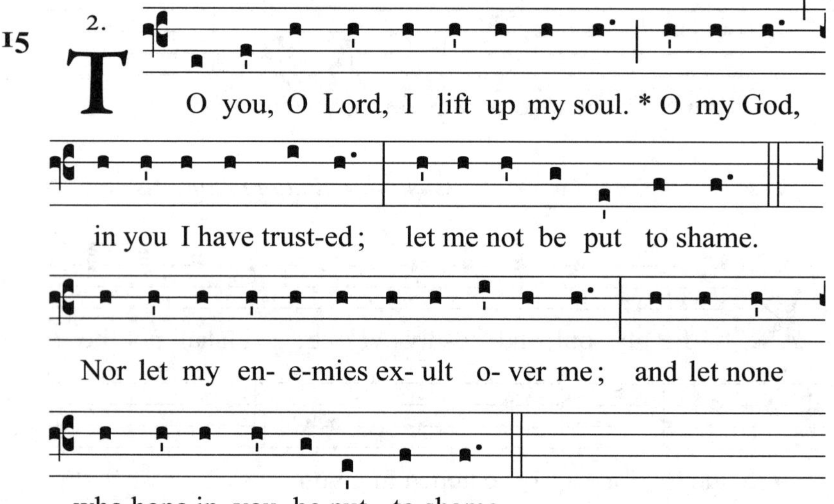
2.
T O you, O Lord, I lift up my soul. * O my God,
in you I have trust-ed; let me not be put to shame.
Nor let my en- e-mies ex- ult o- ver me; and let none
who hope in you be put to shame.

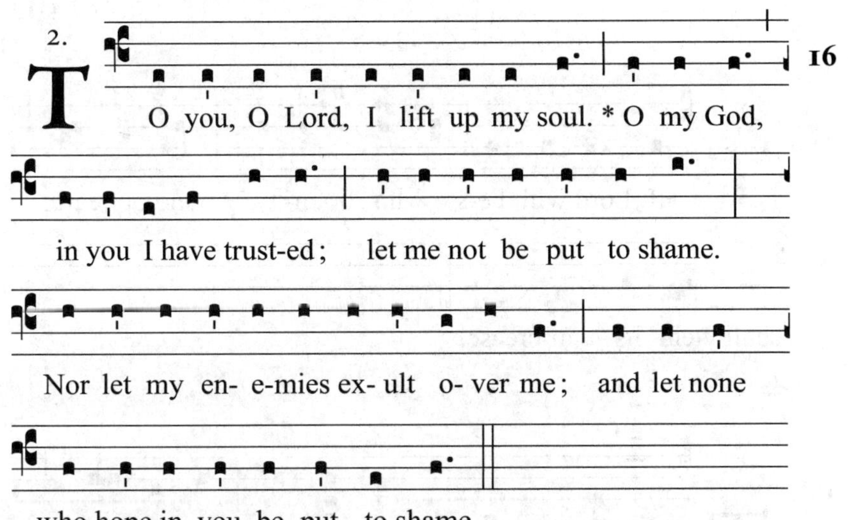
- iv -
2.
16
TO you, O Lord, I lift up my soul. * O my God,
in you I have trust-ed; let me not be put to shame.
Nor let my en- e-mies ex- ult o- ver me; and let none
who hope in you be put to shame.

COMMUNION ANTIPHON *Dominus dabit benignitatem.*
Ps 84:13

- i -

17 I. THE Lord will be-stow his boun- ty, * and our earth shall yield its in-crease.

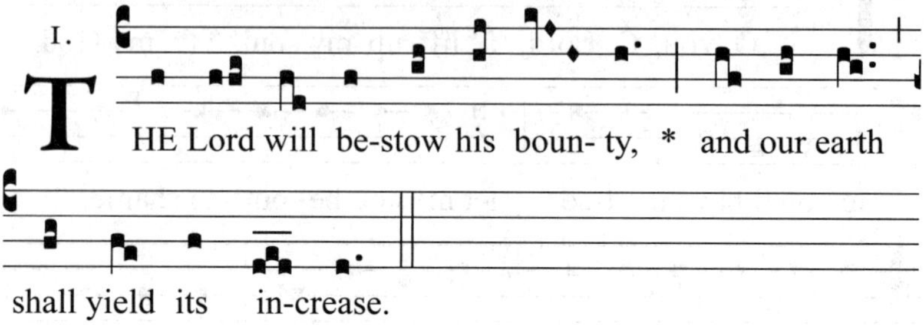

- ii -

18 I. THE Lord will be-stow his boun-ty, * and our earth shall yield its in-crease.

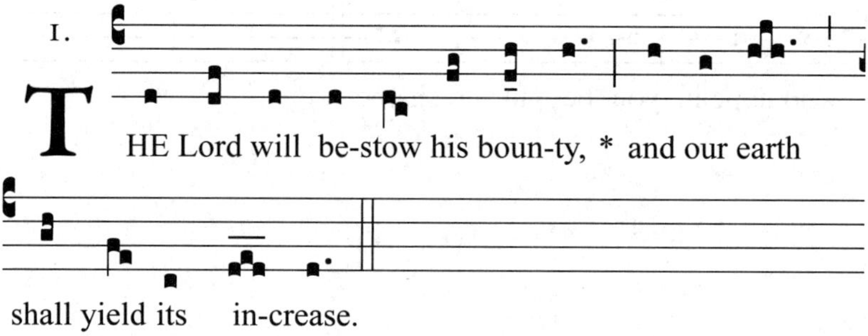

VERSES *Benedixisti, Domine, terram tuam. Ps* 84:2. 3

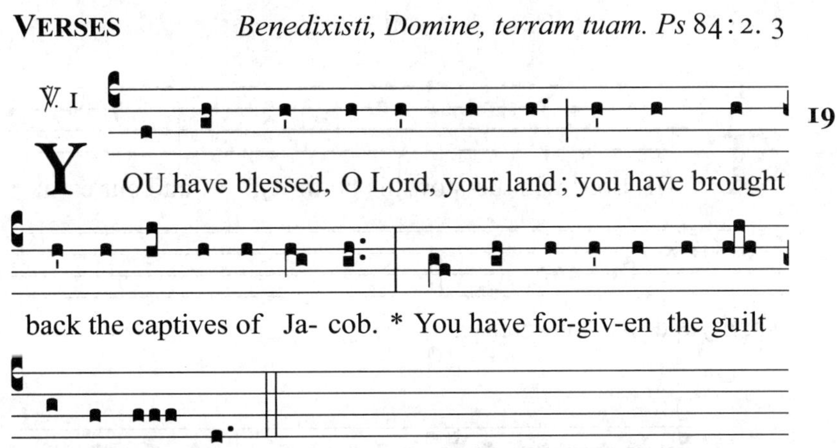
℣. 1
YOU have blessed, O Lord, your land; you have brought
19
back the captives of Ja- cob. * You have for-giv-en the guilt
of your peo- ple.

Ostende nobis, Domine, misericordiam tuam. Ps 84:8

℣. 2
SHOW us, O Lord, your mer- cy, * and grant us your
20
sal- va- tion.

Audiam quid loquatur. Ps 84:9

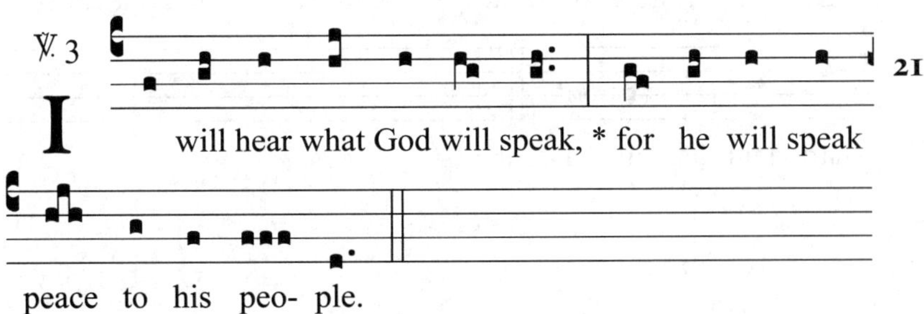
℣. 3
I will hear what God will speak, * for he will speak
21
peace to his peo- ple.

- iii -

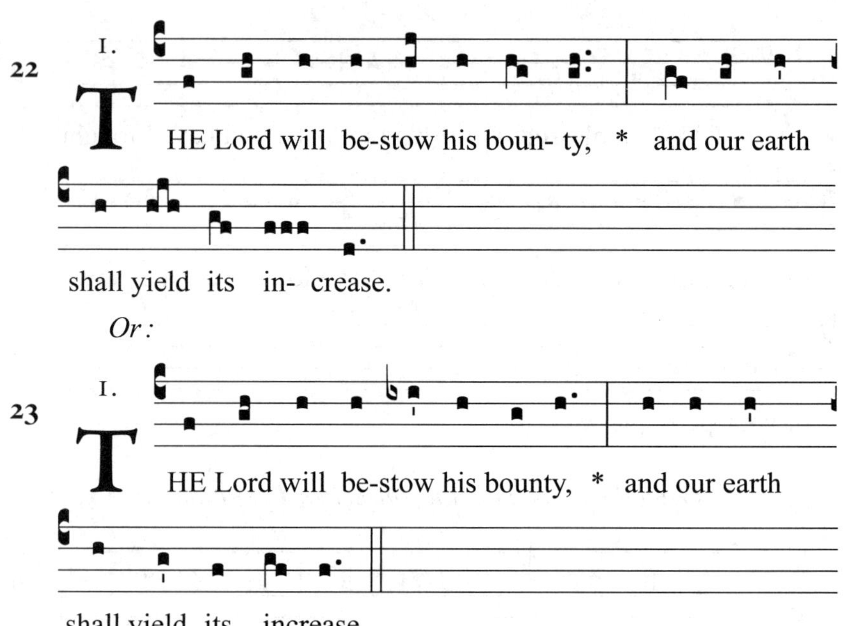
22
I.
THE Lord will be-stow his boun- ty, * and our earth
shall yield its in- crease.
Or:
23
I.
THE Lord will be-stow his bounty, * and our earth
shall yield its increase.

- iv -

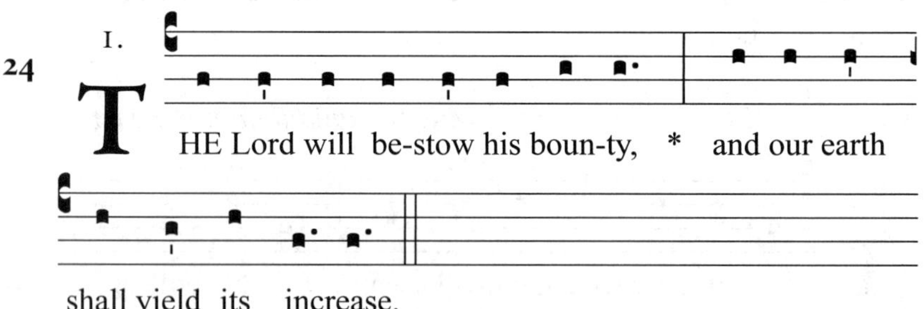
24
I.
THE Lord will be-stow his boun-ty, * and our earth
shall yield its increase.

SECOND SUNDAY OF ADVENT

Entrance Antiphon *Populus Sion. Cf. Is* 30:19.30

- i -

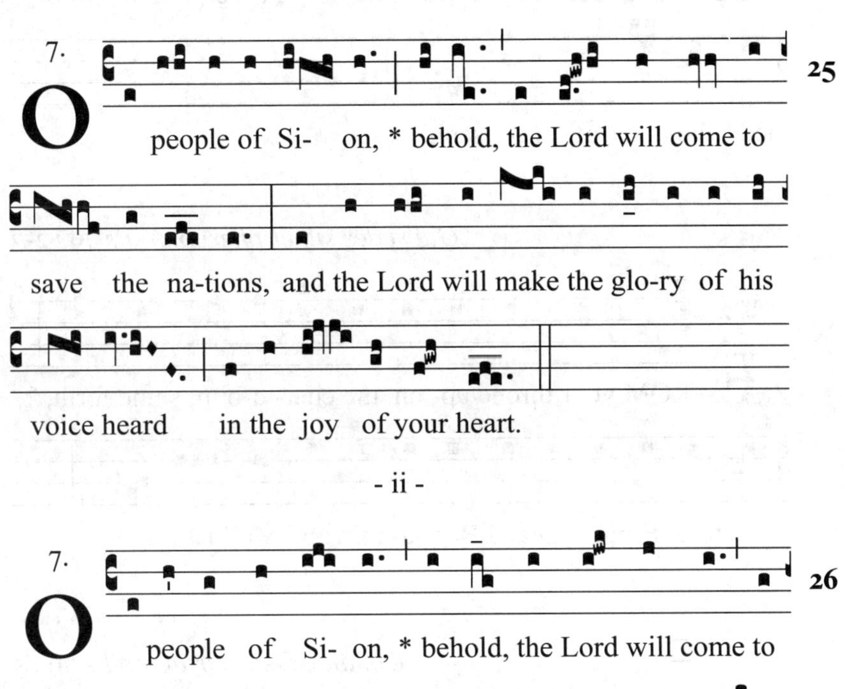
7.
25
O people of Si- on, * behold, the Lord will come to
save the na-tions, and the Lord will make the glo-ry of his
voice heard in the joy of your heart.

- ii -

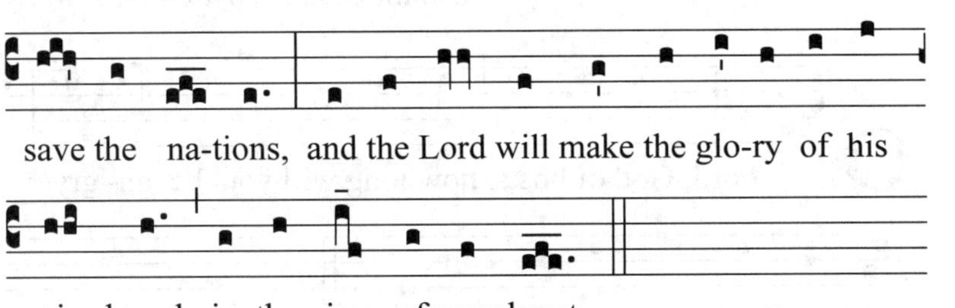
7.
26
O people of Si- on, * behold, the Lord will come to
save the na-tions, and the Lord will make the glo-ry of his
voice heard in the joy of your heart.

VERSES *Qui regis Israel, intende. Ps* 79 : 2

27

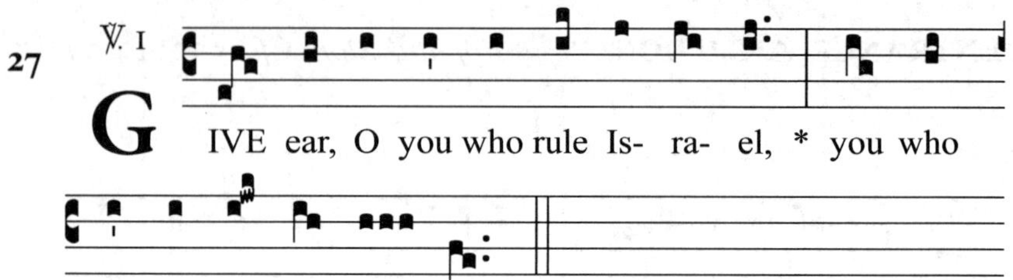
℣. 1
GIVE ear, O you who rule Is- ra- el, * you who
lead the flock of Jo- seph.

Qui sedes super cherubim. Ps 79 : 2-3

28

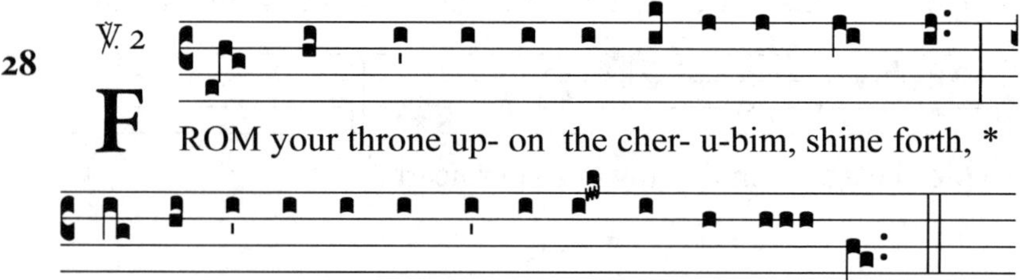
℣. 2
FROM your throne up- on the cher- u-bim, shine forth, *
be-fore E-phra-im and Ben-ja- min and Ma- nas- seh.

Domine, Deus virtutum. Ps 79 : 5

29

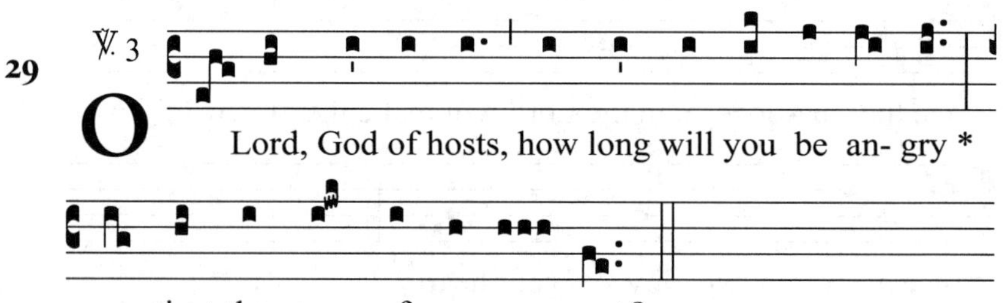
℣. 3
O Lord, God of hosts, how long will you be an- gry *
a-gainst the prayer of your ser- vant?

- iii -

7.
30
O peo-ple of Si- on, * behold, the Lord will come to
save the na-tions, and the Lord will make the glo-ry of his
voice heard in the joy of your heart.

iv

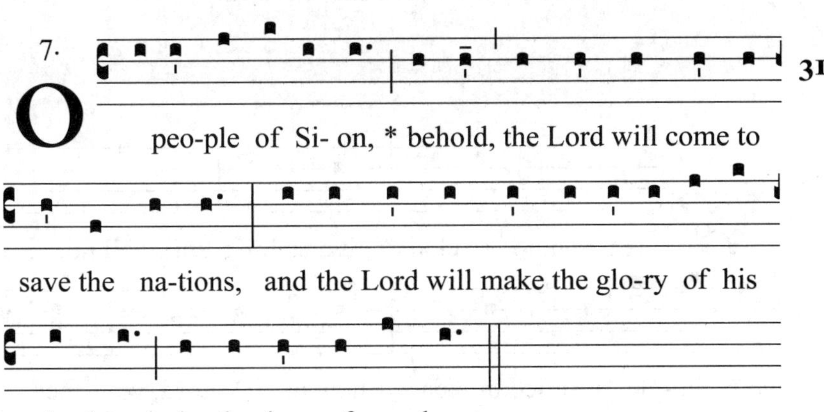
7.
31
O peo-ple of Si- on, * behold, the Lord will come to
save the na-tions, and the Lord will make the glo-ry of his
voice heard in the joy of your heart.

Offertory Antiphon *Deus, tu convertens. Ps* 84 : 7-8

- i -

32
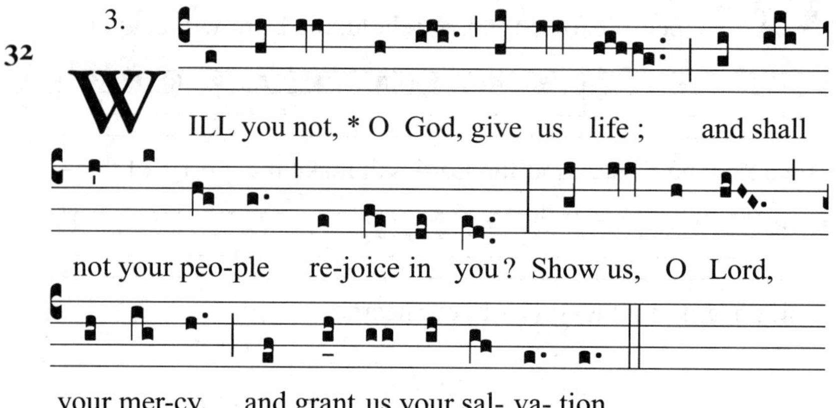
3.
WILL you not, * O God, give us life ; and shall
not your peo-ple re-joice in you ? Show us, O Lord,
your mer-cy, and grant us your sal- va- tion.

- ii -

33 3.

WILL you not, O God, * give us life ; and shall not your peo-ple re-joice in you ? Show us, O Lord, your mer-cy, and grant us your sal- va- tion.

VERSES *Benedixisti, Domine, terram tuam. Ps* 84:2. 3

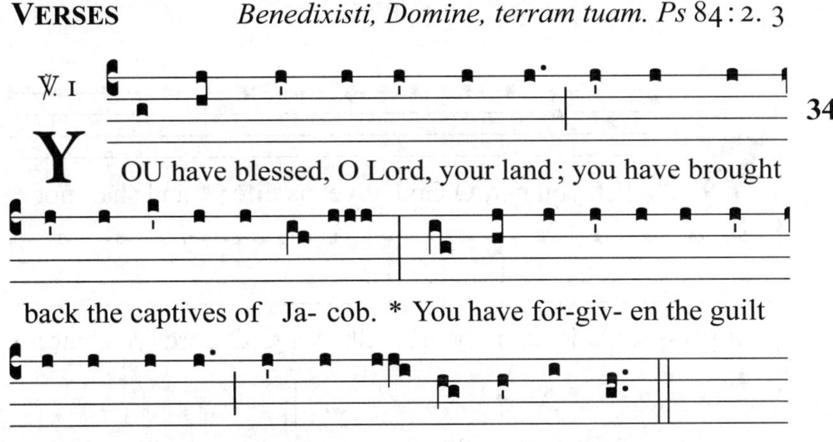
℣. 1
YOU have blessed, O Lord, your land; you have brought
34
back the captives of Ja- cob. * You have for-giv- en the guilt
of your peo-ple; you have cov-ered all their sins.

Converte nos, Deus. Ps 84:5

℣. 2
COn-vert us, O God our sav- ior, * and turn a- way
35
your an- ger from us.

Audiam quid loquatur. Ps 84:9

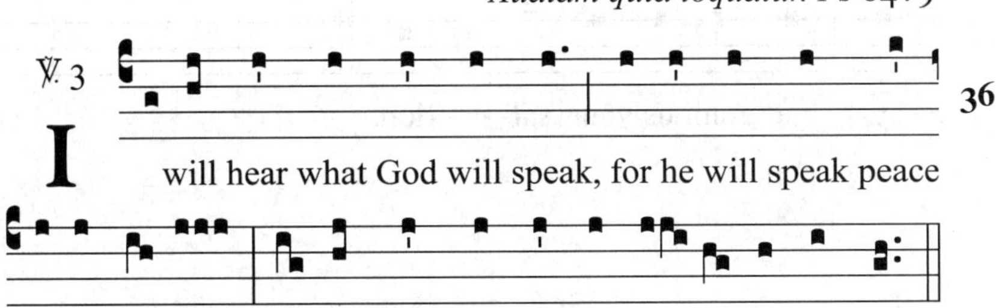
℣. 3
I will hear what God will speak, for he will speak peace
36

to his peo-ple, * and to those who are con-vert-ed to the heart.

- iii -

37

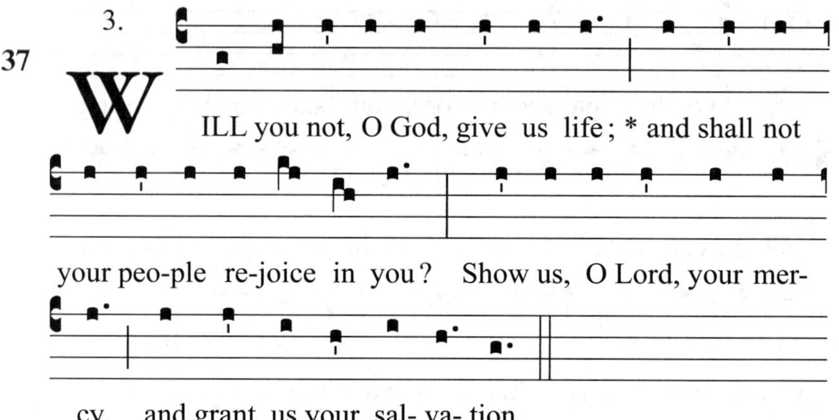
3.
WILL you not, O God, give us life; * and shall not
your peo-ple re-joice in you? Show us, O Lord, your mer-
cy, and grant us your sal- va- tion.

- iv -

38

3.
WILL you not, O God, give us life; * and shall not
your peo-ple re-joice in you? Show us, O Lord, your mer-
cy, and grant us your sal- va- tion.

COMMUNION ANTIPHON *Ierusalem, surge. Bar* 5:5; 4:36

- i -

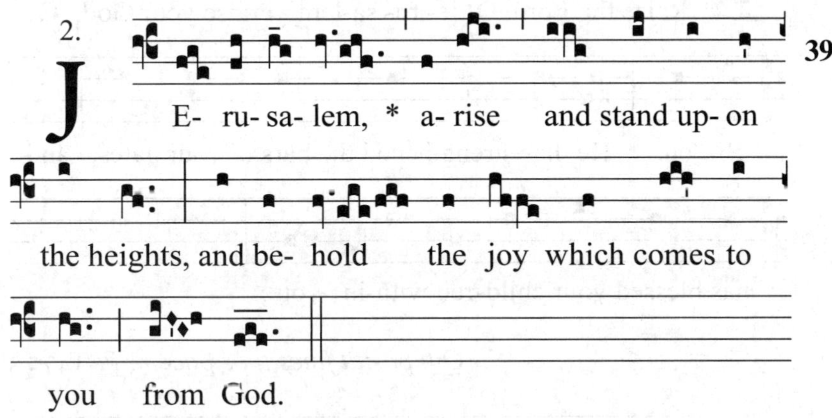
2.
39
JE- ru- sa- lem, * a- rise and stand up- on
the heights, and be- hold the joy which comes to
you from God.

- ii -

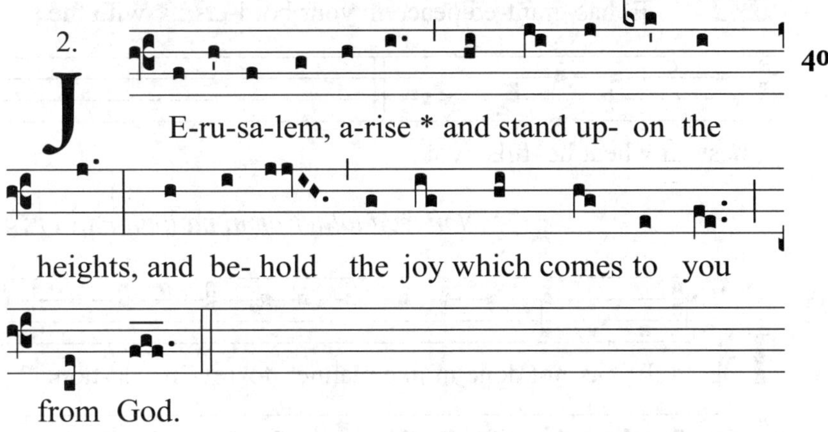
2.
40
JE-ru-sa-lem, a-rise * and stand up- on the
heights, and be- hold the joy which comes to you
from God.

VERSES *Lauda, Jerusalem, Dominum. Ps* 147 : 1

41 ℣. 1

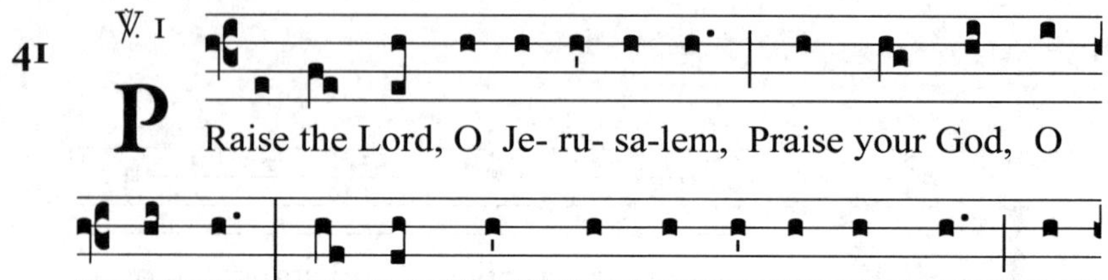

P Raise the Lord, O Je- ru- sa-lem, Praise your God, O

Si- on. * He has strengthened the bars of your gates, and

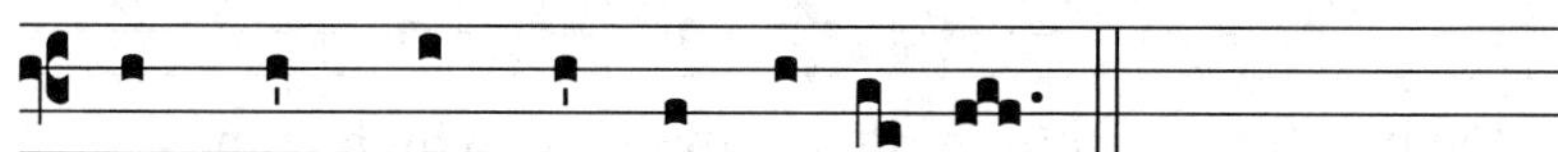

has blessed your child-ren with-in you.

Qui posuit fines tuos pacem. Ps 147 : 3

42 ℣. 2

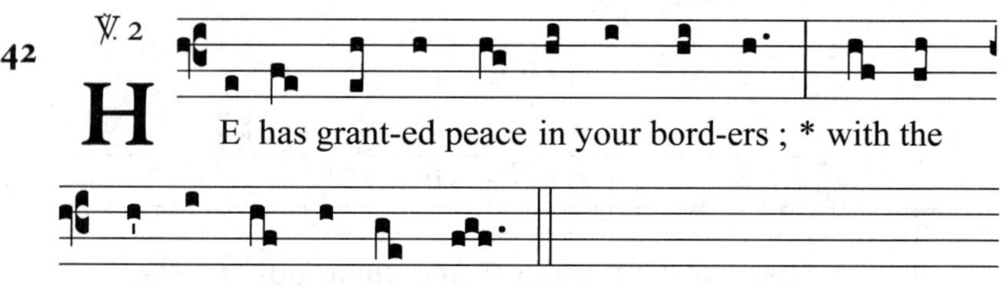

H E has grant-ed peace in your bord-ers ; * with the

best of wheat he fills you.

Non fecit taliter omni nationi. Ps 147 : 9

43 ℣. 3

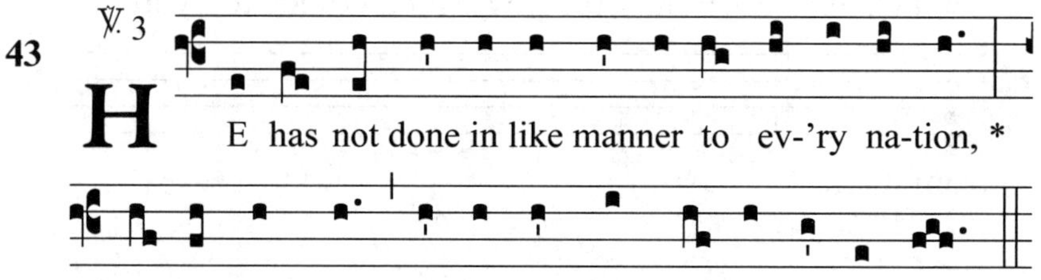

H E has not done in like manner to ev-'ry na-tion, *

and his judgments he has not made man- i- fest to them.

- iii -

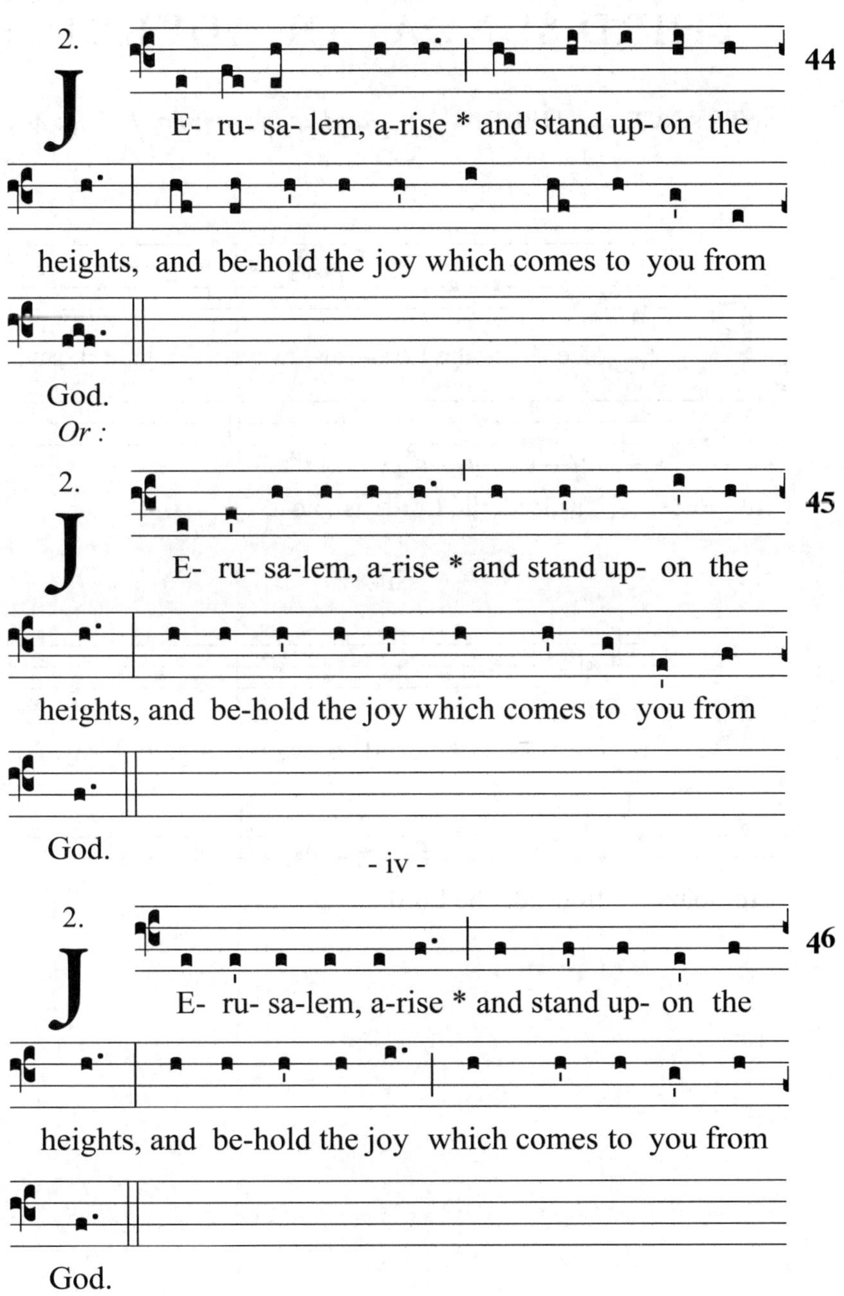
2.
J E- ru- sa- lem, a-rise * and stand up- on the
44
heights, and be-hold the joy which comes to you from
God.
Or :
2.
J E- ru- sa-lem, a-rise * and stand up- on the
45
heights, and be-hold the joy which comes to you from
God.
- iv -
2.
J E- ru- sa-lem, a-rise * and stand up- on the
46
heights, and be-hold the joy which comes to you from
God.

THIRD SUNDAY OF ADVENT

Entrance Antiphon *Gaudete in Domino. Phil* 4 : 4-5

- i -

47

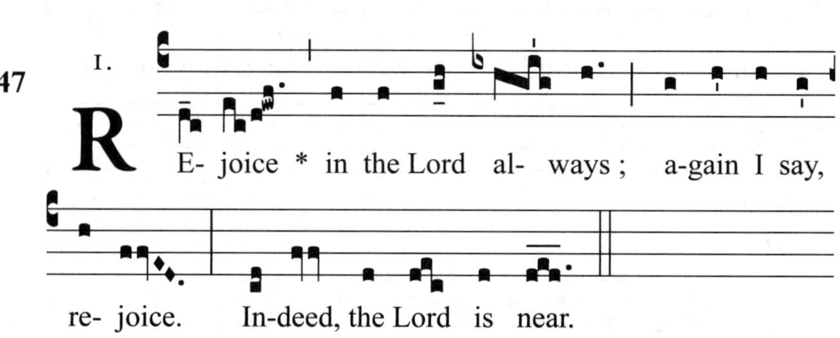
I.
R E- joice * in the Lord al- ways ; a-gain I say,
re- joice. In-deed, the Lord is near.

- ii -

48

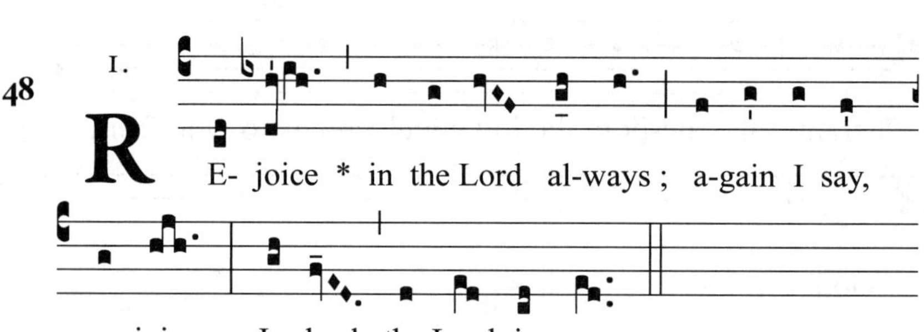
I.
R E- joice * in the Lord al-ways ; a-gain I say,
re- joice. In-deed, the Lord is near.

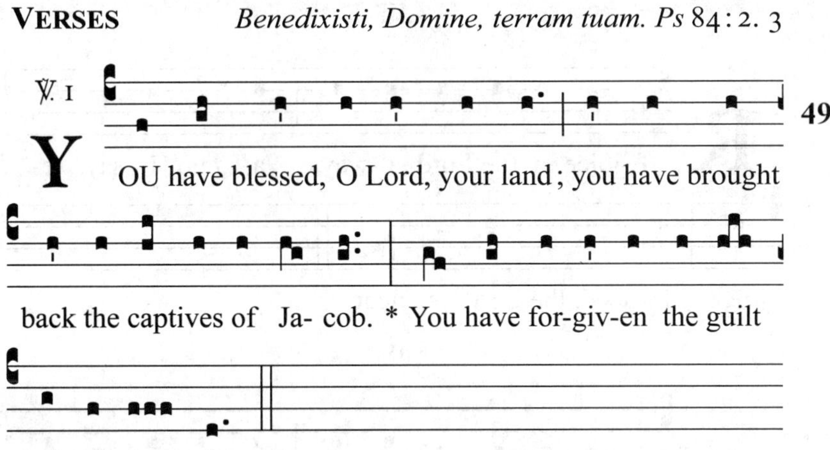
VERSES
Benedixisti, Domine, terram tuam. Ps 84:2. 3
℣. 1
49
YOU have blessed, O Lord, your land; you have brought
back the captives of Ja- cob. * You have for-giv-en the guilt
of your peo- ple.

Converte nos, Deus. Ps 84:5

℣. 2
50
COn-vert us, O God our sav- ior, * and turn a- way
your an- ger from us.

Audiam quid loquatur. Ps 84:9

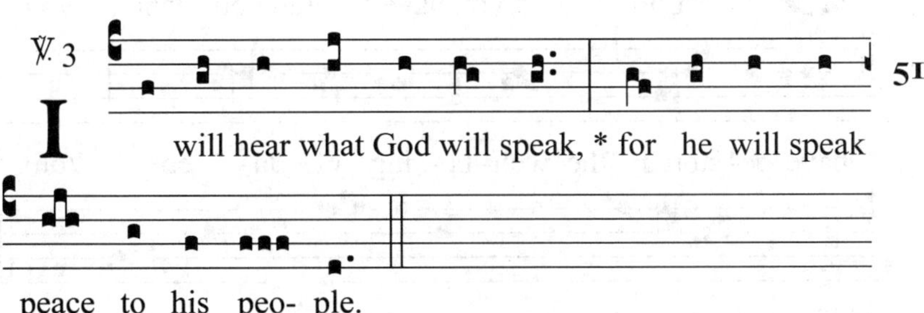
℣. 3
51
I will hear what God will speak, * for he will speak
peace to his peo- ple.

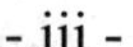
- iii -

52

1.
R
E-joice in the Lord al-ways; * a- gain I say, re-
joice. In-deed, the Lord is near.

- iv -

53

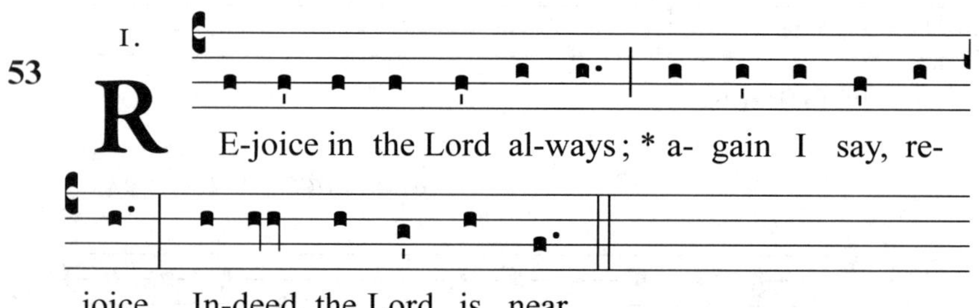
1.
R
E-joice in the Lord al-ways; * a- gain I say, re-
joice. In-deed, the Lord is near.

OFFERTORY ANTIPHON *Benedixisti, Domine. Ps* 84:2

- i -

54

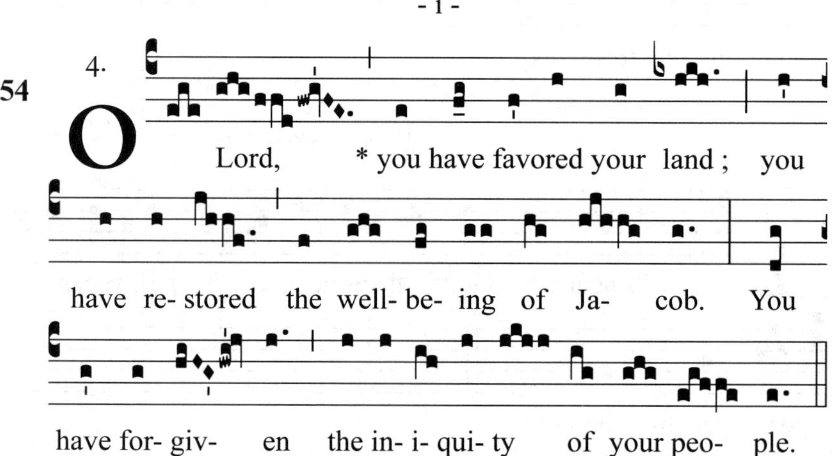
4.
O
Lord, * you have favored your land; you
have re- stored the well- be- ing of Ja- cob. You
have for- giv- en the in- i- qui- ty of your peo- ple.

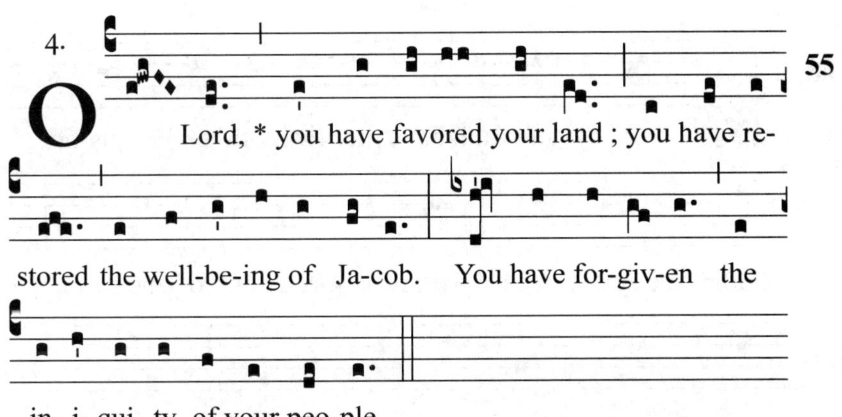
- ii -
4.
55
O Lord, * you have favored your land ; you have restored the well-be-ing of Ja-cob. You have for-giv-en the
in- i- qui- ty of your peo-ple.

VERSES *Converte nos, Deus. Ps* 84:5

℣. 1
56
COn-vert us, O God our Sav-ior ; * and turn a-way your
an- ger from us.

Audiam quid loquatur. Ps 84:9

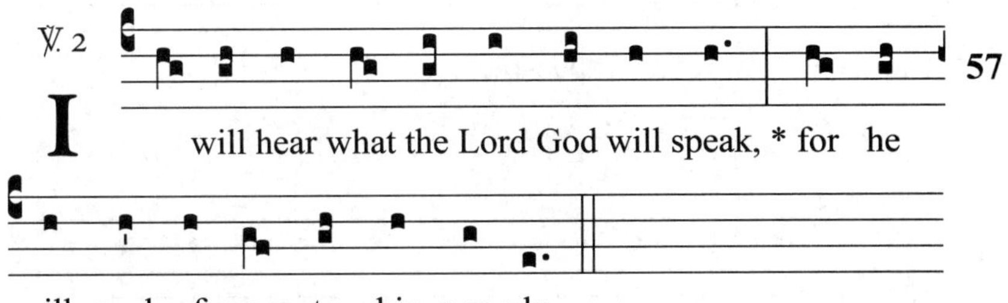
℣. 2
57
I will hear what the Lord God will speak, * for he
will speak of peace to his peo-ple.

Misericordia et veritas. Ps 84:11-12

58

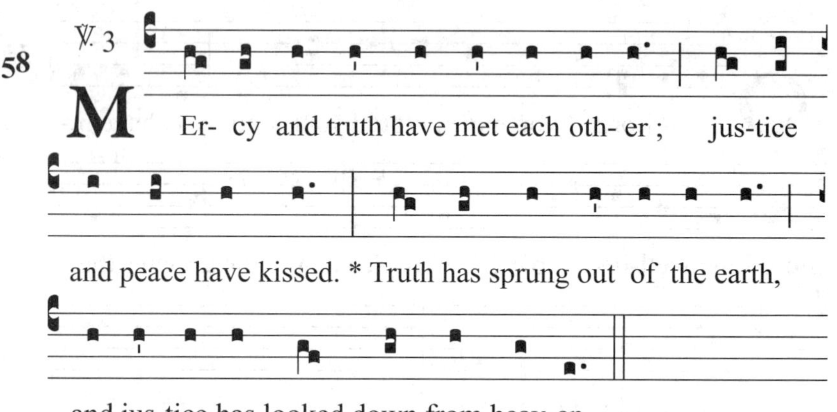
℣. 3
MErcy and truth have met each oth- er ; jus-tice
and peace have kissed. * Truth has sprung out of the earth,
and jus-tice has looked down from heav-en.

\- iii -

59

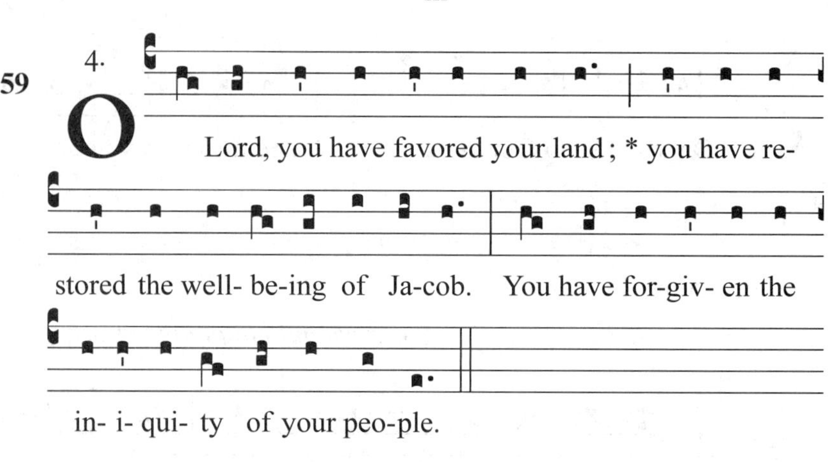
4.
O Lord, you have favored your land ; * you have restored the well- be-ing of Ja-cob. You have for-giv- en the
in- i- qui- ty of your peo-ple.

Or :

60

4.
O Lord, you have favored your land ; * you have restored the well- be-ing of Ja-cob. You have for-giv- en the

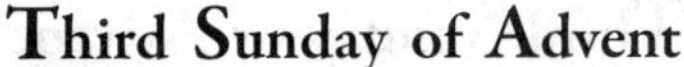

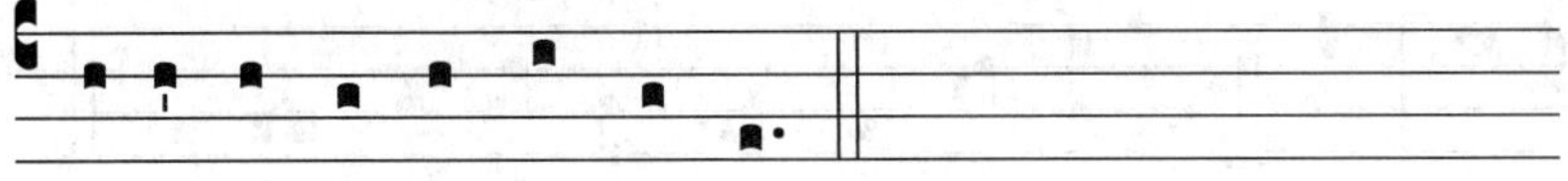
in- i- qui- ty of your peo-ple.

- iv -

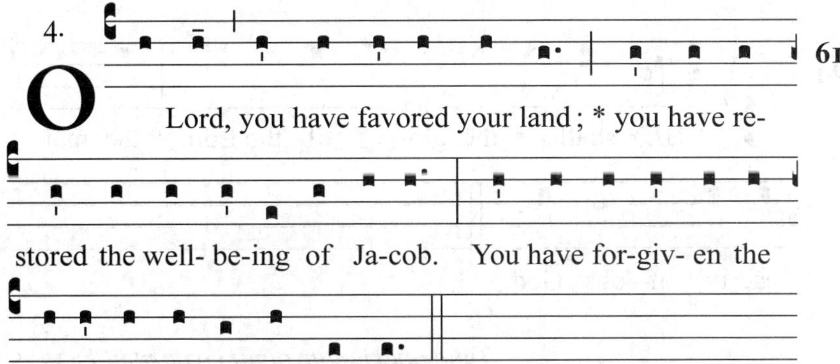
4.
O Lord, you have favored your land; * you have re-
61
stored the well- be-ing of Ja-cob. You have for-giv- en the
in- i- qui- ty of your peo-ple.

COMMUNION ANTIPHON *Dicite : Pusillanimes. Cf. Is* 35 : 4

- i -

7.
SAY to the faint of heart : * Be strong and do not
62
fear. Be-hold, our God will come, and he will
save us.

- ii -

7.

SAY to the faint of heart : * Be strong and do not 63

fear. Be-hold, our God will come, and he will save us.

VERSES *Ipsi videbunt gloriam Domini. Is* 35 : 2

64 ℣. 1

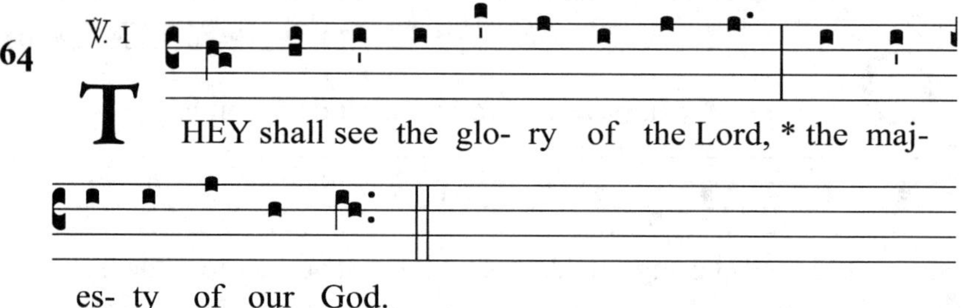

THEY shall see the glo- ry of the Lord, * the maj- es- ty of our God.

Tunc aperientur oculi cæcorum. Is 35 : 5

65 ℣. 2

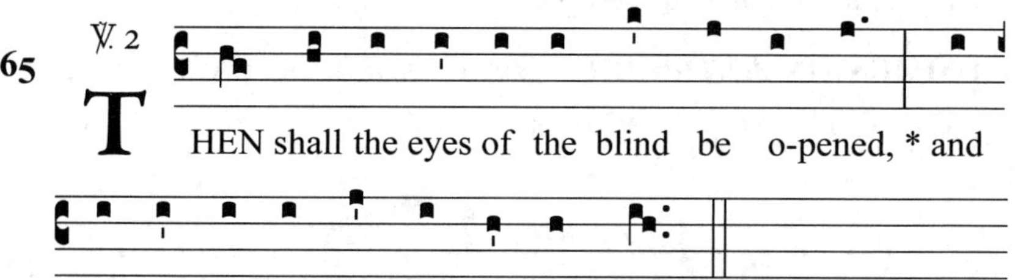

THEN shall the eyes of the blind be o-pened, * and the ears of the deaf shall be un-stopped.

Scissæ sunt in deserto aquæ. Is 35 : 6

66 ℣. 3

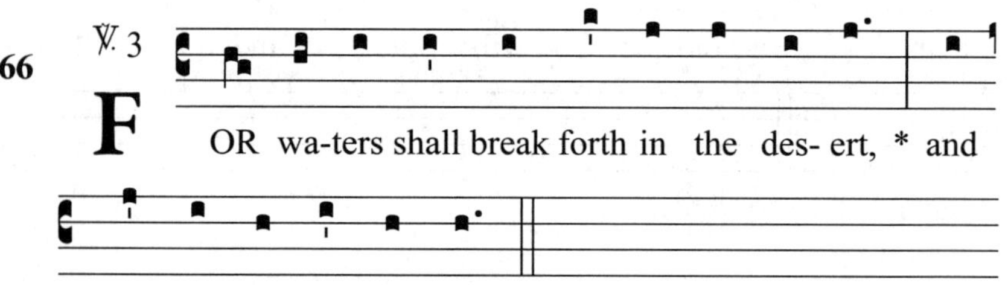

FOR wa-ters shall break forth in the des- ert, * and streams in the wild- er- ness.

- iii -

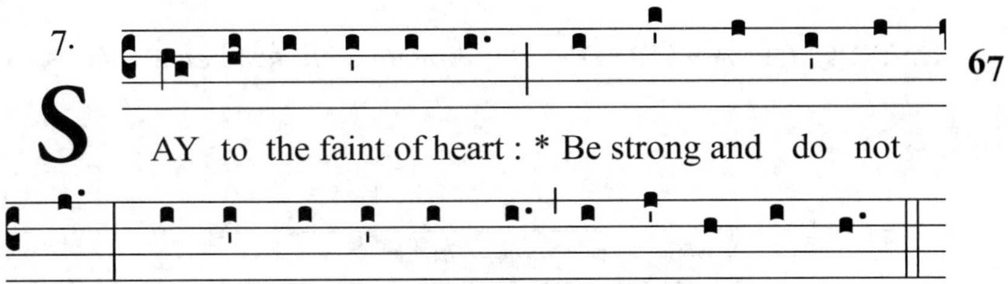
7.
67
SAY to the faint of heart : * Be strong and do not

fear. Be-hold, our God will come, and he will save us.

- iv -

7.
68
SAY to the faint of heart : * Be strong and do not

fear. Be-hold, our God will come, and he will save us.

FOURTH SUNDAY OF ADVENT

Entrance Antiphon *Rorate cæli desuper. Cf. Is* 45:8

- i -

69

I.
DROP down dew * from a- bove, you heav-ens, and
let the clouds rain down the Just One ; let the earth
be o- pened and bring forth a Sav- ior.

- ii -

70

I.
DROP down dew * from a- bove, you heav-ens, and
let the clouds rain down the Just One ; let the earth be
o- pened and bring forth a Sav- ior.

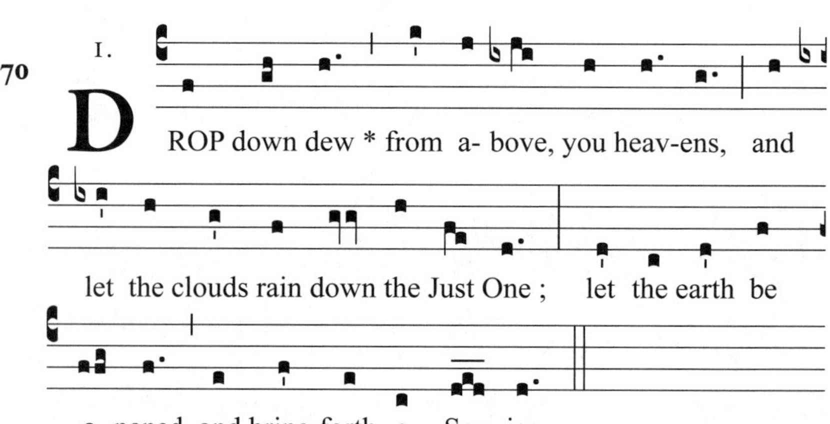

Verses

Cœli enarrant gloriam Dei. Ps 18:2

℣. 1
THE heavens show forth the glo- ry of God, * and
the fir-ma-ment de-clares the work of his hands.

71

Dies diei eructat verbum. Ps 18:3

℣. 2
DAY un- to day con-veys the mes-sage, * and night
un- to night im-parts know-ledge.

72

In sole posuit. Ps 18:6

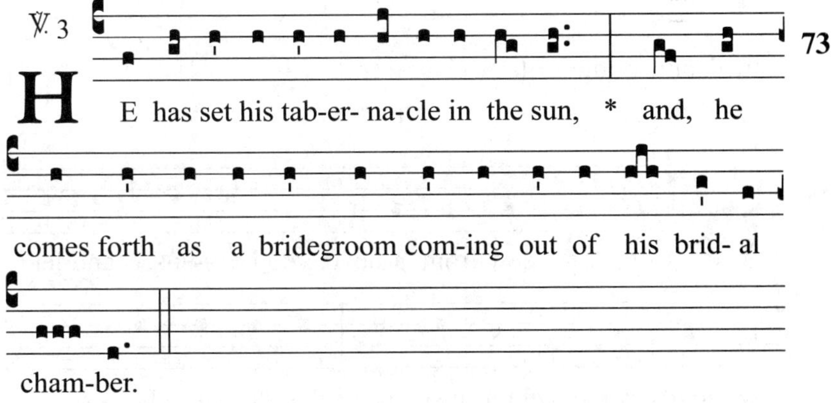
℣. 3
HE has set his tab-er- na-cle in the sun, * and, he
comes forth as a bridegroom com-ing out of his brid- al
cham-ber.

73

- iii -
74
I.
DROP down dew from a-bove, you heav-ens, * and let
the clouds rain down the Just One ; let the earth be o-
pened and bring forth a Sav- ior.
Or :
75
I.
DROP down dew from a-bove, you heav-ens, * and let
the clouds rain down the Just One ; let the earth be o-
pened and bring forth a Sav- ior.
- iv -
76
I.
DROP down dew from a-bove, you heav-ens, * and let
the clouds rain down the Just One ; let the earth be o-

pened and bring forth a Sav- ior.

OFFERTORY ANTIPHON *Ave Maria. Lk* 1 : 28. 42

- i -

8.
77
H AIL, Mar- y, * full of grace ; the Lord is
with you ; bless-ed are you a-mong wo-men, and
bless-ed is the fruit of your womb.

- ii -

8.
78
H AIL, Mar- y, * full of grace ; the Lord is with you ;
bless-ed are you a-mong wo-men, and bless-ed is the fruit of
your womb.

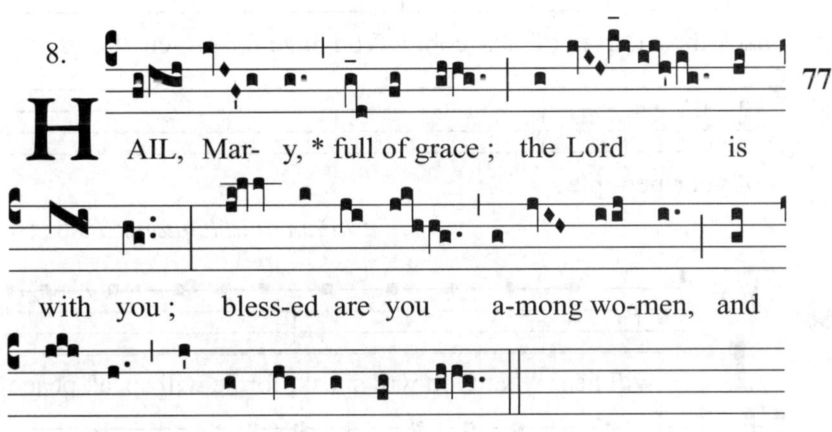

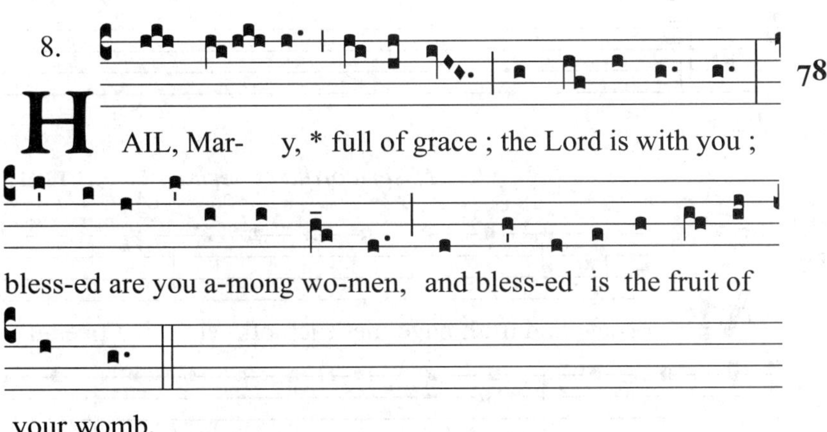

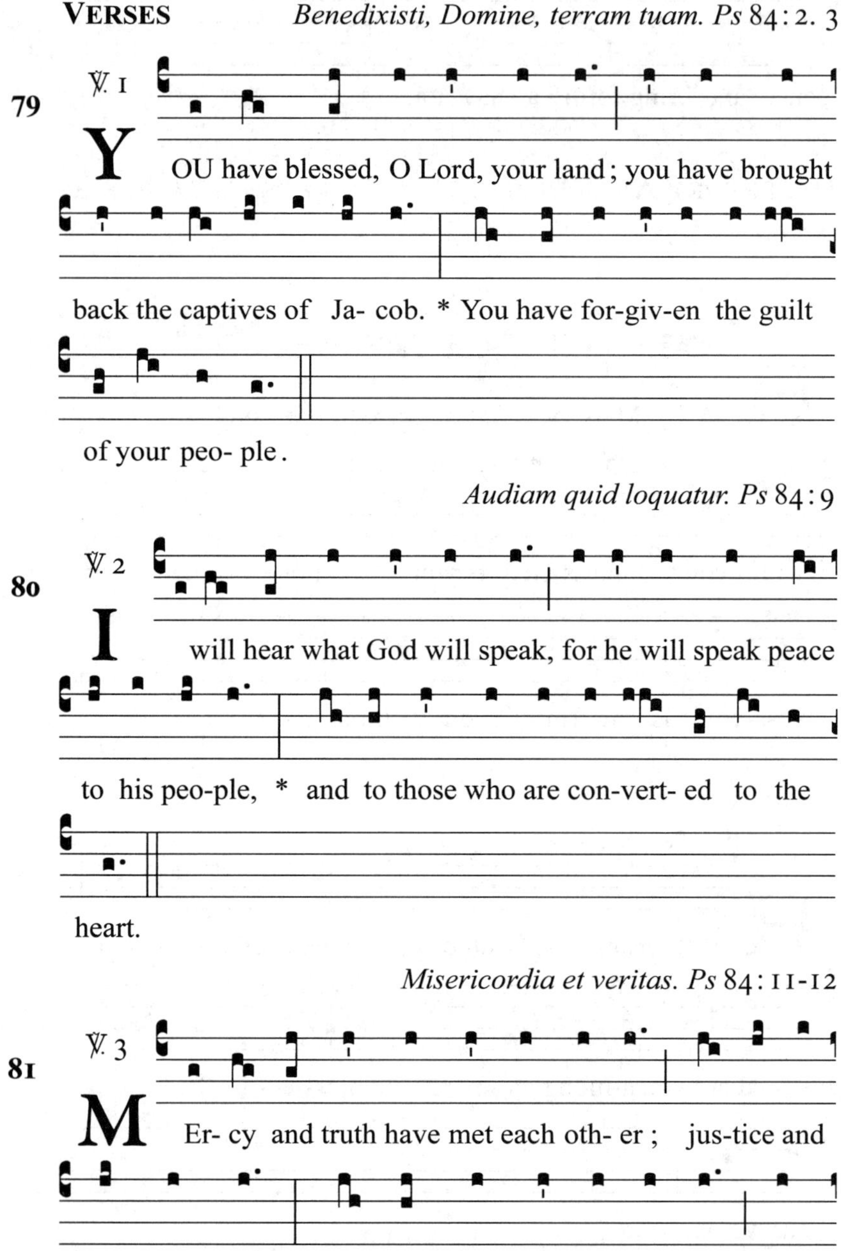
VERSES
Benedixisti, Domine, terram tuam. Ps 84:2. 3
79 ℣. 1
YOU have blessed, O Lord, your land; you have brought
back the captives of Ja- cob. * You have for-giv-en the guilt
of your peo- ple.
Audiam quid loquatur. Ps 84:9
80 ℣. 2
I will hear what God will speak, for he will speak peace
to his peo-ple, * and to those who are con-vert- ed to the
heart.
Misericordia et veritas. Ps 84:11-12
81 ℣. 3
MEr- cy and truth have met each oth- er; jus-tice and
peace have kissed. * Truth has sprung out of the earth, and

jus-tice has looked down from heav-en.

- iii -

8.
82
HAIL, Mar- y, full of grace; * the Lord is with you;
bless-ed are you a-mong wom-en, and bless-ed is the
fruit of your womb.

Or :

8.
83
HAIL, Mar-y, full of grace ; * the Lord is with you ; bless-
ed are you a-mong wo-men, and bless-ed is the fruit of
your womb.

- iv -

8.
84
HAIL, Mar-y, full of grace ; * the Lord is with you ; bless-

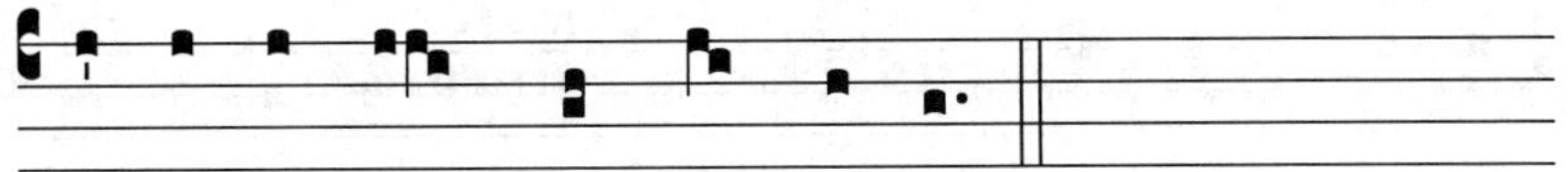

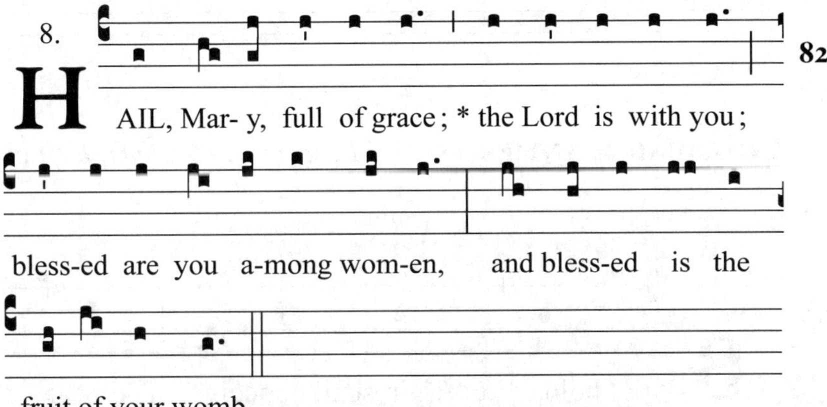

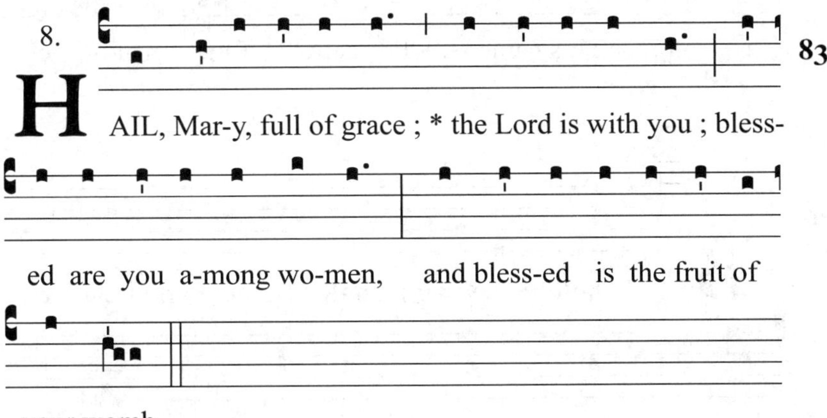

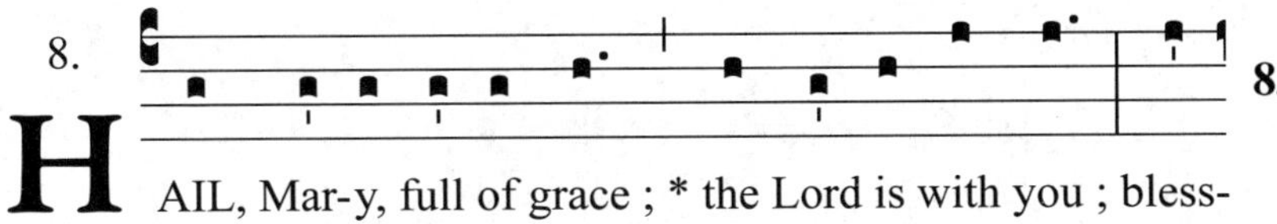

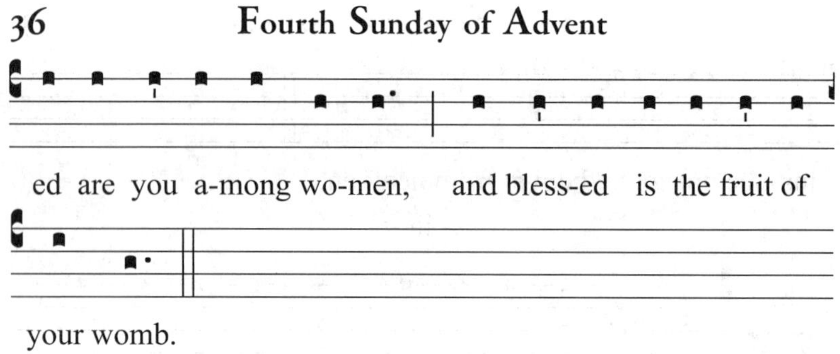
ed are you a-mong wo-men, and bless-ed is the fruit of
your womb.

Communion Antiphon *Ecce, virgo concipiet. Is* 7:14

- i -

85 I.

BE- hold, * a Virgin shall conceive and bear a son ; and his name will be called Em- man-u- el.

- ii -

86 I.

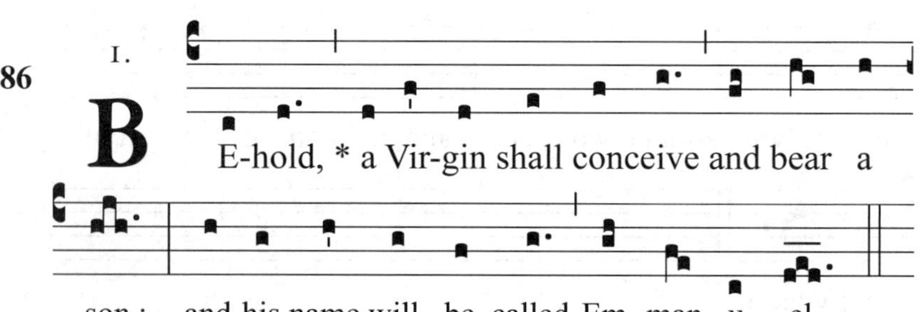
B
E-hold, * a Vir-gin shall conceive and bear a
son ; and his name will be called Em- man- u- el.

VERSES *Cæli enarrant gloriam Dei. Ps* 18:2

℣. 1
87
THE heavens show forth the glo- ry of God, * and
the fir-ma-ment de-clares the work of his hands.

Dies diei eructat verbum. Ps 18:3

℣. 2
88
DAY un- to day con-veys the mes-sage, * and night
un- to night im-parts know-ledge.

In sole posuit. Ps 18:6

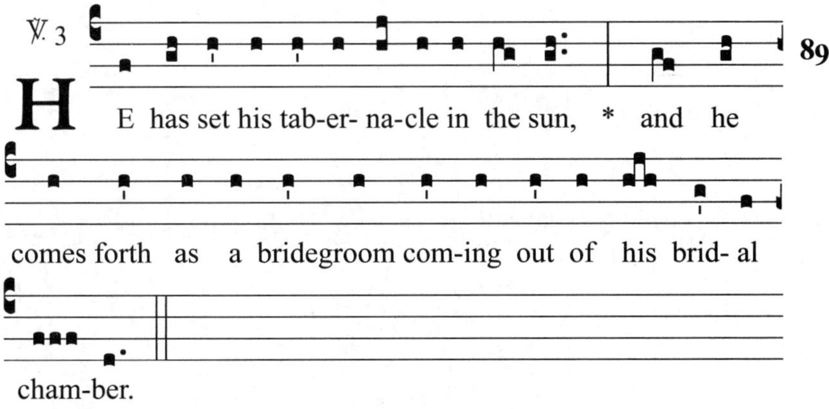
℣. 3
89
HE has set his tab-er- na-cle in the sun, * and he
comes forth as a bridegroom com-ing out of his brid- al
cham-ber.

- iii -

90

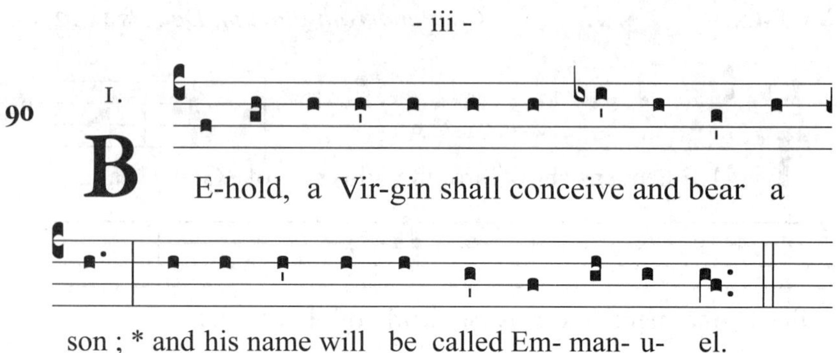
I.
BE-hold, a Vir-gin shall conceive and bear a
son ; * and his name will be called Em- man- u- el.

- iv -

91

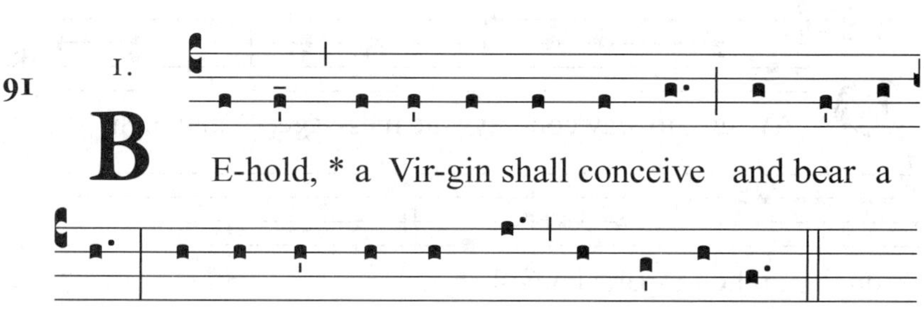
I.
BE-hold, * a Vir-gin shall conceive and bear a
son ; and his name will be called Em-man- u- el.

CHRISTMAS TIME

25 December

THE NATIVITY OF THE LORD [CHRISTMAS]

Solemnity

At the Vigil Mass

ENTRANCE ANTIPHON *Hodie scietis. Cf. Ex* 16 : 6-7

- i -

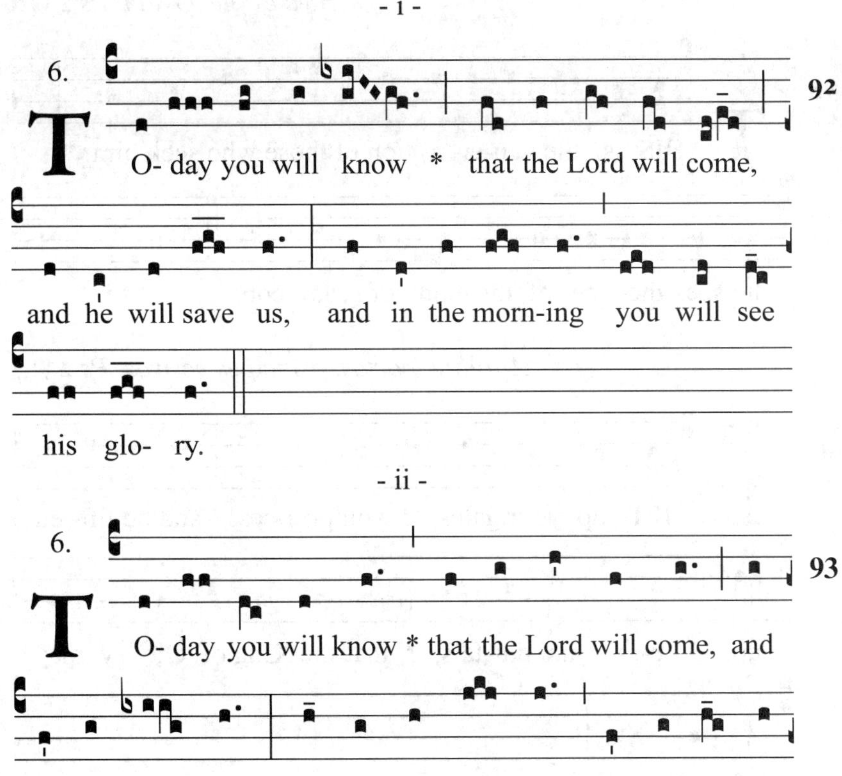
6.
92
TO- day you will know * that the Lord will come,
and he will save us, and in the morn-ing you will see
his glo- ry.
- ii -
6.
93
TO- day you will know * that the Lord will come, and
he will save us, and in the morn-ing you will see his

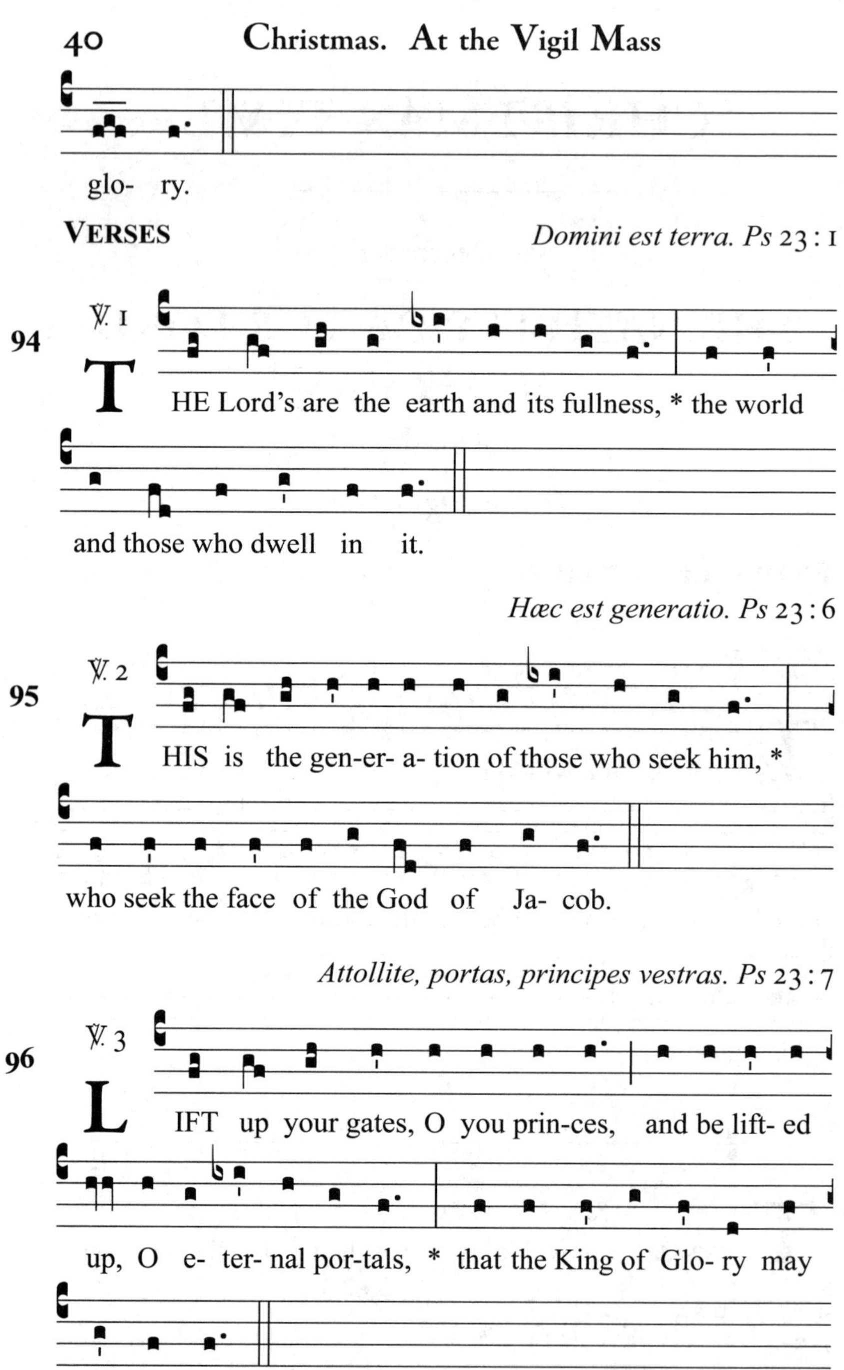
glo- ry.
VERSES
Domini est terra. Ps 23 : 1
℣. 1
94
THE Lord's are the earth and its fullness, * the world
and those who dwell in it.
Hæc est generatio. Ps 23 : 6
℣. 2
95
THIS is the gen-er- a- tion of those who seek him, *
who seek the face of the God of Ja- cob.
Attollite, portas, principes vestras. Ps 23 : 7
℣. 3
96
LIFT up your gates, O you prin-ces, and be lift- ed
up, O e- ter- nal por-tals, * that the King of Glo- ry may
en- ter in.

- iii -

6.
97
TO- day you will know that the Lord will come, and
he will save us, * and in the morn-ing you will see his
glo- ry.
Or :
6.
98
TO- day you will know that the Lord will come, and
he will save us, * and in the morn-ing you will see his
glo- ry.
- iv -
6.
99
TO- day you will know that the Lord will come, * and
he will save us. And in the morn-ing you will see his

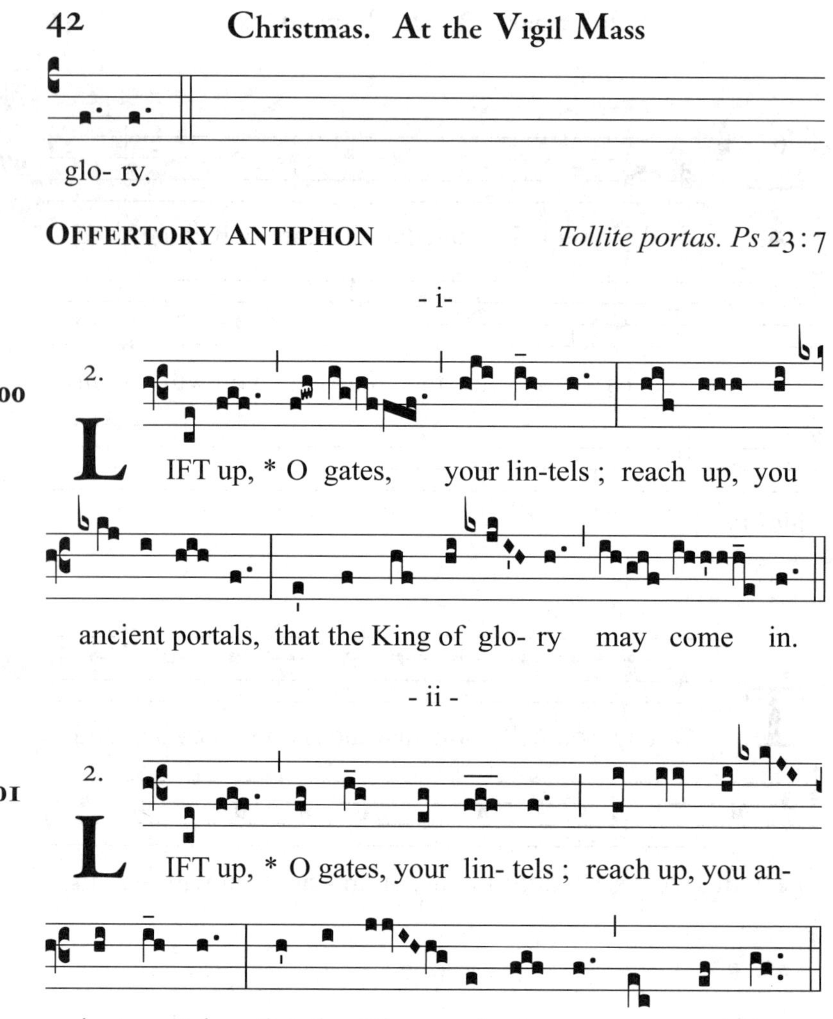
glo- ry.
Offertory Antiphon *Tollite portas. Ps* 23:7
- i-
100
2.
LIFT up, * O gates, your lin-tels ; reach up, you
ancient portals, that the King of glo- ry may come in.
- ii -
101
2.
LIFT up, * O gates, your lin- tels ; reach up, you ancient por-tals, that the King of glo- ry may come in.

VERSES *Domini est terra. Ps* 23 : 1

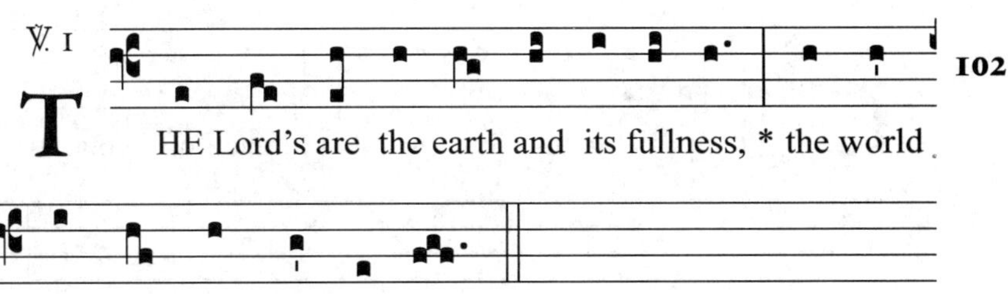

℣. 1 THE Lord's are the earth and its fullness, * the world and those who dwell in it. 102

Quis ascendet in montem Domini. Ps 23 : 3-4

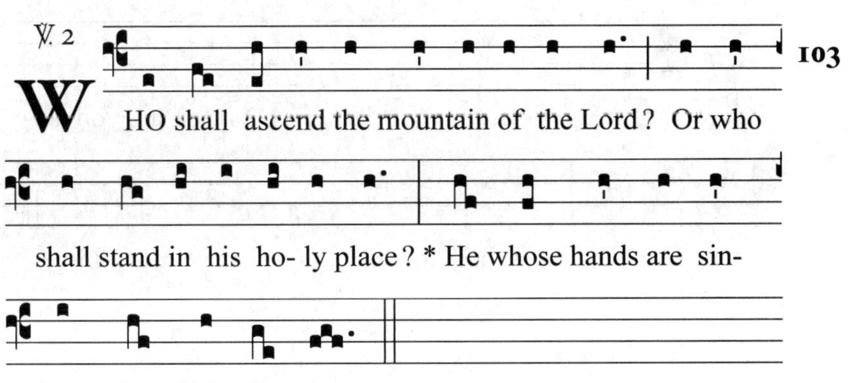

℣. 2 WHO shall ascend the mountain of the Lord? Or who shall stand in his ho- ly place? * He whose hands are sin- less, whose heart is clean. 103

Hæc est generatio. Ps 23 : 6

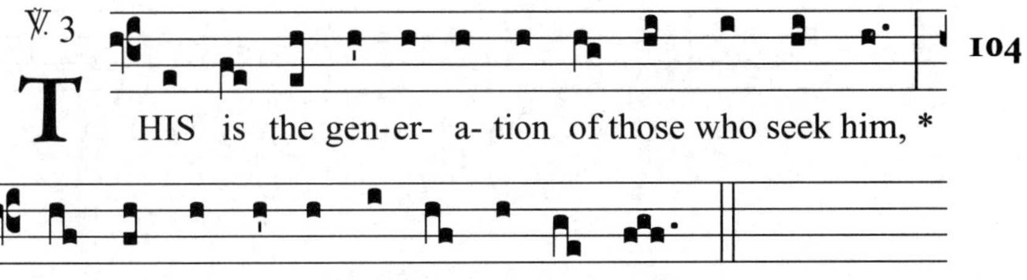

℣. 3 THIS is the gen-er- a- tion of those who seek him, * who seek the face of the God of Ja- cob. 104

- iii -

105

2.
LIFT up, O gates, your lin-tels ; * reach up, you ancient por-tals, that the King of glo- ry may come in.

Or :

106

2.
LIFT up, O gates, your lin- tels ; * reach up, you ancient por-tals, that the King of glo- ry may come in.

- iv -

107

2.
LIFT up, O gates, your lin- tels ; * reach up, you ancient por-tals, that the King of glo- ry may come in.

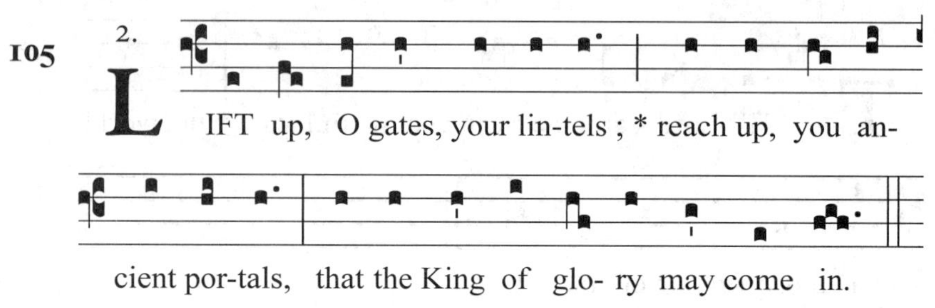

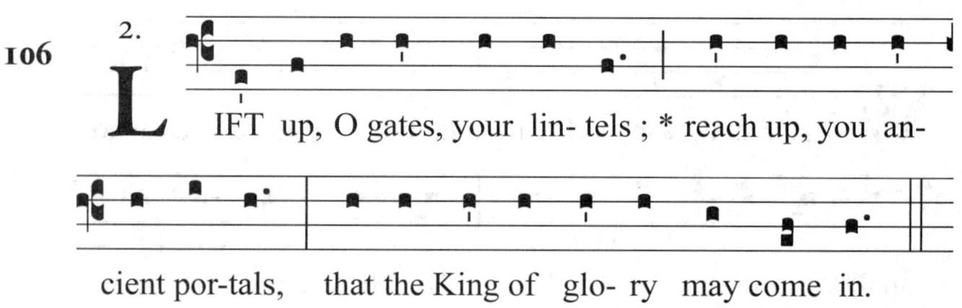

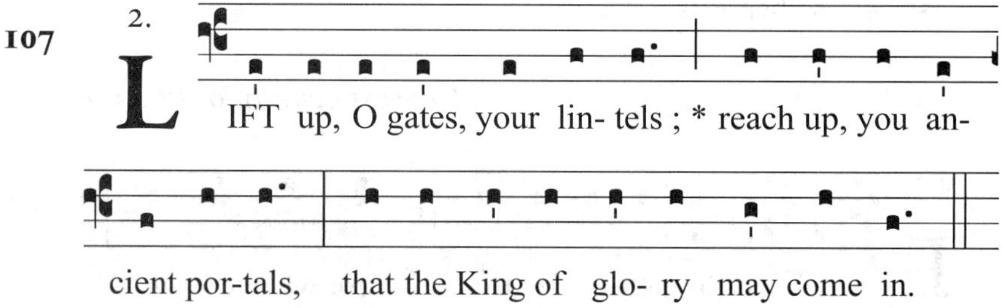

COMMUNION ANTIPHON *Revelabitur gloria. Cf. Is* 40:5

- i -

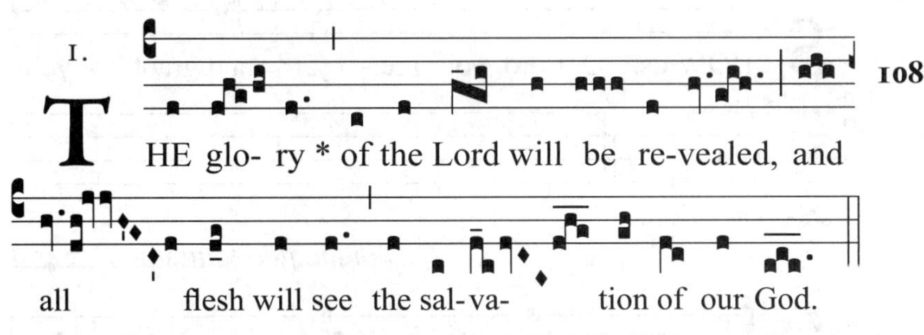
I.
THE glo- ry * of the Lord will be re-vealed, and
108
all flesh will see the sal-va- tion of our God.

- ii -

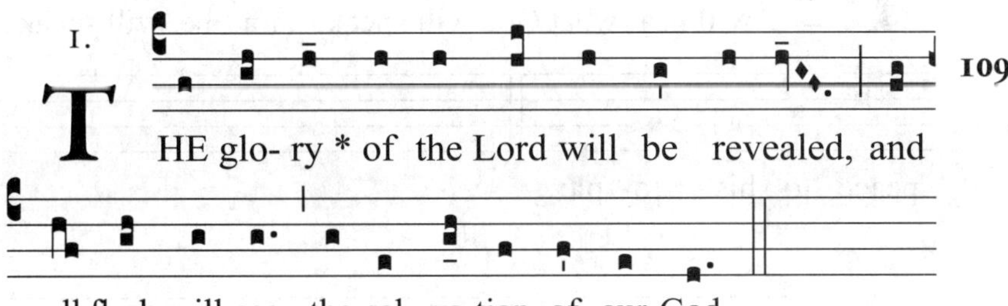
I.
THE glo- ry * of the Lord will be revealed, and
109
all flesh will see the sal- va-tion of our God.

VERSES *Benedixisti, Domine, terram tuam. Ps* 84:2. 3

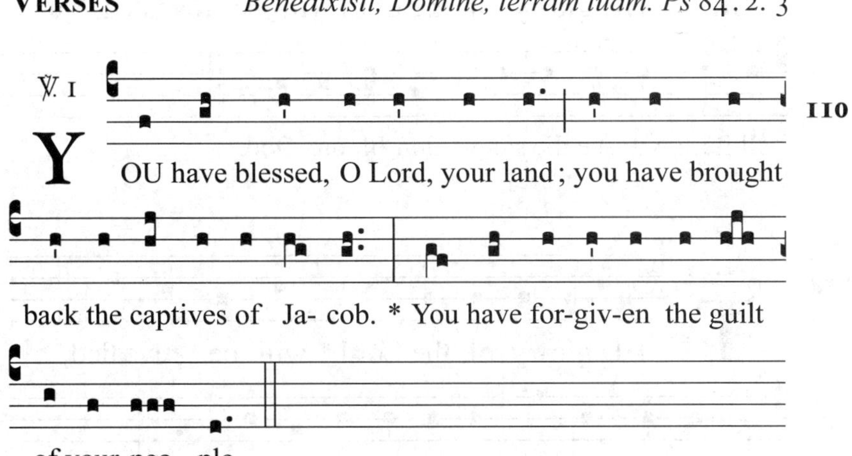
℣. 1
YOU have blessed, O Lord, your land; you have brought
110
back the captives of Ja- cob. * You have for-giv-en the guilt
of your peo- ple.

Ostende nobis, Domine, misericordiam tuam. Ps 84:8

111

℣. 2
SHOW us, O Lord, your mer- cy, * and grant us your
sal- va- tion.

Audiam quid loquatur. Ps 84:9

112

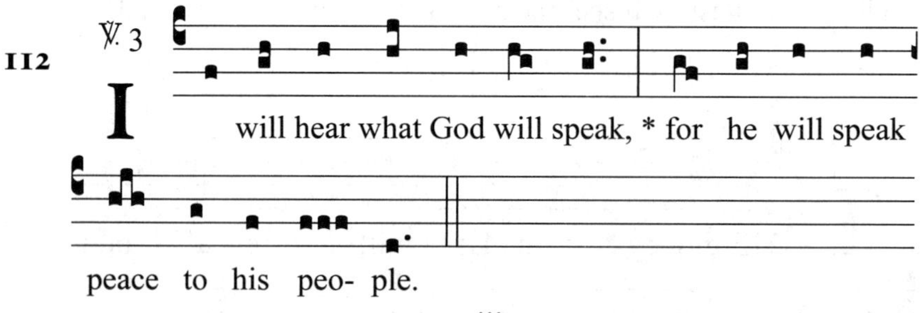
℣. 3
I will hear what God will speak, * for he will speak
peace to his peo- ple.

\- iii -

113

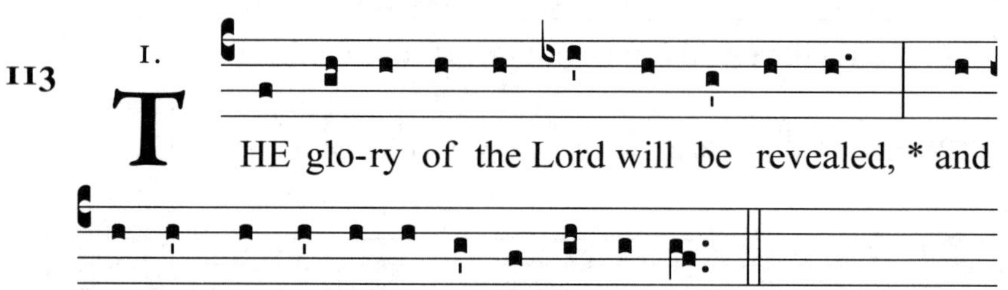
I.
THE glo-ry of the Lord will be revealed, * and
all flesh will see the sal-va-tion of our God.

\- iv -

114

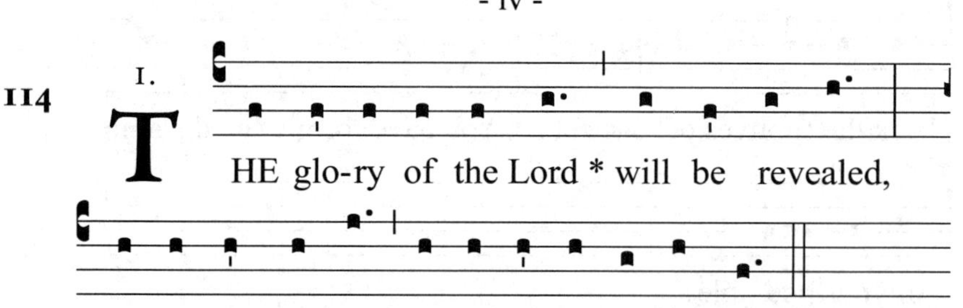
I.
THE glo-ry of the Lord * will be revealed,
and all flesh will see the sal-va-tion of our God.

At the Mass during the Night

Entrance Antiphon *Dominus dixit ad me. Ps* 2:7

- i -

2.
T
HE Lord said to me: * You are my Son. It is
115

I who have be- got- ten you this day.

- ii -

2.
T
HE Lord said to me: * You are my Son. It is
116

I who have be- got- ten you this day.

Verses *Quare fremuerunt gentes. Ps* 2:1

℣. 1
W
HY have the na-tions raged, * and the peo-ple de-
117

vised vain things?

Servite Domino in timore. Ps 2:11-12

118

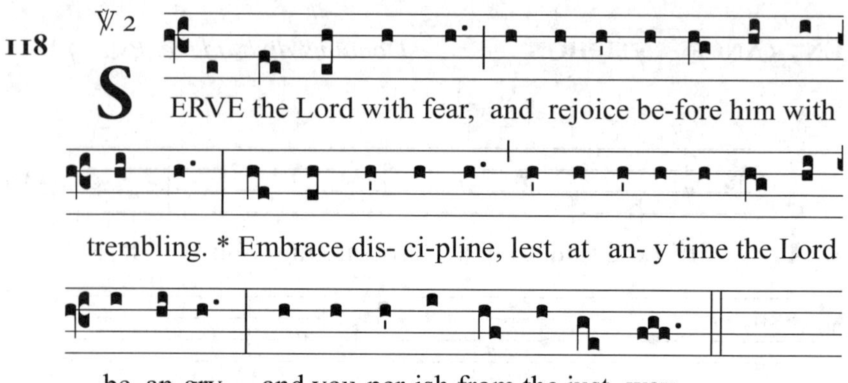
℣. 2
SERVE the Lord with fear, and rejoice be-fore him with
trembling. * Embrace dis- ci-pline, lest at an- y time the Lord
be an-gry, and you per-ish from the just way.

Cum exarserit in brevi ira eius. Ps 2:13

119

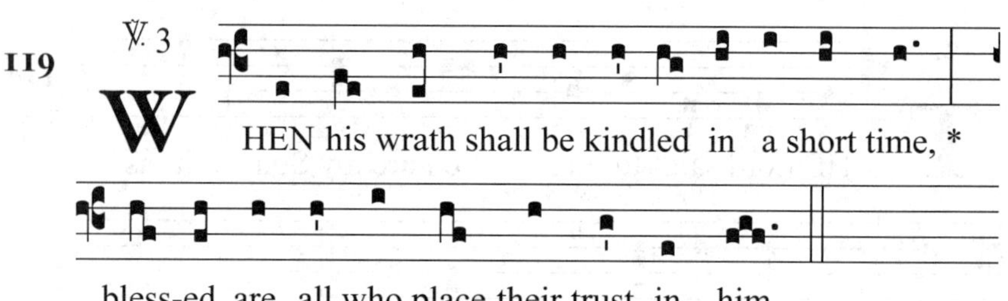
℣. 3
WHEN his wrath shall be kindled in a short time, *
bless-ed are all who place their trust in him.

- iii -

120

2.
THE Lord said to me: * You are my Son. It is
I who have be- got- ten you this day.

- iv -

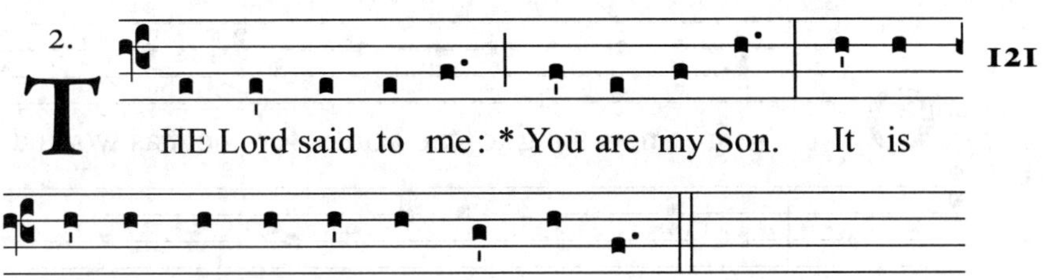
2.
THE Lord said to me: * You are my Son. It is
121
I who have be- got- ten you this day.

Or :

ENTRANCE ANTIPHON *Gaudeamus omnes.*

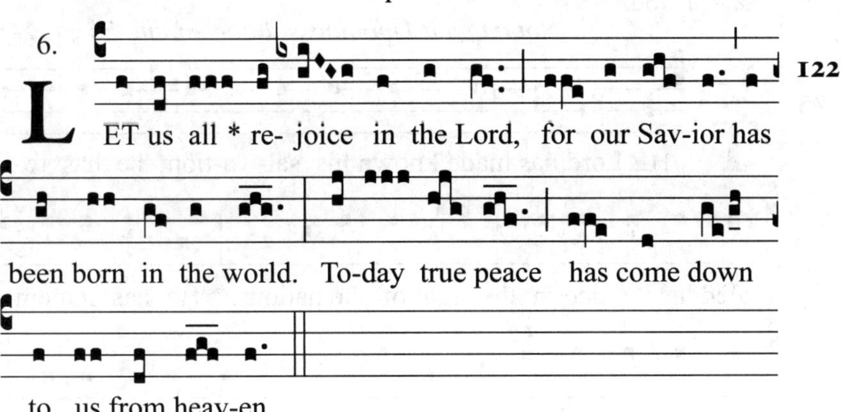
- i -
6.
LET us all * re- joice in the Lord, for our Sav-ior has
122
been born in the world. To-day true peace has come down
to us from heav-en.

- ii -

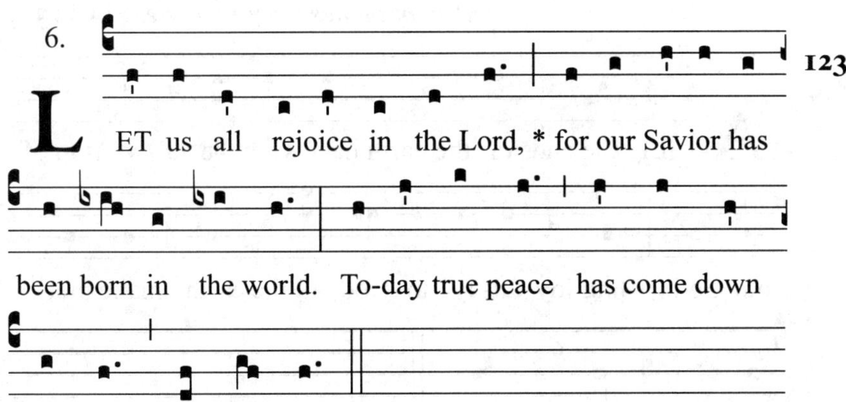
6.
LET us all rejoice in the Lord, * for our Savior has
123
been born in the world. To-day true peace has come down
to us from heav- en.

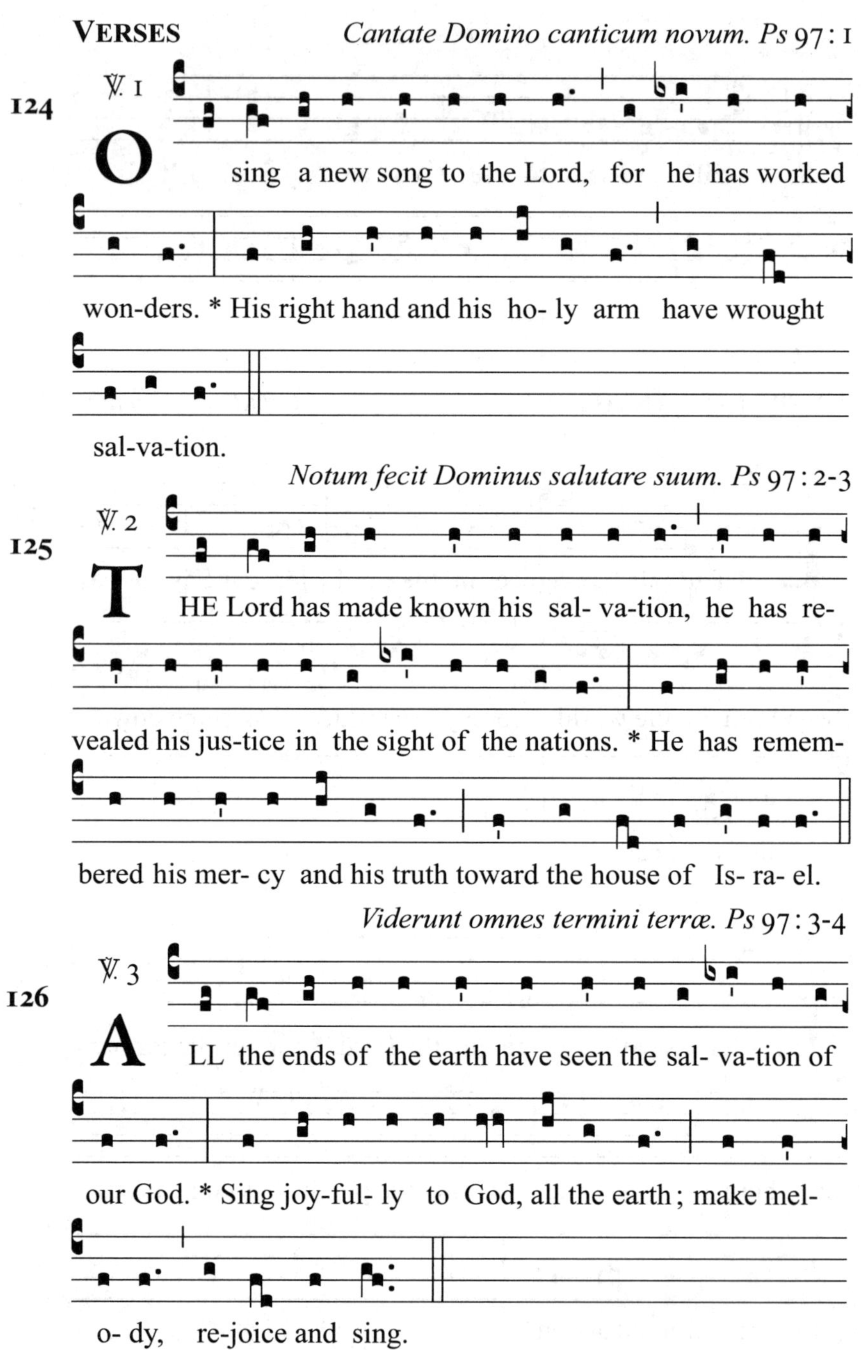
VERSES
Cantate Domino canticum novum. Ps 97 : 1
124
℣. 1
O sing a new song to the Lord, for he has worked
won-ders. * His right hand and his ho- ly arm have wrought
sal-va-tion.
Notum fecit Dominus salutare suum. Ps 97 : 2-3
125
℣. 2
THE Lord has made known his sal- va-tion, he has revealed his jus-tice in the sight of the nations. * He has remembered his mer- cy and his truth toward the house of Is- ra- el.
Viderunt omnes termini terræ. Ps 97 : 3-4
126
℣. 3
ALL the ends of the earth have seen the sal- va-tion of
our God. * Sing joy-ful- ly to God, all the earth; make mel-
o- dy, re-joice and sing.

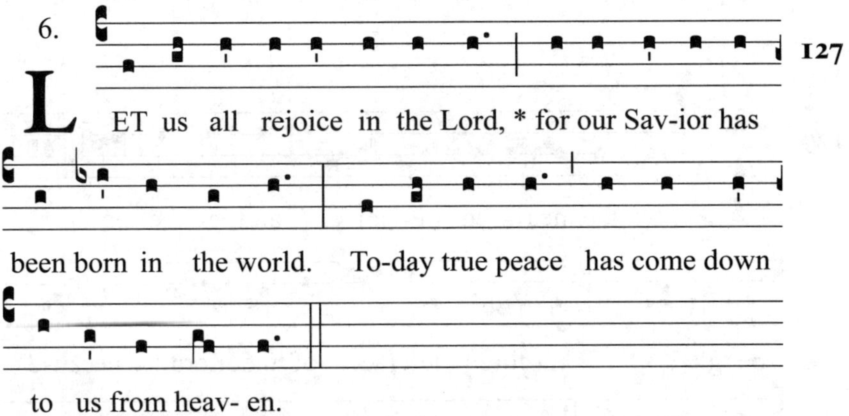

6. 127

LET us all rejoice in the Lord, * for our Sav-ior has been born in the world. To-day true peace has come down to us from heav- en.

- iv -

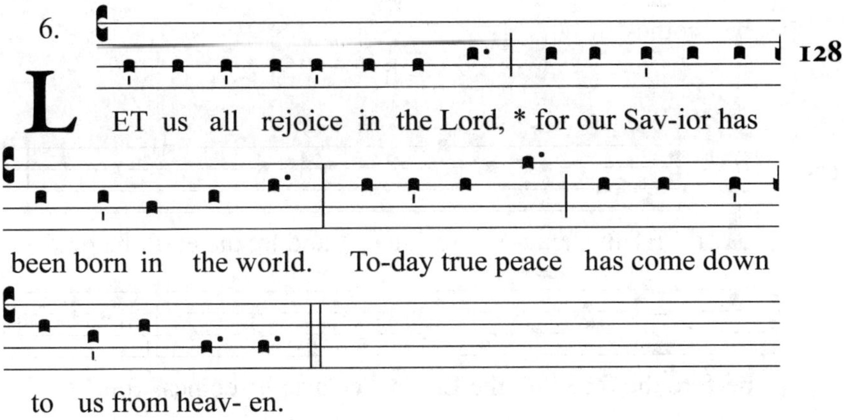

6. 128

LET us all rejoice in the Lord, * for our Sav-ior has been born in the world. To-day true peace has come down to us from heav- en.

OFFERTORY *Lætentur cæli. Ps* 95:11

- i -

129

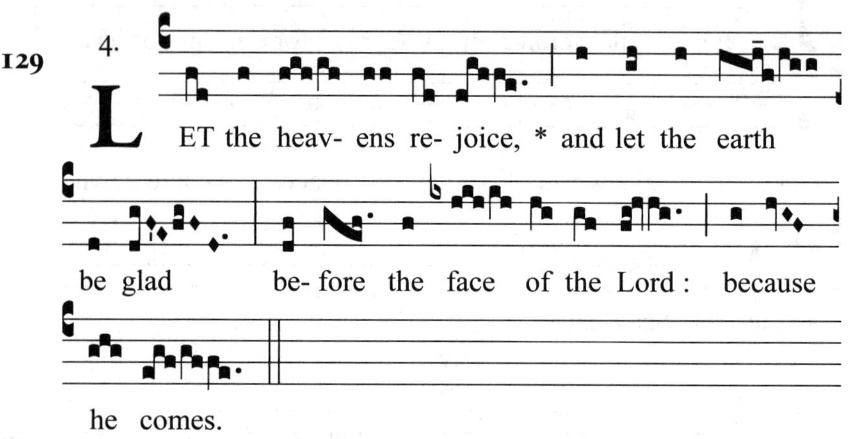
4.
LET the heav- ens re- joice, * and let the earth
be glad be- fore the face of the Lord : because
he comes.

- ii -

130

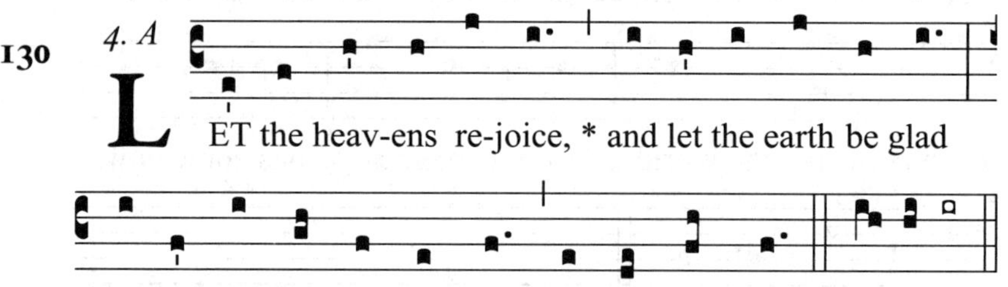
4. A
LET the heav-ens re-joice, * and let the earth be glad
be-fore the face of the Lord : because he comes. Tone 4. A.

When psalm verses are sung with this antiphon using the Gregorian tone on the page opposite, the tone is chanted transposed a fourth above the final, as indicated in the incipit following the antiphon above.

VERSES. *Annuntiate inter gentes. Ps* 95:3

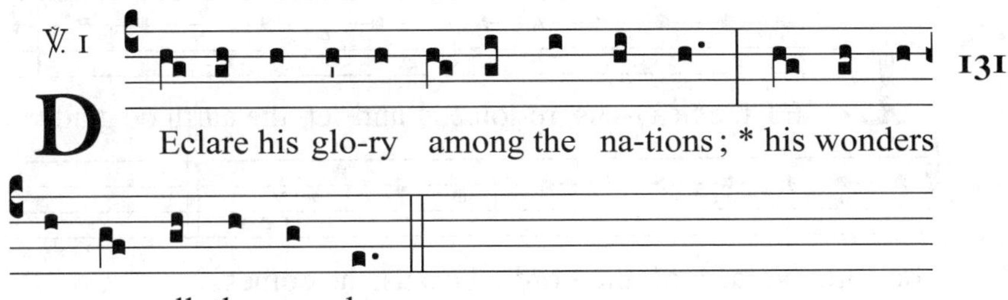
℣. 1
131
DEclare his glo-ry among the na-tions; * his wonders
a-mong all the peo-ples.

Afferte Domino. Ps 95:7

℣. 2
132
BRing to the Lord, you fam- i- lies of the na-tions, *
bring to the Lord glo- ry and hon-or.

Tollite hostias. Ps 95:8-9

℣. 3
133
BRing up sac- ri- fic- es, and come in- to his courts; *
a-dore the Lord in his ho- ly court.

134
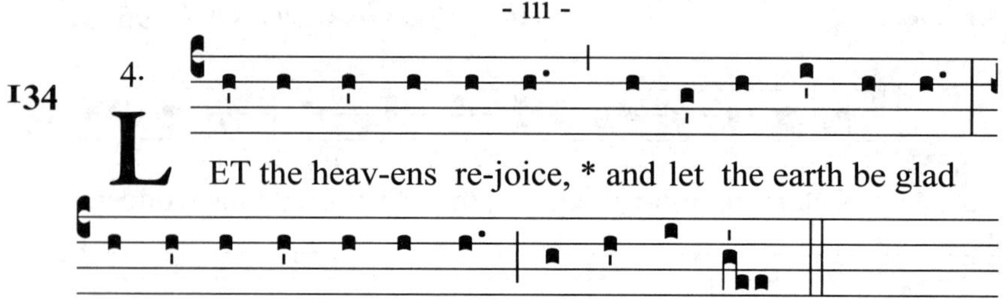
- iii -
4.
LET the heav-ens re-joice, * and let the earth be glad

be-fore the face of the Lord : because he comes.

135
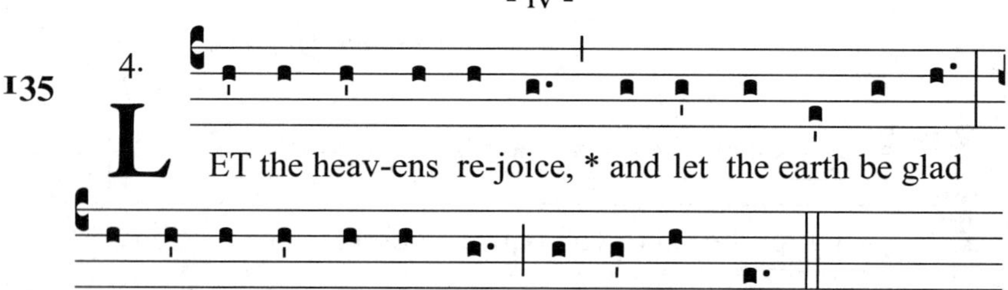
- iv -
4.
LET the heav-ens re-joice, * and let the earth be glad

be-fore the face of the Lord : because he comes.

Communion Antiphon *Verbum caro factum est. Jn* 1 : 14

136
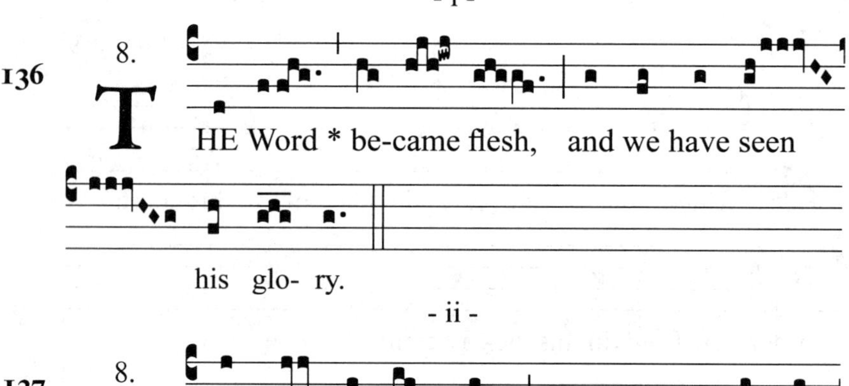
- i -
8.
THE Word * be-came flesh, and we have seen
his glo- ry.

137

- ii -
8.
THE Word became flesh, * and we have seen his
glo- ry.

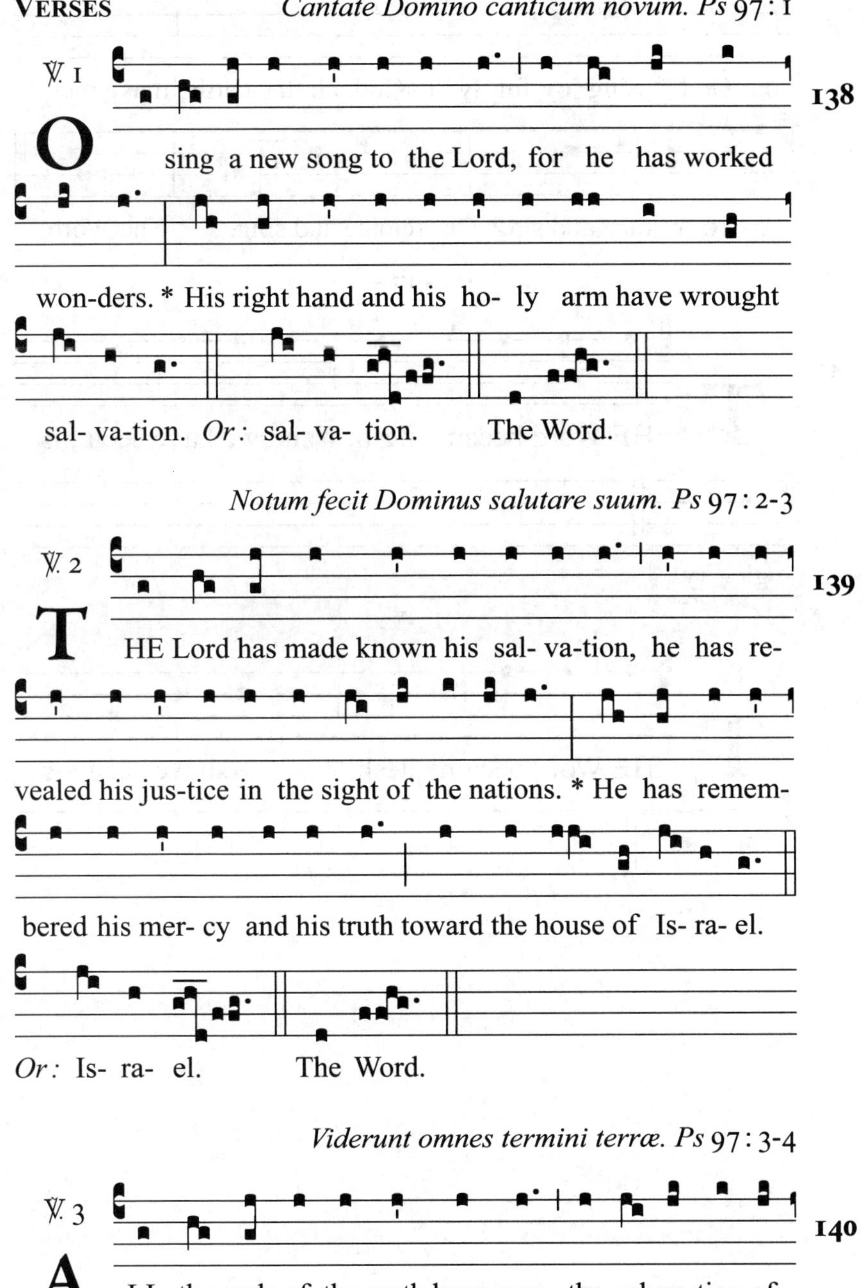
VERSES
Cantate Domino canticum novum. Ps 97 : 1
℣. 1
138
O sing a new song to the Lord, for he has worked
won-ders. * His right hand and his ho- ly arm have wrought
sal- va-tion. Or: sal- va- tion. The Word.
Notum fecit Dominus salutare suum. Ps 97 : 2-3
℣. 2
139
THE Lord has made known his sal- va-tion, he has revealed his jus-tice in the sight of the nations. * He has remembered his mer- cy and his truth toward the house of Is- ra- el.
Or: Is- ra- el. The Word.
Viderunt omnes termini terræ. Ps 97 : 3-4
℣. 3
140
ALL the ends of the earth have seen the sal-va-tion of

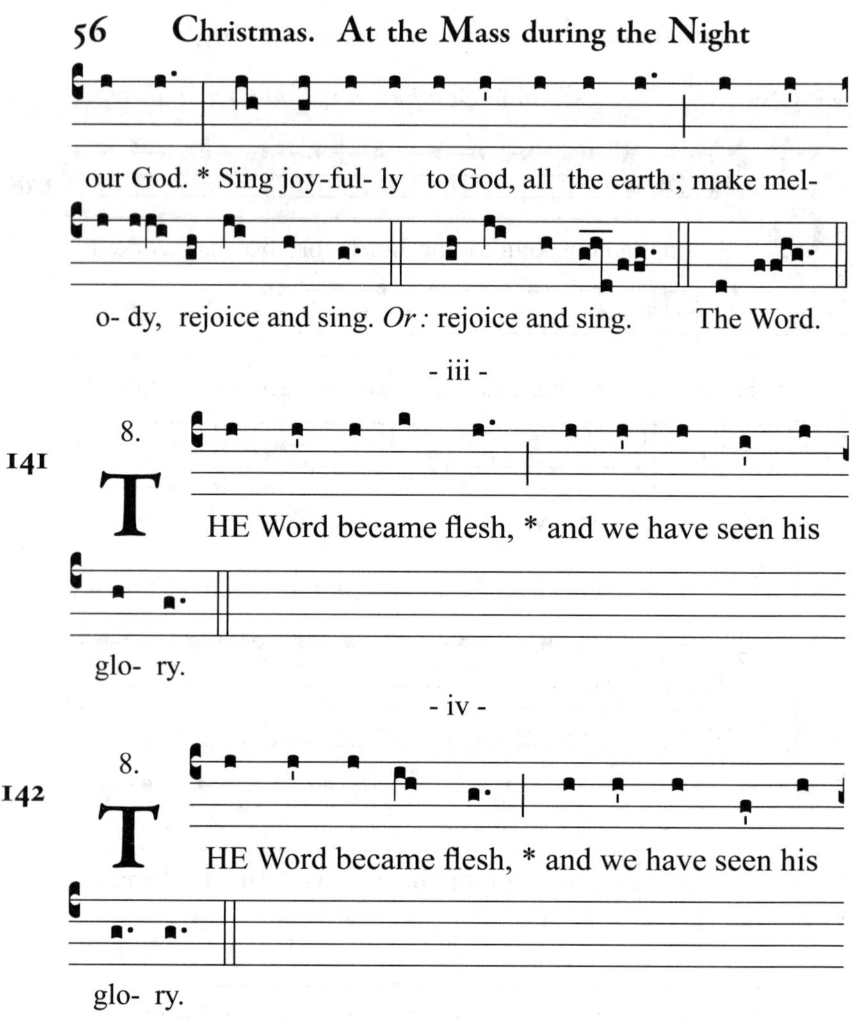
our God. * Sing joy-ful- ly to God, all the earth; make mel-
o- dy, rejoice and sing. *Or:* rejoice and sing. The Word.
- iii -
141
8.
THE Word became flesh, * and we have seen his
glo- ry.
- iv -
142
8.
THE Word became flesh, * and we have seen his
glo- ry.

At the Mass at Dawn

ENTRANCE ANTIPHON *Lux fulgebit.*

Cf. Is 9:1. 5; Lk 1:33

- i -

8.

T O-day * a light will shine up- on us, for the Lord 143

is born for us; and he will be called Won-drous God,

Prince of peace, Father of fu-ture a- ges: and his reign

will be with-out end.

- ii -

8.

T O- day a light will shine up- on us, * for the Lord 144

is born for us; and he will be called Wondrous God,

Prince of peace, Fa-ther of fu-ture a- ges: and his reign

will be with-out end.

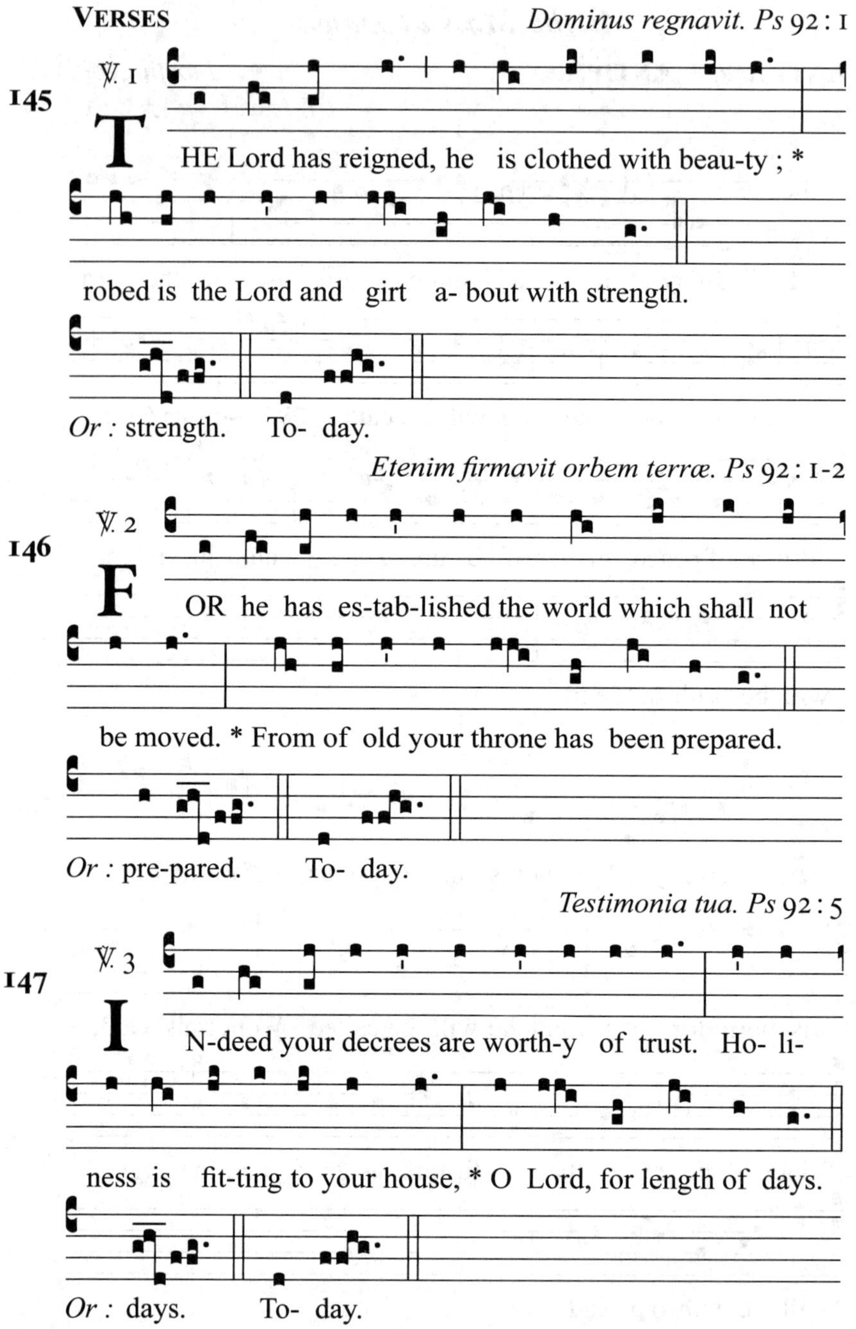
VERSES
Dominus regnavit. Ps 92 : 1
145
℣. 1
THE Lord has reigned, he is clothed with beau-ty ; *
robed is the Lord and girt a- bout with strength.
Or : strength. To- day.
Etenim firmavit orbem terræ. Ps 92 : 1-2
146
℣. 2
FOR he has es-tab-lished the world which shall not
be moved. * From of old your throne has been prepared.
Or : pre-pared. To- day.
Testimonia tua. Ps 92 : 5
147
℣. 3
IN-deed your decrees are worth-y of trust. Ho- li-
ness is fit-ting to your house, * O Lord, for length of days.
Or : days. To- day.

- iii -

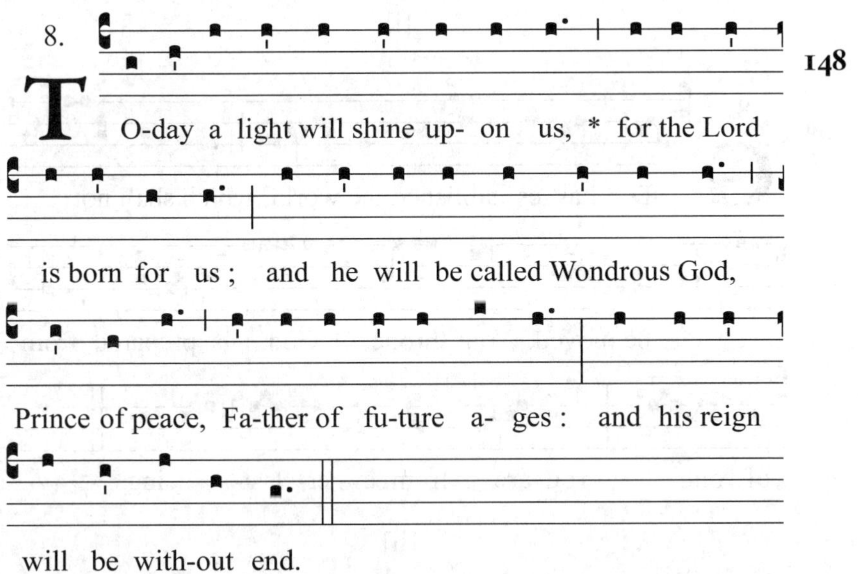
8.
148
TO-day a light will shine up- on us, * for the Lord
is born for us ; and he will be called Wondrous God,
Prince of peace, Fa-ther of fu-ture a- ges : and his reign
will be with-out end.

- iv -

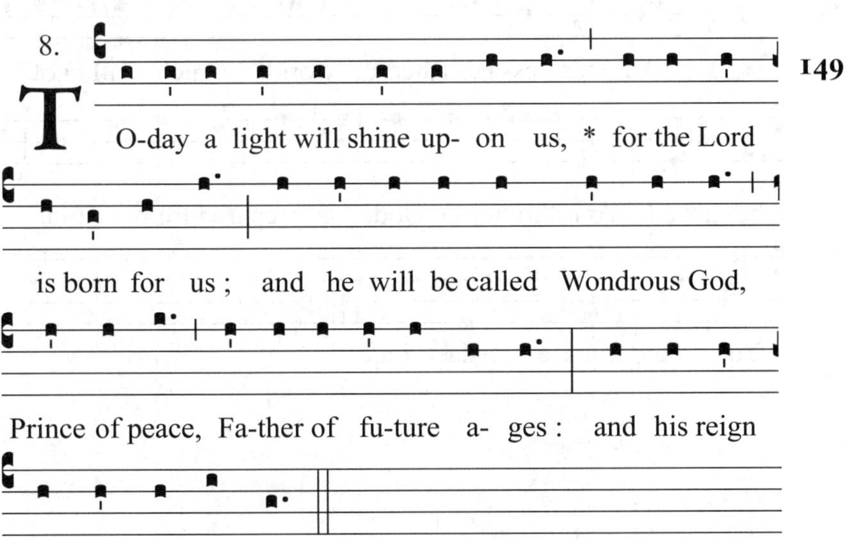
8.
149
TO-day a light will shine up- on us, * for the Lord
is born for us ; and he will be called Wondrous God,
Prince of peace, Fa-ther of fu-ture a- ges : and his reign
will be with-out end.

OFFERTORY *Deus enim firmavit. Ps* 92:1-2

[i]

150

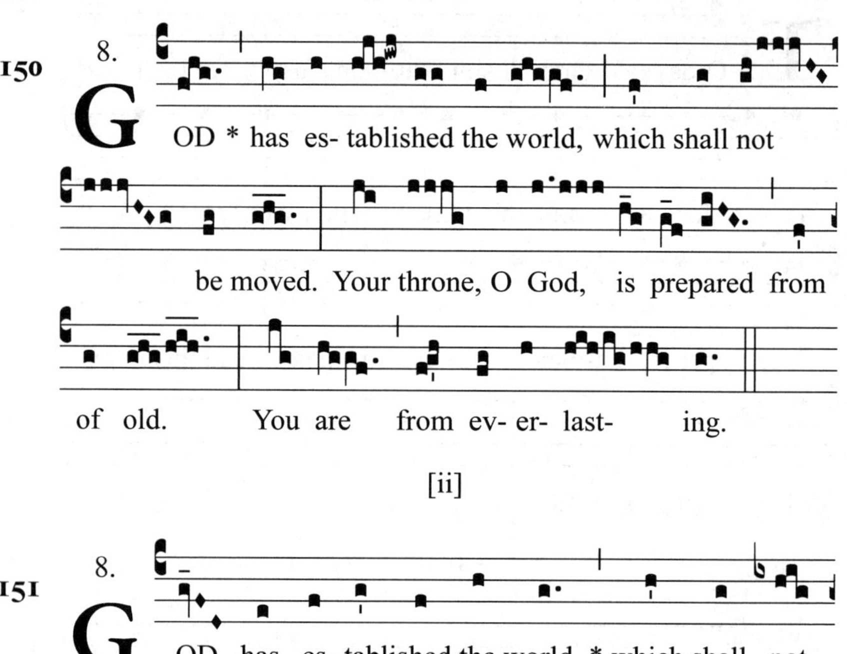
8.
GOD * has es- tablished the world, which shall not
be moved. Your throne, O God, is prepared from
of old. You are from ev- er- last- ing.

[ii]

151

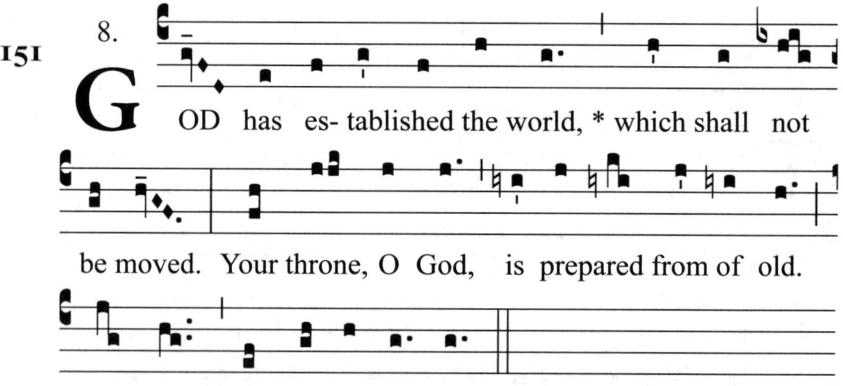
8.
GOD has es- tablished the world, * which shall not
be moved. Your throne, O God, is prepared from of old.
You are from ev- er-last- ing.

VERSES *Dominus regnavit. Ps* 92 : 1

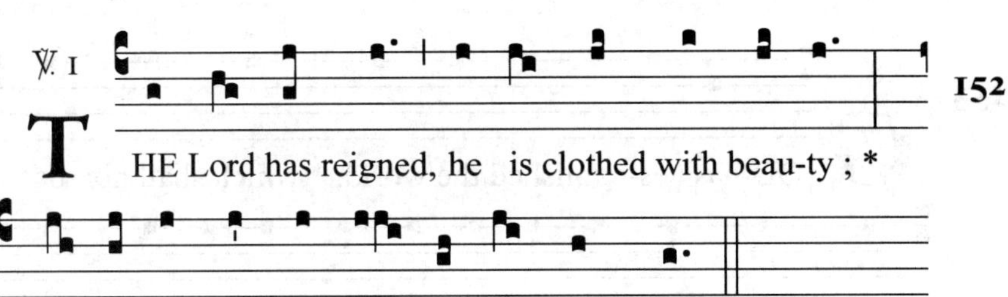

℣. 1
THE Lord has reigned, he is clothed with beau-ty ; *
robed is the Lord and girt a- bout with strength.
152

Etenim firmavit orbem terræ. Ps 92 : 1-2

℣. 2
FOR he has es-tab-lished the world which shall not
be moved. * From of old your throne has been prepared.
153

Testimonia tua. Ps 92 : 5

℣. 3
IN-deed your decrees are worth-y of trust. Ho- li-
ness is fit-ting to your house, * O Lord, for length of days.
154

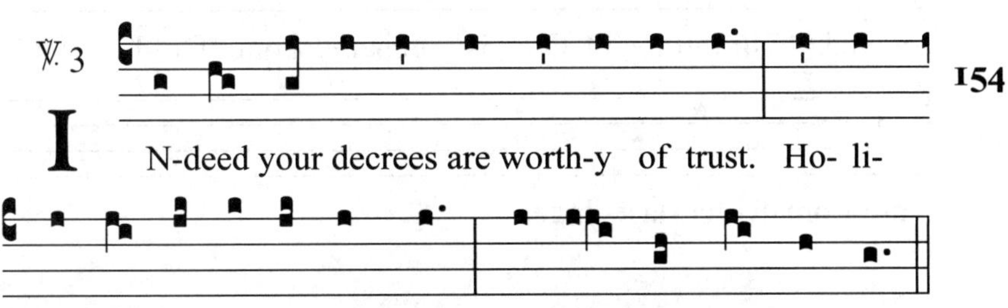

- iii -

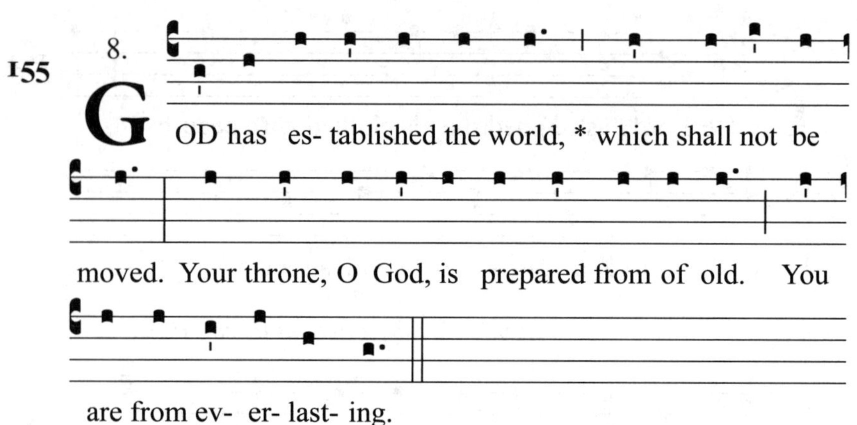
155
8.
GOD has es- tablished the world, * which shall not be
moved. Your throne, O God, is prepared from of old. You
are from ev- er- last- ing.

- iv -

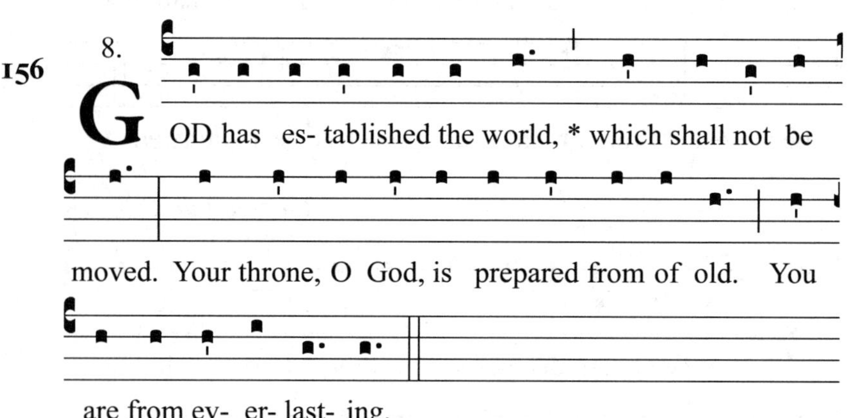
156
8.
GOD has es- tablished the world, * which shall not be
moved. Your throne, O God, is prepared from of old. You
are from ev- er- last- ing.

COMMUNION ANTIPHON *Exsulta, filia Sion. Cf. Zec* 9:9

- i -

4.
R E- joice, * O Daughter Si- on; lift up praise,
Daughter Je- ru- sa- lem: Behold, your King will come,
the Ho- ly One and Sav- ior of the world.

157

- ii -

4.
R E-joice, O Daughter Si- on; * lift up praise,
Daughter Je- ru- sa- lem: Be- hold, your King will come,
the Ho- ly One and Sav- ior of the world.

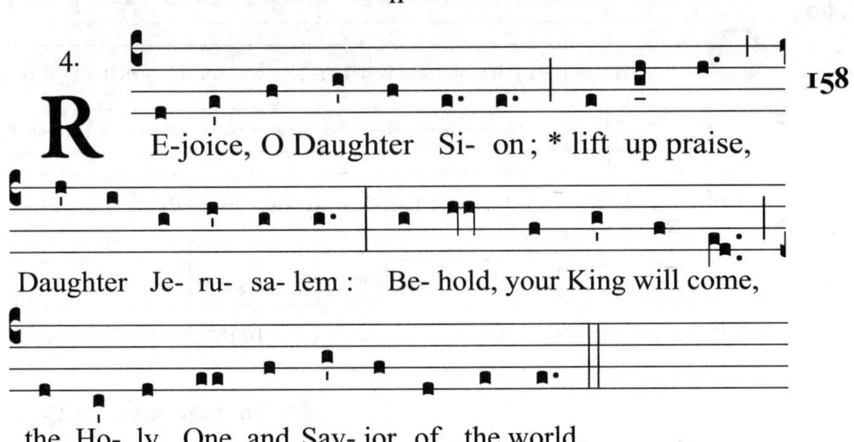

158

VERSES *Benedicam Dominum. Ps* 33:2-3

159

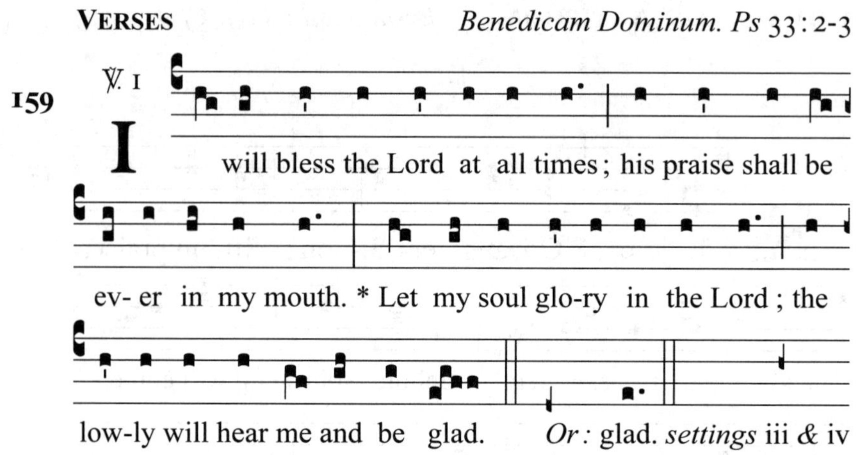
℣. 1
I will bless the Lord at all times; his praise shall be
ev- er in my mouth. * Let my soul glo-ry in the Lord; the
low-ly will hear me and be glad. *Or:* glad. *settings* iii & iv

Magnificate Dominum mecum. Ps 33:4-5

160

℣. 2
O mag-ni- fy the Lord with me, let us to-geth-er ex-
tol his name. * I sought the Lord, and he answered me and
de-liv-ered me from all my fears. *Or:* fears. *settings* iii & iv

Accedite ad eum. Ps 33:6

161

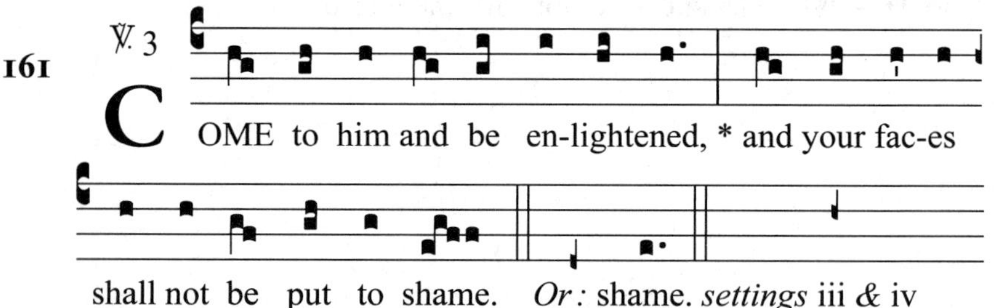
℣. 3
COME to him and be en-lightened, * and your fac-es
shall not be put to shame. *Or:* shame. *settings* iii & iv

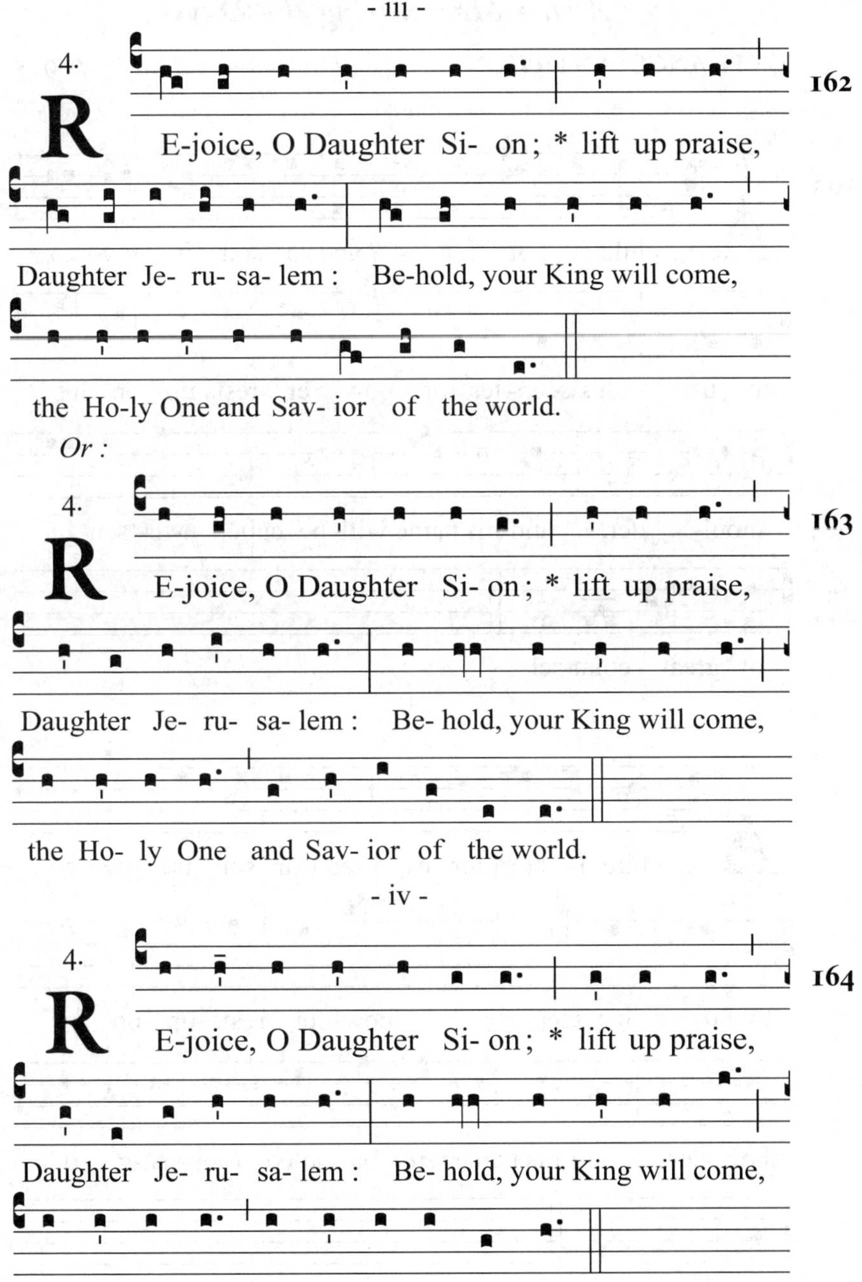
- iii -
4.
162
R E-joice, O Daughter Si- on ; * lift up praise,
Daughter Je- ru- sa- lem : Be-hold, your King will come,
the Ho-ly One and Sav- ior of the world.
Or :
4.
163
R E-joice, O Daughter Si- on ; * lift up praise,
Daughter Je- ru- sa- lem : Be- hold, your King will come,
the Ho- ly One and Sav- ior of the world.
- iv -
4.
164
R E-joice, O Daughter Si- on ; * lift up praise,
Daughter Je- ru- sa- lem : Be- hold, your King will come,
the Ho- ly One and Sav- ior of the world.

At the Mass during the Day

Entrance Antiphon *Puer natus est nobis. Is* 9:5

- i -

165

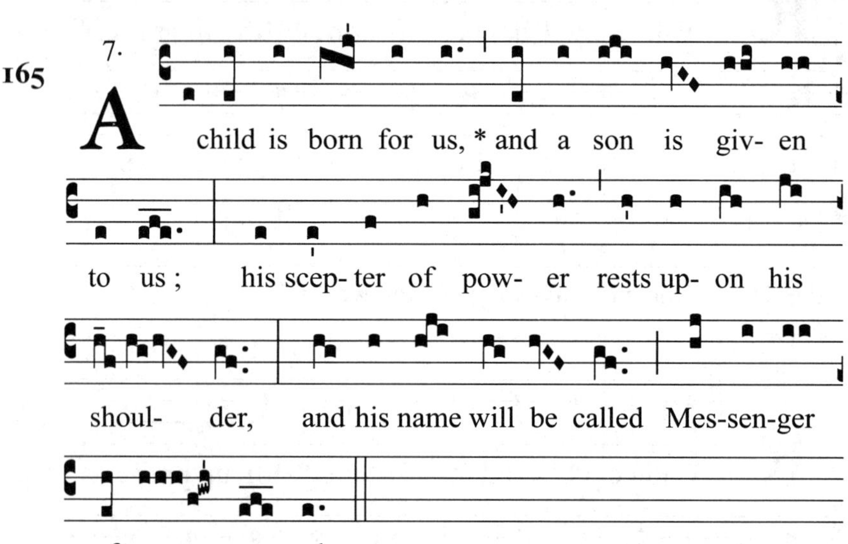
7.
A child is born for us, * and a son is giv- en
to us ; his scep- ter of pow- er rests up- on his
shoul- der, and his name will be called Mes-sen-ger
of great coun-sel.

- ii -

166

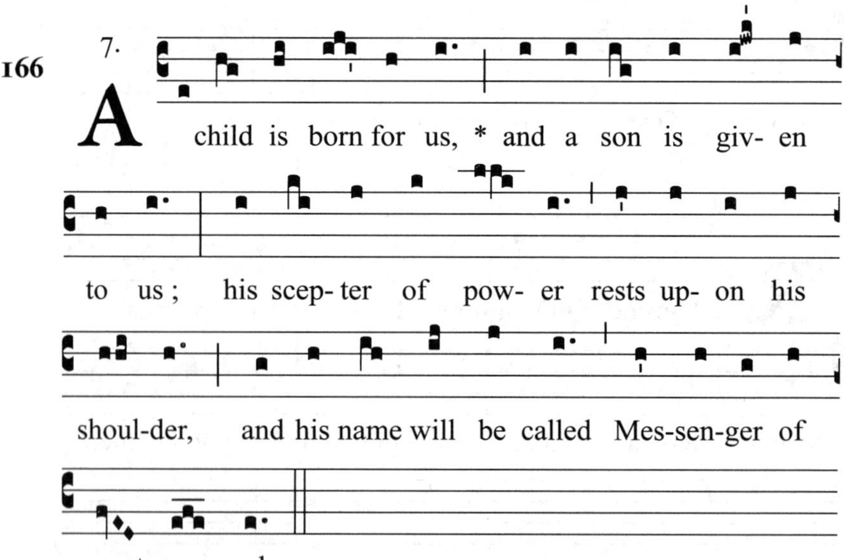
7.
A child is born for us, * and a son is giv- en
to us ; his scep- ter of pow- er rests up- on his
shoul-der, and his name will be called Mes-sen-ger of
great coun- sel.

VERSES *Cantate Domino canticum novum. Ps* 97 : 1

℣. 1
167
O sing a new song to the Lord, for he has worked
won-ders. * His right hand and his ho- ly arm have wrought
sal- va- tion.
Notum fecit Dominus salutare suum. Ps 97 : 2-3
℣. 2
168
THE Lord has made known his sal- va-tion, he has revealed his justice in the sight of the nations. * He has remembered his mer-cy and his truth toward the house of Is- ra- el.
Viderunt omnes termini terræ. Ps 97 : 3-4
℣. 3
169
ALL the ends of the earth have seen the sal-va-tion of
our God. * Sing joy-ful- ly to God, all the earth; make mel-
o- dy, re-joice and sing.

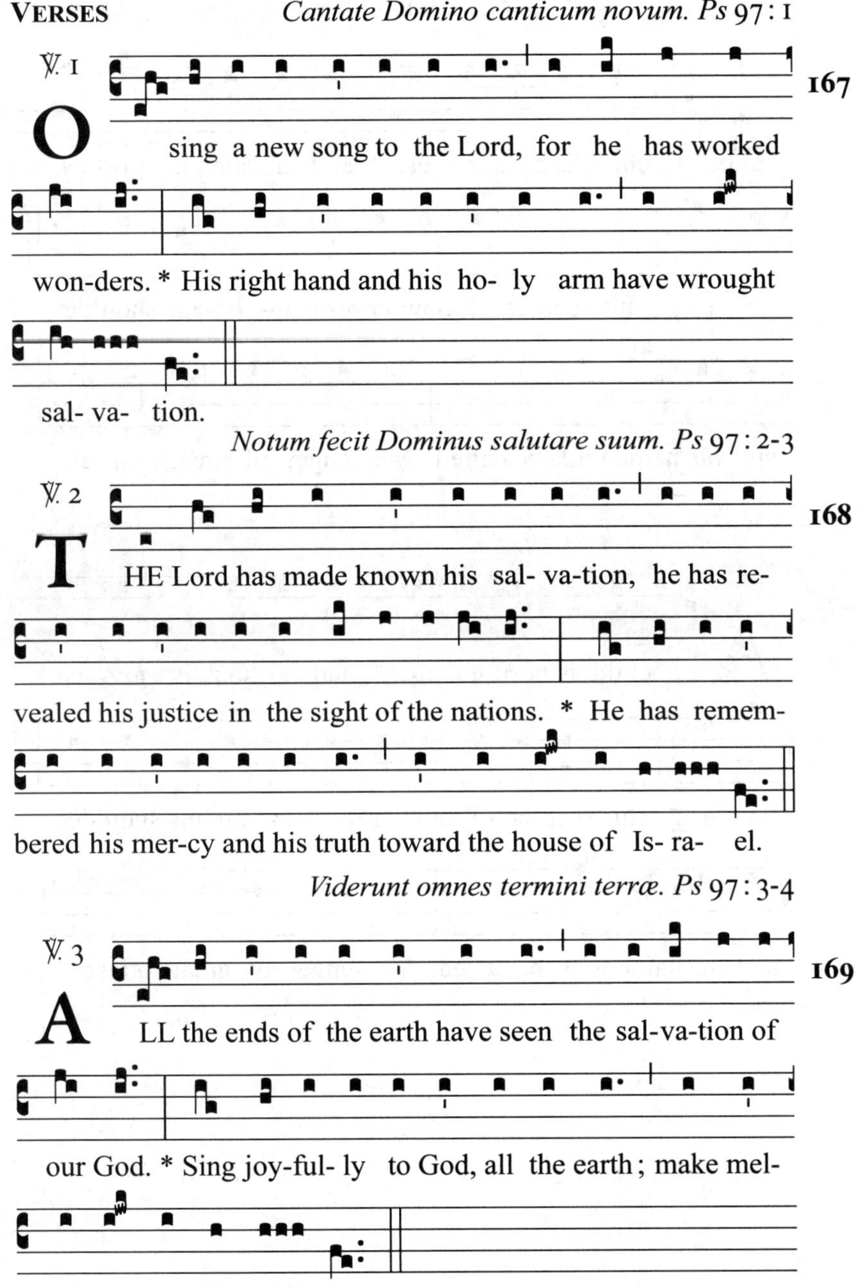

- iii -

170

7.
A child is born for us, * and a son is giv- en
to us ; his scepter of pow-er rests up- on his shoulder,
and his name will be called Messenger of great counsel.

- iv -

171

7.
A child is born for us, * and a son is giv- en
to us ; his scepter of pow-er rests up- on his shoulder,
and his name will be called Messenger of great counsel.

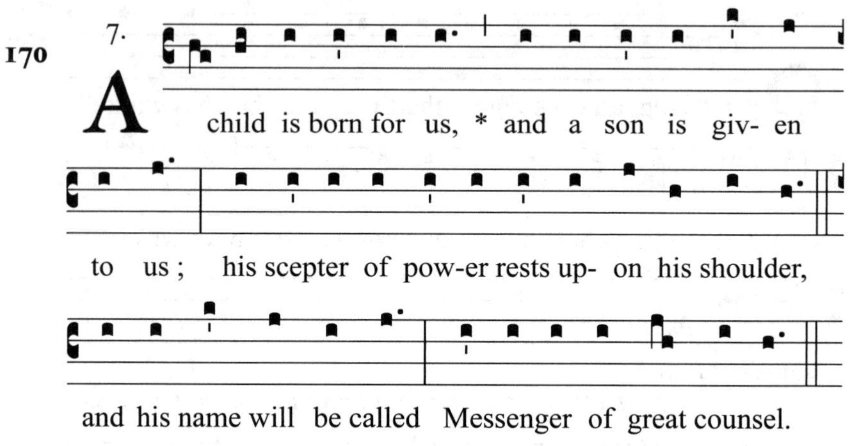

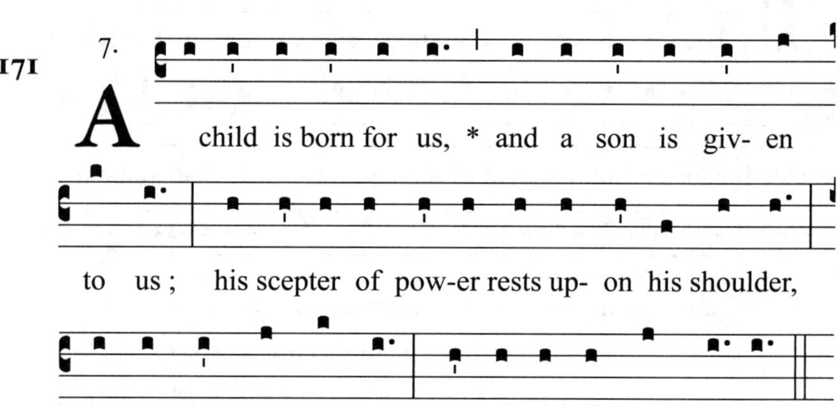

OFFERTORY *Tui sunt cæli. Ps* 88 : 12. 15a

- i -

4.
172
YOurs are * the heav- ens, and yours is the earth,
the world and the ful-ness there- of you have found- ed :
jus- tice and judg- ment are the foun- da- tion
of your throne.

- ii -

4.
173
YOurs are the heav-ens, * and yours is the earth, the
world and the fulness there-of you have found-ed : jus-tice
and judg-ment are the foun-da-tion of your throne.

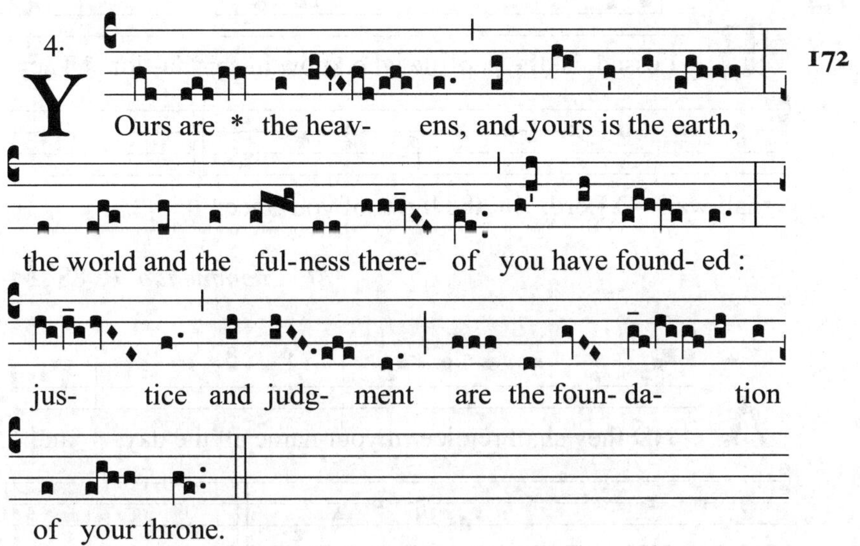

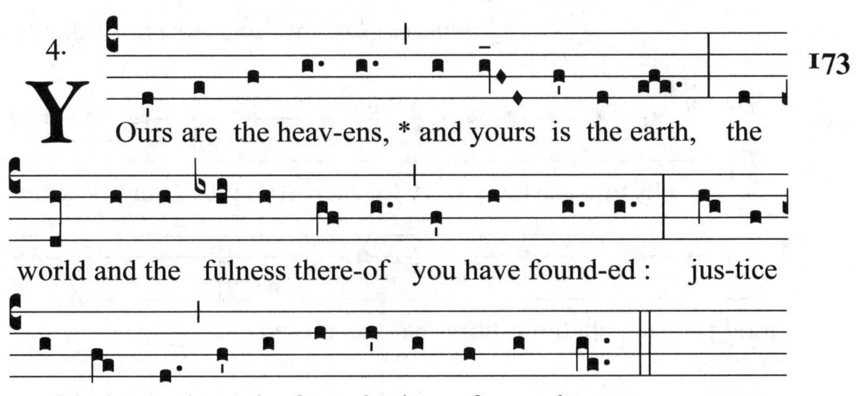

VERSES *Beatus populus. Ps* 88 : 16

174

℣. 1
BLessed is the peo-ple who know ju- bi- la-tion. * They
shall walk O Lord, in the light of your face.

Et in nomine tuo. Ps 88 : 17

175

℣. 2
AND they shall rejoice in your name all the day, * and
in your jus-tice they shall be ex-alt-ed.

Quoniam gloria virtutis eorum. Ps 88 : 18

176

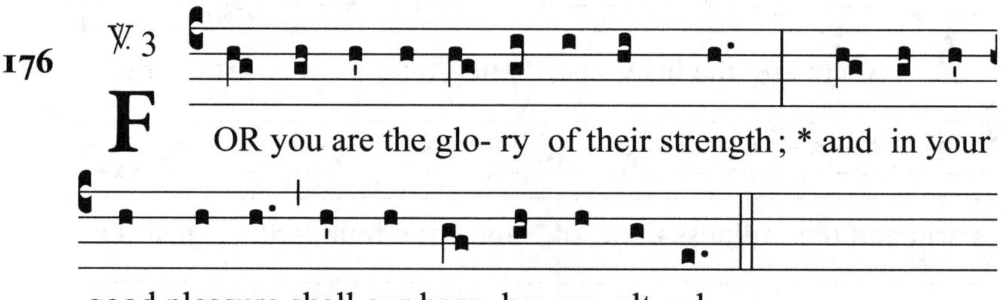
℣. 3
FOR you are the glo- ry of their strength ; * and in your
good pleasure shall our horn be ex- alt- ed.

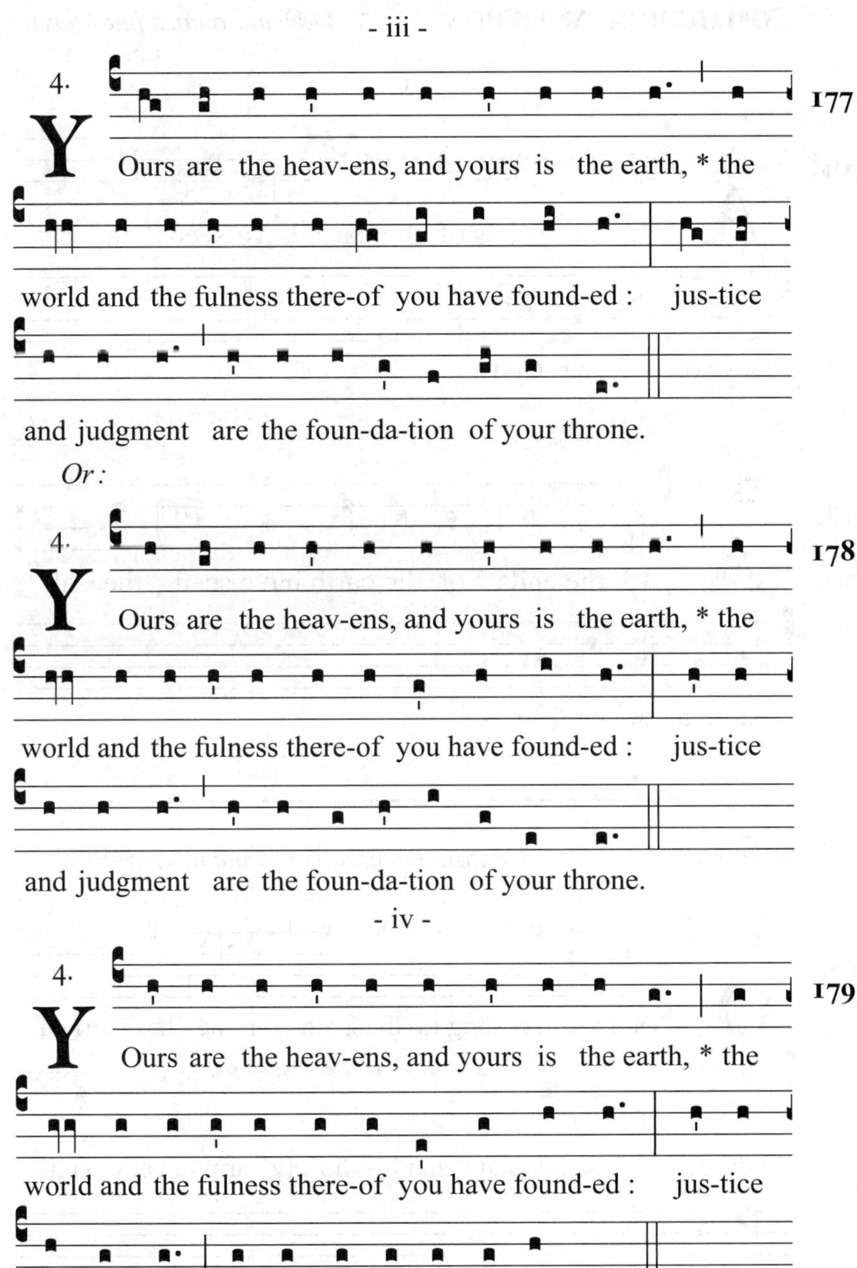
- iii -
4.
177
Yours are the heav-ens, and yours is the earth, * the
world and the fulness there-of you have found-ed : jus-tice
and judgment are the foun-da-tion of your throne.
Or:
4.
178
Yours are the heav-ens, and yours is the earth, * the
world and the fulness there-of you have found-ed : jus-tice
and judgment are the foun-da-tion of your throne.
- iv -
4.
179
Yours are the heav-ens, and yours is the earth, * the
world and the fulness there-of you have found-ed : jus-tice
and judgment are the foun-da-tion of your throne.

COMMUNION ANTIPHON *Viderunt omnes fines terræ.*
Cf. Ps 97:3

- i -

180

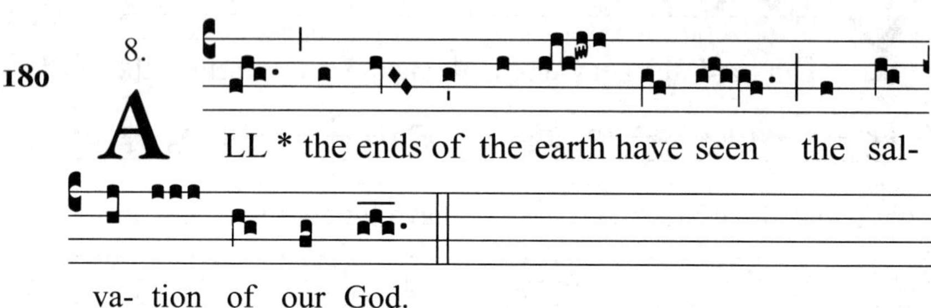
8.
A
LL * the ends of the earth have seen the sal-
va- tion of our God.

- ii -

181

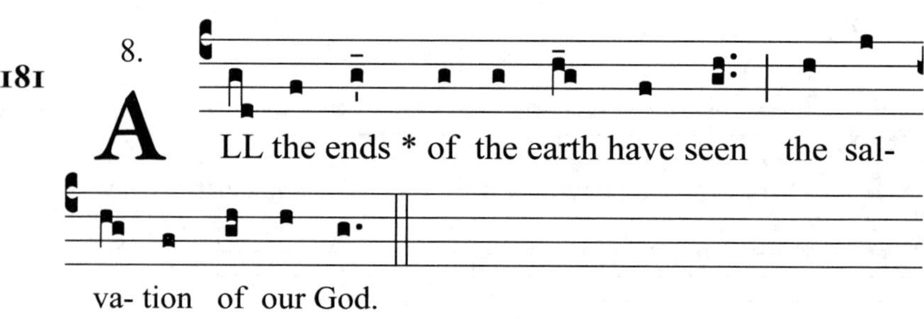
8.
A
LL the ends * of the earth have seen the sal-
va- tion of our God.

VERSES *Cantate Domino canticum novum. Ps* 97:1

182

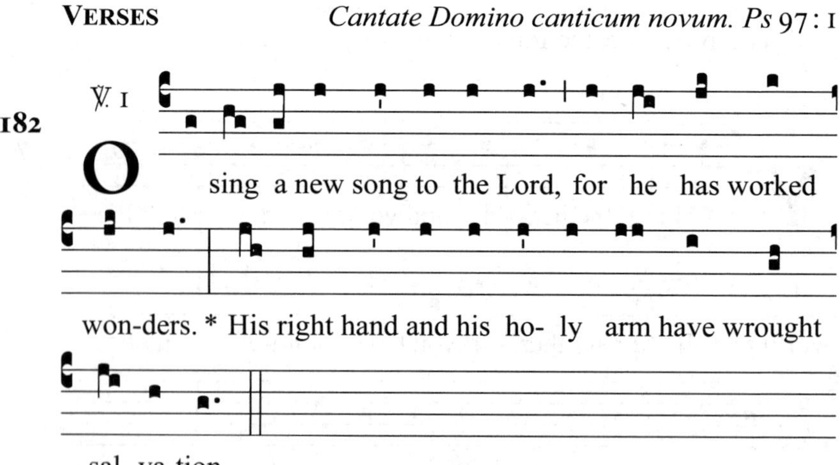
℣. 1
O
sing a new song to the Lord, for he has worked
won-ders. * His right hand and his ho- ly arm have wrought
sal- va-tion.

Notum fecit Dominus salutare suum. Ps 97 : 2-3

℣. 2
183
THE Lord has made known his sal- va-tion, he has revealed his jus-tice in the sight of the nations. * He has remembered his mer- cy and his truth toward the house of Is- ra- el.

Viderunt omnes termini terræ. Ps 97 : 3-4

℣. 3
184
ALL the ends of the earth have seen the sal-va-tion of
our God. * Sing joy-ful- ly to God, all the earth ; make mel-
o- dy, re-joice and sing.

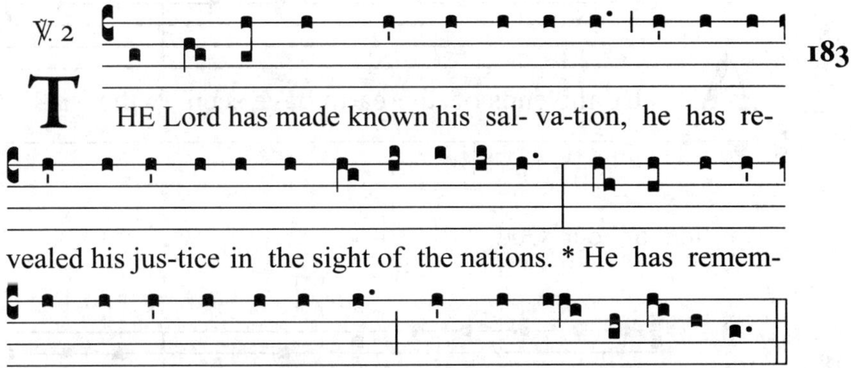

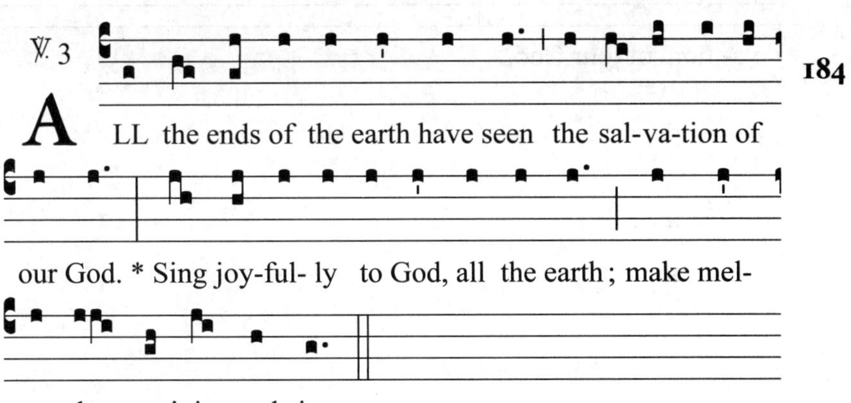

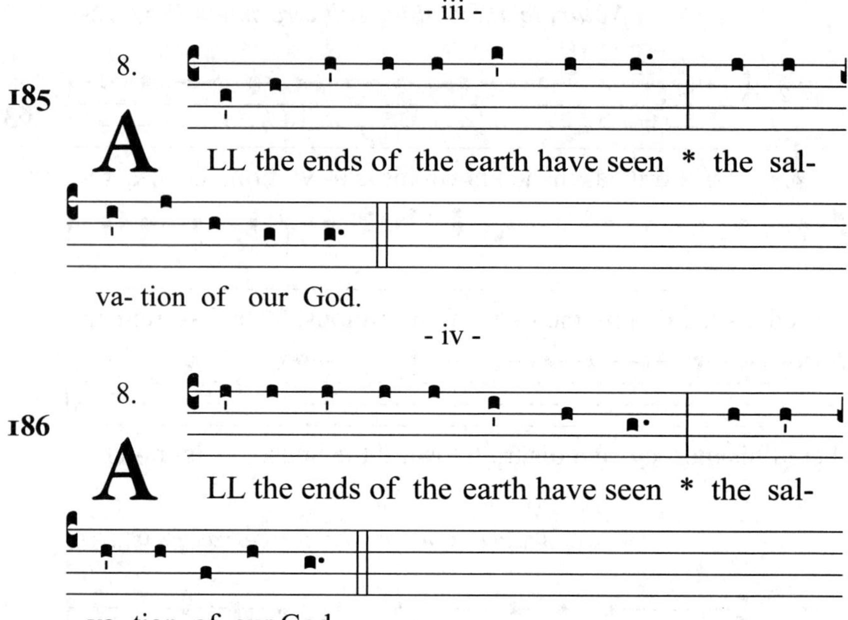
- iii -
185
8.
ALL the ends of the earth have seen * the sal-
va- tion of our God.
- iv -
186
8.
ALL the ends of the earth have seen * the sal-
va- tion of our God.

The Sunday within the Octave of the Nativity of the Lord [Christmas], or, if there is no Sunday, December 30.

THE HOLY FAMILY OF JESUS, MARY AND JOSEPH

Feast

ENTRANCE ANTIPHON *Venerunt pastores festinantes.* *Lk* 2:16

- i -

8.
THE shepherds * went in haste, and found Mar- y and
Jo-seph and the In- fant ly- ing in a man-ger.
187

- ii -

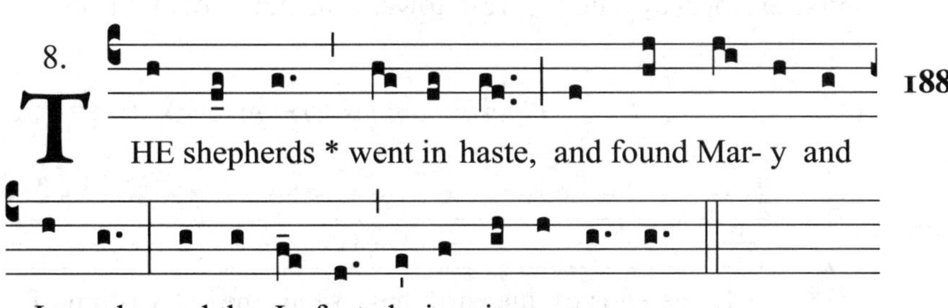
8.
THE shepherds * went in haste, and found Mar- y and
Jo-seph and the In-fant ly-ing in a man-ger.
188

VERSES *Cantate Domino canticum novum. Ps* 97:1

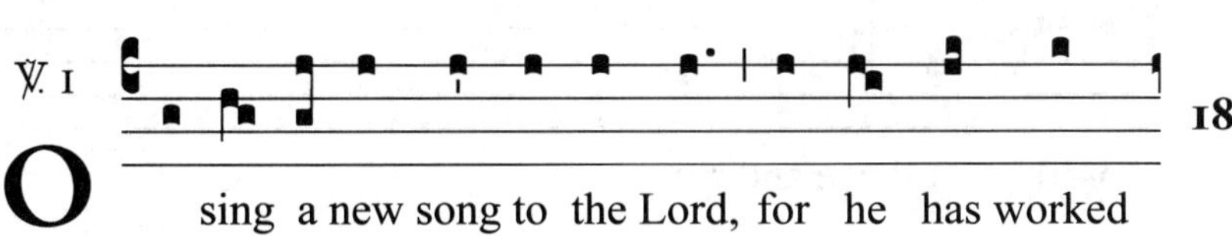
℣. 1
O sing a new song to the Lord, for he has worked
189

won-ders. * His right hand and his ho- ly arm have wrought
sal- va-tion.

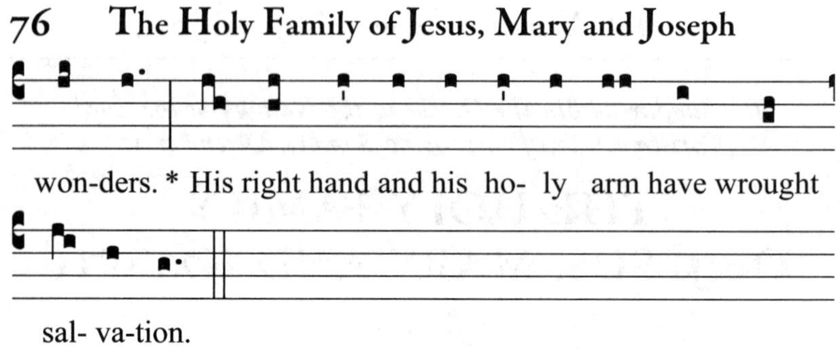

Notum fecit Dominus salutare suum. Ps 97 : 2-3

190

℣. 2
THE Lord has made known his sal- va-tion, he has revealed his jus-tice in the sight of the nations. * He has remembered his mer- cy and his truth toward the house of Is- ra- el.

Viderunt omnes termini terræ. Ps 97 : 3-4

191

℣. 3
ALL the ends of the earth have seen the sal-va-tion of
our God. * Sing joy-ful- ly to God, all the earth; make mel-
o- dy, re-joice and sing.

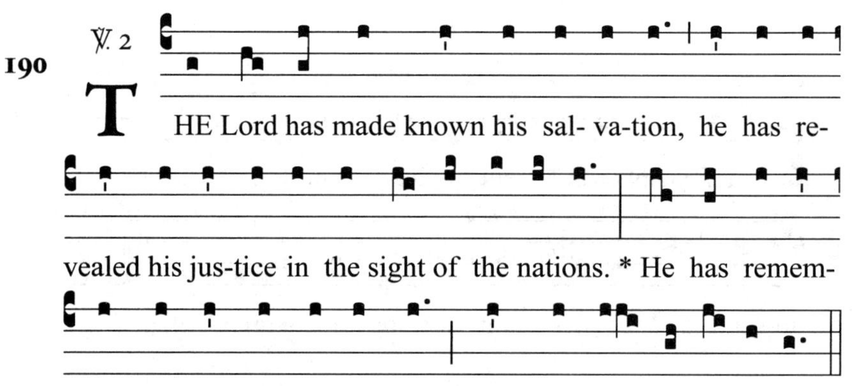

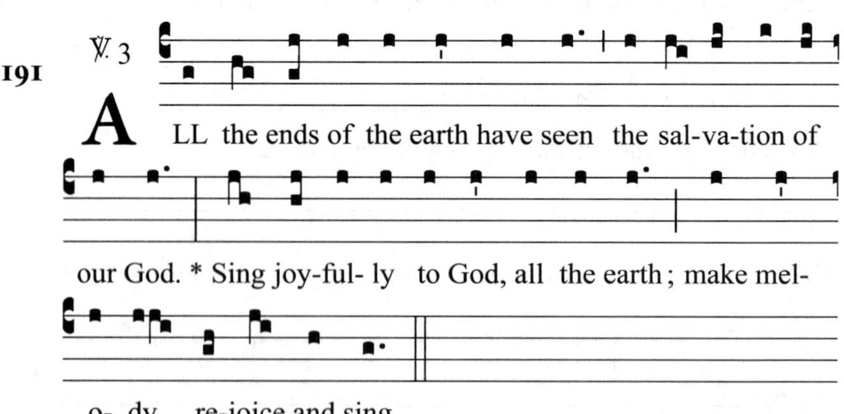

- iii -

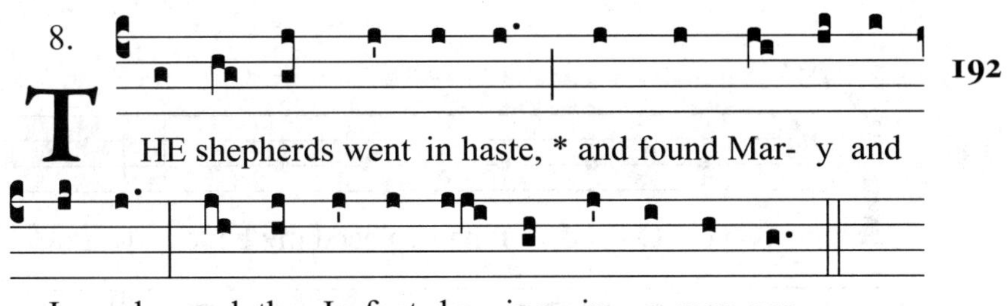
8.
192
THE shepherds went in haste, * and found Mar- y and
Jo-seph and the In-fant ly- ing in a man-ger.

Or:

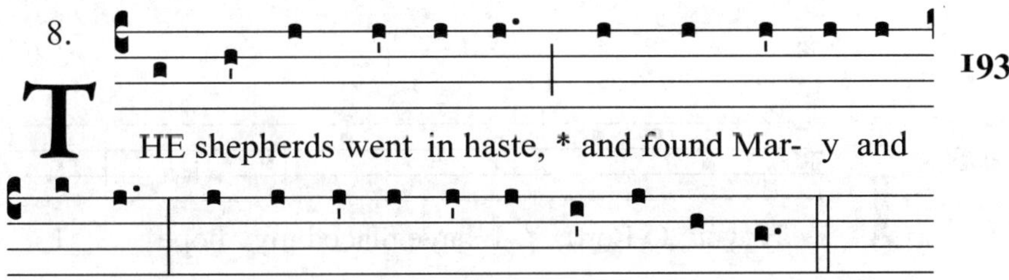
8.
193
THE shepherds went in haste, * and found Mar- y and
Jo-seph and the In-fant ly- ing in a man-ger.

- iv -

8.
194
THE shepherds went in haste, * and found Mar- y and
Jo-seph and the In-fant ly- ing in a man-ger.

OFFERTORY ANTIPHON *In te speravi, Domine.*
Ps 30 : 15. 16

- i -

195

2.
IN you, O Lord, * I have placed my hope ; I said,
You are my God, my times are in your hands.

- ii -

196

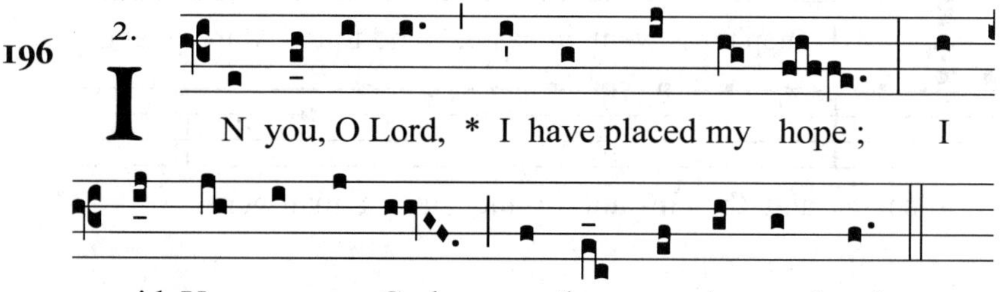
2.
IN you, O Lord, * I have placed my hope ; I
said, You are my God, my times are in your hands.

VERSES *In te, Domine, speravi. Ps* 30 : 2

℣. 1
I N you, O Lord, have I hoped, let me nev- er be
confound-ed, * de- liv- er me in your jus-tice.

197

Inclina ad me aurem tuam. Ps 30 : 3. 4

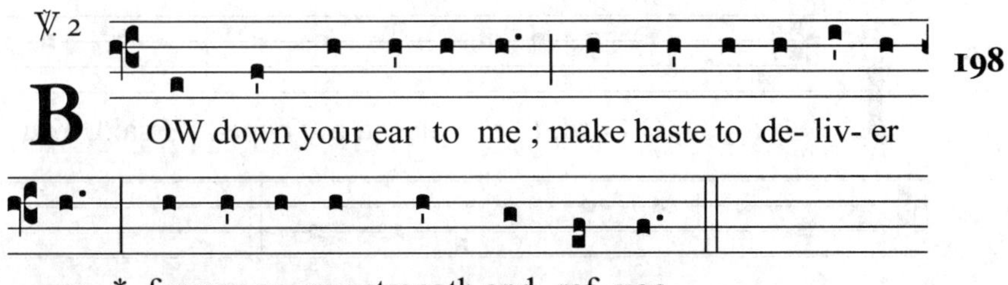
℣. 2
B OW down your ear to me ; make haste to de- liv- er
me, * for you are my strength and ref- uge.

198

In manus tuas, Domine. Ps 30 : 6

℣. 3
I N- to your hands I commend my spir- it, * for you
have redeemed me, O Lord, O God of truth.

199

- iii -

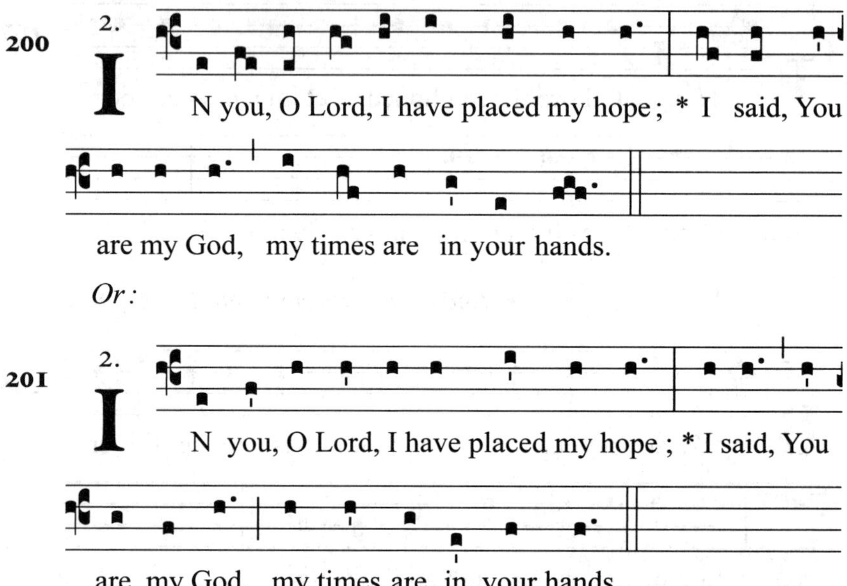
200
2.
IN you, O Lord, I have placed my hope; * I said, You
are my God, my times are in your hands.
Or:
201
2.
IN you, O Lord, I have placed my hope ; * I said, You
are my God, my times are in your hands.

- iv -

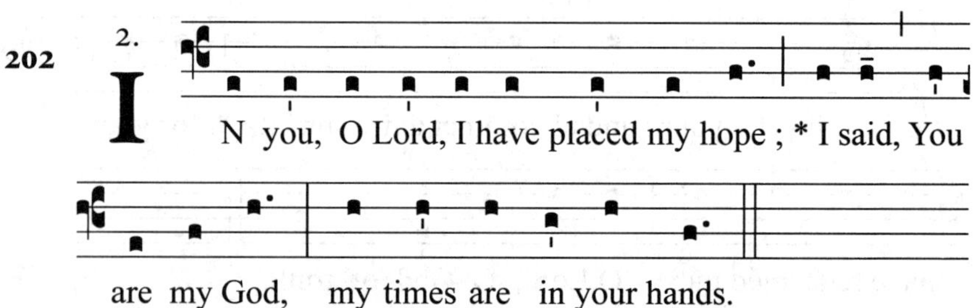
202
2.
IN you, O Lord, I have placed my hope ; * I said, You
are my God, my times are in your hands.

COMMUNION ANTIPHON *Deus noster in terris.*
Bar 3:38

- i -

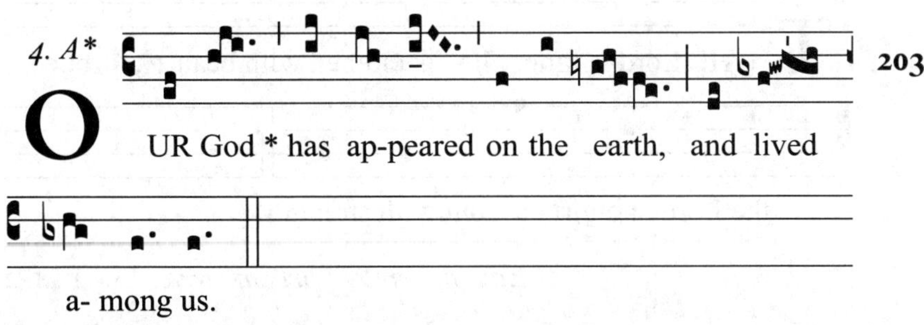
4. A*
O
UR God * has ap-peared on the earth, and lived
a- mong us.
203

- ii -

4. A*
O
UR God * has appeared on the earth, and lived among
us.
204

VERSES *Dominus regnavit, decorem indutus est. Ps* 92 : 1

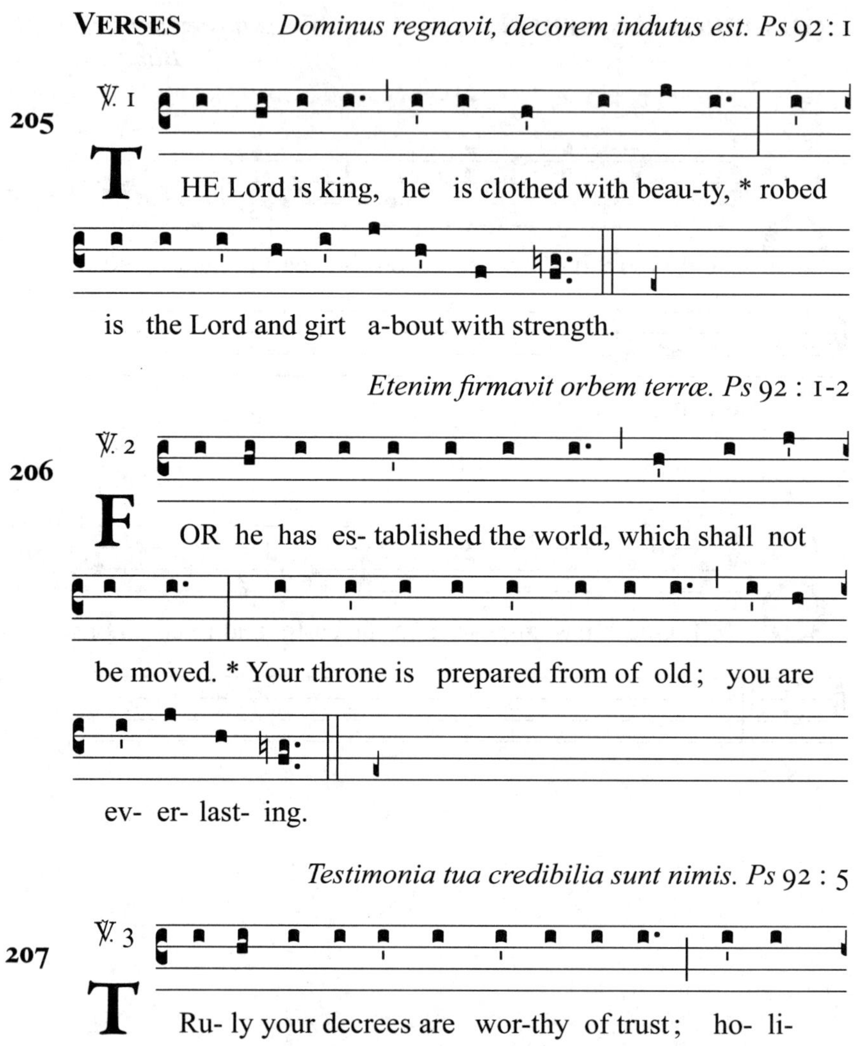
205
℣. 1
THE Lord is king, he is clothed with beau-ty, * robed
is the Lord and girt a-bout with strength.
Etenim firmavit orbem terræ. Ps 92 : 1-2
206
℣. 2
FOR he has es- tablished the world, which shall not
be moved. * Your throne is prepared from of old; you are
ev- er- last- ing.
Testimonia tua credibilia sunt nimis. Ps 92 : 5
207
℣. 3
TRu- ly your decrees are wor-thy of trust; ho- li-

ness be- fits your house, * O Lord, for length of days.

- iii -

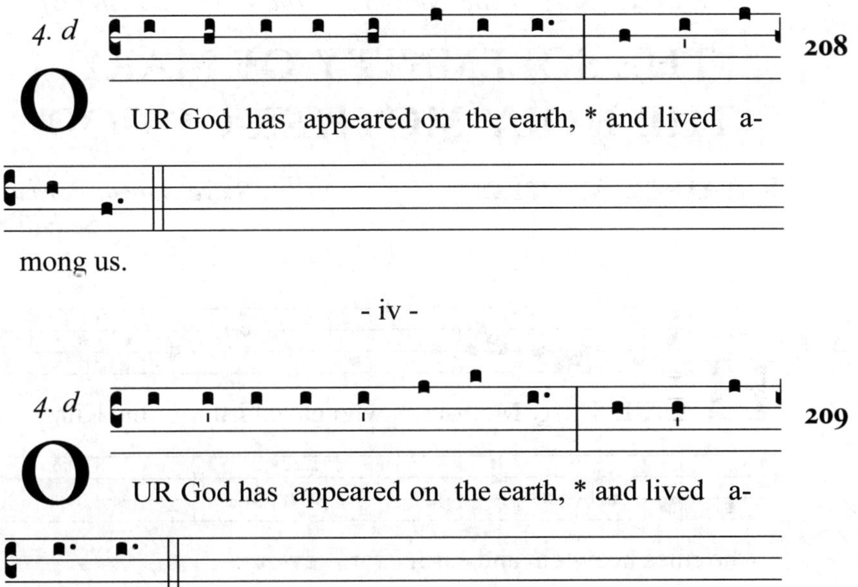
4. d
208
OUR God has appeared on the earth, * and lived a-
mong us.
- iv -
4. d
209
OUR God has appeared on the earth, * and lived a-
mong us.

January 1

The Octave Day of the Nativity of the Lord [Christmas]

THE SOLEMNITY OF MARY, THE HOLY MOTHER OF GOD

ENTRANCE ANTIPHON *Salve, sancta Parens.*
Sedulius

- i -

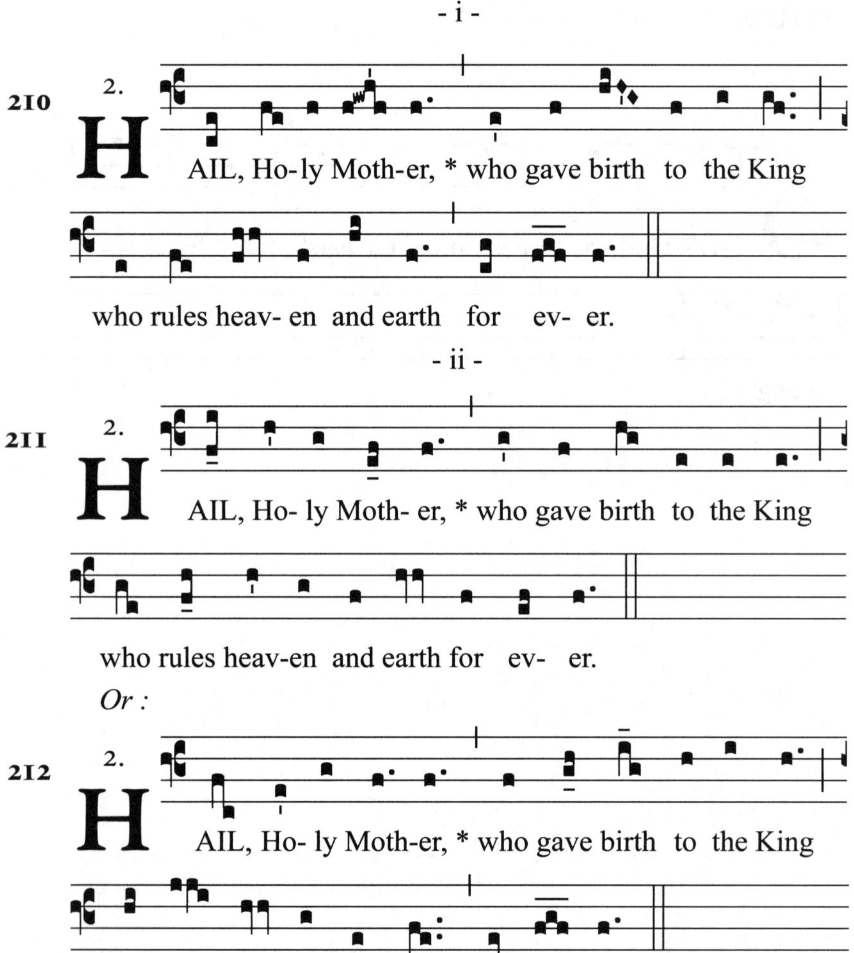
210
2.
HAIL, Ho-ly Moth-er, * who gave birth to the King
who rules heav- en and earth for ev- er.
- ii -
211
2.
HAIL, Ho- ly Moth- er, * who gave birth to the King
who rules heav-en and earth for ev- er.
Or :
212
2.
HAIL, Ho- ly Moth-er, * who gave birth to the King
who rules heav-en and earth for ev- er.

VERSES *Eructavit cor meum verbum bonum. Ps* 44:2

℣. 1 MY heart o- ver-flows with a good-ly theme; * to 213

the king I must speak the song that I have made.

Et concupiscet rex decorem tuum. Ps 44:12

℣. 2 THE king shall great-ly de- sire your beau- ty, * for 214

he is the Lord your God, and him they shall a- dore.

Omnis gloria eius. Ps 44:14

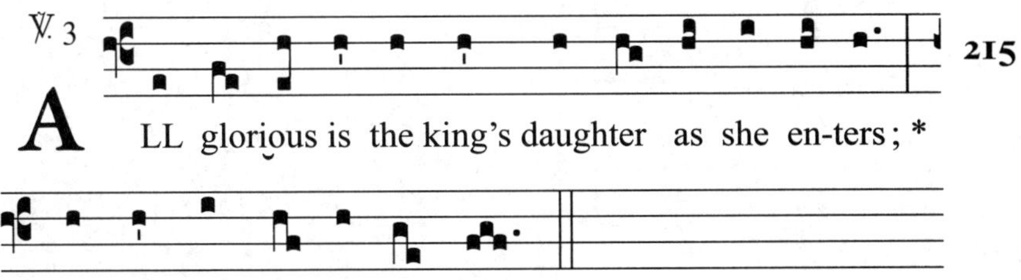

℣. 3 ALL glorious is the king's daughter as she en-ters; * 215

her robes are threaded with gold.

- iii -

216

2.
HAIL, Ho-ly Moth-er, * who gave birth to the King

who rules heav-en and earth for ev- er.

- iv -

217

2.
HAIL, Ho- ly Moth-er, * who gave birth to the King

who rules heav-en and earth for ev- er.

Or:

Lux fulgebit.
Cf. Is 9: 1. 5; Lk 1: 33

- i -

8. 218

T O-day * a light will shine up- on us, for the Lord is born for us; and he will be called Won-drous God, Prince of peace, Father of fu-ture a- ges: and his reign will be with-out end.

- ii -

8. 219

T O- day a light will shine up- on us, * for the Lord is born for us; and he will be called Wondrous God, Prince of peace, Fa-ther of fu-ture a- ges: and his reign will be with-out end.

VERSES *Dominus regnavit, decorem indutus est. Ps* 92 : 1

220

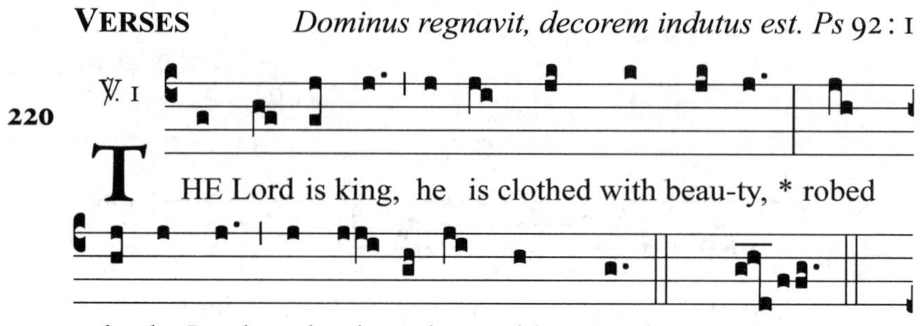
℣. 1
THE Lord is king, he is clothed with beau-ty, * robed
is the Lord and girt a-bout with strength. *Or :* strength.

Use the first ending when returning to antiphon [ii] *or verse that begins on* Sol.
Use the second ending when returning to the antiphon [i] *that begins on* Re.

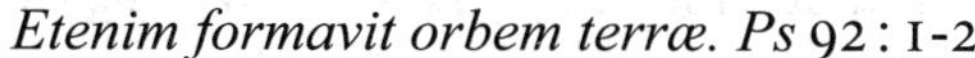
Etenim formavit orbem terræ. Ps 92 : 1-2

221

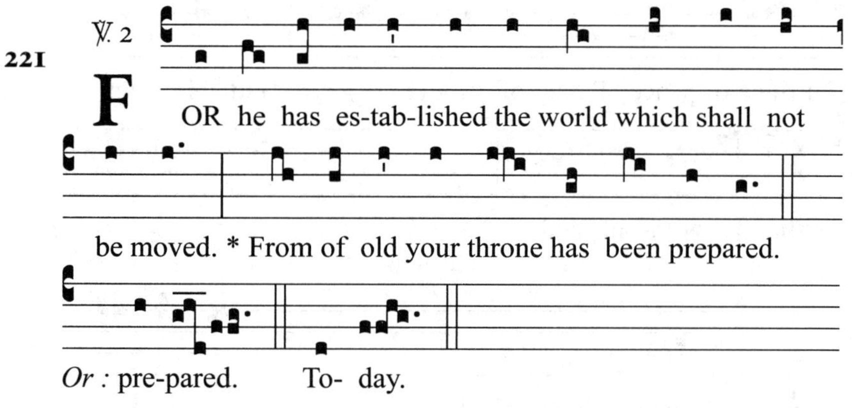
℣. 2
FOR he has es-tab-lished the world which shall not
be moved. * From of old your throne has been prepared.
Or : pre-pared. To- day.

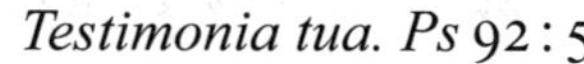
Testimonia tua. Ps 92 : 5

222

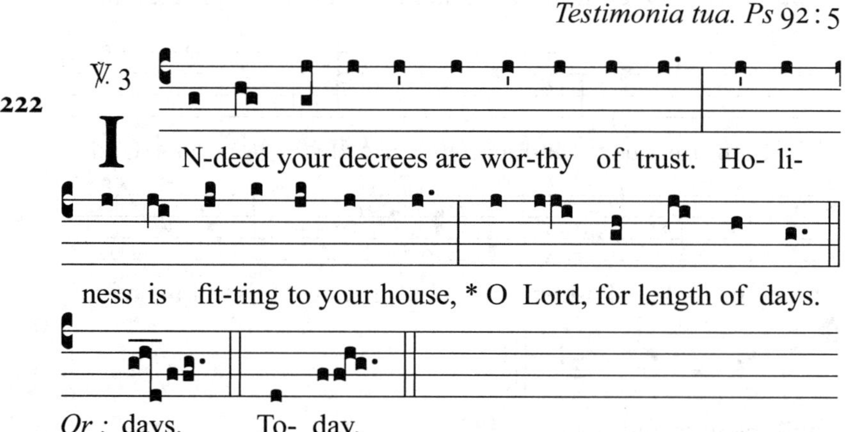
℣. 3
IN-deed your decrees are wor-thy of trust. Ho- li-
ness is fit-ting to your house, * O Lord, for length of days.
Or : days. To- day.

- iii -

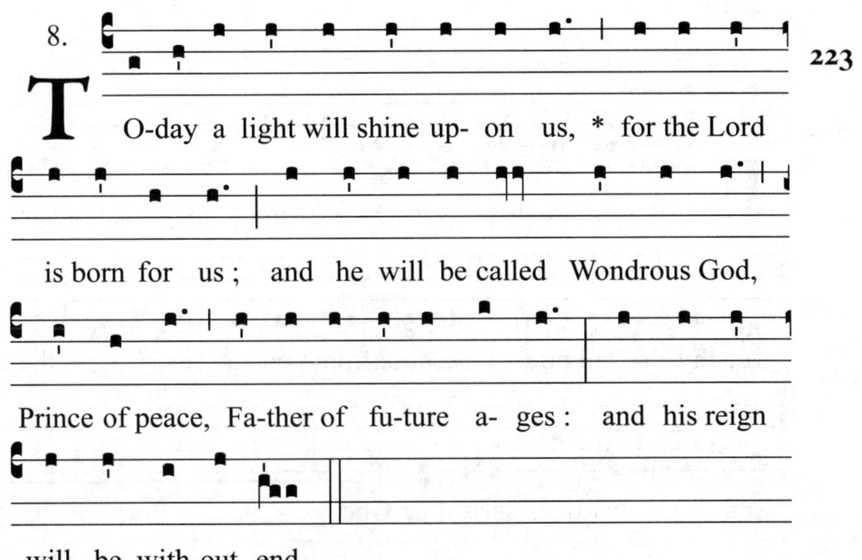
8.
223
T O-day a light will shine up- on us, * for the Lord
is born for us ; and he will be called Wondrous God,
Prince of peace, Fa-ther of fu-ture a- ges : and his reign
will be with-out end.

- iv -

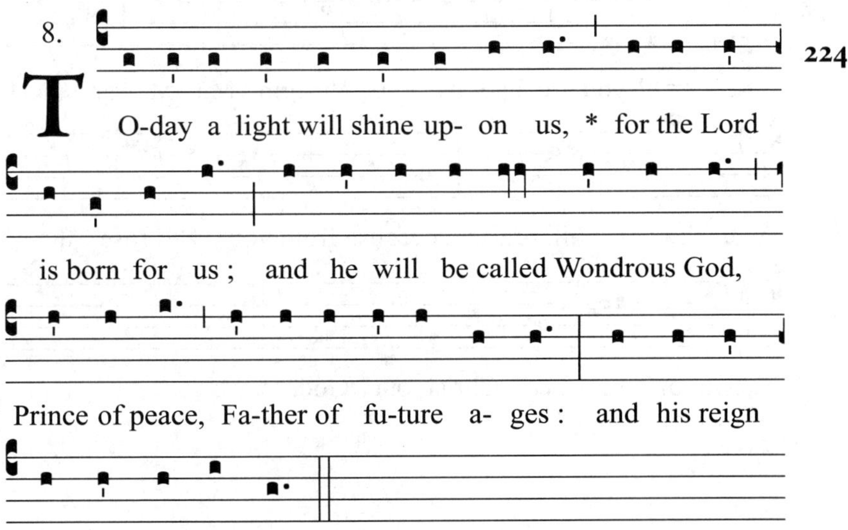
8.
224
T O-day a light will shine up- on us, * for the Lord
is born for us ; and he will be called Wondrous God,
Prince of peace, Fa-ther of fu-ture a- ges : and his reign
will be with-out end.

OFFERTORY ANTIPHON *Felix namque es.*

- i -

225 1.

FOR you are hap- py, * O Vir-gin Mar- y, and most wor-thy of all praise: because from you a- rose the sun of Jus-tice, Christ our God.

- ii -

226 1.

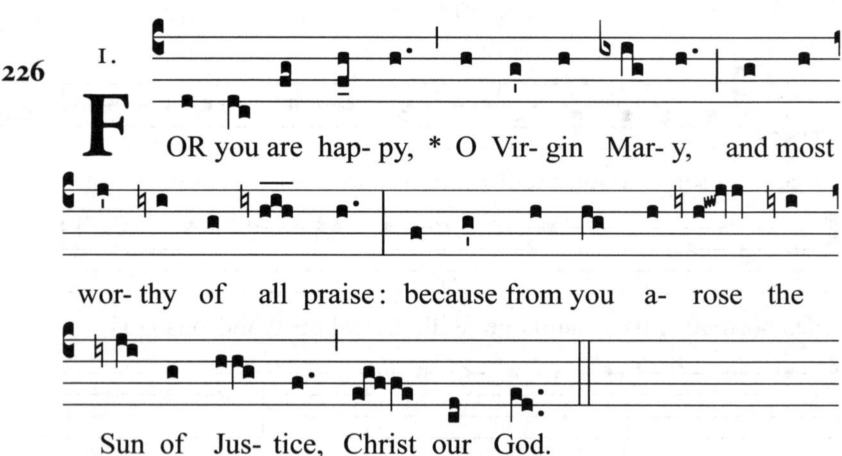
FOR you are hap- py, * O Vir- gin Mar- y, and most
wor- thy of all praise: because from you a- rose the
Sun of Jus- tice, Christ our God.

VERSES *Cantate Domino canticum novum. Ps* 97 : 1

℣. 1
227
O sing a new song to the Lord, for he has worked
won-ders. * His right hand and his ho- ly arm have wrought
sal- va- tion.

Recordatus est misericordiæ suæ. Ps 97 : 3

℣. 2
228
HE has remembered his mer-cy and truth toward the
house of Is- ra- el. * All the ends of the earth have seen
the sal- va- tion of our God.

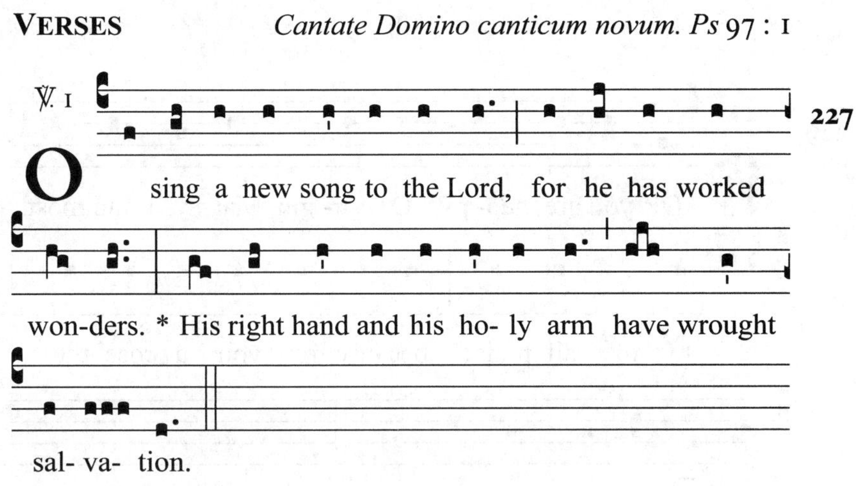

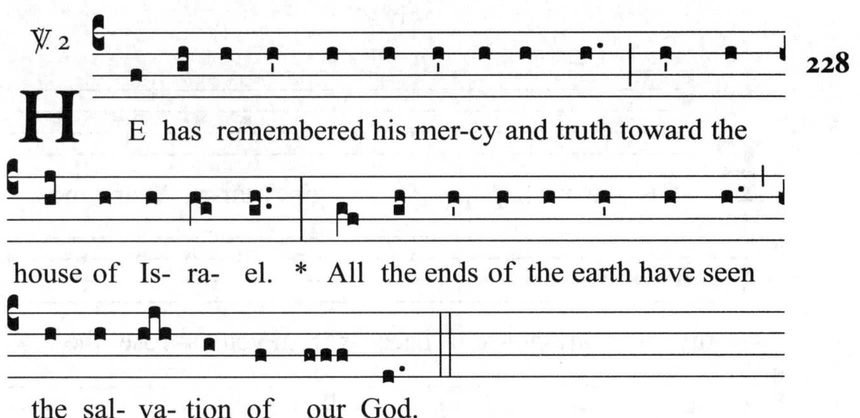

- iii -

229

I.
FOR you are hap- py, O Vir- gin Mar- y, * and most
wor- thy of all praise: because from you a- rose the
Sun of Jus-tice, Christ our God.

- iv -

230

I.
FOR you are hap- py, O Vir- gin Mar- y, * and most
wor-thy of all praise: because from you a- rose the
Sun of Jus-tice, Christ our God.

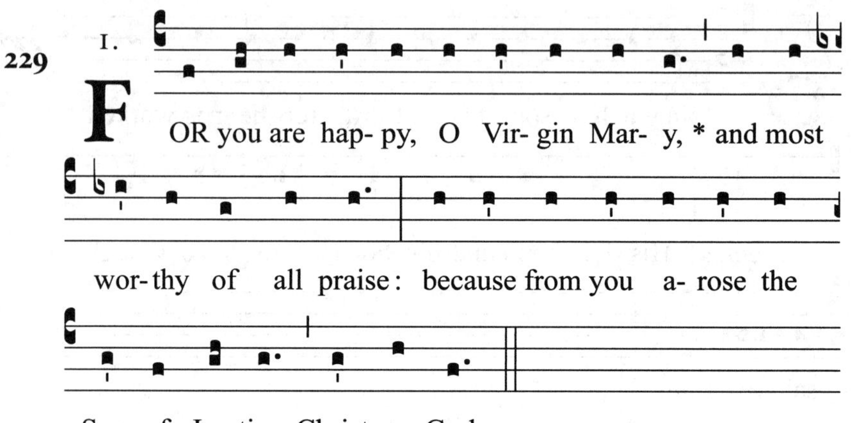

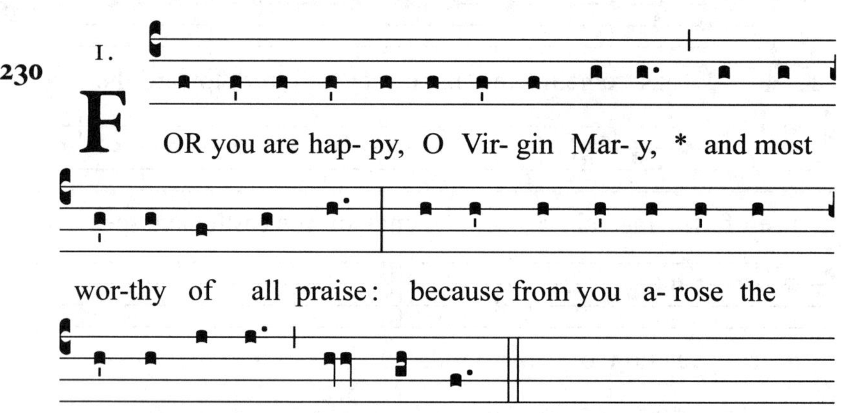

COMMUNION ANTIPHON *Iesus Christus heri et hodie.*
Heb 13:8

- i -

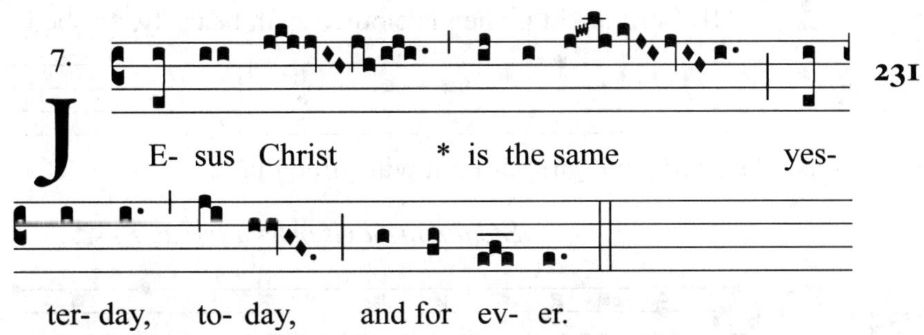
7.
J
E- sus Christ * is the same yes-
ter- day, to- day, and for ev- er.
231

- ii -

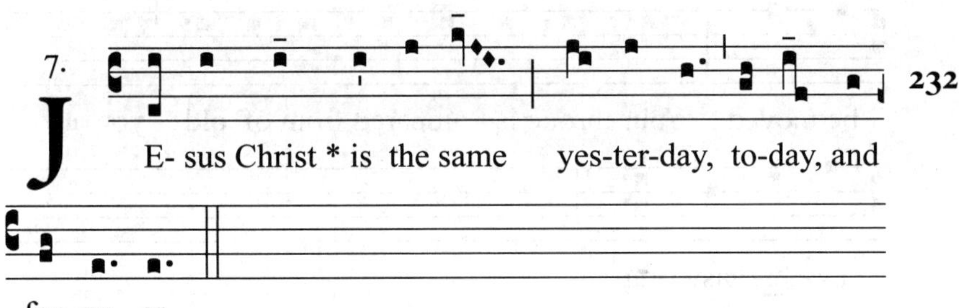
7.
J
E- sus Christ * is the same yes-ter-day, to-day, and
for ev- er.
232

VERSES *Dominus regnavit, decorem indutus est. Ps* 92 : 1

233

℣. 1
THE Lord is king, he is clothed with beau- ty, * robed
is the Lord and girt a- bout with strength.

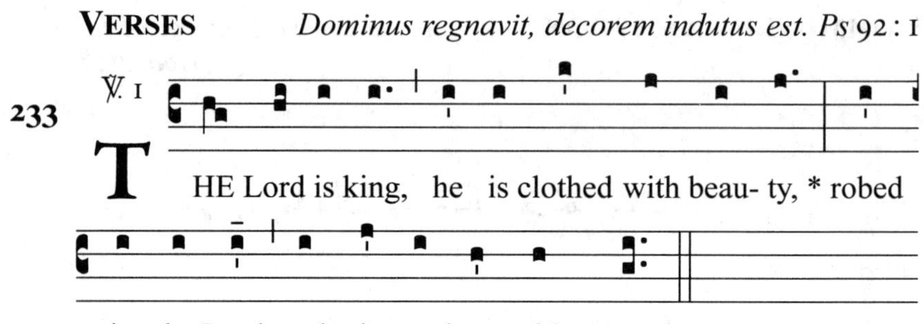

Etenim firmavit orbem terræ. Ps 92 : 1-2

234

℣. 2
FOR he has es- tablished the world, which shall not
be moved. * Your throne is prepared from of old; you are
ev- er- last- ing.

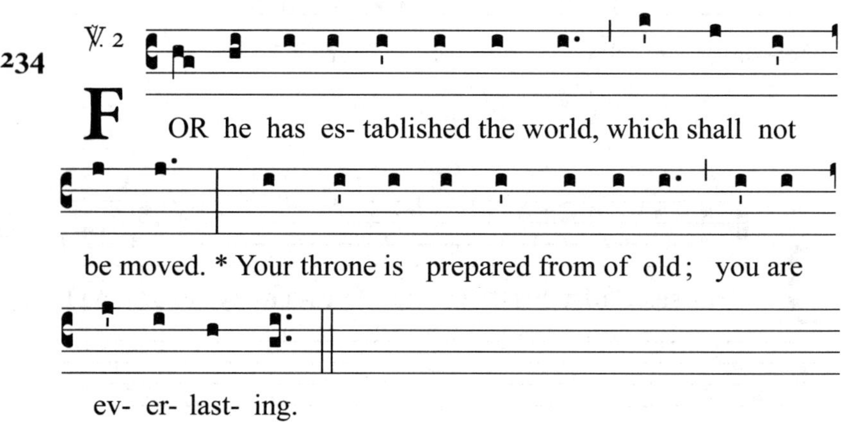

Testimonia tua credibilia sunt nimis. Ps 92 : 5

235

℣. 3
TRu- ly your decrees are wor-thy of trust; ho- li-
ness be- fits your house, * O Lord, for length of days.

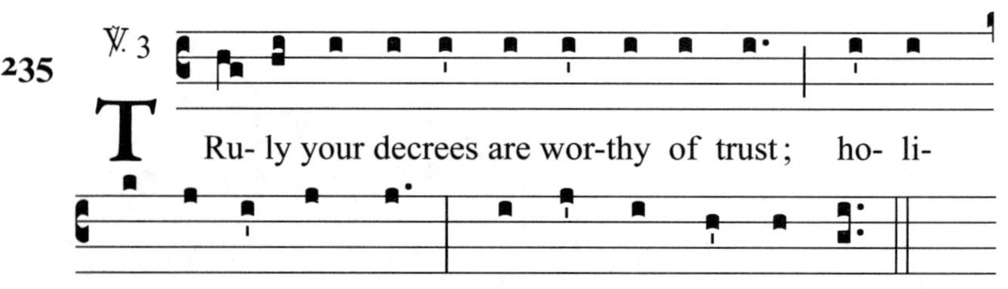

- iii -

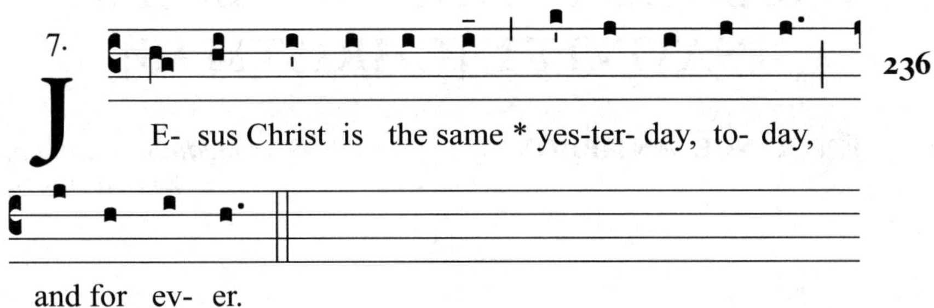
7.
JEsus Christ is the same * yes-ter-day, to-day,
and for ev-er.
236

- iv -

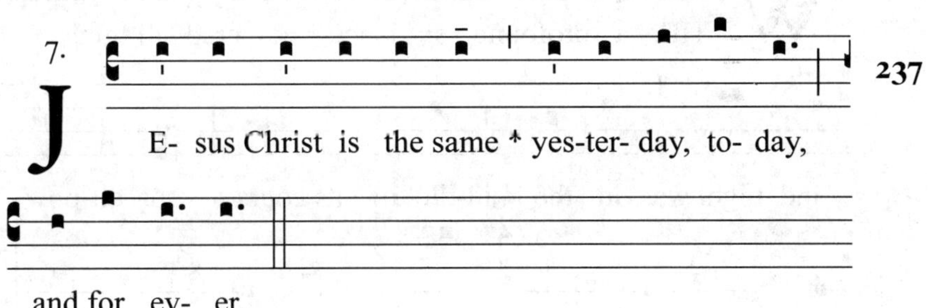
7.
JEsus Christ is the same * yes-ter-day, to-day,
and for ev-er.
237

SECOND SUNDAY AFTER THE NATIVITY [CHRISTMAS]

Entrance Antiphon *Dum medium silentium.*
Wis 18:14-15

- i -

238

8.
WHEN a profound si- lence * cov-ered all things
and night was in the mid-dle of its course, your all-pow-
er- ful Word, O Lord, bound-ed from heav-en's roy- al throne.

- ii -

239

8.
WHEN a profound si- lence * covered all things
and night was in the mid-dle of its course, your all-pow-
er- ful Word, O Lord, bound-ed from heav-en's roy- al throne.

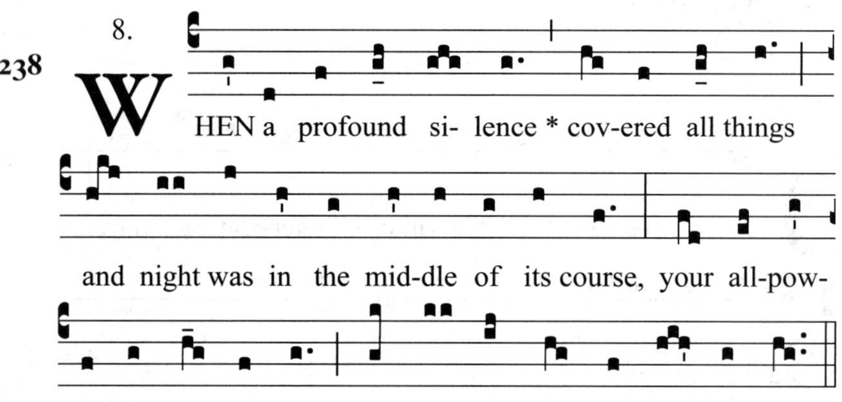

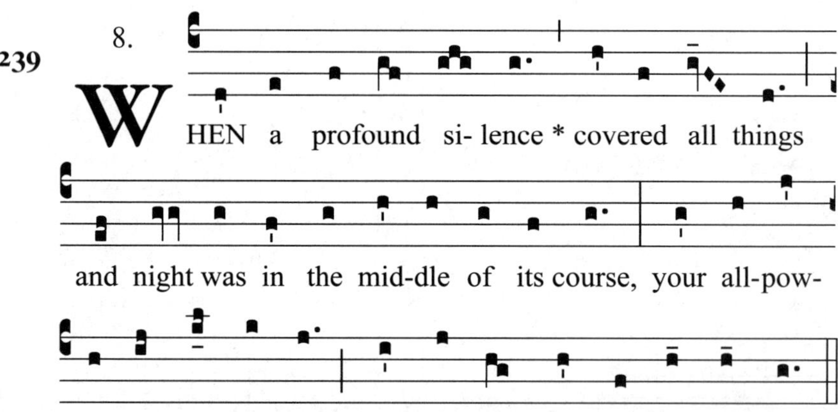

VERSES *Dominus regnavit, decorem indutus est. Ps* 92 : 1

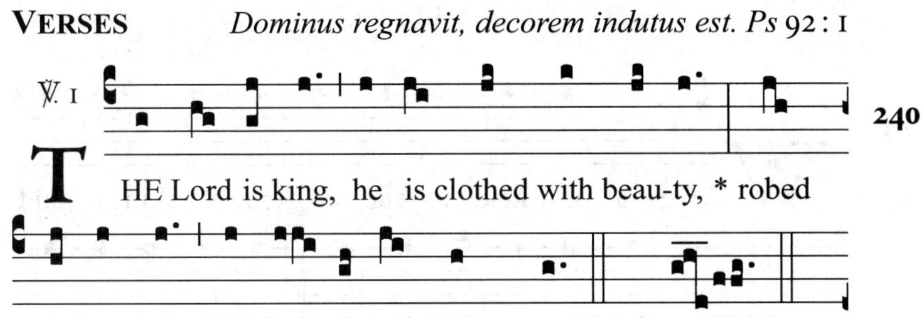
℣. 1
THE Lord is king, he is clothed with beau-ty, * robed

240

is the Lord and girt a-bout with strength. *Or :* strength.

Use the first ending when another Psalm verse that begins on Sol *follows. Use the second ending when returning to the antiphon.*

Etenim formavit orbem terræ. Ps 92 : 1-2

℣. 2 FOR he has es-tab-lished the world which shall not 241

be moved. * From of old your throne has been prepared.

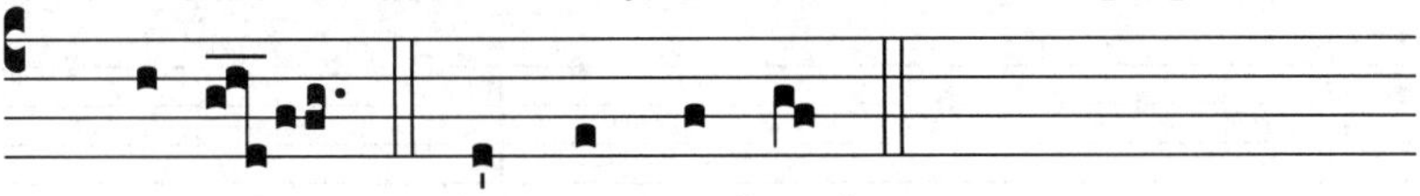

Or : pre-pared. When a profound.

Testimonia tua. Ps 92 : 5

℣. 3 IN-deed your decrees are wor-thy of trust. Ho- li- 242

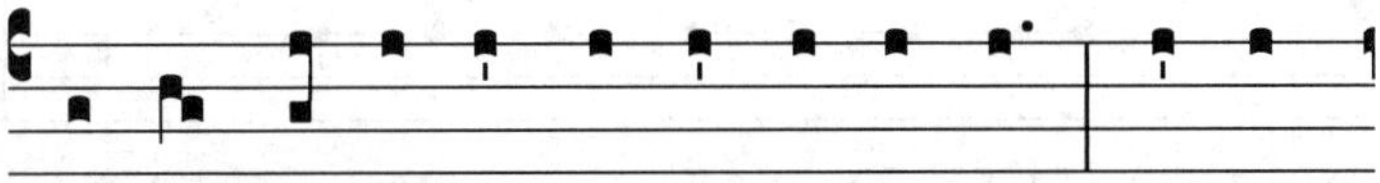

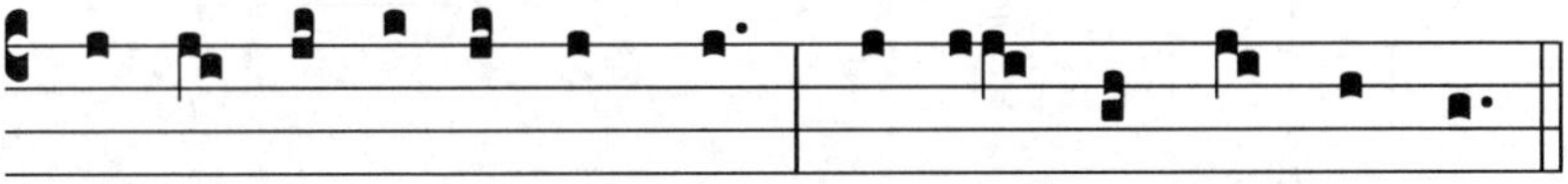

ness is fit-ting to your house, * O Lord, for length of days.

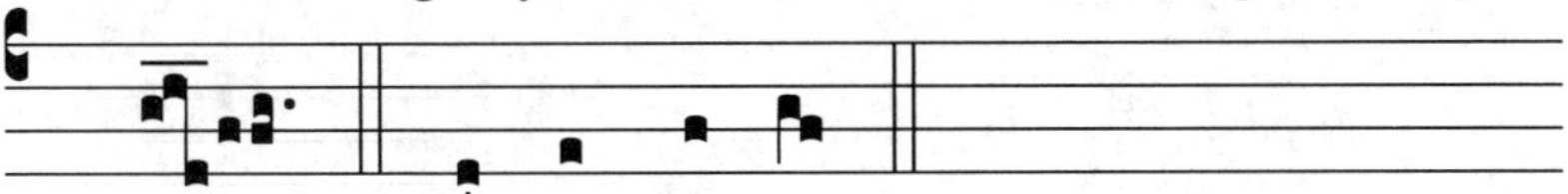

Or : pre-pared. When a profound.

- iii -

243 8.

WHEN a profound si-lence cov-ered all things * and night was in the mid-dle of its course, your all-pow-er- ful Word, O Lord, bound-ed from heav-en's roy- al throne.

- iv -

244 8.

WHEN a profound si-lence cov-ered all things * and night was in the mid-dle of its course, your all-pow-er- ful Word, O Lord, bound-ed from heav-en's roy- al throne.

OFFERTORY ANTIPHON *Benedic, anima mea, Dominum.*
Ps 102 : 2. 5

- i -

5.
245
BLESS the Lord, * O my soul, and nev- er for-
get all he has done for you ; and your youth shall
be re- newed like the ea- gle's.

- ii -

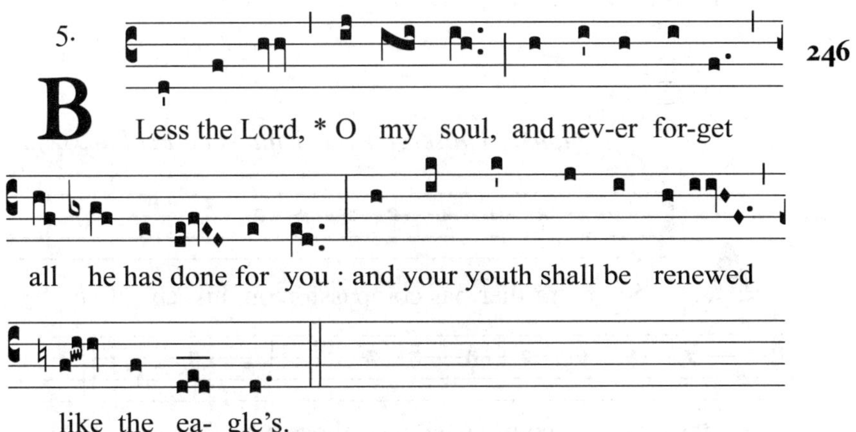
5.
246
BLess the Lord, * O my soul, and nev-er for-get
all he has done for you : and your youth shall be renewed
like the ea- gle's.

VERSES *Miserator et misericors Dominus. Ps* 102:8

247 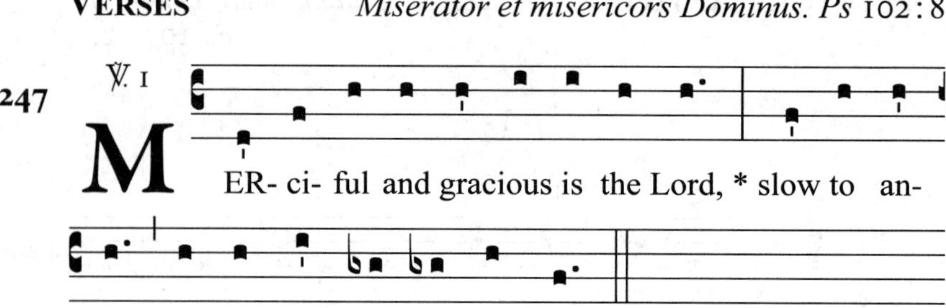
℣. 1
MERCIFUL and gracious is the Lord, * slow to an-

ger and a-bound-ing in kind-ness.

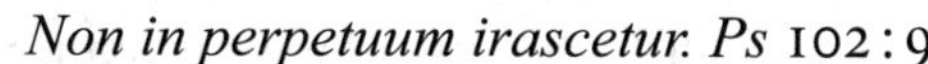
Non in perpetuum irascetur. Ps 102:9

248 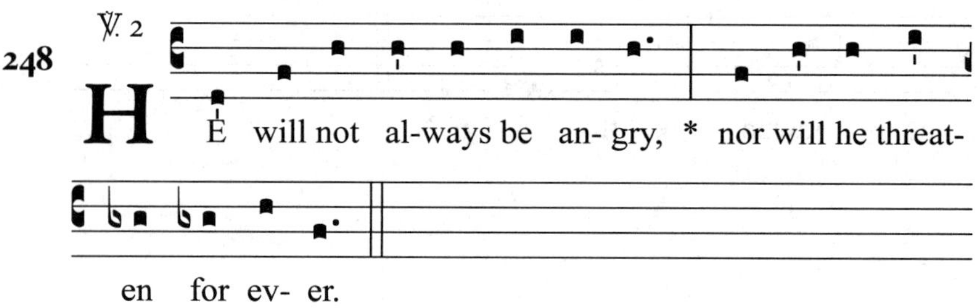
℣. 2
HE will not al-ways be an- gry, * nor will he threat-
en for ev- er.

Quomodo miseretur pater filiorum. Psalm 102:13

249 
℣. 3
AS a fa-ther has compassion on his chil-dren, *

so the Lord has com-pas-sion on those who fear him.

- iii -

5.
250
BLESS the Lord, O my soul, * and nev-er for- get
all he has done for you ; and your youth shall be renewed like the ea- gle's.

Or:

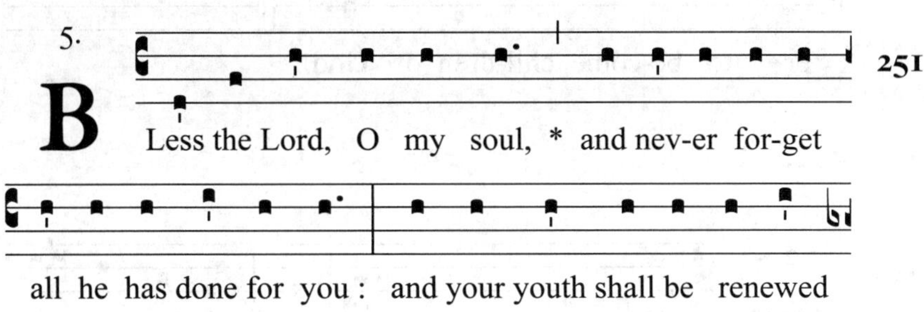
5.
251
BLess the Lord, O my soul, * and nev-er for-get
all he has done for you : and your youth shall be renewed
like the ea- gle's.

- iv -

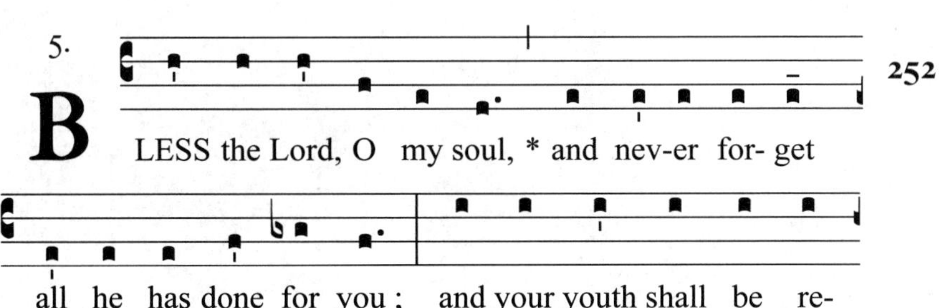
5.
252
BLESS the Lord, O my soul, * and nev-er for- get
all he has done for you ; and your youth shall be re-

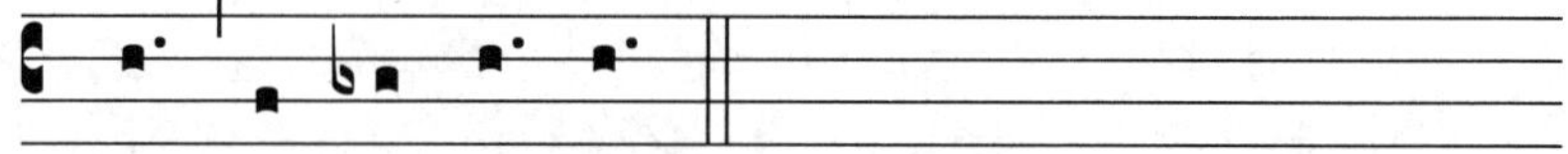

newed like the ea- gle's.

COMMUNION ANTIPHON *Omnibus qui receperunt eum.*
Cf. Jn 1 : 12

- i -

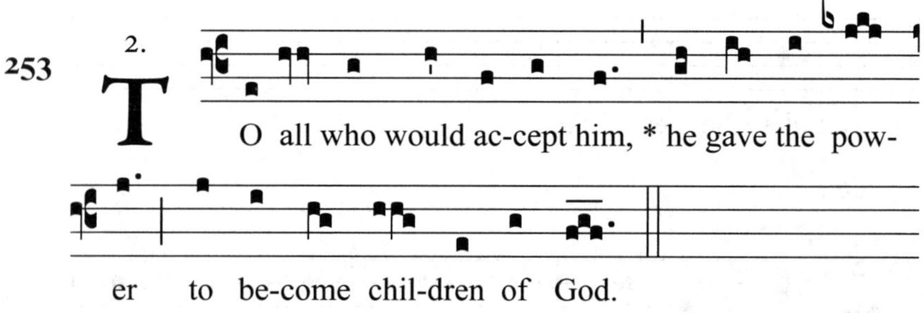
253
2.
TO all who would ac-cept him, * he gave the pow-
er to be-come chil-dren of God.

- ii -

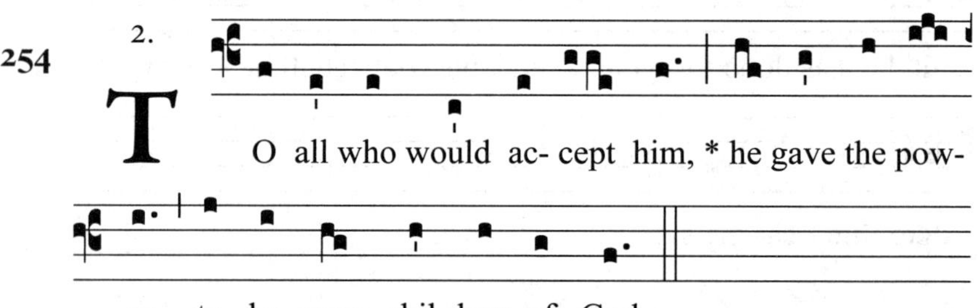
254
2.
TO all who would ac- cept him, * he gave the pow-
er to be-come chil-dren of God.

VERSES *Domine, Dominus noster.* Ps 8 : 2

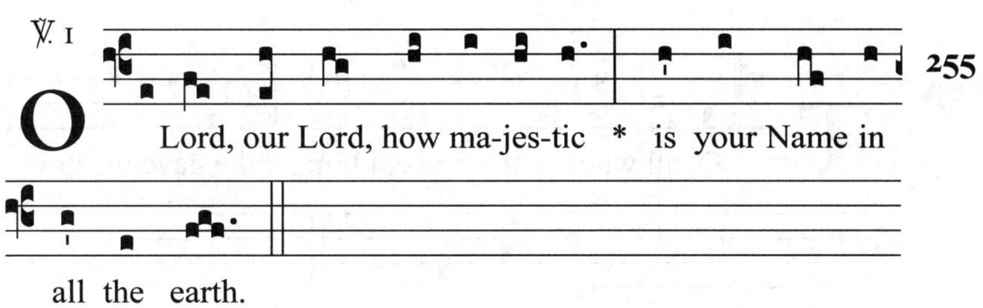
℣. 1
255
O Lord, our Lord, how ma-jes-tic * is your Name in
all the earth.

Quid est homo, quod memor es eius? Ps 8 : 5

℣. 2
256
WHAT is man that you should be mind-ful of him, *
or the son of man, that you should care for him?

Minuitsi eum paulo minus ab angelis. Ps 8 : 6

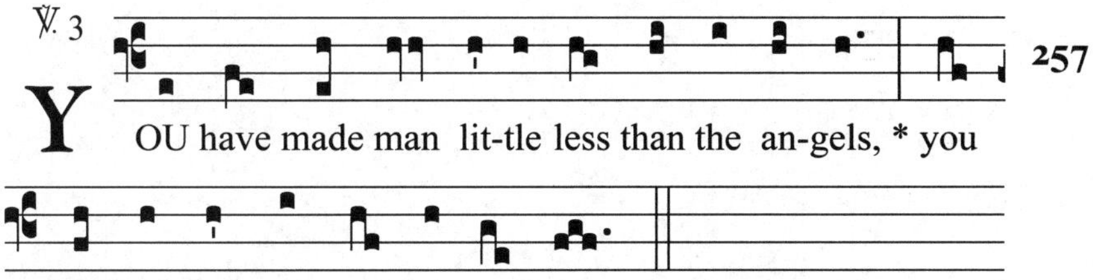
℣. 3
257
YOU have made man lit-tle less than the an-gels, * you
have put all things un- der his feet.

- iii -

258

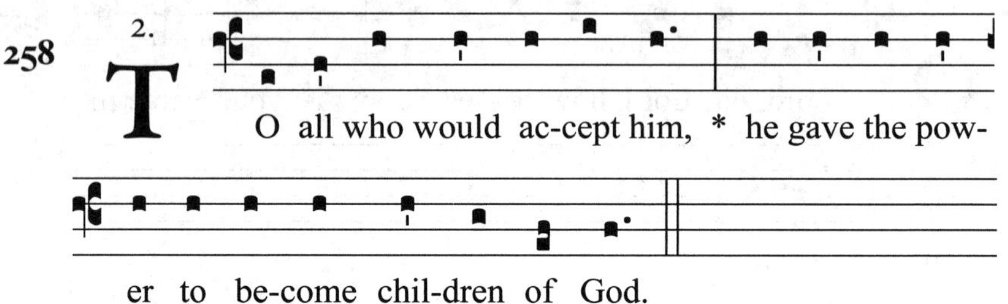
2.
TO all who would ac-cept him, * he gave the pow-
er to be-come chil-dren of God.

- iv -

259

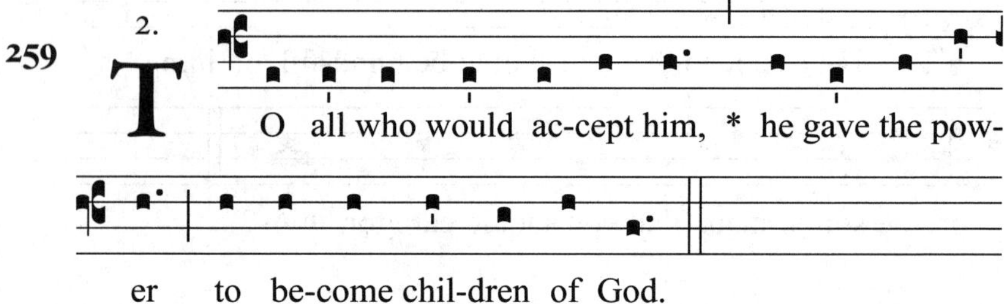
2.
TO all who would ac-cept him, * he gave the pow-
er to be-come chil-dren of God.

January 6

Sunday between January 2 and January 8
[In the Dioceses of the United States]

THE EPIPHANY OF THE LORD

Solemnity

At the Vigil Mass

Entrance Antiphon *Surge, Ierusalem. Cf. Bar* 5:5

- i -

7. A-RISE, Je- ru- sa- lem, * and look to the East and 260
see your chil- dren gath-ered from the ris- ing to the
set-ting of the sun.

- ii -

7. A-RISE, Je- ru- sa- lem, * and look to the East and 261
see your chil-dren gathered from the ris- ing to the setting of the sun.

VERSES *Deus, iudicium tuum regi da. Ps* 71 : 2

262
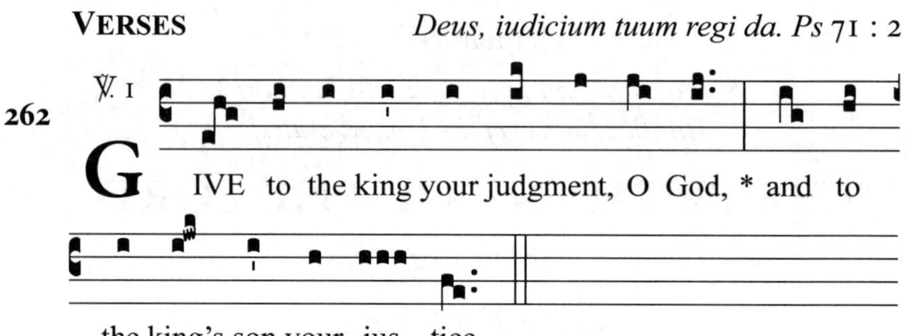
℣. 1
GIVE to the king your judgment, O God, * and to
the king's son your jus- tice.

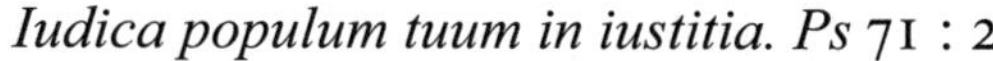
Iudica populum tuum in iustitia. Ps 71 : 2

263

℣. 2
THAT he may gov-ern your peo-ple with jus-tice, * and
your poor in right judg-ment.

Et adorabunt eum. Ps 71 : 11

264
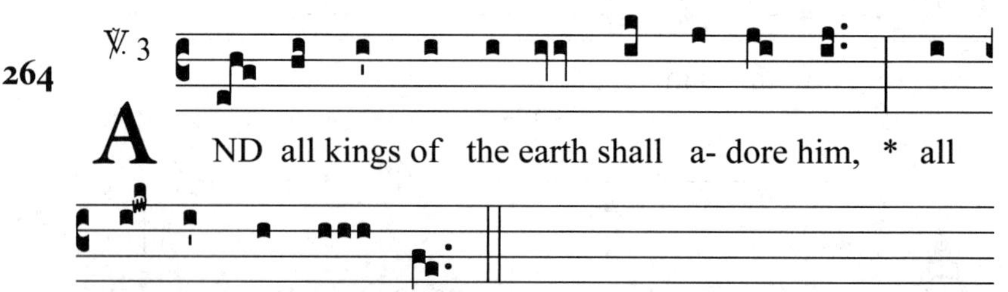
℣. 3
AND all kings of the earth shall a- dore him, * all
na-tions shall serve him.

- iii -

7.
265
A -RISE, Je- ru- sa- lem, * and look to the East and
see your chil-dren gathered from the ris- ing to the set-ting
of the sun.
- iv -
7.
266
A -RISE, Je- ru- sa- lem, * and look to the East and
see your chil-dren gathered from the ris- ing to the set-ting
of the sun.

Offertory Antiphon *Regis Tharsis. Ps* 71 : 10. 11

- i -

267
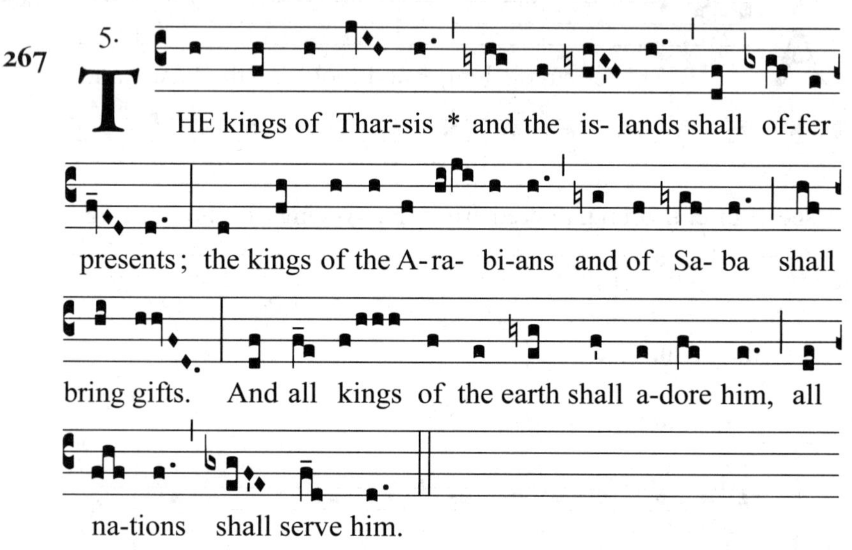
5.
THE kings of Thar-sis * and the is- lands shall of-fer
presents; the kings of the A-ra- bi-ans and of Sa- ba shall
bring gifts. And all kings of the earth shall a-dore him, all
na-tions shall serve him.

- ii -

268
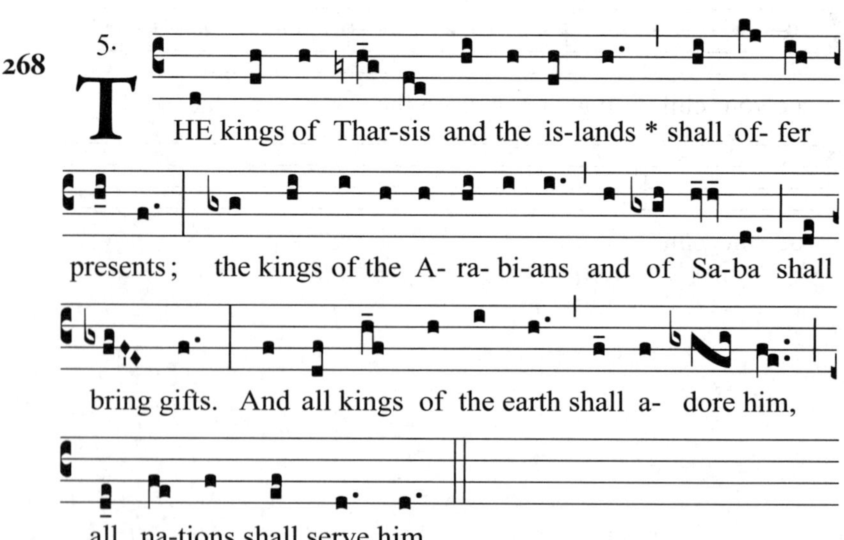
5.
THE kings of Thar-sis and the is-lands * shall of- fer
presents; the kings of the A- ra- bi-ans and of Sa-ba shall
bring gifts. And all kings of the earth shall a- dore him,
all na-tions shall serve him.

VERSES

Deus, iudicium tuum regi da. Ps 71 : 2

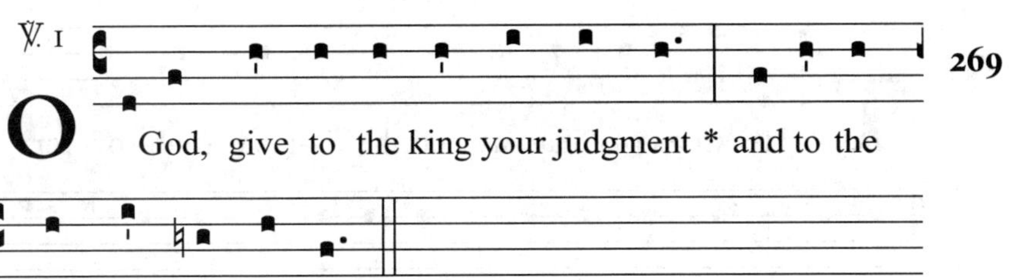
℣. 1
O God, give to the king your judgment * and to the
king's son your jus-tice.

269

Iudica populum tuum in iustitia. Ps 71 : 2

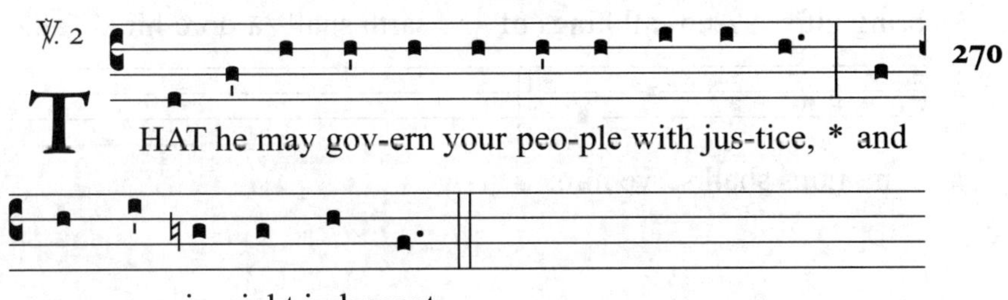
℣. 2
THAT he may gov-ern your peo-ple with jus-tice, * and
your poor in right judgment.

270

Et adorabunt eum. Ps 71 : 11

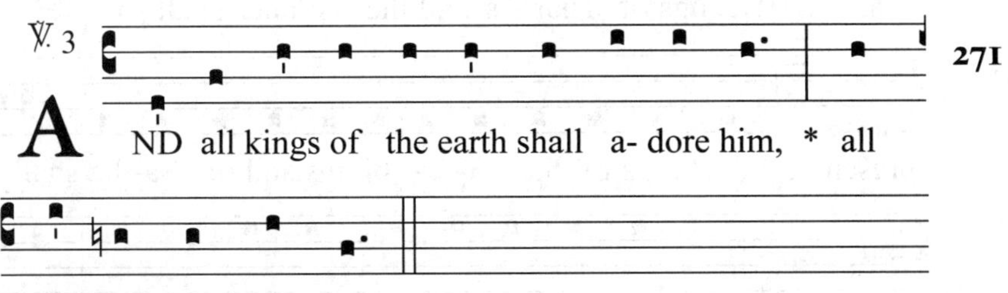
℣. 3
AND all kings of the earth shall a- dore him, * all
na-tions shall serve him.

271

- iii -

272

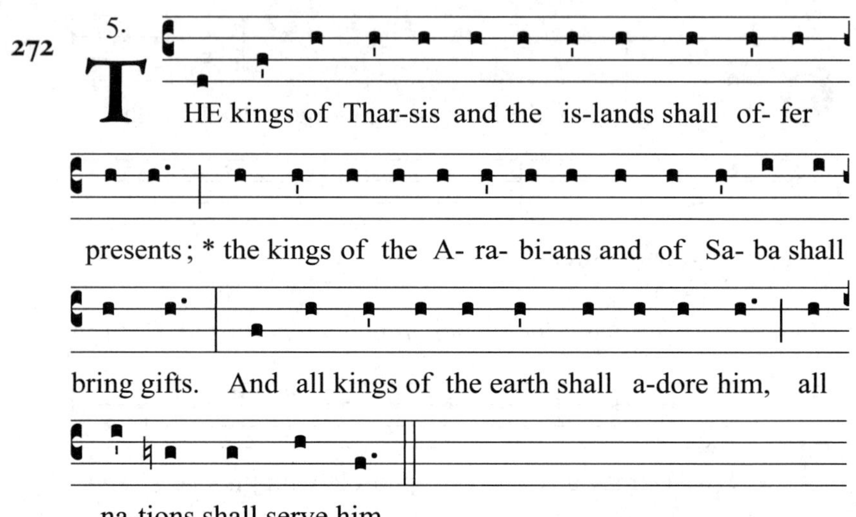

5.
THE kings of Thar-sis and the is-lands shall of- fer
presents; * the kings of the A- ra- bi-ans and of Sa- ba shall
bring gifts. And all kings of the earth shall a-dore him, all
na-tions shall serve him.

- iv -

273

5.
THE kings of Thar-sis and the is-lands shall of- fer
presents; * the kings of the A- ra- bi-ans and of Sa- ba shall
bring gifts. And all kings of the earth shall a-dore him, all
na-tions shall serve him.

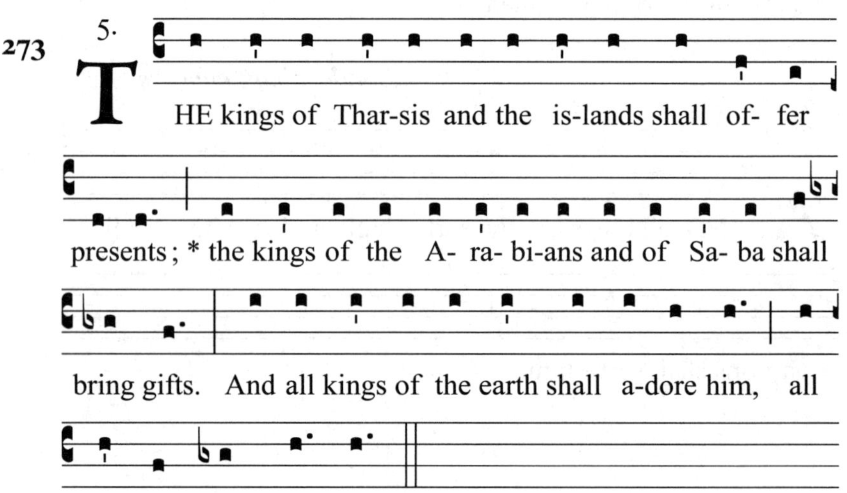

If psalm verses p. 109 *are used with this setting, sing te flat.*

COMMUNION ANTIPHON *Claritas Dei illuminavit.*
Cf. Rev 21:23

- i -
8.
THE bright-ness of God * il- lu-mined the ho- ly
274
cit- y Je- ru- sa- lem, and the nations will walk
by its light.
- ii -
8.
THE brightness of God * il- lu-mined the ho- ly
275
cit- y Je- ru- sa- lem, and the na-tions will walk by its
light.

VERSES *Lux orta est iusto. Ps* 96 : 11

276
℣. 1
LIght is ris- en for the just one, * and joy for the up-
right of heart.

Exaltate Dominum Deum nostrum. Ps 98 : 9

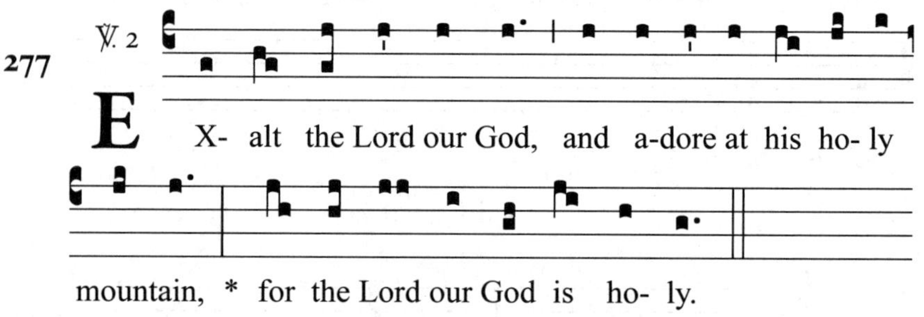
277
℣. 2
EX- alt the Lord our God, and a-dore at his ho- ly
mountain, * for the Lord our God is ho- ly.

Viderunt omnes termini terræ. Ps 97 : 3-4

278
℣. 3
ALL the ends of the earth have seen the sal-va-tion of
our God. * Sing joy-ful- ly to God, all the earth; make mel-
o- dy, rejoice and sing.

- iii -

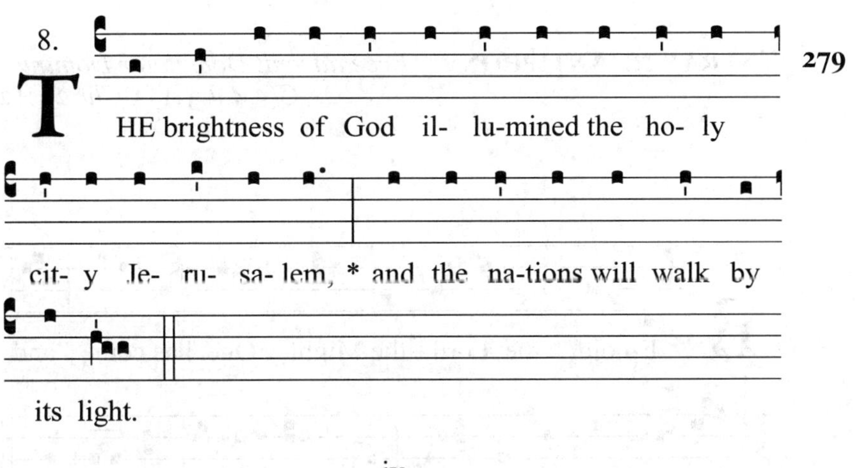
8.
279
THE brightness of God il- lu-mined the ho- ly
cit- y Je- ru- sa- lem, * and the na-tions will walk by
its light.

- iv

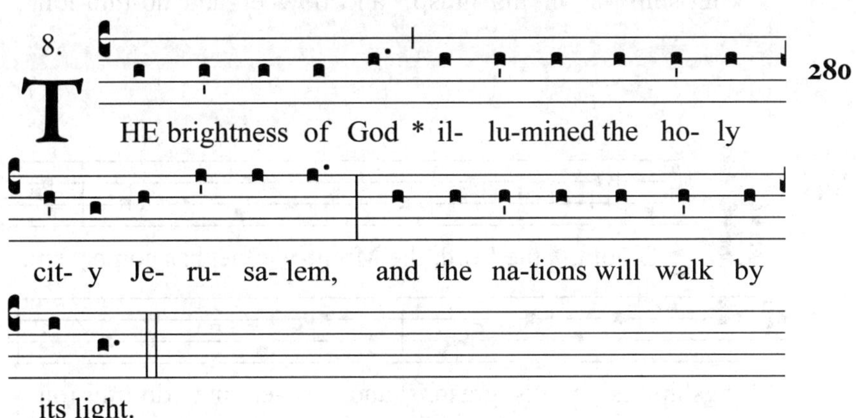
8.
280
THE brightness of God * il- lu-mined the ho- ly
cit- y Je- ru- sa- lem, and the na-tions will walk by
its light.

At the Mass during the Day

Entrance Antiphon *Ecce advenit Dominator Dominus.*
Cf. Mal 3:1; 1 *Chr* 29:12

- i -

281

2.
BE-hold, * the Lord, the Might-y One, has come; and
king-ship is in his grasp, and pow-er and do-min-ion.

- ii -

282

2.
BE-hold, * the Lord, the Might-y One, has come; and
kingship is in his grasp, and pow-er and do-min-ion.

VERSES *Deus, iudicium tuum regi da. Ps* 71 : 2

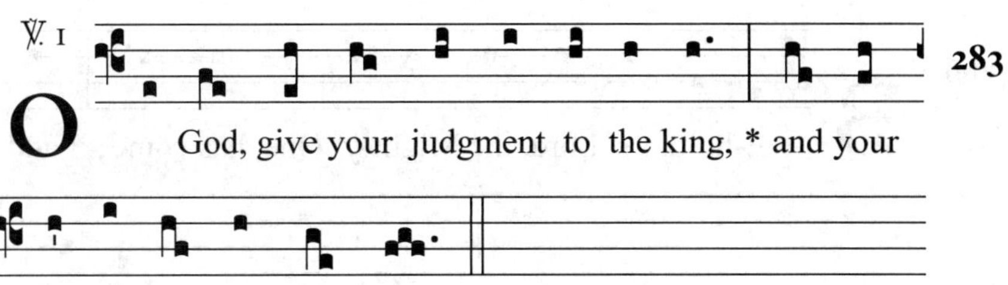
℣. 1
283
O God, give your judgment to the king, * and your
jus-tice to the king's son.

Iudica populum tuum in iustitia. Ps 71 : 2

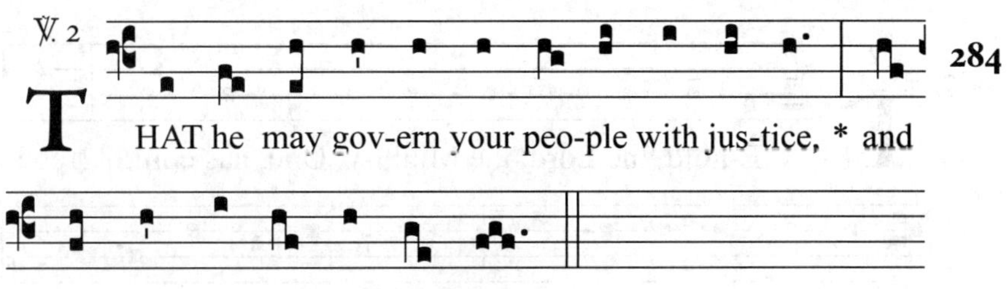
℣. 2
284
THAT he may gov-ern your peo-ple with jus-tice, * and
your poor ones in right judg-ment.

Iudicabit pauperes populi. Ps 71 : 4

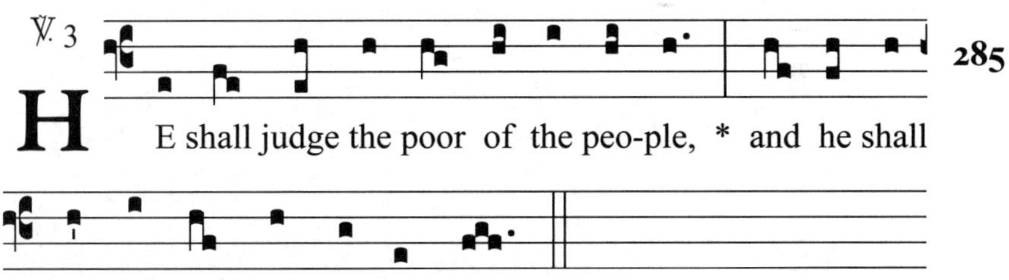
℣. 3
285
HE shall judge the poor of the peo-ple, * and he shall
save the chil-dren of the poor.

- iii -

286

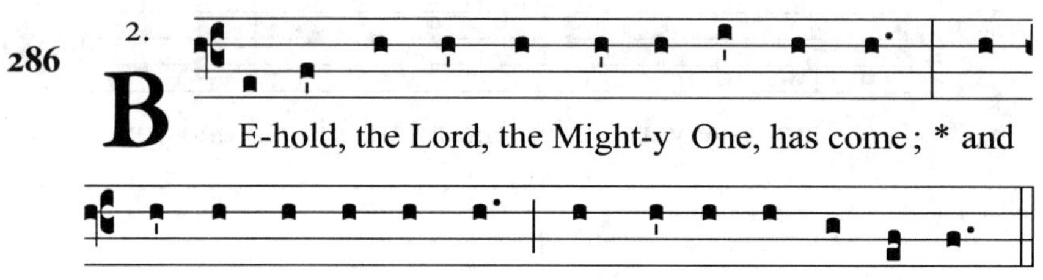
2.
BE-hold, the Lord, the Might-y One, has come; * and

kingship is in his grasp, and pow-er and do-min-ion.

- iv -

287

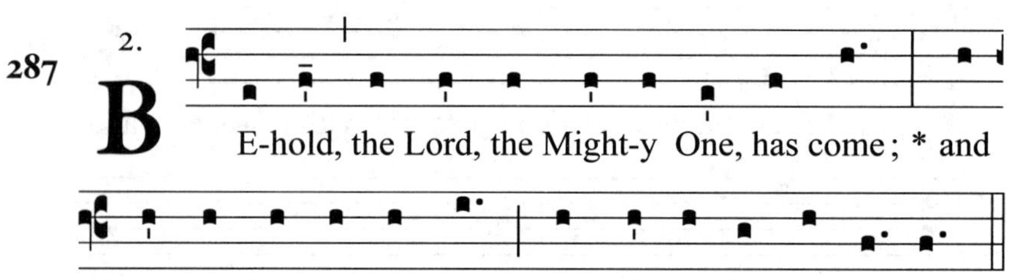
2.
BE-hold, the Lord, the Might-y One, has come; * and

kingship is in his grasp, and pow-er and do-min-ion.

OFFERTORY ANTIPHON *Regis Tharsis. Ps* 71 : 10. 11

- i -

5.
288
T
HE kings of Thar-sis * and the is- lands shall of-fer
presents ; the kings of the A-ra- bi-ans and of Sa- ba shall
bring gifts. And all kings of the earth shall a-dore him, all
na-tions shall serve him.

- ii -

5.
289
T
HE kings of Thar-sis and the is-lands * shall of- fer
presents ; the kings of the A- ra- bi-ans and of Sa-ba shall
bring gifts. And all kings of the earth shall a- dore him,
all na-tions shall serve him.

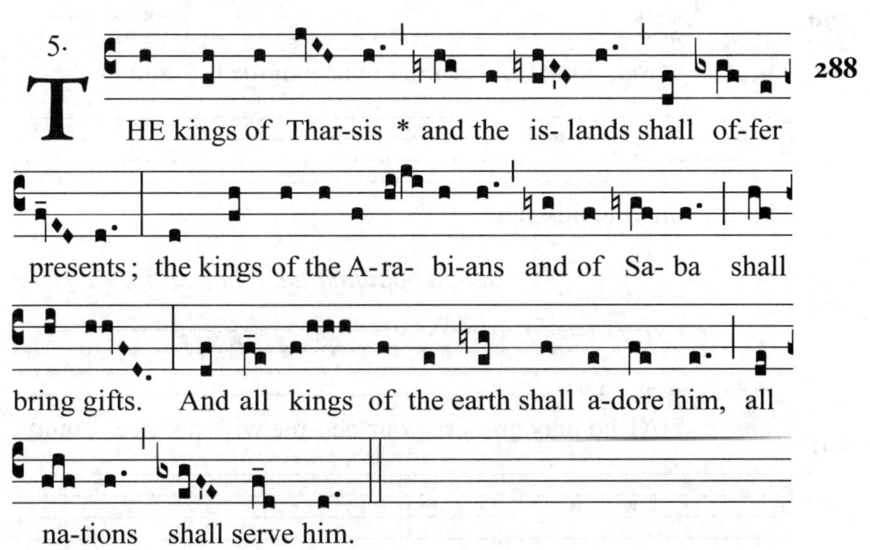

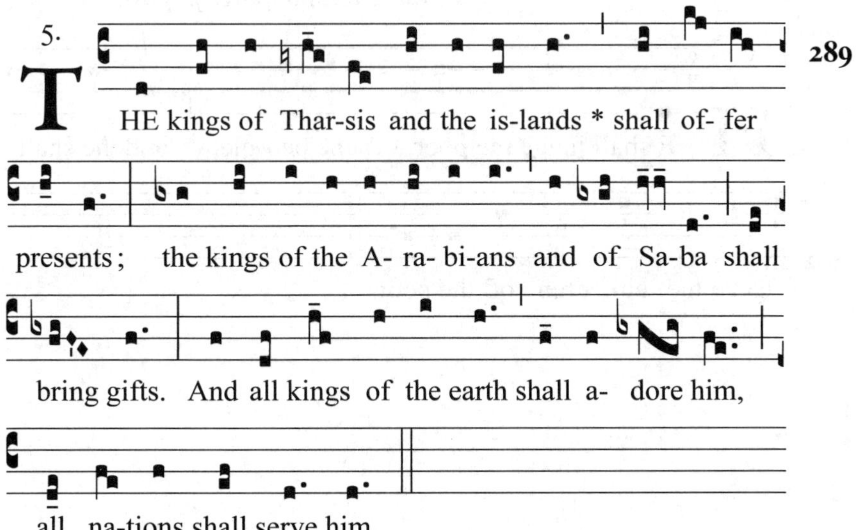

VERSES *Deus, iudicium tuum regi da. Ps* 71 : 2

290
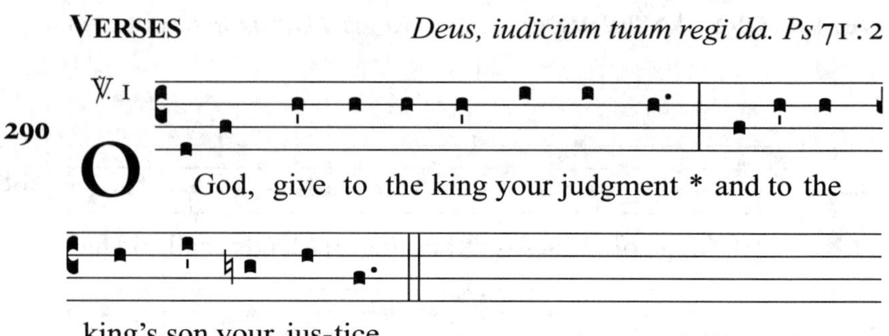
℣. 1
O God, give to the king your judgment * and to the
king's son your jus-tice.

Iudica populum tuum in iustitia. Ps 71 : 2

291
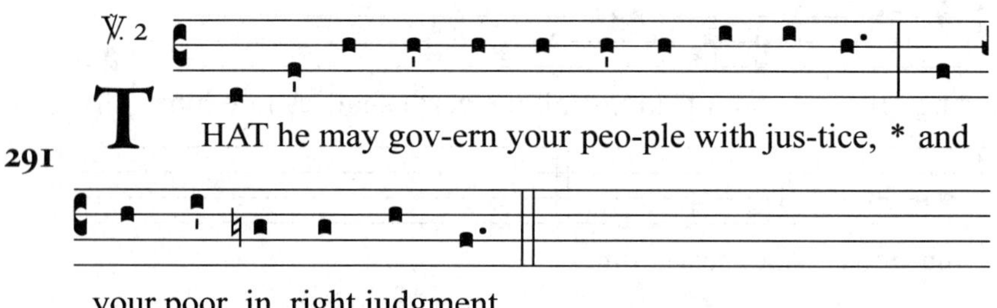
℣. 2
THAT he may gov-ern your peo-ple with jus-tice, * and
your poor in right judgment.

Iudicabit pauperes populi. Ps 71 : 4

292
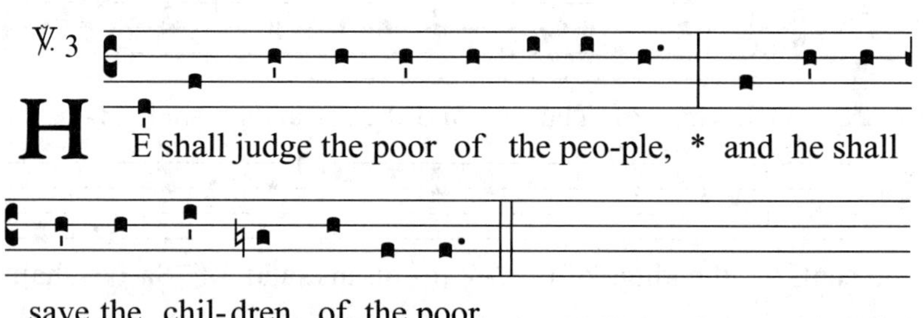
℣. 3
HE shall judge the poor of the peo-ple, * and he shall
save the chil-dren of the poor.

- iii -

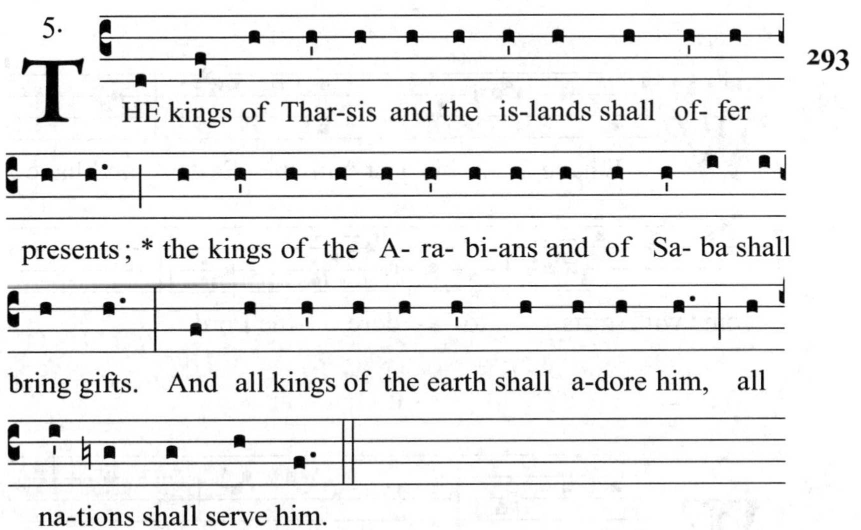

5.
293
THE kings of Thar-sis and the is-lands shall of- fer
presents; * the kings of the A- ra- bi-ans and of Sa- ba shall
bring gifts. And all kings of the earth shall a-dore him, all
na-tions shall serve him.

- iv -

5.
294
THE kings of Thar-sis and the is-lands shall of- fer
presents; * the kings of the A- ra- bi-ans and of Sa- ba shall
bring gifts. And all kings of the earth shall a-dore him, all
na-tions shall serve him.

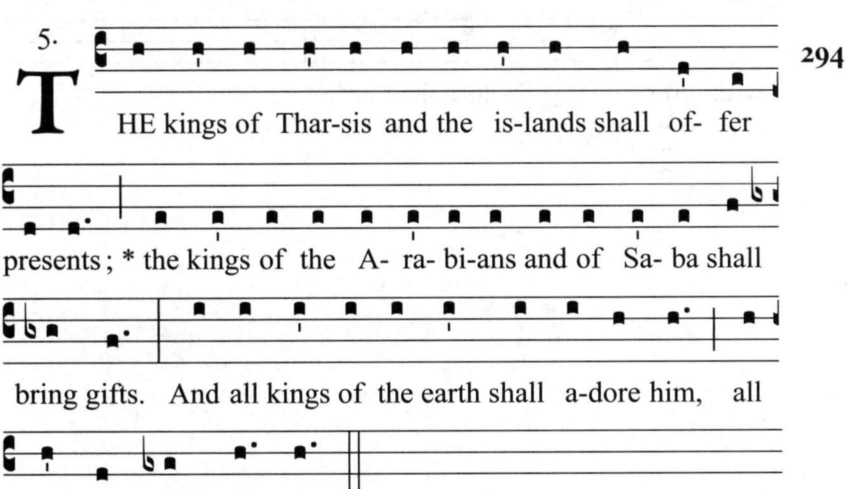

If psalm verses p. 118 *are used with this setting, sing te flat.*

Communion Antiphon *Vidimus stellam eius.*
Cf. Mt 2:2

- i -

295
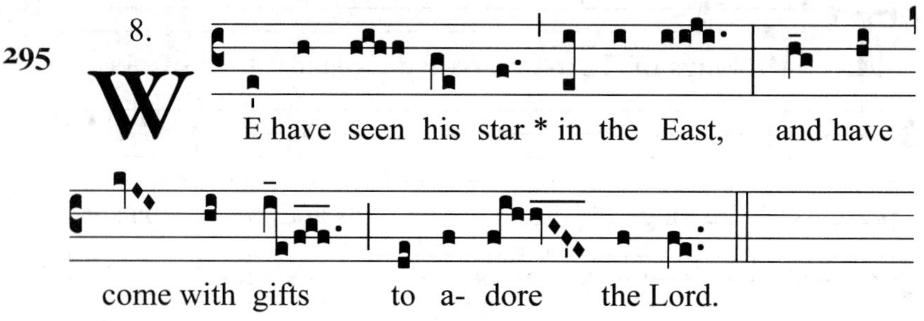
8.
W
E have seen his star * in the East, and have
come with gifts to a- dore the Lord.

- ii -

296
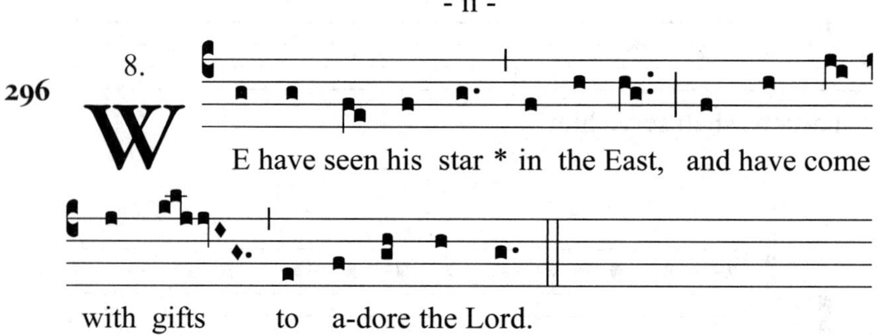
8.
W
E have seen his star * in the East, and have come
with gifts to a-dore the Lord.

VERSES *Lux orta est iusto. Ps* 96:11

℣. 1
297
LIght is ris- en for the just one, * and joy for the up-
right of heart.

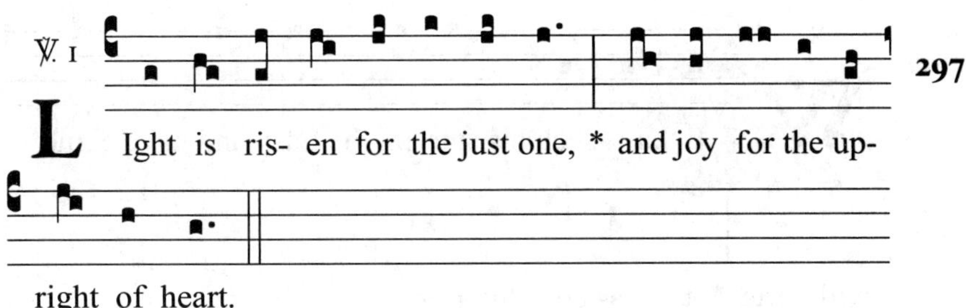

Exaltate Dominum Deum nostrum. Ps 98:9

℣. 2
298
EX- alt the Lord our God, and a-dore at his ho- ly
mountain, * for the Lord our God is ho- ly.

Viderunt omnes termini terræ. Ps 97:3-4

℣. 3
299
ALL the ends of the earth have seen the sal-va-tion of
our God. * Sing joy-ful- ly to God, all the earth; make mel-
o- dy, rejoice and sing.

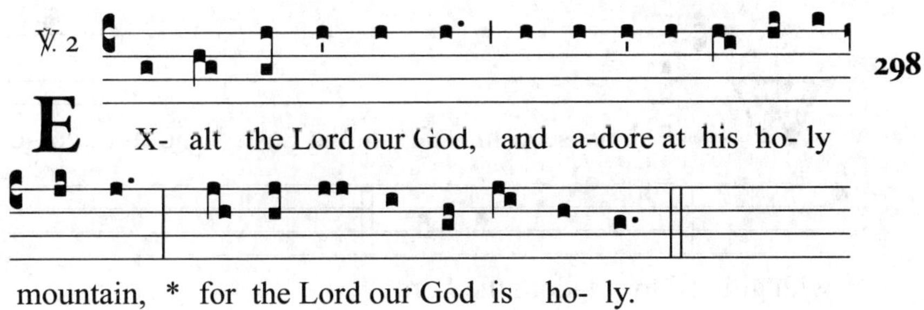

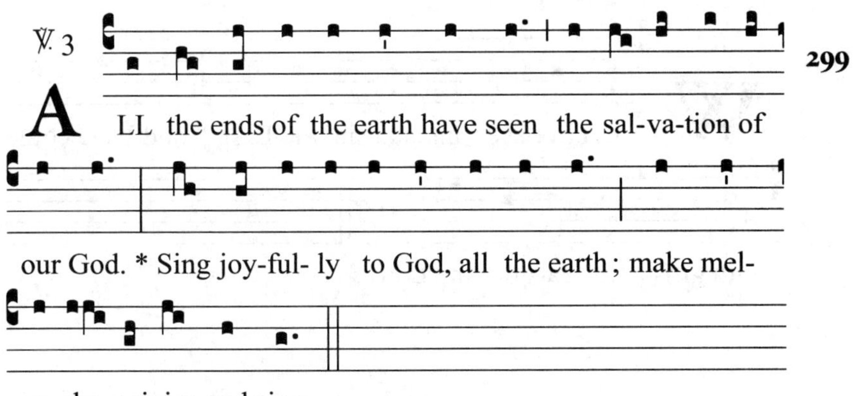

- iii -

300

8.
WE have seen his star in the East, and have come
with gifts * to a- dore the Lord.

Or:

301

8.
WE have seen his star in the East, * and have come
with gifts to a-dore the Lord.

- iv -

302

8.
WE have seen his star in the East, * and have come
with gifts to a-dore the Lord.

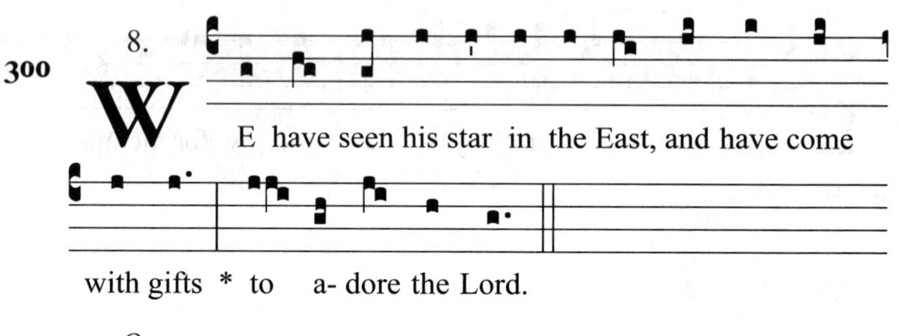

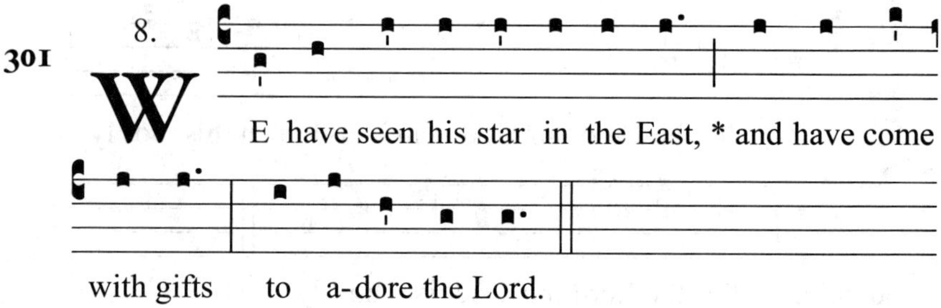

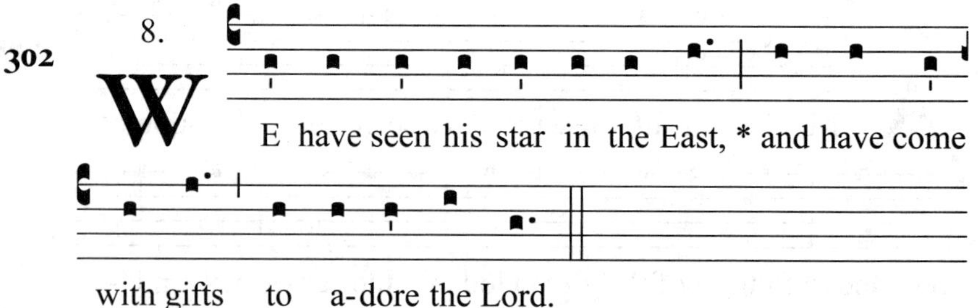

Sunday after the Epiphany of the Lord

THE BAPTISM OF THE LORD

ENTRANCE ANTIPHON *Baptizato Domino.*
Cf. Mt 3:16-17

- i -

7. 303

A F- ter * the Lord was bap-tized, the heav-ens were

opened, and the Spir- it de-scend-ed u- pon him like a

dove, and the voice of the Fa-ther thundered: This is my

be-lov- ed Son, with whom I am well pleased.

- ii -

7. 304

A F- ter * the Lord was bap-tized, the heav-ens were

opened, and the Spir- it de-scend-ed u- pon him like a

dove, and the voice of the Fa-ther thundered: This is my

be-lov- ed Son, with whom I am well pleased.

Verses *Cantate Domino canticum novum.* Ps 97:1

305 ℣. 1 O sing a new song to the Lord, for he has worked 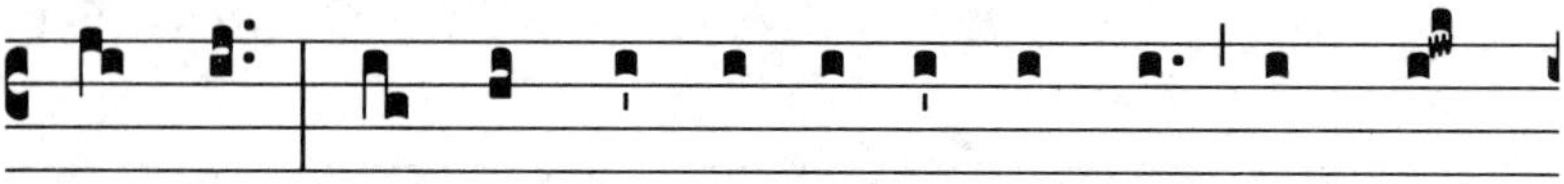 won-ders. * His right hand and his ho- ly arm have wrought 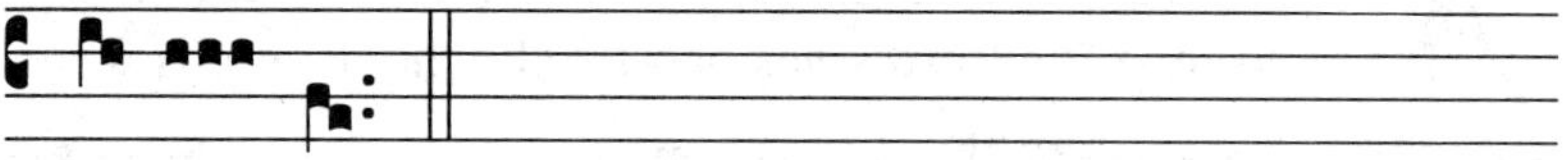 sal- va- tion.

Notum fecit Dominus salutare suum. Ps 97:2

306 ℣. 2 THE Lord has made known his sal- va-tion, he has re-  vealed his justice in the sight of the nations. * He has remem- bered his mer-cy and his truth toward the house of Is- ra- el.

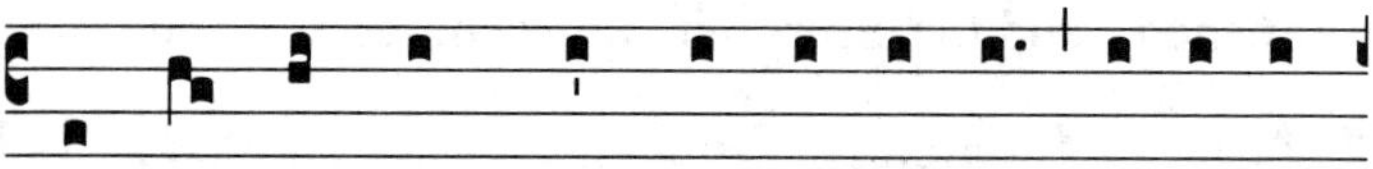

Viderunt omnes termini terræ. Ps 97:3-4

307 ℣. 3 ALL the ends of the earth have seen the sal-va-tion of  our God. * Sing joy-ful- ly to God, all the earth; make mel- o- dy, re-joice and sing.

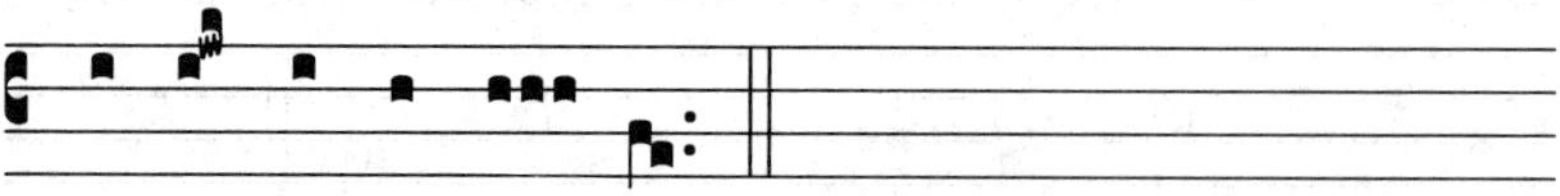

- iii -

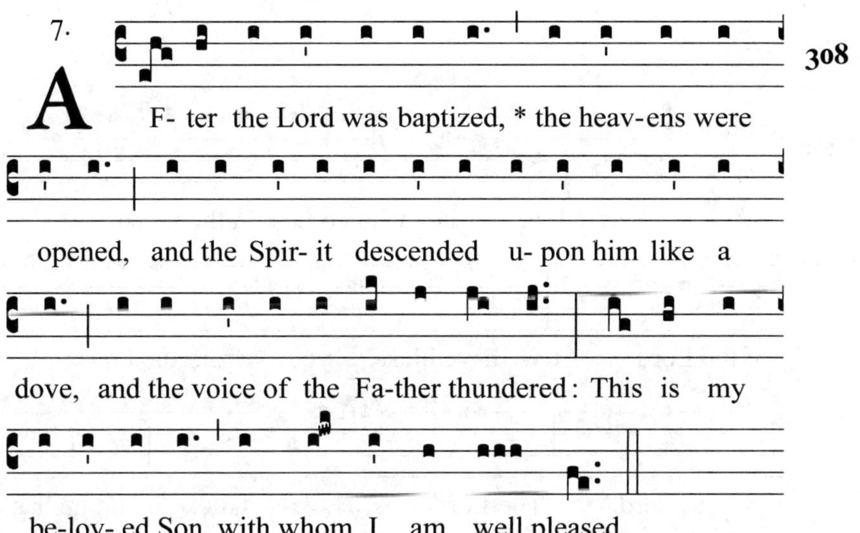
7.
308
A F- ter the Lord was baptized, * the heav-ens were
opened, and the Spir- it descended u- pon him like a
dove, and the voice of the Fa-ther thundered: This is my
be-lov- ed Son, with whom I am well pleased.

- iv -

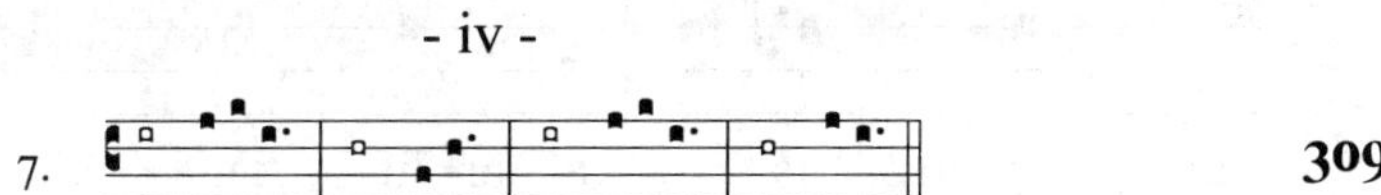
7.

309

After the Lord was baptized, / the heav- | *ens were* **o**-pened, *
and the Spirit descended upon him like | *a* **dove**,
and the voice of the | *Fa-ther* **thun**-dered:
This is my beloved Son, / with whom I am | *well* **pleased**.

OFFERTORY ANTIPHON *Benedictus qui venit.*
Ps 117:26. 27

- i -

310 8.

Bless-ed is he * who comes in the name of the Lord. We have blest you from the house of the Lord. The Lord is God, and he has shown up-on us, al- le- lu- ia, al- le- lu- ia.

- ii -

311 8.

Bless-ed is he * who comes in the name of the Lord. We have blessed you from the house of the Lord. The Lord is God, and he has shown up- on us, al- le-

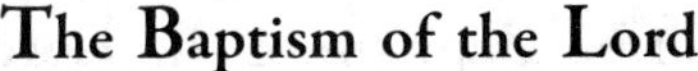

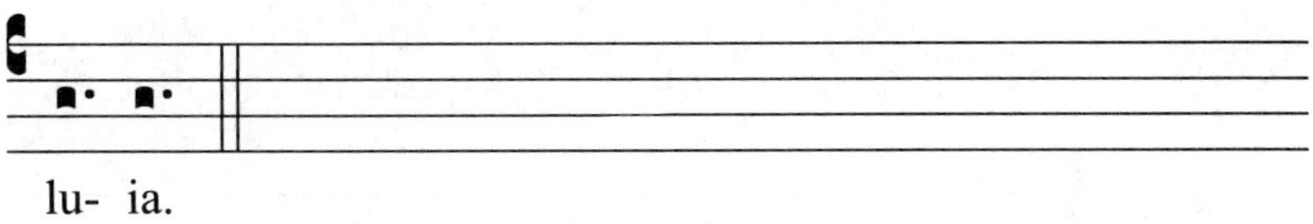
lu- ia.

VERSES *Lapidem, quem reprobaverunt. Psalm* 117:22

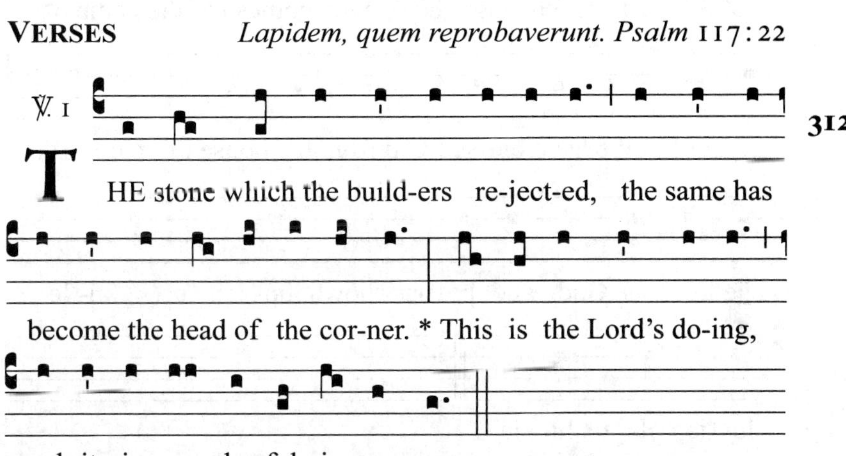
℣. 1
THE stone which the build-ers re-ject-ed, the same has
become the head of the cor-ner. * This is the Lord's do-ing,
and it is won-der-ful in our eyes.
312

Deus meus es tu, et confitebor tibi. Psalm 117:28

℣. 2
YOU are my God, and I will praise you; you are my
God, and I will ex- alt you. * I will praise you be-cause
you have heard me and have be-come my sal- va-tion.
313

- iii -

314

8.
B
Less- ed is he * who comes in the name of
the Lord. We have blessed you from the house of the Lord.
The Lord is God, and he has shown up- on us, al- le-
lu- ia, al- le- lu- ia.

- iv -

315

8.
B
Less- ed is he * who comes in the name of
the Lord. We have blessed you from the house of the Lord.
The Lord is God, and he has shown up- on us, al- le-
lu- ia, al- le- lu- ia.

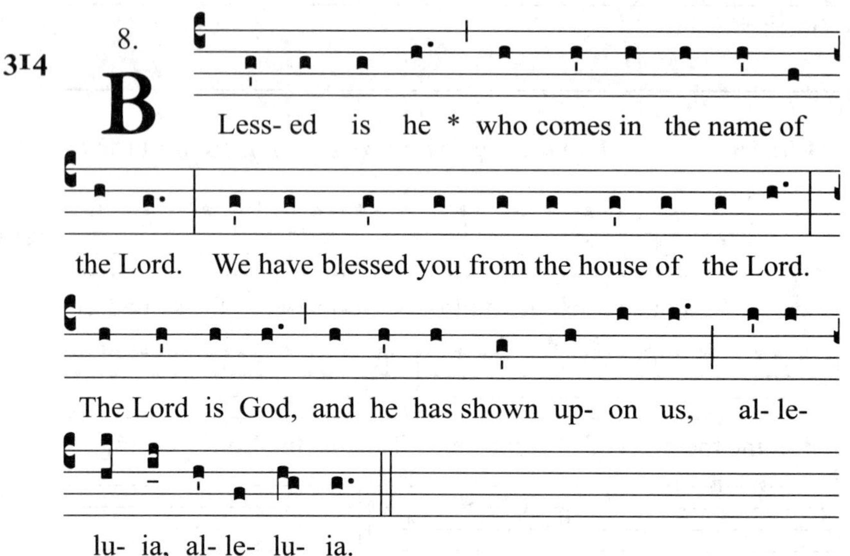

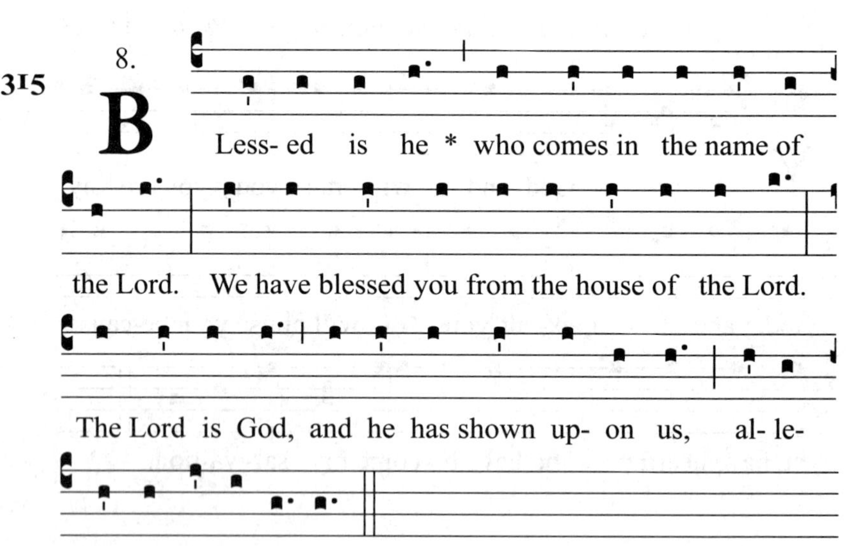

Communion Antiphon *Ecce de quo dicebat.*
Jn 1:32. 34

- i -

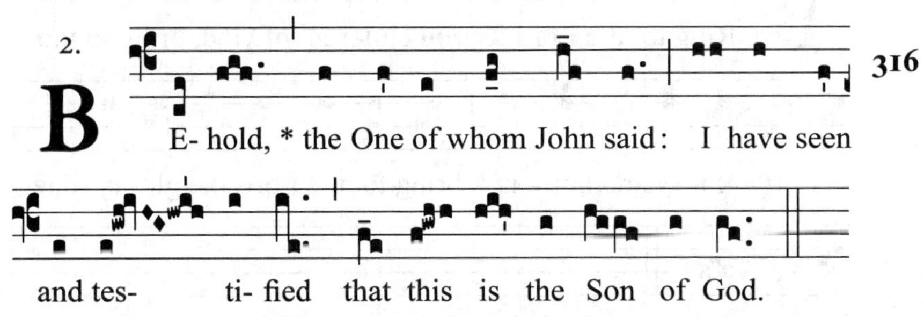
2.
B E- hold, * the One of whom John said: I have seen
and tes- ti- fied that this is the Son of God.

316

- ii -

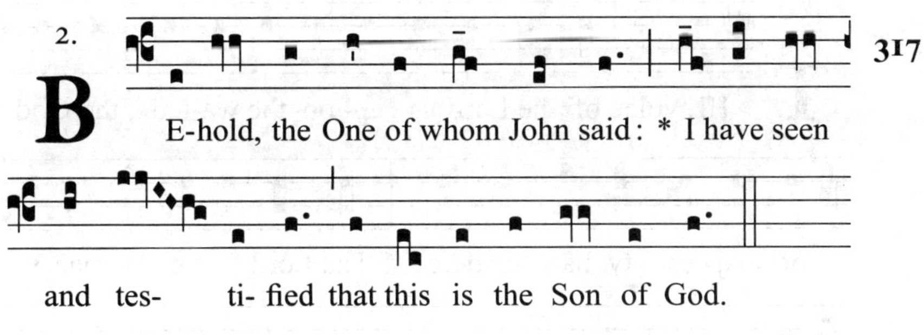
2.
B E-hold, the One of whom John said: * I have seen
and tes- ti- fied that this is the Son of God.

317

Or :

Omnes qui in Christo. Gal 3:27

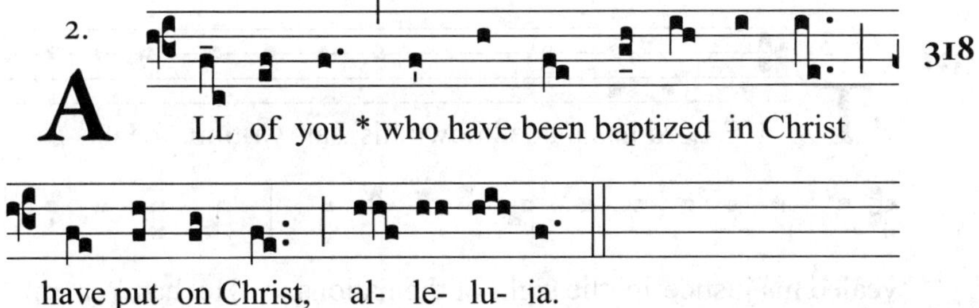
2.
A LL of you * who have been baptized in Christ
have put on Christ, al- le- lu- ia.

318

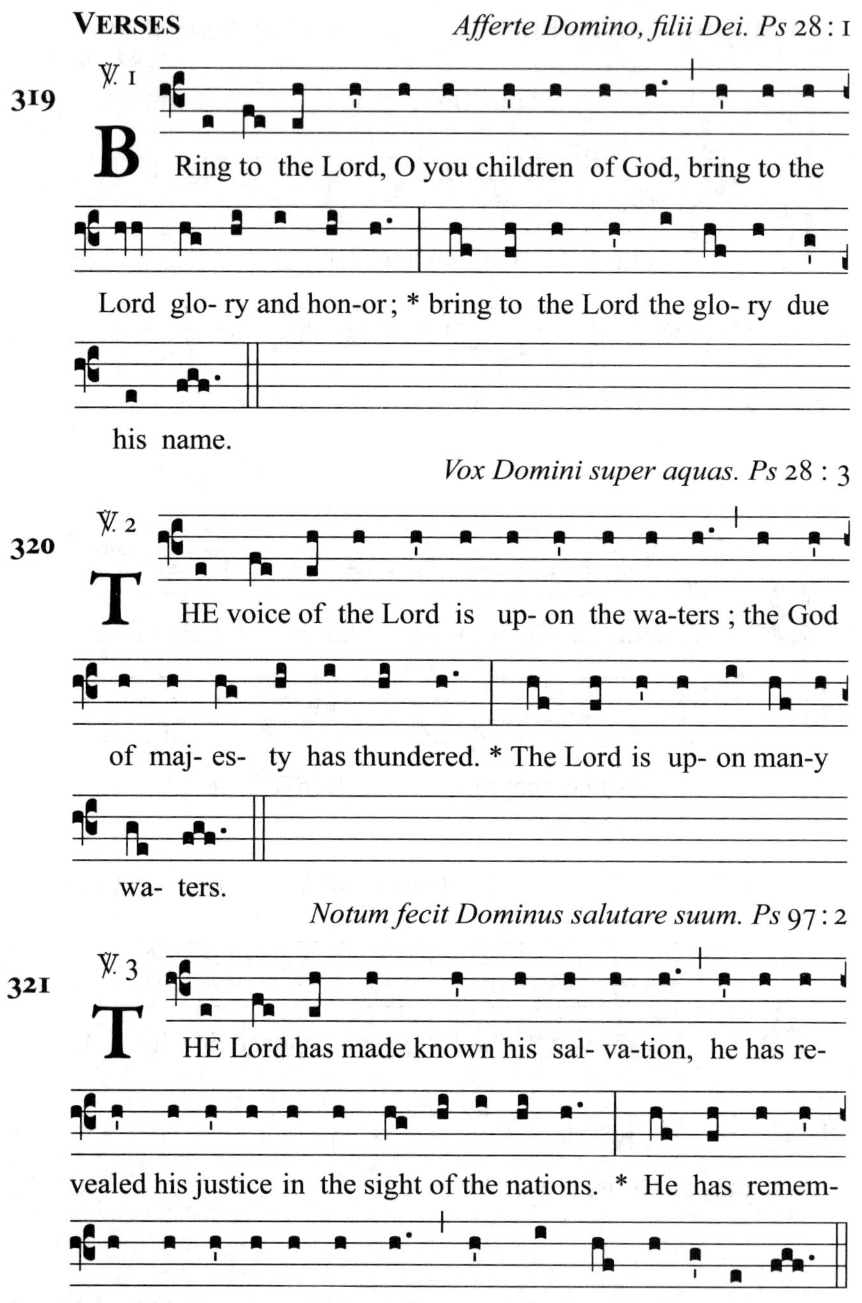
VERSES
Afferte Domino, filii Dei. Ps 28 : 1
319
℣. 1
BRing to the Lord, O you children of God, bring to the
Lord glo- ry and hon-or; * bring to the Lord the glo- ry due
his name.
Vox Domini super aquas. Ps 28 : 3
320
℣. 2
THE voice of the Lord is up- on the wa-ters ; the God
of maj- es- ty has thundered. * The Lord is up- on man-y
wa- ters.
Notum fecit Dominus salutare suum. Ps 97 : 2
321
℣. 3
THE Lord has made known his sal- va-tion, he has revealed his justice in the sight of the nations. * He has remembered his mercy and his truth toward the house of Is- ra- el.

- iii -

2.
BE- hold, the One of whom John said : * I have seen
and tes- ti-fied that this is the Son of God.

322

Or :

2.
BE- hold, the One of whom John said : * I have seen
and tes- ti- fied that this is the Son of God.

323

Or :

2.
ALL of you who have been bap-tized in Christ *
have put on Christ, al- le- lu- ia.

324

- iv -

2.
BE- hold, the One of whom John said : * I have seen

325

and tes- ti- fied that this is the Son of God.

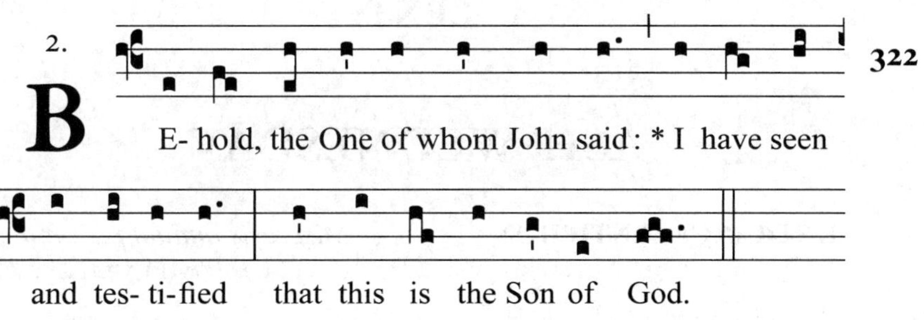

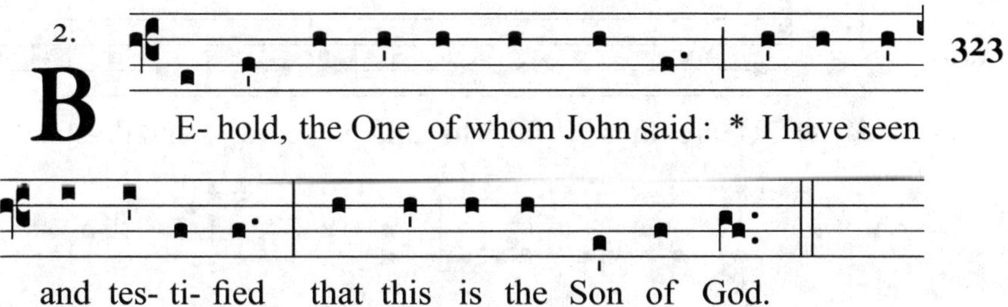

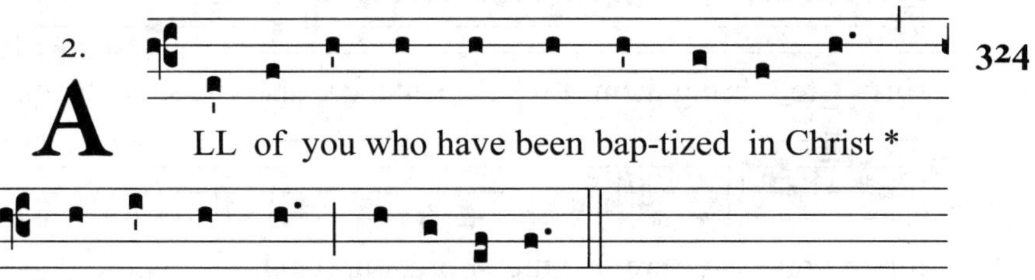

LENT

ASH WEDNESDAY

Entrance Antiphon *Misereris omnium, Domine.*
Cf. Wis 11:24. 25. 27

- i -

326

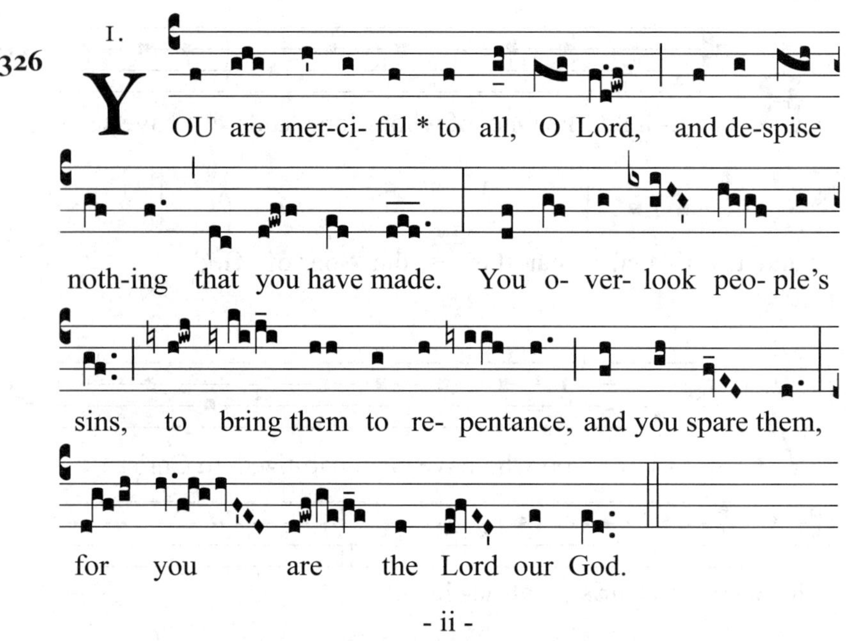
I.
YOU are mer-ci- ful * to all, O Lord, and de-spise
noth-ing that you have made. You o- ver- look peo- ple's
sins, to bring them to re- pentance, and you spare them,
for you are the Lord our God.

- ii -

327

I.
YOU are mer-ci-ful to all, O Lord, * and despise nothing
that you have made. You o- ver-look peo-ple's sins, to bring

them to re-pentance, and you spare them, for you are the Lord
our God.

VERSES *Miserere mei, Deus. Ps* 56:2

℣. 1
HAVE mer-cy on me, O God, have mer-cy on me, *
328
for in you my soul has tak- en ref- uge.

Exaltare super cælos, Deus. Ps 56:6

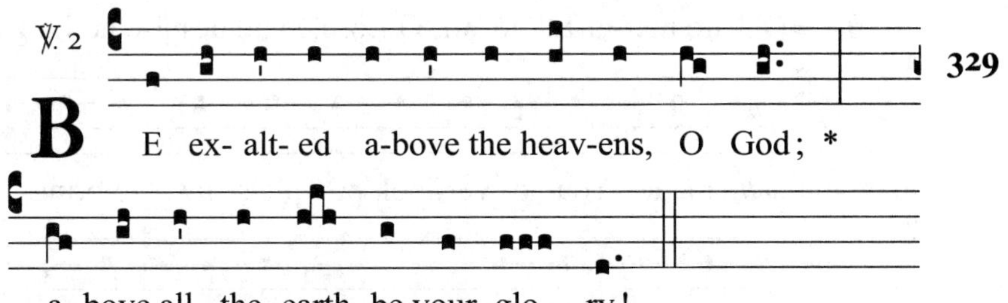
℣. 2
BE ex- alt- ed a-bove the heav-ens, O God; *
329
a- bove all the earth be your glo- ry!

- iii -

330

I.
YOU are mer-ci-ful to all, O Lord, * and despise nothing
that you have made. You o- ver-look peo-ple's sins, to bring
them to re-pentance, and you spare them, for you are the
Lord our God.

- iv -

331

I.
YOU are mer-ci-ful to all, O Lord, * and despise nothing
that you have made. You o- ver-look peo-ple's sins, to bring
them to re-pentance, and you spare them, for you are the Lord
our God.

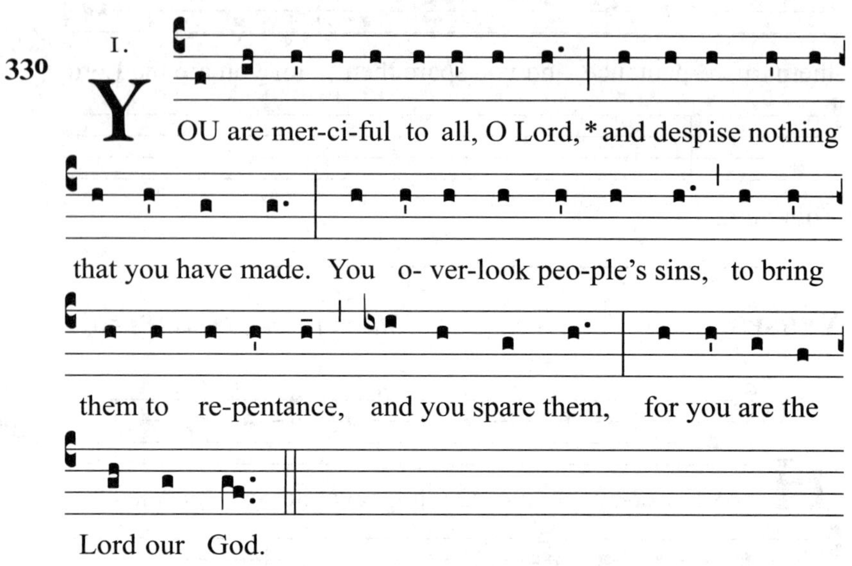

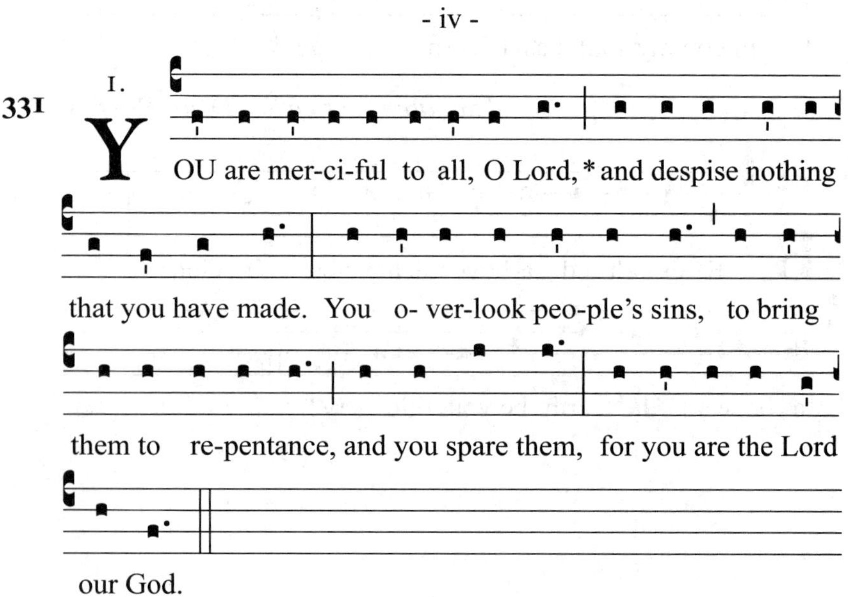

BLESSING AND DISTRIBUTION OF ASHES

ANTIPHON 1

Immutemur habitu, in cinere et cilicio.

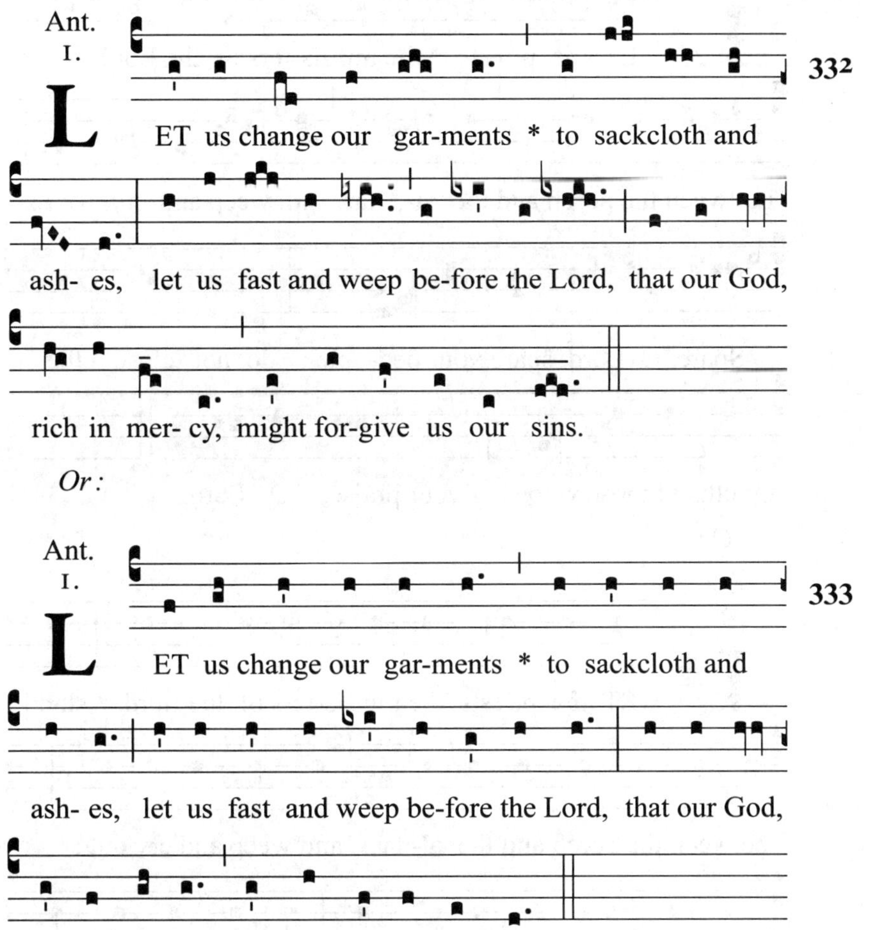
Ant. I.
LET us change our gar-ments * to sackcloth and
332
ash- es, let us fast and weep be-fore the Lord, that our God,
rich in mer- cy, might for-give us our sins.
Or:
Ant. I.
LET us change our gar-ments * to sackcloth and
333
ash- es, let us fast and weep be-fore the Lord, that our God,
rich in mer-cy, might for-give us our sins.

ANTIPHON 2

Inter vestibulum et altare. Cf Jl 2:17; *Est* 4:17

334

335

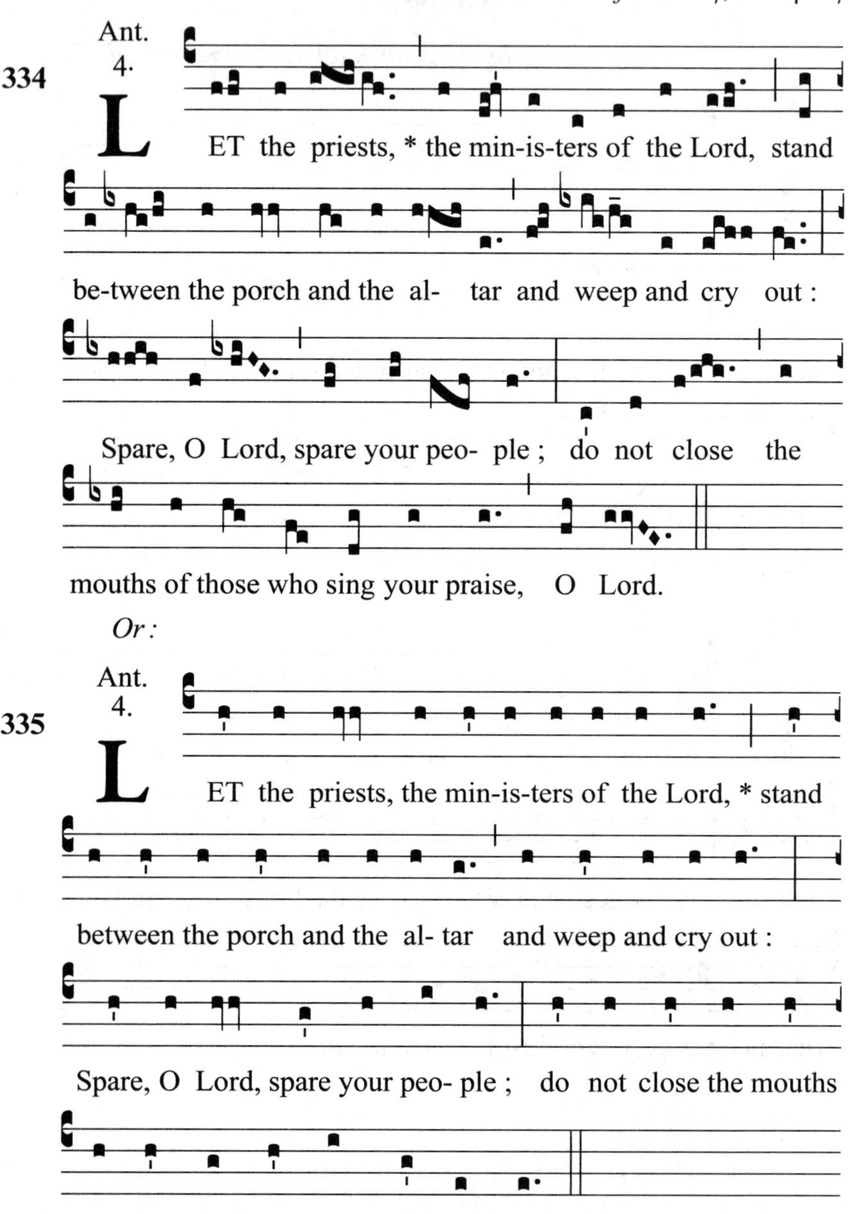
Ant.
4.
LET the priests, * the min-is-ters of the Lord, stand
be-tween the porch and the al- tar and weep and cry out :
Spare, O Lord, spare your peo- ple ; do not close the
mouths of those who sing your praise, O Lord.
Or :
Ant.
4.
LET the priests, the min-is-ters of the Lord, * stand
between the porch and the al- tar and weep and cry out :
Spare, O Lord, spare your peo- ple ; do not close the mouths
of those who sing your praise, O Lord.

ANTIPHON 3

Dele, Domine, iniquitatem meam. Ps 50:3

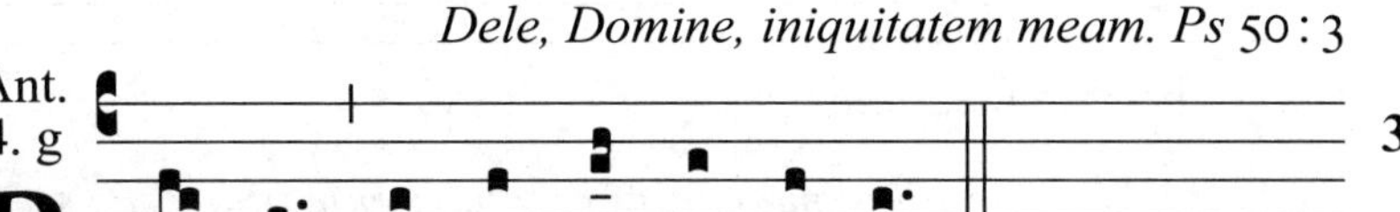
Ant.
4. g

336

B Lot out * my transgressions, O Lord.

VERSES *Miserere mei, Deus. Ps* 50:3

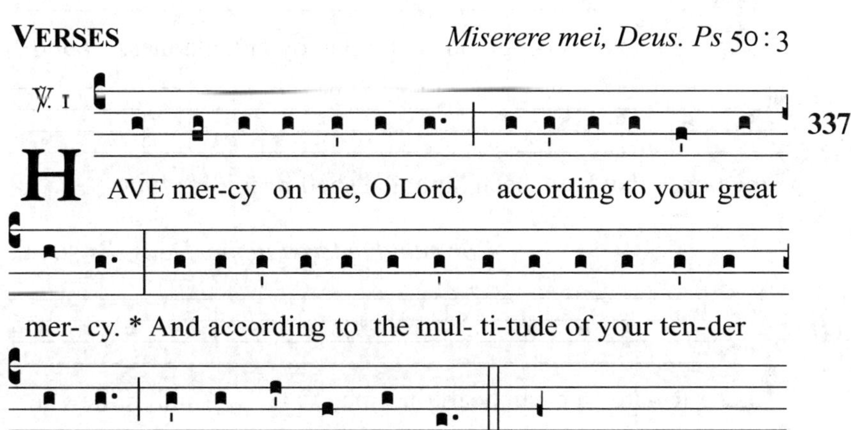
℣. 1
HAVE mer-cy on me, O Lord, according to your great
mer- cy. * And according to the mul- ti-tude of your ten-der

337

mer-cies, blot out my transgressions. *Ant.*

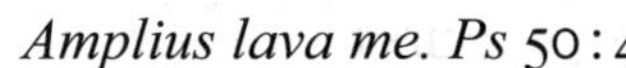

Amplius lava me. Ps 50:4

℣. 2
WASH me yet more from my in- i- qui- ty, * and
cleanse me from my sin. *Ant.*

338

Quoniam iniquitatem meam ego cognosco. Ps 50:5

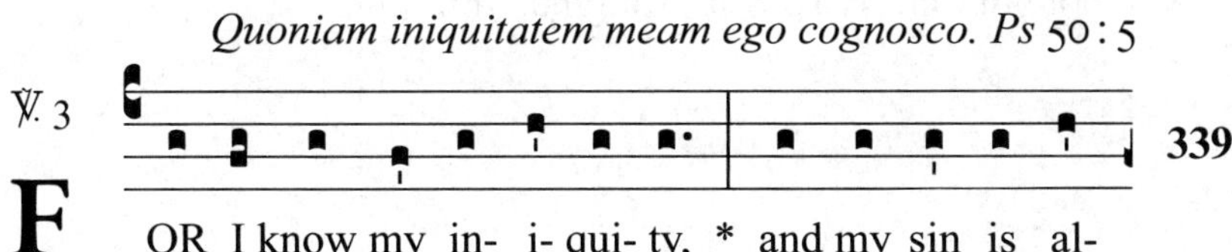
℣. 3
FOR I know my in- i- qui- ty, * and my sin is al-

339

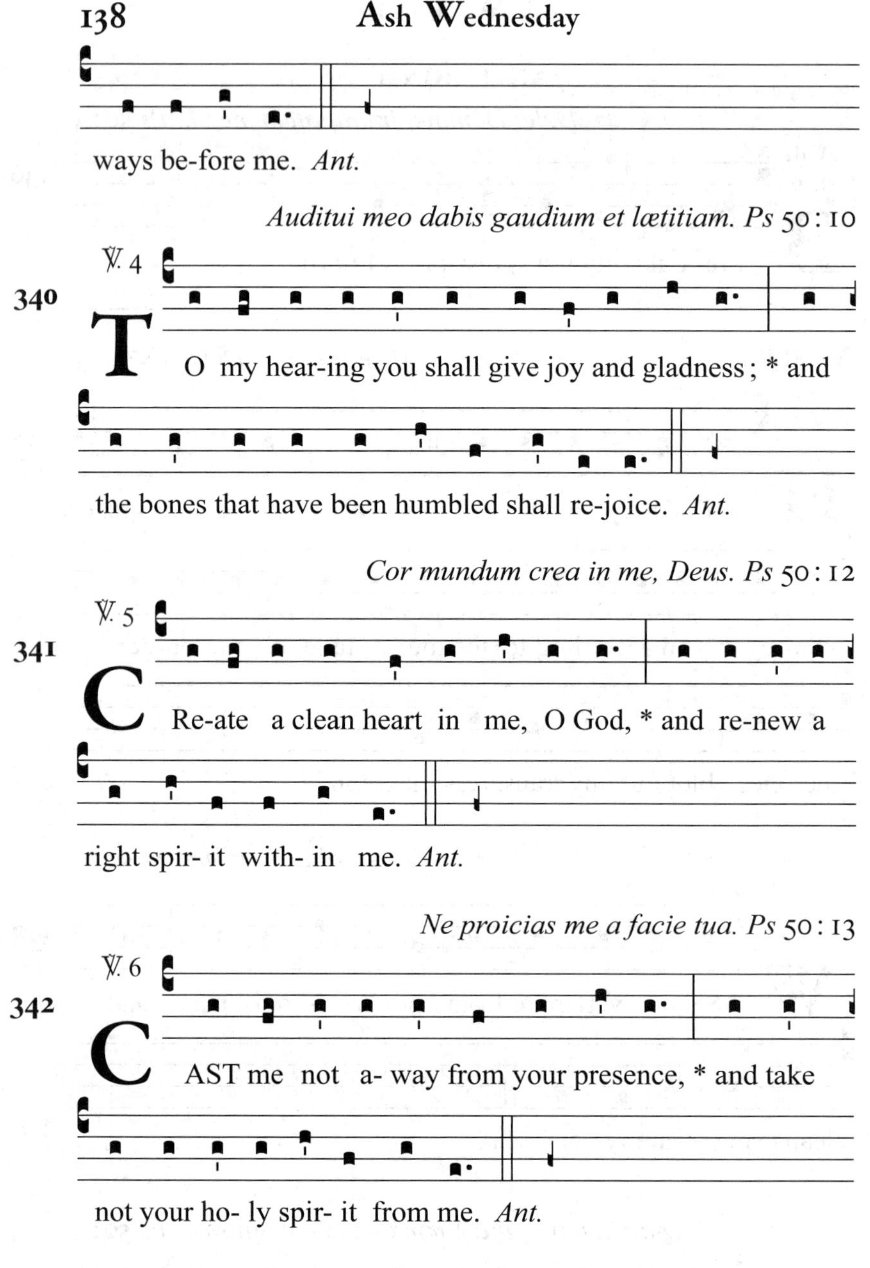
ways be-fore me. Ant.
Auditui meo dabis gaudium et lætitiam. Ps 50:10
℣. 4
340
TO my hear-ing you shall give joy and gladness; * and
the bones that have been humbled shall re-joice. Ant.
Cor mundum crea in me, Deus. Ps 50:12
℣. 5
341
CRe-ate a clean heart in me, O God, * and re-new a
right spir- it with- in me. Ant.
Ne proicias me a facie tua. Ps 50:13
℣. 6
342
CAST me not a- way from your presence, * and take
not your ho- ly spir- it from me. Ant.

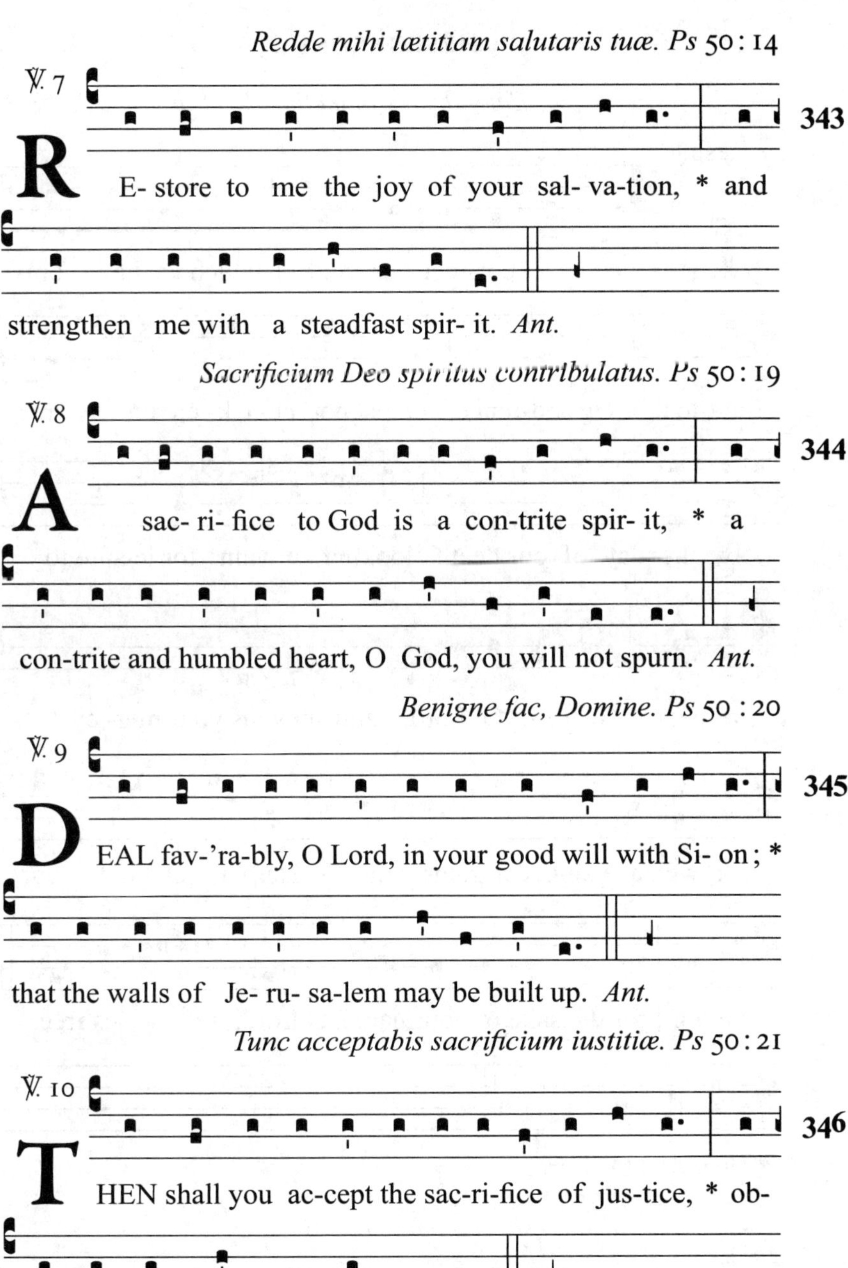
Redde mihi lætitiam salutaris tuæ. Ps 50 : 14
℣. 7 343
RE- store to me the joy of your sal- va-tion, * and
strengthen me with a steadfast spir- it. *Ant.*
Sacrificium Deo spiritus contribulatus. Ps 50 : 19
℣. 8 344
A sac- ri- fice to God is a con-trite spir- it, * a
con-trite and humbled heart, O God, you will not spurn. *Ant.*
Benigne fac, Domine. Ps 50 : 20
℣. 9 345
DEAL fav-'ra-bly, O Lord, in your good will with Si- on ; *
that the walls of Je- ru- sa-lem may be built up. *Ant.*
Tunc acceptabis sacrificium iustitiæ. Ps 50 : 21
℣. 10 346
THEN shall you ac-cept the sac-ri-fice of jus-tice, * ob-

la-tions and whole burnt of- fer- ings. *Ant.*

Responsory

Emendemus in melius. Cf. Bar 3:2; *Ps* 78:9

347

Resp.
2.
LET us cor-rect our faults † which we have com-
mit-ted in ig- no-rance, let us not be tak- en un- awares
by the day of our death, looking in vain for leisure to
re-pent. * Hear us, O Lord, and show us your mer- cy,
for we have sinned a-gainst you. ℣. Help us, O God our
Savior ; for the sake of your name, O Lord, set us free.
* Hear us, O Lord.

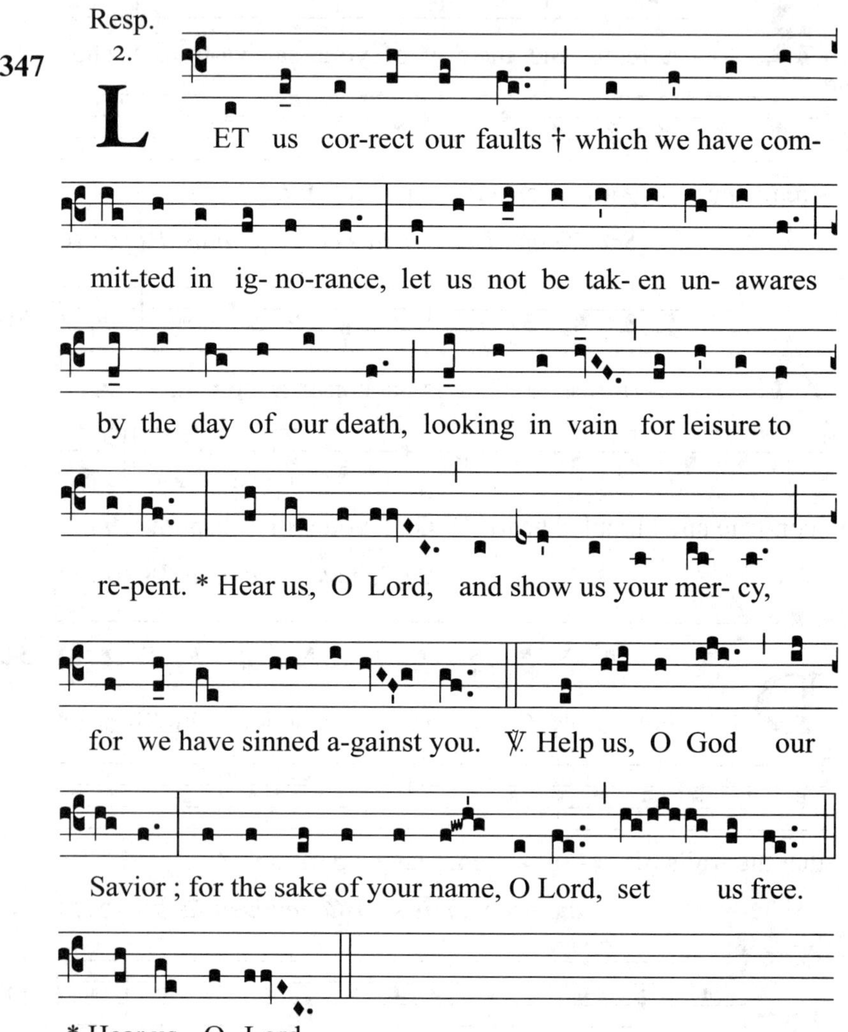

Or:

Resp. 2.
LET us correct our faults † which we have com- 348
mit-ted in ig-norance, let us not be tak-en un- a-wares
by the day of our death, looking in vain for leisure to
re-pent. * Hear us, O Lord, and show us your mer- cy,
for we have sinned against you. ℣. Help us, O God our
Sav-ior ; for the sake of your name, O Lord, set us free.

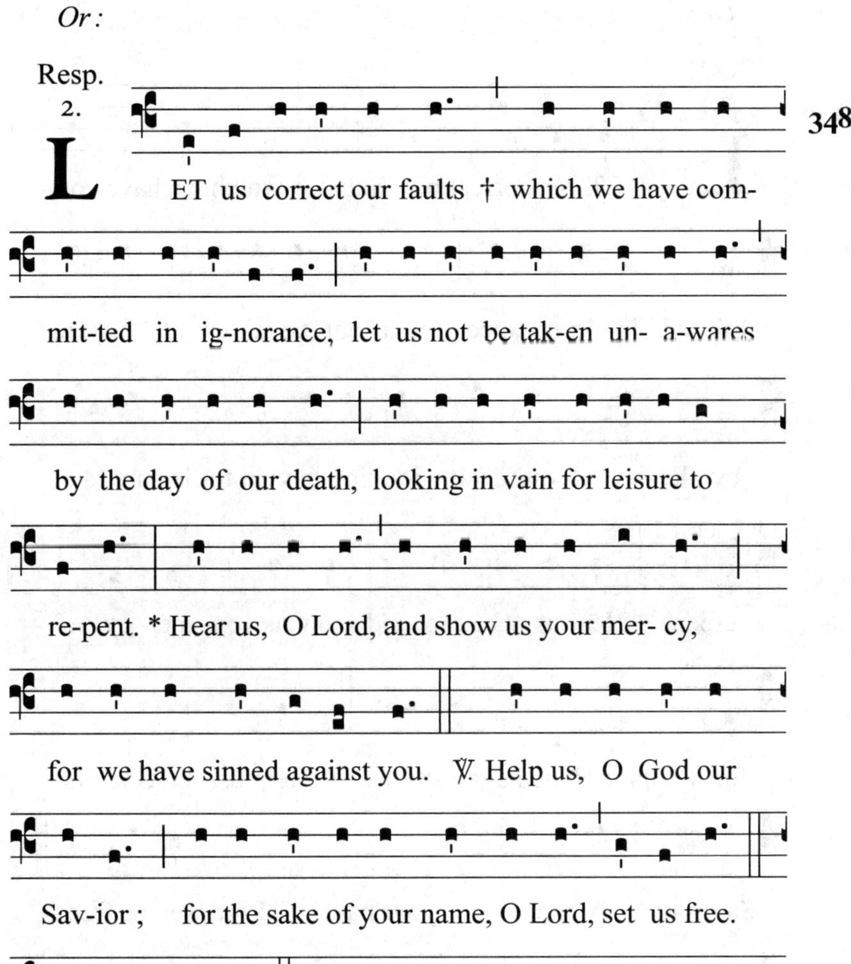

* Hear us, O Lord.

Or:

Resp.
2.

349

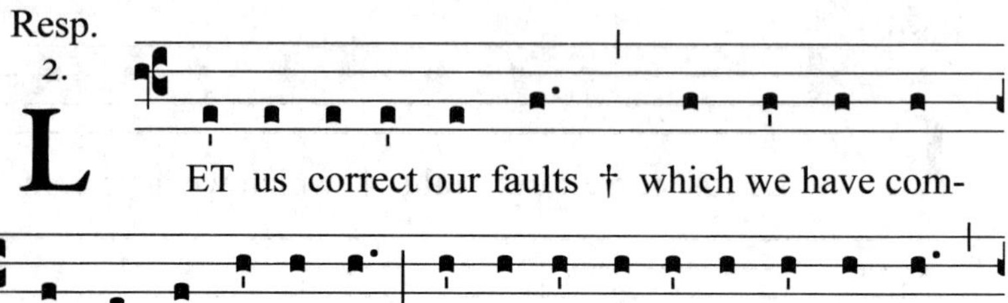

LET us correct our faults † which we have com-

mit-ted in ig-norance, let us not be tak-en un- a-wares

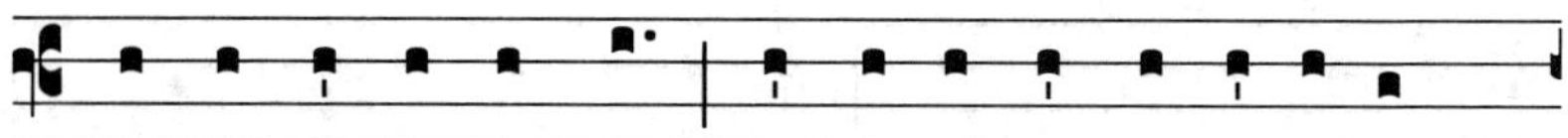

by the day of our death, looking in vain for leisure to

re-pent. * Hear us, O Lord, and show us your mer- cy,

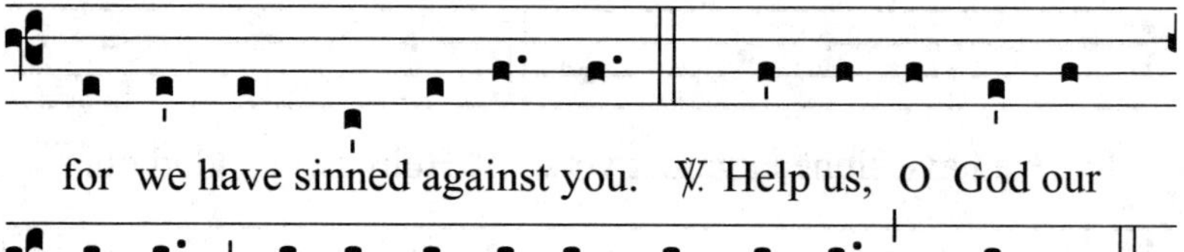

for we have sinned against you. ℣. Help us, O God our

Sav-ior ; for the sake of your name, O Lord, set us free.

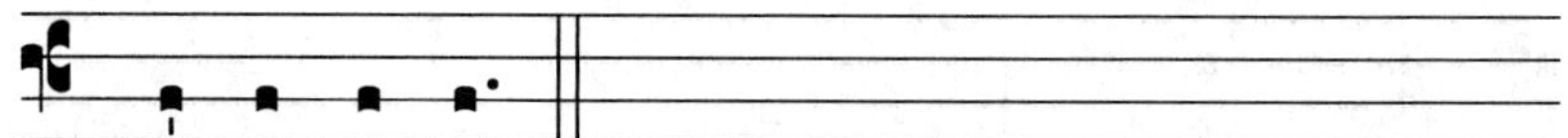

* Hear us, O Lord.

OFFERTORY ANTIPHON *Exaltabo te, Domine.*
Ps 29:2-3

- i -

2.
350
I will ex- tol you, O Lord, * for you have up-held
me, and have not let my en- e-mies re-joice o- ver me.
O Lord, I have cried to you, and you have healed me.

- ii -

2.
351
I will ex- tol you, O Lord, * for you have up-held
me, and have not let my en- e- mies re-joice o- ver me.
O Lord, I have cried to you, and you have healed me.

VERSES *Domine, eduxisti. Ps* 29:4

352
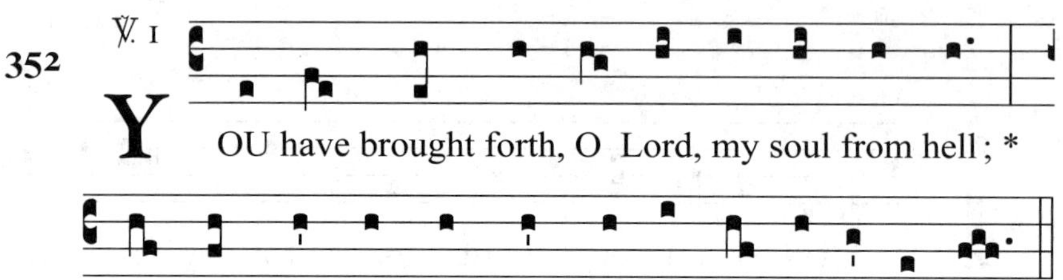
℣. 1
YOU have brought forth, O Lord, my soul from hell; *
you have saved me from those who go down in- to the pit.

Audivit Dominus. Ps 29:11-12

353
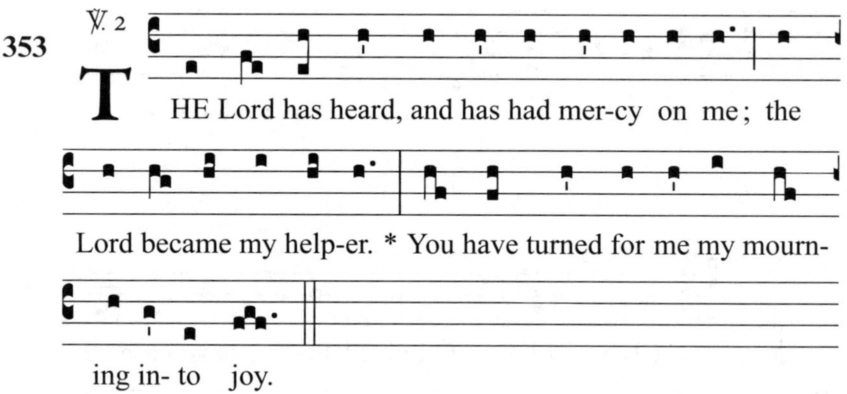
℣. 2
THE Lord has heard, and has had mer-cy on me; the
Lord became my help-er. * You have turned for me my mourning in- to joy.

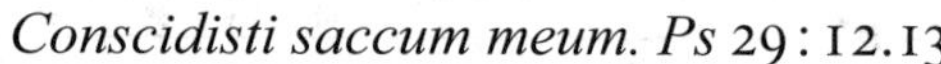
Conscidisti saccum meum. Ps 29:12.13

354
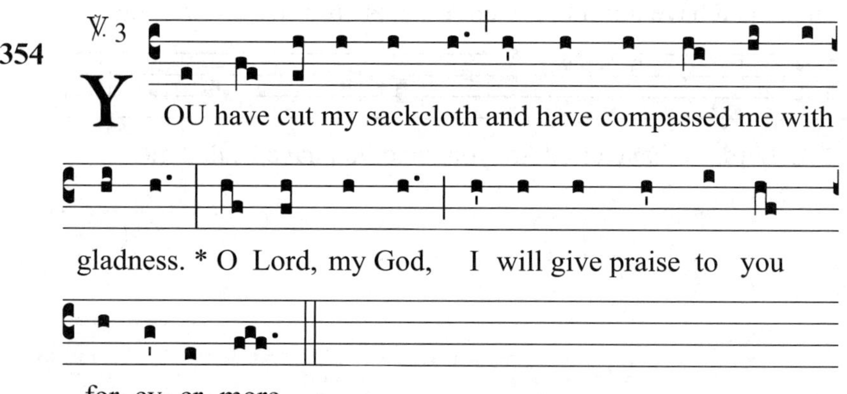
℣. 3
YOU have cut my sackcloth and have compassed me with
gladness. * O Lord, my God, I will give praise to you
for ev- er- more.

- iii -

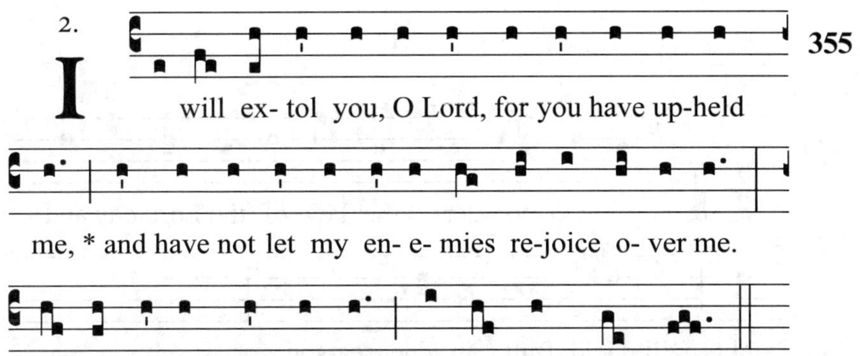

2.
355
I will ex- tol you, O Lord, for you have up-held
me, * and have not let my en- e- mies re-joice o- ver me.

O Lord, I have cried to you, and you have healed me.

- iv -

2.
356
I will ex- tol you, O Lord, * for you have up-held
me, and have not let my en- e- mies re-joice o- ver me.

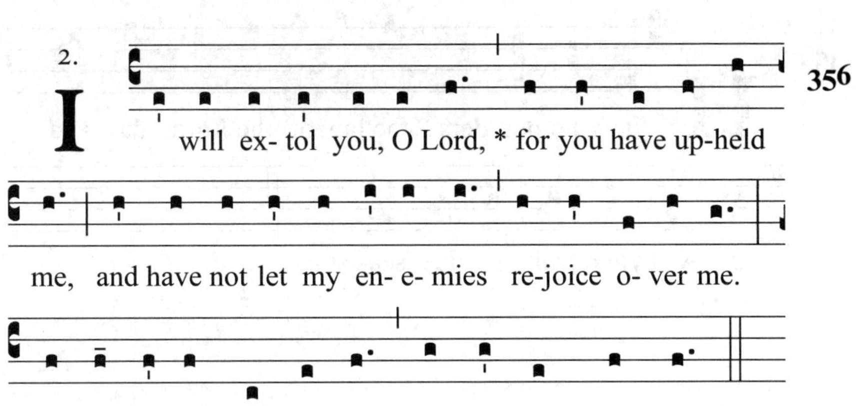

O Lord, I have cried to you, and you have healed me.

COMMUNION ANTIPHON *Qui meditabitur in lege Domini.*
Ps 1:2-3

- i -

357

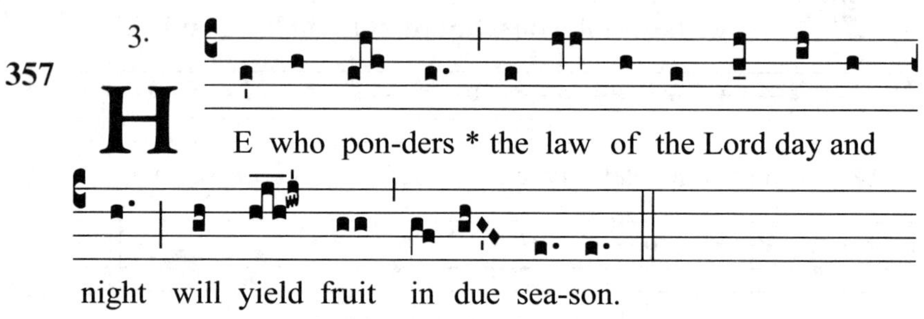
3.
HE who pon-ders * the law of the Lord day and
night will yield fruit in due sea-son.

- ii -

358

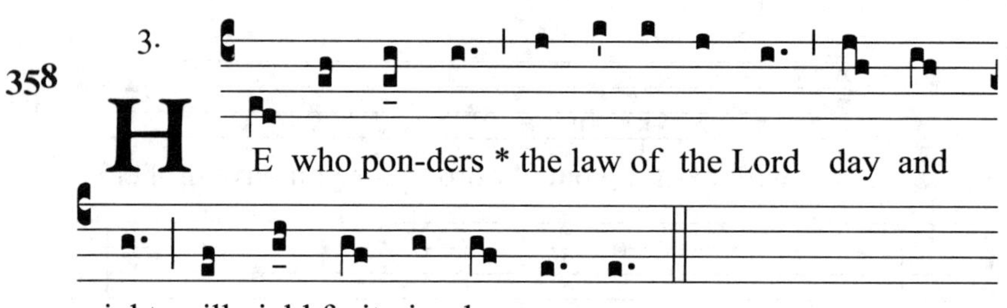
3.
HE who pon-ders * the law of the Lord day and
night will yield fruit in due sea- son.

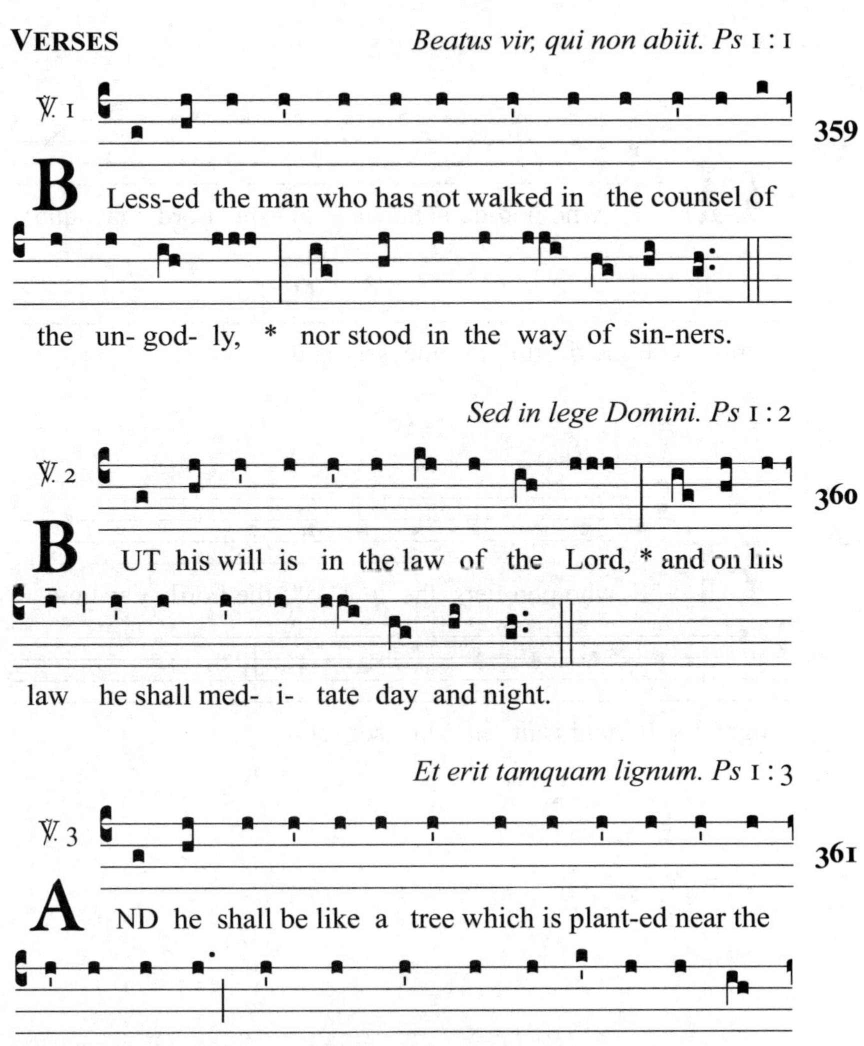
VERSES
Beatus vir, qui non abiit. Ps 1 : 1
℣. 1
359
BLess-ed the man who has not walked in the counsel of
the un- god- ly, * nor stood in the way of sin-ners.
Sed in lege Domini. Ps 1 : 2
℣. 2
360
BUT his will is in the law of the Lord, * and on his
law he shall med- i- tate day and night.
Et erit tamquam lignum. Ps 1 : 3
℣. 3
361
AND he shall be like a tree which is plant-ed near the
running wa-ters, which shall bring forth its fruit in due sea-

son, * and whose leaves shall nev- er fade.

- iii -

362

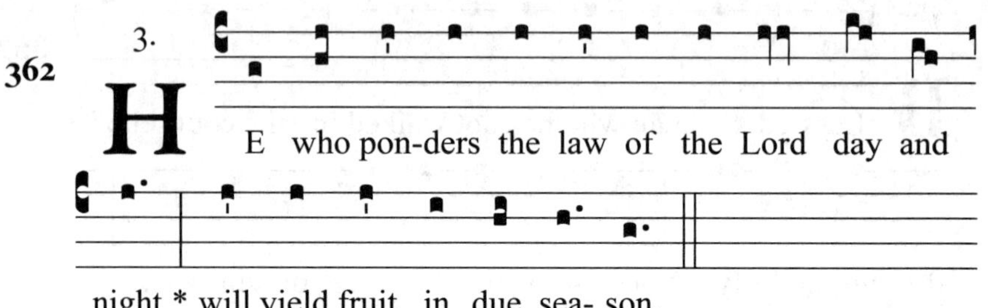
3.
HE who pon-ders the law of the Lord day and
night * will yield fruit in due sea- son.

- iv -

363

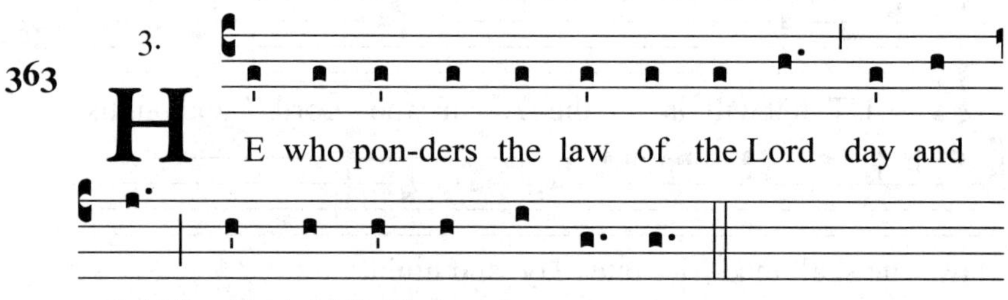
3.
HE who pon-ders the law of the Lord day and
night * will yield fruit in due sea- son.

FIRST SUNDAY OF LENT

Entrance Antiphon *Invocabit me.* *Ps* 90:15-16

- i -

8.
W
HEN he calls on me, * I will an- swer him ; I
will de- liv- er him and give him glo- ry, I will grant
him length of days.

364

- ii -

8.
W
HEN he calls on me, * I will answer him ; I
will de- liv- er him and give him glo- ry, I will grant him
length of days.

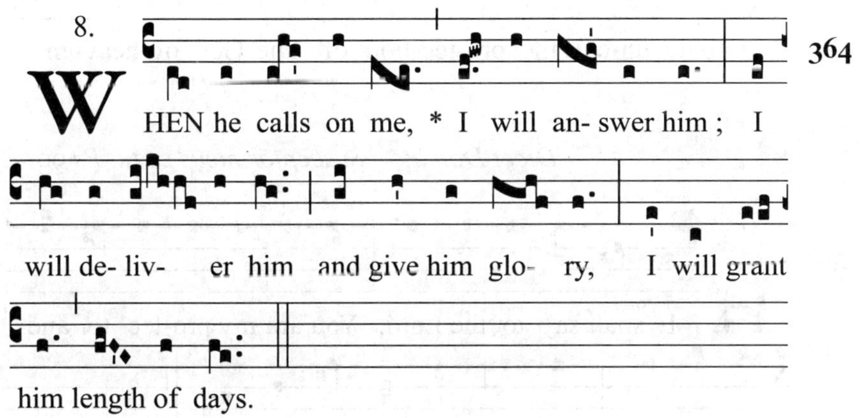

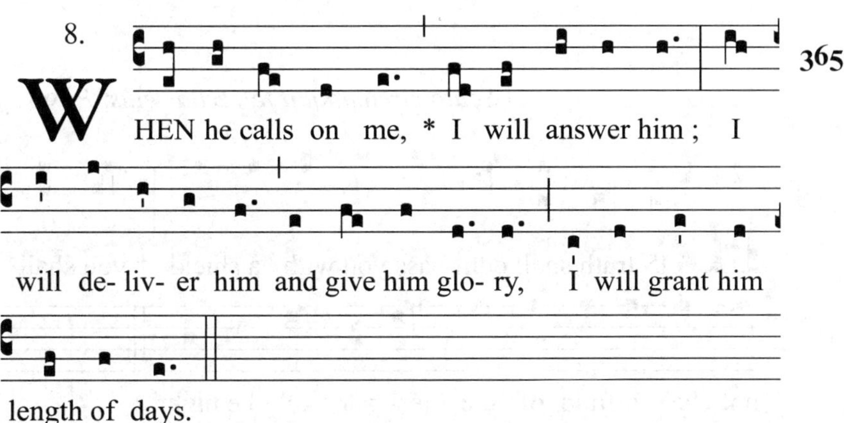

365

VERSES *Qui habitat in adiutorio Altissimi. Ps* 90 : 1

366

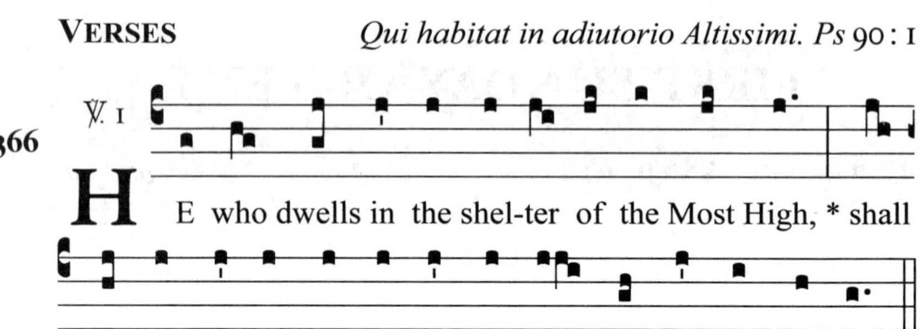
℣. 1
HE who dwells in the shel-ter of the Most High, * shall
a- bide un-der the pro-tec-tion of the God of heav-en.

Dicet Domino : Susceptor meus es tu. Ps 90 : 2

367

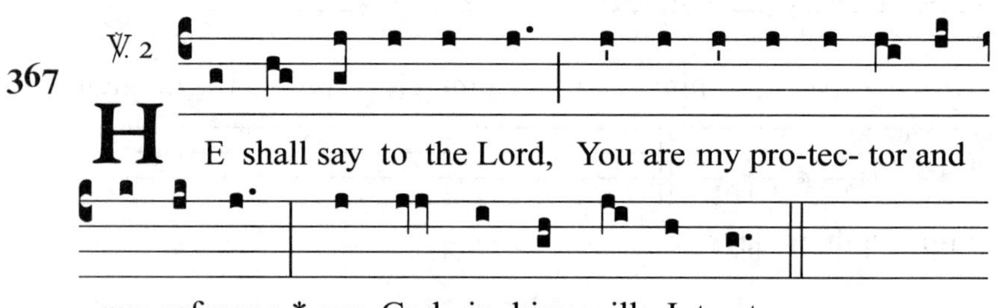
℣. 2
HE shall say to the Lord, You are my pro-tec- tor and
my ref-uge ; * my God, in him will I trust.

Scuto circumdabit te veritas eius. Ps 90 : 5

368

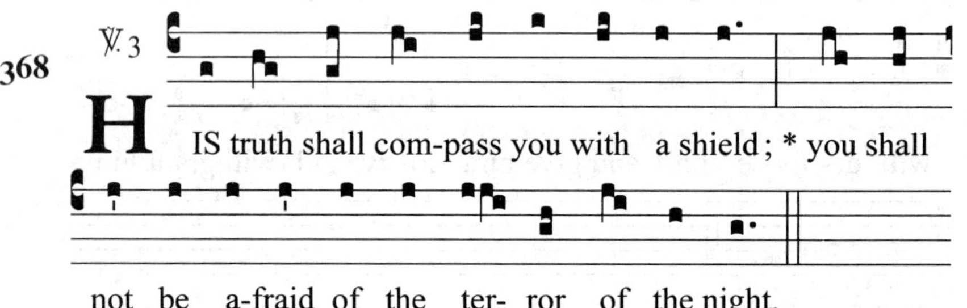
℣. 3
HIS truth shall com-pass you with a shield ; * you shall
not be a-fraid of the ter- ror of the night.

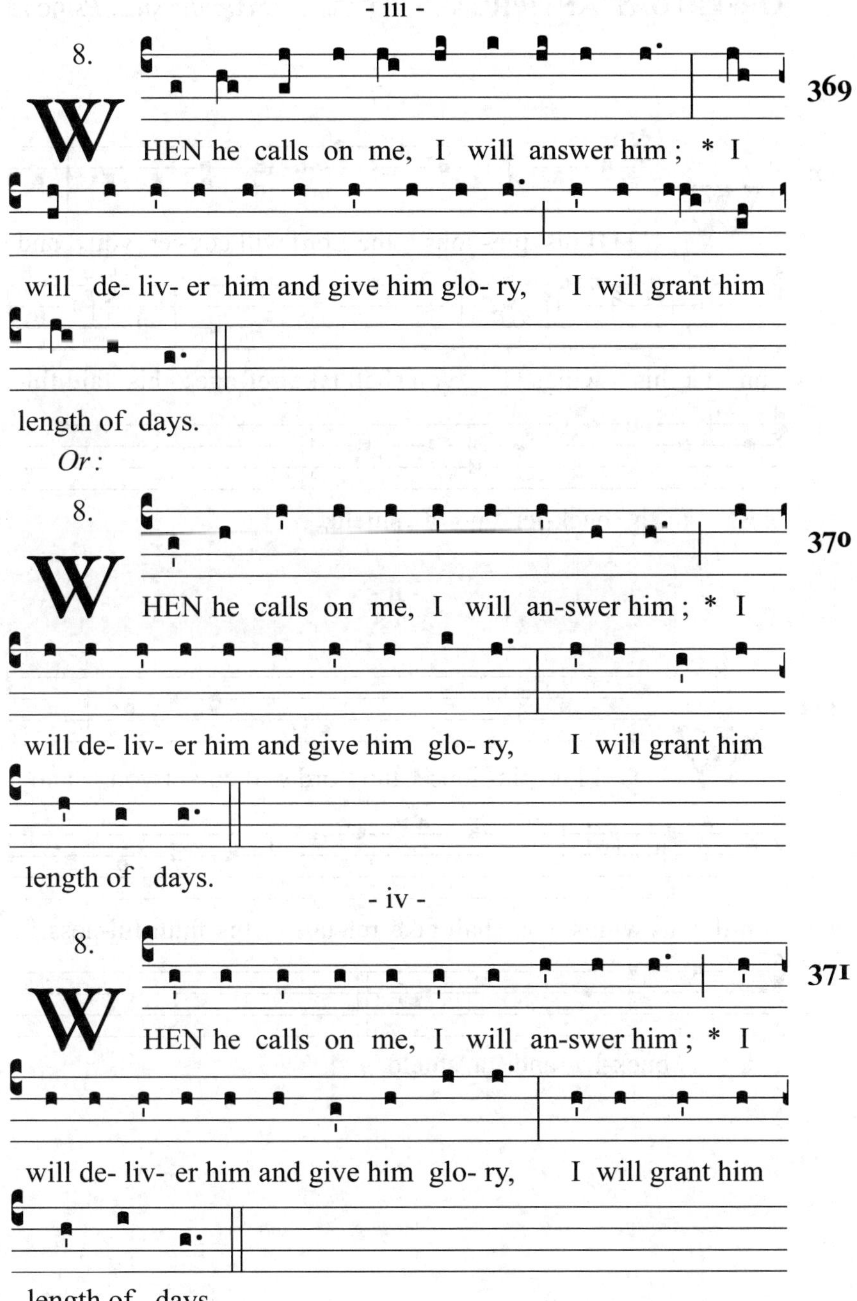
- iii -
8.
369
WHEN he calls on me, I will answer him ; * I
will de- liv- er him and give him glo- ry, I will grant him
length of days.
Or:
8.
370
WHEN he calls on me, I will an-swer him ; * I
will de- liv- er him and give him glo- ry, I will grant him
length of days.
- iv -
8.
371
WHEN he calls on me, I will an-swer him ; * I
will de- liv- er him and give him glo- ry, I will grant him
length of days.

Offertory Antiphon *Scapulis suis. Ps* 90:4

\- i -

372

8.
WITH his pin- ions * the Lord will cov- er you, and
un- der his wings you shall take ref-uge; his faithful-
ness is a buck-ler and a shield.

\- ii -

373

8.
WITH his pin- ions * the Lord will cov-er you, and
un-der his wings you shall take ref-uge ; his faith-ful-ness
is a buck-ler and a shield.

VERSES

Qui habitat in adiutorio Altissimi. Ps 90 : 1

℣. 1
374
HE who dwells in the shel-ter of the Most High, * shall

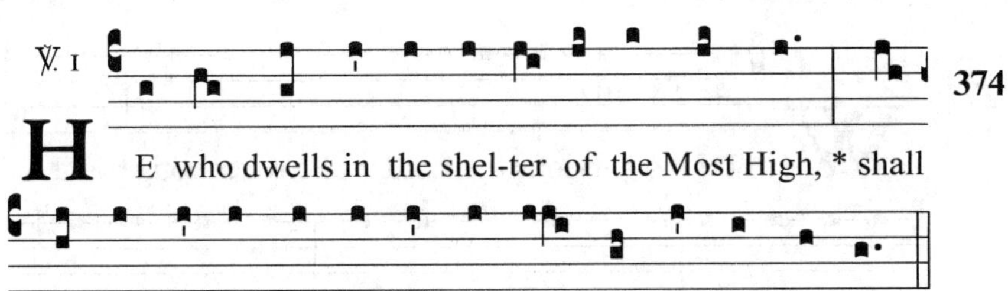

a- bide un-der the pro-tec-tion of the God of heav-en.

Dicet Domino : Susceptor meus es tu. Ps 90 : 2

℣. 2
375
HE shall say to the Lord, You are my pro-tec- tor and

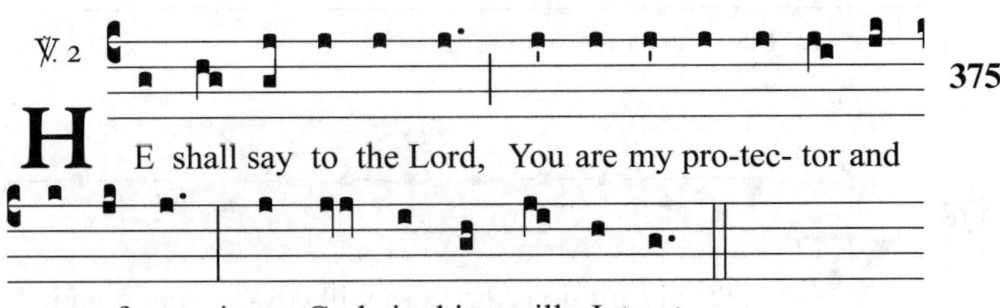

my ref-uge ; * my God, in him will I trust.

Scuto circumdabit te veritas eius. Ps 90 : 5

℣. 3
376
HIS truth shall com-pass you with a shield ; * you shall

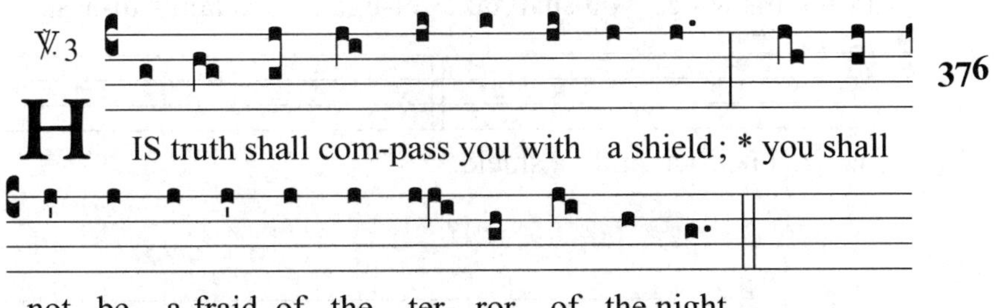

not be a-fraid of the ter- ror of the night.

- iii -

377
8.
WITH his pin-ions the Lord will cov- er you, * and
un-der his wings you shall take ref-uge ; his faith-ful-ness
is a buck-ler and a shield.
Or :
378
8.
WITH his pin-ions the Lord will cov- er you, * and
un-der his wings you shall take ref-uge ; his faith-ful-ness
is a buck-ler and a shield.
- iv -
379
8.
WITH his pin-ions the Lord will cov- er you, * and

un-der his wings you shall take ref-uge ; his faith-ful-ness

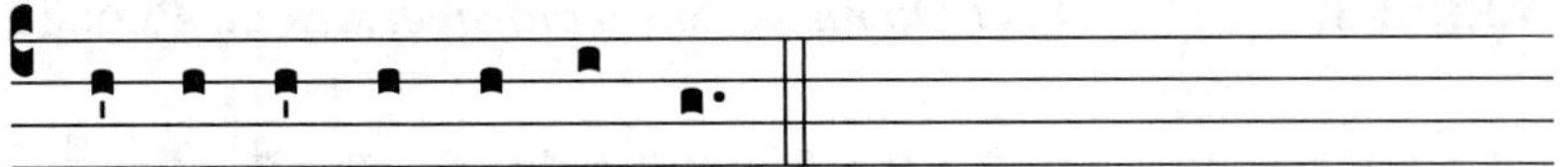
is a buck-ler and a shield.

COMMUNION ANTIPHON *Non in pane solo. Mt* 4:4

- i -

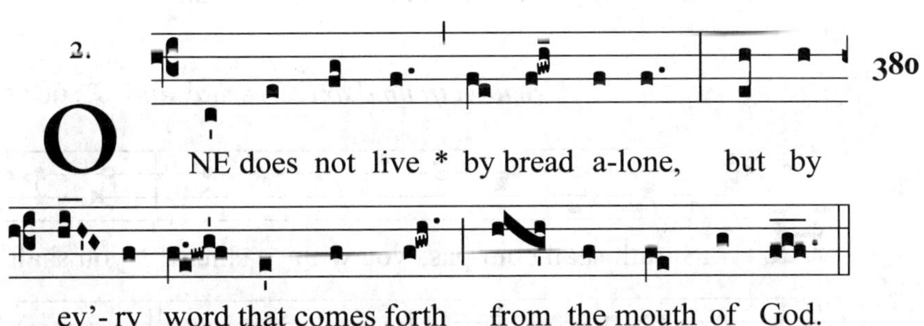
2.
O
NE does not live * by bread a-lone, but by
380
ev'-ry word that comes forth from the mouth of God.

- ii -

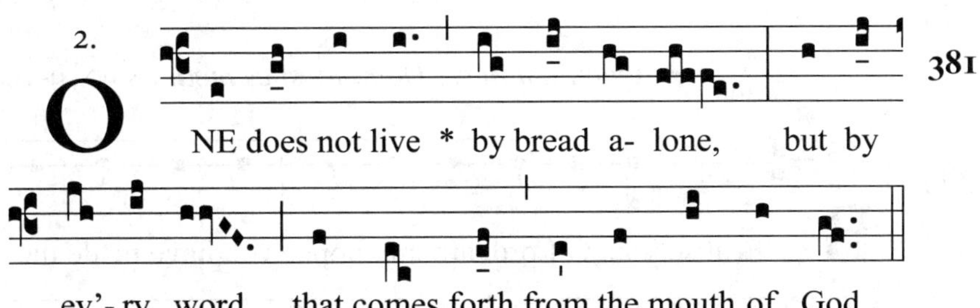
2.
O
NE does not live * by bread a- lone, but by
381
ev'-ry word that comes forth from the mouth of God.

VERSES *Dicet Domino : Susceptor meus es tu. Ps* 90 : 2

382 
℣. 1
HE shall say to the Lord, You are my pro-tec- tor and
my ref-uge ; * my God, in him will I trust.

Scuto circumdabit te veritas eius. Ps 90 : 5

383 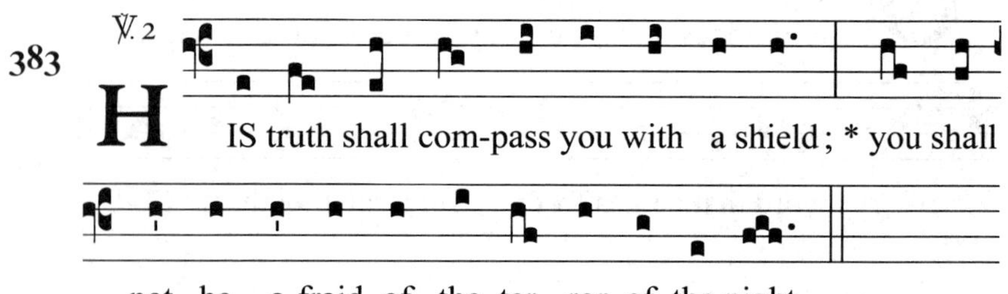
℣. 2
HIS truth shall com-pass you with a shield ; * you shall
not be a-fraid of the ter- ror of the night.

Quoniam tu es, Domine, spes mea. Ps 90 : 9-10

384 
℣. 3
BEcause you, O Lord, are my hope ; you have made the
Most High your ref- uge. * There shall no e- vil come to
you.

- iii -

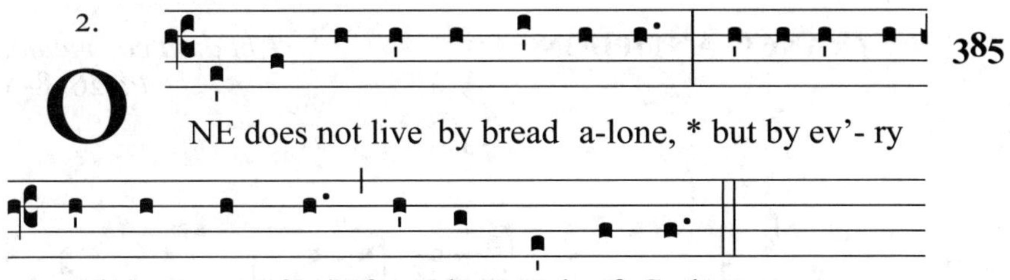
2.
385
O
NE does not live by bread a-lone, * but by ev'- ry
word that comes forth from the mouth of God.

- iv -

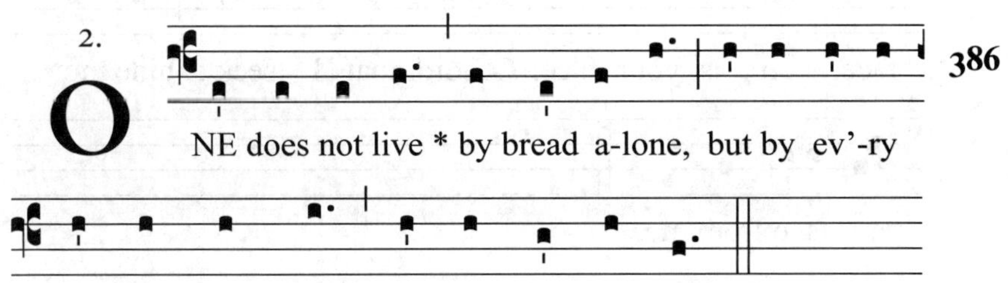
2.
386
O
NE does not live * by bread a-lone, but by ev'-ry
word that comes forth from the mouth of God.

SECOND SUNDAY OF LENT

Entrance Antiphon *Tibi dixit cor meum.*
Ps 26:8-9

- i -

387

3.
OF you * my heart has spo-ken : Seek his
face. It is your face, O Lord, that I seek ; hide not
your face from me.

- ii -

388

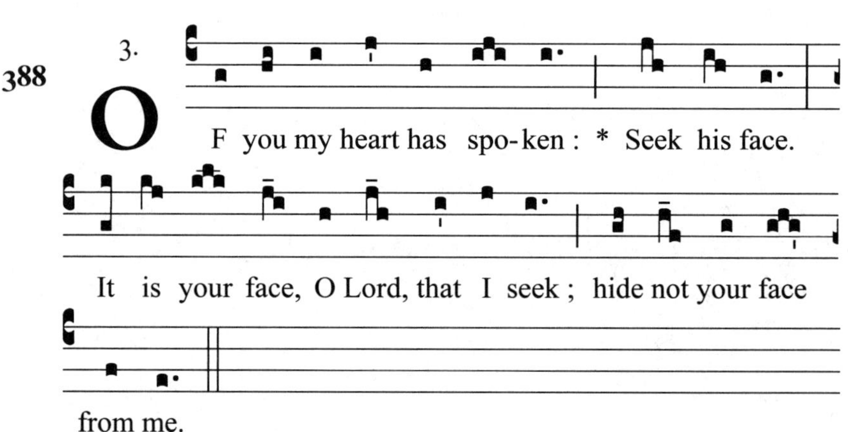
3.
OF you my heart has spo-ken : * Seek his face.
It is your face, O Lord, that I seek ; hide not your face
from me.

VERSES *Dominus illuminatio mea. Ps* 26 : 1

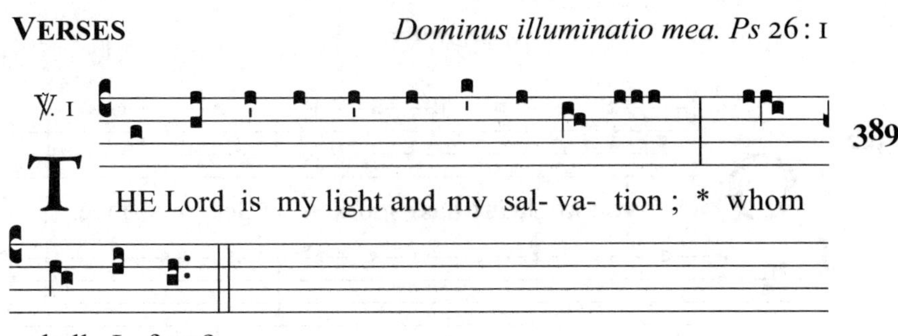
℣. 1
THE Lord is my light and my sal- va- tion ; * whom
shall I fear ?

389

Dominus protector vitæ meæ. Ps 26 : 1

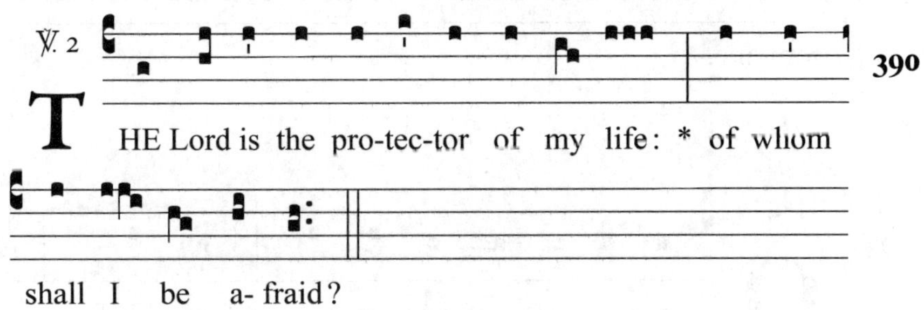
℣. 2
THE Lord is the pro-tec-tor of my life : * of whom
shall I be a- fraid ?

390

Exaudi, Domine, vocem meam. Ps 26 : 7

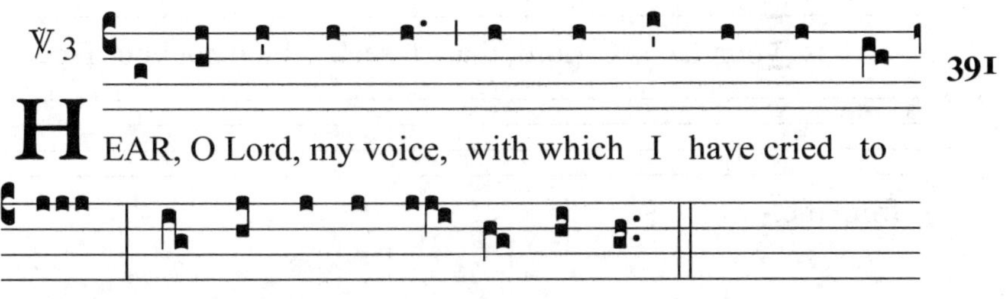
℣. 3
HEAR, O Lord, my voice, with which I have cried to
you ; * have mer- cy on me and hear me.

391

- iii -

392

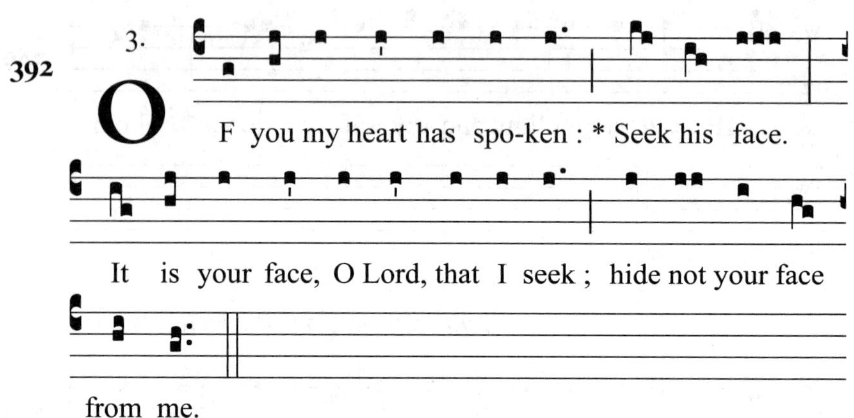
3.
OF you my heart has spo-ken : * Seek his face.
It is your face, O Lord, that I seek ; hide not your face
from me.

- iv -

393

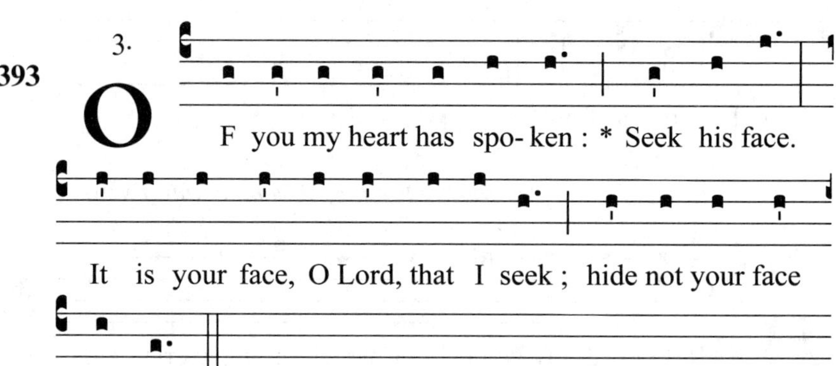
3.
OF you my heart has spo- ken : * Seek his face.
It is your face, O Lord, that I seek ; hide not your face
from me.

Or :

ENTRANCE ANTIPHON *Reminiscere miserationum tuarum.*
Ps 24:6. 2. 22

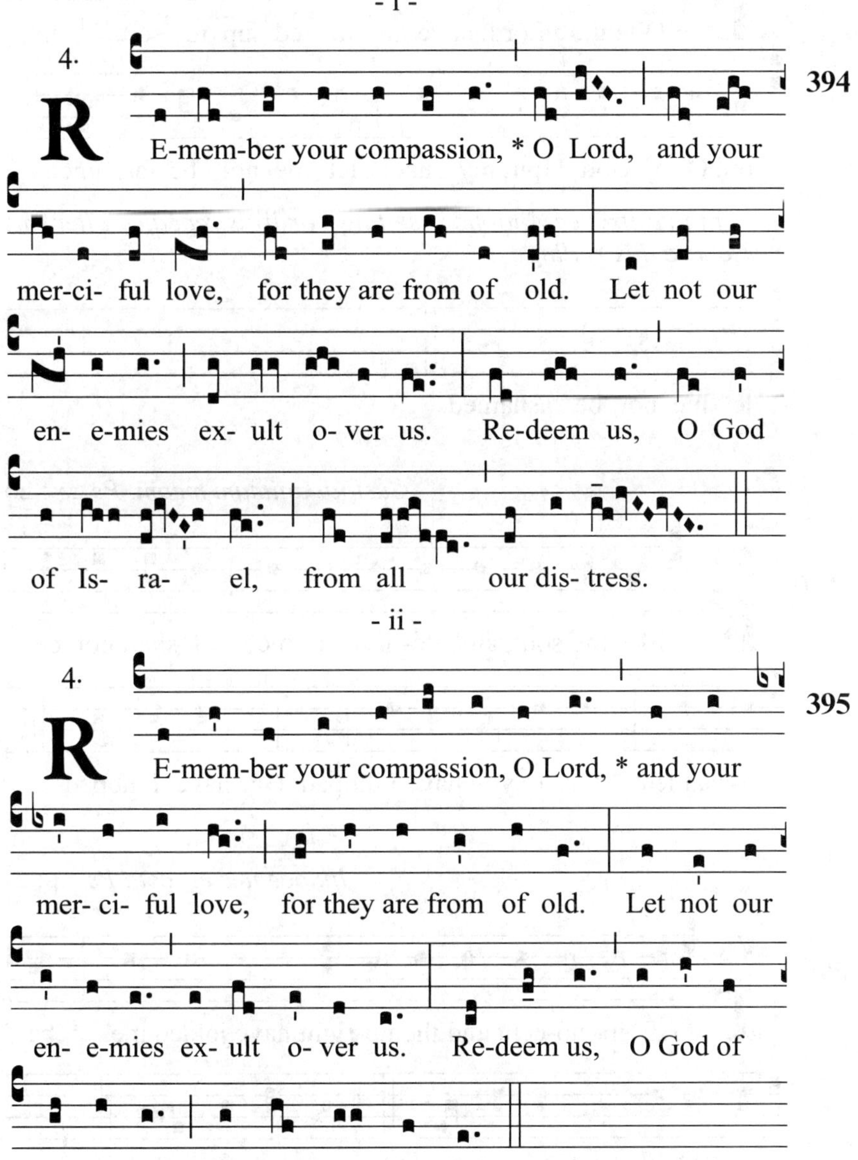
- i -
4.
R E-mem-ber your compassion, * O Lord, and your
394
mer-ci- ful love, for they are from of old. Let not our
en- e-mies ex- ult o- ver us. Re-deem us, O God
of Is- ra- el, from all our dis- tress.
- ii -
4.
R E-mem-ber your compassion, O Lord, * and your
395
mer- ci- ful love, for they are from of old. Let not our
en- e-mies ex- ult o- ver us. Re-deem us, O God of
Is- ra- el, from all our dis-tress.

VERSES *Ad te levavi animam meam. Ps* 24:1

396

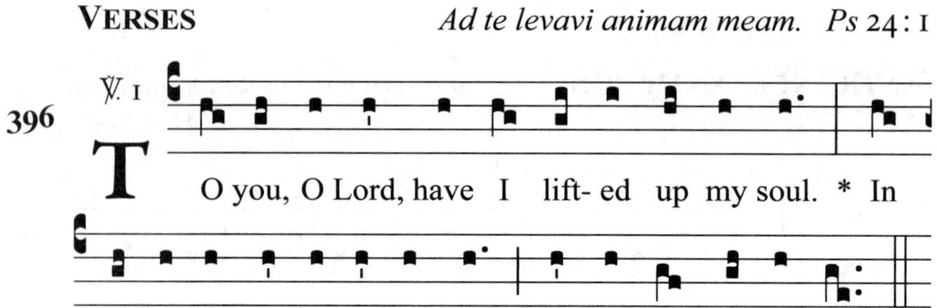
℣. 1
TO you, O Lord, have I lift- ed up my soul. * In
you, O my God, I put my trust; let me not be ashamed.

If the Entrance Antiphon (setting i or ii) is repeated after this verse, use this ending:

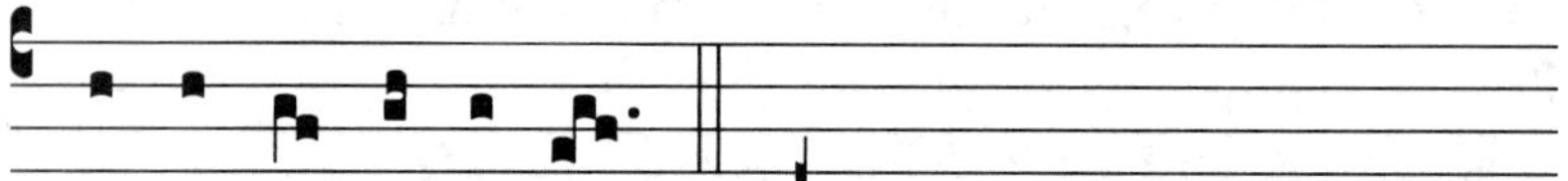
let me not be ashamed.

Custodi animam meam. Ps 24:20

397

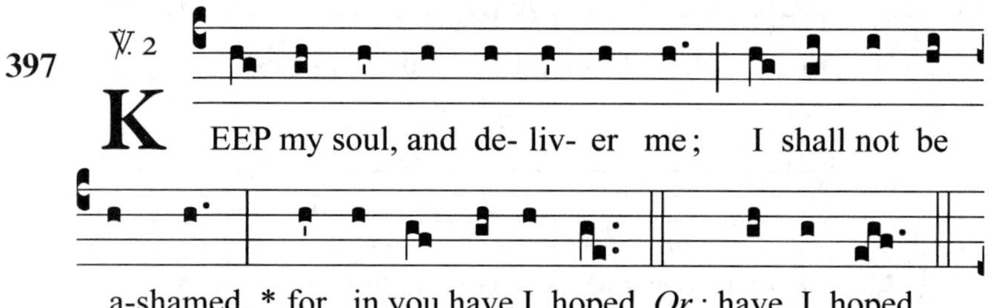
℣. 2
KEEP my soul, and de- liv- er me; I shall not be
a-shamed, * for in you have I hoped. Or: have I hoped.

Innocentes et recti. Ps 24:21

398

℣. 3
THE in- no-cent and the up-right have joined me, * because I have wait- ed on you. Or: wait- ed on you.

- iii -

4. 399

R E-mem-ber your compassion, O Lord, * and your
mer- ci- ful love, for they are from of old. Let not our
en- e-mies ex- ult o- ver us. Re-deem us, O God of
Is- ra- el, from all our dis-tress.

- iv -

4. 400

REmember your compassion, O Lord, * and your merciful love, for they are from of old. Let not our enemies exult over us. Redeem us, O God of Israel, from all our distress.

Offertory Antiphon *Meditabor in mandatis tuis.*
Ps 118:47-48

- i -

401

2.
I will de-light * in your commands, which I love
exceeding-ly ; and I will lift up my hands to your commands, which I love.

- ii -

402

2.
I will de-light * in your commands, which I love
exceeding- ly; and I will lift up my hands to your commands, which I love.

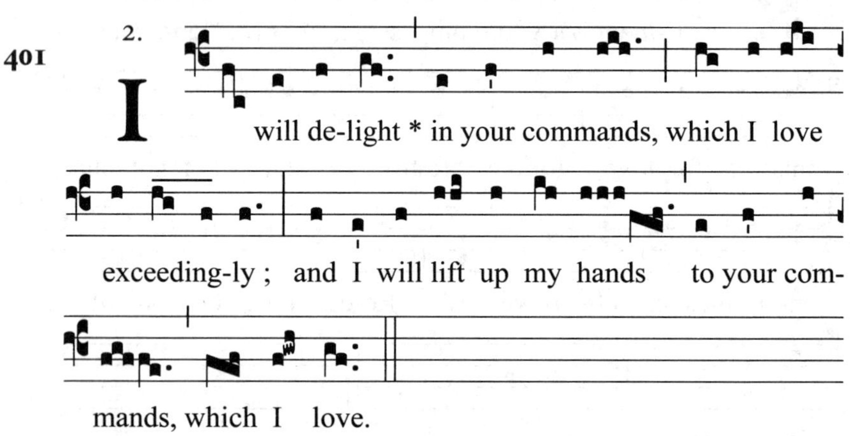

VERSES *Memor esto verbi tui. Ps* 118:49

℣. 1

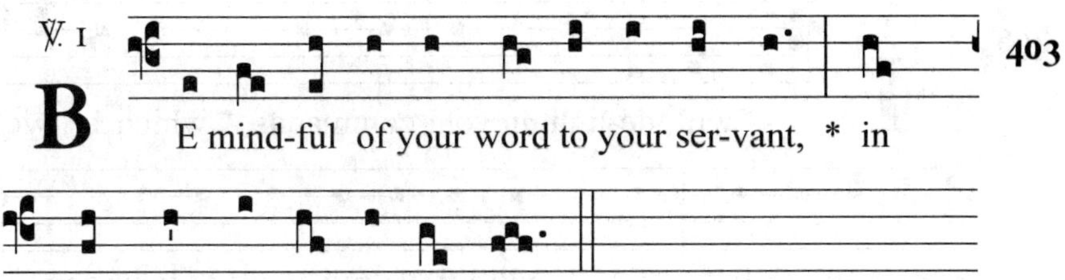

403

B E mind-ful of your word to your ser-vant, * in which you have giv- en me hope.

Hæc me consolata est. Ps 118:50

℣. 2

404

T HIS is my comfort in my af-flic-tion: * that your promise has giv- en me life.

Memor fui iudiciorum tuorum. Ps 118:52

℣. 3

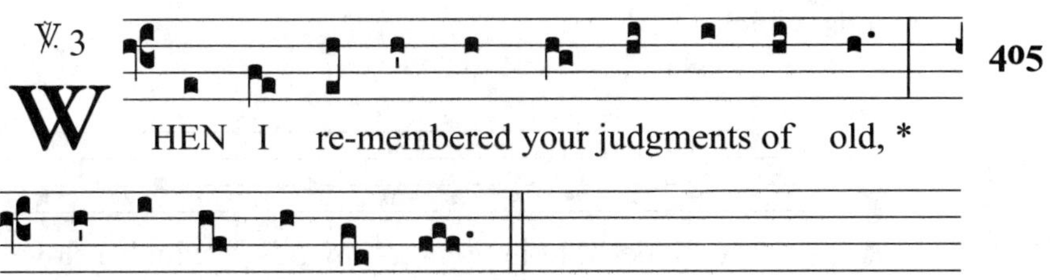

405

W HEN I re-membered your judgments of old, * these, O Lord, consoled me.

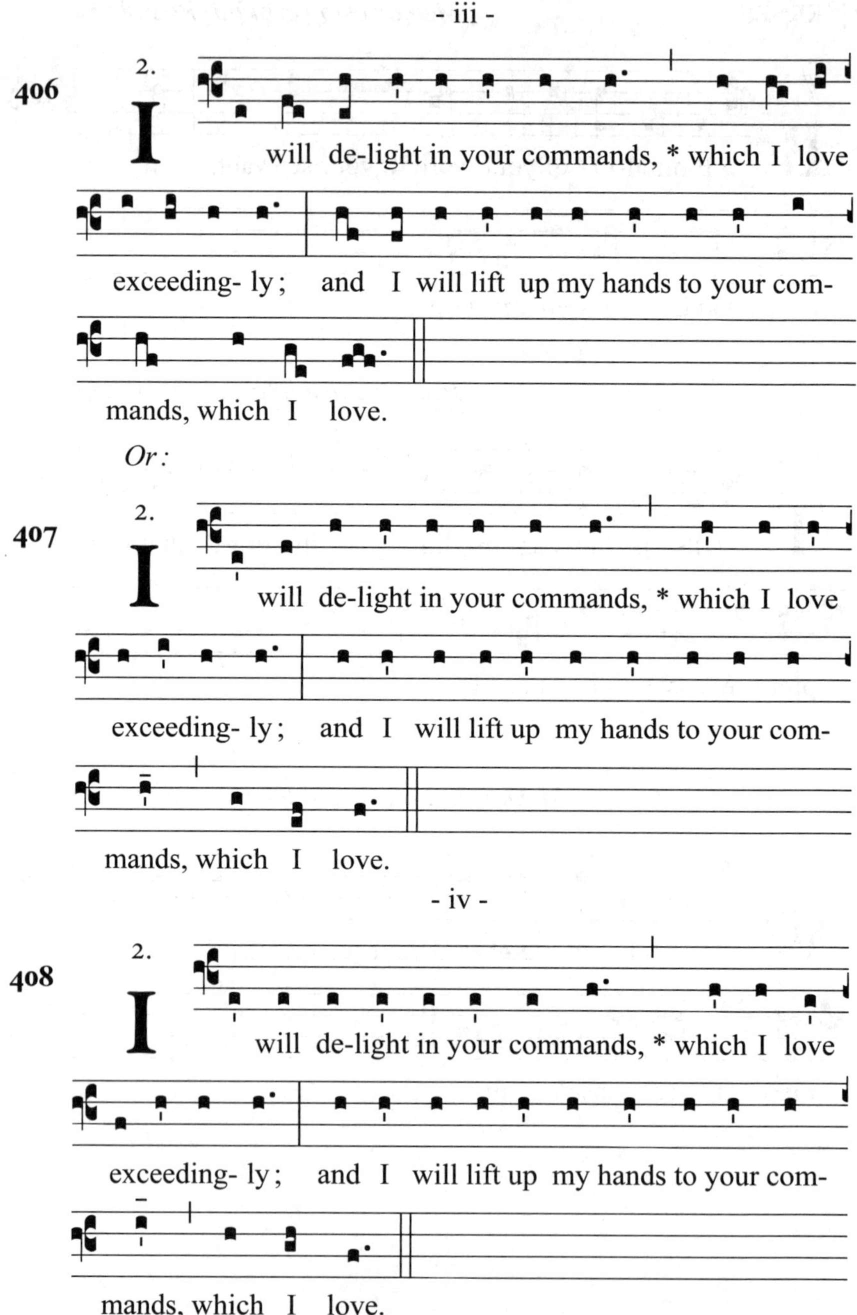
- iii -
406
2.
I will de-light in your commands, * which I love exceeding- ly; and I will lift up my hands to your com- mands, which I love.
Or:
407
2.
I will de-light in your commands, * which I love exceeding- ly; and I will lift up my hands to your com- mands, which I love.
- iv -
408
2.
I will de-light in your commands, * which I love exceeding- ly; and I will lift up my hands to your com- mands, which I love.

Communion Antiphon *Hic est Filius meus dilectus.*
Mt 17:5

- i -

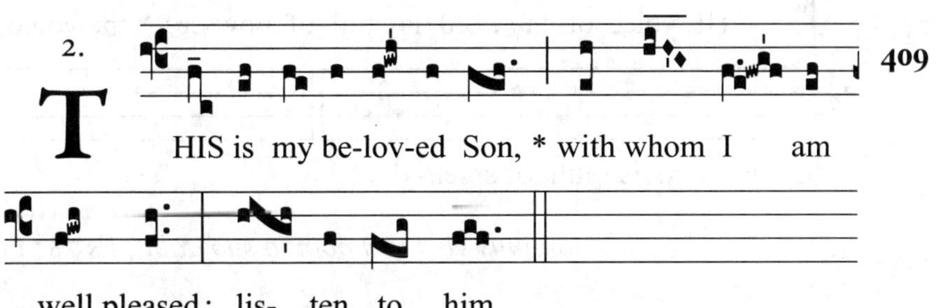
2.
THIS is my be-lov-ed Son, * with whom I am
409
well pleased; lis- ten to him.

- ii -

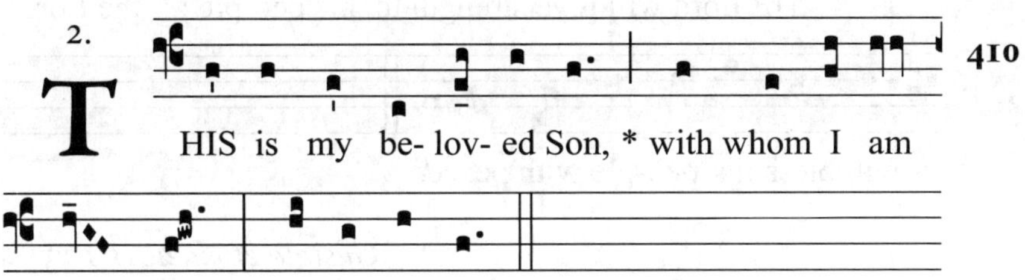
2.
THIS is my be- lov- ed Son, * with whom I am
410

well pleased; lis-ten to him.

VERSES *Vox Domini in virtute. Ps* 28:4

411
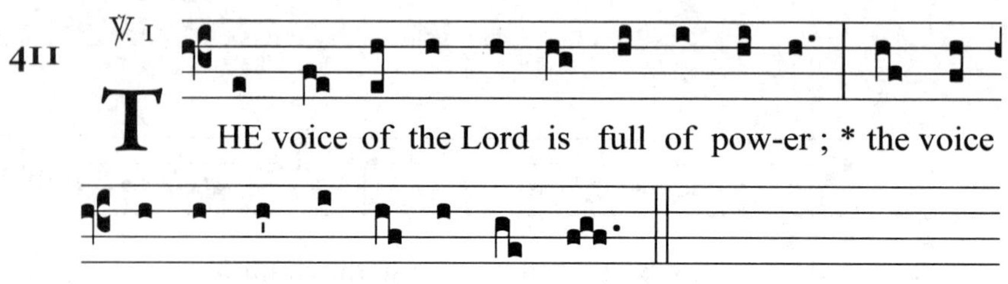
℣. 1
THE voice of the Lord is full of pow-er ; * the voice

of the Lord is full of splen- dor.

Dominus virtutem populo suo dabit. Ps 28:11

412
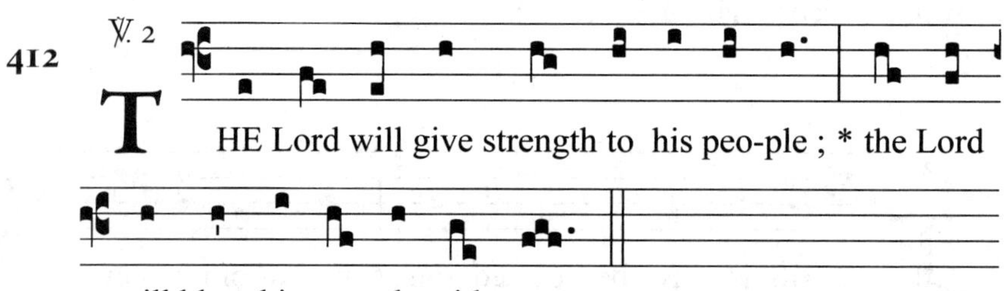
℣. 2
THE Lord will give strength to his peo-ple ; * the Lord
will bless his peo-ple with peace.

Gustate et videte. Ps 33:9

℣. 3
O taste and see how gracious the Lord is ; * bless-ed

413

the man who takes ref- uge in him.

- iii -

2.
THIS is my be-lov- ed Son, * with whom I am
414
well pleased; lis- ten to him.

- iv -

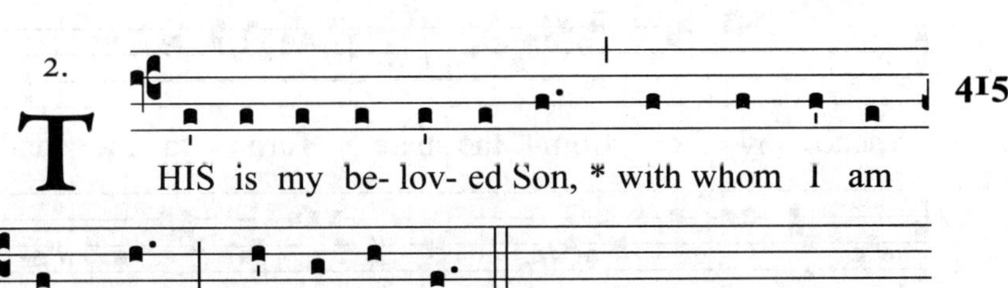
2.
THIS is my be- lov- ed Son, * with whom I am
415
well pleased; lis- ten to him.

THIRD SUNDAY OF LENT

ENTRANCE ANTIPHON *Oculi mei semper ad Dominum.*
Ps 24:15-16

- i -

416

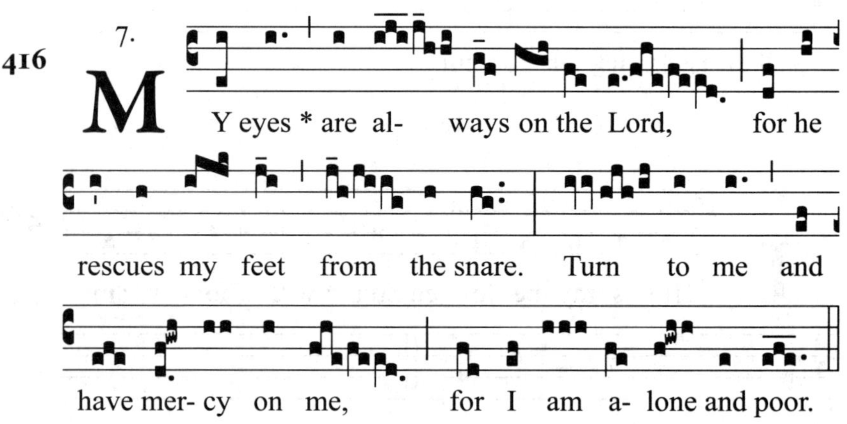
7.
MY eyes * are al- ways on the Lord, for he
rescues my feet from the snare. Turn to me and
have mer- cy on me, for I am a- lone and poor.

- ii -

417

7.
MY eyes * are always on the Lord, for he rescues
my feet from the snare. Turn to me and have mer- cy
on me, for I am a- lone and poor.

VERSES *Ad te levavi animam meam. Ps* 24 : 1

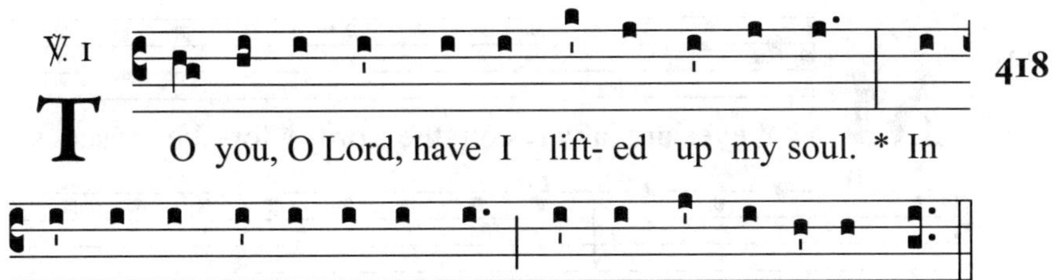
℣. 1
418
TO you, O Lord, have I lift- ed up my soul. * In
you, O my God, I put my trust; let me not be put to shame.

Vias tuas, Domine, demonstra mihi. Ps 24 : 4

℣. 2
419
YOUR ways, O Lord, make known to me, * and teach
me your paths.

Custodi animam meam. Ps 24 : 20

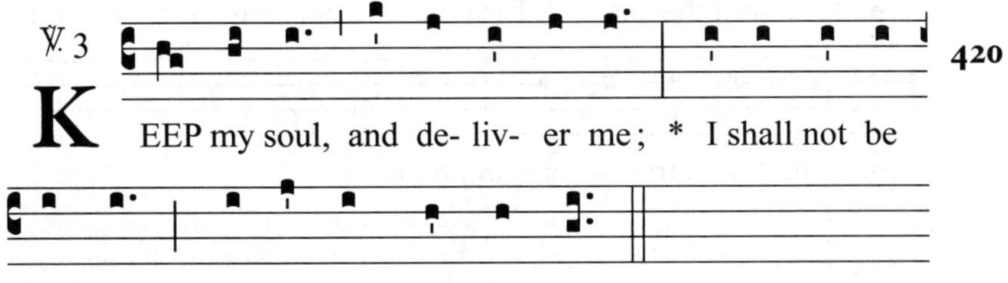
℣. 3
420
KEEP my soul, and de- liv- er me; * I shall not be
ashamed, for I have hoped in you.

- iii -

421

7.
MY eyes are always on the Lord, * for he rescues
my feet from the snare. Turn to me and have mer- cy on
me, for I am a- lone and poor.

- iv -

422

7.
MY eyes are always on the Lord, * for he rescues
my feet from the snare. Turn to me and have mer- cy on
me, for I am a- lone and poor.

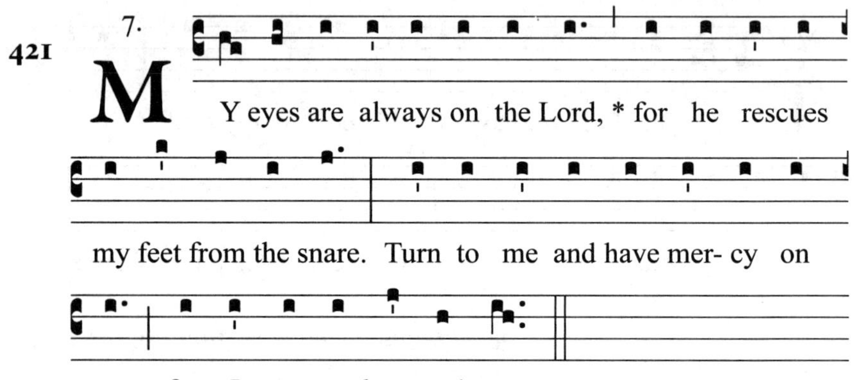

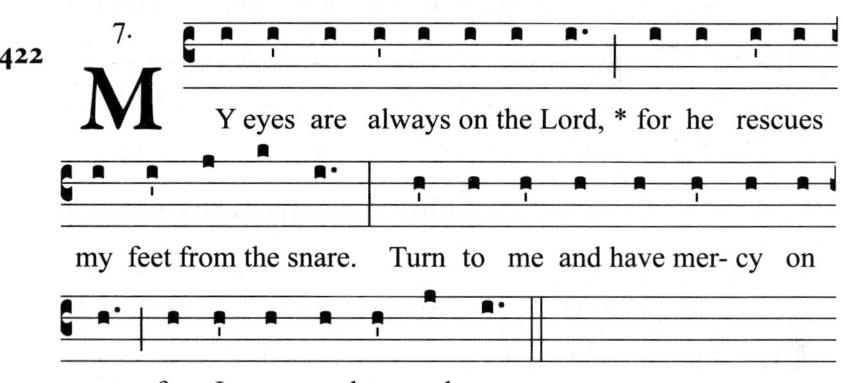

Or :

Entrance Antiphon *Cum sanctificatus fuero in vobis.*
Ez 36:23-26

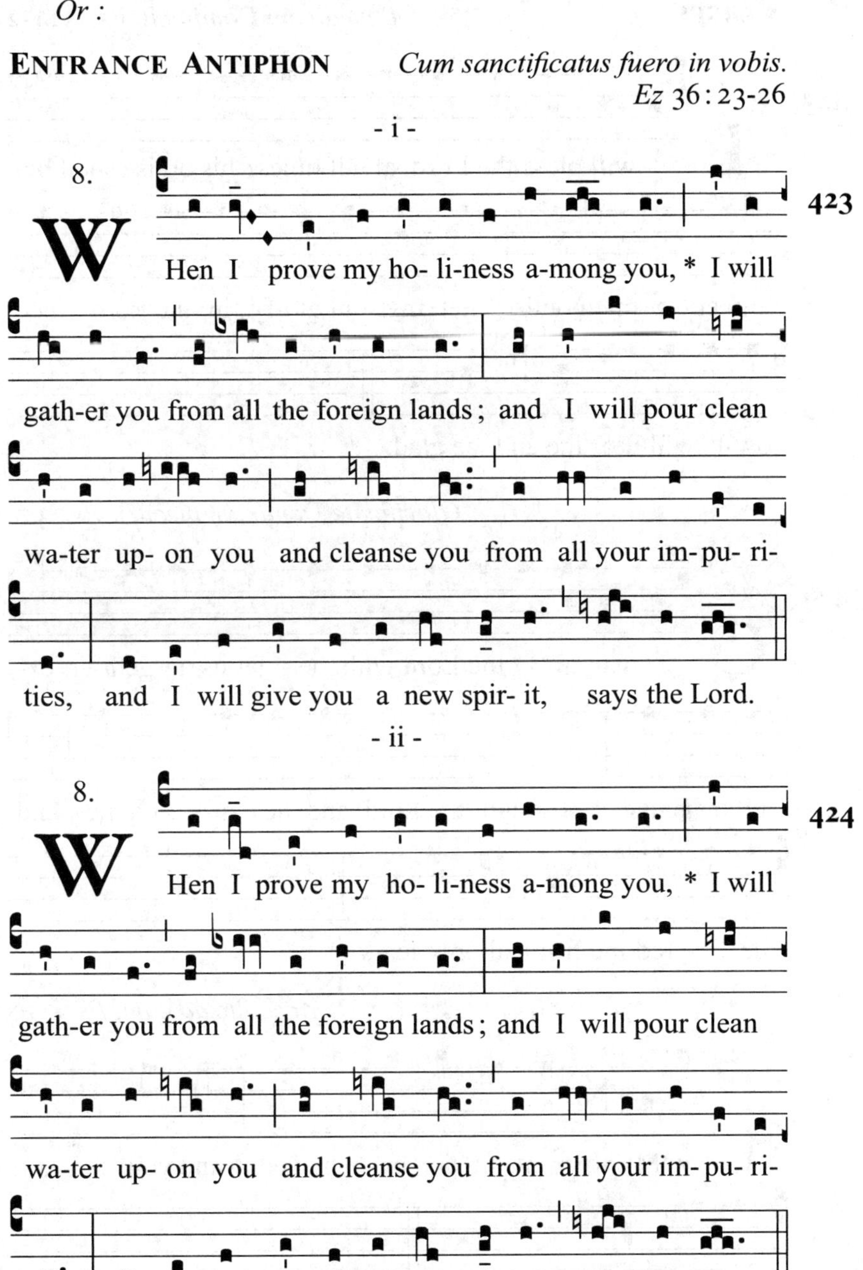
- i -
8.
W Hen I prove my ho- li-ness a-mong you, * I will
423
gath-er you from all the foreign lands; and I will pour clean
wa-ter up- on you and cleanse you from all your im-pu- ri-
ties, and I will give you a new spir- it, says the Lord.
- ii -
8.
W Hen I prove my ho- li-ness a-mong you, * I will
424
gath-er you from all the foreign lands; and I will pour clean
wa-ter up- on you and cleanse you from all your im-pu- ri-
ties, and I will give you a new spir- it, says the Lord.

VERSES *Benedicam Dominum. Ps* 33:1-2

425

℣. 1
I will bless the Lord at all times; his praise shall be
ev- er in my mouth. * Let my soul glo-ry in the Lord; the
low-ly will hear me and be glad.

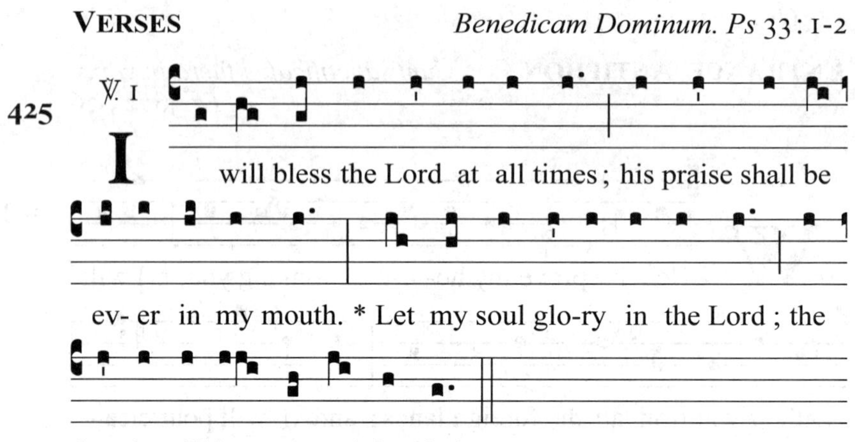

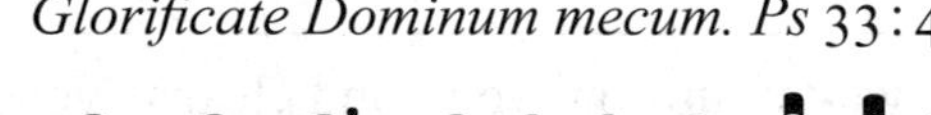

Glorificate Dominum mecum. Ps 33:4

426

℣. 2
O mag-ni- fy the Lord with me, let us to-geth-er ex-
tol his name. * I sought the Lord, and he answered me and
de-liv-ered me from all my fears.

Accedite ad eum. Ps 33:6

427

℣. 3
COME to him and be en-lightened, * and your fac-es
shall not be put to shame.

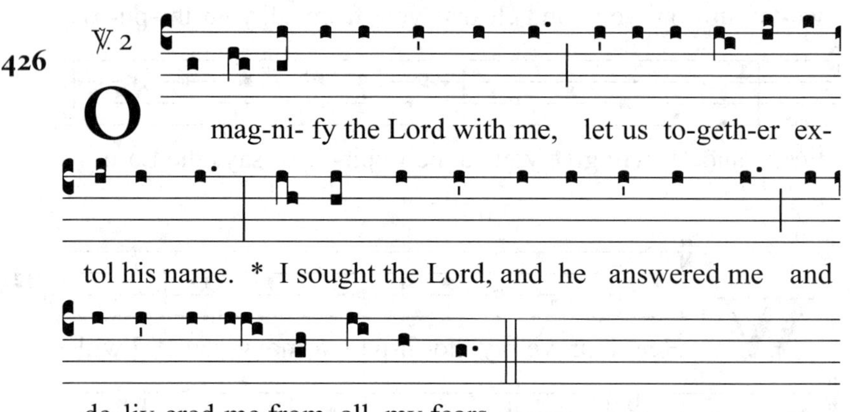

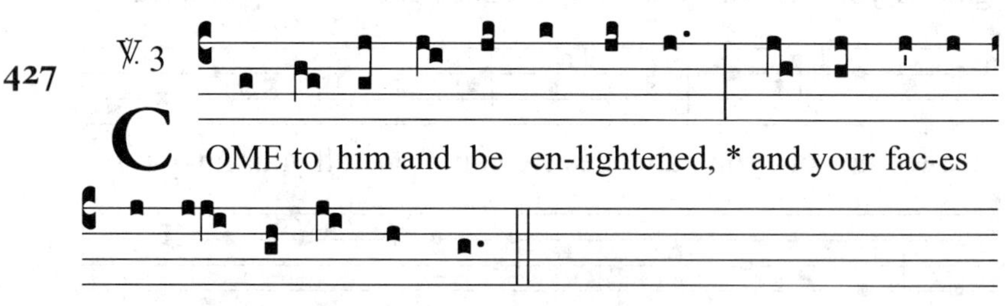

- iii -

8.
428
WHen I prove my ho- li-ness a-mong you, * I will
gath-er you from all the foreign lands; and I will pour clean
wa-ter up- on you and cleanse you from all your im-pu- ri-
ties, and I will give you a new spir- it, says the Lord.

Or :

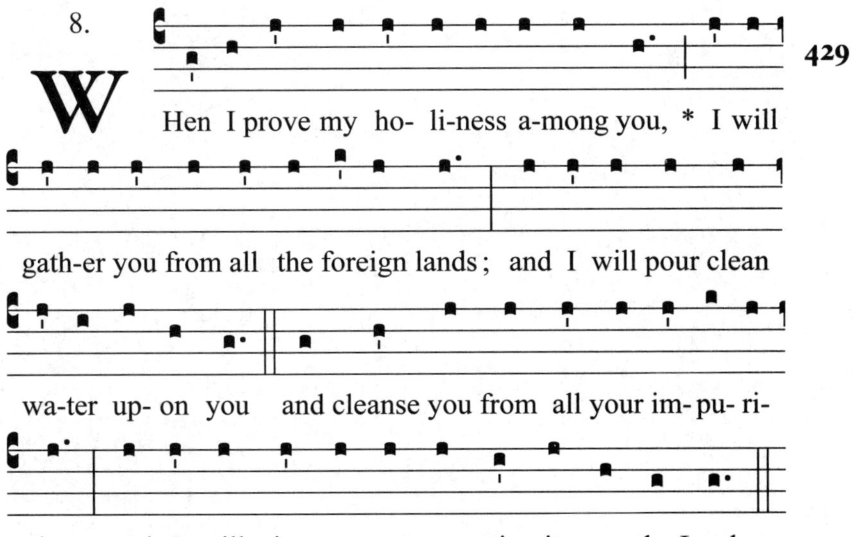
8.
429
WHen I prove my ho- li-ness a-mong you, * I will
gath-er you from all the foreign lands; and I will pour clean
wa-ter up- on you and cleanse you from all your im-pu- ri-
ties, and I will give you a new spir- it, says the Lord.

430

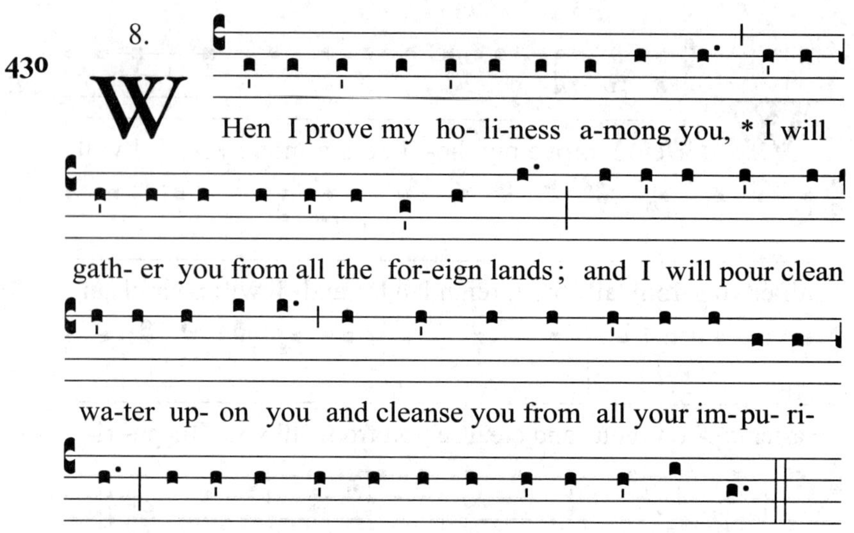
- iv -
8.
WHen I prove my ho- li-ness a-mong you, * I will
gath- er you from all the for-eign lands; and I will pour clean
wa-ter up- on you and cleanse you from all your im- pu- ri-
ties, and I will give you a new spir- it, says the Lord.

OFFERTORY ANTIPHON *Iustitiæ Domini rectæ.*
Ps 18:9. 10. 11. 12

- i -

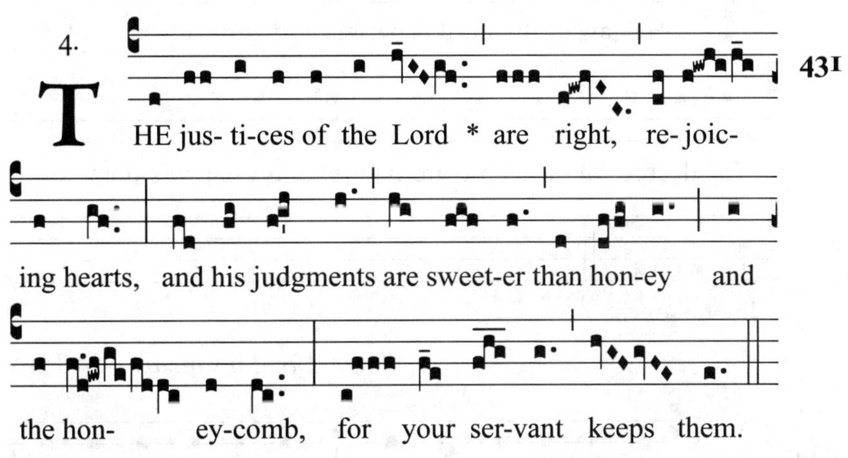
4.
T
HE jus- ti-ces of the Lord * are right, re- joic-
ing hearts, and his judgments are sweet-er than hon-ey and
the hon- ey-comb, for your ser-vant keeps them.
431

- ii -

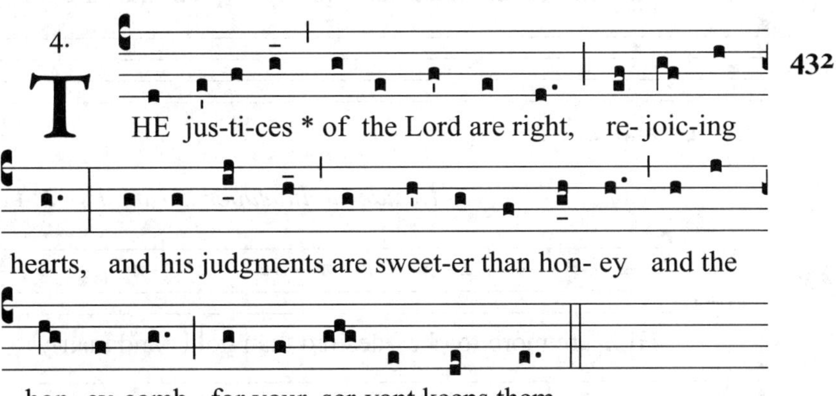
4.
T
HE jus-ti-ces * of the Lord are right, re- joic-ing
hearts, and his judgments are sweet-er than hon- ey and the
hon- ey-comb, for your ser-vant keeps them.
432

VERSES *Lex Domini immaculata. Ps* 18:8

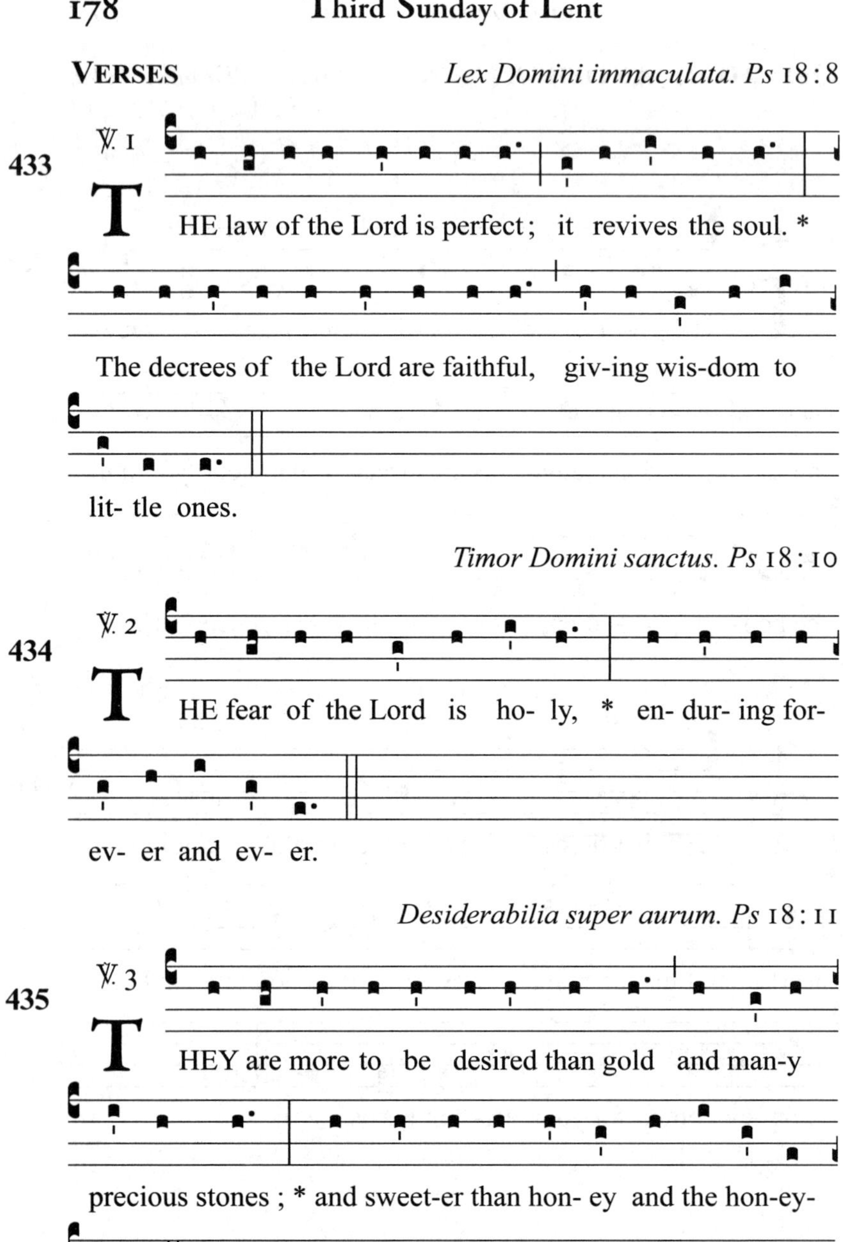
433
℣. 1
THE law of the Lord is perfect; it revives the soul. *
The decrees of the Lord are faithful, giv-ing wis-dom to
lit- tle ones.
Timor Domini sanctus. Ps 18:10
434
℣. 2
THE fear of the Lord is ho- ly, * en- dur- ing for-
ev- er and ev- er.
Desiderabilia super aurum. Ps 18:11
435
℣. 3
THEY are more to be desired than gold and man-y
precious stones; * and sweet-er than hon- ey and the hon-ey-
comb.

- iii -

4.
THE jus- ti-ces of the Lord are right, re- joic- ing
hearts, * and his judgments are sweet-er than hon- ey and the
hon-ey-comb, for your ser-vant keeps them.

436

- iv -

4.
THE jus- ti-ces of the Lord are right, re- joic- ing
hearts, * and his judgments are sweet-er than hon- ey and the
hon-ey-comb, for your ser-vant keeps them.

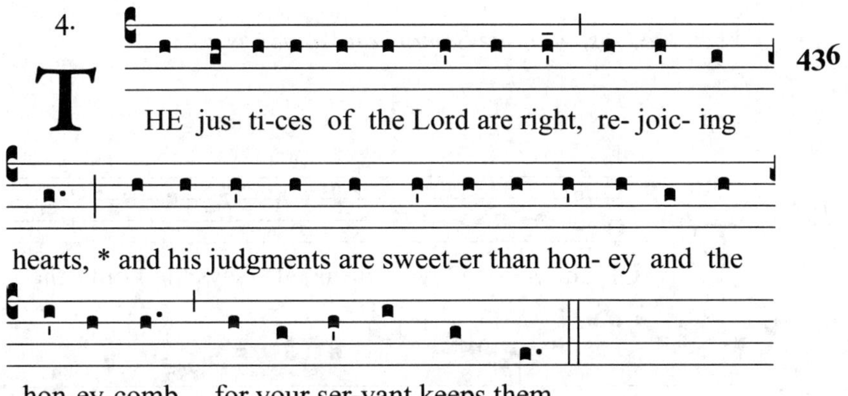

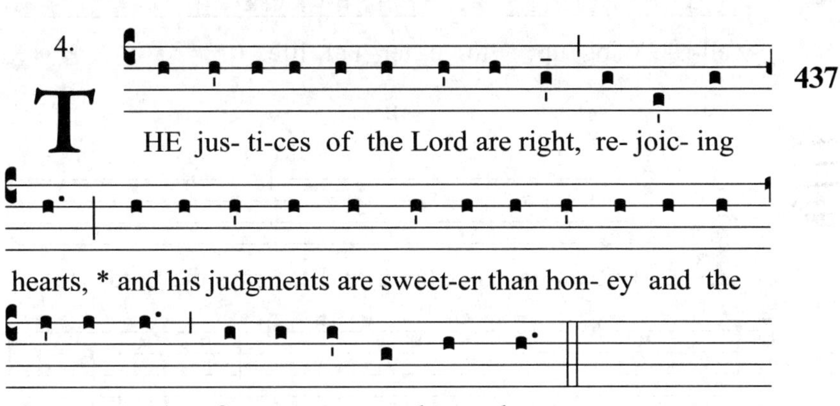

437

COMMUNION ANTIPHON *Qui biberit aquam.*
Jn 4:13-14

When the Gospel of the Samaritan Woman is read:

- i -

438
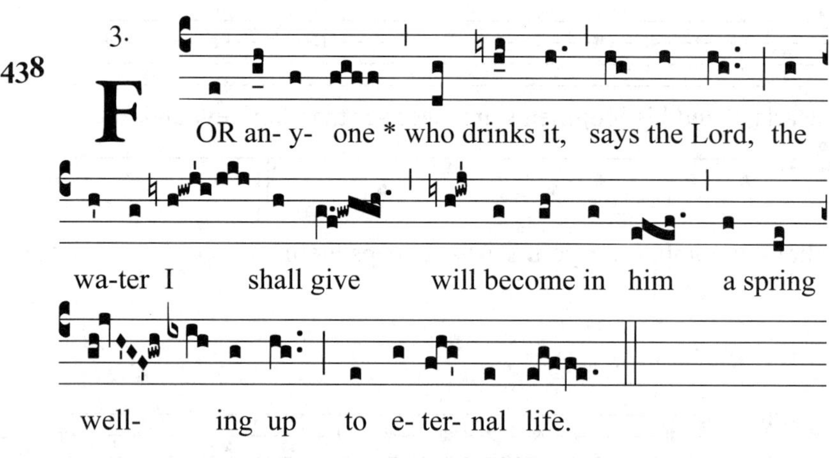
3.
FOR an- y- one * who drinks it, says the Lord, the
wa-ter I shall give will become in him a spring
well- ing up to e- ter- nal life.

- ii -

439
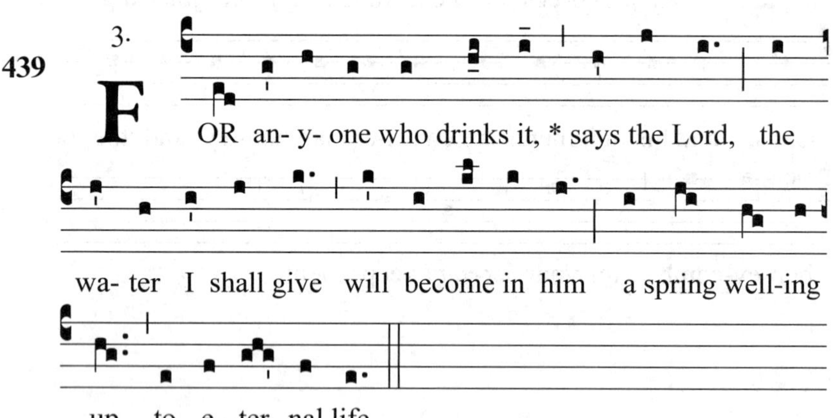
3.
FOR an- y- one who drinks it, * says the Lord, the
wa- ter I shall give will become in him a spring well-ing
up to e- ter- nal life.

VERSES *Deus, Deus meus, ad te de luce vigilo. Ps* 62 : 2-3

℣. 1 440

O God, my God, to you do I watch at break of day. For you my soul has thirst-ed, * my flesh faints for you, as in a dry and wea-ry land where no wa- ter is.

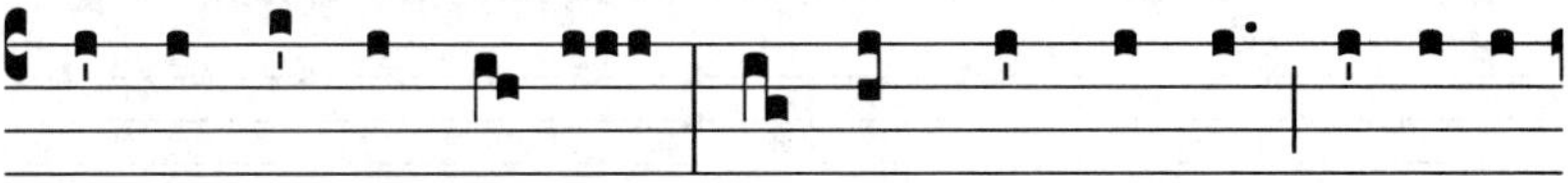

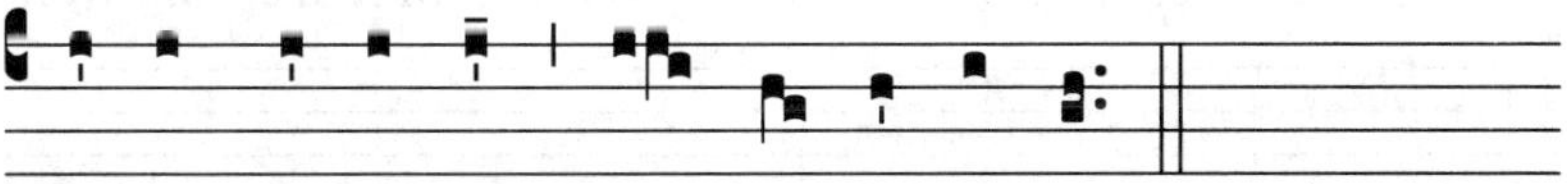

Sic benedicam te in vita mea. Ps 62 : 5

℣. 2 441

THUS will I bless you all my life long, * and in your name I will lift up my hands.

Quia fuisti adiutor meus. Ps 62 : 8-9

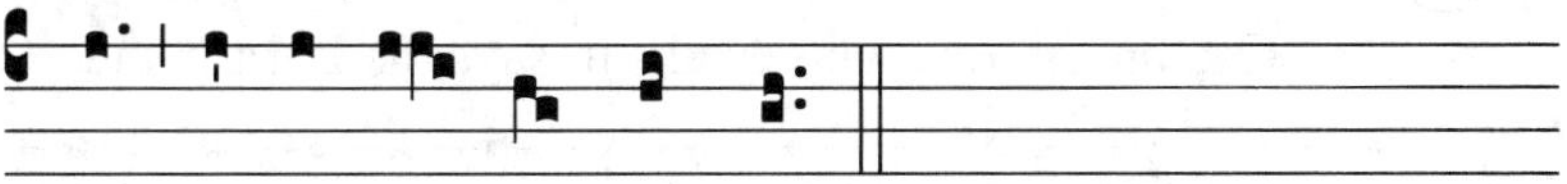

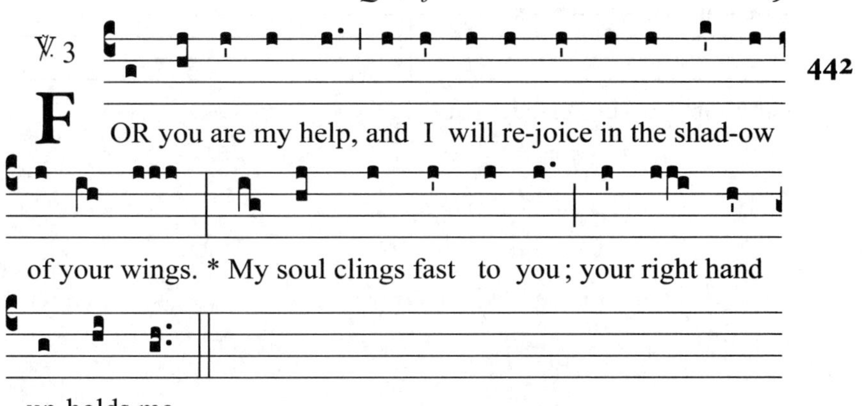
℣. 3
442
FOR you are my help, and I will re-joice in the shad-ow
of your wings. * My soul clings fast to you; your right hand
up-holds me.

- iii -

443

3.
FOR an- y- one who drinks it, says the Lord, * the
wa- ter I shall give will become in him a spring well-
ing up to e- ter-nal life.

Or:

444

3.
FOR an- y- one who drinks it, says the Lord, * the
wa- ter I shall give will become in him a spring well-
ing up to e- ter-nal life.

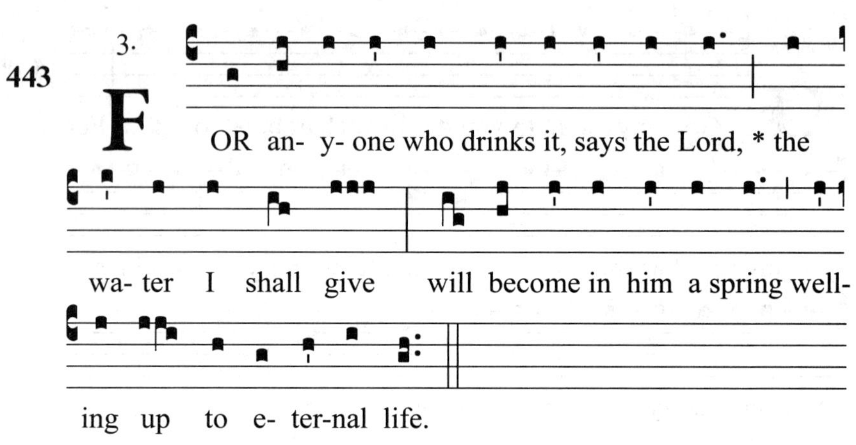

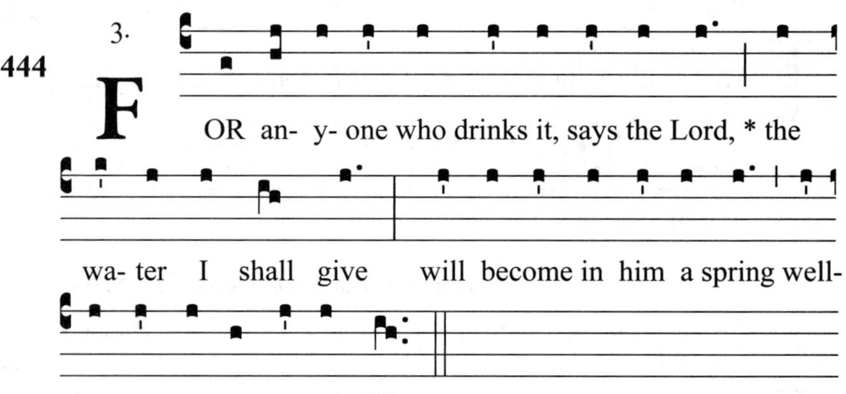

- iv -

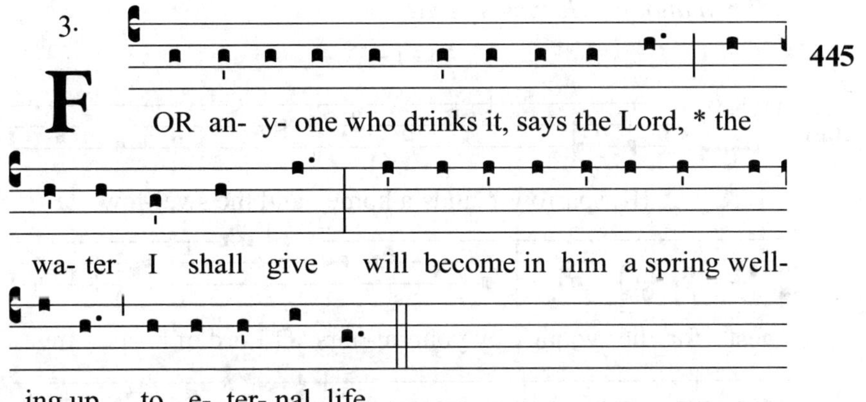
3.
445
FOR an- y- one who drinks it, says the Lord, * the
wa- ter I shall give will become in him a spring well-
ing up to e- ter- nal life.

COMMUNION ANTIPHON *Passer invenit sibi domum.*
Ps 83:4-5

When another Gospel is read:

- i -

446
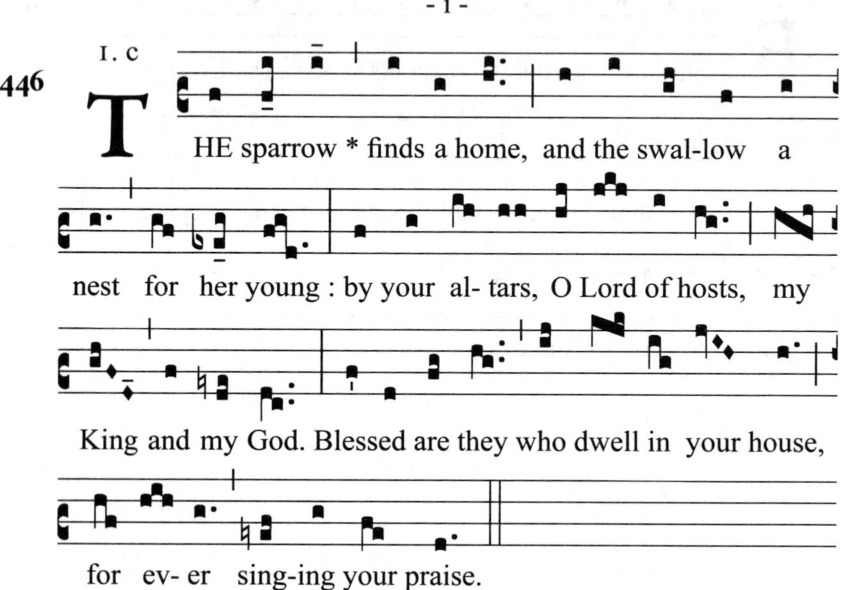
I. c
THE sparrow * finds a home, and the swal-low a
nest for her young : by your al- tars, O Lord of hosts, my
King and my God. Blessed are they who dwell in your house,
for ev- er sing-ing your praise.

- ii -

447
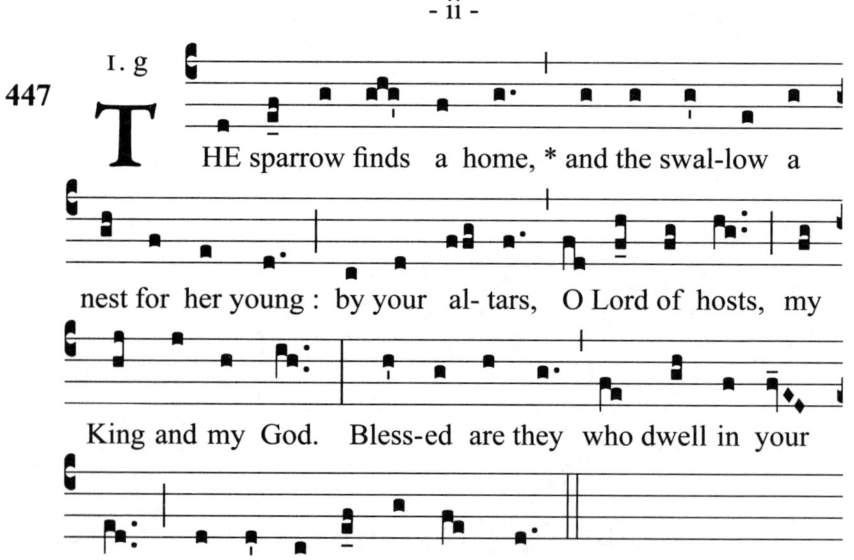
I. g
THE sparrow finds a home, * and the swal-low a
nest for her young : by your al- tars, O Lord of hosts, my
King and my God. Bless-ed are they who dwell in your
house, for ev- er sing-ing your praise.

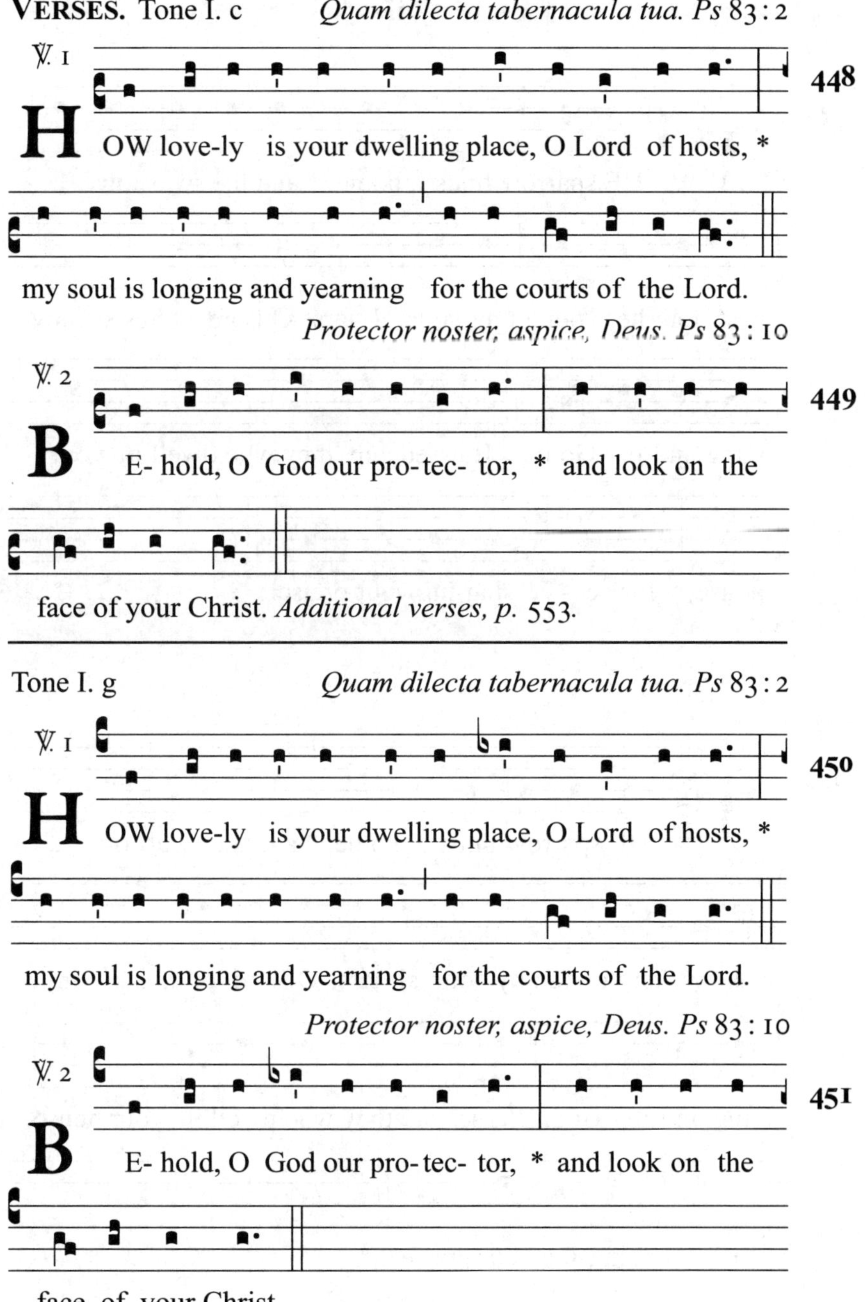
VERSES. Tone I. c *Quam dilecta tabernacula tua. Ps* 83 : 2
℣. 1
448
HOW love-ly is your dwelling place, O Lord of hosts, *
my soul is longing and yearning for the courts of the Lord.
Protector noster, aspice, Deus. Ps 83 : 10
℣. 2
449
BE- hold, O God our pro-tec- tor, * and look on the
face of your Christ. *Additional verses, p.* 553.
Tone I. g *Quam dilecta tabernacula tua. Ps* 83 : 2
℣. 1
450
HOW love-ly is your dwelling place, O Lord of hosts, *
my soul is longing and yearning for the courts of the Lord.
Protector noster, aspice, Deus. Ps 83 : 10
℣. 2
451
BE- hold, O God our pro-tec- tor, * and look on the
face of your Christ.

- iii -

452

I.
THE sparrow finds a home, * and the swal-low a
nest for her young : by your al- tars, O Lord of hosts, my
King and my God. Blessed are they who dwell in your
house, for ev- er sing-ing your praise.

- iv -

453

I.
THE sparrow finds a home, * and the swal-low a
nest for her young : by your al- tars, O Lord of hosts, my
King and my God. Blessed are they who dwell in your house,
for ev- er sing-ing your praise.

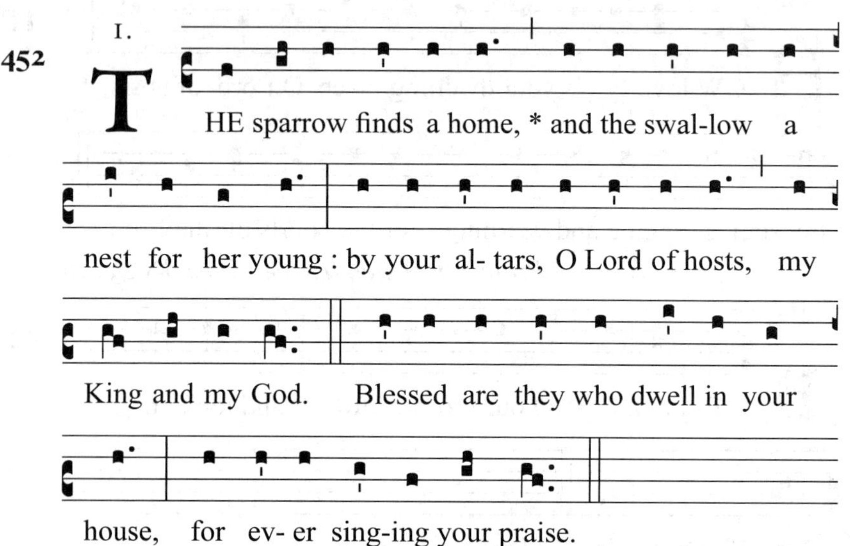

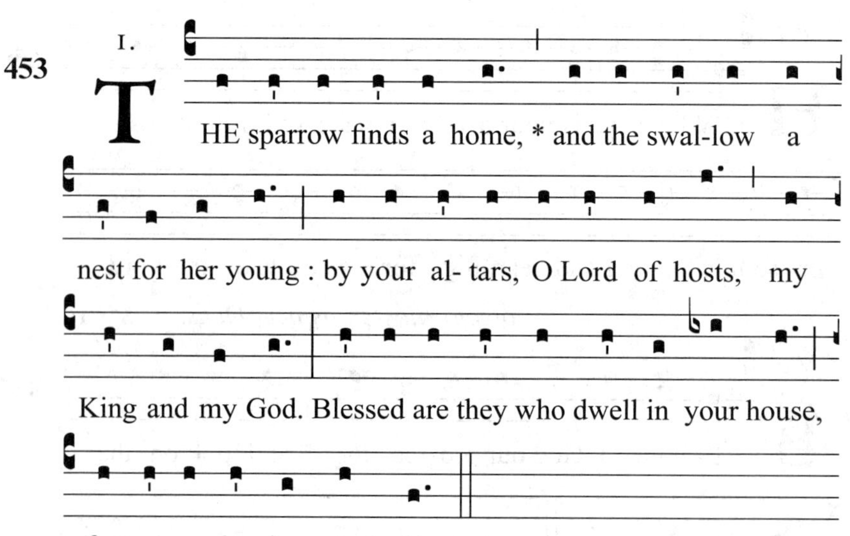

FOURTH SUNDAY OF LENT

Entrance Antiphon *Lætare, Ierusalem.*
Is 66:10-11

- i -

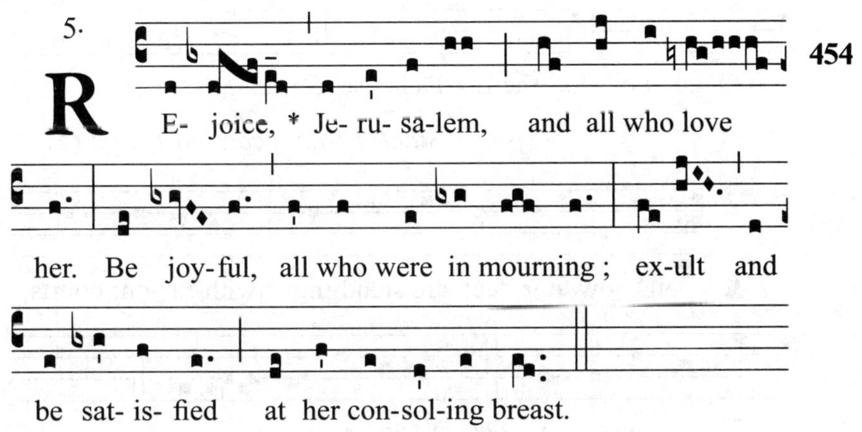
5.
454
REjoice, * Je-ru-sa-lem, and all who love her. Be joy-ful, all who were in mourning; ex-ult and be sat-is-fied at her con-sol-ing breast.

- ii -

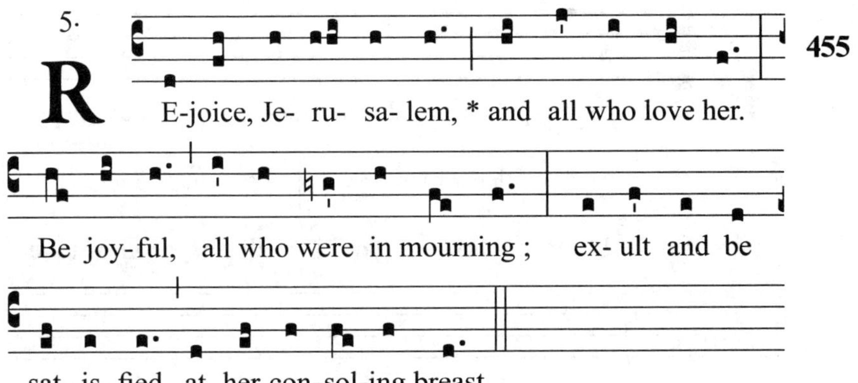
5.
455
REjoice, Je-ru-sa-lem, * and all who love her. Be joy-ful, all who were in mourning; ex-ult and be sat-is-fied at her con-sol-ing breast.

VERSES *Lætatus sum. Ps* 121:1

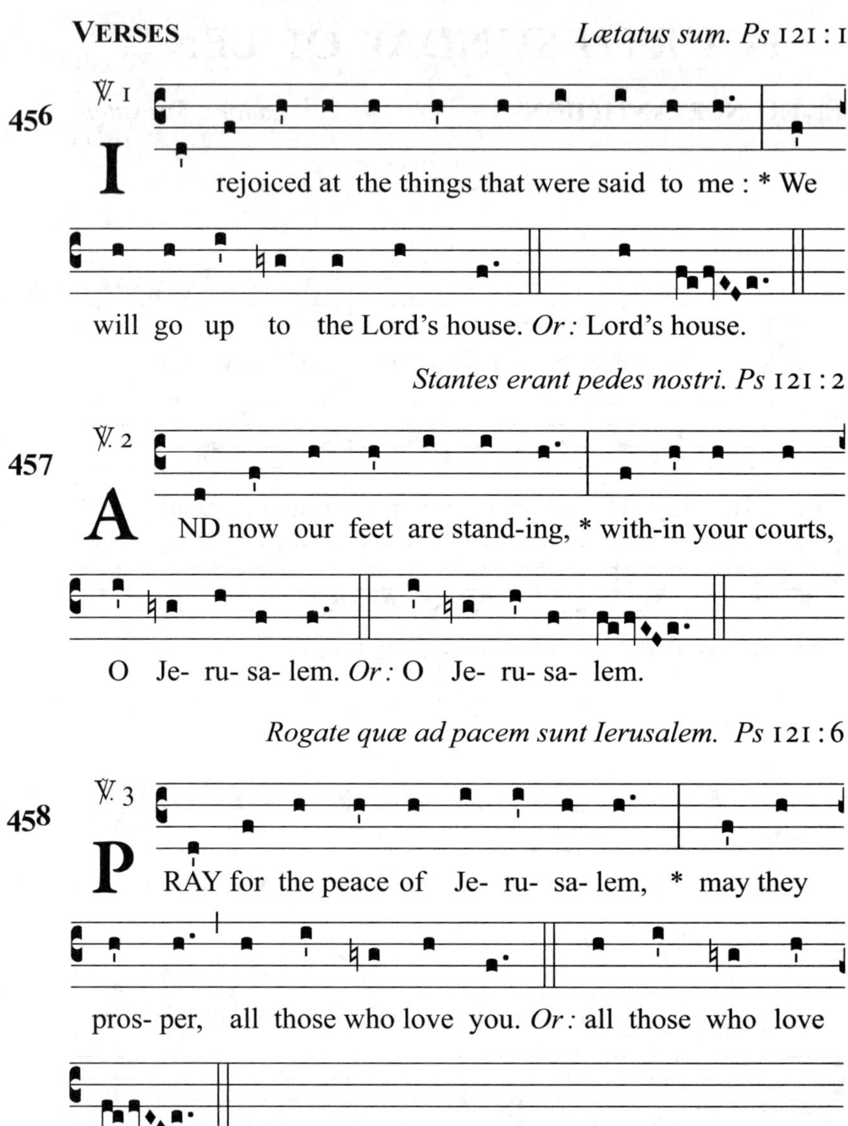
456
℣. 1
I rejoiced at the things that were said to me: * We will go up to the Lord's house. *Or:* Lord's house.
Stantes erant pedes nostri. Ps 121:2
457
℣. 2
AND now our feet are stand-ing, * with-in your courts, O Je- ru- sa- lem. *Or:* O Je- ru- sa- lem.
Rogate quæ ad pacem sunt Ierusalem. Ps 121:6
458
℣. 3
PRAY for the peace of Je- ru- sa- lem, * may they pros- per, all those who love you. *Or:* all those who love you.

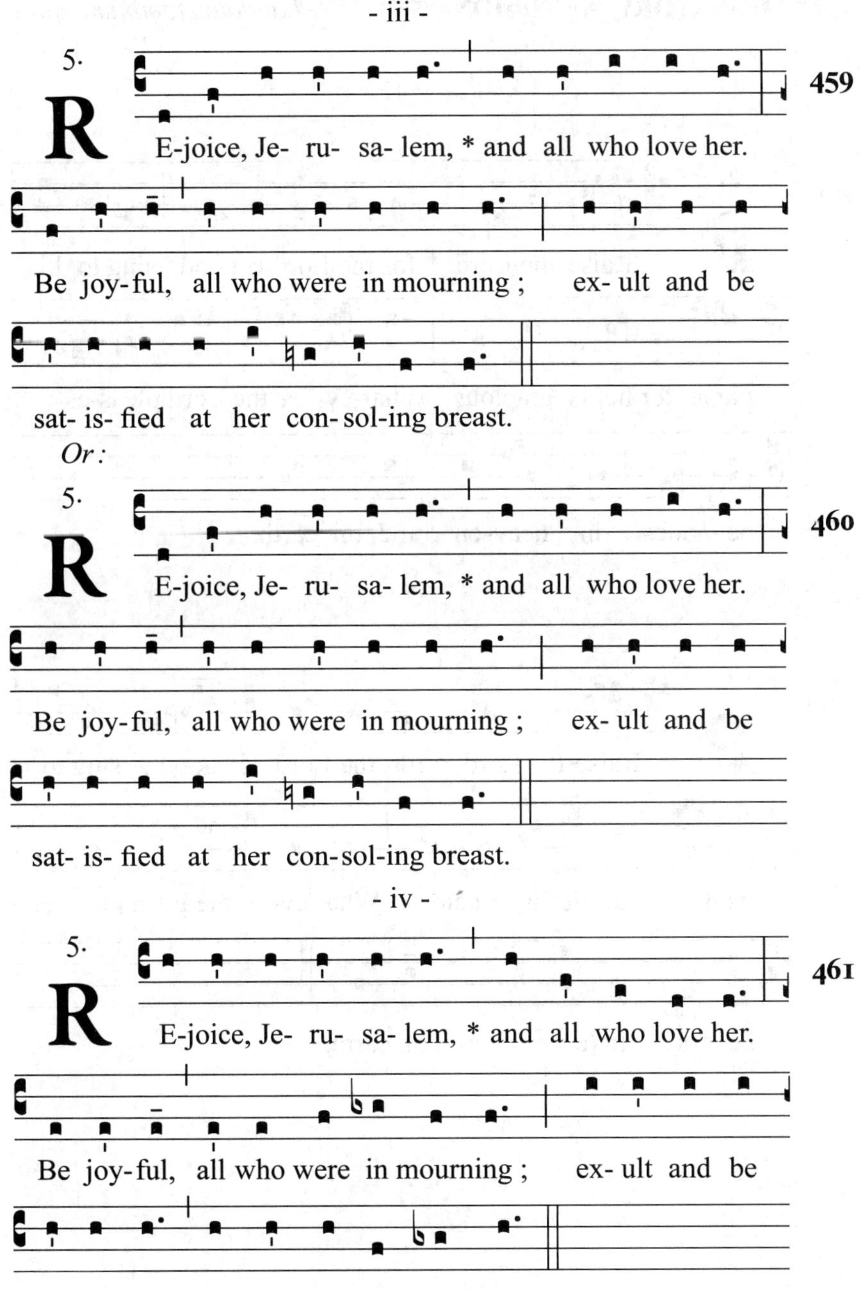
- iii -
5.
R
E-joice, Je- ru- sa- lem, * and all who love her.
459
Be joy-ful, all who were in mourning ; ex- ult and be
sat- is- fied at her con- sol-ing breast.
Or:
5.
R
E-joice, Je- ru- sa- lem, * and all who love her.
460
Be joy-ful, all who were in mourning ; ex- ult and be
sat- is- fied at her con- sol-ing breast.
- iv -
5.
R
E-joice, Je- ru- sa- lem, * and all who love her.
461
Be joy-ful, all who were in mourning ; ex- ult and be
sat- is- fied at her con- sol- ing breast.

OFFERTORY ANTIPHON *Laudate Dominum, quia.*
Ps 134: 3. 6

- i -

462
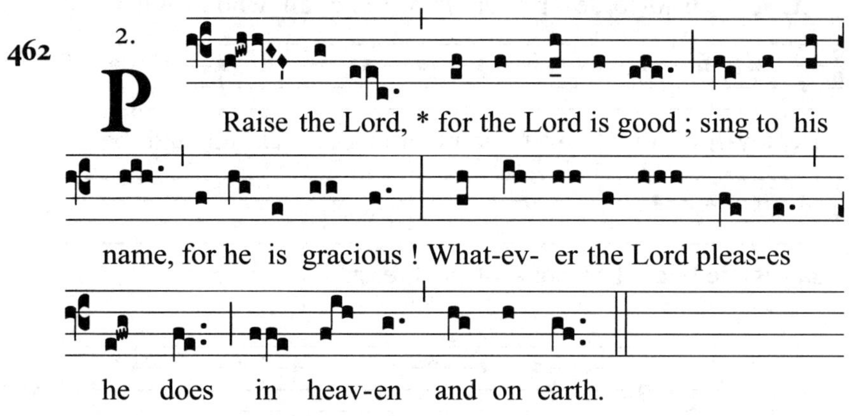
2.
PRaise the Lord, * for the Lord is good ; sing to his
name, for he is gracious ! What-ev- er the Lord pleas-es
he does in heav-en and on earth.

- ii -

463
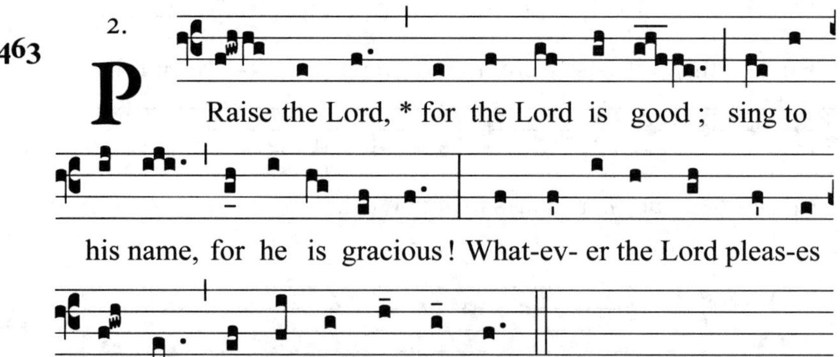
2.
PRaise the Lord, * for the Lord is good ; sing to
his name, for he is gracious ! What-ev- er the Lord pleas-es
he does in heav-en and on earth.

VERSES *Quia ego cognovi. Ps* 134:5-6

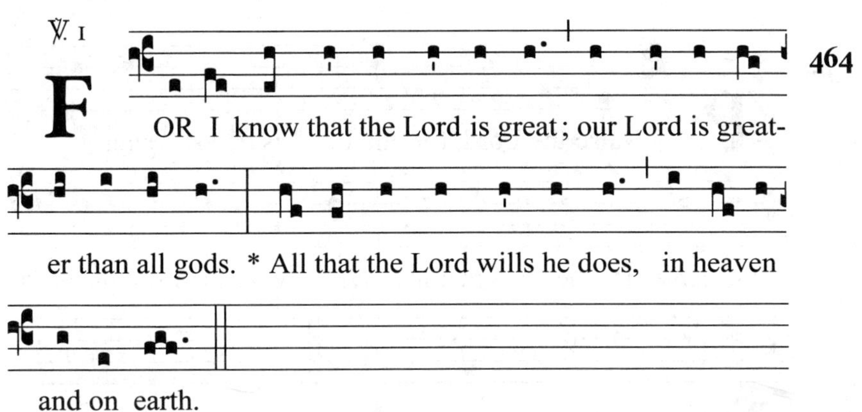
℣. 1
464
FOR I know that the Lord is great; our Lord is great-
er than all gods. * All that the Lord wills he does, in heaven
and on earth.

Domine, nomen tuum. Ps 134:13

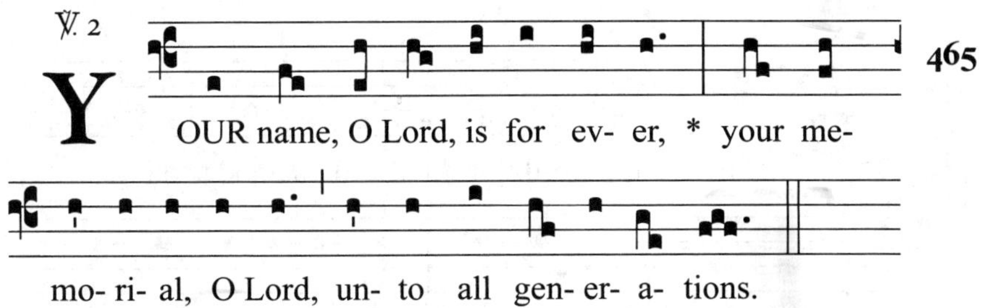
℣. 2
465
YOUR name, O Lord, is for ev- er, * your me-
mo- ri- al, O Lord, un- to all gen- er- a- tions.

Benedictus Dominus ex Sion. Ps 134:21

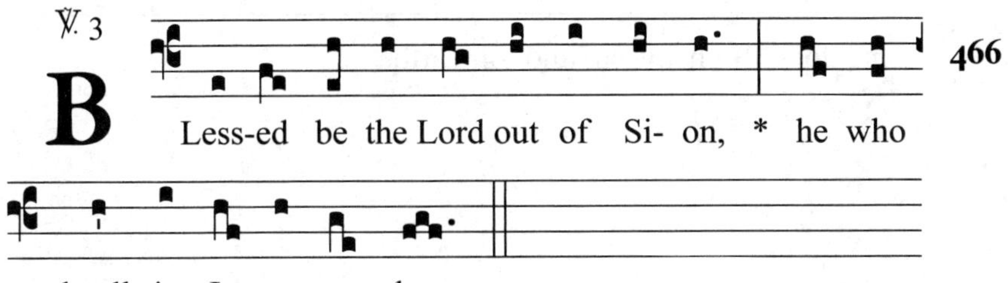
℣. 3
466
BLess-ed be the Lord out of Si- on, * he who
dwells in Je- ru- sa- lem.

- iii -

467

2.
P
Raise the Lord, for the Lord is good; * sing to
his name, for he is gracious! What-ev- er the Lord pleas-es
he does in heav-en and on earth.

- iv -

468

2.
P
Rraise the Lord, for the Lord is good; * sing to
his name, for he is gracious! What-ev- er the Lord pleases
he does in heav-en and on earth.

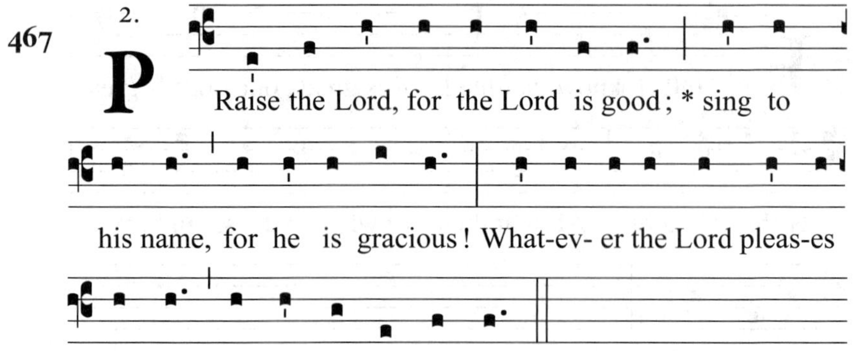

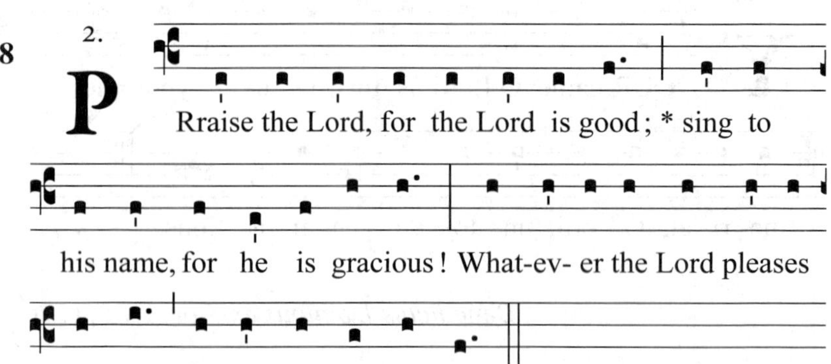

COMMUNION ANTIPHON *Dominus linivit oculos meos.*
Jn 9:11. 38

When the Gospel of the man born blind is read :

- i -

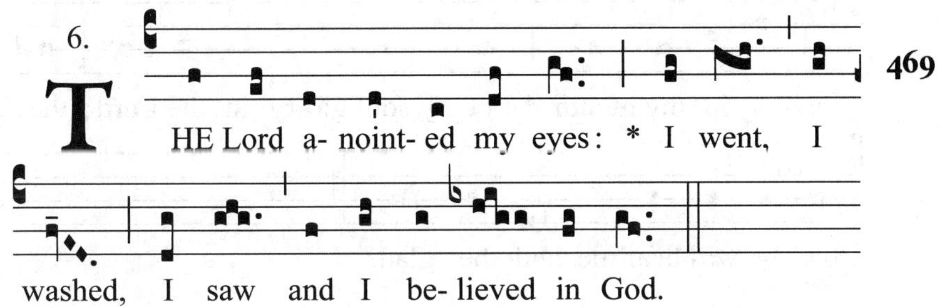
6.
THE Lord a- noint- ed my eyes: * I went, I
washed, I saw and I be- lieved in God.
469

- ii -

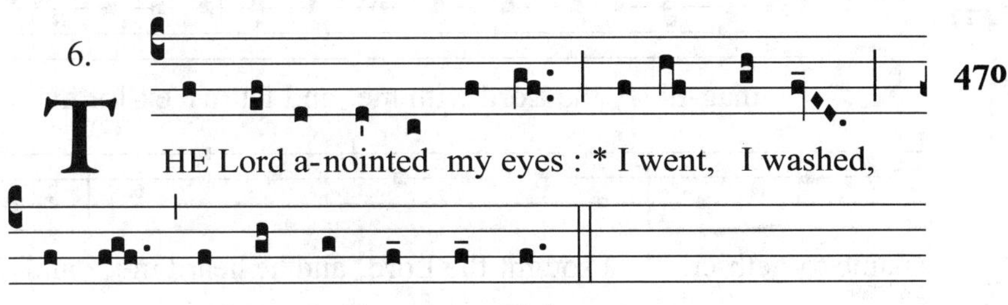
6.
THE Lord a-nointed my eyes : * I went, I washed,
I saw and I believed in God.
470

VERSES *Benedicam Dominum. Ps* 33 : 1-2

471
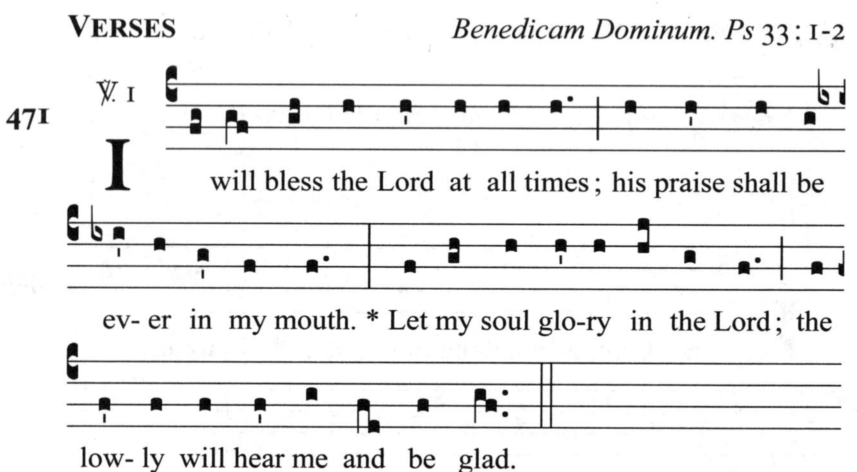
℣. 1
I will bless the Lord at all times; his praise shall be
ev- er in my mouth. * Let my soul glo-ry in the Lord; the
low- ly will hear me and be glad.

Glorificate Dominum mecum. Ps 33 : 4

472
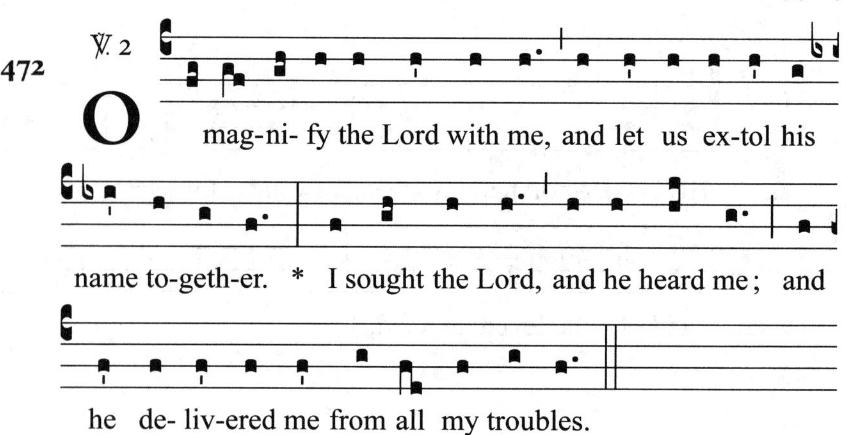
℣. 2
O mag-ni- fy the Lord with me, and let us ex-tol his
name to-geth-er. * I sought the Lord, and he heard me; and
he de- liv-ered me from all my troubles.

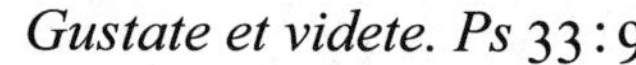
Gustate et videte. Ps 33 : 9

473

℣. 3
O taste and see how gracious the Lord is; * bless-ed
the man who hopes in him.

- iii -

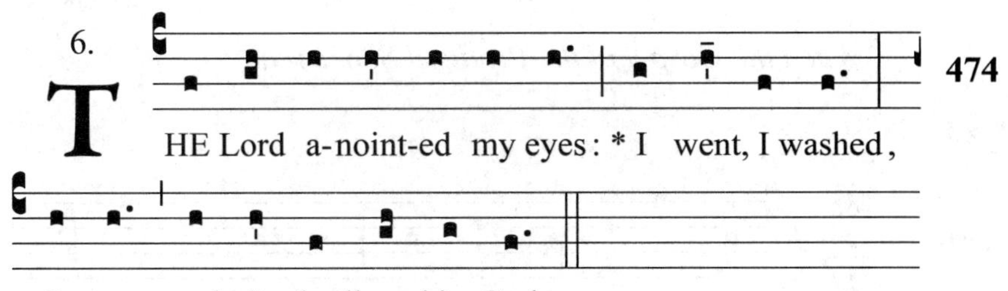
6.
474
THE Lord a-noint-ed my eyes: * I went, I washed,
I saw and I be-lieved in God.

- iv -

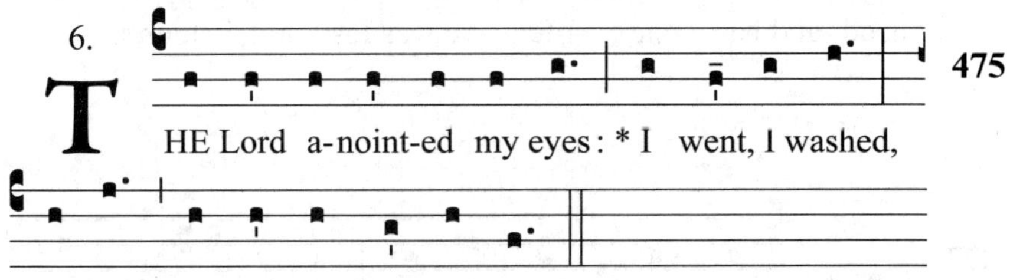
6.
475
THE Lord a-noint-ed my eyes: * I went, I washed,
I saw and I be-lieved in God.

COMMUNION ANTIPHON *Oportet te, fili, gaudere.* *Lk* 15:32

When the Gospel of the Prodigal Son is read:

- i -

476 
8.
YOU must re-joice, my son, * for your broth-er was
dead and has come to life; he was lost and is found.

- ii -

477 
8.
YOU must re-joice, my son, * for your broth-er was
dead and has come to life; he was lost and is found.

VERSES *Benedicam Dominum. Ps* 33 : 1-2

℣. 1
478
I will bless the Lord at all times; his praise shall be
ev- er in my mouth. * Let my soul glo-ry in the Lord ; the
low-ly will hear me and be glad.

Glorificate Dominum mecum. Ps 33 : 4

℣. 2
479
O mag-ni- fy the Lord with me, let us to-geth-er ex-
tol his name. * I sought the Lord, and he answered me and
de-liv-ered me from all my fears.

Accedite ad eum. Ps 33 : 6

℣. 3
480
COME to him and be en-lightened, * and your fac-es
shall not be put to shame.

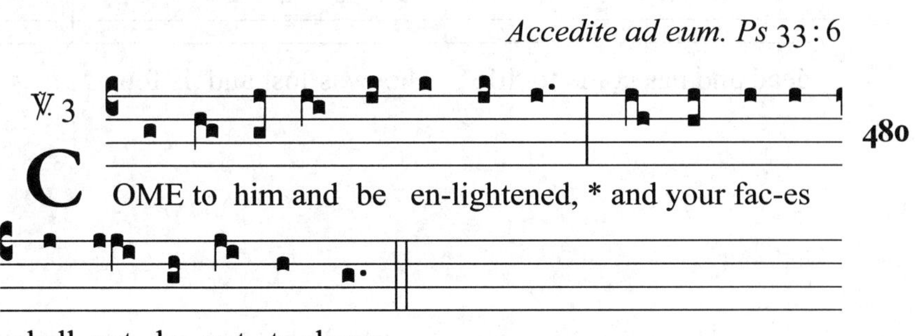

- iii -

481

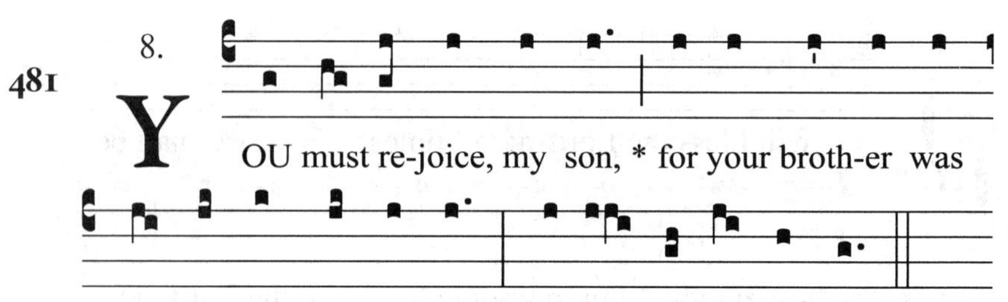

8.
YOU must re-joice, my son, * for your broth-er was

dead and has come to life ; he was lost and is found.

Or:

482

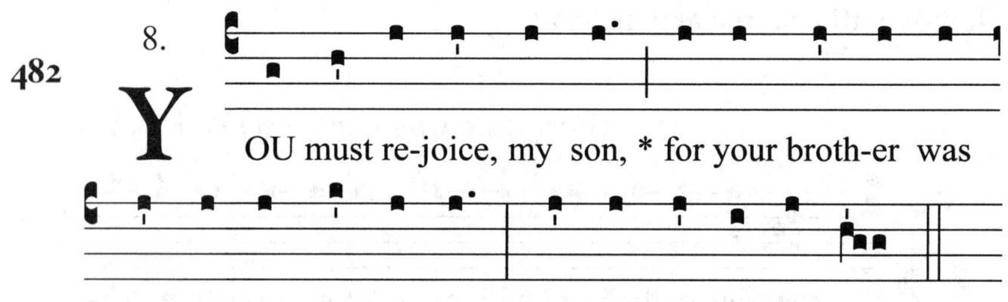

8.
YOU must re-joice, my son, * for your broth-er was

dead and has come to life ; he was lost and is found.

- iv -

483

8.
YOU must re-joice, my son, * for your broth-er was

dead and has come to life ; he was lost and is found.

COMMUNION ANTIPHON *Ierusalem, quae ædificatur.*
Ps 121 : 3-4

When another Gospel is read :

- i -

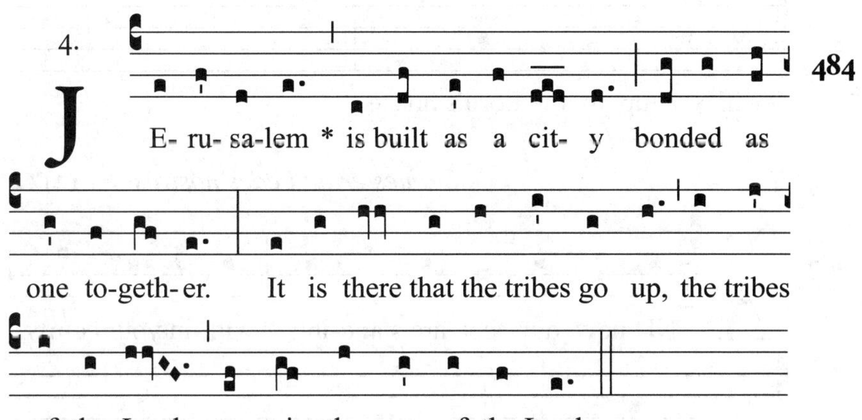
4.
J E- ru- sa-lem * is built as a cit- y bonded as
one to-geth- er. It is there that the tribes go up, the tribes
of the Lord, to praise the name of the Lord.

484

- ii -

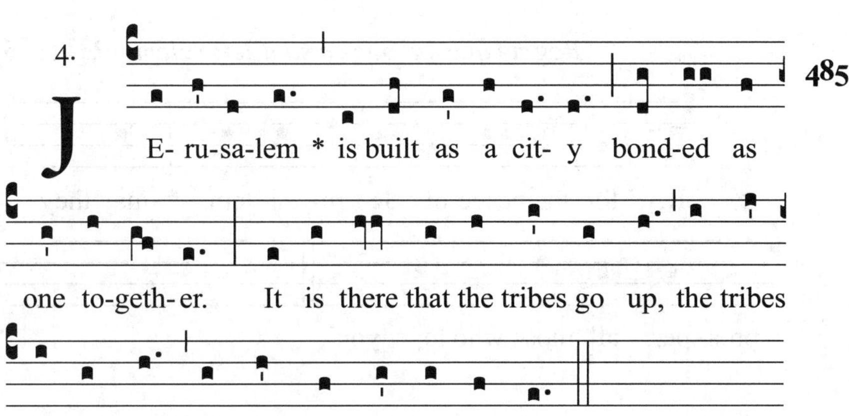
4.
J E- ru-sa-lem * is built as a cit- y bond-ed as
one to-geth- er. It is there that the tribes go up, the tribes
of the Lord, to praise the name of the Lord.

485

VERSES *Lætatus sum. Ps* 121 : 1

486

℣. 1
I rejoiced at the things that were said to me : * We
will go up to the Lord's house.

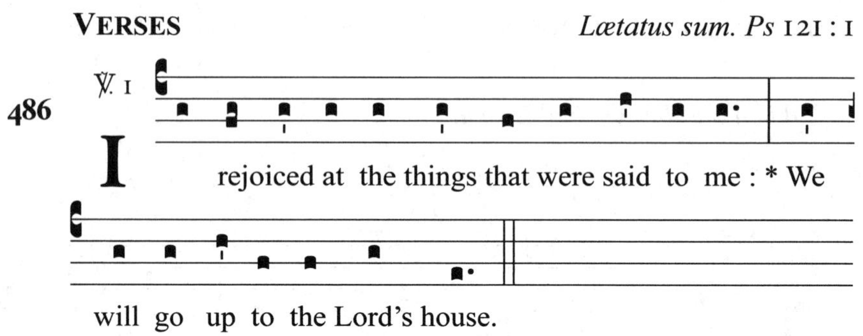

Stantes erant pedes nostros. Ps 121 : 2

487

℣. 2
AND now our feet are stand-ing, * with-in your courts,
O Je- ru- sa- lem.

Rogate quæ ad pacem sunt Ierusalem. Ps 121 : 6

488

℣. 3
PRAY for the peace of Je- ru- sa- lem, * may they
pros- per, all those who love you.

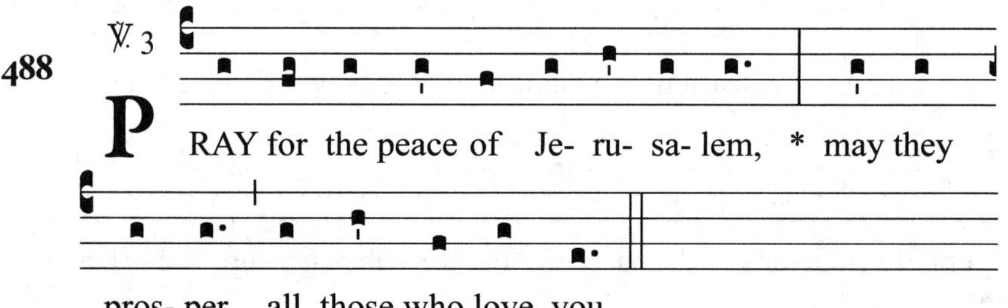

- iii -

4.
JE- ru- sa-lem is built as a cit- y * bond-ed as
one to-geth- er. It is there that the tribes go up, the tribes
of the Lord, to praise the name of the Lord.

489

- iv -

4.
JE- ru- sa-lem is built as a cit- y * bond-ed as
one to-geth- er. It is there that the tribes go up, the tribes
of the Lord, to praise the name of the Lord.

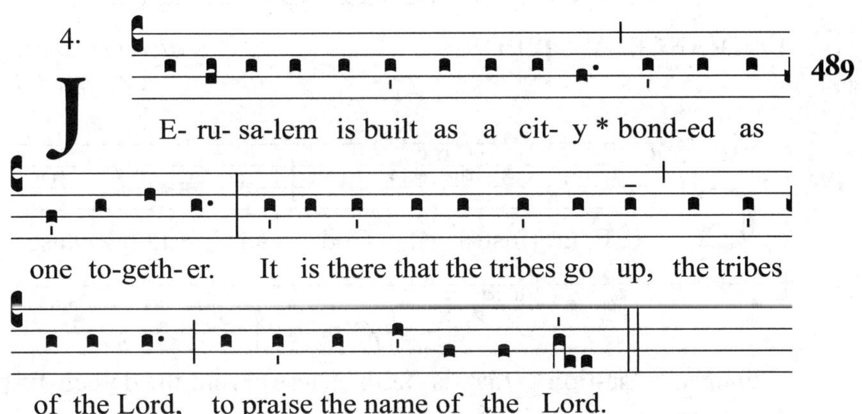

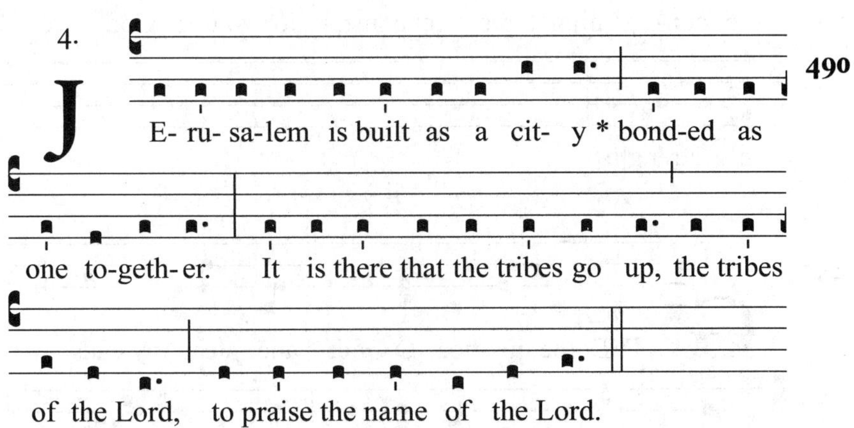

490

FIFTH SUNDAY OF LENT

Entrance Antiphon *Iudica me, Deus.*
Ps 42:1-2

- i -

491

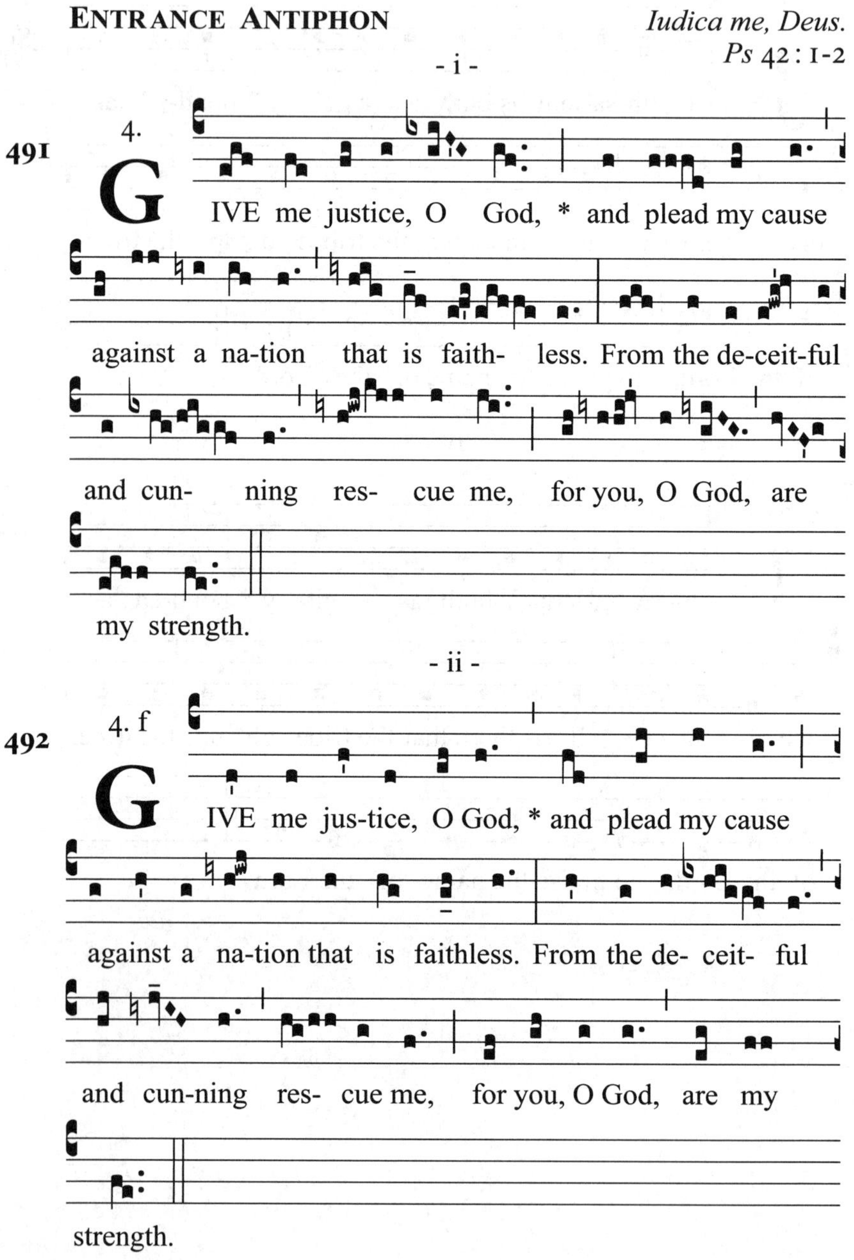
4.
GIVE me justice, O God, * and plead my cause
against a nation that is faith- less. From the de-ceit-ful
and cun- ning res- cue me, for you, O God, are
my strength.
- ii -
492
4. f
GIVE me jus-tice, O God, * and plead my cause
against a na-tion that is faithless. From the de- ceit- ful
and cun-ning res- cue me, for you, O God, are my
strength.

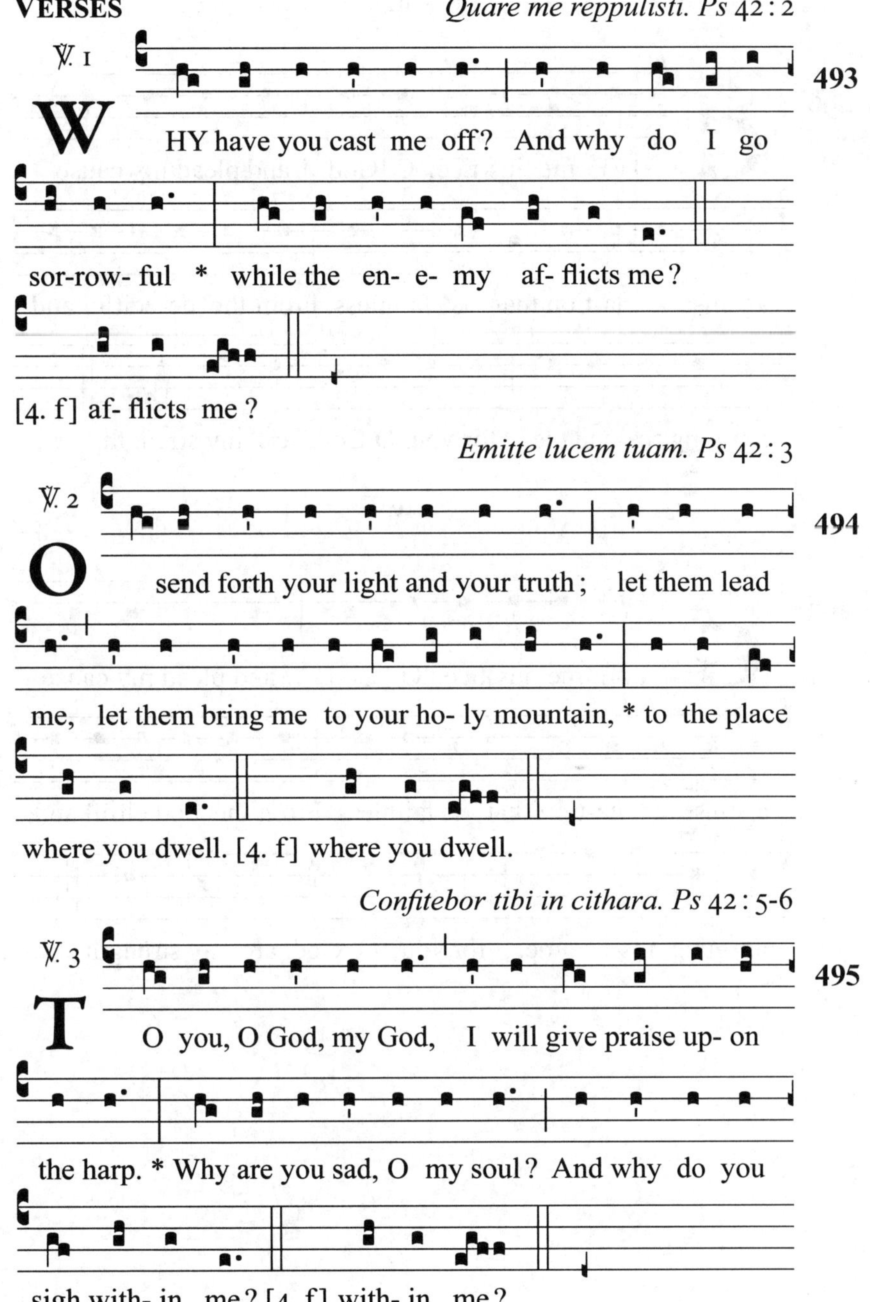
VERSES
Quare me reppulisti. Ps 42 : 2
℣. 1
493
WHY have you cast me off? And why do I go
sor-row- ful * while the en- e- my af- flicts me?
[4. f] af- flicts me?
Emitte lucem tuam. Ps 42 : 3
℣. 2
494
O send forth your light and your truth; let them lead
me, let them bring me to your ho- ly mountain, * to the place
where you dwell. [4. f] where you dwell.
Confitebor tibi in cithara. Ps 42 : 5-6
℣. 3
495
TO you, O God, my God, I will give praise up- on
the harp. * Why are you sad, O my soul? And why do you
sigh with- in me? [4. f] with- in me?

- iii -

496

4.
GIVE me jus-tice, O God, * and plead my cause
against a na-tion that is faithless. From the de-ceitful and
cun-ning res-cue me, for you, O God, are my strength.

- iv -

497

4.
GIVE me jus-tice, O God, * and plead my cause
against a na-tion that is faithless. From the de-ceitful and
cun-ning res-cue me, for you, O God, are my strength.

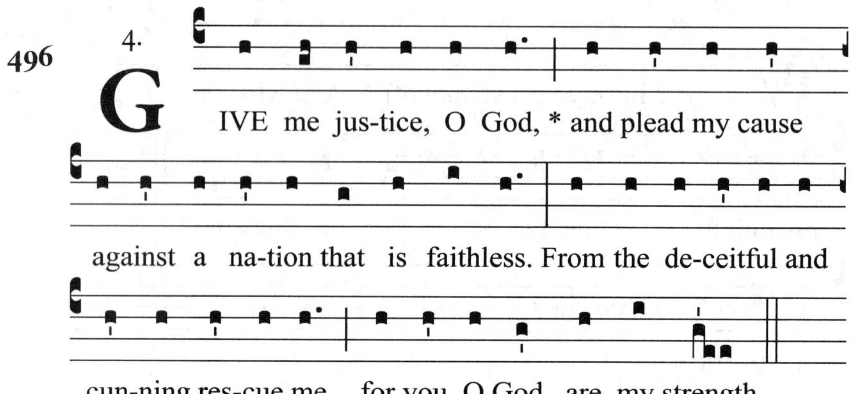

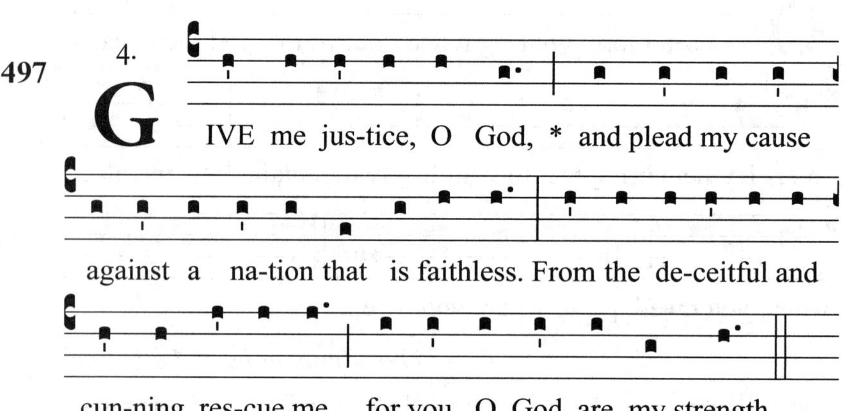

Offertory Antiphon *Confitebor tibi, Domine.*
Ps 118:7. 10. 17. 25

- i -

I.

I will praise you, O Lord, * with an upright heart. 498

Deal boun-ti-f'lly with your ser-vant, that I may live and

keep your words. En-liv- en me ac-cord-ing to your word,

O Lord.

- ii -

I.

I will praise you, O Lord, * with an upright heart. 499

Deal boun-ti- f'lly with your ser-vant, that I may live and

keep your words. En- liv- en me ac-cord-ing to your word,

O Lord.

VERSES *Viam veritatis elegi. Ps* 118 : 30-31

500
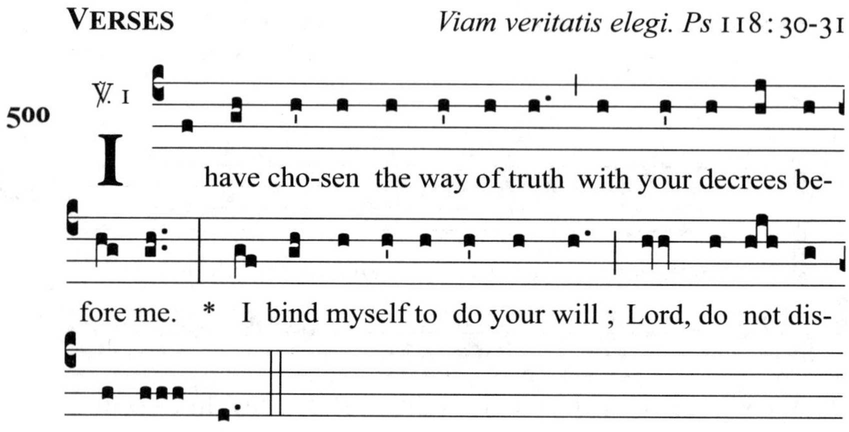
℣. 1
I have cho-sen the way of truth with your decrees be-
fore me. * I bind myself to do your will ; Lord, do not dis-
ap-point me.

Averte oculos meos. Ps 118 : 37-38

501
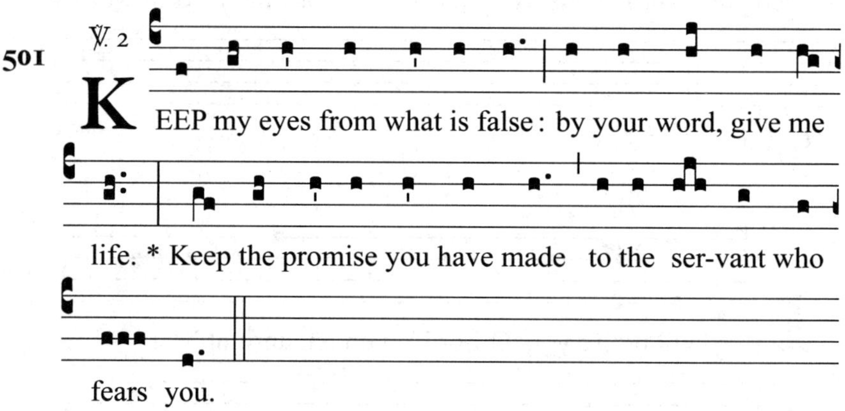
℣. 2
KEEP my eyes from what is false : by your word, give me
life. * Keep the promise you have made to the ser-vant who
fears you.

Memor fui iudiciorum tuorum. Ps 118 : 52

502
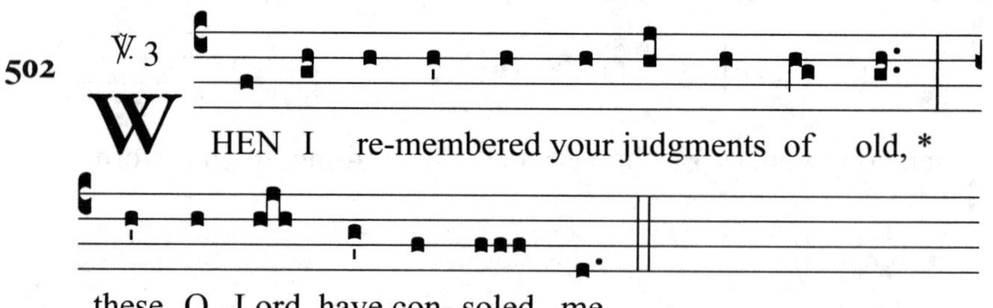
℣. 3
WHEN I re-membered your judgments of old, *
these, O Lord, have con- soled me.

- iii -

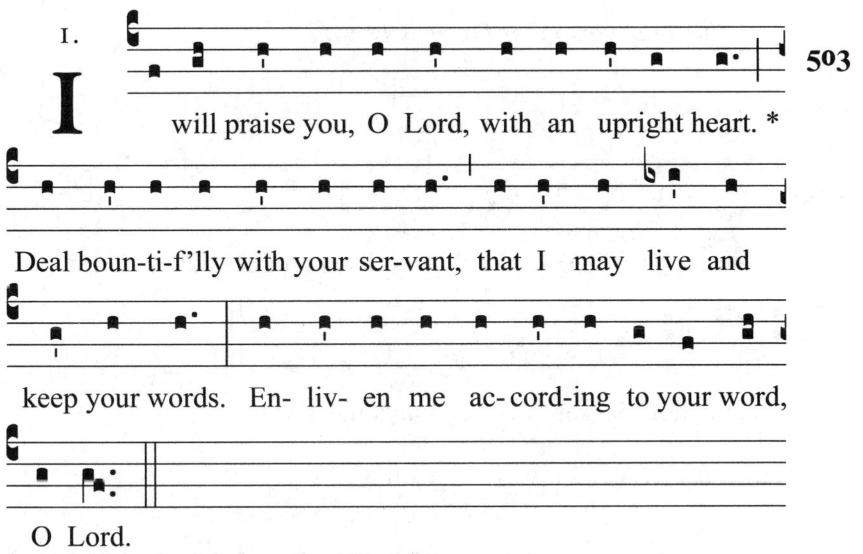
1.
503
I will praise you, O Lord, with an upright heart. *
Deal boun-ti-f'lly with your ser-vant, that I may live and
keep your words. En- liv- en me ac-cord-ing to your word,
O Lord.

- iv -

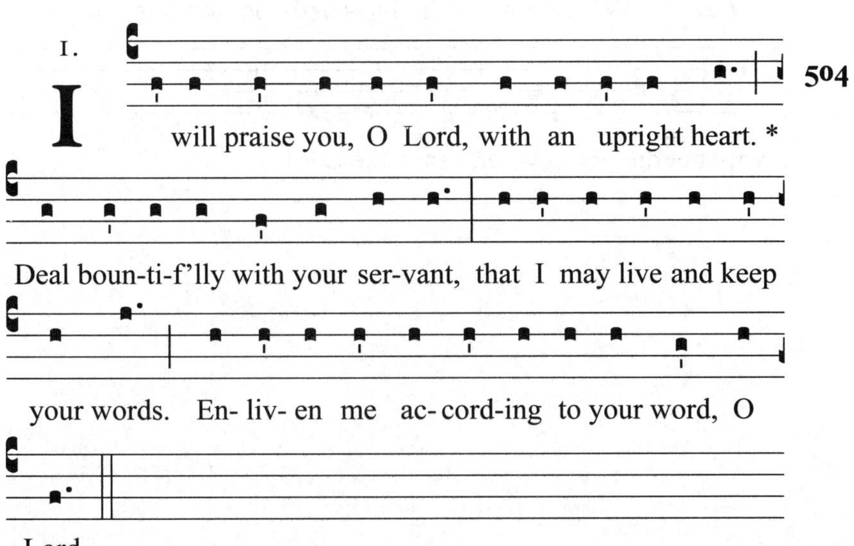
1.
504
I will praise you, O Lord, with an upright heart. *
Deal boun-ti-f'lly with your ser-vant, that I may live and keep
your words. En- liv- en me ac- cord-ing to your word, O
Lord.

COMMUNION ANTIPHON *Omnis qui vivit.*
Jn 11 : 26

When the Gospel of Lazarus is read :

- i -

505
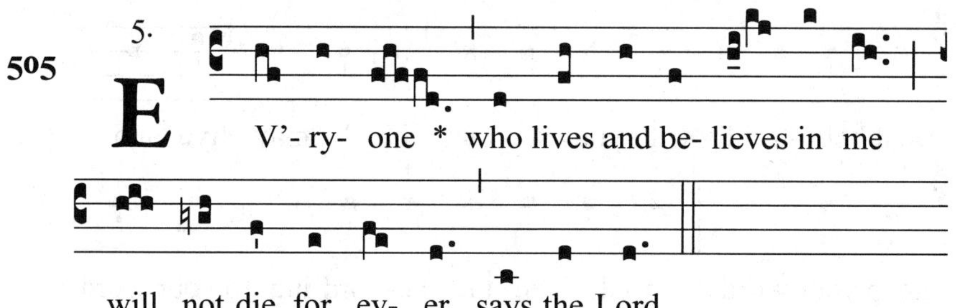
5.
E
V'- ry- one * who lives and be- lieves in me
will not die for ev- er, says the Lord.

- ii -

506

5.
E
V'- ry- one * who lives and be-lieves in me
will not die for ev- er, says the Lord.

VERSES *Benedicam Dominum. Ps* 33 : 1-2

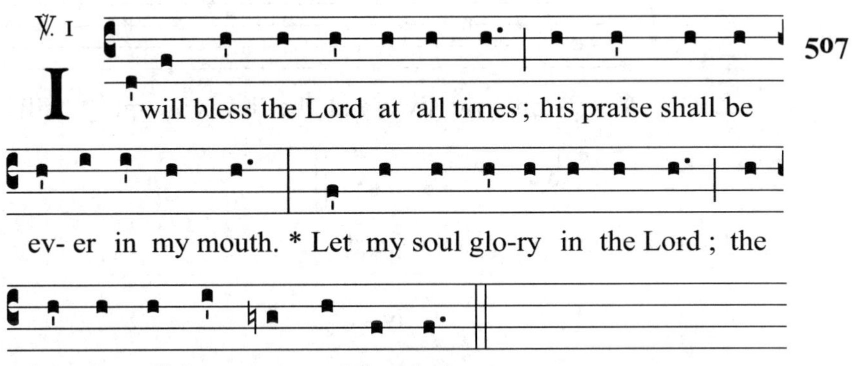
℣. 1
507
I will bless the Lord at all times; his praise shall be
ev- er in my mouth. * Let my soul glo-ry in the Lord; the
low- ly will hear me and be glad.

Glorificate Dominum mecum. Ps 33 : 4

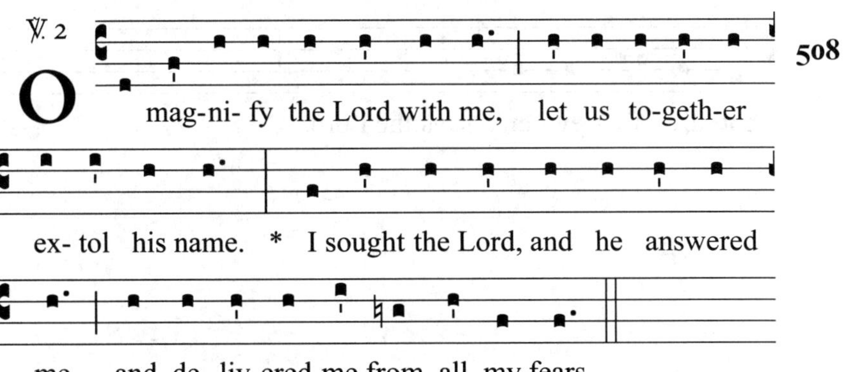
℣. 2
508
O mag-ni- fy the Lord with me, let us to-geth-er
ex- tol his name. * I sought the Lord, and he answered
me and de- liv-ered me from all my fears.

Gustate et videte. Ps 33 : 9

℣. 3
509
O taste and see how gracious the Lord is; * bless-ed
the man who hopes in him.

- iii -

510

5.
E V'- ry- one who lives and be-lieves in me * will
not die for ev- er, says the Lord.

- iv -

511

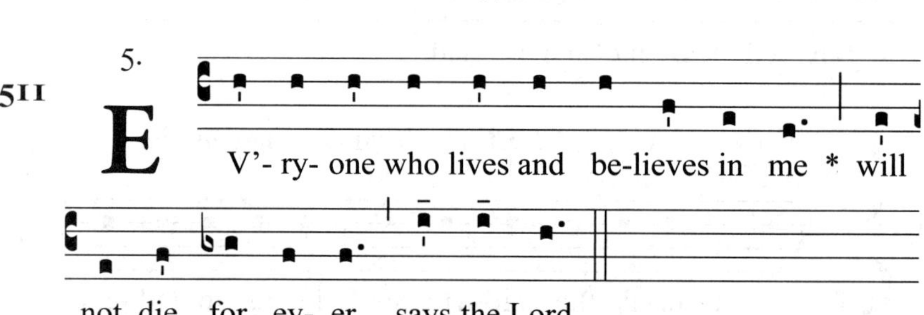
5.
E V'- ry- one who lives and be-lieves in me * will
not die for ev- er, says the Lord.

COMMUNION ANTIPHON *Nemo te condemnavit, mulier?*
Jn 8:10-11

When the Gospel of the Adulterous Woman is read:

- i -

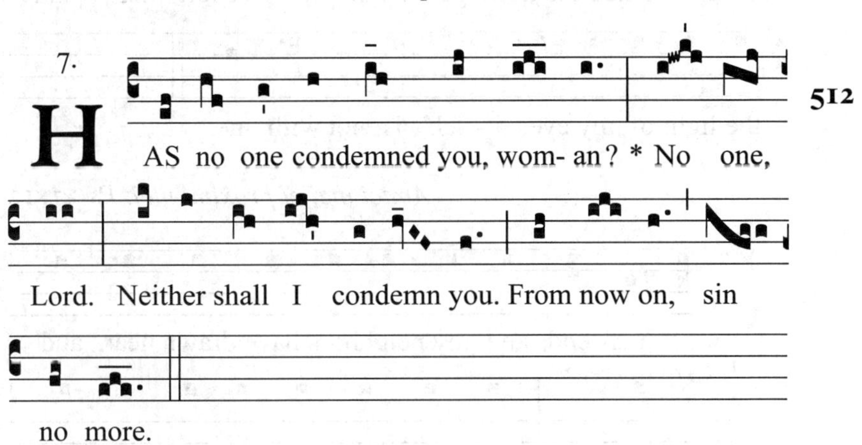
7.
HAS no one condemned you, wom- an? * No one,
Lord. Neither shall I condemn you. From now on, sin
no more.

512

- ii -

7.
HAS no one condemned you, wom- an? * No one,
Lord. Neither shall I condemn you. From now on, sin no more.

513

VERSES *Cor meum conturbatum est. Ps* 37:11

514

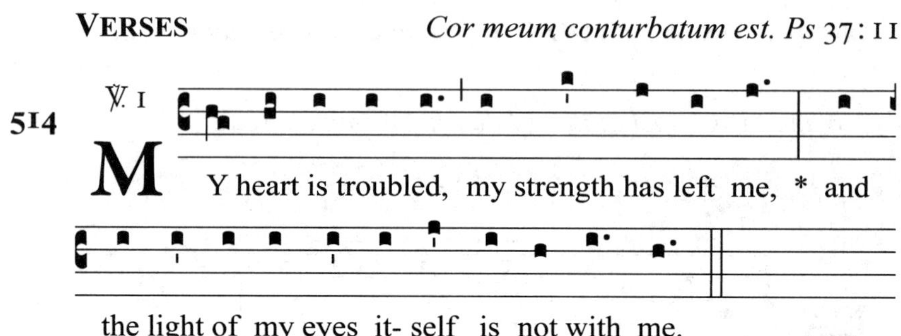
℣. 1
MY heart is troubled, my strength has left me, * and
the light of my eyes it- self is not with me.

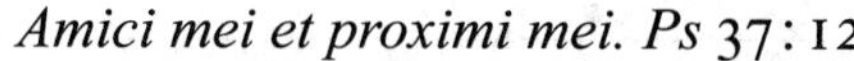
Amici mei et proximi mei. Ps 37:12

515

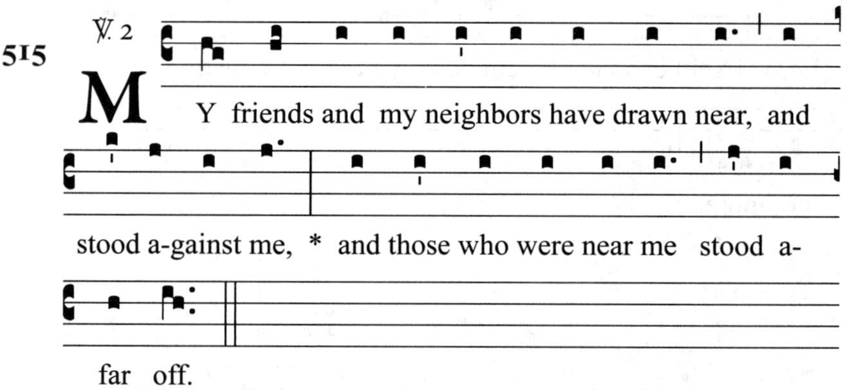
℣. 2
MY friends and my neighbors have drawn near, and
stood a-gainst me, * and those who were near me stood a-
far off.

Quoniam in te, Domine, speravi. Ps 37:16

516

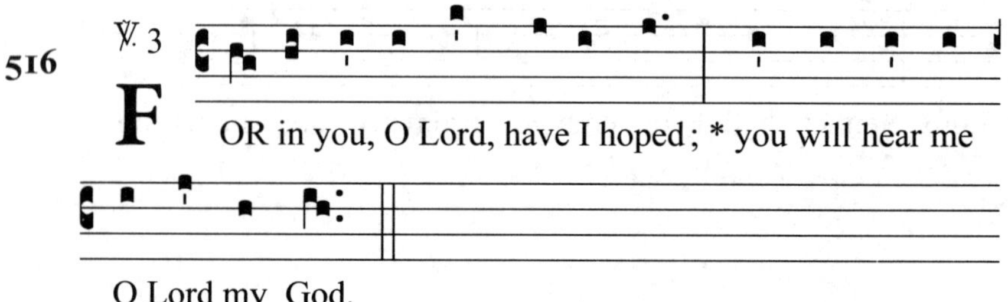
℣. 3
FOR in you, O Lord, have I hoped; * you will hear me
O Lord my God.

- iii -

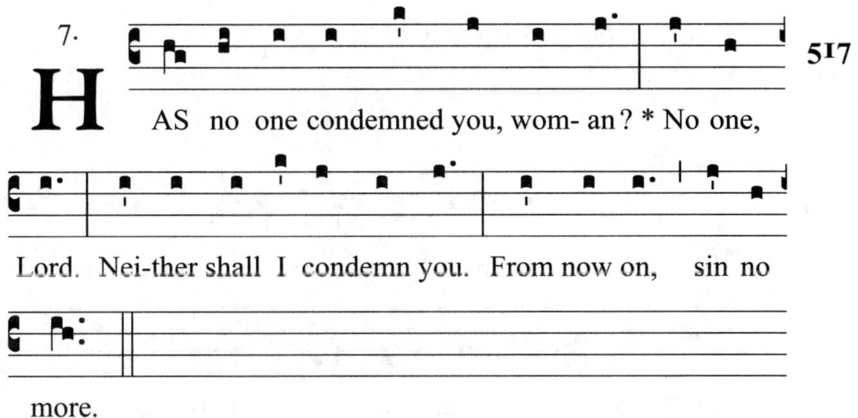
7.
HAS no one condemned you, wom- an? * No one,
517
Lord. Nei-ther shall I condemn you. From now on, sin no
more.

- iv -

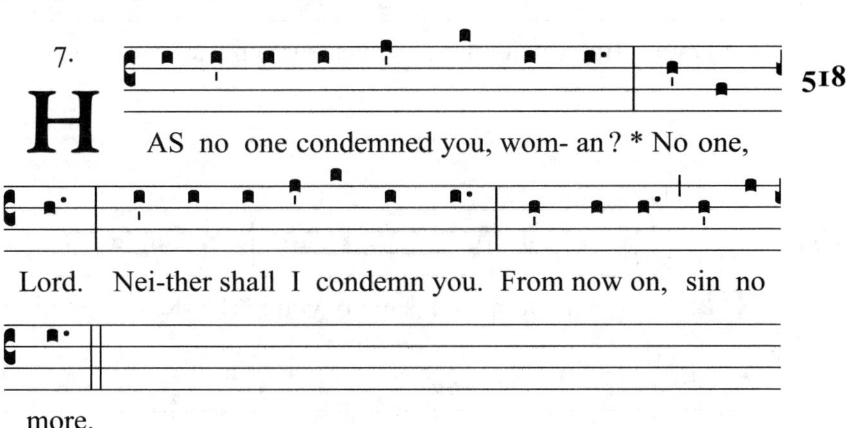
7.
HAS no one condemned you, wom- an? * No one,
518
Lord. Nei-ther shall I condemn you. From now on, sin no
more.

COMMUNION ANTIPHON *Amen, amen dico vobis.*
Jn 12:24

When another Gospel is read :

- i -

519

8.
A - men, a- men * I say to you : Un-less a grain
of wheat falls to the ground and dies, it remains a sin-
gle grain. But if it dies, it bears much fruit.

- ii -

520

8.
A - men, a- men I say to you : * Un-less a grain
of wheat falls to the ground and dies, it remains a sin-
gle grain. But if it dies, it bears much fruit.

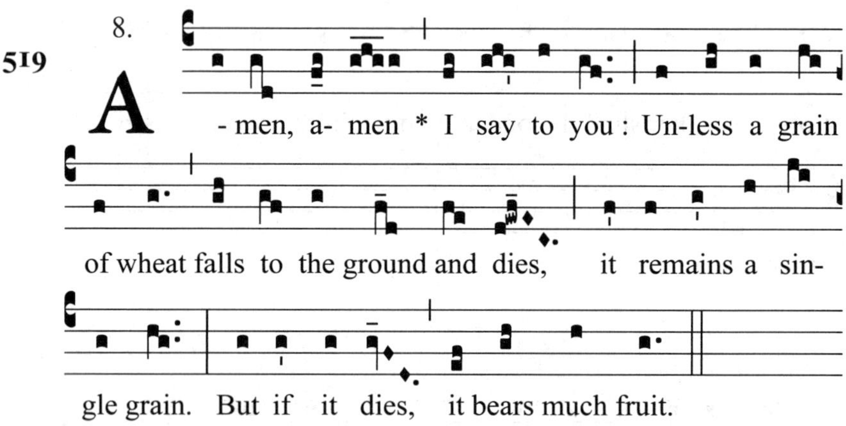

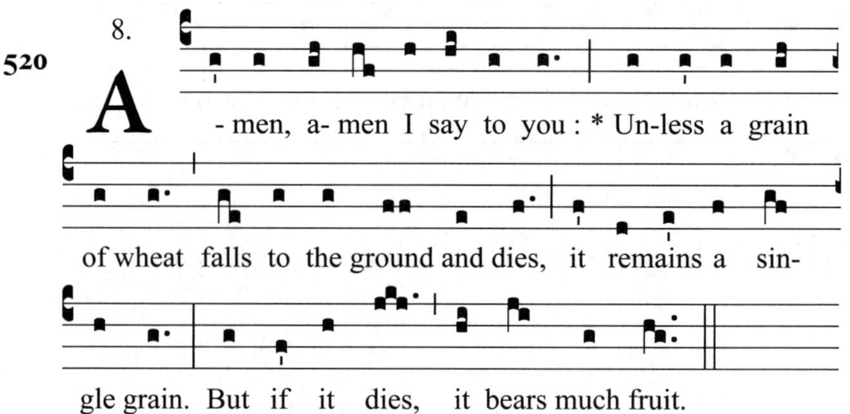

VERSES *Benedicam Dominum. Ps* 33 : 1-2

℣. 1
521
I will bless the Lord at all times; his praise shall be
ev- er in my mouth. * Let my soul glo-ry in the Lord ; the
low-ly will hear me and be glad.

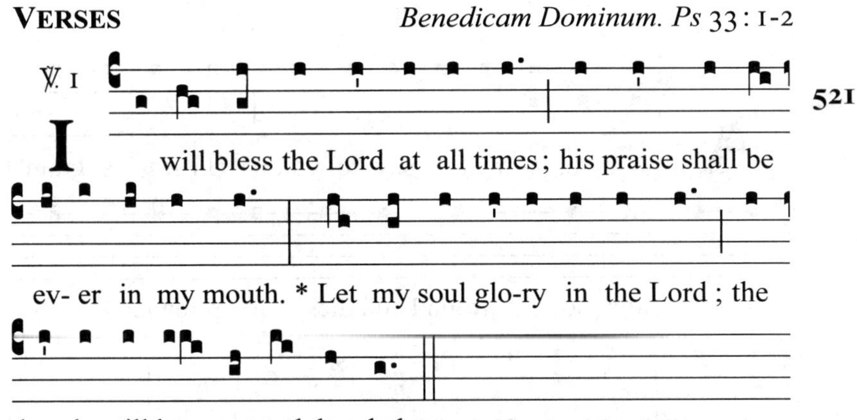

Glorificate Dominum mecum. Ps 33 : 4

℣. 2
522
O mag-ni- fy the Lord with me, let us to-geth-er ex-
tol his name. * I sought the Lord, and he answered me and
de-liv-ered me from all my fears.

Gustate et videte. Ps 33 : 9

℣. 3
523
O taste and see how gracious the Lord is ; * bless-ed
the man who hopes in him.

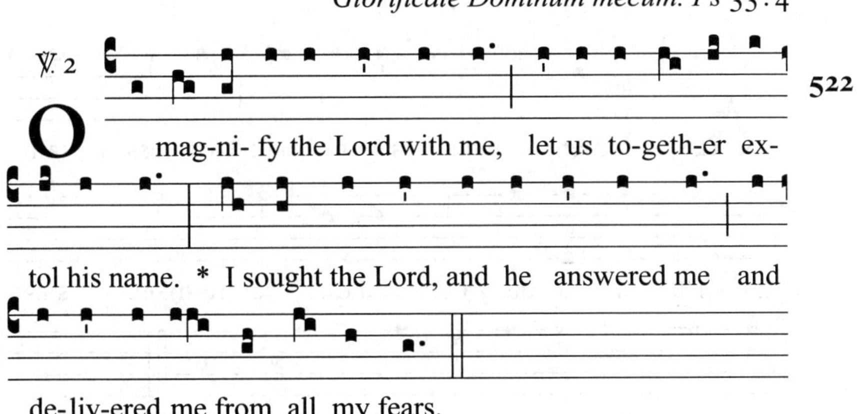

- iii -

524

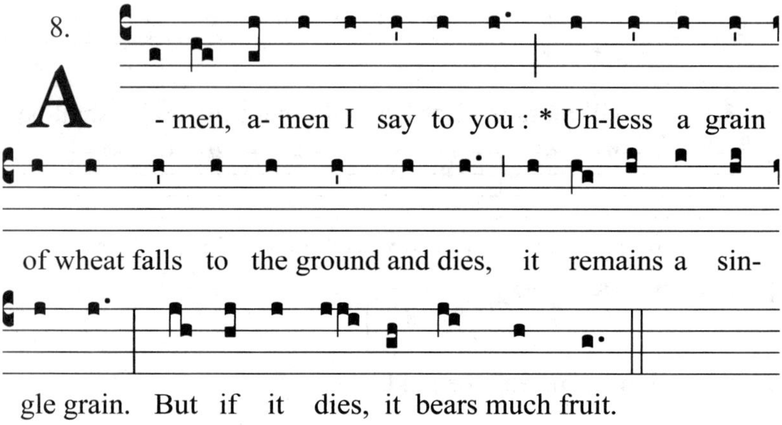

8.

A - men, a- men I say to you : * Un-less a grain of wheat falls to the ground and dies, it remains a sin-gle grain. But if it dies, it bears much fruit.

Or :

525

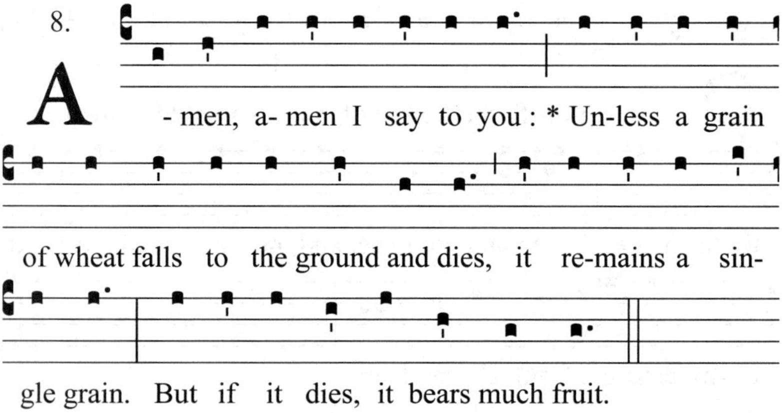

8.

A - men, a- men I say to you : * Un-less a grain of wheat falls to the ground and dies, it re-mains a sin-gle grain. But if it dies, it bears much fruit.

- iv -

526

8.

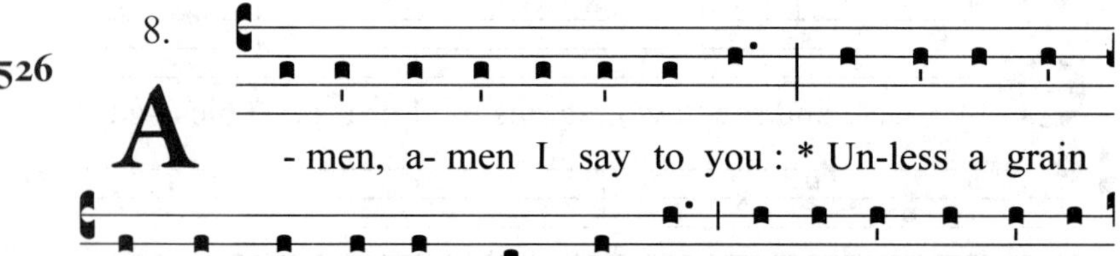

A - men, a- men I say to you : * Un-less a grain of wheat falls to the ground and dies, it remains a sin-gle

grain. But if it dies, it bears much fruit.

COMMUNION ANTIPHON *Qui mihi ministrat.*
Jn 12:26

When another Gospel is read :

- i -

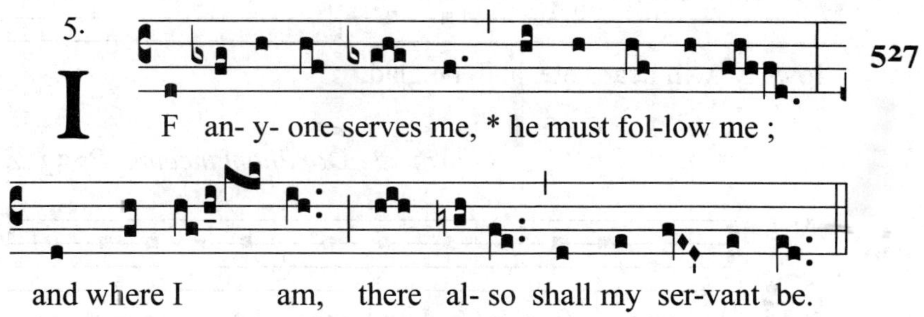
5.
IF an- y- one serves me, * he must fol-low me ;
527
and where I am, there al- so shall my ser-vant be.

- ii -

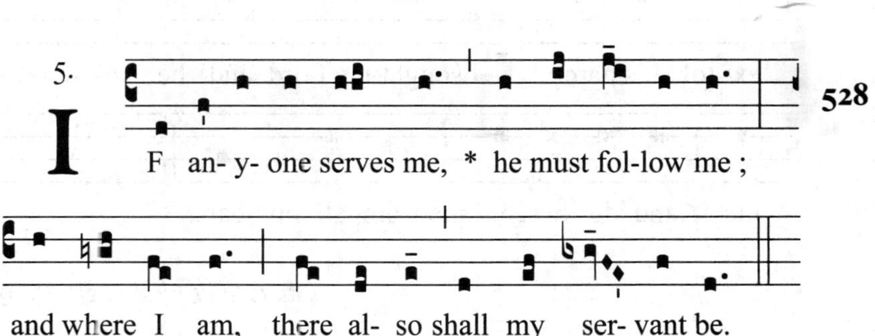
5.
IF an- y- one serves me, * he must fol-low me ;
528
and where I am, there al- so shall my ser- vant be.

VERSES *Benedicam Dominum. Ps* 33:1-2

529

℣. 1
I will bless the Lord at all times; his praise shall be
ev- er in my mouth. * Let my soul glo-ry in the Lord; the
low- ly will hear me and be glad.

Glorificate Dominum mecum. Ps 33:4

530

℣. 2
O mag-ni- fy the Lord with me, let us to-geth-er
ex- tol his name. * I sought the Lord, and he answered
me and de- liv-ered me from all my fears.

Gustate et videte. Ps 33:9

531

℣. 3
O taste and see how gracious the Lord is; * bless-ed
the man who hopes in him.

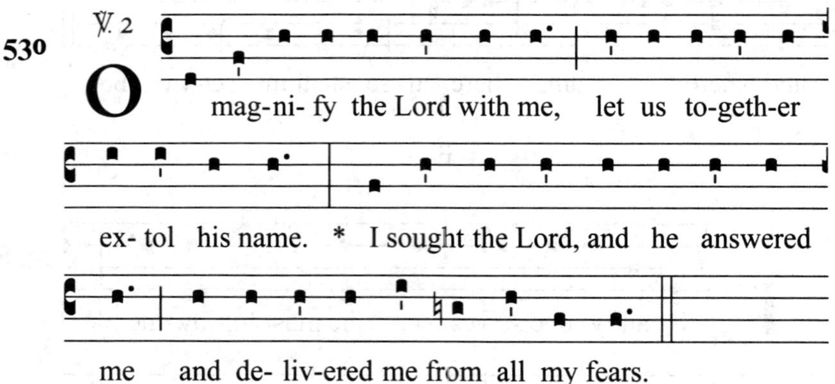

- iii -

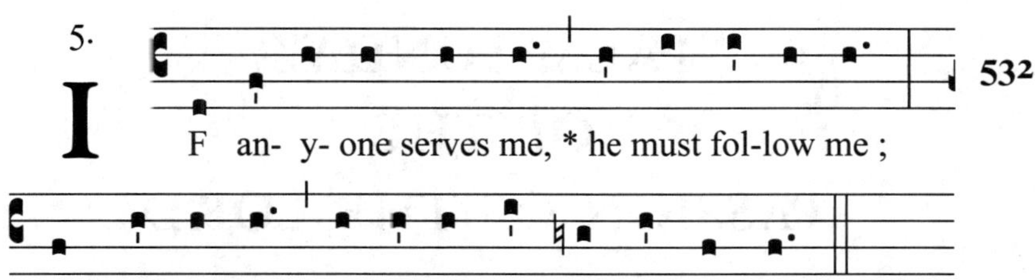
5.
IF an- y- one serves me, * he must fol-low me ;
532

and where I am, there al- so shall my ser-vant be.

Or :

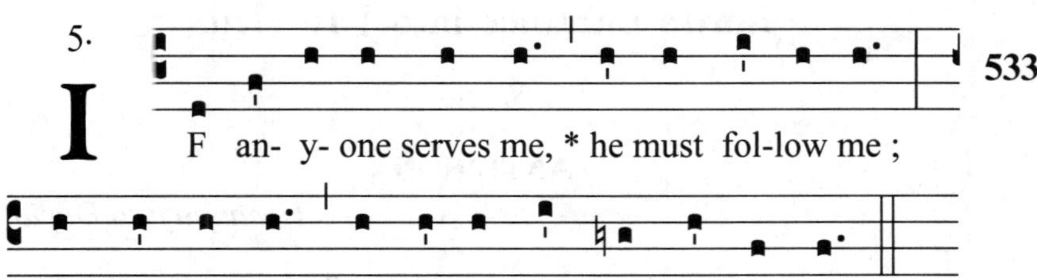
5.
IF an- y- one serves me, * he must fol-low me ;
533

and where I am, there al- so shall my ser-vant be.

- iv -

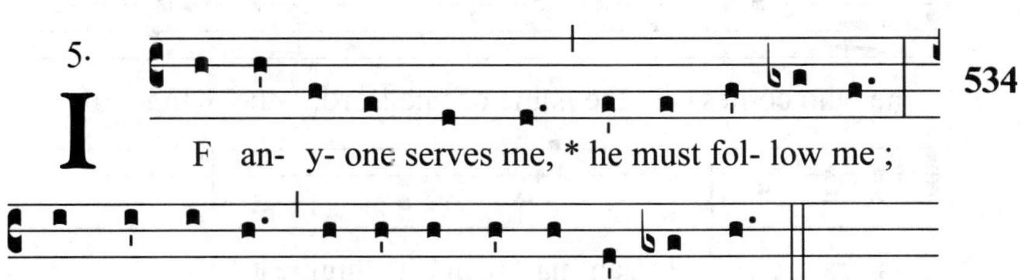
5.
IF an- y- one serves me, * he must fol- low me ;
534

and where I am, there al- so shall my ser-vant be.

HOLY WEEK

PALM SUNDAY OF THE PASSION OF THE LORD

The Commemoration of the Lord's Entrance into Jerusalem

Statio

ANTIPHON

Hosanna filio David.

535

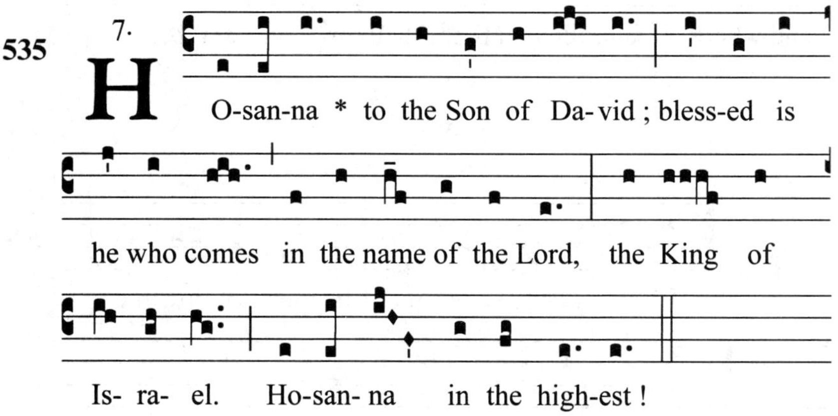
7.
H O-san-na * to the Son of Da-vid; bless-ed is
he who comes in the name of the Lord, the King of
Is- ra- el. Ho-san- na in the high-est!

Procession

INVITATION

536

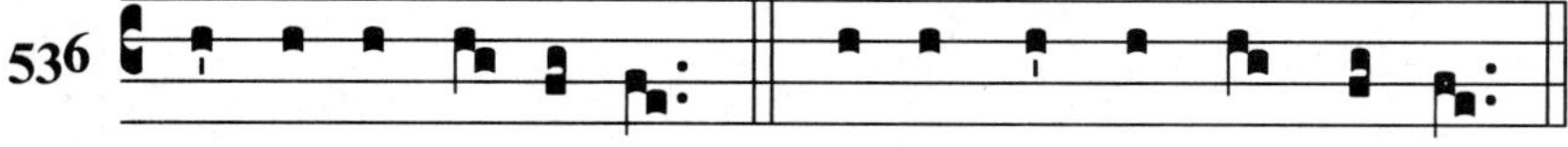
Let us go forth in peace. ℟. In the name of Christ. A- men.

ANTIPHON I

Pueri Hebrœorum.

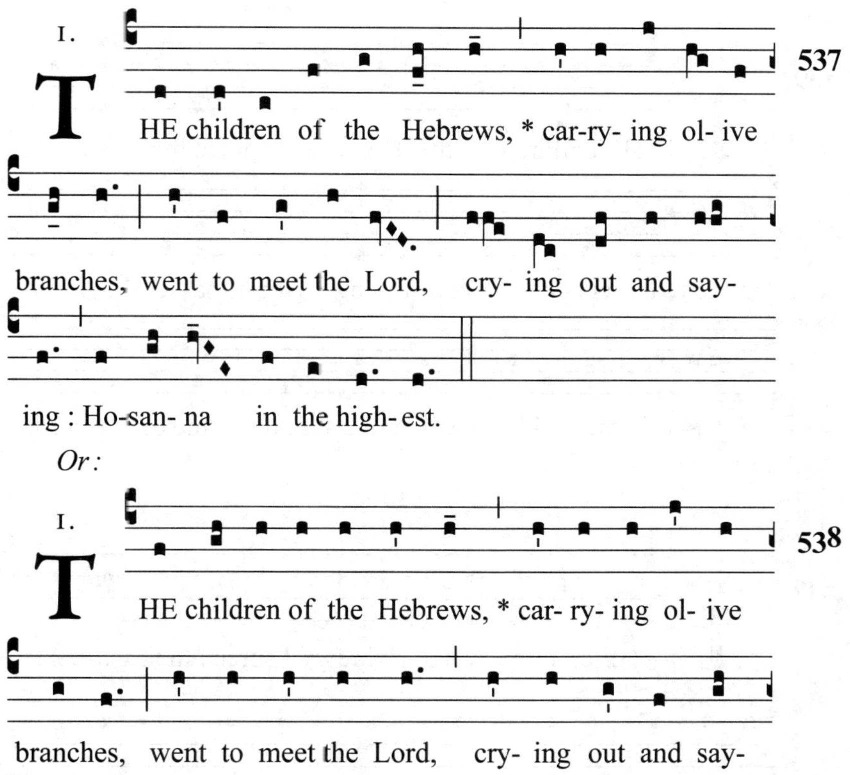
1.
537
THE children of the Hebrews, * car-ry- ing ol- ive
branches, went to meet the Lord, cry- ing out and say-
ing : Ho-san- na in the high- est.
Or:
1.
538
THE children of the Hebrews, * car- ry- ing ol- ive
branches, went to meet the Lord, cry- ing out and say-

ing : Ho-san- na in the high- est.

ANTIPHON 2

- i -

539 I.

THE children of the Hebrews * spread their garments on the road, cry-ing out and say-ing : Hosan-na to the Son of Da-vid ; blessed is he who comes in the name of the Lord.

- iii -

540

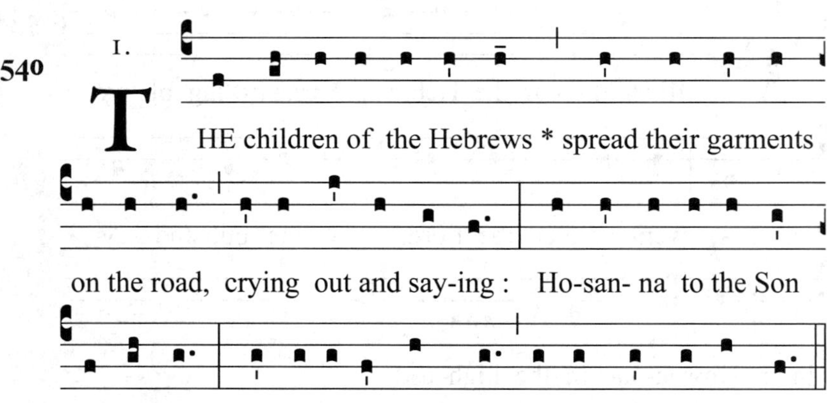
I.
THE children of the Hebrews * spread their garments
on the road, crying out and say-ing : Ho-san- na to the Son
of Da-vid ; blessed is he who comes in the name of the Lord.

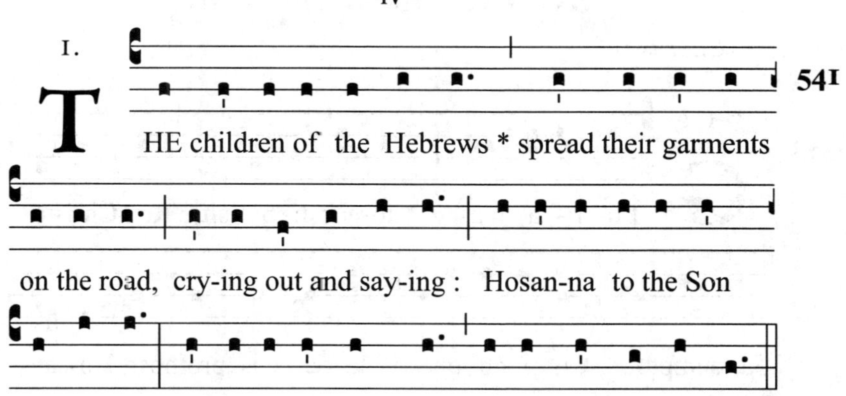
- iv -
1.
541
THE children of the Hebrews * spread their garments
on the road, cry-ing out and say-ing : Hosan-na to the Son
of Da-vid ; blessed is he who comes in the name of the Lord.

Hymn to Christ the King

Chorus :

542

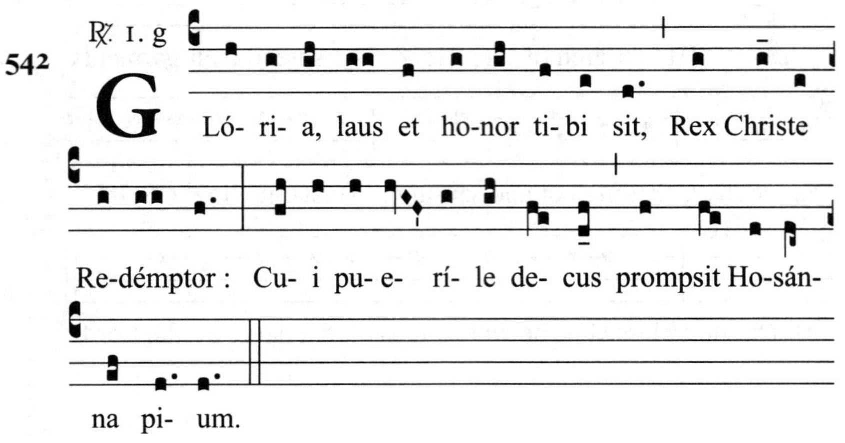
℟. I. g
GLó- ri- a, laus et ho-nor ti- bi sit, Rex Christe
Re-démptor : Cu- i pu- e- rí- le de- cus prompsit Ho-sán-
na pi- um.

All repeat : Gloria, laus . . .

For the verses in Latin, cf. The Parish Book of Chant.

543

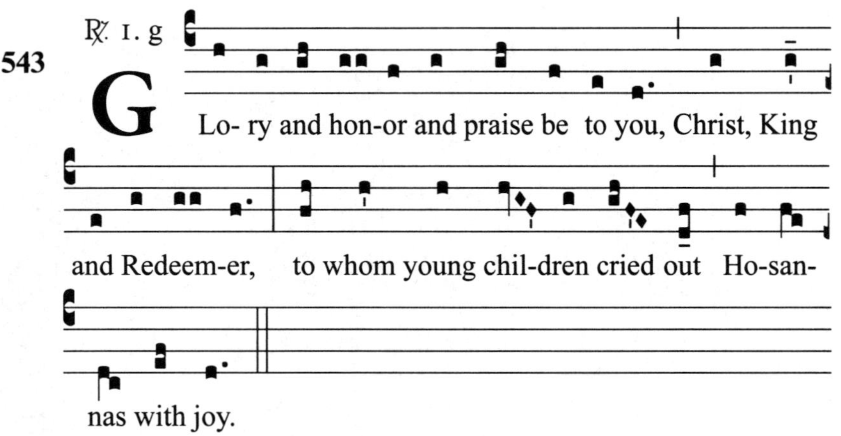
℟. I. g
GLo- ry and hon-or and praise be to you, Christ, King
and Redeem-er, to whom young chil-dren cried out Ho-san-
nas with joy.

All repeat : Glory and honor . . .

Verses

I. g 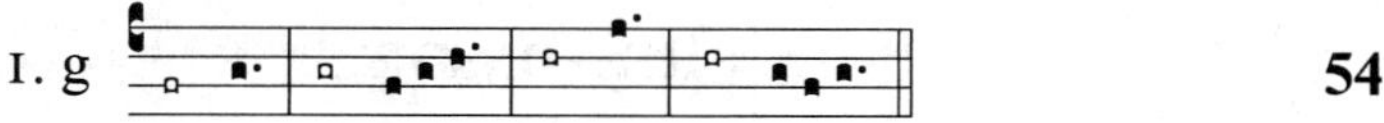 544

Chorus :

Israel's King are | **you**,
King David's magnif- | *i-cent* **off**-spring ;
you are the ruler who | **come**
blest in the name | *of the* **Lord**.

All repeat : Glory and honor . . .

Chorus :

Heavenly hosts on | **high**
unite in sing- | *ing your* **prais**-es ;
men and women on | **earth**
and all crea- | *tion join* **in**.

All repeat : Glory and honor . . .

Chorus :

Bearing branches of | **palm**,
Hebrews come crowding to | **greet** you ;
see how with prayers and | **hymns**
we come to pay | *you our* **vows**.

All repeat : Glory and honor . . .

Chorus :

They offered gifts of praise to | **you**,
so near | *to your* **Pas**-sion ;
see how we sing this song | **now**
to you / reign- | *ing on* **high**.

All repeat : Glory and honor . . .

Chorus :

Those you were pleased to ac- | **cept** ;
now accept our gifts | *of de*-**vo**-tion,
good and merciful | **King**,
lover of all | *that is* **good**.

All repeat : Glory and honor . . .

As the Procession Enters the Church

RESPONSORY

- i -

545

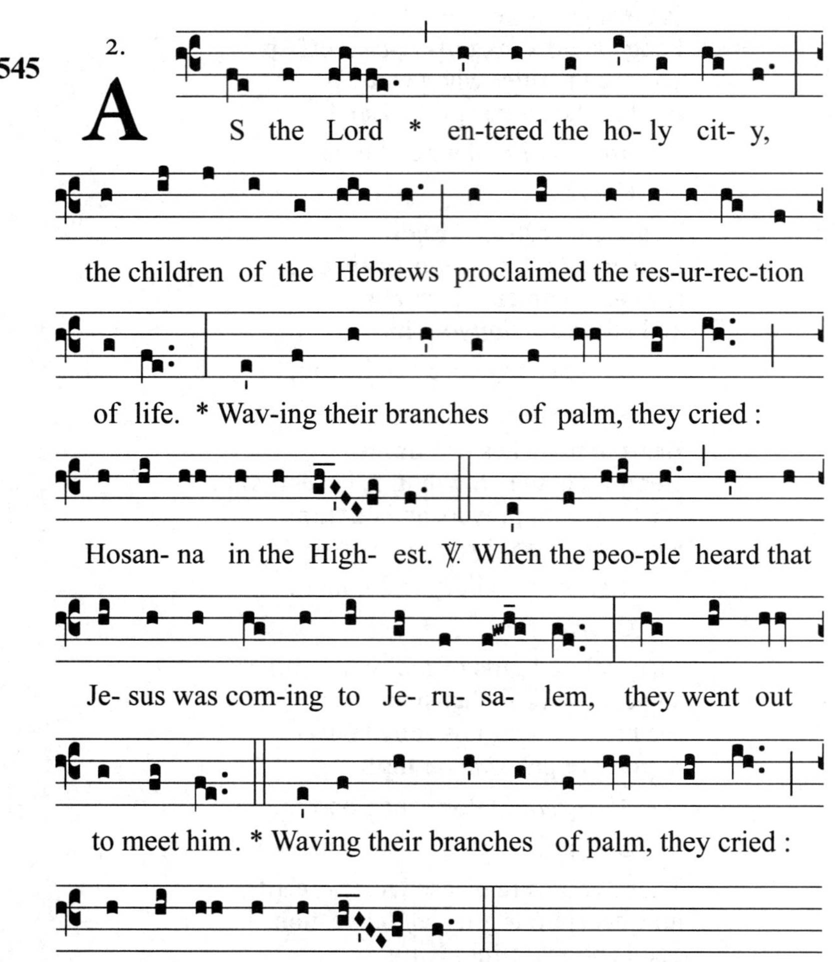
2.
AS the Lord * en-tered the ho- ly cit- y,
the children of the Hebrews proclaimed the res-ur-rec-tion
of life. * Wav-ing their branches of palm, they cried :
Hosan- na in the High- est. ℣. When the peo-ple heard that
Je- sus was com-ing to Je- ru- sa- lem, they went out
to meet him. * Waving their branches of palm, they cried :
Ho-san- na in the High- est.

- iii -

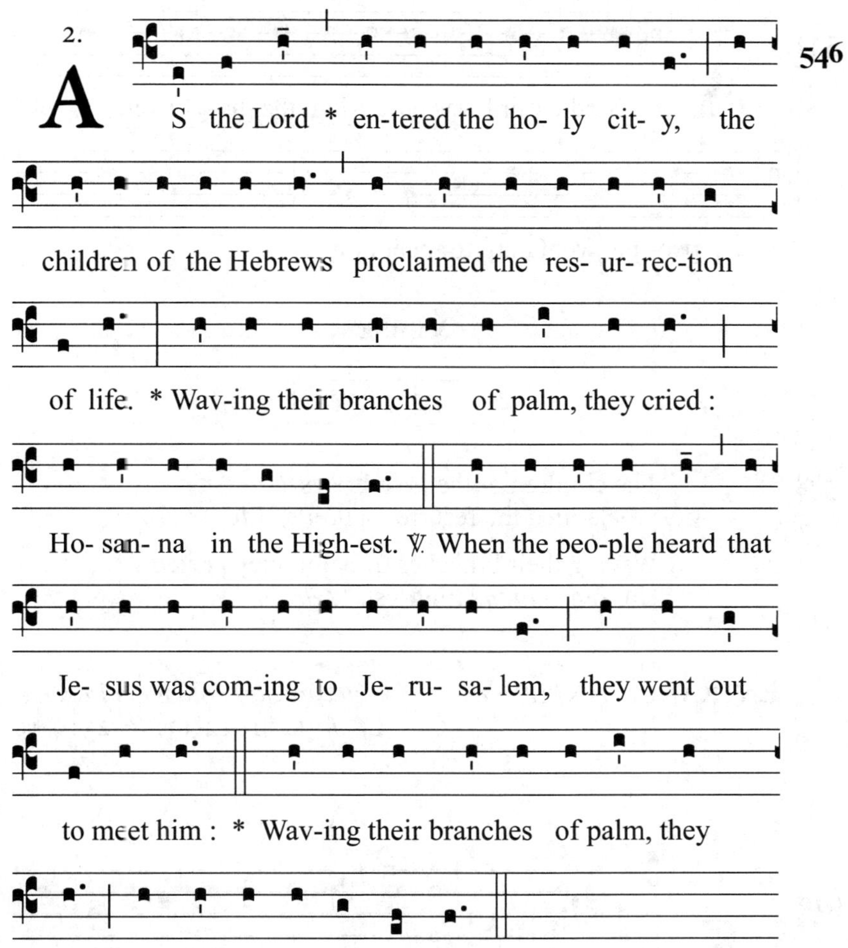
2.
546
AS the Lord * en-tered the ho- ly cit- y, the
children of the Hebrews proclaimed the res- ur- rec-tion
of life. * Wav-ing their branches of palm, they cried :
Ho- san- na in the High-est. ℣. When the peo-ple heard that
Je- sus was com-ing to Je- ru- sa- lem, they went out
to meet him : * Wav-ing their branches of palm, they
cried : Ho- san- na in the High-est.

Refrain

547 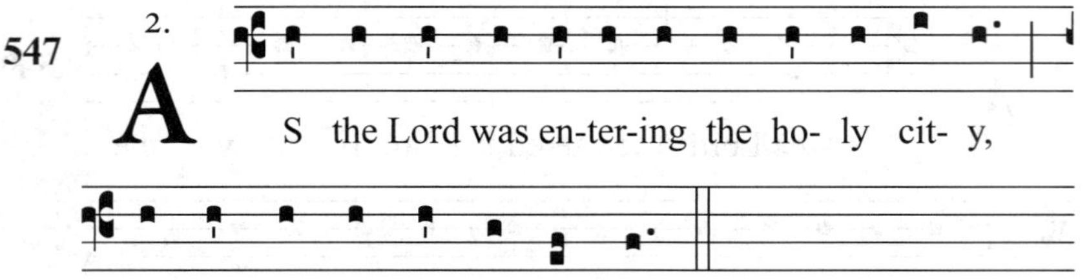
2.
AS the Lord was en-ter-ing the ho- ly cit- y,
the peo- ple went out to meet him.

Verses

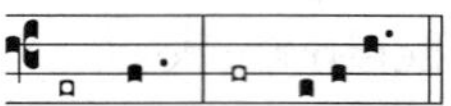

548 The children of the | **He**-brews *
proclaimed the resurrec- | *tion of* **life**. *Refrain.*

Waving their branches of palm, they | **cried** : *
Hosanna | *in the* **high**-est. *Refrain.*

Entrance Antiphon *Ante sex dies sollemnis Paschæ.*
Cf. Jn 12:1. 12-13; *Ps* 23:9-10

- i -

549 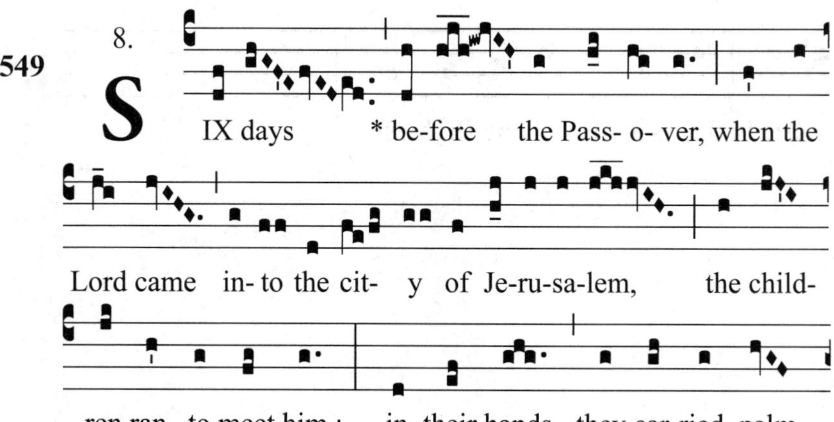
8.
SIX days * be-fore the Pass- o- ver, when the
Lord came in- to the cit- y of Je-ru-sa-lem, the child-
ren ran to meet him ; in their hands they car-ried palm

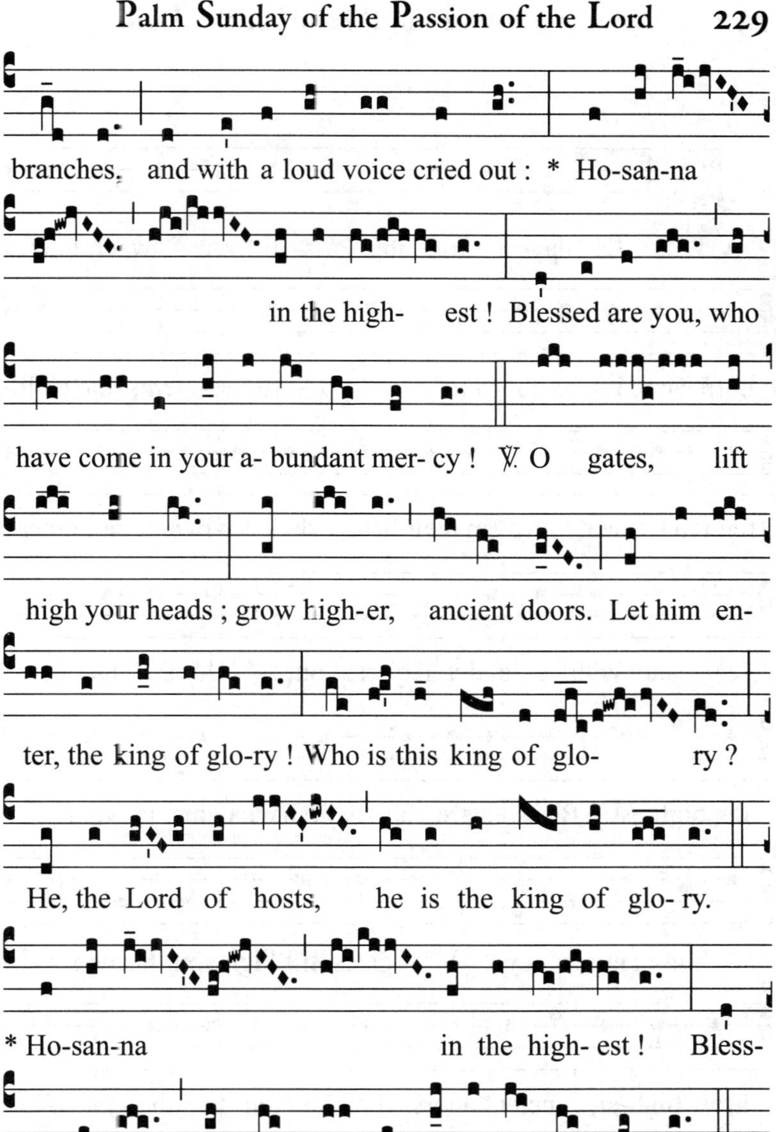
branches, and with a loud voice cried out : * Ho-san-na
in the high- est ! Blessed are you, who
have come in your a- bundant mer- cy ! ℣. O gates, lift
high your heads ; grow high-er, ancient doors. Let him en-
ter, the king of glo-ry ! Who is this king of glo- ry ?
He, the Lord of hosts, he is the king of glo- ry.
* Ho-san-na in the high- est ! Bless-
ed are you, who have come in your a- bundant mer- cy !

- iii -

550

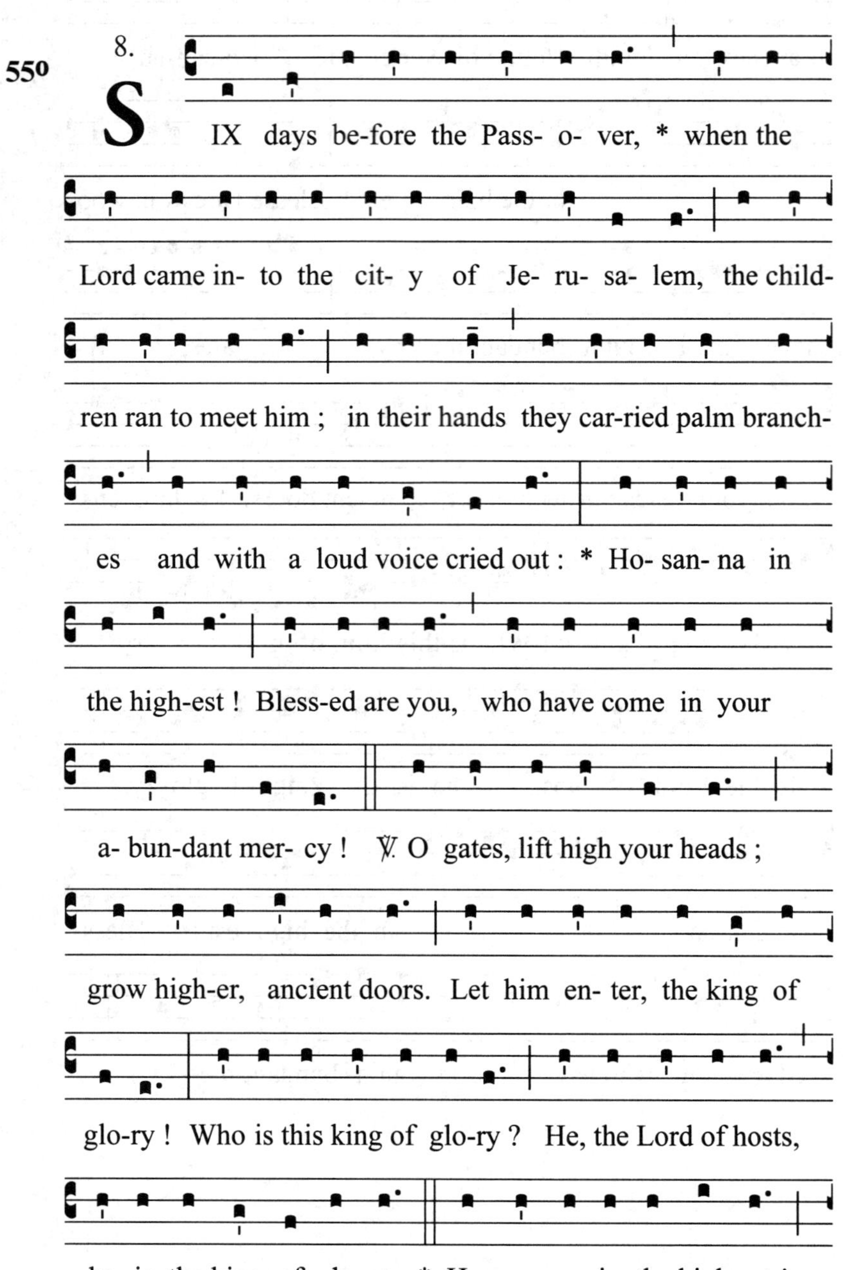
8.
SIX days be-fore the Pass- o- ver, * when the
Lord came in- to the cit- y of Je- ru- sa- lem, the child-
ren ran to meet him ; in their hands they car-ried palm branches and with a loud voice cried out : * Ho- san- na in
the high-est ! Bless-ed are you, who have come in your
a- bun-dant mer- cy ! ℣. O gates, lift high your heads ;
grow high-er, ancient doors. Let him en- ter, the king of
glo-ry ! Who is this king of glo-ry ? He, the Lord of hosts,
he is the king of glo- ry. * Ho- san- na in the high-est !

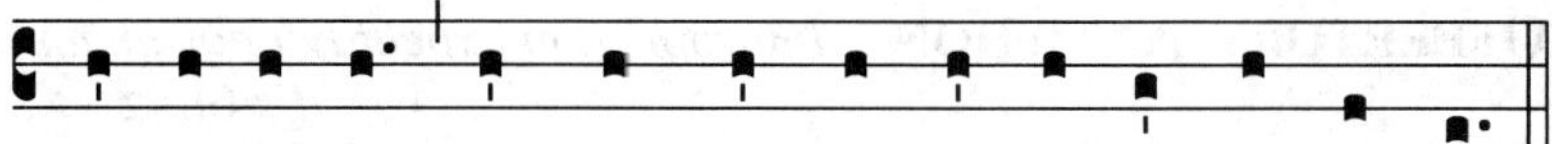

Blessed are you, who have come in your a- bundant mer- cy !

Or :

REFRAIN

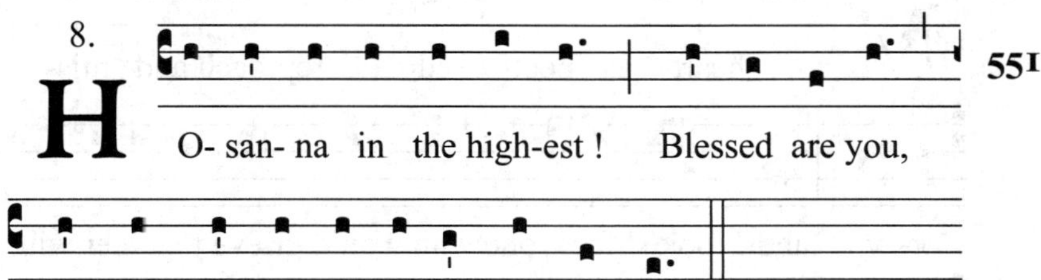
8.
H
O- san- na in the high-est ! Blessed are you,
551

who have come in your a-bun-dant mer- cy.

VERSES

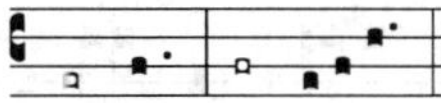

1. Six days before the Passover /
when the Lord came into the city of Je- | **ru**-sa-lem, *
the children | *ran to* **meet** him. *Refrain.* 552

2. In their hands they carried palm | **branch**-es *
and with a loud | *voice cried* **out** : *Refrain.*

3. O gates, lift high your heads ; /
grow higher, ancient | **doors**. *
Let him enter, the | *king of* **glo**-ry ! *Refrain.*

4. Who is this king of glory ? /
He, the LORD of | **hosts**, *
he is the | *king of* **glo**-ry. *Refrain.*

OFFERTORY ANTIPHON *Improperium expectavit cor meum.*
Ps 68:21-22

- i -

553

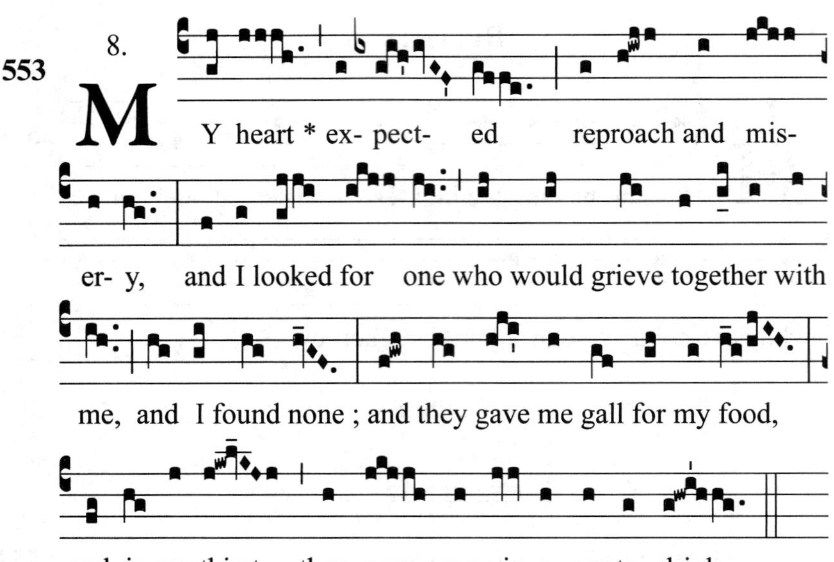
8.
MY heart * ex- pect- ed reproach and mis-
er- y, and I looked for one who would grieve together with
me, and I found none ; and they gave me gall for my food,
and in my thirst they gave me vin- e- gar to drink.

- ii -

554

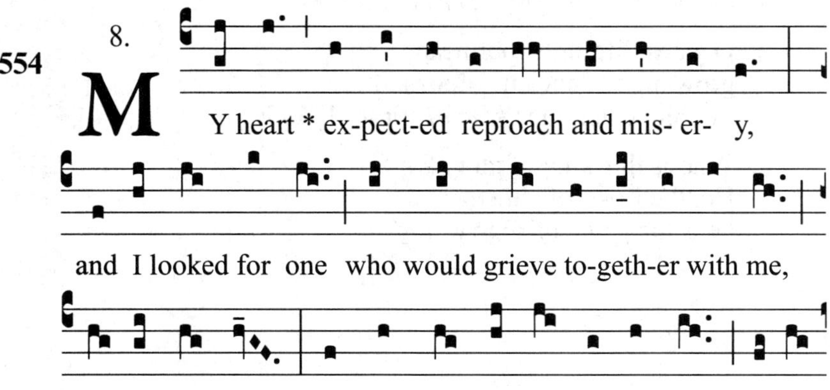
8.
MY heart * ex-pect-ed reproach and mis- er- y,
and I looked for one who would grieve to-geth-er with me,
and I found none; and they gave me gall for my food, and in

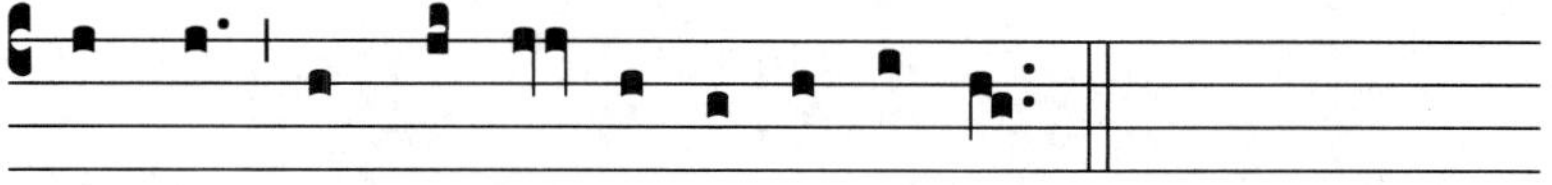

my thirst they gave me vin- e- gar to drink.

VERSES *Ego sum pauper et dolens. Ps* 68 : 30

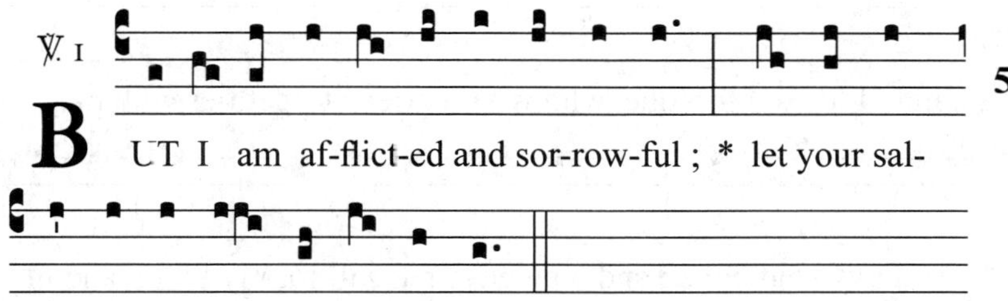
℣. 1
BUT I am af-flict-ed and sor-row-ful ; * let your sal-

555

va-tion, O God, set me on high.

Laudabo nomen Dei. Ps 68 : 31

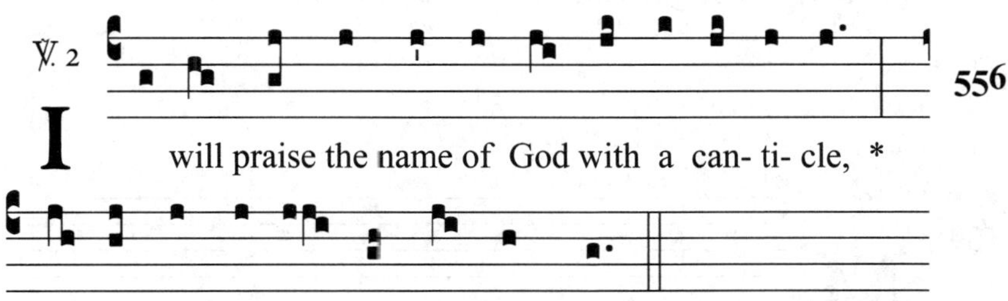
℣. 2
I will praise the name of God with a can- ti- cle, *

556

and I will mag- ni- fy him with praise.

Videant pauperes. Ps 68 : 33

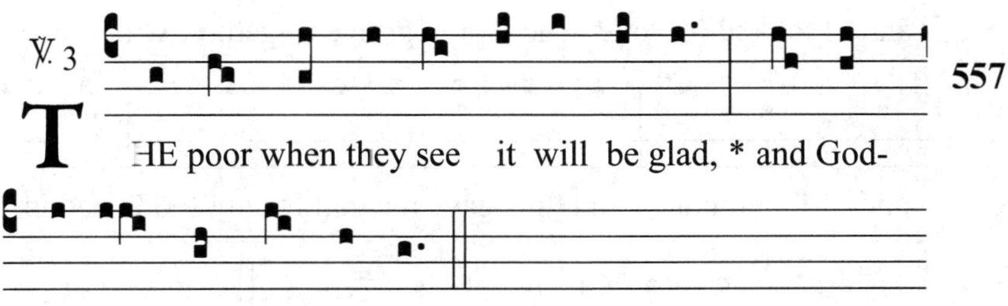
℣. 3
THE poor when they see it will be glad, * and God-

557

seek- ing hearts will re-vive.

- iii -

558

8.
MY heart ex-pect-ed reproach and mis- er- y, *
and I looked for one who would grieve to-geth-er with me,
and I found none ; and they gave me gall for my food, and in
my thirst they gave me vin- e- gar to drink.

- iv -

559

8.
MY heart ex-pect-ed reproach and mis- er- y, *
and I looked for one who would grieve to-geth-er with me,
and I found none ; and they gave me gall for my food, and in
my thirst they gave me vin- e- gar to drink.

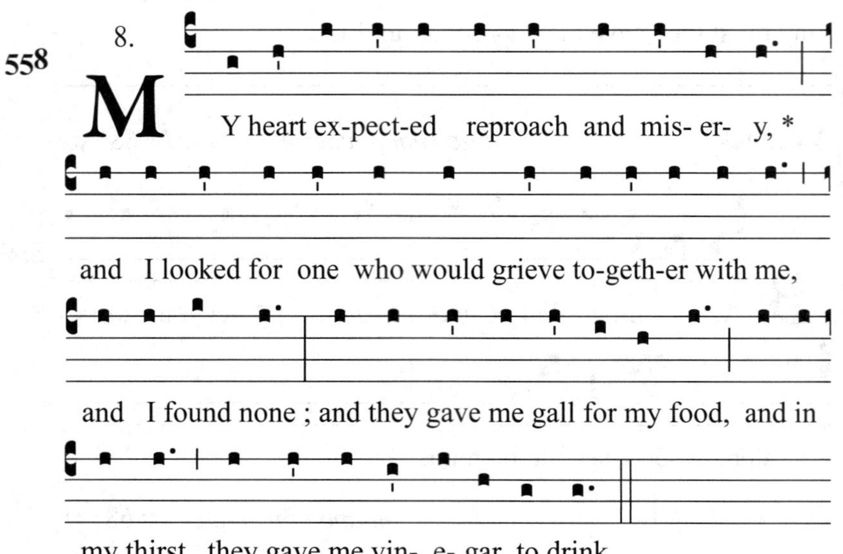

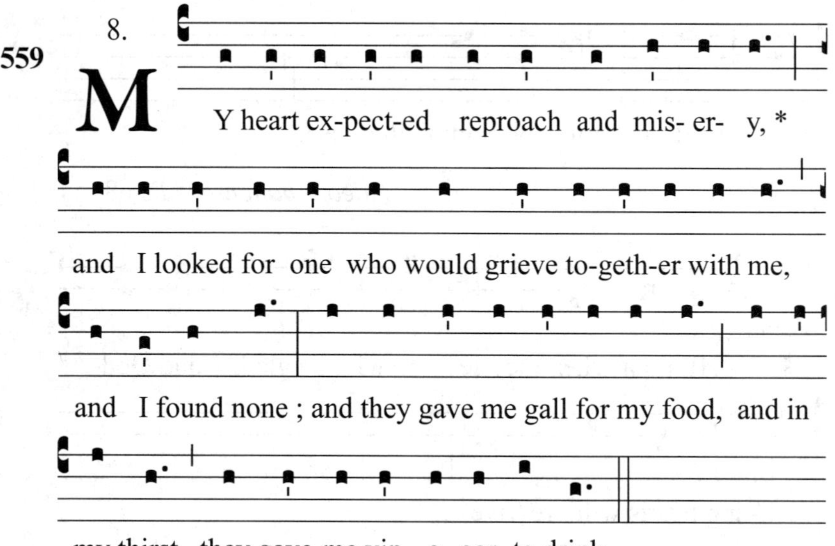

COMMUNION *Mt* 26:42

Pater, si non potest.

- i -

8.
F A- ther, * if this chalice can-not pass without my
drinking it, your will be done.
560

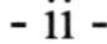

- ii -

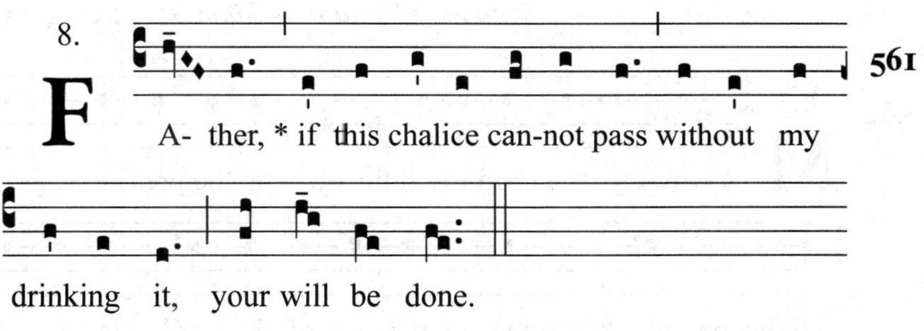
8.
F A- ther, * if this chalice can-not pass without my
drinking it, your will be done.
561

VERSES *Credidi, propter quod locutus sum. Ps* 115:10

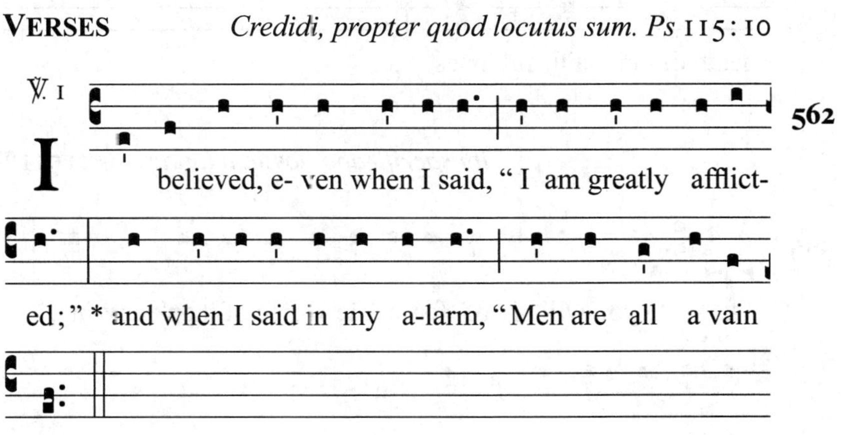
℣. 1
I believed, e- ven when I said, " I am greatly afflict-
ed;" * and when I said in my a-larm, "Men are all a vain
hope."
562

Quid retribuam Domino. Ps 115: 12-13

563
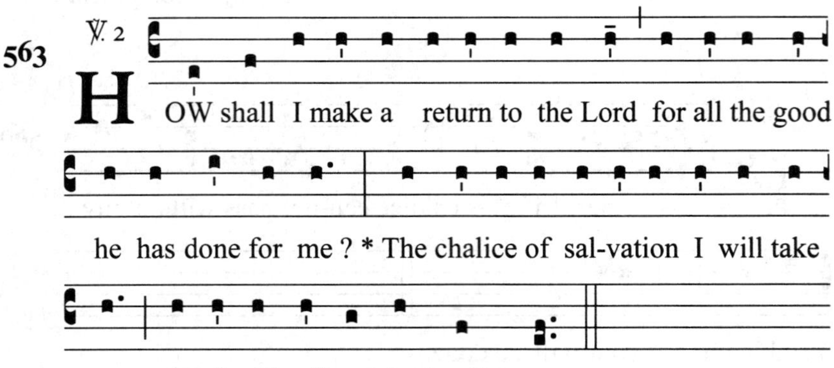
℣. 2
HOW shall I make a return to the Lord for all the good
he has done for me ? * The chalice of sal-vation I will take
up, and I will call on the Lord's name.

Vota mea Domino reddam. Ps 115: 14-15

564
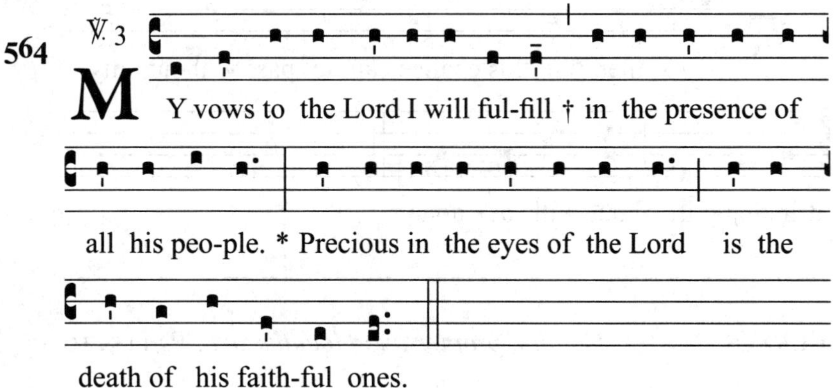
℣. 3
MY vows to the Lord I will ful-fill † in the presence of
all his peo-ple. * Precious in the eyes of the Lord is the
death of his faith-ful ones.

Tibi sacrificabo hostiam laudis. Ps 115: 17

565
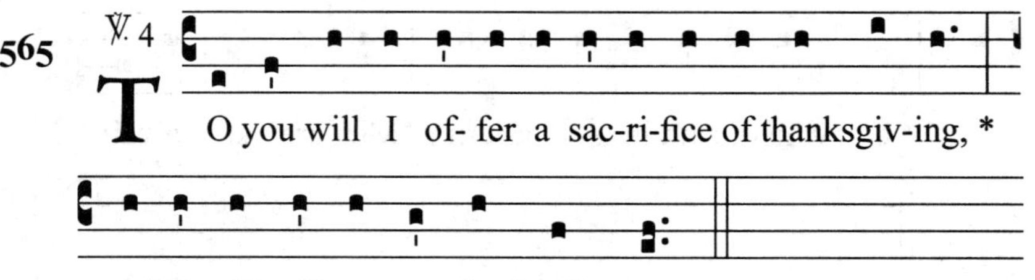
℣. 4
TO you will I of- fer a sac-ri-fice of thanksgiv-ing, *
and I will call up- on the Lord's name.

- iii -

8.
566
FAther, if this chalice cannot pass * with-out my
drinking it, your will be done.

- iv -

8.
567
FAther, if this chalice cannot pass * with-out my
drinking it, your will be done.

Thursday of Holy Week

The Chrism Mass

Entrance Antiphon *Iesus Christus fecit nos.*
Rv 1:6

- i -

568

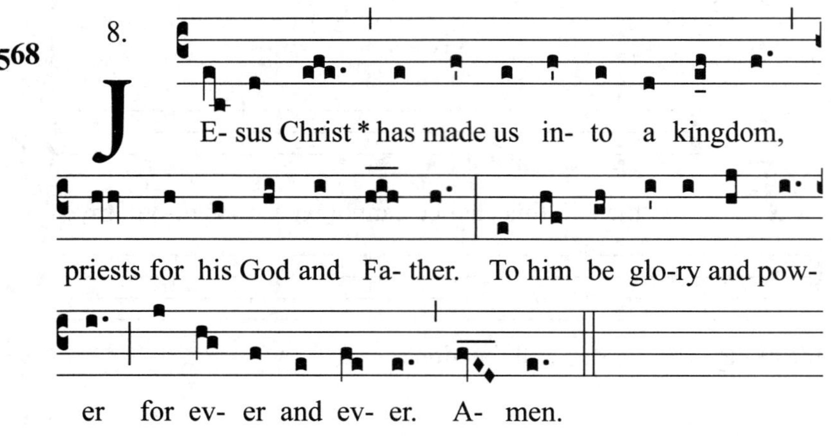
8.
J E- sus Christ * has made us in- to a kingdom,
priests for his God and Fa- ther. To him be glo-ry and pow-
er for ev- er and ev- er. A- men.

- iii -

569

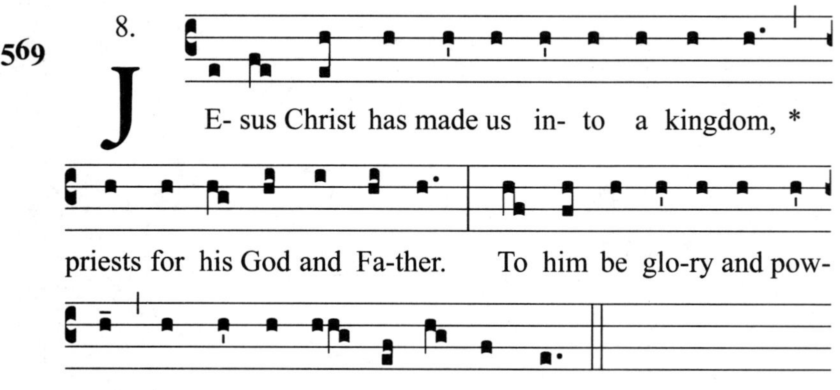
8.
J E- sus Christ has made us in- to a kingdom, *
priests for his God and Fa-ther. To him be glo-ry and pow-
er for ev- er and ev- er. A- men.

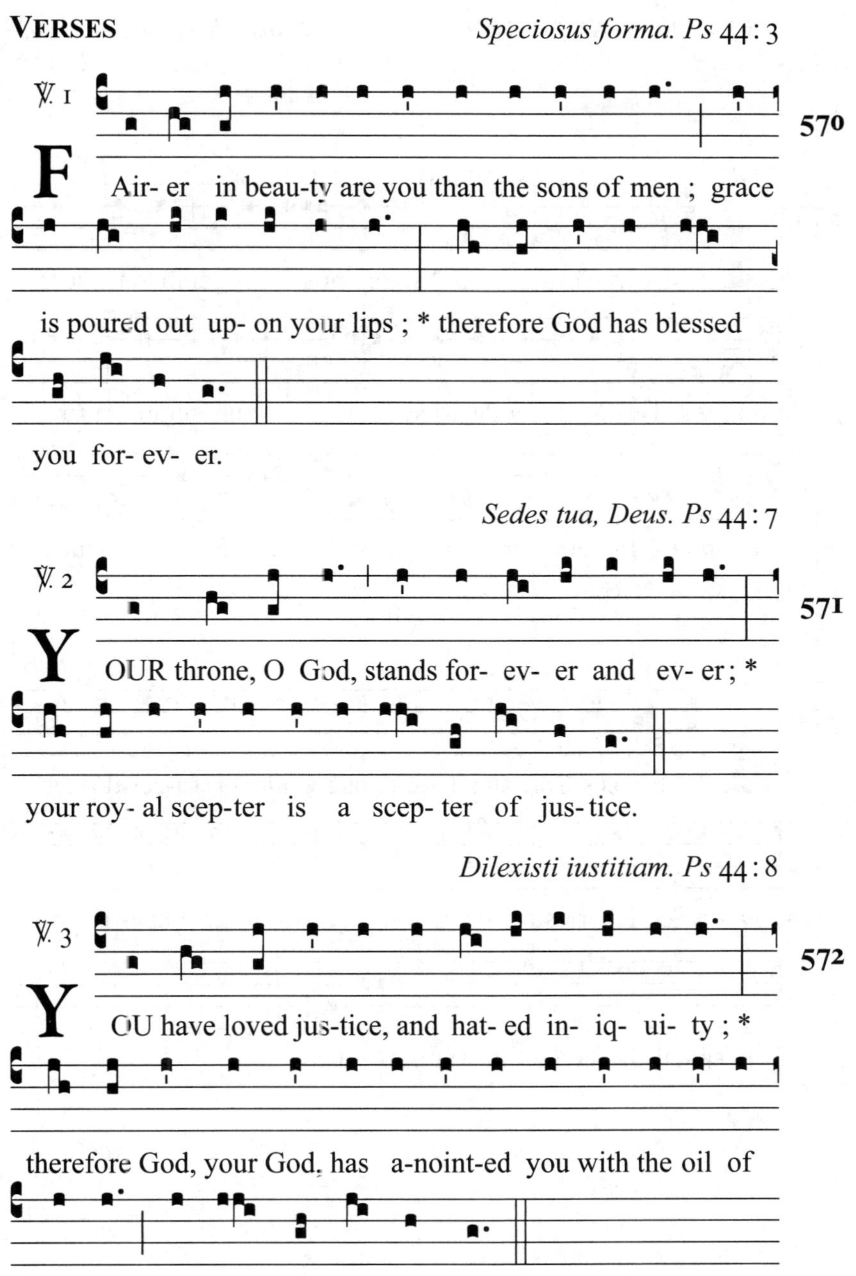
VERSES
Speciosus forma. Ps 44:3
℣. 1
570
FAir- er in beau-ty are you than the sons of men ; grace
is poured out up- on your lips ; * therefore God has blessed
you for- ev- er.
Sedes tua, Deus. Ps 44:7
℣. 2
571
YOUR throne, O God, stands for- ev- er and ev- er ; *
your roy- al scep-ter is a scep- ter of jus- tice.
Dilexisti iustitiam. Ps 44:8
℣. 3
572
YOU have loved jus-tice, and hat- ed in- iq- ui- ty ; *
therefore God, your God, has a-noint-ed you with the oil of
gladness a- bove your fel- low kings.

ENTRANCE ANTIPHON *Jesus Christ has made us.*
Rv 1:6

- i -

573

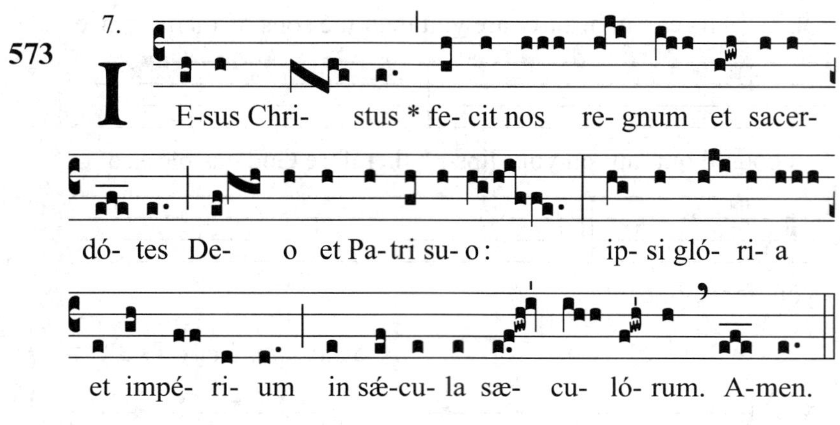
7.
IEsus Christus * fecit nos regnum et sacerdótes Deo et Patri suo: ipsi glória et impérium in sǽcula sæculórum. Amen.

- iii -

574

7.
IEsus Christus fecit nos regnum et sacerdótes Deo et Patri suo: * ipsi glória et impérium in sǽcula sæculórum. Amen.

VERSES

For you were slain. Rv 5:9

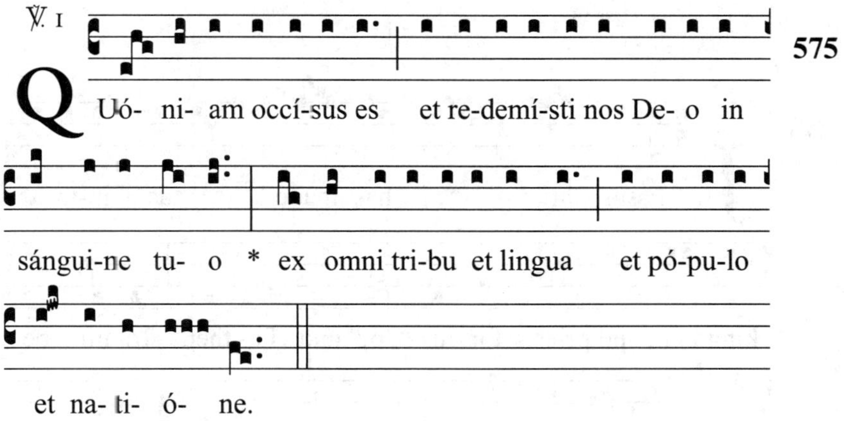
℣. 1
575
QUóniam occísus es et redemísti nos Deo in sánguine tuo * ex omni tribu et lingua et pópulo et natióne.

The Lamb that was slain is worthy. Rv 5:12

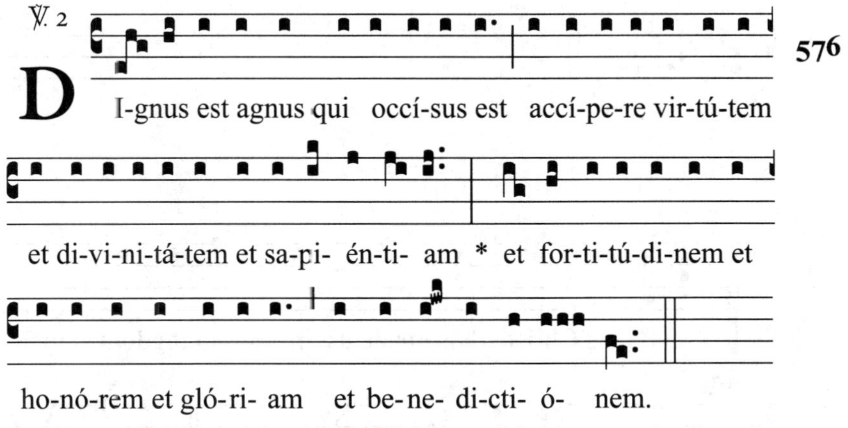
℣. 2
576
DIgnus est agnus qui occísus est accípere virtútem et divinitátem et sapiéntiam * et fortitúdinem et honórem et glóriam et benedictiónem.

And have made us to our God. Rv 5:12

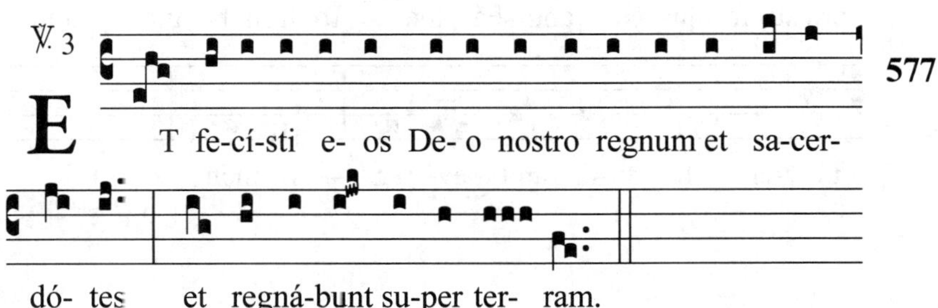
℣. 3
577
ET fecísti eos Deo nostro regnum et sacerdótes et regnábunt super terram.

Entrance Antiphon *Iesus Christus fecit nos.*
Rv 1:6

- i -

578

7.
JEsus Christ * has made us into a kingdom, and priests for his God and Father. To him be glory and power for ever and ever. Amen.

- ii -

579

7.
JEsus Christ * has made us into a kingdom and priests for his God and Father. To him be glory and power for ever and ever. Amen.

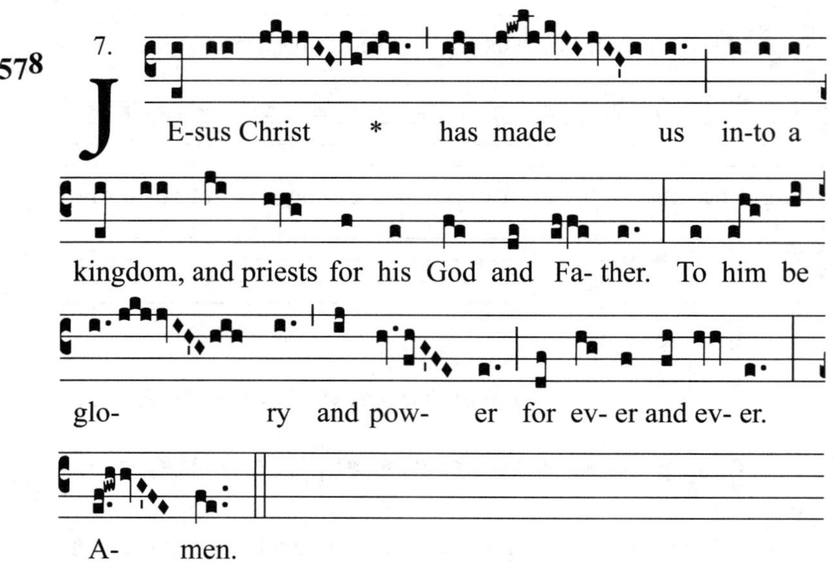

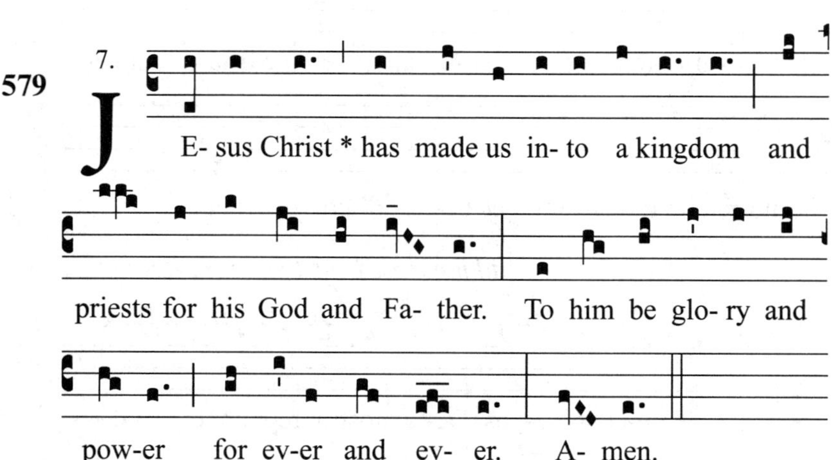

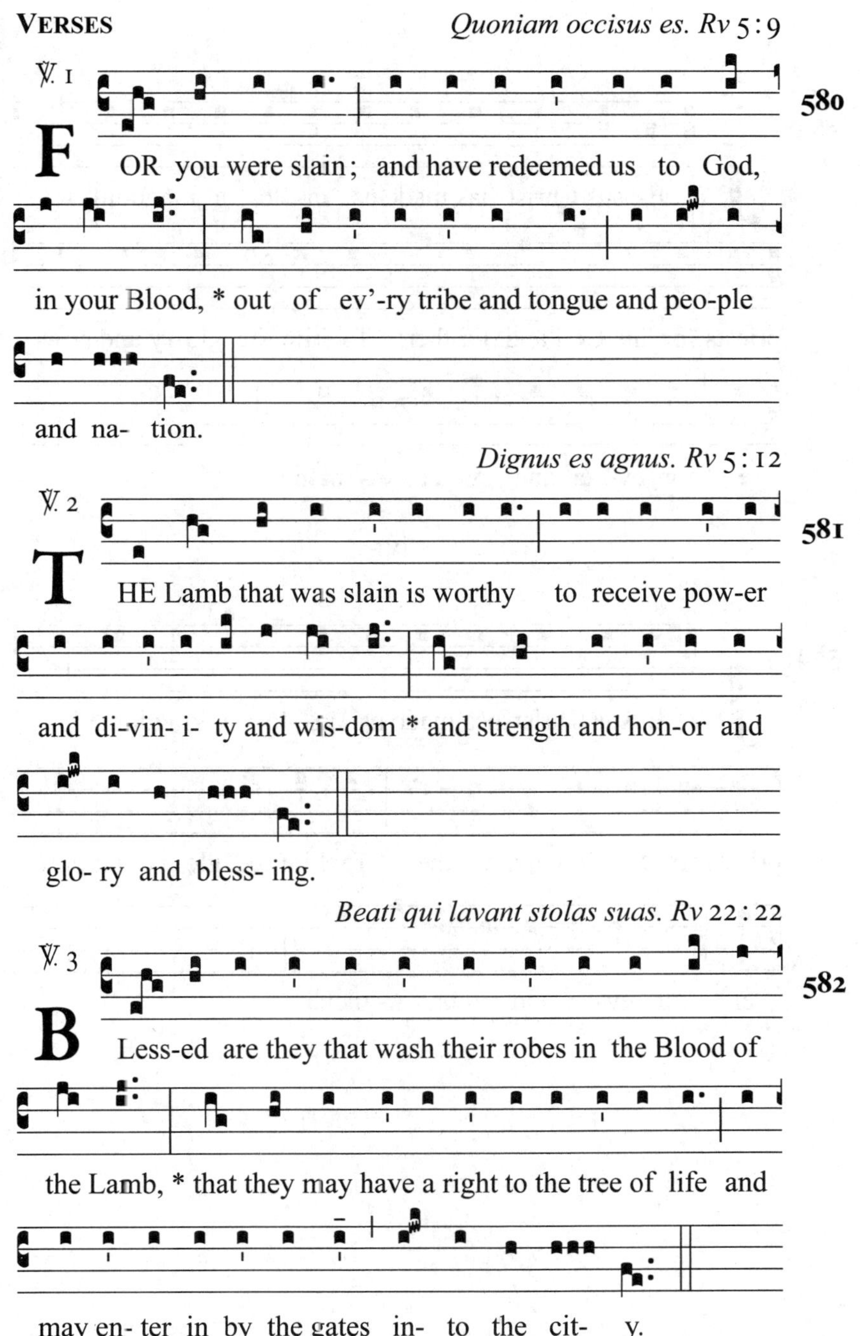
VERSES
Quoniam occisus es. Rv 5:9
℣. 1
580
FOR you were slain; and have redeemed us to God,
in your Blood, * out of ev'-ry tribe and tongue and peo-ple
and na- tion.
Dignus es agnus. Rv 5:12
℣. 2
581
THE Lamb that was slain is worthy to receive pow-er
and di-vin- i- ty and wis-dom * and strength and hon-or and
glo- ry and bless- ing.
Beati qui lavant stolas suas. Rv 22:22
℣. 3
582
BLess-ed are they that wash their robes in the Blood of
the Lamb, * that they may have a right to the tree of life and
may en- ter in by the gates in- to the cit- y.

- iii -

583

7.
J
E- sus Christ has made us in- to a kingdom, *
priests for his God and Fa-ther. To him be glo-ry and pow-
er for ev- er and ev- er. A- men.

- iv -

584

7.
J
E- sus Christ has made us in- to a kingdom, *
priests for his God and Fa-ther. To him be glo- ry and pow-
er for ev- er and ev- er. A- men.

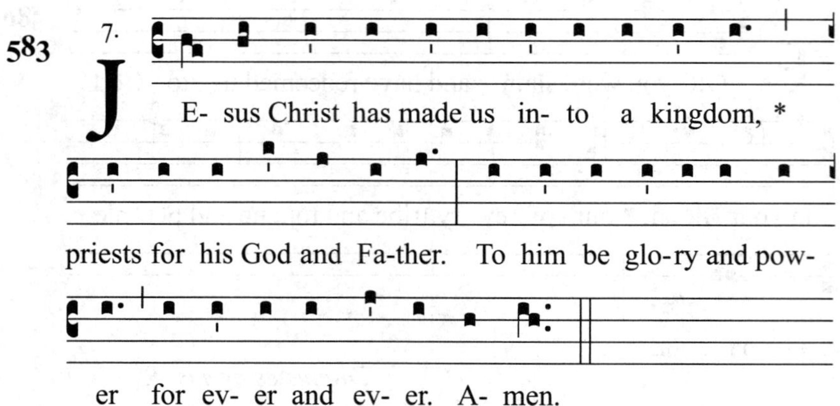

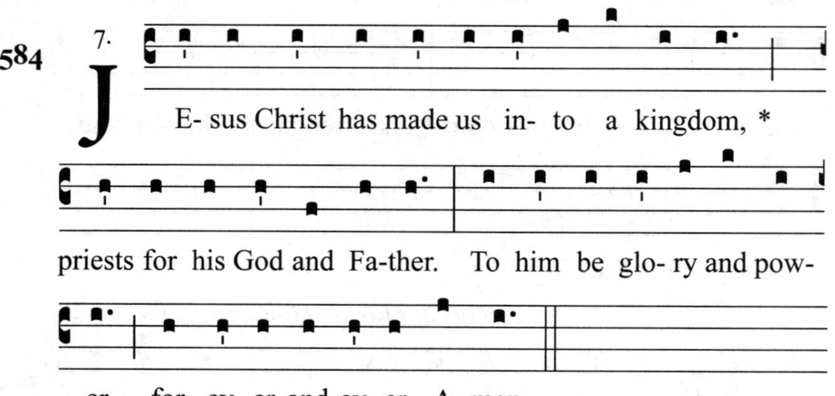

Hymn

The Blessing of the Holy Oils

Two Cantors sing the following verse :

2.
O Redeemer, hear this anthem As we sing with
585

one ac-cord.

The Choir repeats this verse. The two Cantors then sing the following verses :

1. Sacred will become this bounty
That a fruitful tree once bore
When we bear it in procession
Unto you, our Saving Lord.

O Redeemer, hear this anthem
As we sing with one accord.

2. Consecrate, O King of heaven,
Olive oil, a living sign ;
Let it thwart the demons' power,
Lend to it your strength divine.

O Redeemer, hear this anthem
As we sing with one accord.

3. By this Chrism, men and women
Are renewed as they are sealed.
And our glory, once so wounded,
Now at last through grace is healed.

O Redeemer, hear this anthem
As we sing with one accord.

4. When the sacred font has taken
All the stains of sin away,
On those foreheads now anointed,
Send your gifts, O Lord, we pray.

O Redeemer, hear this anthem
As we sing with one accord.

5. Lord, who came from God the Father
In the Virgin's womb to rest,
Grant us light, and let not perish
Those who share this Chrism blest.

O Redeemer, hear this anthem
As we sing with one accord.

6. May this day be always festive
For all ages, we implore ;
Sanctify the praise we offer,
Let us bless you evermore.

O Redeemer, hear this anthem
As we sing with one accord.

VERSES

586
1. Sacred will become this bounty That a fruitful tree once bore
When we bear it in procession Un-to you, our Saving Lord.
587
2. Consecrate, O King of heaven, Olive oil, a liv-ing sign ; Let
it thwart the demons' power, Lend to it your strength divine.
588
3. By this Chrism, men and women Are renewed as they are
sealed, And our glo- ry, once so wounded, Now at last

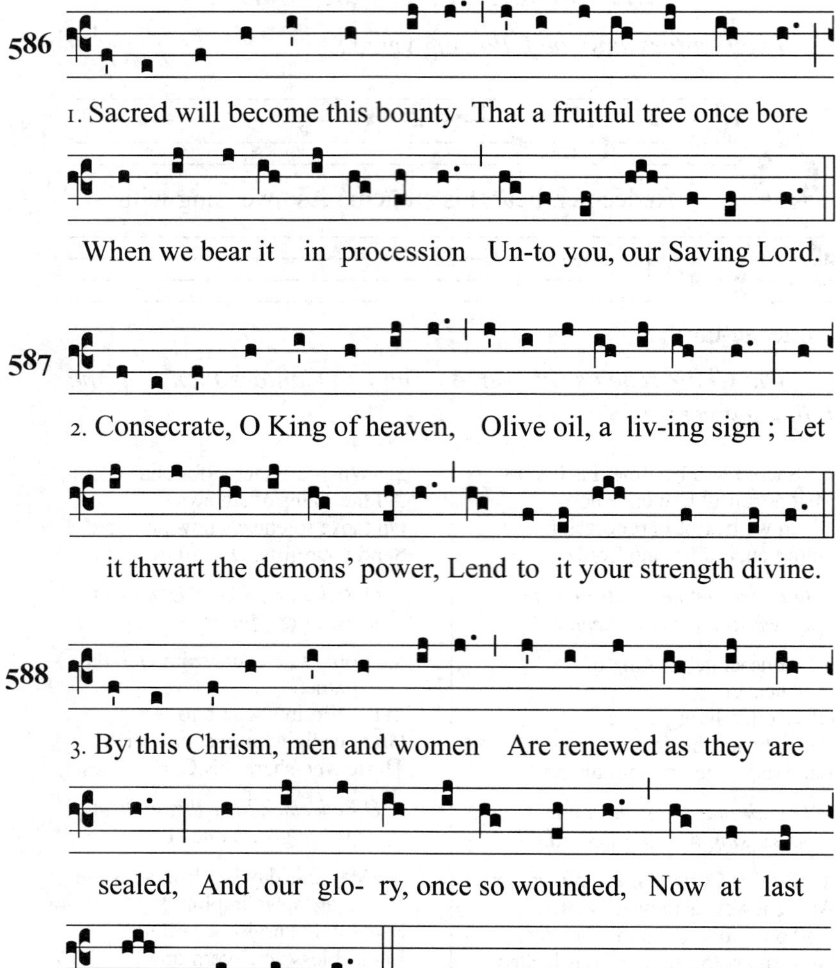

through grace is healed.

VERSES

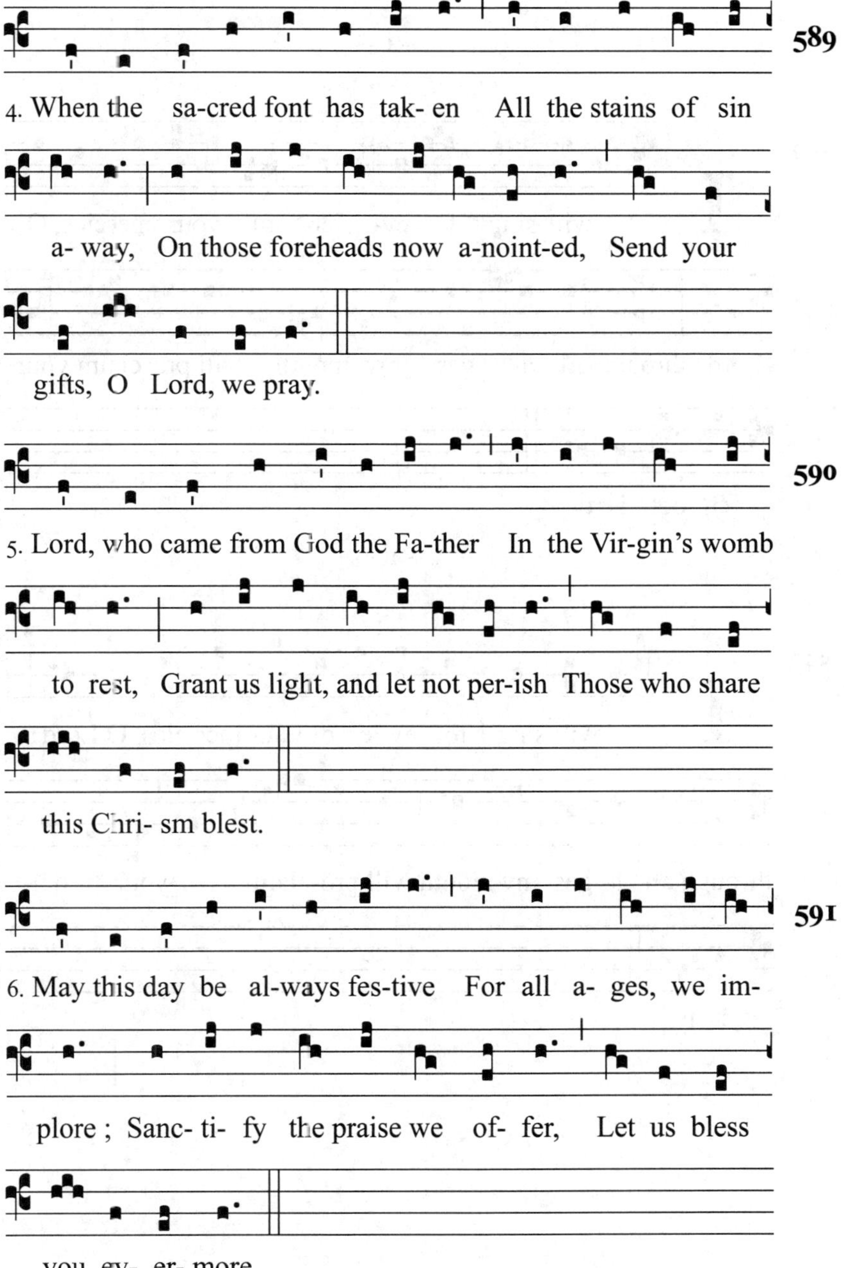
589
4. When the sa-cred font has tak- en All the stains of sin
a- way, On those foreheads now a-noint-ed, Send your
gifts, O Lord, we pray.
590
5. Lord, who came from God the Fa-ther In the Vir-gin's womb
to rest, Grant us light, and let not per-ish Those who share
this Chri- sm blest.
591
6. May this day be al-ways fes-tive For all a- ges, we implore; Sanc- ti- fy the praise we of- fer, Let us bless
you ev- er- more.

COMMUNION ANTIPHON *Misericordias Domini.*
Ps 88 : 2

- i -

592

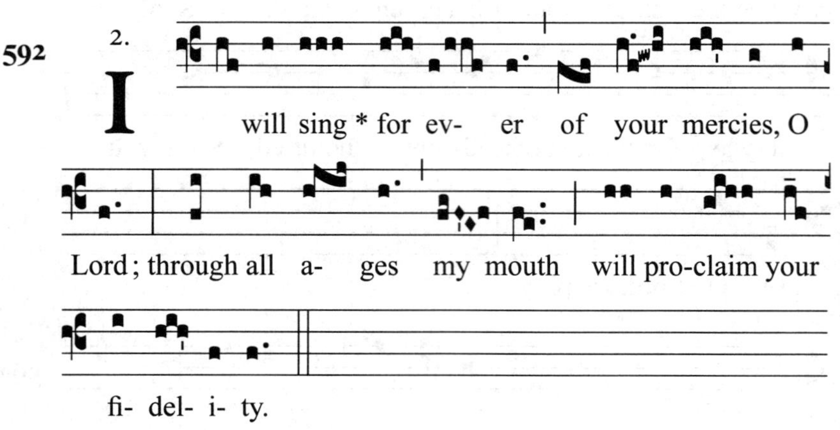
2.
I will sing * for ev- er of your mercies, O
Lord; through all a- ges my mouth will pro-claim your
fi- del- i- ty.

- ii -

593

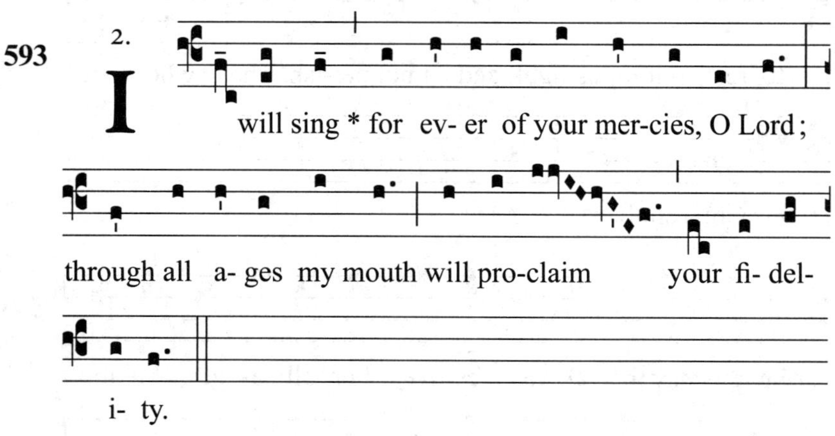
2.
I will sing * for ev- er of your mer-cies, O Lord;
through all a- ges my mouth will pro-claim your fi- del-
i- ty.

VERSES *Beatus populus. Ps* 88 : 16

℣. 1
BLessed is the people who know ju- bi- la-tion. * They
594
shall walk, O Lord, in the light of your face.

Et in nomine tuo. Ps 88 : 17

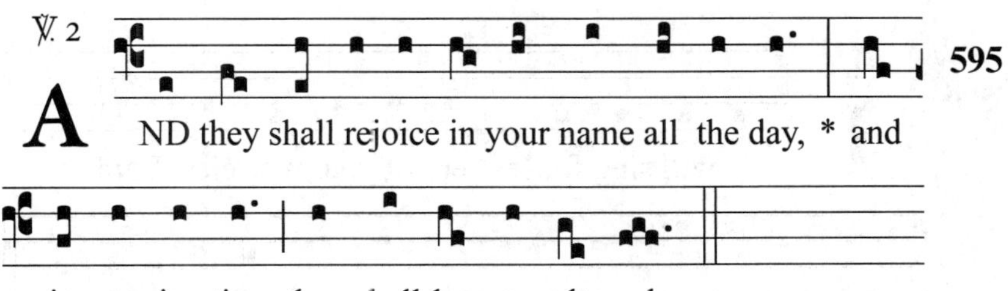
℣. 2
AND they shall rejoice in your name all the day, * and
595
in your jus-tice they shall be ex- alt- ed.

Quoniam gloria virtutis eorum. Ps 88 : 18

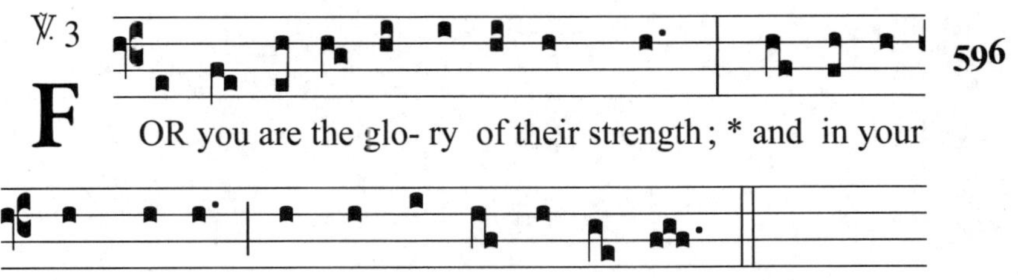
℣. 3
FOR you are the glo- ry of their strength; * and in your
596
good pleasure shall our horn be ex- alt- ed.

- iii -

597

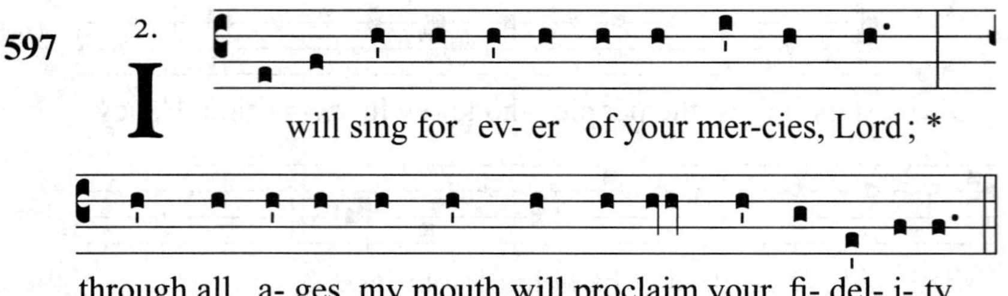
2.
I will sing for ev- er of your mer-cies, Lord; *
through all a- ges my mouth will proclaim your fi- del- i- ty.

- iv -

598

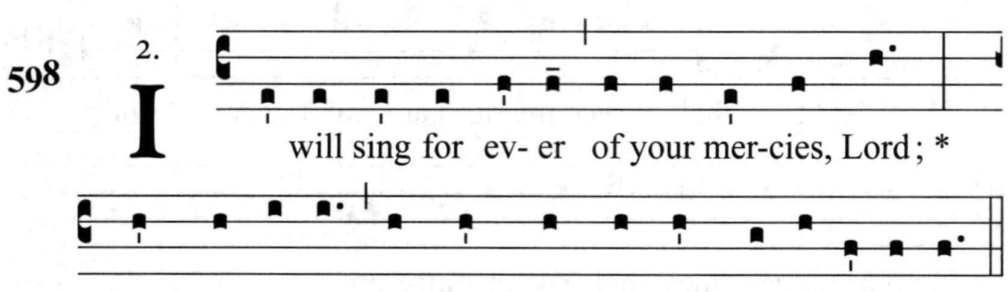
2.
I will sing for ev- er of your mer-cies, Lord; *
through all a- ges my mouth will proclaim your fi-del- i- ty.

THE SACRED PASCHAL TRIDUUM

Thursday of the Lord's Supper

At the Evening Mass

Entrance Antiphon *Nos autem gloriari. Cf. Gal* 6:14

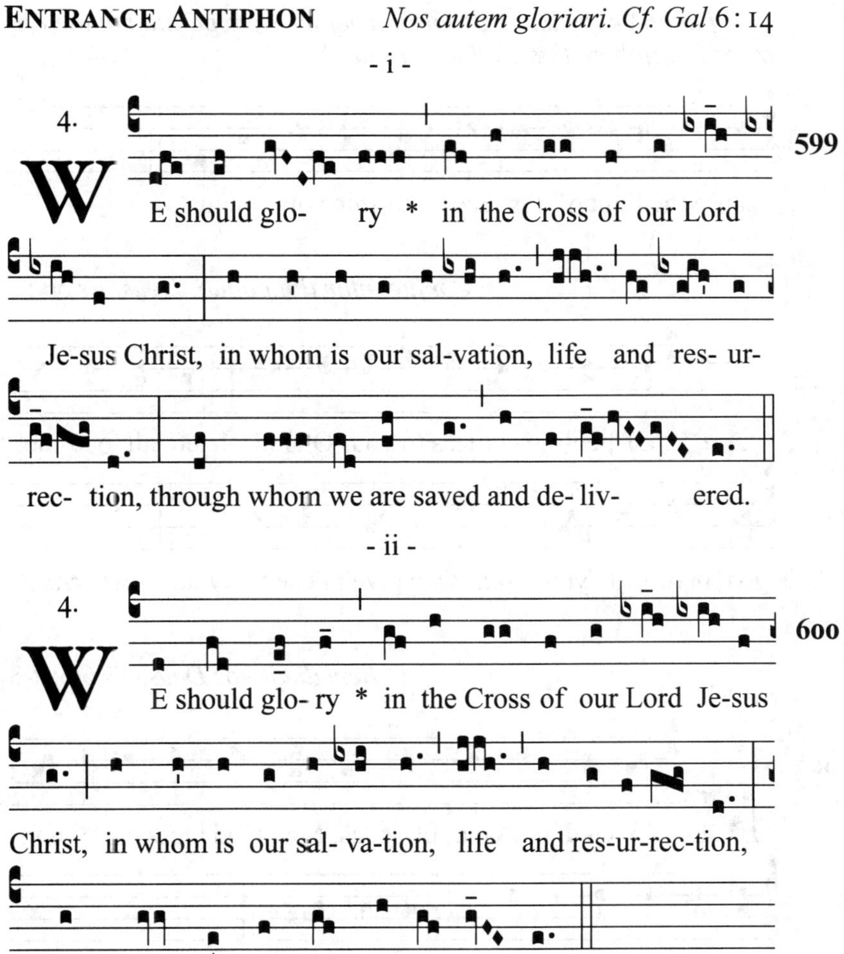

- i -
4.
599
WE should glo- ry * in the Cross of our Lord
Je-sus Christ, in whom is our sal-vation, life and res- ur-
rec- tion, through whom we are saved and de- liv- ered.
- ii -
4.
600
WE should glo- ry * in the Cross of our Lord Je-sus
Christ, in whom is our sal- va-tion, life and res-ur-rec-tion,
through whom we are saved and de- liv- ered.

VERSES *Deus misereatur nostri. Ps* 66 : 2

601

℣. 1
MAY God have mer-cy up- on us, and bless us ; * may
he cause the light of his face to shine up- on us. *Ant.*

If another Psalm verse follows before the repetition of the Entrance Antiphon, this ending is used:

cause the light of his face to shine up- on us.

Confiteantur tibi populi, Deus. Ps 66 : 4

602
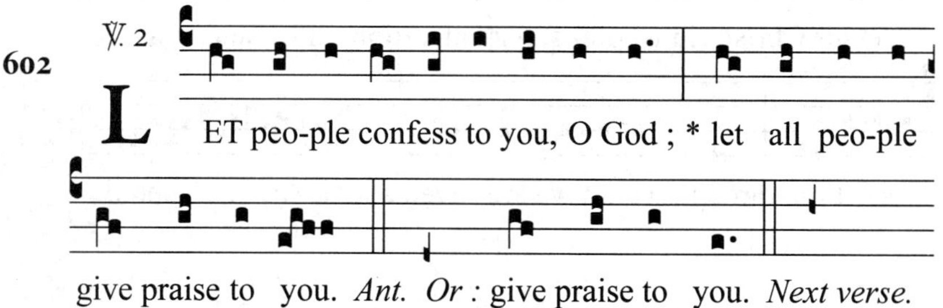
℣. 2
LET peo-ple confess to you, O God ; * let all peo-ple
give praise to you. *Ant.* *Or :* give praise to you. *Next verse.*

Benedicat nos Deus. Ps 66 : 7-8

603
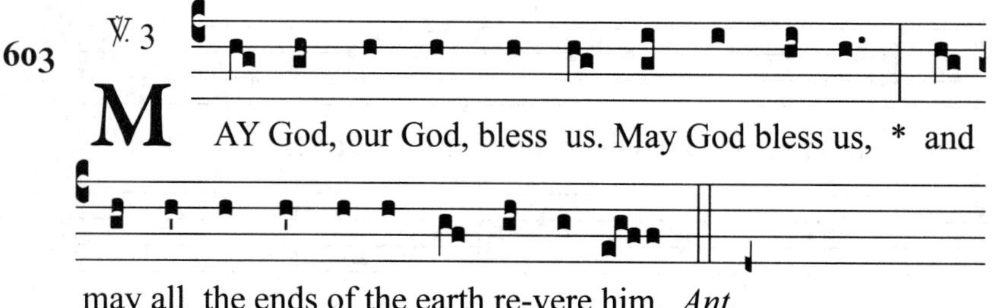
℣. 3
MAY God, our God, bless us. May God bless us, * and
may all the ends of the earth re-vere him. *Ant.*

- iii -

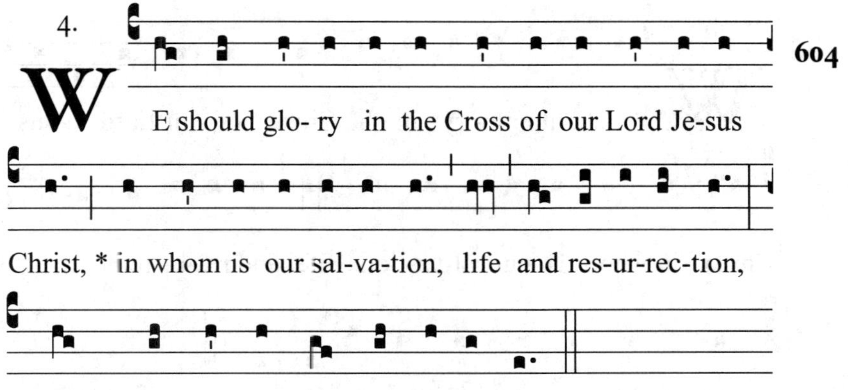
4.
604
WE should glo- ry in the Cross of our Lord Je-sus
Christ, * in whom is our sal-va-tion, life and res-ur-rec-tion,
through whom we are saved and de-liv-ered.

Or:

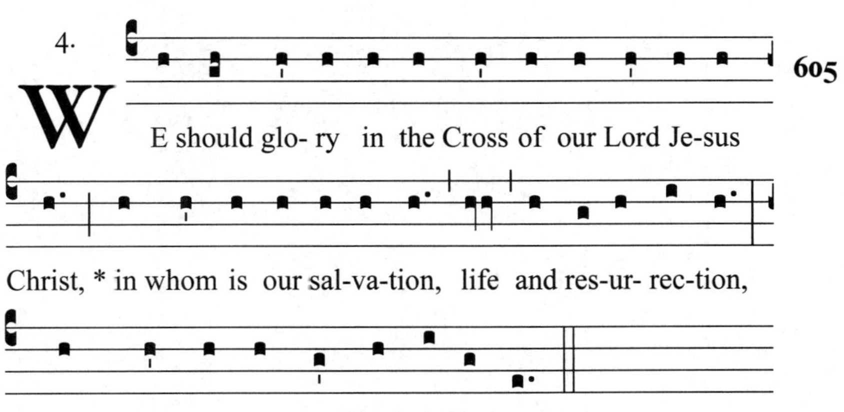
4.
605
WE should glo- ry in the Cross of our Lord Je-sus
Christ, * in whom is our sal-va-tion, life and res-ur- rec-tion,
through whom we are saved and de-liv-ered.

- iv -

606 4.

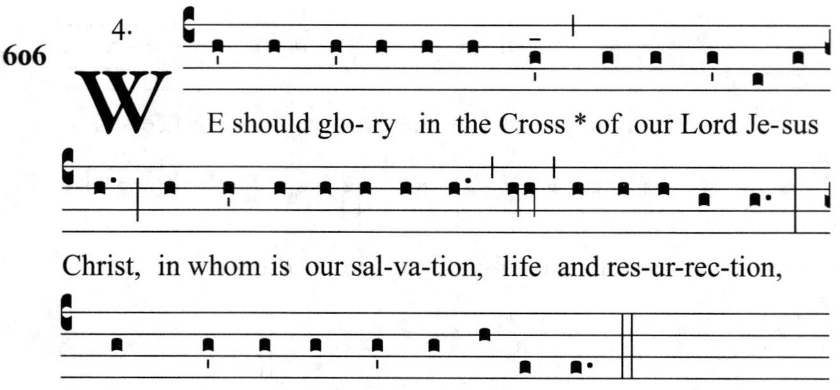
WE should glo- ry in the Cross * of our Lord Je-sus
Christ, in whom is our sal-va-tion, life and res-ur-rec-tion,
through whom we are saved and de-liv-ered.

The Washing of Feet

Postquam surrexit Dominus a cena. Cf. Jn 13:4. 5. 15

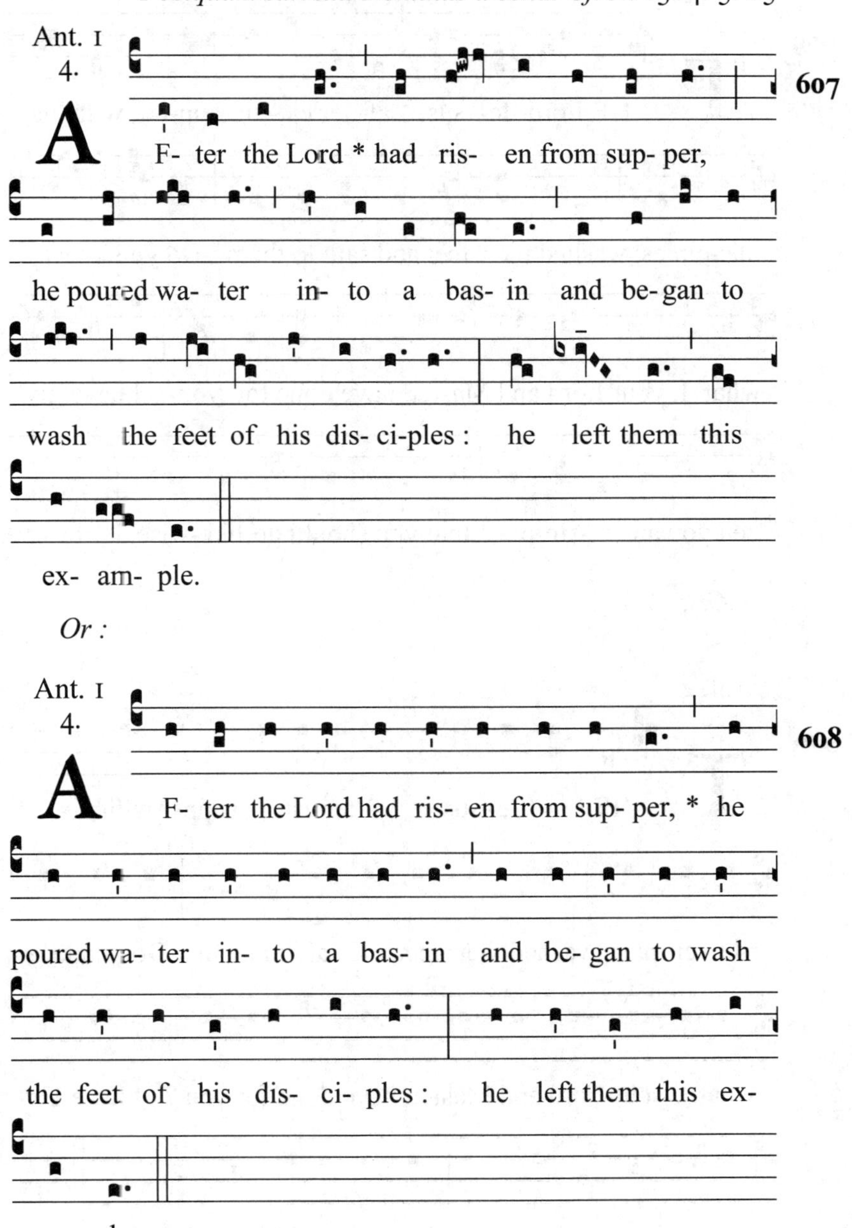
Ant. I
4.
607
AFter the Lord * had risen from supper,
he poured water into a basin and began to
wash the feet of his disciples: he left them this
example.
Or:
Ant. I
4.
608
AFter the Lord had risen from supper, * he
poured water into a basin and began to wash
the feet of his disciples: he left them this example.

Dominus Iesus, postquam cenavit. Cf. Jn 13 : 12. 13. 15

609

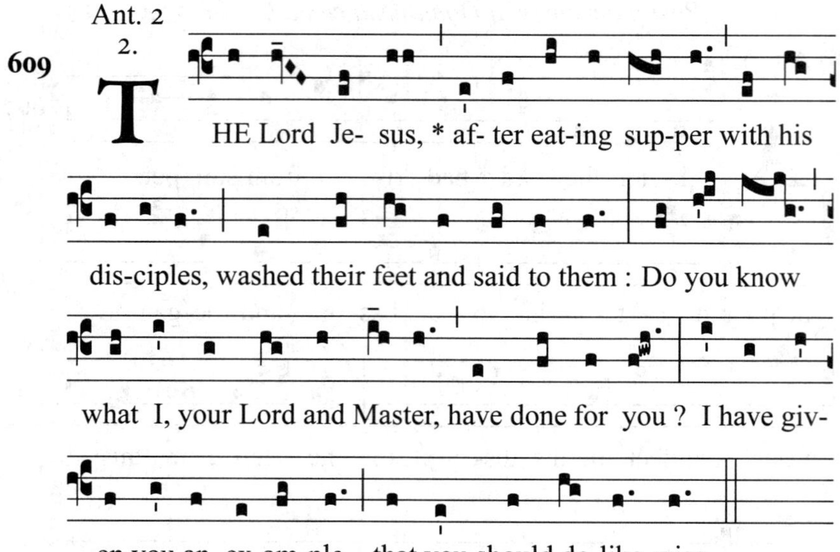
Ant. 2
2.
THE Lord Je- sus, * af- ter eat-ing sup-per with his
dis-ciples, washed their feet and said to them : Do you know
what I, your Lord and Master, have done for you ? I have giv-
en you an ex-am-ple, that you should do like-wise.

Or :

610

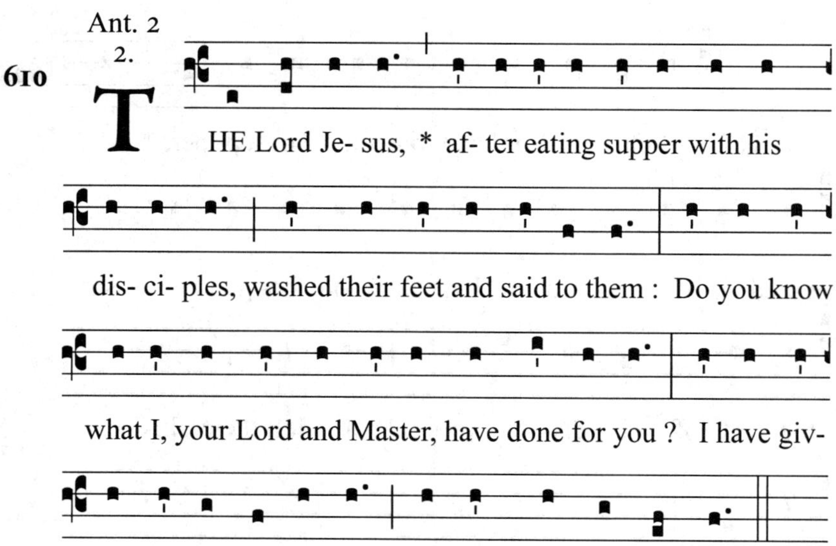
Ant. 2
2.
THE Lord Je- sus, * af- ter eating supper with his
dis- ci- ples, washed their feet and said to them : Do you know
what I, your Lord and Master, have done for you ? I have giv-
en you an ex- am-ple, that you should do like-wise.

Domine, tu mihi lavas pedes? Jn 13:6. 7. 8

Ant. 3
5.

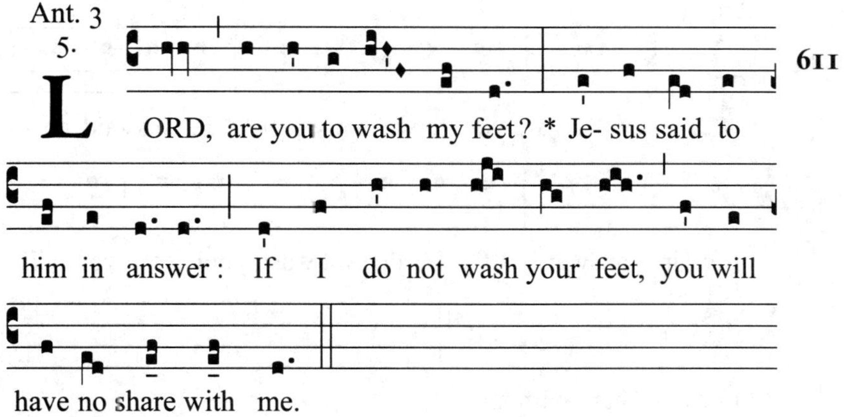
611
LORD, are you to wash my feet? * Je- sus said to
him in answer: If I do not wash your feet, you will
have no share with me.

VERSE 1

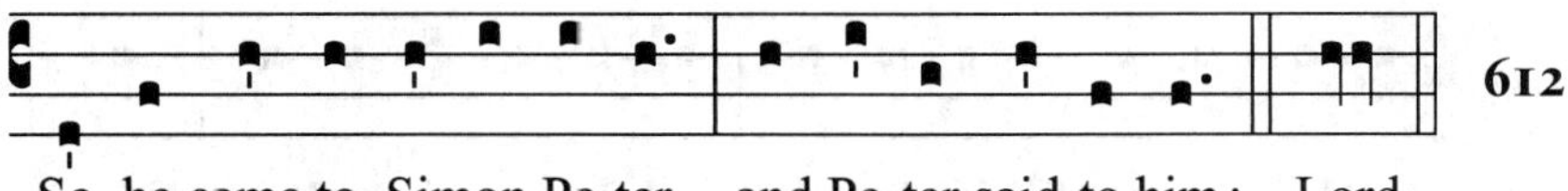
612
So he came to Simon Pe-ter and Pe-ter said to him: Lord.

VERSE 2

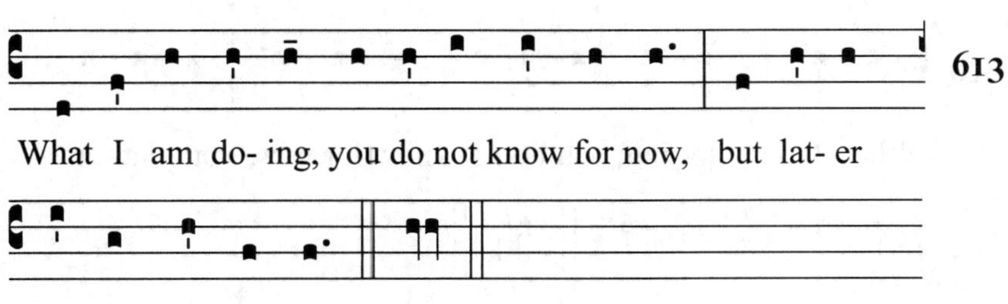
613
What I am do- ing, you do not know for now, but lat- er
you will come to know. Lord.

Or :

614

Ant. 3
5.
LORD, are you to wash my feet? * Je- sus said to
him in answer : If I do not wash your feet, you will
have no share with me.

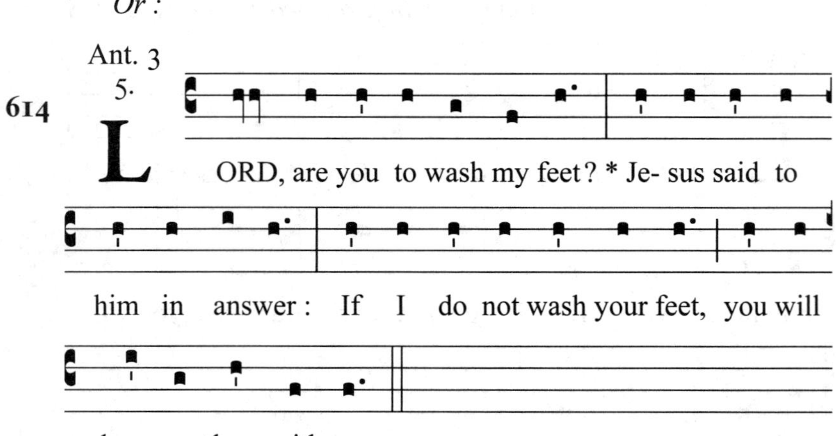

VERSE 1

615

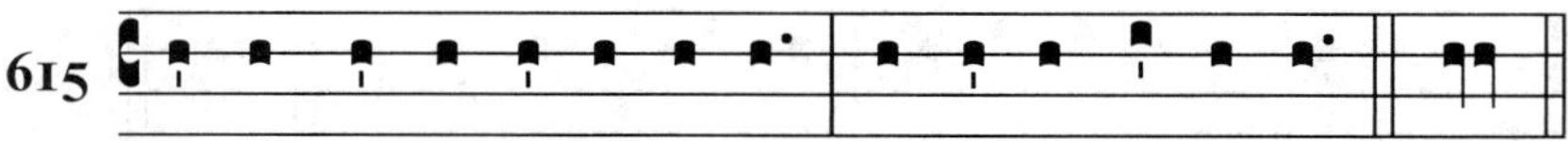

So he came to Simon Pe-ter and Pe-ter said to him : Lord.

VERSE 2

616

What I am do- ing, you do not know for now, but lat- er
you will come to know. Lord.

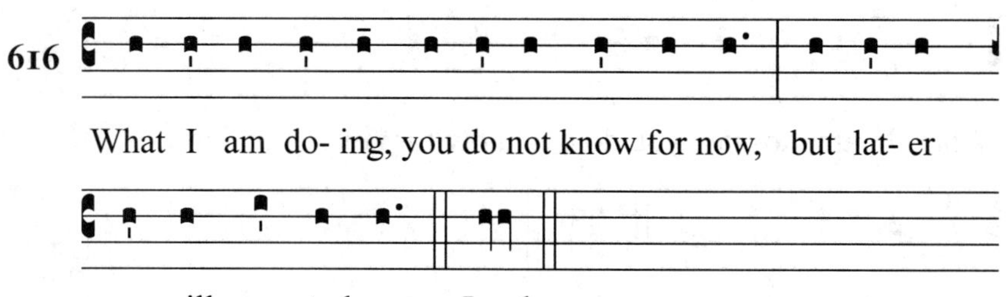

Si ego, Dominus et Magister vester. Cf. Jn 13 : 14

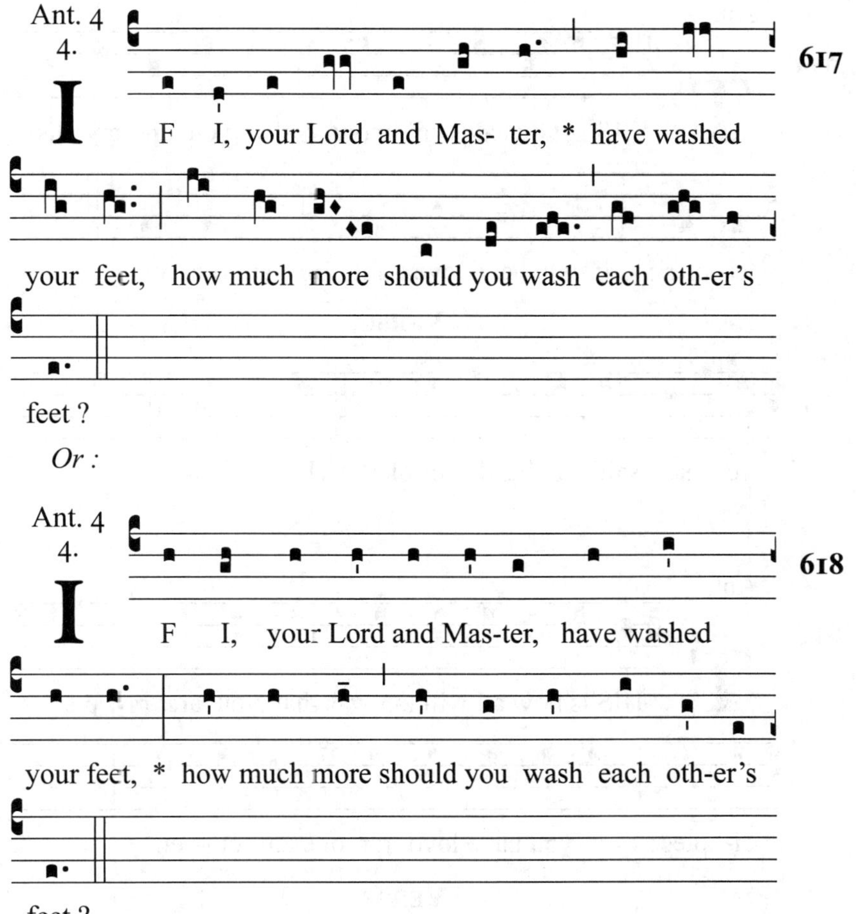
Ant. 4
4.
IF I, your Lord and Mas- ter, * have washed
617
your feet, how much more should you wash each oth-er's
feet ?
Or :
Ant. 4
4.
IF I, your Lord and Mas-ter, have washed
618
your feet, * how much more should you wash each oth-er's
feet ?

In hoc cognoscent omnes. Jn 13 : 35

619 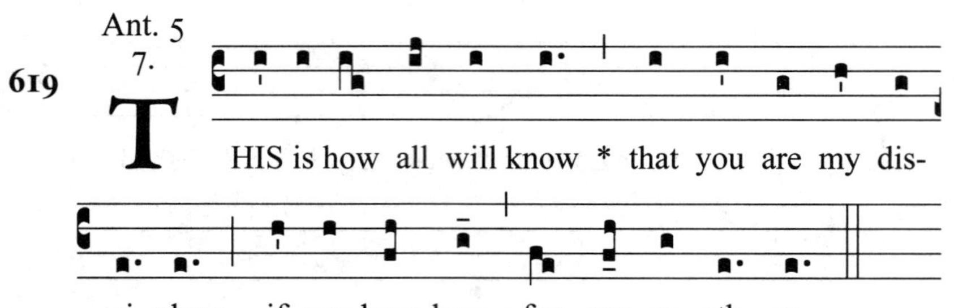
Ant. 5
7.
THIS is how all will know * that you are my dis-
ci- ples : if you have love for one an- oth- er.

VERSE

620 

Je- sus said to his dis- ci-ples : This is how.

Or :

621 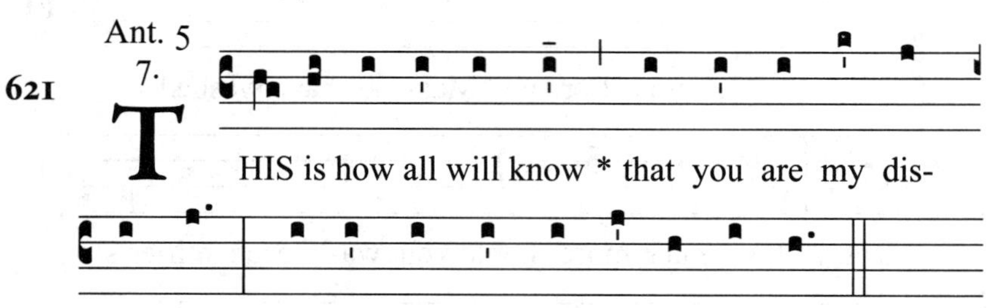
Ant. 5
7.
THIS is how all will know * that you are my dis-

ci- ples : if you have love for one an- oth- er.

VERSE

622 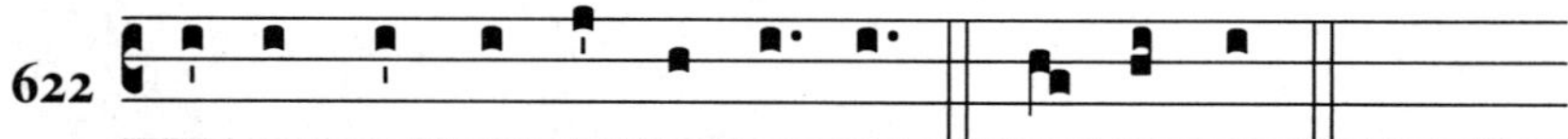

Je- sus said to his dis- ci- ples : This is how.

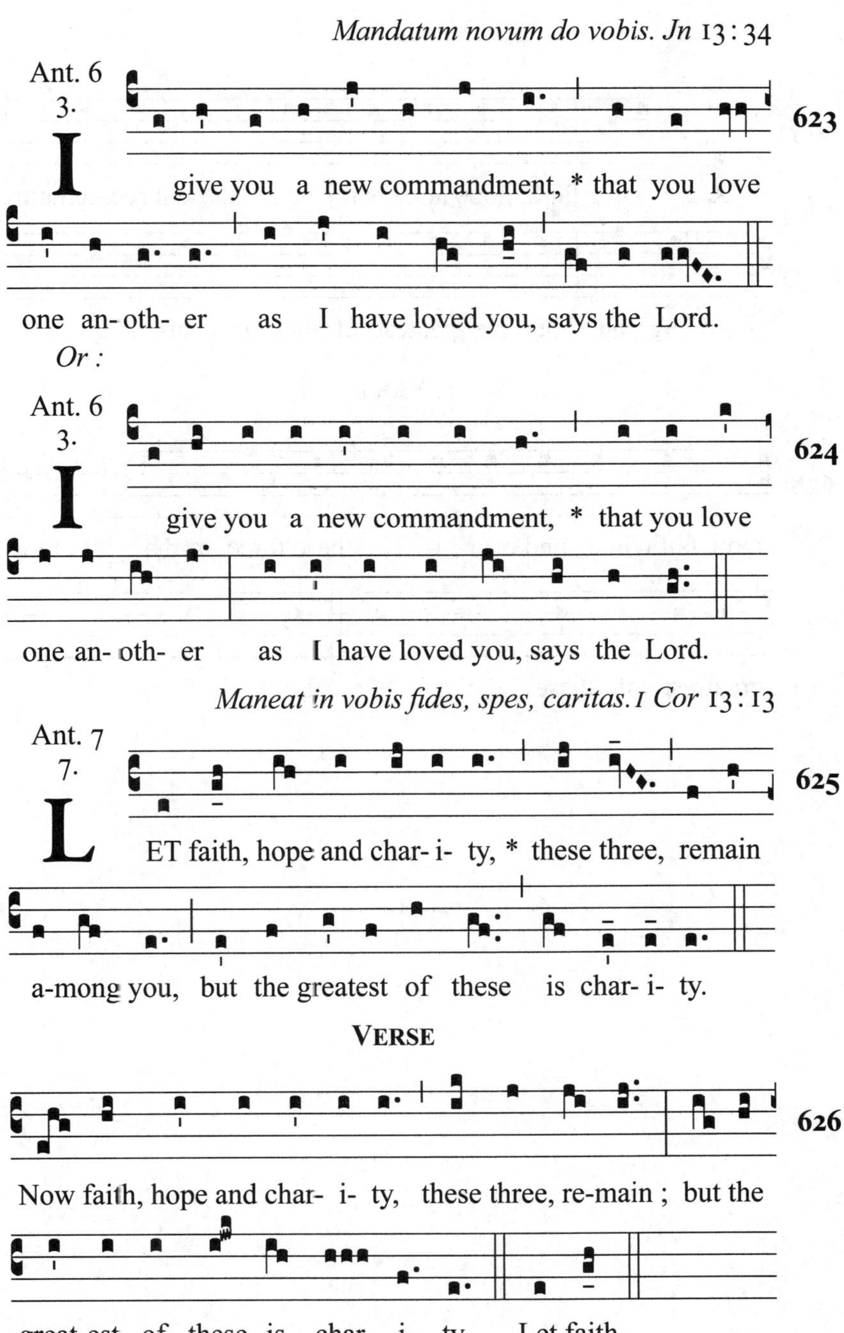
Mandatum novum do vobis. Jn 13:34
Ant. 6
3.
I give you a new commandment, * that you love
one an- oth- er as I have loved you, says the Lord.
623
Or :
Ant. 6
3.
I give you a new commandment, * that you love
one an- oth- er as I have loved you, says the Lord.
624
Maneat in vobis fides, spes, caritas. 1 Cor 13:13
Ant. 7
7.
LET faith, hope and char- i- ty, * these three, remain
a-mong you, but the greatest of these is char- i- ty.
625
VERSE
Now faith, hope and char- i- ty, these three, re-main ; but the
great-est of these is char- i- ty. Let faith.
626

Or :

627

Ant. 7
7.
LET faith, hope and char- i- ty, * these three, remain
a-mong you, but the greatest of these is char- i- ty.

VERSE

628

Now faith, hope and char- i- ty, these three, re-main ; but the
great-est of these is char- i- ty. Let faith.

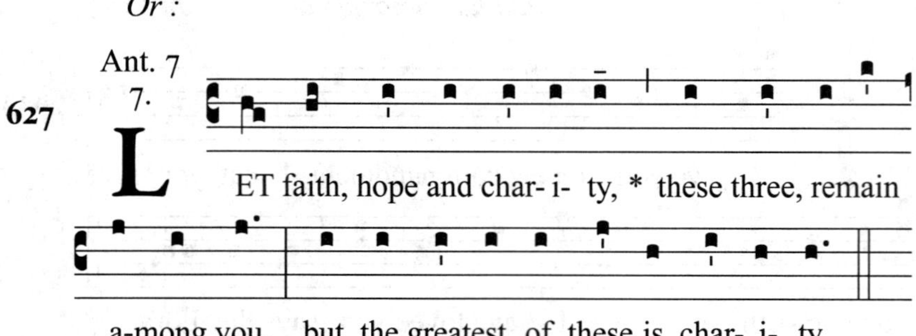

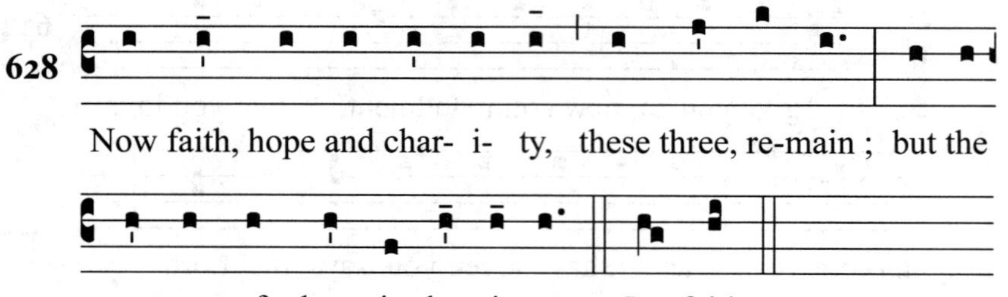

The Liturgy of the Eucharist

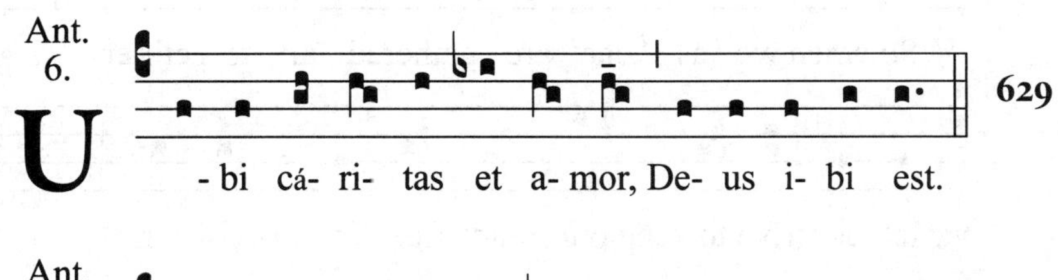
Ant.
6.
U -bi cá- ri- tas et a- mor, De- us i- bi est.
629

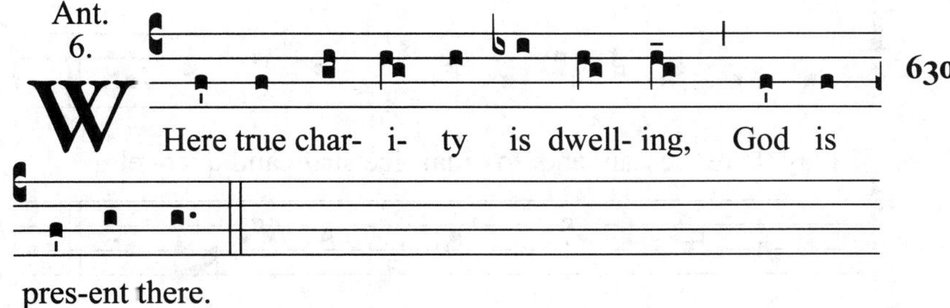
Ant.
6.
W Here true char- i- ty is dwell- ing, God is
630
pres-ent there.

VERSES

631

℣. By the love of Christ we have been brought to-geth-er :

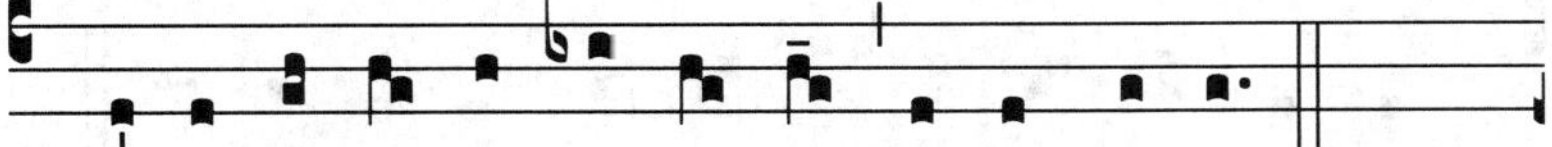

℣. let us find in him our gladness and our pleasure ;

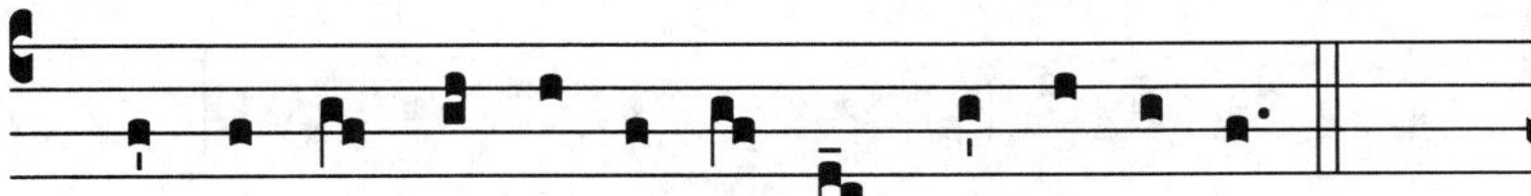

℣. may we love him and re-vere him, God the liv-ing,

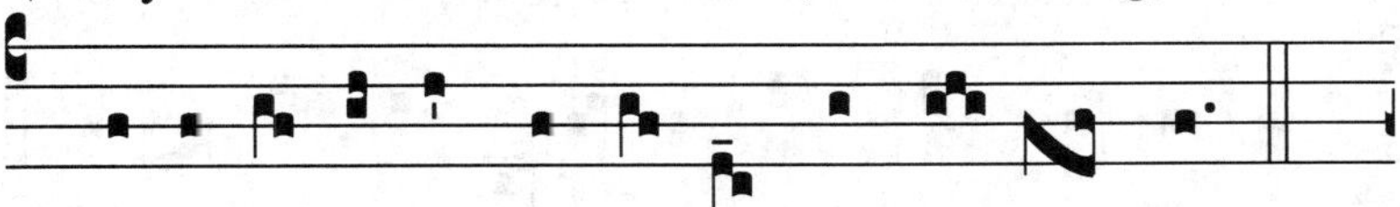

℣. and in love respect each oth- er with sin- cere hearts. *Ant.*

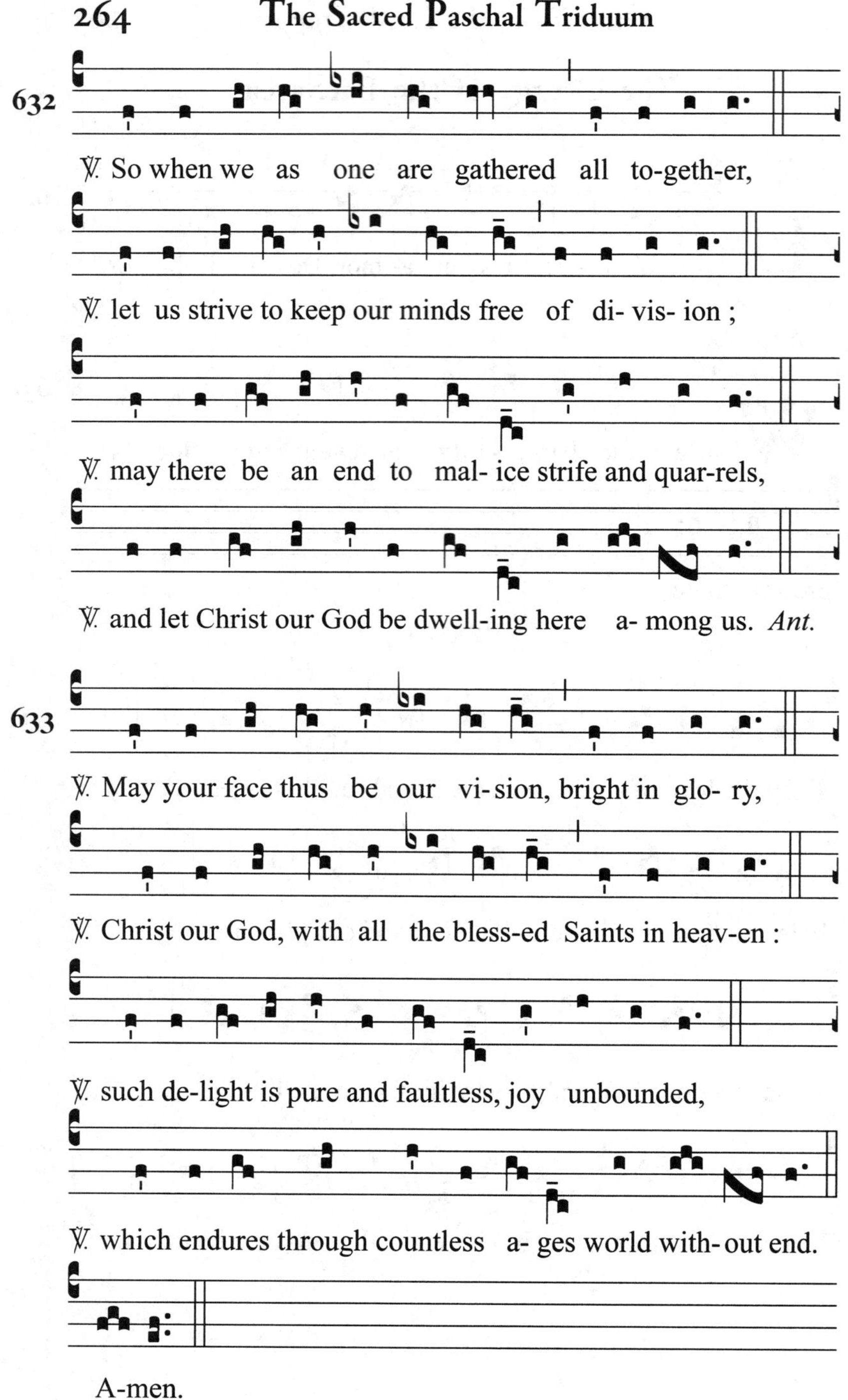
632
℣. So when we as one are gathered all to-geth-er,
℣. let us strive to keep our minds free of di- vis- ion ;
℣. may there be an end to mal- ice strife and quar-rels,
℣. and let Christ our God be dwell-ing here a- mong us. *Ant.*
633
℣. May your face thus be our vi- sion, bright in glo- ry,
℣. Christ our God, with all the bless-ed Saints in heav-en :
℣. such de-light is pure and faultless, joy unbounded,
℣. which endures through countless a- ges world with- out end.
A-men.

COMMUNION *Hoc corpus.* I *Cor* 11:24-25

- i -

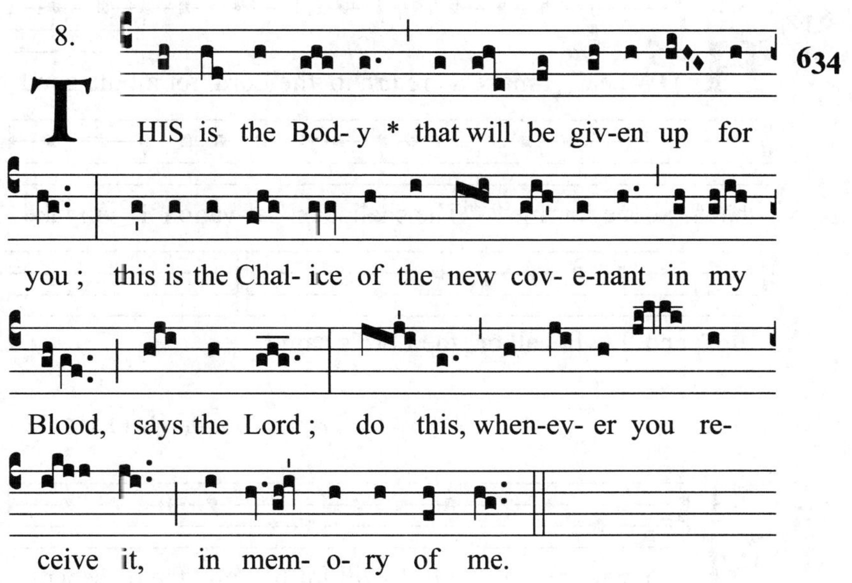
8.
THIS is the Bod- y * that will be giv-en up for
634
you ; this is the Chal- ice of the new cov- e-nant in my
Blood, says the Lord ; do this, when-ev- er you receive it, in mem- o- ry of me.

VERSES *Credidi, propter quod locutus sum. Ps* 115:10

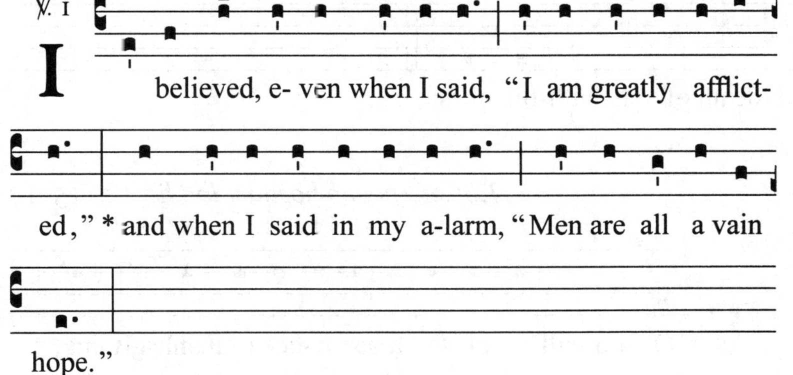
℣. 1
I believed, e- ven when I said, "I am greatly afflict-
ed," * and when I said in my a-larm, "Men are all a vain
hope."

635

Quid retribuam Domino. Ps 115:12-13

636

℣. 2
HOW shall I make a return to the Lord for all the good
he has done for me ? * The chalice of sal-vation I will take
up, and I will call on the Lord's name.

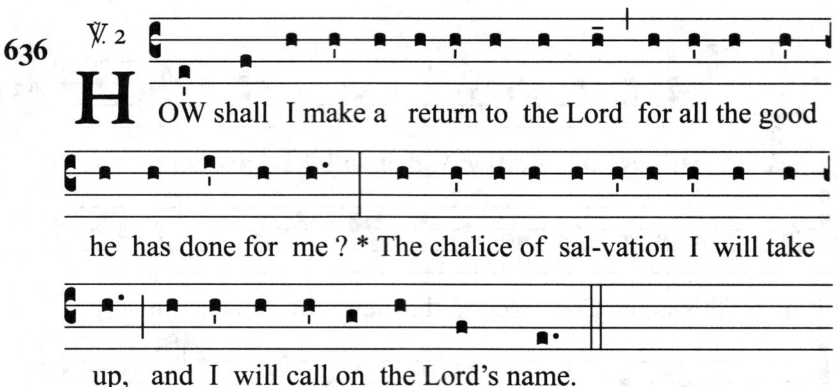

Vota mea reddam. Ps 115:14-15

637

℣. 3
MY vows to the Lord I will ful-fill † in the presence
of all his peo-ple. * Precious in the eyes of the Lord is the
death of his faith-ful ones.

Tibi sacrficabo hostiam laudis. Ps 115:17

638

℣. 4
TO you will I of- fer a sac-ri-fice of thanksgiv-ing, *
and I will call up- on the Lord's name.

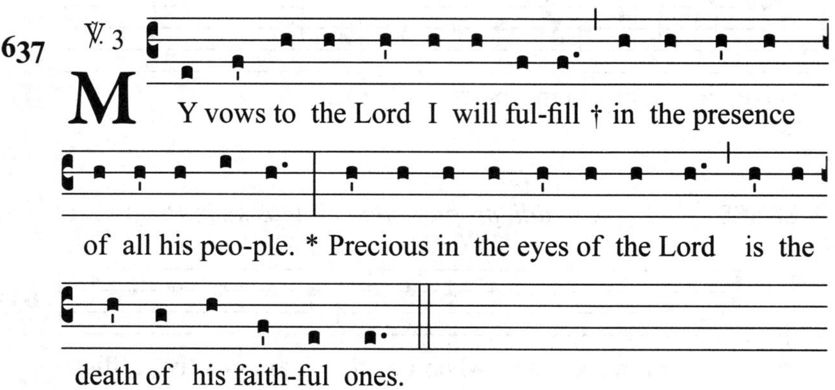

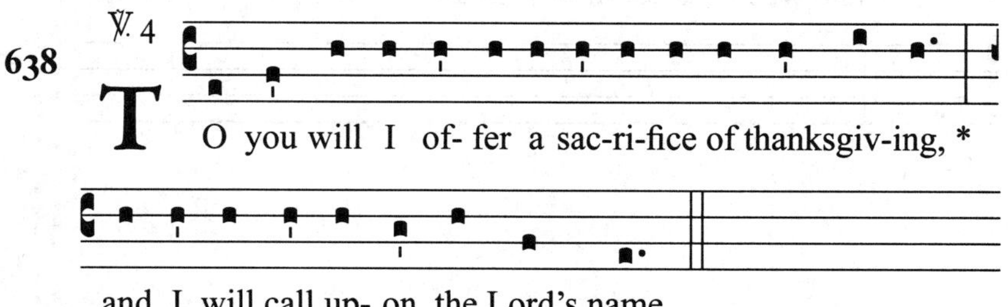

- iii -

8.
THIS is the Bod- y that will be giv- en up for
you ; * this is the Chal-ice of the new cov-e-nant in my
Blood, says the Lord ; do this, when-ev- er you receive it,
in mem'- ry of me.

639

- iv -

8.
THIS is the Bod- y * that will be giv-en up for
you ; this is the Chal-ice of the new cov-e-nant in my
Blood, says the Lord ; do this, when-ev- er you receive it,
in mem-o- ry of me.

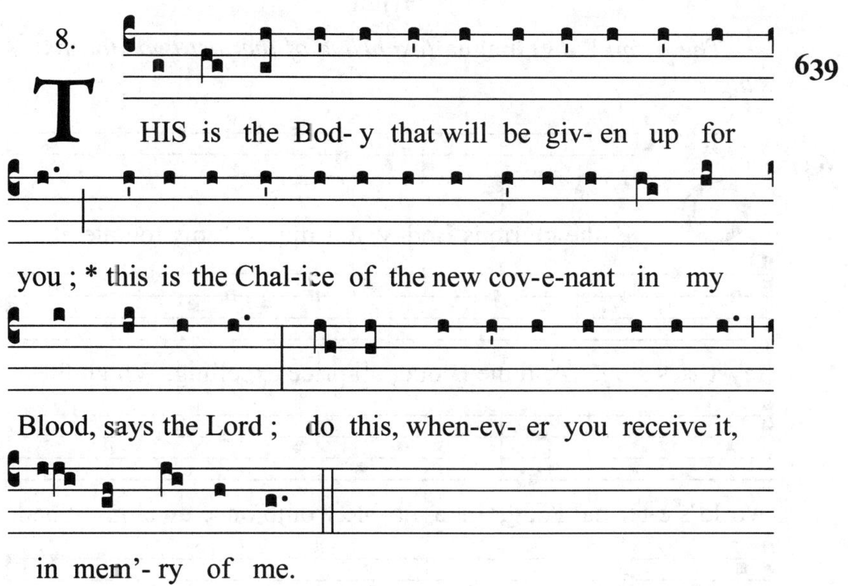

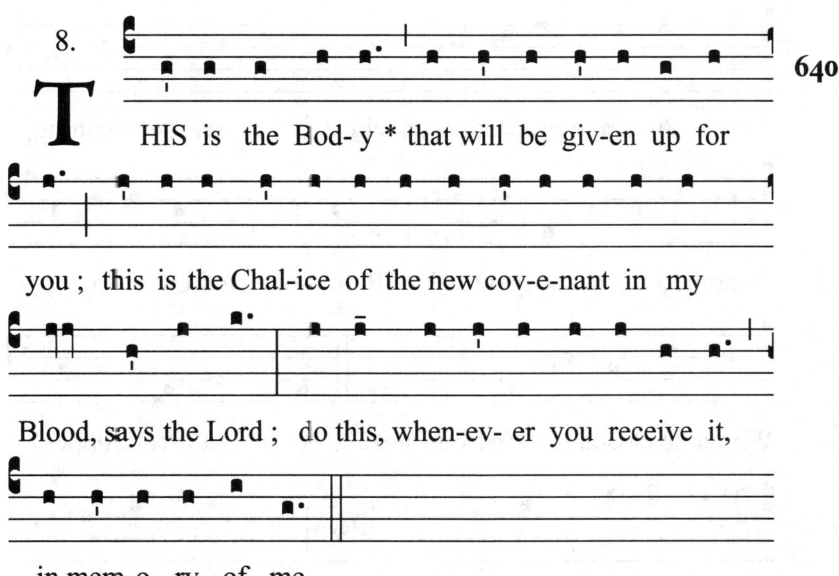

640

The Transfer of the Blessed Sacrament

Hymn

The hymn Pange lingua *(exclusive of the last two stanzas) is sung.*

641

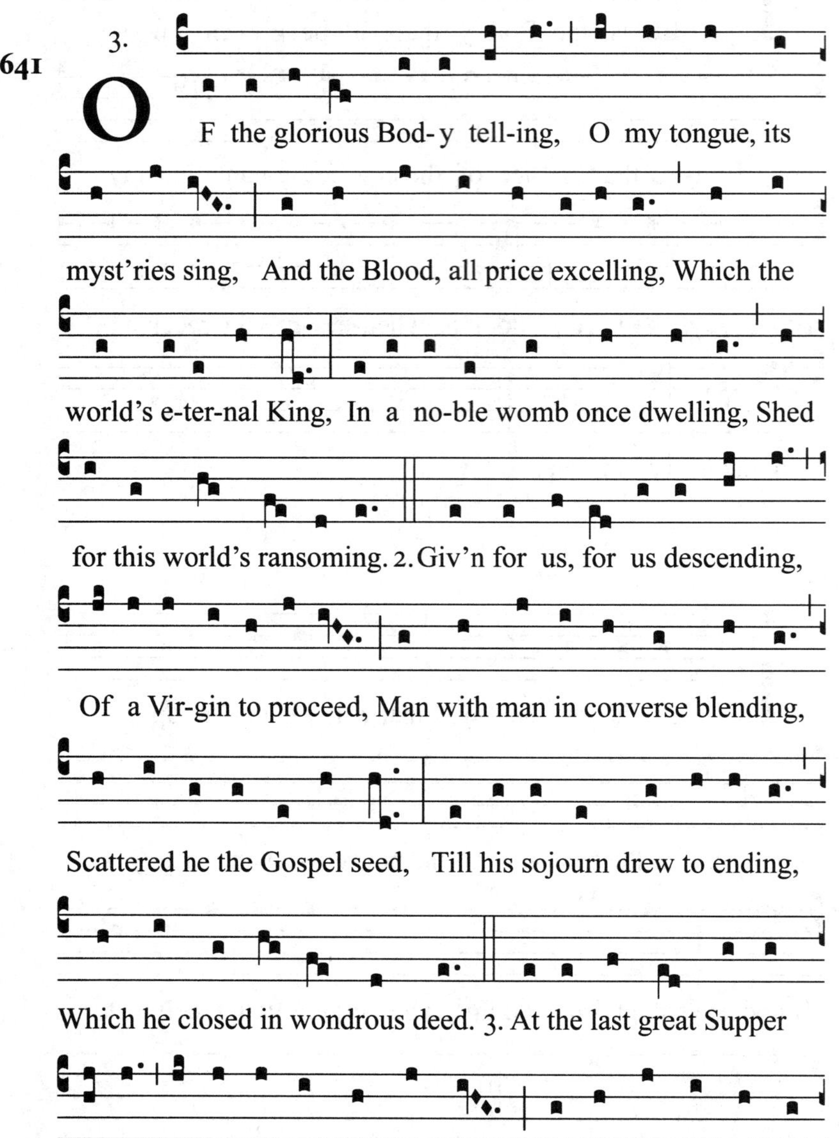
3.
OF the glorious Bod-y tell-ing, O my tongue, its
myst'ries sing, And the Blood, all price excelling, Which the
world's e-ter-nal King, In a no-ble womb once dwelling, Shed
for this world's ransoming. 2. Giv'n for us, for us descending,
Of a Vir-gin to proceed, Man with man in converse blending,
Scattered he the Gospel seed, Till his sojourn drew to ending,
Which he closed in wondrous deed. 3. At the last great Supper
ly-ing Circled by his brethren's band, Meekly with the law com-

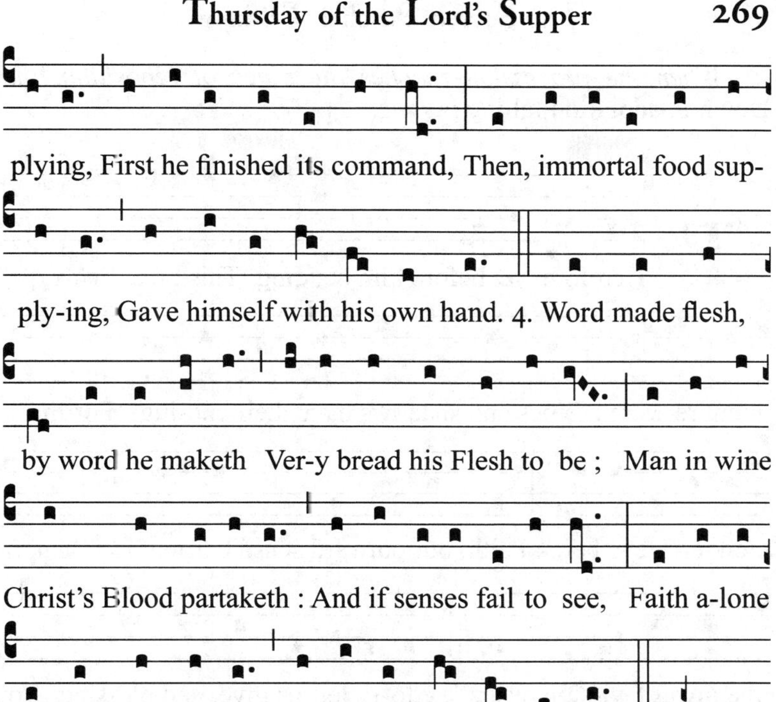
plying, First he finished its command, Then, immortal food sup-
ply-ing, Gave himself with his own hand. 4. Word made flesh,
by word he maketh Ver-y bread his Flesh to be ; Man in wine
Christ's Blood partaketh : And if senses fail to see, Faith a-lone
the true heart waketh To behold the mys-ter- y.

When the procession reaches the place of reposition, the Down in adoration falling *is sung.*

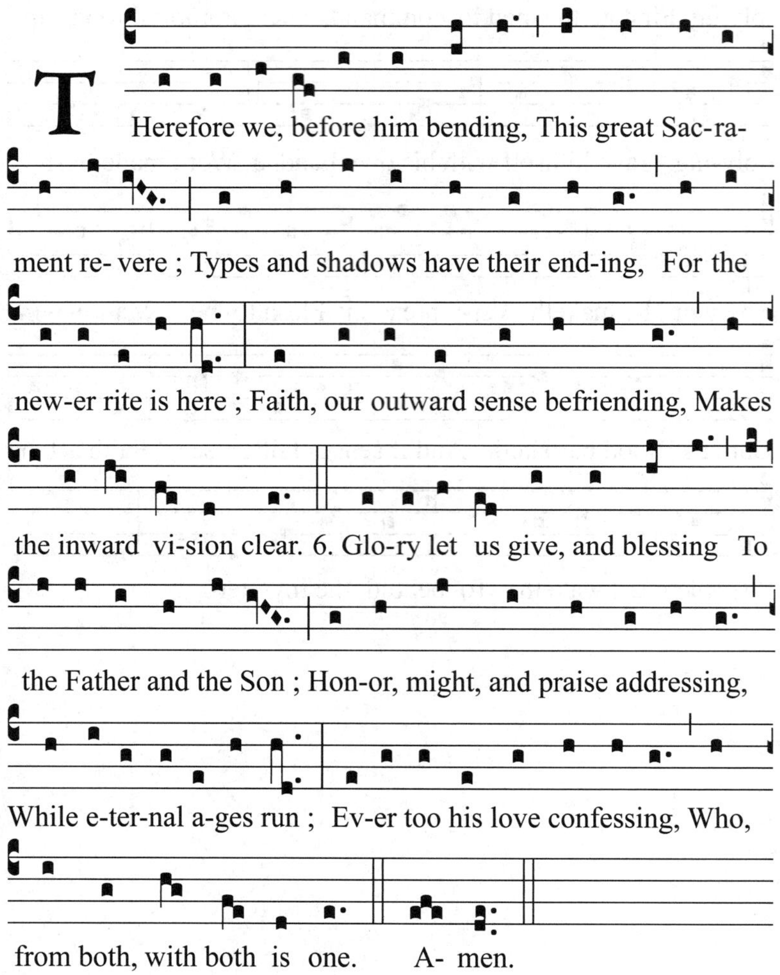
T
Herefore we, before him bending, This great Sac-ra-
ment re- vere ; Types and shadows have their end-ing, For the
new-er rite is here ; Faith, our outward sense befriending, Makes
the inward vi-sion clear. 6. Glo-ry let us give, and blessing To
the Father and the Son ; Hon-or, might, and praise addressing,
While e-ter-nal a-ges run ; Ev-er too his love confessing, Who,
from both, with both is one. A- men.

Another version:

Hymn

The hymn Pange lingua *(exclusive of the last two stanzas) is sung.*

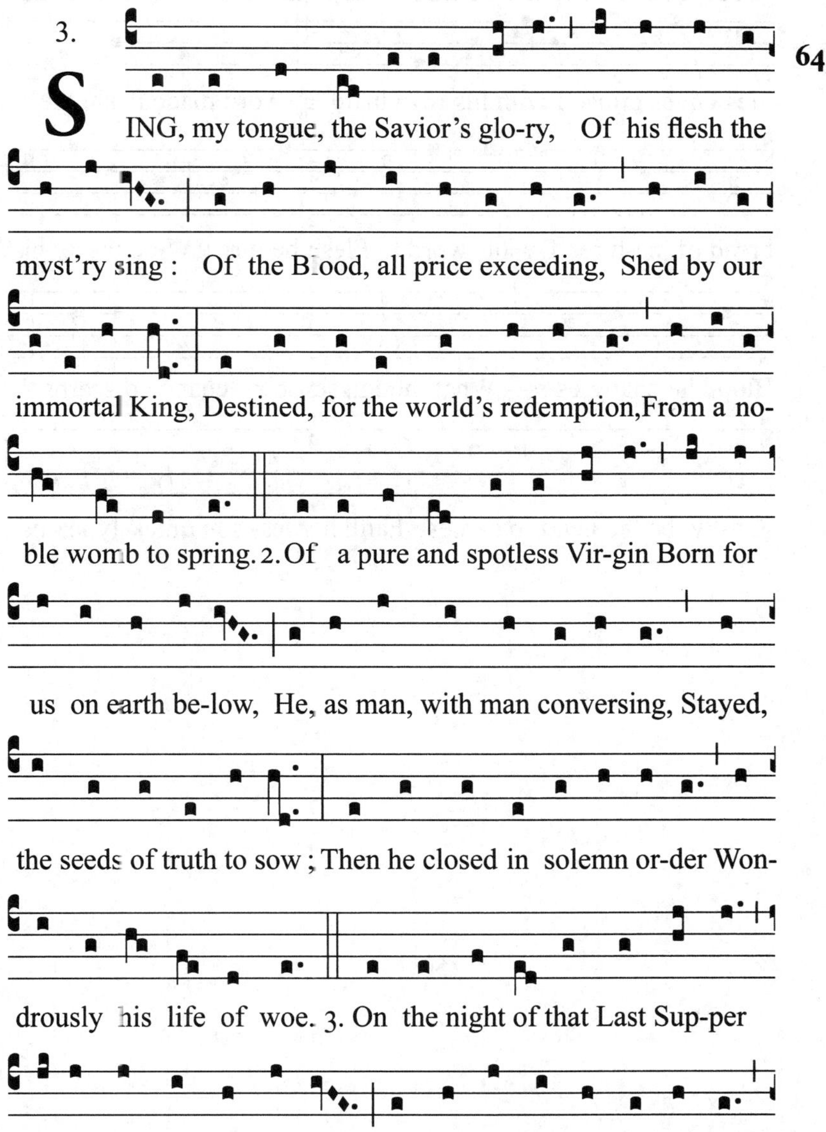
3.
642
SING, my tongue, the Savior's glo-ry, Of his flesh the
myst'ry sing : Of the Blood, all price exceeding, Shed by our
immortal King, Destined, for the world's redemption,From a no-
ble womb to spring. 2. Of a pure and spotless Vir-gin Born for
us on earth be-low, He, as man, with man conversing, Stayed,
the seeds of truth to sow ; Then he closed in solemn or-der Won-
drously his life of woe. 3. On the night of that Last Sup-per
Seated with his cho-sen band, He, the Paschal vic-tim eat-ing,

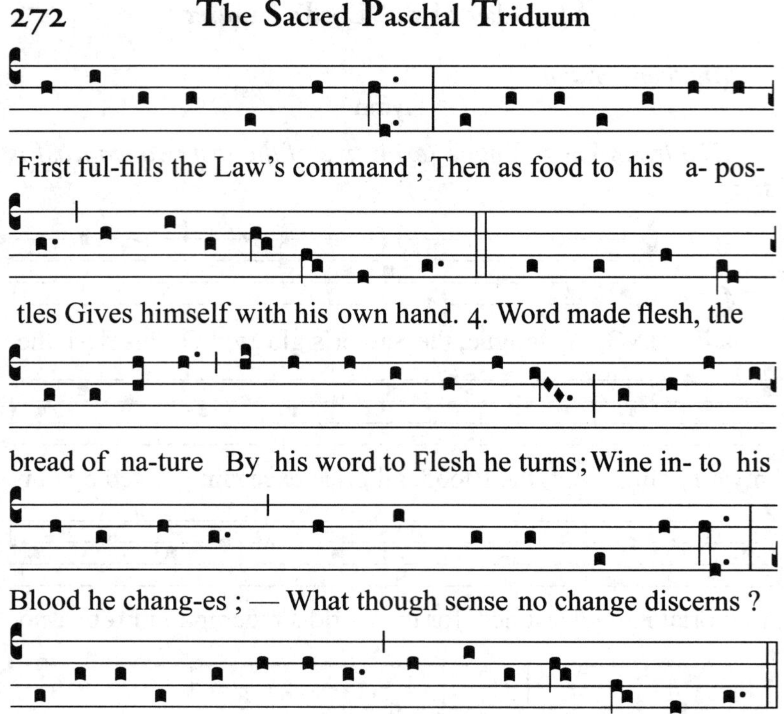
First ful-fills the Law's command ; Then as food to his a- pos-
tles Gives himself with his own hand. 4. Word made flesh, the
bread of na-ture By his word to Flesh he turns; Wine in- to his
Blood he chang-es ; — What though sense no change discerns ?
On- ly be the heart in earnest Faith her les- son quick-ly learns.

When the procession reaches the place of reposition, the Down in adoration falling *is sung.*

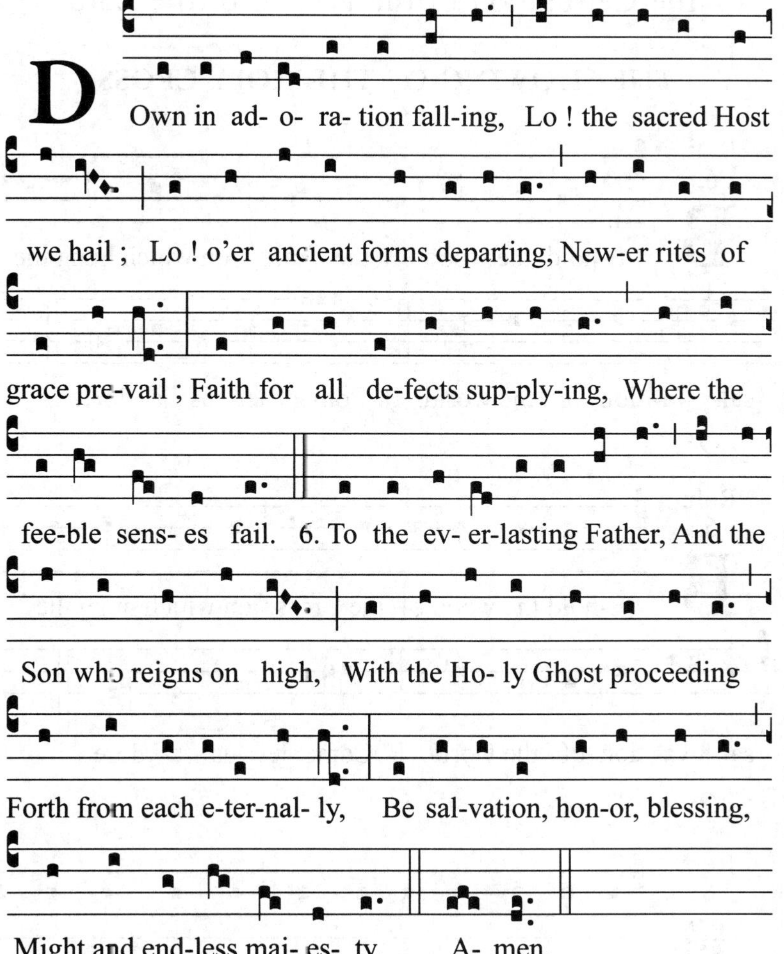
D
Own in ad- o- ra- tion fall-ing, Lo ! the sacred Host
we hail ; Lo ! o'er ancient forms departing, New-er rites of
grace pre-vail ; Faith for all de-fects sup-ply-ing, Where the
fee-ble sens- es fail. 6. To the ev- er-lasting Father, And the
Son who reigns on high, With the Ho- ly Ghost proceeding
Forth from each e-ter-nal- ly, Be sal-vation, hon-or, blessing,
Might and end-less maj- es- ty. A- men.

Friday of the Passion of the Lord

The Celebration of the Passion of the Lord

THE SHOWING OF THE HOLY CROSS

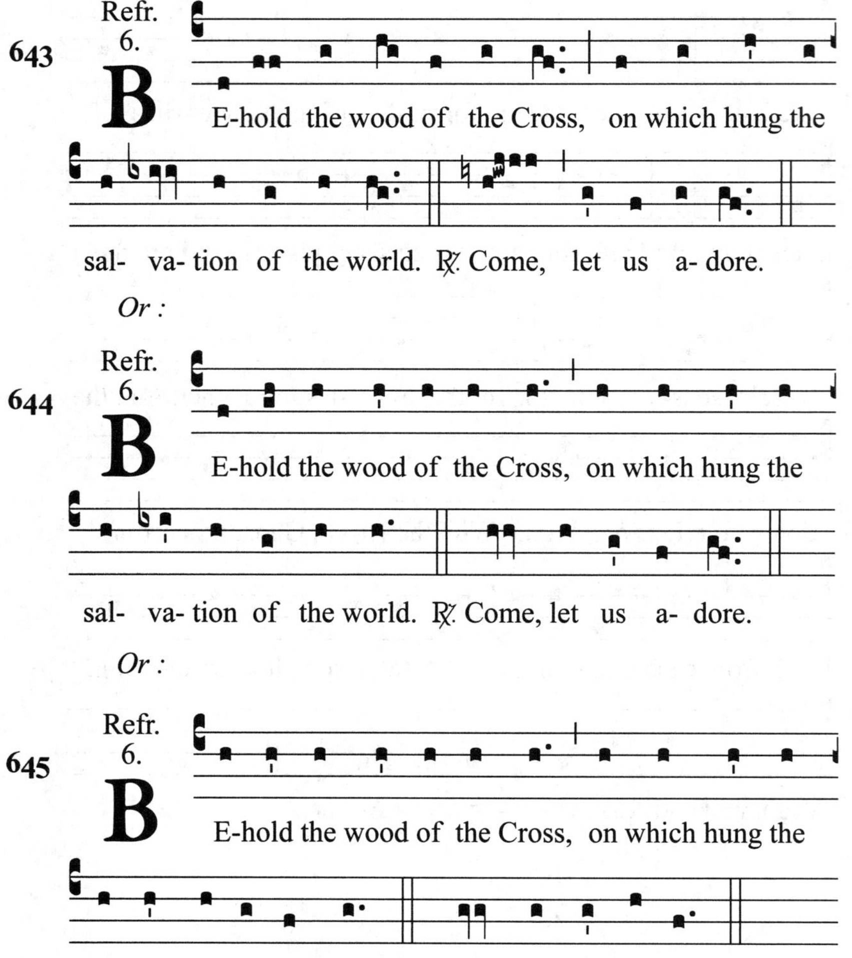
643
Refr. 6.
BEhold the wood of the Cross, on which hung the
sal- va- tion of the world. ℟. Come, let us a- dore.
Or :
644
Refr. 6.
BEhold the wood of the Cross, on which hung the
sal- va- tion of the world. ℟. Come, let us a- dore.
Or :
645
Refr. 6.
BEhold the wood of the Cross, on which hung the
sal- va- tion of the world. ℟. Come, let us a-dore.

Or :

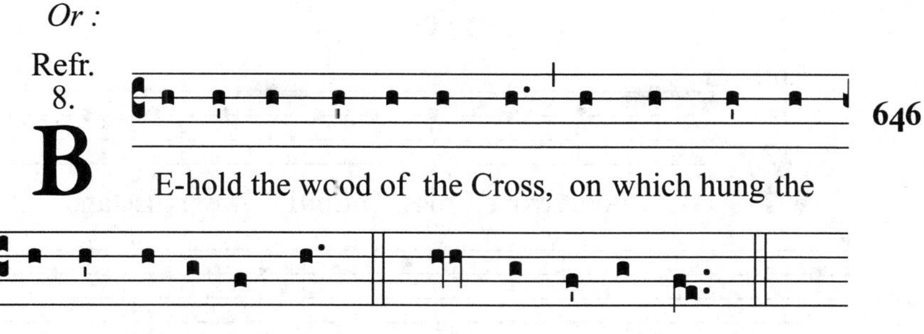
Refr.
8.
646
BE-hold the wood of the Cross, on which hung the
sal- va- tion of the world. ℟. Come, let us a- dore.

THE ADORATION OF THE HOLY CROSS

- i -

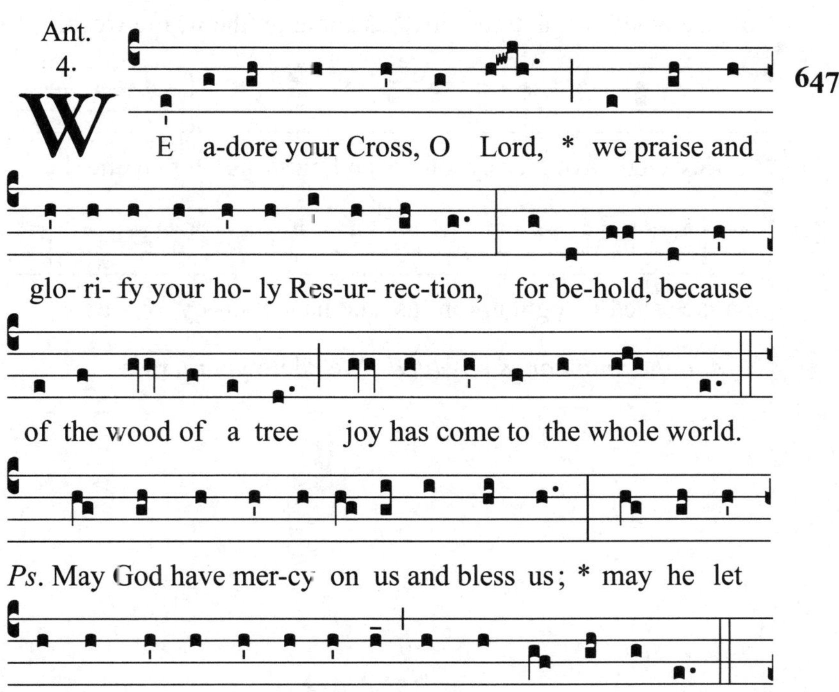
Ant.
4.
647
WE a-dore your Cross, O Lord, * we praise and
glo- ri- fy your ho- ly Res-ur- rec-tion, for be-hold, because
of the wood of a tree joy has come to the whole world.
Ps. May God have mer-cy on us and bless us; * may he let
his face shed its light up-on us and have mer- cy on us.

And the antiphon is repeated : We adore your Cross.

- iii -

648 Ant. 4.

WE a-dore your Cross, O Lord, * we praise and
glo- ri- fy your ho- ly Res- ur- rec-tion, for behold, because
of the wood of a tree joy has come to the whole world.
Ps. May God have mer-cy on us and bless us; * may he let
his face shed its light up-on us and have mer- cy on us.

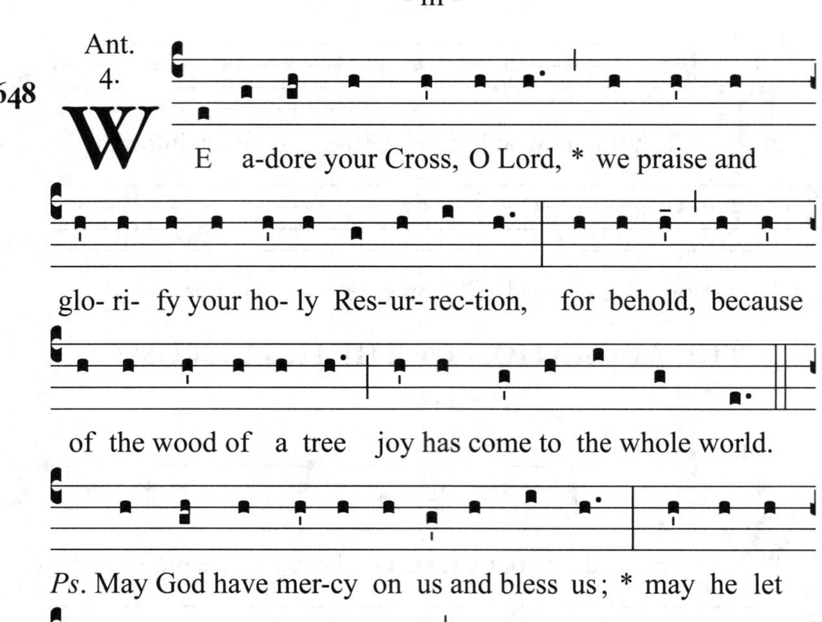

And the antiphon is repeated : We adore your Cross.

- iv -

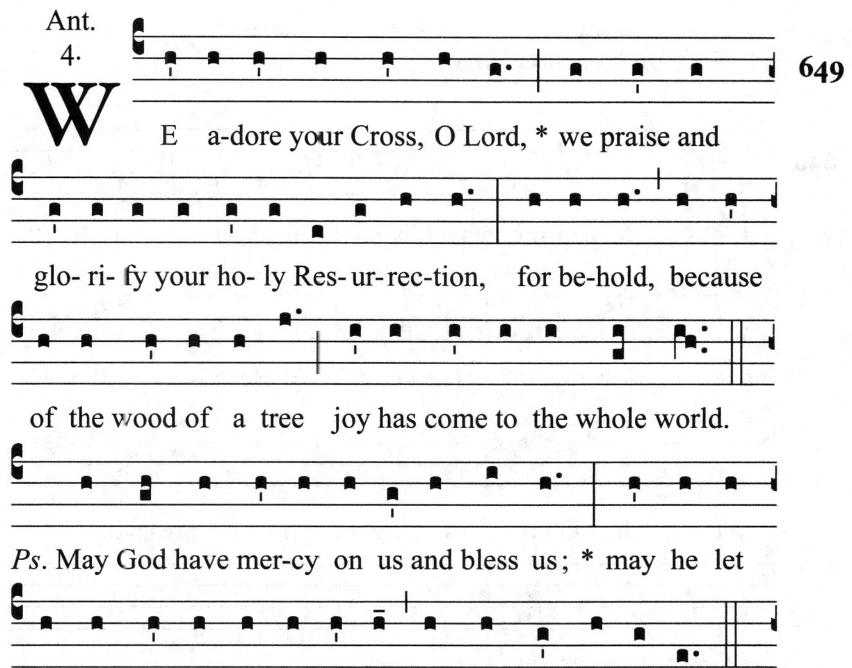

And the antiphon is repeated: We adore your Cross.

REPROACHES

I

First and second choirs :

650

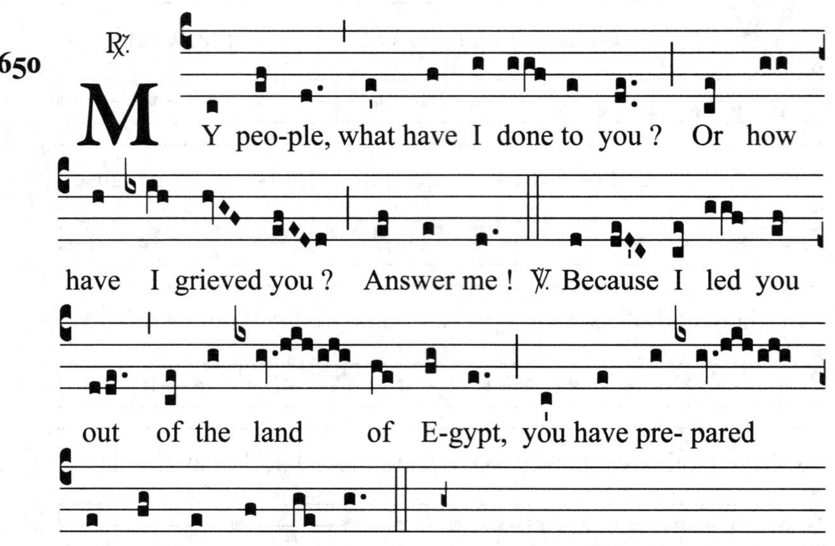
℟.
MY peo-ple, what have I done to you? Or how
have I grieved you? Answer me! ℣. Because I led you
out of the land of E-gypt, you have pre- pared
a Cross for your Sav-ior.

First choir : *Second choir :*

HAgi- os o The- ós,
HO-ly is God,

First choir :

HAgi- os Ischy-rós,

Second choir :

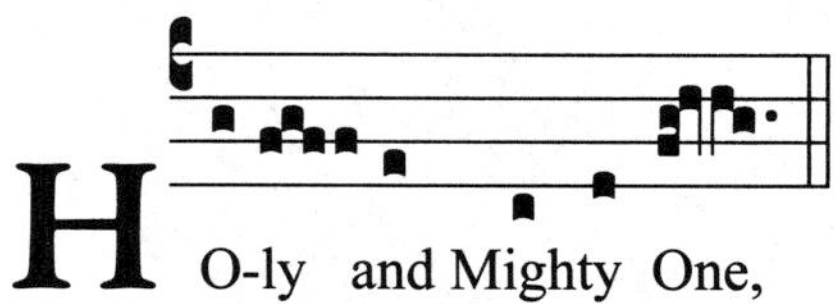
HO-ly and Mighty One,

Note : In the Hagios *first* te *flat, then* ti *natural to the end.*

First choir :

HAgi- os Athá-na- tos, e- lé- i- son
hi- más.

Second choir :

HOly and Immor-tal One, have mer- cy
on us.

First and second choirs :

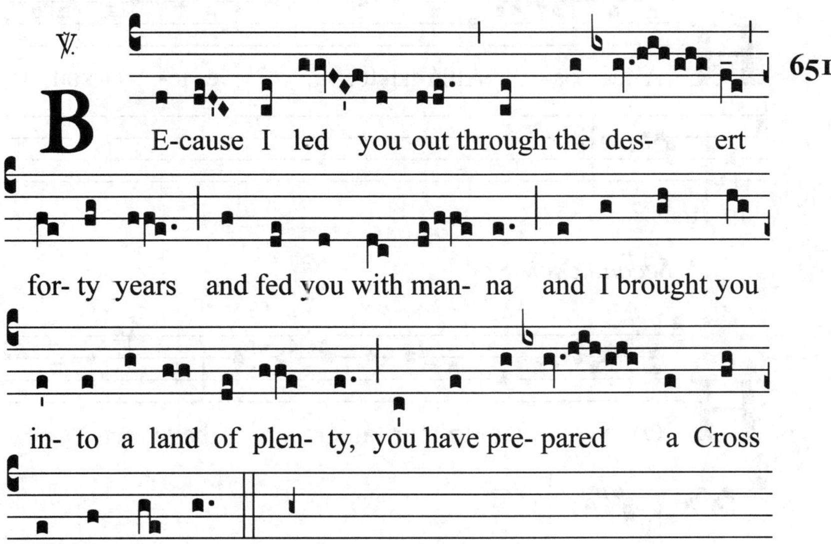
℣.
BEcause I led you out through the des- ert
651
for- ty years and fed you with man- na and I brought you
in- to a land of plen- ty, you have pre- pared a Cross
for your Sav- ior.

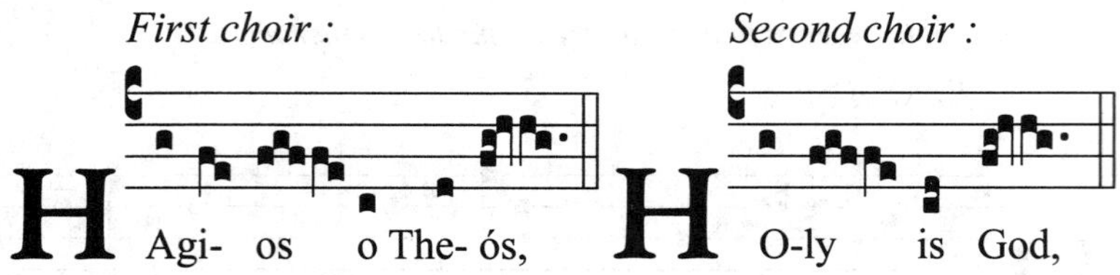
First choir :
HAgi- os o The- ós,
Second choir :
HO-ly is God,

First choir :

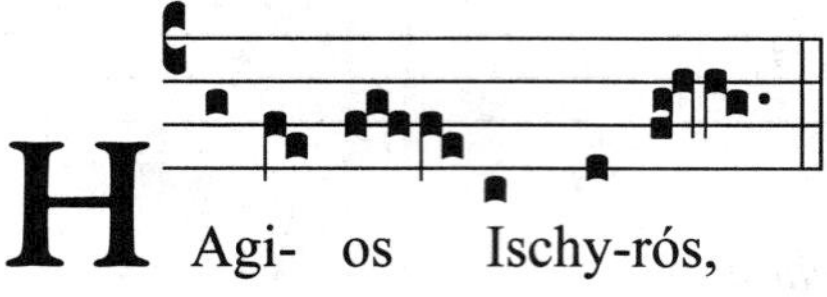
HAgi- os Ischy-rós,

Second choir :

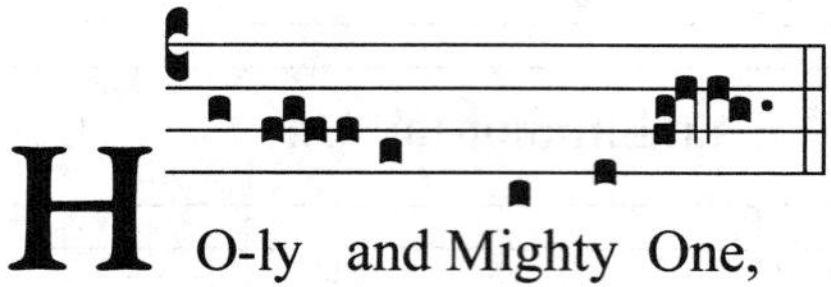
HO-ly and Mighty One,

First choir :

HA-gi- os Athá-na-tos, e- lé- i-son
hi- más.

Second choir :

HO- ly and Immor-tal One, have mer- cy
on us.

First and second choirs :

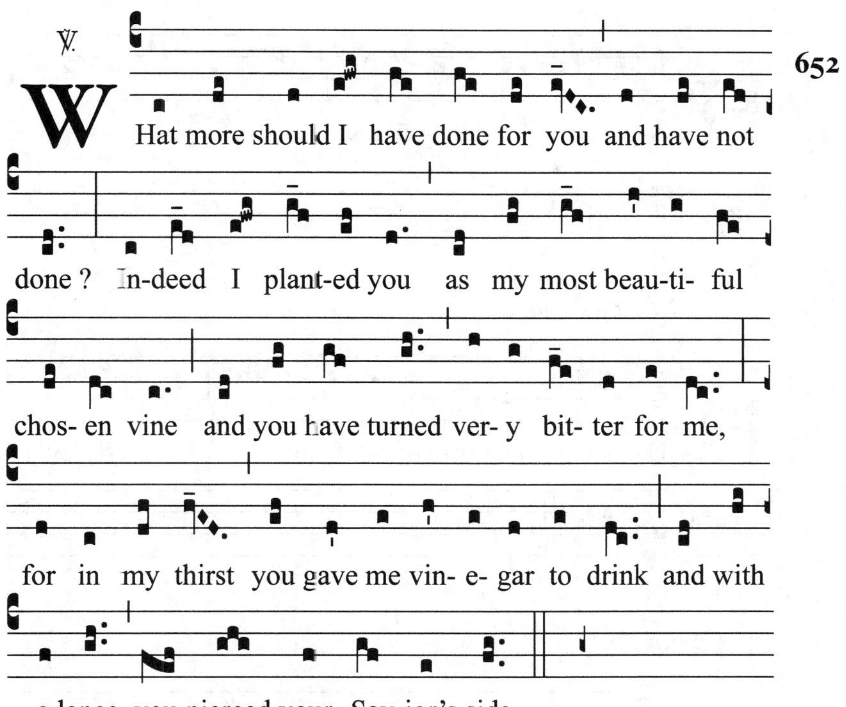
℣.
WHat more should I have done for you and have not done? In-deed I plant-ed you as my most beau-ti- ful chos- en vine and you have turned ver- y bit- ter for me, for in my thirst you gave me vin- e- gar to drink and with a lance you pierced your Sav-ior's side.

652

First choir :

Second choir :

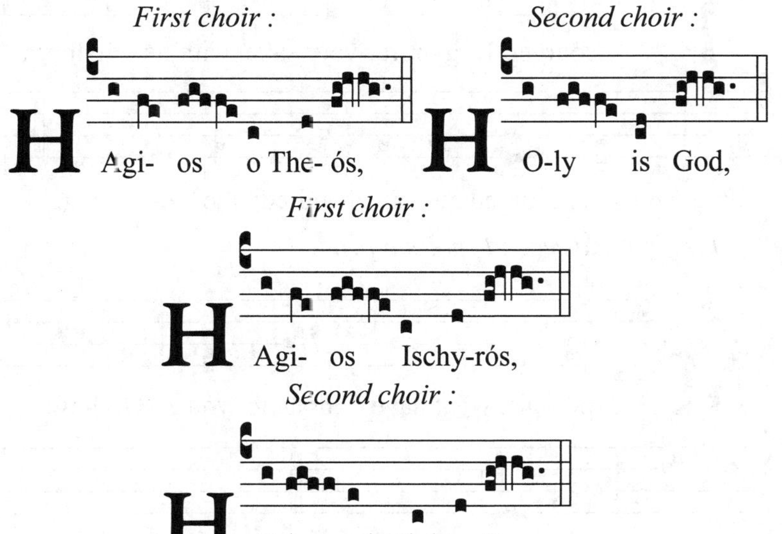
HAgi- os o The- ós,
HO-ly is God,
First choir :
HAgi- os Ischy-rós,
Second choir :
HO-ly and Mighty One,

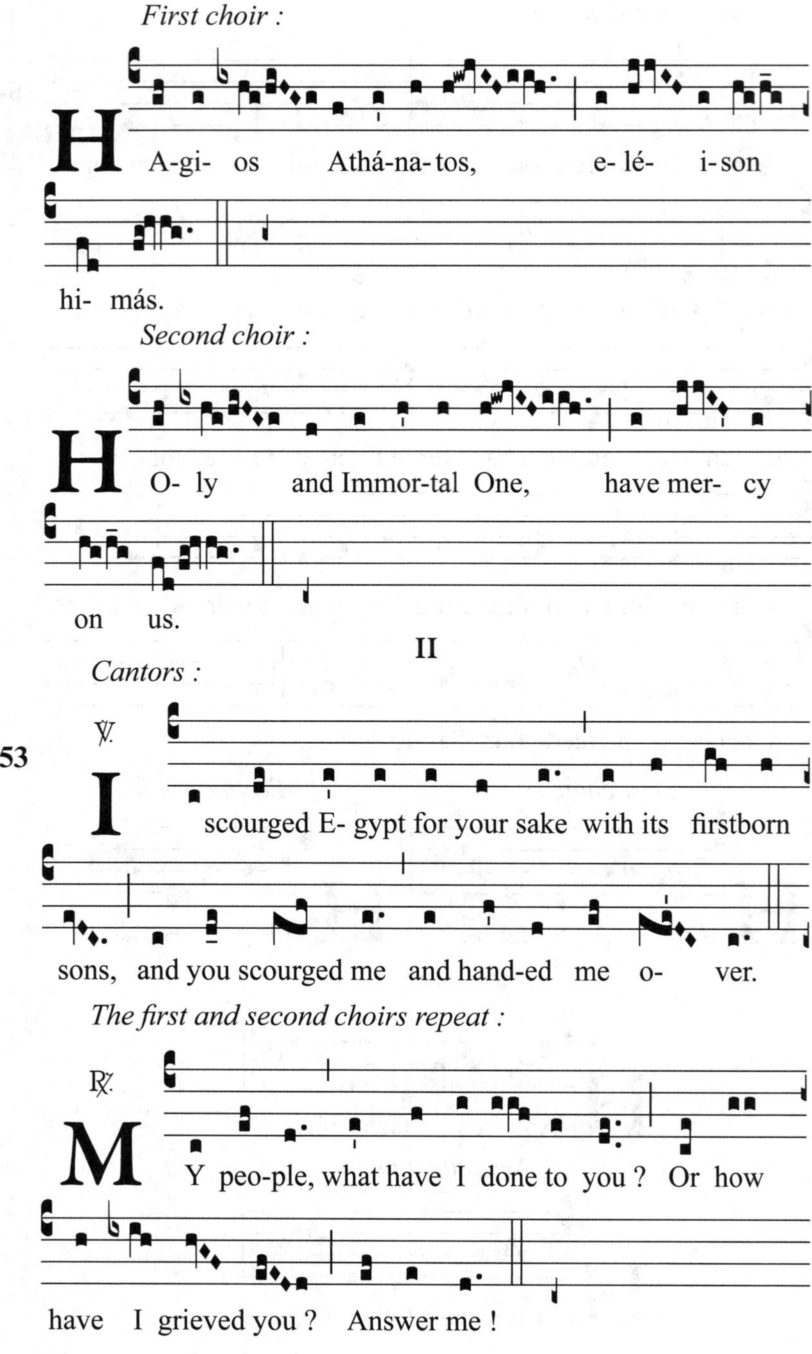
First choir :
H A-gi- os Athá-na-tos, e- lé- i-son
hi- más.
Second choir :
H O- ly and Immor-tal One, have mer- cy
on us.
II
Cantors :
653 ℣. I scourged E- gypt for your sake with its firstborn
sons, and you scourged me and hand-ed me o- ver.
The first and second choirs repeat :
℟. M Y peo-ple, what have I done to you ? Or how
have I grieved you ? Answer me !

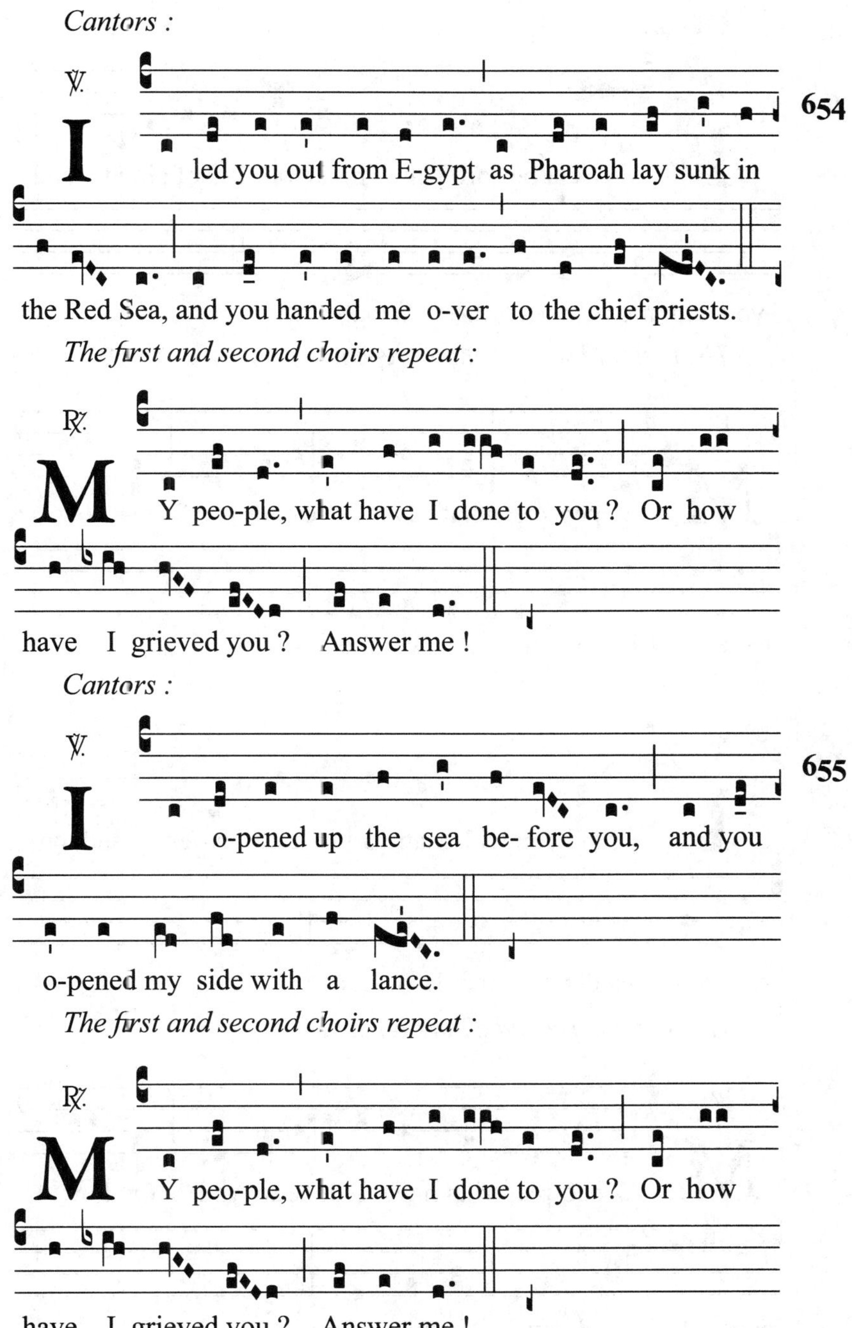
Cantors :
℣. I led you out from E-gypt as Pharoah lay sunk in 654
the Red Sea, and you handed me o-ver to the chief priests.
The first and second choirs repeat :
℟. MY peo-ple, what have I done to you ? Or how
have I grieved you ? Answer me !
Cantors :
℣. I o-pened up the sea be- fore you, and you 655
o-pened my side with a lance.
The first and second choirs repeat :
℟. MY peo-ple, what have I done to you ? Or how
have I grieved you ? Answer me !

Cantors :

656
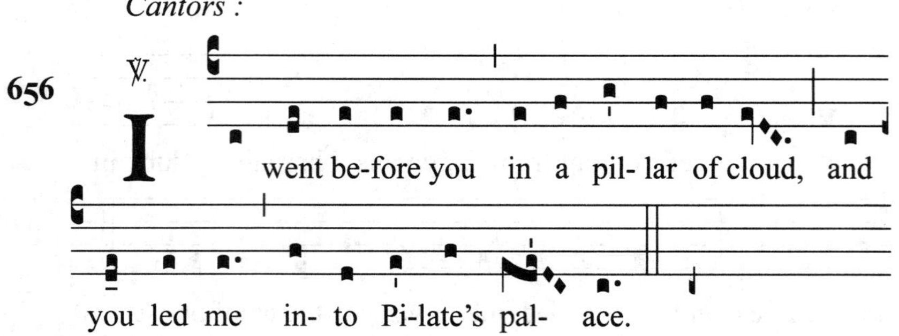
℣.
I went be-fore you in a pil- lar of cloud, and
you led me in- to Pi-late's pal- ace.

The first and second choirs repeat :

℟.
MY peo-ple, what have I done to you ? Or how
have I grieved you ? Answer me !

Cantors :

657

℣.
I fed you with man-na in the des- ert, and on
me you rained blows and lash- es.

The first and second choirs repeat :

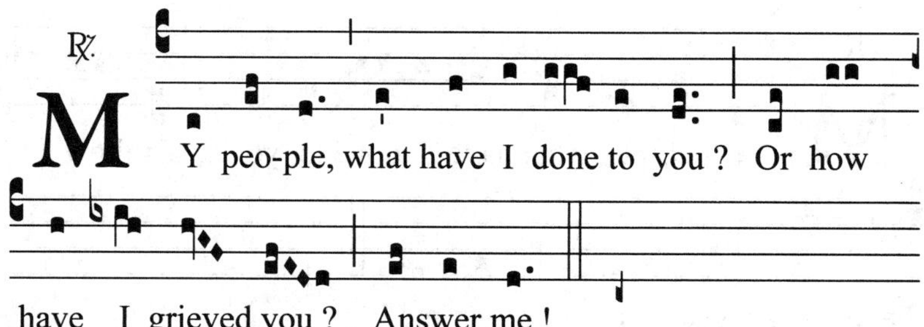
℟.
MY peo-ple, what have I done to you ? Or how
have I grieved you ? Answer me !

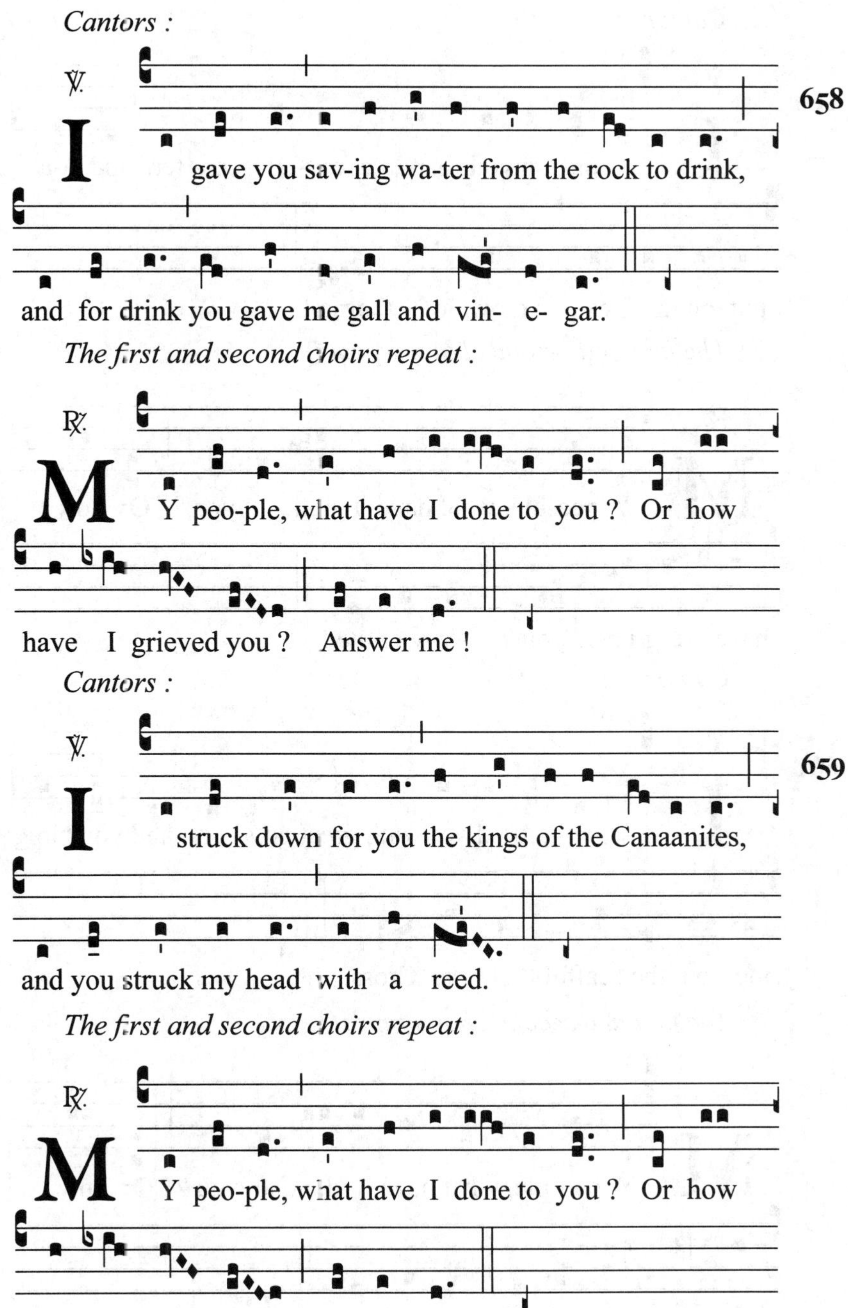
Cantors :
℣. I gave you sav-ing wa-ter from the rock to drink, 658
and for drink you gave me gall and vin- e- gar.
The first and second choirs repeat :
℟. MY peo-ple, what have I done to you ? Or how
have I grieved you ? Answer me !
Cantors :
℣. I struck down for you the kings of the Canaanites, 659
and you struck my head with a reed.
The first and second choirs repeat :
℟. MY peo-ple, what have I done to you ? Or how
have I grieved you ? Answer me !

Cantors :

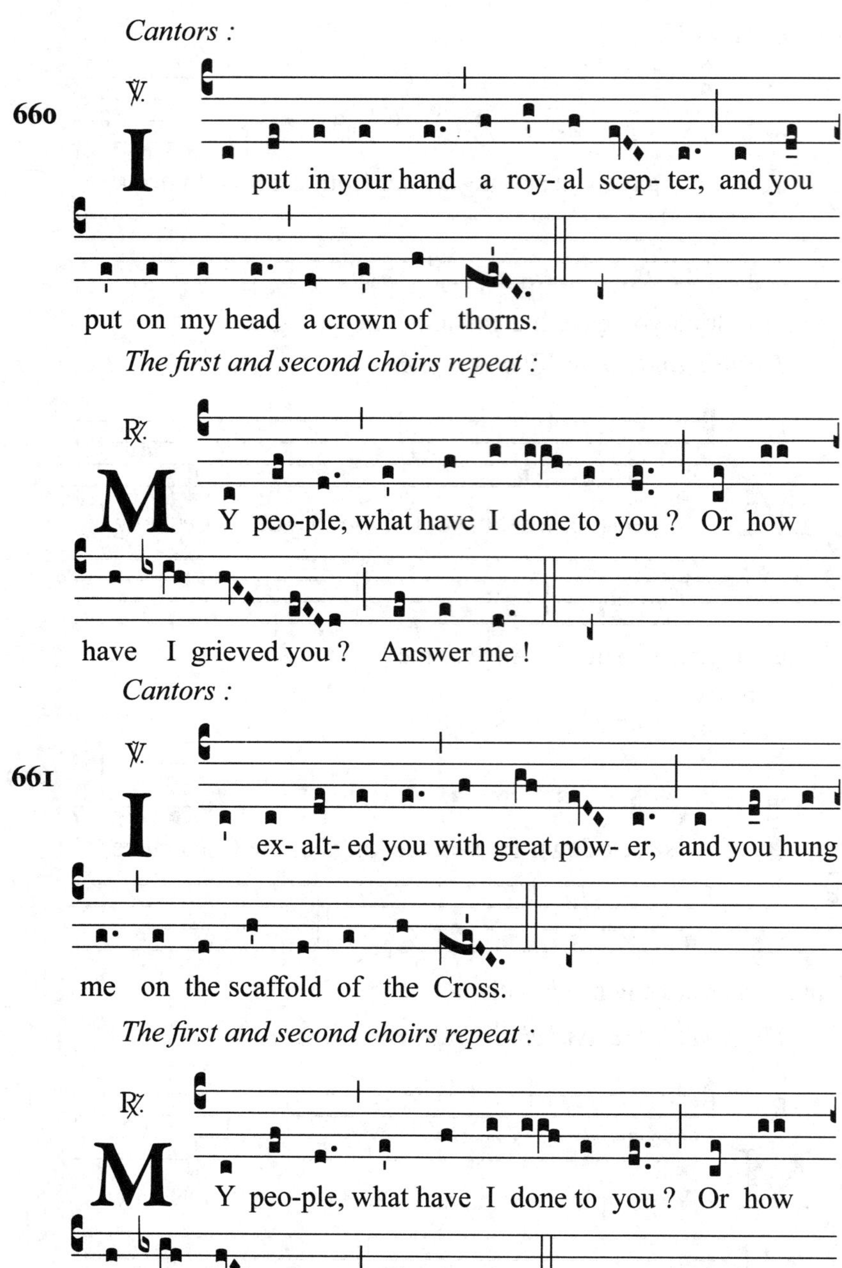
660
℣.
I put in your hand a roy- al scep- ter, and you put on my head a crown of thorns.
The first and second choirs repeat :
℟.
MY peo-ple, what have I done to you ? Or how have I grieved you ? Answer me !
Cantors :
661
℣.
I ex- alt- ed you with great pow- er, and you hung me on the scaffold of the Cross.
The first and second choirs repeat :
℟.
MY peo-ple, what have I done to you ? Or how have I grieved you ? Answer me !

THE ADORATION OF THE HOLY CROSS

Alternate setting

Ant. 4.
662
WE a-dore your Cross, O Lord, * we praise and
glo- ri- fy your ho- ly Res- ur- rec-tion, for behold, because
of the wood of a tree joy has come to the whole world.
Ps. May God have mer-cy on us and bless us ; * may he let
his face shed its light up-on us and have mer- cy on us.

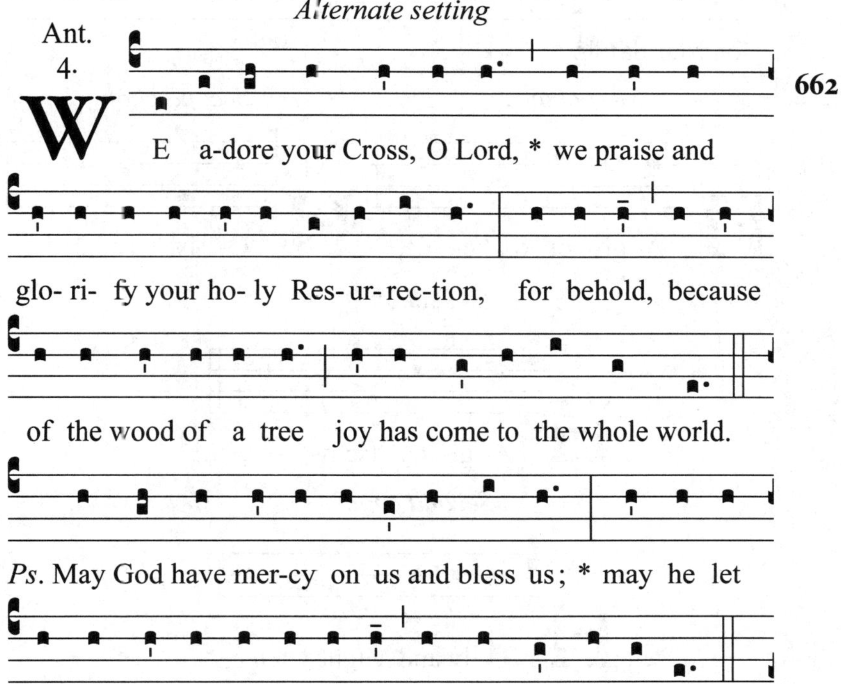

And the antiphon is repeated : We adore your Cross.

REPROACHES

I

First and second choirs :

℟.
663
MY peo-ple, what have I done to you ? Or how
have I grieved you ? Answer me ! ℣. Because I led you
out of the land of E-gypt, you have pre-pared a Cross

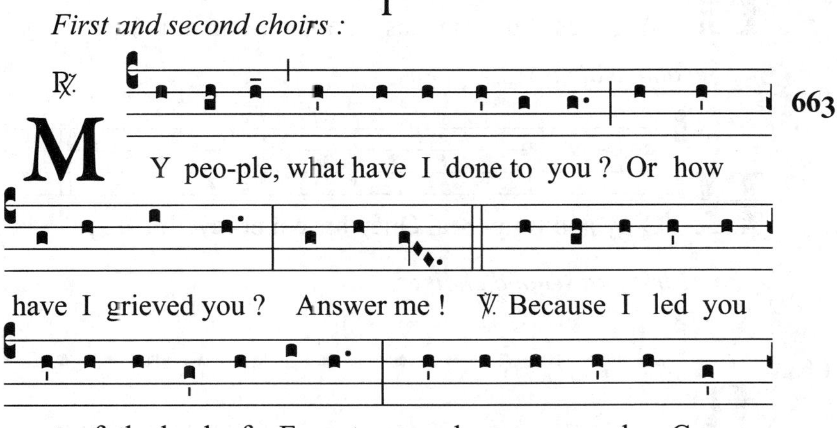

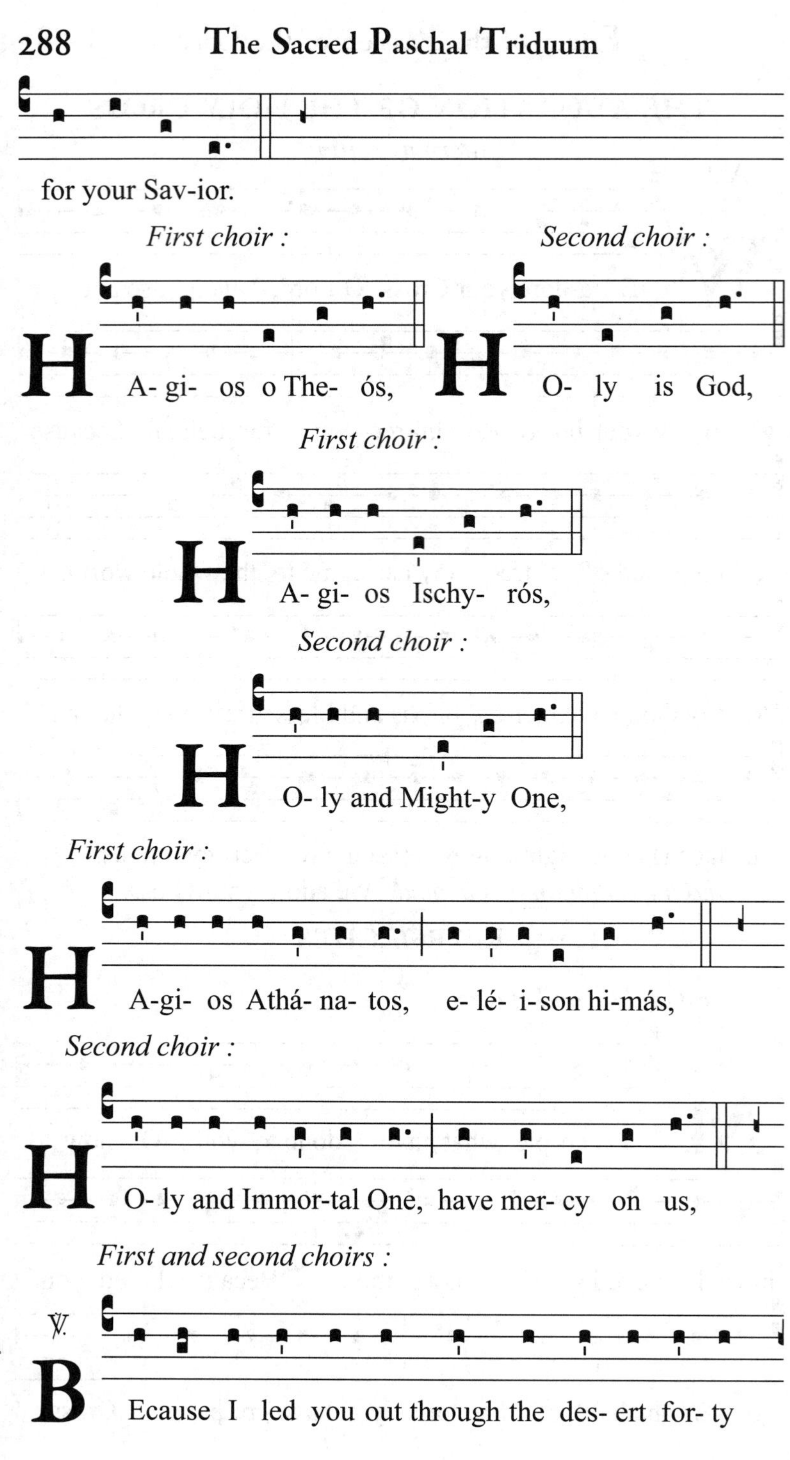
for your Sav-ior.
First choir :
Second choir :
HAgi-os o The-ós,
HOly is God,
First choir :
HAgi-os Ischy-rós,
Second choir :
HOly and Might-y One,
First choir :
HAgi-os Athá-na-tos, e-lé-i-son hi-más,
Second choir :
HOly and Immor-tal One, have mer-cy on us,
First and second choirs :
664 ℣.
BEcause I led you out through the des-ert for-ty

years and fed you with man-na and brought you in- to
a land of plen- ty, you have pre-pared a Cross for your
Sa-vior
First choir :
Second choir :
H A- gi- os o The- ós,
H O- ly is God,
First choir :
H A- gi- os Ischy- rós,
Second choir :
H O- ly and Might-y One,

First choir :

H A-gi- os Athá- na- tos, e- lé- i-son hi- más.

Second choir :

H O- ly and Immor-tal One, have mer- cy on us.

First and second choirs :

665

℣.
WHat more should I have done for you and have not
done ? In-deed, I plant-ed you as my most beau- ti- ful
chos-en vine and you have turned ver- y bit-ter for me,
for in my thirst you gave me vin- e- gar to drink and with
a lance you pierced your Sav-ior's side.

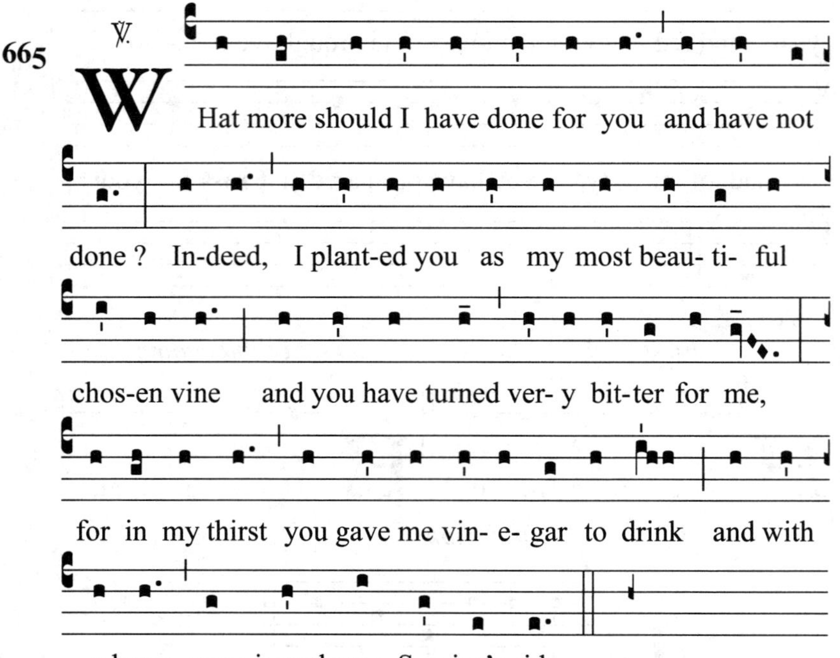

First choir :
Second choir :
H A- gi- os o The- ós,
H O- ly is God,
First choir :
H A- gi- os Ischy- rós,
Second choir :
H O- ly and Might-y One,
First choir :
H A-gi- os Athá- na- tos, e- lé- i- son hi-más.
Second choir :
H O- ly and Immor-tal One, have mer- cy on us.

II

Cantors :

666 ℣. I scourged E- gypt for your sake with its firstborn sons, and you scourged me and hand-ed me o- ver.

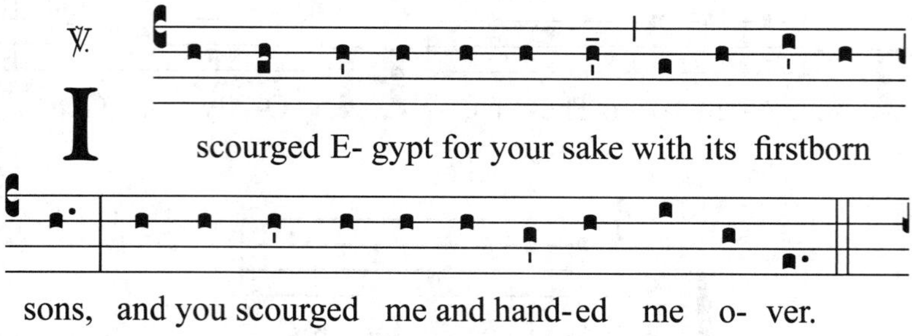

The first and second choirs repeat :

℟. MY peo-ple, what have I done to you? Or how have I grieved you? Answer me!

Cantors :

667 ℣. I led you from E-gypt as Pharoah lay sunk in the Red Sea, and you handed me o- ver to the chief priests.

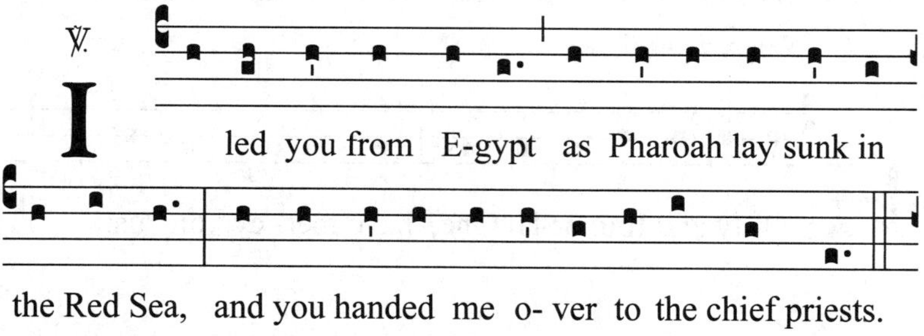

The first and second choirs repeat :

℟. MY peo-ple, what have I done to you? Or how have I grieved you? Answer me!

Cantors :

℣.
I o-pened up the sea be-fore you, and you
668

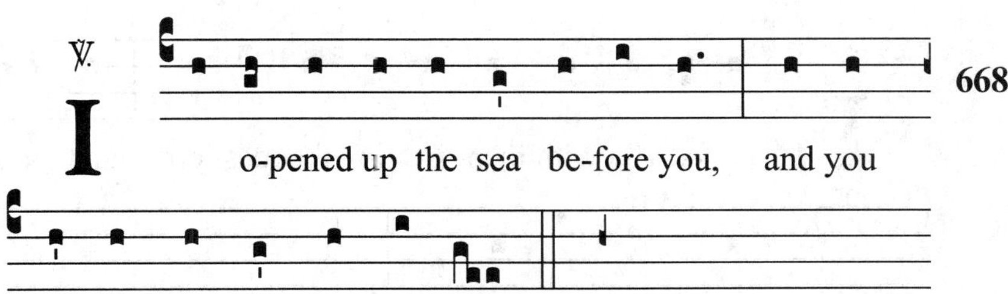

o-pened my side with a lance.

The first and second choirs repeat :

℟.
MY peo-ple, what have I done to you ? Or how

have I grieved you ? Answer me !

Cantors :

℣.
I went be-fore you in a pil- lar of cloud, and
669

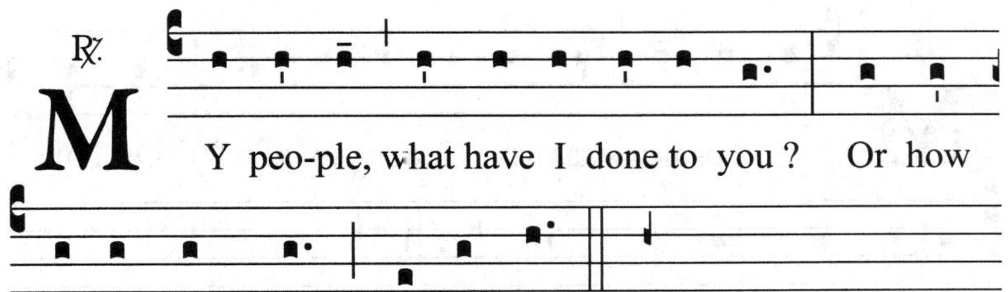

you led me in- to Pi- late's pal-ace.

The first and second choirs repeat :

℟.
MY peo-ple, what have I done to you ? Or how

have I grieved you ? Answer me !

Cantors :

670

℣.
I fed you with man- na in the des- ert, and on
me you rained blows and lash- es.

The first and second choirs repeat :

℟.
MY peo-ple, what have I done to you ? Or how
have I grieved you ? Answer me !

Cantors :

671

℣.
I gave you sav-ing wa-ter from the rock to drink,
and for drink you gave me gall and vin- e- gar.

The first and second choirs repeat :

℟.
MY peo-ple, what have I done to you ? Or how
have I grieved you ? Answer me !

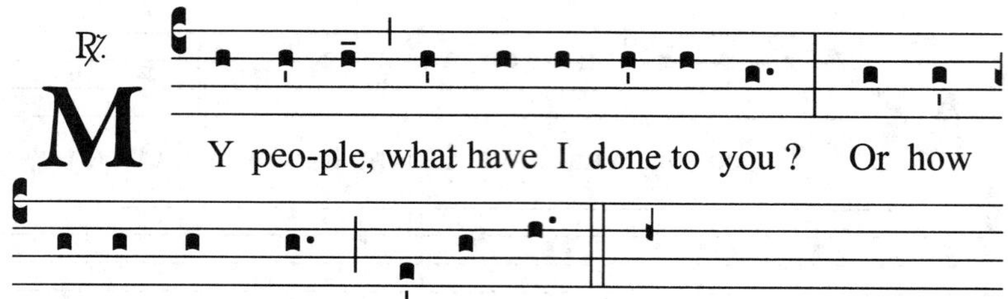

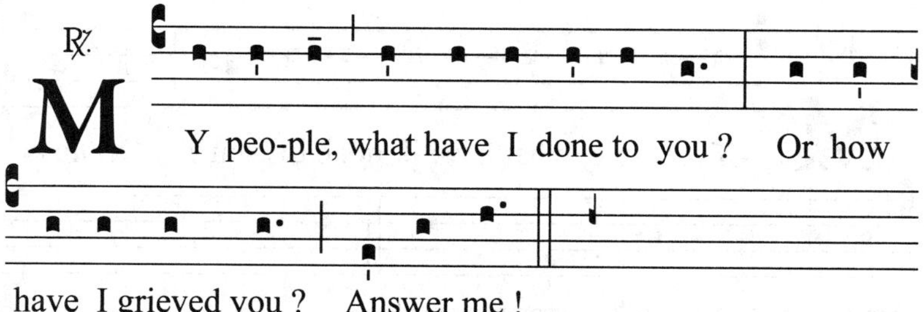

Cantors :

℣.
I struck down for you the kings of the Canaanites,
672

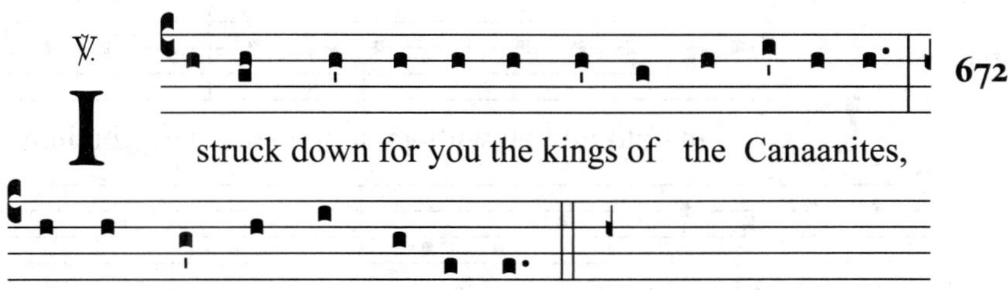

and you struck my head with a reed.

The first and second choirs repeat :

℟.
MY peo-ple, what have I done to you? Or how

have I grieved you? Answer me!

Cantors :

℣.
I put in your hand a roy- al scep-ter, and you
673

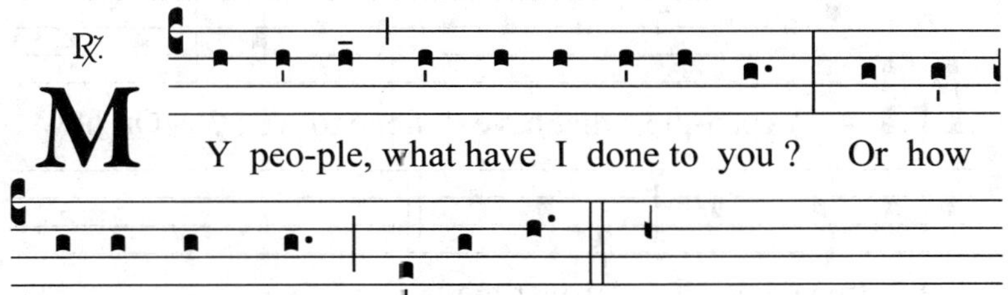

put on my head a crown of thorns.

The first and second choirs repeat :

℟.
MY peo-ple, what have I done to you? Or how

have I grieved you? Answer me!

Cantors :

674 ℣.

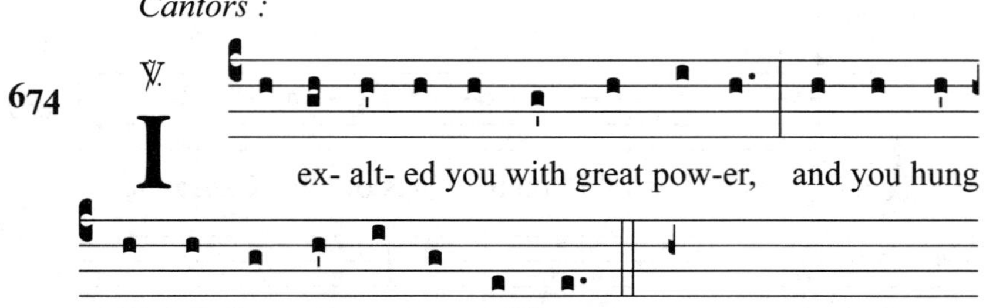
I ex- alt- ed you with great pow-er, and you hung

me on the scaffold of the Cross.

The first and second choirs repeat :

℟.

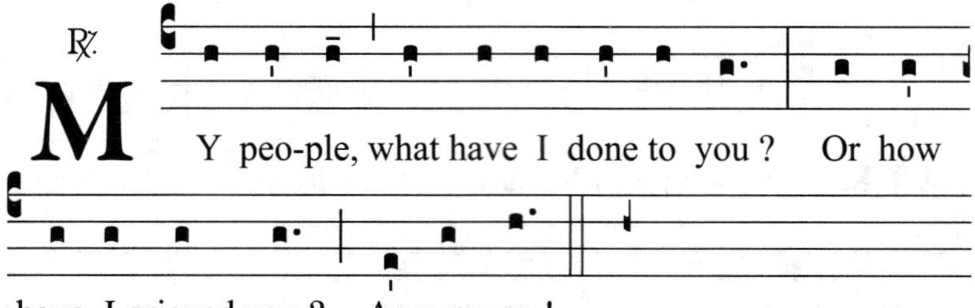
MY peo-ple, what have I done to you ? Or how

have I grieved you ? Answer me !

Hymn

Venantius Fortunatus (6th cent.)

675 1.

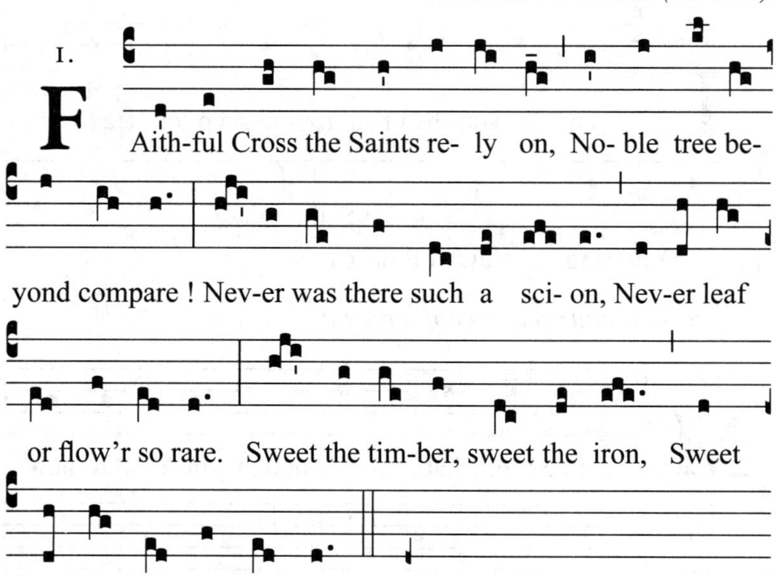
FAith-ful Cross the Saints re- ly on, No- ble tree be-
yond compare ! Nev-er was there such a sci- on, Nev-er leaf
or flow'r so rare. Sweet the tim-ber, sweet the iron, Sweet
the bur- den that they bear !

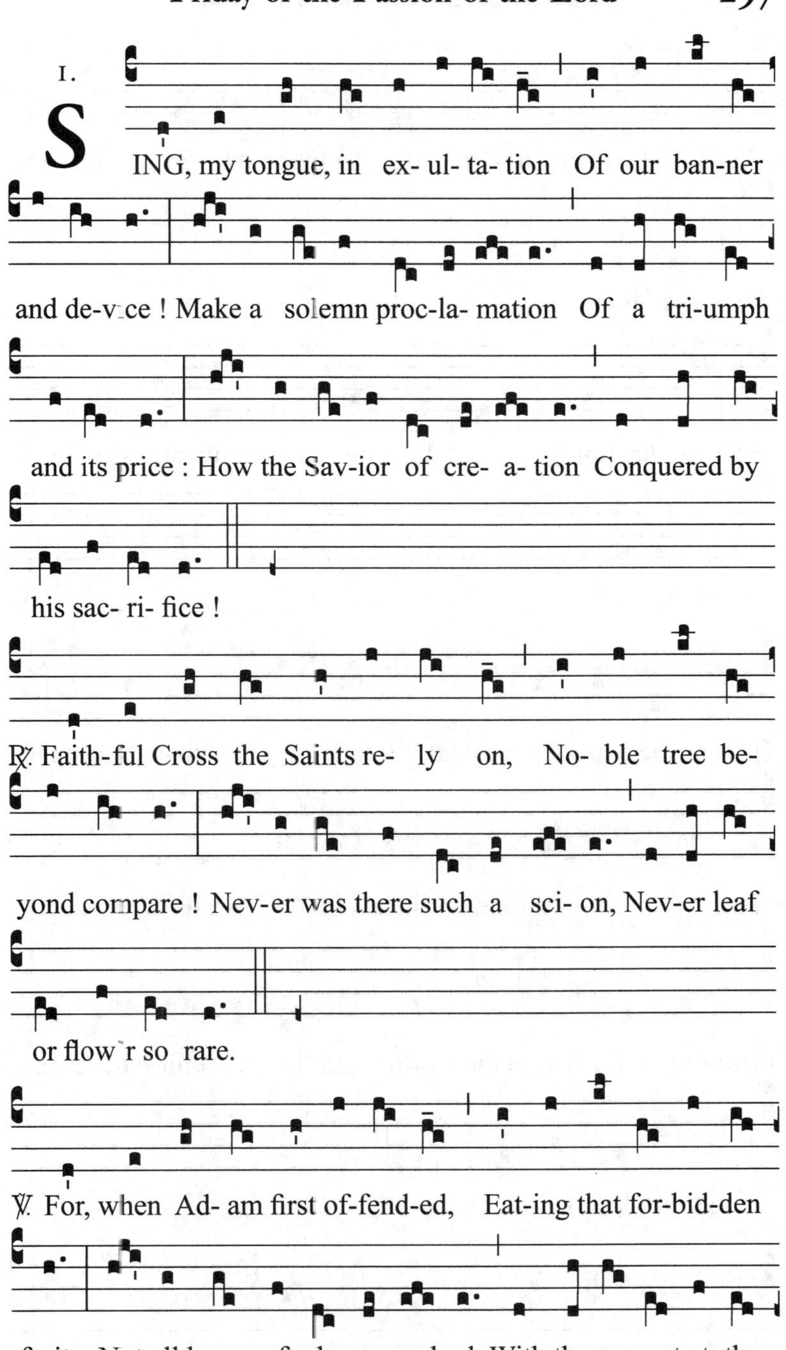
1.
SING, my tongue, in ex- ul- ta- tion Of our ban-ner
and de-vice ! Make a solemn proc-la- mation Of a tri-umph
and its price : How the Sav-ior of cre- a- tion Conquered by
his sac- ri- fice !
℟. Faith-ful Cross the Saints re- ly on, No- ble tree beyond compare ! Nev-er was there such a sci- on, Nev-er leaf
or flow'r so rare.
℣. For, when Ad- am first of-fend-ed, Eat-ing that for-bid-den
fruit, Not all hopes of glo- ry end-ed With the serpent at the

root : Bro-ken na-ture would be mend-ed By a sec-ond
tree and shoot.
* Sweet the tim-ber, sweet the iron, Sweet the bur- den that
they bear !
℣. Thus the tempt-er was out-wit-ted By a wis-dom deeper
still : Rem- e- dy and ail-ment fit- ted, Means to cure and
means to kill ; That the world might be ac- quit-ted, Christ
would do his Fa- ther's will.
℟. Faith-ful Cross the Saints re- ly on, No- ble tree be-

yond compare ! Nev-er was there such a sci- on, Nev-er leaf
or flow'r so rare.
℣. So the Fa-ther, out of pit- y For our self-in-flict-ed doom,
Sent him from the heav'n-ly cit- y When the ho- ly time
had come : He, the Son and the Al-might-y, Took our flesh in
Mar- y's womb.
* Sweet the tim-ber, sweet the iron, Sweet the bur- den that
they bear !
℣. Hear a ti- ny ba- by cry- ing, Found-er of the seas and

strands ; See his vir-gin Moth-er ty- ing Cloth a-round his feet
and hands ; Find him in a man-ger ly- ing Tight-ly wrapped
in swaddling bands !
℟. Faith-ful Cross the Saints re- ly on, No- ble tree beyond compare ! Nev-er was there such a sci- on, Nev-er leaf
or flow'r so rare.
℣. So he came, the long-ex-pect-ed, Not in glo- ry, not to
reign ; On- ly born to be re- ject- ed, Choosing hun-ger, toil
and pain, Till the scaffold was e- rect- ed And the Pas-

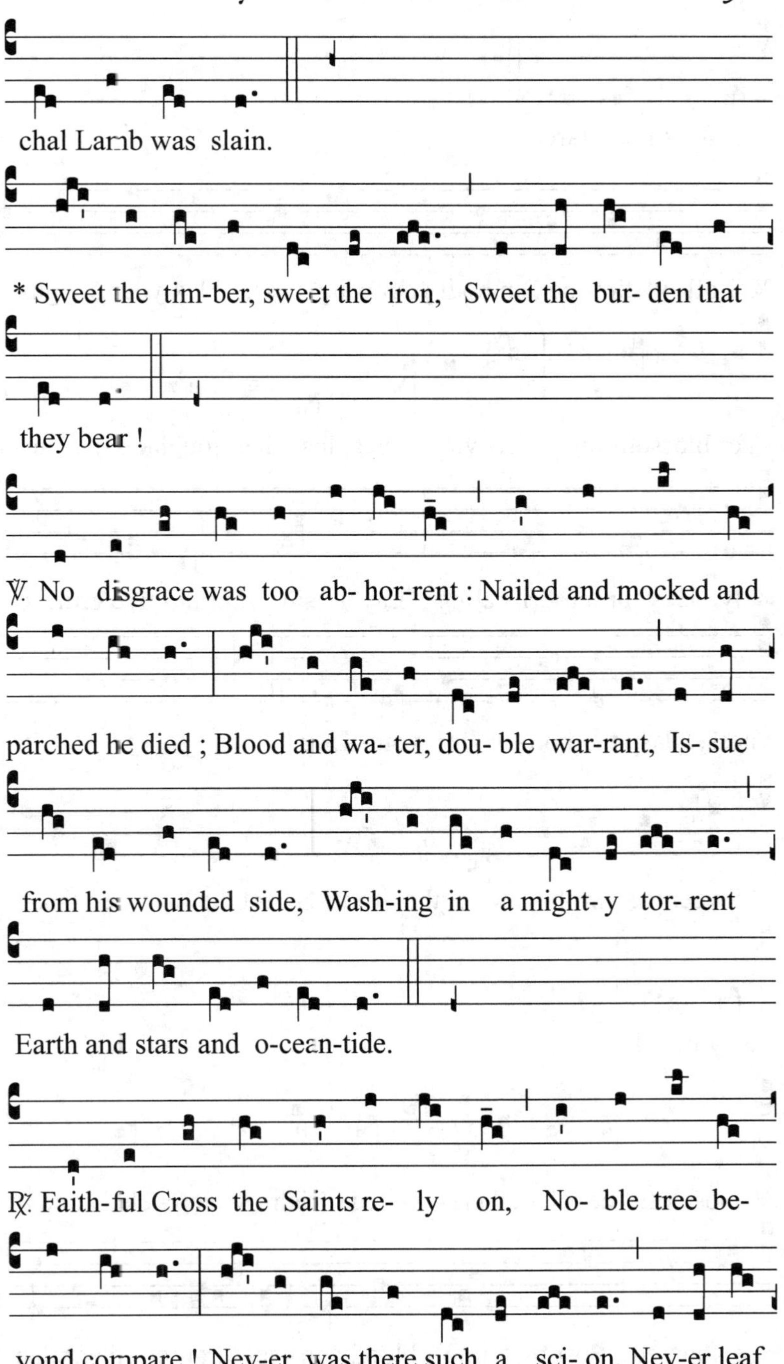
chal Lamb was slain.
* Sweet the tim-ber, sweet the iron, Sweet the bur- den that
they bear !
℣. No disgrace was too ab- hor-rent : Nailed and mocked and
parched he died ; Blood and wa- ter, dou- ble war-rant, Is- sue
from his wounded side, Wash-ing in a might- y tor- rent
Earth and stars and o-cean-tide.
℟. Faith-ful Cross the Saints re- ly on, No- ble tree beyond compare ! Nev-er was there such a sci- on, Nev-er leaf

or flow'r so rare.
℣. Loft- y tim- ber, smooth your roughness, Flex your boughs
for blossom-ing ; Let your fi-bers lose their toughness, Gent-
ly let your ten-drils cling ; Lay a- side your na- tive gruff-
ness, Clasp the bod- y of your King !
* Sweet the tim-ber, sweet the iron, Sweet the bur- den that
they bear !
℣. No-blest tree of all cre- a- ted, Rich- ly jew- eled and
embossed : Post by Lamb's blood con- se- crat- ed ; Spar that

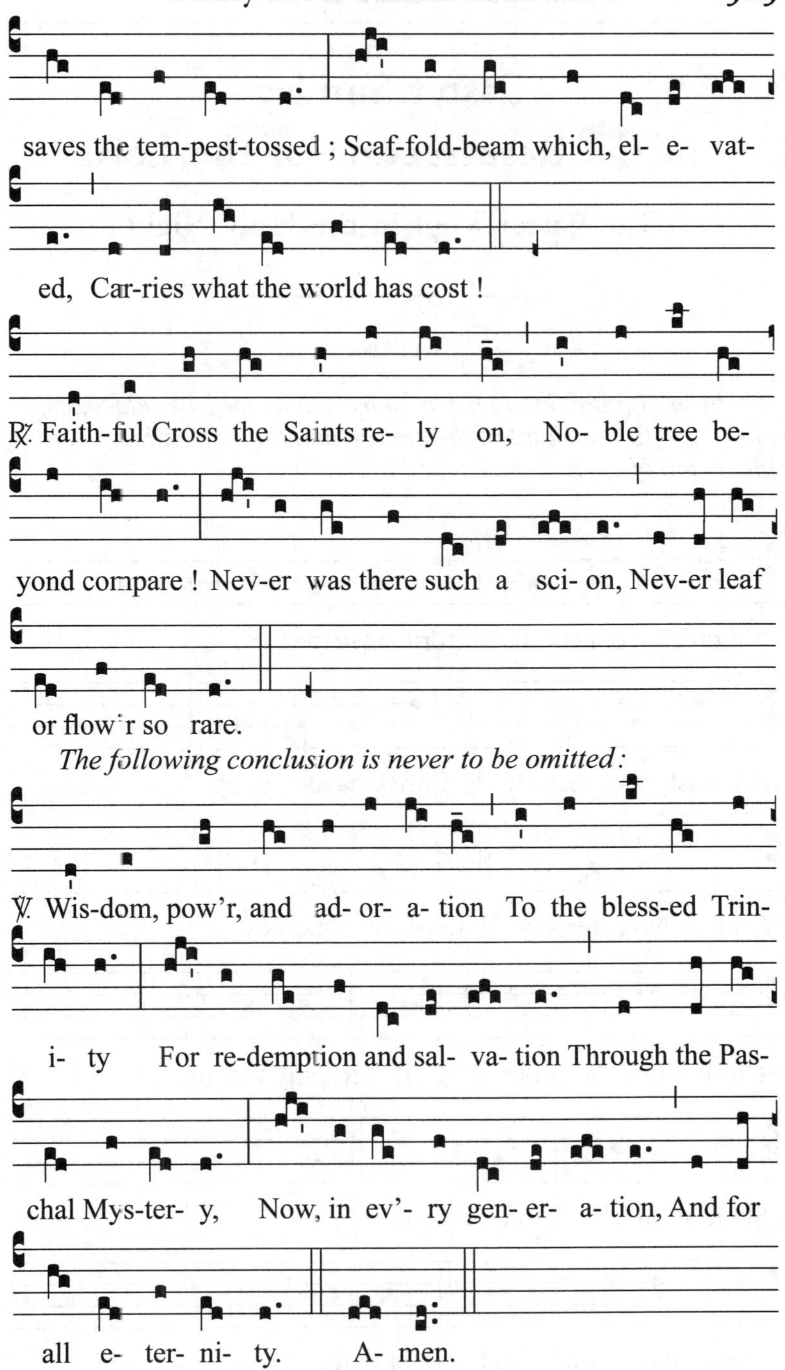
saves the tem-pest-tossed ; Scaf-fold-beam which, el- e- vat-
ed, Car-ries what the world has cost !
℟. Faith-ful Cross the Saints re- ly on, No- ble tree beyond compare ! Nev-er was there such a sci- on, Nev-er leaf
or flow'r so rare.
The following conclusion is never to be omitted:
℣. Wis-dom, pow'r, and ad- or- a- tion To the bless-ed Trin-
i- ty For re-demption and sal- va- tion Through the Paschal Mys-ter- y, Now, in ev'- ry gen- er- a- tion, And for
all e- ter- ni- ty. A- men.

Easter Sunday of the Resurrection of the Lord

The Easter Vigil in the Holy Night

LITANY

In the Litany the names of some Saints may be added, especially the Titular Saint of the church and the Patron Saints of the place and of those to be baptized.

676

℣. Lord, have mer- cy. ℟. Lord, have mer- cy.
℣. Christ, have mer- cy. ℟. Christ, have mer- cy.
℣. Lord, have mer- cy. ℟. Lord, have mer- cy.
Ho- ly Mar-y, Moth-er of **God**, ℟. pray for us.
Saint **Mich**ael, ℟. pray for us.
Ho-ly An-gels of **God**, ℟. pray for us.

Saint John the **Bap**tist, ℟. pray for us.
Saint **Jo**seph, ℟. pray for us.
Saint Peter and Saint **Paul**, ℟. pray for us.
Saint **An**drew, ℟. pray for us.
Saint **John**, ℟. pray for us.

Saint Mar- y **Mag**-*da*-lene, ℟. Pray for us.

Saint **Ste**phen, ℟. pray for us.
Saint Ignatius of **An***ti*och, ℟. pray for us.
Saint **Law**rence, ℟. pray for us.
Saint Perpetua and Saint Fe**lic***i*ty, ℟. pray for us.
Saint **Ag**nes, ℟. pray for us.
Saint **Greg***o*ry, ℟. pray for us.
Saint Au**gus**tine, ℟. pray for us.
Saint Atha**na**sius, ℟. pray for us.
Saint **Ba**sil, ℟. pray for us.
Saint **Ma**rtin, ℟. pray for us.
Saint **Ben**edict, ℟. pray for us.
Saint Francis and Saint **Dom***i*nic, ℟. pray for us.
Saint Francis **Xa**vier, ℟. pray for us.
Saint John Vi**an**ney, ℟. pray for us.
Saint Catherine of Siena, ℟. pray for us.
Saint Teresa of **Je**sus, ℟. pray for us.
All holy men and women, Saints of **God**, ℟. pray for us.

Lord, be mer-ci- ful, ℟. Lord, de-liv- er us, we pray.

From all e- vil, ℟. Lord, de- liv- er us, we pray.

From ev'-ry sin, ℟. Lord, de- liv- er us, we pray.

From ev- er-last-ing death, ℟. Lord, de- liv- er us, we pray.

By your In-car-na-tion, ℟. Lord, de-liv- er us, we pray.

By your Death and Res-ur-rec-tion, ℟. Lord, de- liv- er us, we pray.

By the outpouring of the Ho- ly Spir- it, ℟. Lord, de- liv- er us, we pray.

Be mer-ci-ful to us sin-ners. ℟. Lord, we ask you, hear our prayer.

If there are candidates to be baptized:

Bring these cho-sen ones to new birth through the grace of Baptism, ℟. Lord, we ask you, hear our prayer.

If there is no one to be baptized:

Make this font ho- ly by your grace for the new birth of your

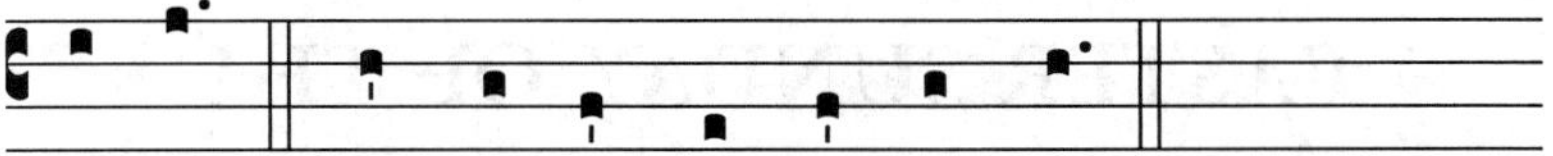

children. ℟. Lord, we ask you, hear our prayer.

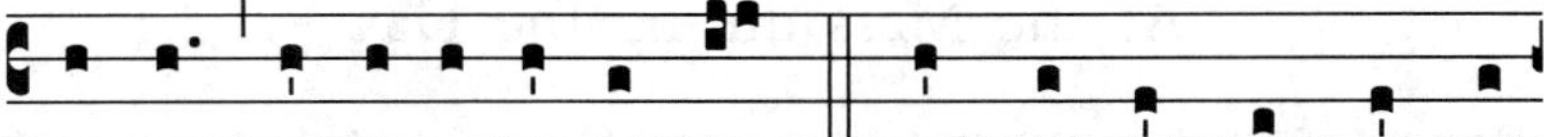

Je- sus, Son of the liv-ing God, ℟. Lord, we ask you, hear our

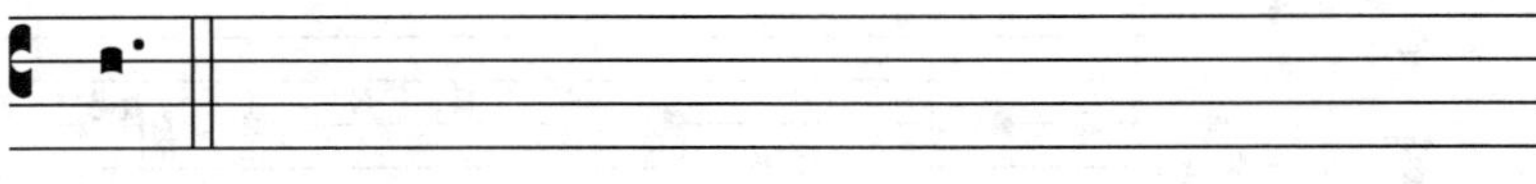

prayer.

Christ, hear us. ℟. Christ, hear us.

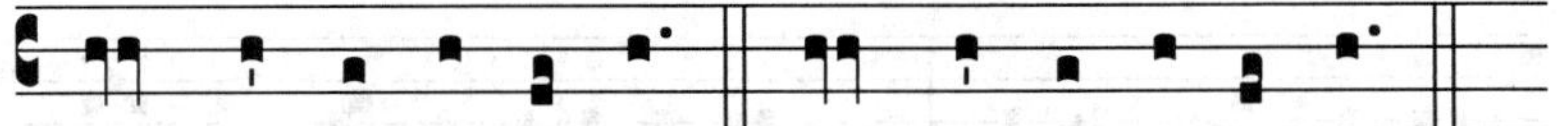

Christ, gracious-ly hear us. ℟. Christ, gracious-ly hear us.

ACCLAMATION

The candle is lifted out of the water, as the people acclaim:

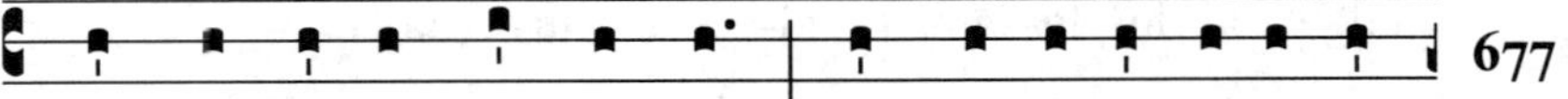 677

Springs of wa-ter, bless the Lord; praise and ex-alt him a-bove

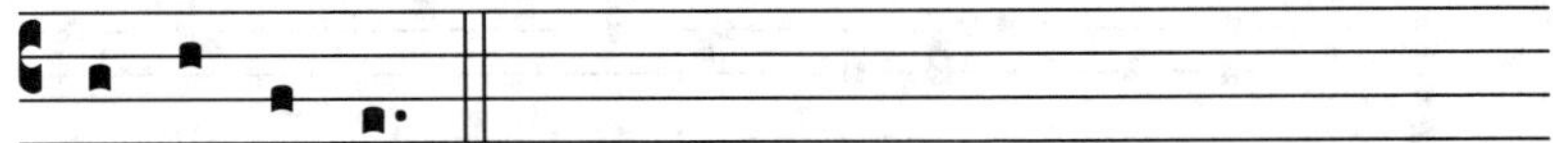

all for ev- er.

SPRINKLING WITH HOLY WATER

I saw water, p. 972.

OFFERTORY

The right hand of the Lord, p. 438.

COMMUNION

Christ our Passover, p. 317.

EASTER SUNDAY OF THE RESURRECTION OF THE LORD

At the Mass during the Day

ENTRANCE ANTIPHON *Resurrexi. Ps* 138:18. 5. 6

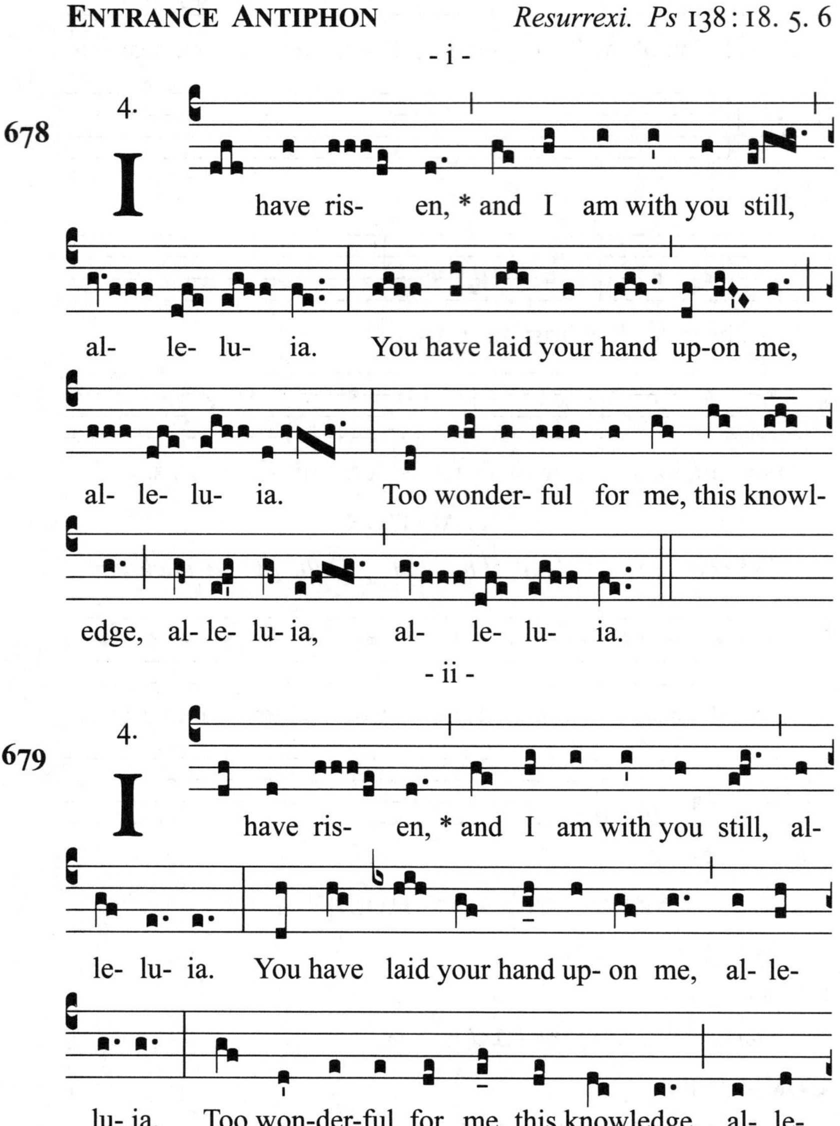

- i -
678
4.
I have ris- en, * and I am with you still,
al- le- lu- ia. You have laid your hand up-on me,
al- le- lu- ia. Too wonder- ful for me, this knowledge, al- le- lu- ia, al- le- lu- ia.
- ii -
679
4.
I have ris- en, * and I am with you still, al-
le- lu- ia. You have laid your hand up- on me, al- le-
lu- ia. Too won-der-ful for me, this knowledge, al- le-

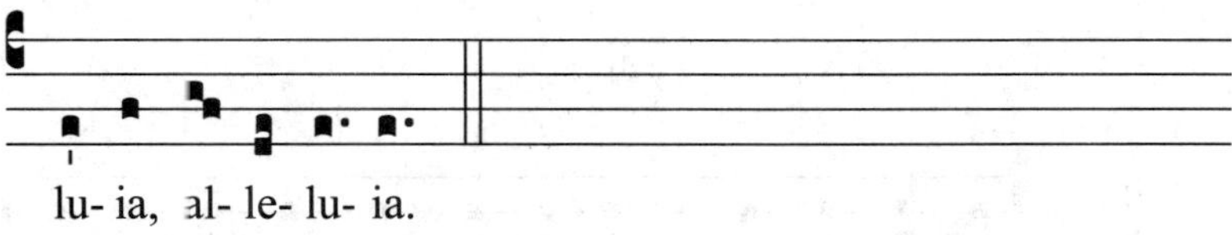
lu- ia, al- le- lu- ia.

VERSES *Domine, probasti me. Ps* 138:1-2

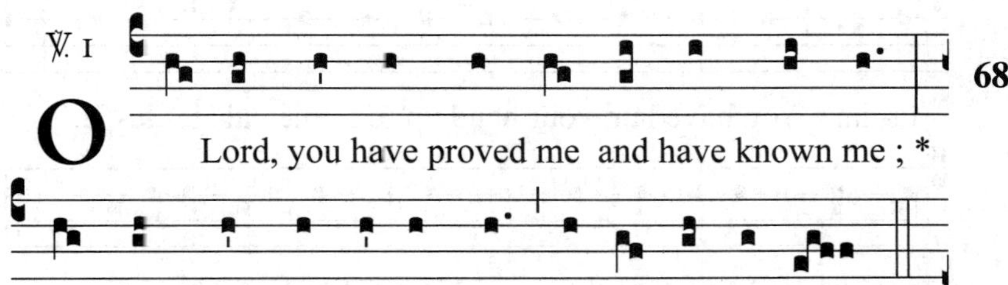
℣. 1
680
O Lord, you have proved me and have known me ; *
you have known my go-ing down, and my ris- ing up. *Ant.*

If another Psalm verse follows before the repetition of the Offertory Antiphon, this ending is used :

and my ris-ing up.

Intellexisti cogitationes meas. Psalm 138:3

℣. 2
681
YOU have un-derstood my thoughts a- far off; * my
paths and my ways you have searched out. *Ant.*

If another Psalm verse follows before the repetition of the Entrance Antiphon, this ending is used :

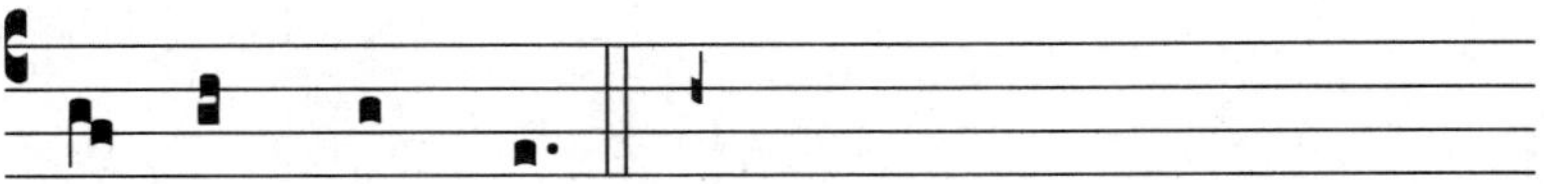
you have searched out.

- iii -

682

4.
I have ris- en, * and I am with you still, al- le-
lu- ia. You have laid your hand up- on me, al- le- lu- ia.
Too wonderful for me, this knowledge, al-le-lu- ia, al-le-lu- ia.

Or:

683

4.
I have ris- en, * and I am with you still, al- le-
lu- ia. You have laid your hand up- on me, al- le- lu- ia.
Too wonderful for me, this knowledge, al-le-lu- ia, al- le-lu- ia.

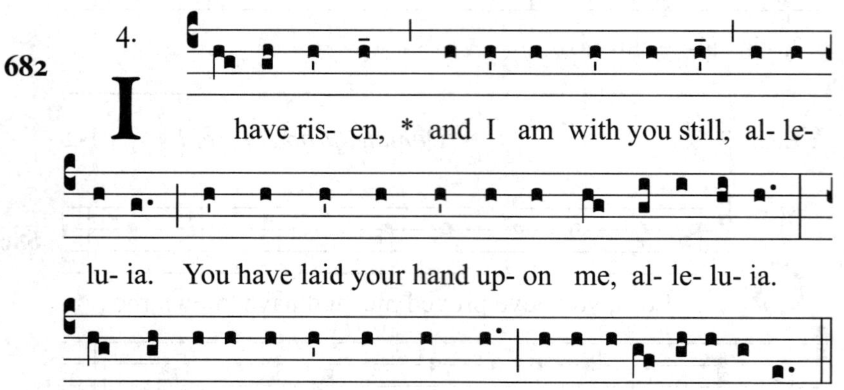

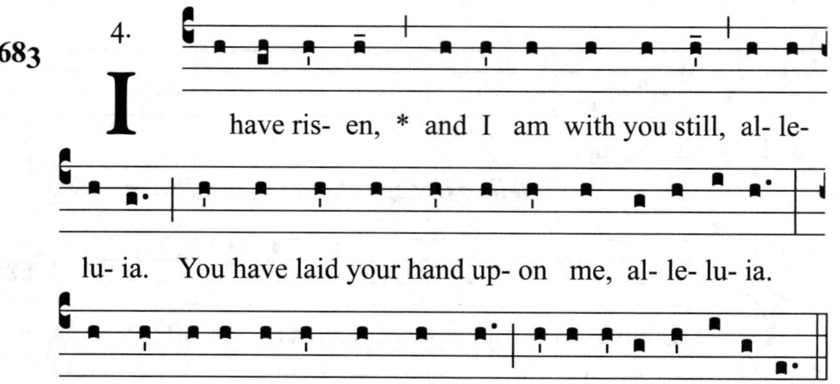

Or:

ENTRANCE ANTIPHON *Surrexit Dominus vere.*
Lk 24:34; *cf. Rv* 1:6

- i -

7.
THE Lord is tru-ly ris- en, * al-le- lu- ia. To him
684
be glo-ry and pow-er for all the ag- es of e- ter- ni- ty,
al-le- lu- ia, al- le- lu- ia, al-le- lu- ia.
- ii -
7.
THE Lord is tru- ly ris- en, * al- le- lu- ia. To him
685
be glo-ry and pow-er for all the ag-es of e- ter- ni- ty, al-
le- lu- ia, al- le- lu- ia, al- le- lu- ia.

VERSES

Quoniam occisus es. Rv 5:9

686

℣. 1
FOR you were slain; and have redeemed us to God,
in your Blood, * out of ev'-ry tribe and tongue and peo-ple
and na- tion.
Dignus es agnus. Rv 5:12
℣. 2
687
THE Lamb that was slain is worthy to receive pow-er
and di-vin- i- ty and wis-dom * and strength and hon-or and
glo- ry and bless- ing.
Beati qui lavant stolas suas. Rv 22:22
℣. 3
688
BLess-ed are they that wash their robes in the Blood of
the Lamb, * that they may have a right to the tree of life and
may en- ter in by the gates in- to the cit- y.

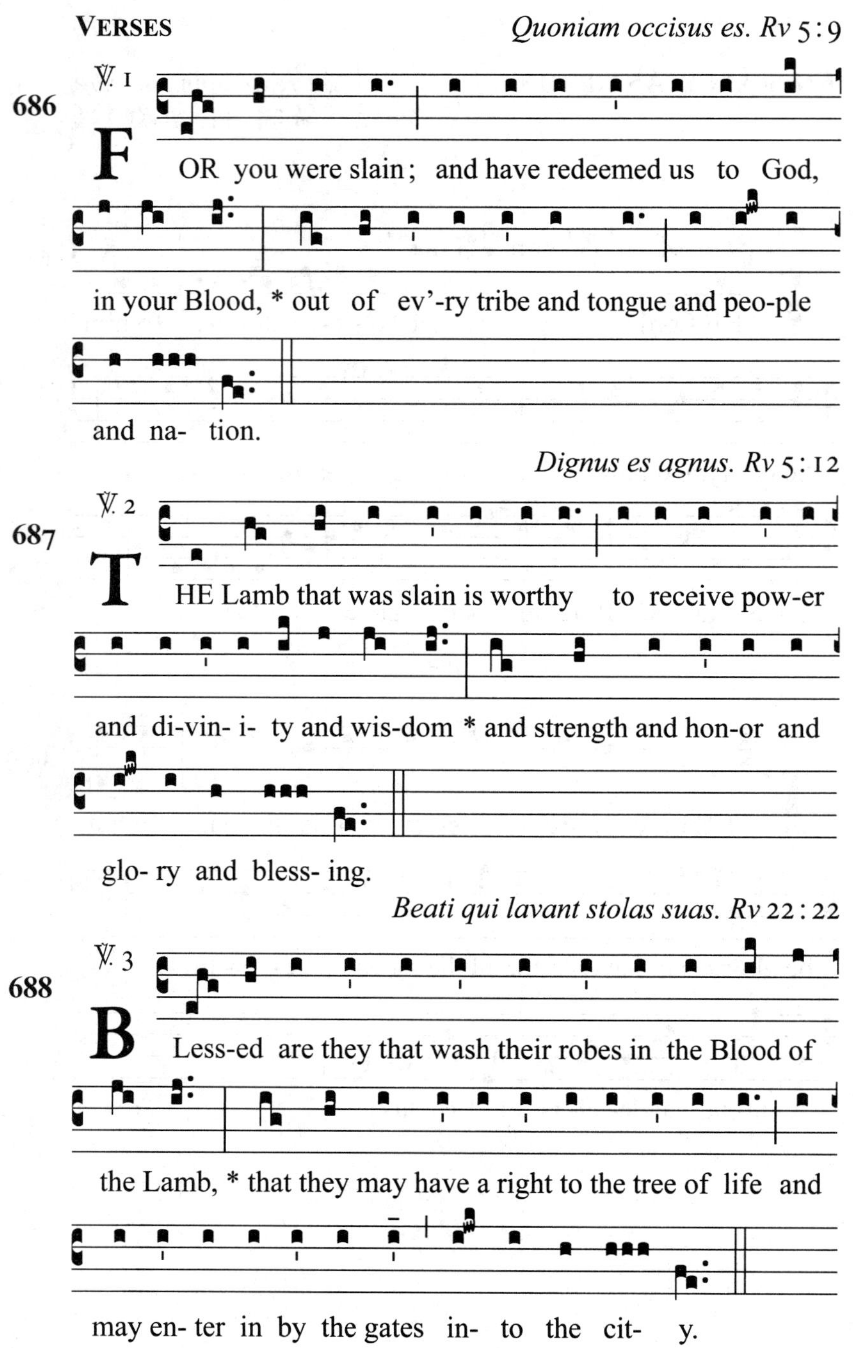

- iii -

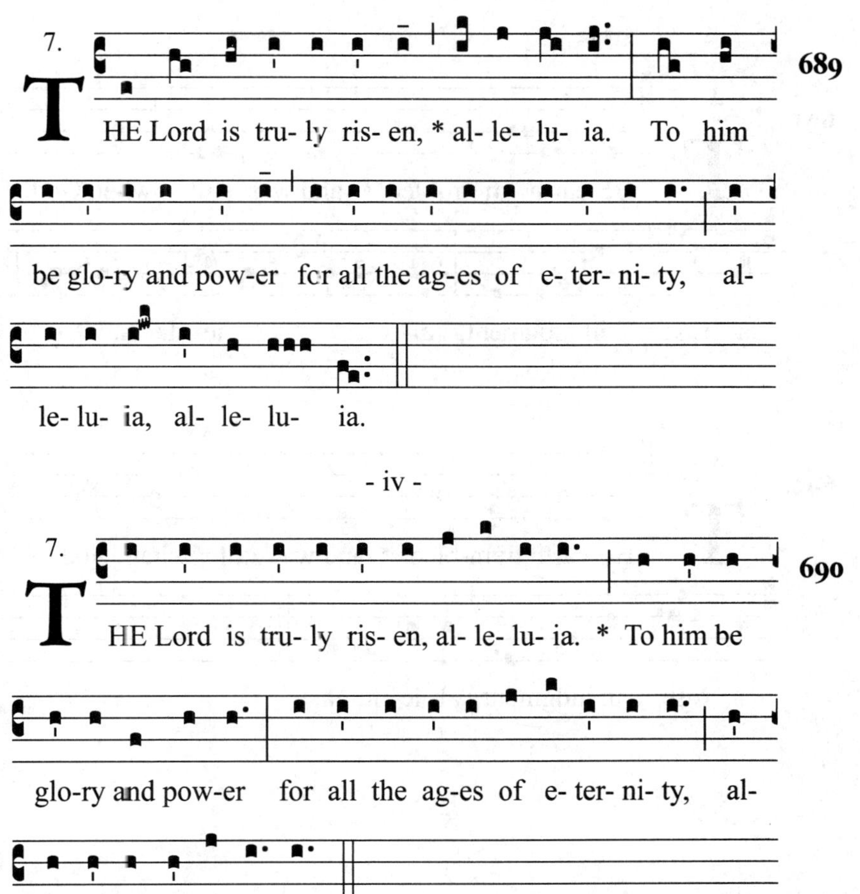
7.
689
THE Lord is tru- ly ris- en, * al- le- lu- ia. To him
be glo-ry and pow-er for all the ag-es of e- ter- ni- ty, al-
le- lu- ia, al- le- lu- ia.
- iv -
7.
690
THE Lord is tru- ly ris- en, al- le- lu- ia. * To him be
glo-ry and pow-er for all the ag-es of e- ter- ni- ty, al-
le- lu- ia, al- le- lu- ia.

OFFERTORY ANTIPHON *Ps* 75:9. 10

- i -

691 4.

THE earth trem-bled * and was still when God a- rose in judgment, al- le- lu- ia.

- ii -

692 4.

THE earth trem-bled * and was still when God a- rose in judgment, al- le- lu- ia.

VERSES *Notus in Iudea Deus. Ps* 75 : 2-3

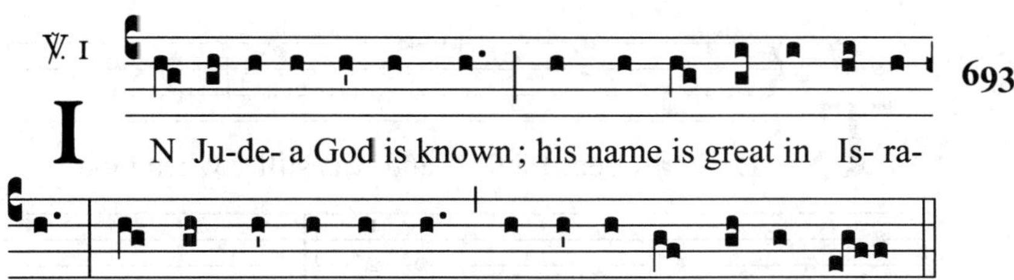
℣. 1
693
IN Ju-de- a God is known; his name is great in Is- ra-

el. * And his place is in peace, and his a-bode in Si- on. *Ant.*

If another Psalm verse follows before the repetition of the Offertory Antiphon, this ending is used :

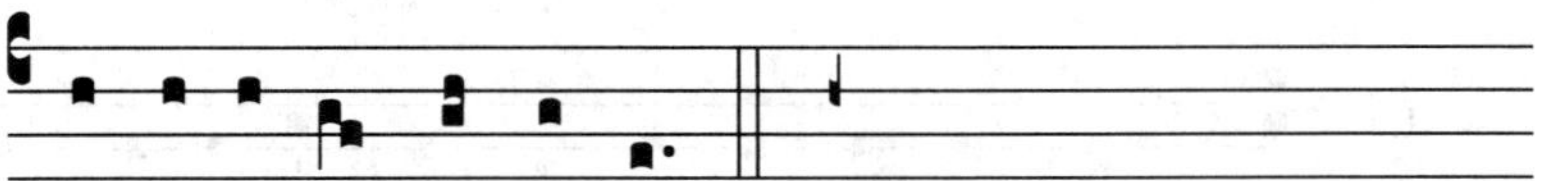

and his a-bode in Si- on.

Vovete, et redite Domino Deo vestro. Ps 75 : 12

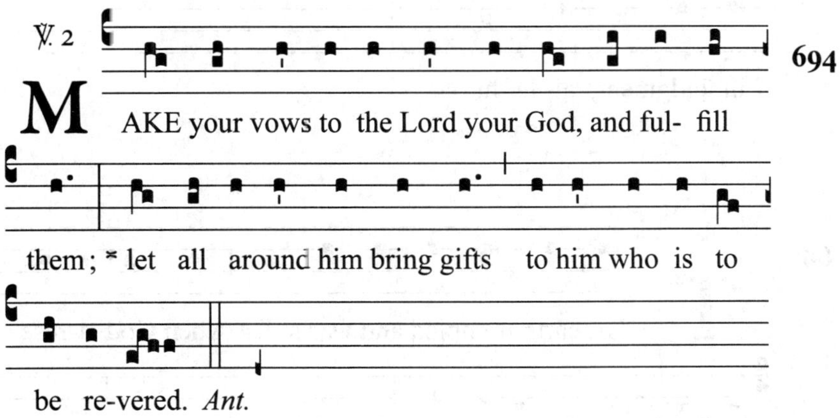
℣. 2
694
MAKE your vows to the Lord your God, and ful- fill
them; * let all around him bring gifts to him who is to
be re-vered. *Ant.*

Or:

695

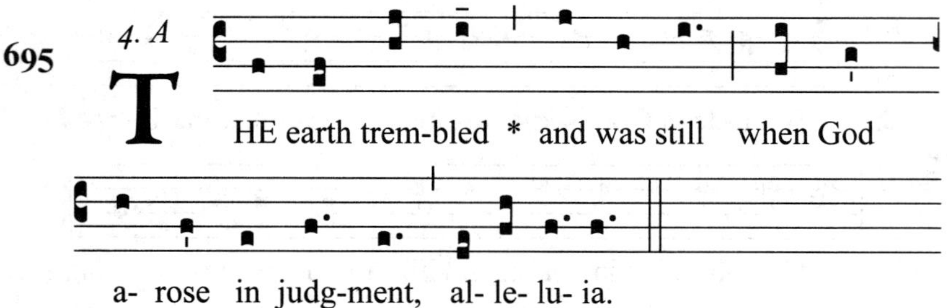
4. A
THE earth trem-bled * and was still when God
a- rose in judg-ment, al- le- lu- ia.

- iii -

696

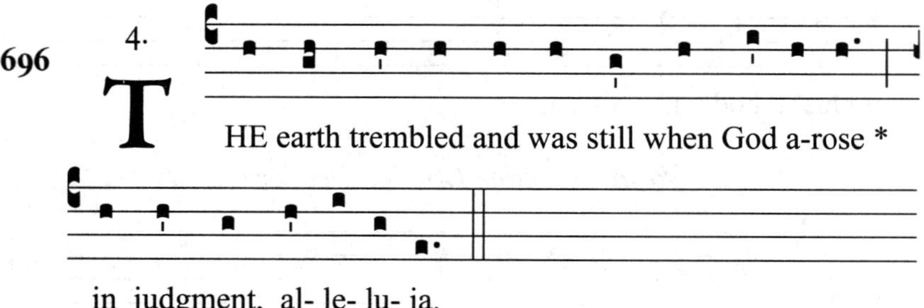
4.
THE earth trembled and was still when God a-rose *
in judgment, al- le- lu- ia.

- iv -

697

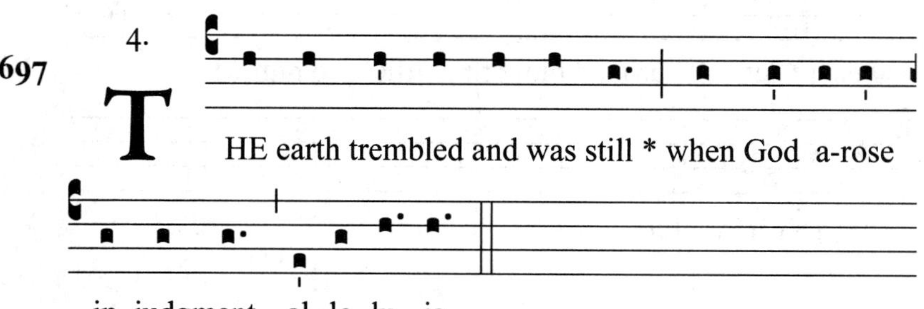
4.
THE earth trembled and was still * when God a-rose
in judgment, al- le- lu- ia.

COMMUNION ANTIPHON *Pascha nostrum.* 1 *Cor* 5:7. 8

- i -

6.
698
CHrist our Pass- c- ver * has been sac-ri- ficed, al-le-
lu- ia ; there- fore let us keep the feast with the
un-leavened bread of pu- ri- ty and truth, al- le-
lu- ia, al- le- lu- ia, al- le- lu- ia.

- ii -

6.
699
CHrist our Pass- o- ver * has been sac- ri-ficed, al- le-
lu- ia : therefore let us keep the feast with the unleavened
bread of pu- ri- ty and truth, al- le- lu- ia.

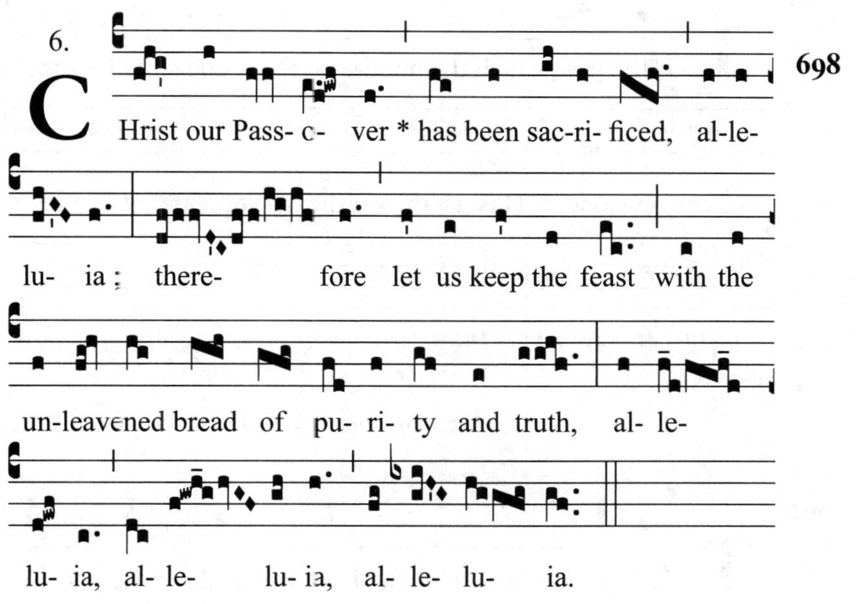

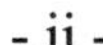

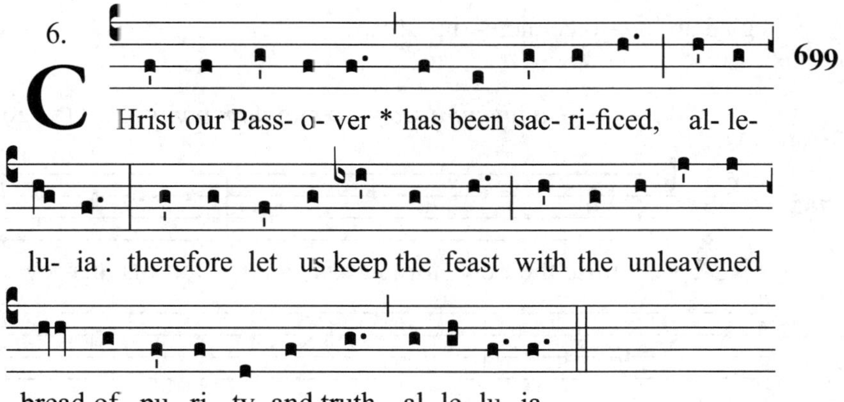

VERSES *Lapidem quem reprobaverunt ædificantes. Ps* 117:22

700
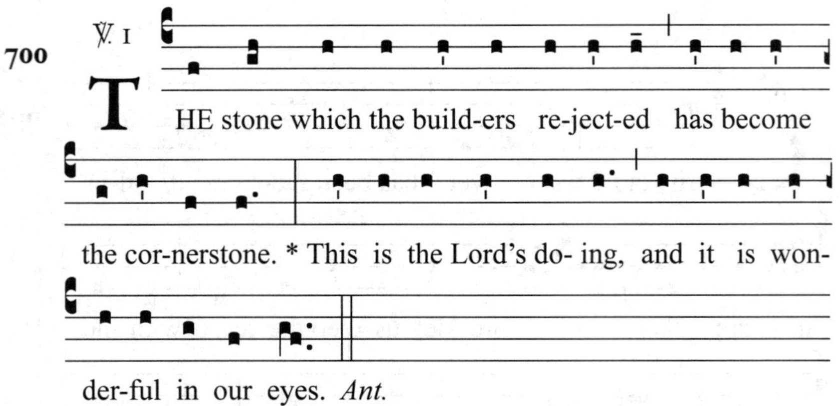
℣. 1
THE stone which the build-ers re-ject-ed has become
the cor-nerstone. * This is the Lord's do- ing, and it is won-
der-ful in our eyes. Ant.

Hæc dies quam fecit Dominus. Ps 117:24

701
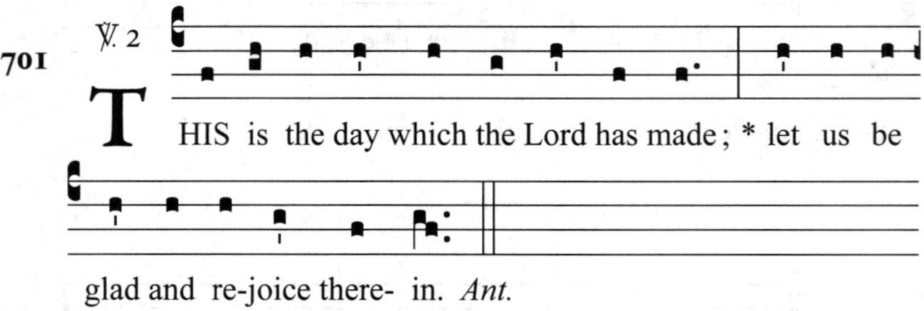
℣. 2
THIS is the day which the Lord has made; * let us be
glad and re-joice there- in. Ant.

Confitemini Domino quoniam bonus. Ps 117:29

702
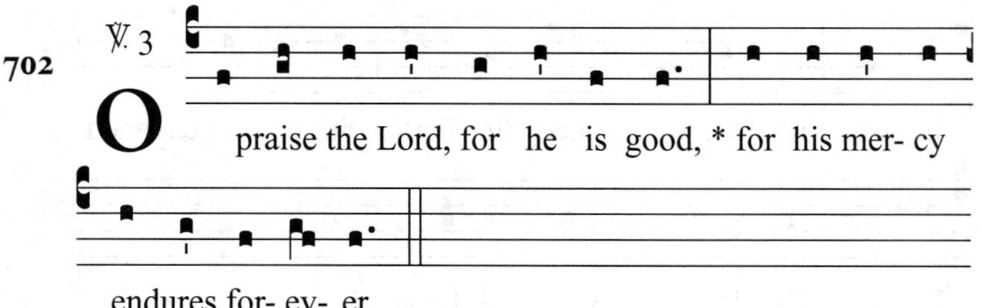
℣. 3
O praise the Lord, for he is good, * for his mer- cy
endures for- ev- er.

- iii -
6.
703
CHrist our Pass- o- ver has been sac-ri-ficed, * al- le-
lu- ia ; therefore let us keep the feast with the un-leavened bread of pu- ri- ty and truth, al- le- lu- ia, al- le-
lu- ia.
- iv -
6.
704
CHrist our Pass- o- ver has been sac-ri-ficed, * al- le-
lu- ia ; therefore let us keep the feast with the un-leavened bread of pur- i- ty and truth, al- le- lu- ia, al- le-
lu- ia.

SECOND SUNDAY OF EASTER
(*or* of Divine Mercy)

ENTRANCE ANTIPHON *Quasimodo geniti infantes.*
1 *Pt* 2:2

- i -
705
6.
LIKE newborn in- fants, * al- le- lu- ia, you must
long for the pure, spir-i-tual milk, that in him you may grow
to sal- va- tion, al-le- lu- ia, al- le- lu- ia, al-le-
lu- ia.
- ii -
706
6.
LIKE newborn in-fants, * al- le- lu- ia, you must
long for the pure, spir-i-tual milk, that in him you may grow
to sal-va-tion, al- le- lu- ia, al- le- lu- ia.

VERSES *Exsultate Deo, adiutori nostro.* Ps 80 : 1

Use the 6 g *ending for* (i), *the* 6 F *ending for* (ii, iii and iv.), or when another psalm verse follows immediately.

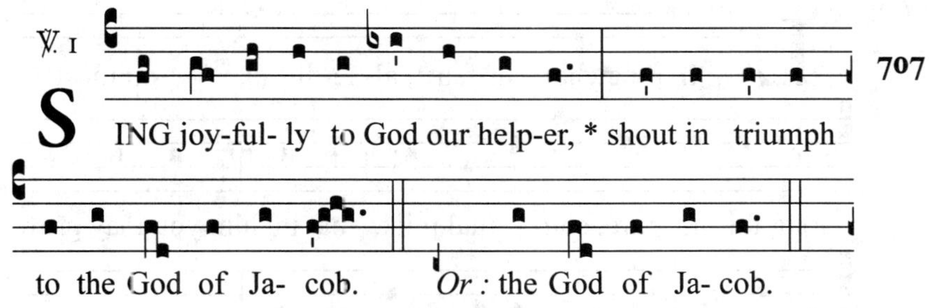
℣. 1
707
SING joy-ful- ly to God our help-er, * shout in triumph
to the God of Ja- cob. *Or :* the God of Ja- cob.

Summite psalmum, et date tympanum. Ps 80 : 3

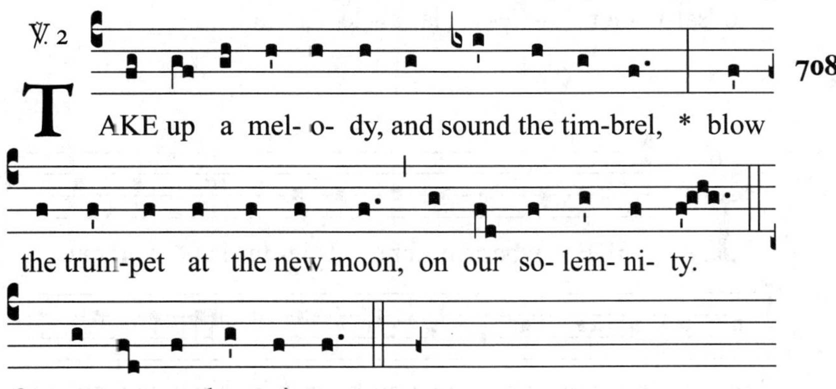
℣. 2
708
TAKE up a mel- o- dy, and sound the tim-brel, * blow
the trum-pet at the new moon, on our so- lem- ni- ty.
Or : on our so- lem- ni- ty.

Et cibavit eos ex adipe frumenti. Ps 80 : 17

℣. 3
709
AND with the fin- est wheat he fed them * and with
hon-ey out of the rock he filled them.
Or : he filled them.

- iii -

710

6.
LIKE newborn in-fants, al- le- lu- ia, * you must
long for the pure, spir- i- tual milk, that in him you may grow
to sal-va-tion, al- le- lu- ia, al- le- lu- ia.

- iv -

711

6.
LIKE newborn in-fants, al- le- lu- ia, * you must
long for the pure, spir- i- tual milk, that in him you may grow
to sal- va-tion, al- le- lu- ia, al- le- lu- ia.

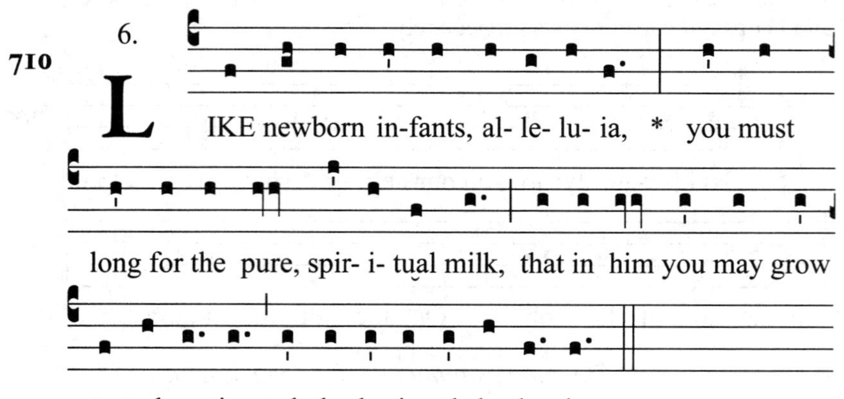

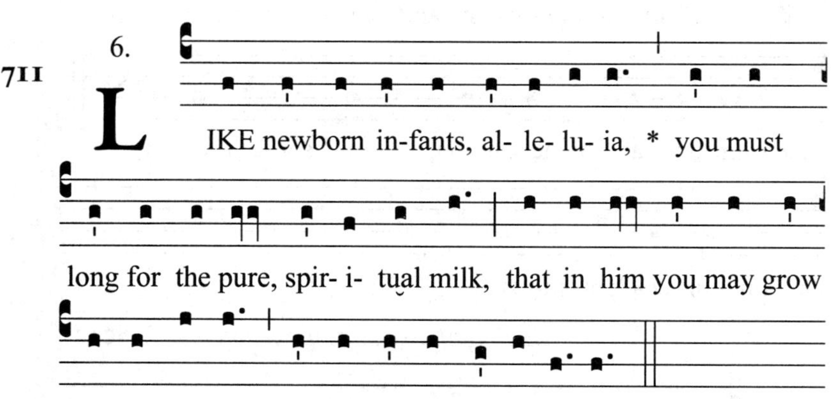

Or :

Accipite iucunditatem.
4 *Esdr* 2 : 36-37

- i -

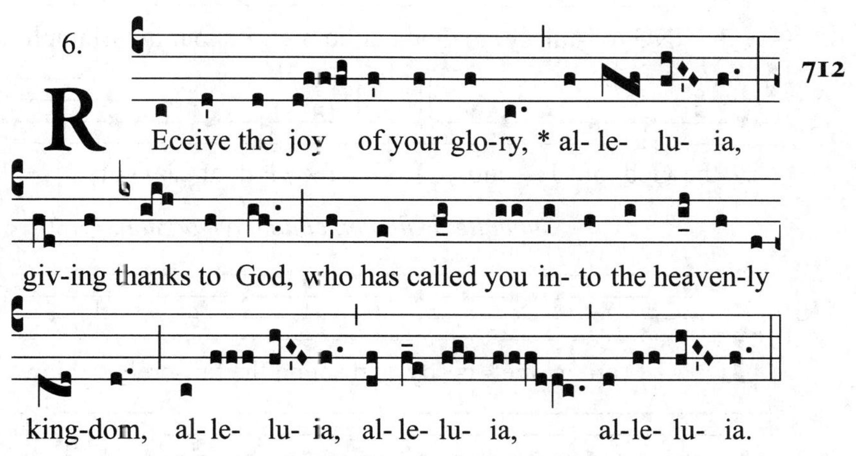
6.
712
R Eceive the joy of your glo-ry, * al- le- lu- ia,
giv-ing thanks to God, who has called you in- to the heaven-ly
king-dom, al- le- lu- ia, al- le- lu- ia, al- le- lu- ia.

- ii -

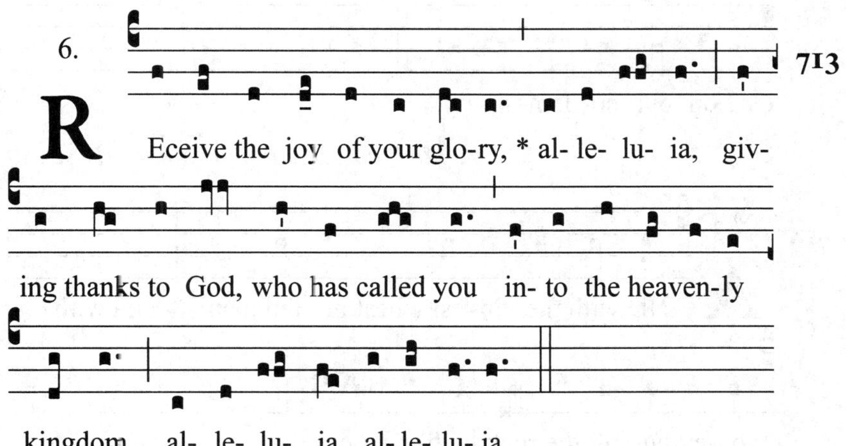
6.
713
R Eceive the joy of your glo-ry, * al- le- lu- ia, giv-
ing thanks to God, who has called you in- to the heaven-ly
kingdom, al- le- lu- ia, al- le- lu- ia.

VERSES *Exsultate Deo, adiutori nostro.* Ps 80 : 1

Use the 6 g *ending for* (i), *the* 6 F *ending for* (ii, iii and iv.), or when another psalm verse follows immediately.

714

℣. 1
SING joy-ful- ly to God our help-er, * shout in triumph
to the God of Ja- cob. *Or :* the God of Ja- cob.

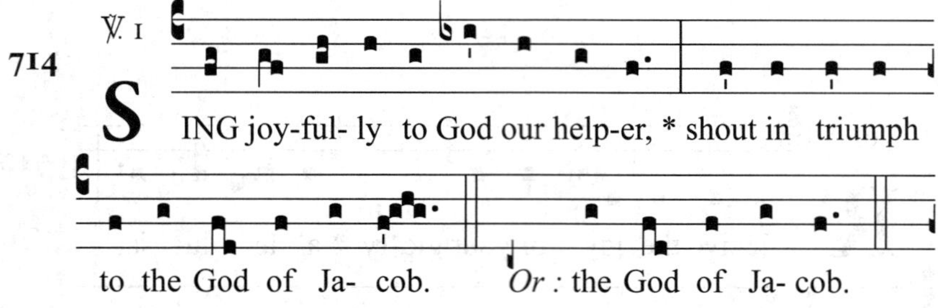

Summite psalmum, et date tympanum. Ps 80 : 3

715

℣. 2
TAKE up a mel- o- dy, and sound the tim-brel, * blow
the trum-pet at the new moon, on our so- lem- ni- ty.
Or : on our so- lem- ni- ty.

Et cibavit eos ex adipe frumenti. Ps 80 : 17

716

℣. 3
AND with the fin- est wheat he fed them * and with
hon-ey out of the rock he filled them.
Or : he filled them.

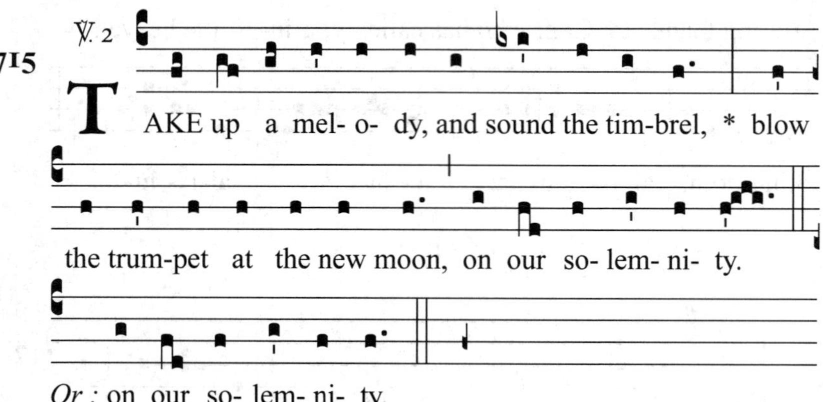

- iii -

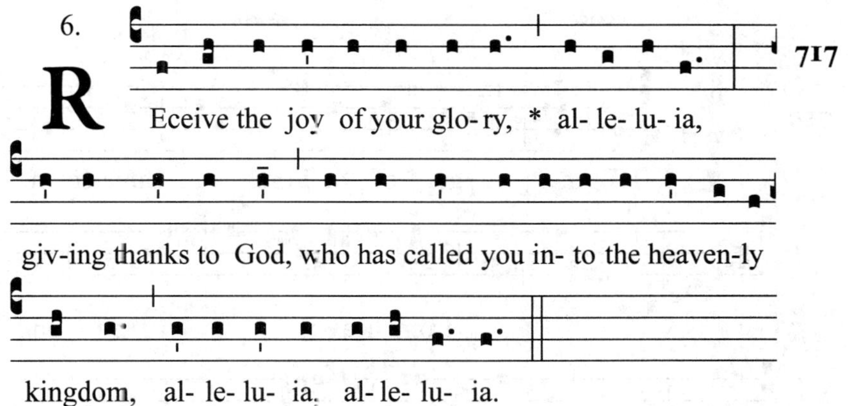
6.
R
Eceive the joy of your glo- ry, * al- le- lu- ia,
717
giv-ing thanks to God, who has called you in- to the heaven-ly
kingdom, al- le- lu- ia. al- le- lu- ia.

- iv -

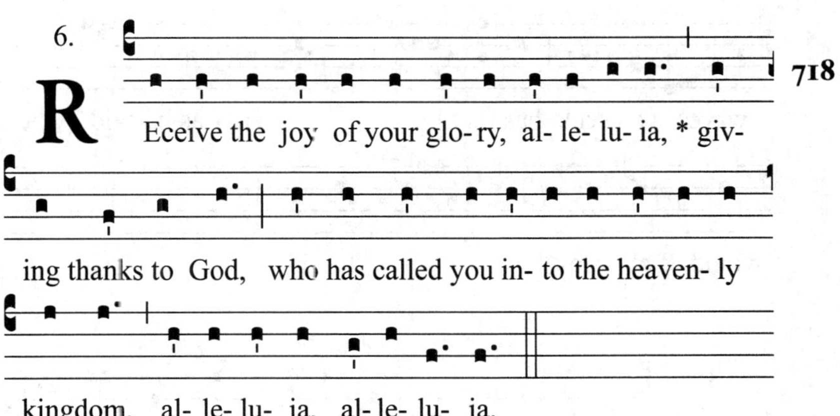
6.
R
Eceive the joy of your glo- ry, al- le- lu- ia, * giv-
718
ing thanks to God, who has called you in- to the heaven- ly
kingdom, al- le- lu- ia. al- le- lu- ia.

Offertory Antiphon *Angelus Domini descendit.*
Mt 28:2. 5. 6

- i -
719
8.
THE An- gel * of the Lord came down
from heav- en and
said to the wom- en : “ The One
whom you seek has ris- en as he said he
would, ” al- le- lu- ia.
- ii -
8.
THE An-gel of the Lord * came down from heaven
720
and said to the wom-en : “ The One whom you seek has ris-en,
as he said he would, ” al- le- lu- ia, al- le- lu- ia.

VERSES *Lapidem quem reprobaverunt ædificantes.* *Ps* 117:22

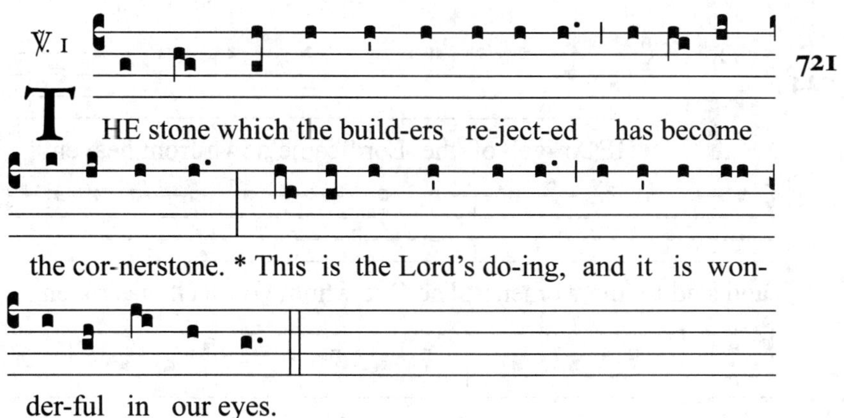
℣. 1
THE stone which the build-ers re-ject-ed has become
721
the cor-nerstone. * This is the Lord's do-ing, and it is won-
der-ful in our eyes.

Hæc dies quam fecit Dominus. *Ps* 117:24

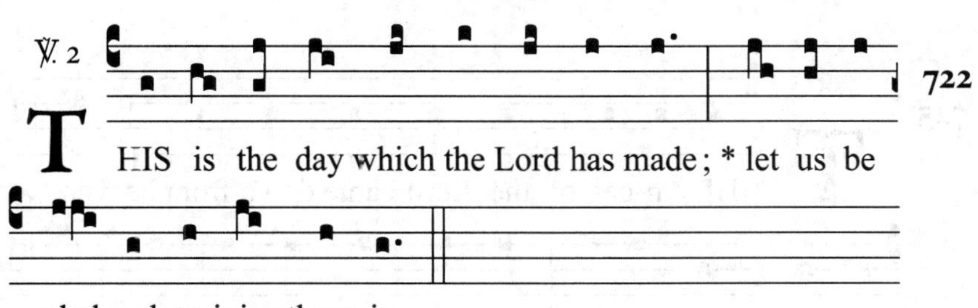
℣. 2
THIS is the day which the Lord has made; * let us be
722
glad and re-joice there-in.

Deus meus es tu, et confitebor tibi. *Ps* 117:28

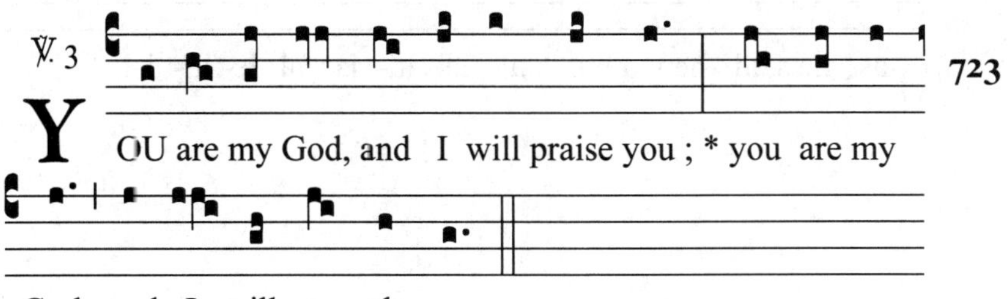
℣. 3
YOU are my God, and I will praise you ; * you are my
723
God, and I will ex- alt you.

- iii -

724

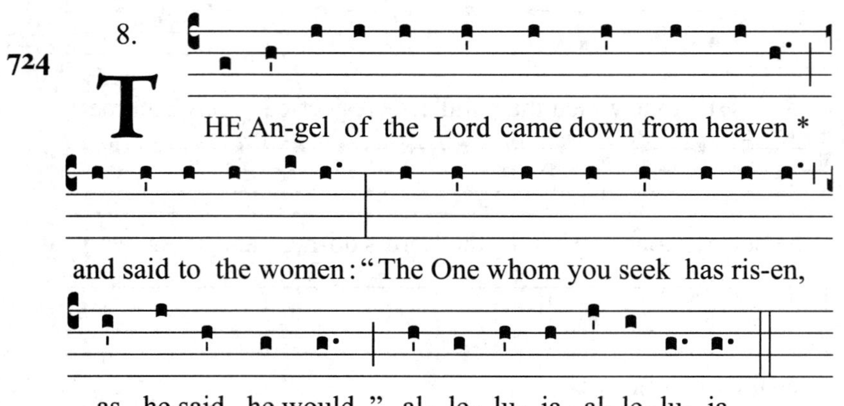

- iv -

725

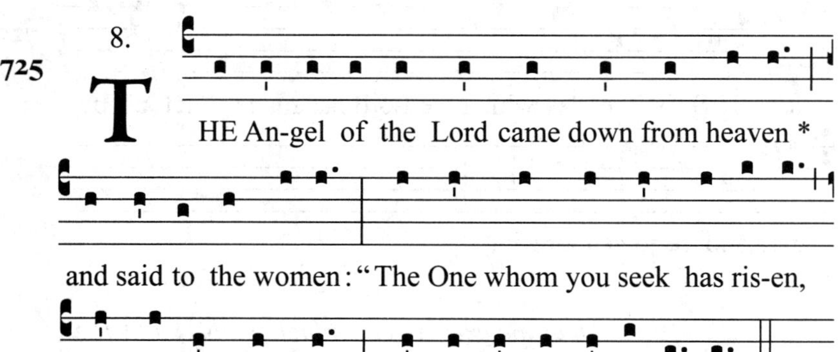

COMMUNION ANTIPHON *Mitte manum tuam.*
Jn 20:27

- i -

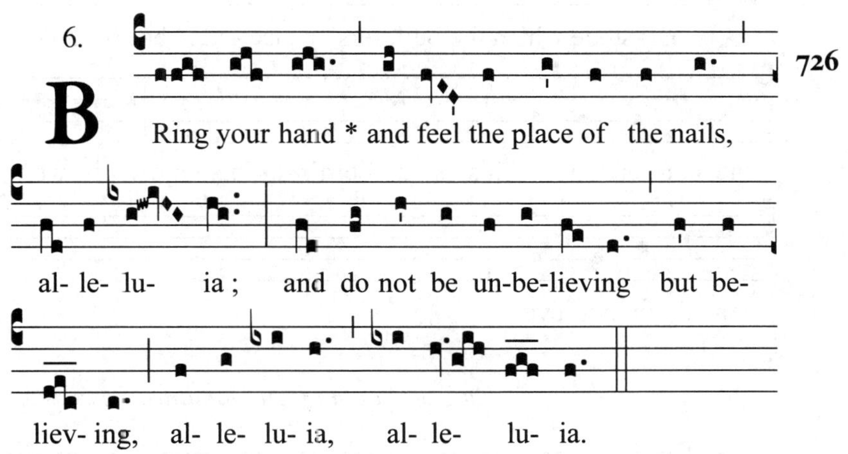
6.
726
BRing your hand * and feel the place of the nails,
al- le- lu- ia ; and do not be un-be-lieving but be-
liev- ing, al- le- lu- ia, al- le- lu- ia.

- ii -

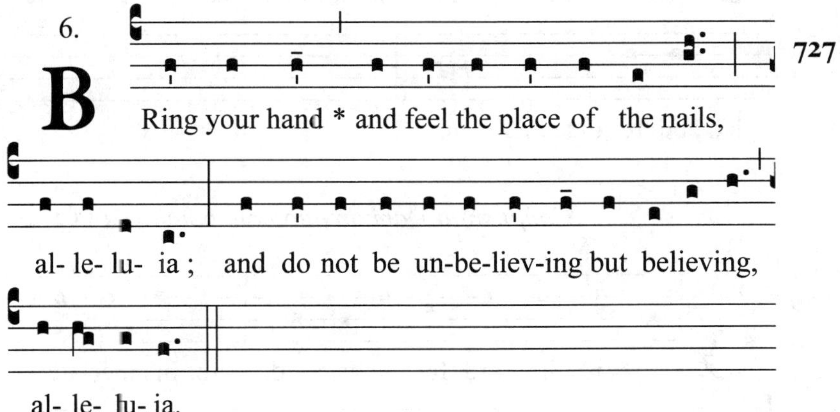
6.
727
BRing your hand * and feel the place of the nails,
al- le- lu- ia ; and do not be un-be-liev-ing but believing,
al- le- lu- ia.

VERSES *Lapidem quem reprobaverunt ædificantes. Ps* 117:22

728 ℣. 1 THE stone which the build-ers re-ject-ed has become the cor-nerstone. * This is the Lord's do-ing, and it is won-der-ful in our eyes.

Hæc dies quam fecit Dominus. Ps 117:24

729 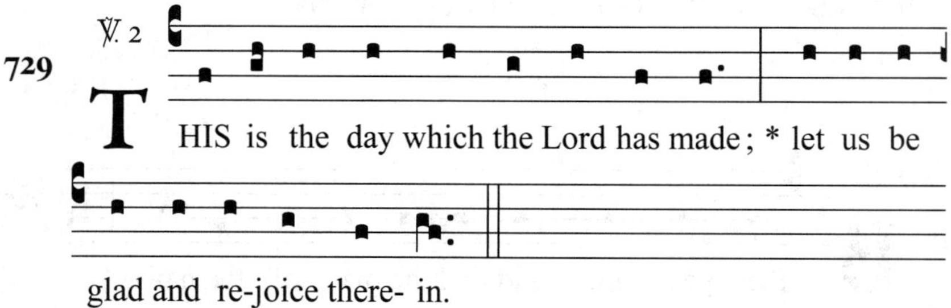
℣. 2
THIS is the day which the Lord has made; * let us be
glad and re-joice there- in.

Confitemini Domino quoniam bonus. Ps 117:29

730 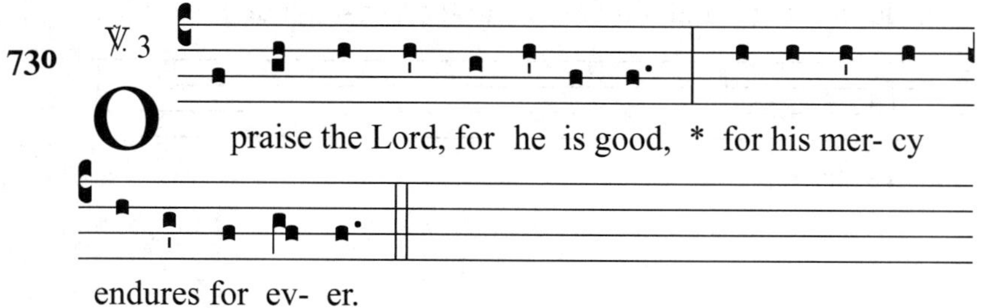
℣. 3
O praise the Lord, for he is good, * for his mer- cy
endures for ev- er.

- iii -

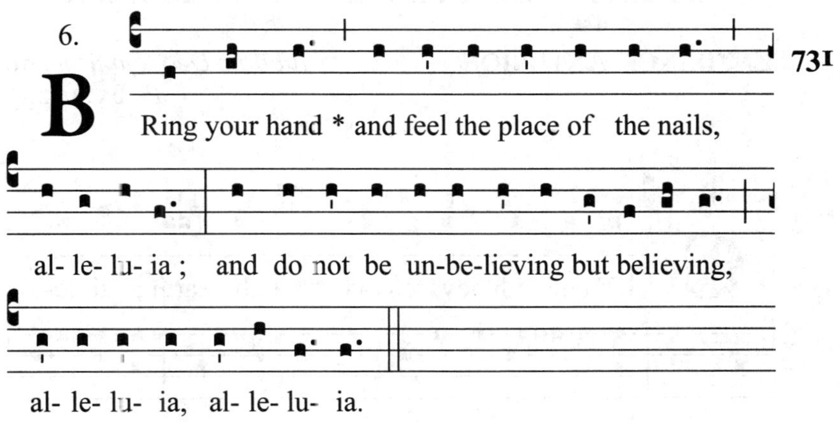
6.
731
BRing your hand * and feel the place of the nails,
al- le- lu- ia ; and do not be un-be-lieving but believing,
al- le- lu- ia, al- le- lu- ia.

- iv -

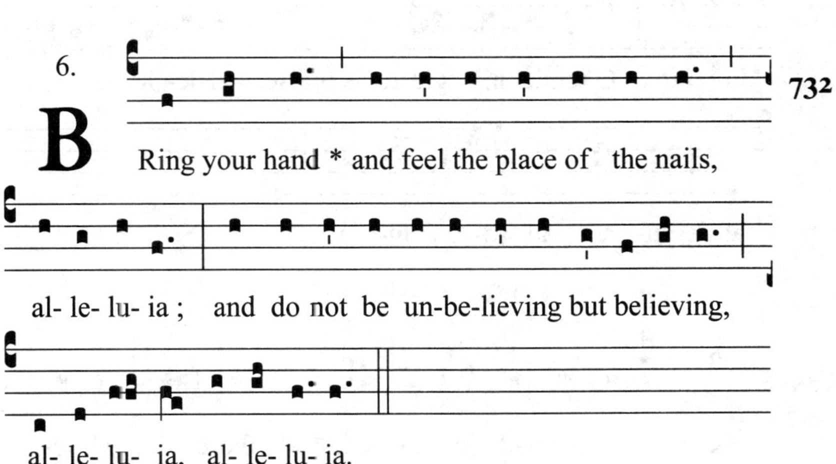
6.
732
BRing your hand * and feel the place of the nails,
al- le- lu- ia ; and do not be un-be-lieving but believing,
al- le- lu- ia, al- le- lu- ia.

THIRD SUNDAY OF EASTER

ENTRANCE ANTIPHON *Iubilate Deo, omnis terra.*
Ps 65:1. 2. 3

- i -

733 8. CRY out with joy to God, * all the earth; al- le- lu- ia; O sing to the glo- ry of his name, al-le- lu- ia. O render him glo-rious praise, al-le- lu- ia, al- le- lu- ia, al- le- lu- ia.

- ii -

734 8. CRY out with joy to God, * all the earth; al- le- lu- ia. O sing to the glo-ry of his name, al-le- lu- ia; O render him glo-rious praise, al-le- lu- ia, al-le- lu- ia.

VERSES *Dicite Deo : quam terribila sunt. Ps* 65 : 3-4

℣. 1 735

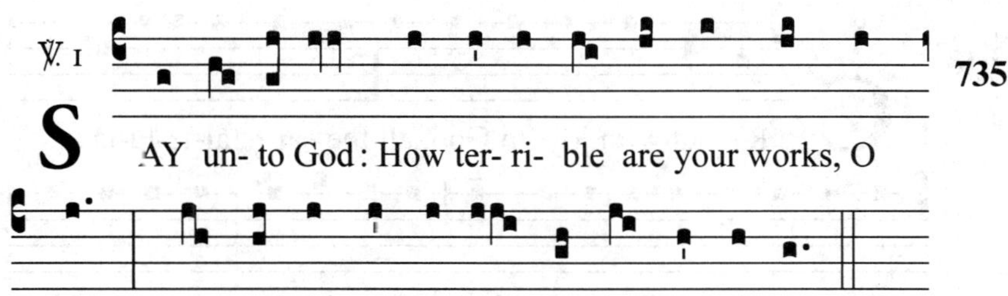

SAY un- to God : How ter- ri- ble are your works, O

Lord ! * Let all the earth a- dore you and sing to you.

Benedicite, gentes, Deum nostrum. Ps 65 : 8

℣. 2 736

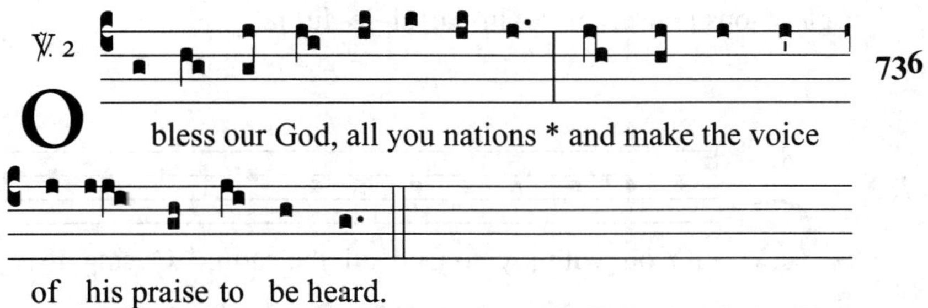

O bless our God, all you nations * and make the voice

of his praise to be heard.

Introibo in domum tuam. Ps 65 : 13-14

℣. 3 737

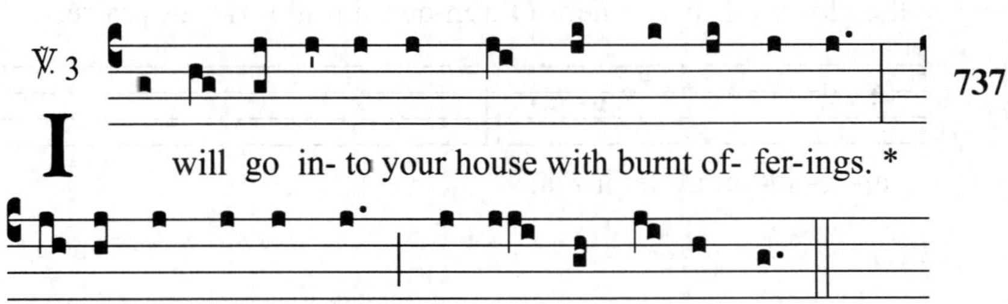

I will go in- to your house with burnt of- fer-ings. *

I will pay you my vows which my lips have ut-tered.

- iii -

738

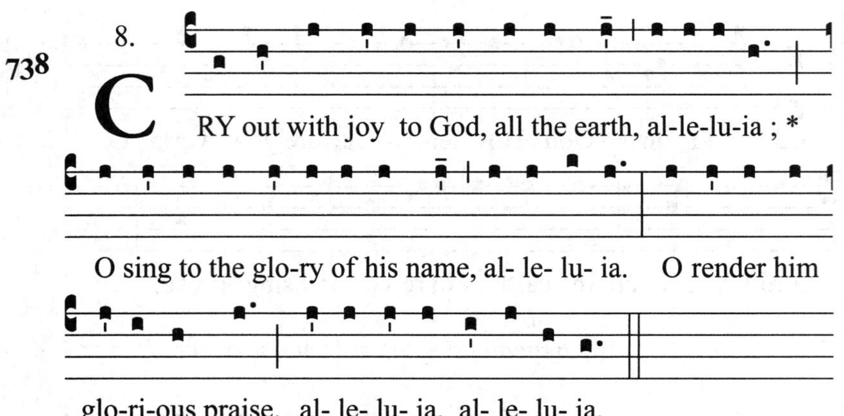
8.
CRY out with joy to God, all the earth, al-le-lu-ia ; *
O sing to the glo-ry of his name, al- le- lu- ia. O render him
glo-ri-ous praise, al- le- lu- ia, al- le- lu- ia.

- iv -

739

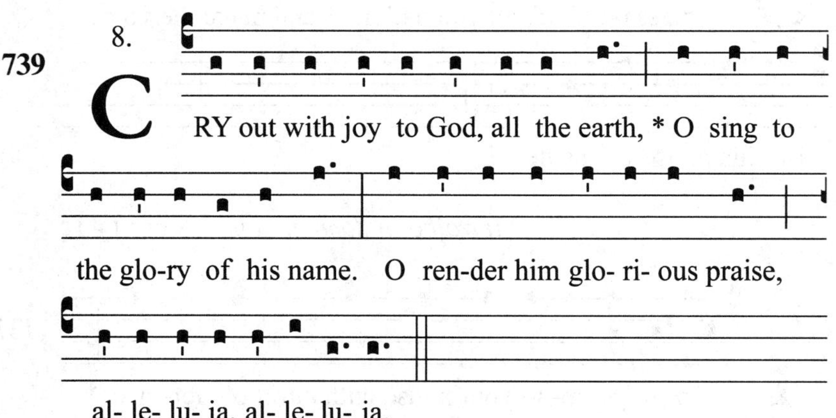
8.
CRY out with joy to God, all the earth, * O sing to
the glo-ry of his name. O ren-der him glo- ri- ous praise,
al- le- lu- ia, al- le- lu- ia.

OFFERTORY ANTIPHON *Lauda, anima mea, Dominum.*
Ps 145:2

- i -

4. PRaise the Lord, * O my soul, all my life I 740

will praise the Lord, I will sing praise to my God as

long as I shall live, al- le- lu- ia.

- ii -

4. PRaise the Lord, * O my soul, all my life I will 741

praise the Lord, I will sing praise to my God as long as

I shall live, al- le- lu- ia.

Or:

4. PRaise the Lord, O my soul, * all my life I will 742

praise the Lord, I will sing praise to my God as long as

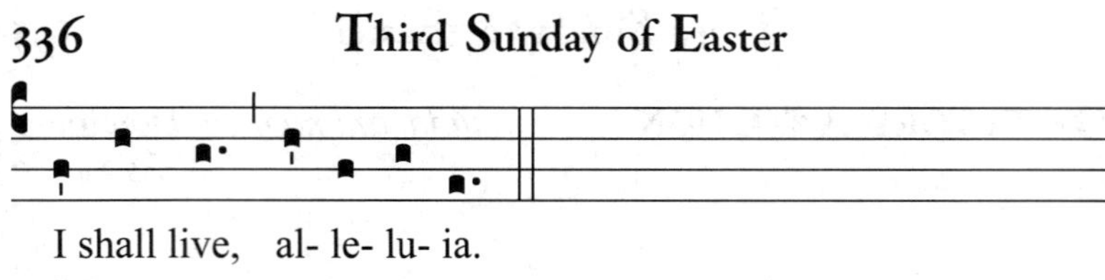
I shall live, al- le- lu- ia.

VERSES *Beatus, cuius Deus Iacob. Ps* 145:5

743

℣. 1
BLess-ed is he who has the God of Ja-cob as his
help-er, * whose hope is in the Lord his God.

Qui fecit cælum et terram. Ps 145:5-6

744
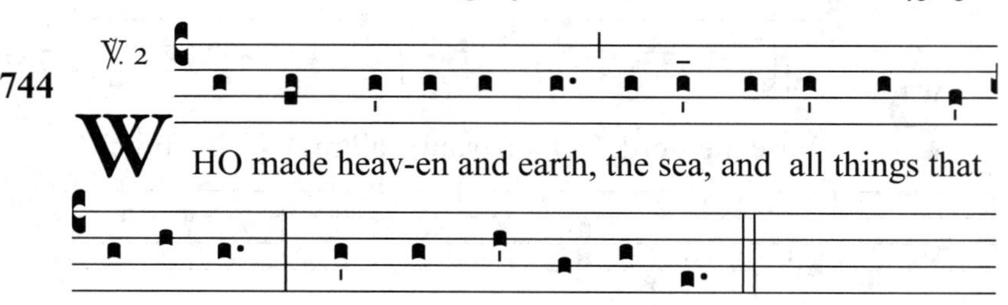
℣. 2
WHO made heav-en and earth, the sea, and all things that
are in them. * Who keeps truth for ev- er.

Regnabit Dominus in sæcula. Ps 145:10

745
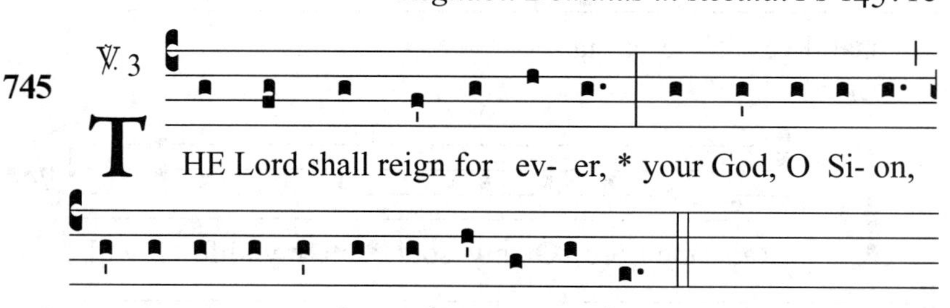
℣. 3
THE Lord shall reign for ev- er, * your God, O Si- on,
un- to gen- er- a- tion and gen-er- a- tion.

- iii -

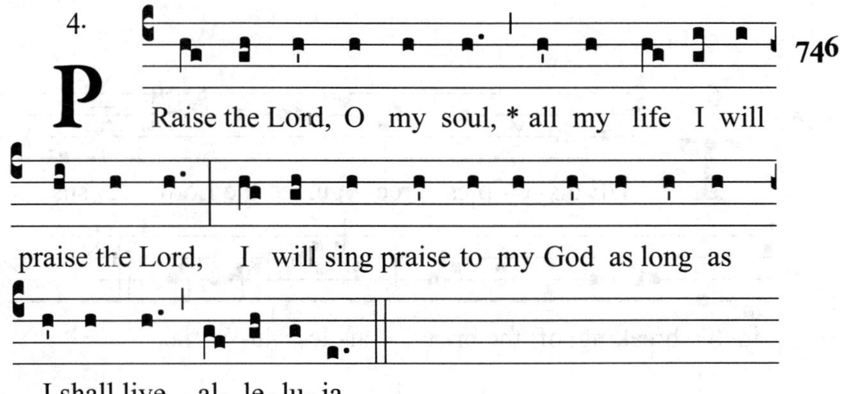
4.
746
PRaise the Lord, O my soul, * all my life I will
praise the Lord, I will sing praise to my God as long as
I shall live, al- le- lu- ia.

- iv -

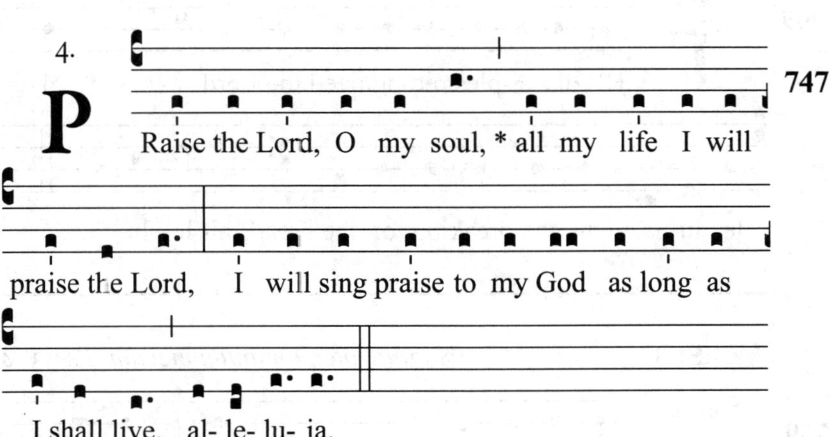
4.
747
PRaise the Lord, O my soul, * all my life I will
praise the Lord, I will sing praise to my God as long as
I shall live, al- le- lu- ia.

COMMUNION ANTIPHON *Cognoverunt discipuli.* *Lk* 24:35

- i -

748
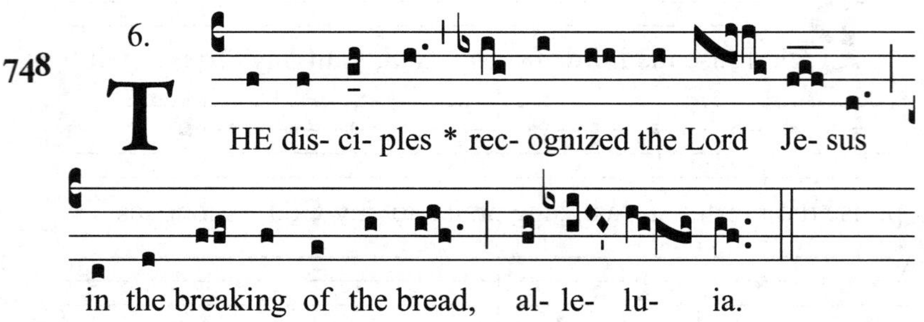
6.
THE dis- ci- ples * rec- ognized the Lord Je- sus
in the breaking of the bread, al- le- lu- ia.

- ii -

749
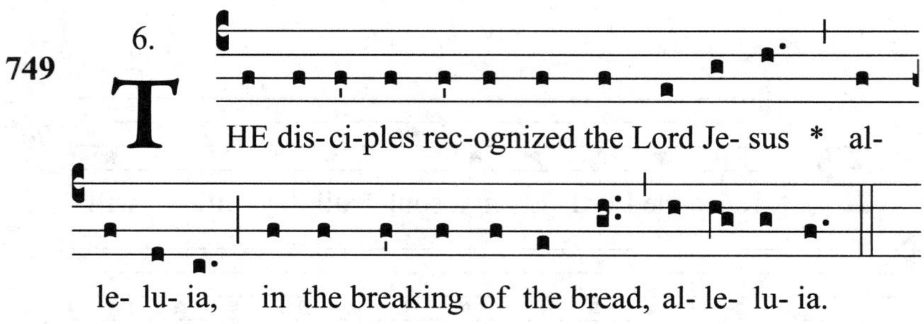
6.
THE dis-ci-ples rec-ognized the Lord Je- sus * al-
le- lu- ia, in the breaking of the bread, al- le- lu- ia.

VERSES *Magnificate Dominum mecum. Ps* 33:4

750
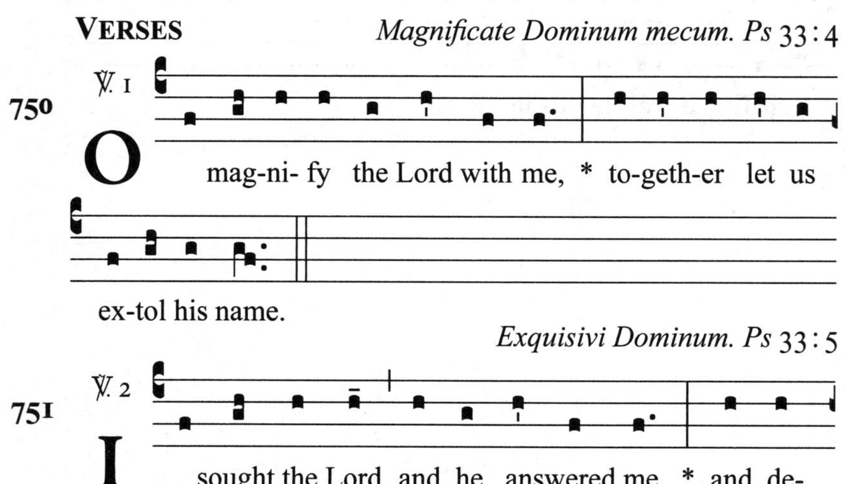
℣. 1
O mag-ni- fy the Lord with me, * to-geth-er let us
ex-tol his name.
Exquisivi Dominum. Ps 33:5
℣. 2
I sought the Lord, and he answered me, * and de-

751

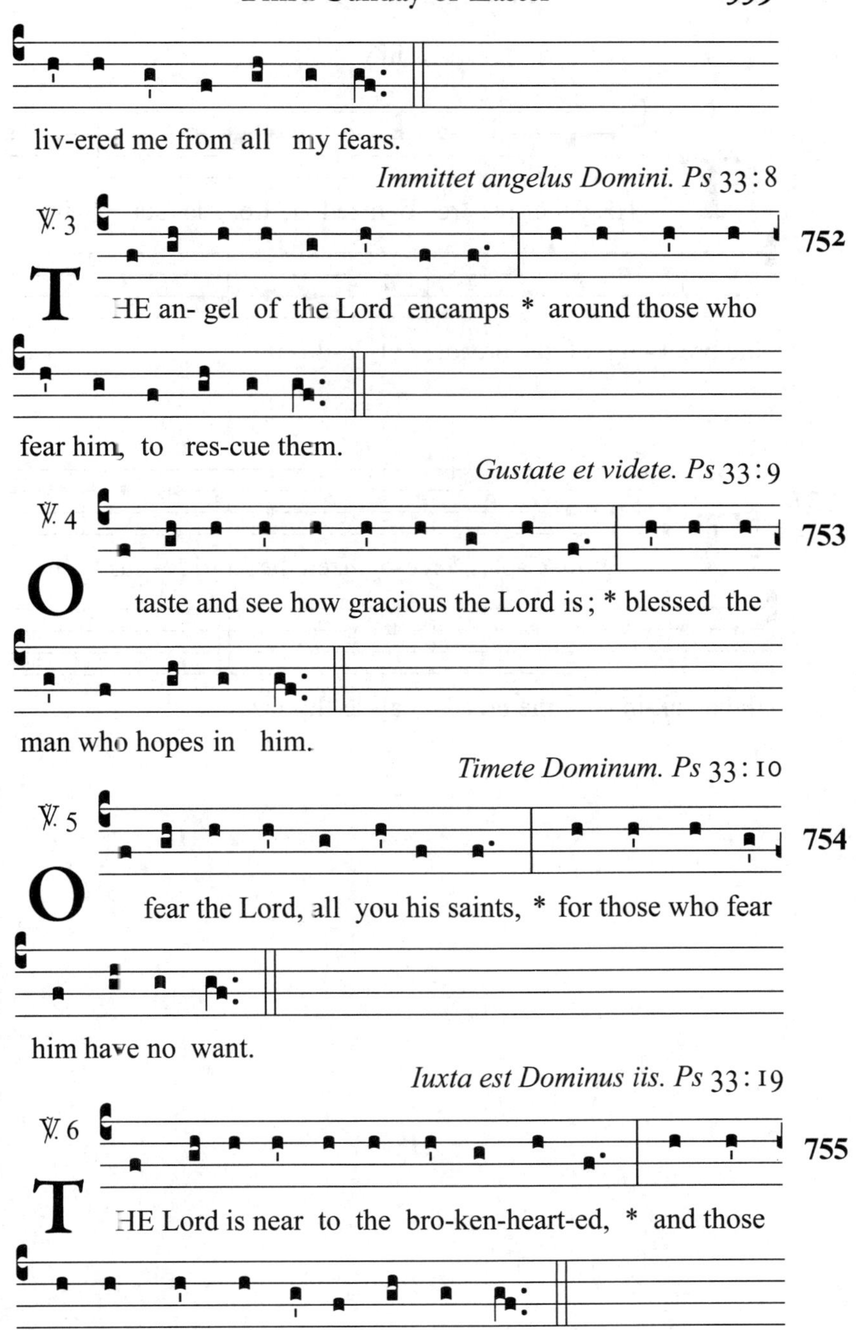
liv-ered me from all my fears.
Immittet angelus Domini. Ps 33:8
℣. 3
THE an- gel of the Lord encamps * around those who
752
fear him, to res-cue them.
Gustate et videte. Ps 33:9
℣. 4
O taste and see how gracious the Lord is; * blessed the
753
man who hopes in him.
Timete Dominum. Ps 33:10
℣. 5
O fear the Lord, all you his saints, * for those who fear
754
him have no want.
Iuxta est Dominus iis. Ps 33:19
℣. 6
THE Lord is near to the bro-ken-heart-ed, * and those
755
who are crushed in spir- it he will save.

- iii -

756

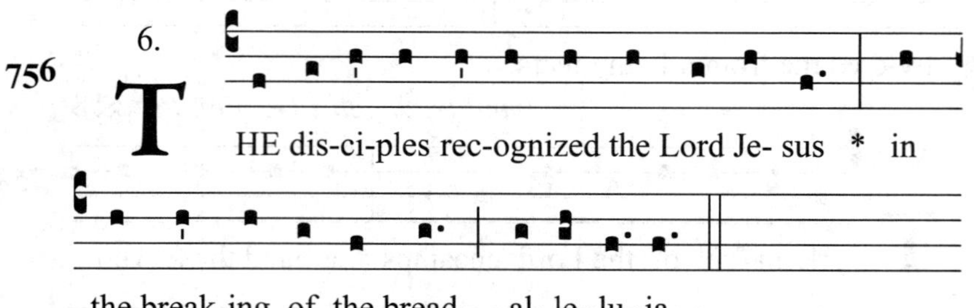
6.
THE dis-ci-ples rec-ognized the Lord Je- sus * in
the break-ing of the bread, al- le- lu- ia.

- iv -

757

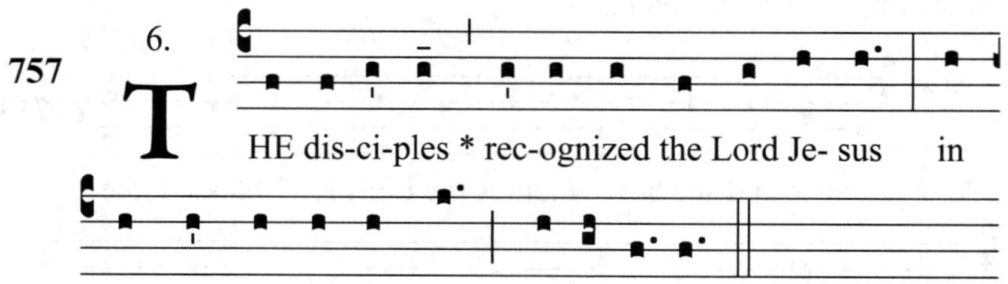
6.
THE dis-ci-ples * rec-ognized the Lord Je- sus in
the break-ing of the bread, al- le- lu- ia.

Option for Year B: *Oportebat Christum pati.*
Lk 24:46-47

- i -
8.
T HE Christ * had to suf- fer and on the
758
third day rise
from the dead; in his name re- pen-
tance and re- mis- sion of sins must be preached to all
the na- tions, al- le- lu- ia.
- ii -
8.
T HE Christ had to suf- fer * and on the third day
759
rise from the dead; in his name re-pentance and re-mission of
sins must be preached to all the nations, al- le- lu- ia.

VERSES *Lapidem quem reprobaverunt ædificantes.* *Ps* 117:22

760

℣. 1
THE stone which the build-ers re-ject-ed has become
the cor-nerstone. * This is the Lord's do-ing, and it is won-
der-ful in our eyes.

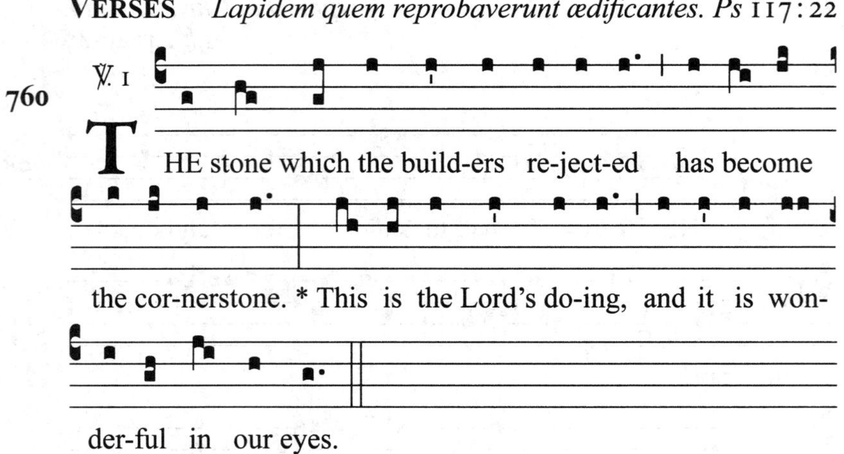

Hæc dies quam fecit Dominus. *Ps* 117:24

761

℣. 2
THIS is the day which the Lord has made; * let us be
glad and re-joice there-in.

Deus meus es tu, et confitebor tibi. *Ps* 117:28

762

℣. 3
YOU are my God, and I will praise you ; * you are my
God, and I will ex- alt you.

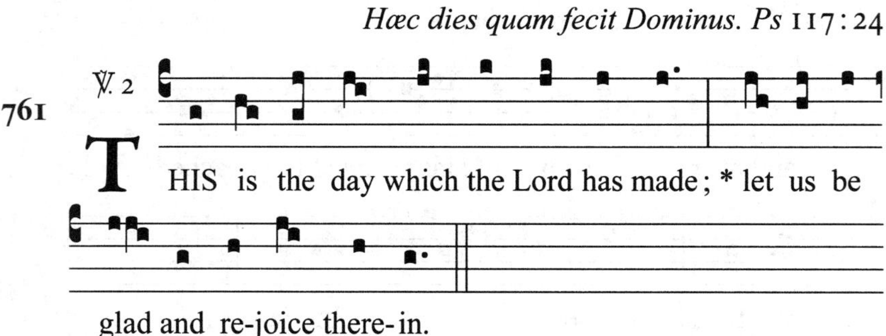

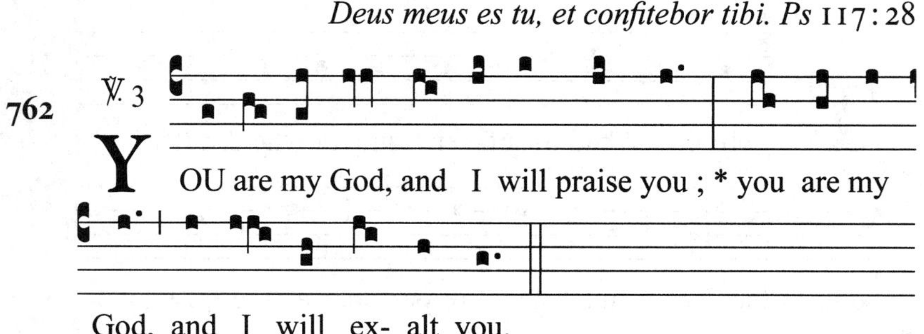

- iii -

8.
THE Christ had to suf- fer * and on the third day
rise from the dead; in his name re-pentance and re-mission
of sins must be preached to all the na- tions, al- le- lu- ia.

763

- iv -

8.
THE Christ had to suf- fer * and on the third day
rise from the dead ; in his name re-pentance and re-mission
of sins must be preached to all the nations, al- le- lu- ia.

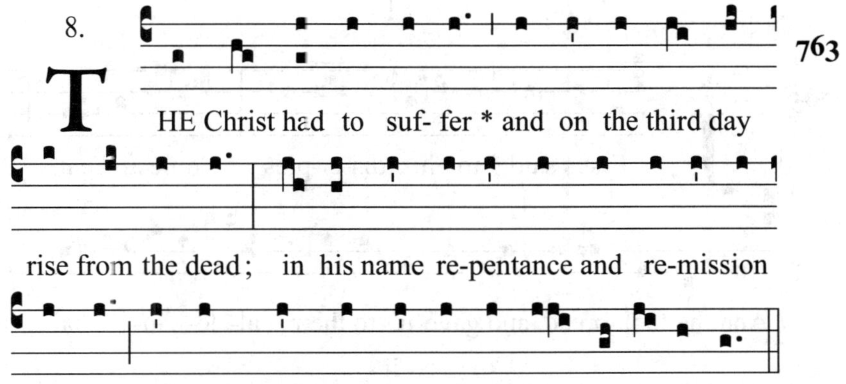

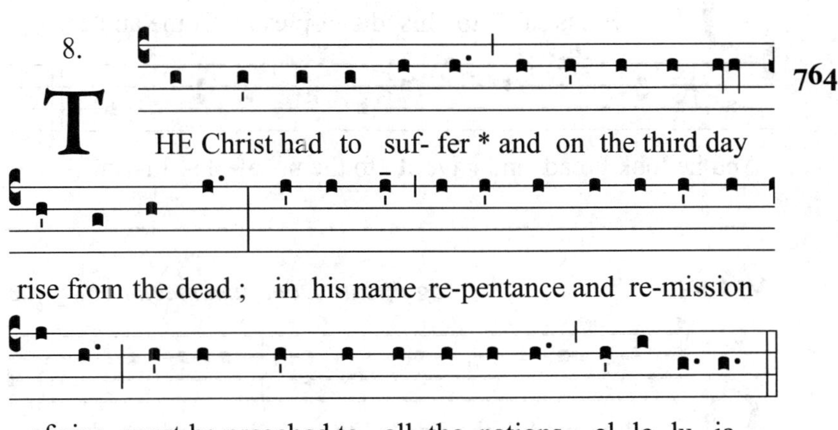

764

Option for Year C : *Dixit Iesus discipulis suis.*
Jn 21 : 12-13

- i -

765 6.

JEsus said * to his dis-ci-ples : * Come and eat.
And he took bread and gave it to them, al- le- lu- ia.

- ii -

766 6.

JEsus said to his dis-ci-ples : * Come and eat.
And he took bread and gave it to them, al- le- lu- ia.

VERSES *Magnificate Dominum mecum. Ps* 33 : 4

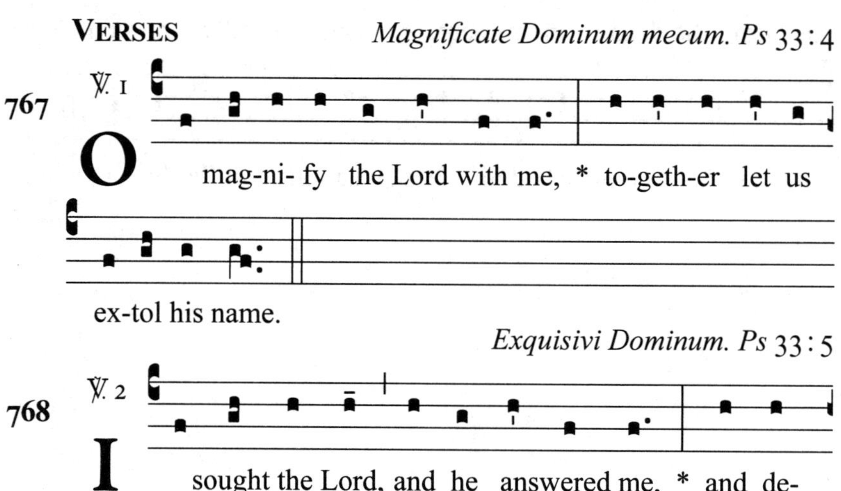
767 ℣. 1
O mag-ni- fy the Lord with me, * to-geth-er let us
ex-tol his name.
Exquisivi Dominum. Ps 33 : 5
768 ℣. 2
I sought the Lord, and he answered me, * and de-

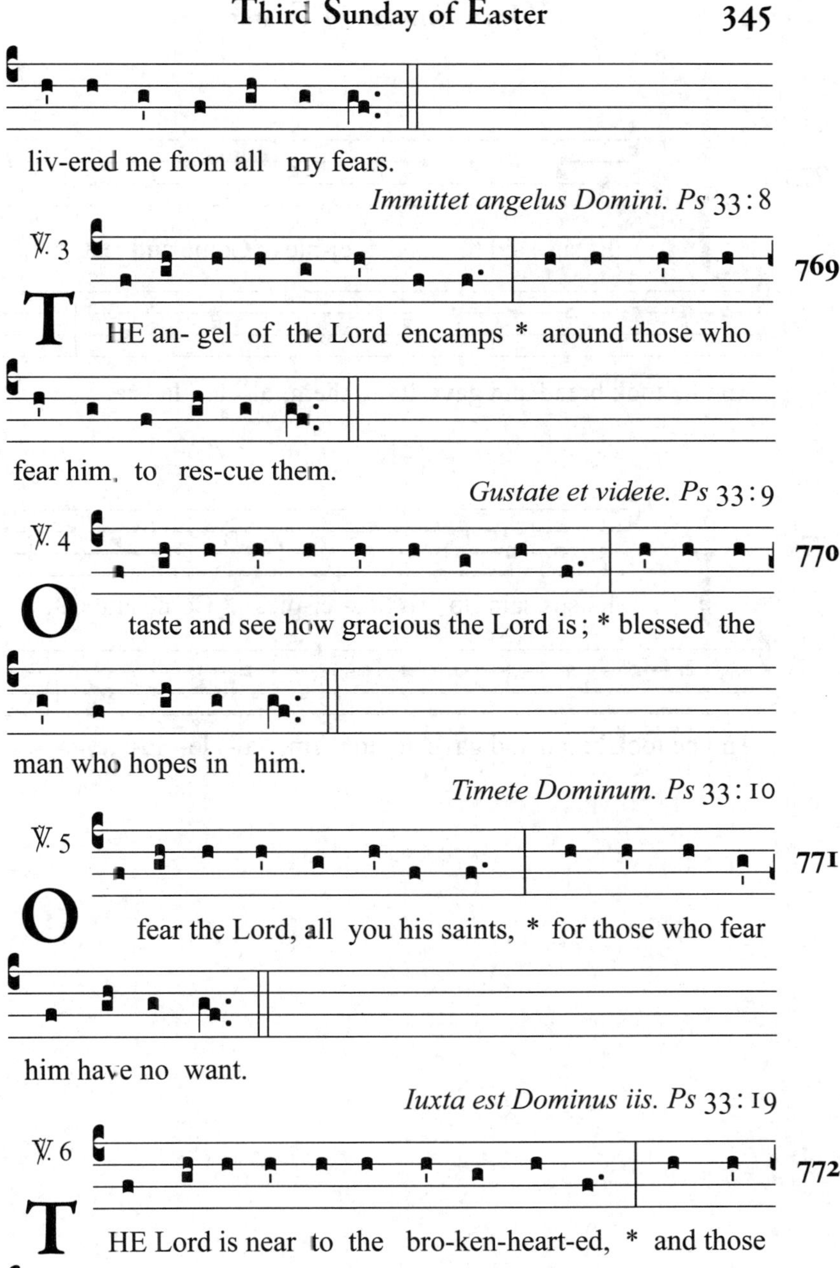
liv-ered me from all my fears.
Immittet angelus Domini. Ps 33:8
℣. 3
THE an- gel of the Lord encamps * around those who
769
fear him, to res-cue them.
Gustate et videte. Ps 33:9
℣. 4
O taste and see how gracious the Lord is; * blessed the
770
man who hopes in him.
Timete Dominum. Ps 33:10
℣. 5
O fear the Lord, all you his saints, * for those who fear
771
him have no want.
Iuxta est Dominus iis. Ps 33:19
℣. 6
THE Lord is near to the bro-ken-heart-ed, * and those
772
who are crushed in spir- it he will save.

- iii -

773

6.
JEsus said to his dis- ci-ples : Come and eat. *

And he took bread and gave it to them, al- le- lu- ia.

- iv -

774

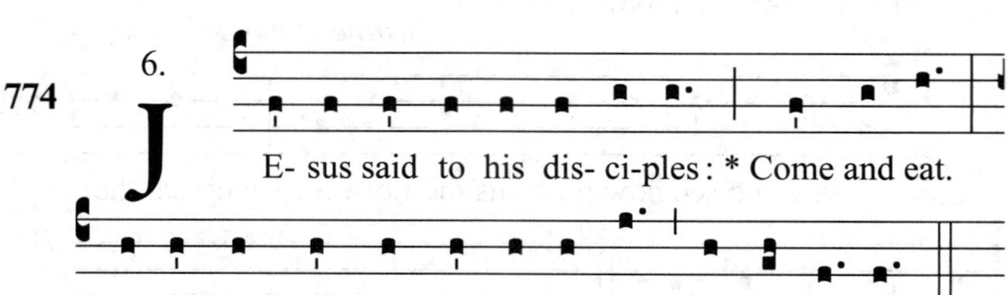
6.
JEsus said to his dis- ci-ples : * Come and eat.

And he took bread and gave it to them, al- le- lu- ia.

FOURTH SUNDAY OF EASTER

Entrance Antiphon *Misericordia Domini.*
Ps 32:5-6

- i -

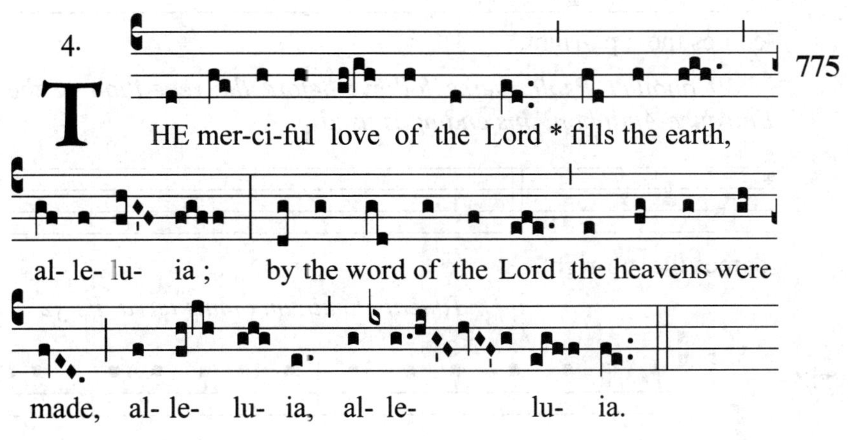
4.
THE mer-ci-ful love of the Lord * fills the earth,
775
al- le- lu- ia ; by the word of the Lord the heavens were
made, al- le- lu- ia, al- le- lu- ia.

- ii -

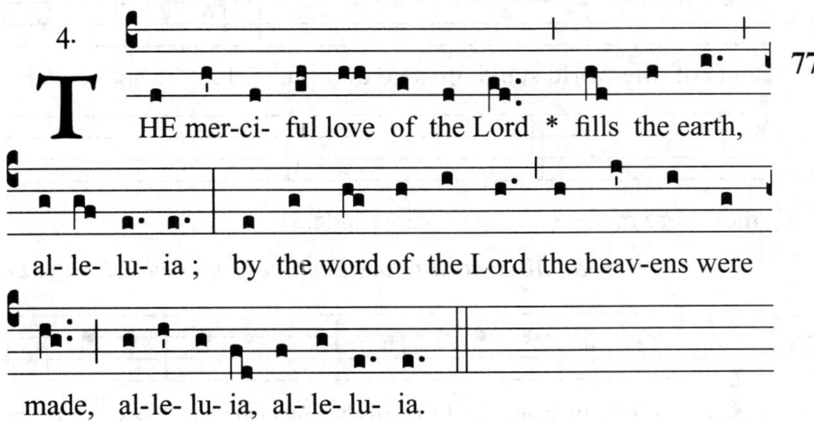
4.
THE mer-ci- ful love of the Lord * fills the earth,
776
al- le- lu- ia ; by the word of the Lord the heav-ens were
made, al-le- lu- ia, al- le- lu- ia.

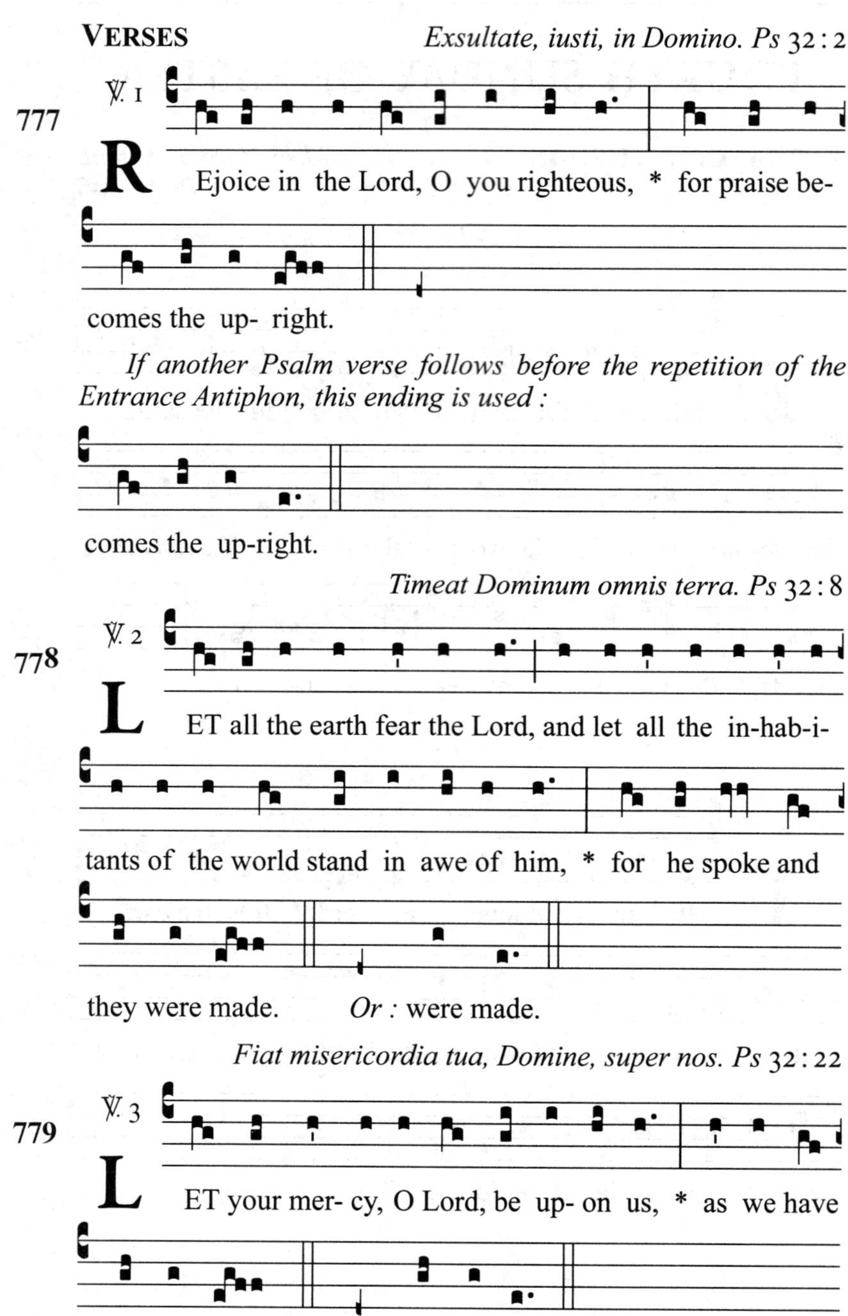
VERSES
Exsultate, iusti, in Domino. Ps 32 : 2
777
℣. 1
REjoice in the Lord, O you righteous, * for praise becomes the up- right.
If another Psalm verse follows before the repetition of the Entrance Antiphon, this ending is used :
comes the up-right.
Timeat Dominum omnis terra. Ps 32 : 8
778
℣. 2
LET all the earth fear the Lord, and let all the in-hab-i-
tants of the world stand in awe of him, * for he spoke and
they were made.
Or : were made.
Fiat misericordia tua, Domine, super nos. Ps 32 : 22
779
℣. 3
LET your mer- cy, O Lord, be up- on us, * as we have
hoped in you.
Or : hoped in you.

- iii -

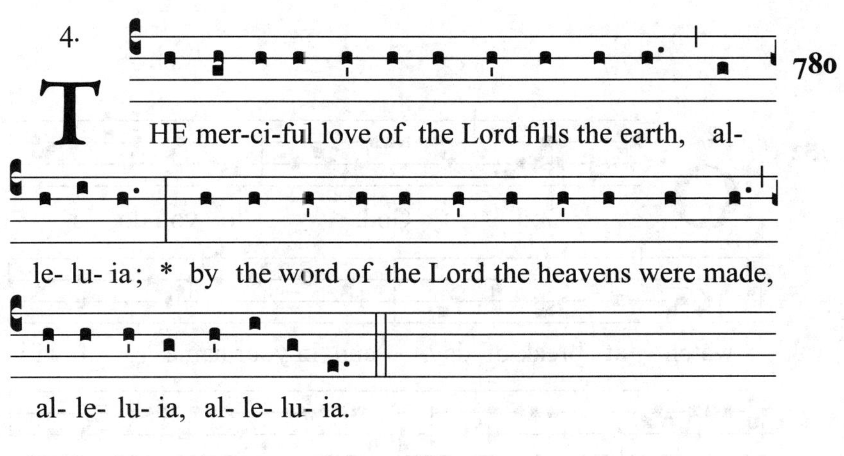
4.
780
THE mer-ci-ful love of the Lord fills the earth, al-
le- lu- ia; * by the word of the Lord the heavens were made,
al- le- lu- ia, al- le- lu- ia.

- iv -

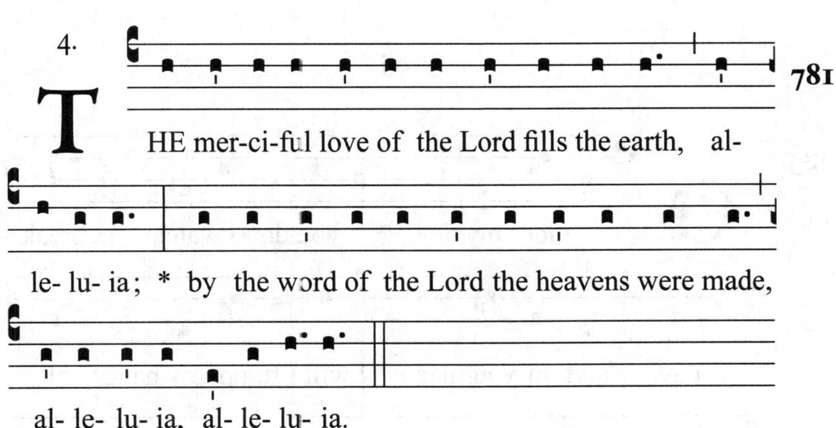
4.
781
THE mer-ci-ful love of the Lord fills the earth, al-
le- lu- ia; * by the word of the Lord the heavens were made,
al- le- lu- ia, al- le- lu- ia.

Offertory Antiphon *Deus, Deus meus, ad te.*
Ps 62:2. 5

- i -

782

2.
O God, * my God, to you do I
watch at break of day, and in your name I will
lift up my hands, al-le- lu- ia.

- ii -

783
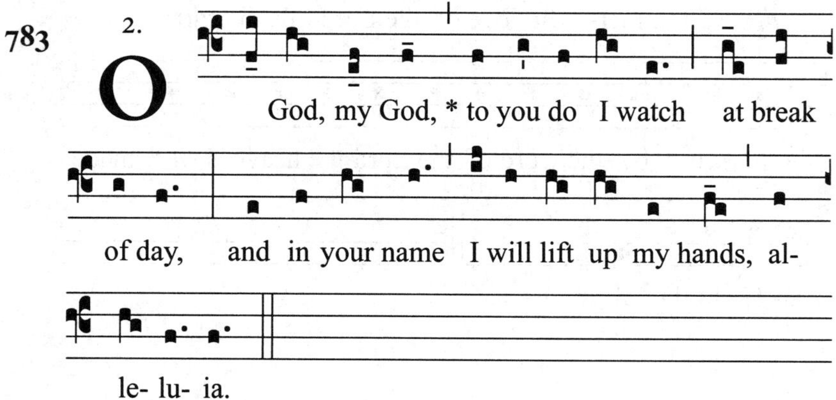
2.
O God, my God, * to you do I watch at break
of day, and in your name I will lift up my hands, al-
le- lu- ia.

Verses *Deus, Deus meus, ad te de luce vigilo.* Ps 62 : 2-3

℣. 1
784
O God, my God, to you do I watch at break of day. *
For you my soul has thirst-ed, my flesh faints for you, as

in a dry and wea-ry land where no wa- ter is.

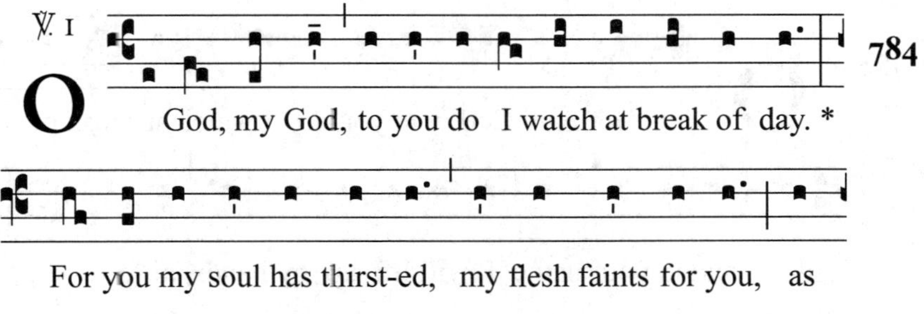

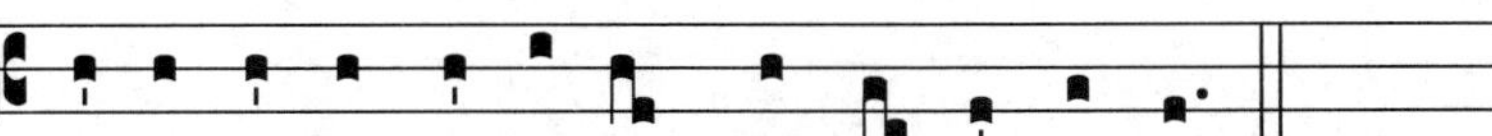

Sic benedicam te in vita mea. Ps 62 : 5

℣. 2
785
THUS will I bless you all my life long, * and in your
name I will lift up my hands.

Quia fuisti adiutor meus. Ps 62 : 8-9

℣. 3
786
FOR you are my help, and I will re-joice in the shad-
ow of your wings. * My soul clings fast to you; your right
hand up-holds me.

- iii -

787

2.
O God, my God, * to you do I watch at break of
day, and in your name I will lift up my hands, al-le-lu-ia.

Or:

788

2.
O God, my God, * to you do I watch at break of
day, and in your name I will lift up my hands, al-le-lu-ia.

- iv -

789

2.
O God, my God, * to you do I watch at break of
day, and in your name I will lift up my hands, al-le-lu-ia.

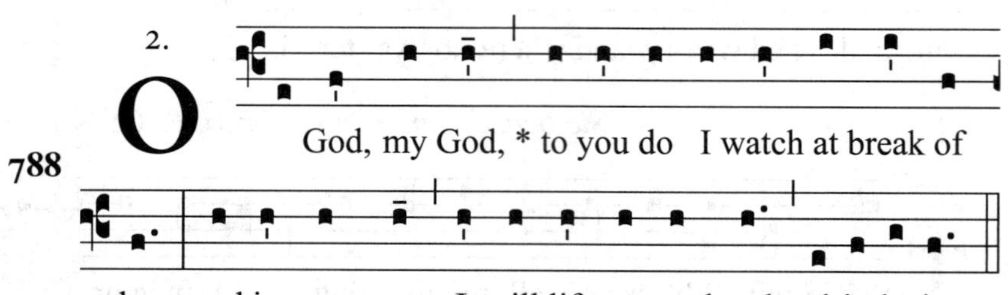

COMMUNION ANTIPHON *Surrexit Pastor bonus.*

- i -

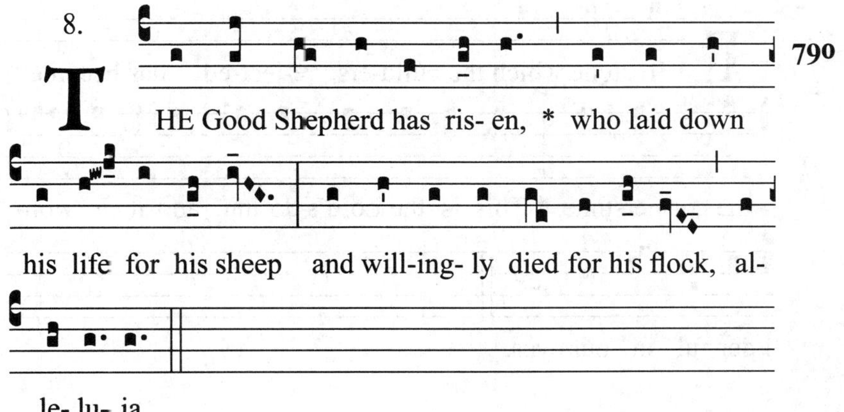
8.
THE Good Shepherd has ris- en, * who laid down
his life for his sheep and will-ing- ly died for his flock, al-
le- lu- ia.
790

- ii -

8.
THE Good Shepherd has ris- en, * who laid down
his life for his sheep and will-ing- ly died for his flock, al-
le- lu- ia.
791

VERSES *Lapidem quem reprobaverunt ædificantes. Ps* 117:22

792 ℣. 1

THE stone which the build-ers re-ject-ed has become the cor-nerstone. * This is the Lord's do-ing, and it is won-der-ful in our eyes.

Hæc dies quam fecit Dominus. Ps 117:24

793 ℣. 2

THIS is the day which the Lord has made; * let us be
glad and re-joice there-in.

Deus meus es tu, et confitebor tibi. Ps 117:28

794 ℣. 3

YOU are my God, and I will praise you; * you are my
God, and I will ex- alt you.

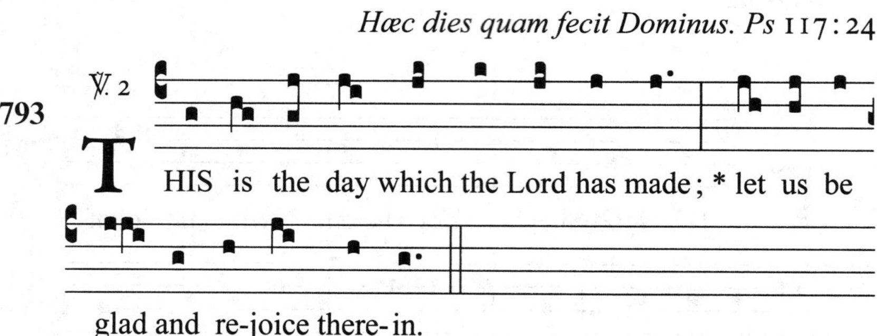

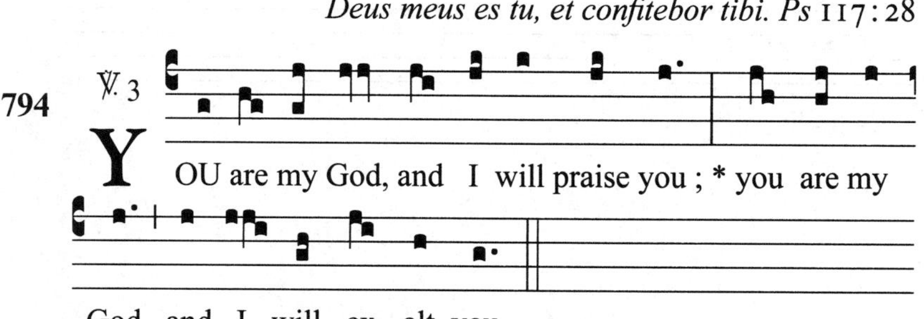

- iii -

8.
795
THE Good Shepherd has ris- en, * who laid down
his life for his sheep and will-ing- ly died for his flock, al-
le- lu- ia.
Or:
8.
796
THE Good Shepherd has ris- en, * who laid down
his life for his sheep and will-ing- ly died for his flock, al-
le- lu- ia.
- iv -
8.
797
THE Good Shepherd has ris- en, * who laid down
his life for his sheep and will-ing- ly died for his flock, al-
le- lu- ia.

FIFTH SUNDAY OF EASTER

Entrance Antiphon *Cantate Domino canticum novum.*
Ps 97:1.2

- i -
798
6.
O sing a new song * to the Lord, al- le- lu- ia;
for he has worked wonders, al- le- lu- ia; in the
sight of the na- tions he has shown his de- liv- erance, al- le-
lu- ia, al- le- lu- ia.
- ii -
799
6.
O sing a new song to the Lord, * al- le- lu- ia; for
he has worked won- ders, al- le- lu- ia; in the sight of the
nations he has shown his de-liv-erance, al- le-lu- ia, al-le-lu-ia.

VERSES *Cantate Domino canticum novum. Ps* 97 : 1

℣. 1
800
O sing a new song to the Lord, for he has worked
won-ders. * His right hand and his ho- ly arm have wrought
sal-va-tion.
℣. 2
801
THE Lord has made known his sal- va-tion, he has revealed his jus-tice in the sight of the nations. * He has remembered his mer- cy and his truth toward the house of Is- ra- el.
℣. 3
802
ALL the ends of the earth have seen the sal- va-tion of
our God. * Sing joy-ful- ly to God, all the earth; make mel-
o- dy, re-joice and sing.

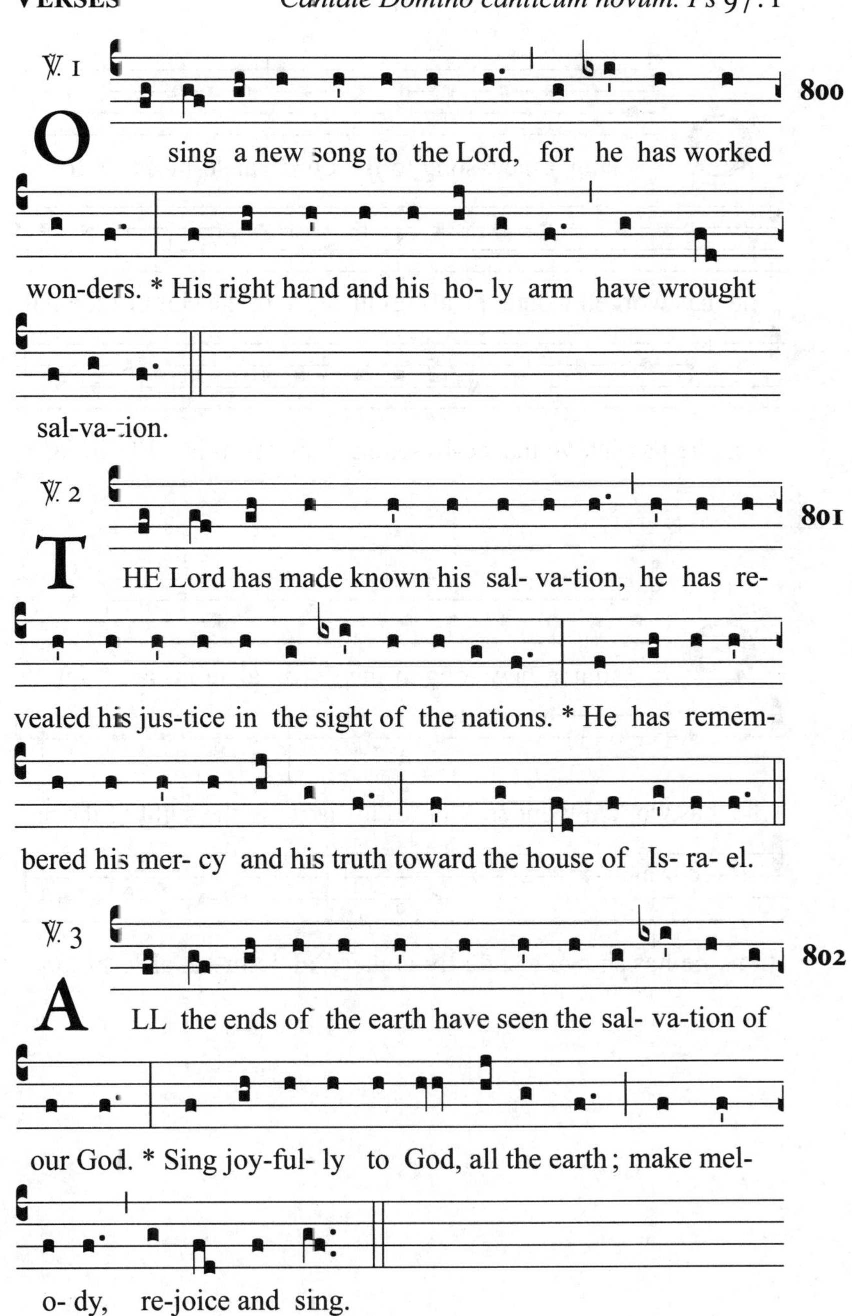

- iii -

803

6.

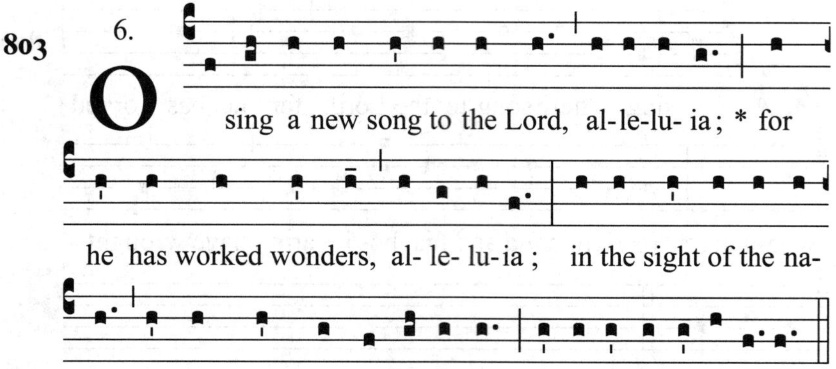

O sing a new song to the Lord, al-le-lu- ia ; * for
he has worked wonders, al- le- lu-ia ; in the sight of the na-

tions he has shown his de-liv-erance, al- le-lu- ia, al-le-lu-ia.

804

- iv -

6.

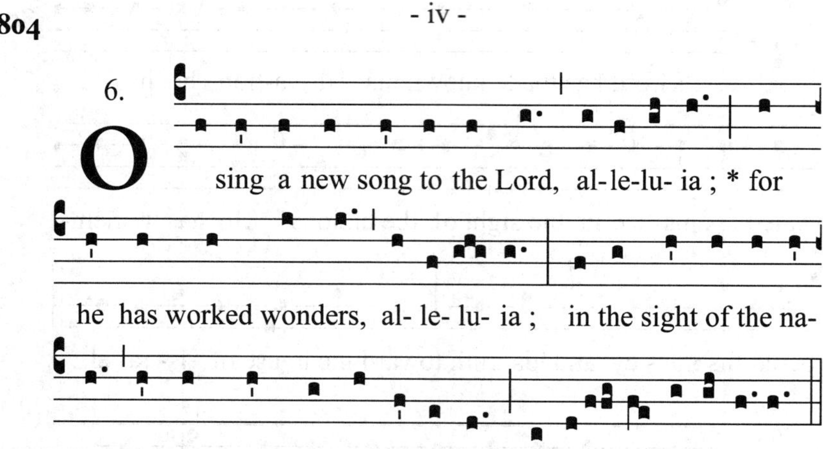

O sing a new song to the Lord, al-le-lu- ia ; * for
he has worked wonders, al- le- lu- ia ; in the sight of the na-

tions he has shown his de-liv-erance, al- le-lu- ia, al-le-lu-ia.

OFFERTORY ANTIPHON *Iubilate Deo, omnis terra.*
Ps 65:1. 2. 16

- i -
1.
805
S Hout with joy * to God, all the earth; sing a psalm
to his name. Come and hear, all who fear God, and I will
tell you what great things the Lord has done for my soul,
al- le- lu- ia.
- ii -
1.
806
S Hout with joy * to God, all the earth; sing a psalm
to his name. Come and hear, all who fear God, and I will
tell you what great things the Lord has done for my soul,
al- le- lu- ia.

VERSES *Benedicite, gentes, Deum nostrum. Ps* 65:8

807 ℣. 1

O bless our God, you na-tions, and make the voice of his praise to be heard. * Who has set my soul to live, and has kept my feet from stumbling.

Introibo in domum tuam. Ps 65:13-14

808 ℣. 2

I will go in- to your house with burnt of-fer-ings ; I will pay you my vows, * which my lips have ut-tered, and my mouth has spo-ken, when I was in trou- ble.

Iniquitatem si aspexi in corde meo. Ps 65:18-19

809 ℣. 3

WERE I to cher-ish e- vil in my heart, the Lord would not hear. * But God has heard, and has at-tend-ed to the voice of my sup-pli- ca- tion.

- iii -

I.
810
SHout with joy to God, all the earth; * sing a psalm
to his name. Come and hear, all who fear God, and I will
tell you what great things the Lord has done for my soul, al-
le- lu- ia.
- iv -
I.
811
SHout with joy to God, all the earth; * sing a psalm
to his name. Come and hear, all who fear God, and I will
tell you what great things the Lord has done for my soul, al-
le- lu- ia.

COMMUNION ANTIPHON *Ego sum vitis vera. Jn* 15:5

- i -

812

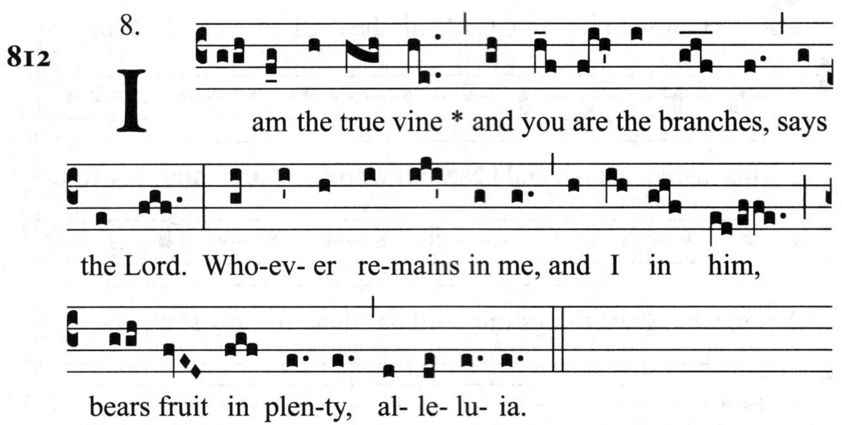
8.
I am the true vine * and you are the branches, says
the Lord. Who-ev- er re-mains in me, and I in him,
bears fruit in plen-ty, al- le- lu- ia.

- ii -

813

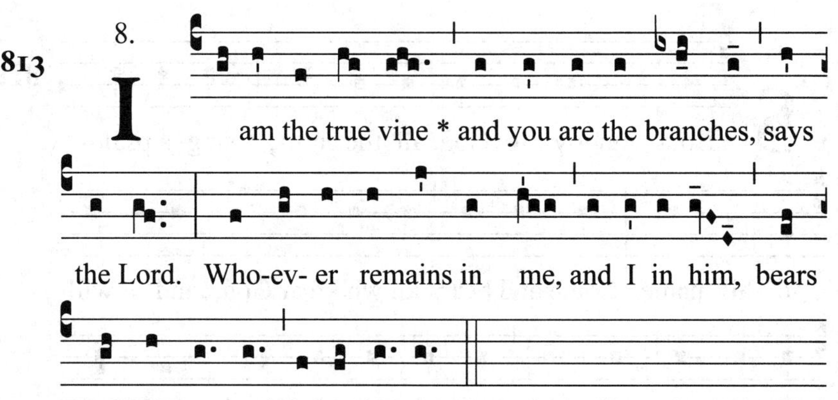
8.
I am the true vine * and you are the branches, says
the Lord. Who-ev- er remains in me, and I in him, bears
fruit in plen- ty, al- le- lu- ia.

VERSES *Deus virtutum, convertere. Ps* 79 : 15-16

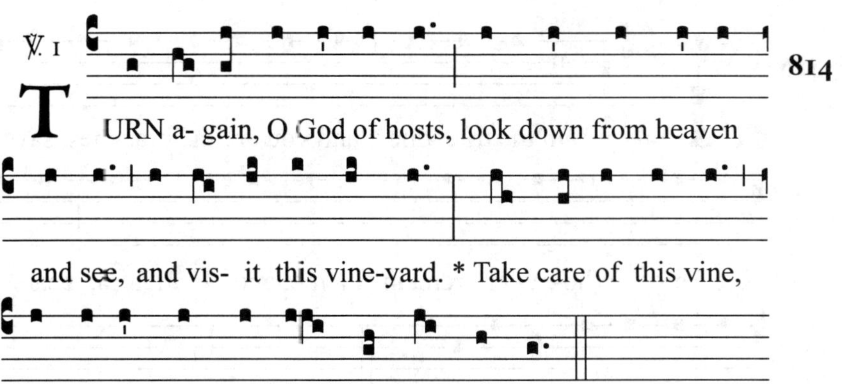
℣. 1
TURN a- gain, O God of hosts, look down from heaven
and see, and vis- it this vine-yard. * Take care of this vine,
and protect what your right hand has plant-ed.

814

Fiat manus tua super virum dexteræ tuæ. Ps 79 : 18-20

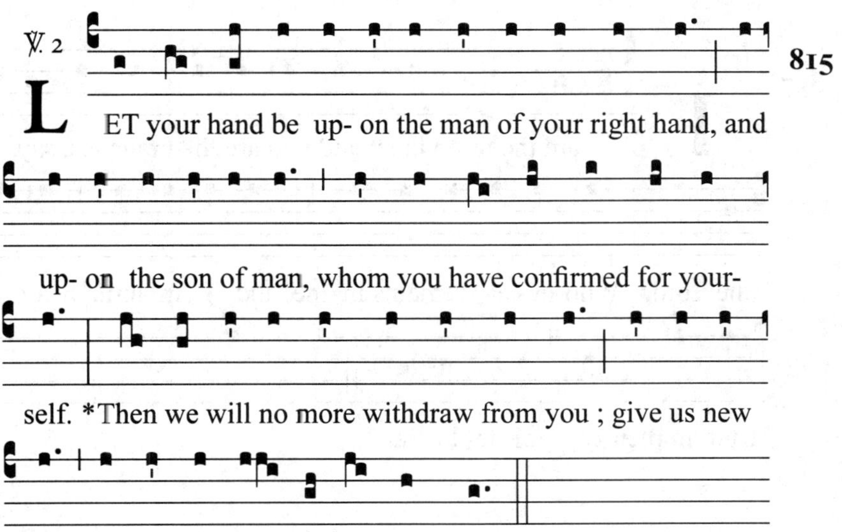
℣. 2
LET your hand be up- on the man of your right hand, and
up- on the son of man, whom you have confirmed for yourself. *Then we will no more withdraw from you ; give us new
life, and we will call up- on your name.

815

Cf. also verses of Ps 117, *p.* 354.

- iii -

816

8.
I am the true vine * and you are the branches, says
the Lord. Who-ev- er remains in me, and I in him, bears
fruit in plen-ty, al- le- lu- ia.

- iv -

817

8.
I am the true vine * and you are the branches, says
the Lord. Who-ev- er remains in me, and I in him, bears
fruit in plen-ty, al- le- lu- ia.

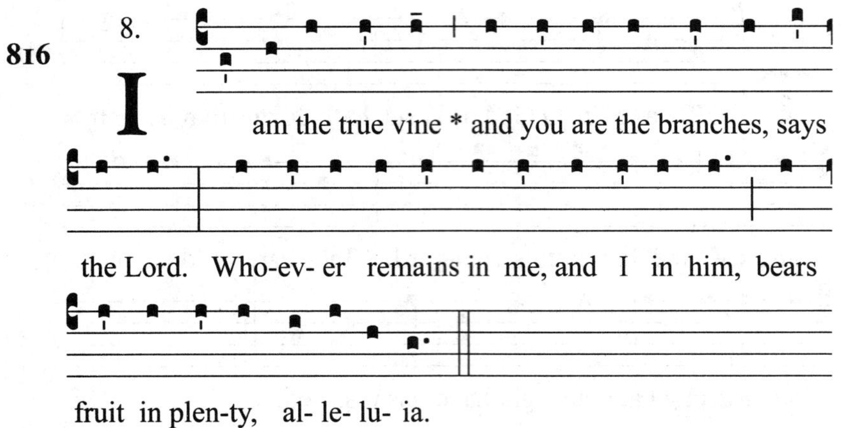

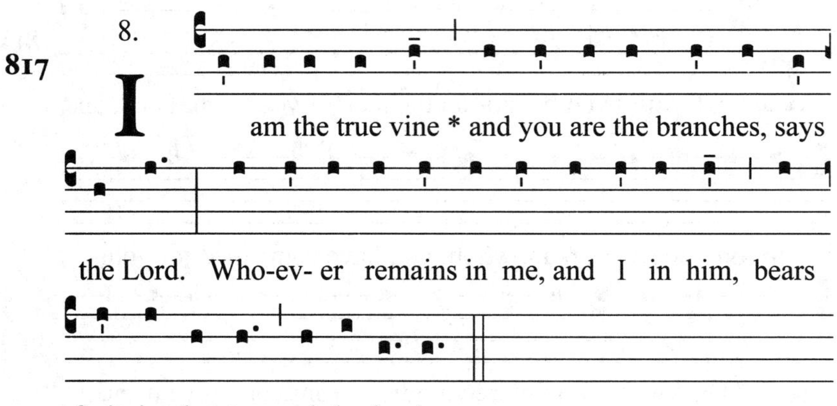

SIXTH SUNDAY OF EASTER

ENTRANCE ANTIPHON *Vocem iucunditatis annunitate.*
Is 48 : 20

- i -

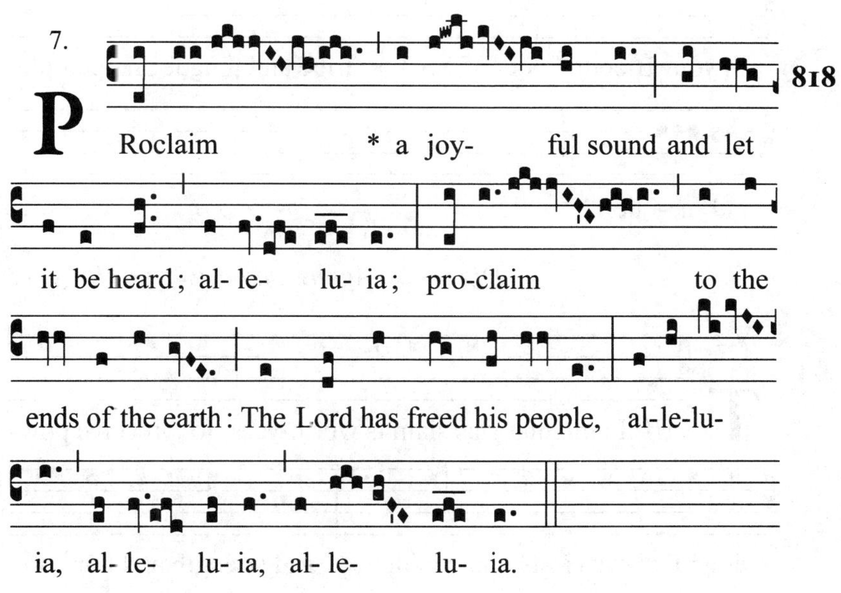
7.
818
PRoclaim * a joy- ful sound and let
it be heard; al- le- lu- ia; pro-claim to the
ends of the earth: The Lord has freed his people, al-le-lu-
ia, al- le- lu- ia, al- le- lu- ia.

- ii -

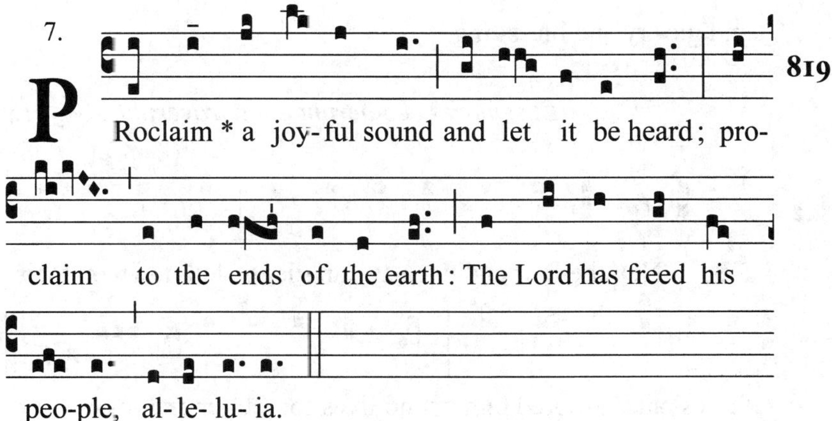
7.
819
PRoclaim * a joy-ful sound and let it be heard; proclaim to the ends of the earth: The Lord has freed his
peo-ple, al- le- lu- ia.

VERSES *Quoniam occisus es. Rv* 5:9

820
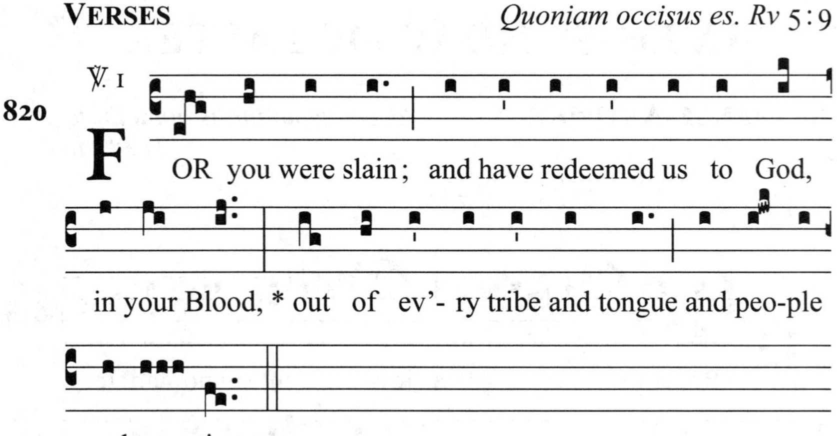
℣. 1
FOR you were slain; and have redeemed us to God,
in your Blood, * out of ev'- ry tribe and tongue and peo-ple
and na- tion.

Dignus est Agnus qui occisus est. Rv 5:12

821
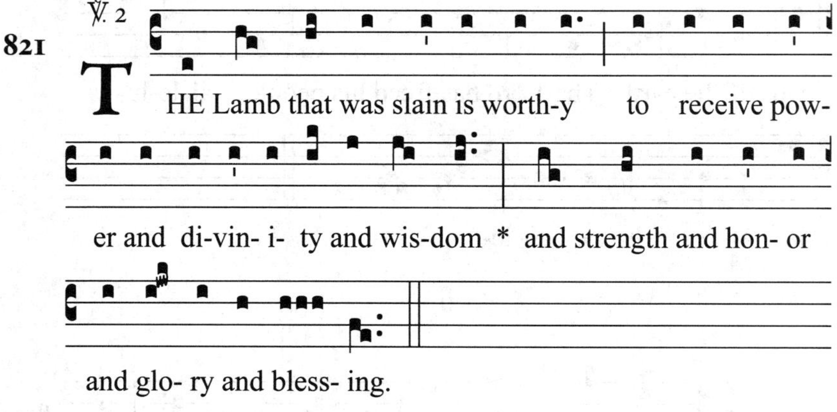
℣. 2
THE Lamb that was slain is worth-y to receive pow-
er and di-vin- i- ty and wis-dom * and strength and hon- or
and glo- ry and bless- ing.

Et seniores ceciderunt et adoraverunt. Rv 5:14

822
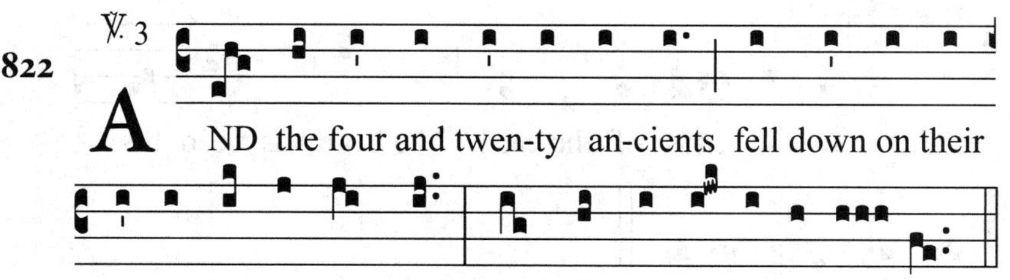
℣. 3
AND the four and twen-ty an-cients fell down on their
fac-es and a-dored him * who lives for ev- er and ev- er.

- iii -

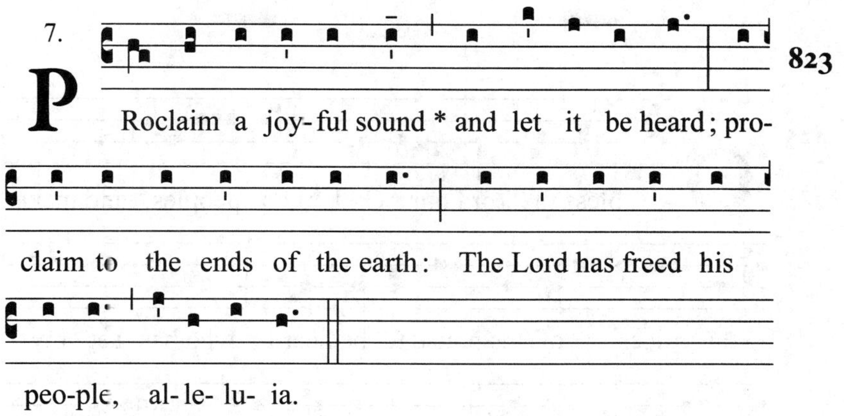
7.
823
PRoclaim a joy-ful sound * and let it be heard; proclaim to the ends of the earth: The Lord has freed his
peo-ple, al-le-lu-ia.

- iv -

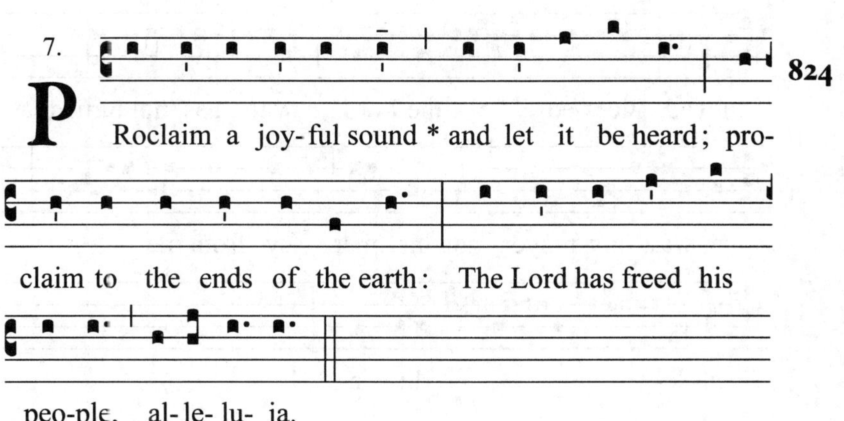
7.
824
PRoclaim a joy-ful sound * and let it be heard; proclaim to the ends of the earth: The Lord has freed his
peo-ple, al-le-lu-ia.

OFFERTORY ANTIPHON *Benedicite, gentes, Dominum.*
Ps 65:8-9. 20

- i -

825 2.

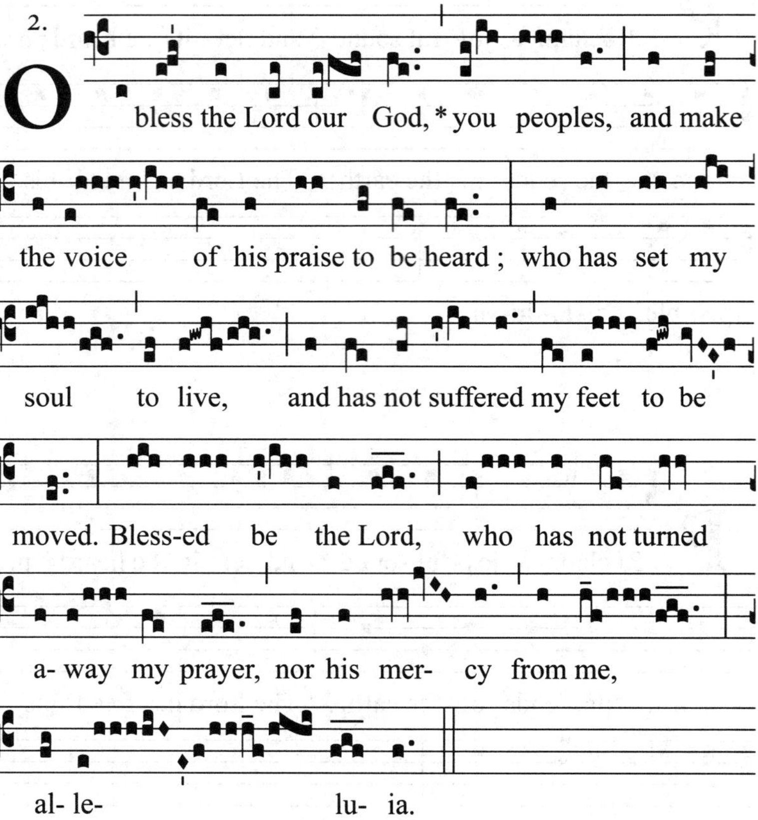

O bless the Lord our God, * you peoples, and make
the voice of his praise to be heard; who has set my
soul to live, and has not suffered my feet to be
moved. Bless-ed be the Lord, who has not turned
a- way my prayer, nor his mer- cy from me,
al- le- lu- ia.

- ii -

826

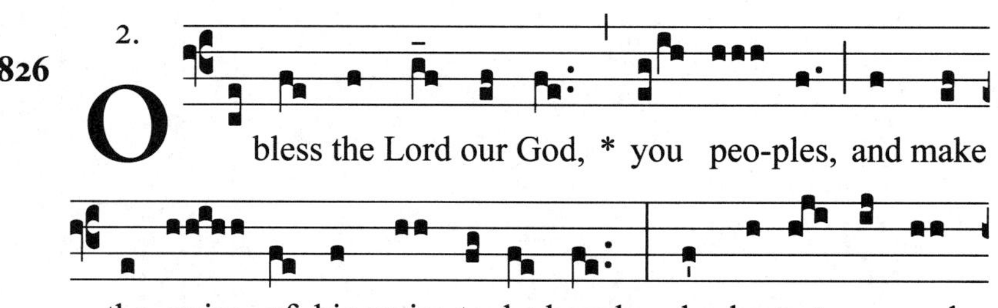
2.
O bless the Lord our God, * you peo-ples, and make
the voice of his praise to be heard; who has set my soul

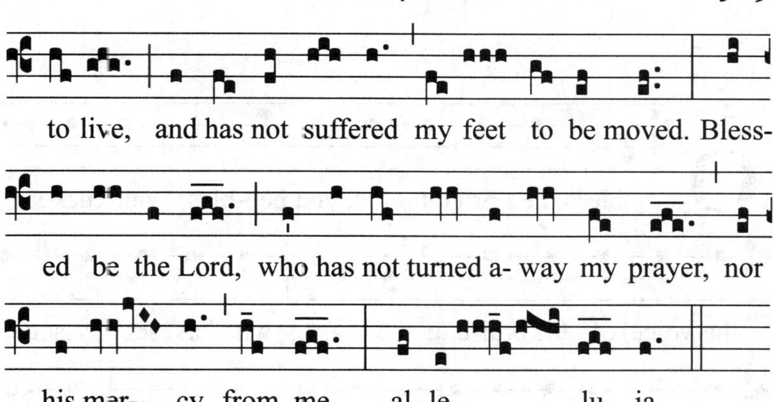
to live, and has not suffered my feet to be moved. Bless-
ed be the Lord, who has not turned a- way my prayer, nor
his mer- cy from me, al- le- lu- ia.

VERSES *Iubilate Deo, omnis terra. Ps* 65 : 1-2

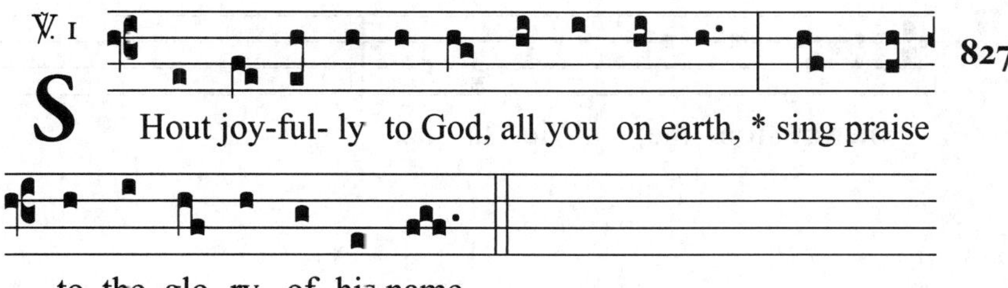
℣. 1
S Hout joy-ful- ly to God, all you on earth, * sing praise
to the glo- ry of his name.
827

Dicite Deo : quam terribilia sunt. Ps 65 : 3-4

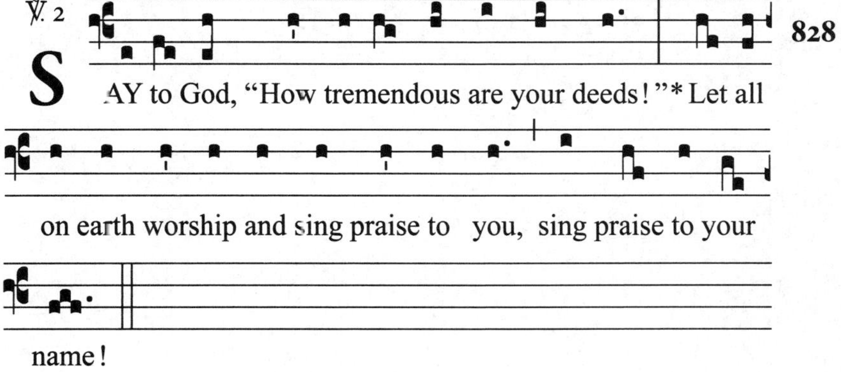
℣. 2
S AY to God, "How tremendous are your deeds!"* Let all
on earth worship and sing praise to you, sing praise to your
name!
828

- iii -

829

2.
O bless the Lord our God, you peo-ples, * and make
the voice of his praise to be heard ; who has set my soul
to live, and has not suffered my feet to be moved. Blessed
be the Lord, who has not turned a- way my prayer, nor his
mer-cy from me, al- le- lu- ia.

- iv -

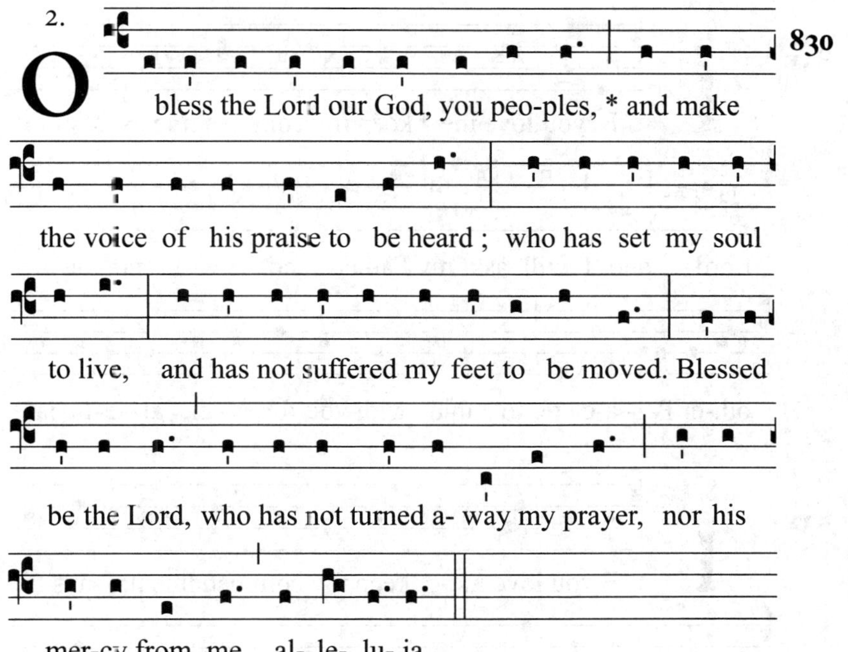
2.
830
O bless the Lord our God, you peo-ples, * and make
the voice of his praise to be heard ; who has set my soul
to live, and has not suffered my feet to be moved. Blessed
be the Lord, who has not turned a- way my prayer, nor his
mer-cy from me, al- le- lu- ia.

Communion Antiphon *Si diligitis me. Jn* 14:15-16

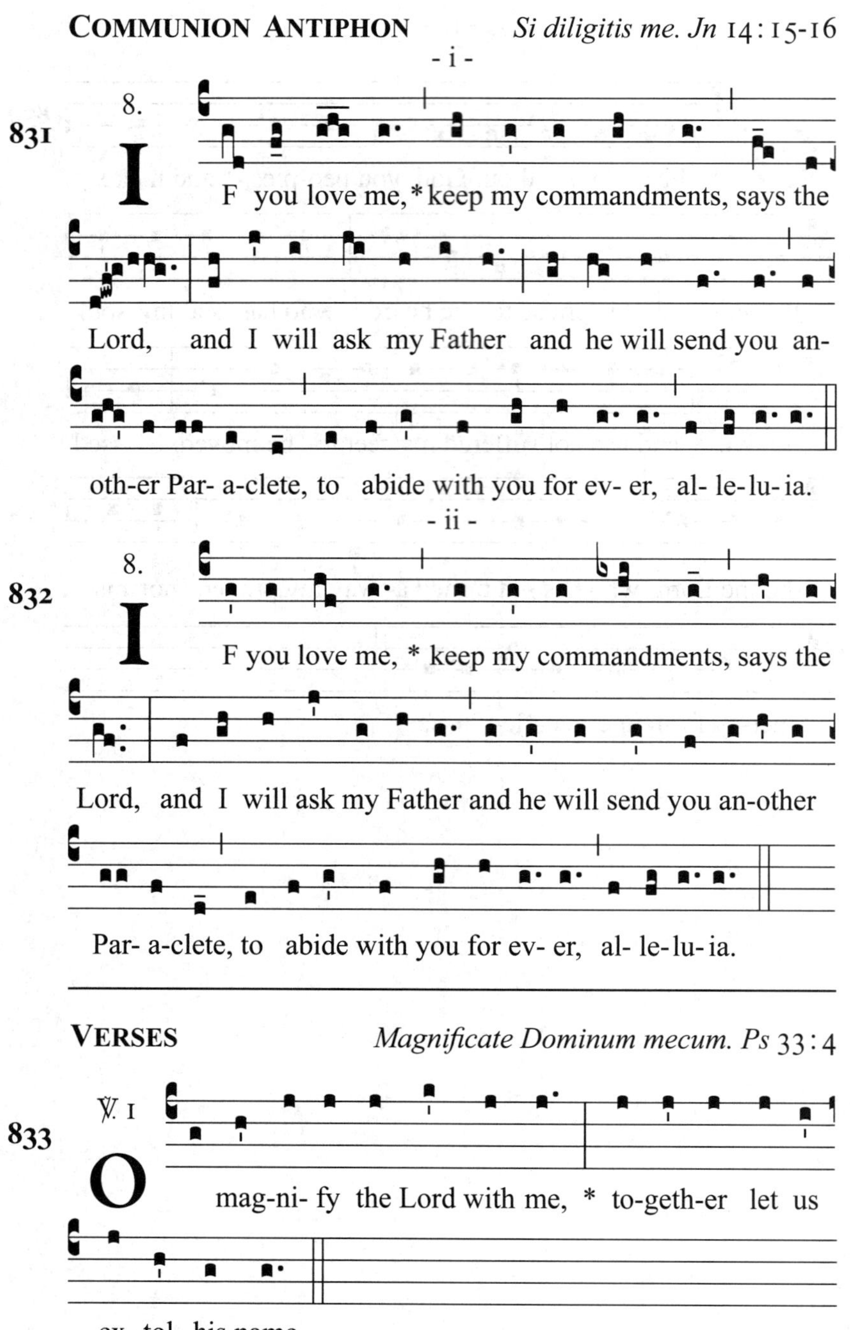
- i -
831
8.
IF you love me, * keep my commandments, says the
Lord, and I will ask my Father and he will send you an-
oth-er Par- a-clete, to abide with you for ev- er, al- le-lu-ia.
- ii -
832
8.
IF you love me, * keep my commandments, says the
Lord, and I will ask my Father and he will send you an-other
Par- a-clete, to abide with you for ev- er, al- le-lu-ia.

Verses *Magnificate Dominum mecum. Ps* 33:4

833 ℣. 1 O mag-ni- fy the Lord with me, * to-geth-er let us ex- tol his name.

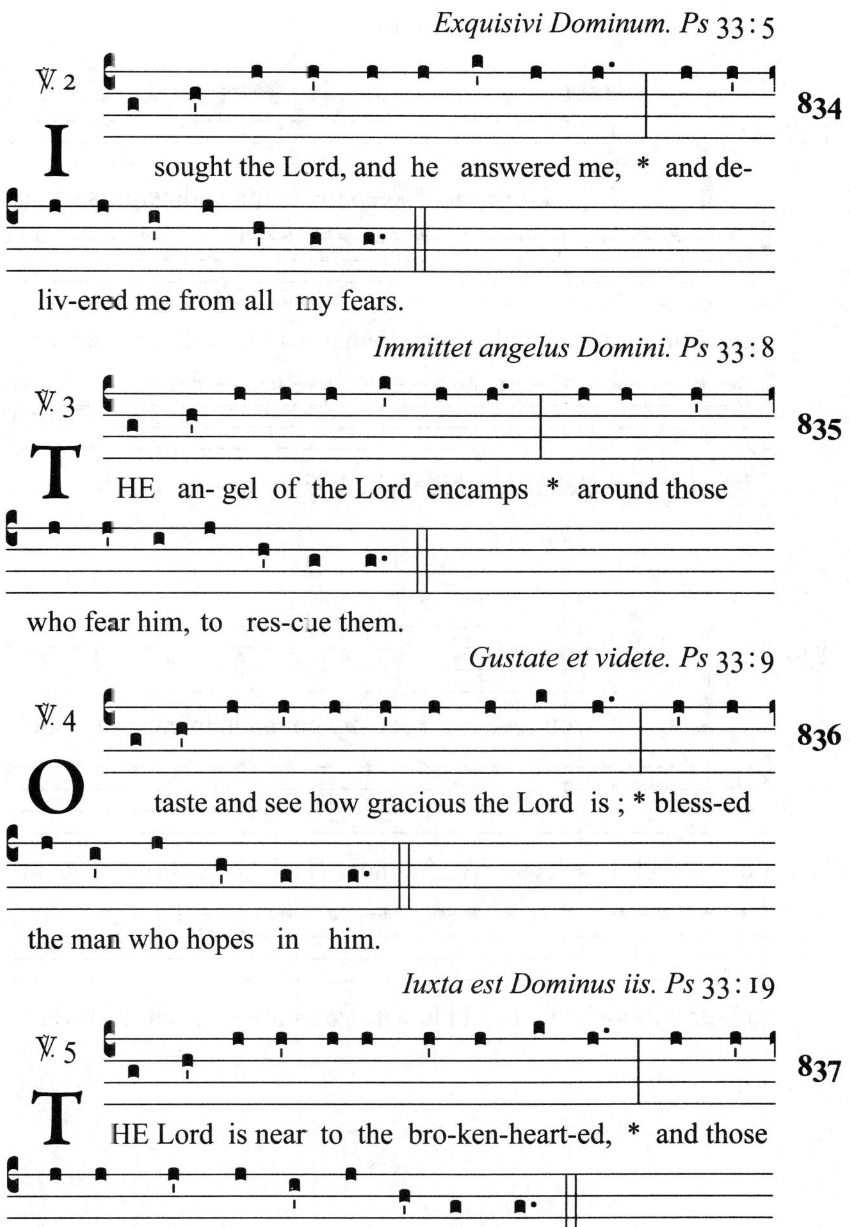
Exquisivi Dominum. Ps 33:5
℣. 2
834
I sought the Lord, and he answered me, * and de-
liv-ered me from all my fears.
Immittet angelus Domini. Ps 33:8
℣. 3
835
THE an- gel of the Lord encamps * around those
who fear him, to res-cue them.
Gustate et videte. Ps 33:9
℣. 4
836
O taste and see how gracious the Lord is ; * bless-ed
the man who hopes in him.
Iuxta est Dominus iis. Ps 33:19
℣. 5
837
THE Lord is near to the bro-ken-heart-ed, * and those
who are crushed in spir- it he will save.

Cf. also the solemn tone for Ps 33, *p.* 415.

- iii -

838

8.
IF you love me, * keep my commandments, says
the Lord, and I will ask my Father and he will send you an-
oth-er Par- a-clete, to abide with you for ev- er, al- le-lu- ia.

- iv -

839

8.
IF you love me, keep my commandments, says the
Lord, * and I will ask my Fa-ther and he will send you an-
oth-er Par- a-clete, to abide with you for ev-er, al- le- lu- ia.

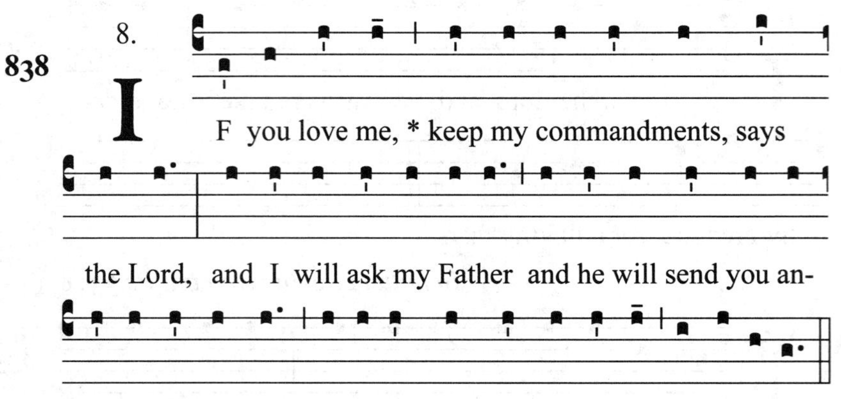

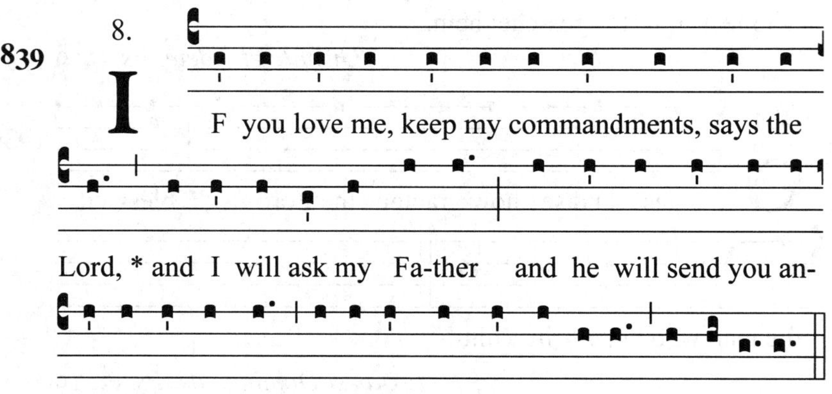

THE ASCENSION OF THE LORD

At the Vigil Mass

ENTRANCE ANTIPHON *Regna terrœ, cantate Domino.*
Ps 67:33. 35

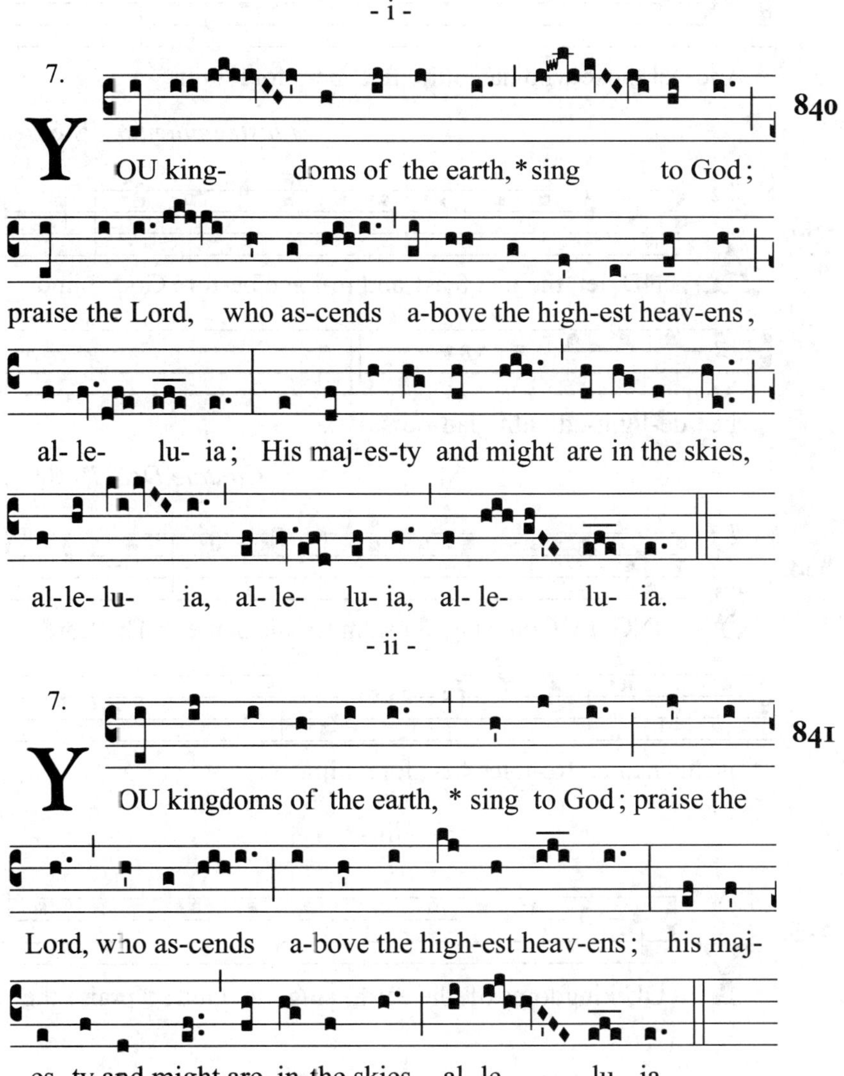
- i -
7.
840
YOU king- doms of the earth, * sing to God;
praise the Lord, who as-cends a-bove the high-est heav-ens,
al- le- lu- ia; His maj-es-ty and might are in the skies,
al-le- lu- ia, al- le- lu- ia, al- le- lu- ia.
- ii -
7.
841
YOU kingdoms of the earth, * sing to God; praise the
Lord, who as-cends a-bove the high-est heav-ens; his maj-
es- ty and might are in the skies, al- le- lu- ia.

VERSES *Exsurgat Deus. Ps* 67:2

842

℣. 1 LET God a-rise, and let his en- e-mies be scat-tered. * And let those who hate him flee be- fore him.

Et iusti epulentur. Ps 67:4

843
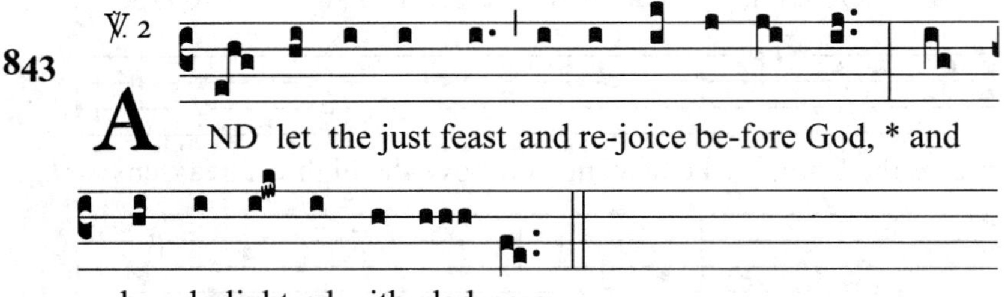
℣. 2 AND let the just feast and re-joice be-fore God, * and be de-light-ed with glad-ness.

Cantate Deo. Ps 67:5

844
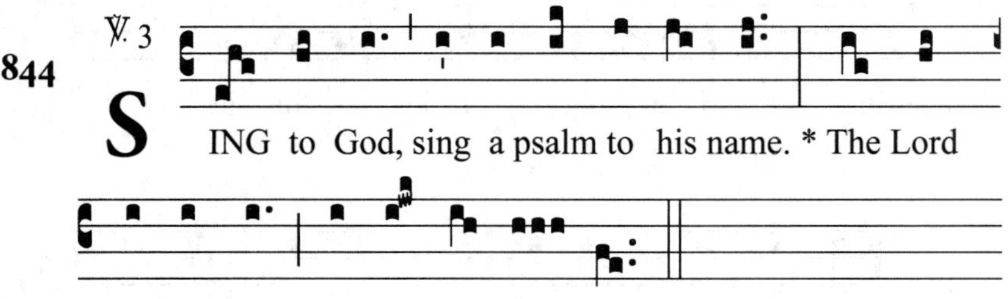
℣. 3 SING to God, sing a psalm to his name. * The Lord is his name. Re-joice be- fore him.

- iii -

845
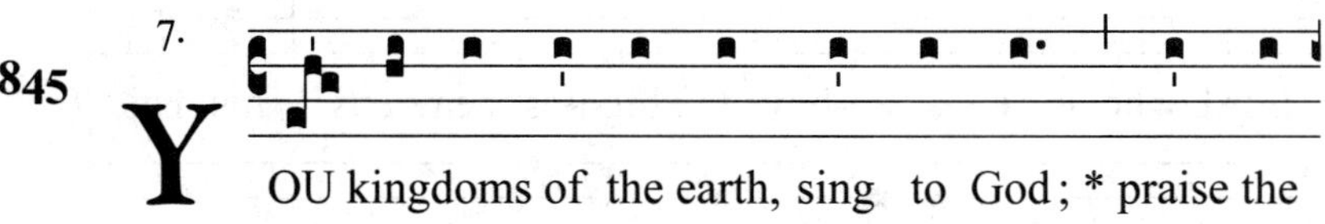
7. YOU kingdoms of the earth, sing to God; * praise the

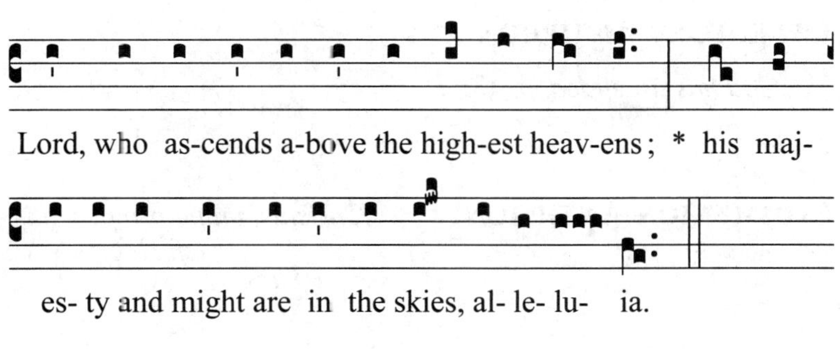
Lord, who as-cends a-bove the high-est heav-ens ; * his maj-
es- ty and might are in the skies, al- le- lu- ia.

Or :

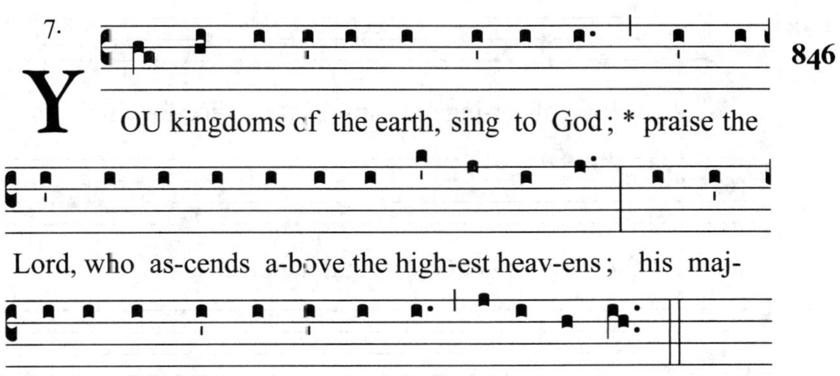
7.
846
YOU kingdoms of the earth, sing to God ; * praise the
Lord, who as-cends a-bove the high-est heav-ens ; his maj-
es- ty and might are in the skies, al- le- lu- ia.

- iv -

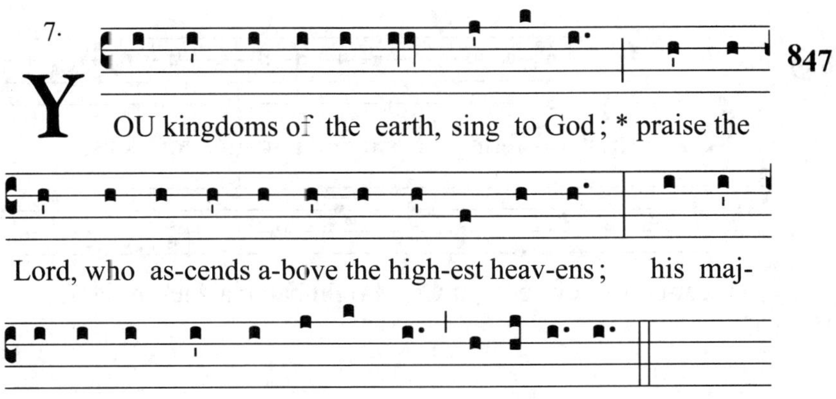
7.
847
YOU kingdoms of the earth, sing to God ; * praise the
Lord, who as-cends a-bove the high-est heav-ens ; his maj-
es- ty and might are in the skies, al- le- lu- ia.

OFFERTORY ANTIPHON

God has ascended, p. 384.

COMMUNION ANTIPHON *Christus, unum pro peccatis.*
Cf. Hebr 10: 12

- i -

848

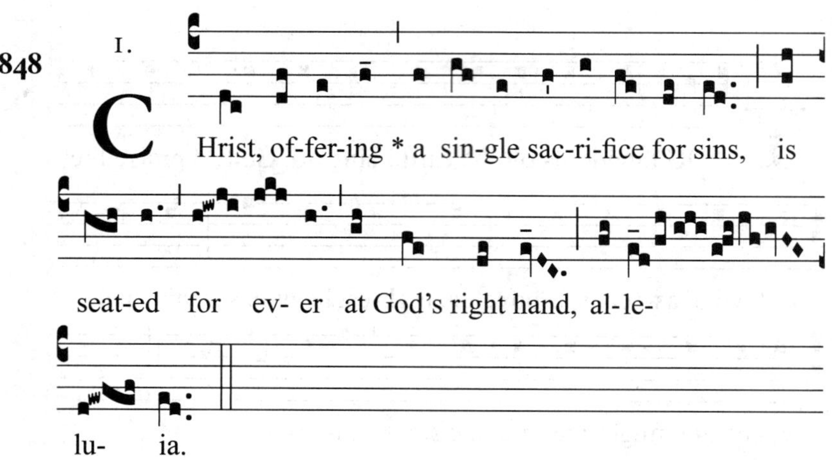
I.
CHrist, of-fer-ing * a sin-gle sac-ri-fice for sins, is
seat-ed for ev- er at God's right hand, al-le-
lu- ia.

- ii -

849

I.
CHrist, of- fering * a single sac-ri-fice for sins,
is seat-ed for ev- er at God's right hand, al- le- lu- ia.

VERSES *Quoniam occisus es. Rv* 5:9

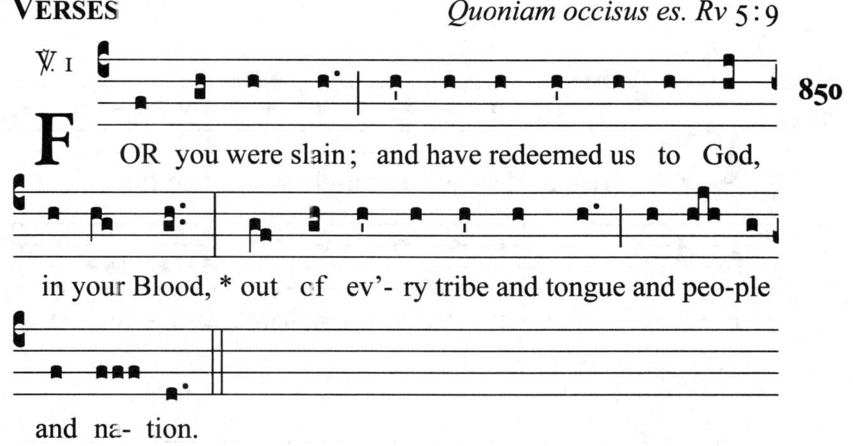

℣. 1
FOR you were slain; and have redeemed us to God,
in your Blood, * out of ev'- ry tribe and tongue and peo-ple
and na- tion.

850

Dignus est Agnus qui occisus est. Rv 5:12

℣. 2
THE Lamb that was slain is wor-thy to receive pow-
er and di-vin- i- ty and wis-dom * and strength and hon- or
and glo- ry and bless-ing.

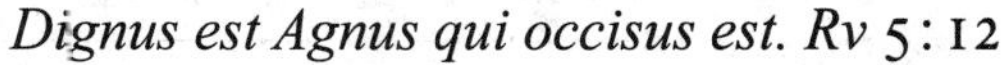

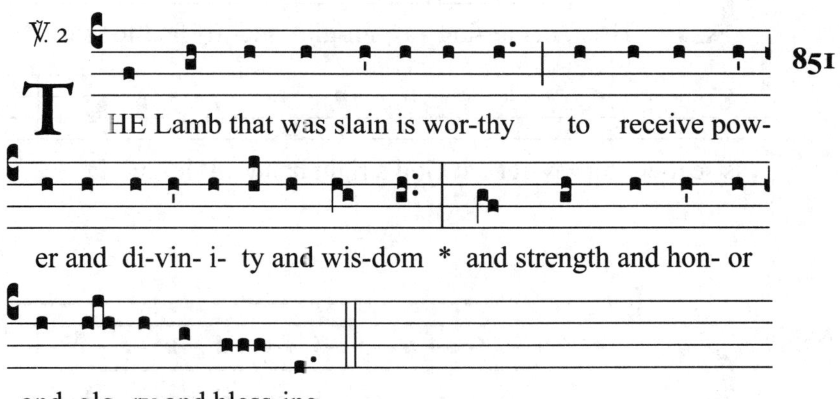

851

Et seniores ceciderunt et adoraverunt. Rv 5:14

℣. 3
THE four and twen-ty an-cients fell down on their
fac-es and a-dored him * who lives for ev- er and ev- er.

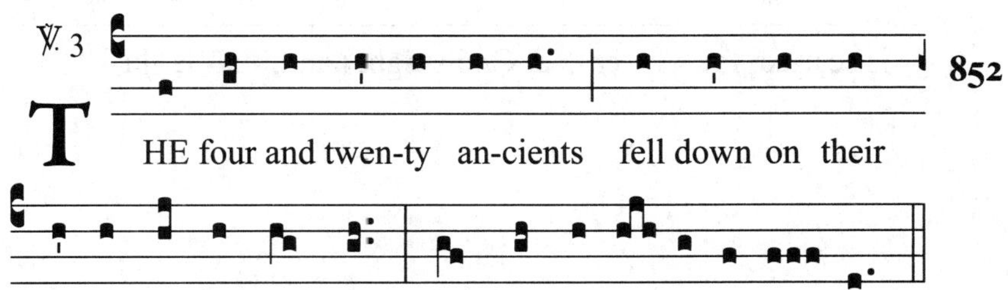

852

- iii -

853

I.
CHrist, of- fer-ing a sin-gle sac- ri-fice for sins, *
is seat-ed for ev- er at God's right hand, al- le- lu- ia.

Or :

854

I.
CHrist, of- fer-ing a sin-gle sac- ri- fice for sins, *
is seat-ed for ev- er at God's right hand, al- le- lu- ia.

- iv -

855

I.
CHrist, of- fer-ing a sin-gle sac- ri- fice for sins, *
is seat-ed for ev- er at God's right hand, al- le- lu- ia.

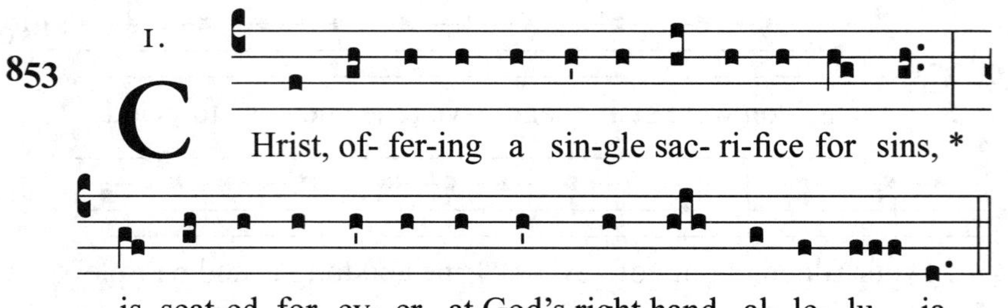

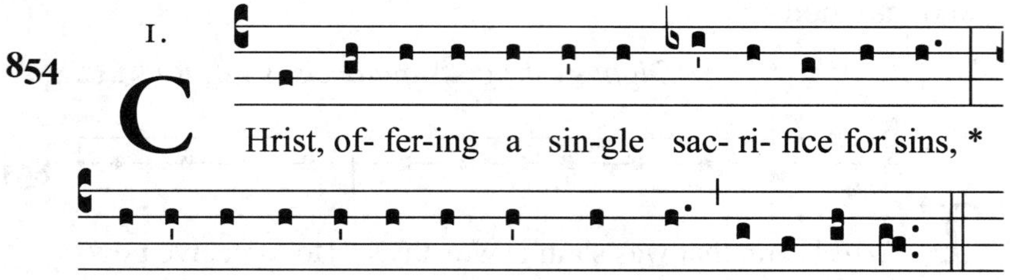

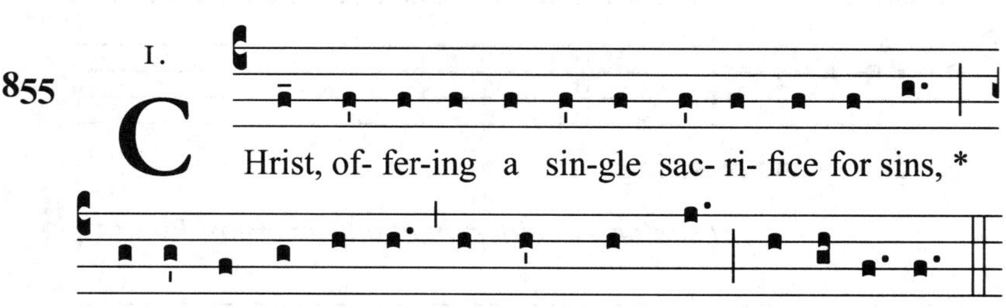

THE ASCENSION OF THE LORD

At the Mass during the Day

Entrance Antiphon *Viri Galilæi. Acts* 1:11

- i -

7.

MEN of Gal- i- lee, * why gaze in won-der at the heav-ens ? al- le- lu- ia ; This Je- sus whom you saw as-cending in- to heav-en will re- turn as you saw him go, al- le- lu- ia, al- le- lu- ia, al- le- lu- ia. 856

- ii -

7.

MEN of Gal- i- lee, * why gaze in wonder at the heav-ens ? This Je- sus whom you saw as-cend- ing in- to heav-en will re-turn as you saw him go, al- le- lu- ia 857

VERSES *Omnes gentes, plaudite manibus. Ps* 46:2

858

℣. 1
O clap your hands, all you na-tions, * shout un- to
God with loud cries of glad- ness.

Elegit nobis hereditatem suam. Ps 46:5-6

859
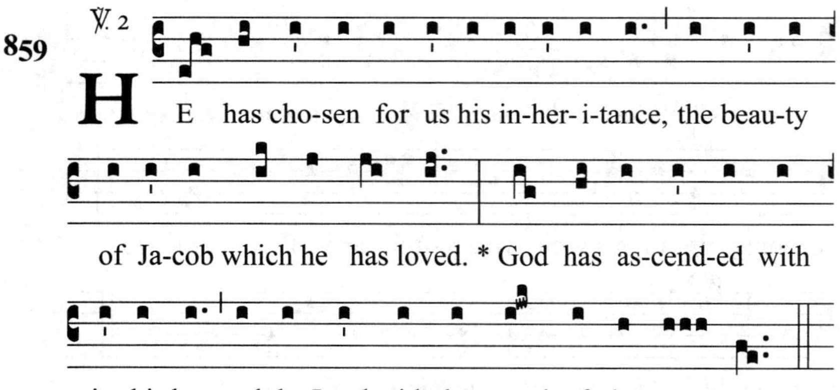
℣. 2
HE has cho-sen for us his in-her- i-tance, the beau-ty
of Ja-cob which he has loved. * God has as-cend-ed with
ju- bi- lee, and the Lord with the sound of the trum- pet.

Psallite Deo nostro, psallite. Ps 46:7

860
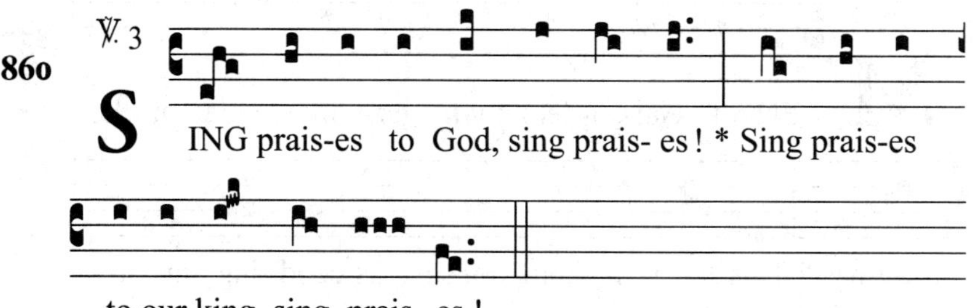
℣. 3
SING prais-es to God, sing prais- es ! * Sing prais-es
to our king, sing prais- es !

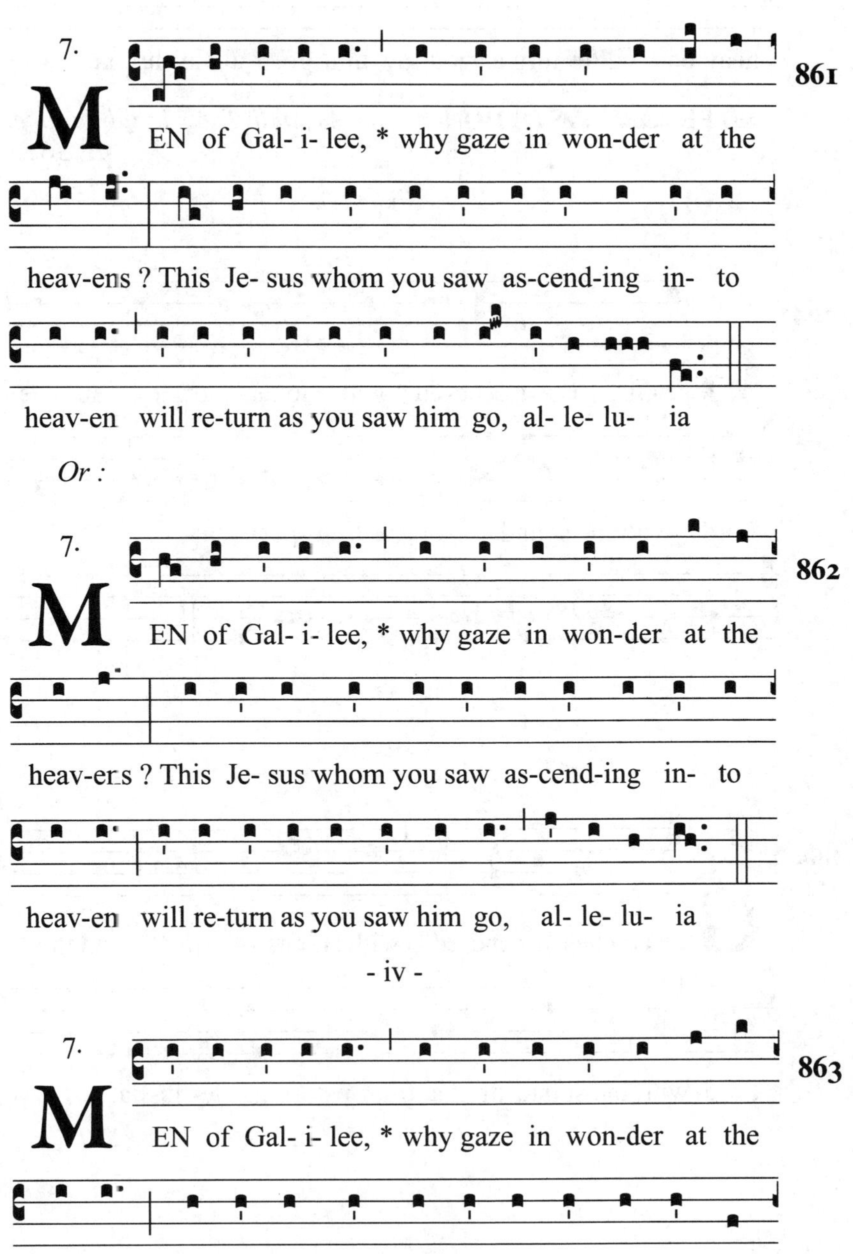
- iii -
7.
861
MEN of Gal- i- lee, * why gaze in won-der at the
heav-ens ? This Je- sus whom you saw as-cend-ing in- to
heav-en will re-turn as you saw him go, al- le- lu- ia
Or :
7.
862
MEN of Gal- i- lee, * why gaze in won-der at the
heav-ens ? This Je- sus whom you saw as-cend-ing in- to
heav-en will re-turn as you saw him go, al- le- lu- ia
- iv -
7.
863
MEN of Gal- i- lee, * why gaze in won-der at the
heav-ens ? This Je- sus whom you saw as-cend-ing in- to

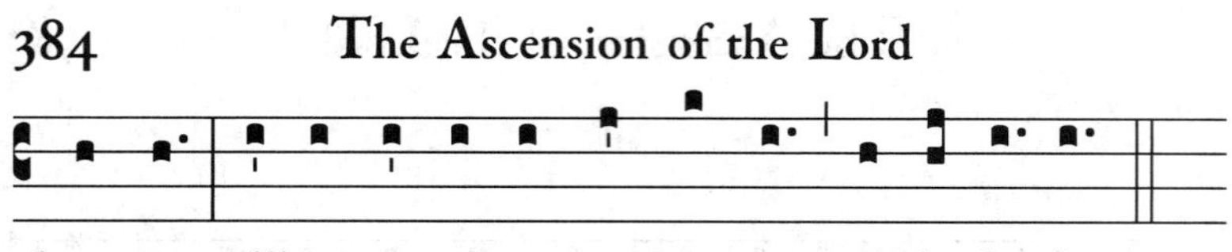

heav-en will re-turn as you saw him go, al- le- lu- ia

OFFERTORY ANTIPHON *Ascendit Deus in iubilatione.*
Ps 46:6

- i -

864
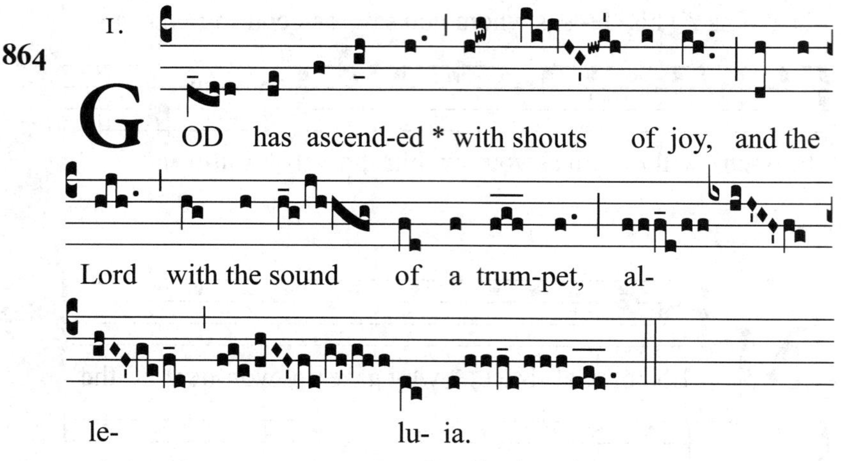
I.
GOD has ascend-ed * with shouts of joy, and the
Lord with the sound of a trum-pet, al-
le- lu- ia.

- ii -

865
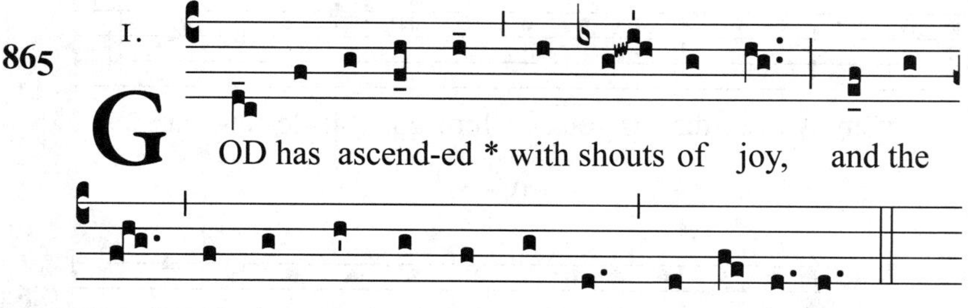
I.
GOD has ascend-ed * with shouts of joy, and the
Lord with the sound of a trum-pet, al- le- lu- ia.

VERSES *Omnes gentes, plaudite manibus. Ps* 46 : 2

℣. 1
866
O clap your hands, all you na-tions, * shout un- to
God with loud cries of glad- ness.

Elegit nobis hereditatem suam. Ps 46 : 5-6

℣. 2
867
HE has cho-sen for us his in-her-i-tance, the beau-ty
of Ja-cob which he has loved. * God has as-cend-ed with
ju- bi- lee, and the Lord with the sound of the trum- pet.

Psallite Deo nostro, psallite. Ps 46 : 7

℣. 3
868
SING prais-es to God, sing prais- es ! * Sing prais- es
to our king, sing prais- es !

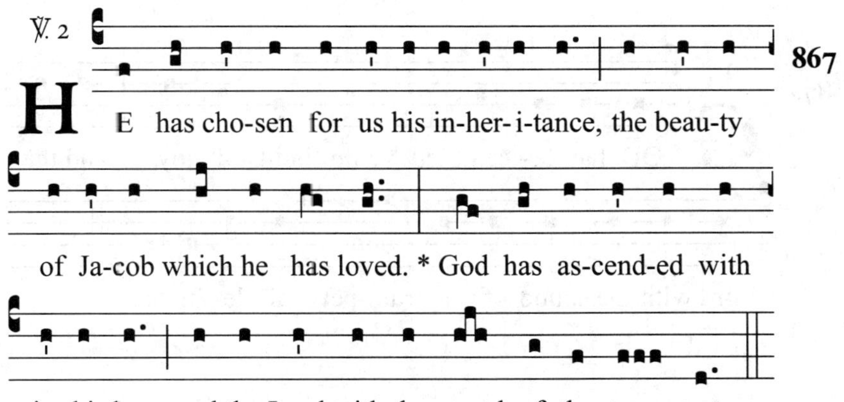

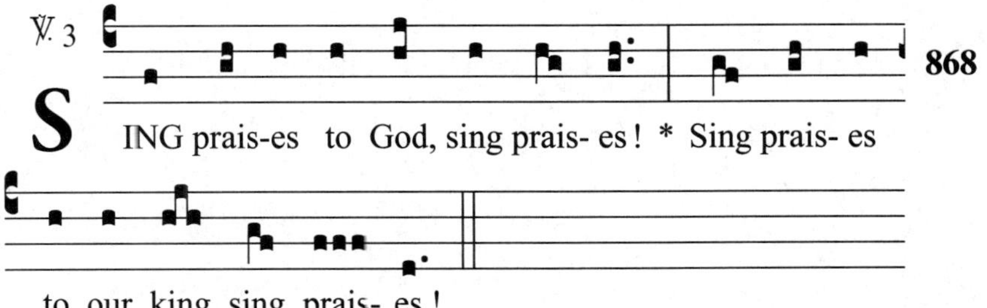

- iii -

869

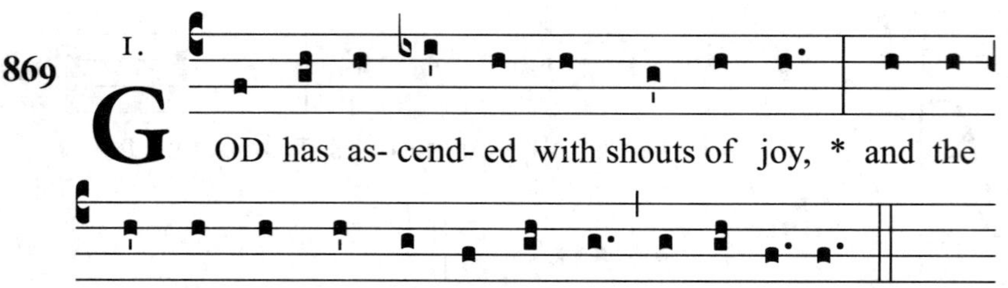
I.
GOD has as- cend- ed with shouts of joy, * and the
Lord with the sound of a trum-pet, al- le- lu- ia.

- iv -

870

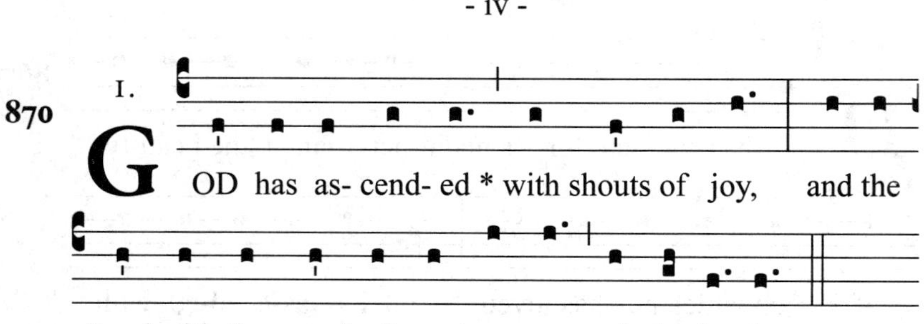
I.
GOD has as- cend- ed * with shouts of joy, and the
Lord with the sound of a trum-pet, al- le- lu- ia.

COMMUNION ANTIPHON *Ecce ego vobiscum sum. Mt* 28:20

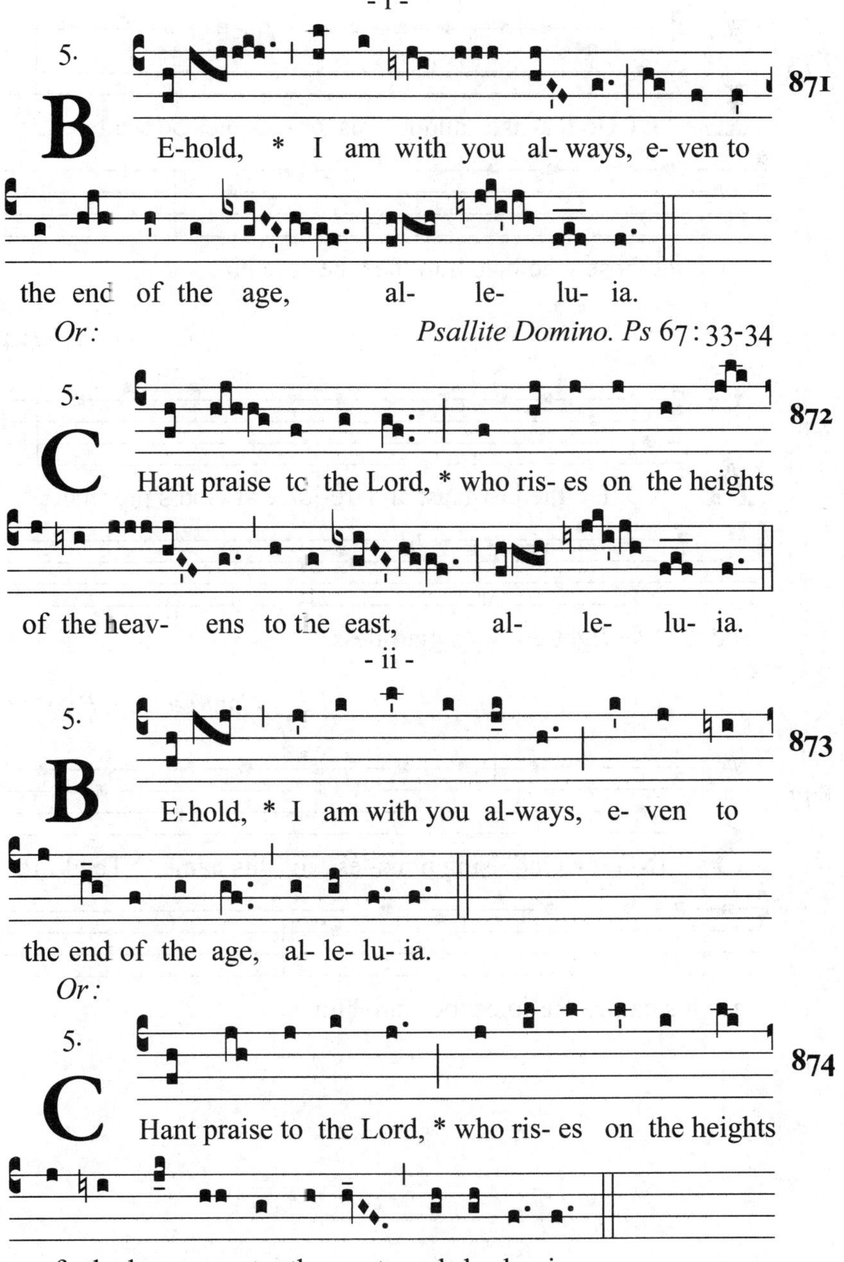
- i -
5.
871
BEhold, * I am with you al- ways, e- ven to
the end of the age, al- le- lu- ia.
Or: Psallite Domino. Ps 67:33-34
5.
872
CHant praise to the Lord, * who ris- es on the heights
of the heav- ens to the east, al- le- lu- ia.
- ii -
5.
873
BEhold, * I am with you al-ways, e- ven to
the end of the age, al- le- lu- ia.
Or:
5.
874
CHant praise to the Lord, * who ris- es on the heights
of the heav-ens to the east, al- le- lu- ia.

VERSES

Exsurgat Deus. Ps 67:2

875

℣. 1
LET God a-rise, and let his en- e-mies be scattered. *
And let those who hate him flee be-fore him.

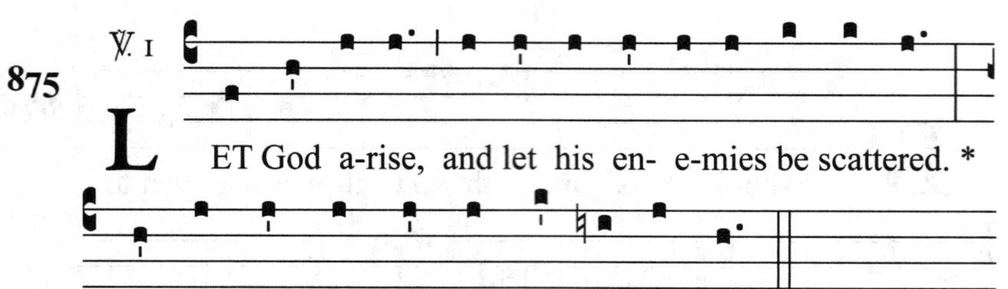

Et iusti epulentur. Ps 67:4

876

℣. 2
AND let the just feast and re-joice at God's presence, *
and be de-light-ed with glad-ness.

Cantate Deo. Ps 67:5

877

℣. 3
SING to God, sing prais- es to his name. * The Lord
is his name. Re-joice be- fore him.

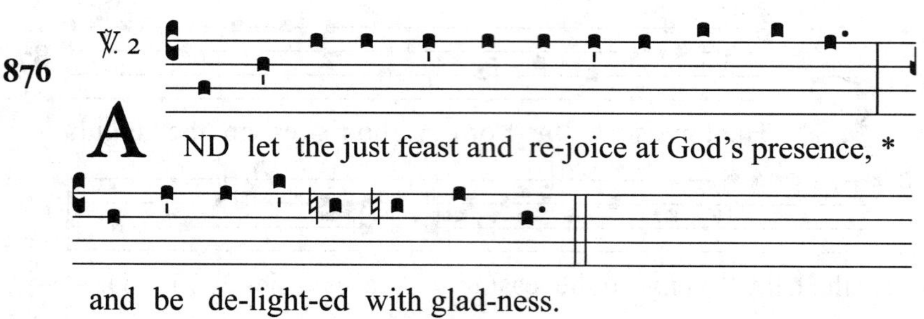

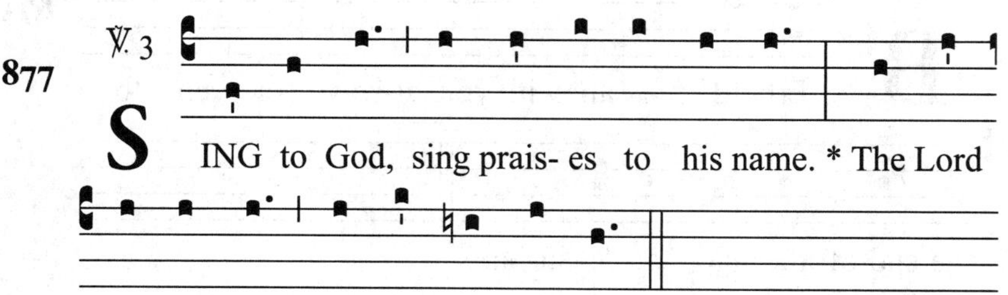

- iii -

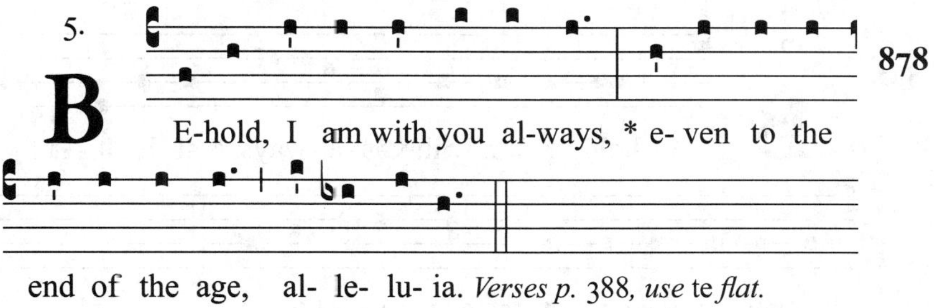

5. BEhold, I am with you al-ways, * e- ven to the 878

end of the age, al- le- lu- ia. *Verses p.* 388, *use* te *flat.*

Or:

5. CHant praise to the Lord, * who ris- es on the heights 879

of the heav-ens to the east, al- le- lu- ia.

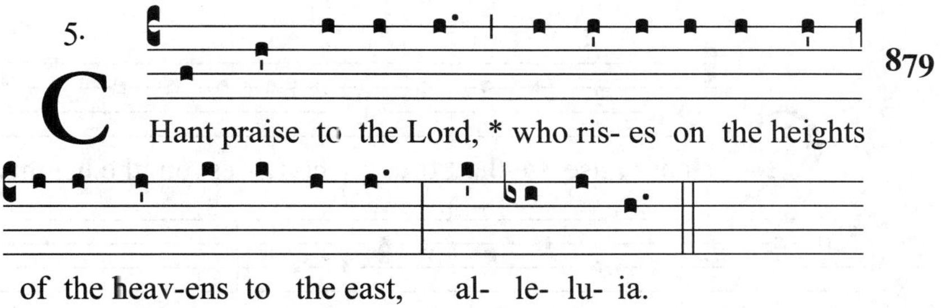

Verses p. 388, *use* te *flat.*

- iv -

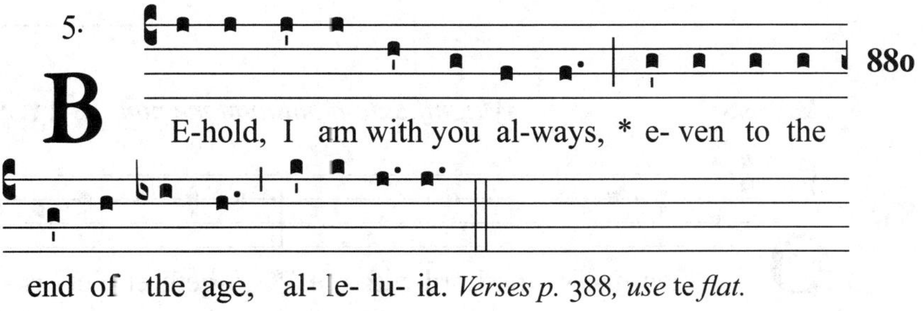

5. BEhold, I am with you al-ways, * e- ven to the 880

end of the age, al- le- lu- ia. *Verses p.* 388, *use* te *flat.*

Or:

5. 881

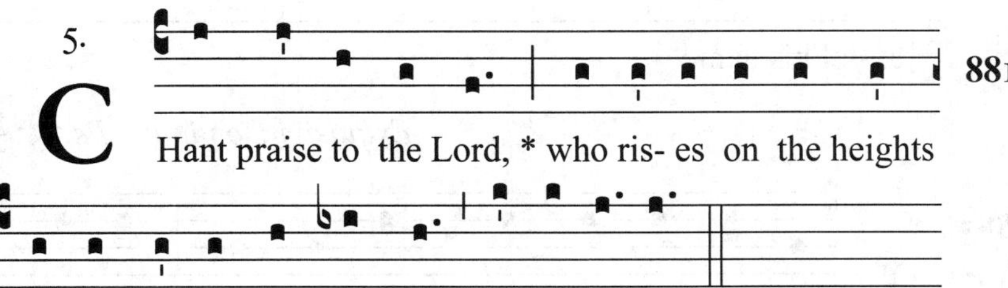
CHant praise to the Lord, * who ris- es on the heights

of the heavens to the east, al- le- lu- ia.

Verses p. 406, *use* te *flat.*

- i -

882

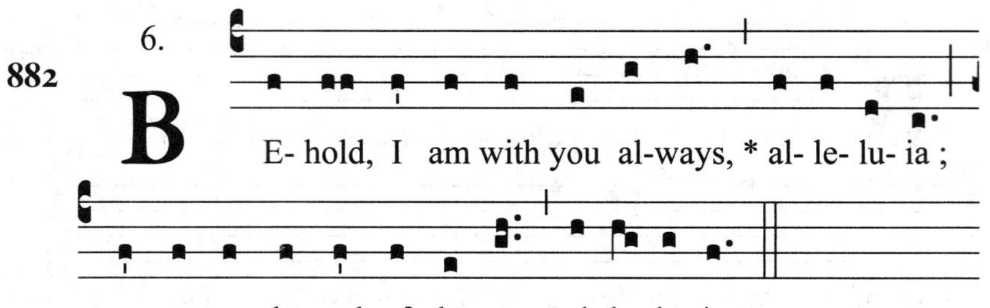
6.
BEhold, I am with you al-ways, * al- le- lu- ia ;
e- ven to the end of the age, al- le- lu- ia.

- iii -

883

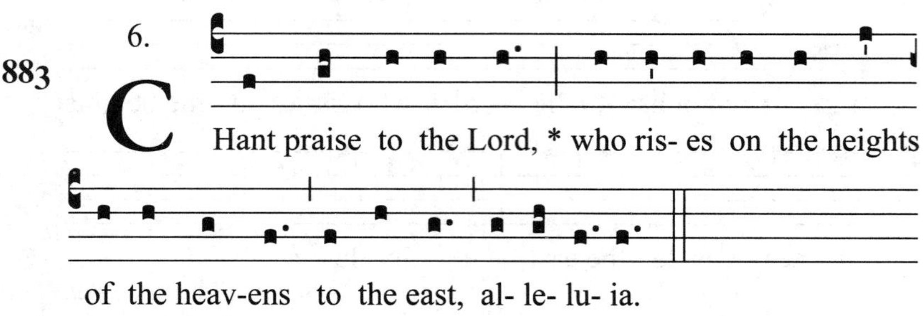
6.
CHant praise to the Lord, * who ris- es on the heights
of the heav-ens to the east, al- le- lu- ia.

VERSES *Magnificate Dominum mecum. Ps* 33:4

884

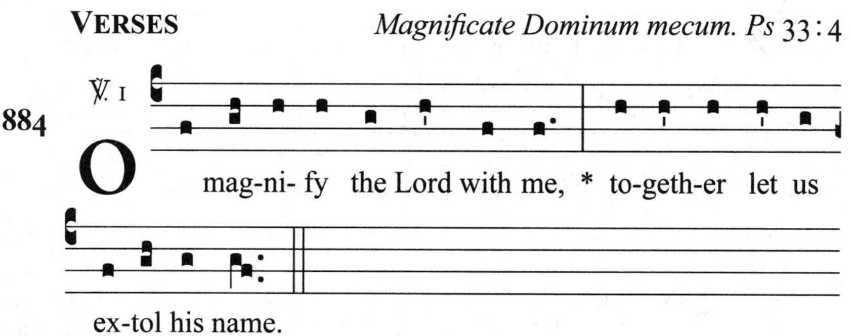
℣. 1
O mag-ni- fy the Lord with me, * to-geth-er let us
ex-tol his name.

Exquisivi Dominum. Ps 33:5

885

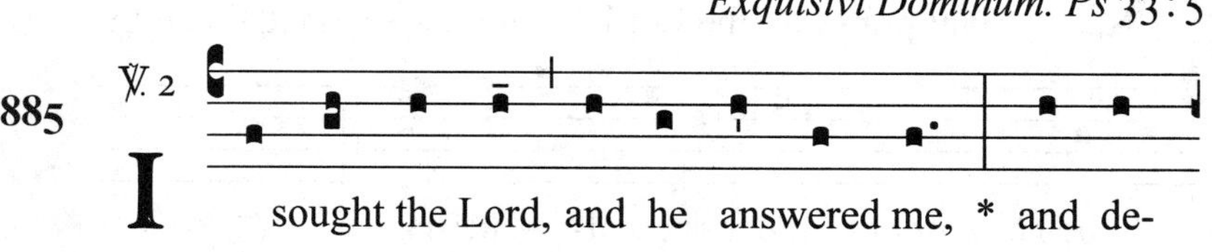
℣. 2
I sought the Lord, and he answered me, * and de-

liv-ered me from all my fears.

Immittet angelus Domini. Ps 33:8

℣. 3 THE an- gel of the Lord encamps * around those who 886

fear him, to res-cue them.

Gustate et videte. Ps 33:9

℣. 4 O taste and see how gracious the Lord is; * blessed the 887

man who hopes in him.

Timete Dominum. Ps 33:10

℣. 5 O fear the Lord, all you his saints, * for those who fear 888

him have no want.

Iuxta est Dominus iis. Ps 33:19

℣. 6 THE Lord is near to the bro-ken-heart-ed, * and those 889

who are crushed in spir- it he will save.

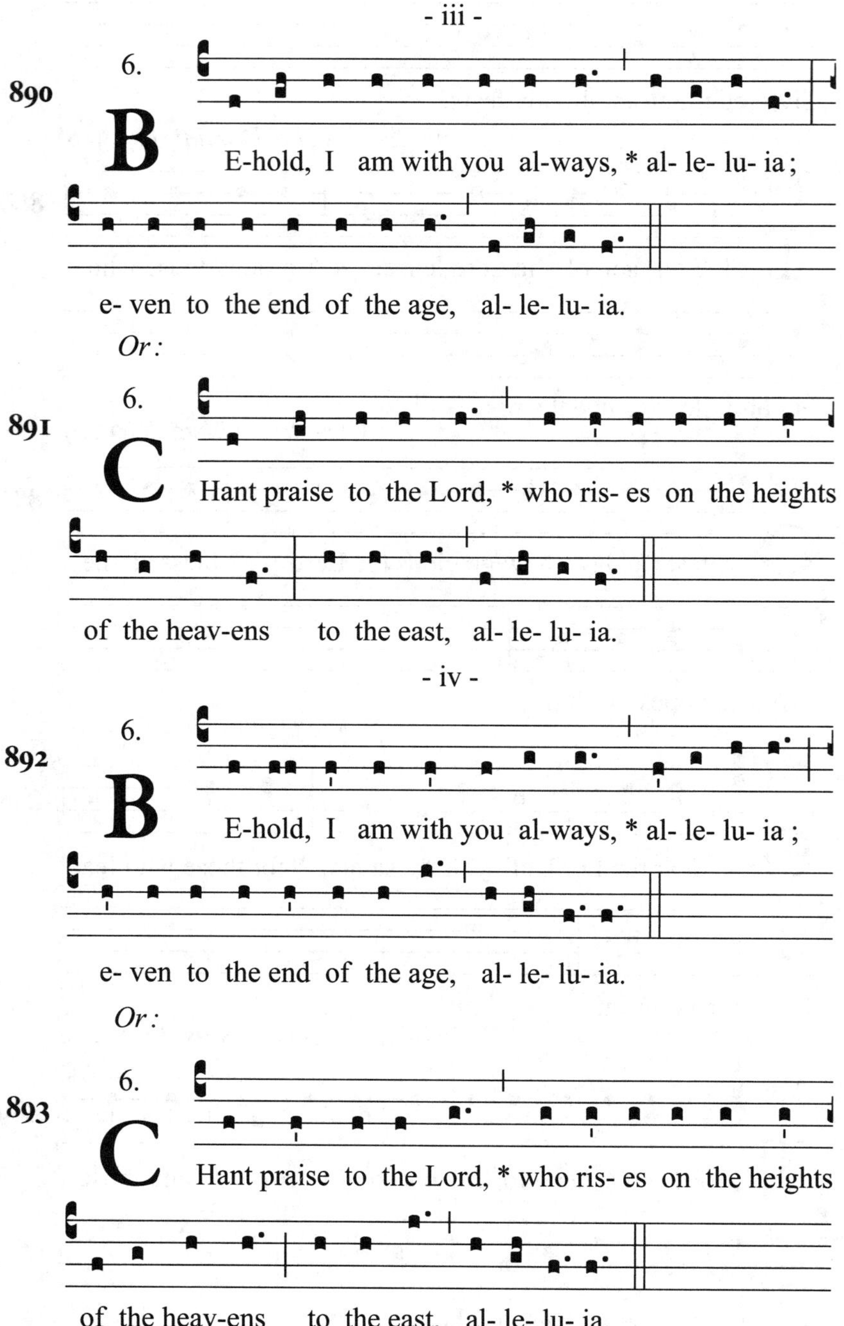
- iii -
890
6.
BEhold, I am with you al-ways, * al- le- lu- ia;
e- ven to the end of the age, al- le- lu- ia.
Or:
891
6.
CHant praise to the Lord, * who ris- es on the heights
of the heav-ens to the east, al- le- lu- ia.
- iv -
892
6.
BEhold, I am with you al-ways, * al- le- lu- ia ;
e- ven to the end of the age, al- le- lu- ia.
Or:
893
6.
CHant praise to the Lord, * who ris- es on the heights
of the heav-ens to the east, al- le- lu- ia.

SEVENTH SUNDAY OF EASTER

ENTRANCE ANTIPHON *Exaudi, Domine, vocem meam.*
Ps 26:7-9

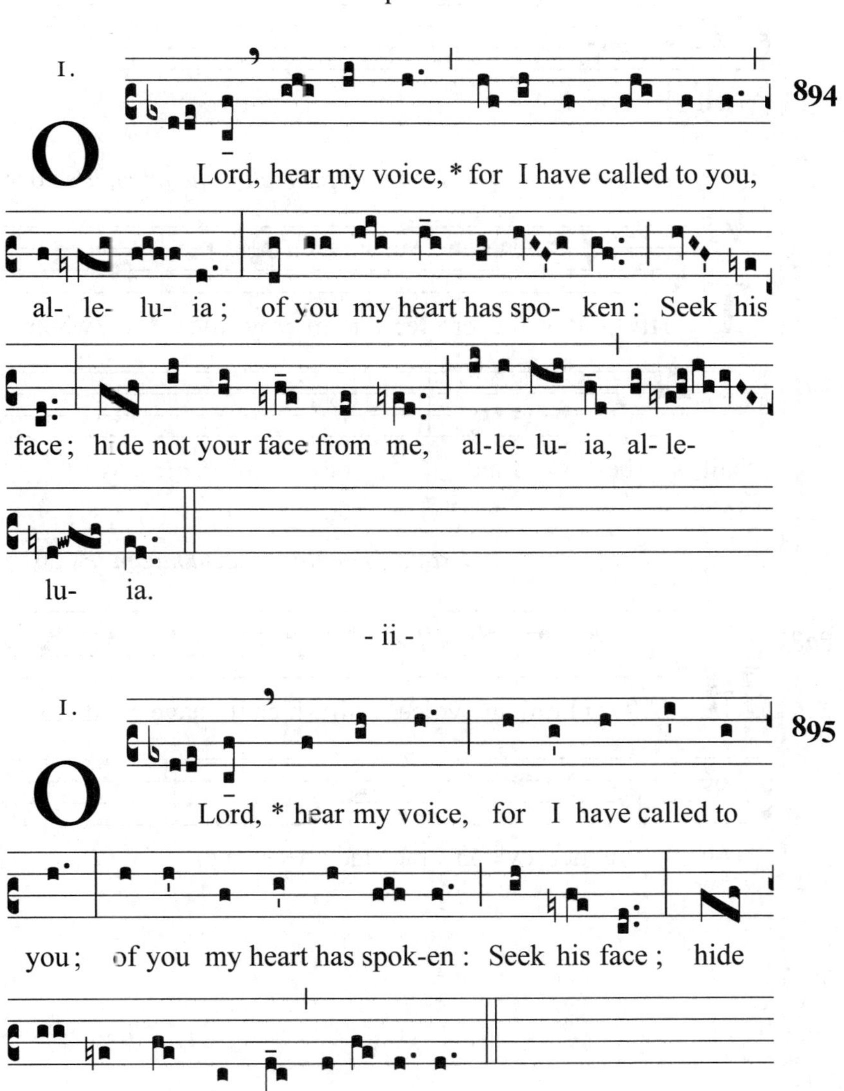
- i -
I.
894
O Lord, hear my voice, * for I have called to you,
al- le- lu- ia ; of you my heart has spo- ken : Seek his
face ; hide not your face from me, al-le- lu- ia, al- le-
lu- ia.
- ii -
I.
895
O Lord, * hear my voice, for I have called to
you ; of you my heart has spok-en : Seek his face ; hide
not your face from me, al-le- lu- ia.

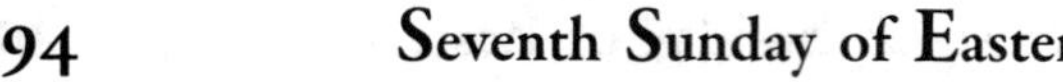

VERSES *Dominus illuminatio mea. Ps* 26:1

896
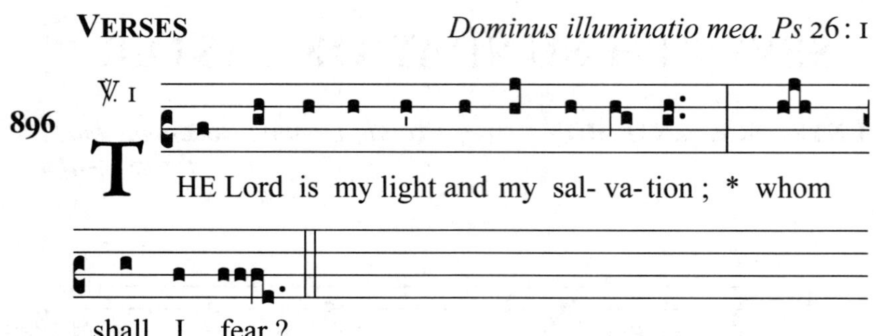
℣. 1
THE Lord is my light and my sal- va- tion ; * whom
shall I fear ?

Dominus protector vitæ meæ. Ps 26:1

897

℣. 2
THE Lord is the pro-tec-tor of my life : * of whom
shall I be a- fraid ?

Exaudi, Domine, vocem meam. Ps 26:7

898

℣. 3
HEAR, O Lord, my voice, with which I have cried to
you ; * have mer- cy on me and hear me.

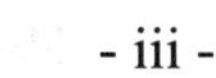

- iii -

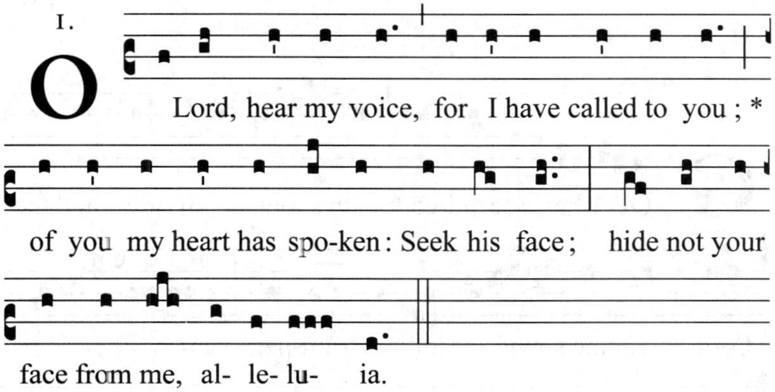

1\.

O Lord, hear my voice, for I have called to you; * 899

of you my heart has spo-ken: Seek his face; hide not your

face from me, al- le- lu- ia.

Or:

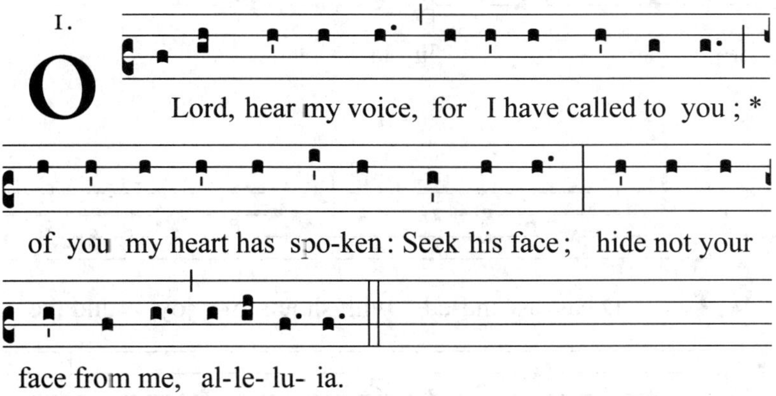

1\.

O Lord, hear my voice, for I have called to you; * 900

of you my heart has spo-ken: Seek his face; hide not your

face from me, al-le- lu- ia.

- iv -

1\.

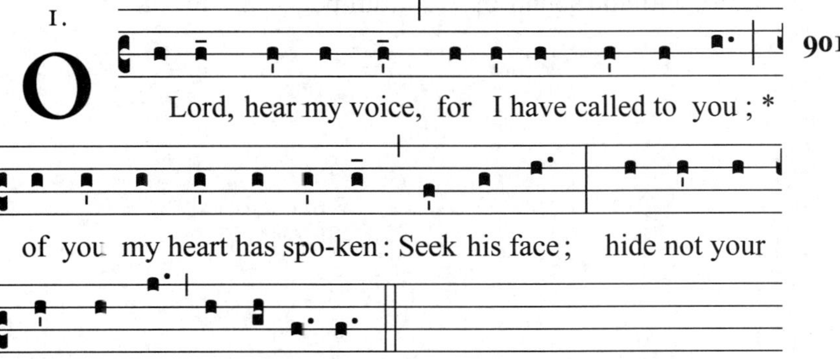

O Lord, hear my voice, for I have called to you; * 901

of you my heart has spo-ken: Seek his face; hide not your

face from me, al- le- lu- ia.

Offertory Antiphon *Ascendit Deus in iubilatione.* *Ps* 46:6

- i -

902

I.
GOD has ascend-ed * with shouts of joy, and the
Lord with the sound of a trum-pet, al-
le- lu- ia.

- ii -

903

I.
GOD has ascend-ed * with shouts of joy, and the
Lord with the sound of a trum-pet, al- le- lu- ia.

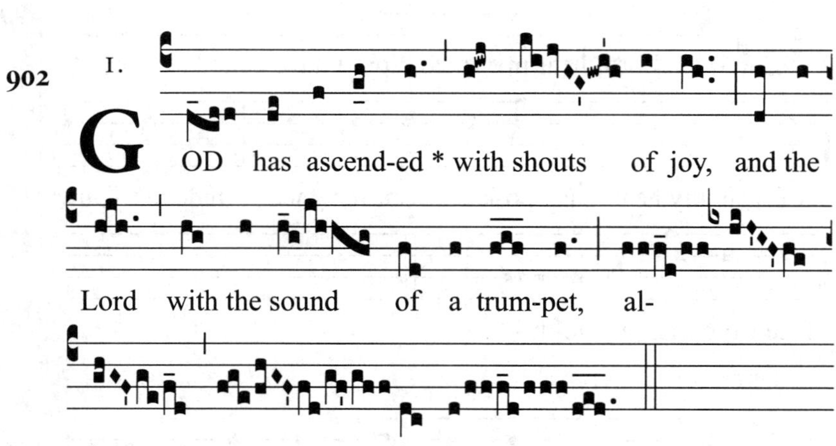

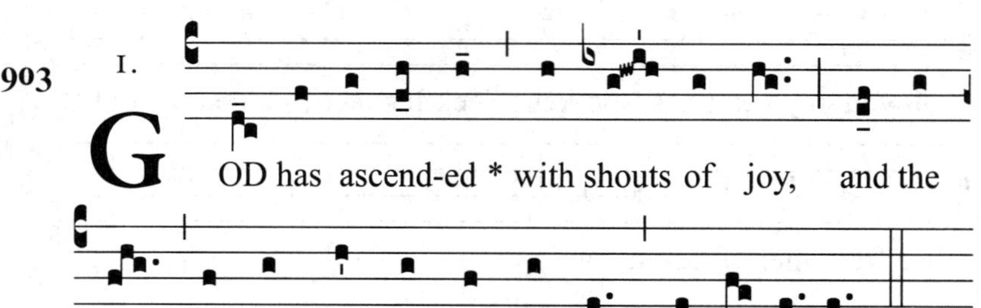

VERSES *Omnes gentes, plaudite manibus. Ps* 46:2

℣. 1
904
O clap your hands, all you na-tions, * shout un- to
God with loud cries of glad- ness.

Elegit nobis hereditatem suam. Ps 46:5-6

℣. 2
905
HE has cho-sen for us his in-her- i-tance, the beau-ty
of Ja-cob which he has loved. * God has as-cend-ed with
ju- bi- lee, and the Lord with the sound of the trum- pet.

Psallite Deo nostro, psallite. Ps 46:7

℣. 3
906
SING prais-es to God, sing prais- es ! * Sing prais- es
to our king, sing prais- es !

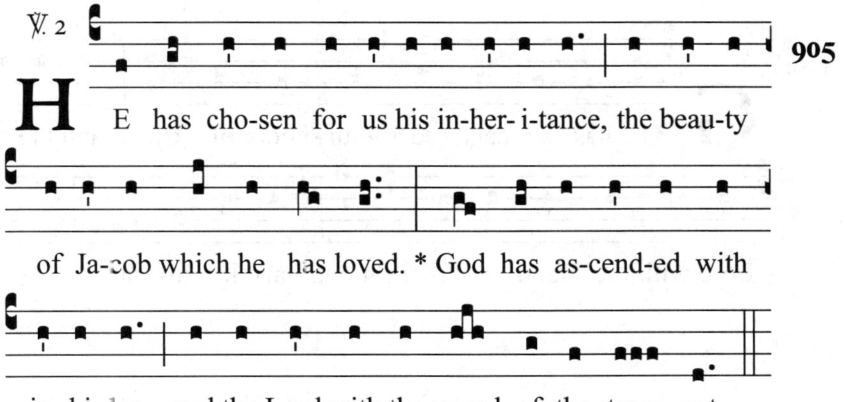

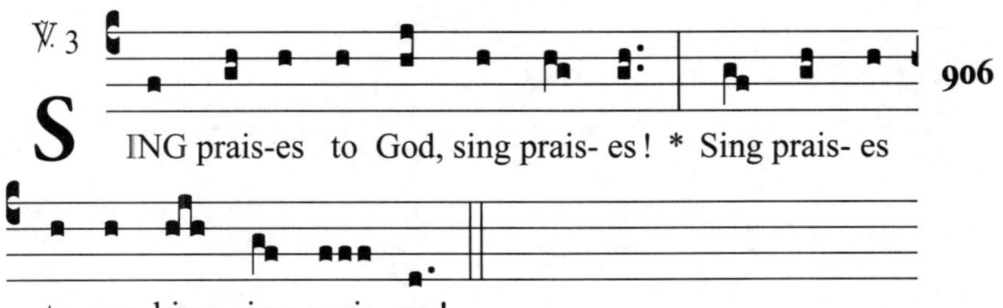

- iii -

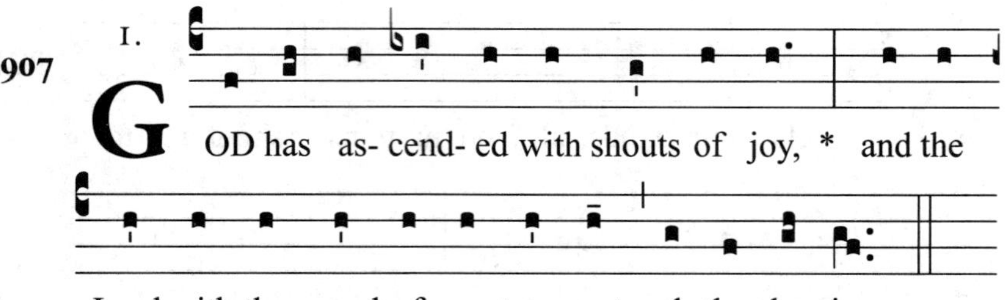
907
1.
GOD has as- cend- ed with shouts of joy, * and the

Lord with the sound of a trum-pet, al- le- lu- ia.

- iv -

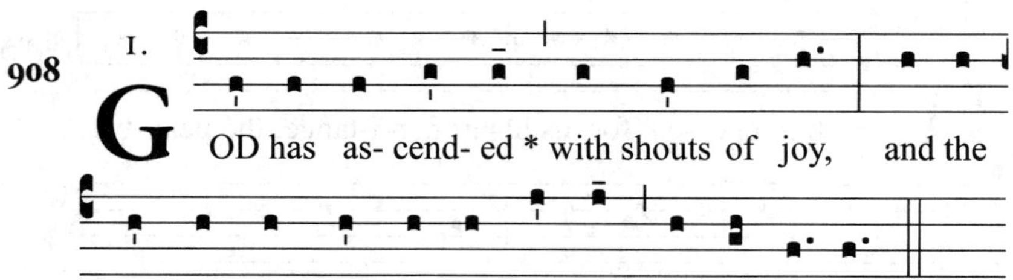
908
1.
GOD has as- cend- ed * with shouts of joy, and the

Lord with the sound of a trum-pet, al- le- lu- ia.

COMMUNION ANTIPHON *Rogo, Pater.*
Jn 17:22

- i -

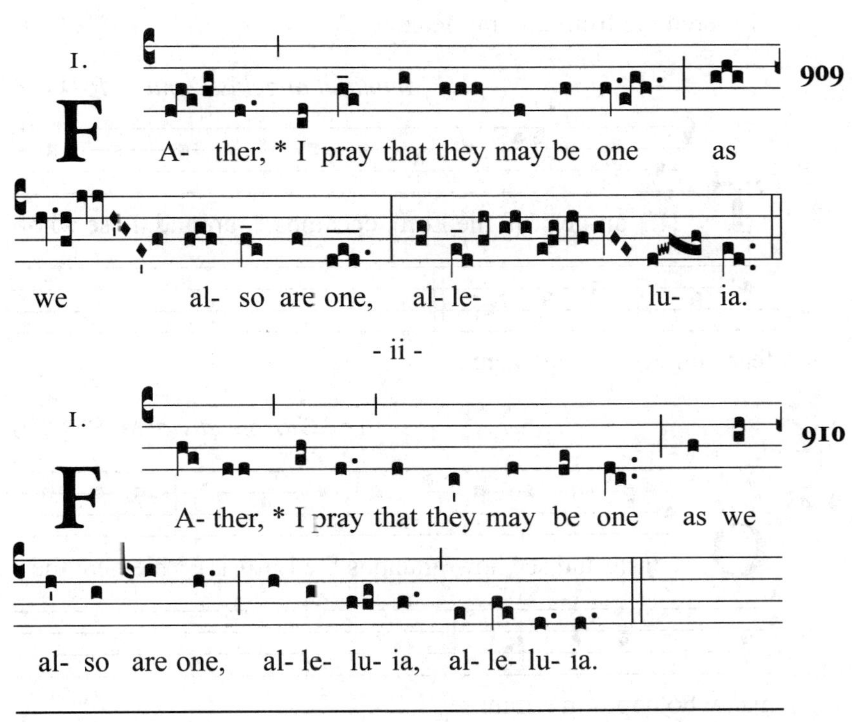
I.
909
FA- ther, * I pray that they may be one as
we al- so are one, al- le- lu- ia.
- ii -
I.
910
FA- ther, * I pray that they may be one as we
al- so are one, al- le- lu- ia, al- le- lu- ia.

VERSES *Magnificate Dominum mecum. Ps* 33:4

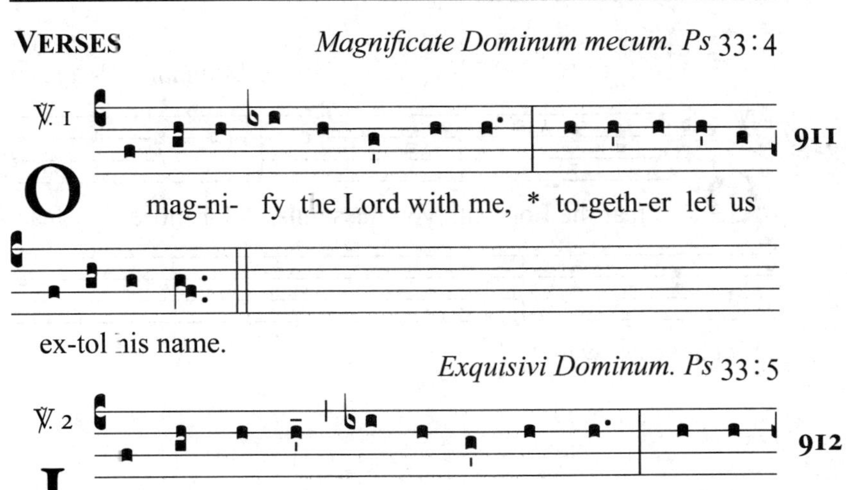
℣. 1
911
O mag-ni- fy the Lord with me, * to-geth-er let us
ex-tol his name.
Exquisivi Dominum. Ps 33:5
℣. 2
912
I sought the Lord, and he answered me, * and de-

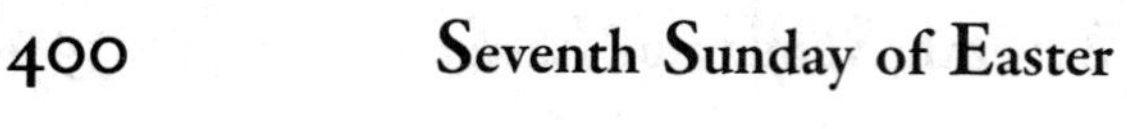

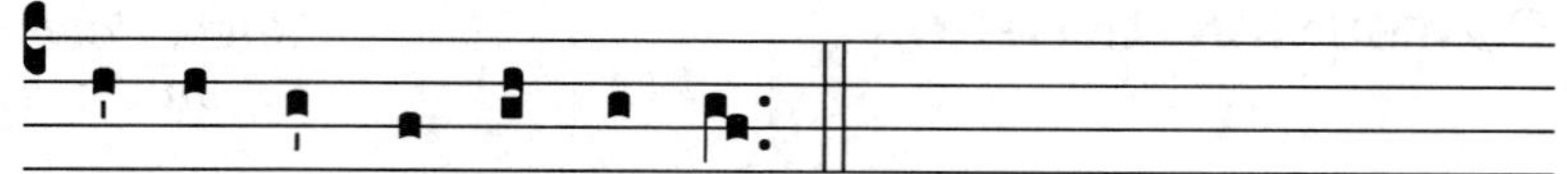

liv-ered me from all my fears.

Immittet angelus Domini. Ps 33:8

913

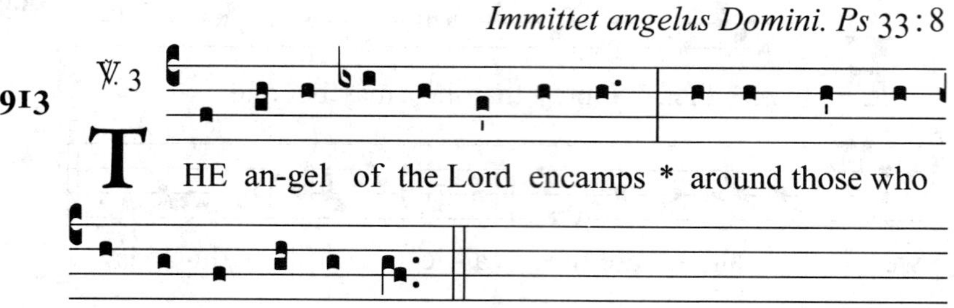

℣. 3 THE an-gel of the Lord encamps * around those who fear him, to res-cue them.

Gustate et videte. Ps 33:9

914

℣. 4 O taste and see how gracious the Lord is; * blessed the man who hopes in him.

Timete Dominum. Ps 33:10

915

℣. 5 O fear the Lord, all you his saints, * for those who fear him have no want.

- iii -

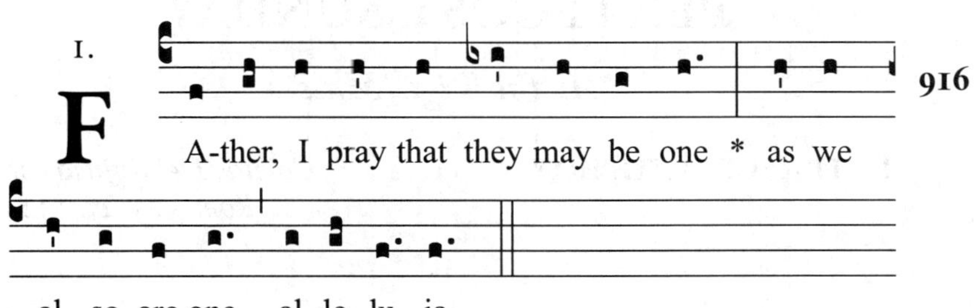
1.
916
F A-ther, I pray that they may be one * as we
al- so are one, al- le- lu- ia.

- iv -

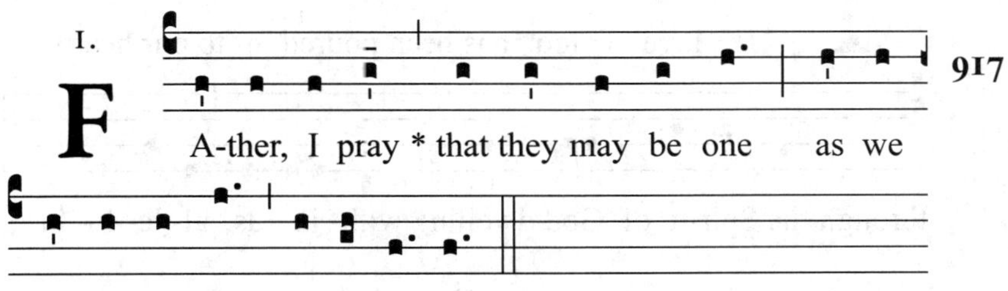
1.
917
F A-ther, I pray * that they may be one as we
al- so are one, al- le- lu- ia.

PENTECOST SUNDAY

At the Vigil Mass

Entrance Antiphon *Caritas Dei diffusa est.*
Rom 5:5; *cf.* 8:11

- i -

918
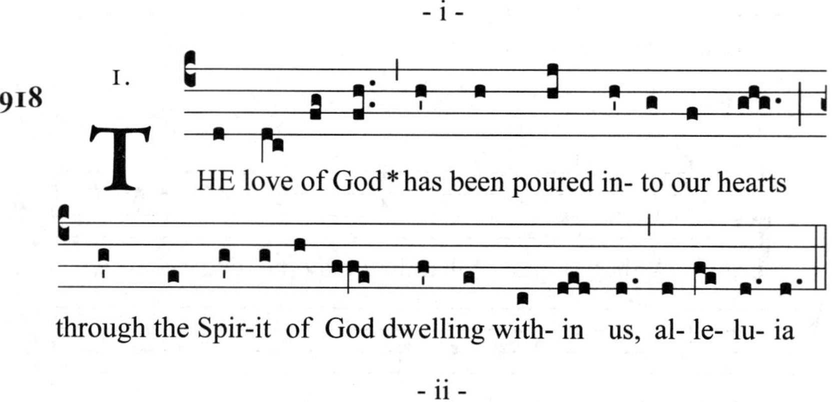
I.
THE love of God * has been poured in- to our hearts
through the Spir-it of God dwelling with- in us, al- le- lu- ia

- ii -

919
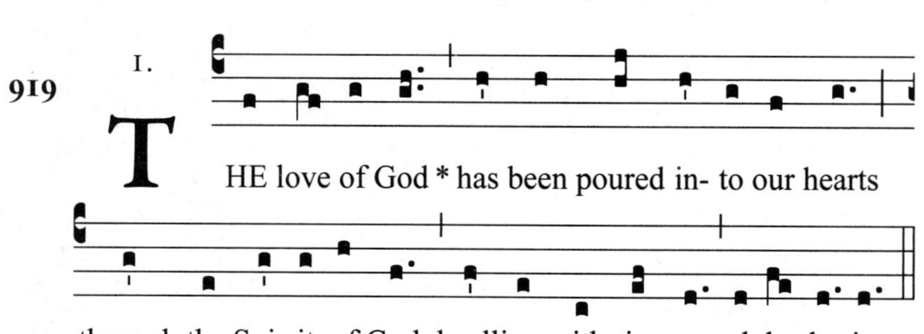
I.
THE love of God * has been poured in- to our hearts
through the Spir-it of God dwelling with- in us, al- le- lu- ia

VERSES *Miserator et misericors Dominus. Ps* 102:8

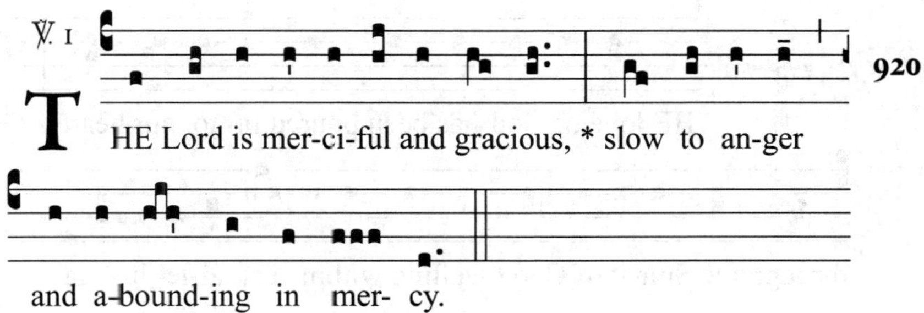
℣. 1
920
THE Lord is mer-ci-ful and gracious, * slow to an-ger
and a-bound-ing in mer- cy.

Non in perpetuum irascetur. Ps 102:9

℣. 2
921
HE will not al-ways be an- gry, * nor will he threat-
en for ev- er.

Misericordia autem Domini. Ps 102:17

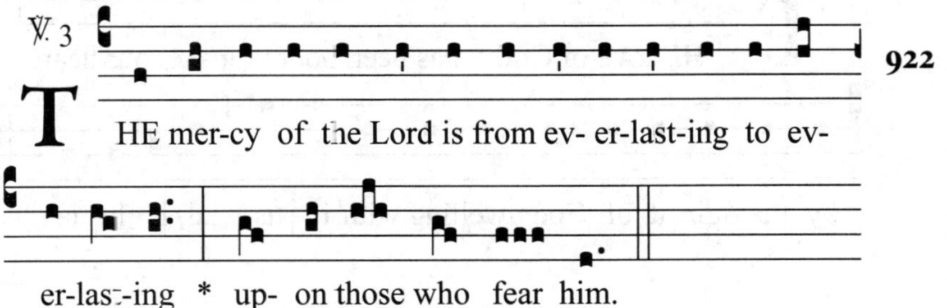
℣. 3
922
THE mer-cy of the Lord is from ev- er-last-ing to ev-
er-last-ing * up- on those who fear him.

- iii -

923
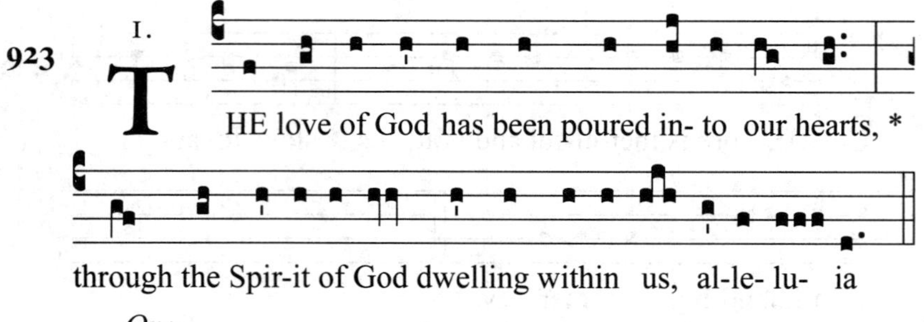
I.
THE love of God has been poured in- to our hearts, *
through the Spir-it of God dwelling within us, al-le- lu- ia

Or:

924

I.
THE love of God has been poured in- to our hearts, *
by the Spir- it of God dwelling with- in us, al- le-lu- ia

- iv -

925
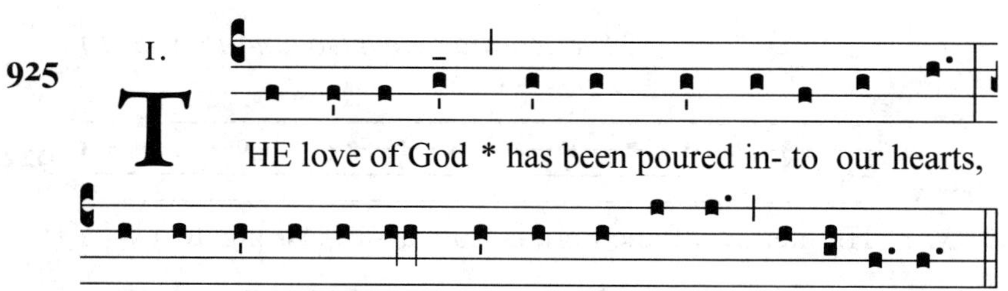
I.
THE love of God * has been poured in- to our hearts,
by the Spir- it of God dwelling with-in us, al- le- lu- ia

Offertory Antiphon

Confirm, O God, p. 411.

Communion Antiphon *Ultimo festivitatis die.*
Jn 7:37

- i -

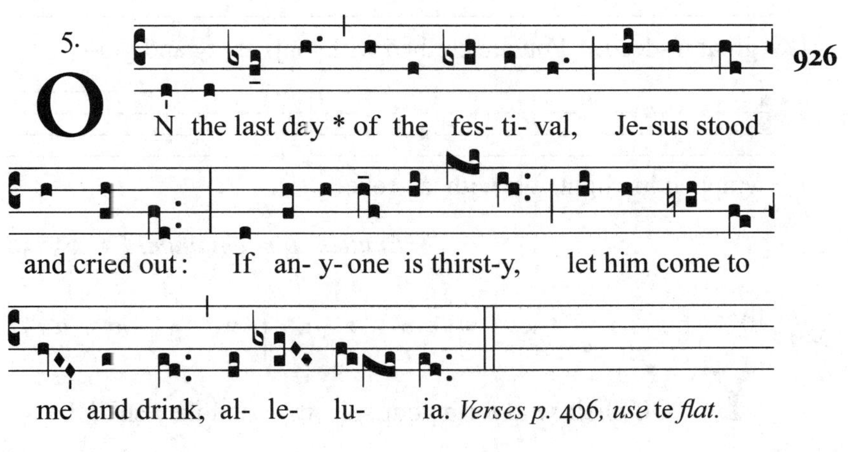
5.
926
ON the last day * of the fes- ti- val, Je-sus stood
and cried out: If an- y- one is thirst-y, let him come to
me and drink, al- le- lu- ia.
Verses p. 406, *use* te *flat.*

- ii -

Ti *natural throughout:*

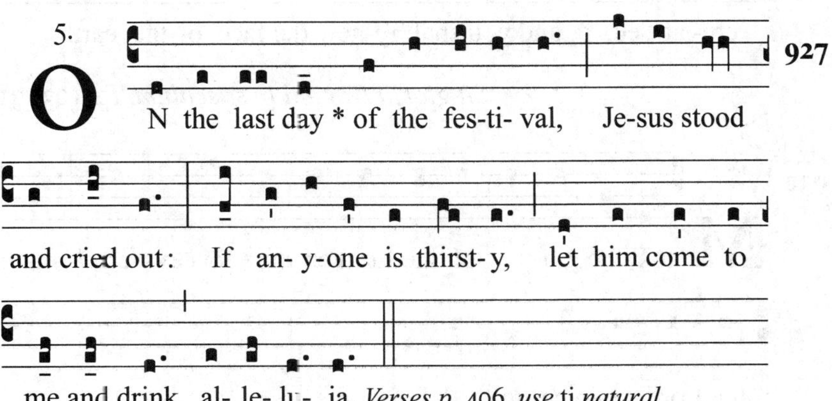
5.
927
ON the last day * of the fes-ti- val, Je-sus stood
and cried out: If an- y-one is thirst- y, let him come to
me and drink, al- le- lu- ia.
Verses p. 406, *use* ti *natural.*

VERSES *Benedic, anima mea, Domino. Ps* 103:1

928 

℣. 1

BLESS the Lord, O my soul. O Lord my God, you are

great in-deed. * You are clothed with maj- es- ty and glo-ry,

wrapped in light as with a robe.

Emittes spiritum tuum. Ps 103:30

929 

℣. 2

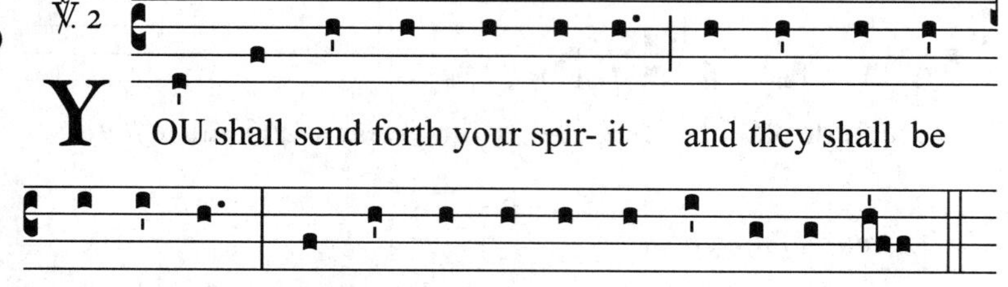

YOU shall send forth your spir- it and they shall be

cre- at- ed, * and you shall re-new the face of the earth.

Sit gloria Domini in saeculum. Ps 103:31

930 

℣. 3

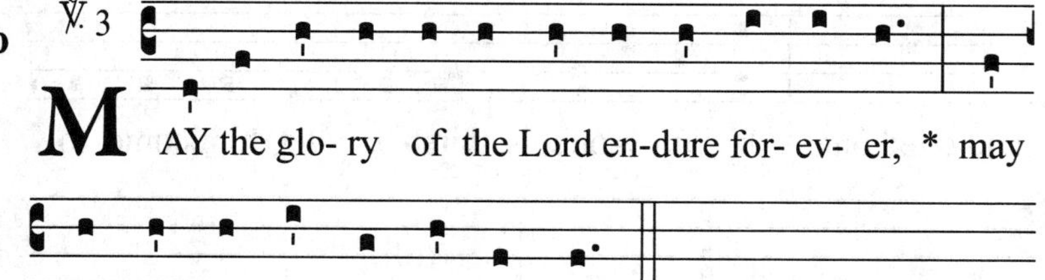

MAY the glo- ry of the Lord en-dure for- ev- er, * may

the Lord re-joice in all his works.

- iii -

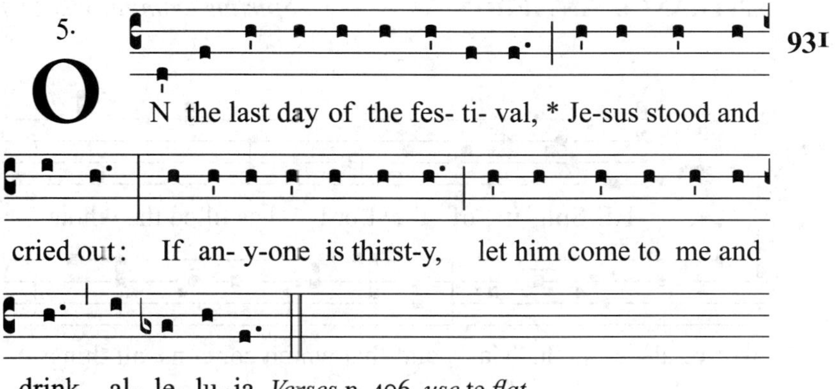

5.
931
ON the last day of the fes- ti- val, * Je-sus stood and
cried out: If an- y-one is thirst-y, let him come to me and
drink, al- le- lu- ia.
Verses p. 406, *use* te *flat.*

- iv -

5.
932
ON the last day of the fes- ti- val, * Je-sus stood
and cried out: If an- y-one is thirst-y, let him come to
me and drink, al- le- lu- ia.
Verses p. 406, *use* te *flat.*

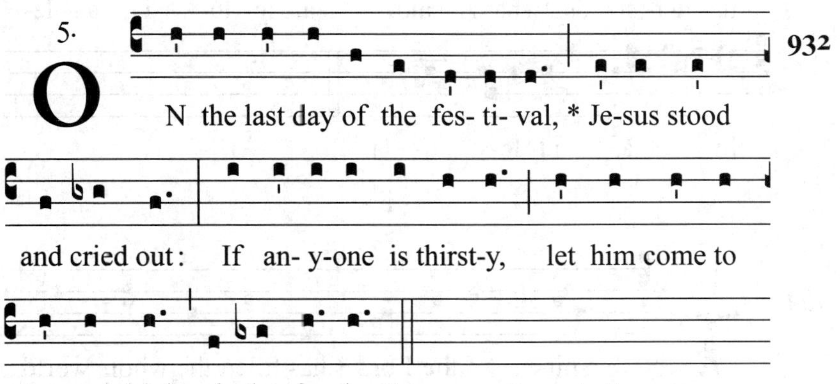

At the Mass during the Day

ENTRANCE ANTIPHON *Spiritus Domini. Wis* 1:7

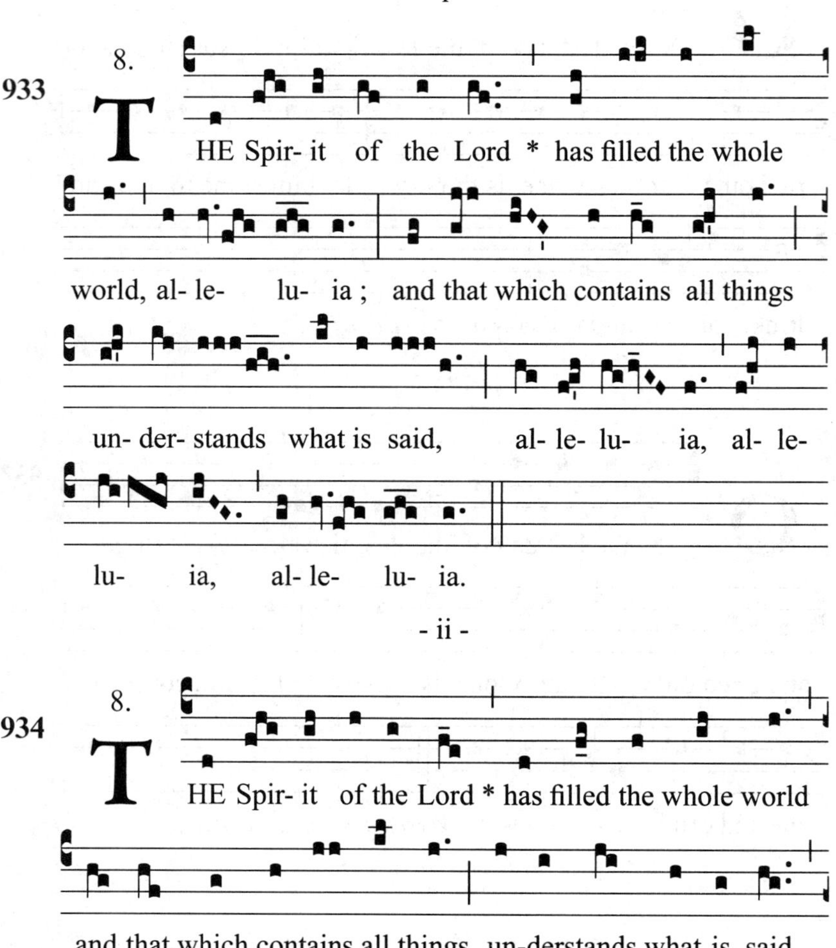
- i -
8.
933
THE Spir- it of the Lord * has filled the whole
world, al- le- lu- ia ; and that which contains all things
un- der- stands what is said, al- le- lu- ia, al- le-
lu- ia, al- le- lu- ia.
- ii -
8.
934
THE Spir- it of the Lord * has filled the whole world
and that which contains all things un-derstands what is said,

al- le- lu- ia.

Note : If the Entrance Antiphon *is repeated after the verse, use the second ending. If another verse follows, use the first ending.*

VERSES *Exsurgat Deus. Ps* 67 : 2

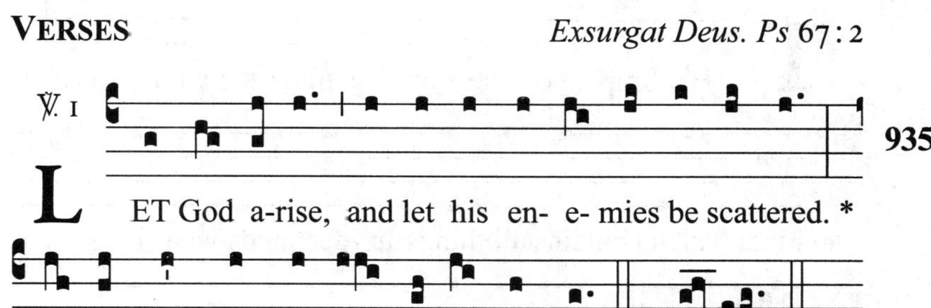
℣. 1
935
LET God a-rise, and let his en- e- mies be scattered. *
And let those who hate him flee be-fore him. *Or :* him.

Et iusti epulentur. Ps 67 : 4

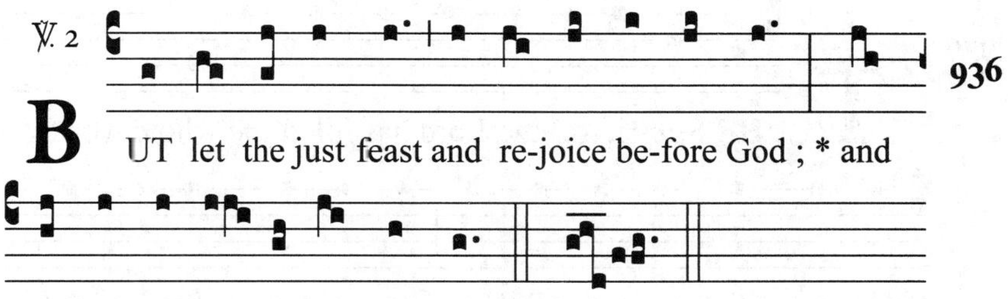
℣. 2
936
BUT let the just feast and re-joice be-fore God ; * and
let them be ju- bi-lant with joy. *Or :* joy.

Cantate Deo. Ps 67 : 5

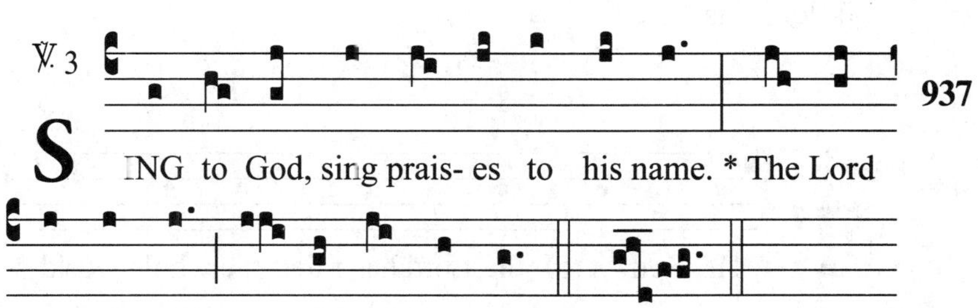
℣. 3
937
SING to God, sing prais- es to his name. * The Lord
is his name. Re-joice be- fore him. *Or :* him.

- iii -

938

8.
THE Spir- it of the Lord has filled the whole world *
and that which contains all things un-derstands what is said,
al- le- lu- ia.

Or:

939

8.
THE Spir- it of the Lord has filled the whole world *
and that which contains all things un-derstands what is said,
al- le- lu- ia.

- iv -

940

8.
THE Spir- it of the Lord has filled the whole world *
and that which contains all things un-derstands what is said,

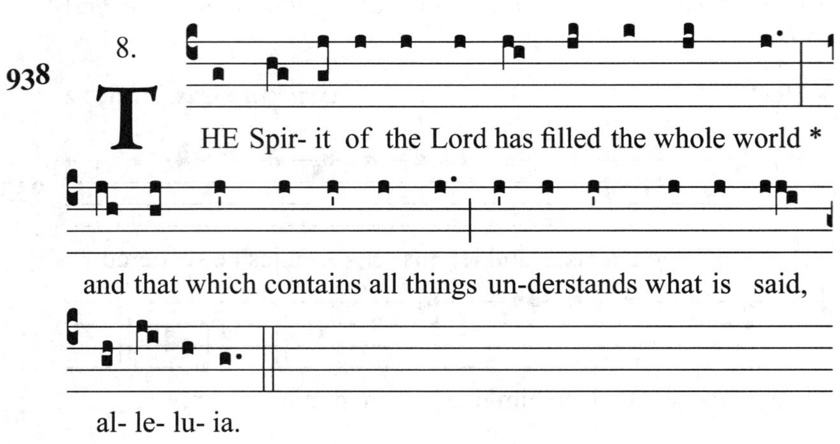

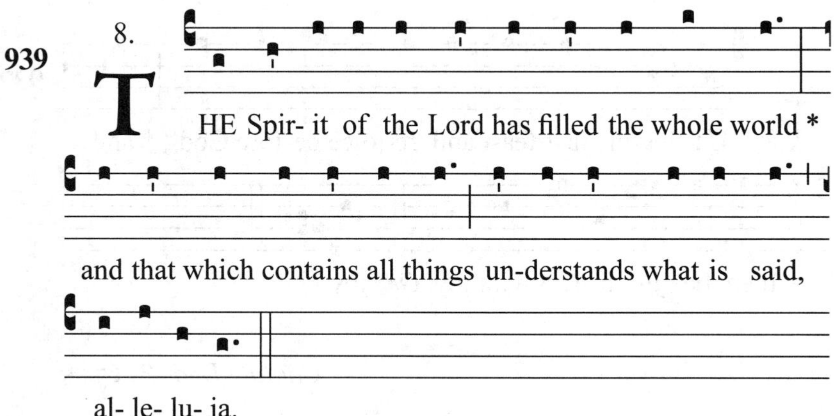

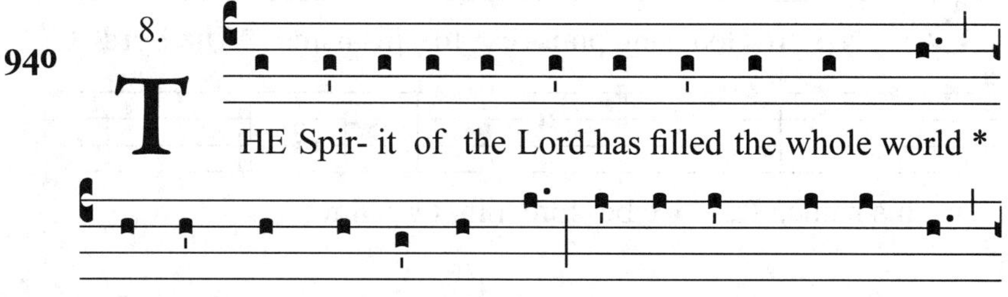

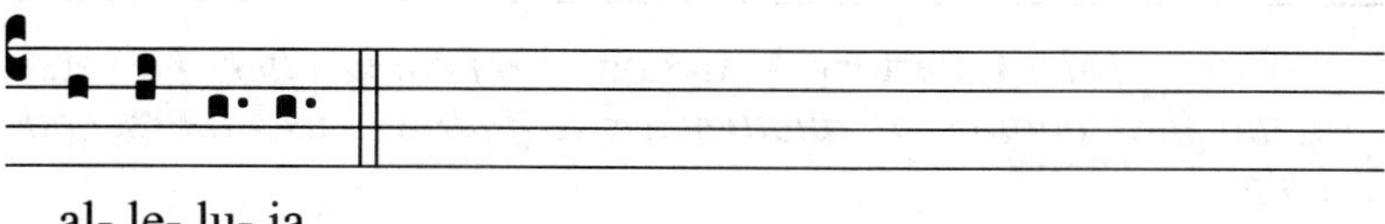
al- le- lu- ia.

OFFERTORY ANTIPHON *Confirma hoc, Deus. Ps* 67:29-30

- i -

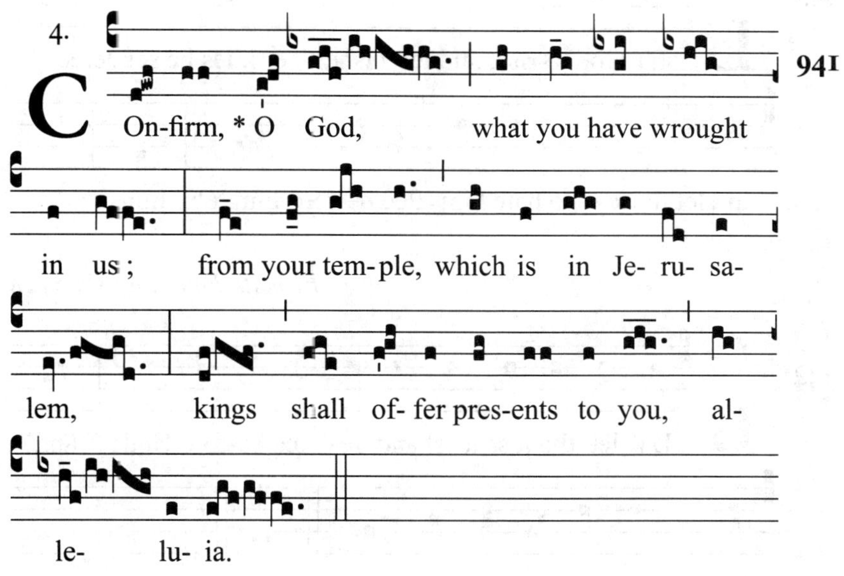
4.
C On-firm, * O God, what you have wrought
941
in us; from your tem-ple, which is in Je- ru- sa-
lem, kings shall of- fer pres-ents to you, al-
le- lu- ia.

- ii -

4.

C On-firm, O God, * what you have wrought in us; from 942

your tem-ple, which is in Je- ru- sa- lem, kings shall of- fer

pres-ents to you, al- le- lu- ia.

Note : If the Offertory Antiphon *is repeated after the verse, use the first ending. If another verse follows, use the second ending.*

VERSES *Exsurgat Deus. Ps* 67 : 2

943

℣. 1
LET God a-rise, and let his en- e- mies be scattered. *

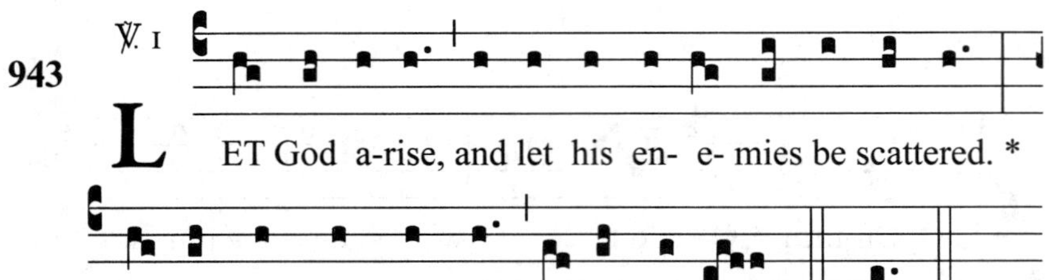

And let those who hate him flee be-fore him. *Or :* him.

Et iusti epulentur. Ps 67 : 4

944

℣. 2
BUT let the just feast and re-joice be-fore God ; * and

let them be ju- bi- lant with joy. *Or :* joy.

Cantate Deo. Ps 67 : 5

945

℣. 3
SING to God, sing prais- es to his name. * The Lord

is his name. Re-joice be-fore him. *Or :* him.

- iii -

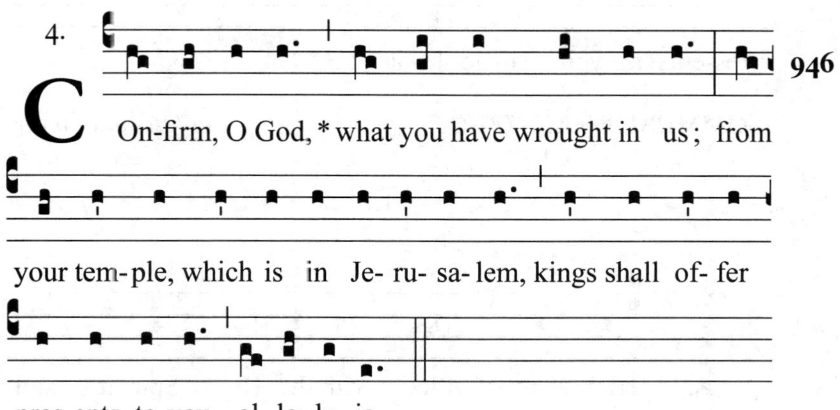
4.
946
C On-firm, O God, * what you have wrought in us; from
your tem-ple, which is in Je- ru- sa- lem, kings shall of- fer
pres-ents to you, al- le- lu- ia.

Or :

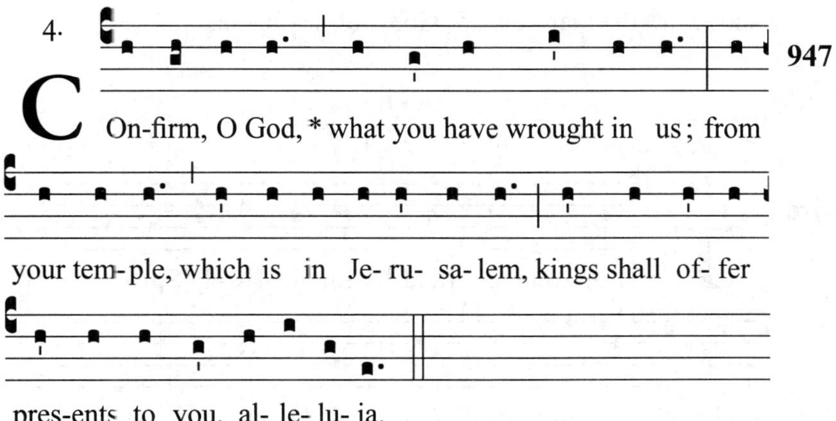
4.
947
C On-firm, O God, * what you have wrought in us; from
your tem-ple, which is in Je- ru- sa- lem, kings shall of- fer
pres-ents to you, al- le- lu- ia.

- iv -

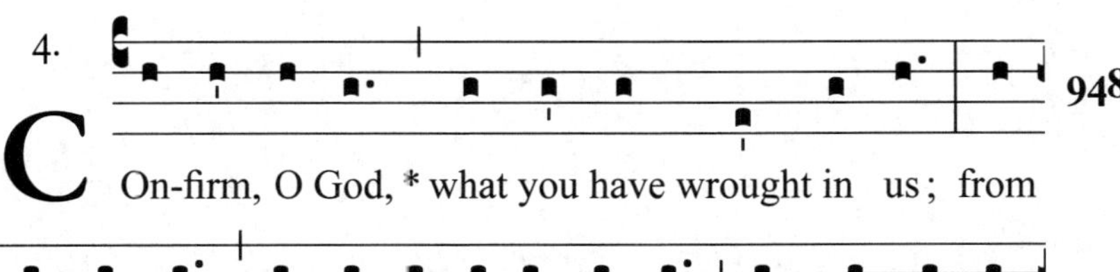
4.
948
C On-firm, O God, * what you have wrought in us; from
your tem-ple, which is in Je- ru- sa- lem, kings shall of- fer

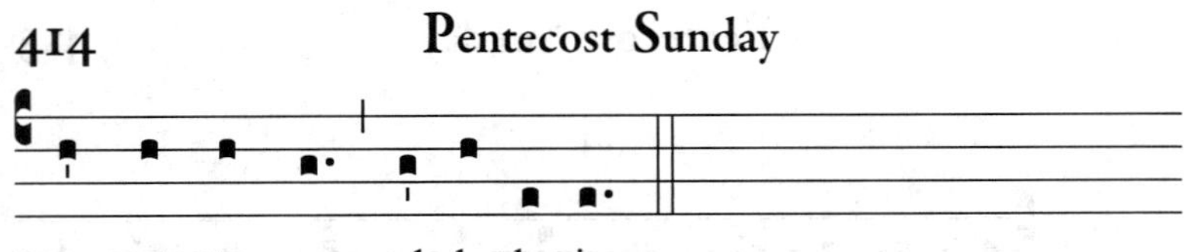
pres-ents to you, al- le- lu- ia.

Communion Antiphon *Repleti sunt omnes.*
Acts 2:4. 11

- i -

949
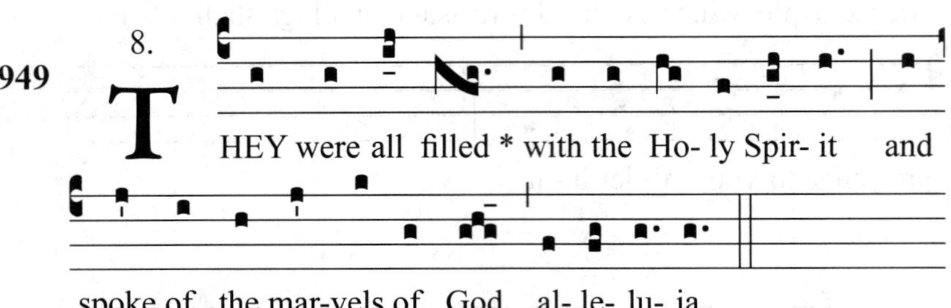
8.
THEY were all filled * with the Ho- ly Spir- it and
spoke of the mar-vels of God, al- le- lu- ia.

- ii -

950
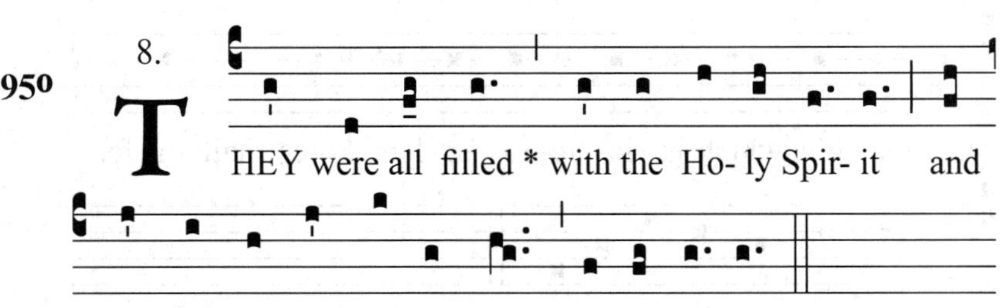
8.
THEY were all filled * with the Ho- ly Spir- it and
spoke of the mar-vels of God, al- le- lu- ia.

VERSES *Benedicam Dominum. Ps* 33 : 1-2

℣. 1
I will bless the Lord at all times; his praise shall be
ev- er in my mouth. * Let my soul glo-ry in the Lord ; the
951

low-ly will hear me and be glad.

Glorificate Dominum mecum. Ps 33 : 4

℣. 2
O mag-ni- fy the Lord with me, let us to-geth-er ex-
tol his name. * I sought the Lord, and he answered me and
952

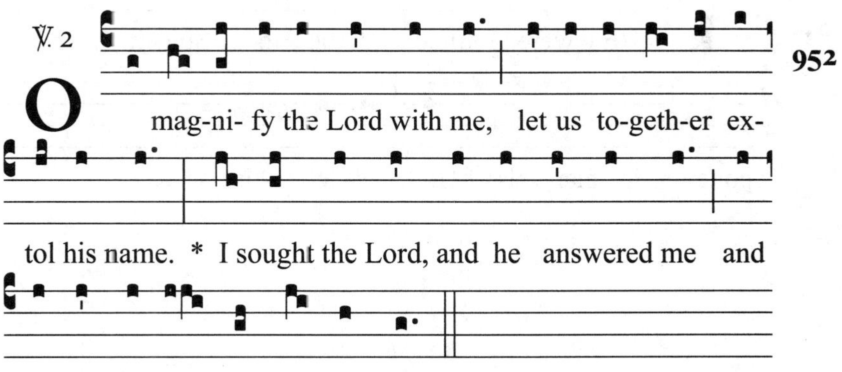

de-liv-ered me from all my fears.

Gustate et videte. Ps 33 : 9

℣. 3
O taste and see how gracious the Lord is ; * bless-ed
953

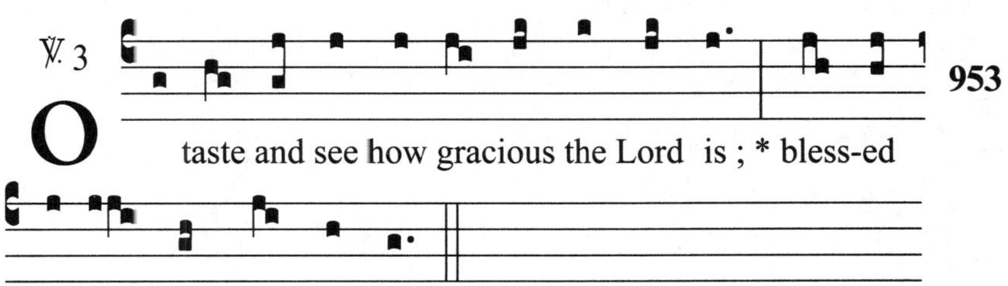

the man who hopes in him.

Cf. also Ps 33, *simple tone, p.* 372.

- iii -

954

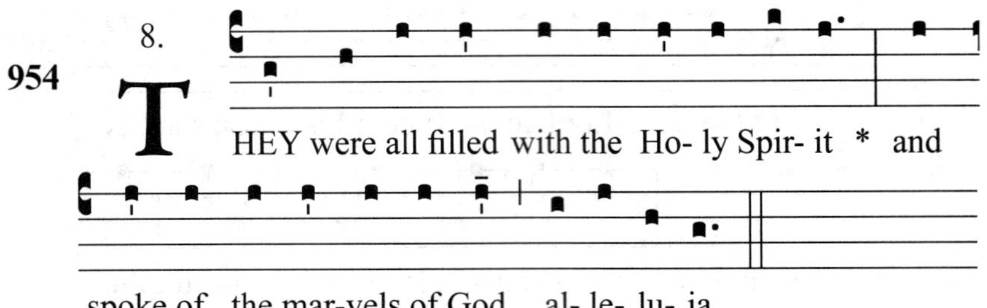
8.
THEY were all filled with the Ho- ly Spir- it * and
spoke of the mar-vels of God, al- le- lu- ia.

- iv -

955

8.
THEY were all filled with the Ho- ly Spir- it * and
spoke of the mar-vels of God, al- le- lu- ia.

FIRST SUNDAY IN ORDINARY TIME

Entrance Antiphon *In excelso throno.*
Cf. Dn 7:9. 10. 13. 14,
and Is 6:1-3

- i -

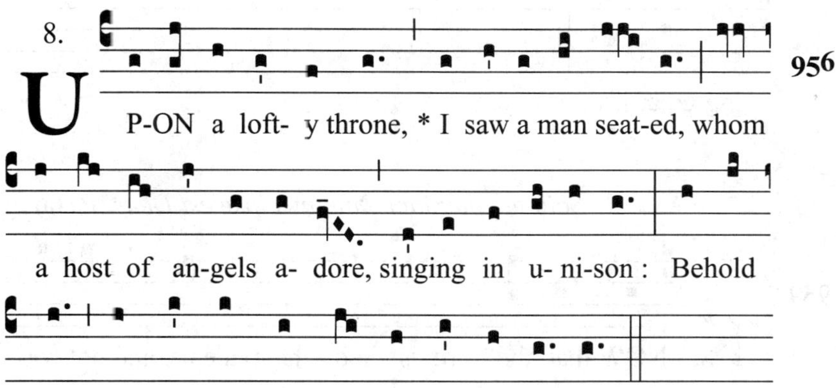
8.
956
UPON a loft- y throne, * I saw a man seat-ed, whom
a host of an-gels a- dore, singing in u- ni-son : Behold

him, the name of whose em-pire is e- ter- nal.

- ii -

8. 957

UPON a loft- y throne, * I saw a man seat-ed, whom

a host of an-gels a- dore, singing in u- ni-son : Behold

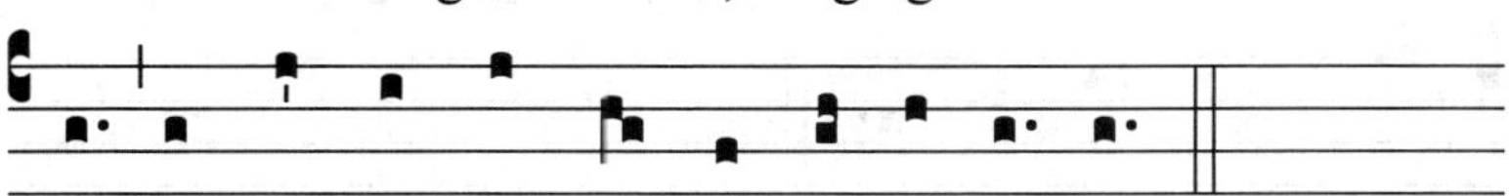

him, the name of whose em-pire is e- ter- nal.

VERSES *Iubilate Deo omnis terra. Ps* 99:2

958
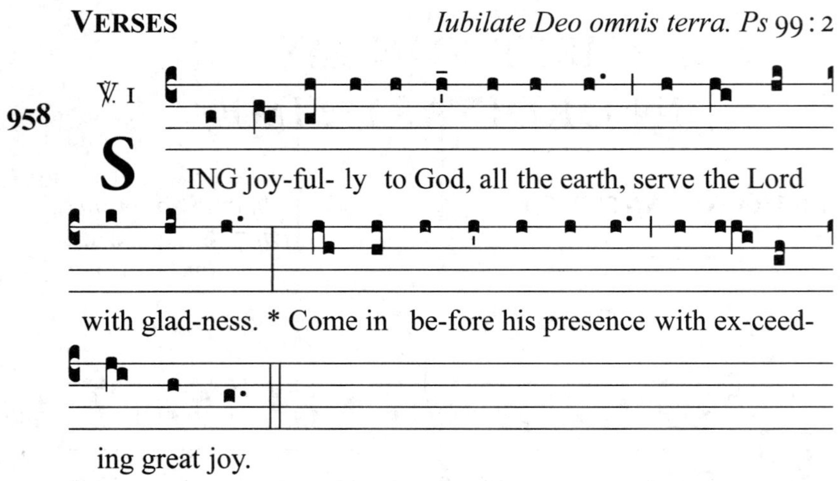
℣. 1
SING joy-ful- ly to God, all the earth, serve the Lord
with glad-ness. * Come in be-fore his presence with ex-ceed-
ing great joy.

Scitote, quoniam Dominus ipse est Deus. Ps 99:3

959
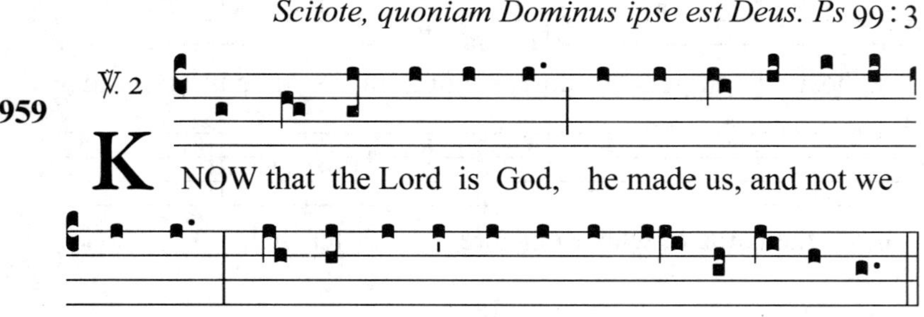
℣. 2
KNOW that the Lord is God, he made us, and not we
ourselves. * We are his peo-ple and the sheep of his pasture.

Introite portas eius. Ps 99:4

960
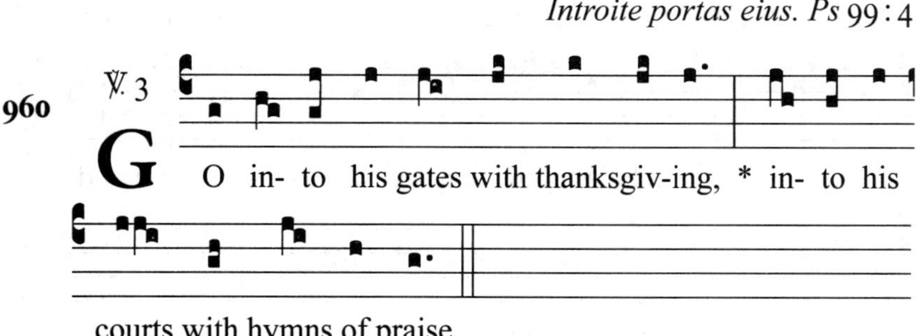
℣. 3
GO in- to his gates with thanksgiv-ing, * in- to his
courts with hymns of praise.

- iii -

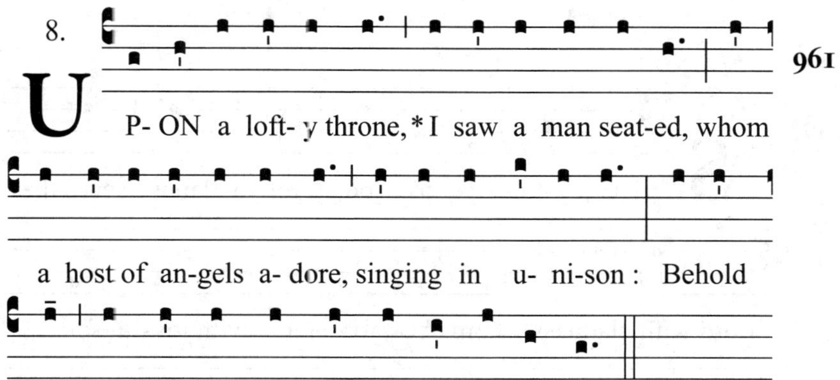
8.
961
UPON a loft-y throne, * I saw a man seat-ed, whom
a host of an-gels a-dore, singing in u-ni-son: Behold
him, the name of whose em-pire is e-ter-nal.

- iv -

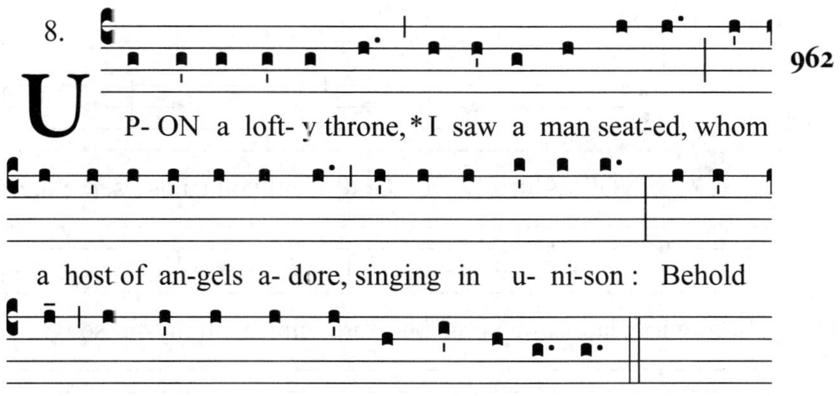
8.
962
UPON a loft-y throne, * I saw a man seat-ed, whom
a host of an-gels a-dore, singing in u-ni-son: Behold
him, the name of whose em-pire is e-ter-nal.

OFFERTORY ANTIPHON *Iubilate Deo, omnis terra. Ps* 99:2

- i -

963

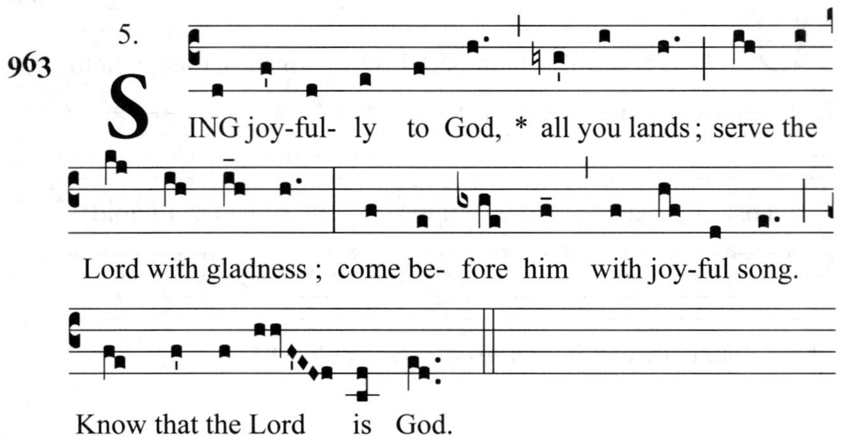
5.
SING joy-ful- ly to God, * all you lands; serve the
Lord with gladness; come be- fore him with joy-ful song.
Know that the Lord is God.

- ii -

964

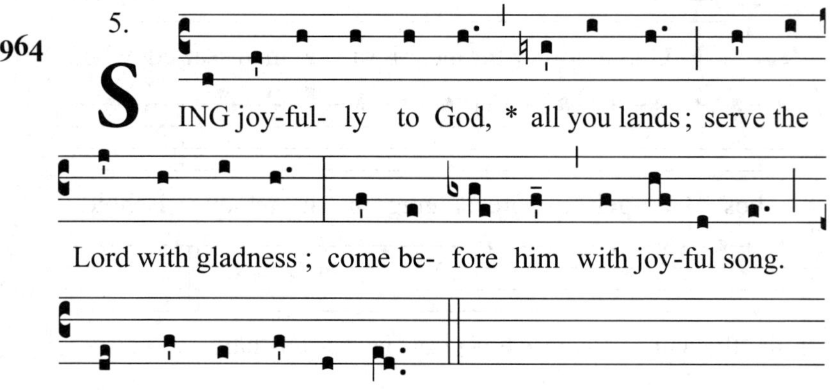
5.
SING joy-ful- ly to God, * all you lands; serve the
Lord with gladness; come be- fore him with joy-ful song.
Know that the Lord is God.

VERSES *Scitote, quoniam Dominus ipse est Deus. Ps* 99:3

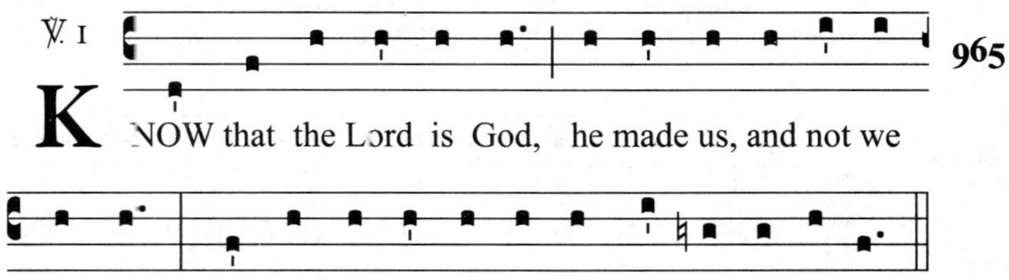
℣. 1
KNOW that the Lord is God, he made us, and not we
ourselves. * We are his peo-ple and the sheep of his pasture.

965

Introite portas eius. Ps 99:4

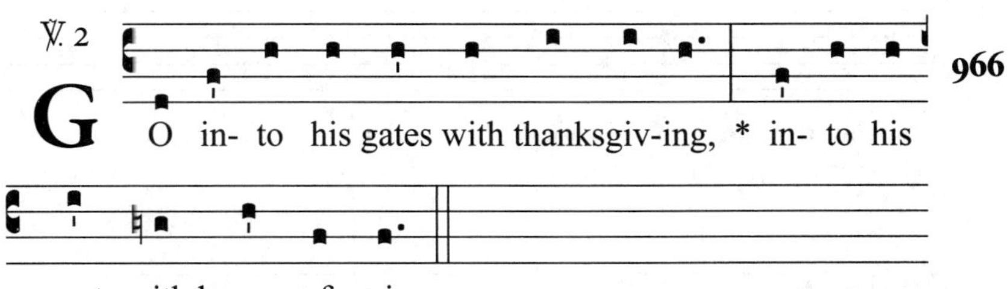
℣. 2
GO in- to his gates with thanksgiv-ing, * in- to his
courts with hymns of praise.

966

Quoniam suavis est Dominus. Ps 99:5

℣. 3
FOR the Lord is good, his mer-cy endures for ev- er, *
and his truth to gen- er- a- tion and gen- er- a- tion.

967

- iii -

When singing this antiphon with the Latin psalm tone (p. 535), use ti *natural; with the English psalm (p. 537) tone, use* te *flat.*

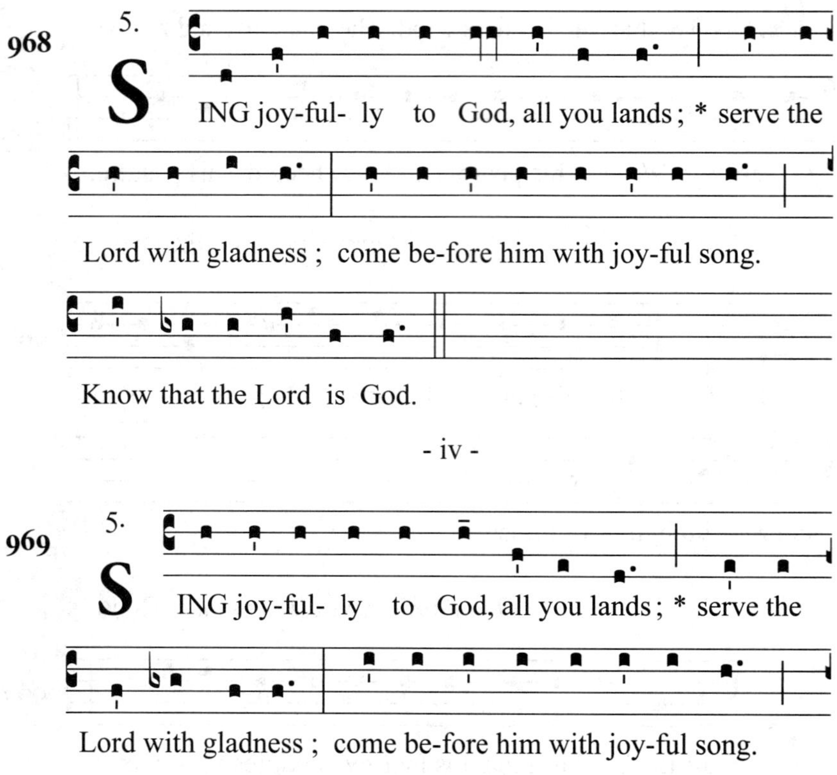
968
5.
SING joy-ful- ly to God, all you lands; * serve the
Lord with gladness ; come be-fore him with joy-ful song.
Know that the Lord is God.
- iv -
969
5.
SING joy-ful- ly to God, all you lands; * serve the
Lord with gladness ; come be-fore him with joy-ful song.

Know that the Lord is God.

COMMUNION ANTIPHON *Domine, apud te.*
Ps 35:10

- i -

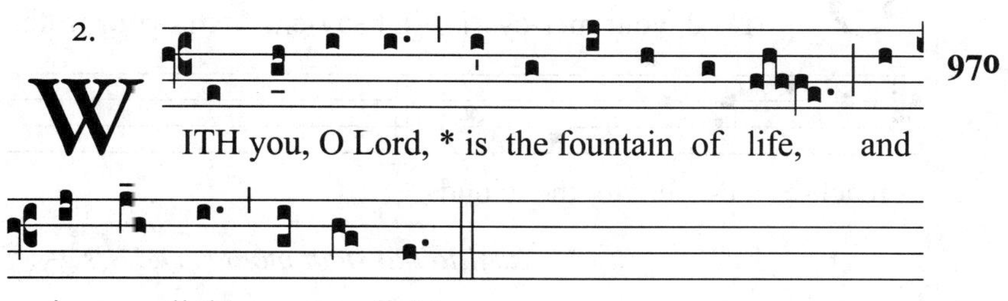
2.
WITH you, O Lord, * is the fountain of life, and
970

in your light we see light.

- ii -

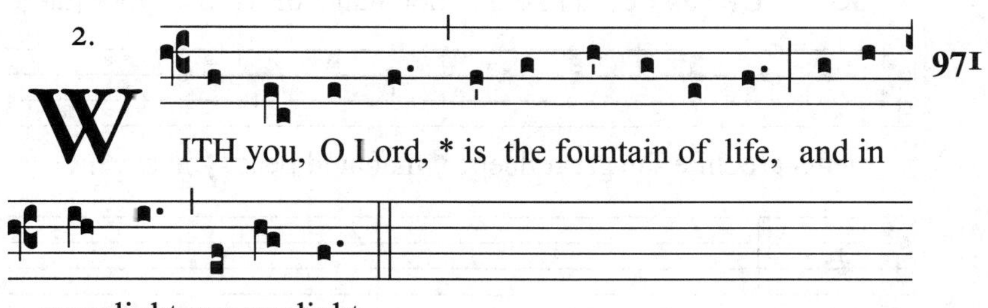
2.
WITH you, O Lord, * is the fountain of life, and in
971

your light we see light.

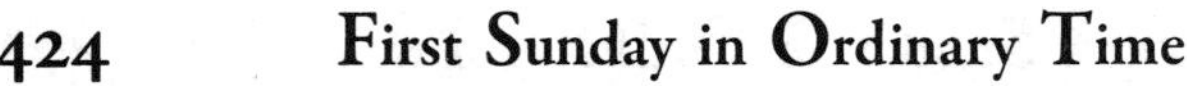

VERSES *Domine, in cælo misericordia tua. Ps* 35 : 6

972 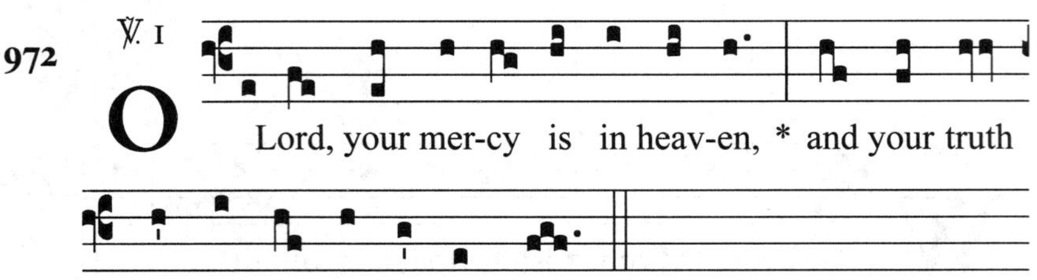
℣. 1
O Lord, your mer-cy is in heav-en, * and your truth

reach-es e- ven to the clouds.

Iustitia tua sicut montes Dei. Ps 35 : 7

973 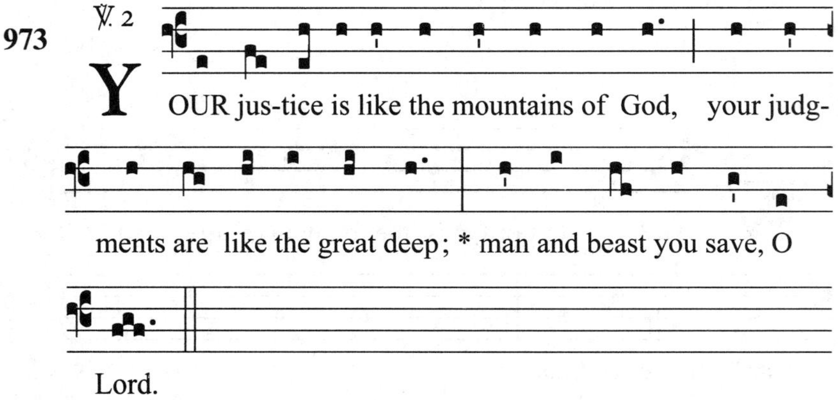
℣. 2
YOUR jus-tice is like the mountains of God, your judgments are like the great deep; * man and beast you save, O
Lord.

Quemadmodum multiplicasti misericordiam tuam. Ps 35 : 7-8

974 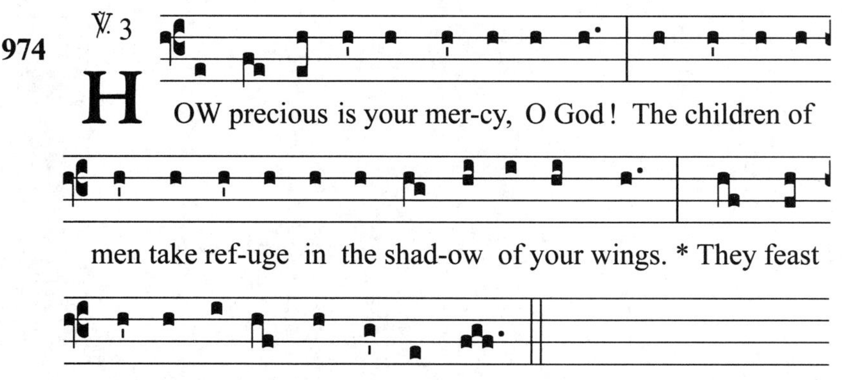
℣. 3
HOW precious is your mer-cy, O God! The children of
men take ref-uge in the shad-ow of your wings. * They feast
on the a- bundance of your house.

- iii -

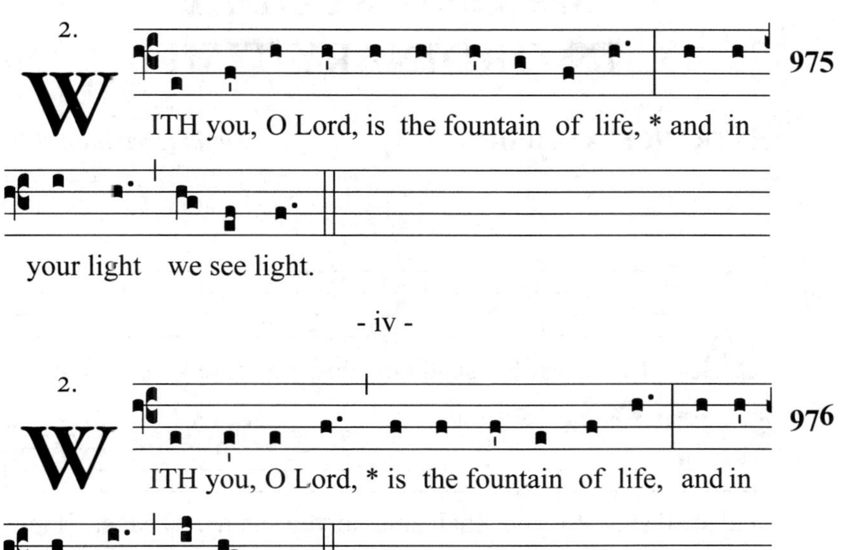
2.
WITH you, O Lord, is the fountain of life, * and in
975
your light we see light.

- iv -

2.
WITH you, O Lord, * is the fountain of life, and in 976

your light we see light.

SECOND SUNDAY IN ORDINARY TIME

ENTRANCE ANTIPHON *Omnis terra adoret te.*
Ps 65:4

- i -

977

8.
ALL the earth * shall bow down be-fore you, O God,
and shall sing to you, shall sing to your name, O Most High !

- ii -

978

8.
ALL the earth * shall bow down be-fore you, O God,
and shall sing to you, shall sing to your name, O Most High !

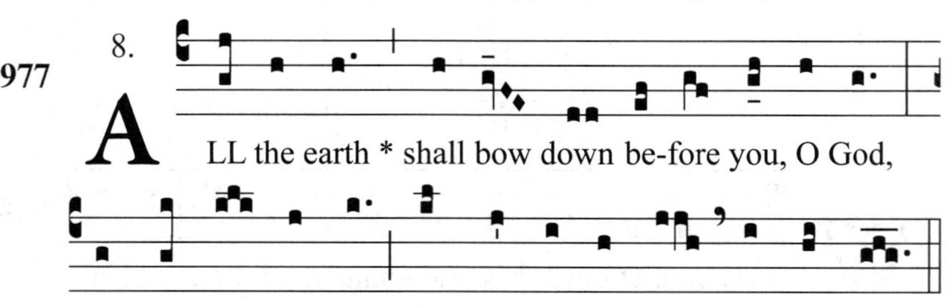

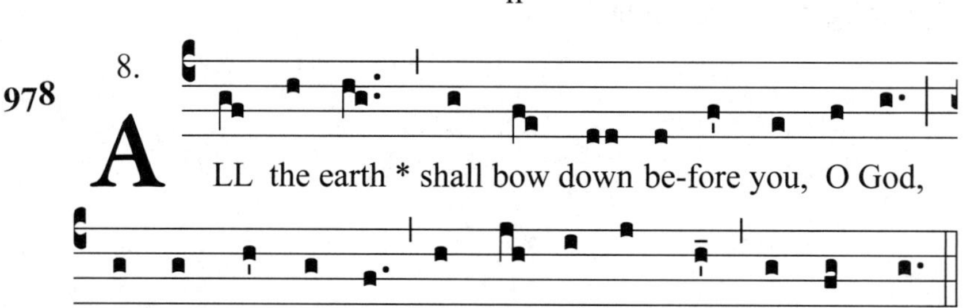

VERSES *Dicite Deo : quam terribila sunt. Ps* 65 : 3-4

℣. 1
979
SAY un- to God : How ter- ri- ble are your works, O

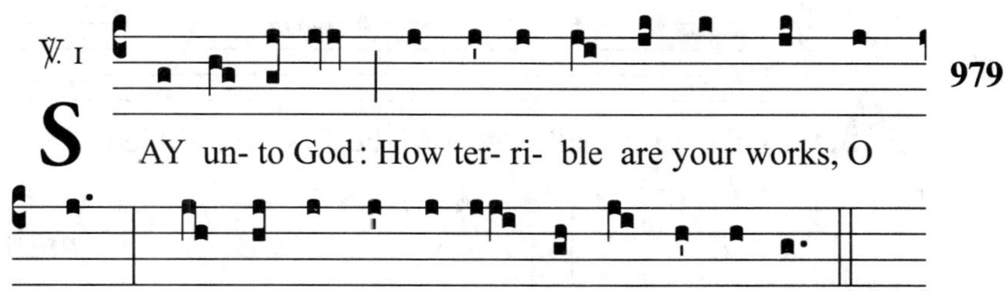

Lord ! * Let all the earth a- dore you and sing to you.

Benedicite, gentes, Deum nostrum. Ps 65 : 8

℣. 2
980
O bless our God, all you nations * and make the voice
of his praise to be heard.

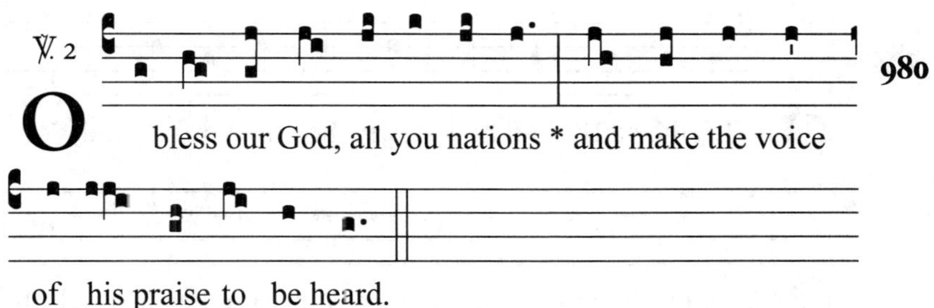

Introibo in domum tuam. Ps 65 : 13-14

℣. 3
981
I will go in- to your house with burnt of- fer-ings. *

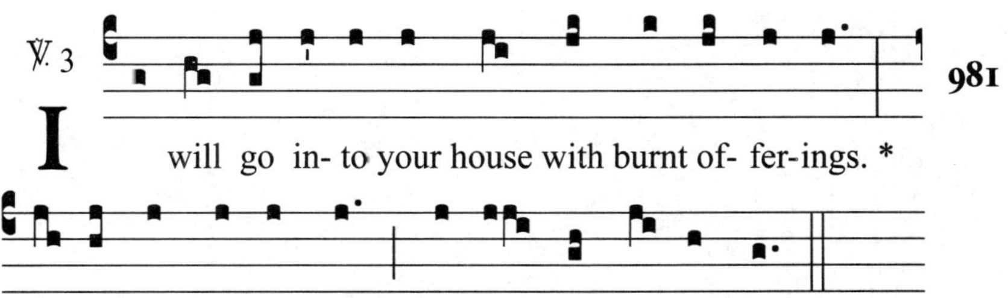

I will pay you my vows which my lips have ut-tered.

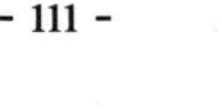

- iii -

982 8.

ALL the earth shall bow down be-fore you, O God, *
and shall sing to you, shall sing to your name, O Most High!

- iv -

983

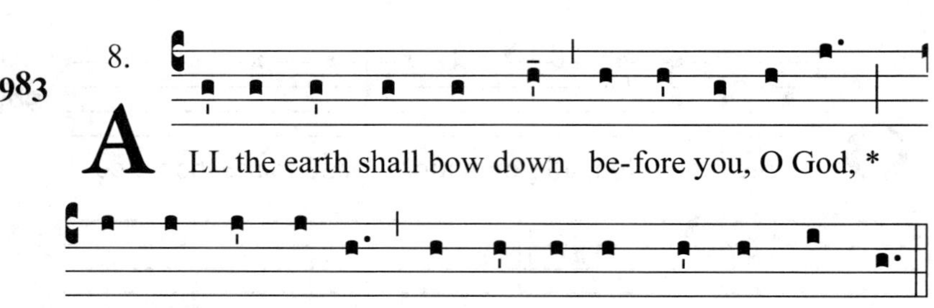

8.
ALL the earth shall bow down be-fore you, O God, *

and shall sing to you, shall sing to your name, O Most High!

Offertory Antiphon *Iubilate Deo, omnis terra.*
Ps 65: 1. 2. 16

- i -

1.
984
SHout with joy * to God, all the earth; sing a psalm
to his name. Come and hear, all who fear God, and I will
tell you what great things the Lord has done for my soul.

- ii -

1.
985
SHout with joy * to God, all the earth; sing a psalm
to his name. Come and hear, all who fear God, and I will
tell you what great things the Lord has done for my soul.

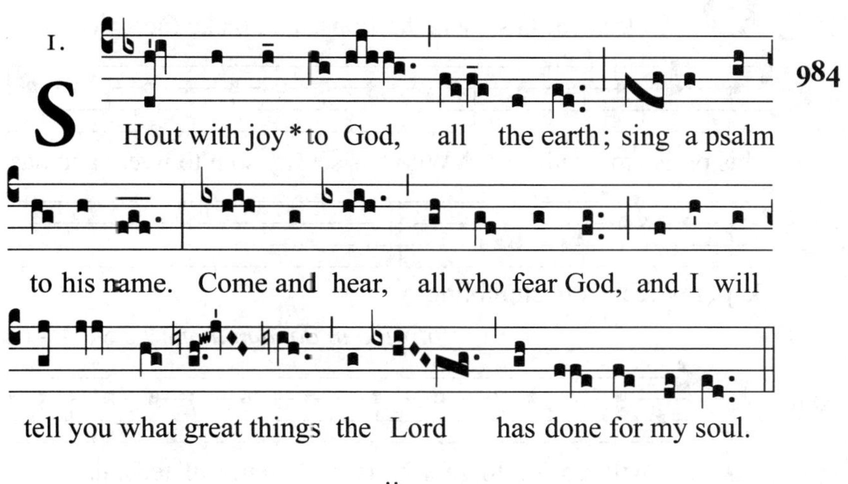

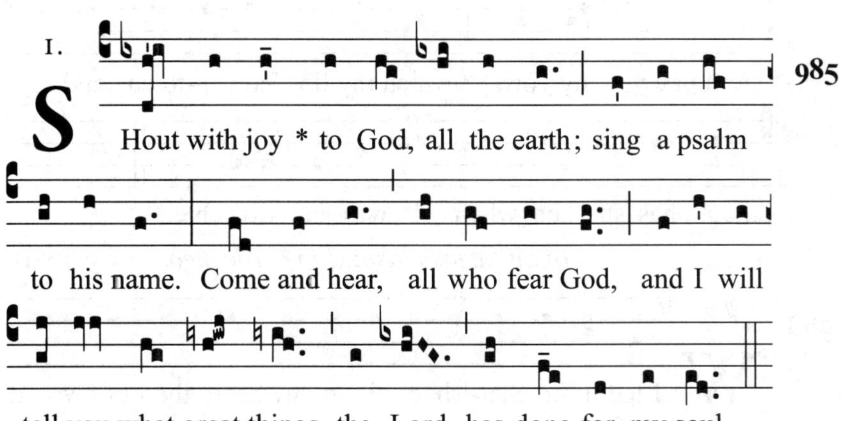

VERSES *Benedicite, gentes, Deum nostrum. Ps* 65:8

986
℣. 1
O bless our God, you na-tions, and make the voice of
his praise to be heard. * Who has set my soul to live, and has
kept my feet from stumbling.
Introibo in domum tuam. Ps 65:13-14
987
℣. 2
I will go in- to your house with burnt of-fer-ings ; I
will pay you my vows, * which my lips have ut-tered, and my
mouth has spo-ken, when I was in trou- ble.
Iniquitatem si aspexi in corde meo. Ps 65:18-19
988
℣. 3
WERE I to cher-ish e- vil in my heart, the Lord would
not hear. * But God has heard, and has at-tend-ed to the voice
of my sup-pli- ca- tion.

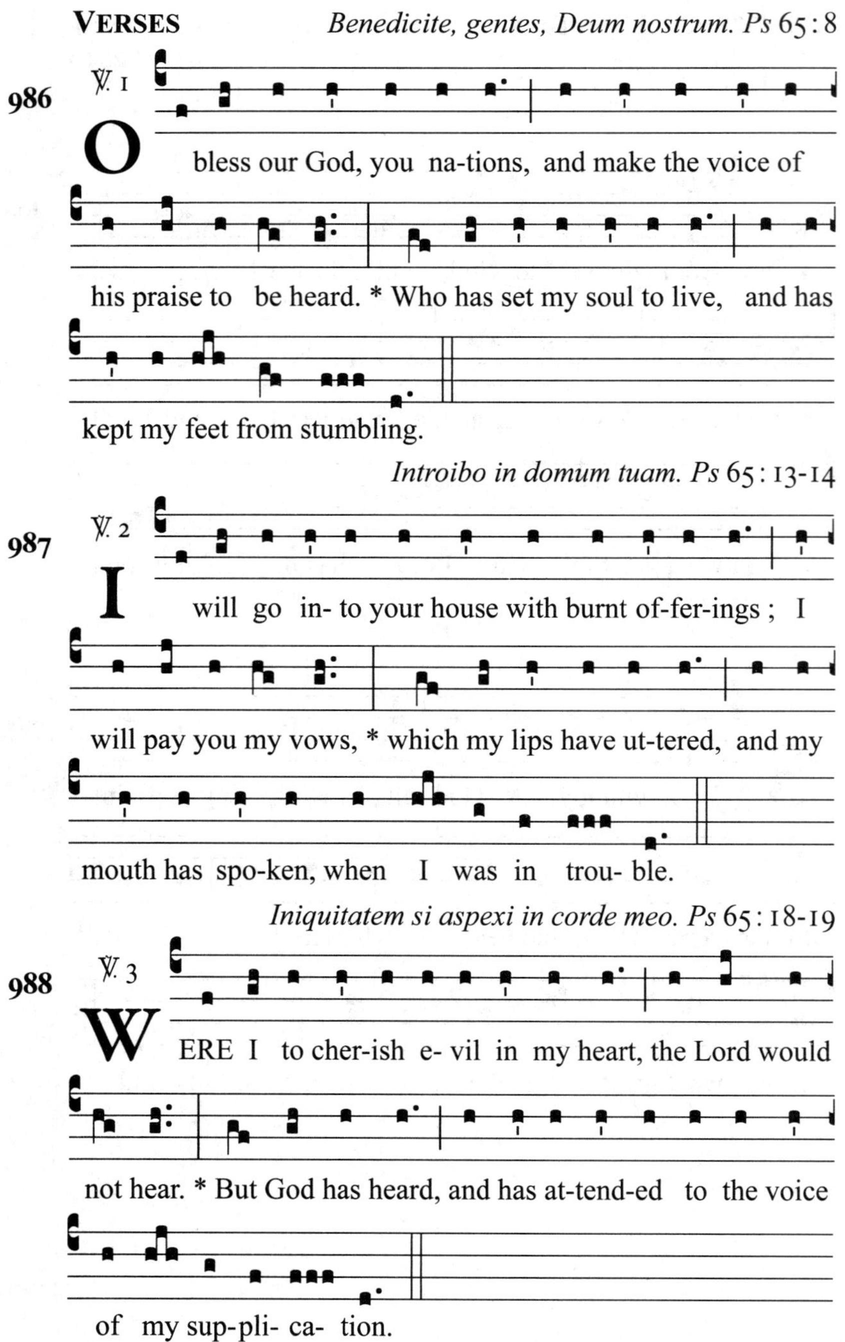

- iii -

1.
989
S Hout with joy to God, all the earth; * sing a psalm
to his name. Come and hear, all who fear God, and I will
tell you what great things the Lord has done for my soul.

- iv -

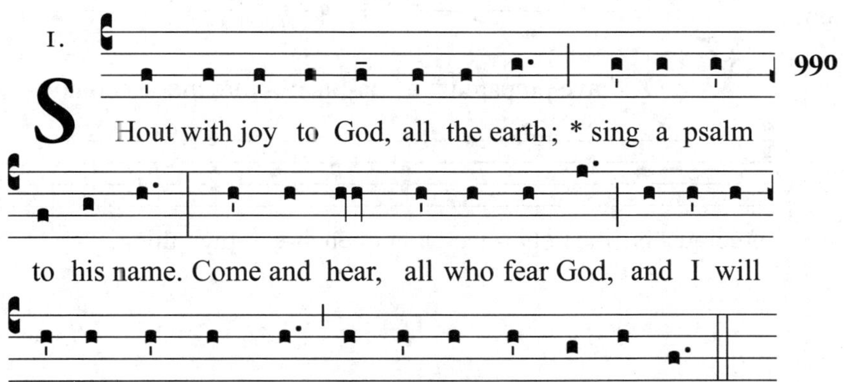
1.
990
S Hout with joy to God, all the earth; * sing a psalm
to his name. Come and hear, all who fear God, and I will
tell you what great things the Lord has done for my soul.

Communion Antiphon *Parasti in conspectu meo.*
Ps 22:5

\- i -

991
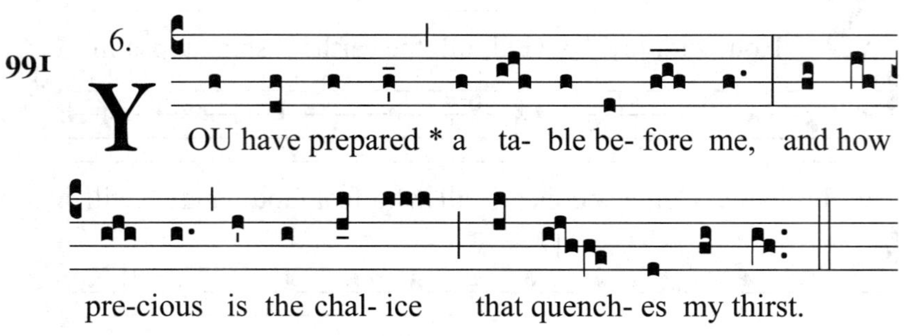
6.
YOU have prepared * a ta- ble be- fore me, and how
pre-cious is the chal- ice that quench- es my thirst.

\- ii -

992
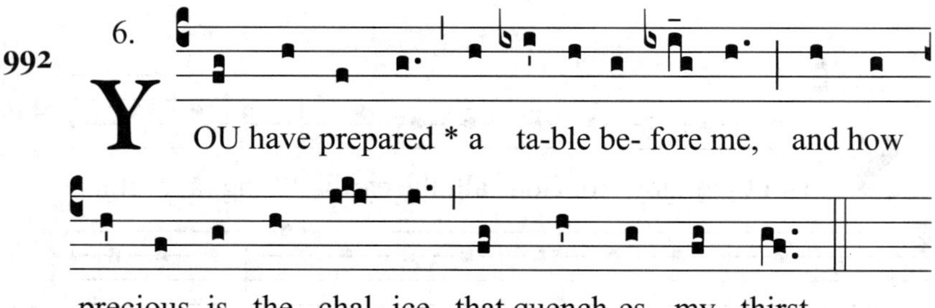
6.
YOU have prepared * a ta-ble be- fore me, and how
precious is the chal- ice that quench-es my thirst.

VERSES

Dominus regit me. Ps 22:1

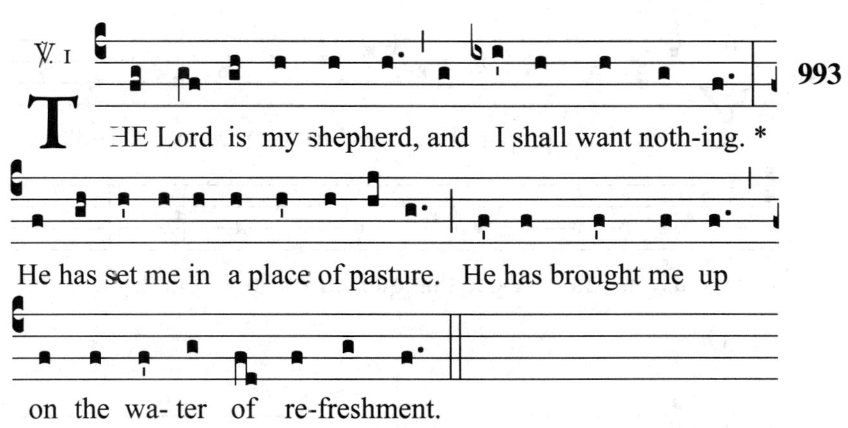
℣. 1
993
THE Lord is my shepherd, and I shall want noth-ing. *
He has set me in a place of pasture. He has brought me up
on the wa- ter of re-freshment.

Nam, et si ambulavero. Ps 22:4

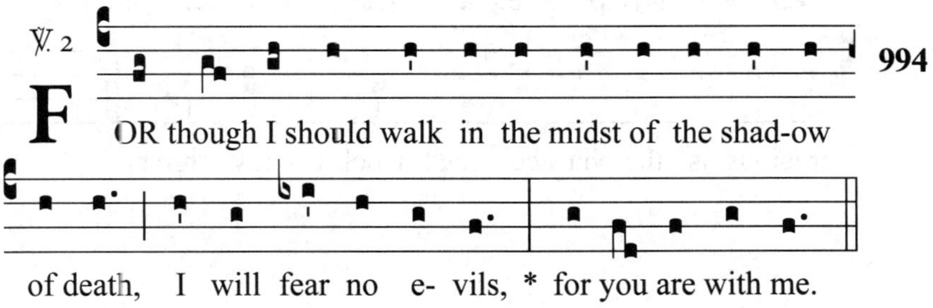
℣. 2
994
FOR though I should walk in the midst of the shad-ow
of death, I will fear no e- vils, * for you are with me.

Parasti in conspectu meo mensam. Ps 22:5

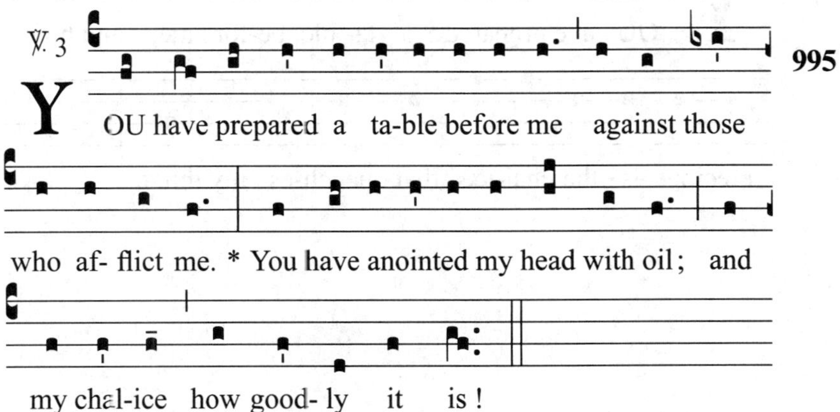
℣. 3
995
YOU have prepared a ta-ble before me against those
who af- flict me. * You have anointed my head with oil; and
my chal-ice how good- ly it is!

- iii -

996

6.
YOU have prepared a ta-ble be-fore me, * and how
precious is the chal-ice that quench-es my thirst.

Or:

997

6.
YOU have prepared a ta-ble be-fore me, * and how
precious is the chal-ice that quench-es my thirst.

- iv -

998

6.
YOU have prepared * a ta- ble be-fore me, and how
precious is the chal-ice that quench-es my thirst.

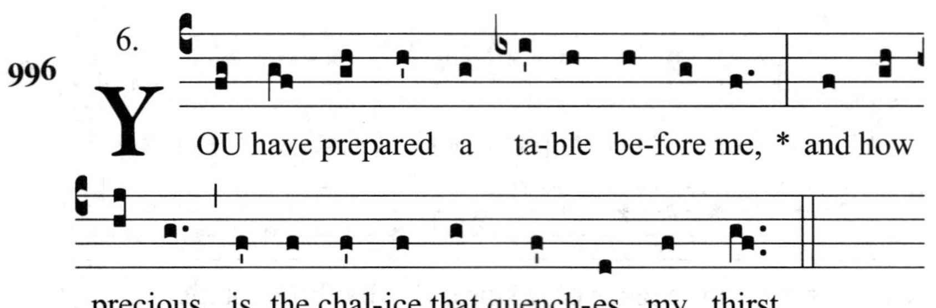

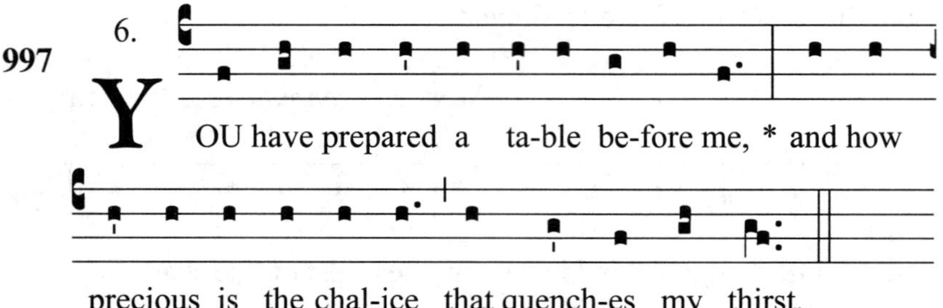

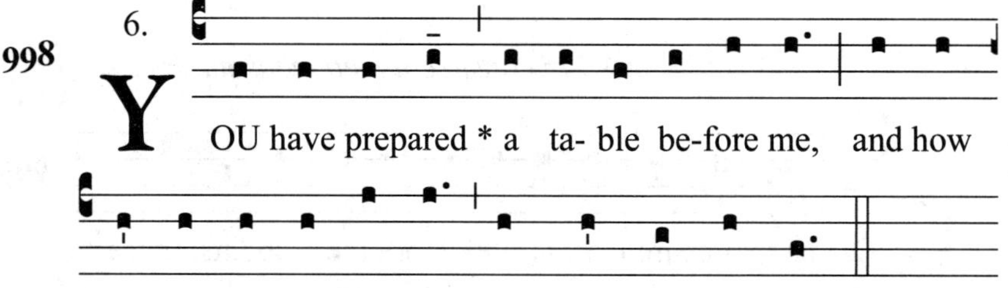

THIRD SUNDAY IN ORDINARY TIME

Entrance Antiphon *Cantate Domino canticum novum.*
Ps 95:1. 6

- i -

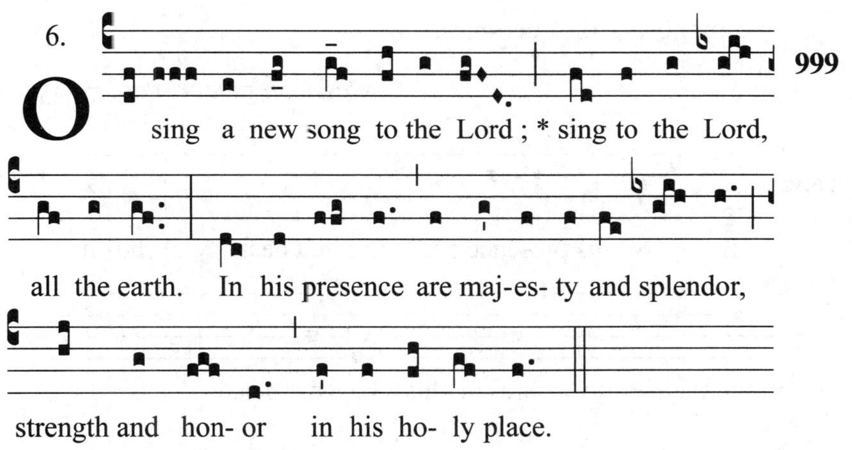
6.
O sing a new song to the Lord; * sing to the Lord,
999
all the earth. In his presence are maj-es- ty and splendor,
strength and hon- or in his ho- ly place.

- ii -

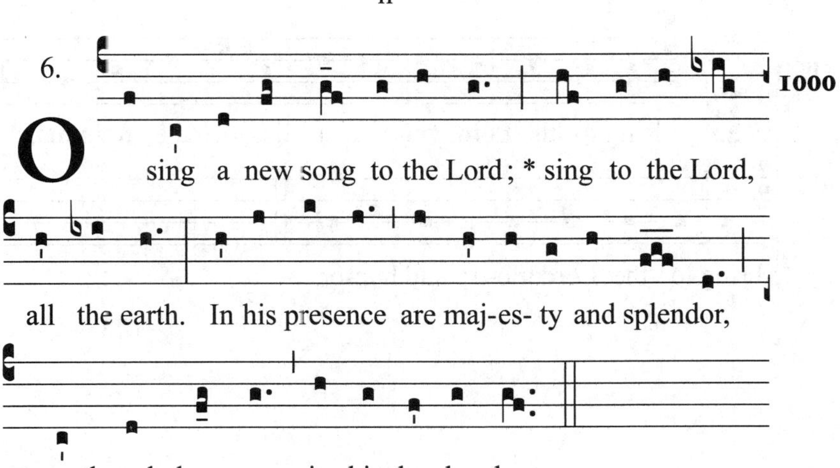
6.
O sing a new song to the Lord; * sing to the Lord,
1000
all the earth. In his presence are maj-es- ty and splendor,
strength and hon- or in his ho- ly place.

VERSES. *Annuntiate inter gentes. Ps* 95:3

1001
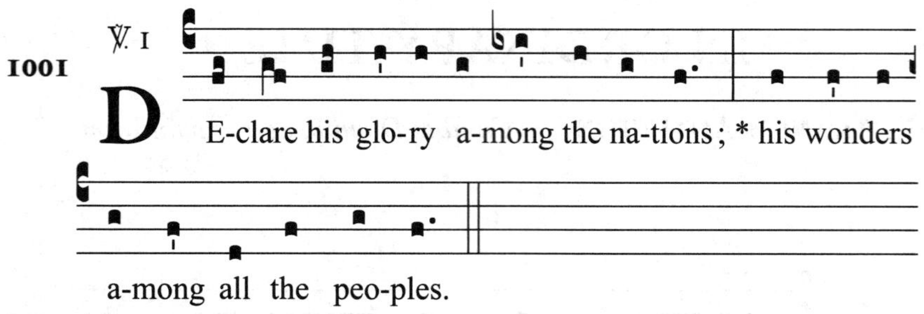
℣. 1
DEclare his glo-ry a-mong the na-tions; * his wonders
a-mong all the peo-ples.

Confessio et pulchritudo. Ps 95:6

1002
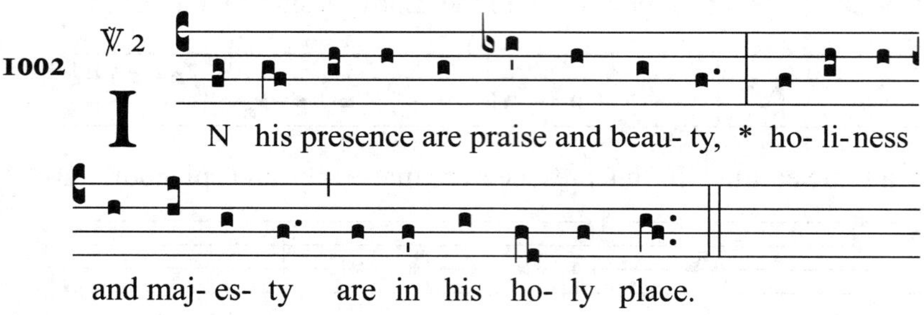
℣. 2
IN his presence are praise and beau- ty, * ho- li-ness
and maj- es- ty are in his ho- ly place.

Afferte Domino. Ps 95:7

1003
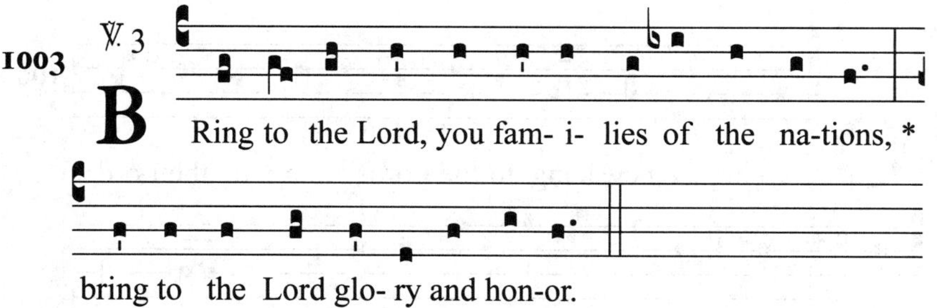
℣. 3
BRing to the Lord, you fam- i- lies of the na-tions, *
bring to the Lord glo- ry and hon-or.

- iii -

6.
O sing a new song to the Lord; * sing to the Lord,
all the earth. In his presence are maj-es-ty and splendor,
strength and hon-or in his ho-ly place.

1004

Or:

6.
O sing a new song to the Lord; * sing to the Lord,
all the earth. In his presence are maj-es-ty and splendor,
strength and hon-or in his ho-ly place.

1005

- iv -

6.
O sing a new song to the Lord; * sing to the Lord,
all the earth. In his presence are maj-es-ty and splendor,

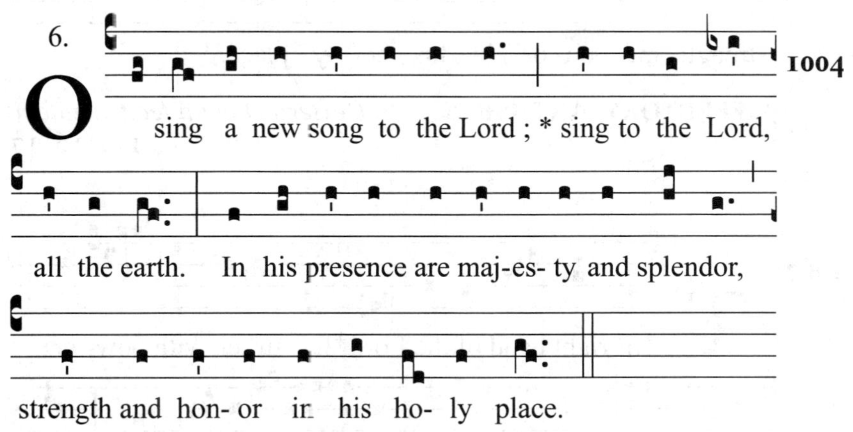

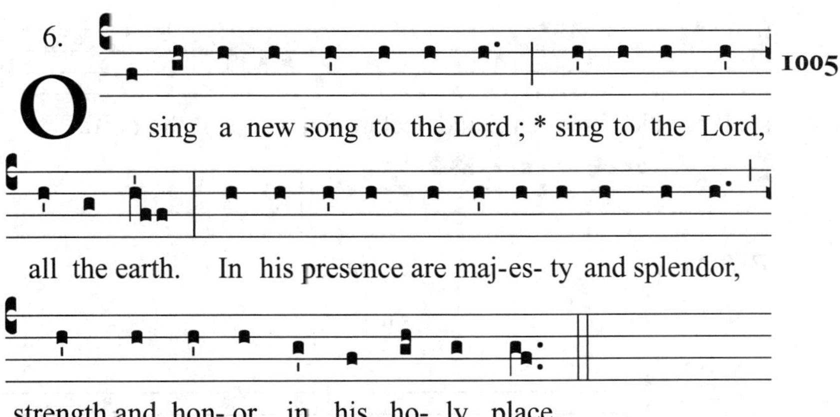

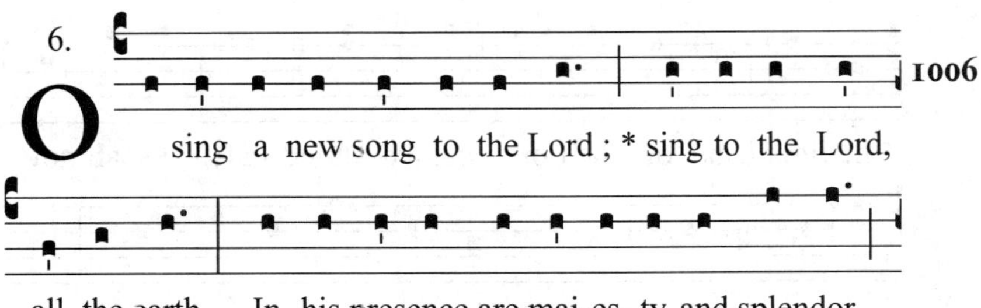

1006

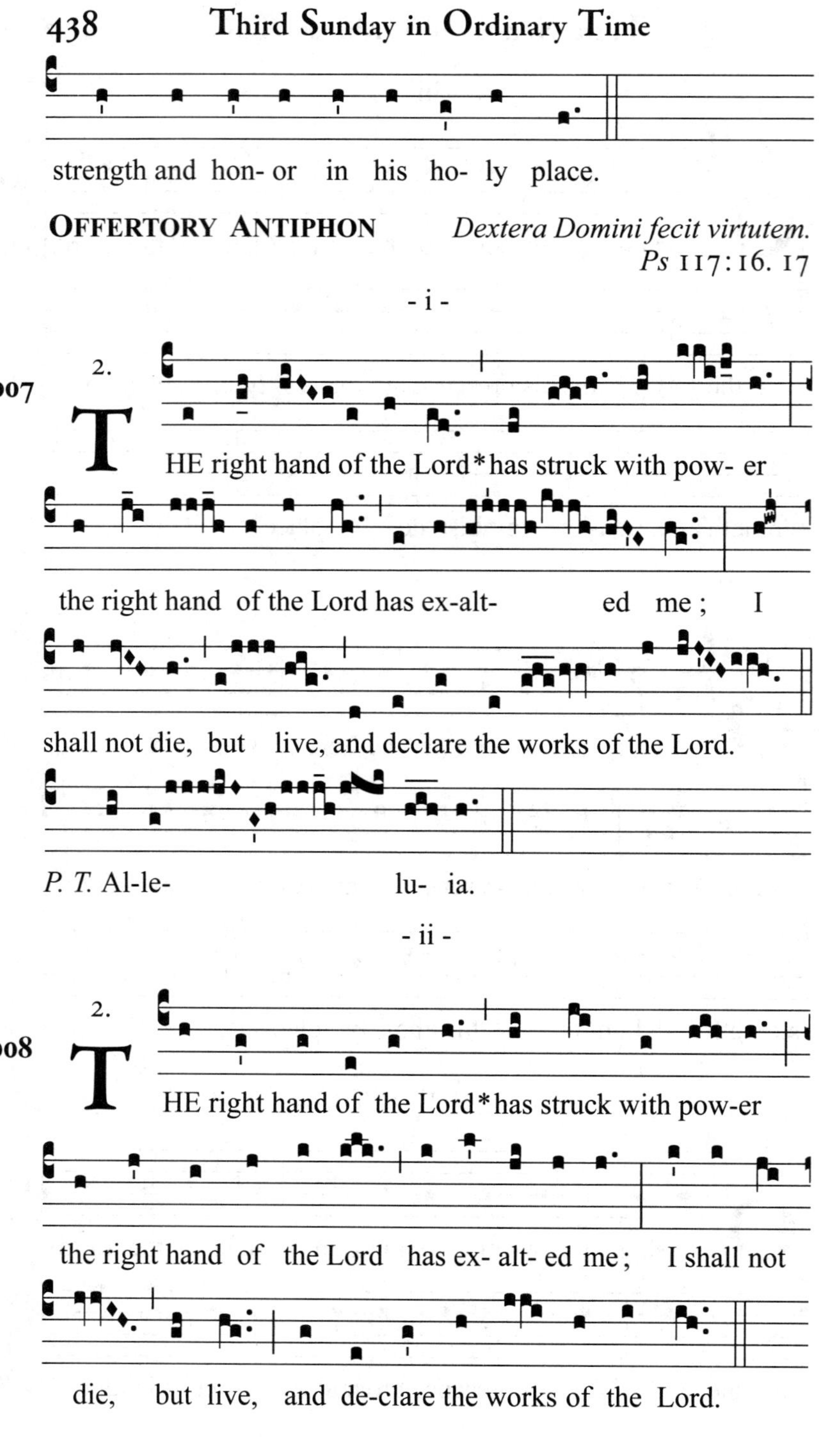
strength and hon- or in his ho- ly place.
OFFERTORY ANTIPHON
Dextera Domini fecit virtutem.
Ps 117:16. 17
- i -
1007
2.
THE right hand of the Lord * has struck with pow- er
the right hand of the Lord has ex-alt- ed me ; I
shall not die, but live, and declare the works of the Lord.
P. T. Al-le- lu- ia.
- ii -
1008
2.
THE right hand of the Lord * has struck with pow-er
the right hand of the Lord has ex- alt- ed me ; I shall not
die, but live, and de-clare the works of the Lord.

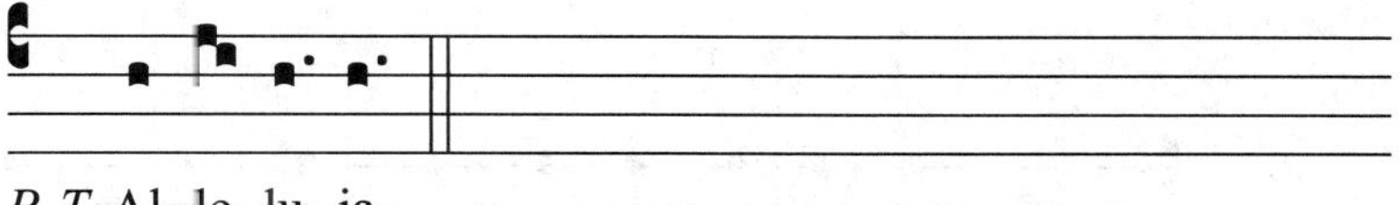
P. T. Al- le- lu- ia.

VERSES
Aperite mihi portas iustitiæ. Ps 117:19
℣. 1
1009
O - pen to me the gates of justice; I will go in- to
them and give praise un- to the Lord, * This is the gate of the

Lord, and the just shall en- ter in- to it.

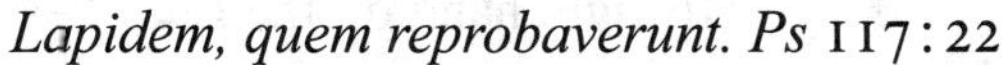
Lapidem, quem reprobaverunt. Ps 117:22

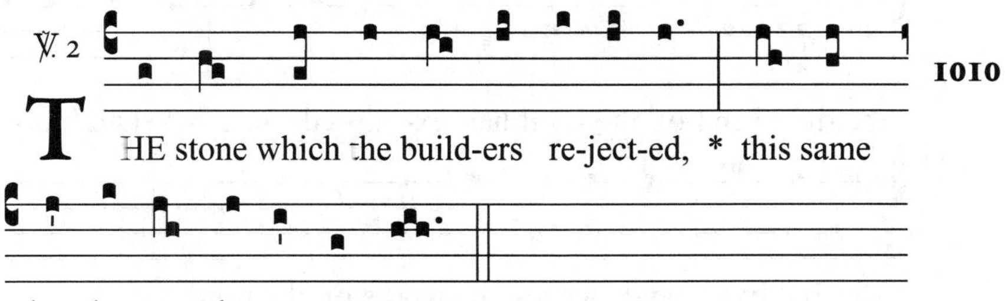
℣. 2
1010
THE stone which the build-ers re-ject-ed, * this same
has become the cor-ner-stone.

Deus meus es tu, et confitebor tibi. Ps 117:28

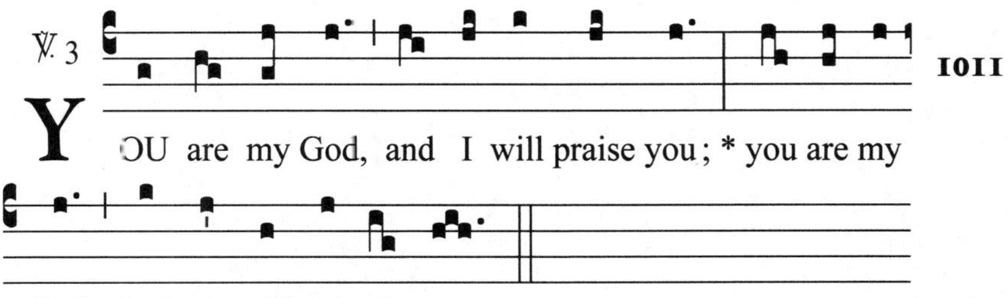
℣. 3
1011
YOU are my God, and I will praise you; * you are my
God, and I will ex- alt you.

- iii -

1012 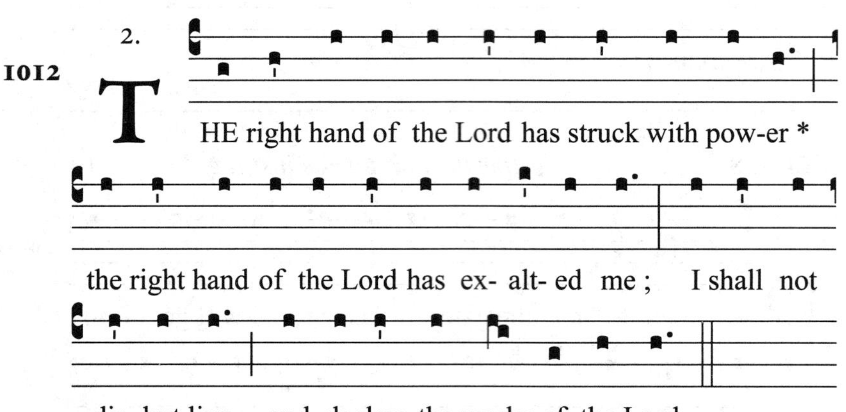
2.
THE right hand of the Lord has struck with pow-er *
the right hand of the Lord has ex- alt- ed me ; I shall not
die, but live, and declare the works of the Lord.

- iv -

1013 2.

THE right hand of the Lord has struck with pow-er *

the right hand of the Lord has ex- alt- ed me ; I shall not

die, but live, and declare the works of the Lord.

COMMUNION ANTIPHON *Accedite ad Dominum.* *Ps* 33:6

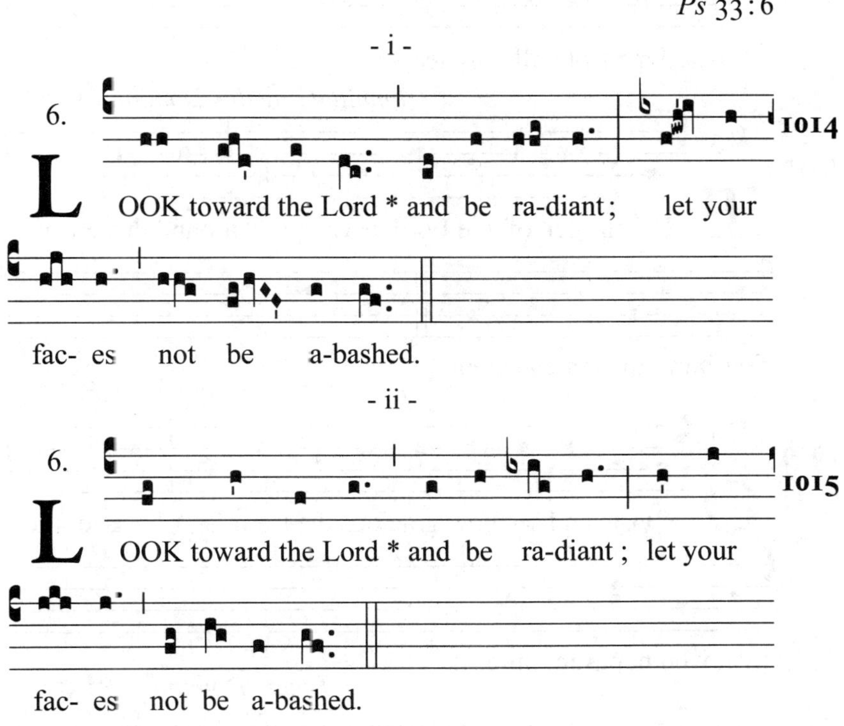
- i -
6.
1014
L OOK toward the Lord * and be ra-diant; let your
fac- es not be a-bashed.
- ii -
6.
1015
L OOK toward the Lord * and be ra-diant; let your
fac- es not be a-bashed.

VERSES *Magnificate Dominum mecum.* *Ps* 33:4

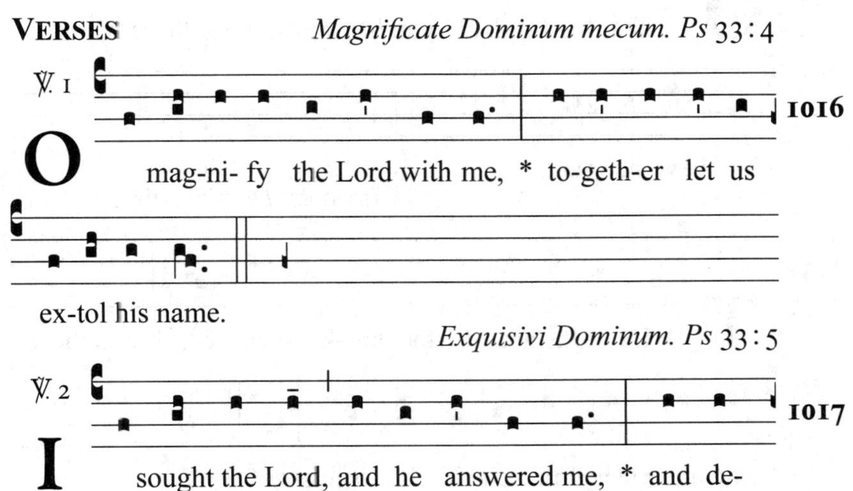
℣. 1
1016
O mag-ni- fy the Lord with me, * to-geth-er let us
ex-tol his name.
Exquisivi Dominum. *Ps* 33:5
℣. 2
1017
I sought the Lord, and he answered me, * and de-

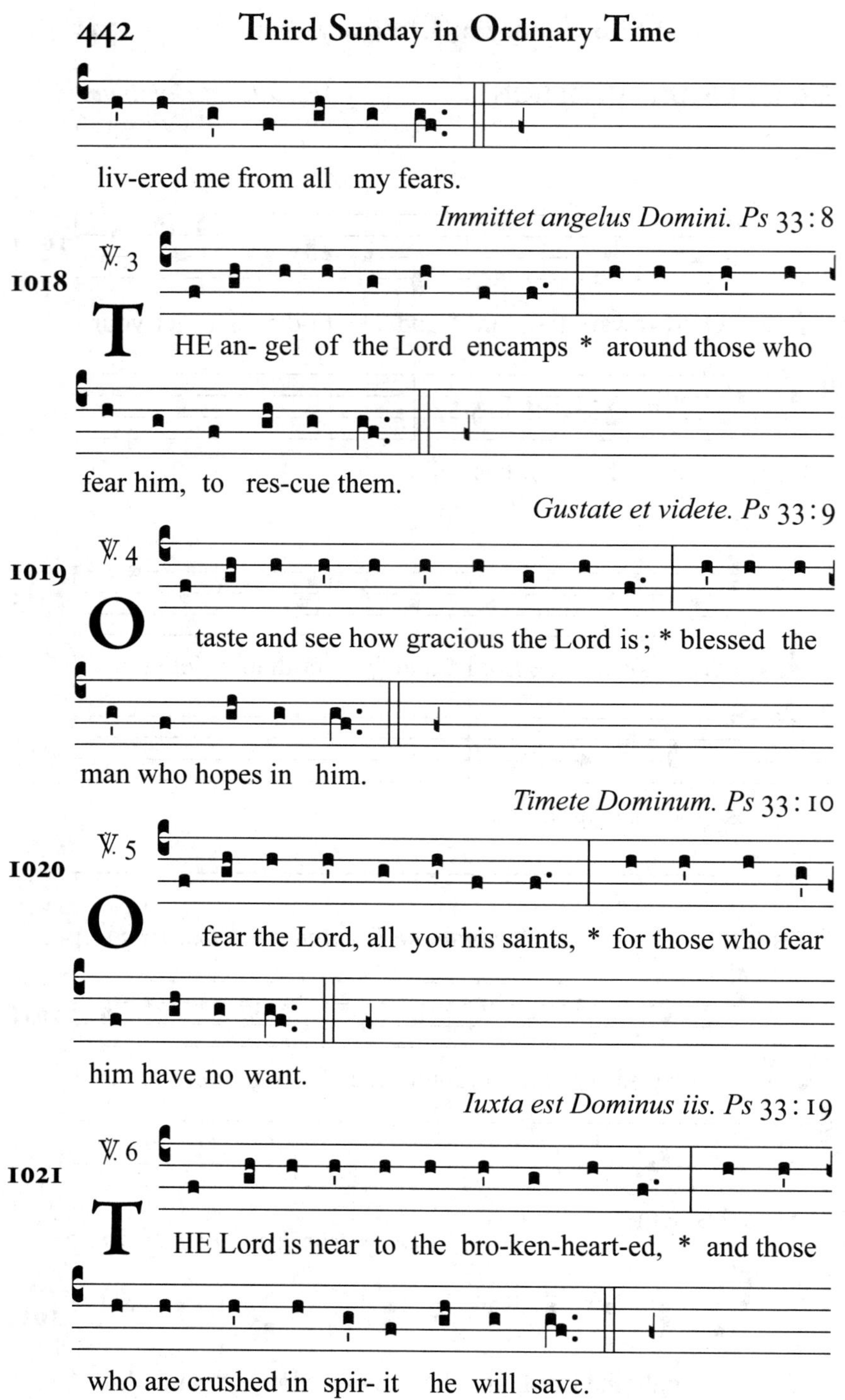
liv-ered me from all my fears.
Immittet angelus Domini. Ps 33 : 8
1018 ℣. 3
THE an- gel of the Lord encamps * around those who
fear him, to res-cue them.
Gustate et videte. Ps 33 : 9
1019 ℣. 4
O taste and see how gracious the Lord is ; * blessed the
man who hopes in him.
Timete Dominum. Ps 33 : 10
1020 ℣. 5
O fear the Lord, all you his saints, * for those who fear
him have no want.
Iuxta est Dominus iis. Ps 33 : 19
1021 ℣. 6
THE Lord is near to the bro-ken-heart-ed, * and those
who are crushed in spir- it he will save.

- iii -

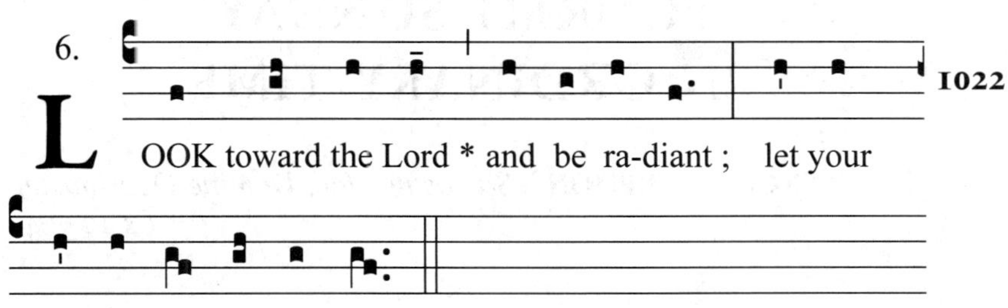

LOOK toward the Lord * and be ra-diant ; let your fac- es not be a-bashed.

- iv -

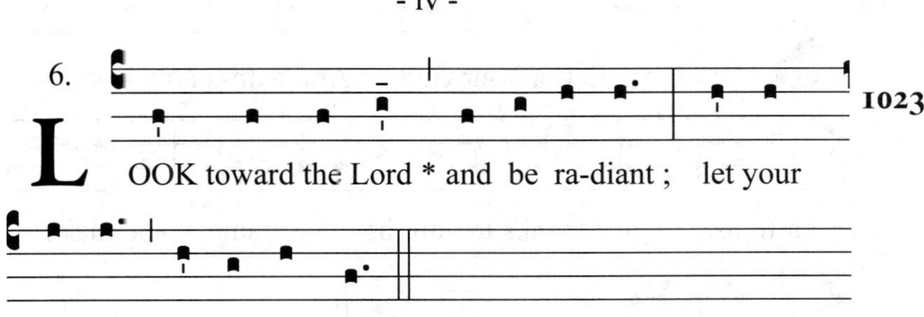

LOOK toward the Lord * and be ra-diant ; let your fac- es not be a-bashed.

FOURTH SUNDAY IN ORDINARY TIME

ENTRANCE ANTIPHON *Salvos nos fac, Domine Deus noster.* *Ps* 105:47

- i -

1024

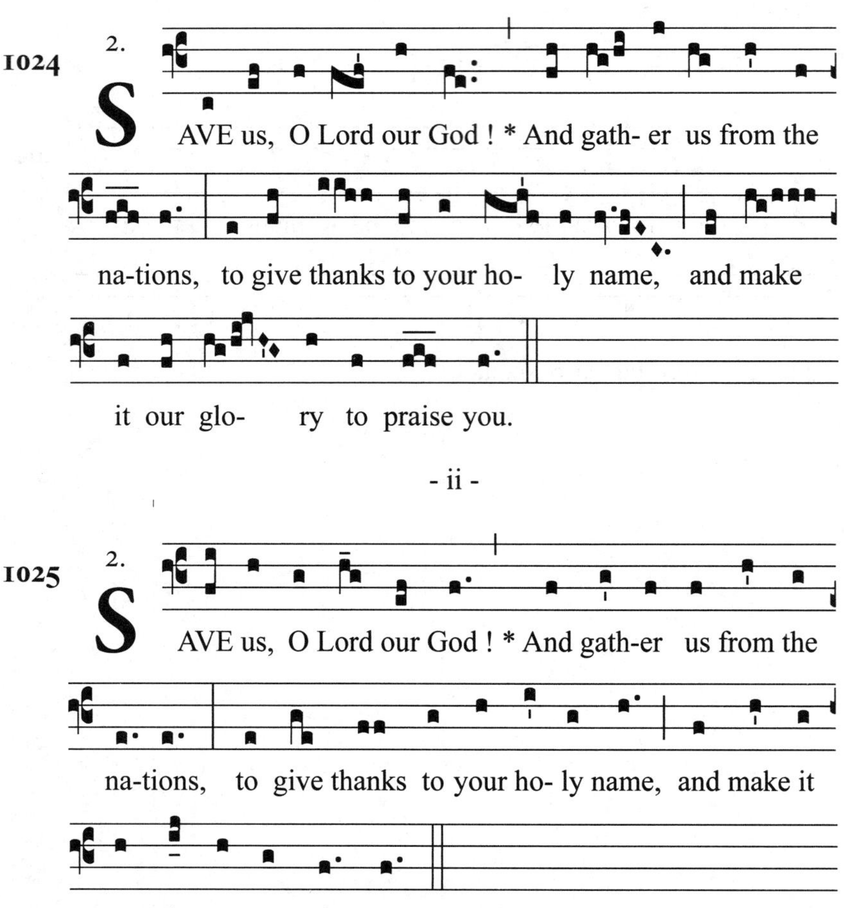

2.
SAVE us, O Lord our God ! * And gath- er us from the
na-tions, to give thanks to your ho- ly name, and make
it our glo- ry to praise you.
- ii -
1025
2.
SAVE us, O Lord our God ! * And gath-er us from the
na-tions, to give thanks to your ho- ly name, and make it
our glo- ry to praise you.

VERSES

Beati, qui custodiunt iudicium. Ps 105:3

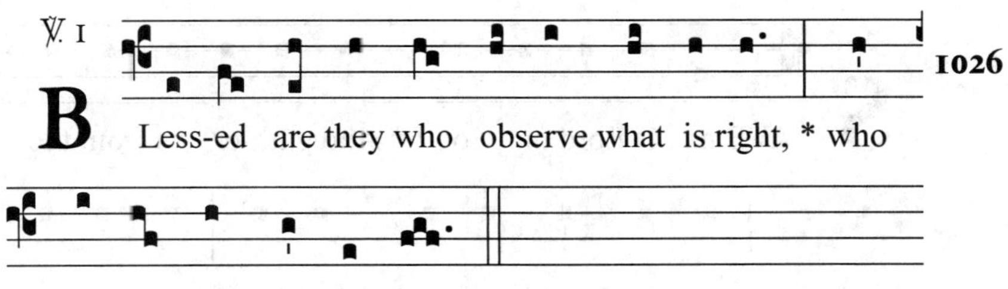
℣. 1
BLess-ed are they who observe what is right, * who
do al- ways what is just.

1026

Memento nostri, Domine. Ps 105:4

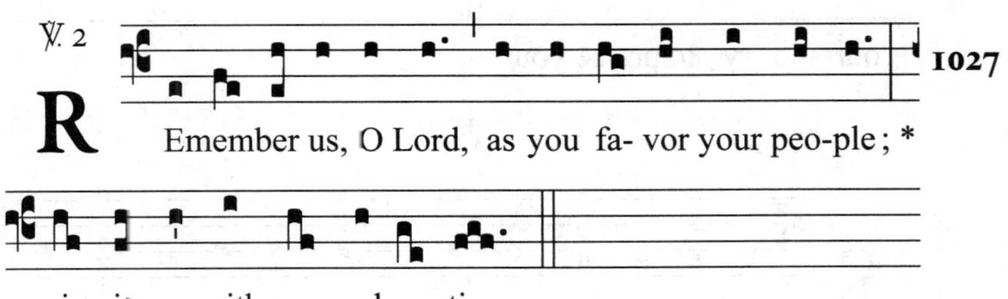
℣. 2
REmember us, O Lord, as you fa- vor your peo-ple; *
vis- it us with your sal-va- tion.

1027

Benedictus Dominus. Ps 105:48

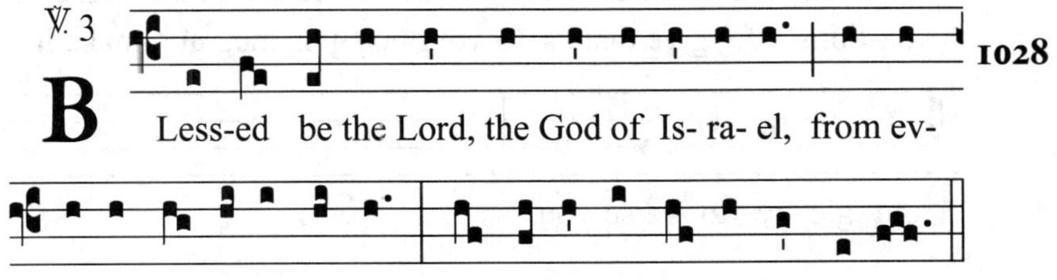
℣. 3
BLess-ed be the Lord, the God of Is- ra- el, from ev-
lasting to ev-er-lasting. * And let all the people say: A-men.

1028

- iii -

1029
2.
SAVE us, O Lord our God ! * And gath-er us from the
na-tions, to give thanks to your ho- ly name, and make it
our glo- ry to praise you.

- iv -

1030
2.
SAVE us, O Lord our God ! * And gath-er us from the
na-tions, to give thanks to your ho- ly name, and make it
our glo- ry to praise you.

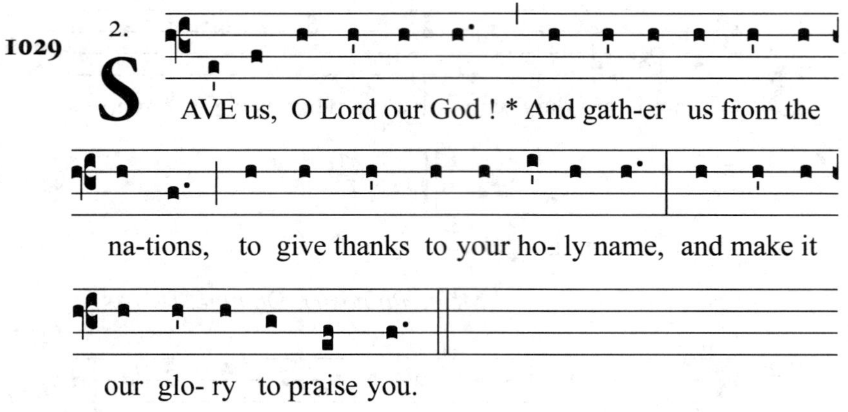

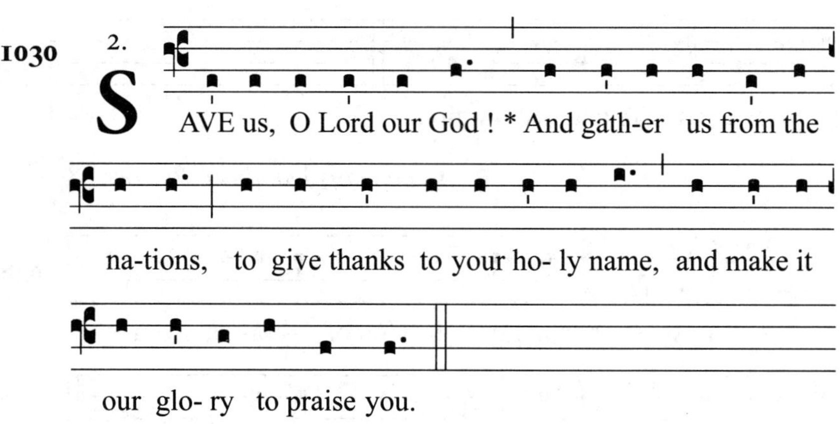

OFFERTORY ANTIPHON *Bonum est confiteri Domino.*
Ps 91:2

- i -

8.
IT is good * to give praise to the Lord, and to
sing to your Name, O Most High.
1031

- ii -

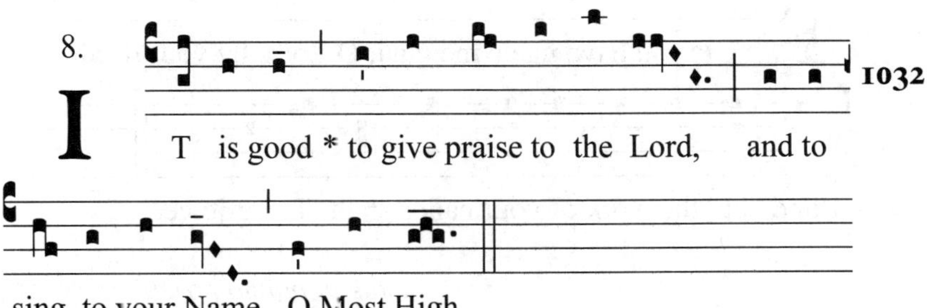
8.
IT is good * to give praise to the Lord, and to
sing to your Name, O Most High.
1032

VERSES *Ad annuntiandum mane misericordiam tuam.* *Ps* 91:3

1033

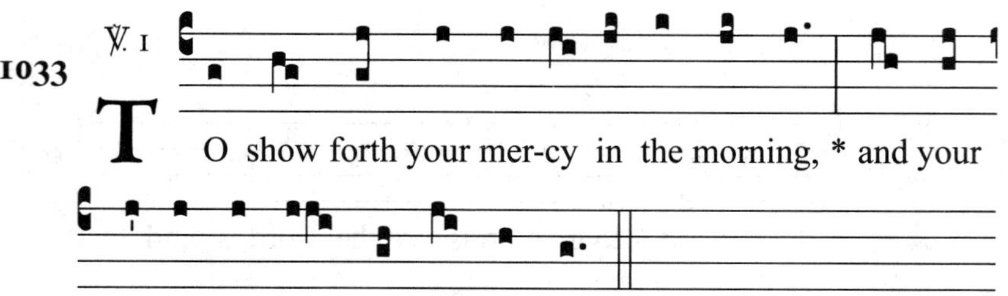
℣. 1
TO show forth your mer-cy in the morning, * and your

truth in the watch- es of the night.

Quia delectasti me, Domine. Ps 91:5

1034

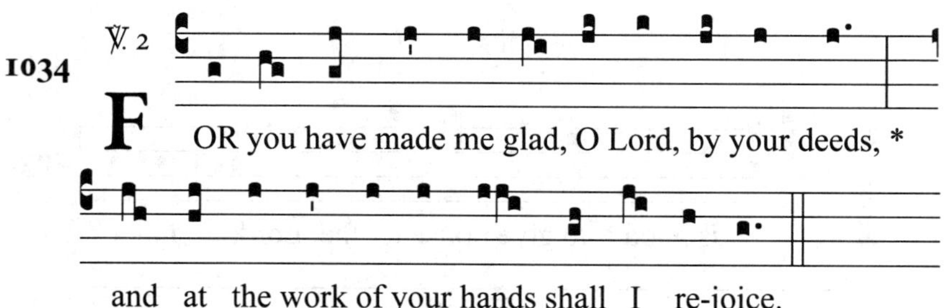
℣. 2
FOR you have made me glad, O Lord, by your deeds, *
and at the work of your hands shall I re-joice.

Iustus ut palma florebit. Ps 91:13

1035

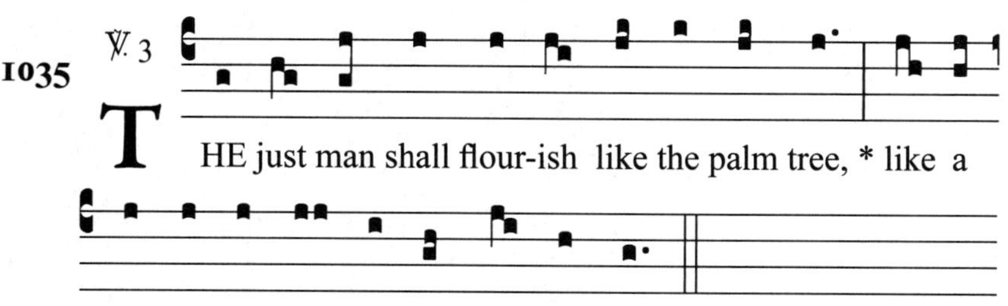
℣. 3
THE just man shall flour-ish like the palm tree, * like a

ce- dar of Leb- a- non shall he grow.

- iii -

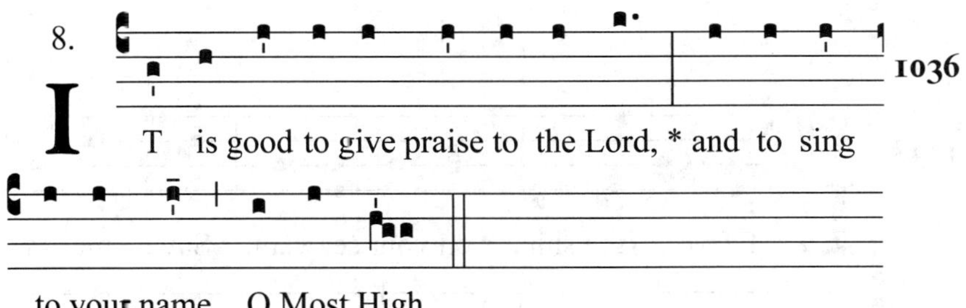
8.
IT is good to give praise to the Lord, * and to sing
to your name, O Most High.

1036

- iv -

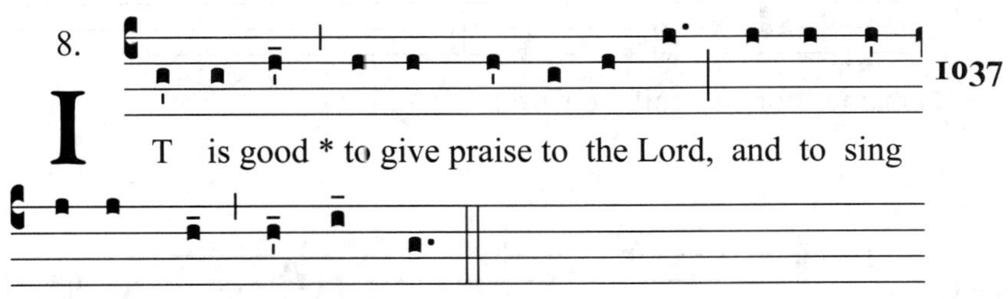
8.
IT is good * to give praise to the Lord, and to sing
to your name, O Most High.

1037

COMMUNION ANTIPHON *Illumina faciem tuam.*
Ps 30:17-18

- i -

1038 I.

LET your face shine * on your ser-vant. Save me in your mer- ci- ful love. O Lord, let me nev-er be put to shame, for I call on you.

- ii -

1039 I.

LET your face shine * on your ser- vant. Save me in your mer-ci- ful love. O Lord, let me nev- er be put to shame, for I call on you.

VERSES *In te, Domine, speravi. Ps* 30 : 2

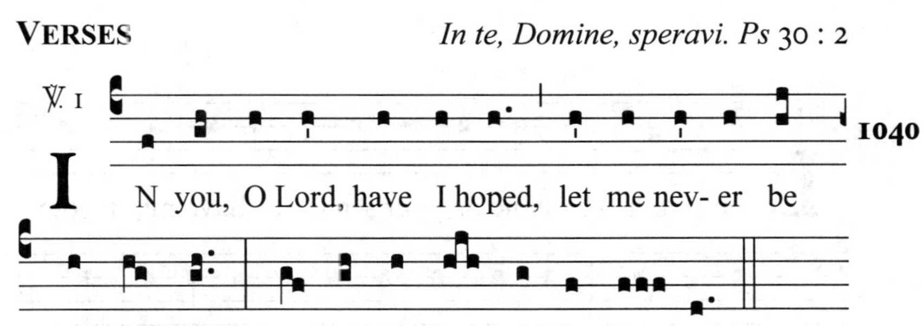
℣. 1
IN you, O Lord, have I hoped, let me nev- er be
1040
confound-ed, * de- liv- er me in your jus-tice.

Inclina ad me aurem tuam. Ps 30 : 3. 4

℣. 2
BOW down your ear to me; make haste to save me, *
1041
for you are my strength and my ref- uge.

Illustra faciem tuam. Ps 30 : 17

℣. 3
LET your face shine up- on your ser- vant; * save me
1042
in your mer- cy. Let me not be con-found-ed.

- iii -

1043

I.
LET your face shine on your ser-vant. * Save me in your
mer- ci- ful love. O Lord, let me nev- er be put to shame,
for I call on you.

- iv -

1044

I.
LET your face shine on your ser-vant. * Save me in your
mer- ci- ful love. O Lord, let me nev- er be put to shame,
for I call on you.

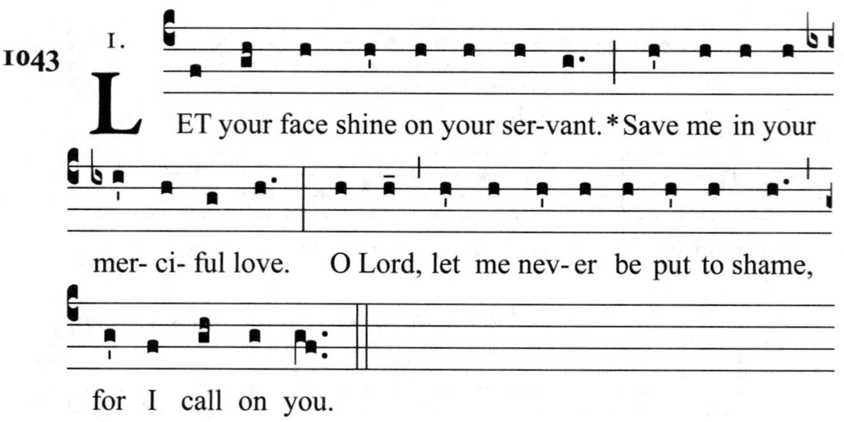

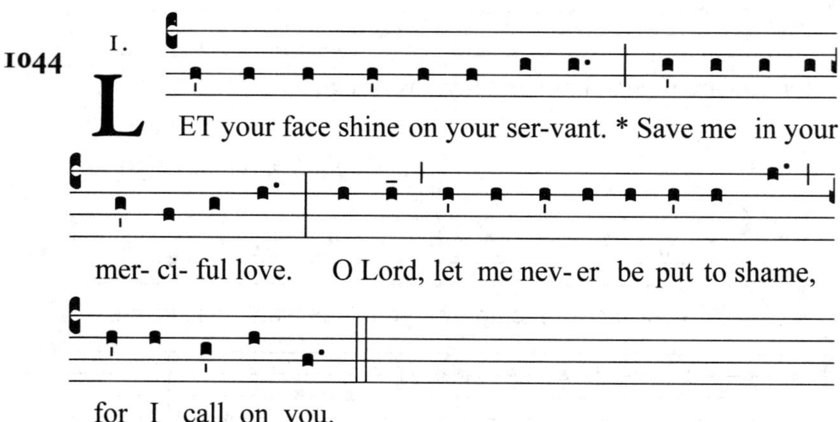

FIFTH SUNDAY IN ORDINARY TIME

ENTRANCE ANTIPHON *Venite, adoremus Deum.*
Ps 94:6-7

- i -

2.
O come, * let us wor-ship God and bow low
1045
before the God who made us, for he is the Lord our God.

- ii -

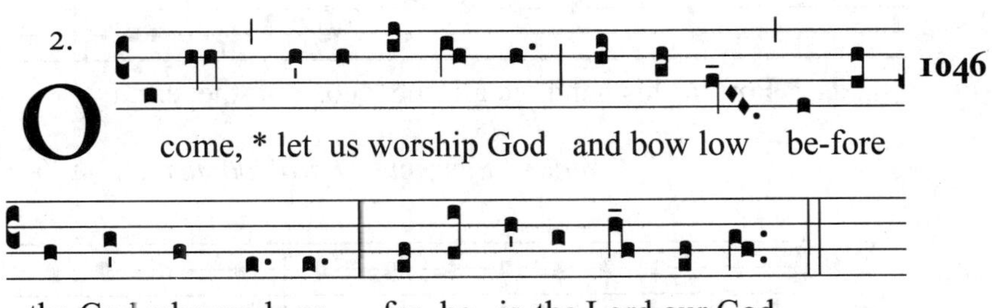
2.
O come, * let us worship God and bow low be-fore
1046
the God who made us, for he is the Lord our God.

VERSES *Venite, exultemus Domino. Ps* 94:1

1047 
℣. 1
O come, let us praise the Lord with joy, let us joy-ful-
ly sing to God our Sav-ior. * Let us come be-fore his presence
with thanksgiv-ing, and make a joyful noise to him with psalms.

Quoniam Deus magnus Dominus. Ps 94:3-4

1048 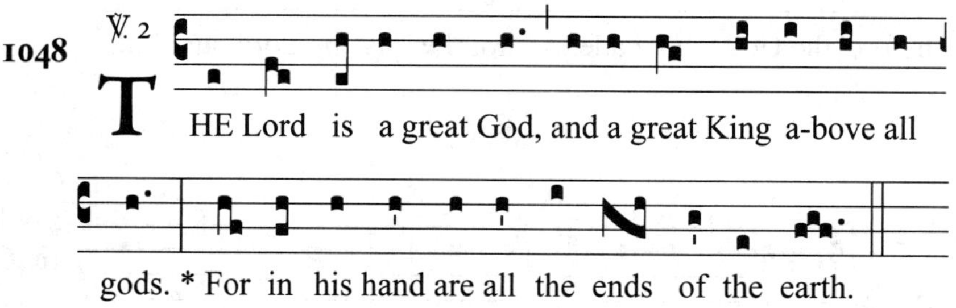
℣. 2
THE Lord is a great God, and a great King a-bove all
gods. * For in his hand are all the ends of the earth.

Venite, adoremus et procidamus. Ps 94:6-7

1049 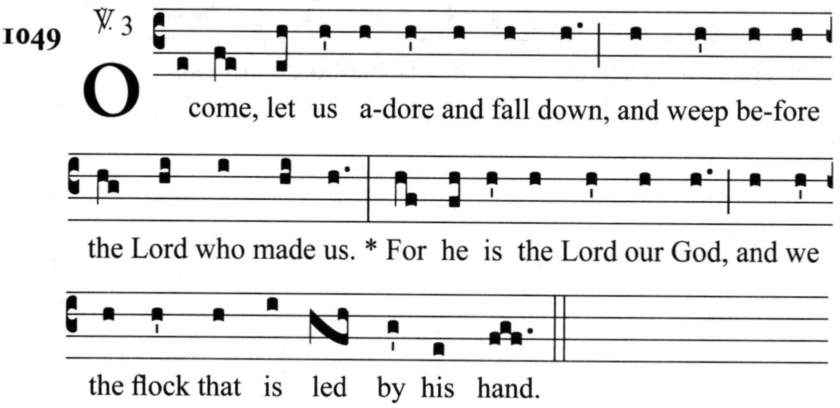
℣. 3
O come, let us a-dore and fall down, and weep be-fore
the Lord who made us. * For he is the Lord our God, and we
the flock that is led by his hand.

- iii -

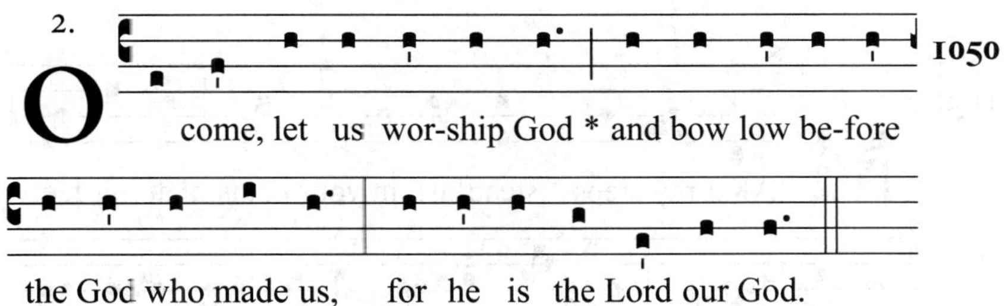
2.
1050
O come, let us wor-ship God * and bow low be-fore
the God who made us, for he is the Lord our God.

- iv -

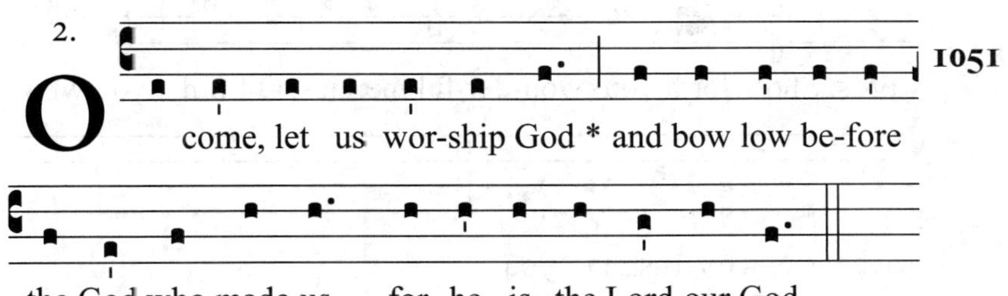
2.
1051
O come, let us wor-ship God * and bow low be-fore
the God who made us, for he is the Lord our God.

OFFERTORY ANTIPHON *Perfice gressus meos.*
Ps 16:5. 6. 7

- i -

1052

4.
MAKE my steps * steadfast in your paths, that my feet
may not fal- ter. In- cline your ear to me, and hear my
words. Show forth your won-der-ful mercies, O Lord, you who
save those who trust in you.

- ii -

1053

4.
MAKE my steps steadfast in your paths, * that my feet
may not fal- ter. In-cline your ear to me, and hear my
words. Show forth your won-der-ful mer-cies, O Lord, you
who save those who trust in you.

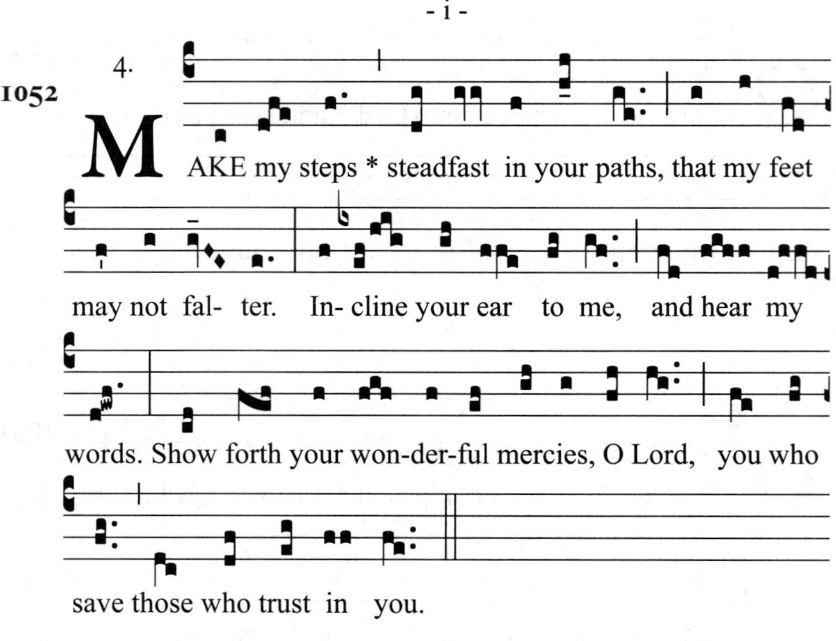

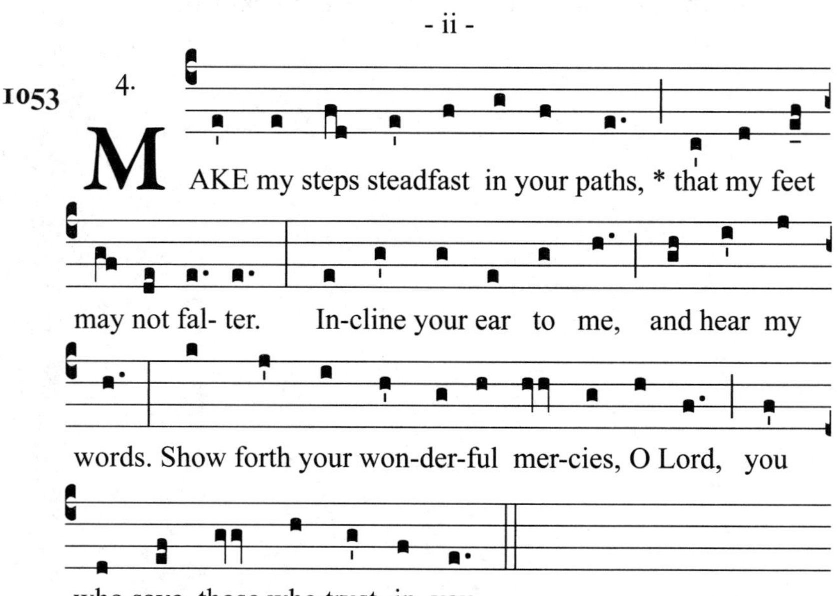

VERSES *Exaudi, Domine, iustitiam meam. Ps* 16:1

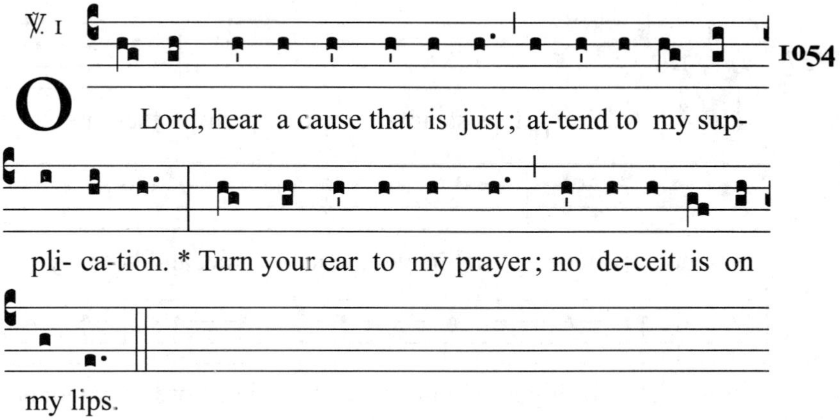

℣. 1 1054

O Lord, hear a cause that is just; at-tend to my sup-
pli- ca-tion. * Turn your ear to my prayer; no de-ceit is on
my lips.

De vultu tuo. Ps 16:2

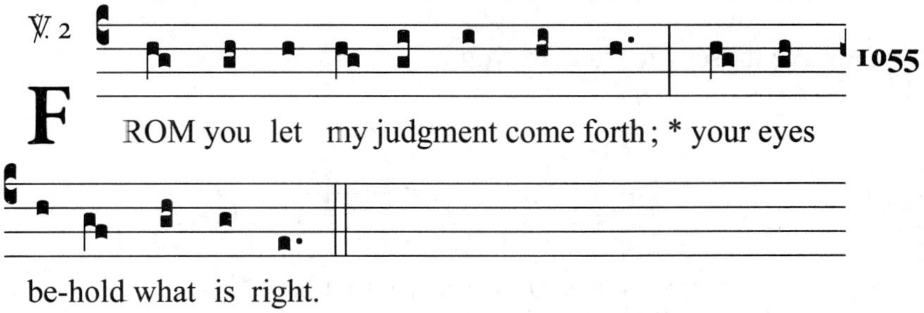

℣. 2 1055

FROM you let my judgment come forth; * your eyes
be-hold what is right.

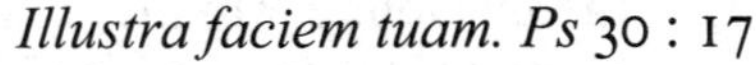
Illustra faciem tuam. Ps 30 : 17

℣. 3
1056
BUT I, in jus-tice shall be-hold your face; * when I

a-wake, I shall be con-tent in your pres-ence.

- iii -

1057
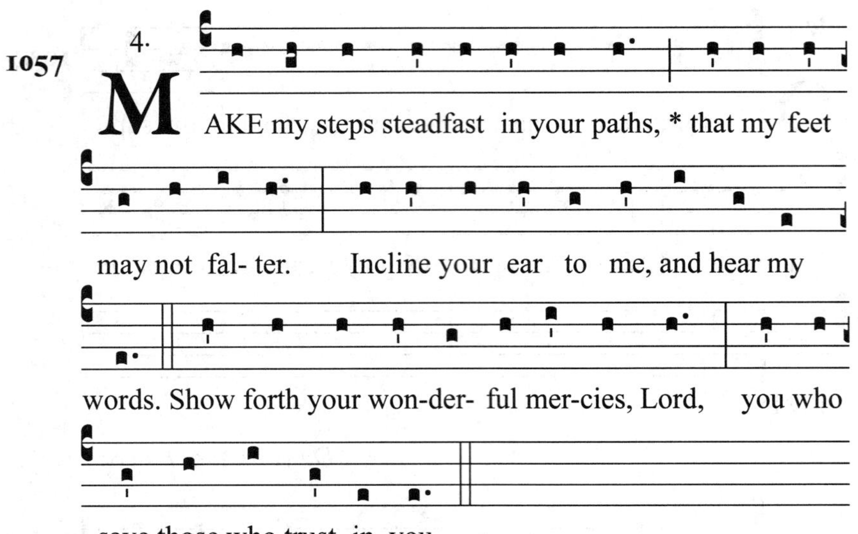
4.
MAKE my steps steadfast in your paths, * that my feet
may not fal- ter. Incline your ear to me, and hear my
words. Show forth your won-der- ful mer-cies, Lord, you who
save those who trust in you.

- iv -

1058 4. E

Make my steps steadfast in your paths, / *
that my feet may not | **fal**-ter.
Incline your ear to me, and | *hear my* **words**.
Show forth your wonderful mercies, O | **Lord**,
you who save / those who trust | *in* **you**.

COMMUNION ANTIPHON *Confiteantur Domino.*
Ps 106:8-9

- i -

6. 1059

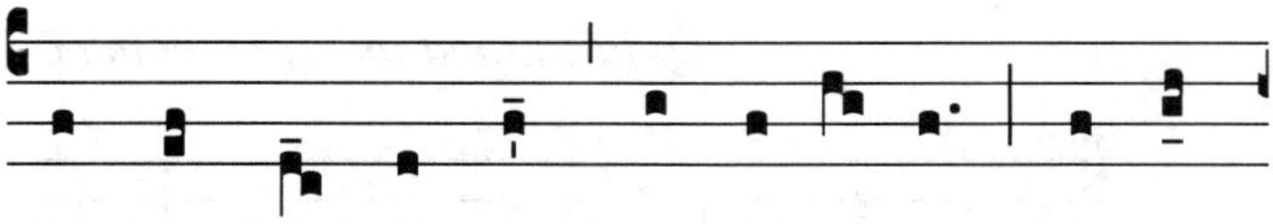

LET them thank the Lord * for his mer-cy, his won-ders for the children of men, for he sat- is-fies the  thirst-y soul, and the hun- gry he fills with good things.

- ii -

6. 1060

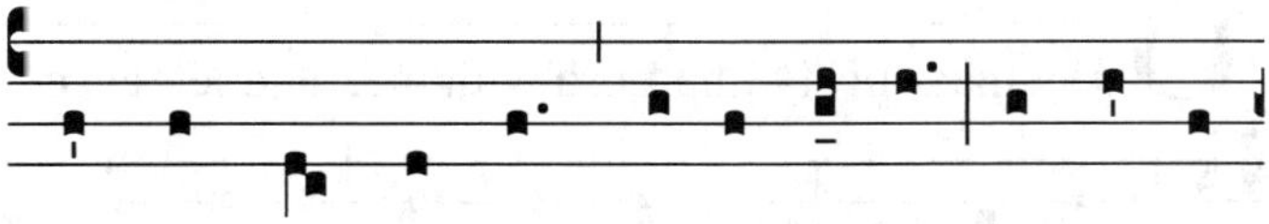

LET them thank the Lord * for his mer-cy, his wonders for the children of men, for he sat- is-fies the thirst-y soul, and the hun-gry he fills with good things.

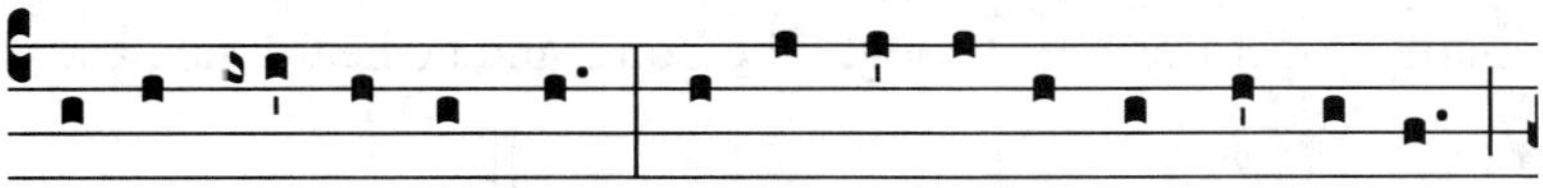

VERSES *Confitemini Domino quoniam bonus. Ps* 106:1

℣. 1 1061

O give glo- ry to the Lord, for he is good, * for his

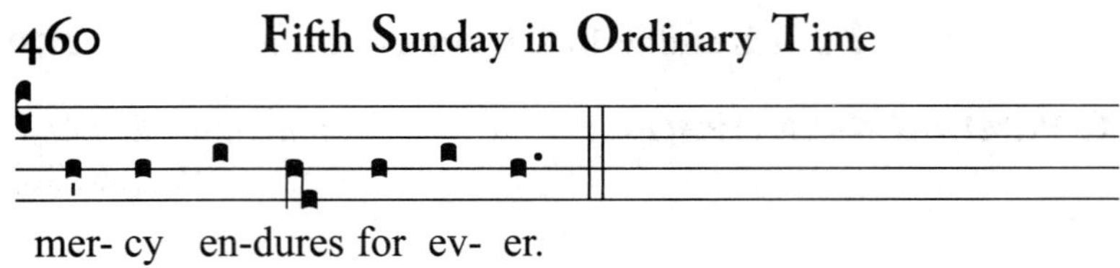
mer- cy en-dures for ev- er.

Quia satiavit animam inanem. Ps 106:9

1062

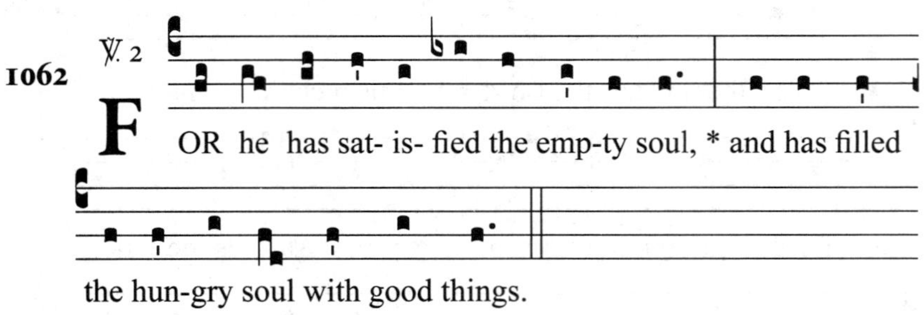
℣. 2
FOR he has sat- is- fied the emp-ty soul, * and has filled
the hun-gry soul with good things.

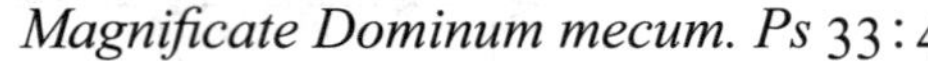
Magnificate Dominum mecum. Ps 33:4

1063

℣. 3
O mag- ni- fy the Lord with me, and let us ex-tol his
name to-geth-er. * I sought the Lord, and he heard me ; and
he de-livered me from all my troubles.

Gustate et videte. Ps 33:9

1064

℣. 4
O taste and see how gra-cious the Lord is ; * blessed
the man who hopes in him.

- iii -

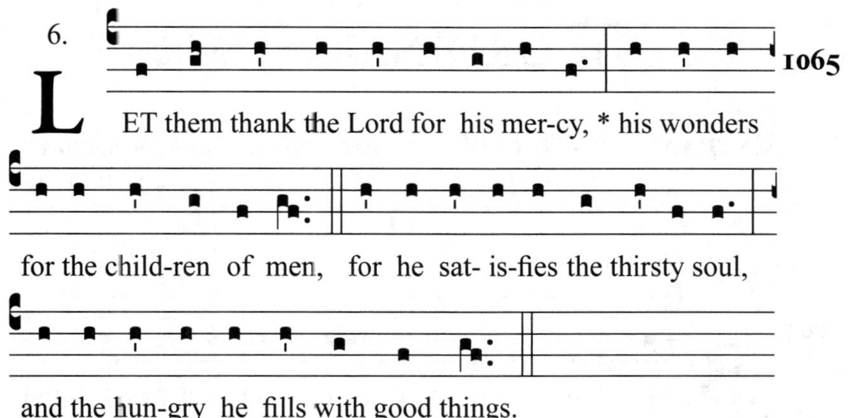
6.
1065
LET them thank the Lord for his mer-cy, * his wonders
for the child-ren of men, for he sat- is-fies the thirsty soul,
and the hun-gry he fills with good things.

- iv -

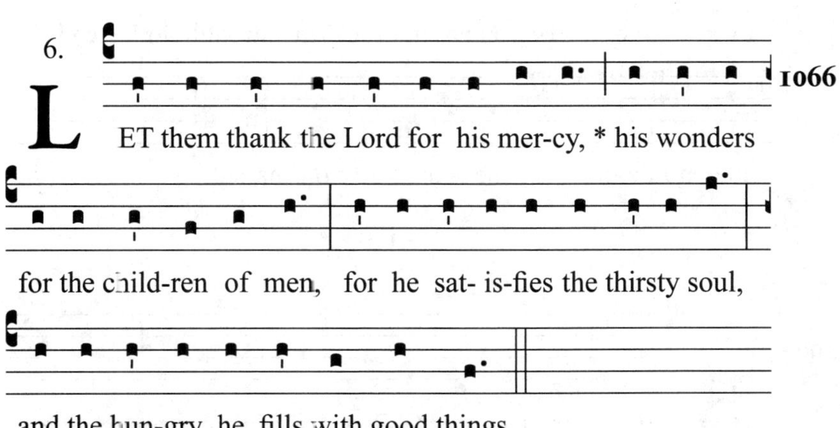
6.
1066
LET them thank the Lord for his mer-cy, * his wonders
for the child-ren of men, for he sat- is-fies the thirsty soul,
and the hun-gry he fills with good things.

SIXTH SUNDAY IN ORDINARY TIME

Entrance Antiphon *Esto mihi in Deum protectorem.*
Ps 30:3. 4. 2

- i -

1067

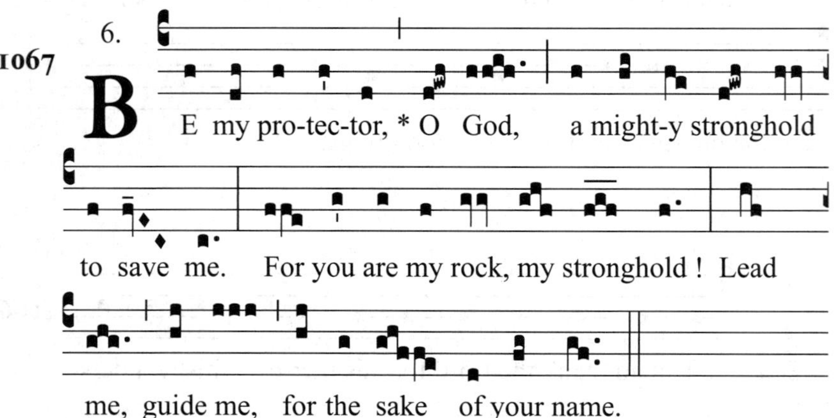
6.
BE my pro-tec-tor, * O God, a might-y stronghold
to save me. For you are my rock, my stronghold! Lead
me, guide me, for the sake of your name.

- ii -

1068

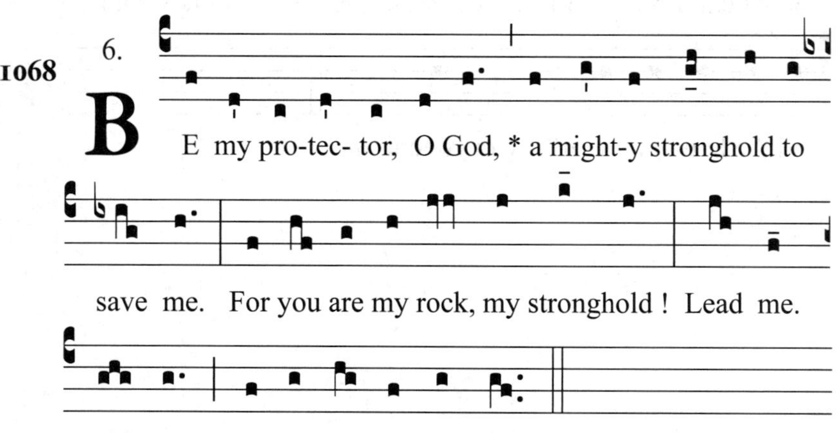
6.
BE my pro-tec- tor, O God, * a might-y stronghold to
save me. For you are my rock, my stronghold! Lead me.
guide me, for the sake of your name.

VERSES *In te, Domine, speravi. Ps* 30 : 2

℣. 1
I N you, O Lord, have I hoped, let me nev- er be
confound-ed, * de- liv- er me in your jus-tice.

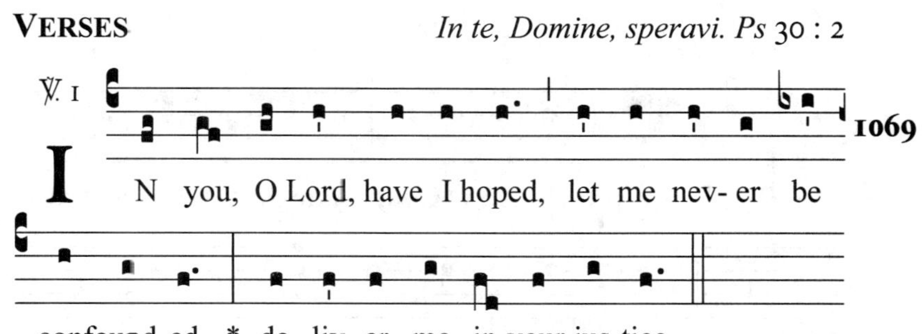

1069

Inclina ad me aurem tuam. Ps 30 : 3. 4

℣. 2
B OW down your ear to me; make haste to de- liv- er
me, * for you are my strength and ref- uge.

1070

In manus tuas, Domine. Ps 30 : 6

℣. 3
I N- to your hands I commend my spir- it, * for you
have redeemed me, O Lord, O God of truth.

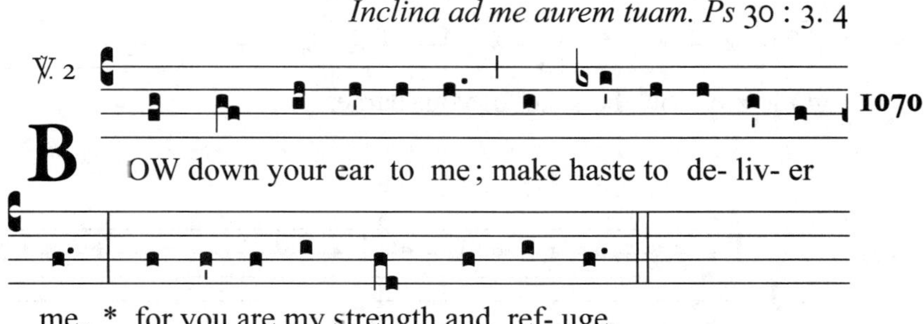

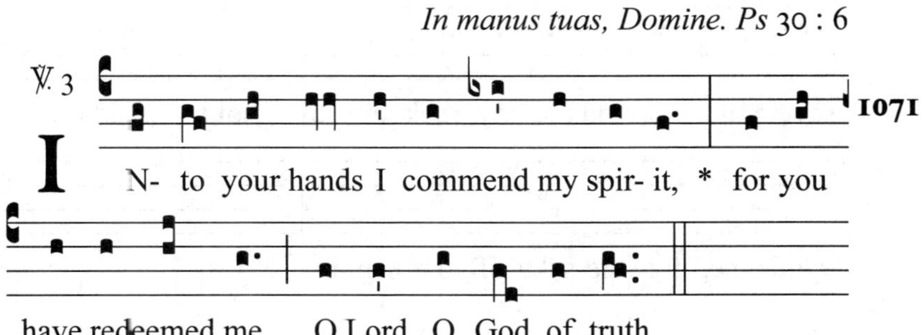

1071

- iii -

1072

6.
BE my pro-tec-tor, O God, * a might-y stronghold to
save me. For you are my rock, my stronghold! Lead me,
guide me, for the sake of your name.

Or:

1073

6.
BE my pro-tec-tor, O God, * a might-y stronghold to
save me. For you are my rock, my stronghold! Lead me,
guide me, for the sake of your name.

- iv -

1074

6.
BE my pro-tec-tor, O God, * a might-y stronghold to
save me. For you are my rock, my stronghold! Lead me,

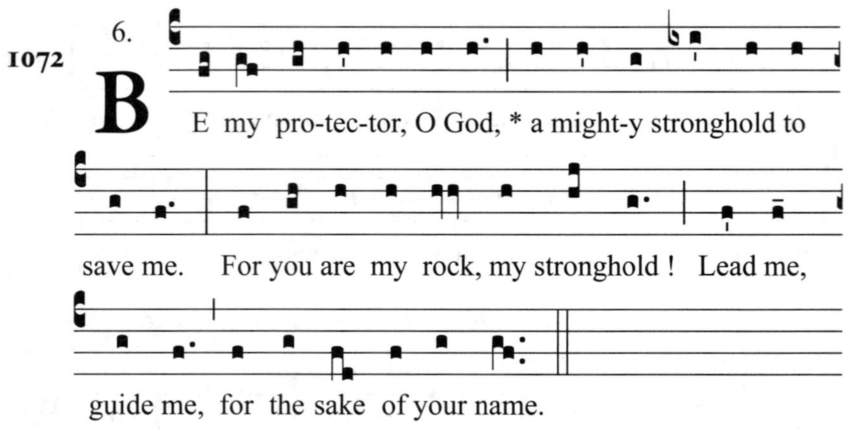

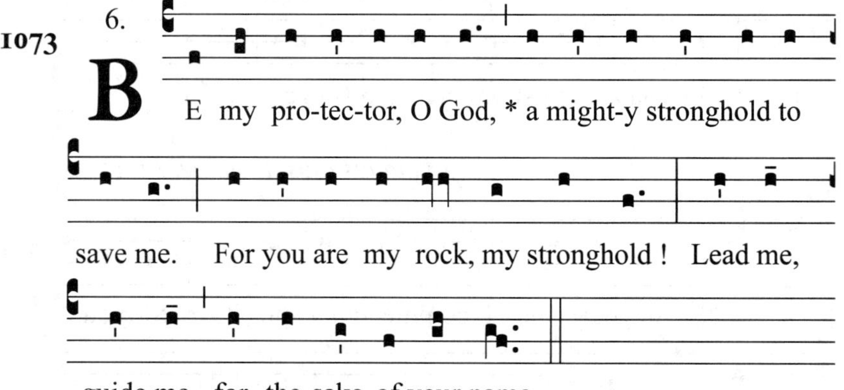

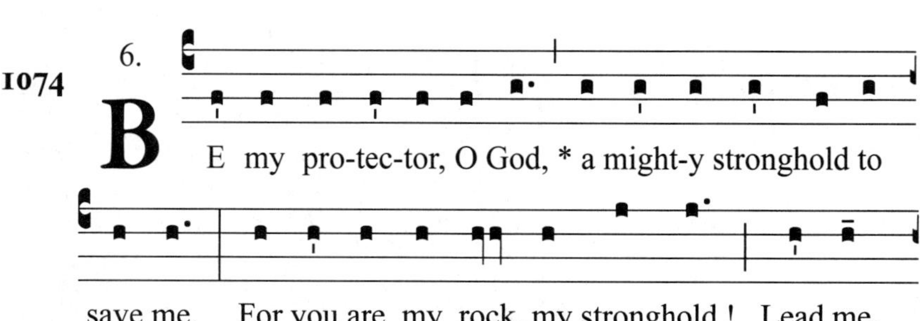

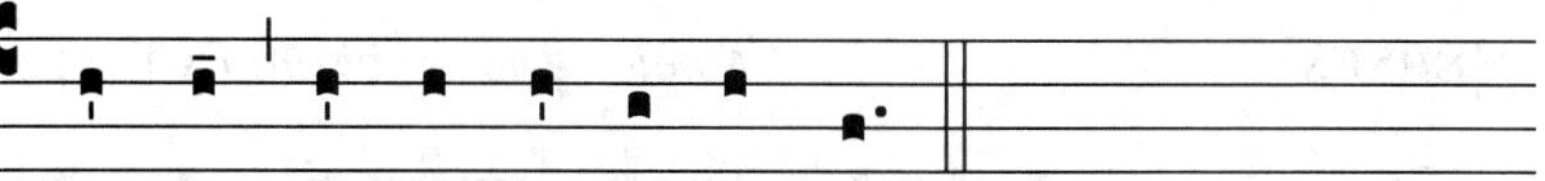

guide me, for the sake of your name.

Offertory Antiphon *Benedictus es, Domine.*
Ps 118: 12.13

- i -

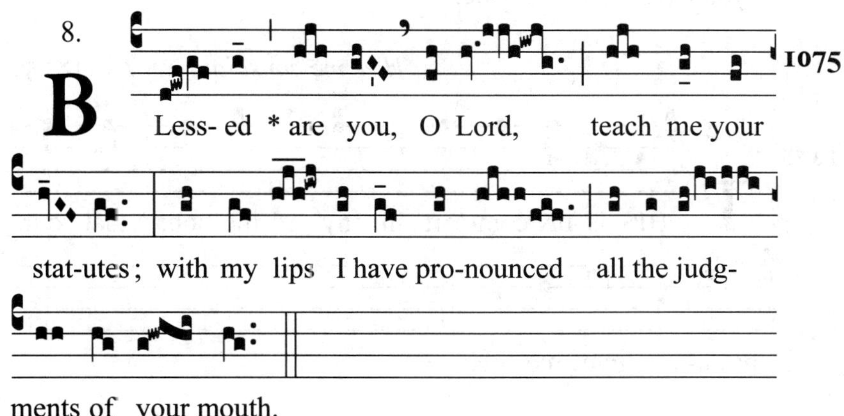
8.
1075
BLess- ed * are you, O Lord, teach me your
stat-utes; with my lips I have pro-nounced all the judgments of your mouth.

- ii -

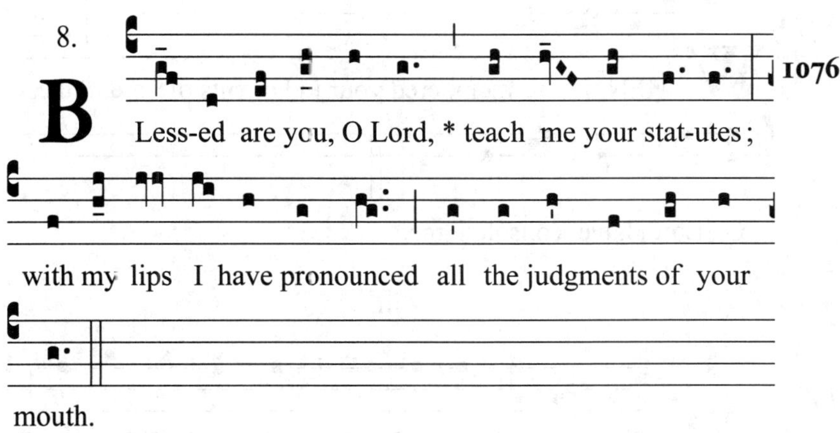
8.
1076
BLess-ed are you, O Lord, * teach me your stat-utes;
with my lips I have pronounced all the judgments of your
mouth.

Verses *Memor esto verbi tui. Ps* 118:49

1077
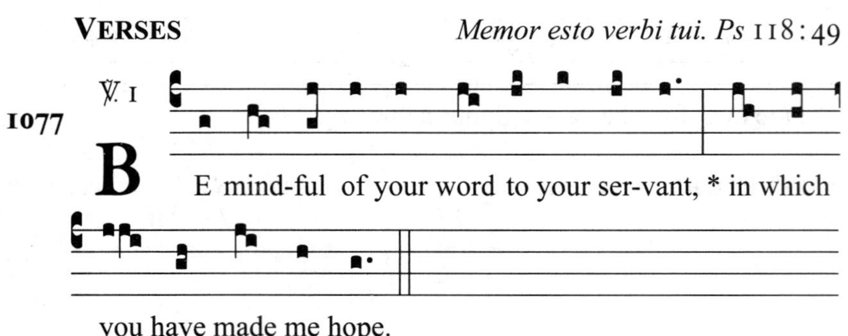
℣. 1
BE mind-ful of your word to your ser-vant, * in which
you have made me hope.

Hæc me consolata est. Ps 118:50

1078
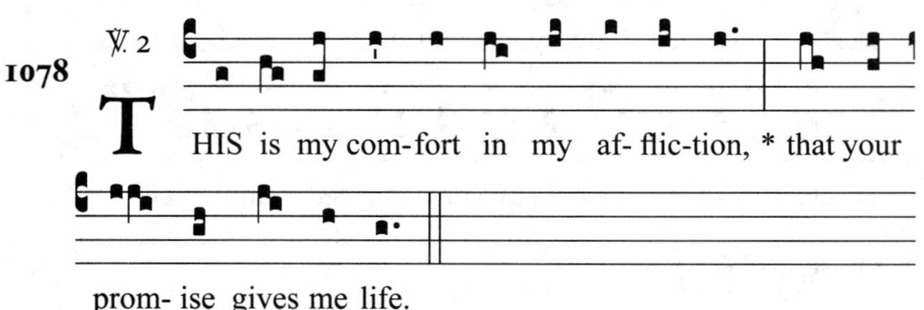
℣. 2
THIS is my com-fort in my af- flic-tion, * that your
prom- ise gives me life.

Memor fui iudiciorum tuorum. Ps 118:52

1079
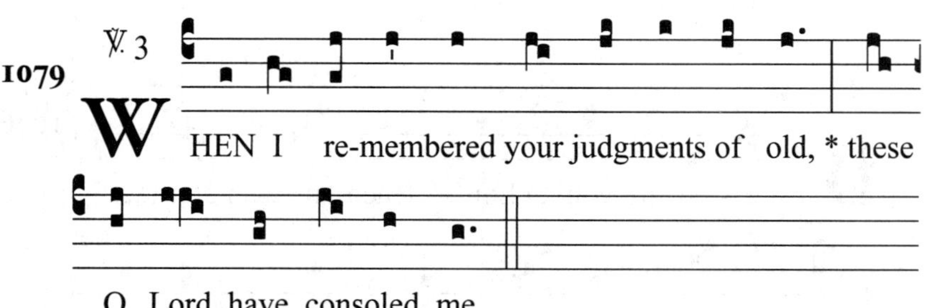
℣. 3
WHEN I re-membered your judgments of old, * these
O Lord, have consoled me.

- iii -

1080
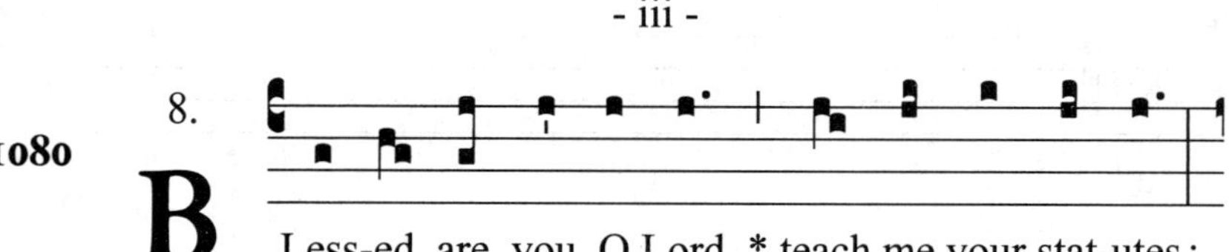
8.
BLess-ed are you, O Lord, * teach me your stat-utes;

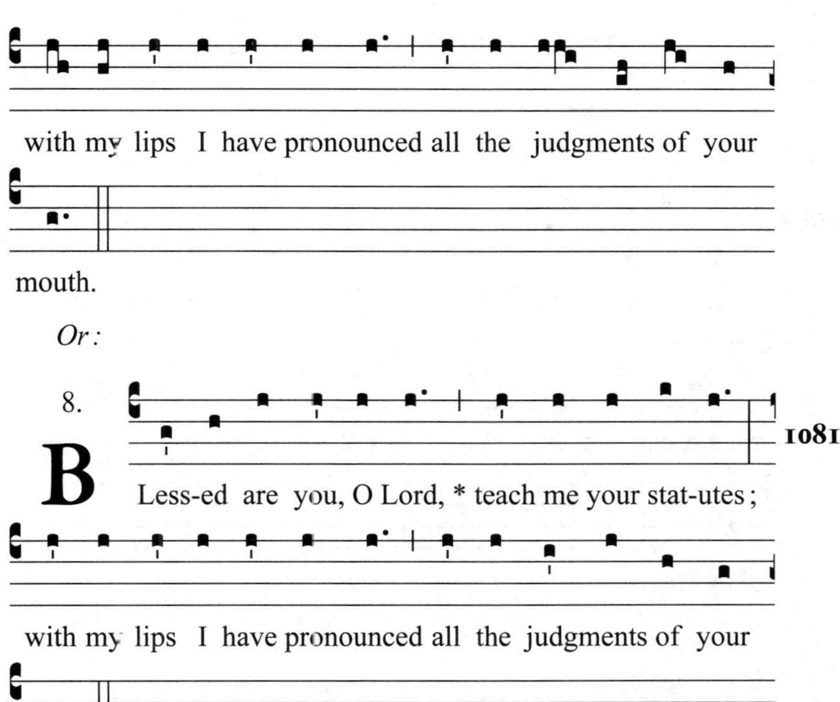
with my lips I have pronounced all the judgments of your
mouth.
Or:
8.
B
Less-ed are you, O Lord, * teach me your stat-utes ; 1081
with my lips I have pronounced all the judgments of your

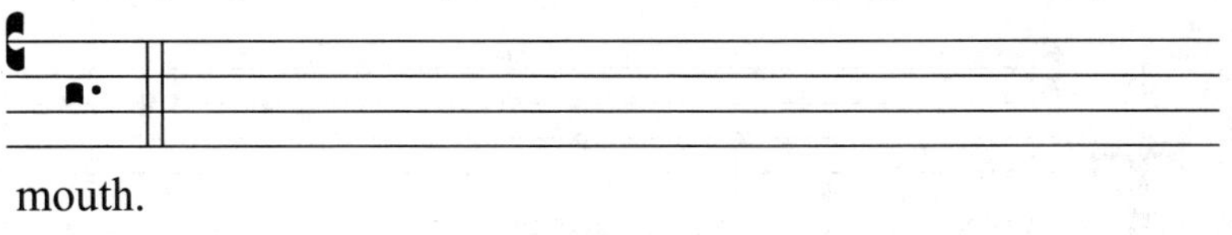
mouth.

- iv -

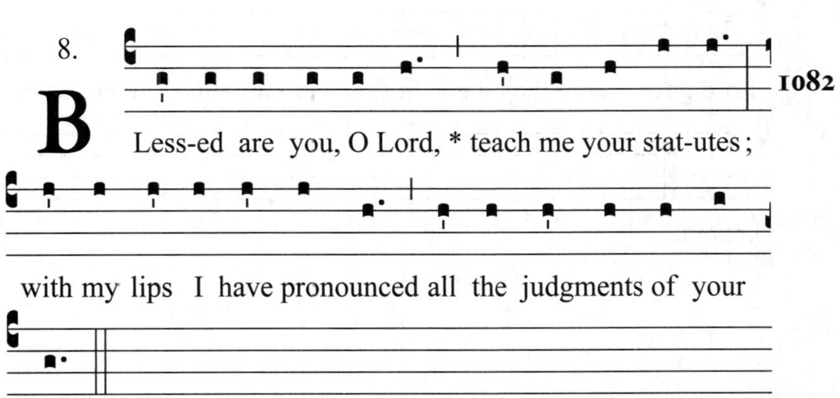
8.
B
Less-ed are you, O Lord, * teach me your stat-utes ; 1082
with my lips I have pronounced all the judgments of your
mouth.

COMMUNION ANTIPHON *Manducaverunt, et saturati sunt.*
Ps 77:29-30

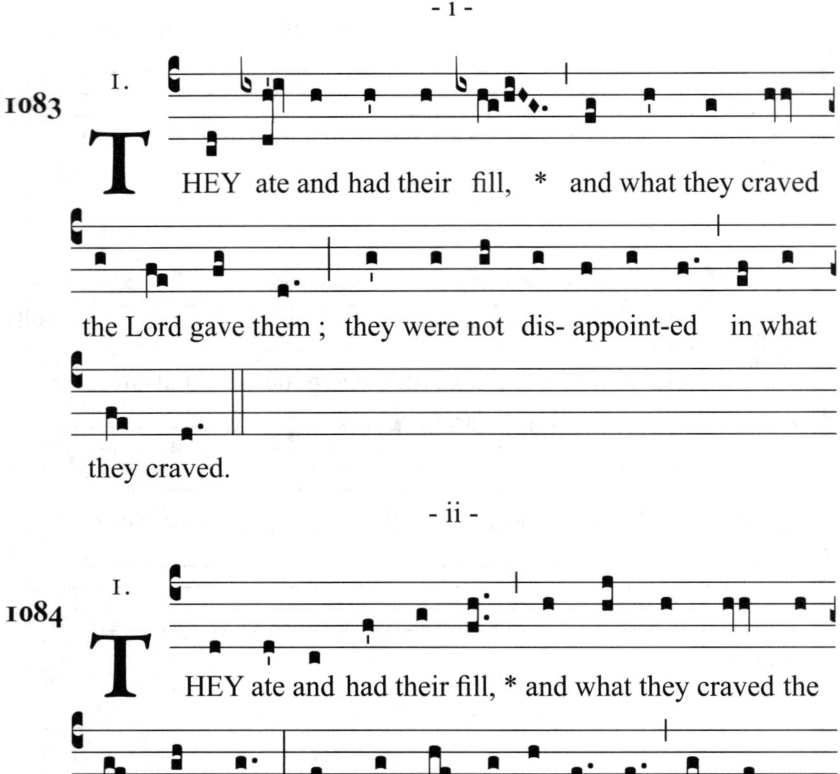
- i -
1083 I.
THEY ate and had their fill, * and what they craved
the Lord gave them ; they were not dis- appoint-ed in what
they craved.
- ii -
1084 I.
THEY ate and had their fill, * and what they craved the
Lord gave them ; they were not dis-appoint-ed in what they
craved.

VERSES

Et pluit illis manna ad manducandum. Ps 77:24

℣. 1
1085
HE rained down man- na up- on them to eat, * and
gave them the bread of heav- en.

Panem angelorum manducavit homo. Ps 77:25

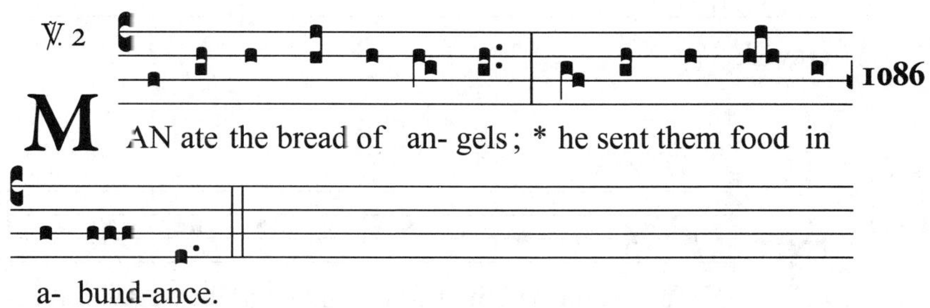
℣. 2
1086
MAN ate the bread of an- gels; * he sent them food in
a- bund-ance.

Et manducaverunt, et saturati sunt nimis. Ps 77:52

℣. 3
1087
HIS peo-ple he led forth like sheep, * and guid-ed them
like a flock in the des- ert.

- iii -

1088

I.
THEY ate and had their fill, * and what they craved the
Lord gave them ; they were not dis-appoint-ed in what they
craved.

- iv -

1089

I.
THEY ate and had their fill, * and what they craved the
Lord gave them ; they were not dis-appoint-ed in what they
craved.

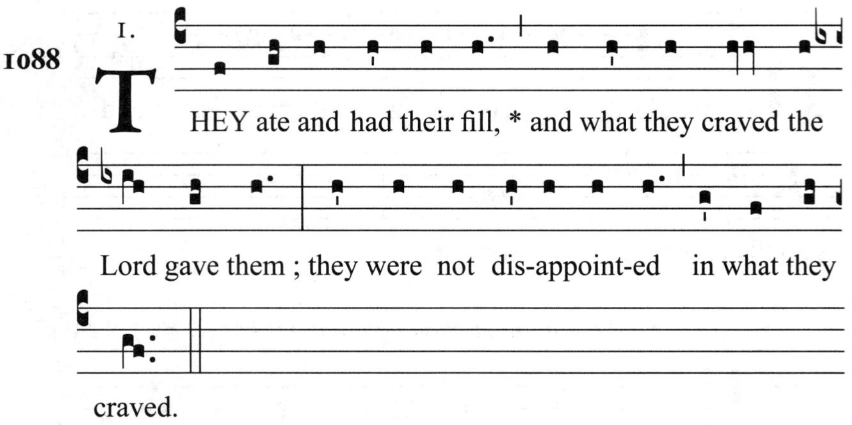

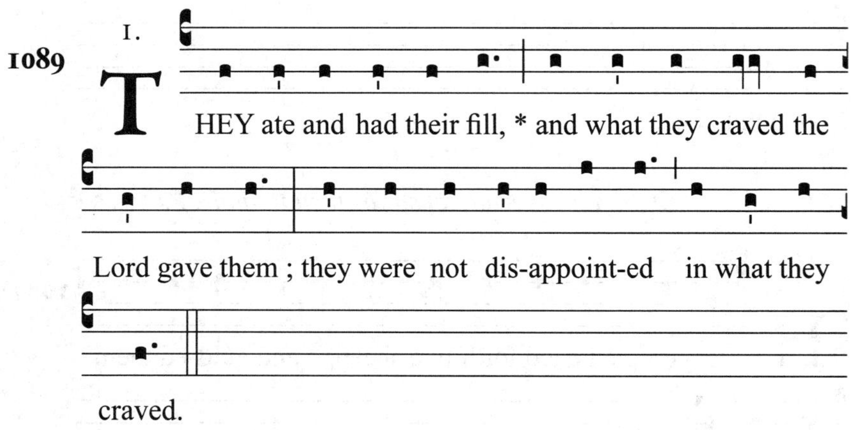

SEVENTH SUNDAY IN ORDINARY TIME

Entrance Antiphon *Domine, in tua misericordia speravi.*
Ps 12:6

- i -

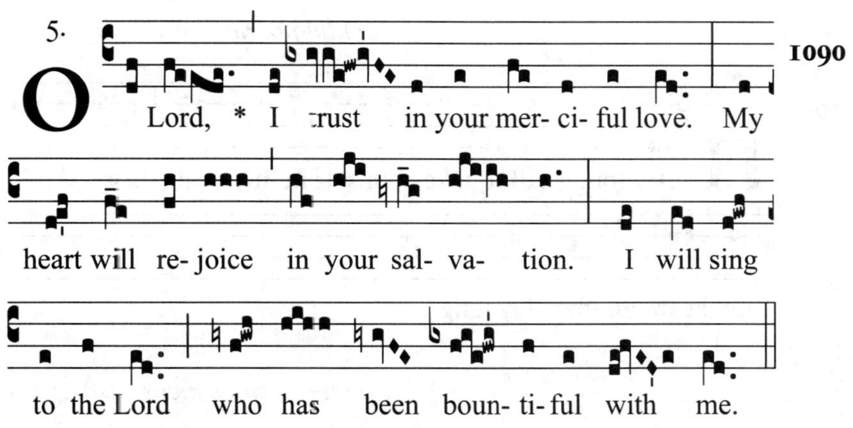
5.
O Lord, * I trust in your mer- ci- ful love. My
1090
heart will re- joice in your sal- va- tion. I will sing
to the Lord who has been boun- ti- ful with me.

- ii -

5.
O Lord, I trust * in your mer- ci- ful love. My
1091
heart will re-joice in your sal-va-tion. I will sing to the
Lord who has been boun- ti- ful with me.

VERSES *Usquequo, Domine. Ps* 12 : 1

1092
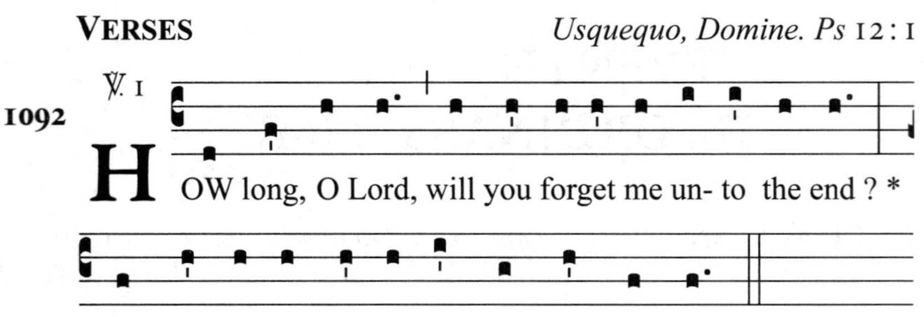
℣. 1
HOW long, O Lord, will you forget me un- to the end ? *
How long do you turn a-way your face from me ?

Quamdiu ponam consilia. Ps 12 : 2

1093
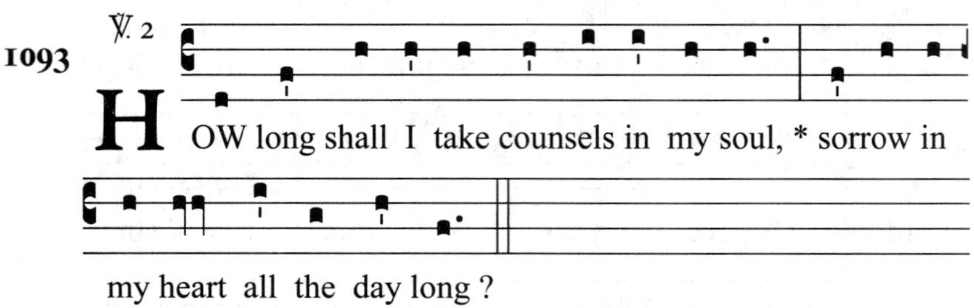
℣. 2
HOW long shall I take counsels in my soul, * sorrow in
my heart all the day long ?

Illumina oculos meos. Ps 12 : 4-5

1094

℣. 3
ENlighten my eyes, that I nev- er sleep in death ; * lest
at an-y time my en- e-my say : I have prevailed against him.

- iii -

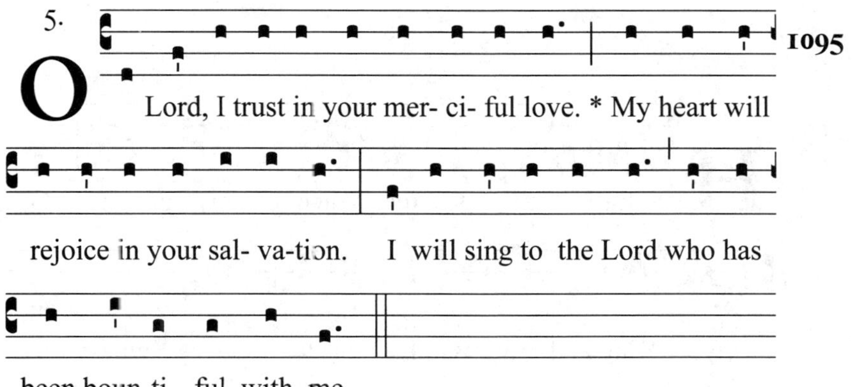
5.
1095
O Lord, I trust in your mer- ci- ful love. * My heart will
rejoice in your sal- va-tion. I will sing to the Lord who has
been boun-ti- ful with me.

- iv -

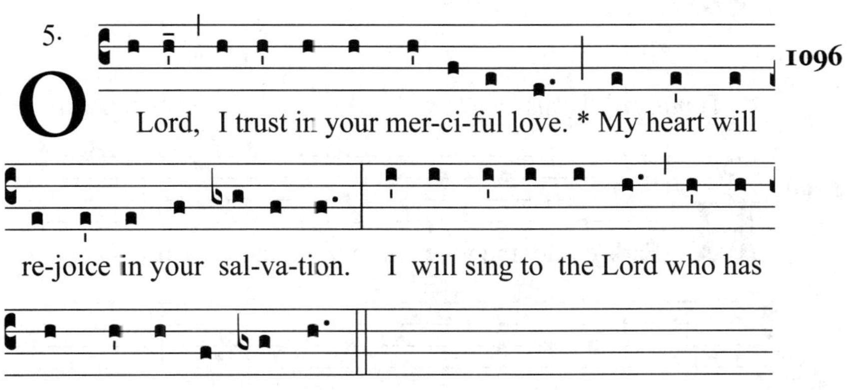
5.
1096
O Lord, I trust in your mer-ci-ful love. * My heart will
re-joice in your sal-va-tion. I will sing to the Lord who has
been boun-ti- ful with me.

If psalm verses on p. 472 *are used with this setting, sing* te *flat.*

OFFERTORY ANTIPHON *Intende voci orationis meæ.*
Ps 5:3-4

- i -

1097
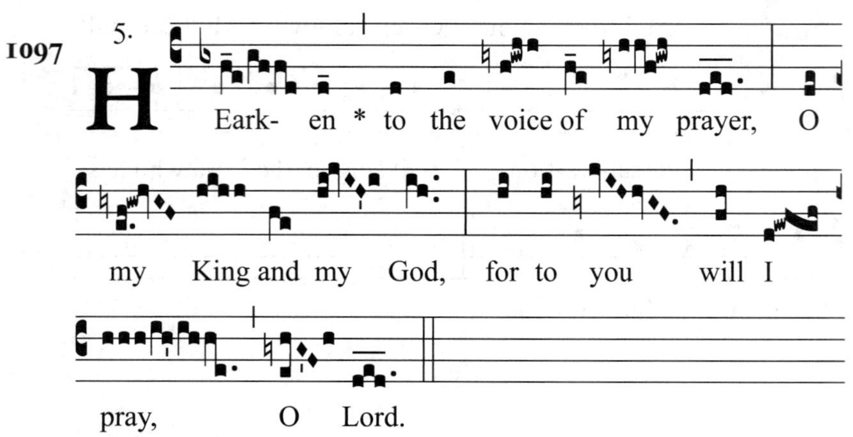
5.
HEark- en * to the voice of my prayer, O
my King and my God, for to you will I
pray, O Lord.

- ii -

Ti *natural throughout*:

1098
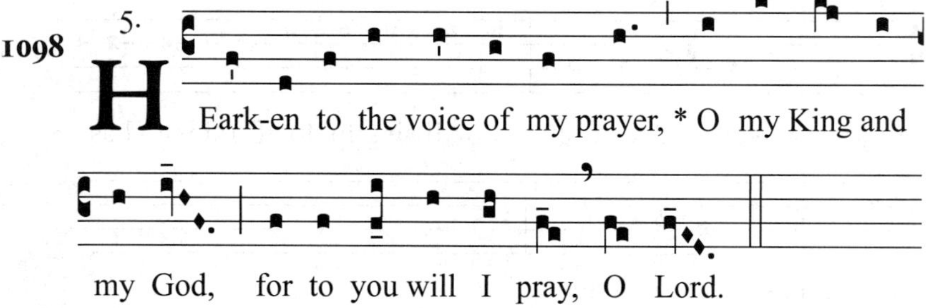
5.
HEark-en to the voice of my prayer, * O my King and
my God, for to you will I pray, O Lord.

VERSES *Domine, mane exaudies vocem meam. Ps* 5:4

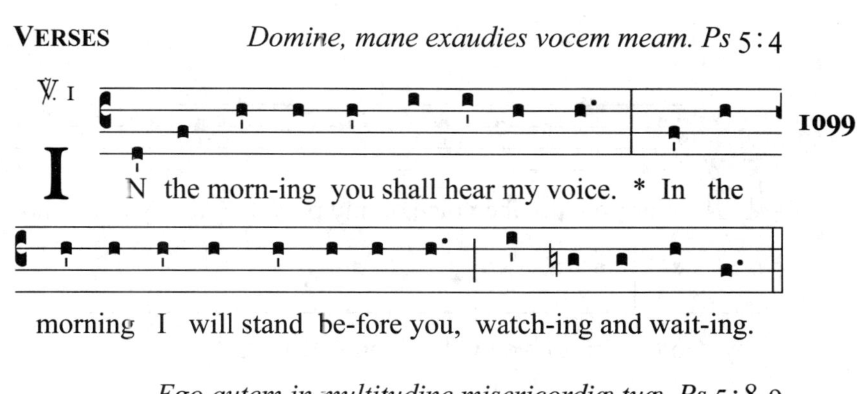
℣. 1
IN the morn-ing you shall hear my voice. * In the
morning I will stand be-fore you, watch-ing and wait-ing.
1099

Ego autem in multitudine misericordiæ tuæ. Ps 5:8-9

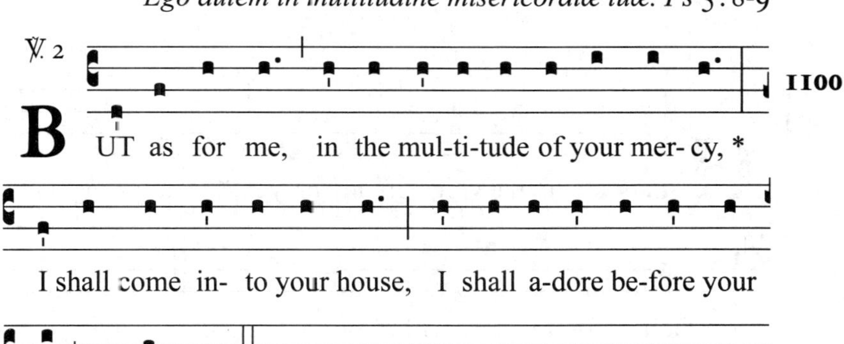
℣. 2
BUT as for me, in the mul-ti-tude of your mer- cy, *
I shall come in- to your house, I shall a-dore be-fore your
ho- ly tem-ple.
1100

Quoniam tu benedices iusto. Ps 5:13

℣. 3
FOR you have blessed the just, O Lord; * as with a
shield of your good will, you have crowned us.
1101

- iii -

1102

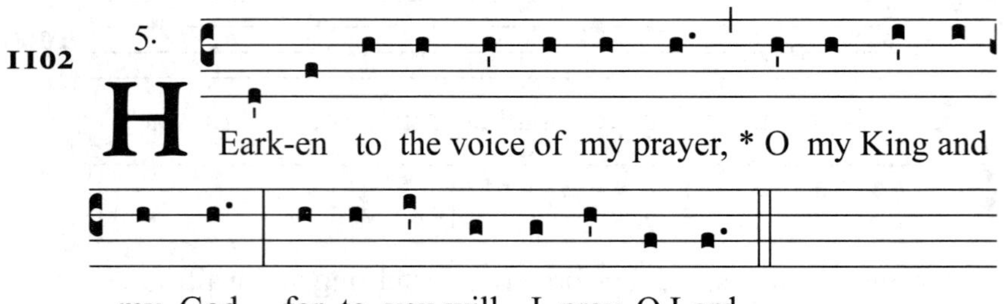
5.
HEark-en to the voice of my prayer, * O my King and
my God, for to you will I pray, O Lord.

- iv -

1103

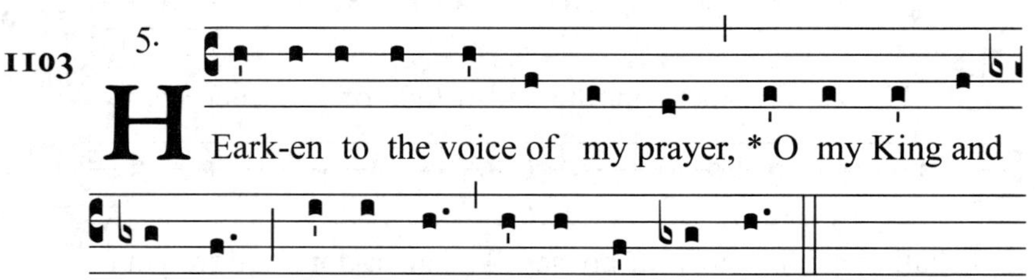
5.
HEark-en to the voice of my prayer, * O my King and
my God, for to you will I pray, O Lord.

If psalm verses on p. 475 *are used with this setting, sing* te *flat.*

COMMUNION ANTIPHON *Narrabo omnia mirabilia tua.*
Ps 9:2-3

- i -

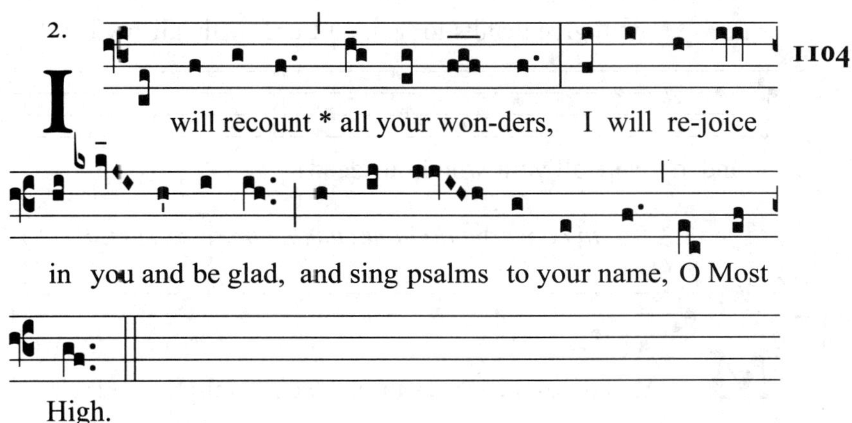
2.
I will recount * all your won-ders, I will re-joice
1104
in you and be glad, and sing psalms to your name, O Most
High.

- ii -

2.
I will recount * all your won-ders, I will re-joice
1105
in you and be glad, and sing psalms to your name, O Most

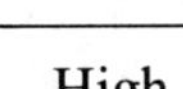
High.

VERSES *Confitebor tibi, Domine. Ps* 9:2

1106 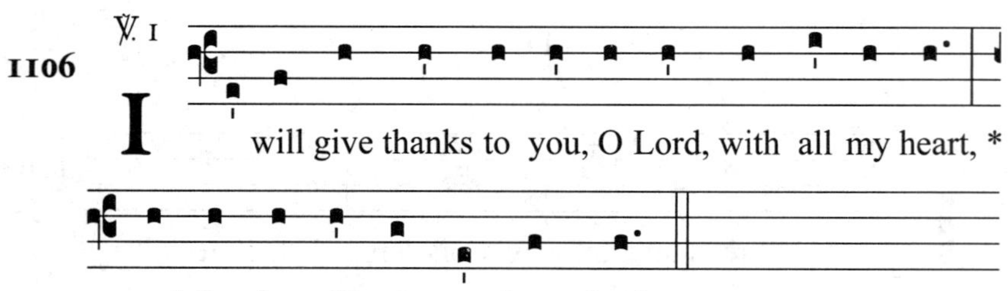
℣. 1
I will give thanks to you, O Lord, with all my heart, *
and de-clare all your wondrous deeds.

In convertendo inimicum meum retrorsum. Ps 9:4

1107 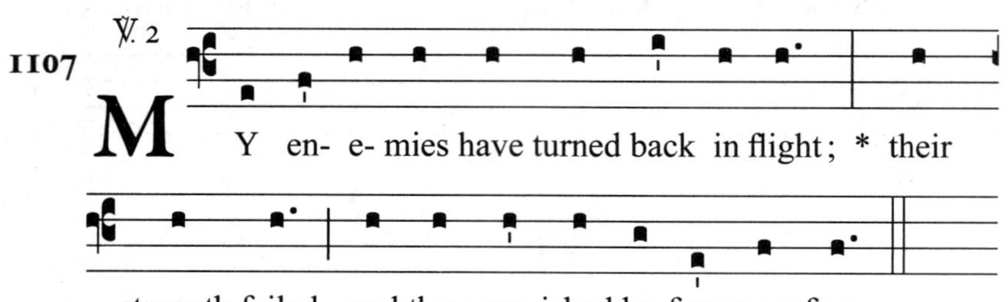
℣. 2
MY en- e- mies have turned back in flight; * their
strength failed, and they per-ished be-fore your face.

Psallite Domino, qui habitat in Sion. Ps 9:12

1108 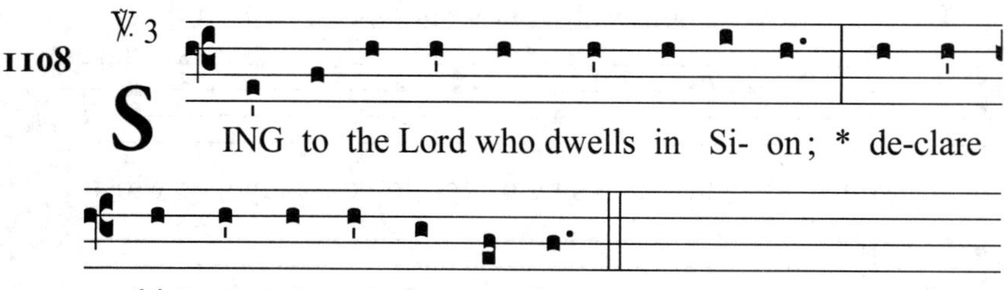
℣. 3
SING to the Lord who dwells in Si- on; * de-clare
his ways a-mong the na- tions.

- iii -

2.
I will recount all your won-ders, * I will re-joice in
1109
you and be glad, and sing psalms to your name, O Most High.

Or:

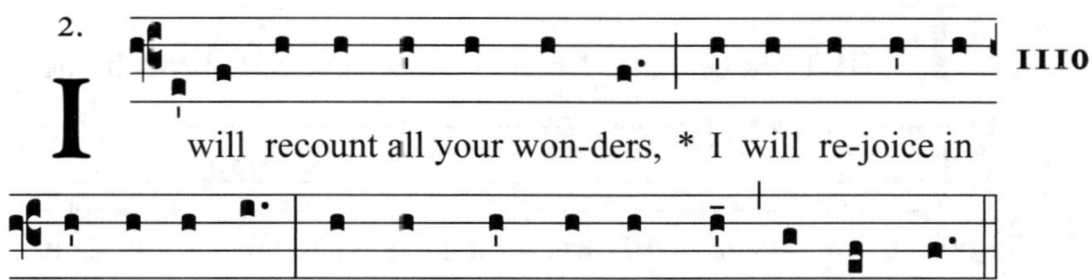
2.
I will recount all your won-ders, * I will re-joice in
1110
you and be glad, and sing psalms to your name, O Most High.

- iv -

2.
I will recount * all your won-ders, I will re-joice in
1111
you and be glad, and sing psalms to your name, O Most High.

EIGHTH SUNDAY IN ORDINARY TIME

ENTRANCE ANTIPHON *Factus est Dominus protector meus.*
Ps 17:19-20

- i -

1112 I.

THE Lord be-came * my pro-tec- tor. * He brought me out to a place of free-dom; he saved me be-cause he de- light- ed in me.

- ii -

1113 I.

THE Lord became my pro-tec- tor. * He brought me out to a place of freedom ; he saved me because he de-light- ed in me.

VERSES *Diligam te, Domine. Ps* 17:2

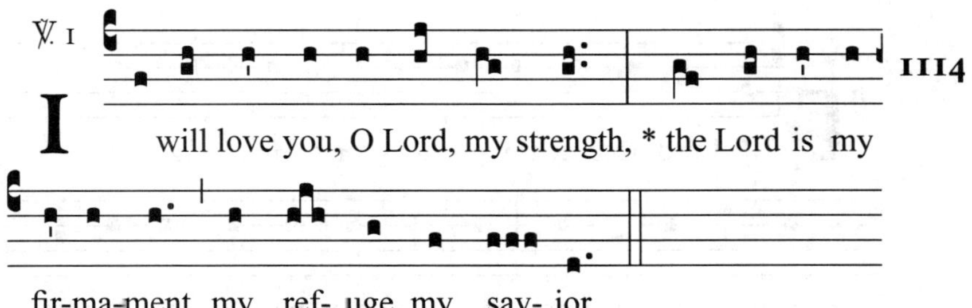
℣. 1
1114
I will love you, O Lord, my strength, * the Lord is my
fir-ma-ment, my ref- uge, my sav- ior.

Misit de summo. Ps 17:17

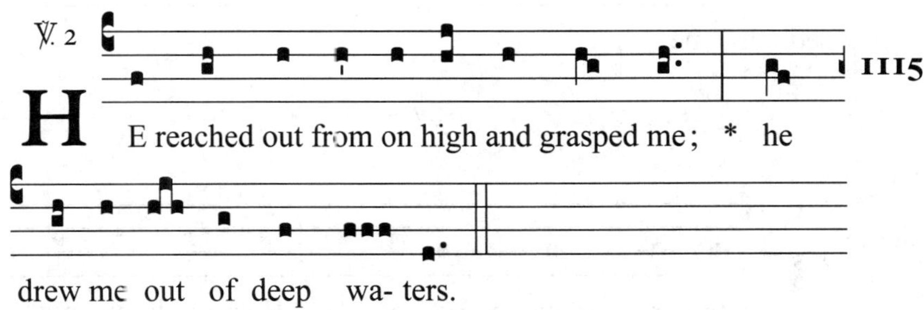
℣. 2
1115
HE reached out from on high and grasped me; * he
drew me out of deep wa- ters.

Quoniam tu illuminas. Ps 17:29

℣. 3
1116
FOR you, O Lord, give light to my lamp; * O my God,
en-light-en my dark-ness.

- iii -

1117

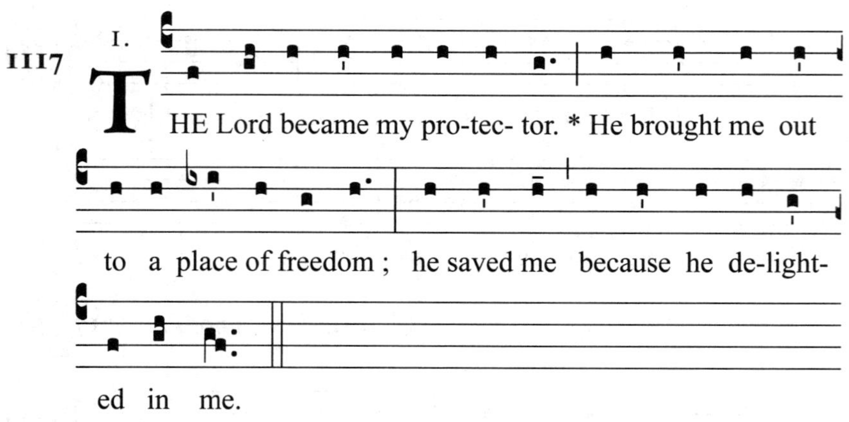
I.
THE Lord became my pro-tec- tor. * He brought me out
to a place of freedom ; he saved me because he de-light-
ed in me.

- iv -

1118

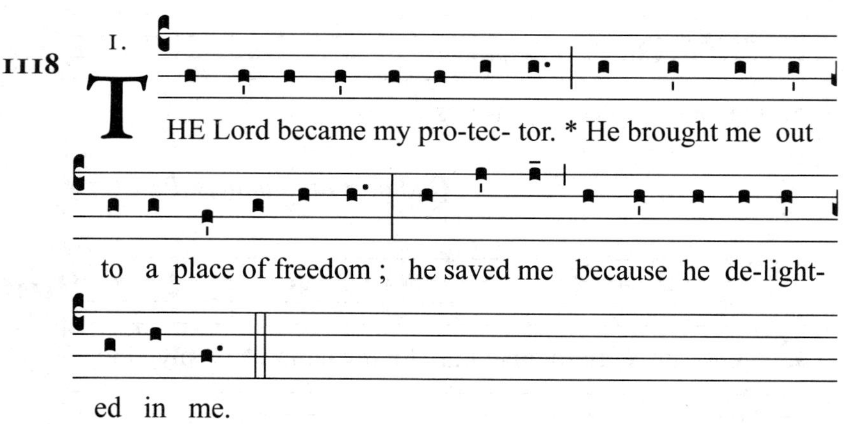
I.
THE Lord became my pro-tec- tor. * He brought me out
to a place of freedom ; he saved me because he de-light-
ed in me.

Offertory Antiphon *Domine, convertere. Ps* 6:5

- i -

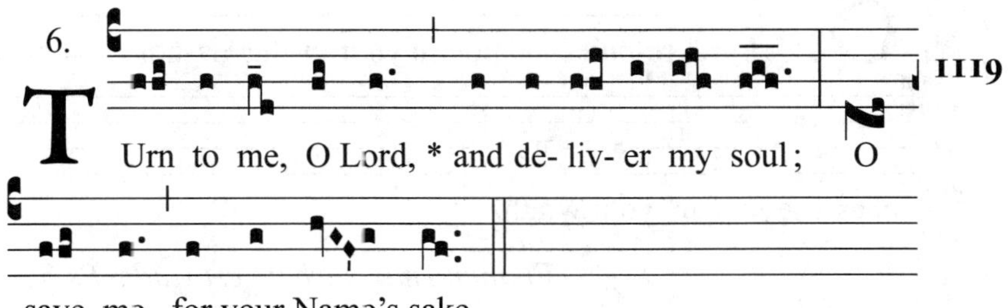
6.
TUrn to me, O Lord, * and de- liv- er my soul; O
save me for your Name's sake.

- ii -

6.
TUrn to me, O Lord, * and de- liv- er my soul; O save
me for your Name's sake.

VERSES *Domine, ne in furore tuo. Ps* 6:2

1121
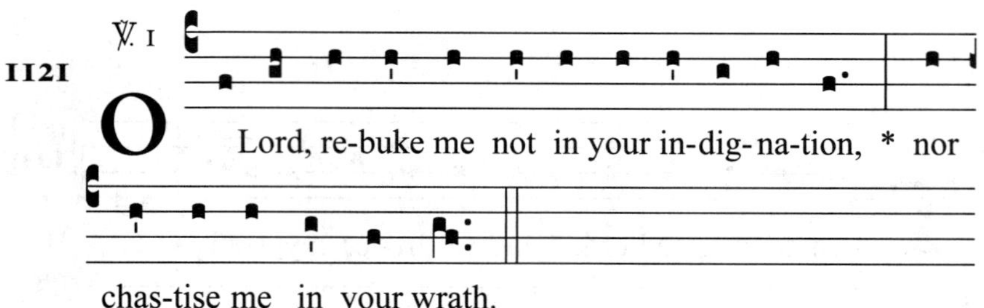
℣. 1
O Lord, re-buke me not in your in-dig-na-tion, * nor
chas-tise me in your wrath.

Et anima mea turbata est valde. Ps 6:4

1122

℣. 2
AND my soul is troubled ex-ceed-ing-ly; * but you, O
Lord, how long?

Exaudivit Dominus deprecationem meam. Ps 6:10

1123

℣. 3
THE Lord has heard my sup-pli-ca-tion; * the Lord
has received my prayer.

- iii -

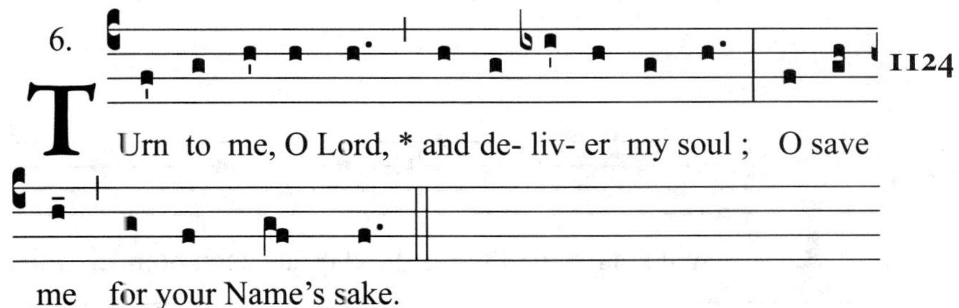
6.
TUrn to me, O Lord, * and de- liv- er my soul ; O save
1124
me for your Name's sake.

- iv -

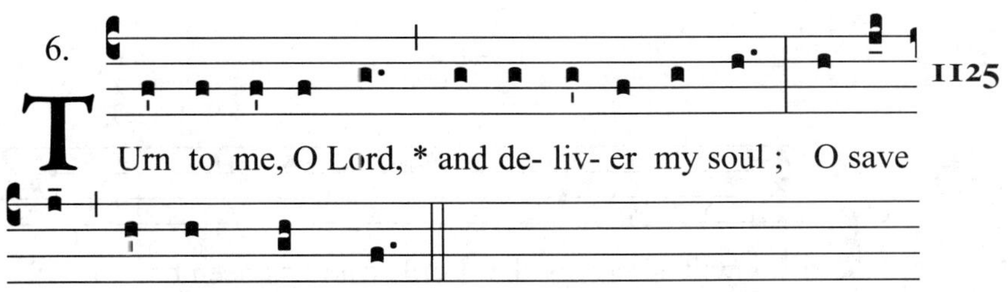
6.
TUrn to me, O Lord, * and de- liv- er my soul ; O save
1125
me for your Name's sake.

COMMUNION *Cantabo Domino. Ps* 12:6

Ti *natural for the antiphons below and psalm verses on p.* 623.

- i -

1126

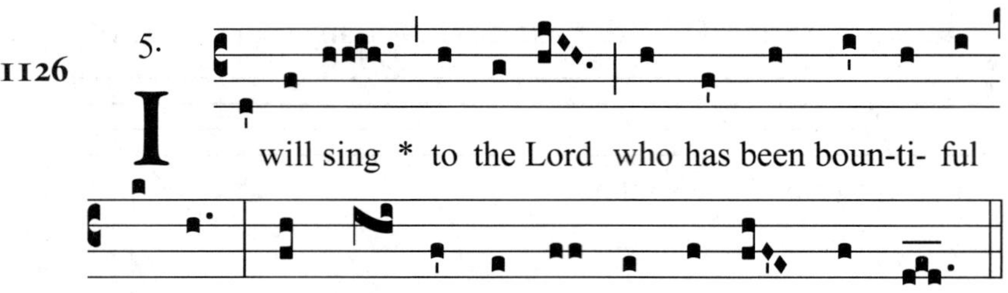
5.
I will sing * to the Lord who has been boun-ti- ful
with me, sing psalms to the name of the Lord Most High.

- ii -

1127

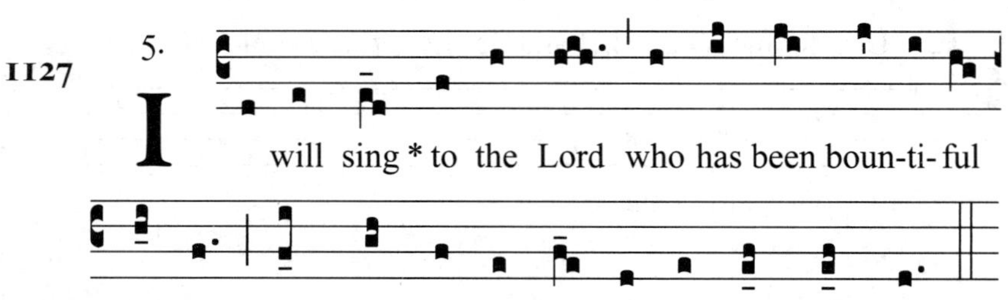
5.
I will sing * to the Lord who has been boun-ti- ful
with me, sing psalms to the name of the Lord Most High.

VERSES *Usquequo, Domine. Ps* 12 : 1

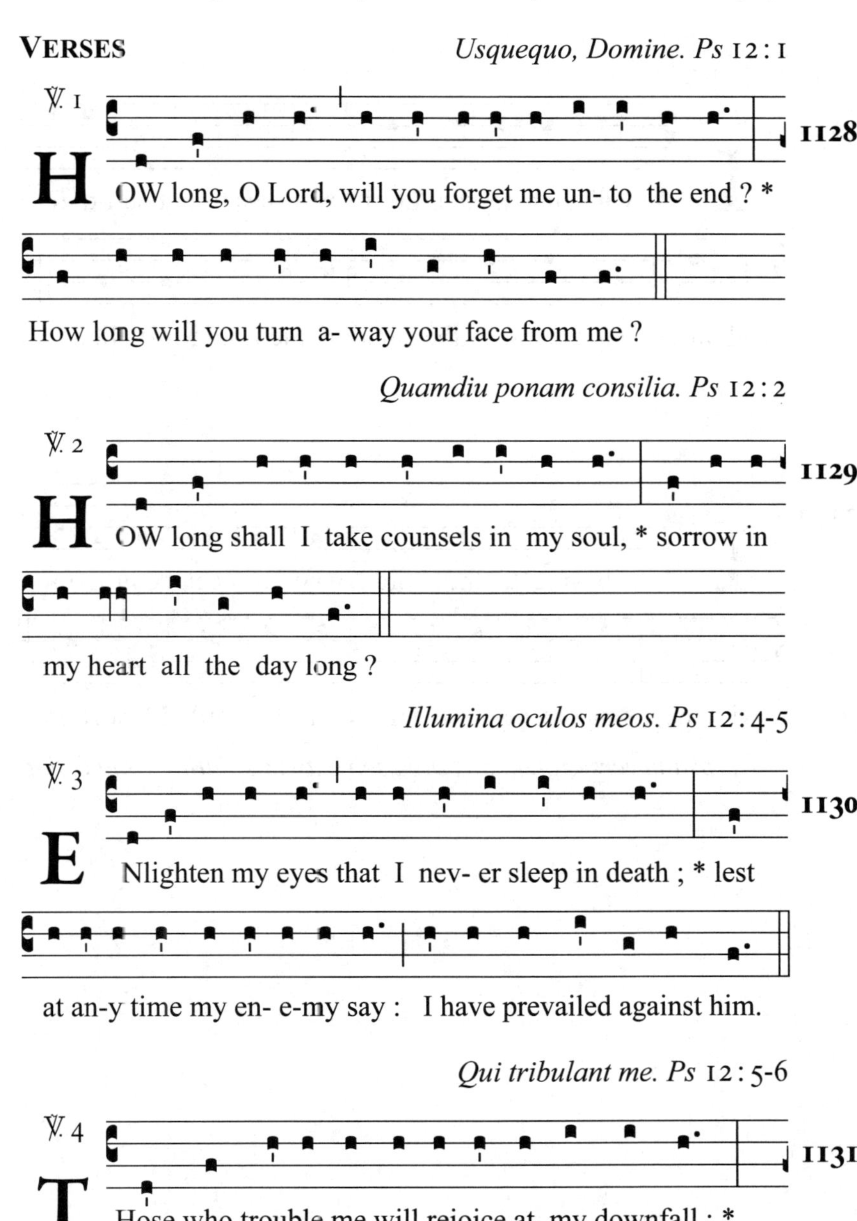
℣. 1
1128
HOW long, O Lord, will you forget me un- to the end ? *
How long will you turn a- way your face from me ?
Quamdiu ponam consilia. Ps 12 : 2
℣. 2
1129
HOW long shall I take counsels in my soul, * sorrow in
my heart all the day long ?
Illumina oculos meos. Ps 12 : 4-5
℣. 3
1130
ENlighten my eyes that I nev- er sleep in death ; * lest
at an-y time my en- e-my say : I have prevailed against him.
Qui tribulant me. Ps 12 : 5-6
℣. 4
1131
THose who trouble me will rejoice at my downfall ; *
but I have trust-ed in your mer-cy.

- iii -

1132

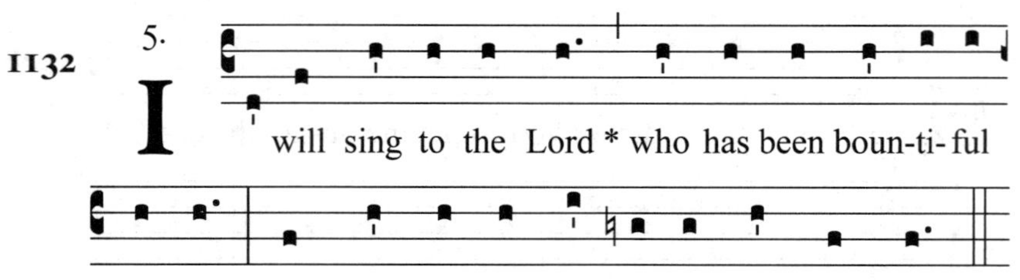

5.
I will sing to the Lord * who has been boun-ti-ful
with me, sing psalms to the name of the Lord Most High.

- iv -

1133

5.
I will sing to the Lord * who has been boun-ti-ful
with me, sing psalms to the name of the Lord Most High.

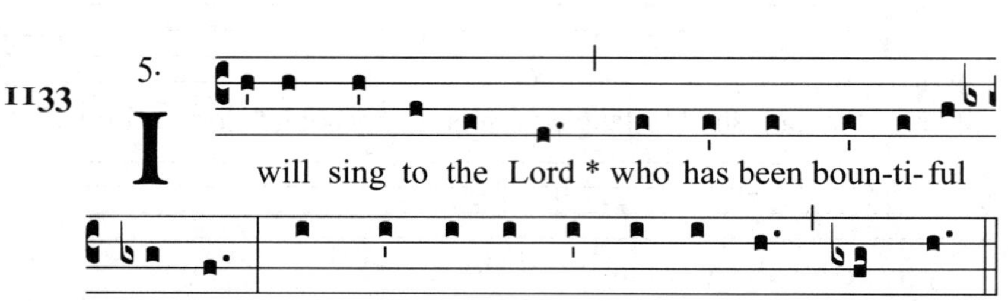

If psalm verses on p. 487 are used with this setting, sing te *flat.*

NINTH SUNDAY IN ORDINARY TIME

Entrance Antiphon *Respice in me, et miserere mei.*
Ps 24:16-18

- i -

6. TUrn to me * and have mer- cy on me, O Lord, for 1134
I am a- lone and poor. See my low- li- ness and
suf- fer-ing and take a-way all my sins, my
God.

- ii -

6. TUrn to me * and have mer- cy on me, O Lord, for 1135
I am a- lone and poor. See my low- li-ness and suf- fer-
ing and take a-way all my sins, my God.

VERSES *Ad te levavi animam meam. Ps* 24: 1-2

1136
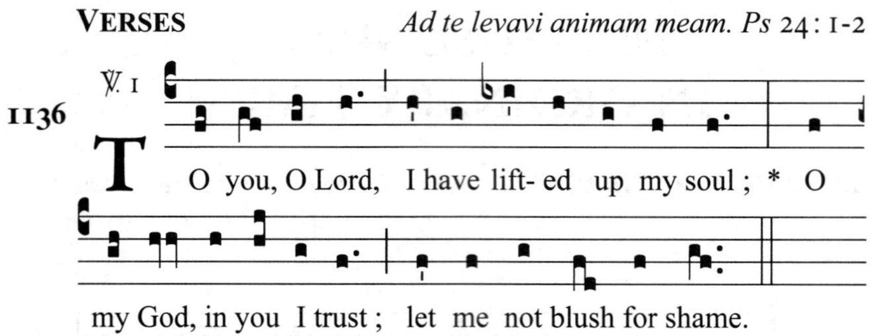
℣. 1
TO you, O Lord, I have lift- ed up my soul ; * O
my God, in you I trust ; let me not blush for shame.

Dirige me in veritate tua. Ps 24: 5

1137

℣. 2
DI- rect me in your truth, and teach me, for you are God
my Sav-ior, * and on you have I wait-ed all the day long.

Respice inimicos meos. Ps 24: 19-20

1138
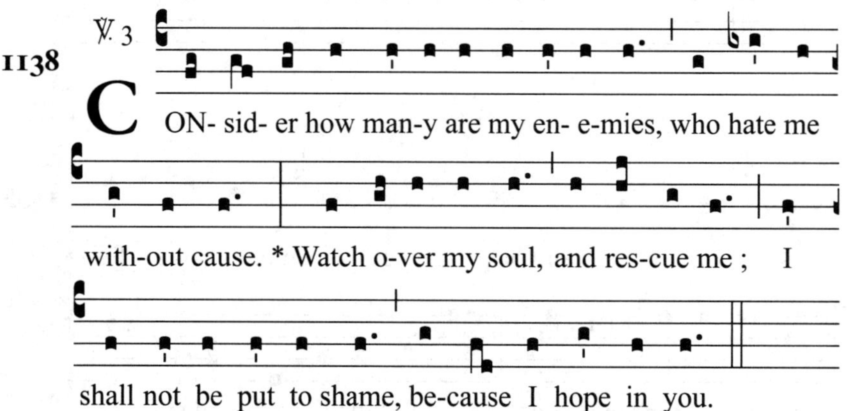
℣. 3
CON- sid- er how man-y are my en- e-mies, who hate me
with-out cause. * Watch o-ver my soul, and res-cue me ; I
shall not be put to shame, be-cause I hope in you.

- iii -

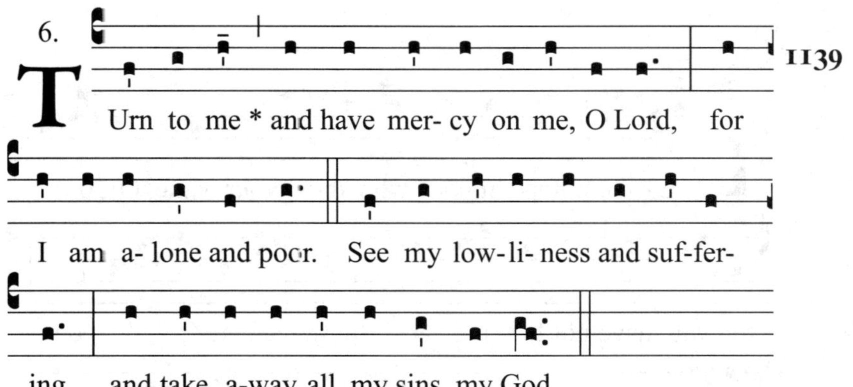
6.
TUrn to me * and have mer- cy on me, O Lord, for 1139
I am a- lone and poor. See my low- li- ness and suf-fer-
ing and take a-way all my sins, my God.

- iv -

6.
TUrn to me and have mer-cy on me, O Lord, * for 1140
I am a- lone and poor. See my low- li- ness and suf- fer-
ing and take a-way all my sins, my God.

Offertory Antiphon *Sperent in te omnes.*
Ps 9:11. 12. 13

- i -

1141
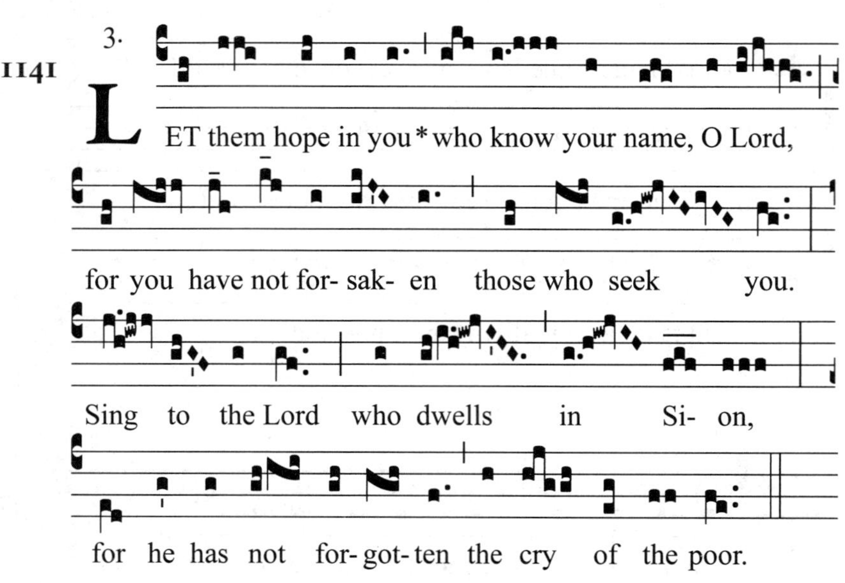
3.
LET them hope in you * who know your name, O Lord,
for you have not for- sak- en those who seek you.
Sing to the Lord who dwells in Si- on,
for he has not for- got- ten the cry of the poor.

- ii -

1142 3.
LET them hope in you * who know your name, O Lord,
for you have not for- sak- en those who seek you. Sing to
the Lord who dwells in Si- on, for he has not for-got-ten
the cry of the poor.

VERSES

Confitebor tibi, Domine. Ps 9 : 2

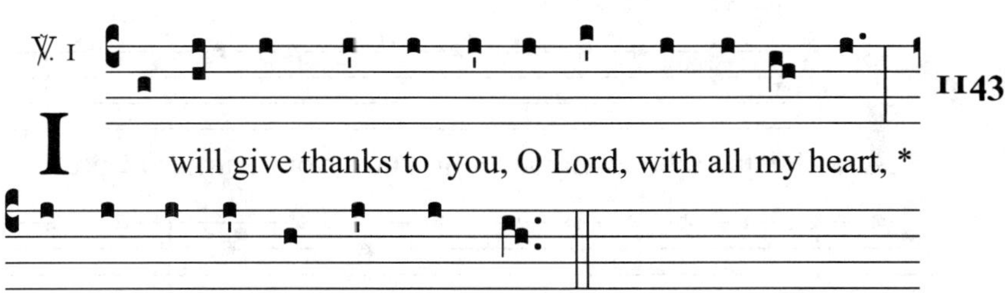
℣. 1
I will give thanks to you, O Lord, with all my heart, *
1143

and de-clare all your wondrous deeds.

Lætabor et exsultabo in te. Ps 9 : 3

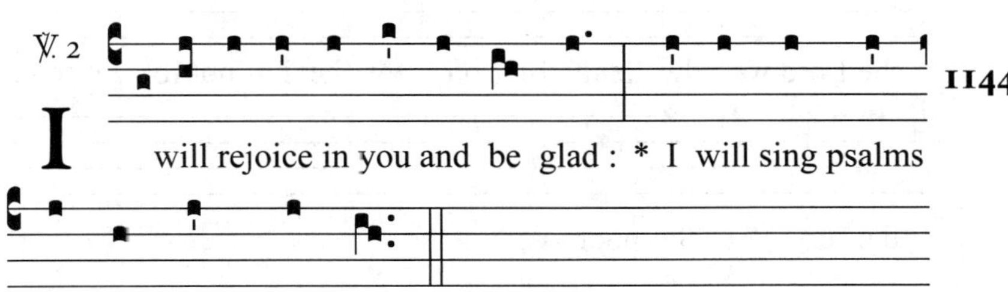
℣. 2
I will rejoice in you and be glad : * I will sing psalms
1144

to your name, Most High.

In convertendo inimicum meum retrorsum. Ps 9 : 4

℣. 3
MY en- e- mies have turned back in flight ; * their
1145

strength failed, and they perished be-fore your face.

- iii -

1146

3.
LET them hope in you * who know your name, O Lord,
for you have not for- sak- en those who seek you. Sing to
the Lord who dwells in Si- on, for he has not for-got-ten
the cry of the poor.

- iv -

1147

3.
LET them hope in you * who know your name, O Lord,
for you have not for- sak- en those who seek you. Sing to
the Lord who dwells in Si- on, for he has not for-got-ten
the cry of the poor.

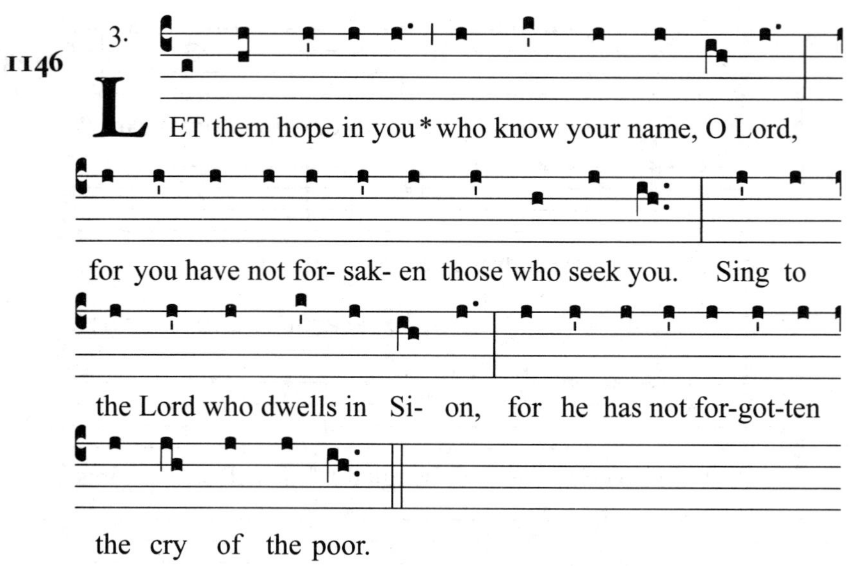

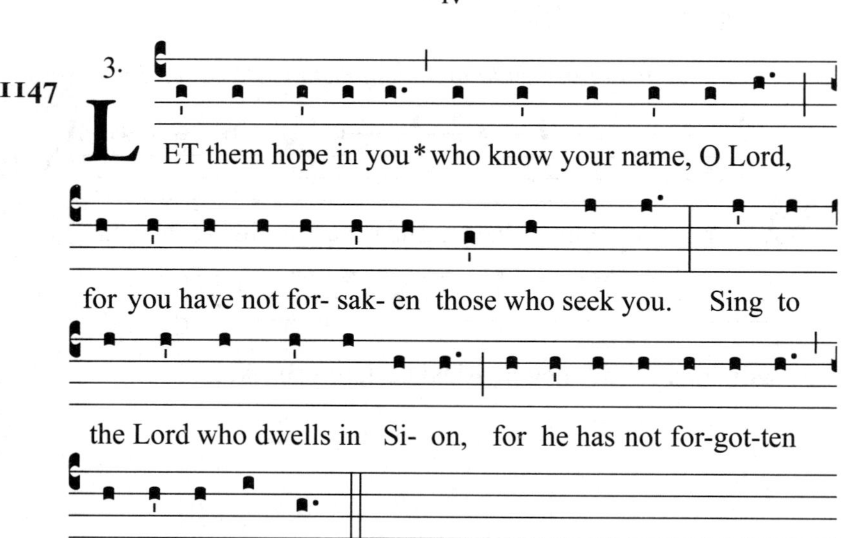

COMMUNION ANTIPHON *Ego clamavi. Ps* 16:6

- i -

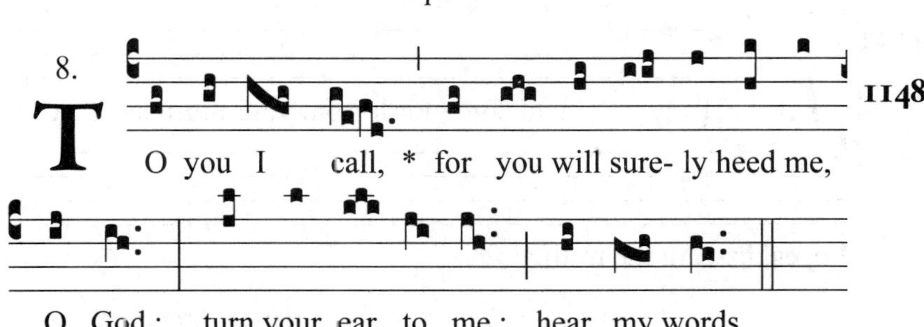
8.
1148
T O you I call, * for you will sure- ly heed me,
O God ; turn your ear to me ; hear my words.

- ii -

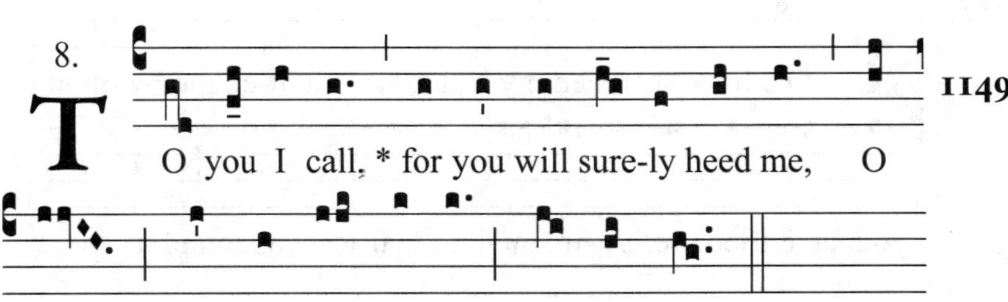
8.
1149
T O you I call, * for you will sure-ly heed me, O
God ; turn your ear to me ; hear my words.

VERSES *Exaudi, Domine, iustitiam meam. Ps* 16:1

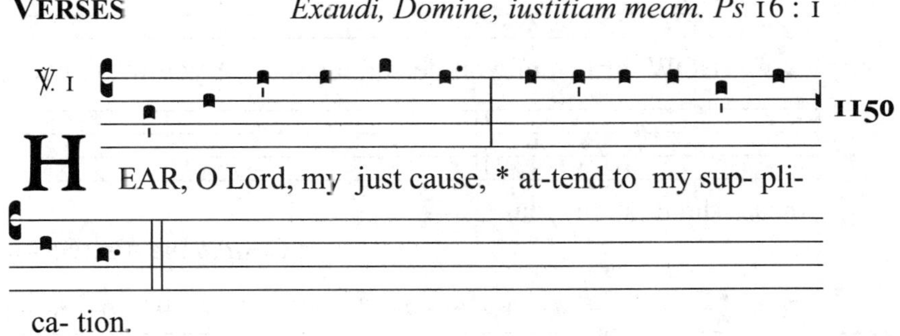
℣. 1
1150
HEAR, O Lord, my just cause, * at-tend to my sup- pli-
ca- tion.

Auribus percipe orationem meam. Psalm 16:1

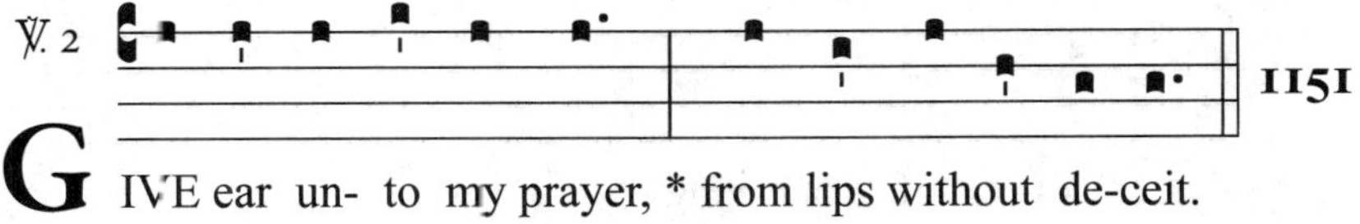
℣. 2
1151
GIVE ear un- to my prayer, * from lips without de-ceit.

De vultu tuo. Ps 16:2

1152
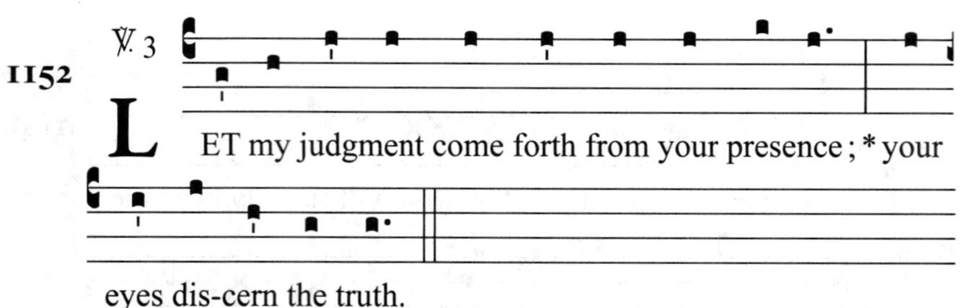
℣. 3
LET my judgment come forth from your presence; * your eyes dis-cern the truth.

Probasti cor meum. Ps 16:3

1153

℣. 4
YOU have searched my heart, and vis-it-ed me by night; * you have tried me by fire, and no mal-ice was found in me.

Mirifica misericordias tuas. Ps 16:7

1154
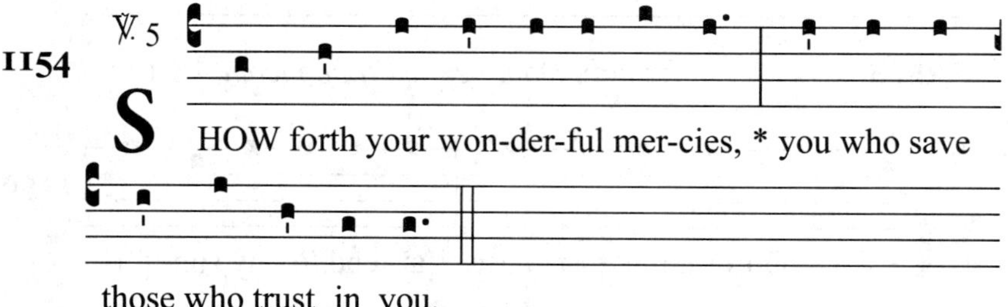
℣. 5
SHOW forth your won-der-ful mer-cies, * you who save those who trust in you.

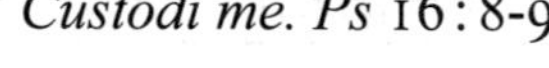
Custodi me. Ps 16:8-9

1155
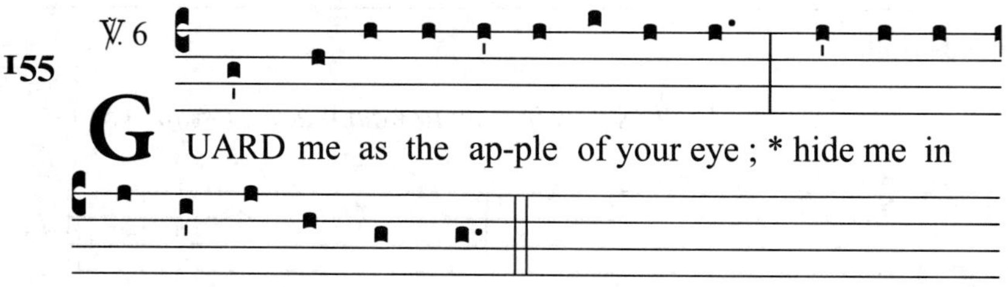
℣. 6
GUARD me as the ap-ple of your eye; * hide me in the shad-ow of your wings.

- iii -

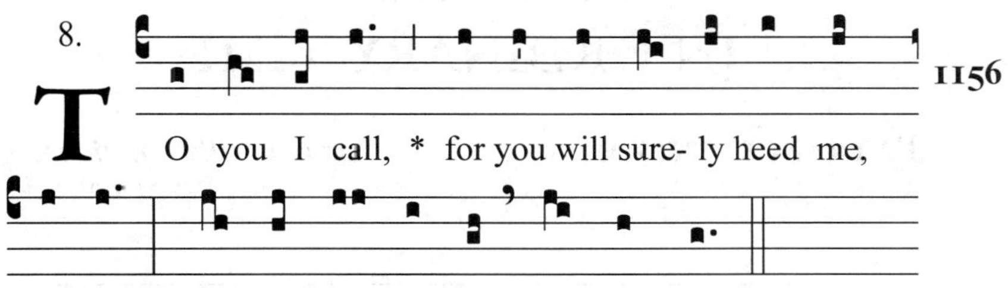
8.
1156
TO you I call, * for you will sure- ly heed me,
O God; turn your ear to me; hear my words.

Or:

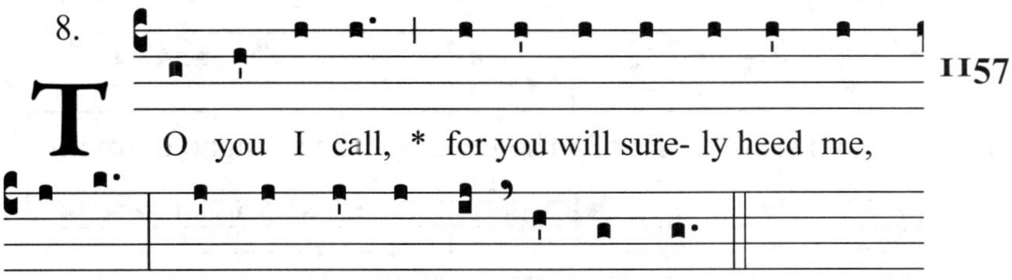
8.
1157
TO you I call, * for you will sure- ly heed me,
O God; turn your ear to me; hear my words.

- iv -

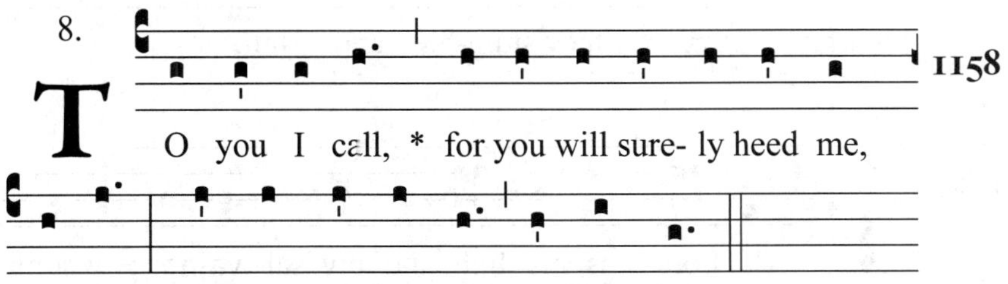
8.
1158
TO you I call, * for you will sure- ly heed me,
O God; turn your ear to me; hear my words.

TENTH SUNDAY IN ORDINARY TIME

ENTRANCE ANTIPHON *Dominus illuminatio mea.*
Ps 26:1-2

- i -

1159 2. THE Lord * is my light and my sal-va- tion; whom shall I fear? The Lord is the stronghold of my life; whom should I dread? When those who do e- vil draw near, they stum-ble and fall.

- ii -

1160 2. THE Lord * is my light and my sal- va-tion; whom shall I fear? The Lord is the stronghold of my life; whom should I dread? When those who do e- vil draw near, they

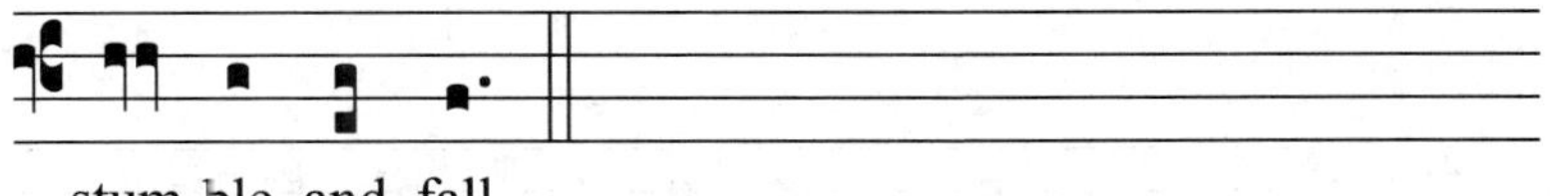
stum-ble and fall.

VERSES *Si consistant adversum me castra. Ps* 26:3

℣. 1
THough an ar- my en-camp a-gainst me, * my heart
1161
shall not fear.

Unam petii a Domino. Ps 26:4

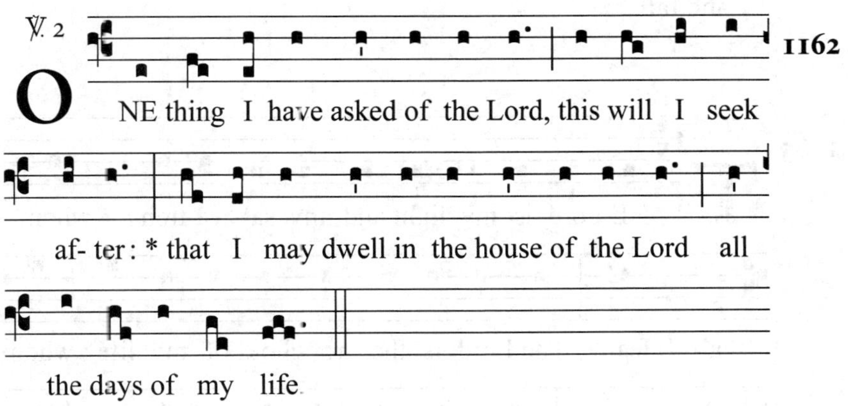
℣. 2
ONE thing I have asked of the Lord, this will I seek
1162
af- ter: * that I may dwell in the house of the Lord all
the days of my life.

Ut videam voluptatem Domini. Ps 26:4-5

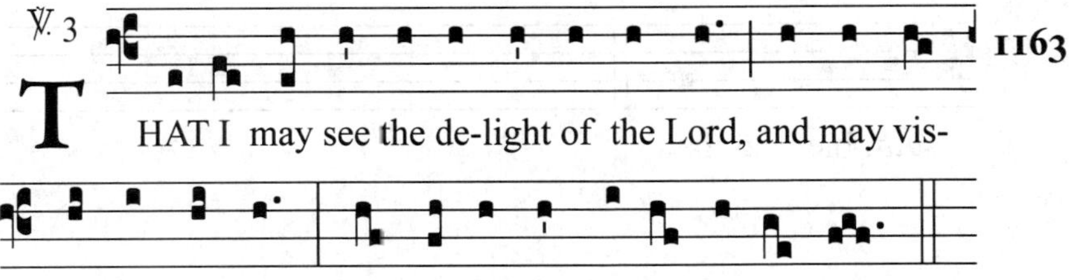
℣. 3
THAT I may see the de-light of the Lord, and may vis-
1163
it his tem-ple. * For he has hid-den me in his tent.

- iii -

1164

2.
THE Lord is my light and my sal-va-tion; * whom shall
I fear? The Lord is the stronghold of my life; whom should
I dread? When those who do e- vil draw near, they stumble
and fall.

- iv -

1165

2.
THE Lord is my light and my sal- va-tion; * whom
shall I fear? The Lord is the stronghold of my life; whom
should I dread? When those who do e- vil draw near, they
stum-ble and fall.

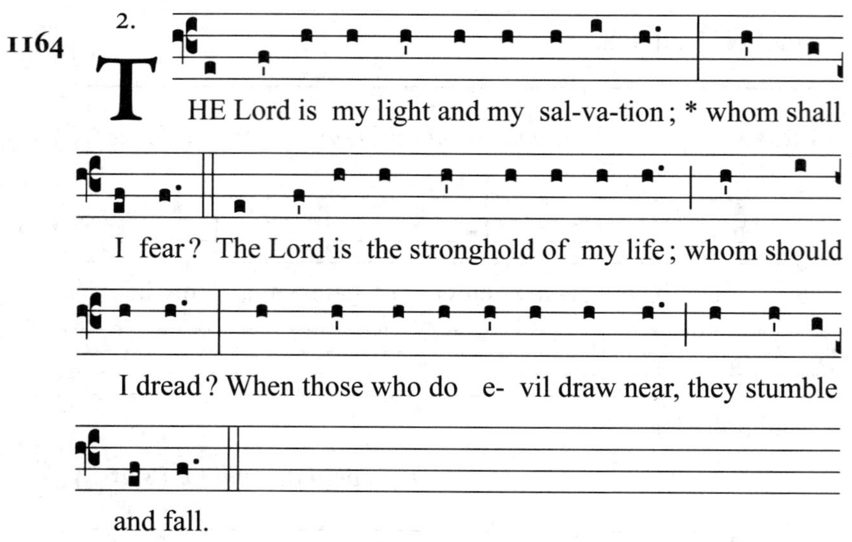

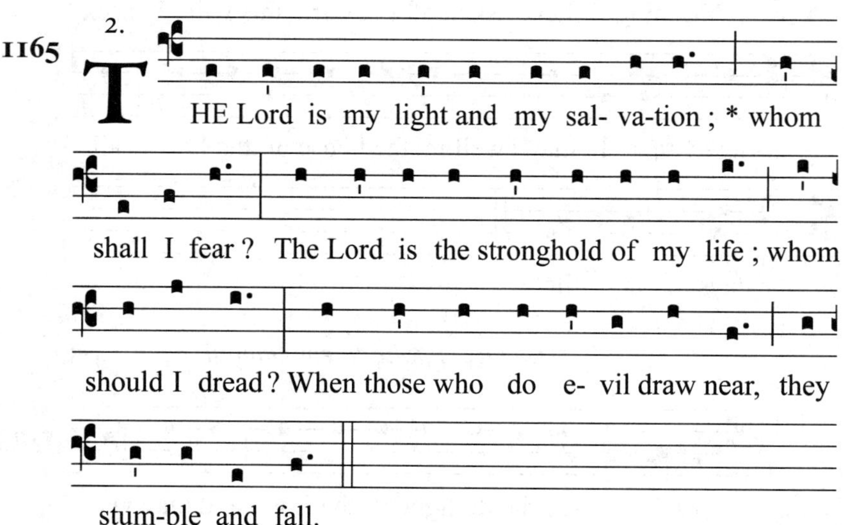

Offertory Antiphon *Illumina oculos meos.*
Ps 12:4-5

- i -

4.
E
N- light- en my eyes, * that I nev- er sleep in
1166
death, lest at an- y time my en- e- my say : I have
prevailed a-gainst him.

- ii -

4.
E
N-light- en my eyes, * that I nev- er sleep in death,
1167
lest at an- y time my en- e- my say : I have prevailed
a-gainst him.

VERSES

Usquequo, Domine. Ps 12:1

1168

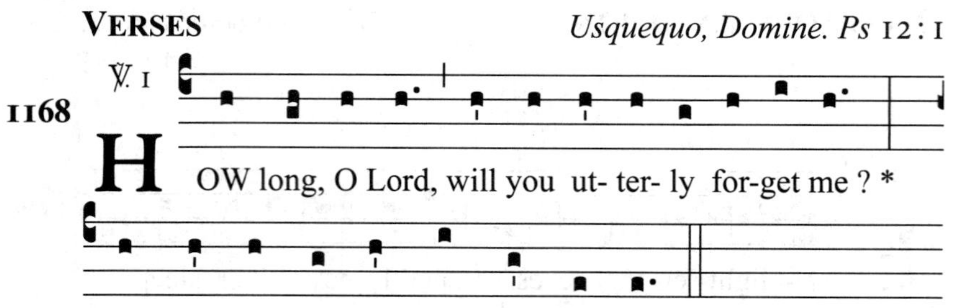
℣. 1
HOW long, O Lord, will you ut- ter- ly for-get me ? *
How long will you hide your face from me ?

Quamdiu ponam consilia. Ps 12:2

1169

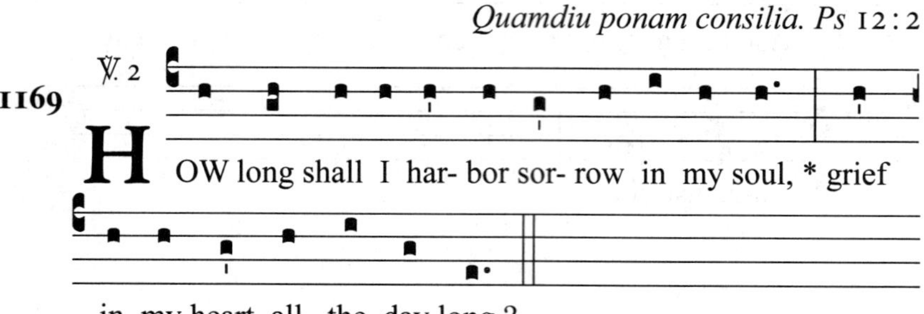
℣. 2
HOW long shall I har- bor sor- row in my soul, * grief
in my heart all the day long ?

Exsultabit cor meum. Ps 12:6

1170

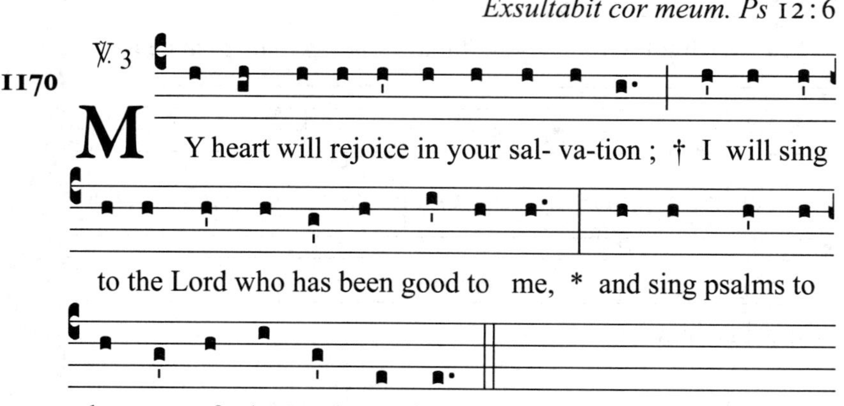
℣. 3
MY heart will rejoice in your sal- va-tion ; † I will sing
to the Lord who has been good to me, * and sing psalms to
the name of the Lord most high.

- iii -

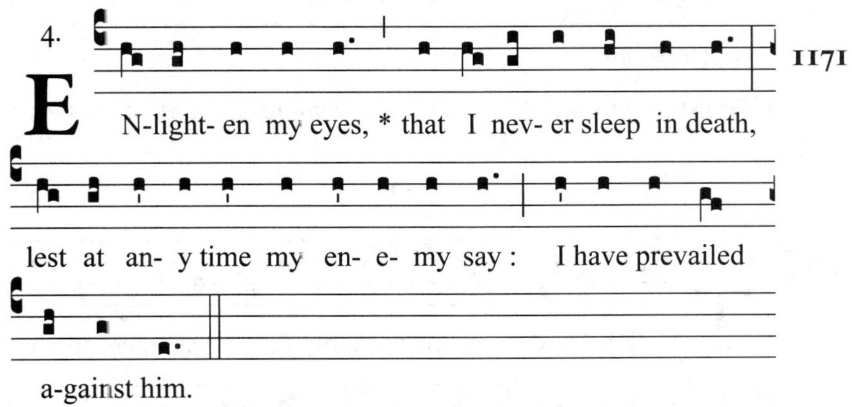
4.
1171
E N-light- en my eyes, * that I nev- er sleep in death,
lest at an- y time my en- e- my say : I have prevailed
a-gainst him.

Or :

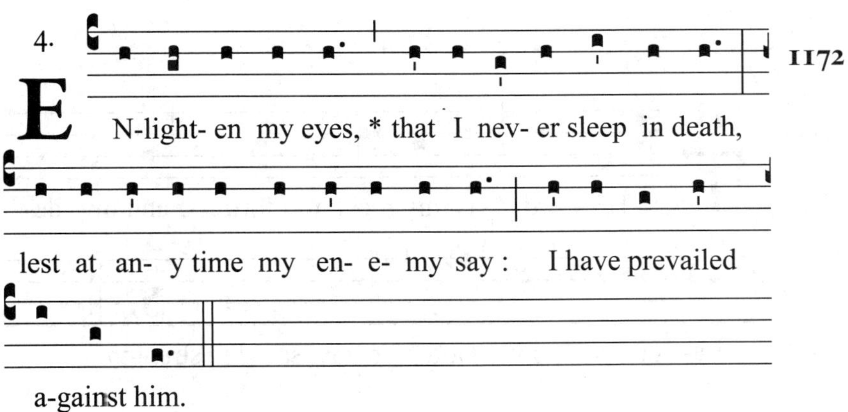
4.
1172
E N-light- en my eyes, * that I nev- er sleep in death,
lest at an- y time my en- e- my say : I have prevailed
a-gainst him.

- iv -

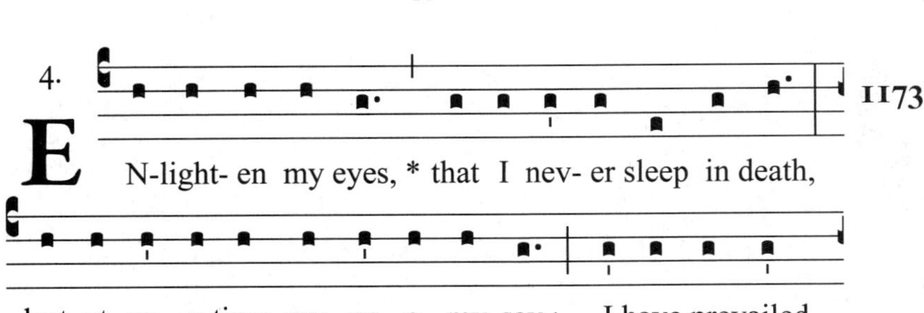
4.
1173
E N-light- en my eyes, * that I nev- er sleep in death,
lest at an- y time my en- e- my say : I have prevailed

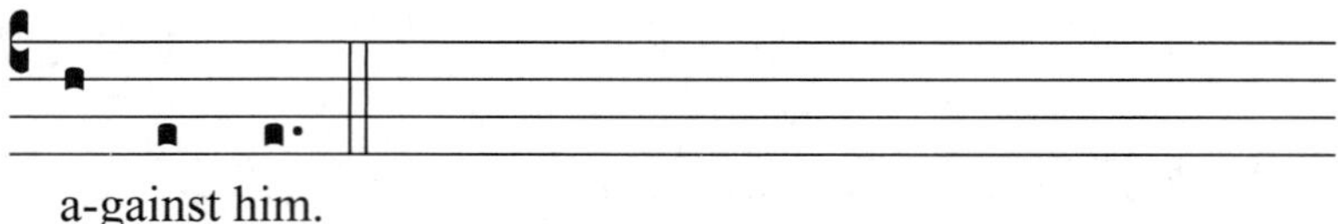
a-gainst him.

COMMUNION ANTIPHON *Dominus firmamentum meum.*
Ps 17:3

- i -

1174
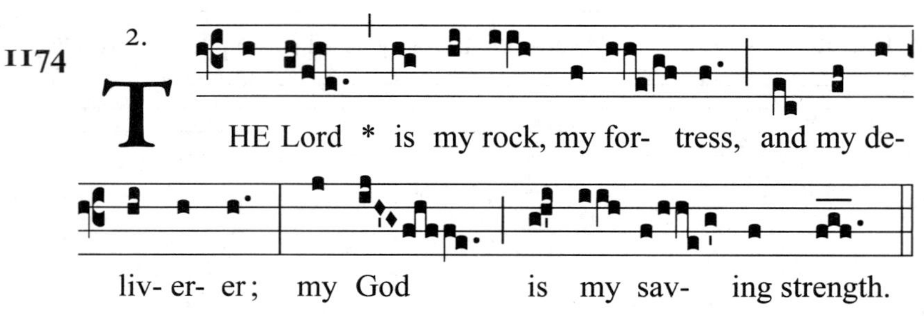
2.
THE Lord * is my rock, my for- tress, and my de-
liv- er- er; my God is my sav- ing strength.

- ii -

1175
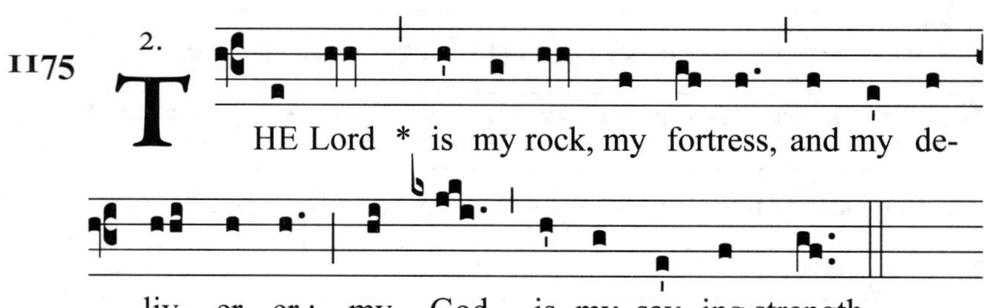
2.
THE Lord * is my rock, my fortress, and my de-
liv- er- er; my God is my sav- ing strength.

VERSES *Laudans invocabo Dominum. Ps* 17:4

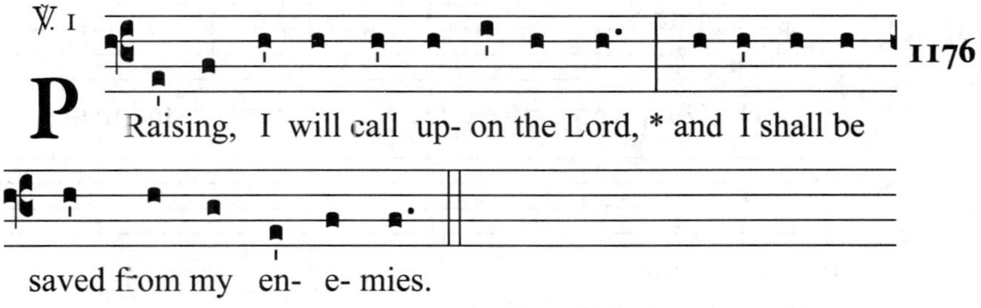
℣. 1
1176
PRaising, I will call up- on the Lord, * and I shall be
saved from my en- e- mies.

In tribulatione mea. Ps 17:7

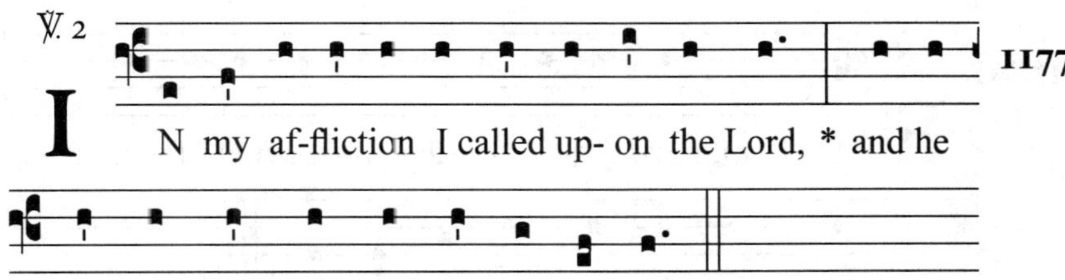
℣. 2
1177
IN my af-fliction I called up- on the Lord, * and he

heard my voice from his ho- ly tem-ple.

Quoniam tu illuminas. Ps 17:29

℣. 3
1178
FOR you give light to my lamp, O Lord ; * O my God,

en-light-en my darkness.

Deus, qui præcinxit me. Ps 17:33

1179 ℣. 4

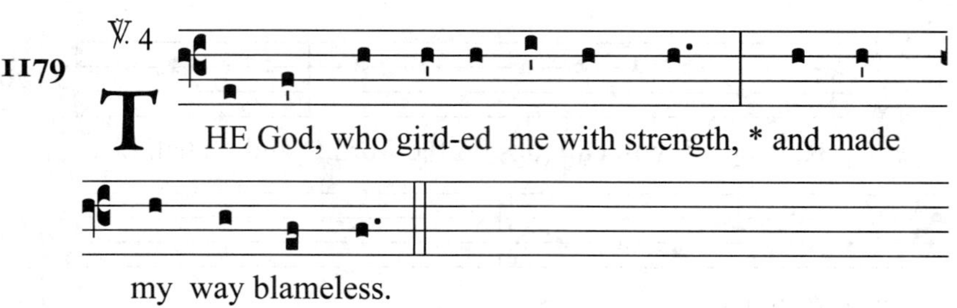
THE God, who gird-ed me with strength, * and made
my way blameless.

Quoniam quis Deus. Ps 17:36

1180 ℣. 5

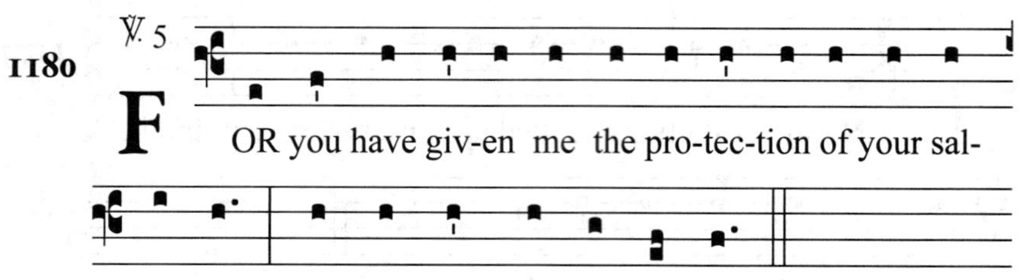
FOR you have giv-en me the pro-tec-tion of your sal-
va- tion, * and your right hand up-held me.

- iii -

2.

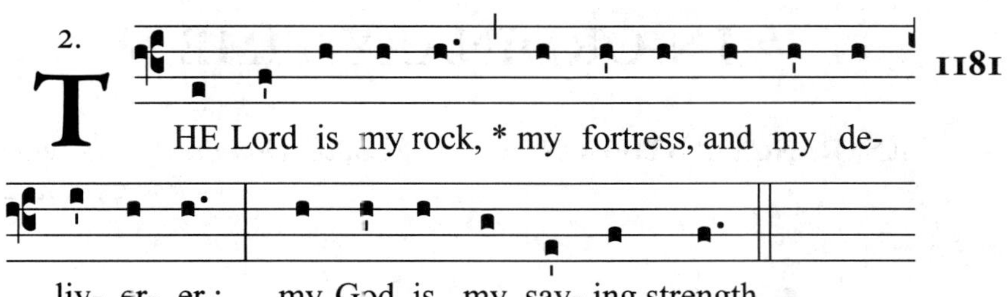
THE Lord is my rock, * my fortress, and my de-
liv- er- er ; my God is my sav- ing strength.

1181

- iv -

2.

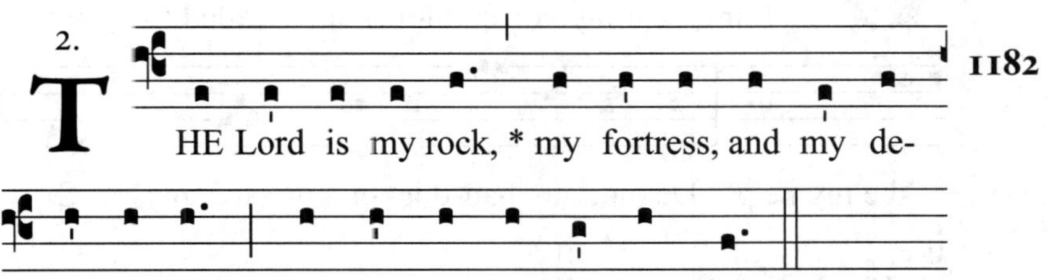
THE Lord is my rock, * my fortress, and my de-
liv- er- er ; my God is my sav- ing strength.

1182

ELEVENTH SUNDAY IN ORDINARY TIME

ENTRANCE ANTIPHON *Exaudi, Dominus . . . adiutor.*
Ps 30:3. 4. 2

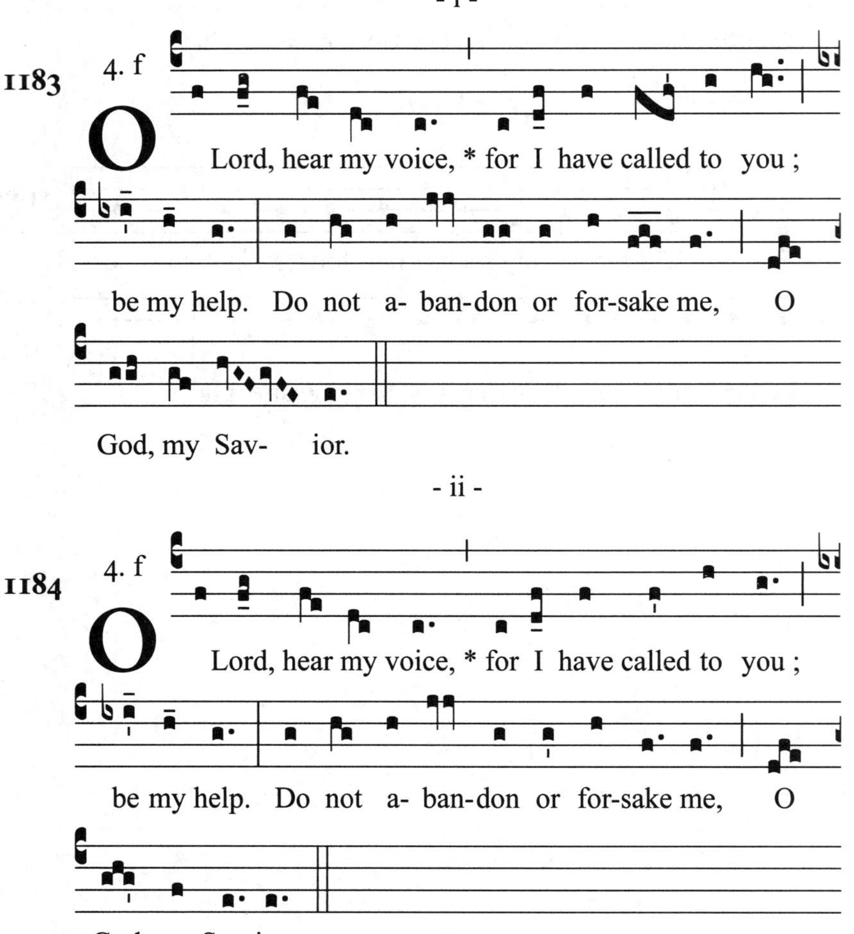
- i -
1183 4. f
O Lord, hear my voice, * for I have called to you;
be my help. Do not a- ban-don or for-sake me, O
God, my Sav- ior.
- ii -
1184 4. f
O Lord, hear my voice, * for I have called to you;
be my help. Do not a- ban-don or for-sake me, O
God, my Sav-ior.

Note · If the Entrance Antiphon *is repeated after the verse, use the second ending. If another verse follows, use the first ending.*

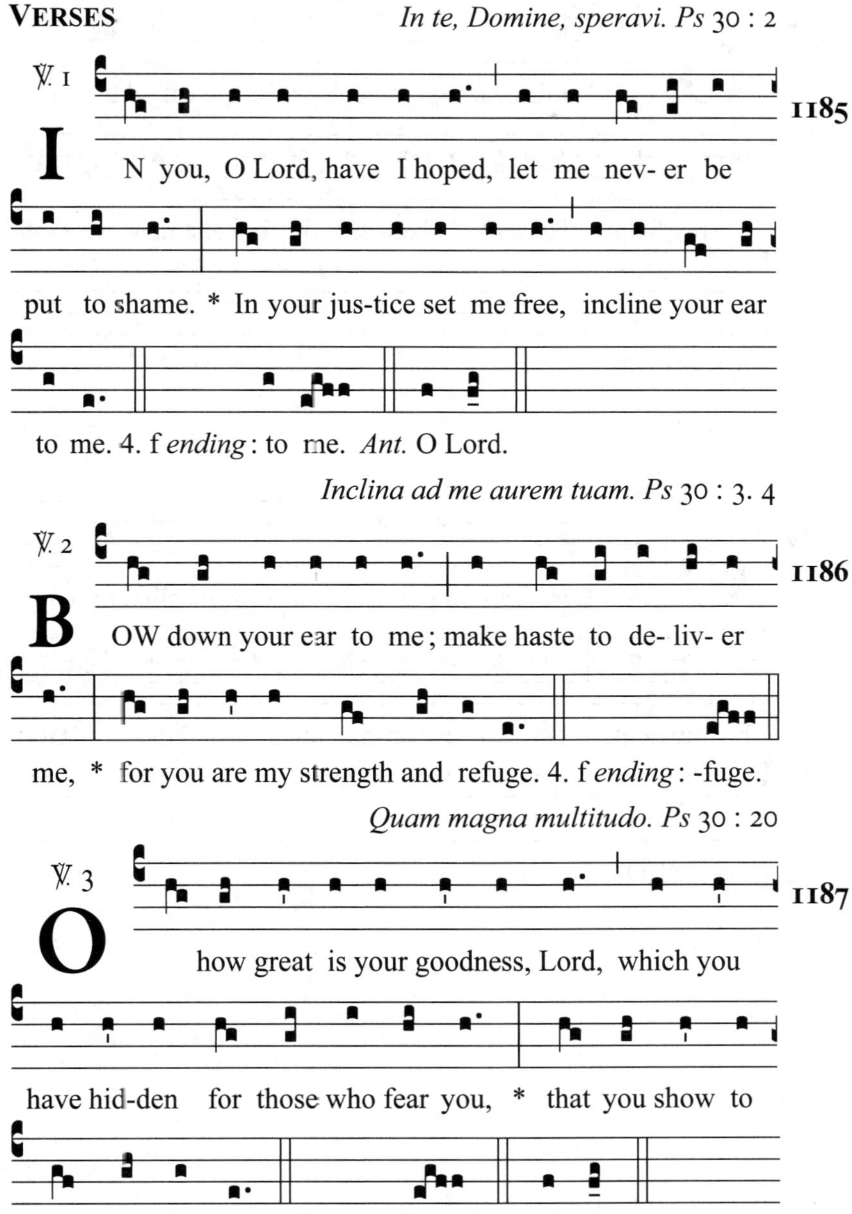
VERSES
In te, Domine, speravi. Ps 30 : 2
℣. 1
1185
IN you, O Lord, have I hoped, let me nev- er be
put to shame. * In your jus-tice set me free, incline your ear
to me. 4. f ending: to me. Ant. O Lord.
Inclina ad me aurem tuam. Ps 30 : 3. 4
℣. 2
1186
BOW down your ear to me; make haste to de- liv- er
me, * for you are my strength and refuge. 4. f ending: -fuge.
Quam magna multitudo. Ps 30 : 20
℣. 3
1187
O how great is your goodness, Lord, which you
have hid-den for those who fear you, * that you show to
those who trust you. 4. f ending: you. Ant. O Lord.

- iii -

1188

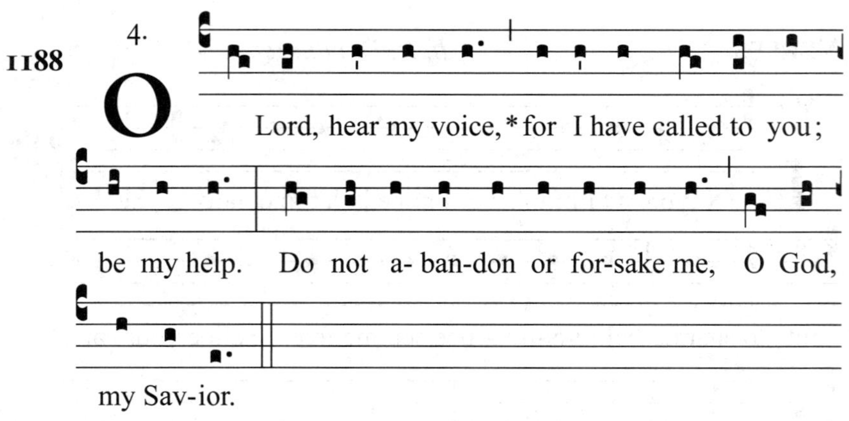
4.
O Lord, hear my voice, * for I have called to you;
be my help. Do not a- ban-don or for-sake me, O God,
my Sav-ior.

Or :

1189

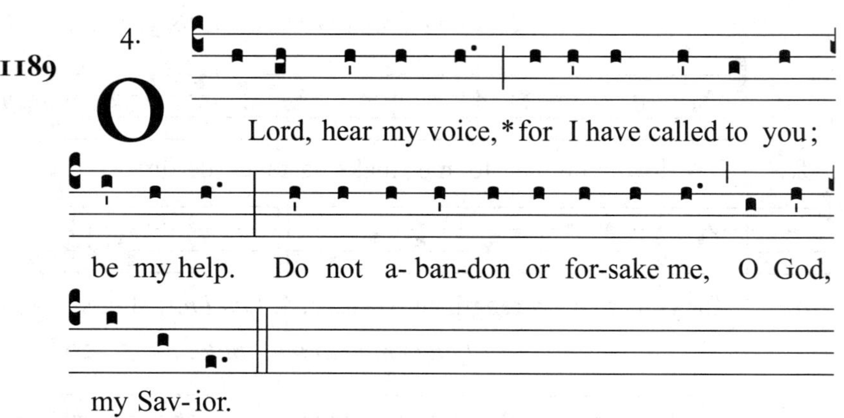
4.
O Lord, hear my voice, * for I have called to you;
be my help. Do not a- ban-don or for-sake me, O God,
my Sav- ior.

- iv -

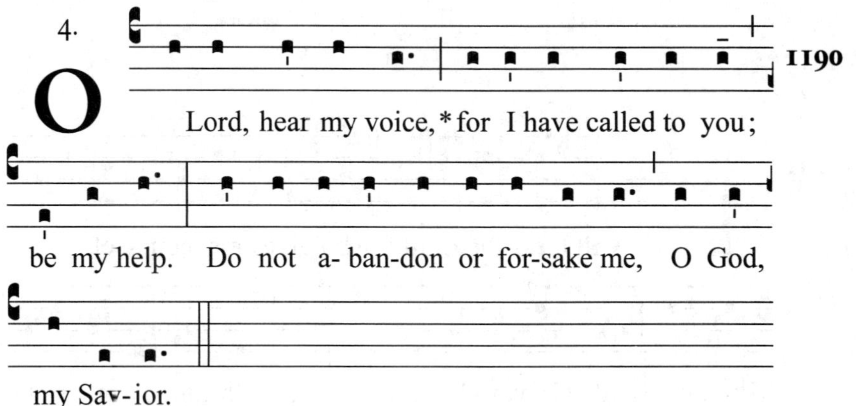
4.
O Lord, hear my voice, * for I have called to you;
1190
be my help. Do not a- ban-don or for-sake me, O God,
my Sav-ior.

OFFERTORY ANTIPHON *Bendicam Dominum.*
Ps 15:7.8

- i -

1191

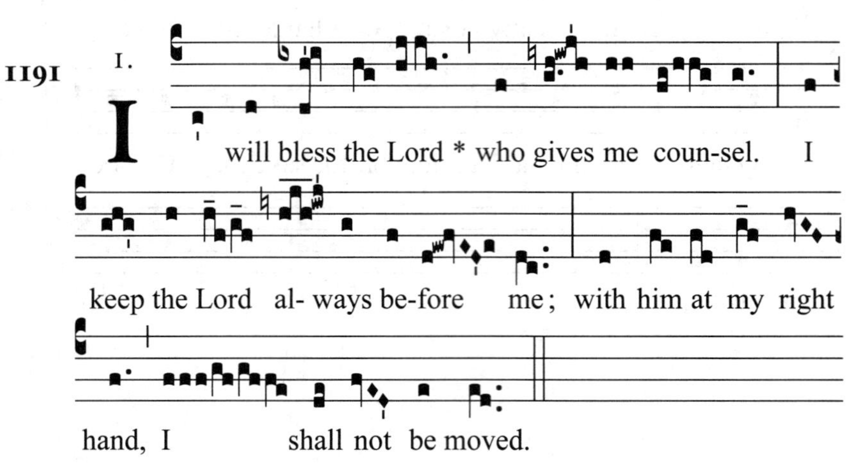
I.
I will bless the Lord * who gives me coun-sel. I
keep the Lord al- ways be-fore me; with him at my right
hand, I shall not be moved.

- ii -

1192

I.
I will bless the Lord * who gives me coun-sel. I
keep the Lord al-ways be-fore me; with him at my right
hand, I shall not be moved.

VERSES *Conserva me, Domine. Ps* 15:1-2

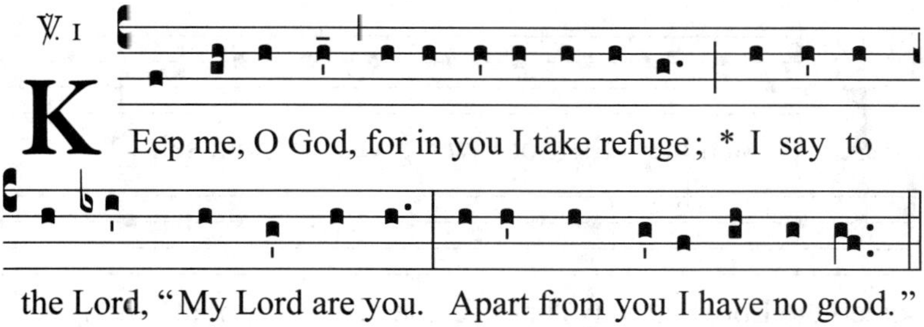

℣. 1 KEep me, O God, for in you I take refuge; * I say to 1193

the Lord, "My Lord are you. Apart from you I have no good."

Sanctis, qui sunt in terra. Ps 15:3

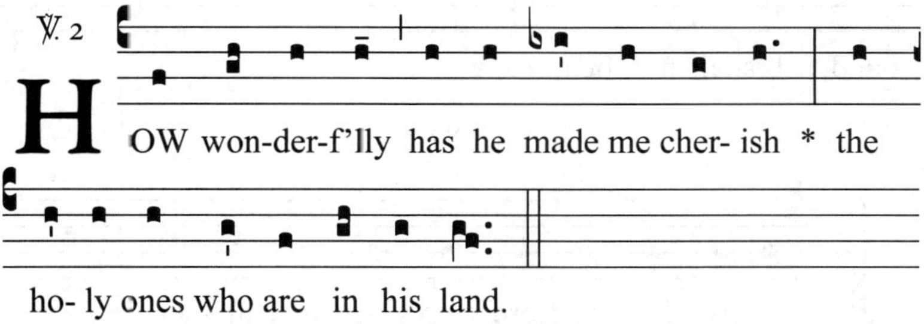

℣. 2 HOW won-der-f'lly has he made me cher- ish * the 1194

ho- ly ones who are in his land.

Propter hoc lætatum est cor meum. Ps 15:9

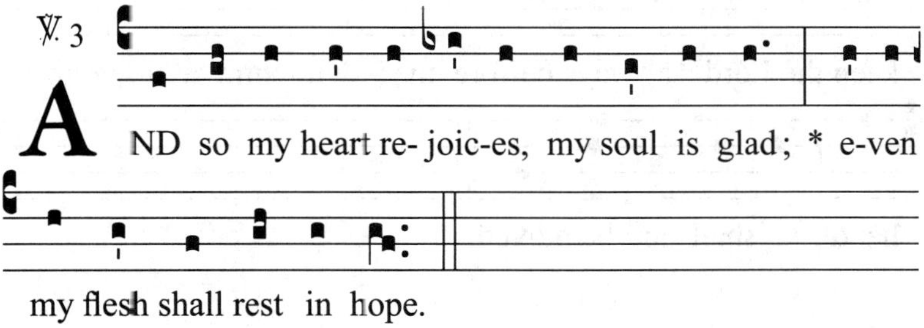

℣. 3 AND so my heart re- joic-es, my soul is glad; * e-ven 1195

my flesh shall rest in hope.

Notas mihi fecisti vias vitæ. Ps 15:11

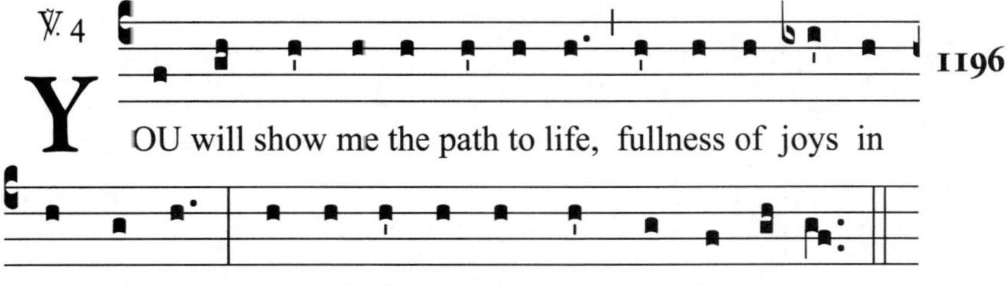

℣. 4 YOU will show me the path to life, fullness of joys in 1196

your presence, * the delights at your right hand for- ev- er.

- iii -

1197

1.
I will bless the Lord who gives me coun-sel. * I
keep the Lord al-ways be-fore me ; with him at my right
hand, I shall not be moved.

- iv -

1198

1.
I will bless the Lord who gives me coun-sel. * I
keep the Lord al-ways be-fore me ; with him at my right
hand, I shall not be moved.

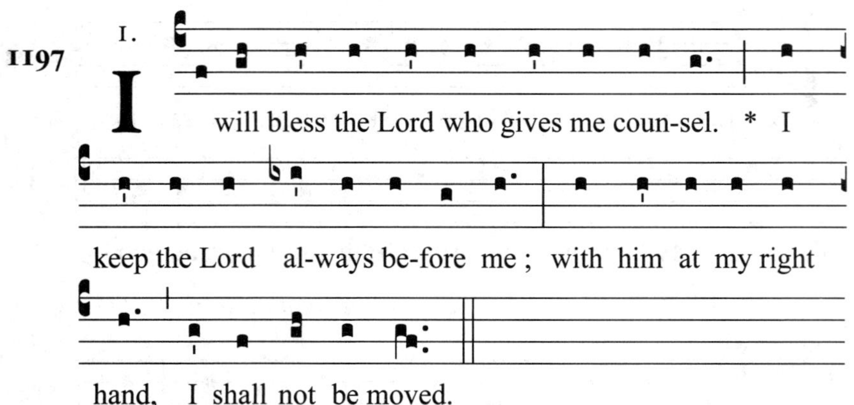

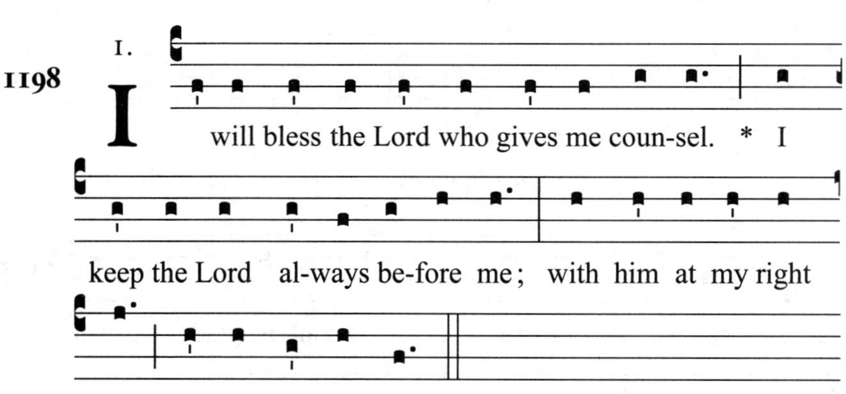

COMMUNION ANTIPHON *Unum petii a Domino.*
Ps 26:4

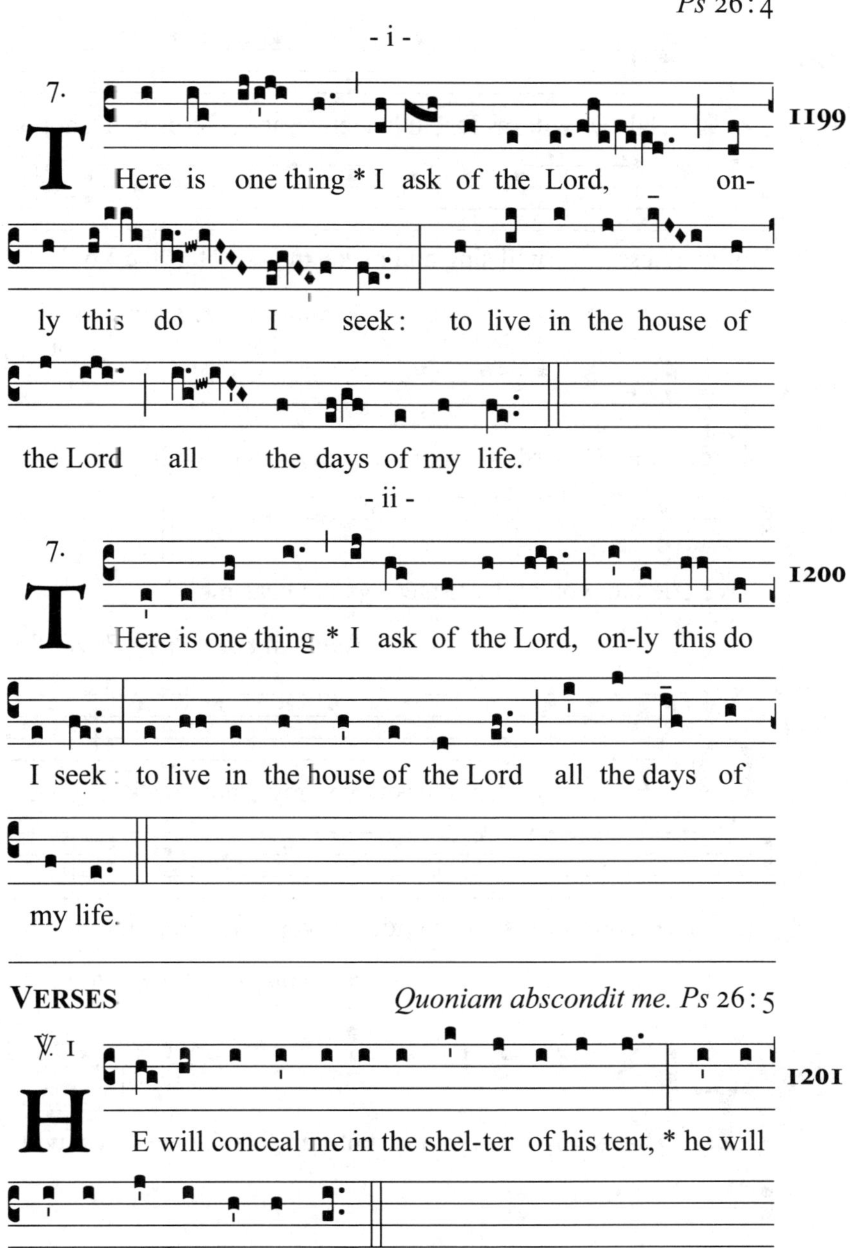
- i -
7.
1199
THere is one thing * I ask of the Lord, only this do I seek: to live in the house of
the Lord all the days of my life.
- ii -
7.
1200
THere is one thing * I ask of the Lord, on-ly this do
I seek: to live in the house of the Lord all the days of
my life.
VERSES *Quoniam abscondit me. Ps* 26:5
℣. 1
1201
HE will conceal me in the shel-ter of his tent, * he will

set me high up- on a rock.

Conserva me, Domine. Ps 26:6

1202
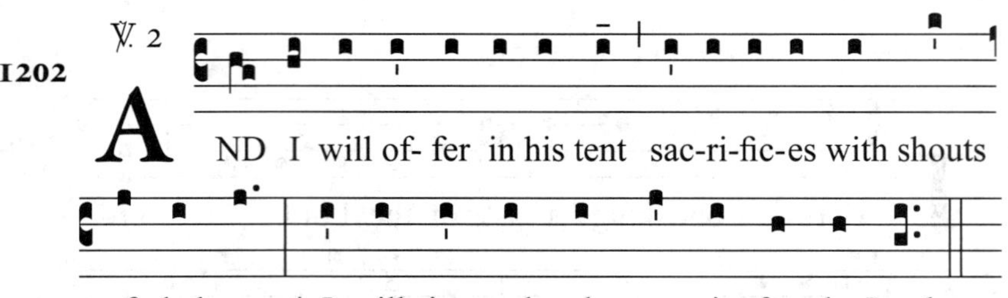
℣. 2
AND I will of- fer in his tent sac-ri-fic-es with shouts
of gladness; * I will sing and make mu- sic for the Lord.

Exaudi, Domine, vocem meam. Ps 26:7

1203
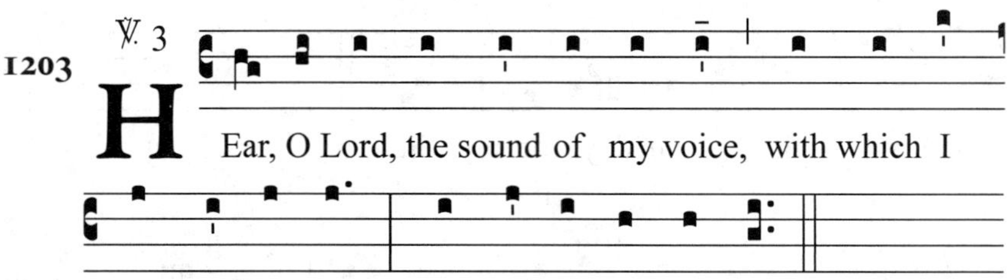
℣. 3
HEar, O Lord, the sound of my voice, with which I
have cried to you; * have mer-cy and hear me.

Tibi dixit cor meum. Ps 26:8-9

1204
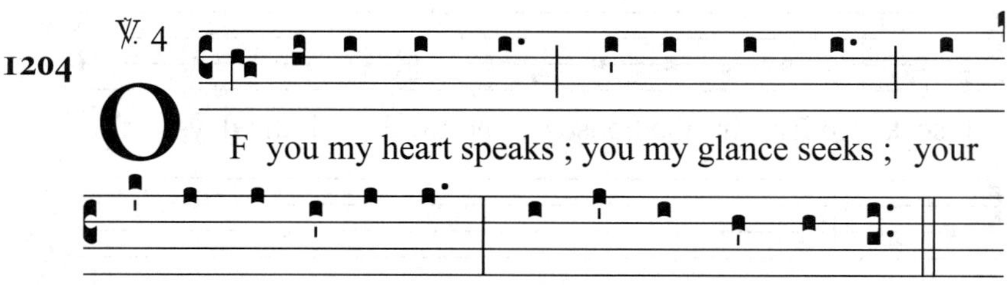
℣. 4
OF you my heart speaks; you my glance seeks; your
presence, O Lord, I seek. * Hide not your face from me.

Quoniam pater meus. Ps 26:10

1205
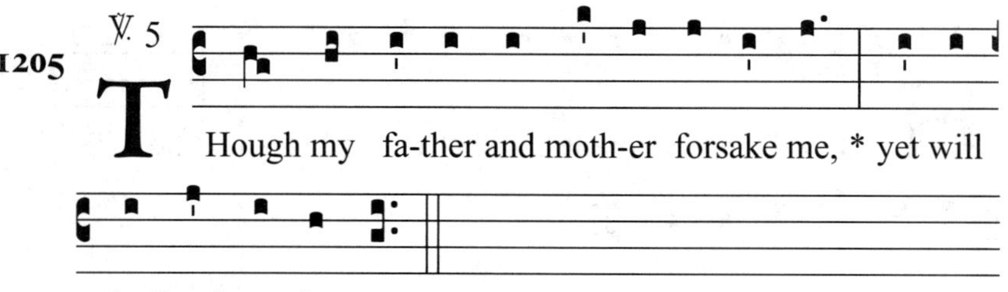
℣. 5
THough my fa-ther and moth-er forsake me, * yet will
the Lord receive me.

- iii -

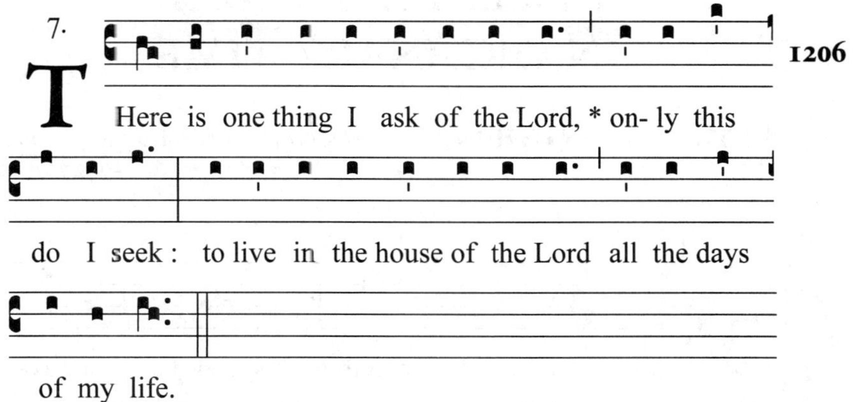
7.
THere is one thing I ask of the Lord, * on- ly this
do I seek : to live in the house of the Lord all the days
of my life.
1206

- iv -

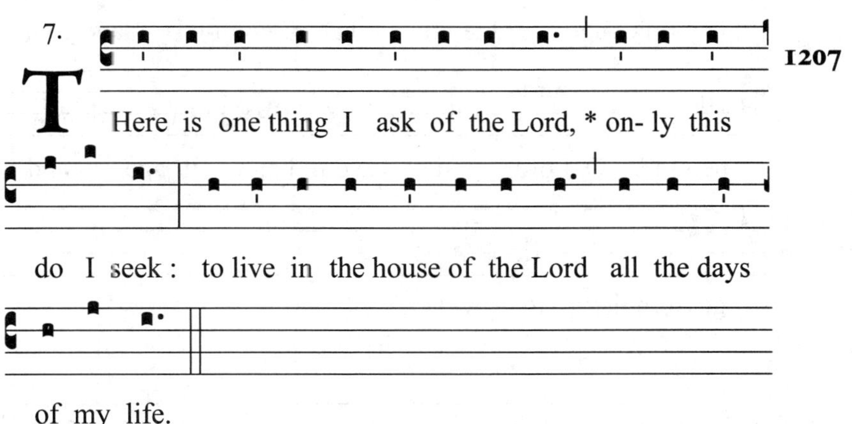
7.
THere is one thing I ask of the Lord, * on- ly this
do I seek : to live in the house of the Lord all the days
of my life.
1207

TWELFTH SUNDAY IN ORDINARY TIME

Entrance Antiphon *Dominus fortitudo plebis tuæ.*
Ps 27:8-9

- i -

1208

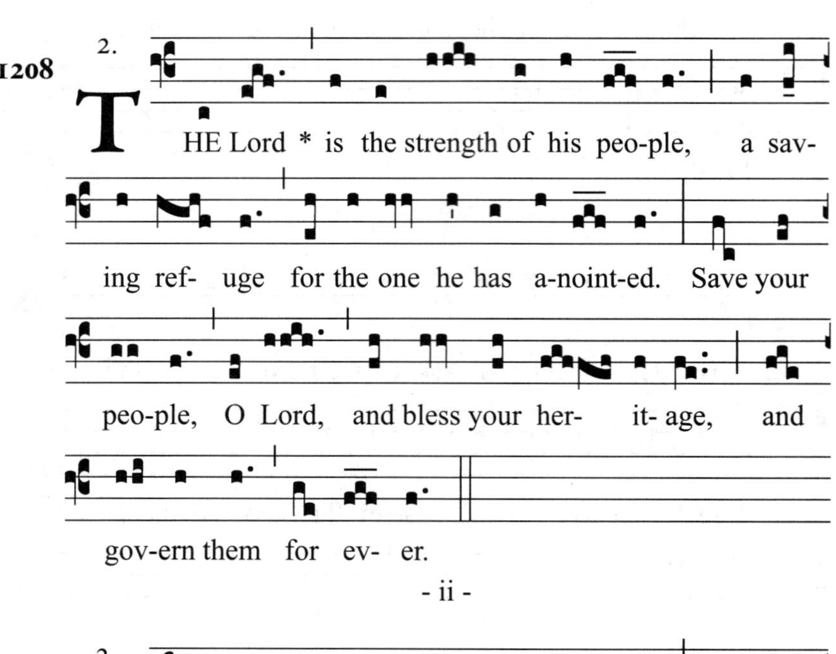
2.
THE Lord * is the strength of his peo-ple, a sav-
ing ref- uge for the one he has a-noint-ed. Save your
peo-ple, O Lord, and bless your her- it- age, and
gov-ern them for ev- er.

- ii -

1209

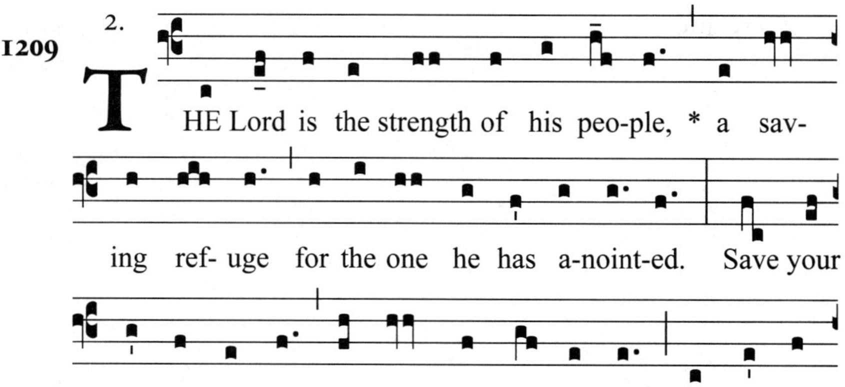
2.
THE Lord is the strength of his peo-ple, * a sav-
ing ref- uge for the one he has a-noint-ed. Save your
peo-ple, O Lord, and bless your her- it- age, and gov-ern

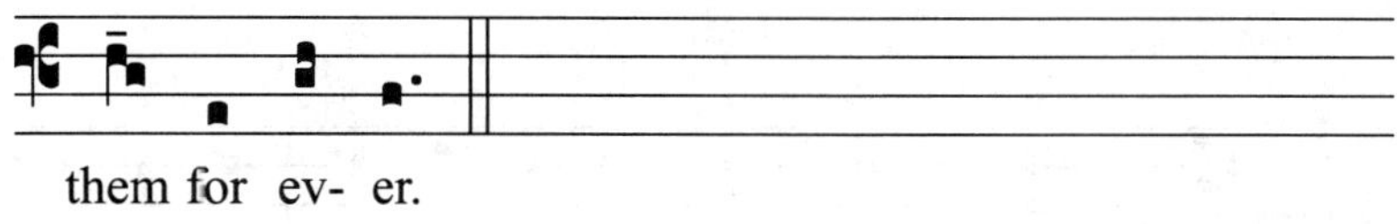
them for ev- er.

VERSES *Ad te, Domine, clamabo. Ps* 27:1

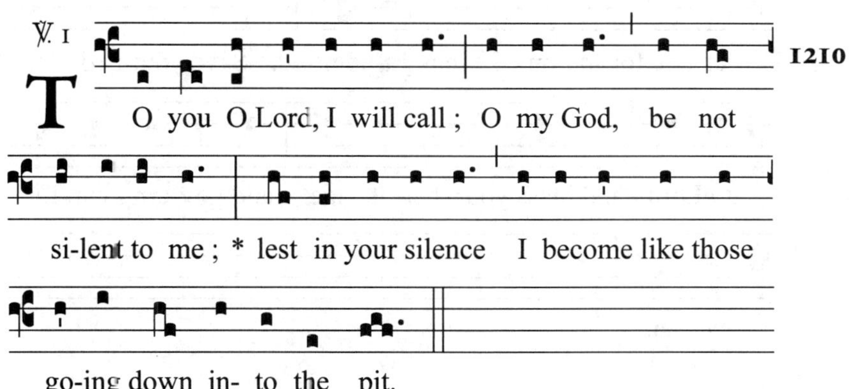
℣. 1
TO you O Lord, I will call ; O my God, be not
si-lent to me ; * lest in your silence I become like those
go-ing down in- to the pit.
1210

Exaudi, Domine, vocem deprecationis meæ. Ps 27:2

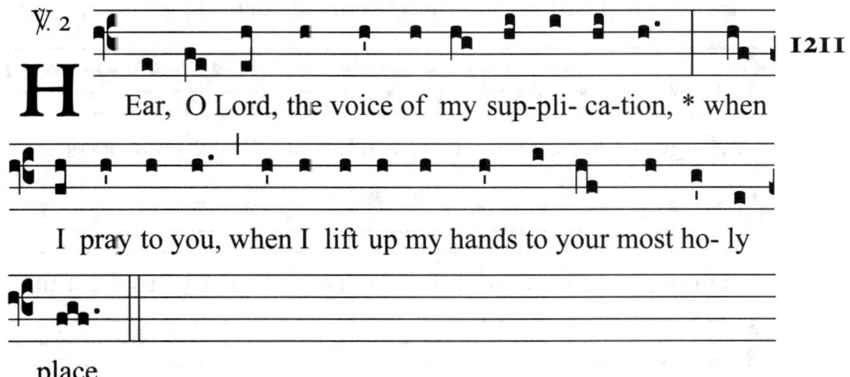
℣. 2
HEar, O Lord, the voice of my sup-pli- ca-tion, * when
I pray to you, when I lift up my hands to your most ho- ly
place.
1211

- iii -

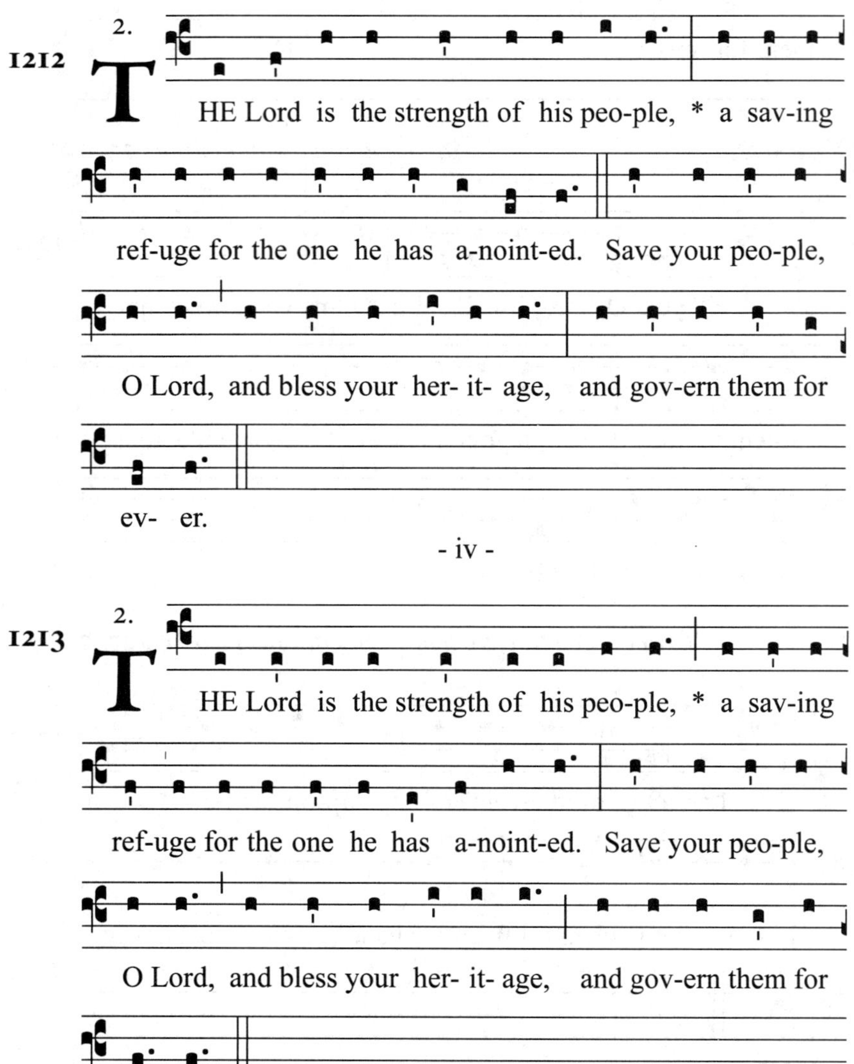
1212
2.
THE Lord is the strength of his peo-ple, * a sav-ing
ref-uge for the one he has a-noint-ed. Save your peo-ple,
O Lord, and bless your her- it- age, and gov-ern them for
ev- er.
- iv -
1213
2.
THE Lord is the strength of his peo-ple, * a sav-ing
ref-uge for the one he has a-noint-ed. Save your peo-ple,
O Lord, and bless your her- it- age, and gov-ern them for
ev- er.

OFFERTORY ANTIPHON *Perfice gressus meos.*
Ps 16:5. 6. 7

- i -

4. 1214

MAKE me * to walk per-fect-ly in your paths, that my
footsteps may not fal- ter. In- cline your ear to
me, and hear my words, show forth your won-der-ful
mer- cies, you who save those who trust in you, O Lord.

- ii -

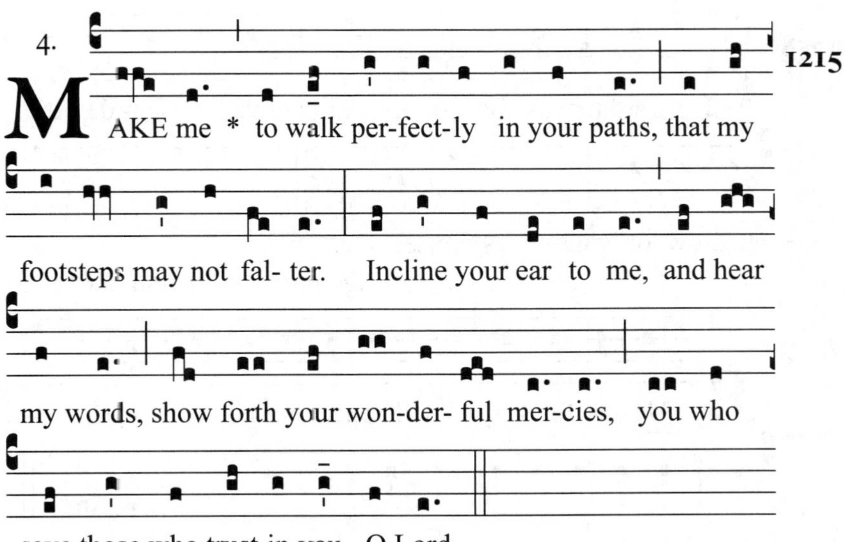
4.
1215
MAKE me * to walk per-fect-ly in your paths, that my
footsteps may not fal- ter. Incline your ear to me, and hear
my words, show forth your won-der- ful mer-cies, you who
save those who trust in you, O Lord.

VERSES *Exaudi, Domine, iustitiam meam.* *Ps* 16:1

1216

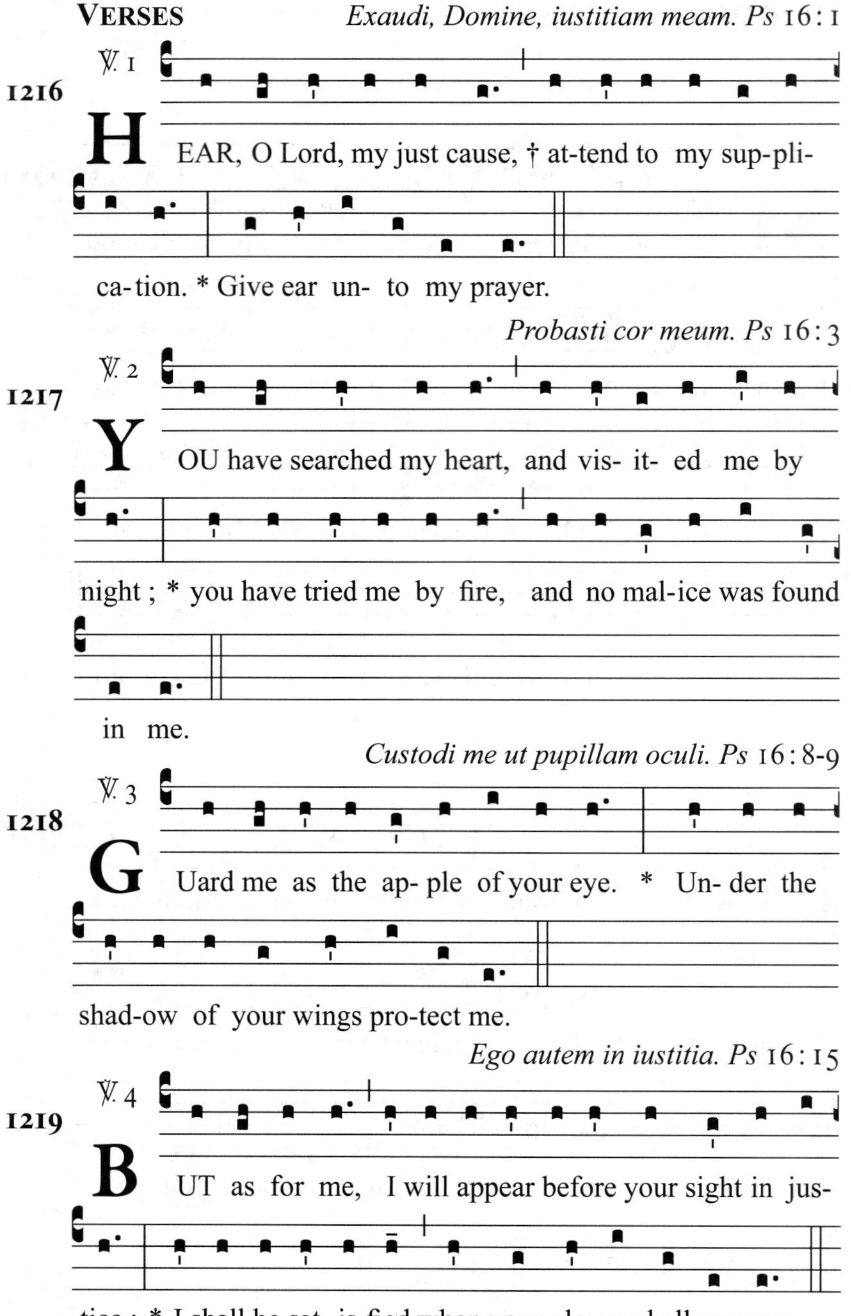
℣. 1
HEAR, O Lord, my just cause, † at-tend to my sup-pli-
ca-tion. * Give ear un- to my prayer.
Probasti cor meum. Ps 16:3
℣. 2
YOU have searched my heart, and vis- it- ed me by
night ; * you have tried me by fire, and no mal-ice was found
in me.
Custodi me ut pupillam oculi. Ps 16:8-9
℣. 3
GUard me as the ap- ple of your eye. * Un- der the
shad-ow of your wings pro-tect me.
Ego autem in iustitia. Ps 16:15
℣. 4
BUT as for me, I will appear before your sight in jus-
tice ; * I shall be sat- is-fied when your glo- ry shall ap-pear.

1217

1218

1219

- iii -

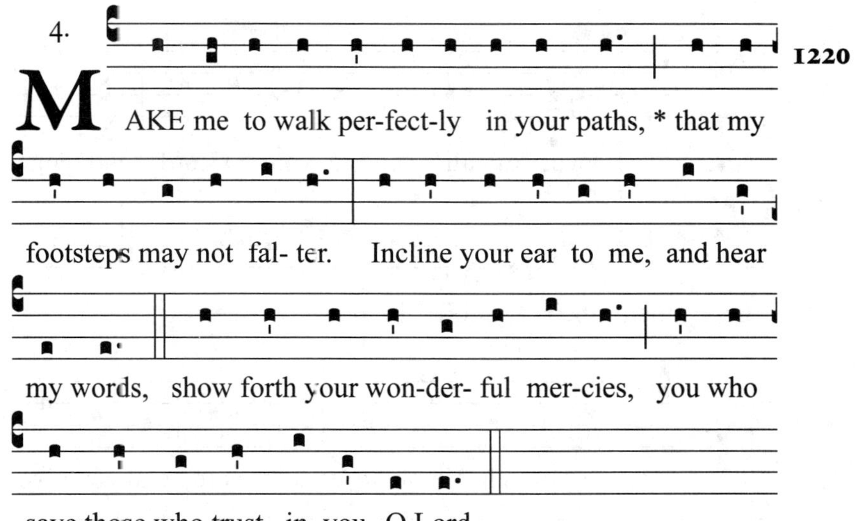
4.
1220
MAKE me to walk per-fect-ly in your paths, * that my
footsteps may not fal- ter. Incline your ear to me, and hear
my words, show forth your won-der- ful mer-cies, you who
save those who trust in you, O Lord.

- iv -

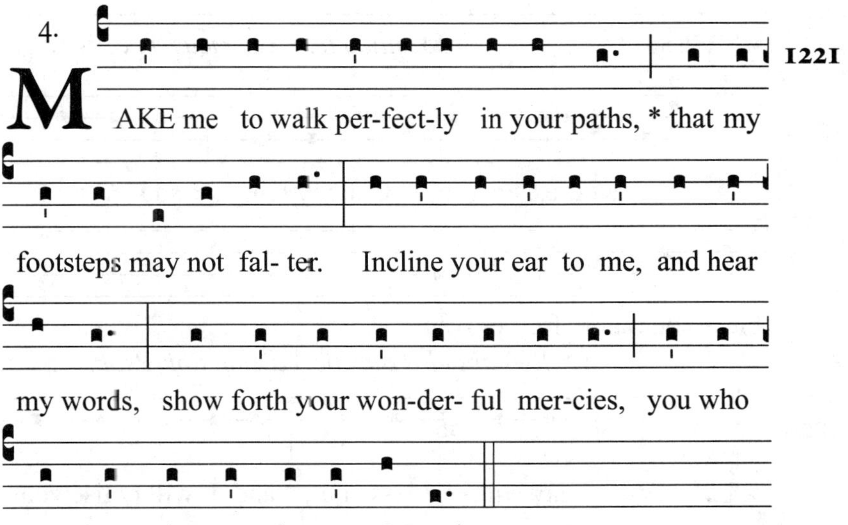
4.
1221
MAKE me to walk per-fect-ly in your paths, * that my
footsteps may not fal- ter. Incline your ear to me, and hear
my words, show forth your won-der- ful mer-cies, you who
save those who trust in you, O Lord.

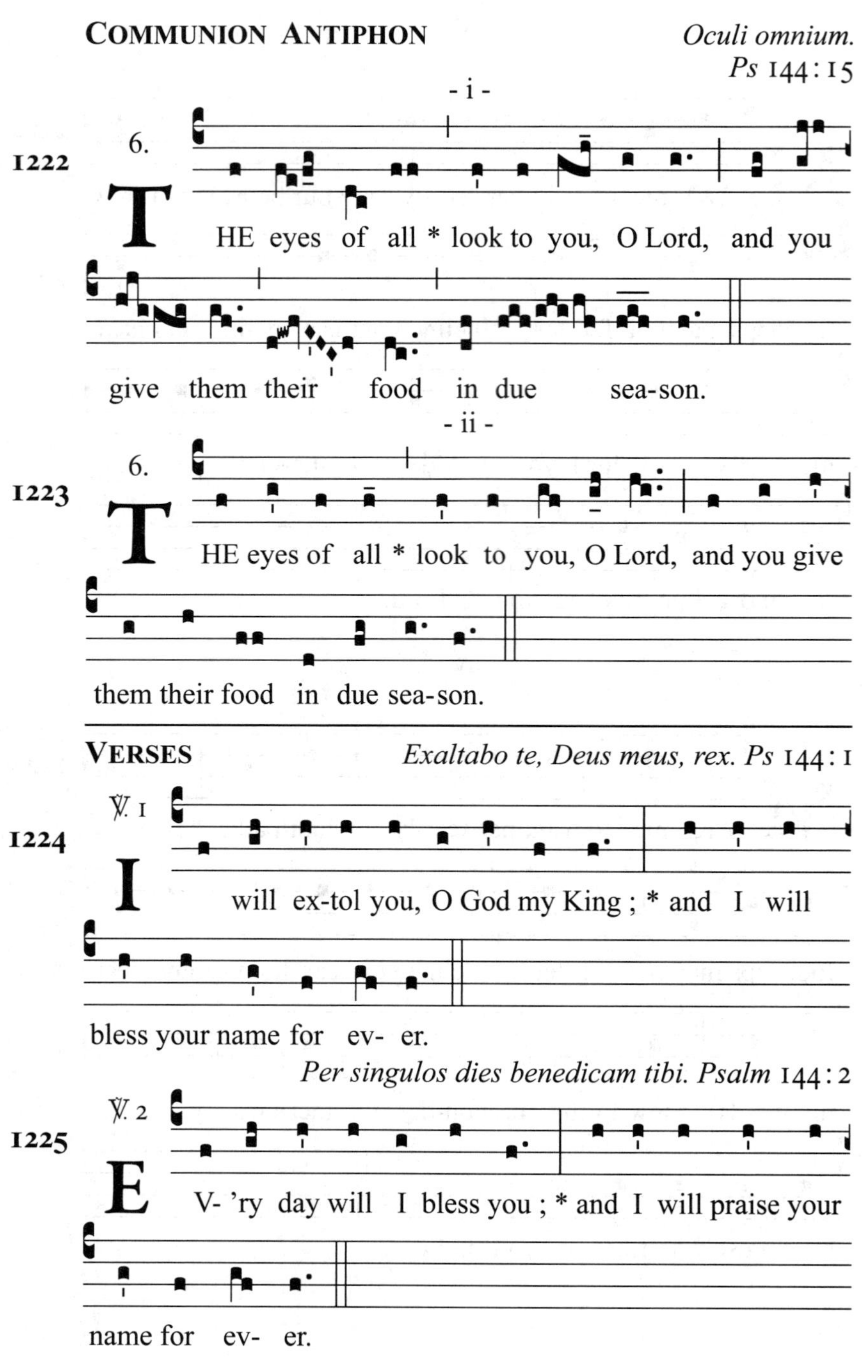
COMMUNION ANTIPHON
Oculi omnium.
Ps 144:15
- i -
1222
6.
THE eyes of all * look to you, O Lord, and you
give them their food in due sea-son.
- ii -
1223
6.
THE eyes of all * look to you, O Lord, and you give
them their food in due sea-son.
VERSES
Exaltabo te, Deus meus, rex. Ps 144:1
1224
℣. 1
I will ex-tol you, O God my King; * and I will
bless your name for ev- er.
Per singulos dies benedicam tibi. Psalm 144:2
1225
℣. 2
EV- 'ry day will I bless you; * and I will praise your
name for ev- er.

Magnus Dominus, et laudabilis nimis. Ps 144:3

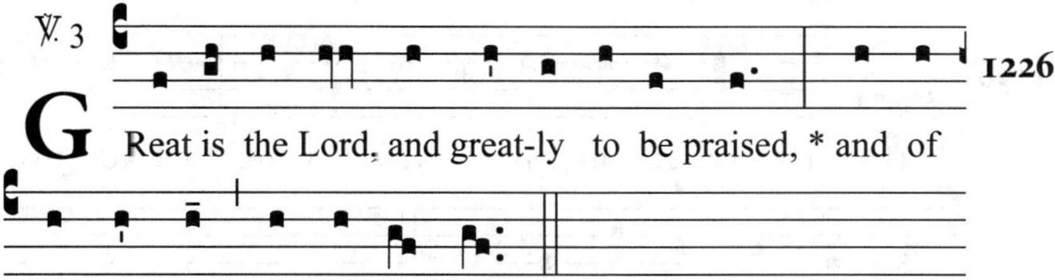
℣. 3
1226
GReat is the Lord, and great-ly to be praised, * and of
his greatness there is no end.

Generatio et generatio. Ps 144:4

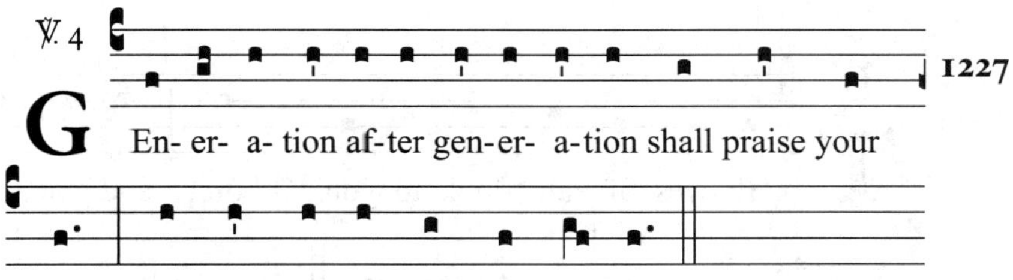
℣. 4
1227
GEn- er- a- tion af-ter gen-er- a-tion shall praise your
works * and they shall de-clare your pow- er.

Magnificentiam gloriæ sanctitatis tuæ. Ps 144:5

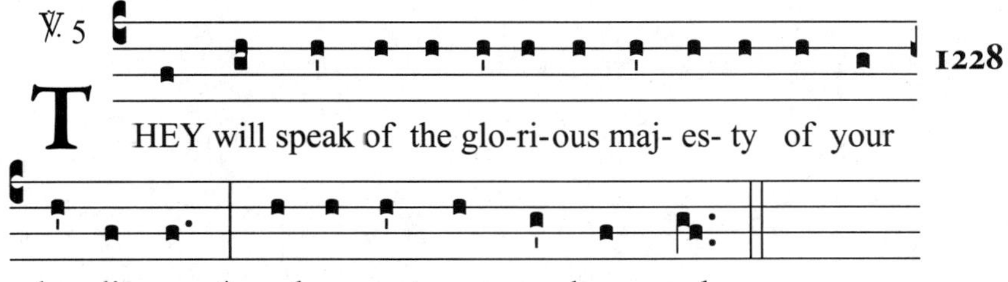
℣. 5
1228
THEY will speak of the glo-ri-ous maj- es- ty of your
ho- li- ness * and recount your wondrous works.

Memoriam abundantiæ suavitatis tuæ. Ps 144:6

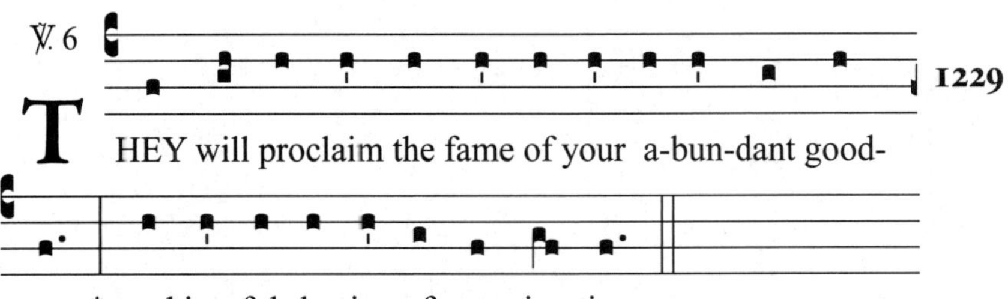
℣. 6
1229
THEY will proclaim the fame of your a-bun-dant goodness * and joy-ful- ly sing of your jus-tice.

- iii -

1230
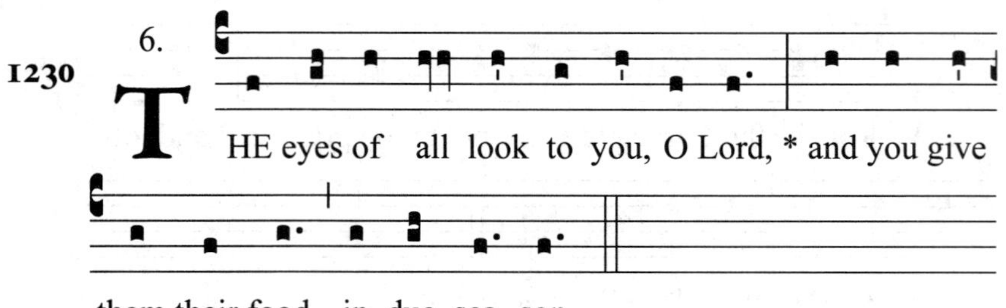
6.
THE eyes of all look to you, O Lord, * and you give

them their food in due sea- son.

- iv -

1231 6.

THE eyes of all * look to you, O Lord, and you

give them their food in due sea-son.

THIRTEENTH SUNDAY IN ORDINARY TIME

ENTRANCE ANTIPHON *Omnes gentes, plaudite manibus.*
Ps 46:2

- i -

6.
ALL peo-ples, * clap your hands. Cry to God with
shouts of joy!
1232

- ii -

6.
ALL peo-ples, clap your hands. * Cry to God with shouts
of joy!
1233

Verses *Quoniam Dominus excelsus. Psalm* 46

1234
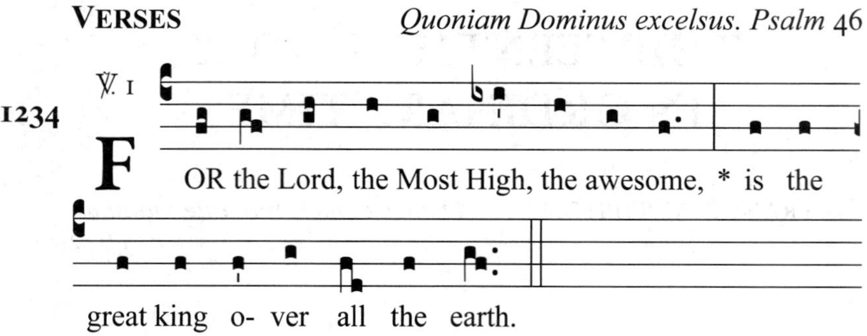
℣. 1
FOR the Lord, the Most High, the awesome, * is the
great king o- ver all the earth.

Psallite Deo nostro, psallite. Psalm 46

1235

℣. 2
SING prais-es to God, sing prais- es ! * Sing prais-es
to our king, sing prais-es !

Quoniam rex omnis terrae Deus . Psalm 46

1236
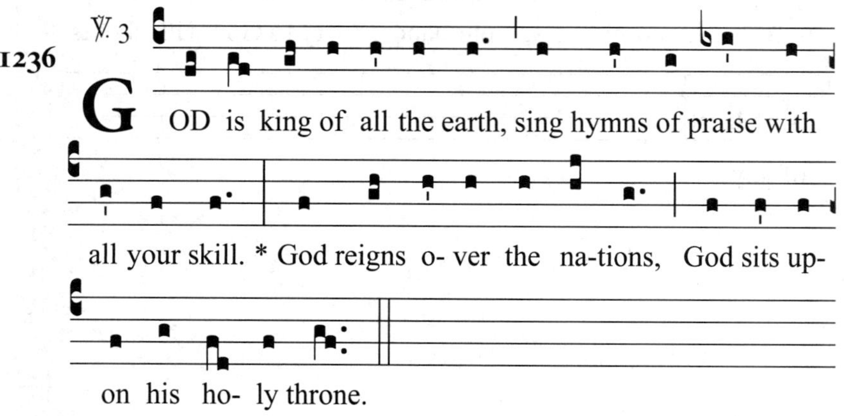
℣. 3
GOD is king of all the earth, sing hymns of praise with
all your skill. * God reigns o- ver the na-tions, God sits up-
on his ho- ly throne.

- iii -

6.
ALL peo-ples, clap your hands. * Cry to God with
shouts of joy!

1237

- iv -

6.
ALL peoples, clap your hands. * Cry to God with shouts
of joy!

1238

OFFERTORY ANTIPHON *Sicut in holocaustis. Daniel* 3:40

- i -

1239 4. d

AS in ho- locausts * of rams and bullocks, and as in
thousands of fat lambs; so let our sac-ri-fice be made in your
sight this day, that it may please you: for there is no con-
fu-sion to them that trust in you, O Lord.

- ii -

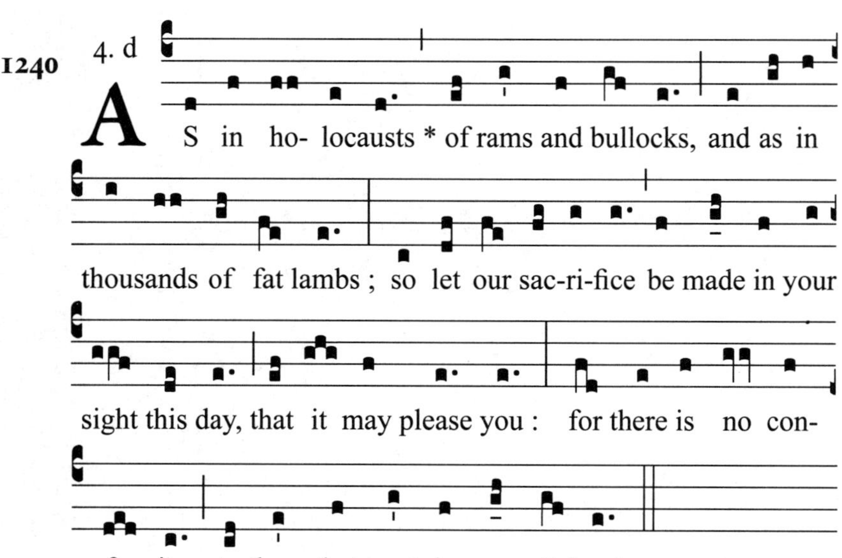
1240
4. d
AS in ho- locausts * of rams and bullocks, and as in
thousands of fat lambs; so let our sac-ri-fice be made in your
sight this day, that it may please you: for there is no con-
fu- sion to them that trust in you, O Lord.

VERSES

Note : If the Offertory Antiphon *is repeated after the verse, use the first ending* (4. d). *If another verse follows, use the second ending* (4. g).

Sacrificium et oblationem noluisti. Ps 39 : 7-8

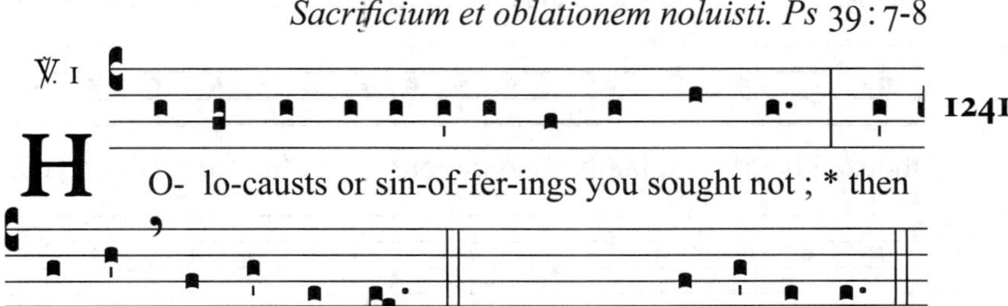
℣. 1
HO- lo-causts or sin-of-fer-ings you sought not ; * then
1241

said I, " Be-hold, I come." 4. g *ending*: "Behold, I come."

In capite libri scriptum est. Psalm 39 : 8-9

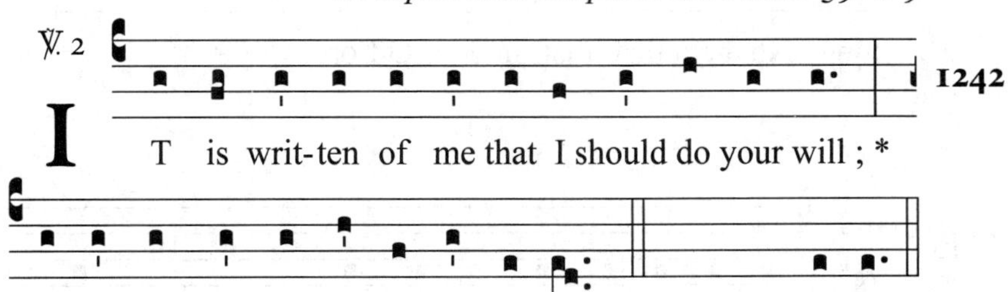
℣. 2
IT is writ-ten of me that I should do your will ; *
1242

to do your will, O God, is my de-light ! 4. g *ending* : delight !

Annuntiavi iustitiam tuam. Ps 39 : 10

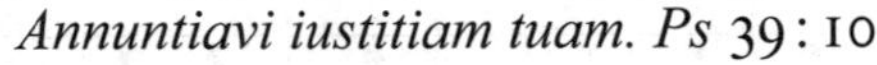

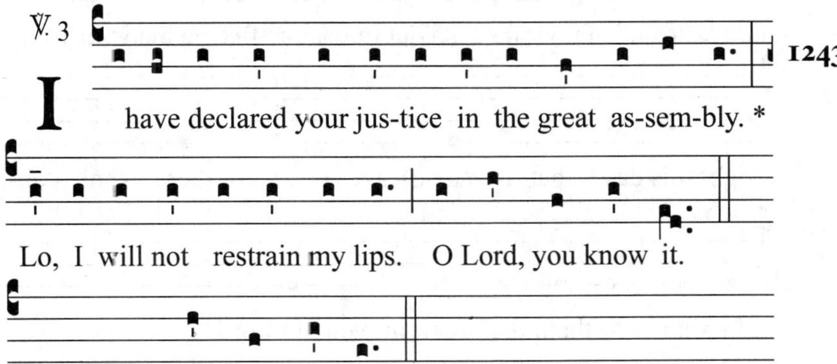
℣. 3
I have declared your jus-tice in the great as-sem-bly. *
1243
Lo, I will not restrain my lips. O Lord, you know it.

4. g *ending* : Lord, you know it.

- iii -

1244

4. g
As in ho- lo-causts of rams and bullocks, * and as in
thousands of fat lambs; so let our sac-ri-fice be made in your
sight this day, that it may please you: for there is no con-fu-
sion to them that trust in you, O Lord.

- iv -

1245

4. g
As in ho- lo-causts of rams and bullocks, * and as in
thousands of fat lambs; so let our sac-ri-fice be made in your
sight this day, that it may please you: for there is no con-
fu-sion to them that trust in you, O Lord.

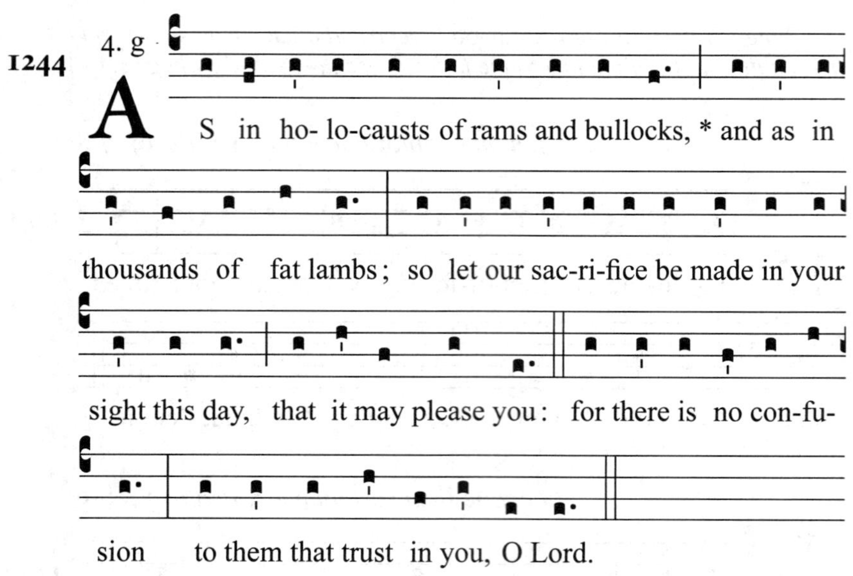

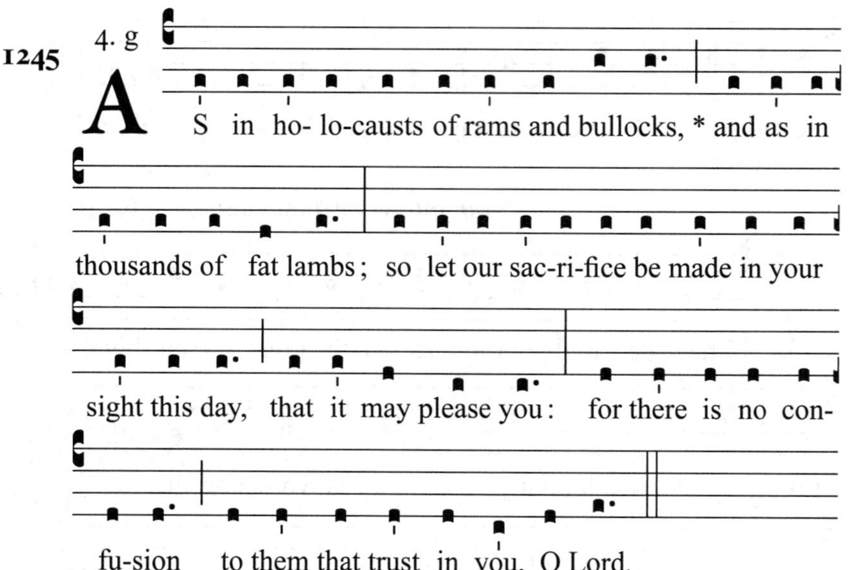

COMMUNION ANTIPHON *Benedic, anima mea, Domino.*
Ps 102:1

- i -

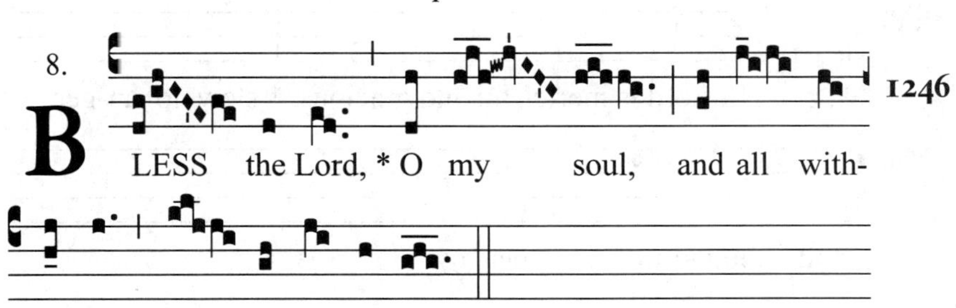
8.
B LESS the Lord, * O my soul, and all with-
1246
in me, bless his ho- ly name.

- ii -

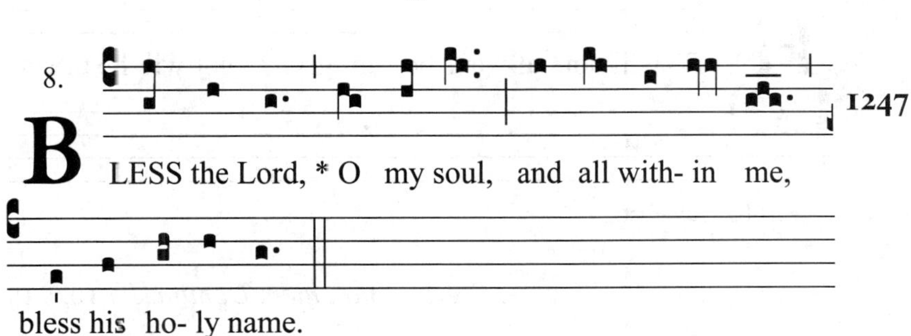
8.
B LESS the Lord, * O my soul, and all with- in me,
1247
bless his ho- ly name.

VERSES *Miserator et misericors Dominus. Ps* 102:8

1248

℣. 1
THE Lord is mer-ci-ful and gracious, * slow to an-ger
and a-bound-ing in mer- cy.

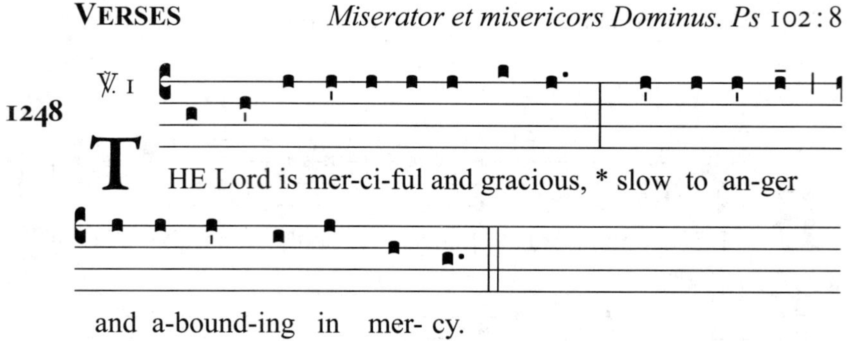

Non in perpetuum irascetur. Ps 102:9

1249

℣. 2
HE will not al-ways be an- gry, * nor will he threat-
en for ev- er.

Misericordia autem Domini. Ps 102:17

1250

℣. 3
THE mer-cy of the Lord is from ev- er-last-ing to ev-
er-last-ing * up- on those who fear him.

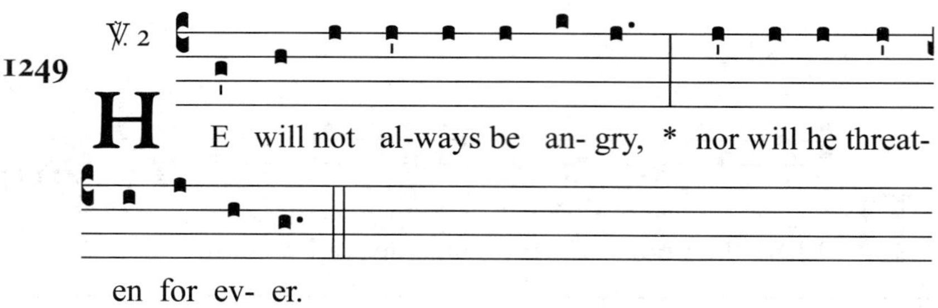

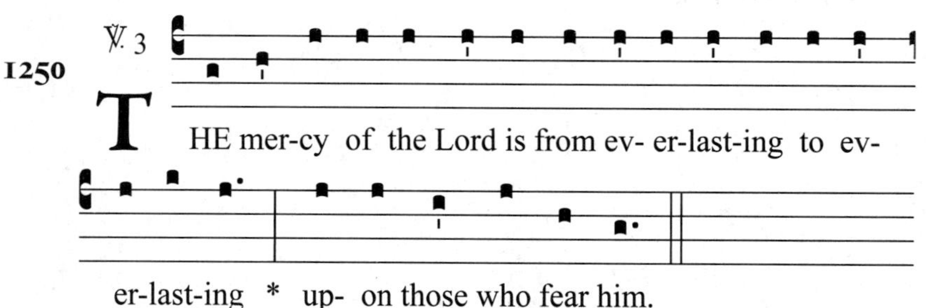

- iii -

8.
1251
BLESS the Lord, O my soul, * and all with- in me,
bless his ho- ly name.

- iv -

8.
1252
BLESS the Lord, O my soul, * and all with- in me,
bless his ho- ly name.

FOURTEENTH SUNDAY IN ORDINARY TIME

ENTRANCE ANTIPHON *Suscepimus, Deus.*
Ps 47:10-11

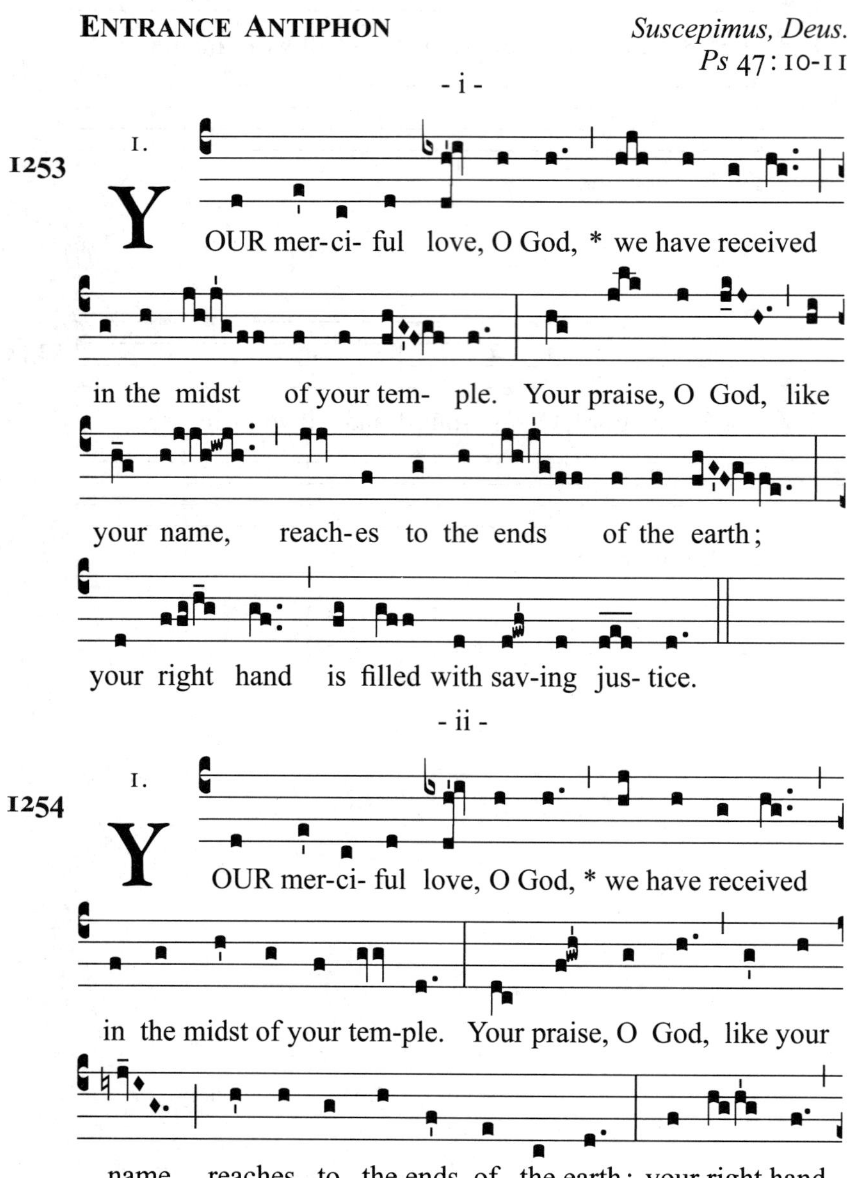
- i -
1253
I.
YOUR mer-ci- ful love, O God, * we have received
in the midst of your tem- ple. Your praise, O God, like
your name, reach-es to the ends of the earth;
your right hand is filled with sav-ing jus- tice.
- ii -
1254
I.
YOUR mer-ci- ful love, O God, * we have received
in the midst of your tem-ple. Your praise, O God, like your
name, reaches to the ends of the earth; your right hand

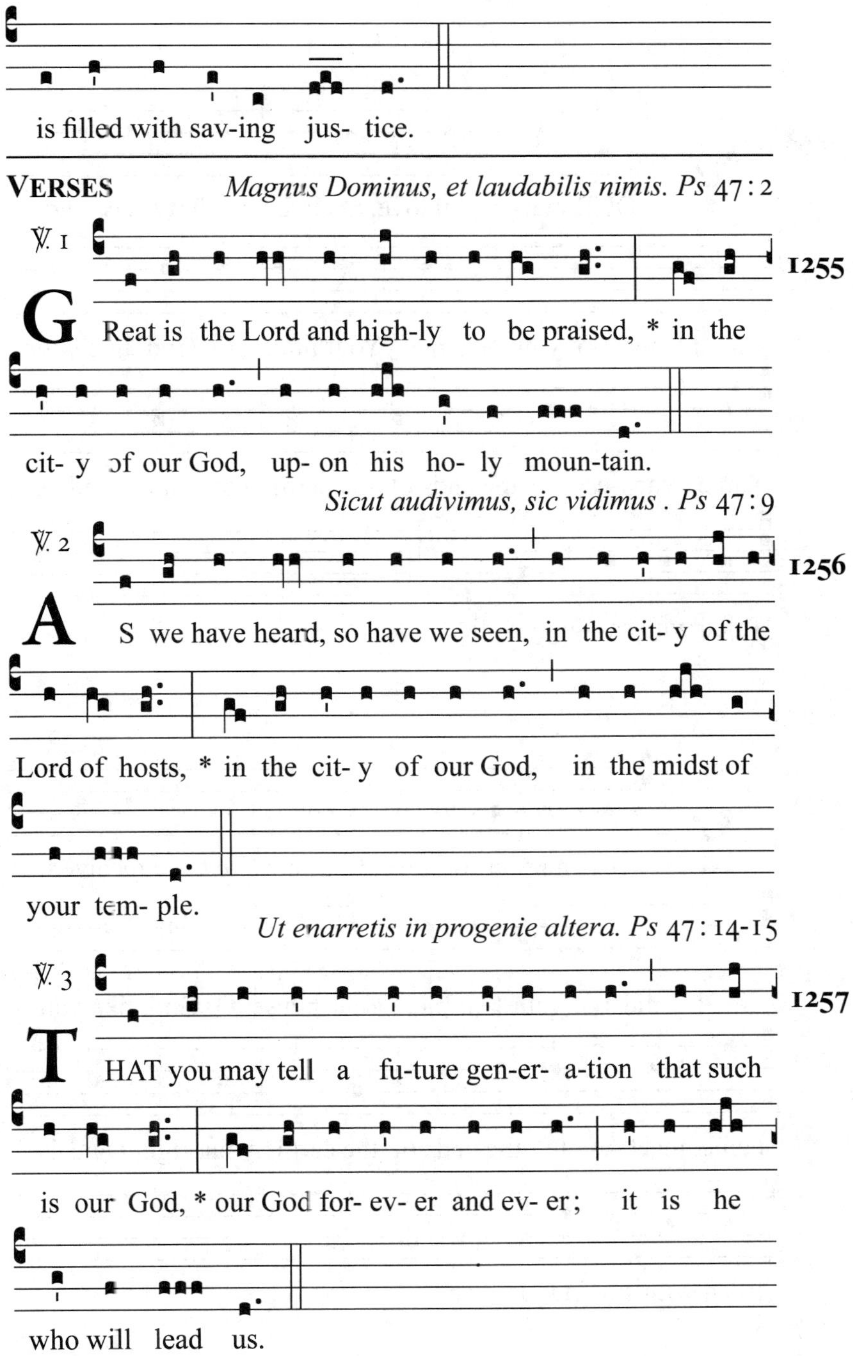
is filled with sav-ing jus- tice.
VERSES
Magnus Dominus, et laudabilis nimis. Ps 47:2
℣. 1
1255
GReat is the Lord and high-ly to be praised, * in the
cit- y of our God, up- on his ho- ly moun-tain.
Sicut audivimus, sic vidimus . Ps 47:9
℣. 2
1256
AS we have heard, so have we seen, in the cit- y of the
Lord of hosts, * in the cit- y of our God, in the midst of
your tem- ple.
Ut enarretis in progenie altera. Ps 47:14-15
℣. 3
1257
THAT you may tell a fu-ture gen-er- a-tion that such
is our God, * our God for- ev- er and ev- er; it is he
who will lead us.

- iii -

1258

I.
YOUR mer- ci- ful love, O God, * we have received
in the midst of your tem-ple. Your praise, O God, like your
name, reach-es to the ends of the earth; your right hand is
filled with sav-ing jus- tice.

- iv -

1259

I.
YOUR mer- ci- ful love, O God, * we have received
in the midst of your tem-ple. Your praise, O God, like your
name, reach-es to the ends of the earth; your right hand is
filled with sav-ing jus- tice.

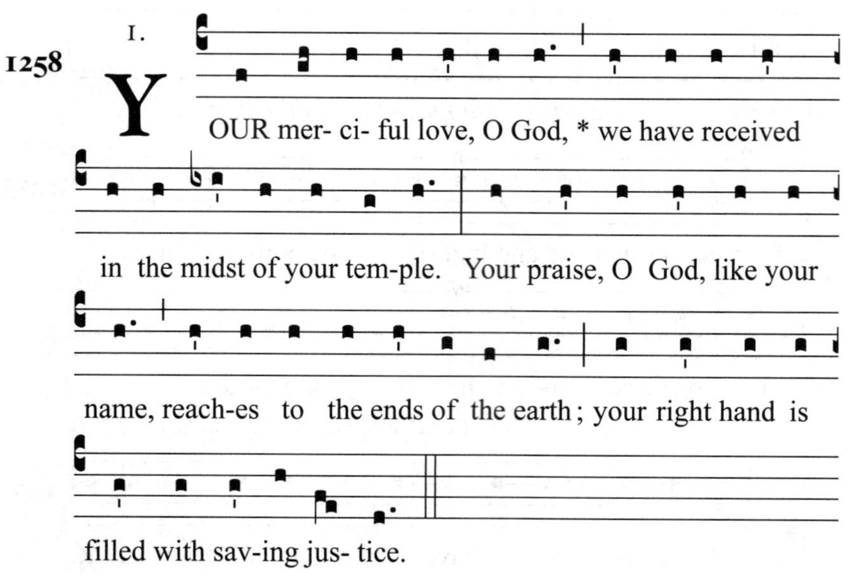

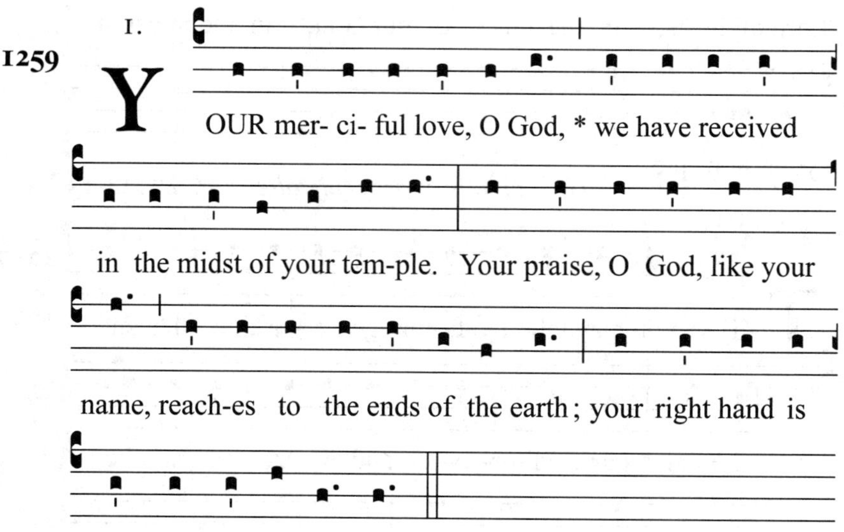

OFFERTORY ANTIPHON

Populum humilem.
Ps 17:28. 32

- i -

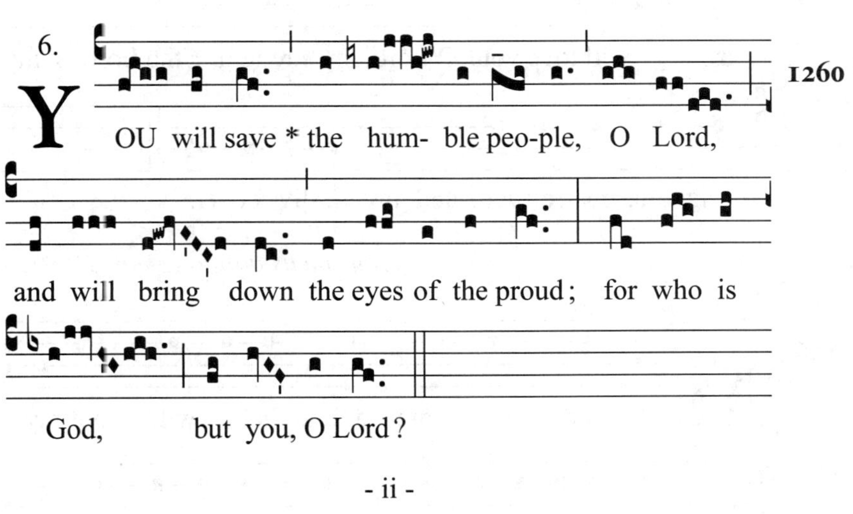
6.
1260
Y OU will save * the hum- ble peo-ple, O Lord,
and will bring down the eyes of the proud; for who is
God, but you, O Lord?

- ii -

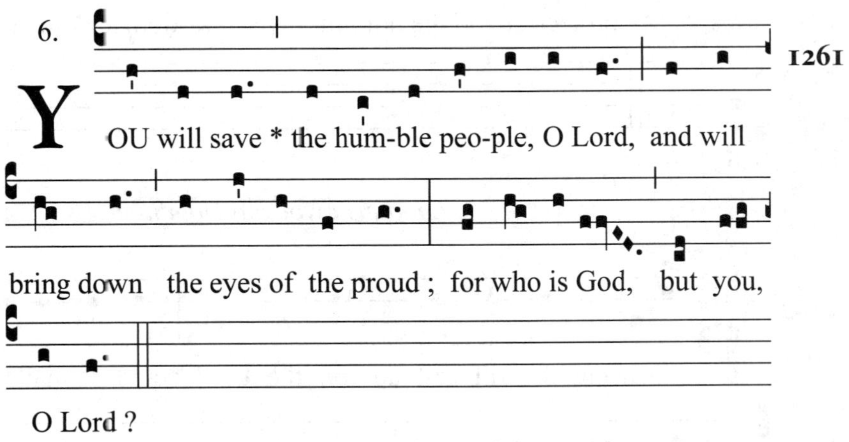
6.
1261
Y OU will save * the hum-ble peo-ple, O Lord, and will
bring down the eyes of the proud; for who is God, but you,
O Lord?

VERSES *Diligam te, Domine. Ps* 17:2

1262

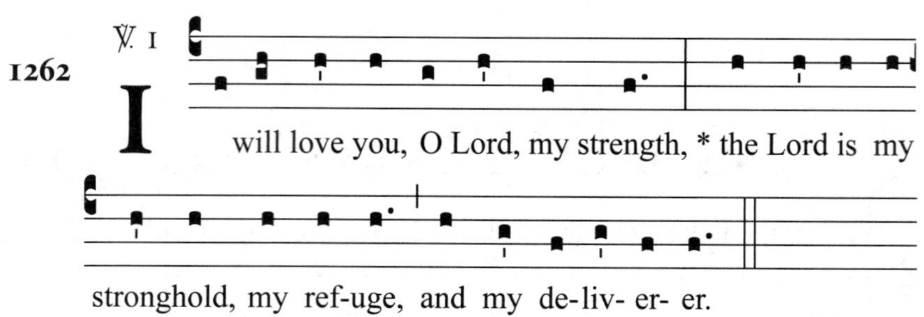
℣. 1
I will love you, O Lord, my strength, * the Lord is my
stronghold, my ref-uge, and my de-liv- er- er.

Deus meus adiutor meus. Ps 17:3

1263

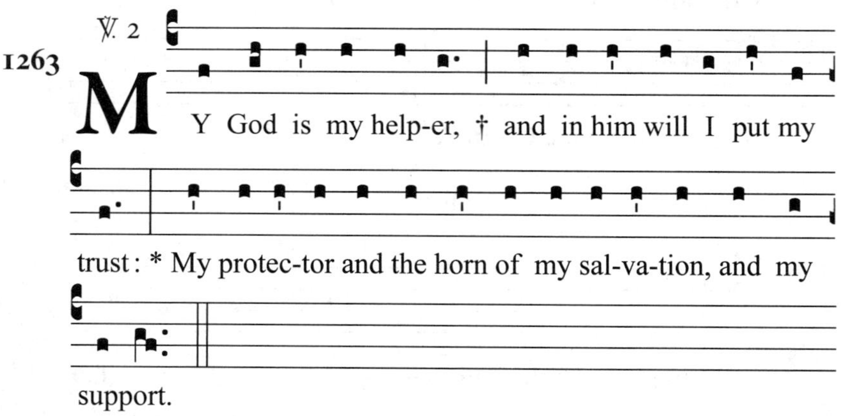
℣. 2
MY God is my help-er, † and in him will I put my
trust: * My protec-tor and the horn of my sal-va-tion, and my
support.

Laudans invocabo Dominum. Ps 17:4

1264

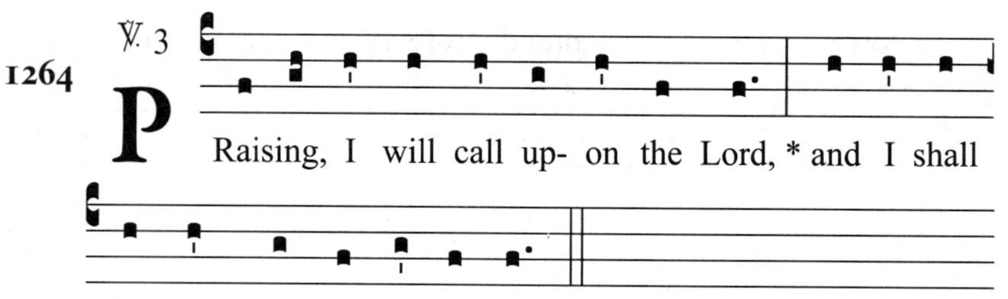
℣. 3
PRaising, I will call up- on the Lord, * and I shall
be saved from my en- e- mies.

- iii -

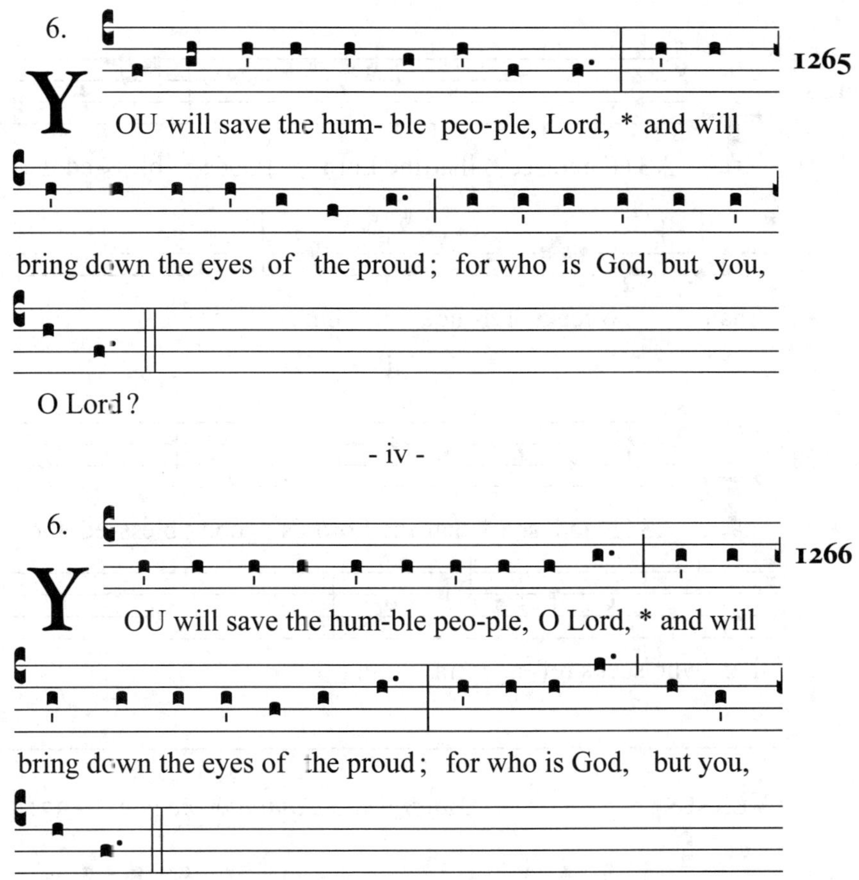
6.
YOU will save the hum- ble peo-ple, Lord, * and will 1265
bring down the eyes of the proud; for who is God, but you,
O Lord?
- iv -
6.
YOU will save the hum-ble peo-ple, O Lord, * and will 1266
bring down the eyes of the proud; for who is God, but you,
O Lord?

Communion Antiphon

Gustate et videte. Ps 33:9

- i -

1267

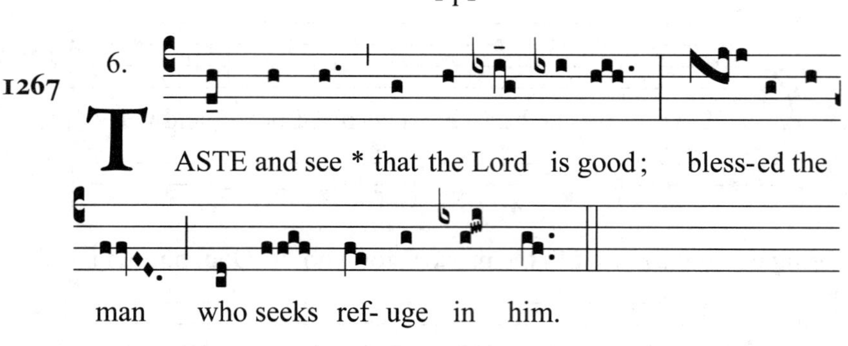
6.
TASTE and see * that the Lord is good; bless-ed the
man who seeks ref- uge in him.

- ii -

1268

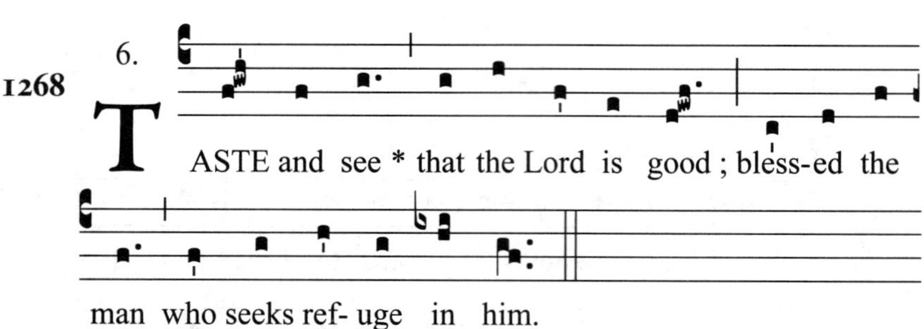
6.
TASTE and see * that the Lord is good ; bless-ed the
man who seeks ref- uge in him.

Verses

Magnificate Dominum mecum. Ps 33:4

1269

1270

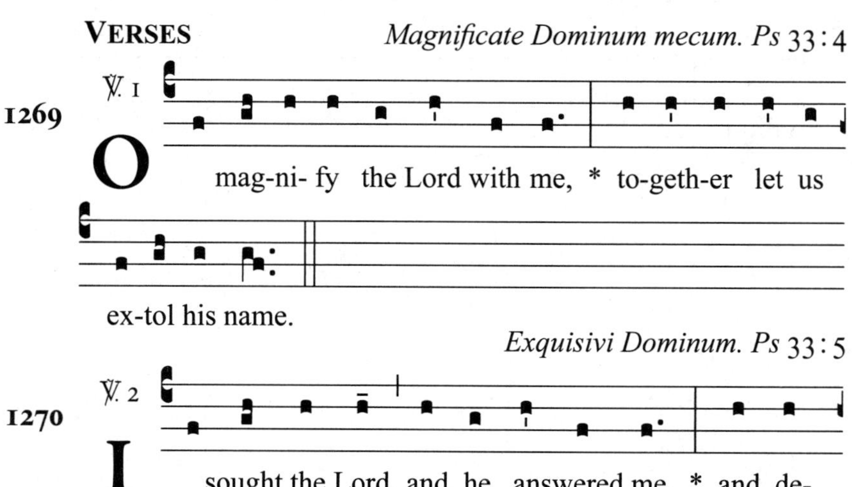
℣. 1
O mag-ni- fy the Lord with me, * to-geth-er let us
ex-tol his name.
Exquisivi Dominum. Ps 33:5
℣. 2
I sought the Lord, and he answered me, * and de-

liv-ered me from all my fears.

Immittet angelus Domini. Ps 33:8

℣. 3 THE an- gel of the Lord encamps * around those who 1271

fear him, to res-cue them.

Gustate et videte. Ps 33:9

℣. 4 O taste and see how gracious the Lord is; * blessed the 1272

man who hopes in him.

Timete Dominum. Ps 33:10

℣. 5 O fear the Lord, all you his saints, * for those who fear 1273

him have no want.

Iuxta est Dominus iis. Ps 33:19

℣. 6 THE Lord is near to the bro-ken-heart-ed, * and those 1274

who are crushed in spir- it he will save.

- iii -

1275

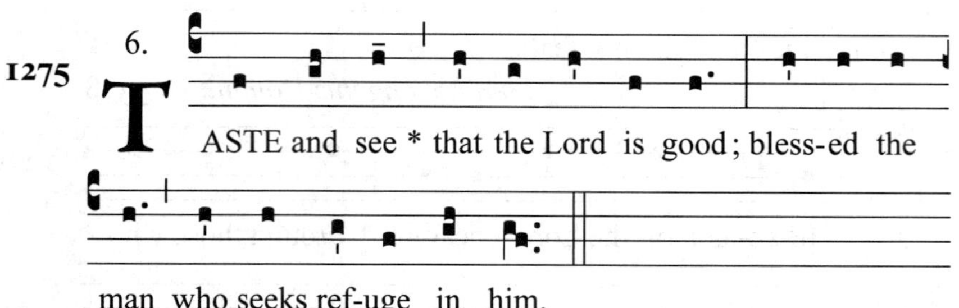
6.
TASTE and see * that the Lord is good; bless-ed the
man who seeks ref-uge in him.

- iv -

1276

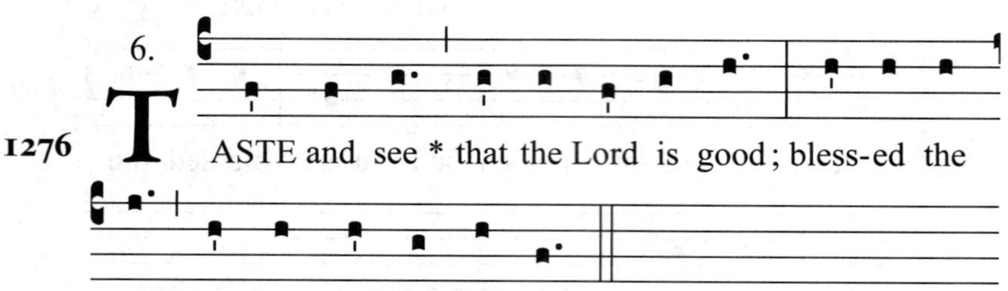
6.
TASTE and see * that the Lord is good; bless-ed the
man who seeks ref- uge in him.

FIFTEENTH SUNDAY IN ORDINARY TIME

ENTRANCE ANTIPHON *Ego autem cum iustitia. Ps* 16 : 15

- i -

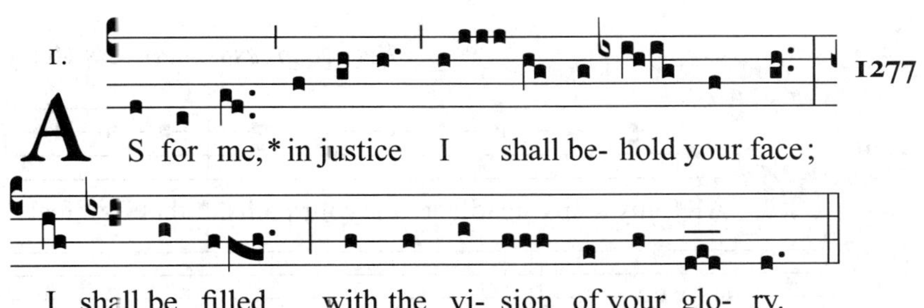
I.
AS for me,* in justice I shall be- hold your face;
1277
I shall be filled with the vi- sion of your glo- ry.

- ii -

I.
AS for me,* in jus-tice I shall be- hold your face;
1278
I shall be filled with the vi- sion of your glo- ry.

VERSES *Exaudi, Domine, iustitiam meam. Ps* 16 : 1

1279 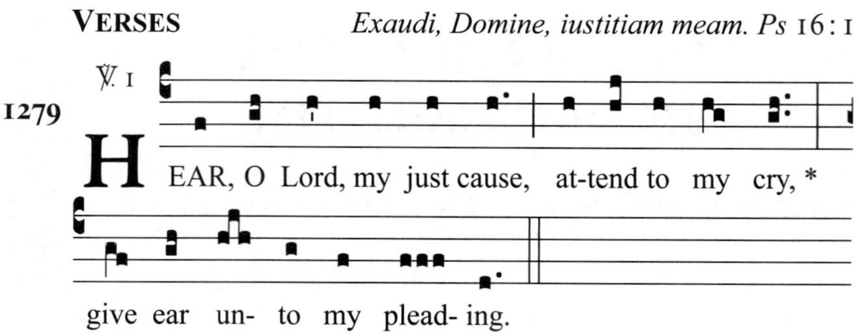
℣. 1
HEAR, O Lord, my just cause, at-tend to my cry, *
give ear un- to my plead- ing.

Perfice gressus meos. Ps 16 : 5

1280 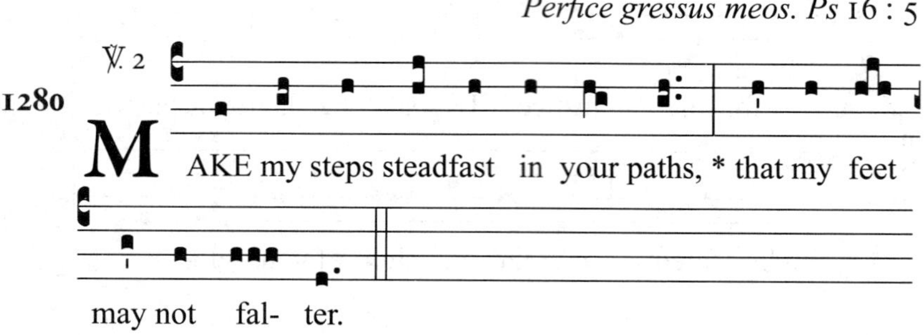
℣. 2
MAKE my steps steadfast in your paths, * that my feet
may not fal- ter.

Custodi me ut pupillam oculi. Ps 16 : 8

1281 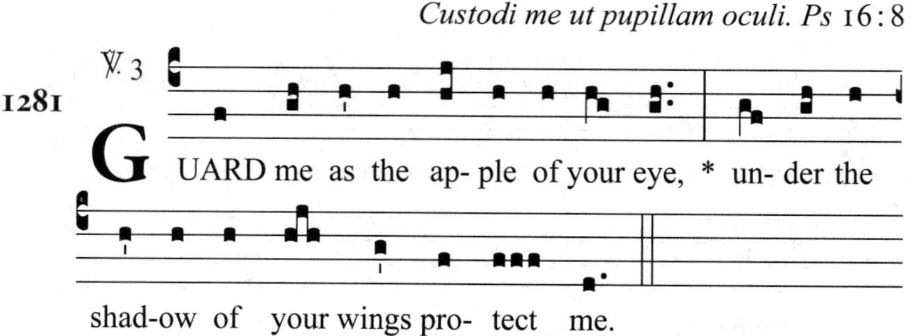
℣. 3
GUARD me as the ap- ple of your eye, * un- der the
shad-ow of your wings pro- tect me.

- iii -

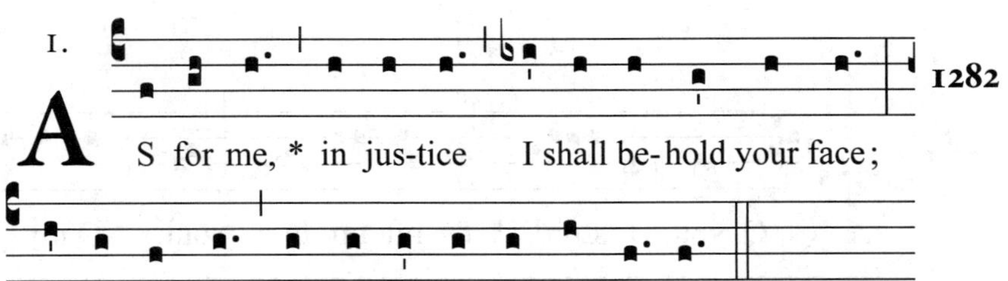
1.
1282
AS for me, * in jus-tice I shall be-hold your face;
I shall be filled with the vi-sion of your glo- ry.

- iv -

1.
1283
AS for me, in jus-tice * I shall be-hold your face;
I shall be filled with the vi-sion of your glo- ry.

Offertory Antiphon *Ad te, Domine, levavi. Ps* 24:1-3

- i -

1284

2.
TO you, O Lord, * I lift up my soul. O my
God, in you I have trust-ed; let me not be put to
shame. Nor let my en- e- mies ex- ult o- ver
me; and let none who hope in you be put to shame.

- ii -

1285

2.
TO you, O Lord, * I lift up my soul. O my
God, in you I have trust- ed; let me not be put to
shame. Nor let my en- e-mies ex- ult o-ver me; and let
none who hope in you be put to shame.

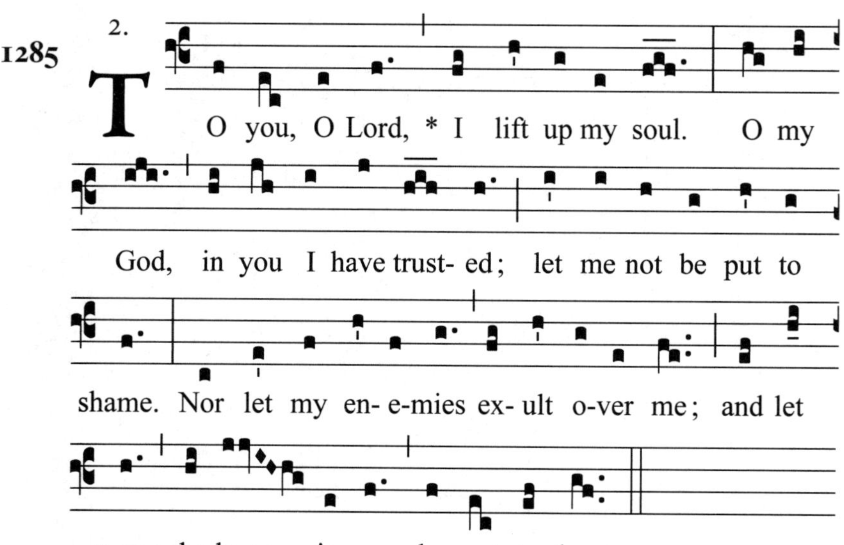

VERSES *Reminiscere miserationum tuarum. Ps* 24 : 6-7

℣. 1
R E-mem-ber your compassion, O Lord, and your mer-
ci- ful love, for they are from of old. * In your mer-ci-ful
love re-member me, because of your goodness, O Lord.
1286

De necessitatibus meis. Ps 24 : 17-18

℣. 2
S ET me free from my distress. See my low- li- ness and
suf-fer-ing, * and take a- way all my sins.
1287

Custodi animam meam. Ps 24 : 20

℣. 3
K EEP my soul, and de- liv- er me; I shall not be
ashamed, * for I have hoped in you.
1288

- iii -

1289

2.
TO you, O Lord, I lift up my soul. * O my God,
in you I have trust-ed; let me not be put to shame.
Nor let my en- e-mies ex- ult o- ver me; and let none
who hope in you be put to shame.

Or:

1290

2.
TO you, O Lord, I lift up my soul. * O my God,
in you I have trust-ed; let me not be put to shame.
Nor let my en- e-mies ex- ult o- ver me; and let none
who hope in you be put to shame.

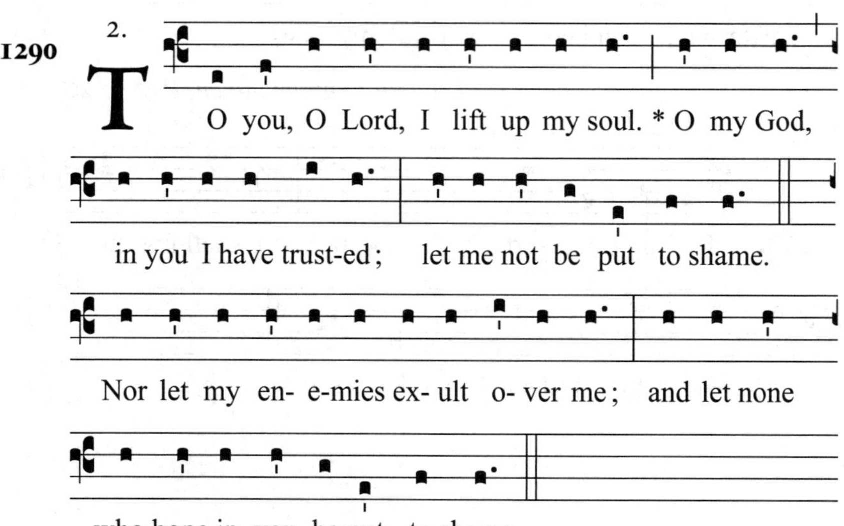

- iv -

2. 1291

TO you, O Lord, I lift up my soul. * O my God,
in you I have trust-ed; let me not be put to shame.
Nor let my en- e-mies ex- ult o- ver me; and let none
who hope in you be put to shame.

COMMUNION ANTIPHON *Paser invenit sibi domum.*
Ps 83:4-5

- i -

1292
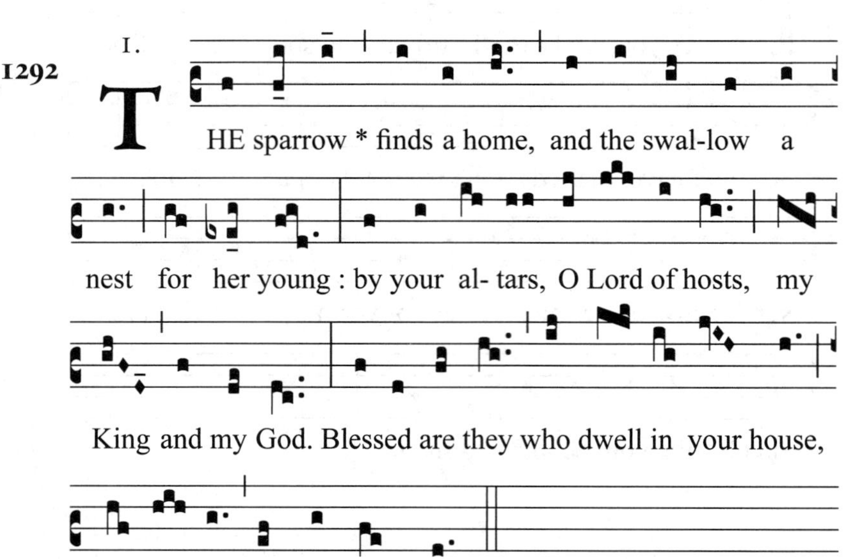
I.
THE sparrow * finds a home, and the swal-low a
nest for her young : by your al- tars, O Lord of hosts, my
King and my God. Blessed are they who dwell in your house,
for ev- er sing-ing your praise.

- ii -

The sparrow finds a home, p. 184

VERSES. *Quam dilecta tabernacula tua. Ps* 83:2

1293
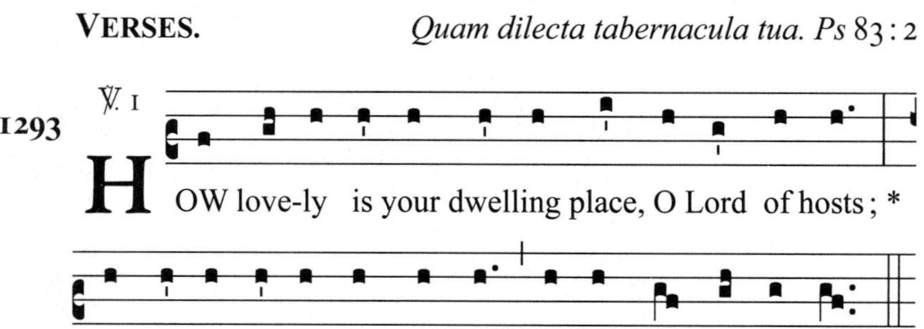
℣. I
HOW love-ly is your dwelling place, O Lord of hosts; *
my soul is longing and yearning for the courts of the Lord.

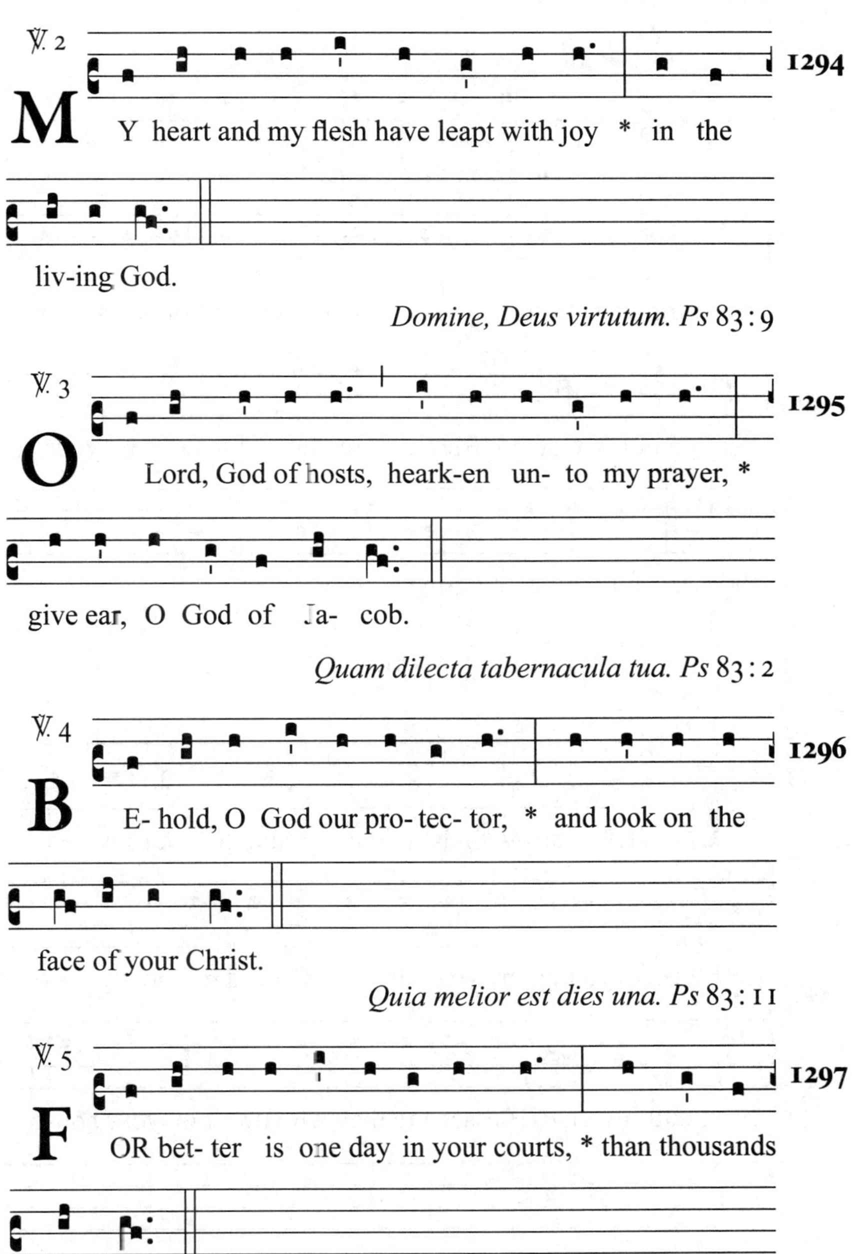
Cor meum et caro mea. Ps 83:3
℣. 2
1294
MY heart and my flesh have leapt with joy * in the
liv-ing God.
Domine, Deus virtutum. Ps 83:9
℣. 3
1295
O Lord, God of hosts, heark-en un- to my prayer, *
give ear, O God of Ja- cob.
Quam dilecta tabernacula tua. Ps 83:2
℣. 4
1296
BE- hold, O God our pro- tec- tor, * and look on the
face of your Christ.
Quia melior est dies una. Ps 83:11
℣. 5
1297
FOR bet- ter is one day in your courts, * than thousands
else-where.

- iii -

1298

I.
THE sparrow finds a home, * and the swal-low a
nest for her young : by your al- tars, O Lord of hosts, my
King and my God. Blessed are they who dwell in your
house, for ev- er sing-ing your praise.

- iv -

1299

I.
THE sparrow finds a home, * and the swal-low a
nest for her young : by your al- tars, O Lord of hosts, my
King and my God. Blessed are they who dwell in your house,
for ev- er sing-ing your praise.

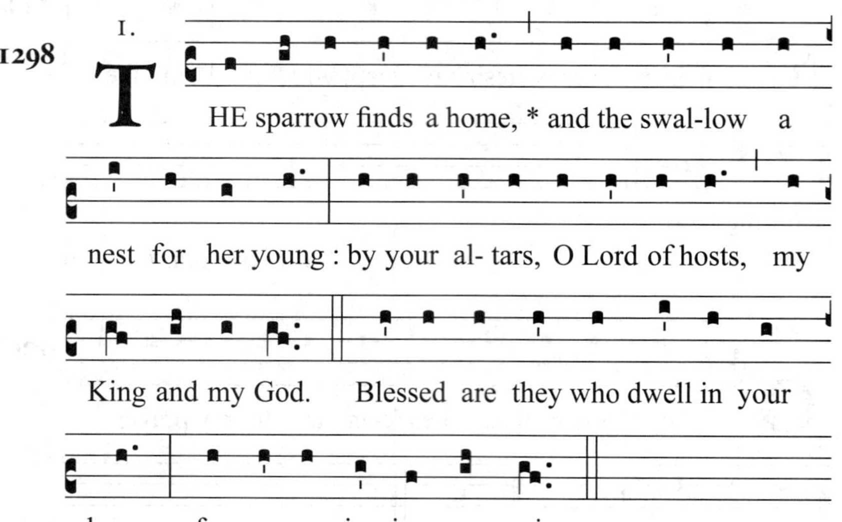

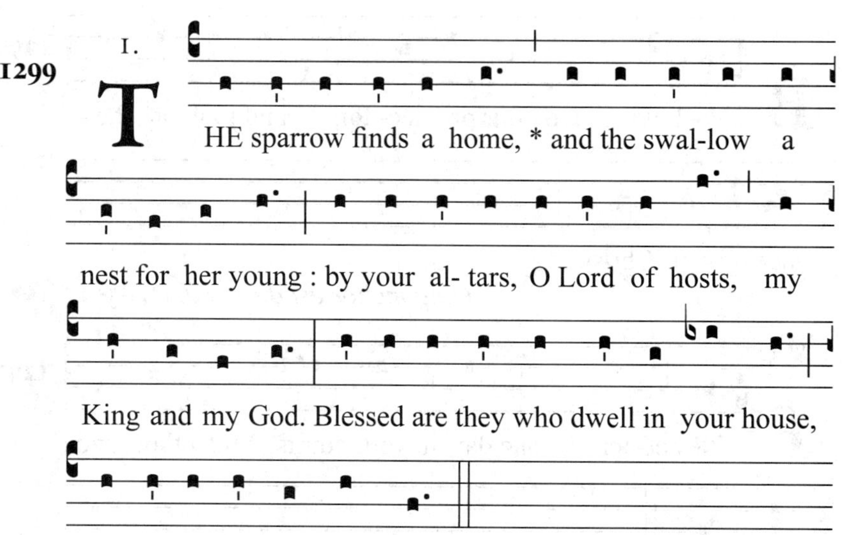

SIXTEENTH SUNDAY IN ORDINARY TIME

ENTRANCE ANTIPHON *Ecce Deus adiuvat me.*
Ps 53 : 6. 8

- i -

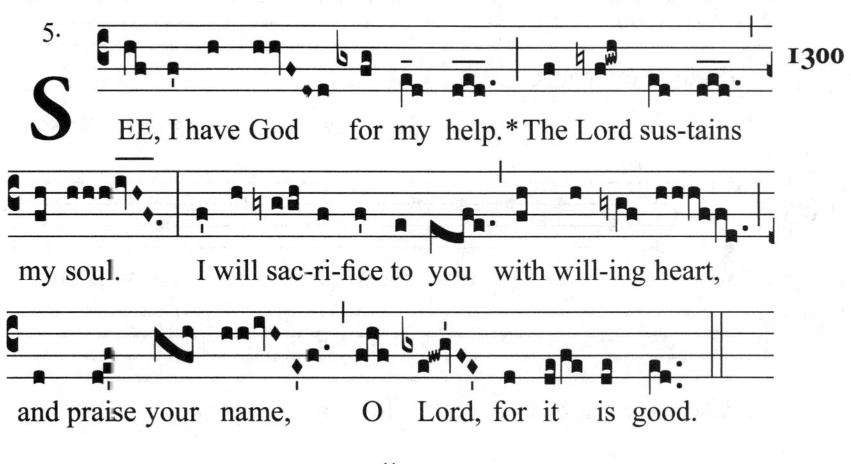
5.
1300
SEE, I have God for my help. * The Lord sus-tains
my soul. I will sac-ri-fice to you with will-ing heart,
and praise your name, O Lord, for it is good.

- ii -

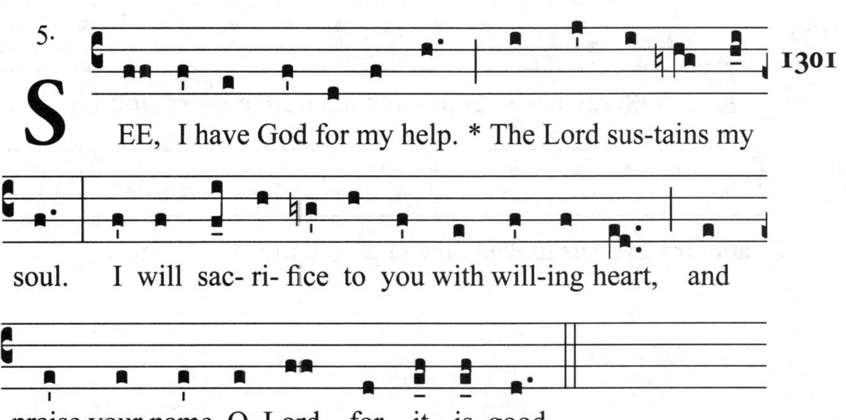
5.
1301
SEE, I have God for my help. * The Lord sus-tains my
soul. I will sac- ri- fice to you with will-ing heart, and
praise your name, O Lord, for it is good.

VERSES

With antiphon -i-, *sing* te *(flat)*; *with antiphon* -ii-, *sing* ti *(natural).*

Deus, in nomine tuo. Ps 53:3

1302 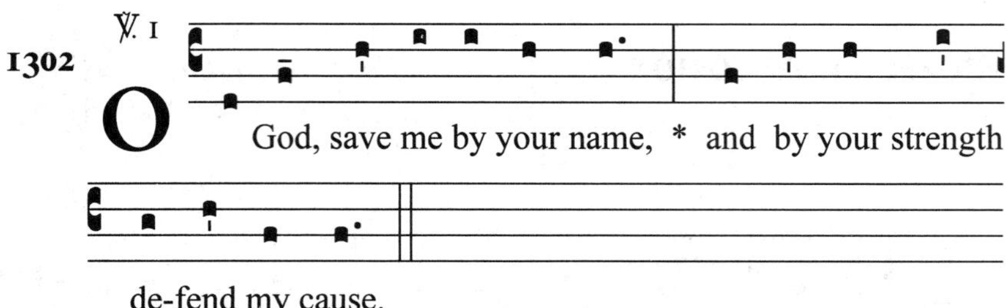
℣. 1
O God, save me by your name, * and by your strength
de-fend my cause.

Voluntarie sacrificabo tibi. Ps 53:8

1303 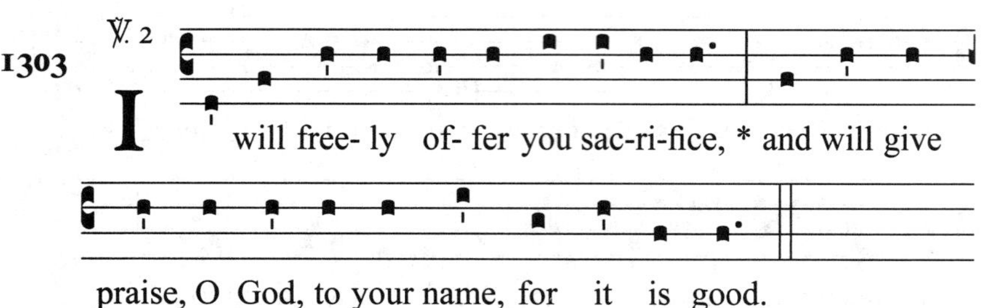
℣. 2
I will free- ly of- fer you sac-ri-fice, * and will give
praise, O God, to your name, for it is good.

Quoniam ex omni tribulatione. Ps 53:8

1304 
℣. 3
FOR you have de- liv-ered me from ev'- ry trou-ble, *
and my eye has looked down up- on my en- e- mies.

- iii -

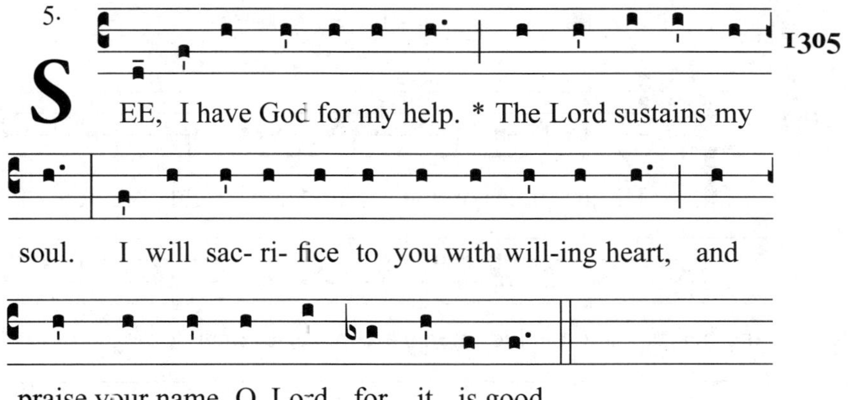
5.
1305
SEE, I have God for my help. * The Lord sustains my
soul. I will sac- ri- fice to you with will-ing heart, and
praise your name, O Lord, for it is good.

- iv -

5.
1306
SEE, I have God for my help. * The Lord sustains my
soul. I will sac- ri- fice to you with will-ing heart, and
praise your name, O Lord, for it is good.

OFFERTORY ANTIPHON *Iustitiæ Domini rectæ.*
Ps 18:9. 10. 11. 12

- i -

1307

4.
THE jus- ti-ces of the Lord * are right, re-joic-
ing hearts, and his judgments are sweet-er than hon-ey and
the hon- ey-comb, for your ser-vant keeps them.

- ii -

1308

4.
THE jus- ti-ces * of the Lord are right, re-joic-ing
hearts, and his judgments are sweet-er than hon- ey and the
hon-ey-comb, for your servant keeps them.

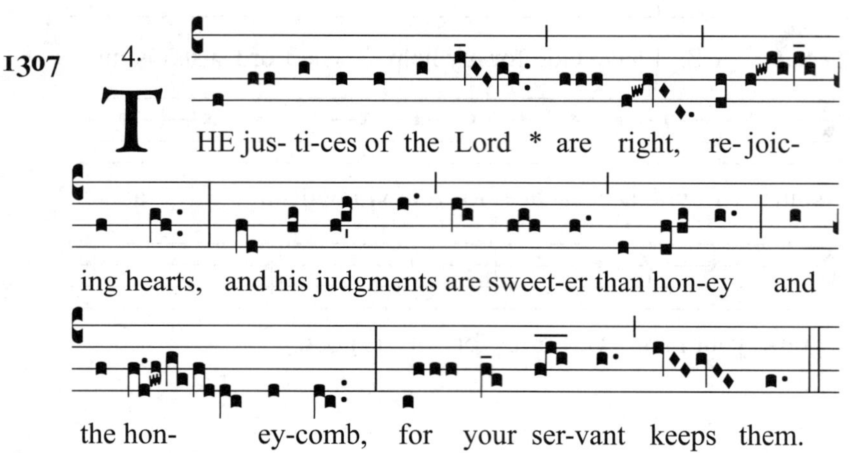

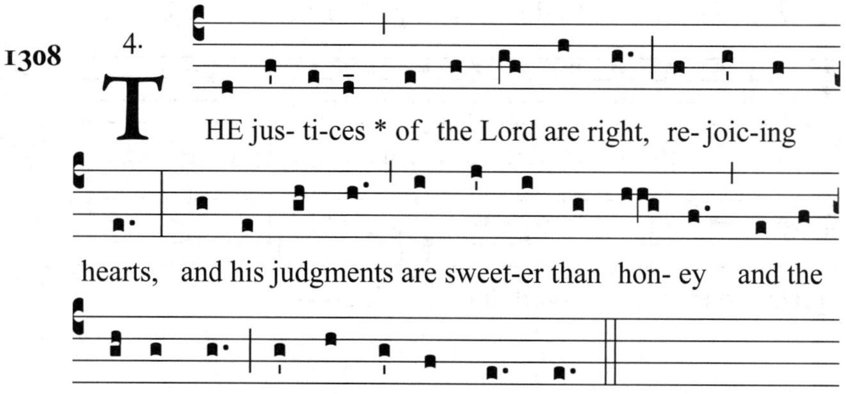

Lex Domini immaculata. Ps 18:8

℣. 1
1309
THE law of the Lord is perfect; it revives the soul. *
The decrees of the Lord are faithful, giv-ing wis-dom to
lit- tle ones.

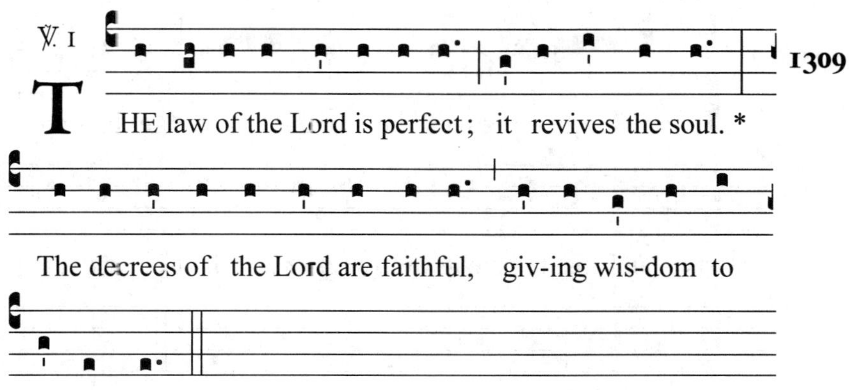

Timor Domini sanctus. Ps 18:10

℣. 2
1310
THE fear of the Lord is ho- ly, * en- dur- ing for-
ev- er and ev- er.

Desiderabilia super aurum. Ps 18:11

℣. 3
1311
THEY are more to be desired than gold and man-y
precious stones; * and sweet-er than hon- ey and the hon-ey-
comb.

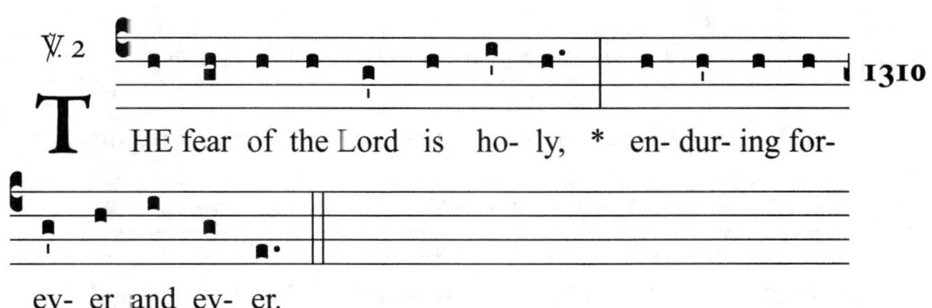

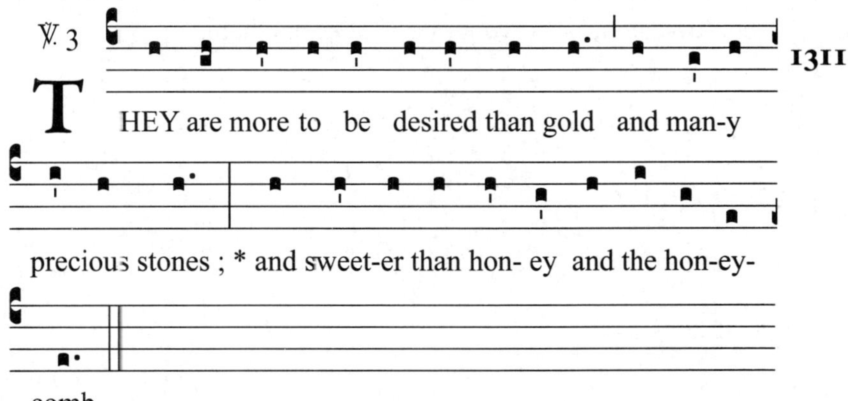

- iii -

1312
4.
T HE jus- ti-ces of the Lord are right, * re-joic-ing
hearts, and his judgments are sweet-er than hon-ey and the
hon- ey-comb, for your ser-vant keeps them.

- iv -

1313
4.
T HE jus- ti-ces of the Lord are right, * re-joic-ing
hearts, and his judgments are sweet-er than hon-ey and the
hon-ey-comb, for your ser-vant keeps them.

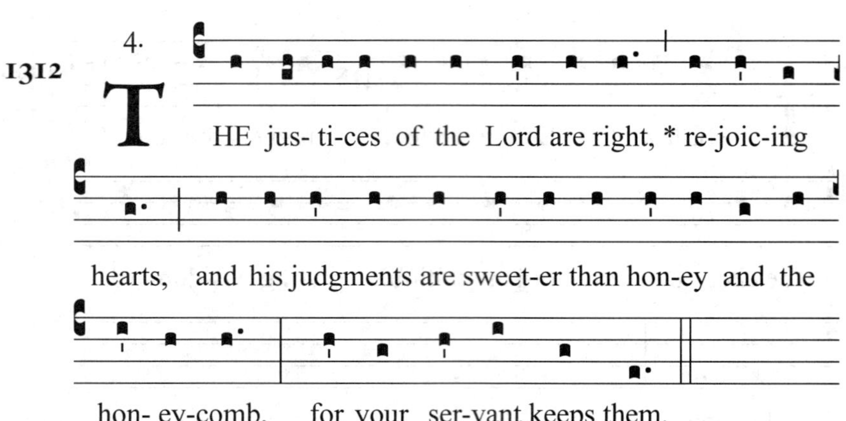

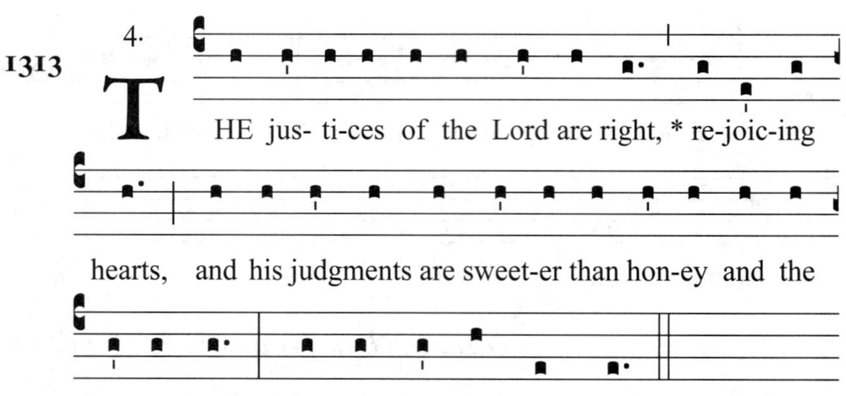

COMMUNION ANTIPHON *Memoriam fecit mirabilium suorum.* *Ps* 110:4-5

- i -

4\. 1314

THE Lord, * the gracious, the mer- ci- ful, has made a me- mo- ri- al of his won-ders ; he gives food to those who fear him.

- ii -

4\. 1315

THE Lord, * the gracious, the mer- ci- ful, has made a me- mo- ri- al of his won-ders ; he gives food to those who fear him.

VERSES *Confitebor tibi, Domine.* *Ps* 110:1

℣. 1 1316

I will praise you, O Lord, with all my heart, * in the com- pa- ny of the just and their as-sem-bly.

Magna opera Domini. Ps 110:2

1317

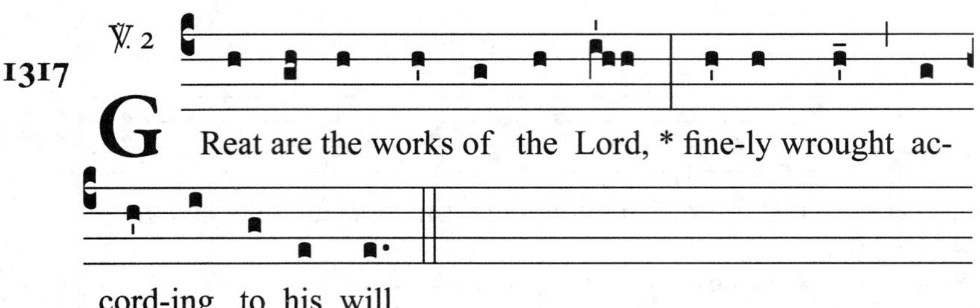
℣. 2
GReat are the works of the Lord, * fine-ly wrought ac-
cord-ing to his will.

Confessio et magnificentia opus eius. Ps 110:3

1318

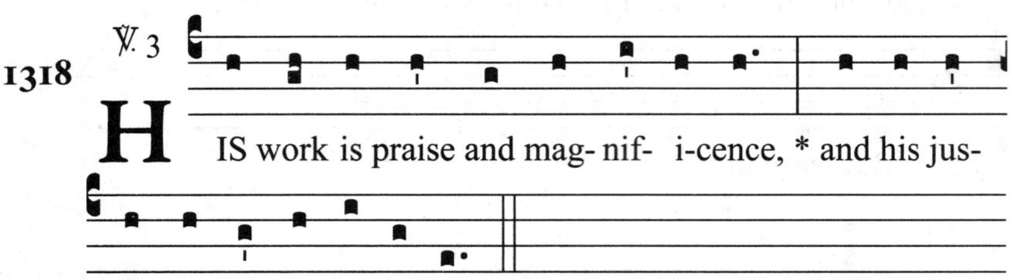
℣. 3
HIS work is praise and mag- nif- i-cence, * and his jus-
tice con-tin-ues for-ev- er.

Memor erit in saeculum testamenti eius. Ps 110:5-6

1319

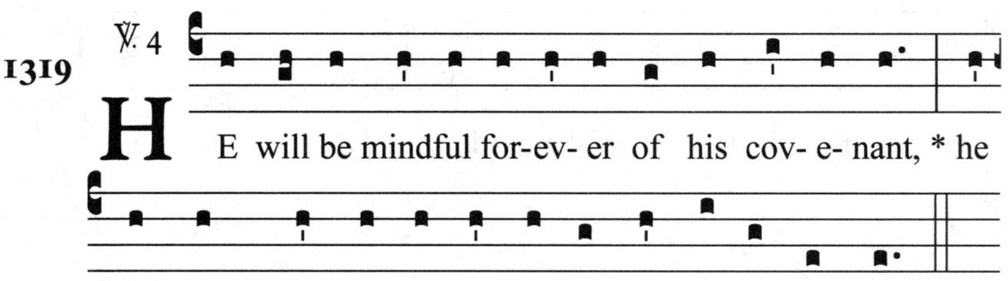
℣. 4
HE will be mindful for-ev- er of his cov- e- nant, * he
will make known to his peo-ple the pow- er of his works.

Fidelia omnia mandata eius. Ps 110:8

1320

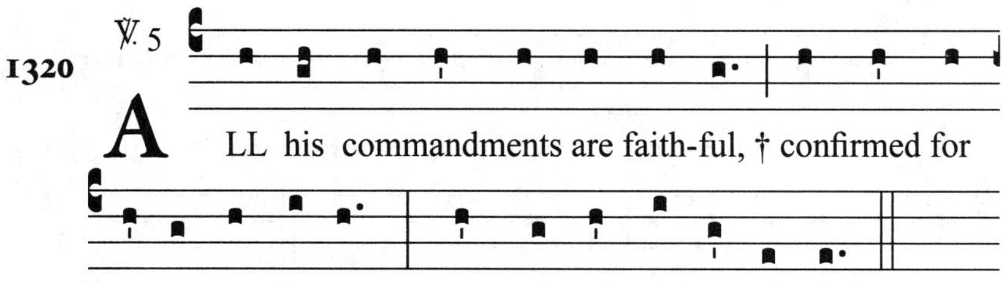
℣. 5
ALL his commandments are faith-ful, † confirmed for
ev- er and ev- er, * wrought in truth and eq- ui- ty.

- iii -

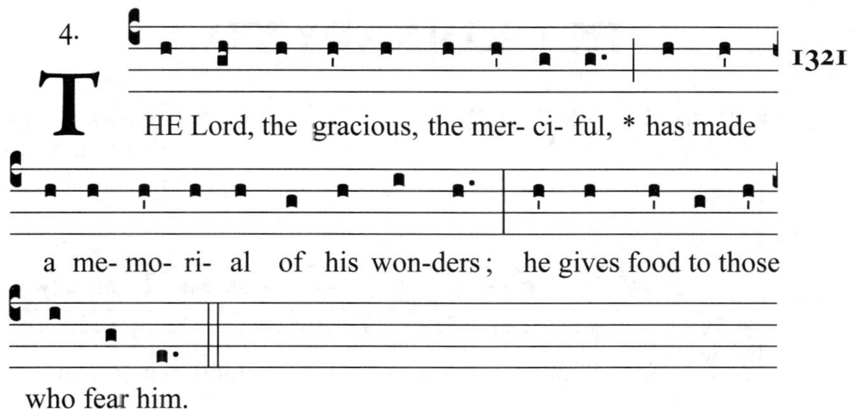
4.
1321
THE Lord, the gracious, the mer- ci- ful, * has made
a me- mo- ri- al of his won-ders; he gives food to those
who fear him.

- iv -

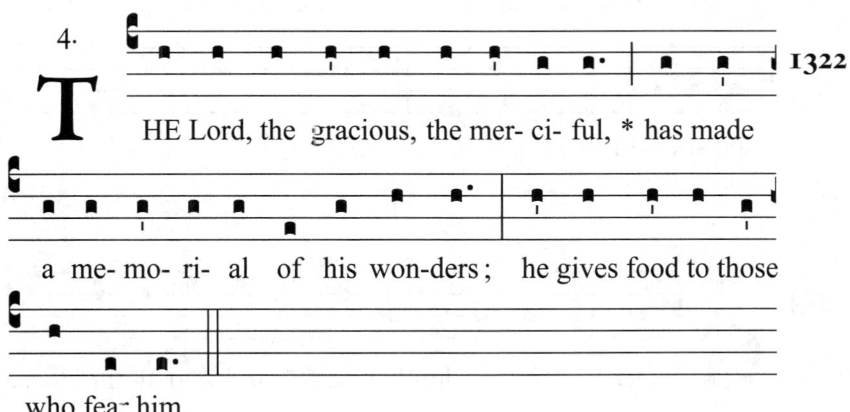
4.
1322
THE Lord, the gracious, the mer- ci- ful, * has made
a me- mo- ri- al of his won-ders; he gives food to those
who fear him.

SEVENTEENTH SUNDAY IN ORDINARY TIME

Entrance Antiphon *Deus in loco sancto suo.*
Ps 67:6-7. 36

- i -

1323

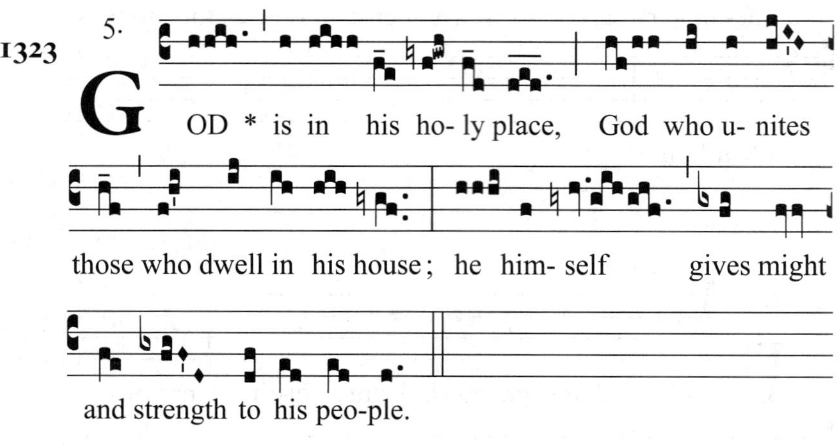
5.
GOD * is in his ho- ly place, God who u- nites
those who dwell in his house; he him- self gives might
and strength to his peo-ple.

- ii -

1324 5.

GOD is in his ho- ly place, * God who u-nites those
who dwell in his house ; he himself gives might and strength
to his peo-ple.

VERSES *Exsurgat Deus. Ps* 67:2

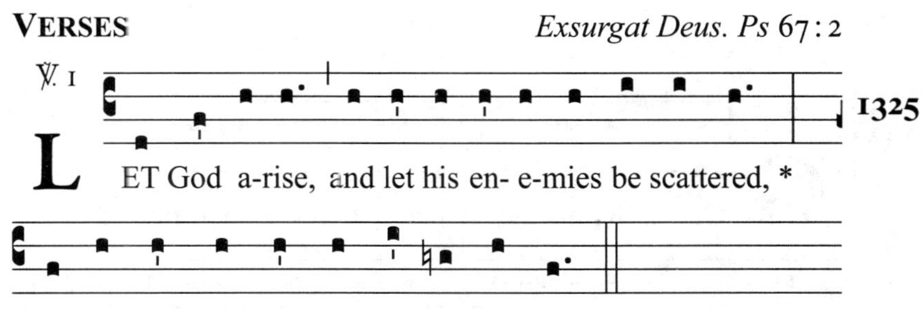
℣. 1
LET God a-rise, and let his en- e-mies be scattered, * 1325
and let them that hate him flee be-fore him.

Et iusti epulentur. Ps 67:4

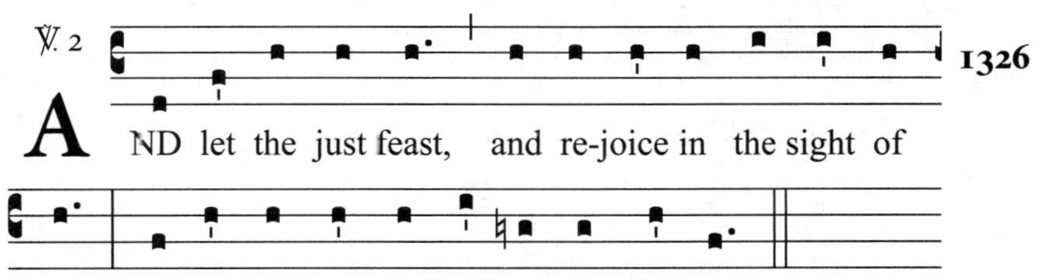
℣. 2
AND let the just feast, and re-joice in the sight of 1326
God, * and let them be de-light-ed with gladness.

Cantate Deo. Ps 67:5

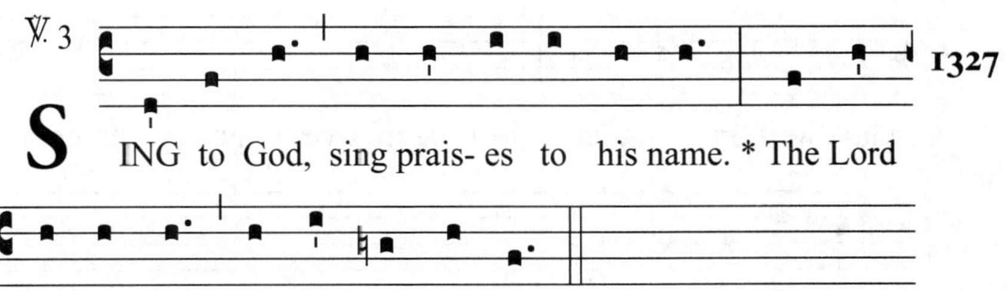
℣. 3
SING to God, sing prais- es to his name. * The Lord 1327
is his name. Re-joice be- fore him.

- iii -

1328

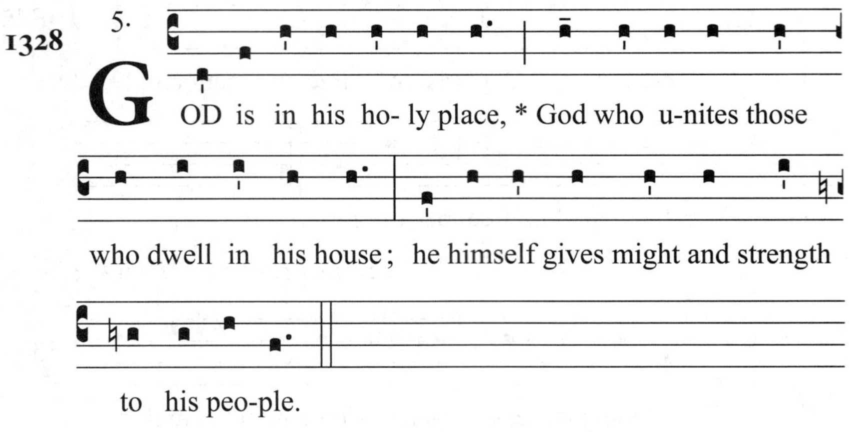

5.
GOD is in his ho- ly place, * God who u-nites those
who dwell in his house; he himself gives might and strength
to his peo-ple.

- iv -

1329

5.
GOD is in his ho- ly place, * God who u-nites those

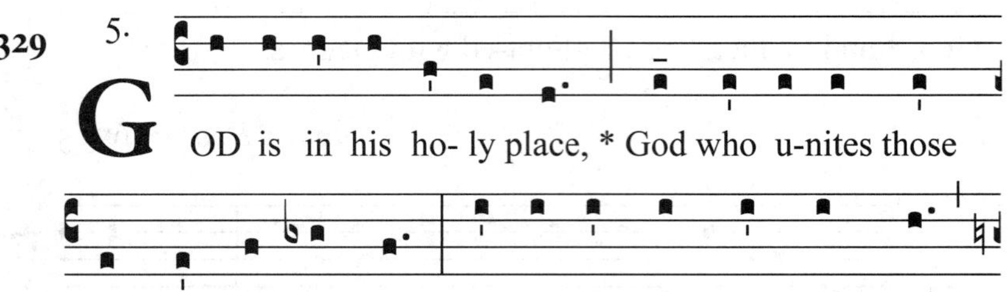

who dwell in his house; he himself gives might and strength

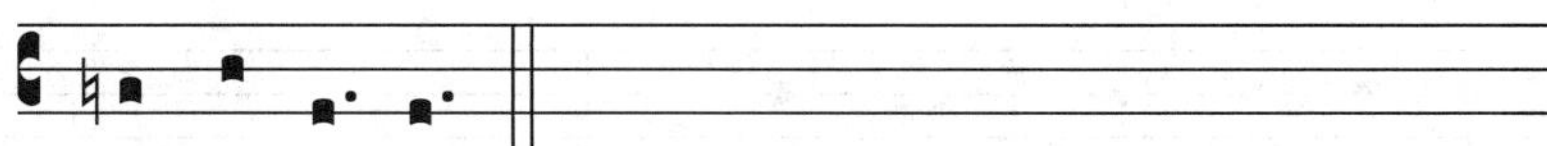

to his peo-ple.

Offertory Antiphon *Exaltabo te, Domine.*
Ps 29:2-3

- i -

2.
I will ex-tol you, O Lord,* for you have up-held
1330
me, and have not let my en- emies re- joice
o- ver me. O Lord, I have cried to you, and you
have healed me.

- ii -

2.
I will ex- tol you, O Lord, * for you have up-held
1331
me, and have not let my en- e- mies re-joice o- ver me.
O Lord, I have cried to you, and you have healed me.

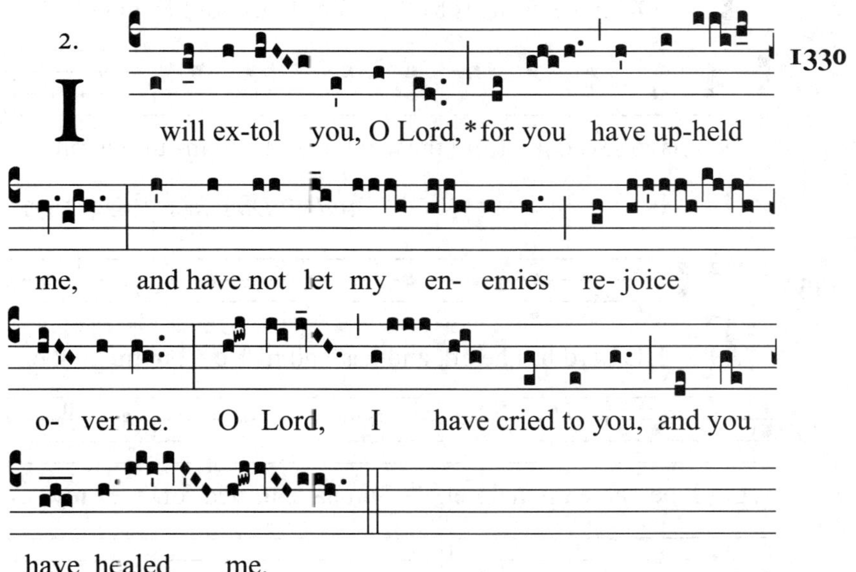

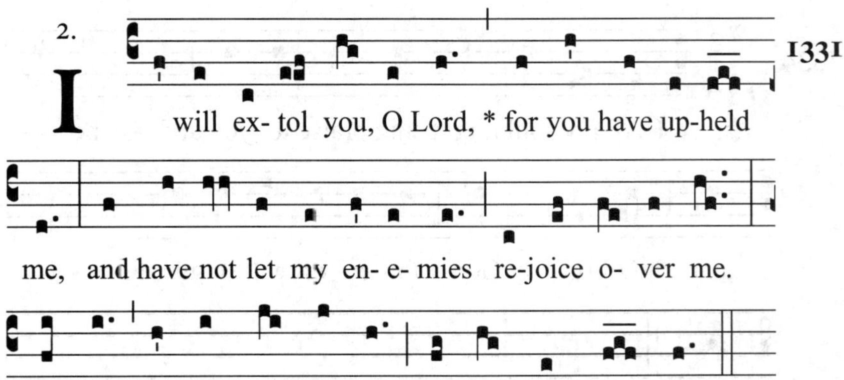

VERSES *Domine, eduxisti. Ps* 29 : 4

1332

℣. 1
YOU have brought forth, O Lord, my soul from hell ; *

you have saved me from those who go down in- to the pit.

Audivit Dominus. Ps 29 : 11-12

1333
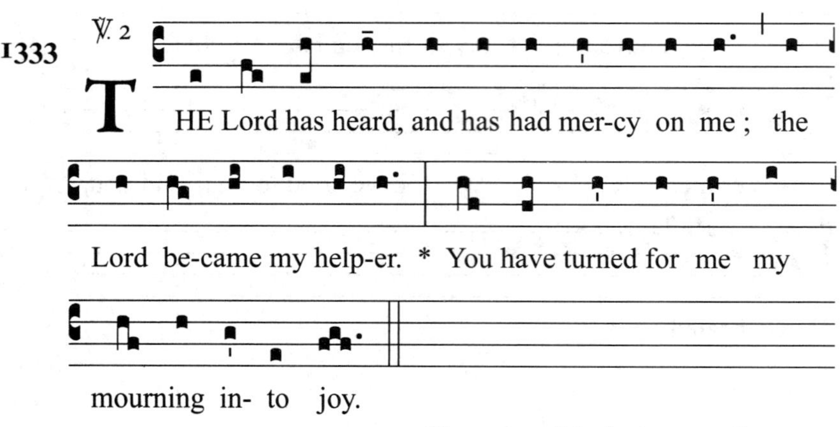
℣. 2
THE Lord has heard, and has had mer-cy on me ; the
Lord be-came my help-er. * You have turned for me my
mourning in- to joy.

Ut cantet tibi gloria mea. Ps 29 : 13

1334
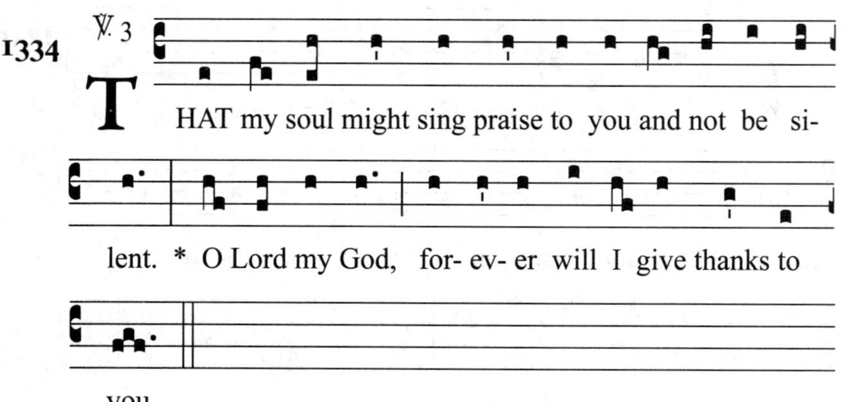
℣. 3
THAT my soul might sing praise to you and not be si-
lent. * O Lord my God, for- ev- er will I give thanks to
you.

- iii -

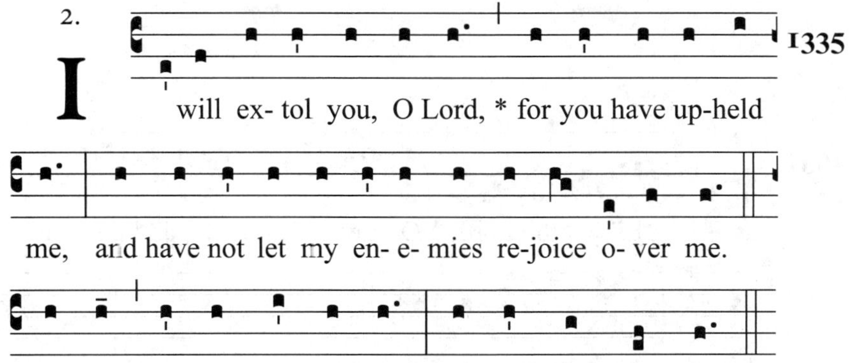

2.
I will ex- tol you, O Lord, * for you have up-held
1335
me, and have not let my en- e- mies re-joice o- ver me.

O Lord, I have cried to you, and you have healed me.

- iv -

2.
I will ex- tol you, O Lord, * for you have up-held
1336
me, and have not let my en- e- mies re-joice o- ver me.

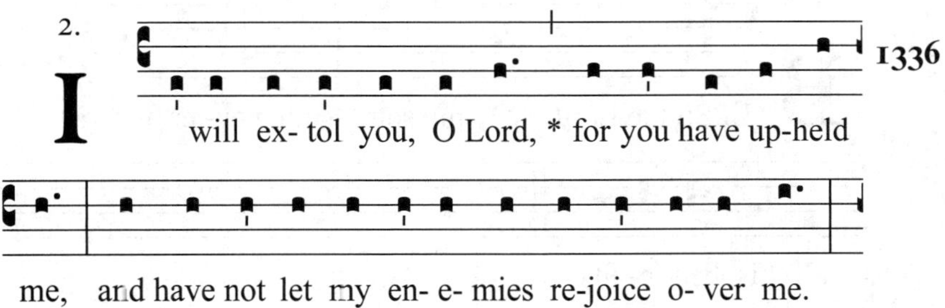

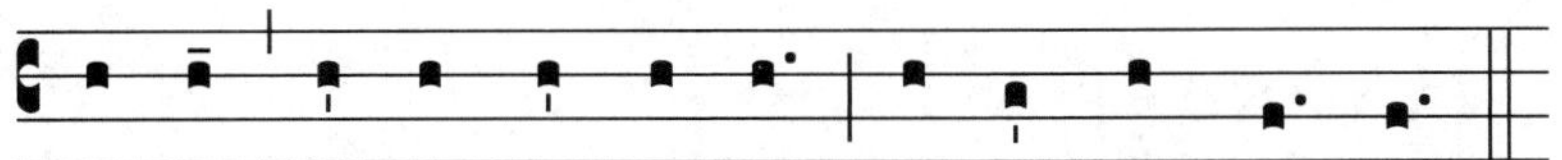

O Lord, I have cried to you, and you have healed me.

COMMUNION ANTIPHON *Benedic, anima mea, Domino.*
Ps 102:2

- i -

1337

8.
BLESS the Lord, * O my soul, and nev- er
for- get all his ben- e- fits.

- ii -

1338
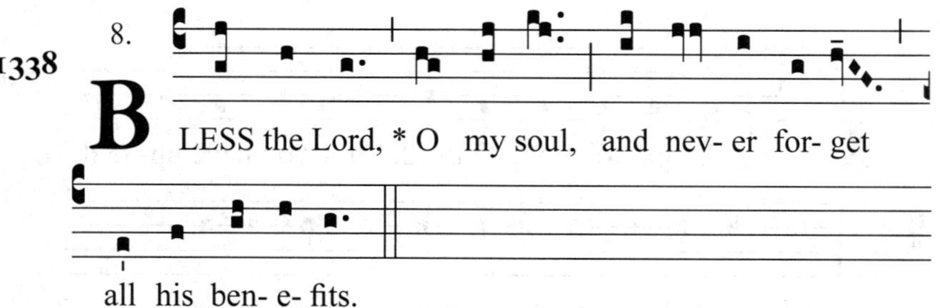
8.
BLESS the Lord, * O my soul, and nev- er for- get
all his ben- e- fits.

VERSES *Miserator et misericors Dominus. Ps* 102:8

℣. 1
1339
THE Lord is mer-ci-ful and gracious, * slow to an-ger
and a-bound-ing in mer- cy.

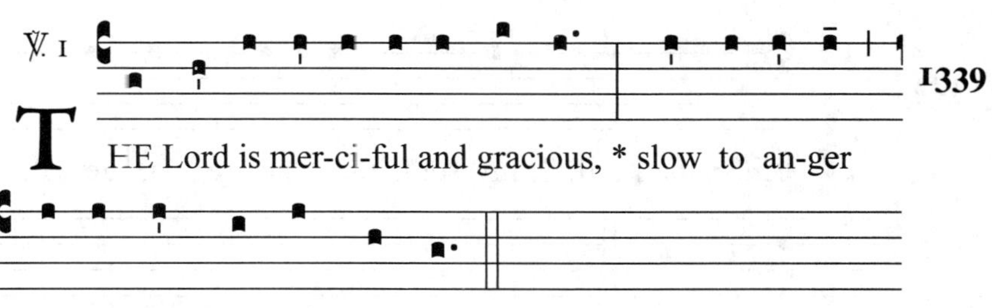

Non in perpetuum irascetur. Ps 102:9

℣. 2
1340
HE will not al-ways be an- gry, * nor will he threat-
en for ev- er.

Misericordia autem Domini. Ps 102:17

℣. 3
1341
THE mer-cy of the Lord is from ev- er-last-ing to ev-
er-last-ing * up- on those who fear him.

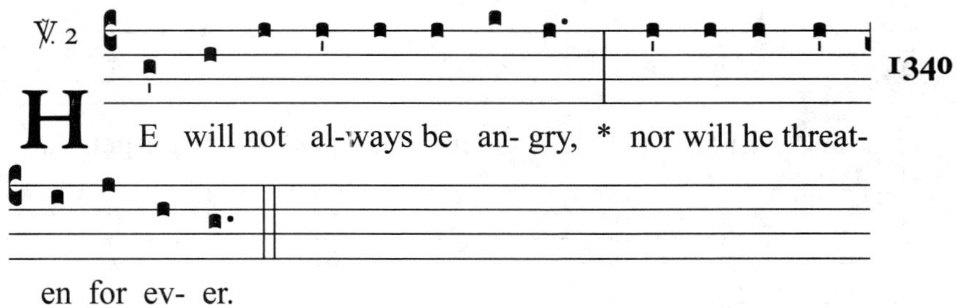

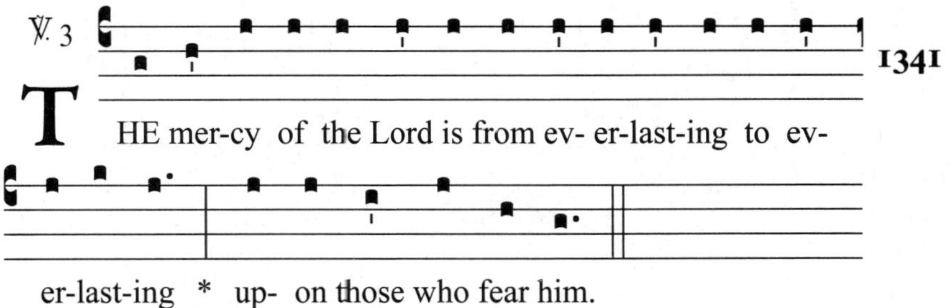

- iii -

1342

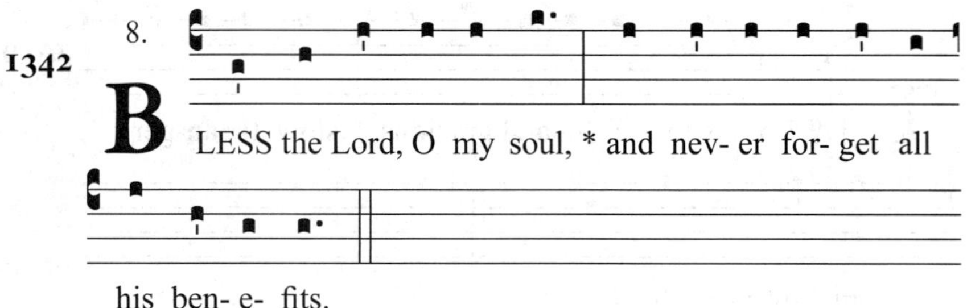
8.
BLESS the Lord, O my soul, * and nev- er for- get all
his ben- e- fits.

- iv -

1343

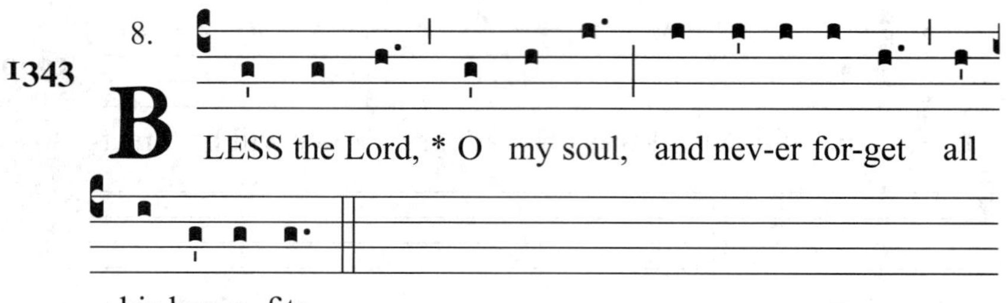
8.
BLESS the Lord, * O my soul, and nev-er for-get all
his ben-e- fits.

EIGHTEENTH SUNDAY IN ORDINARY TIME

Entrance Antiphon *Deus in adiutorium meum.*
Ps 69:2. 6

- i -

8.
1344
O God, * come to my as- sis-tance; O Lord, make
haste to help me! You are my res- cu- er, my help;
O Lord, do not de- lay.

- ii -

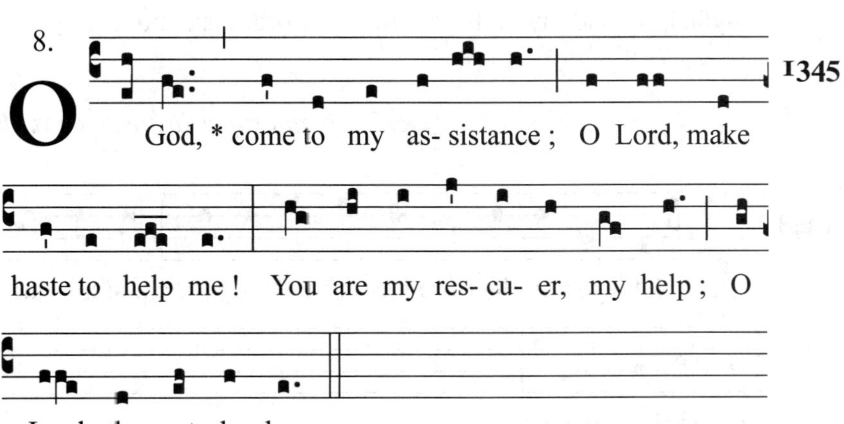
8.
1345
O God, * come to my as- sistance; O Lord, make
haste to help me! You are my res- cu- er, my help; O
Lord, do not de- lay.

VERSES *Exsultent et lætentur in te. Ps* 69:5

1346

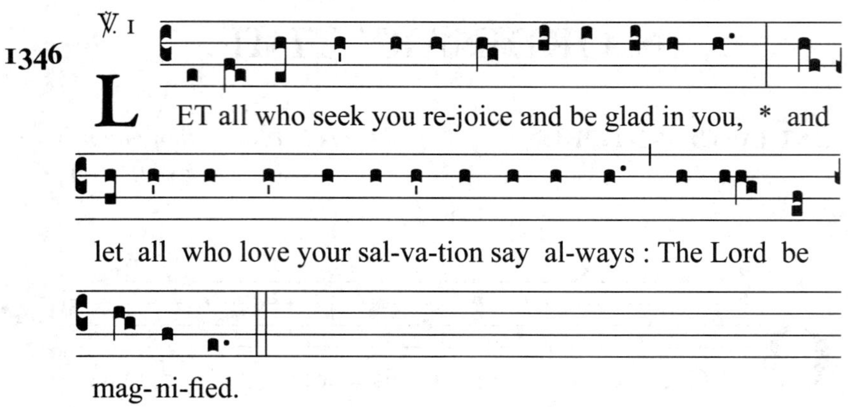
℣. 1
LET all who seek you re-joice and be glad in you, * and
let all who love your sal-va-tion say al-ways : The Lord be
mag-ni-fied.

Ego vero egenus et pauper sum. Ps 69:6

1347

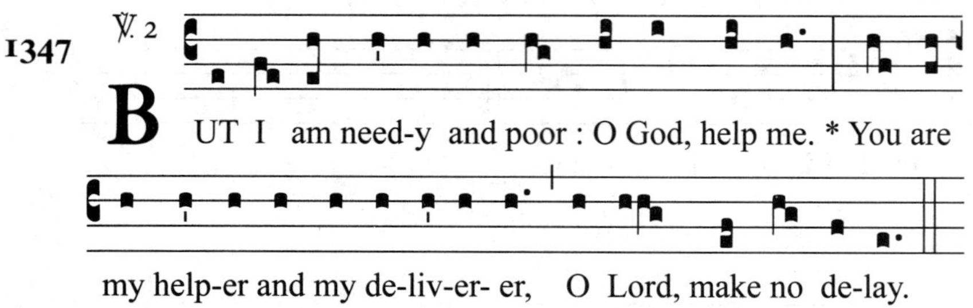
℣. 2
BUT I am need-y and poor : O God, help me. * You are
my help-er and my de-liv-er-er, O Lord, make no de-lay.

Oculi Domini super iustos. Ps 33:16

1348

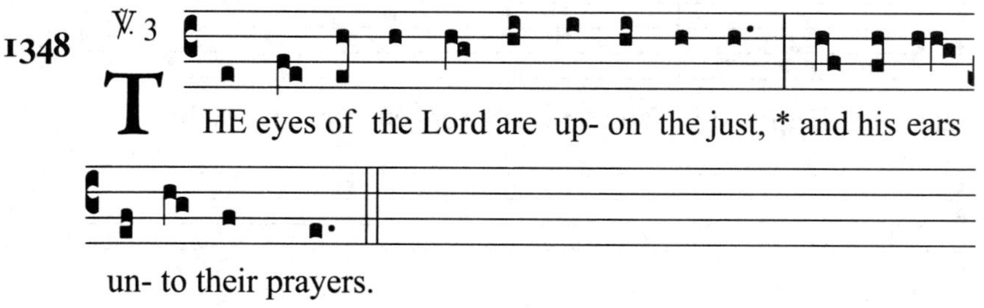
℣. 3
THE eyes of the Lord are up-on the just, * and his ears
un-to their prayers.

- iii -

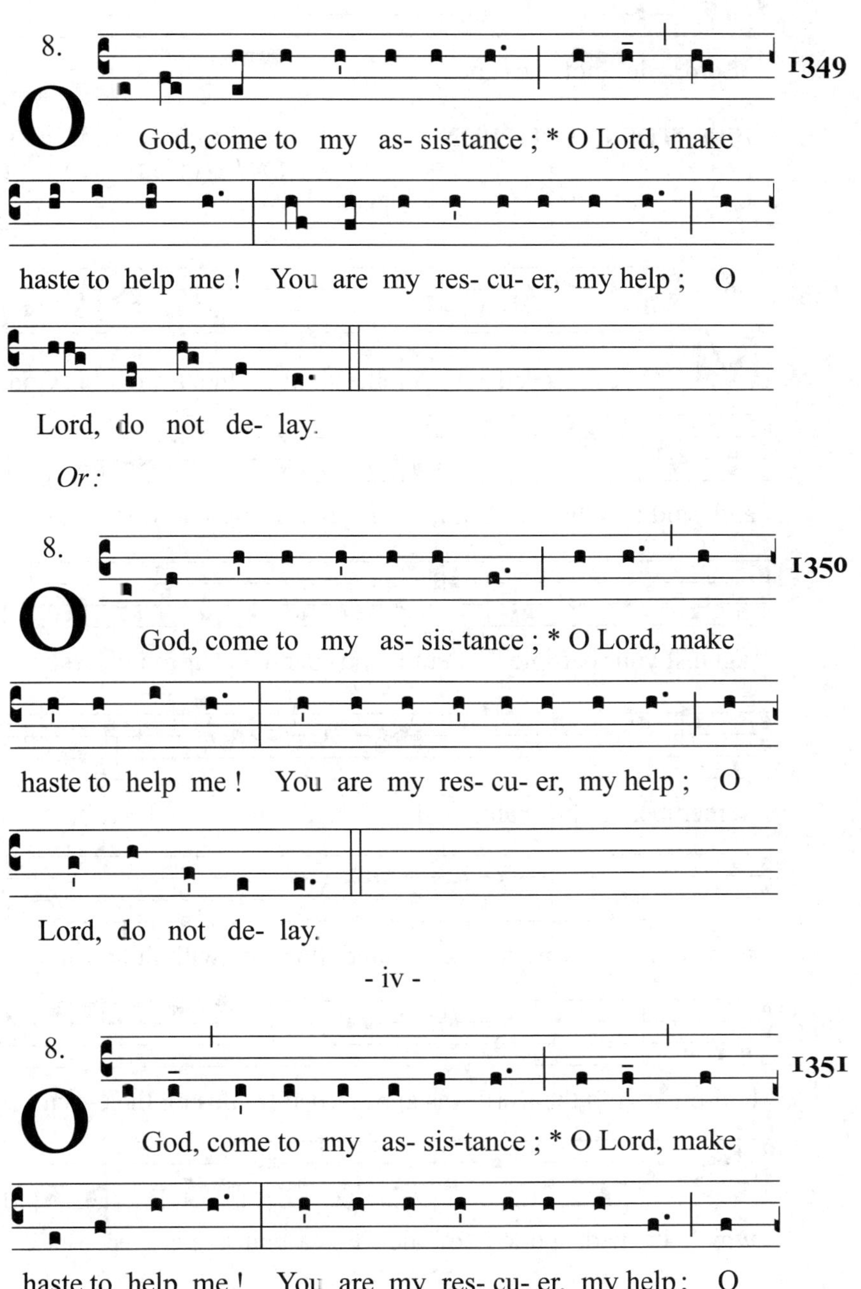
8.
1349
O God, come to my as- sis-tance ; * O Lord, make
haste to help me ! You are my res- cu- er, my help ; O
Lord, do not de- lay.
Or:
8.
1350
O God, come to my as- sis-tance ; * O Lord, make
haste to help me ! You are my res- cu- er, my help ; O
Lord, do not de- lay.
- iv -
8.
1351
O God, come to my as- sis-tance ; * O Lord, make
haste to help me ! You are my res- cu- er, my help ; O

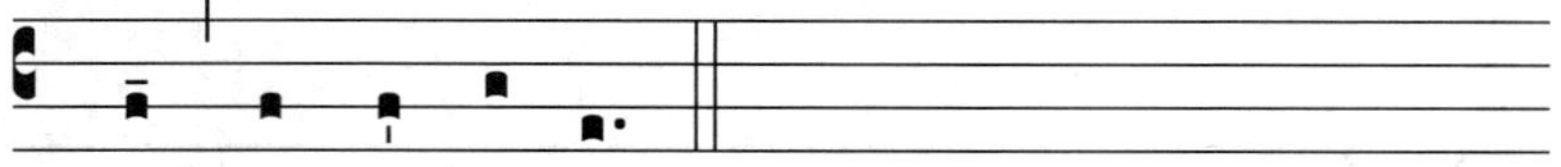
Lord, do not de- lay.

OFFERTORY ANTIPHON *Precatus est Moyses.*
Cf. Ex 32 : 11. 12. 13. 14

- i -

1352 8.

MO-ses prayed * in the sight of the Lord his God,
and said : Why, O Lord, is your in-dig-na- tion kindled
against your peo-ple ? Let the an- ger of your mind cease ;
remember A-bra-ham, I- saac, and Ja- cob,
to whom you swore to give a land flow-ing with milk and
hon-ey. ** And the Lord was appeased from do-ing the e- vil
which he had spo-ken of do- ing a-gainst his peo-ple.

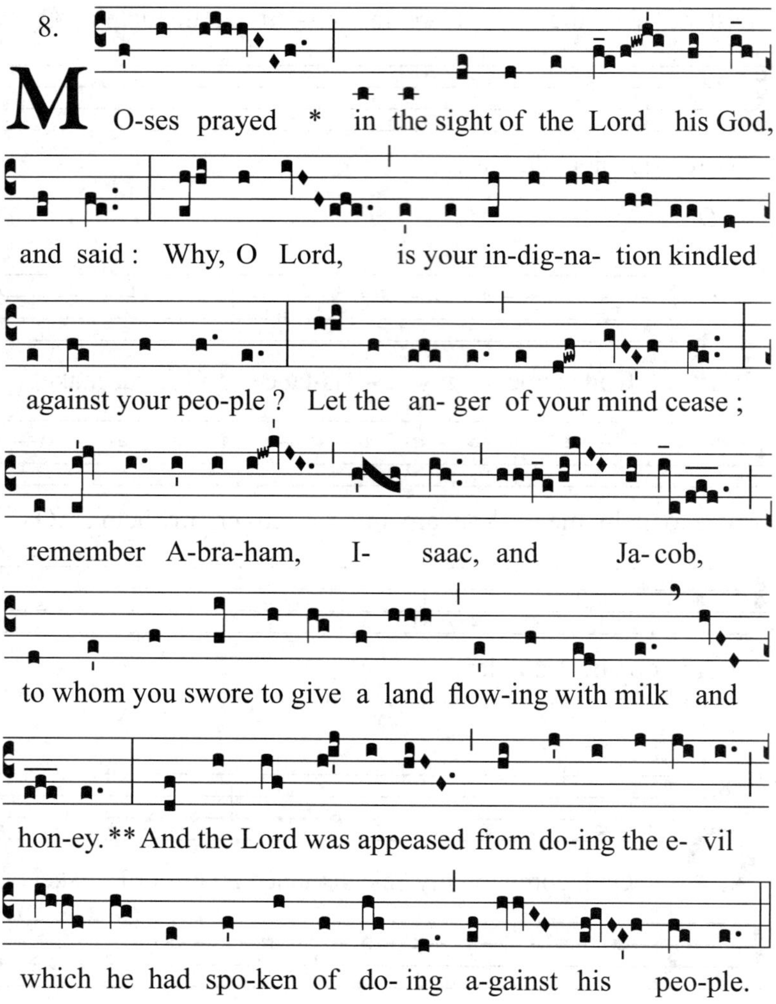

VERSES *Dixit Dominus ad Moysen.*

℣. 1 1353

THE Lord spoke to Mo-ses : You have found grace in

my sight and I know you a-bove all oth- ers. * And Mo-ses,

mak-ing haste, bowed down prostrate un- to the earth, and a-

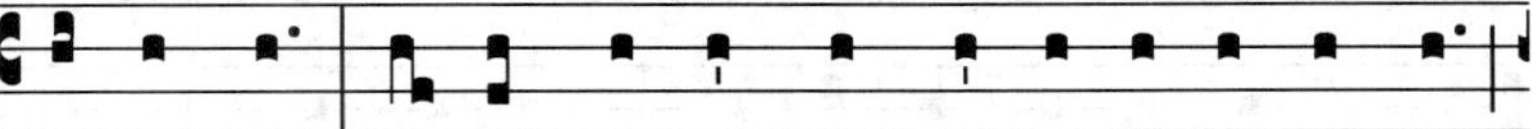

dor-ing, said : I know that you show mer-cy un- to thousands,

taking a-way our in-iq- ui- ty and our sins. ** And the Lord.

Dixit Moyses et Aaron.

℣. 2 1354

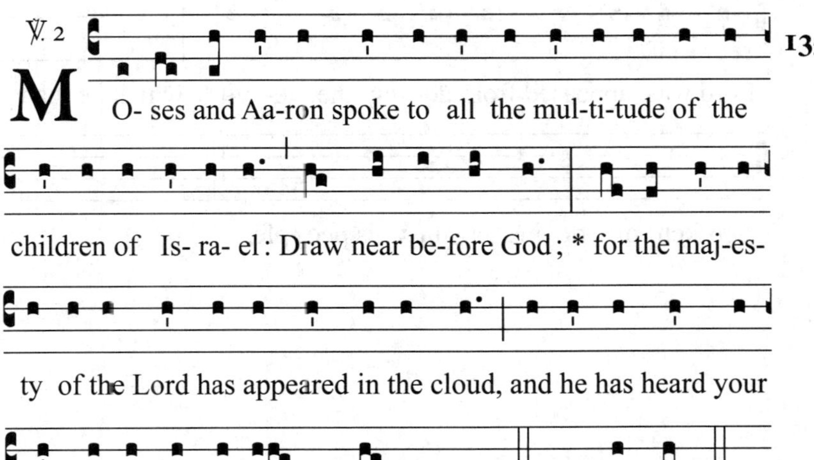

MO- ses and Aa-ron spoke to all the mul-ti-tude of the

children of Is- ra- el : Draw near be-fore God ; * for the maj-es-

ty of the Lord has appeared in the cloud, and he has heard your

murmuring in the time of temp-ta- tion. ** And the Lord.

- ii -

1355

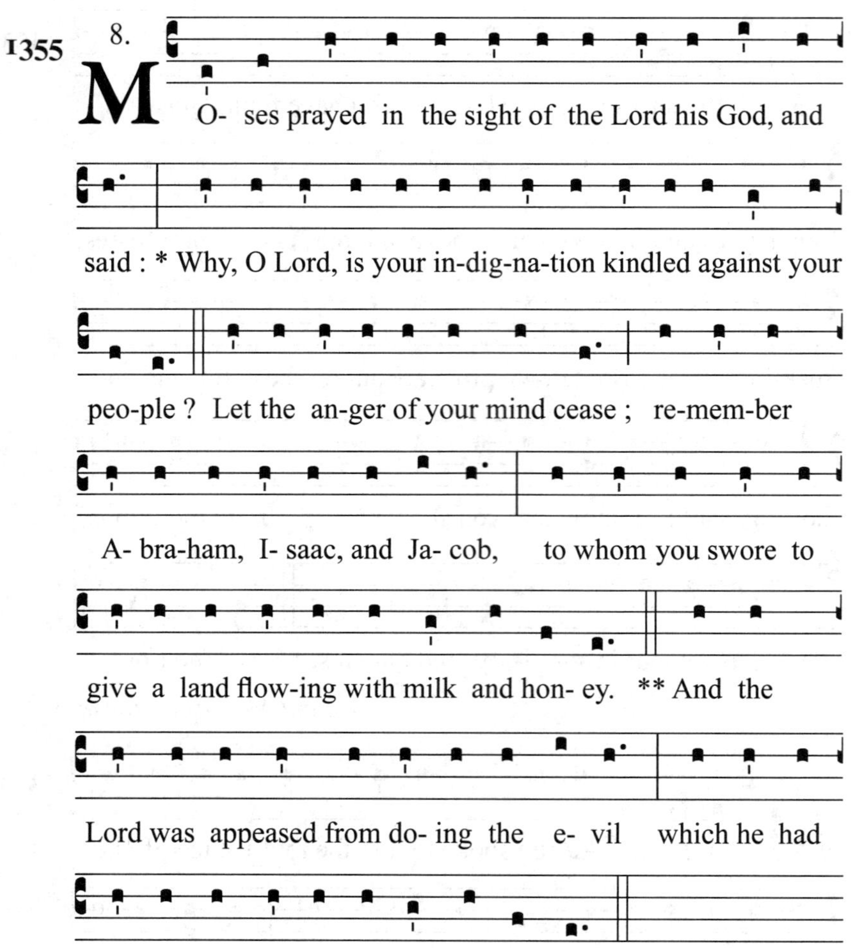

VERSES *Dixit Dominus ad Moysen.*

℣. 1 1356

THE Lord spoke to Mo-ses : You have found grace in

my sight and I know you a-bove all oth- ers. * And Mo-ses,

mak-ing haste, bowed down prostrate un- to the earth, and a-

doring, said : I know that you show mer-cy un- to thousands, *

taking a-way our in-iq- ui- ty and our sins. ** And the Lord.

Dixit Moyses et Aaron.

℣. 2 1357

MO- ses and Aa-ron spoke to all the mul-ti-tude of the

children of Is- ra- el : * Draw near be-fore God ; the maj-es- ty

of the Lord has appeared in the cloud, and he has heard your

mur-mur-ing in the time of temp-ta- tion. ** And the Lord.

Communion Antiphon *Panem de cælo.* *Wis* 16:20

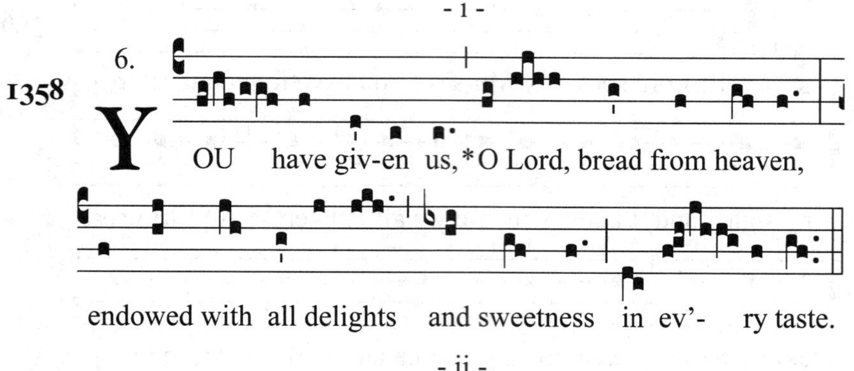

- i -
1358
6.
Y OU have giv-en us, * O Lord, bread from heaven,
endowed with all delights and sweetness in ev'- ry taste.

- ii -
1359
6.
Y OU have giv-en us, O Lord, * bread from heav-en,
endowed with all delights and sweetness in ev'-ry taste.

Verses *Magnificate Dominum mecum. Ps* 33:4

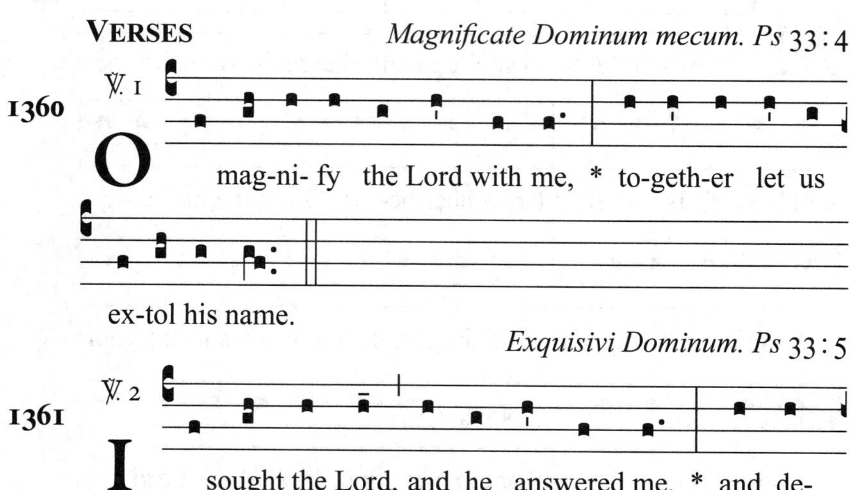

1360
℣. 1
O mag-ni- fy the Lord with me, * to-geth-er let us
ex-tol his name.
Exquisivi Dominum. Ps 33:5
1361
℣. 2
I sought the Lord, and he answered me, * and de-

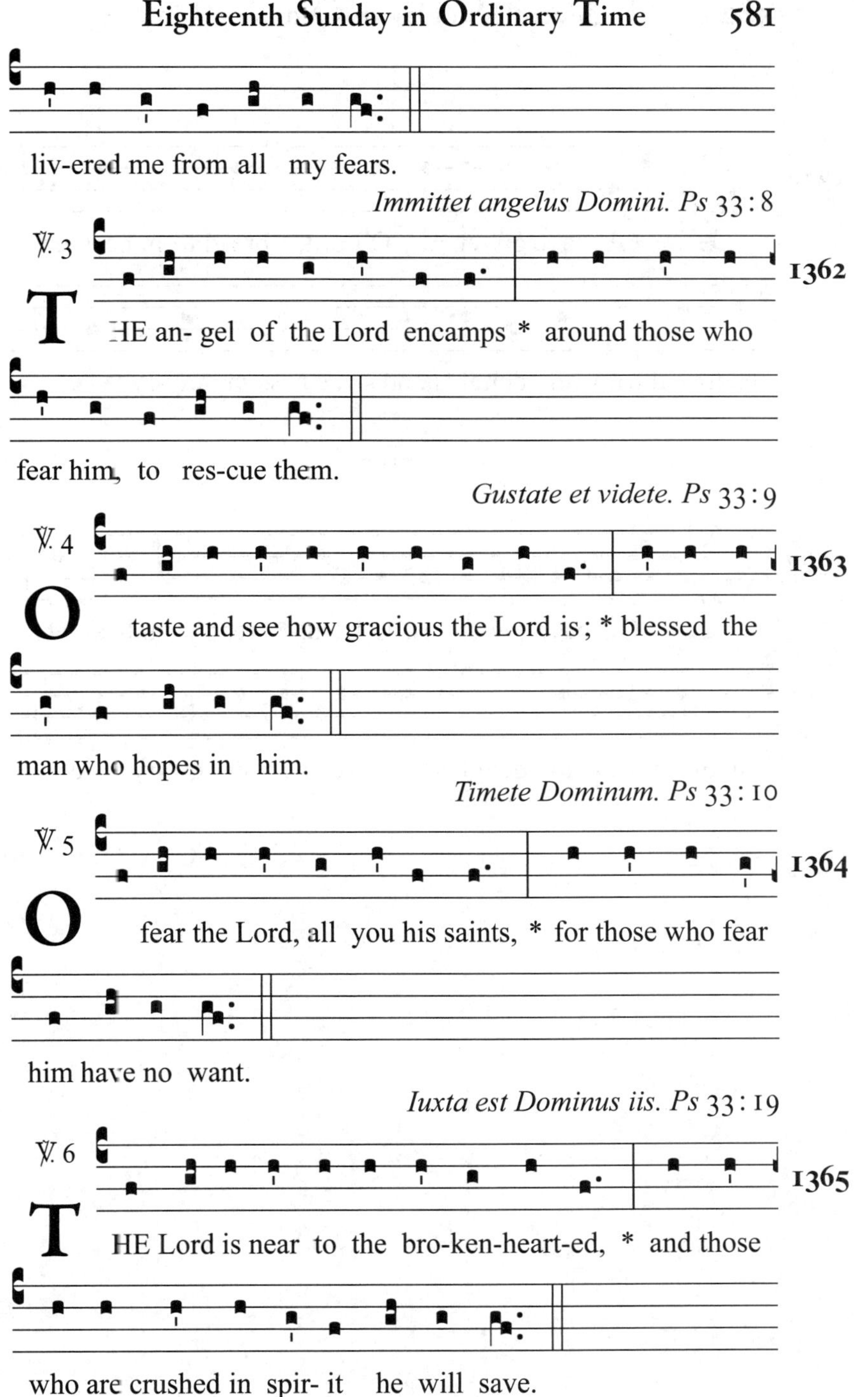
liv-ered me from all my fears.
Immittet angelus Domini. Ps 33:8
℣. 3
THE an- gel of the Lord encamps * around those who 1362
fear him, to res-cue them.
Gustate et videte. Ps 33:9
℣. 4
O taste and see how gracious the Lord is; * blessed the 1363
man who hopes in him.
Timete Dominum. Ps 33:10
℣. 5
O fear the Lord, all you his saints, * for those who fear 1364
him have no want.
Iuxta est Dominus iis. Ps 33:19
℣. 6
THE Lord is near to the bro-ken-heart-ed, * and those 1365
who are crushed in spir- it he will save.

- iii -

1366

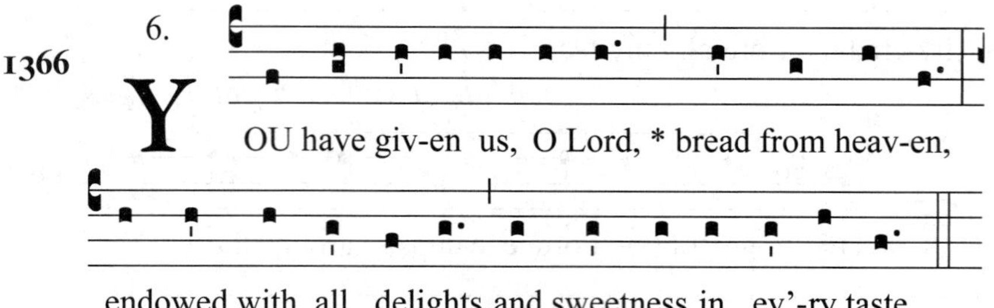
6.
Y OU have giv-en us, O Lord, * bread from heav-en,
endowed with all delights and sweetness in ev'-ry taste.

- iv -

1367

6.
Y OU have giv-en us, O Lord, * bread from heav-en,
endowed with all delights and sweetness in ev'-ry taste.

NINETEENTH SUNDAY IN ORDINARY TIME

ENTRANCE ANTIPHON *Respice, Domine.* *Ps* 73:20. 19. 22. 23

- i -

7. 1368

LOOK to your cov-e-nant, O Lord, * and for- get not the

life of your poor ones for ev- er. A- rise, O God, and

de-fend your cause, and for-get not the cries of those who

seek you.

- ii -

7. 1369

LOOK to your cov-e-nant, O Lord, * and for- get not

the life of your poor ones for ev- er. A- rise, O God, and

de-fend your cause, and for-get not the cries of those who

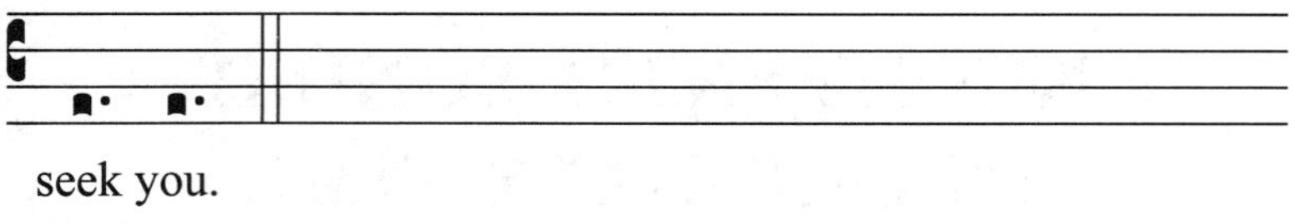
seek you.

VERSES *Ut quid, Deus, repulisit in finem. Ps* 73 : 1

1370

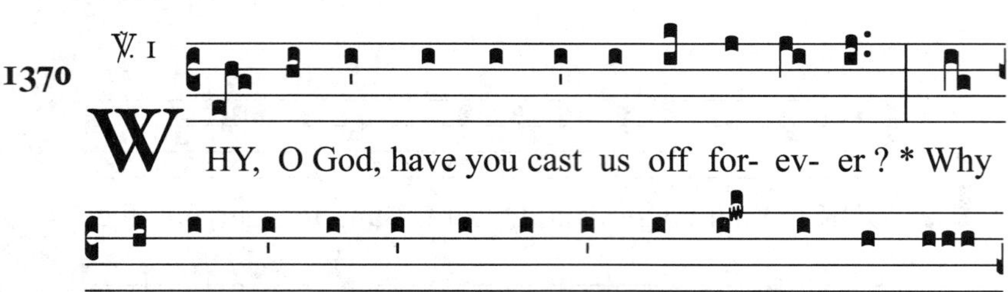
℣. 1
WHY, O God, have you cast us off for- ev- er ? * Why
is your wrath en- kin-dled a-gainst the sheep of your pas-

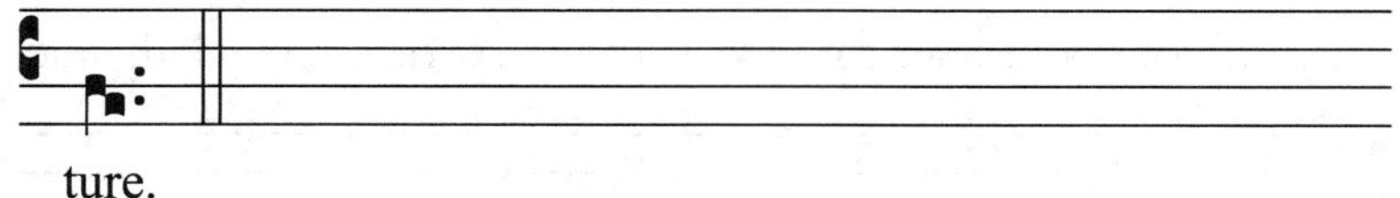
ture.

Ne tradas bestiis animas confitentes tibi. Ps 73 : 19

1371

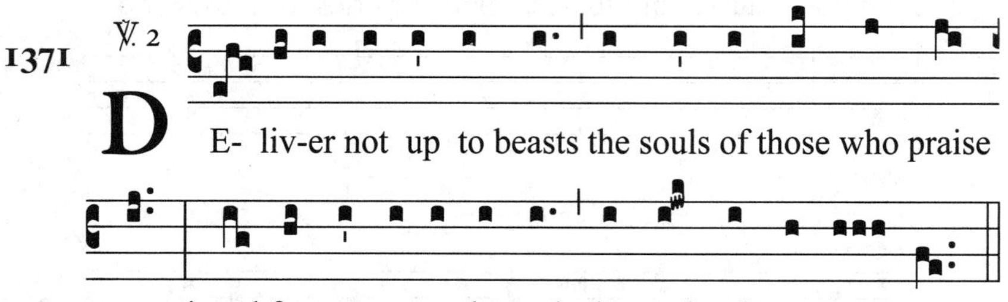
℣. 2
DE- liv-er not up to beasts the souls of those who praise
you ; * and for-get not to the end the souls of your poor ones.

Defecit caro mea et cor meum. Ps 72 : 26

1372

℣. 3
MY flesh and my heart may waste a- way, but God
is the strength of my heart * and my por-tion for ev- er.

- iii -

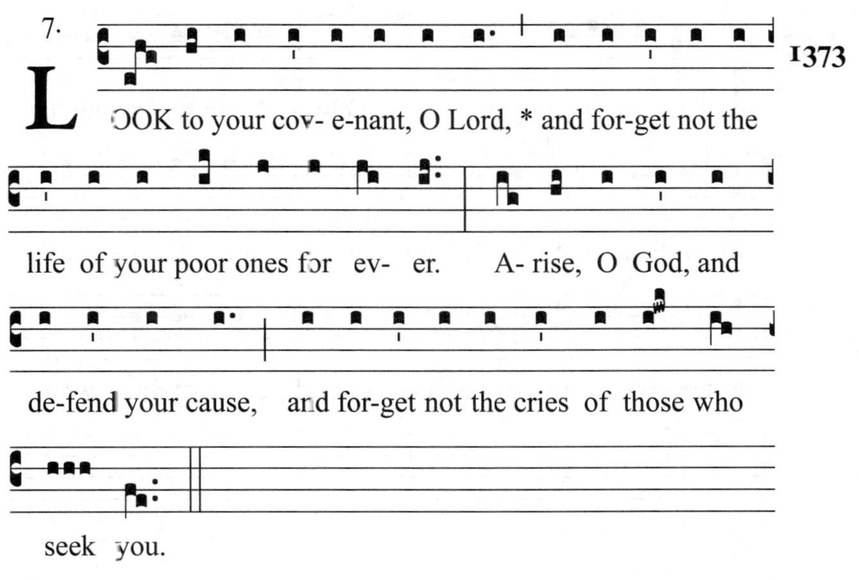
7.
1373
LOOK to your cov- e-nant, O Lord, * and for-get not the
life of your poor ones for ev- er. A- rise, O God, and
de-fend your cause, and for-get not the cries of those who
seek you.

Or:

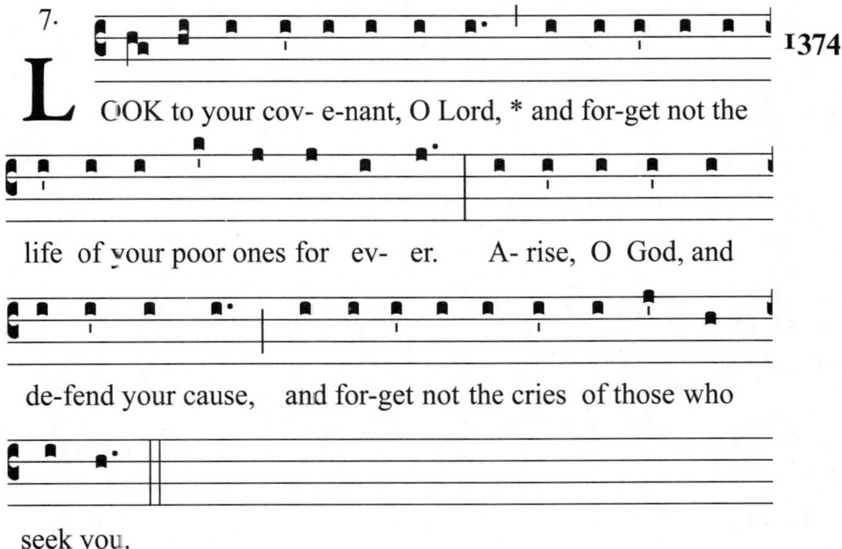
7.
1374
LOOK to your cov- e-nant, O Lord, * and for-get not the
life of your poor ones for ev- er. A- rise, O God, and
de-fend your cause, and for-get not the cries of those who
seek you.

- iv -

1375

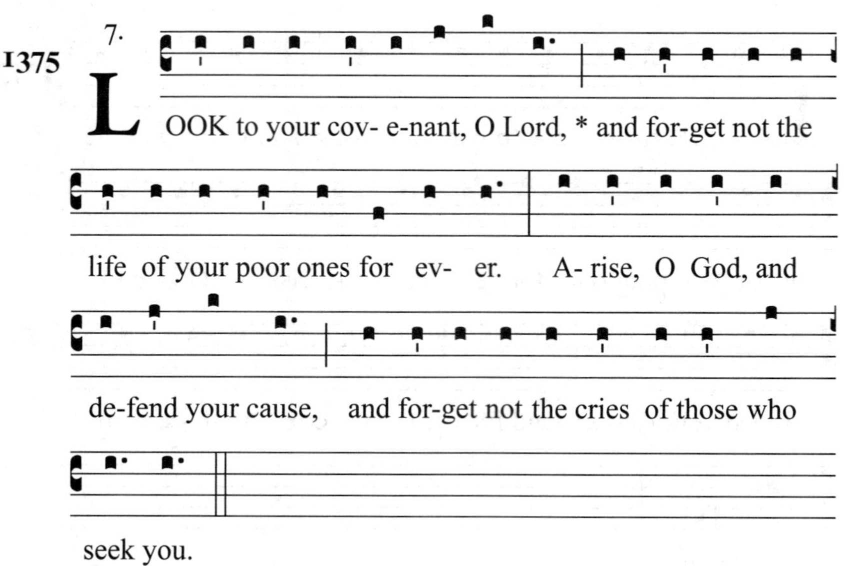
7.
LOOK to your cov- e-nant, O Lord, * and for-get not the
life of your poor ones for ev- er. A- rise, O God, and
de-fend your cause, and for-get not the cries of those who
seek you.

OFFERTORY ANTIPHON *In te speravi, Domine.*
Ps 30:15

- i -

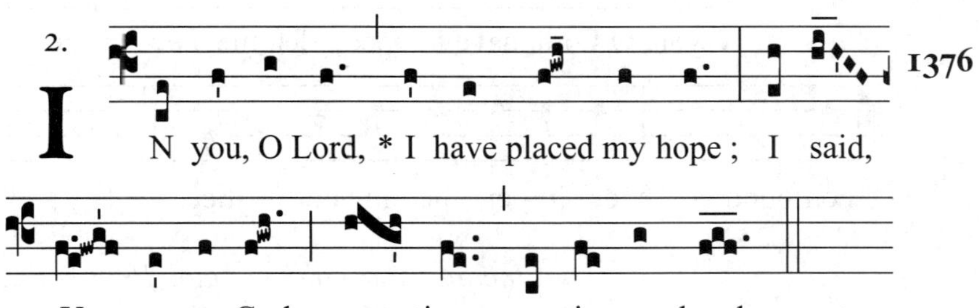
2.
IN you, O Lord, * I have placed my hope ; I said,
You are my God ; my times are in your hands.

1376

- ii -

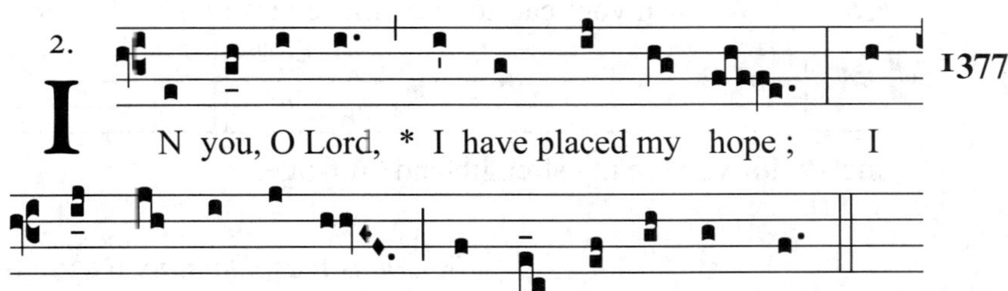
2.
IN you, O Lord, * I have placed my hope ; I
said, You are my God ; my times are in your hands.

1377

VERSES *In te, Domine, speravi.* *Ps* 30 : 2

1378

℣. 1
IN you, O Lord, have I hoped, let me nev- er be
confound-ed, * de- liv- er me in your jus-tice.

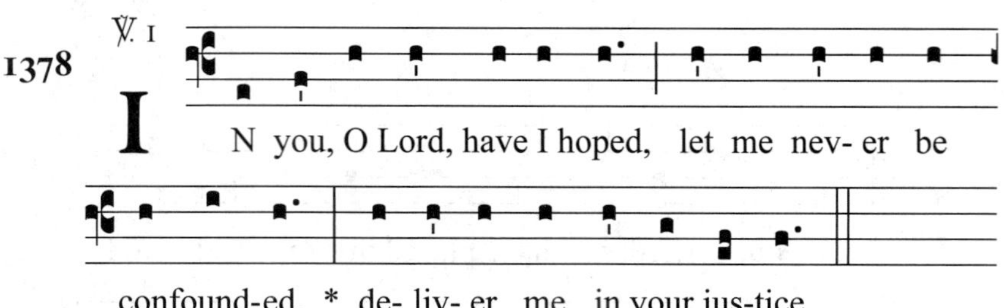

Inclina ad me aurem tuam. *Ps* 30 : 3. 4

1379

℣. 2
BOW down your ear to me ; make haste to de- liv- er
me, * for you are my strength and ref-uge.

In manus tuas, Domine. *Ps* 30 : 6

1380

℣. 3
IN- to your hands I commend my spir- it, * for you
have redeemed me, O Lord, O God of truth.

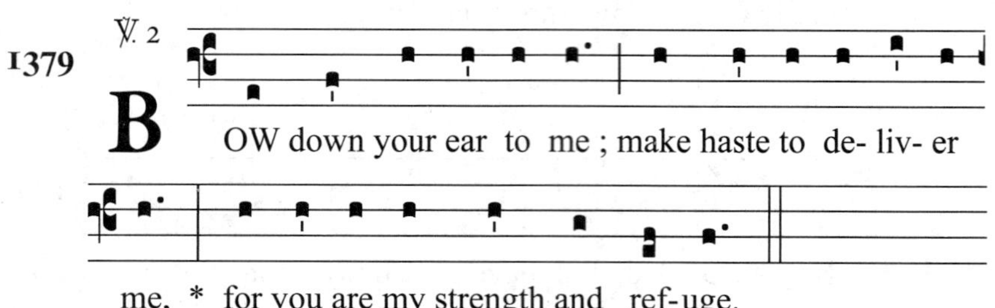

- iii -

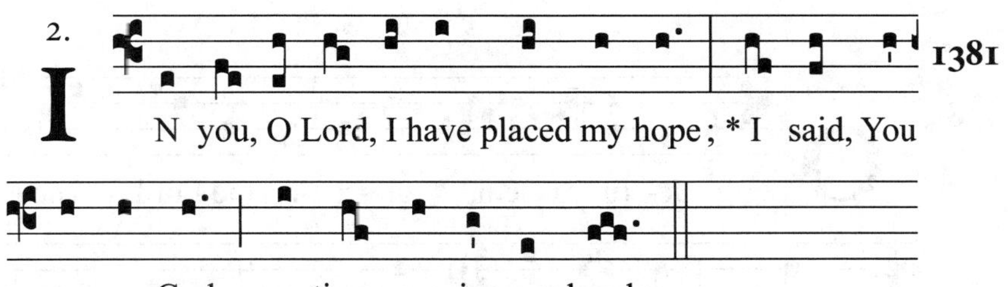
2.
IN you, O Lord, I have placed my hope ; * I said, You
are my God ; my times are in your hands.
1381

Or :

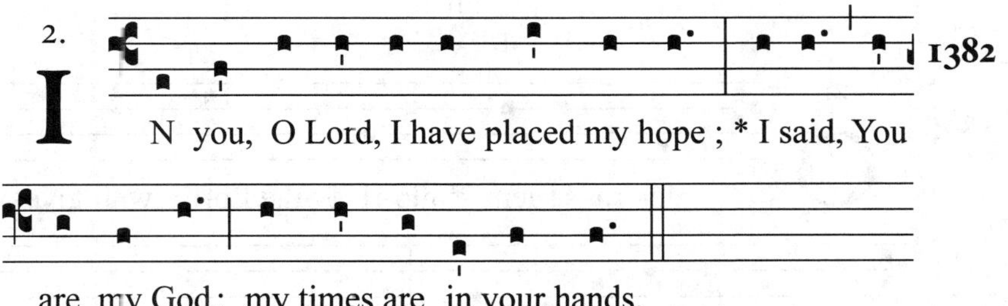
2.
IN you, O Lord, I have placed my hope ; * I said, You
are my God ; my times are in your hands.
1382

- iv -

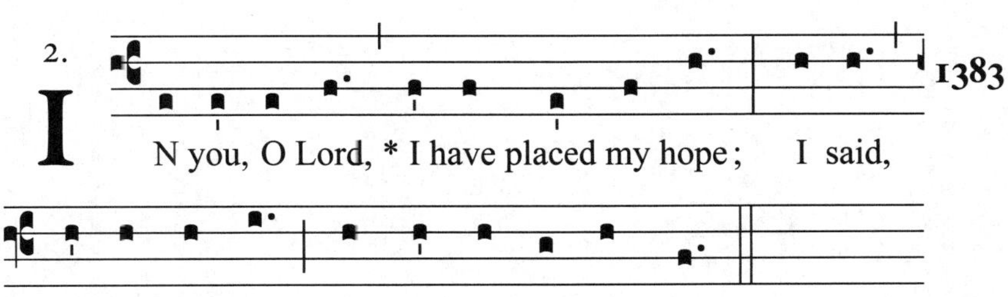
2.
IN you, O Lord, * I have placed my hope ; I said,
You are my God ; my times are in your hands.
1383

COMMUNION ANTIPHON *Lauda, Ierusalem, Dominum.*
Ps 147:12. 14

- i -

1384
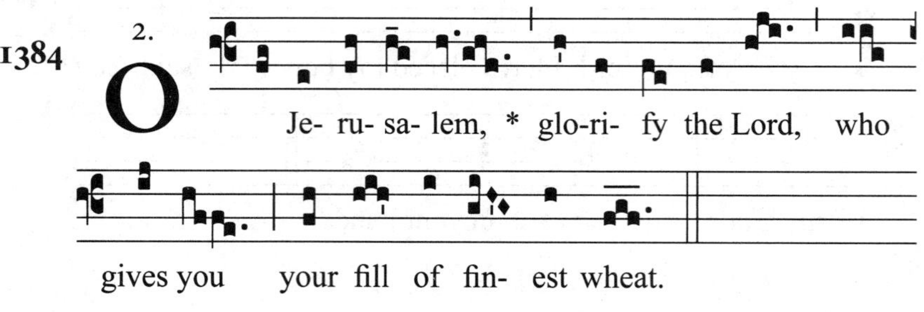
2.
O Je- ru- sa- lem, * glo-ri- fy the Lord, who
gives you your fill of fin- est wheat.

- ii -

1385
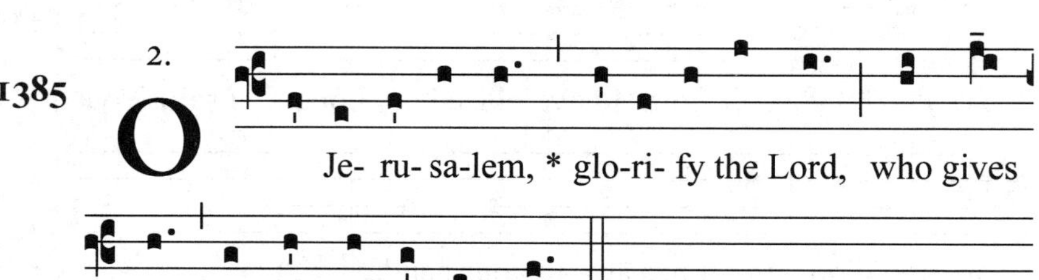
2.
O Je- ru- sa-lem, * glo-ri- fy the Lord, who gives
you your fill of fin-est wheat.

VERSES *Lauda, Jerusalem, Dominum. Ps* 147 : 1

℣. 1
PRaise the Lord, O Je- ru- sa-lem. Praise your God, O
Si- on. * He has strengthened the bars of your gates, and
has blessed your chil-dren with-in you.

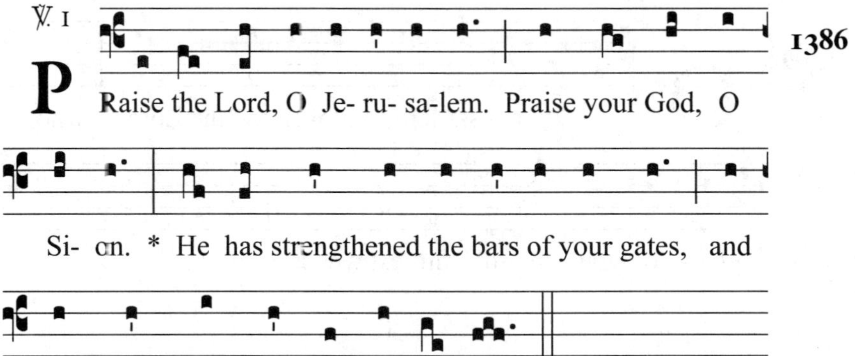

1386

Qui posuit fines tuos pacem. Ps 147 : 4

℣. 2
HE has grant-ed peace in your bor-ders ; * with the
best of wheat he fills you.

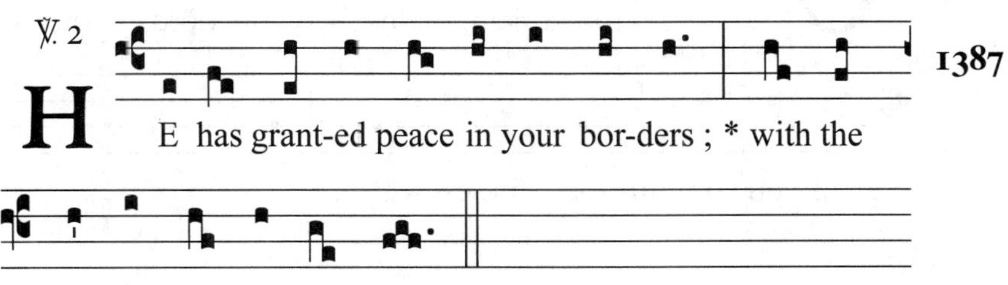

1387

Non fecit taliter omni nationi. Ps 147 : 9

℣. 3
HE has not done in like manner to ev-'ry na-tion, *
and his judgments he has not made man- i- fest to them.

1388

- iii -

1389

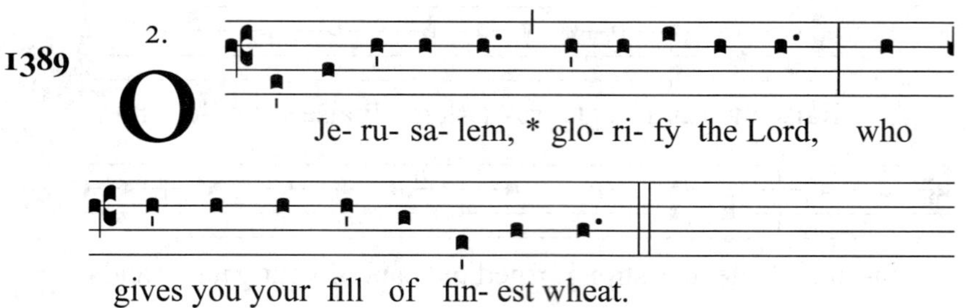
2.
O Je- ru- sa- lem, * glo- ri- fy the Lord, who
gives you your fill of fin- est wheat.

- iv -

1390

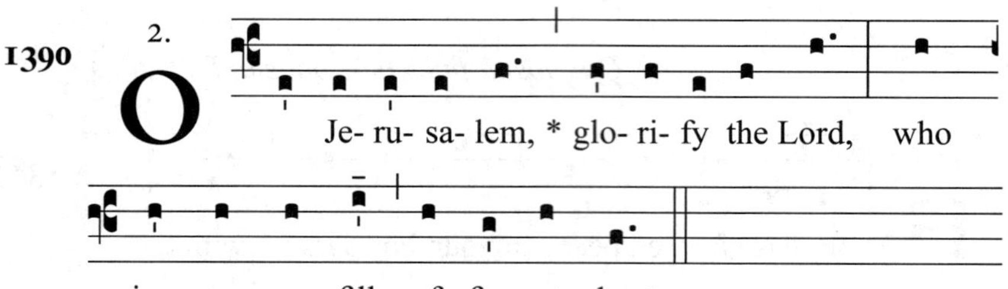
2.
O Je- ru- sa- lem, * glo- ri- fy the Lord, who
gives you your fill of fin- est wheat.

TWENTIETH SUNDAY IN ORDINARY TIME

ENTRANCE ANTIPHON *Protector noster, aspice.*
Ps 83:10-11

- i -

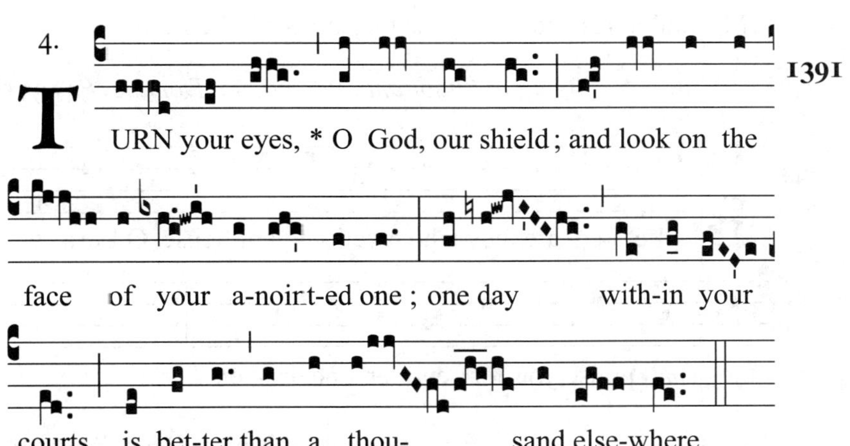
4.
1391
TURN your eyes, * O God, our shield; and look on the
face of your a-noint-ed one; one day with-in your
courts is bet-ter than a thou- sand else-where.

- ii -

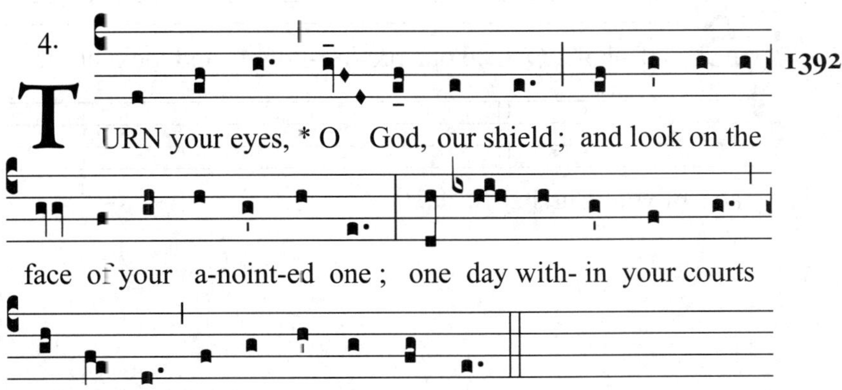
4.
1392
TURN your eyes, * O God, our shield; and look on the
face of your a-noint-ed one; one day with- in your courts
is bet- ter than a thousand elsewhere.

VERSES *Quam dilecta tabernacula tua. Ps 83:2*

1393

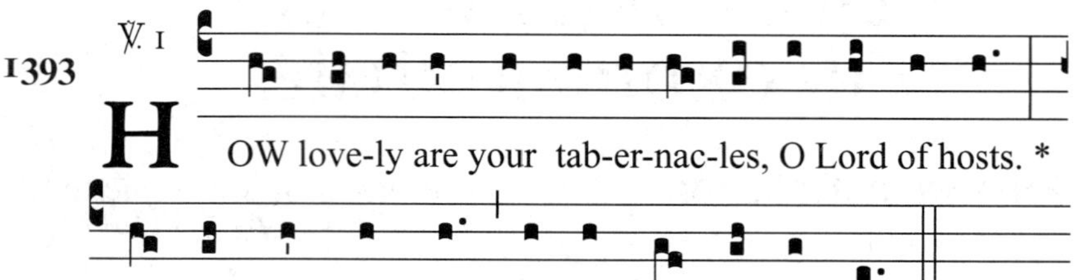
℣. 1
HOW love-ly are your tab-er-nac-les, O Lord of hosts. *

My soul longs and faints for the courts of the Lord.

Beati, qui habitant in domo tua, Domine. Ps 83:5

1394

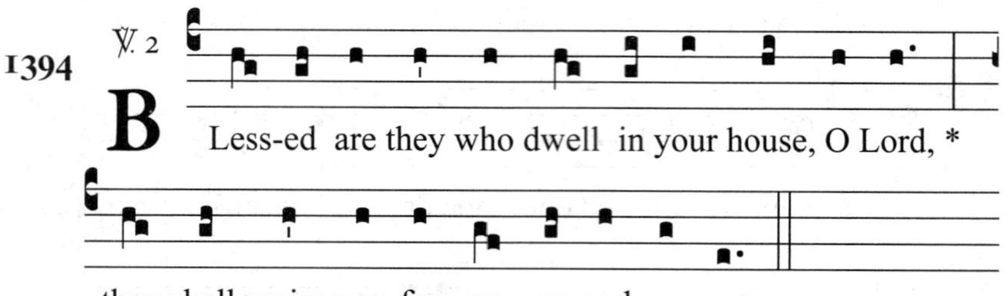
℣. 2
BLess-ed are they who dwell in your house, O Lord, *

they shall praise you for ev- er and ev- er.

Protector noster, aspice, Deus. Ps 83:10

1395

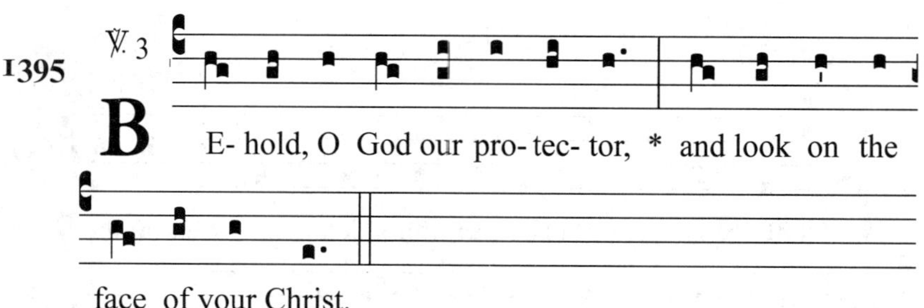
℣. 3
BE- hold, O God our pro- tec- tor, * and look on the
face of your Christ.

- iii -

4.
1396
TURN your eyes, O God, our shield; * and look on the
face of your a-noint-ed one; one day with- in your courts
is bet-ter than a thousand elsewhere.

Or:

4.
1397
TURN your eyes, O God, our shield; * and look on the
face of your a-noint-ed one; one day with- in your courts
is bet-ter than a thousand elsewhere.

- iv -

4.
1398
TURN your eyes, O God, our shield; * and look on the
face of your a-noint-ed one; one day with- in your courts

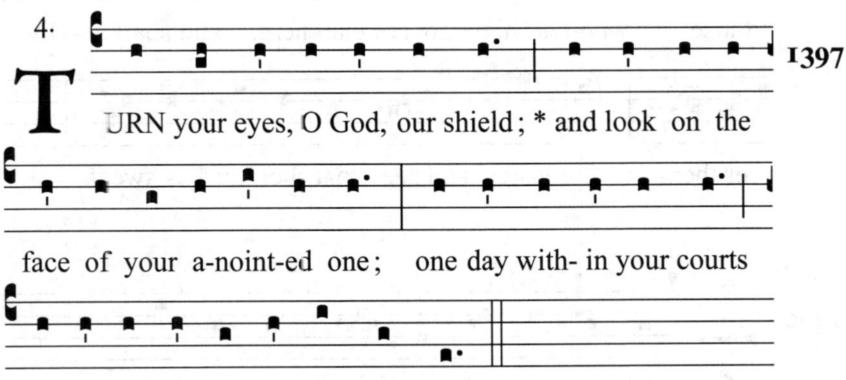

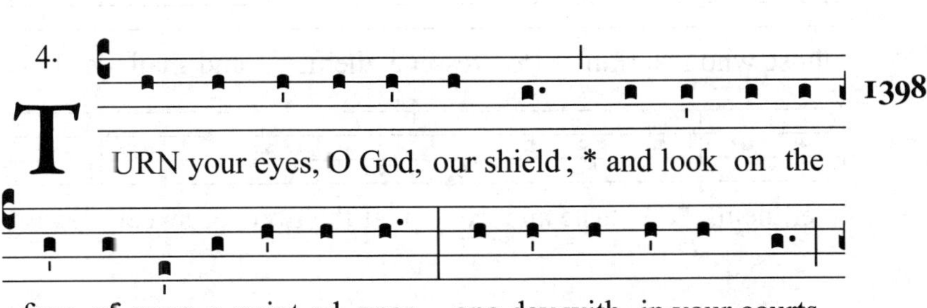

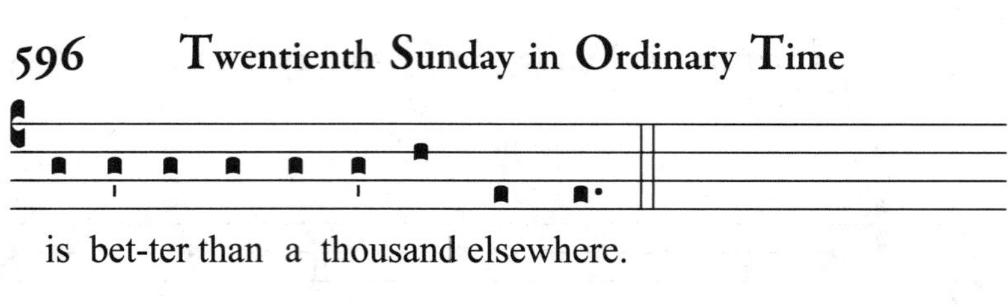
is bet-ter than a thousand elsewhere.

Offertory Antiphon *Immitet angelus Domini.*

Ps 33:8.9

- i -

Use ti *natural throughout except for the word "deliver."*

1399

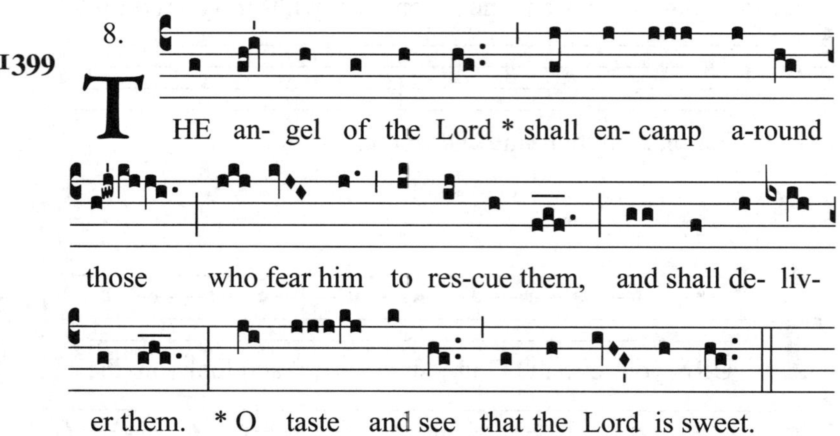
8.
THE an- gel of the Lord * shall en- camp a-round
those who fear him to res-cue them, and shall de- liv-
er them. * O taste and see that the Lord is sweet.

- ii -

1400

8.
THE an- gel of the Lord * shall en-camp a-round
those who fear him to res-cue them, and shall de- liv-
er them. * O taste and see that the Lord is sweet.

VERSES *Benedicam Dominum. Ps* 33:1-2

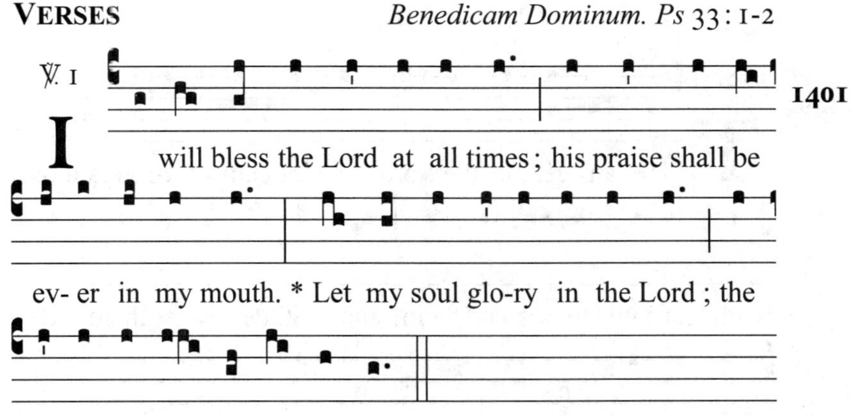
℣. 1
I will bless the Lord at all times; his praise shall be
ev- er in my mouth. * Let my soul glo-ry in the Lord; the
low-ly will hear me and be glad.

1401

The antiphon may be repeated from the beginning, or from * O taste.

Diverte a malo, et fac bonum. Ps 33:15

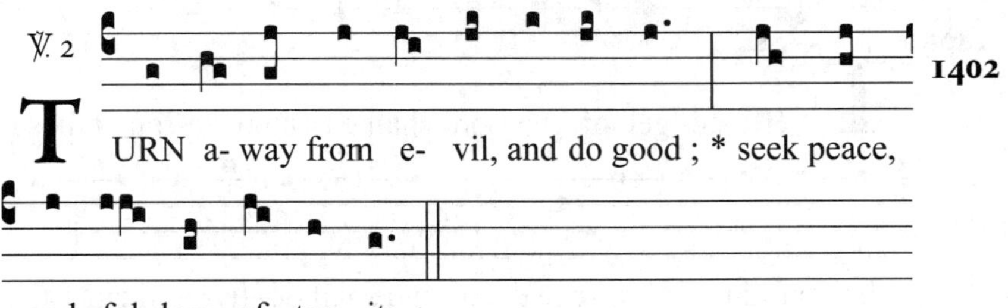
℣. 2
TURN a- way from e- vil, and do good; * seek peace,
and fcl- low af- ter it.

1402

The antiphon may be repeated from the beginning, or from * O taste.

Oculi Domini super iustos. Ps 33:16

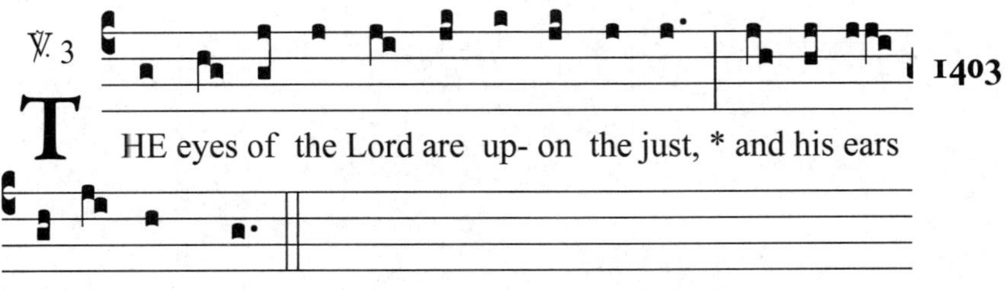
℣. 3
THE eyes of the Lord are up- on the just, * and his ears
un- to their prayers.

1403

The antiphon may be repeated from the beginning, or from * O taste.

- iii -

1404

8.
THE an- gel of the Lord shall en-camp * a-round those
who fear him to res-cue them, and shall de- liv- er them. O
taste and see that the Lord is sweet.
Or:
8.
THE an- gel of the Lord shall en-camp * a-round those

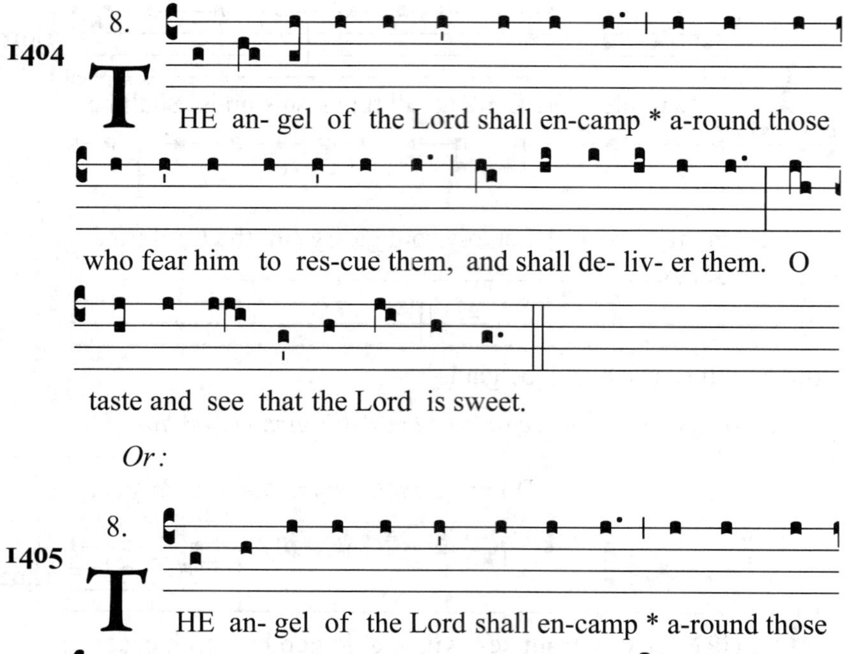

1405

who fear him to res-cue them, and shall de- liv- er them. O

taste and see that the Lord is sweet.

- iv -

8.

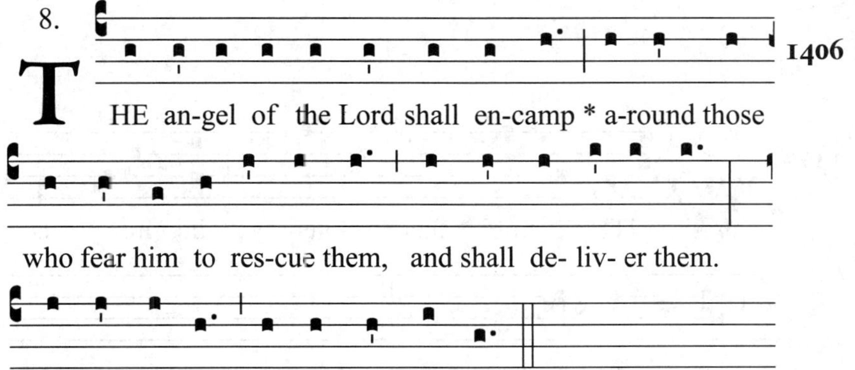
THE an-gel of the Lord shall en-camp * a-round those
who fear him to res-cue them, and shall de- liv- er them.
O taste and see that the Lord is sweet.

1406

COMMUNION ANTIPHON *Apud Dominum misericordia.*
Ps 129:7

- i -

1407
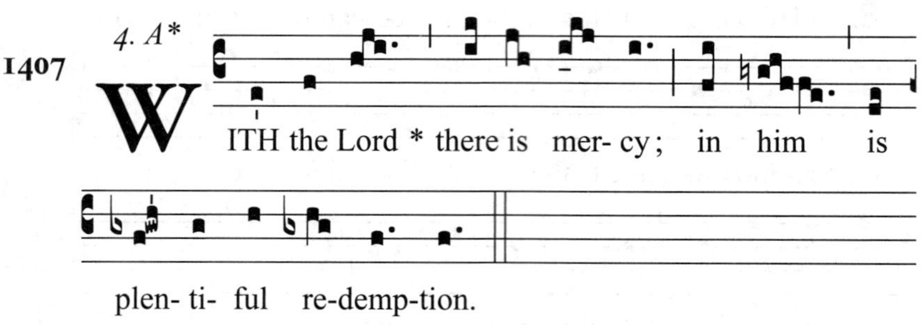
4. A*
WITH the Lord * there is mer- cy; in him is
plen- ti- ful re-demp-tion.

- ii -

1408
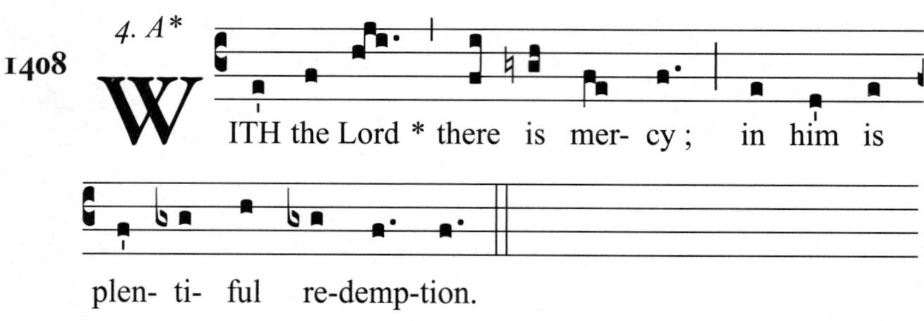
4. A*
WITH the Lord * there is mer- cy; in him is
plen- ti- ful re-demp-tion.

VERSES *De profundis clamavi ad te, Domine. Ps* 129:1-2

1409 ℣. 1

OUT of the depths I have cried to you, O Lord; * Lord,
hear my voice.

Fiant aures tuæ intendentes. *Ps* 129:2

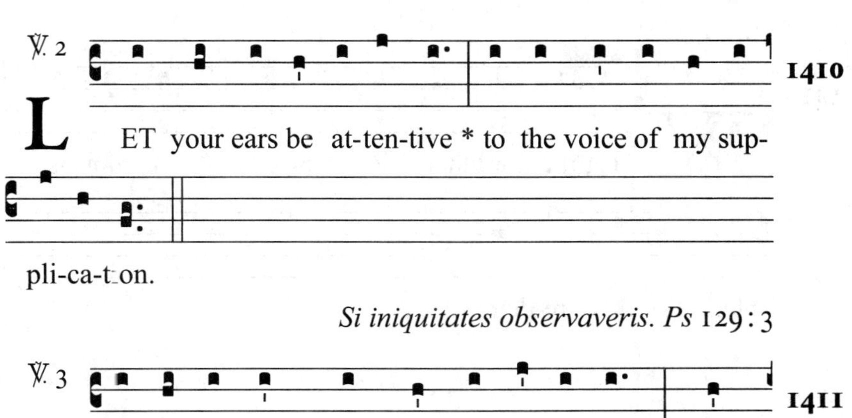
℣. 2
LET your ears be at-ten-tive * to the voice of my sup-
pli-ca-t on.
Si iniquitates observaveris. *Ps* 129:3
℣. 3
IF you, O Lord, should mark in- iq- ui-ties, * Lord,
who shall stand it ?

1410

1411

Sustinuit anima mea in verbo eius. *Ps* 129:4-5

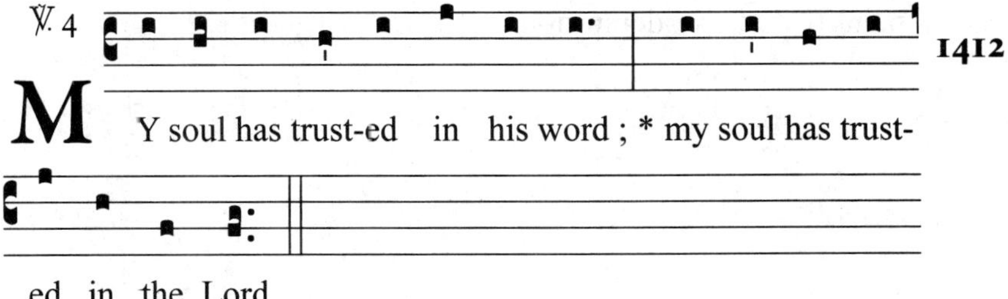
℣. 4
MY soul has trust-ed in his word ; * my soul has trust-
ed in the Lord.

1412

Et ipse redimet Israel. *Ps* 129:7

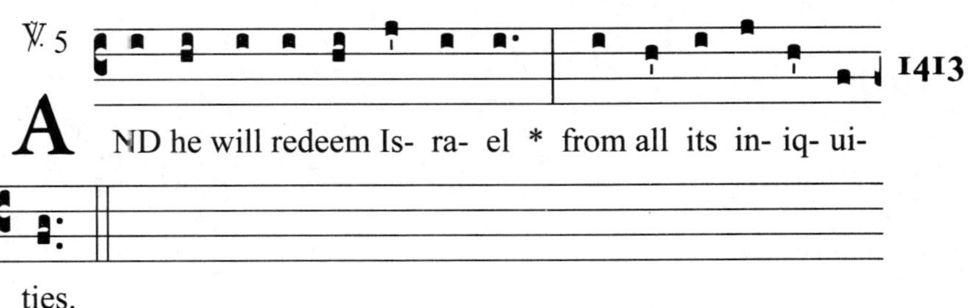
℣. 5
AND he will redeem Is- ra- el * from all its in- iq- ui-
ties.

1413

- iii -

1414 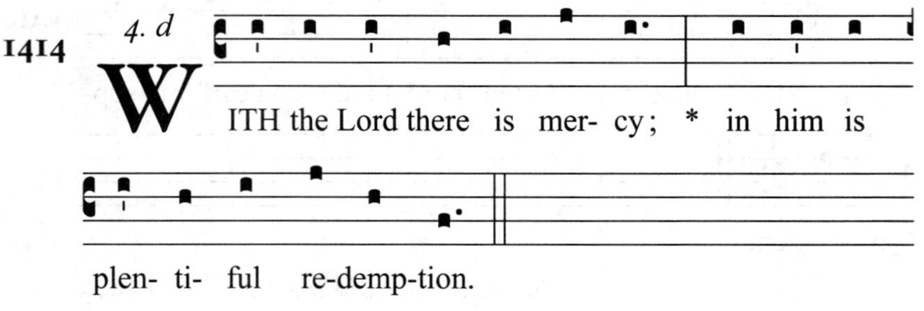
4. d
WITH the Lord there is mer- cy; * in him is
plen- ti- ful re-demp-tion.

- iv -

1415 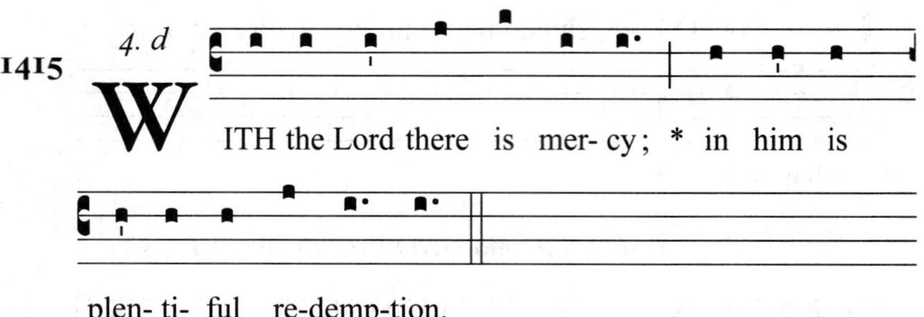
4. d
WITH the Lord there is mer- cy; * in him is
plen- ti- ful re-demp-tion.

TWENTY-FIRST SUNDAY IN ORDINARY TIME

ENTRANCE ANTIPHON *Inclina, Domine, aurem tuam.* *Ps* 85:1-3

- i -

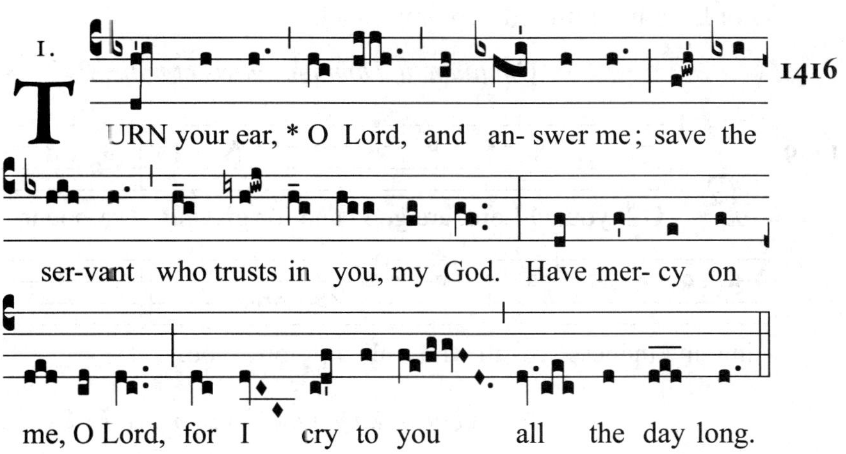
1.
TURN your ear, * O Lord, and an- swer me; save the
ser-vant who trusts in you, my God. Have mer- cy on
me, O Lord, for I cry to you all the day long.
1416

- ii -

1.
TURN your ear, * O Lord, and an-swer me ; save the
ser-vant who trusts in you, my God. Have mer- cy on me,
O Lord, for I cry to you all the day long.
1417

VERSES

Lætifica animam servi tui. Ps 85:4

1418 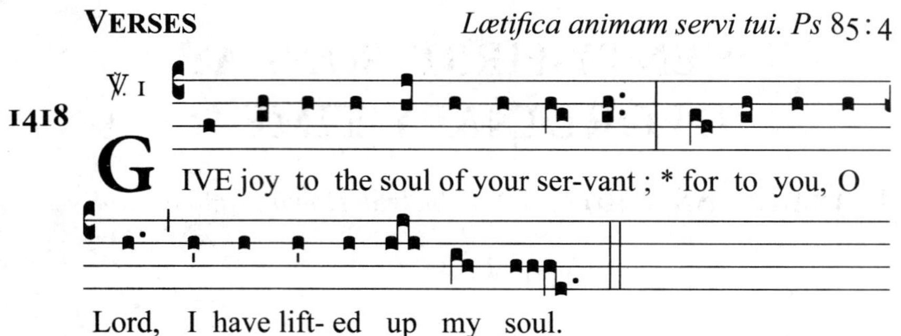
℣. 1
GIVE joy to the soul of your ser-vant ; * for to you, O
Lord, I have lift- ed up my soul.

Quoniam tu, Domine, suavis et mitis. Ps 85:5

1419 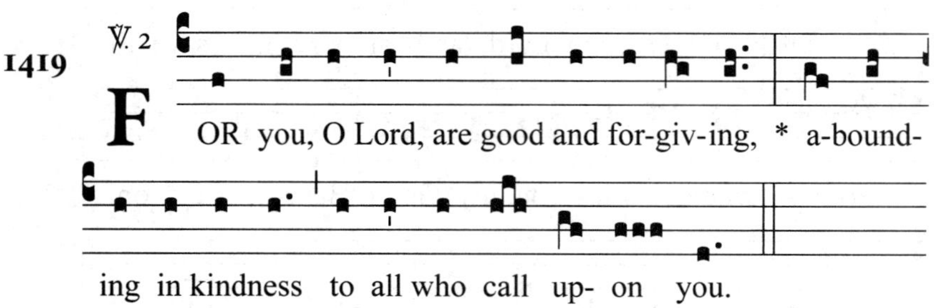
℣. 2
FOR you, O Lord, are good and for-giv-ing, * a-bound-
ing in kindness to all who call up- on you.

Confitebor tibi, Domine, Deus meus. Ps 85:12

1420 
℣. 3
I will praise you, O Lord my God, with all my heart, *
and I will glo- ri- fy your name for- ev- er.

- iii -

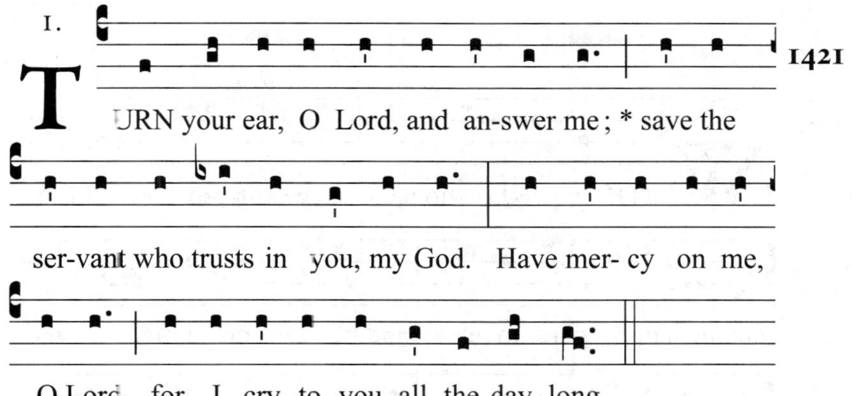
1.
1421
TURN your ear, O Lord, and an-swer me; * save the
ser-vant who trusts in you, my God. Have mer- cy on me,
O Lord, for I cry to you all the day long.

- iv -

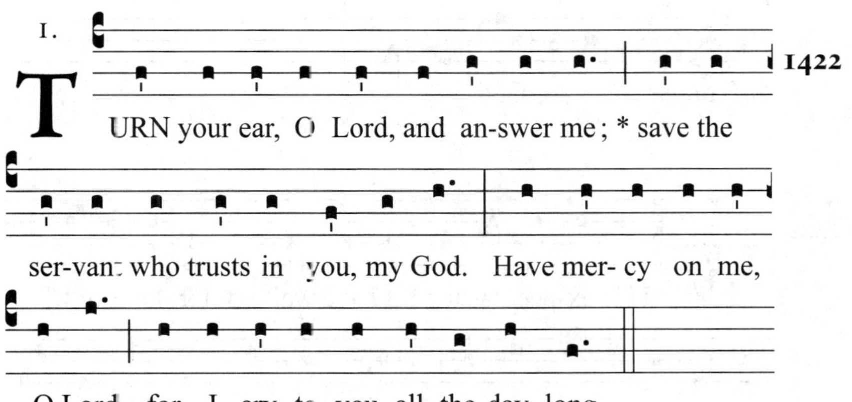
1.
1422
TURN your ear, O Lord, and an-swer me; * save the
ser-vant who trusts in you, my God. Have mer- cy on me,
O Lord, for I cry to you all the day long.

OFFERTORY ANTIPHON *Expectans expectavi Dominum.*
Ps 39:2. 3. 4

- i -

1423
5.
WITH ex-pec-ta- tion * I have wait- ed for the Lord,
and he had re- gard to me, and he heard my prayer, ** and
he put a new can- ti- cle in- to my mouth, a hymn
of praise to God.
- ii -
1424
5.
WITH ex-pec- ta-tion * I have wait-ed for the Lord,
and he had re-gard to me, and he heard my prayer, ** and he
put a new can- ti- cle in- to my mouth, a hymn of praise
to God.

The antiphon may be repeated from the beginning, or from ** And he put.

VERSES *Et statuit super petram pedes meos. Ps* 39 : 3

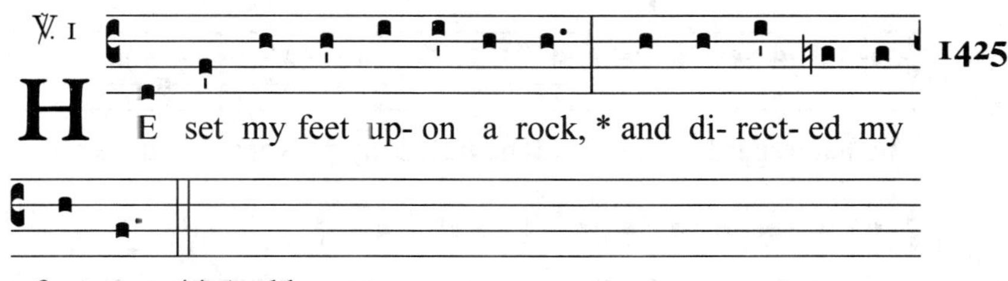
℣. 1
HE set my feet up- on a rock, * and di- rect- ed my
footsteps. ** And he put.
1425

Multa fecisti tu, Domine, Deus meus. Ps 39 : 6. 10

℣. 2
YOU have mul-ti-plied your won-der-ful works, O Lord,
my God, * and in your thoughts, there is no one like to you.
** And he put.
1426

Iustitiam tuam non abscondi. Ps 39 : 10. 11

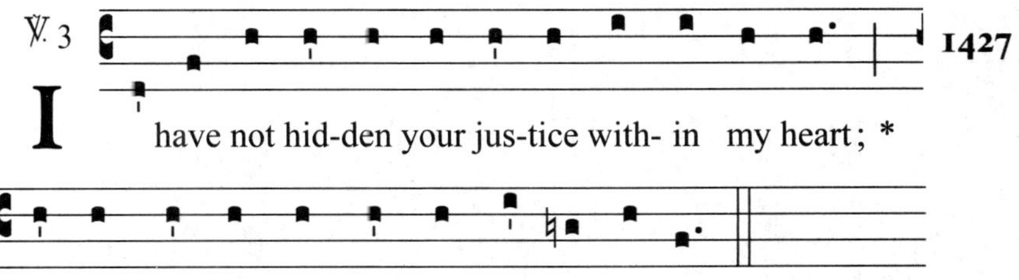
℣. 3
I have not hid-den your jus-tice with- in my heart; *
I have spo-ken your truth and your sal- va-tion. ** And he put.
1427

- iii -

1428

5.
WITH ex-pec-ta-tion I have wait-ed for the Lord, * and
he had regard to me, and he heard my prayer ; and he put
a new can-ti-cle in- to my mouth, a hymn of praise to God.

- iv -

1429

5.
WITH ex-pec-ta-tion I have wait-ed for the Lord, * and
he had re-gard to me, and he heard my prayer ; and he put
a new can-ti-cle in- to my mouth, a hymn of praise to God.

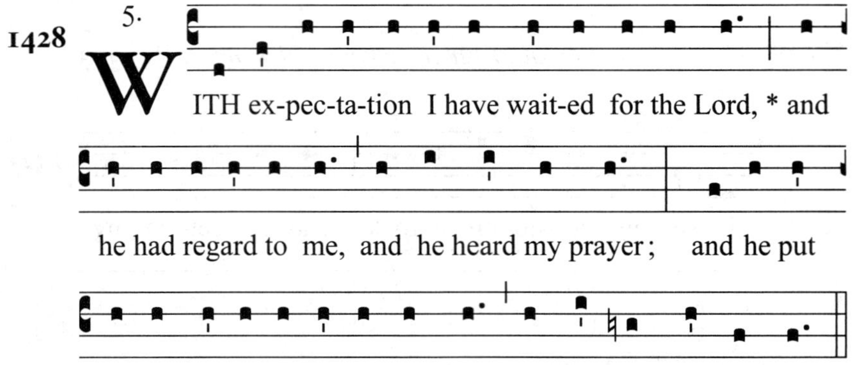

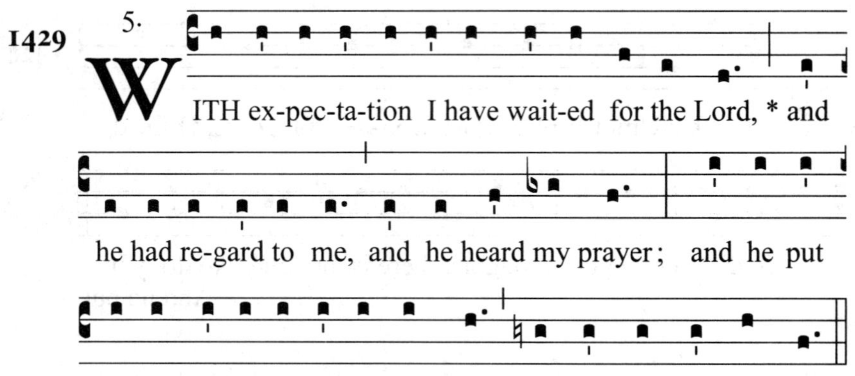

COMMUNION ANTIPHON *Qui manducat carnem meam.*
John 6:51

- i -

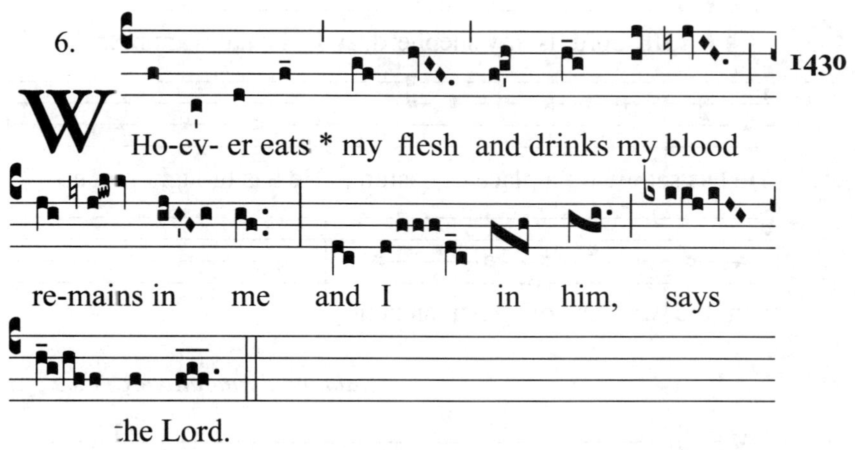
6.
W
Ho-ev- er eats * my flesh and drinks my blood
1430
re-mains in me and I in him, says
the Lord.

- ii -

6.
W
Ho- ev- er eats my flesh * and drinks my blood
1431
re-mains in me and I in him, says the Lord.

VERSES *Dominus regit me. Ps* 22:1

1432

℣. 1
THE Lord is my shepherd, and I shall want noth-ing. *
He has set me in a place of pasture. He has brought me up
on the wa- ter of re-freshment.

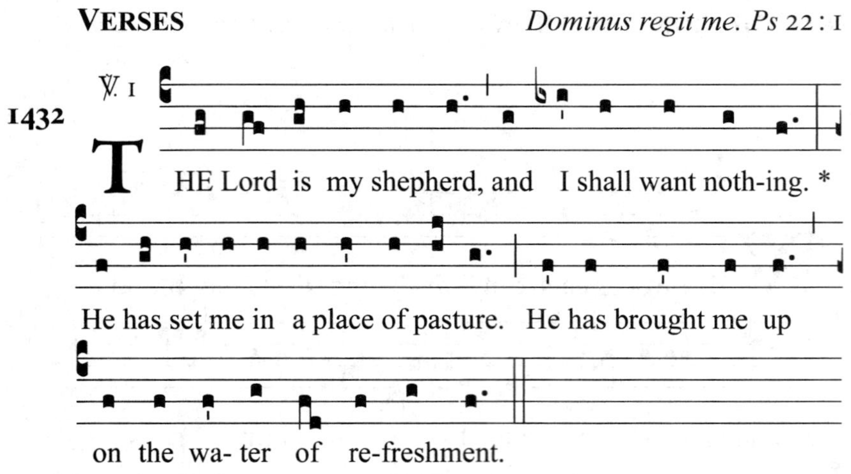

Nam, et si ambulavero. Ps 22:4

1433

℣. 2
FOR though I should walk in the midst of the shad-ow
of death, I will fear no e- vils, * for you are with me.

Parasti inconspectu meo mensam. Ps 22:5

1434

℣. 3
YOU have prepared a ta-ble before me against those
who af- flict me. * You have anointed my head with oil; and
my chal-ice how good- ly it is !

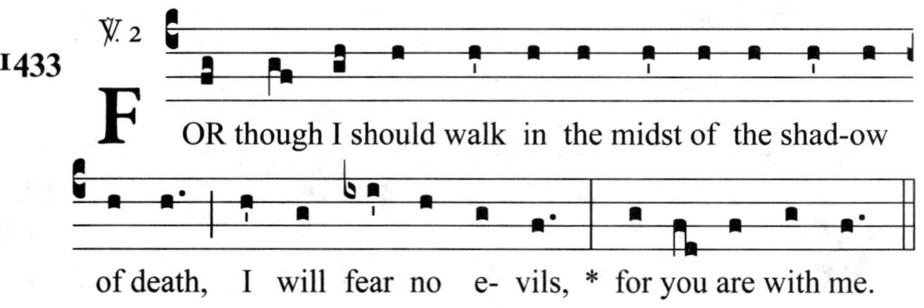

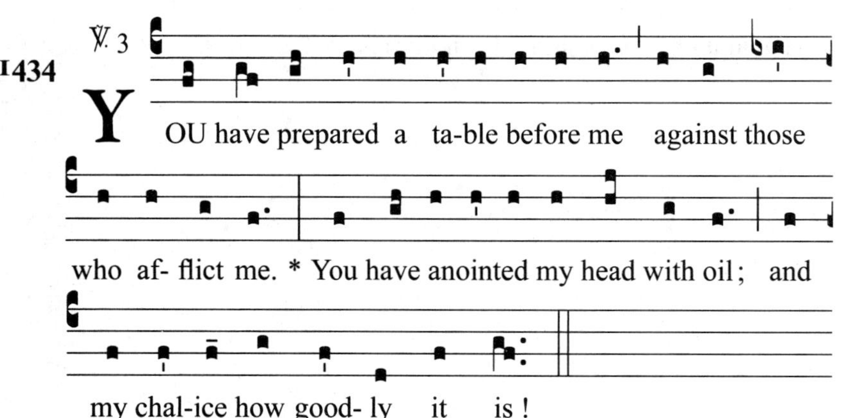

- iii -

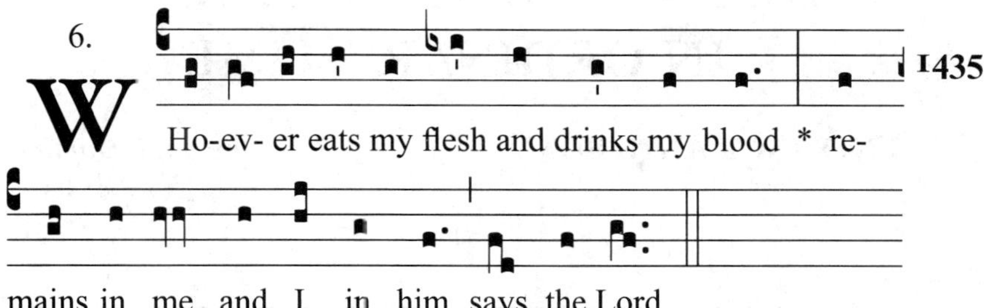
6.
WHo-ev- er eats my flesh and drinks my blood * re-
1435
mains in me and I in him, says the Lord.

Or:

6.
WHo-ev-er eats my flesh * and drinks my blood re-
1436
mains in me and I in him, says the Lord.

- iv -

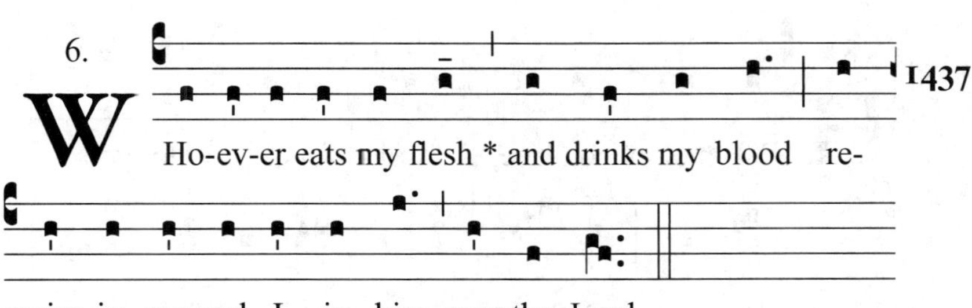
6.
WHo-ev-er eats my flesh * and drinks my blood re-
1437
mains in me and I in him, says the Lord.

TWENTY-SECOND SUNDAY IN ORDINARY TIME

Entrance Antiphon *Miserere mihi, Domine.*
Ps 85:3. 5

- i -

1438

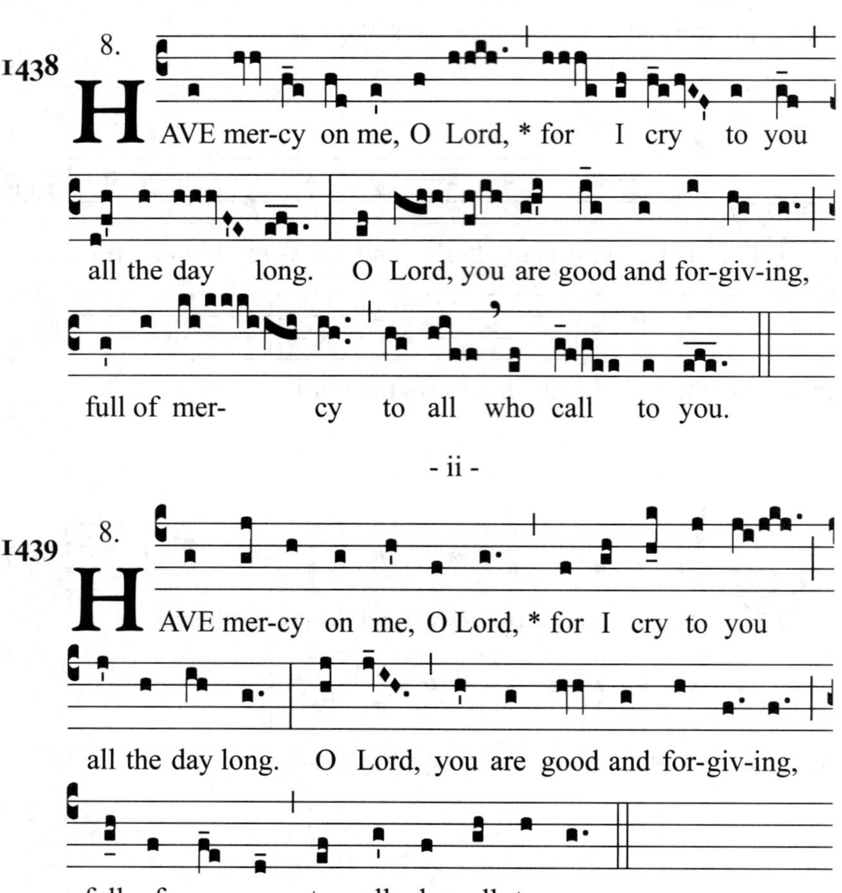
8.
HAVE mer-cy on me, O Lord, * for I cry to you
all the day long. O Lord, you are good and for-giv-ing,
full of mer- cy to all who call to you.
- ii -
8.
HAVE mer-cy on me, O Lord, * for I cry to you
all the day long. O Lord, you are good and for-giv-ing,
full of mer- cy to all who call to you.

1439

VERSES *Inclina aurem tuam et exaudi me. Ps* 85 : 1

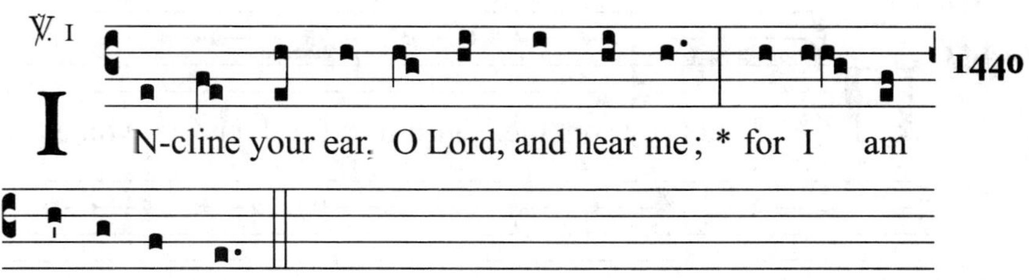
℣. 1
INCLINE your ear, O Lord, and hear me ; * for I am
1440

need-y and poor.

Custodiam animam mean, quoniam sanctus sum. Ps 85 : 2

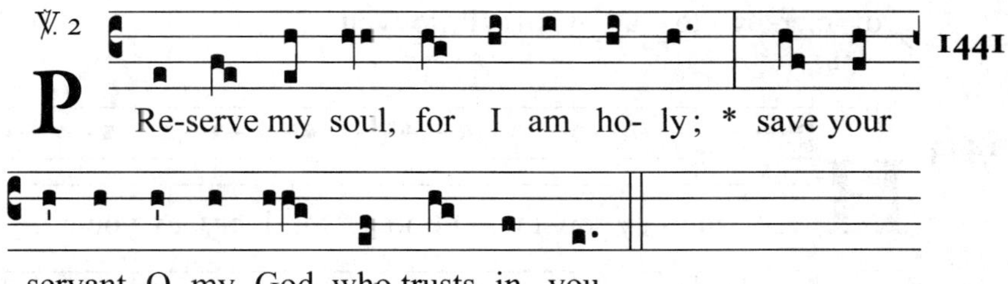
℣. 2
PRe-serve my soul, for I am ho- ly ; * save your
1441
servant, O my God, who trusts in you.

Lætifica animam servi tui. Ps 85 : 4

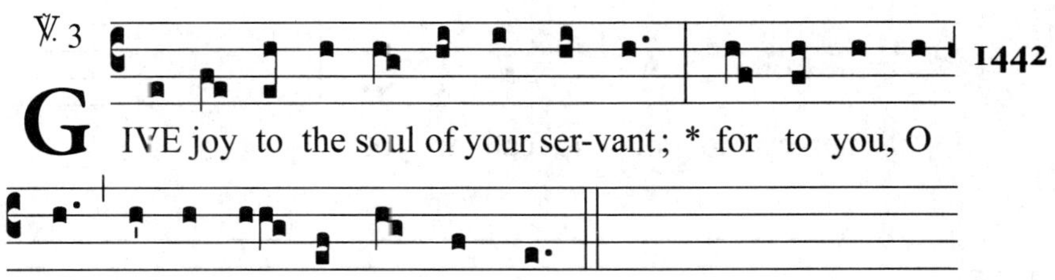
℣. 3
GIVE joy to the soul of your ser-vant ; * for to you, O
1442

Lord, I have lift- ed up my soul.

- iii -

1443

8.
HAVE mer- cy on me, O Lord, * for I cry to you all
the day long. O Lord, you are good and for-giv-ing, full
of mer- cy to all who call to you.
Or:
8.
HAVE mer- cy on me, O Lord, * for I cry to you all
the day long. O Lord, you are good and for-giv-ing, full
of mer- cy to all who call to you.
- iv -
8.
HAVE mer- cy on me, O Lord, * for I cry to you all
the day long. O Lord, you are good and for-giv-ing, full
of mer- cy to all who call to you.

1444

1445

OFFERTORY ANTIPHON *Domine, in auxilium meum respice.*
Ps 39 : 14. 15

- i -
6.
1446
LOOK down, O Lord, * to help me ; let them be con-
found- ed and a- shamed who seek af- ter my soul
to take it a- way ; look down, O Lord, to
help me.
- ii -
6.
1447
LOOK down, O Lord, to help me ; * let them be confound-ed and a-shamed who seek af- ter my soul to take
it a-way ; look down, O Lord, to help me.

VERSES *Exspectans exspectavi Dominum. Ps* 39:2

1448 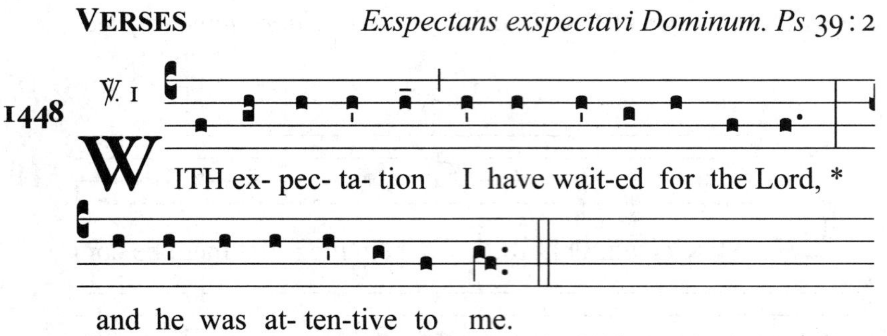
℣. 1
WITH ex- pec- ta- tion I have wait-ed for the Lord, *
and he was at- ten-tive to me.

Avertantur retrorsum et erubescant. Ps 39:15

1449 
℣. 2
LET them be turned backward and be a-shamed, * who
wish e- vil up- on me.

Annuntiavi iustitiam tuam. Ps 39:10

1450 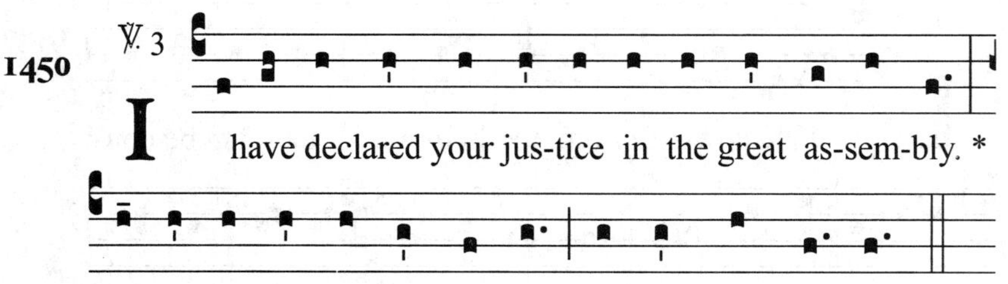
℣. 3
I have declared your jus-tice in the great as-sem-bly. *
Lo, I will not restrain my lips. O Lord, you know it.

- iii -

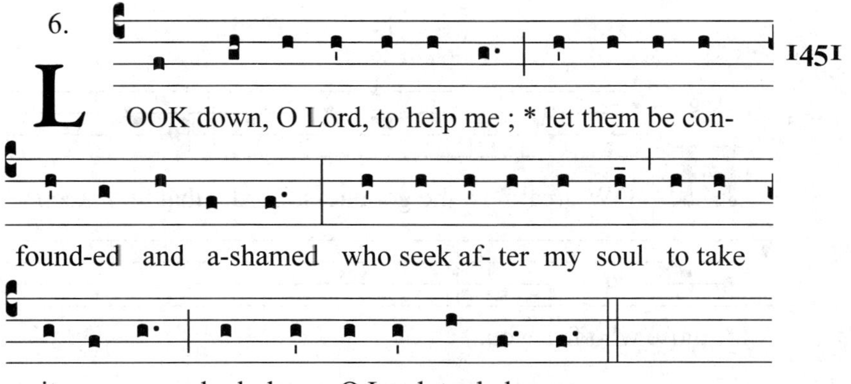
6.
1451
LOOK down, O Lord, to help me ; * let them be confound-ed and a-shamed who seek af- ter my soul to take
it a- way ; look down, O Lord, to help me.

- iv -

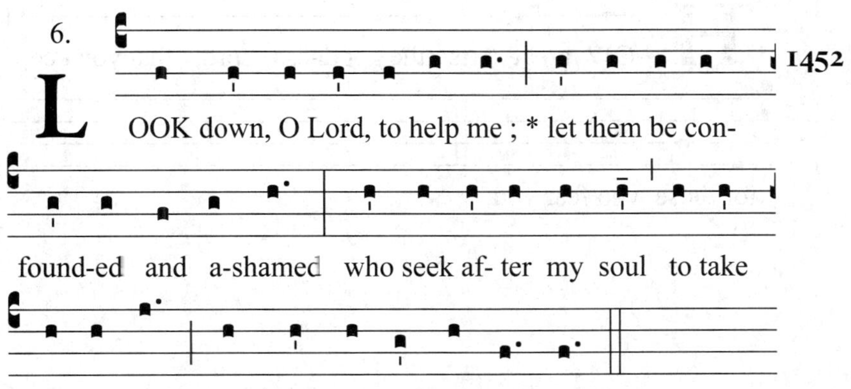
6.
1452
LOOK down, O Lord, to help me ; * let them be confound-ed and a-shamed who seek af- ter my soul to take
it a- way ; look down, O Lord, to help me.

COMMUNION ANTIPHON *Quam magna multitudo.*
Psalm 30:20

- i -

1453

4. g
HOW great * is the goodness, Lord, that you keep
for those who fear you.

- ii -

1454 4. g

HOW great * is the goodness, Lord, that you keep
for those who fear you.

VERSES *In te, Domine, sperávi. Ps* 30:2

1455 ℣. 1

IN you, O Lord, have I hoped, let me nev- er be
confound-ed, * de- liv- er me in your jus-tice.

Inclina ad me aurem tuam. Ps 30 : 3. 4

℣. 2 1456

BOW down your ear to me; make haste to de- liv- er me, * for you are my strength and ref- uge.

In manus tuas commendo spiritum meum. Ps 30 : 6

℣. 3
1457
INTO your hands I com-mend my spir- it, * for
you have redeemed me, O Lord, the God of truth.

Exsultabo et laetabor in misericordia tua. Ps 30 : 8

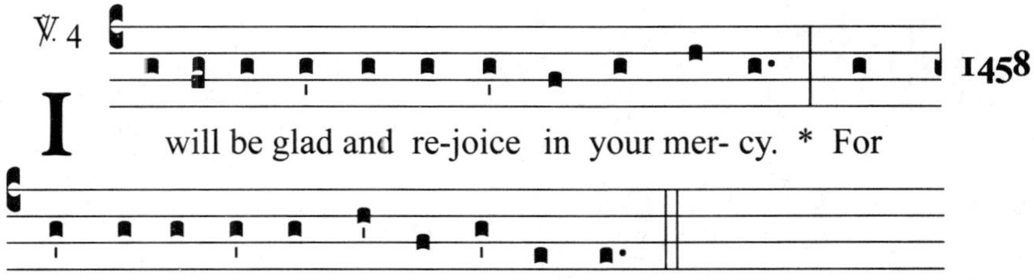
℣. 4
1458
I will be glad and re-joice in your mer- cy. * For
you have re-gard-ed my hu- mil- i- ty.

Ego autem in te speravi. Ps 30 : 15-16

℣. 5
1459
BUT I have put my trust in you, O Lord; * I have
said, You are my God; my lot is in your hands.

- iii -

1460 4. g

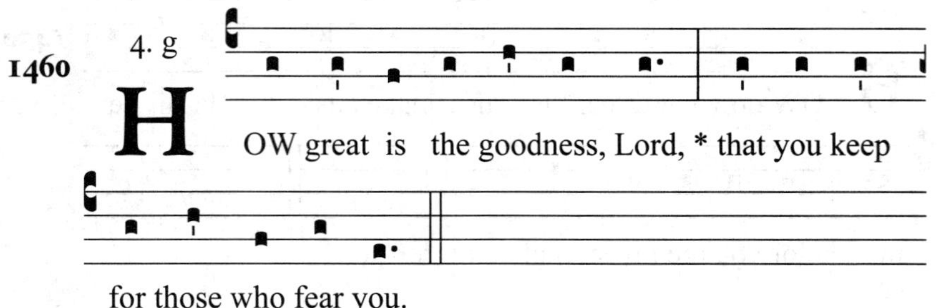
HOW great is the goodness, Lord, * that you keep
for those who fear you.

- iv -

1461 4. g

HOW great is the goodness, Lord, * that you keep for
those who fear you.

TWENTY-THIRD SUNDAY IN ORDINARY TIME

Entrance Antiphon *Iustus es, Domine.*
Ps 118:137. 124

- i -

I. 1462

YOU are just, O Lord, * and your judgment is right ;
treat your ser-vant in ac-cord with your mer-ci- ful love.

- ii -

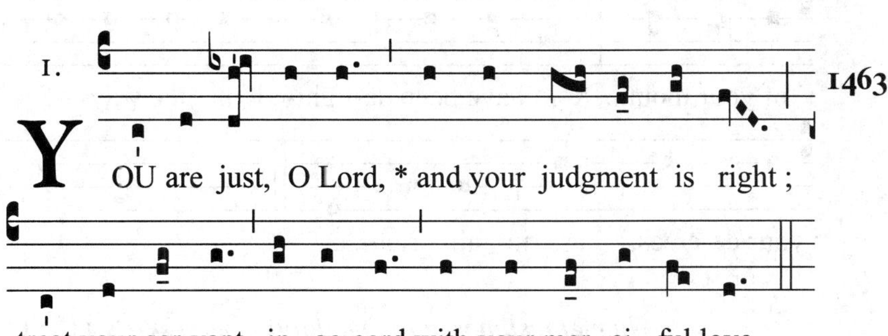
I.
1463
YOU are just, O Lord, * and your judgment is right ;
treat your ser-vant in ac-cord with your mer- ci- ful love.

VERSES *In corde mea abscondi eloquia tua. Ps* 118 : 11-12

1464
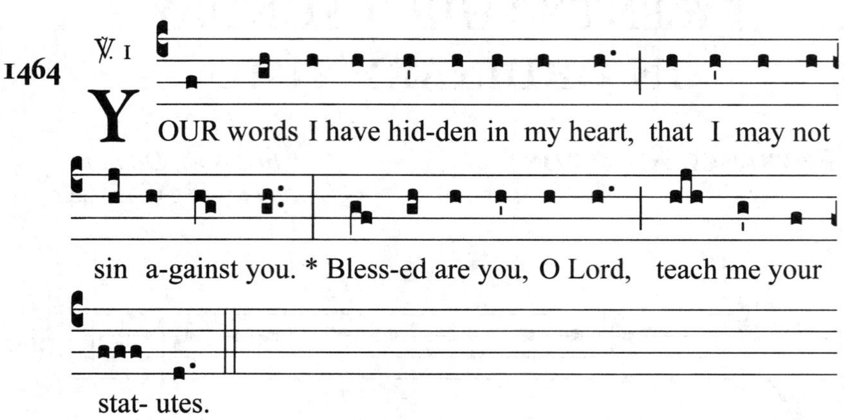
℣. 1
Y OUR words I have hid-den in my heart, that I may not
sin a-gainst you. * Bless-ed are you, O Lord, teach me your
stat- utes.

In labiis meis pronuntiavi. Ps 118 : 13-14

1465
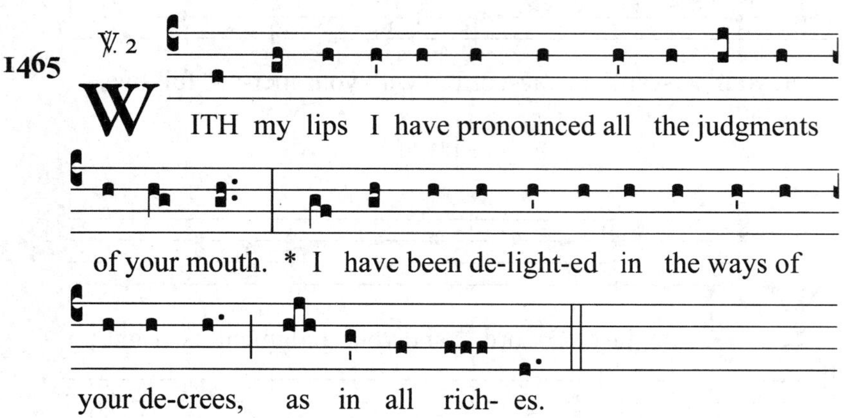
℣. 2
W ITH my lips I have pronounced all the judgments
of your mouth. * I have been de-light-ed in the ways of
your de-crees, as in all rich- es.

Nam et testimonia tua meditatio mea est. Ps 118 : 12

1466

℣. 3
F OR your tes- ti- mo-nies are my med- i- ta- tion, *
and your jus- ti- fi- ca- tions my coun- sel.

- iii -

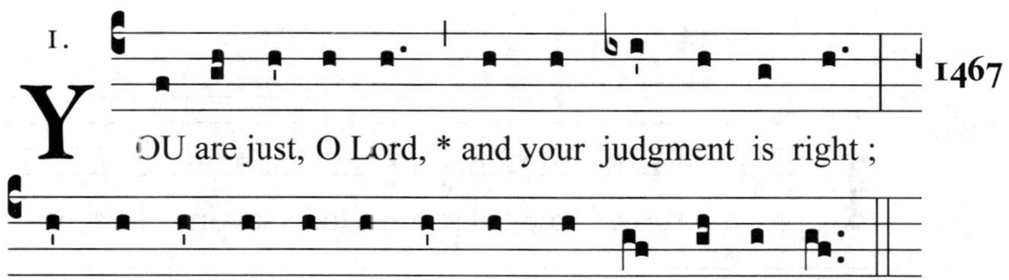
1.
1467
YOU are just, O Lord, * and your judgment is right ;
treat your ser-vant in ac-cord with your mer- ci- ful love.

- iv -

1.
1468
YOU are just, O Lord, * and your judgment is right ;
treat your ser-vant in ac-cord with your mer-ci- ful love.

OFFERTORY ANTIPHON *Oravi Deum meum ego Daniel.*
Dn 9:4. (2.) 17. 19

- i -

1469 4.

I, Dan-iel,*prayed to my God, say-ing: Hear, O Lord, the prayers of your ser-vant; show your face up- on your ho- ly place, and fav'-ra- bly look down up- on this peo- ple up- on whom your name is in-voked, O God.

- ii -

1470

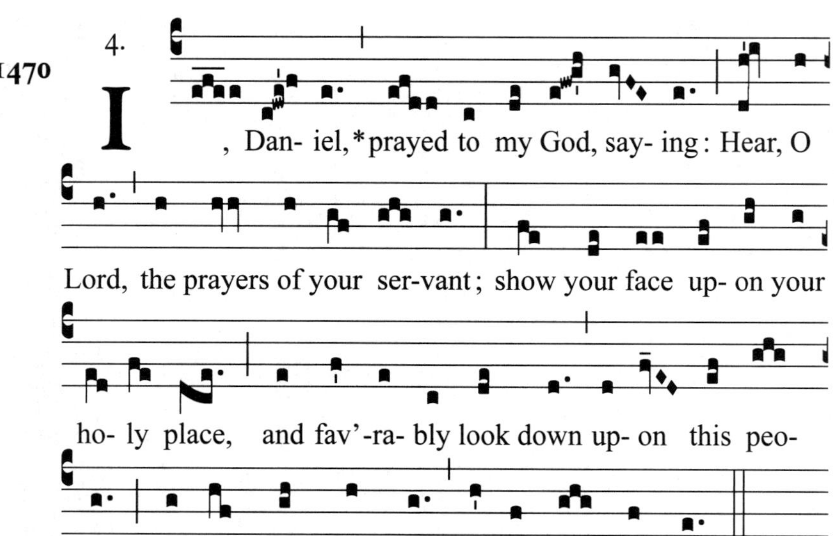
4.
I
, Dan- iel,*prayed to my God, say- ing: Hear, O
Lord, the prayers of your ser-vant; show your face up- on your
ho- ly place, and fav'-ra- bly look down up- on this peo-
ple up- on whom your name is in-voked, O God.

VERSES *Adhuc me loquente. Dn 9:20*

℣. 1

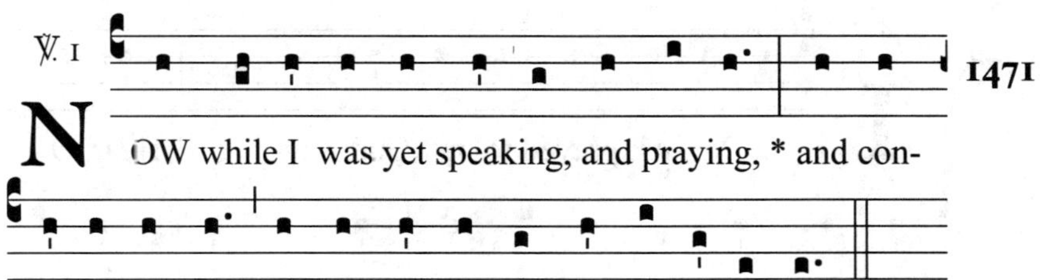
1471
NOW while I was yet speaking, and praying, * and confessing my sins, and the sins of my peo-ple Is- ra- el.

Audivi vocem decentem mihi. Dn 9:20; 10:11

℣. 2

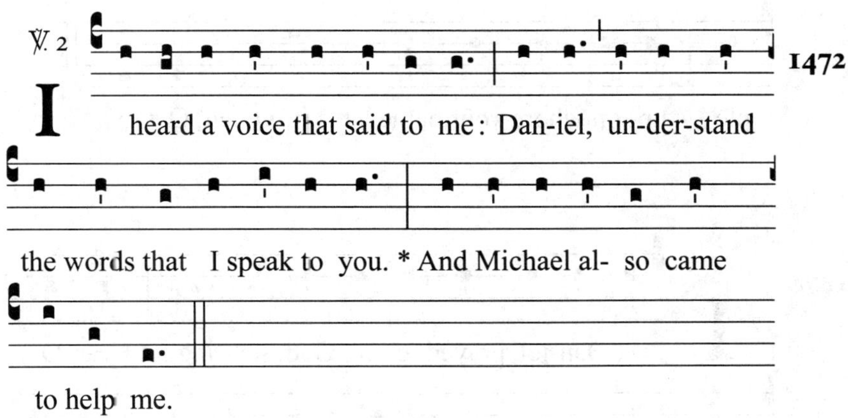
1472
I heard a voice that said to me: Dan-iel, un-der-stand
the words that I speak to you. * And Michael al- so came
to help me.

- iii -

1473

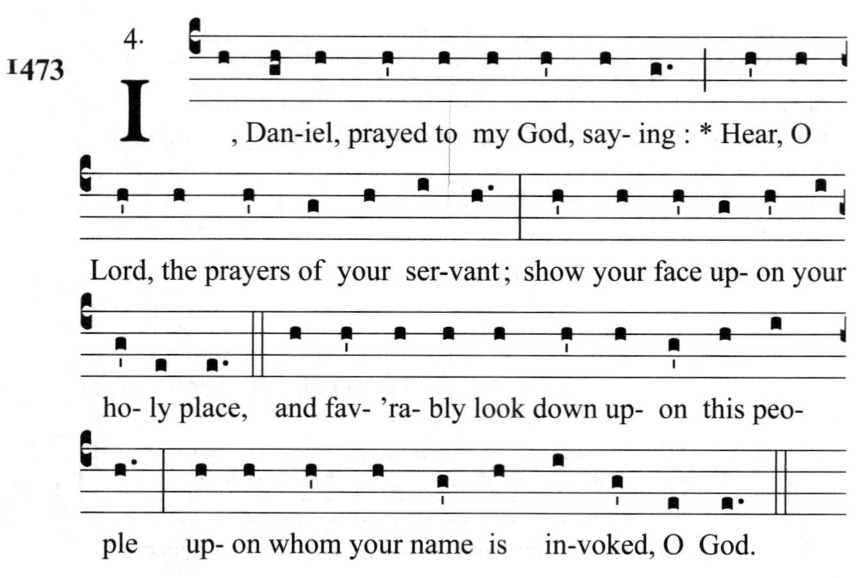

- iv -

1474

4.

I, Dan-iel, prayed to my God, say- ing : * Hear, O

Lord, the prayers of your ser-vant; show your face up- on your

ho- ly place, and fav- 'ra- bly look down up- on this peo-

ple up- on whom your name is in-voked, O God.

COMMUNION ANTIPHON *Quemadmodum desiderat cervus.*
Ps 41 : 2-3

- i -

4. g

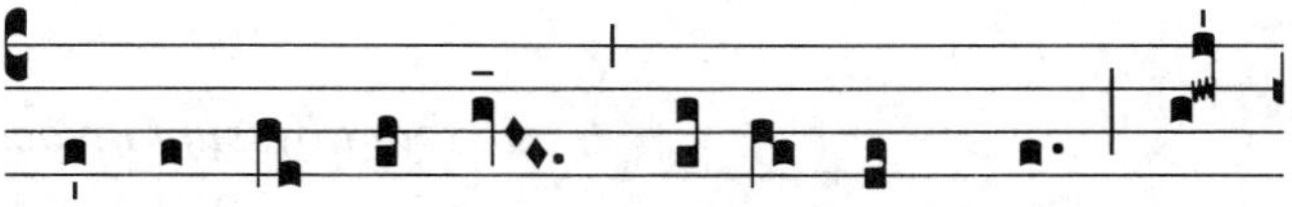

LIKE the deer that yearns * for running streams, so 1475

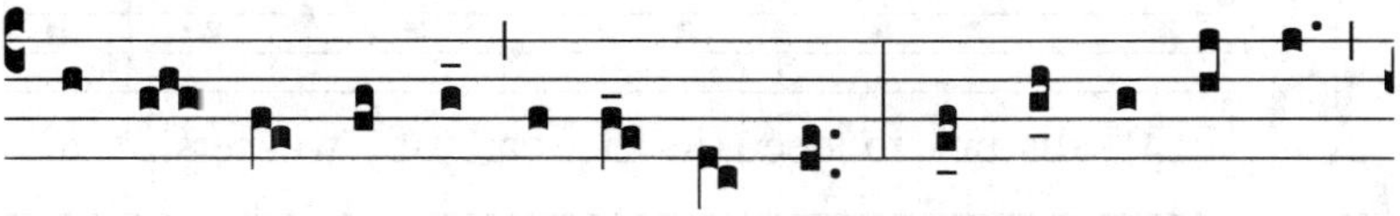

my soul is yearning for you, my God; my soul is thirsting

for God, the liv- ing God.

- ii -

4. g

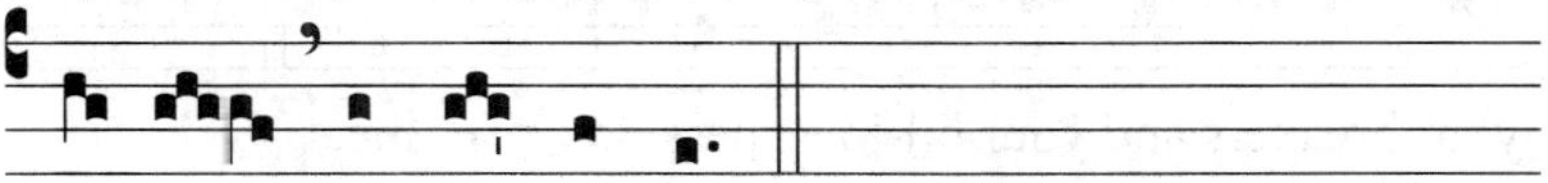

LIKE the deer that yearns for running streams, * so 1476

my soul is yearning for you, my God; my soul is thirsting

for God, the liv-ing God.

VERSES *Spera in Deo. Ps* 41 : 6

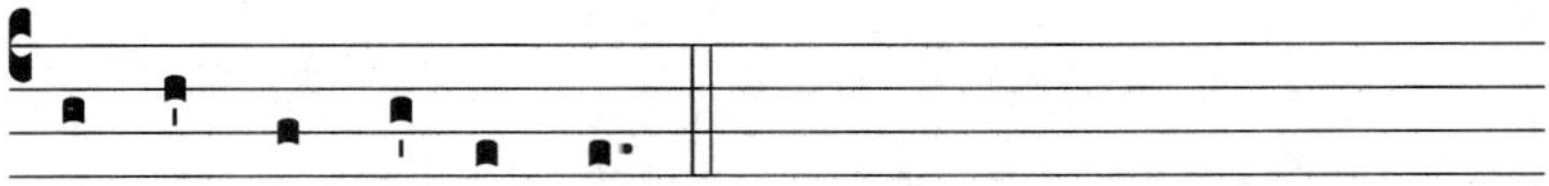

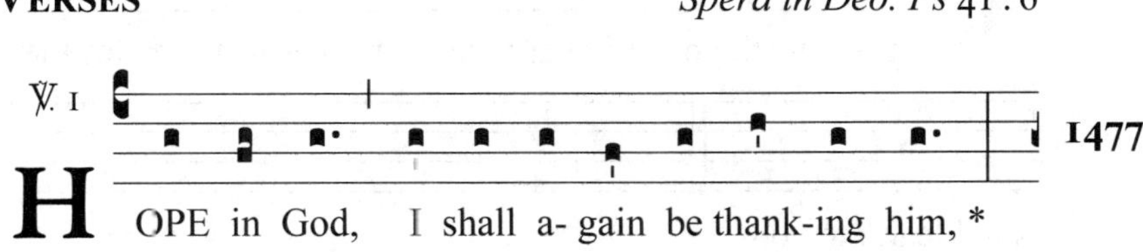
℣. 1
1477
HOPE in God, I shall a- gain be thank-ing him, *

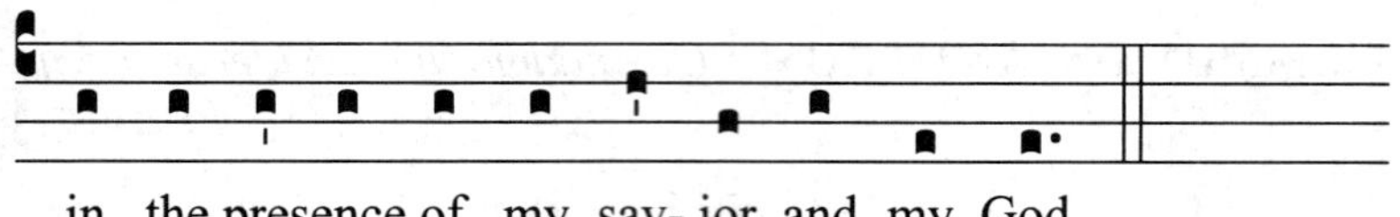
in the presence of my sav- ior and my God.

Abyssys abyssum invocat. Ps 41 : 8

1478 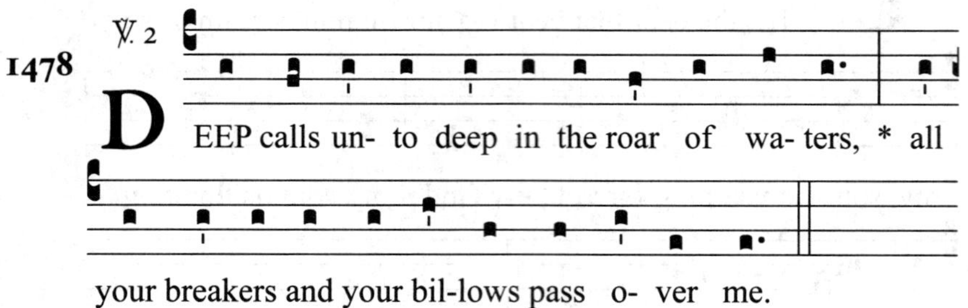
℣. 2
DEEP calls un- to deep in the roar of wa- ters, * all
your breakers and your bil-lows pass o- ver me.

In die mandavit Dominus misericordiam suam. Ps 41 : 9

1479 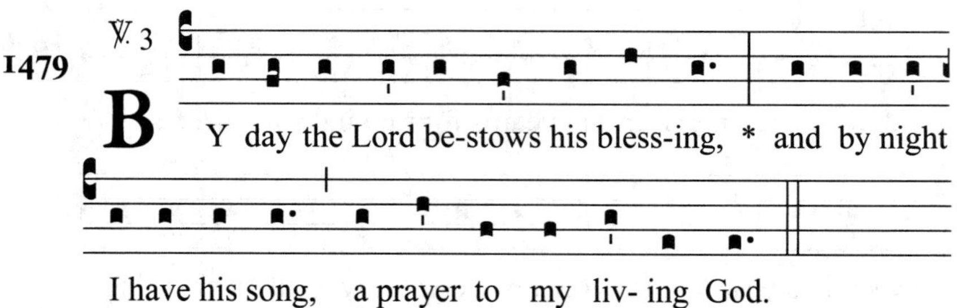
℣. 3
BY day the Lord be-stows his bless-ing, * and by night
I have his song, a prayer to my liv- ing God.

Emitte lucem tuam et veritatem tuam. Ps 42 : 3

1480 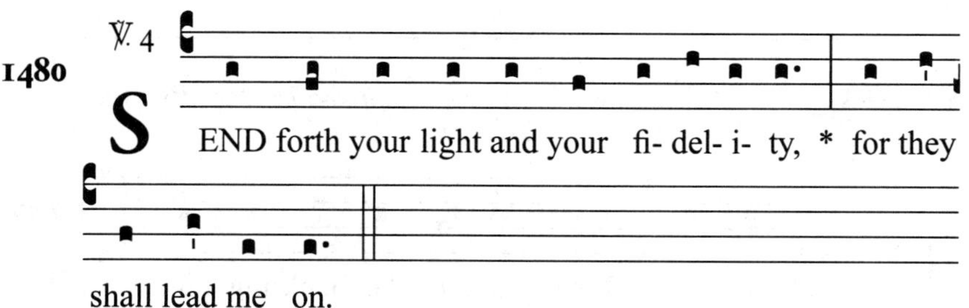
℣. 4
SEND forth your light and your fi- del- i- ty, * for they
shall lead me on.

- iii -

4.
1481
LIKE the deer that yearns for running streams, * so my
soul is yearning for you, my God ; my soul is thirsting for
God, the liv- ing God.

Or:

4. 1482

LIKE the deer that yearns for running streams, * so my soul is yearn-ing for you, my God; my soul is thirsting for God, the liv- ing God.

- iv -

1483

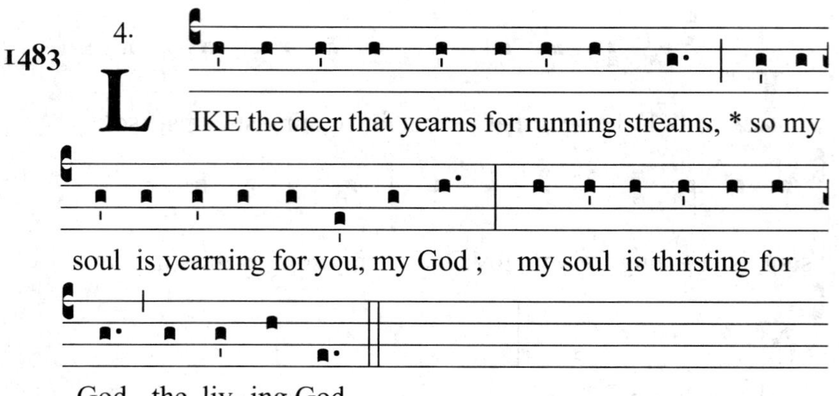
4.
LIKE the deer that yearns for running streams, * so my
soul is yearning for you, my God ; my soul is thirsting for
God, the liv- ing God.

TWENTY-FOURTH SUNDAY IN ORDINARY TIME

Entrance Antiphon *Da pacem, Domine. Cf. Sir* 36:18

- i -

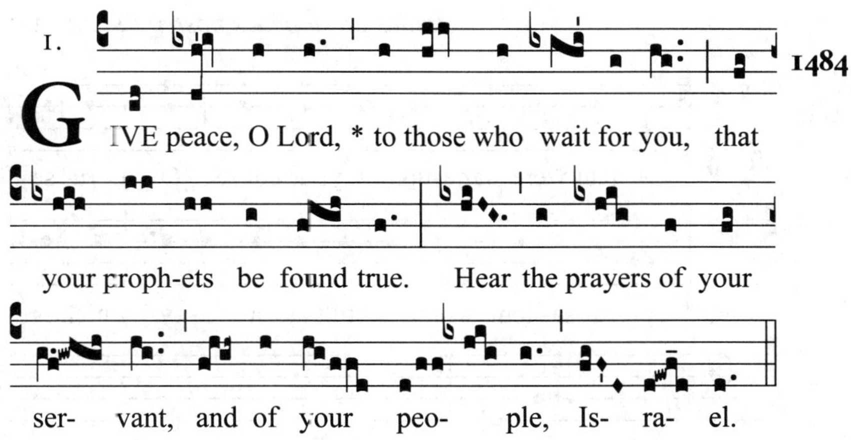
I.
1484
GIVE peace, O Lord, * to those who wait for you, that
your proph-ets be found true. Hear the prayers of your
ser- vant, and of your peo- ple, Is- ra- el.

- ii -

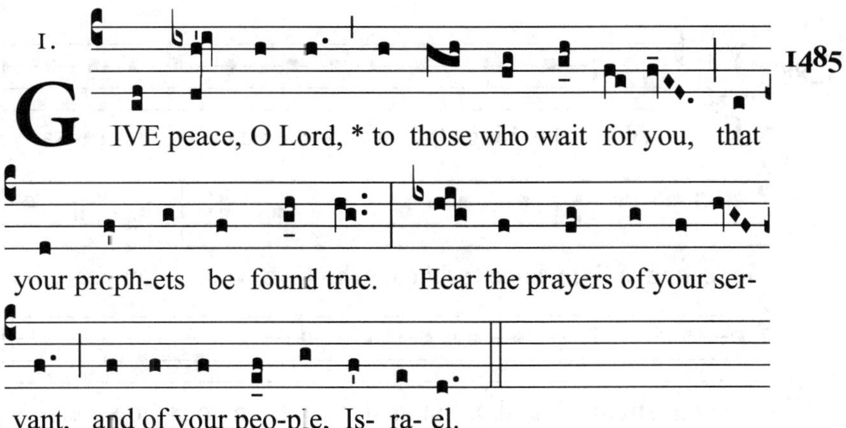
I.
1485
GIVE peace, O Lord, * to those who wait for you, that
your proph-ets be found true. Hear the prayers of your ser-
vant, and of your peo-ple, Is- ra- el.

VERSES *Lætatus sum in his quæ dicta sunt mihi. Ps* 121 : 1

1486
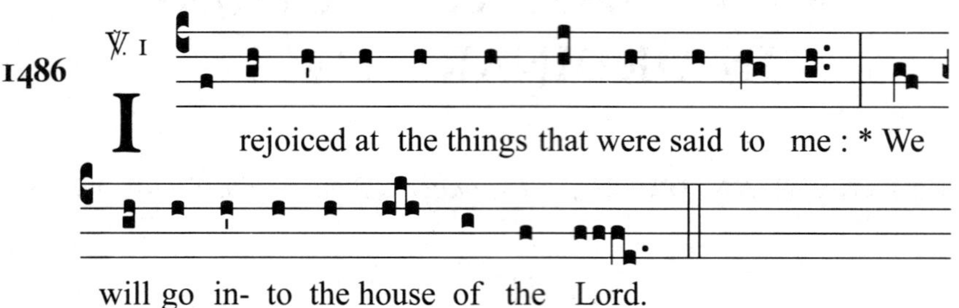
℣. 1
I rejoiced at the things that were said to me : * We
will go in- to the house of the Lord.

Stantes erant pedes nostri. Ps 121 : 2-3

1487
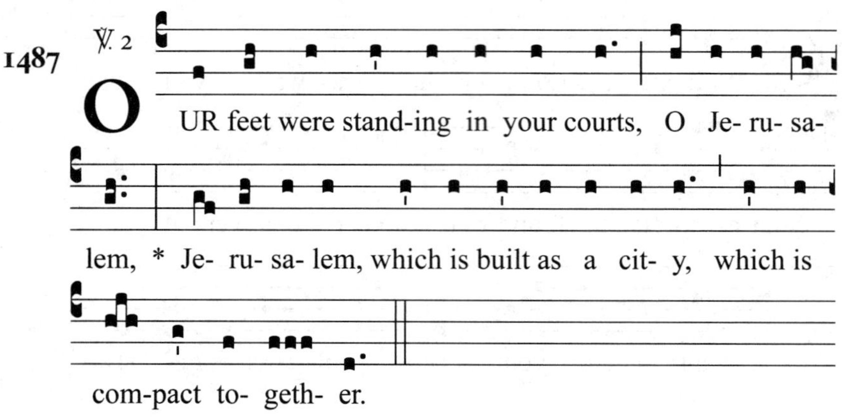
℣. 2
OUR feet were stand-ing in your courts, O Je- ru- sa-
lem, * Je- ru- sa- lem, which is built as a cit- y, which is
com-pact to- geth- er.

Rogate quæ ad pacem sunt Ierusalem. Ps 121 : 6-7

1488
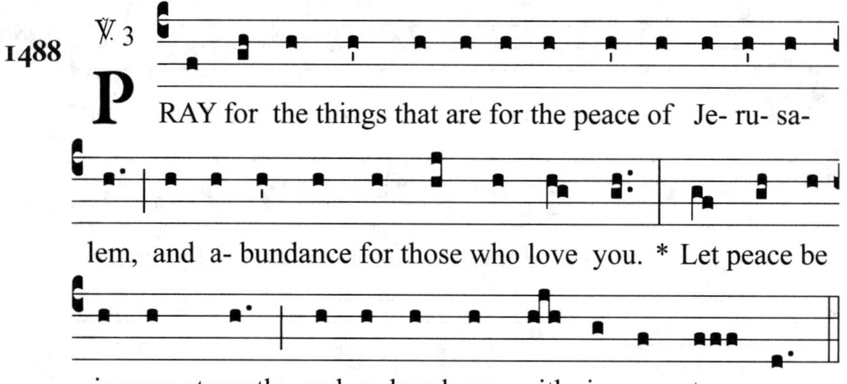
℣. 3
PRAY for the things that are for the peace of Je- ru- sa-
lem, and a- bundance for those who love you. * Let peace be
in your strength, and a- bundance with- in your tow- ers.

- iii -

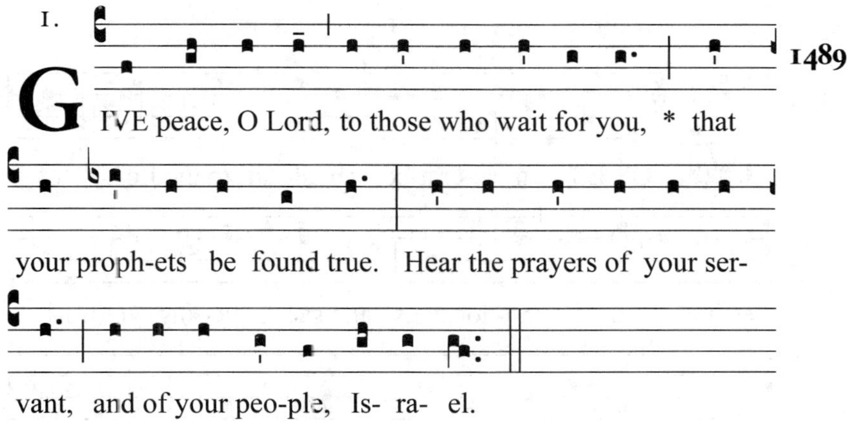
I.
1489
GIVE peace, O Lord, to those who wait for you, * that
your proph-ets be found true. Hear the prayers of your ser-
vant, and of your peo-ple, Is- ra- el.

- iv -

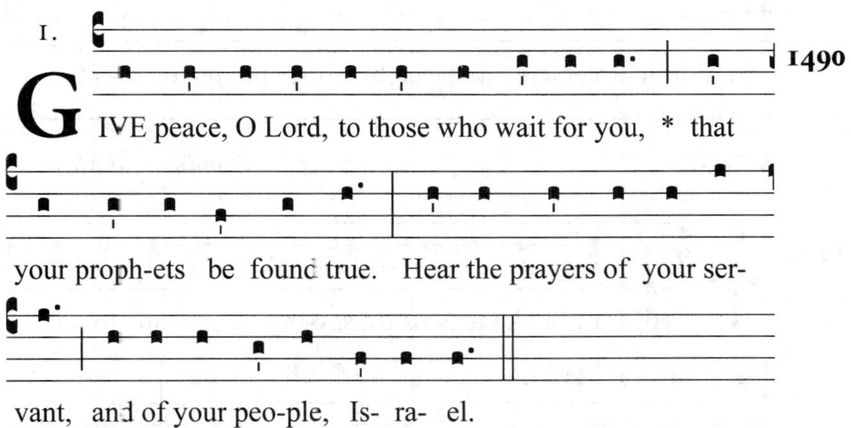
I.
1490
GIVE peace, O Lord, to those who wait for you, * that
your proph-ets be found true. Hear the prayers of your ser-
vant, and of your peo-ple, Is- ra- el.

OFFERTORY ANTIPHON *Sanctificavit Moyses altare Domino.*
Ex 24:4. 5

1491

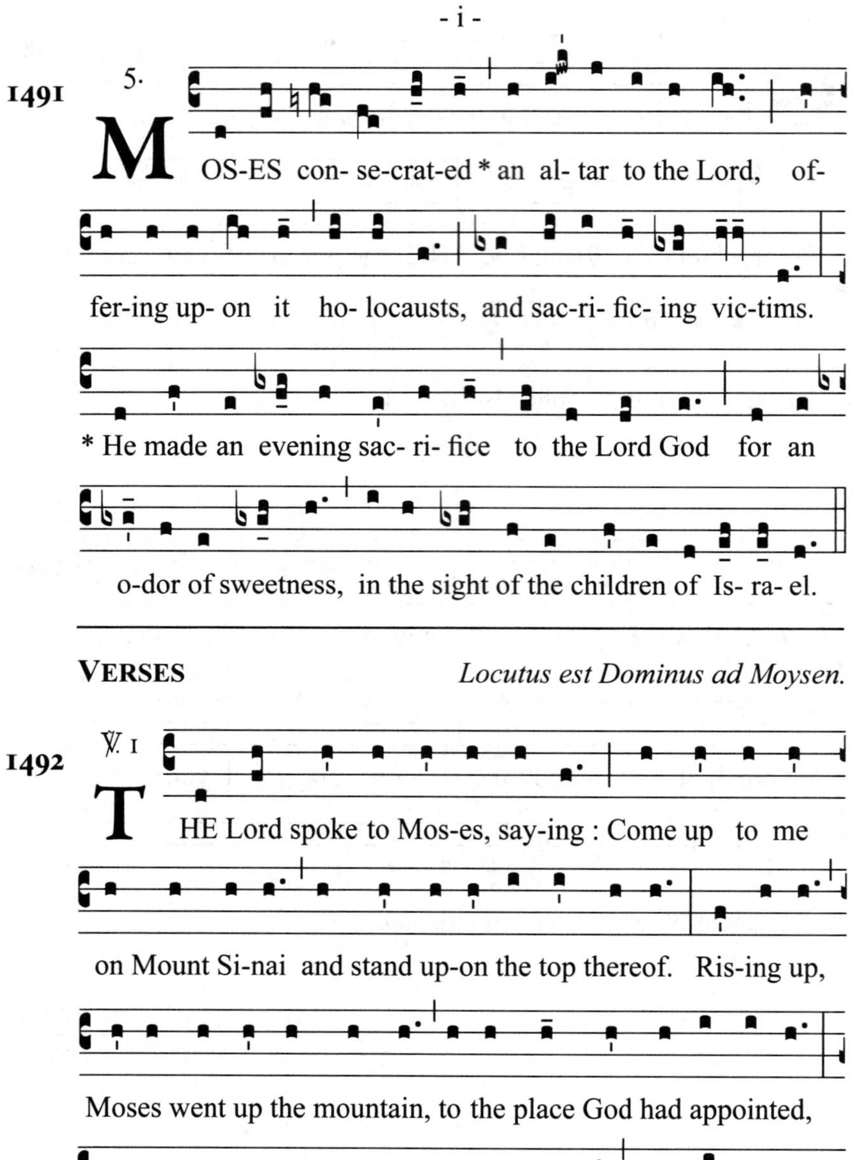
- i -
5.
MOS-ES con- se-crat-ed * an al- tar to the Lord, of-
fer-ing up- on it ho- locausts, and sac-ri- fic- ing vic-tims.
* He made an evening sac- ri- fice to the Lord God for an
o-dor of sweetness, in the sight of the children of Is- ra- el.

VERSES *Locutus est Dominus ad Moysen.*

1492

℣. 1
THE Lord spoke to Mos-es, say-ing : Come up to me
on Mount Si-nai and stand up-on the top thereof. Ris-ing up,
Moses went up the mountain, to the place God had appointed,
and the Lord came down to him in a cloud and stood be-fore

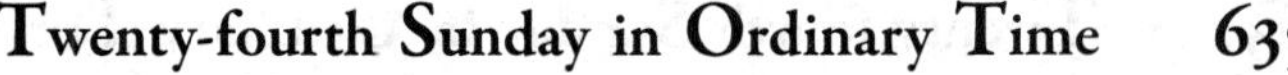

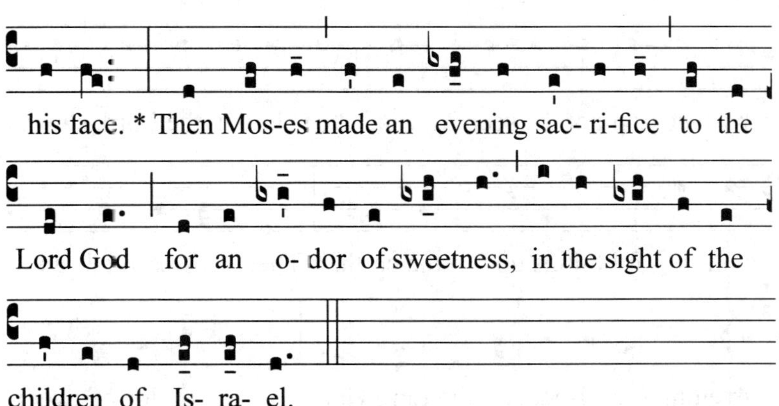
his face. * Then Mos-es made an evening sac- ri-fice to the
Lord God for an o- dor of sweetness, in the sight of the
children of Is- ra- el.

Oravit Moyses Dominum dixit.

℣. 2 MOSES prayed to the Lord, and said : If I have found 1493
fav-or in your sight, show me yourself o-pen-ly, that I may see
you. And the Lord spoke to him, say-ing : Man shall not see me
and live. But stand up-on the rock and my right hand will pro-
tect you, un- til I have passed by. While I am passing by, I
will take a-way my hand, and then you shall see my glo-ry, but

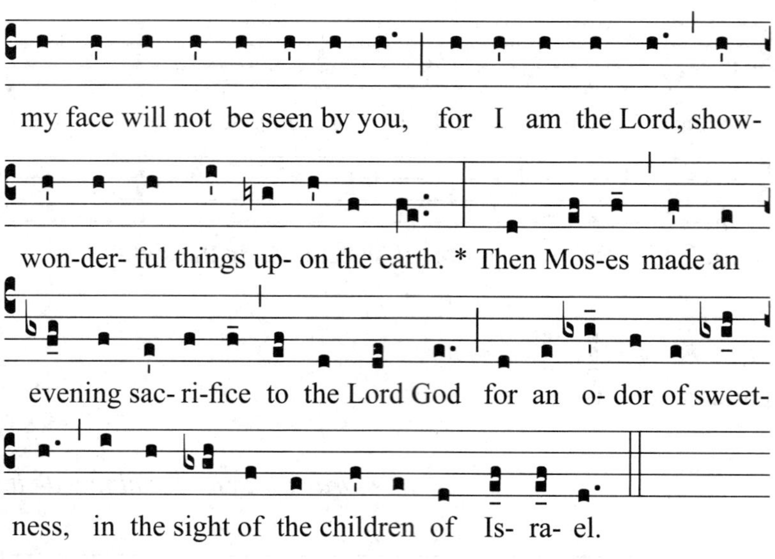
my face will not be seen by you, for I am the Lord, show-
won-der- ful things up- on the earth. * Then Mos-es made an
evening sac- ri-fice to the Lord God for an o- dor of sweetness, in the sight of the children of Is- ra- el.

- iii -

1494 5.
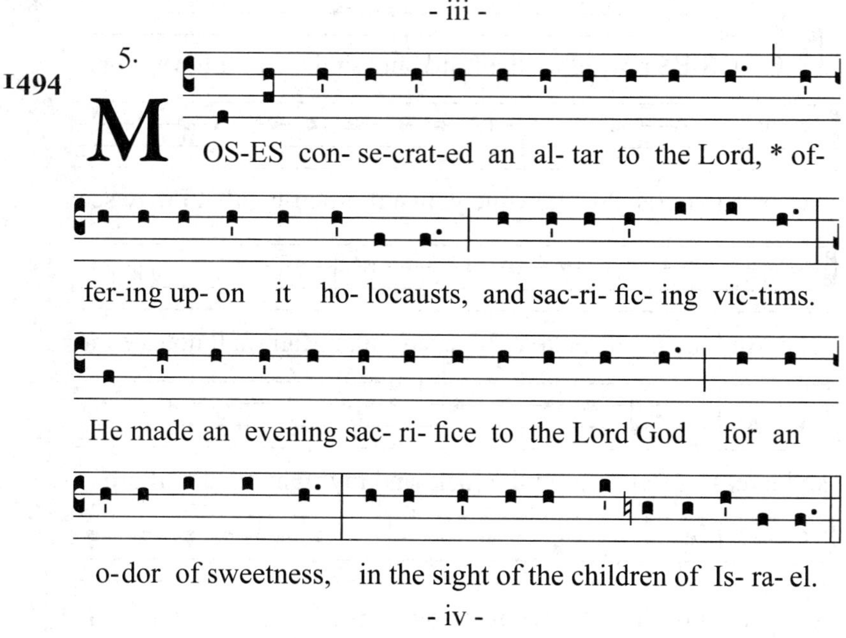
MOS-ES con- se-crat-ed an al- tar to the Lord, * of-
fer-ing up- on it ho- locausts, and sac-ri- fic- ing vic-tims.
He made an evening sac- ri- fice to the Lord God for an
o-dor of sweetness, in the sight of the children of Is- ra- el.

- iv -

1495 5.

MOS-ES con- se-crat-ed an al- tar to the Lord, * of-

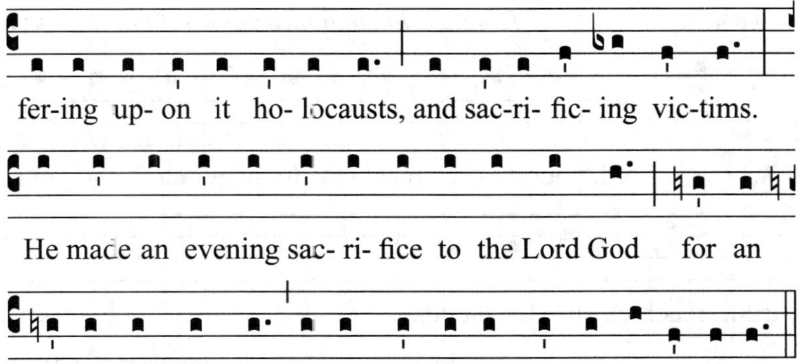
fer-ing up- on it ho- locausts, and sac-ri- fic- ing vic-tims.
He made an evening sac- ri- fice to the Lord God for an

o-dor of sweetness, in the sight of the children of Is- ra- el.

COMMUNION ANTIPHON *Quam pretiosa est.*
Ps 35:8

- i -

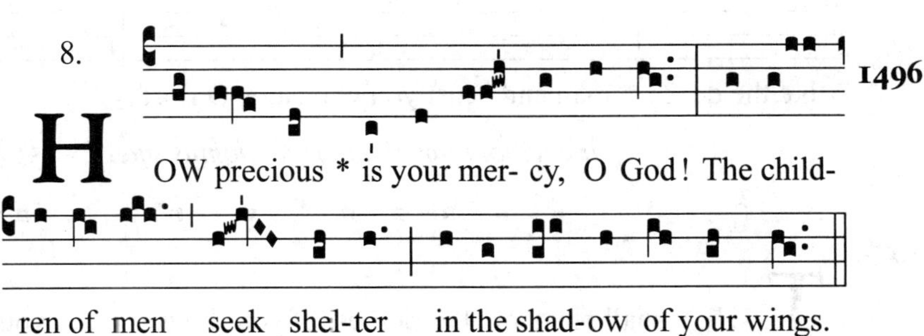
8.
HOW precious * is your mer- cy, O God! The child-
1496
ren of men seek shel-ter in the shad-ow of your wings.

- ii -

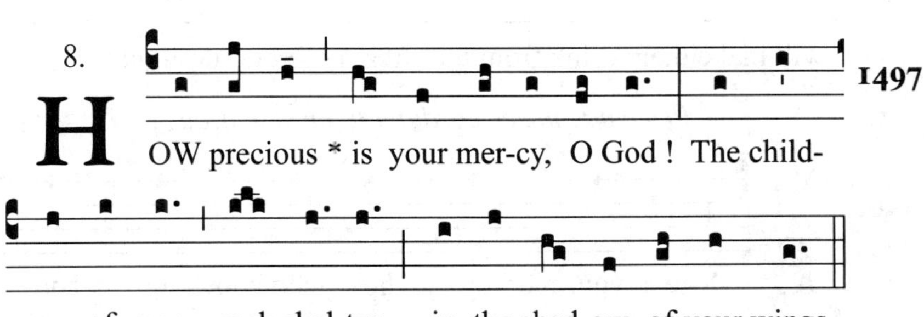
8.
HOW precious * is your mer-cy, O God ! The child-
1497
ren of men seek shel-ter in the shad-ow of your wings.

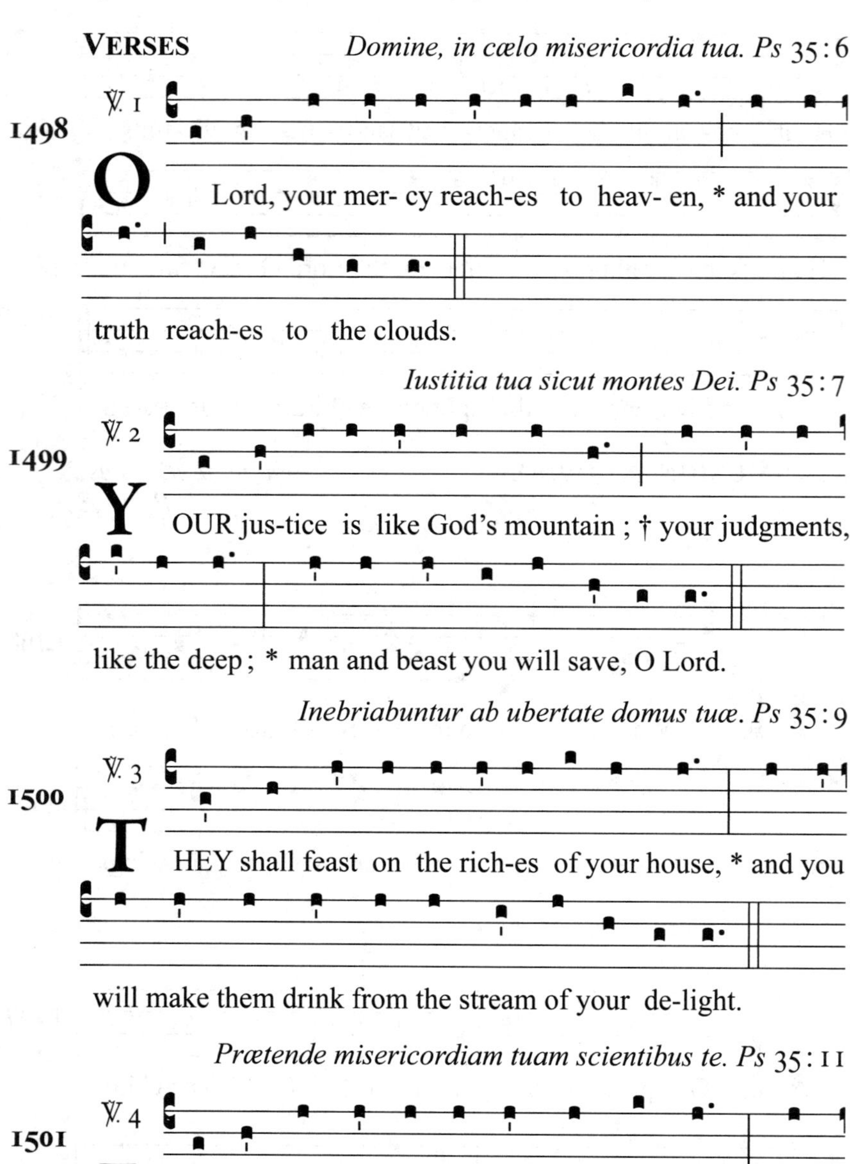
VERSES
Domine, in cælo misericordia tua. Ps 35:6
1498 ℣. 1
O Lord, your mer- cy reach-es to heav- en, * and your truth reach-es to the clouds.
Iustitia tua sicut montes Dei. Ps 35:7
1499 ℣. 2
YOUR jus-tice is like God's mountain ; † your judgments, like the deep; * man and beast you will save, O Lord.
Inebriabuntur ab ubertate domus tuæ. Ps 35:9
1500 ℣. 3
THEY shall feast on the rich-es of your house, * and you will make them drink from the stream of your de-light.
Prætende misericordiam tuam scientibus te. Ps 35:11
1501 ℣. 4

EXtend your mer- cy to those who know you, * and your jus-tice to up-right hearts.

- iii -

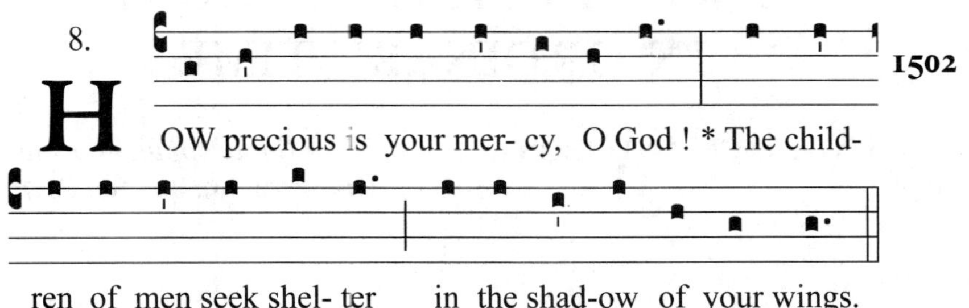
8.
1502
HOW precious is your mer- cy, O God! * The child-
ren of men seek shel- ter in the shad-ow of your wings.

- iv -

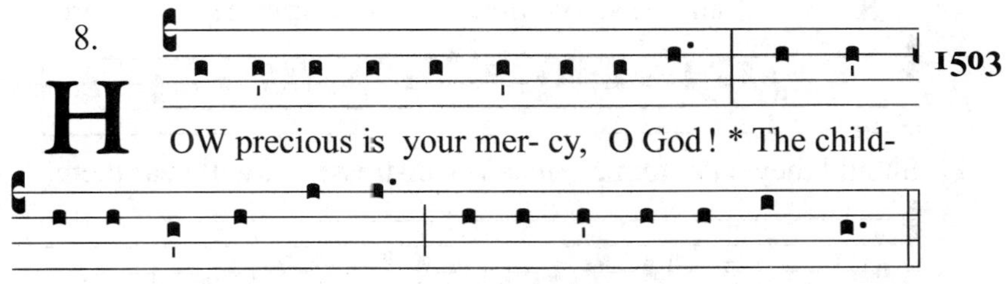
8.
1503
HOW precious is your mer- cy, O God! * The child-
ren of men seek shel- ter in the shad-ow of your wings.

TWENTY-FIFTH SUNDAY IN ORDINARY TIME

Entrance Antiphon *Salus populi ego sum.*
Cf. Ps 36:39. 40. 28; *Ps* 77

- i -

1504 4.

I am the sal-va-tion * of the people, says the Lord.
Should they cry to me in an- y distress, I will hear them,
and I will be their Lord for ev- er.

- ii -

1505

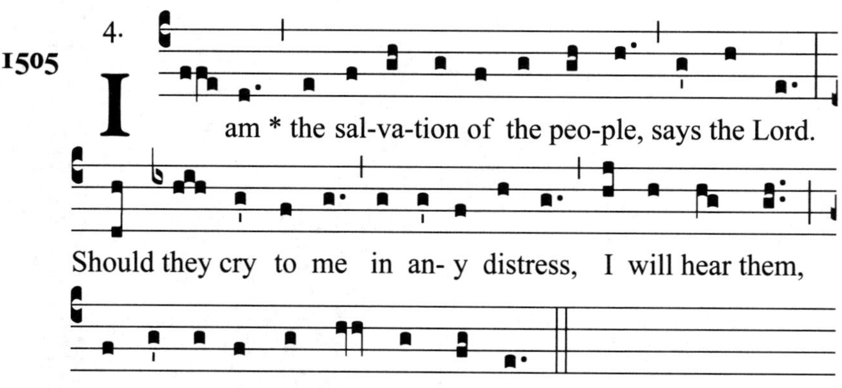
4.
I am * the sal-va-tion of the peo-ple, says the Lord.
Should they cry to me in an- y distress, I will hear them,
and I will be their Lord for ev- er.

VERSES *Attendite popule meus legem meam. Ps* 77 : 1

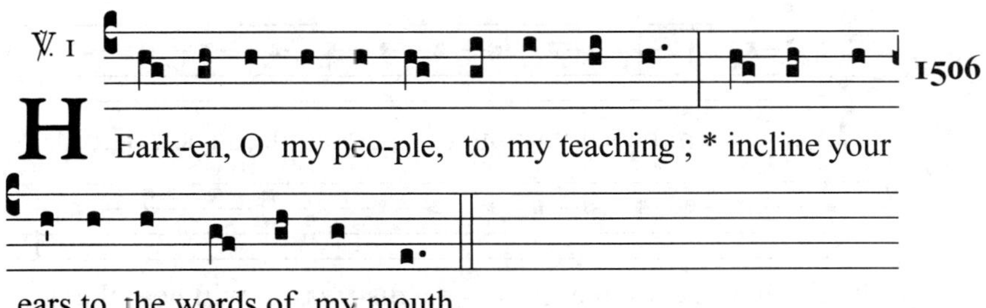
℣. 1
1506
HEark-en, O my peo-ple, to my teaching ; * incline your
ears to the words of my mouth.

Et manducaverunt, et saturati sunt nimis. Ps 77 : 52

℣. 2
1507
HIS peo-ple he led forth like sheep, * and guid-ed them
like a flock in the des-ert.

Sed elegit tribum Judah. Ps 77 : 68. 70

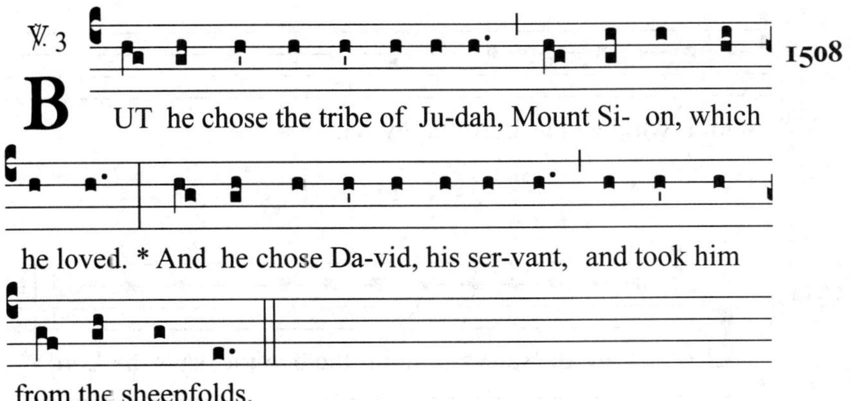
℣. 3
1508
BUT he chose the tribe of Ju-dah, Mount Si- on, which
he loved. * And he chose Da-vid, his ser-vant, and took him
from the sheepfolds.

- iii -

1509

4.
I am the sal-va-tion of the peo-ple, says the Lord. *
Should they cry to me in an- y dis-tress, I will hear them,
and I will be their Lord for ev- er.

Or:

1510

4.
I am the sal-va-tion of the peo-ple, says the Lord. *
Should they cry to me in an- y dis-tress, I will hear them,
and I will be their Lord for ev- er.

- iv -

1511

4.
I am the sal-va-tion of the peo-ple, says the Lord. *
Should they cry to me in an- y dis-tress, I will hear them,

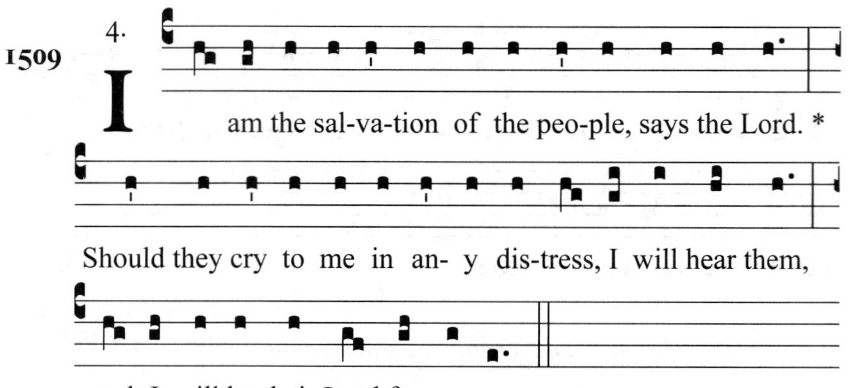

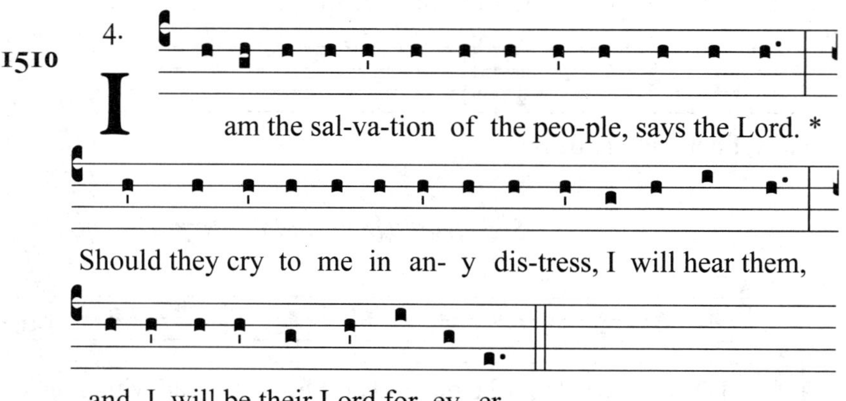

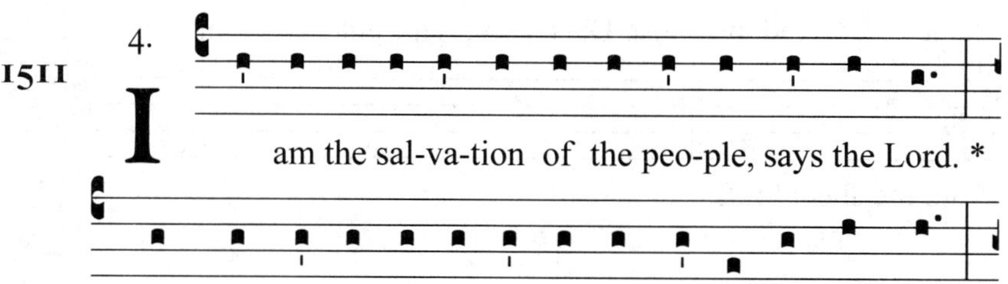

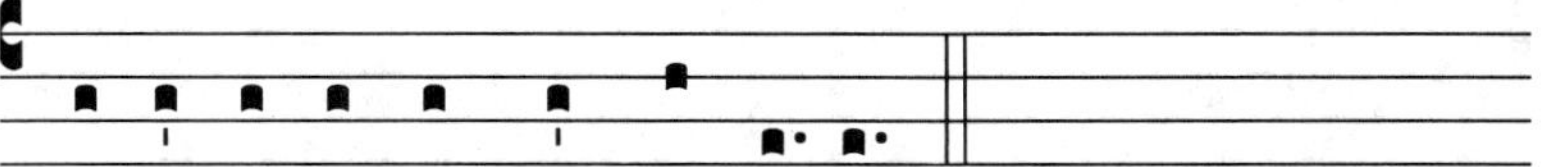

and I will be their Lord for ev- er.

OFFERTORY ANTIPHON

Si ambulavero.
Ps 137:7

- i -

8.

I F I shall walk * in the midst of trib-u- la- tion, you 1512

will give me life, O Lord; and you will stretch forth your hand

a-gainst the wrath of my en- e- mies;* and your right hand

shall save me.

- ii -

8.

I F I shall walk * in the midst of tri-bu- la- tion, you 1513

will give me life, O Lord; and you will stretch forth your hand

a-gainst the wrath of my en- e- mies; and your right hand

shall save me.
VERSES
In quacumque die invocavero te. Ps 137:3
1514
℣. 1
IN what day so- ev- er I shall call up- on you, hear
me. You shall mul- ti- ply strength in my soul. * And your
right hand shall save me.
Adorabo ad templum sanctum tuum. Ps 137:2
1515
℣. 2
I will wor-ship towards your ho- ly tem-ple, and I
will give glo- ry to your ho- ly Name, O Lord, for your mer-
cy and for your truth. * And your right hand shall save me.
Or:
Adorabo ad templum sanctum tuum. Ps 137:2
1516
℣.
I will worship towards your ho- ly tem-ple, * and I

will give glo- ry to your ho- ly Name, O Lord. *Ant.* If I shall.

OFFERTORY ANTIPHON *Si ambulavero. Ps* 137:7

- iii -

8.
1517
IF I shall walk in the midst of tri-bu-la-tion, * you
will give me life, O Lord ; and you will stretch forth your hand
against the wrath of my en- e- mies ; and your right hand
shall save me.

Or:

8.
1518
IF I shall walk in the midst of tri-bu-la-tion, * you
will give me life, O Lord ; and you will stretch forth your hand
against the wrath of my en- e- mies ; and your right hand

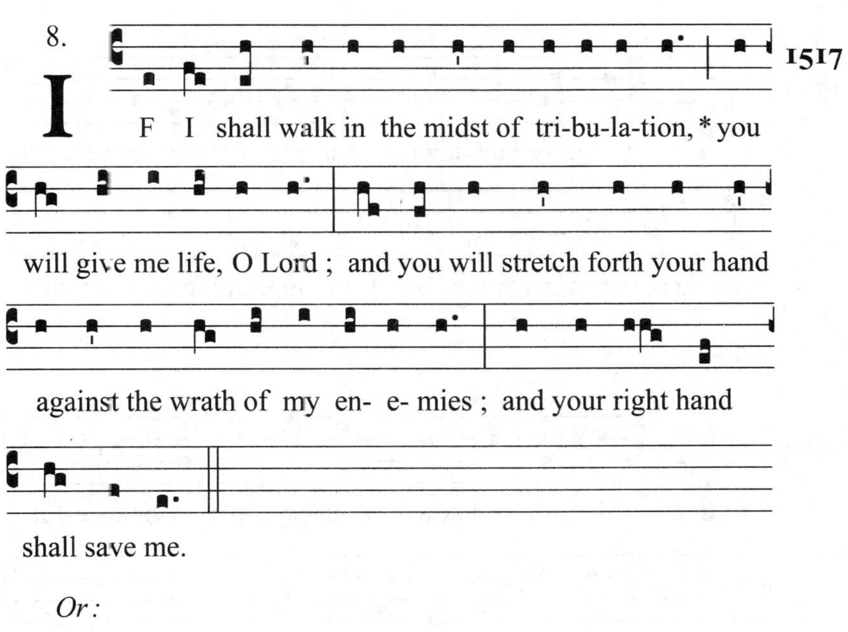

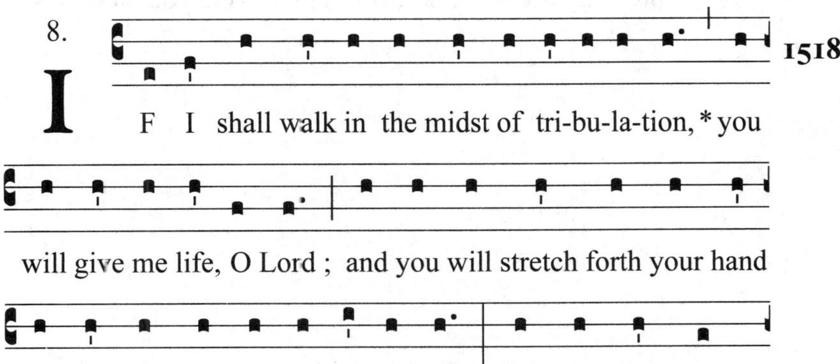

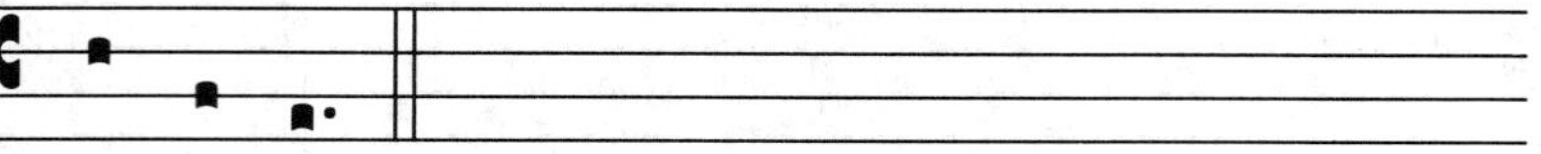

shall save me.

COMMUNION ANTIPHON *Tu mandasti mandata tua.*
Ps 118:4-5

- i -

1519
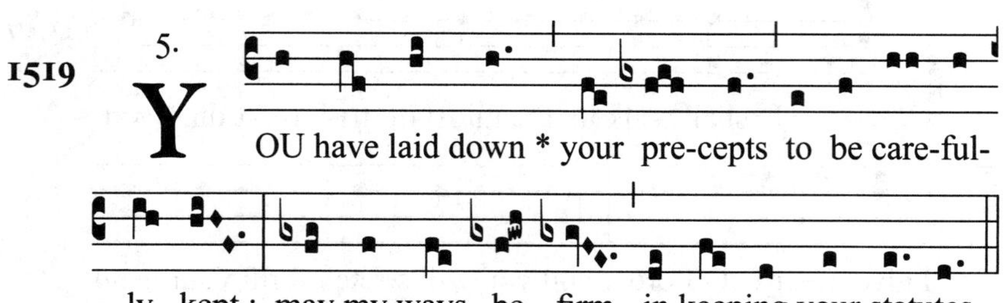
5.
YOU have laid down * your pre-cepts to be care-ful-
ly kept; may my ways be firm in keeping your statutes.

- ii -

1520
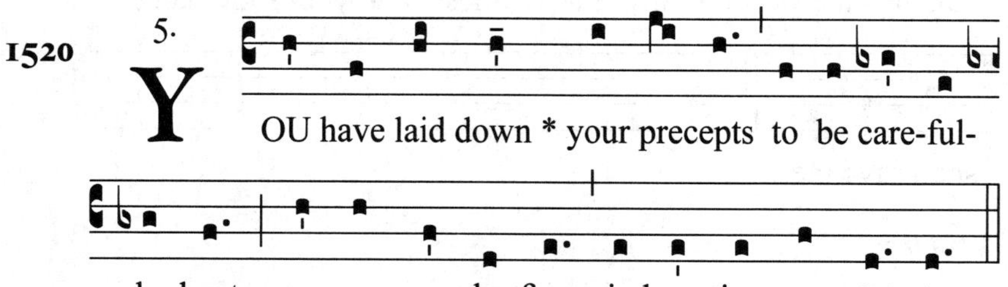
5.
YOU have laid down * your precepts to be care-ful-
ly kept; may my ways be firm in keep-ing your stat-utes.

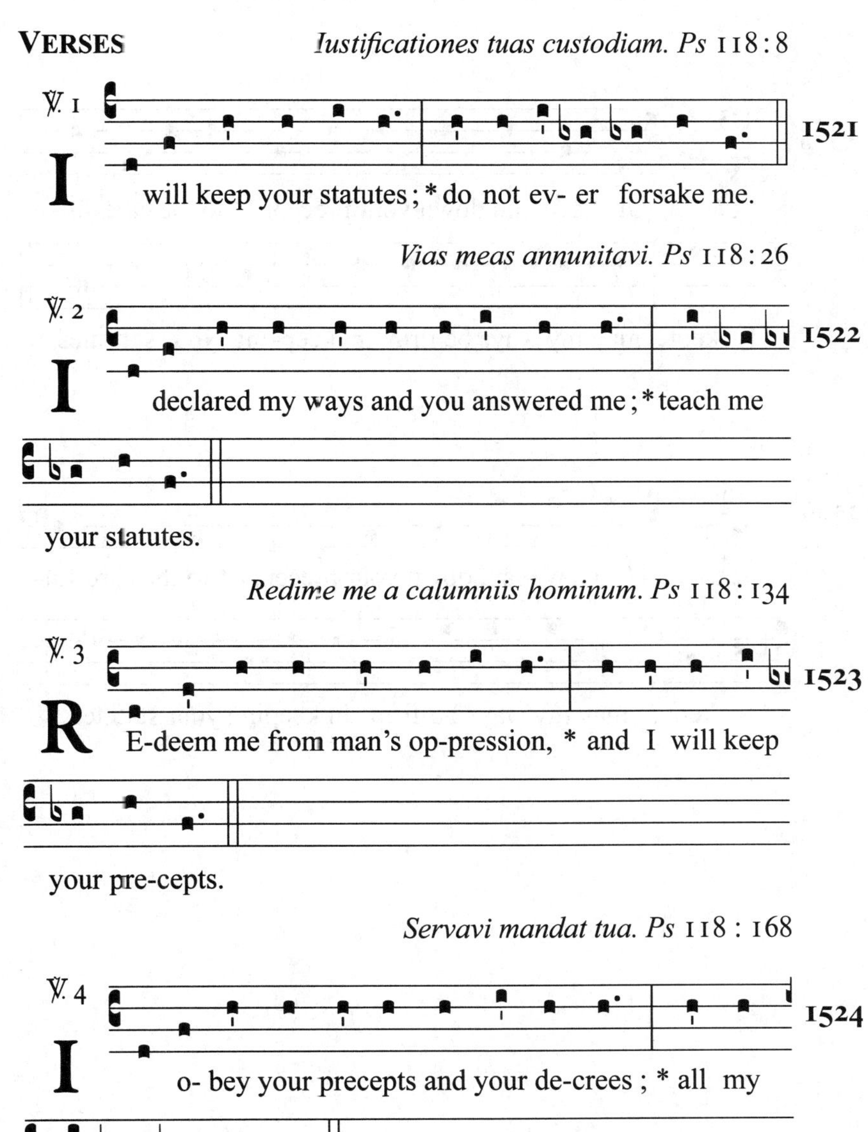
VERSES
Iustificationes tuas custodiam. Ps 118:8
℣. 1
I will keep your statutes; * do not ev- er forsake me.
1521
Vias meas annunitavi. Ps 118:26
℣. 2
I declared my ways and you answered me; * teach me
1522
your statutes.
Redime me a calumniis hominum. Ps 118:134
℣. 3
RE-deem me from man's op-pression, * and I will keep
1523
your pre-cepts.
Servavi mandat tua. Ps 118:168
℣. 4
I o- bey your precepts and your de-crees ; * all my
1524
ways are be-fore you.

- iii -

1525

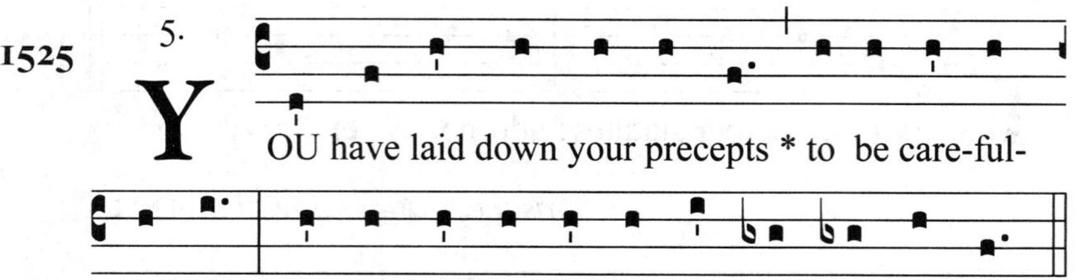
5.
Y
OU have laid down your precepts * to be care-ful-
ly kept; may my ways be firm in keep-ing your stat-utes.

- iv -

1526

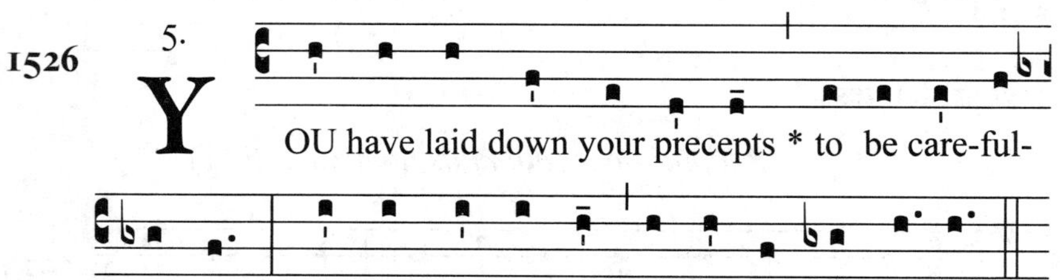
5.
Y
OU have laid down your precepts * to be care-ful-
ly kept ; may my ways be firm in keeping your statutes.

TWENTY-SIXTH SUNDAY IN ORDINARY TIME

ENTRANCE ANTIPHON *Omnia, quæ fecisti nobis.*
Daniel 3 : 31, 29, 30, 43, 42

- i -

3. 1527

ALL that you * have done to us, O Lord, you have
done with true judg-ment, for we have sinned a- gainst
you and not o-beyed your com-mand-ments. But give
glo- ry to your name and deal with us ac-cord-ing
to the boun- ty of your mer- cy.

- ii -

3. 1528

ALL that you * have done to us, O Lord, you have done
with true judgment, for we have sinned a-gainst you and not o-

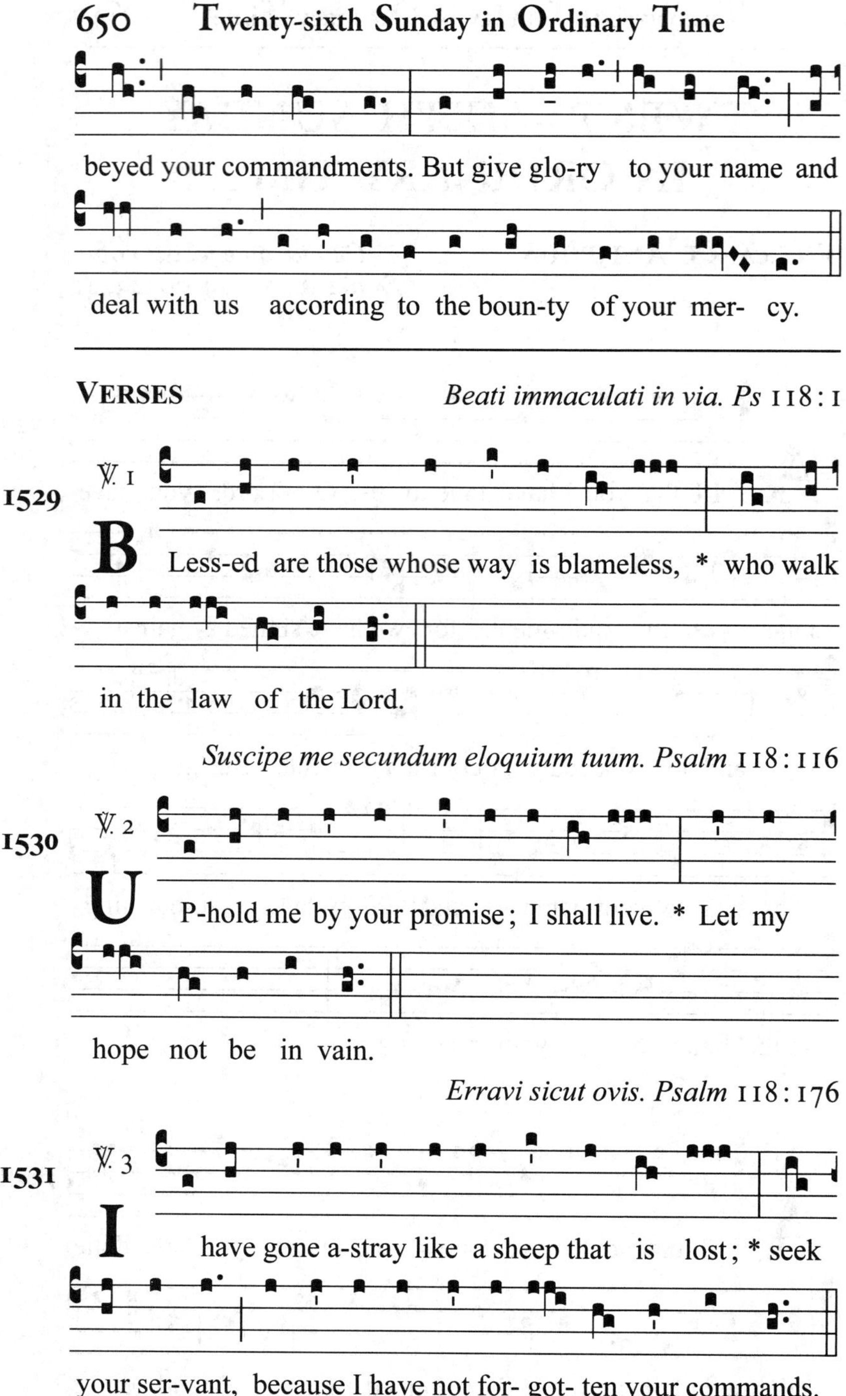
beyed your commandments. But give glo-ry to your name and
deal with us according to the boun-ty of your mer- cy.
VERSES
Beati immaculati in via. Ps 118:1
1529
℣. 1
BLess-ed are those whose way is blameless, * who walk
in the law of the Lord.
Suscipe me secundum eloquium tuum. Psalm 118:116
1530
℣. 2
UP-hold me by your promise; I shall live. * Let my
hope not be in vain.
Erravi sicut ovis. Psalm 118:176
1531
℣. 3
I have gone a-stray like a sheep that is lost; * seek
your ser-vant, because I have not for- got- ten your commands.

- iii -

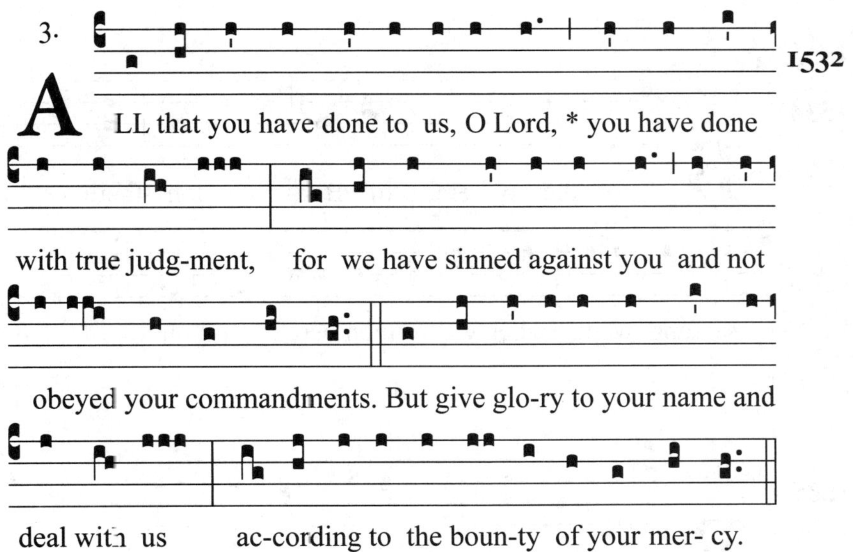
3.
1532
ALL that you have done to us, O Lord, * you have done
with true judg-ment, for we have sinned against you and not
obeyed your commandments. But give glo-ry to your name and
deal with us ac-cording to the boun-ty of your mer- cy.

- iv -

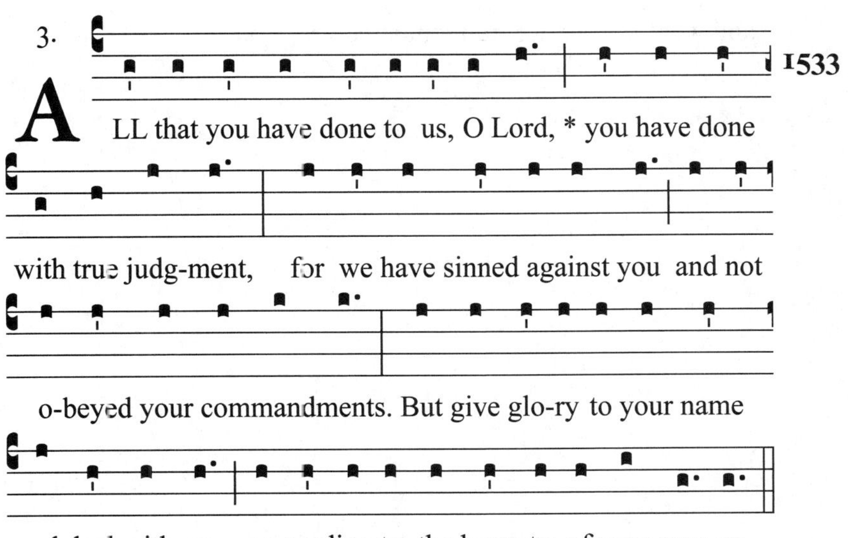
3.
1533
ALL that you have done to us, O Lord, * you have done
with true judg-ment, for we have sinned against you and not
o-beyed your commandments. But give glo-ry to your name
and deal with us ac-cording to the boun-ty of your mer-cy.

Offertory Antiphon *Super flumina Babylonis.*
Ps 136:1

- i -

1534 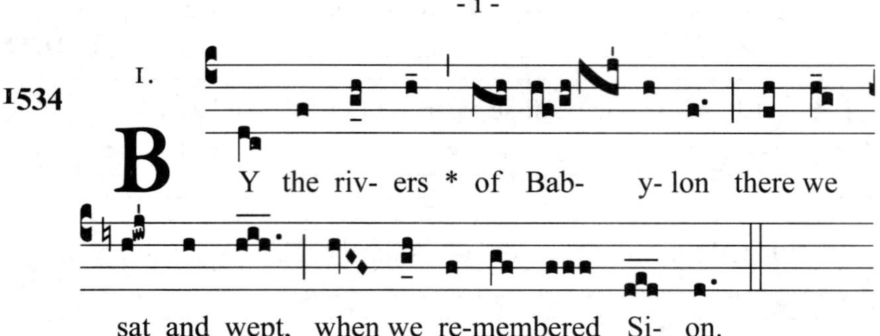
I.
BY the riv- ers * of Bab- y- lon there we
sat and wept, when we re-membered Si- on.

- ii -

1535 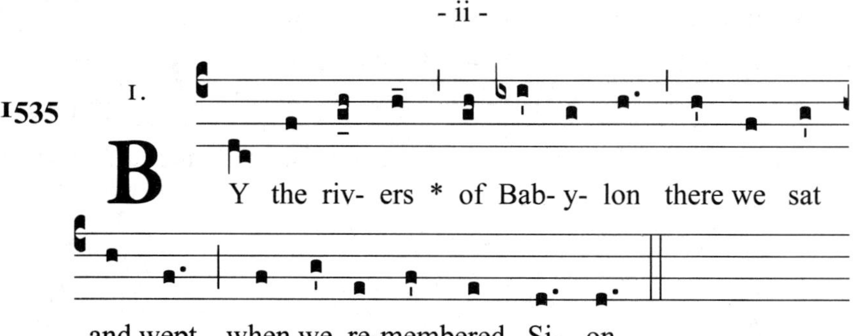
I.
BY the riv- ers * of Bab- y- lon there we sat
and wept, when we re-membered Si- on.

VERSES
Quia illic interrogaverunt nos. Ps 136:3
℣. 1
FOR there our cap-tors asked of us * the lyr- ics of
1536
our songs.

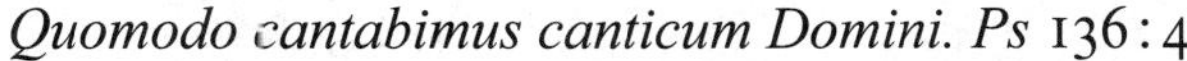
Quomodo cantabimus canticum Domini. Ps 136:4

℣. 2
HOW could we sing the Lord's song * in a foreign land ?
1537

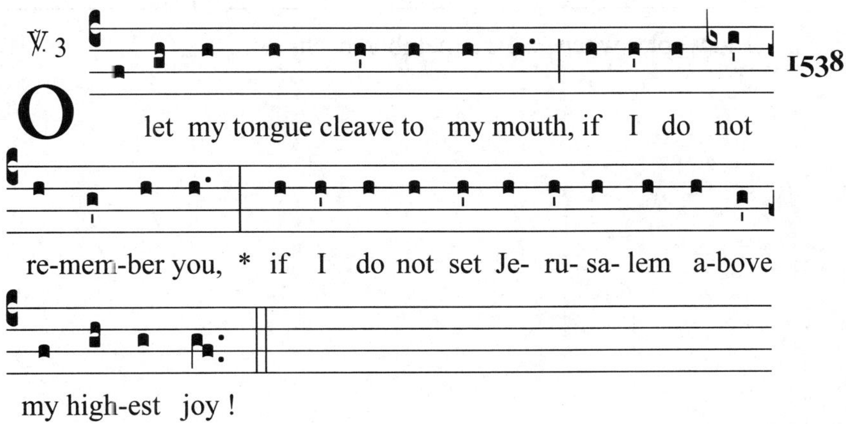
Adhæreat lingua mea faucibus meis. Ps 136:6
℣. 3
O let my tongue cleave to my mouth, if I do not
1538
re-mem-ber you, * if I do not set Je- ru- sa- lem a-bove
my high-est joy !

- iii -

1539

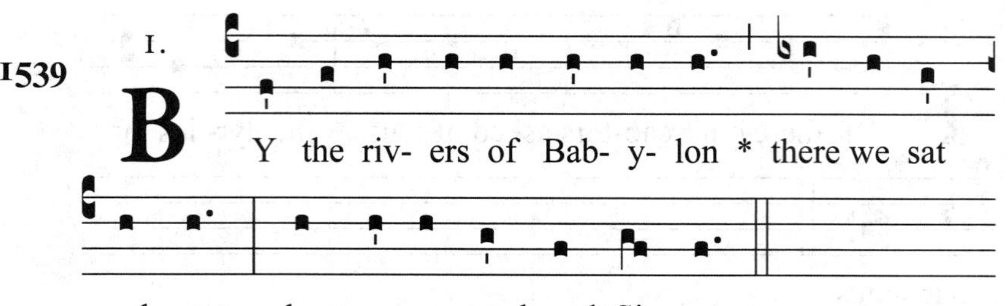
I.
BY the riv- ers of Bab- y- lon * there we sat
and wept, when we re-membered Si- on.

- iv -

1540

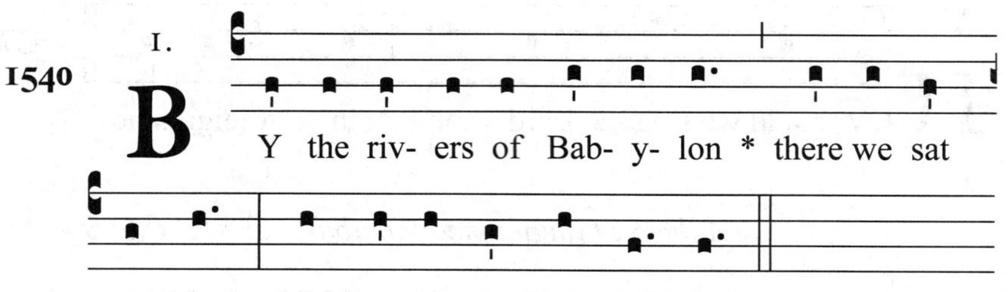
I.
BY the riv- ers of Bab- y- lon * there we sat
and wept, when we re-membered Si- on.

COMMUNION ANTIPHON *Memento verbi tui servo tuo.*
Ps 118:49-50

- i -

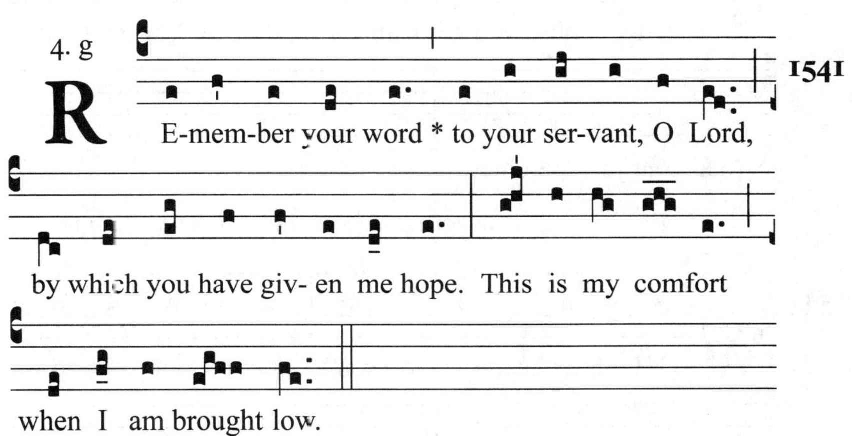
4. g
1541
R
E-mem-ber your word * to your ser-vant, O Lord,
by which you have giv- en me hope. This is my comfort
when I am brought low.

- ii -

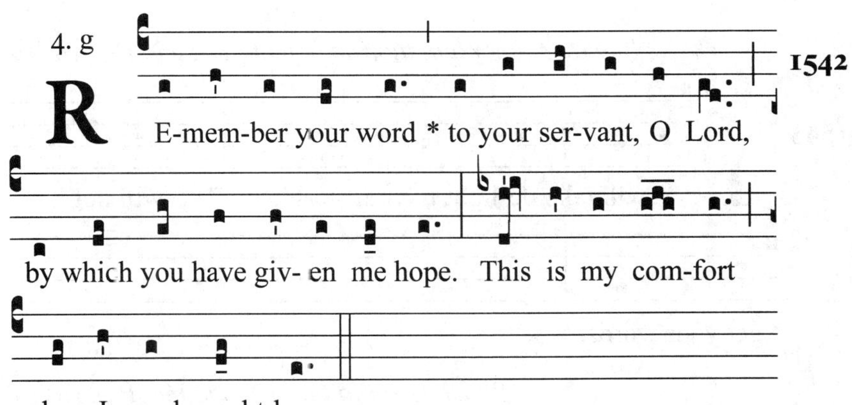
4. g
1542
R
E-mem-ber your word * to your ser-vant, O Lord,
by which you have giv- en me hope. This is my com-fort
when I am brought low.

VERSES *Confitebor tibi in directione cordis. Ps* 118:7

1543

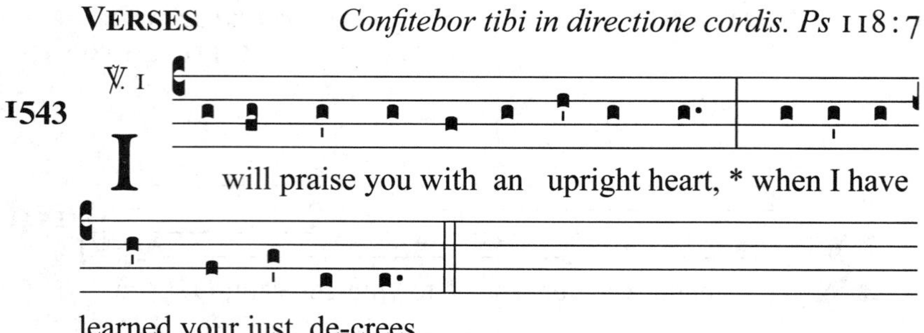
℣. 1
I will praise you with an upright heart, * when I have
learned your just de-crees.

In toto corde meo exquisivi te. Ps 118:10

1544

℣. 2
WITH all my heart I seek you, * let me not wan-der
from your commandments.

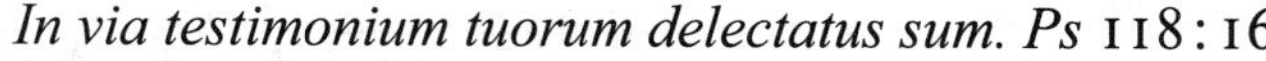
In via testimonium tuorum delectatus sum. Ps 118:16

1545

℣. 3
I will take de-light in your sta-tutes ; * I will not for-
get your words.

Retribue servo tuo, vivifica me. Ps 118:17

1546

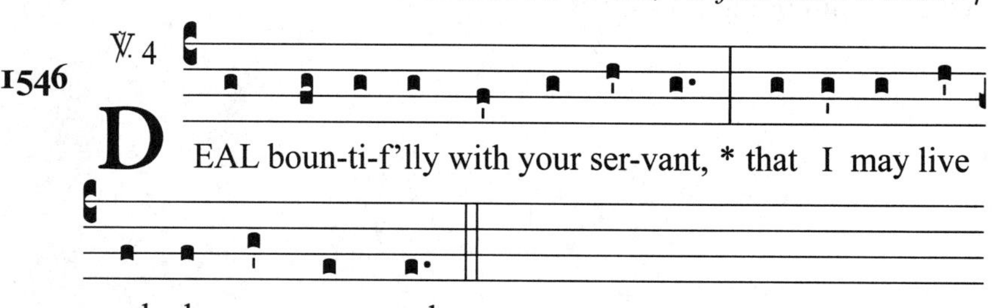
℣. 4
DEAL boun-ti-f'lly with your ser-vant, * that I may live
and ob-serve your words.

- iv -

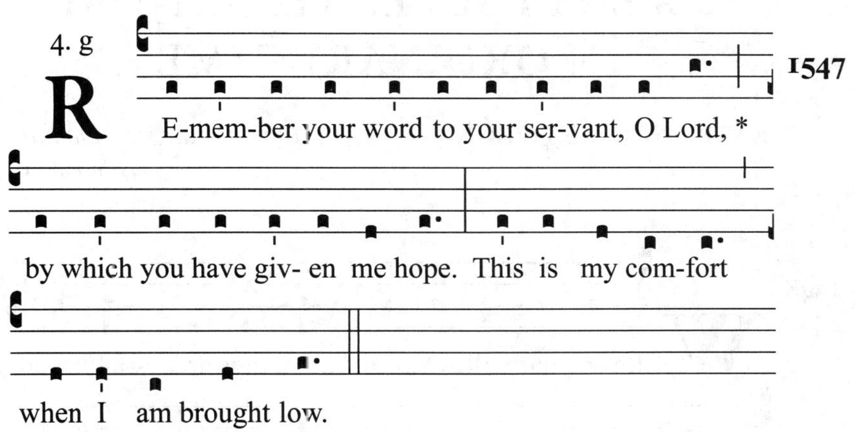
4. g
1547
R E-mem-ber your word to your ser-vant, O Lord, *
by which you have giv- en me hope. This is my com-fort
when I am brought low.

TWENTY-SEVENTH SUNDAY IN ORDINARY TIME

Entrance Antiphon *In voluntate tua, Domine.*
Esther 4:17

- i -

1548

4.
W
Ith-in your will, O Lord,* all things are es-tablished
and there is none that can re- sist your will. For you have
made all things, the heav-en and the earth, and all that is
held with-in the cir- cle of heav-en ; you are the Lord
of all.
- ii -
4.
W
Ith- in your will, O Lord,* all things are es-tablished
and there is none that can re- sist your will. For you have made

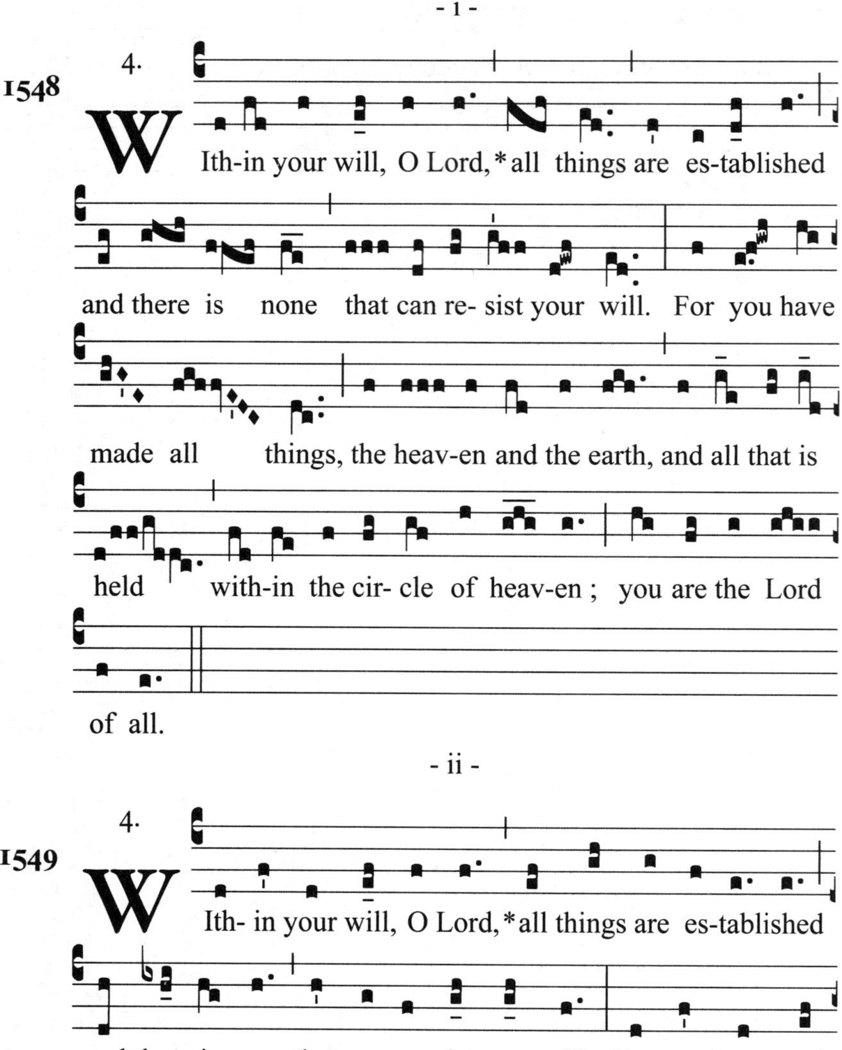

1549

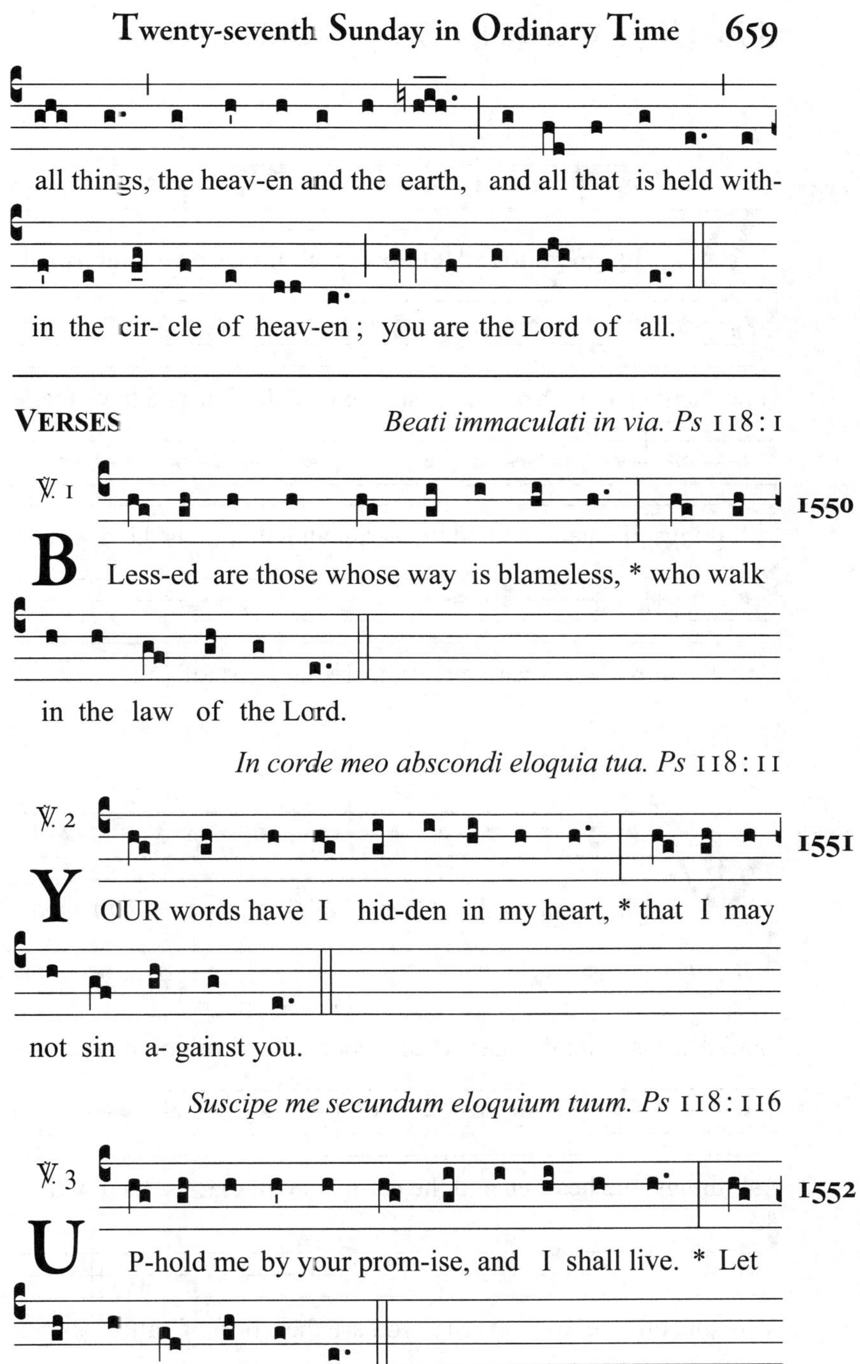
all things, the heav-en and the earth, and all that is held with-
in the cir- cle of heav-en ; you are the Lord of all.
VERSES
Beati immaculati in via. Ps 118:1
℣. 1
B Less-ed are those whose way is blameless, * who walk
1550
in the law of the Lord.
In corde meo abscondi eloquia tua. Ps 118:11
℣. 2
Y OUR words have I hid-den in my heart, * that I may
1551
not sin a- gainst you.
Suscipe me secundum eloquium tuum. Ps 118:116
℣. 3
U P-hold me by your prom-ise, and I shall live. * Let
1552
my hope not be in vain.

- iii -

1553

4.
W
Ith- in your will, O Lord, * all things are es-tablished
and there is none that can re- sist your will. For you have made
all things, the heav-en and the earth, and all that is held with-
in the cir- cle of heav-en; you are the Lord of all.

Or:

1554

4.
W
Ith-in your will, O Lord, * all things are es-tablished
and there is none that can re- sist your will. For you have made
all things, the heav-en and the earth, and all that is held with-
in the cir- cle of heav-en; you are the Lord of all.

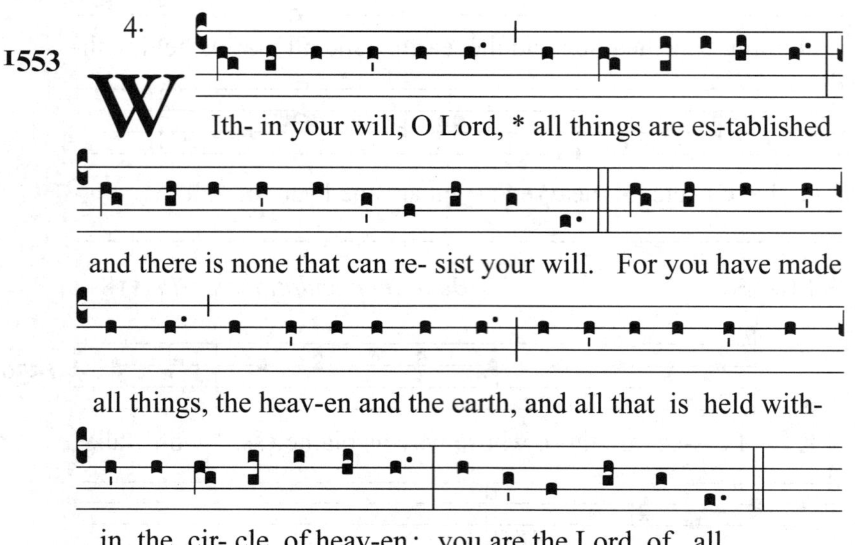

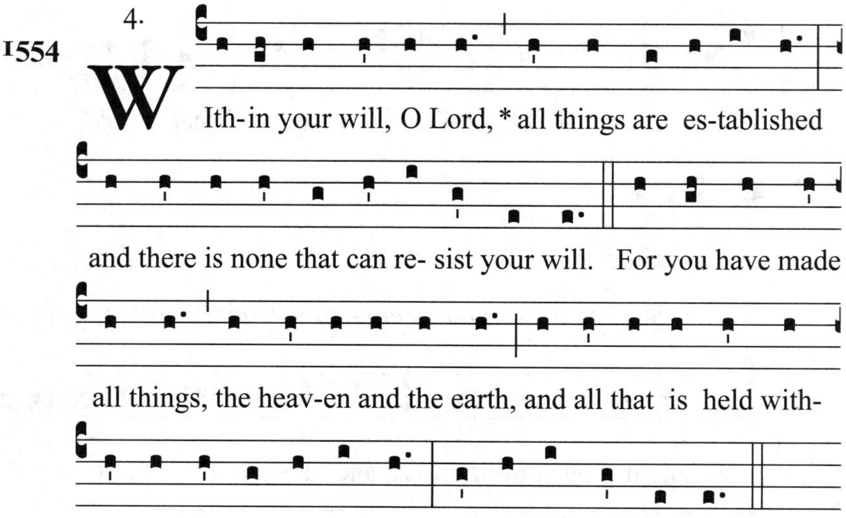

- iv -

4. 1555

Within your will, O Lord, all things are es- | **tab**-lished *
and there is none that can re- | *sist your* **will**.
For you have made all things, / the heaven and the earth, /
and all that is held within the circle of | **heav**-en ;
you are the Lord | *of* **all**.

OFFERTORY ANTIPHON *Vir erat in terra Hus.*
Job 1 *and* 2. 7

- i -

1556

2.
THere was a man * in the land of Hus, whose name
was Job, simple, and upright, and fearing
God, whom Satan besought that he might tempt, and
power was given him from the Lord over his posses-
sions and his flesh ; and he destroyed all his substance
and his children ; and wounded his flesh also with
a grievous ulcer.

VERSES *Utinam appenderentur peccata mea. Job* 6:2-3

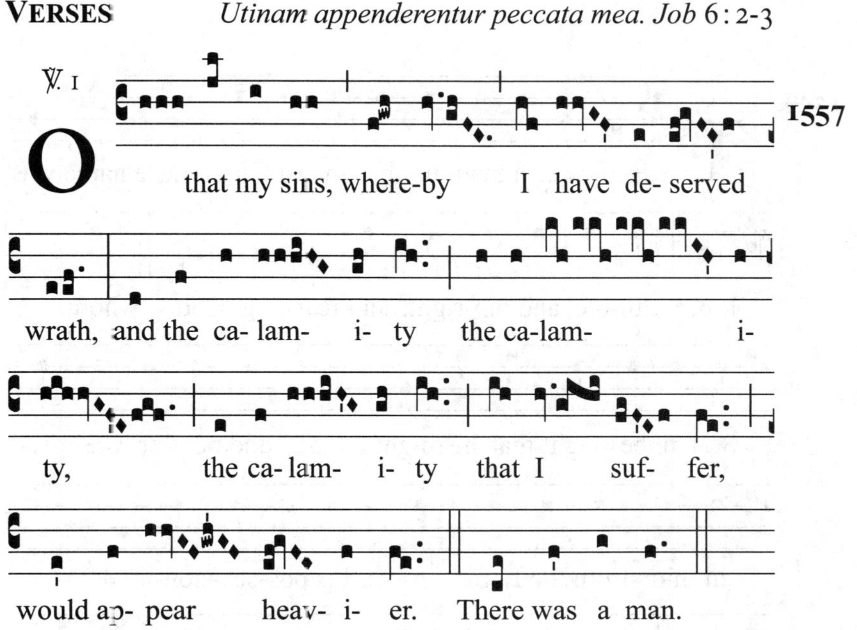
℣. 1
O that my sins, where-by I have de- served
1557
wrath, and the ca- lam- i- ty the ca-lam- i-
ty, the ca- lam- i- ty that I suf- fer,
would ap- pear heav- i- er. There was a man.

Quae est enim, fortituto mea? Job 6:11

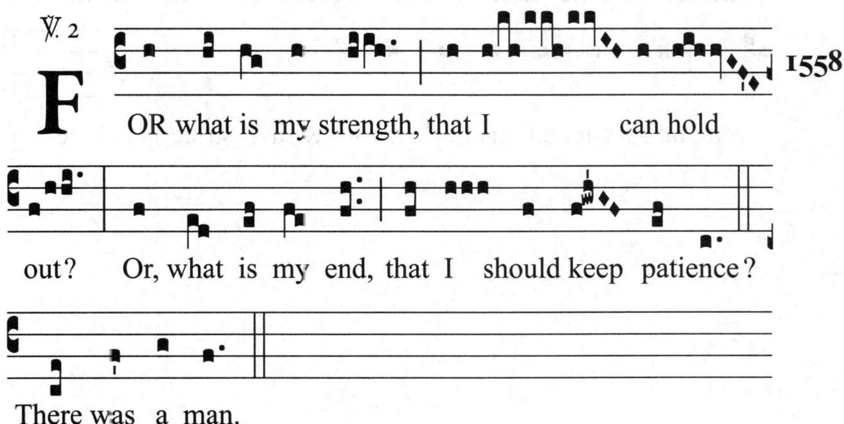
℣. 2
FOR what is my strength, that I can hold
1558
out? Or, what is my end, that I should keep patience?
There was a man.

- iii -

1559 2.

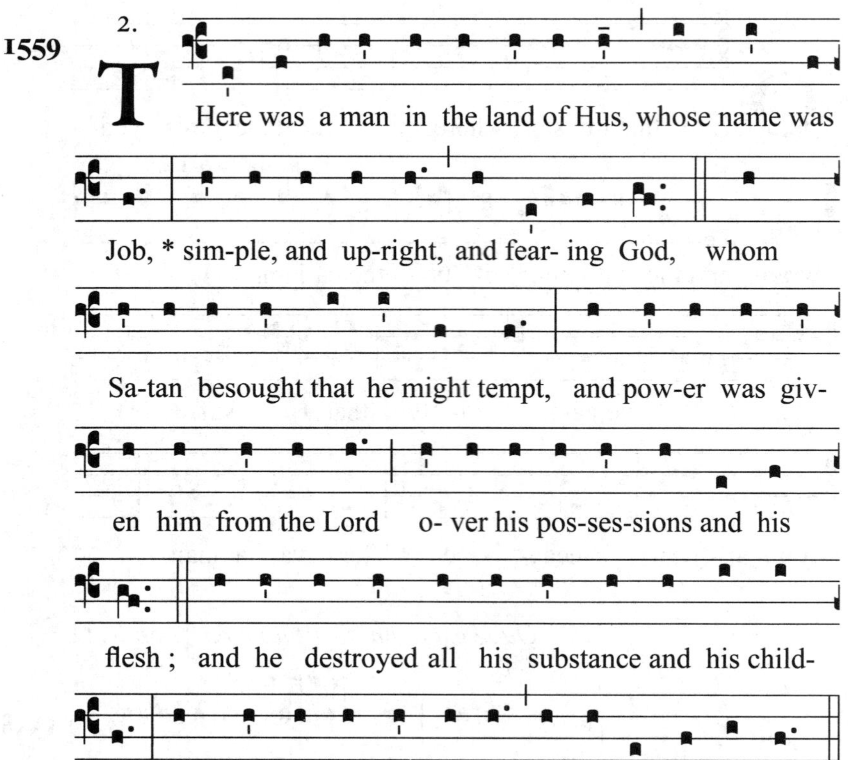
THere was a man in the land of Hus, whose name was
Job, * sim-ple, and up-right, and fear- ing God, whom
Sa-tan besought that he might tempt, and pow-er was giv-
en him from the Lord o- ver his pos-ses-sions and his
flesh ; and he destroyed all his substance and his child-
ren ; and wounded his flesh al- so with a grievous ul- cer.

Numquid fortitudo lapidum est? Job 6:12

℣. 3
F
OR my strength is not the strength of stones, nor
1560
is my flesh of brass. There was a man.

Quoniam non revertetur oculus meus. Job 7:7

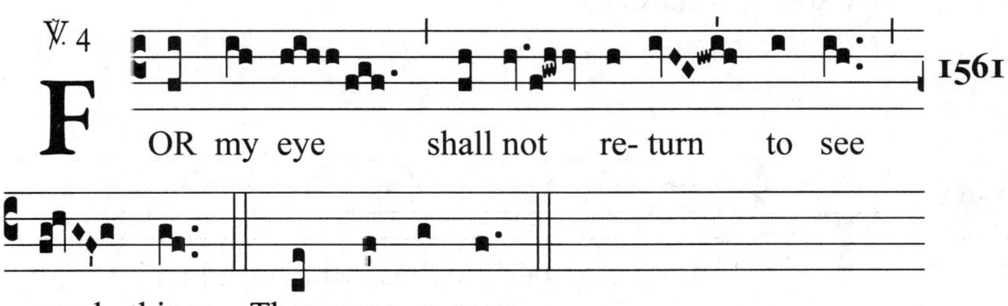
℣. 4
F
OR my eye shall not re- turn to see
1561
good things, There was a man.

COMMUNION ANTIPHON *Bonus est Dominus.*
Lam 3:25

- i -

1562

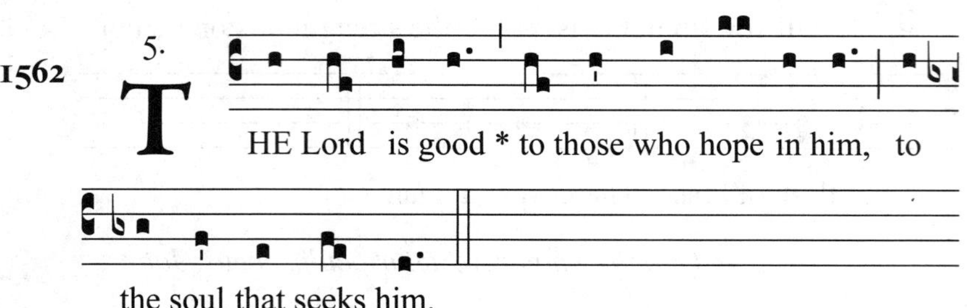
5.
T
HE Lord is good * to those who hope in him, to
the soul that seeks him.

- ii -

1563

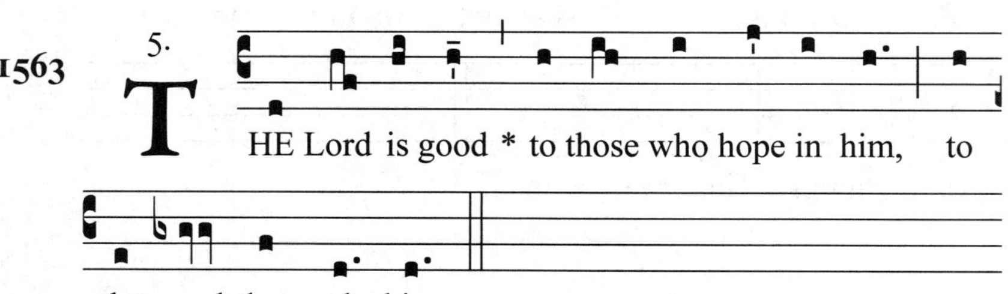
5.
T
HE Lord is good * to those who hope in him, to
the soul that seeks him.

VERSES *Confitebor tibi in directione cordis. Ps* 118:7

℣. 1
I will praise you with an up-right heart, * when I have
learned your just de-crees.
1564

In toto corde meo exquisivi te. Ps 118:10

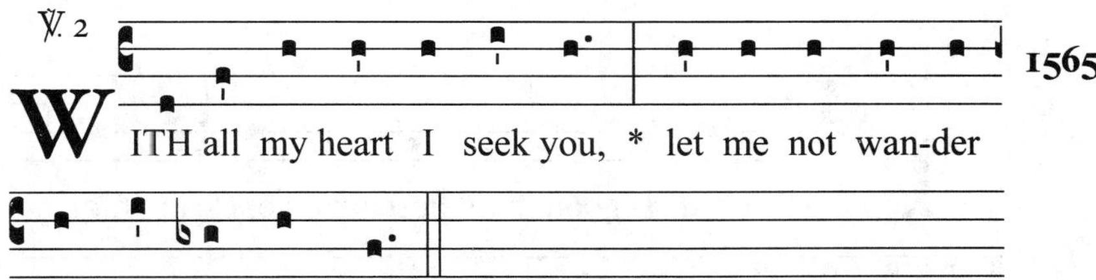

℣. 2
WITH all my heart I seek you, * let me not wan-der
from your commandments.
1565

In via testimonium tuorum delectatus sum. Ps 118:16

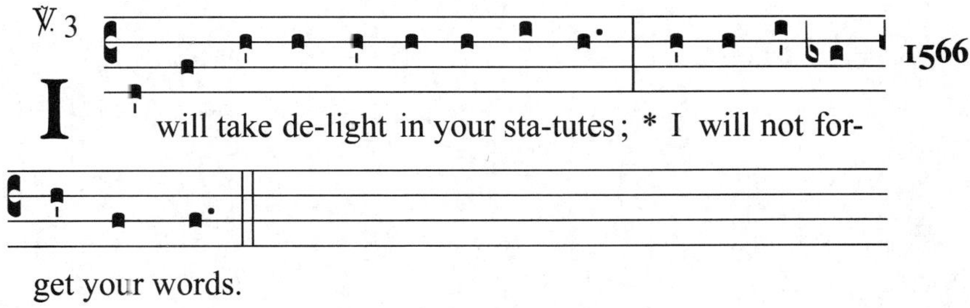

℣. 3
I will take de-light in your sta-tutes; * I will not for-
get your words.
1566

Retribue servo tuo, vivifica me. Ps 118:17

℣. 4
DEAL boun-ti-f'lly with your ser-vant, * that I may live
and ob-serve your words.
1567

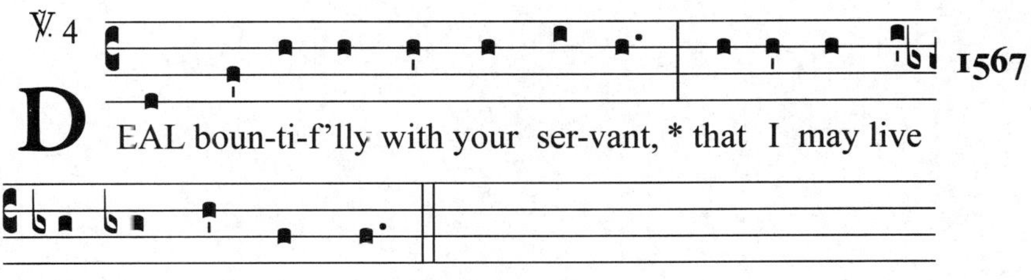

- iii -

1568

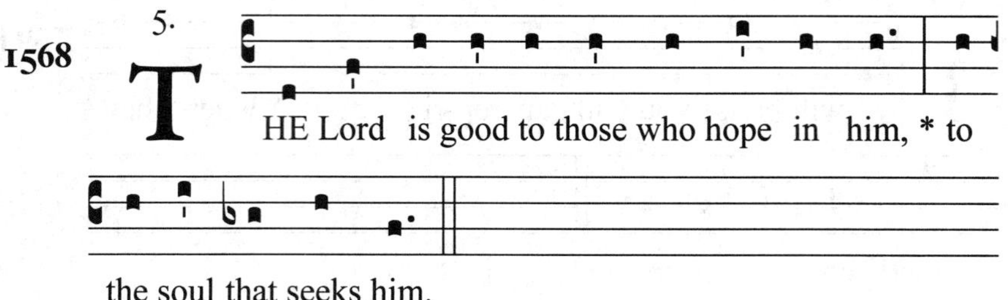
5.
THE Lord is good to those who hope in him, * to
the soul that seeks him.

- iv -

1569

5.
THE Lord is good * to those who hope in him,
to the soul that seeks him.

TWENTY-EIGHTH SUNDAY IN ORDINARY TIME

ENTRANCE ANTIPHON *Si iniquitates observaveris.* *Ps* 129:3-4

- i -

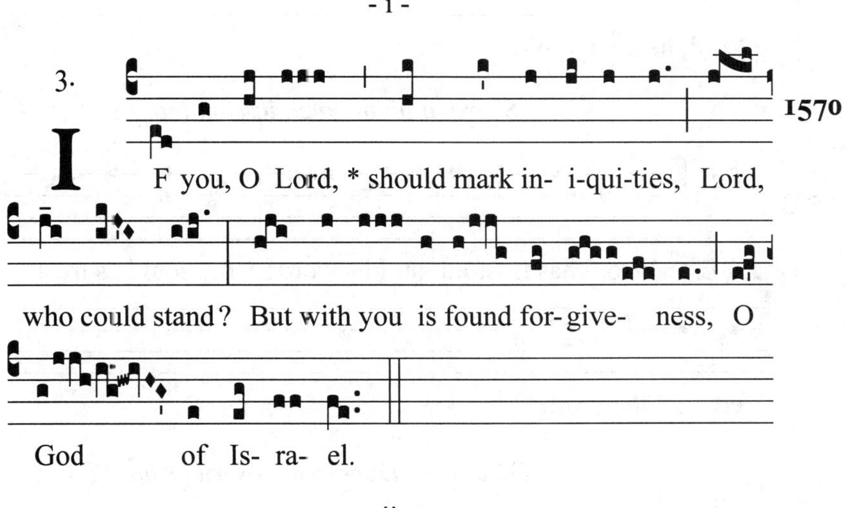
3.
1570
IF you, O Lord, * should mark in- i-qui-ties, Lord,
who could stand? But with you is found for-give- ness, O
God of Is- ra- el.

- ii -

3.
1571
IF you, O Lord, * should mark in- iq- ui-ties, Lord,
who could stand? But with you is found for-give-ness, O
God of Is- ra- el.

VERSES *De profundis clamavi ad te, Domine. Ps* 129:1

1572

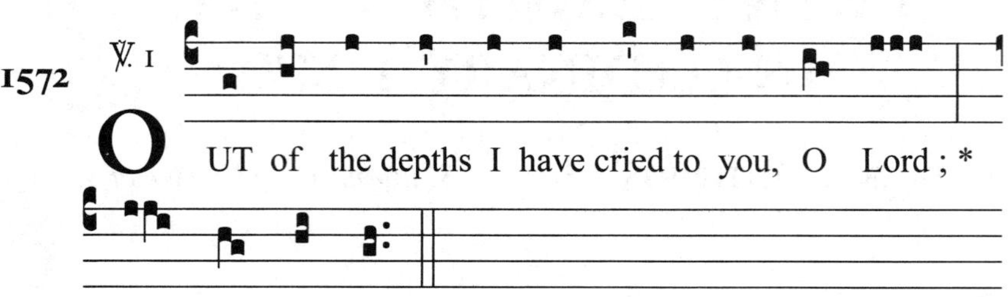

℣. 1 OUT of the depths I have cried to you, O Lord; * Lord, hear my voice.

Speravit anima mea in Domino. Ps 129:4-5

1573

℣. 2 MY soul has trust-ed in his word; * my soul has trust-ed in the Lord.

Quia apud Dominum misericordia. Ps 129:7

1574

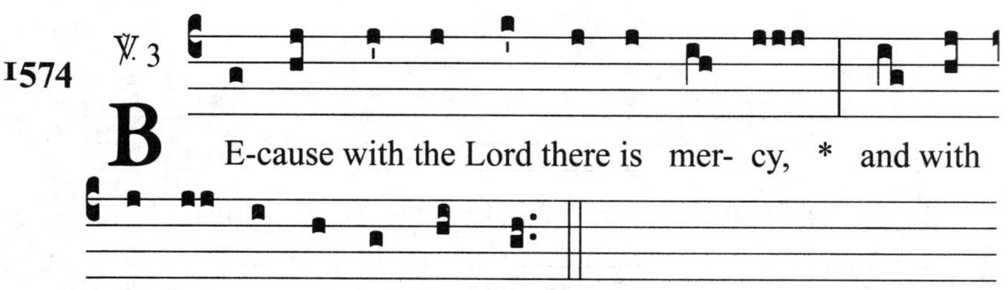

℣. 3 BE-cause with the Lord there is mer- cy, * and with him plen- ti- ful re-demp-tion.

- iii -

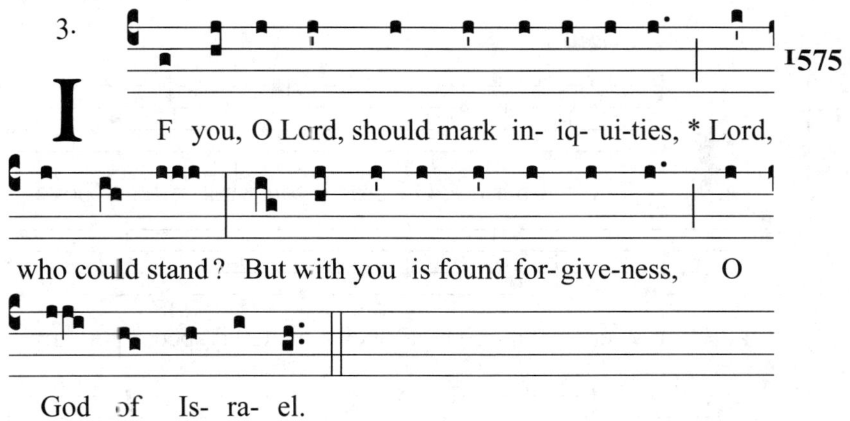
3.
1575
IF you, O Lord, should mark in- iq- ui-ties, * Lord,
who could stand? But with you is found for- give-ness, O
God of Is- ra- el.

- iv -

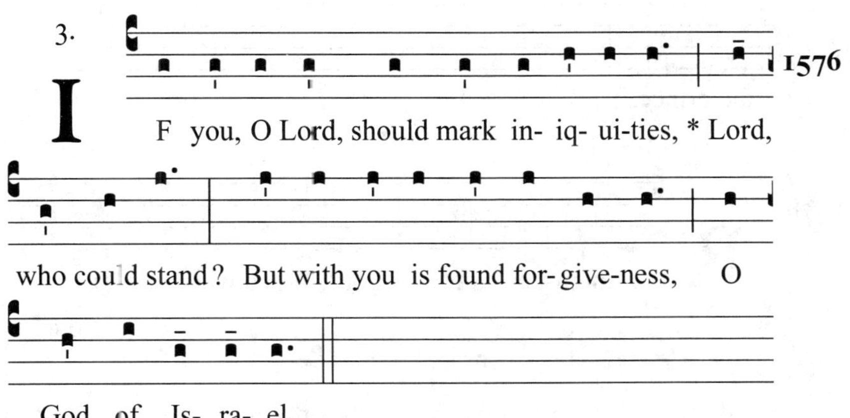
3.
1576
IF you, O Lord, should mark in- iq- ui-ties, * Lord,
who could stand? But with you is found for- give-ness, O
God of Is- ra- el.

OFFERTORY ANTIPHON

Recordare mei, Domine.
Esther 14:12. 13

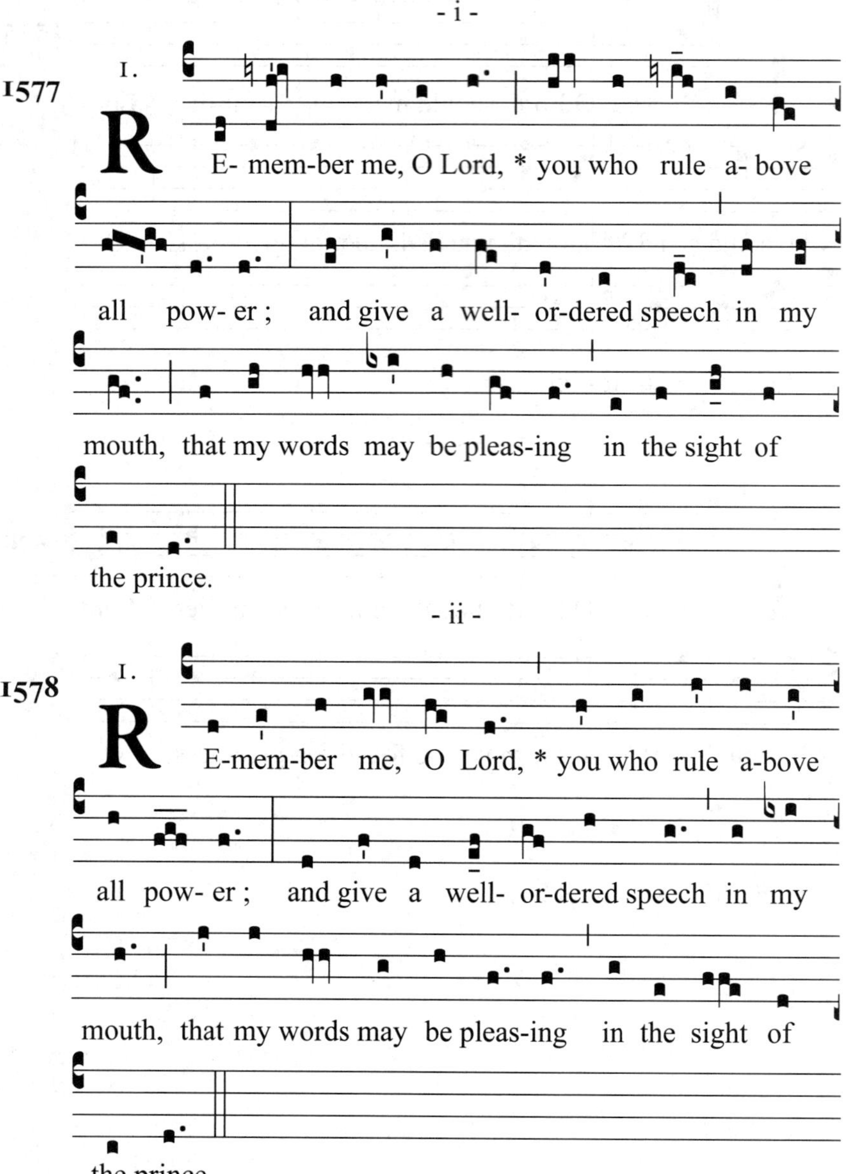
- i -
1577
I.
RE- mem-ber me, O Lord, * you who rule a- bove
all pow- er ; and give a well- or-dered speech in my
mouth, that my words may be pleas-ing in the sight of
the prince.
- ii -
1578
I.
RE-mem-ber me, O Lord, * you who rule a-bove
all pow- er ; and give a well- or-dered speech in my
mouth, that my words may be pleas-ing in the sight of
the prince.

VERSES *Everte cor eius in odium repugnantium nobis.*

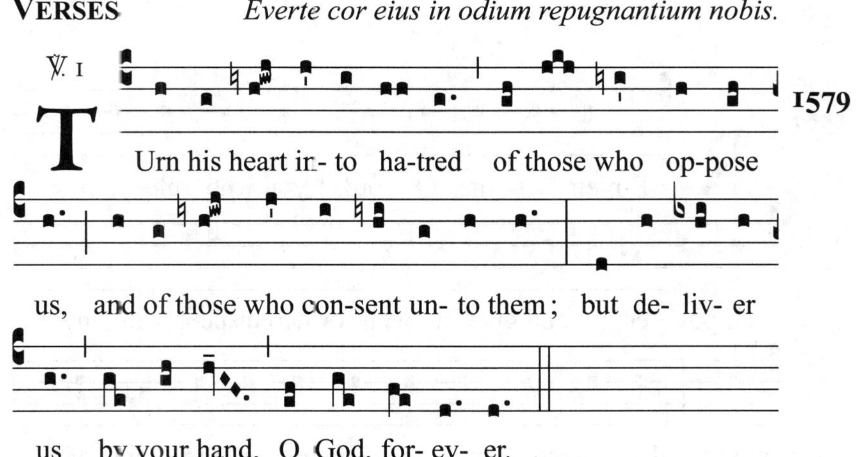
℣. 1
1579
TUrn his heart in- to ha-tred of those who op-pose
us, and of those who con-sent un- to them; but de- liv- er
us by your hand, O God, for- ev- er.

Recordare quod steterim in conspectu tuo. Jer 18 : 20

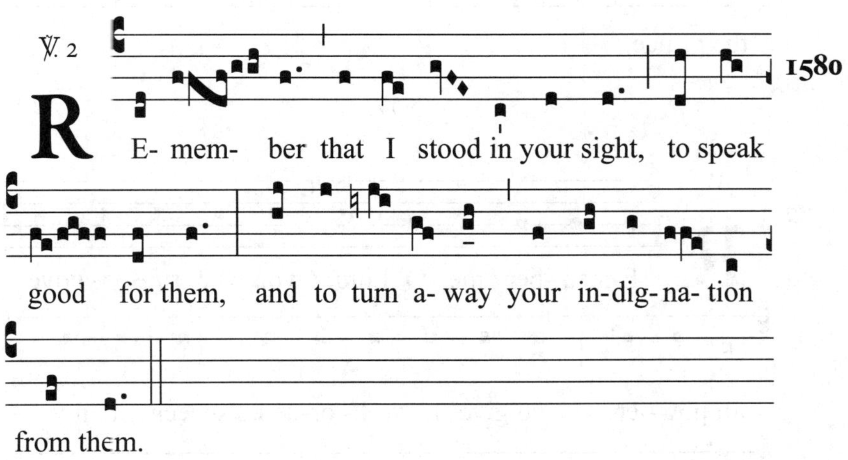
℣. 2
1580
RE- mem- ber that I stood in your sight, to speak
good for them, and to turn a- way your in-dig- na- tion
from them.

- iii -

1581

I.
R
E-mem-ber me, O Lord, * you who rule a- bove
all pow- er; and give a well- or-dered speech in my
mouth, that my words may be pleas-ing in the sight of
the prince.

- iv -

1582

I.
R
E-mem-ber me, O Lord, * you who rule a- bove
all pow- er; and give a well- or-dered speech in my
mouth, that my words may be pleas-ing in the sight of
the prince.

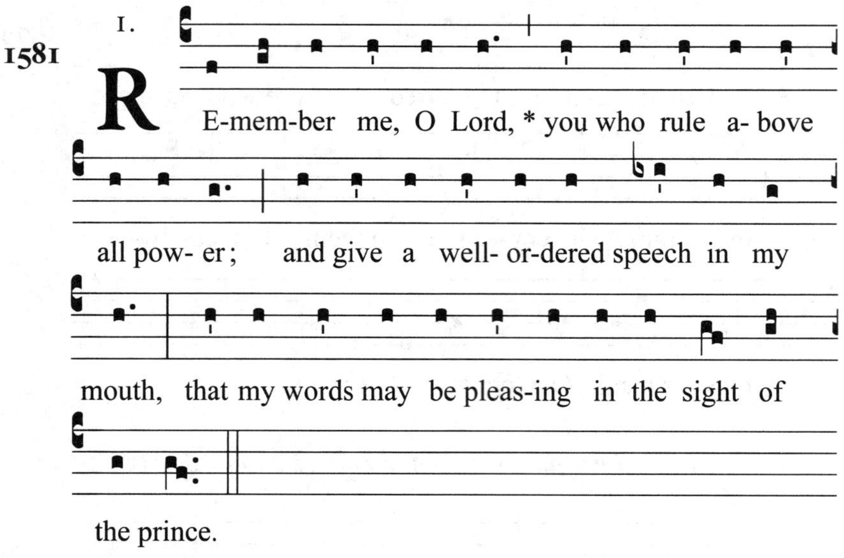

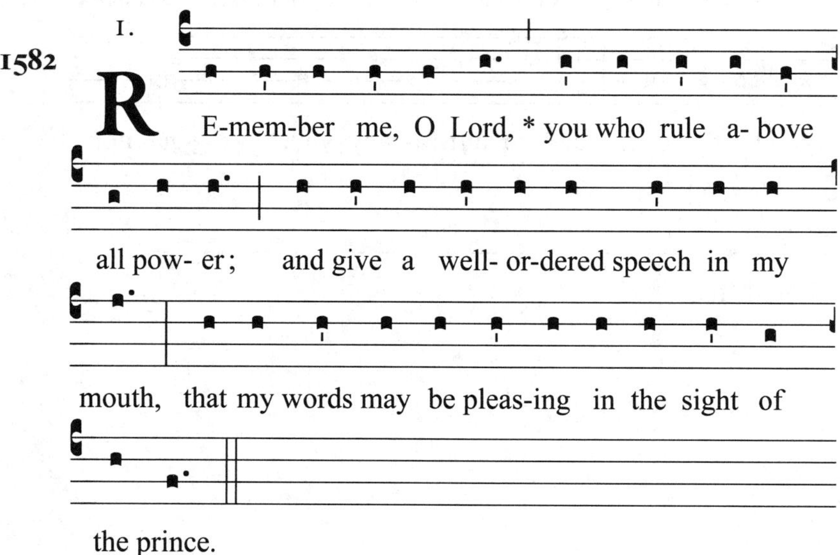

Communion Antiphon *Divites eguerunt et esurierunt.*
Ps 33:11

- i -

7.
THE rich suf- fer want * and go hun-gry, but those
1583
who seek the Lord lack no bless-ing.

- ii -

7.
THE rich suf- fer want * and go hun- gry, but those
1584
who seek the Lord lack no bless-ing.

VERSES *Benedicam Dominum in omni tempore.* Ps 33:2

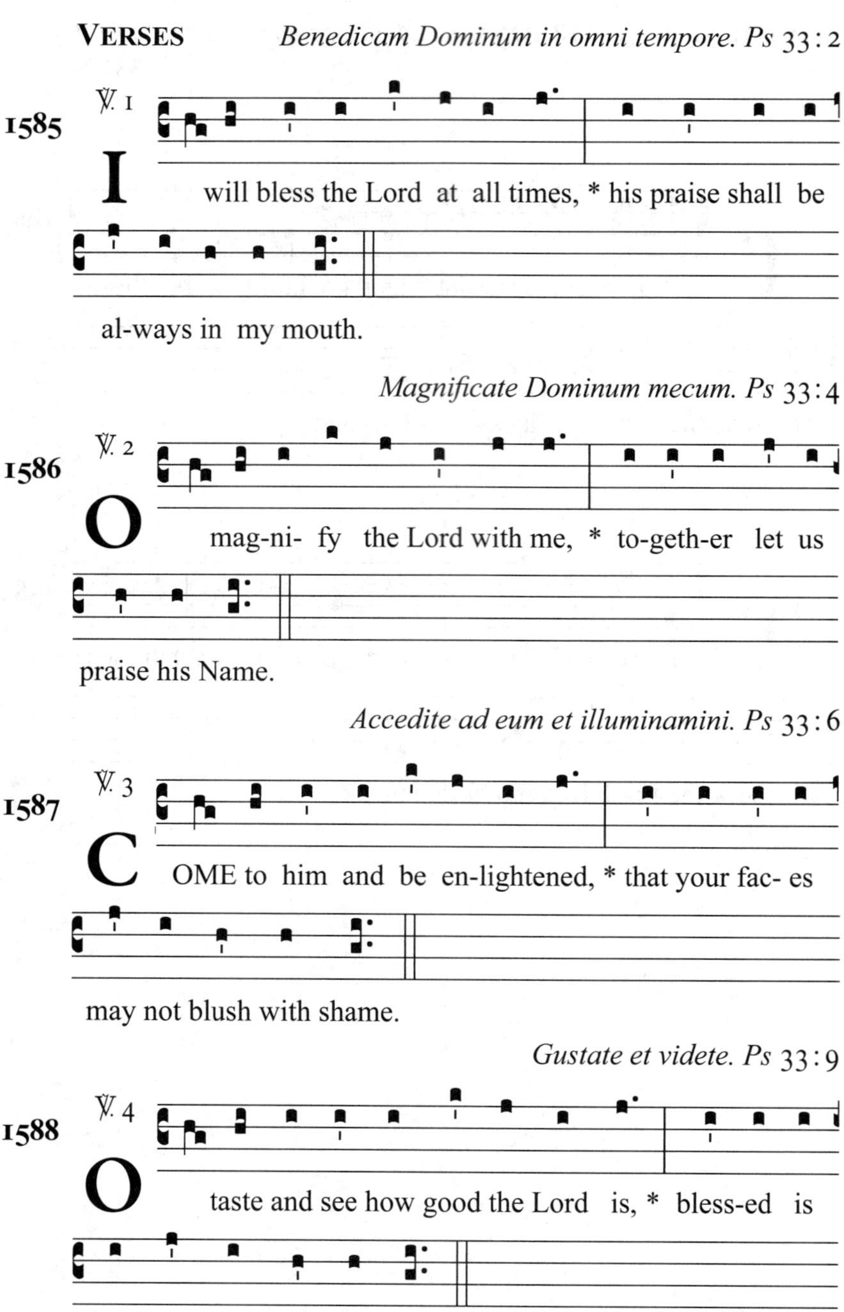
1585
℣. 1
I will bless the Lord at all times, * his praise shall be al-ways in my mouth.
Magnificate Dominum mecum. Ps 33:4
1586
℣. 2
O mag-ni- fy the Lord with me, * to-geth-er let us praise his Name.
Accedite ad eum et illuminamini. Ps 33:6
1587
℣. 3
COME to him and be en-lightened, * that your fac- es may not blush with shame.
Gustate et videte. Ps 33:9
1588
℣. 4
O taste and see how good the Lord is, * bless-ed is the man who hopes in him.

- iii -

7.
THE rich suf- fer want and go hun- gry, * but those
1589

who seek the Lord lack no bless-ing.

- iv -

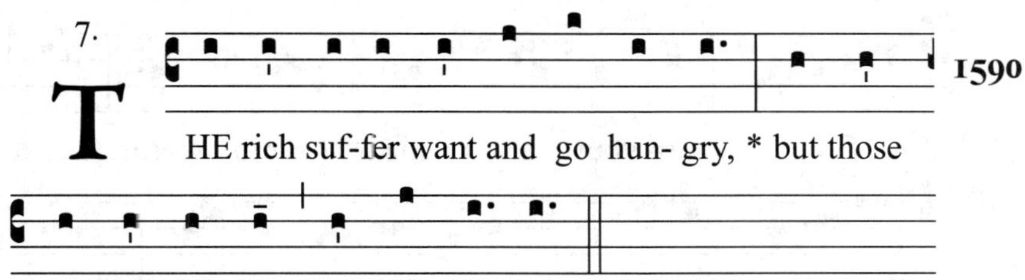
7.
THE rich suf-fer want and go hun- gry, * but those
1590

who seek the Lord lack no bless-ing.

TWENTY-NINTH SUNDAY IN ORDINARY TIME

ENTRANCE ANTIPHON *Ego clamavi, quoniam exaudisti me.*
Psalm 16:6. 8

- i -

Ti *natural throughout, except as marked on "ear to me."*

1591

3.
TO you I call; * for you will sure-ly heed me,
O God; turn your ear to me; hear my words. Guard
me, O Lord, as the ap- ple of your eye; in the
shad- ow of your wings, pro- tect me.

- ii -

1592

3.
TO you I call; * for you will sure- ly heed me, O
God; turn your ear to me; hear my words. Guard me, O Lord,
as the ap-ple of your eye; in the shad- ow of your wings

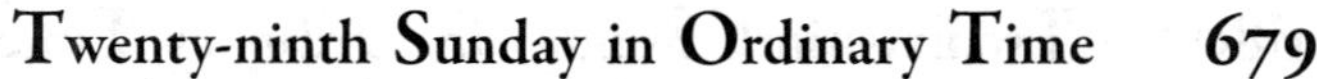

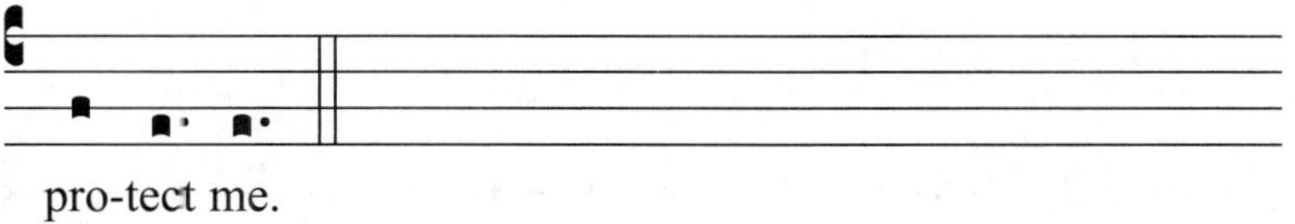
pro-tect me.

VERSES *Exaudi, Domine, iustitiam. Psalm* 16:1

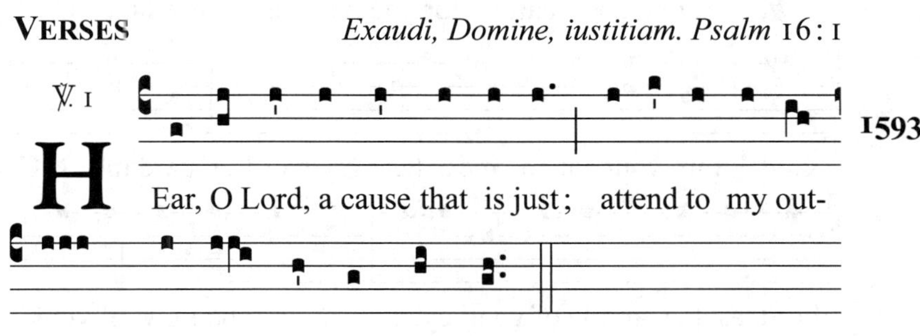
℣. 1
HEar, O Lord, a cause that is just; attend to my out-
cry; * Give ear un- to my prayer.
1593

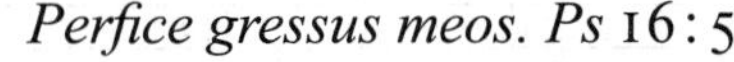
Perfice gressus meos. Ps 16:5

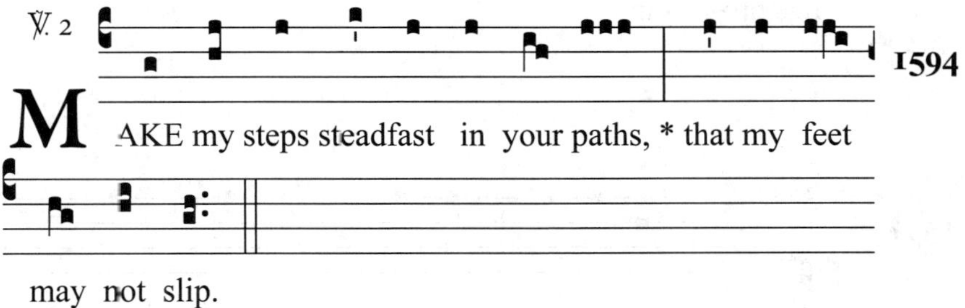
℣. 2
MAKE my steps steadfast in your paths, * that my feet
may not slip.
1594

Ego autem in iustitia. Psalm 16:15

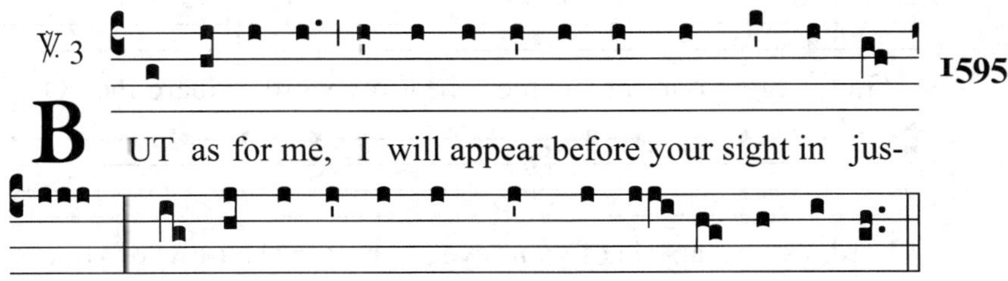
℣. 3
BUT as for me, I will appear before your sight in jus-
tice; * I shall be sat- is-fied when your glo- ry shall appear.
1595

- iii -

1596

3.
TO you I call; * for you will sure-ly heed me, O
God; turn your ear to me; hear my words. Guard me, O
Lord, as the ap-ple of your eye; in the shad-ow of your
wings pro-tect me.

Or:

1597

3.
TO you I call; * for you will sure-ly heed me, O
God; turn your ear to me; hear my words. Guard me, O
Lord, as the ap-ple of your eye; in the shad-ow of your
wings pro-tect me.

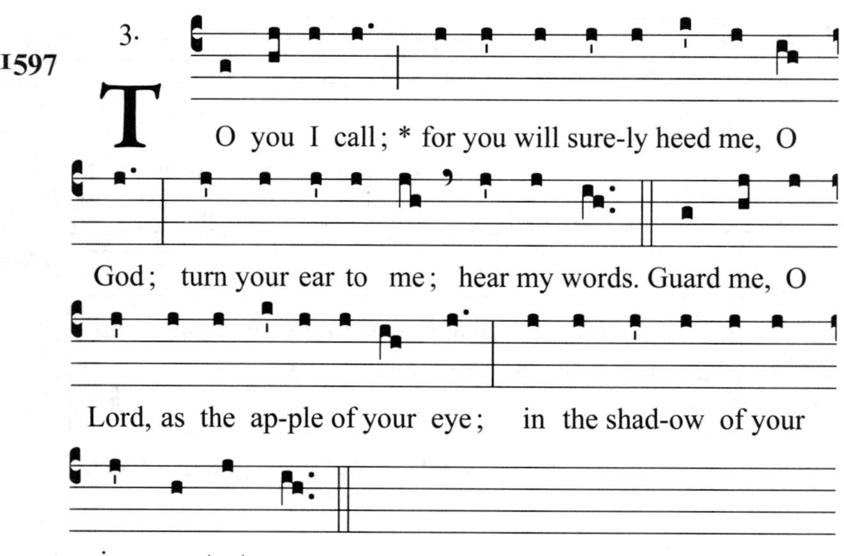

- iv -

1598

To you I call; / for you will surely heed me, O | **God**;
turn your ear to me; / | *hear my* **words**.
Guard me, O Lord, as the apple of your | **eye**;
in the shadow of your wings | *pro*-**tect** me.

Offertory Antiphon *Meditabor in madatis tuis.* *Ps* 118:47. 48

1599
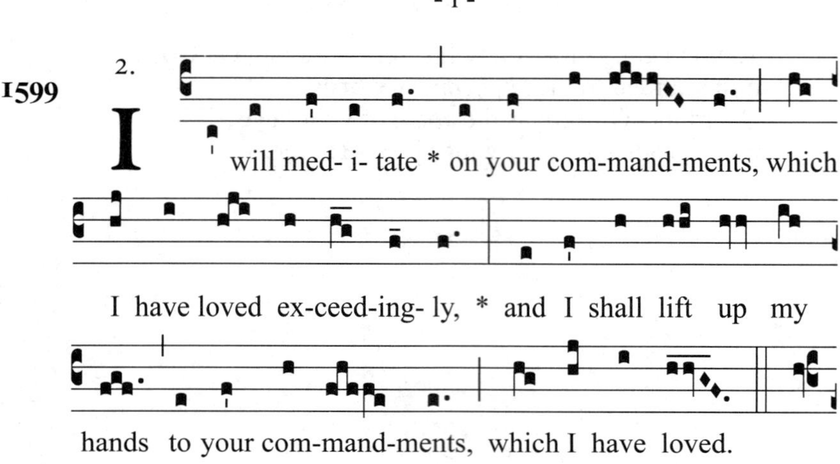
- i -
2.
I will med- i- tate * on your com-mand-ments, which
I have loved ex-ceed-ing- ly, * and I shall lift up my
hands to your com-mand-ments, which I have loved.

Verses *Pars mea Domine, dixi custodire legem tuam.* *Ps* 118:57-58

1600
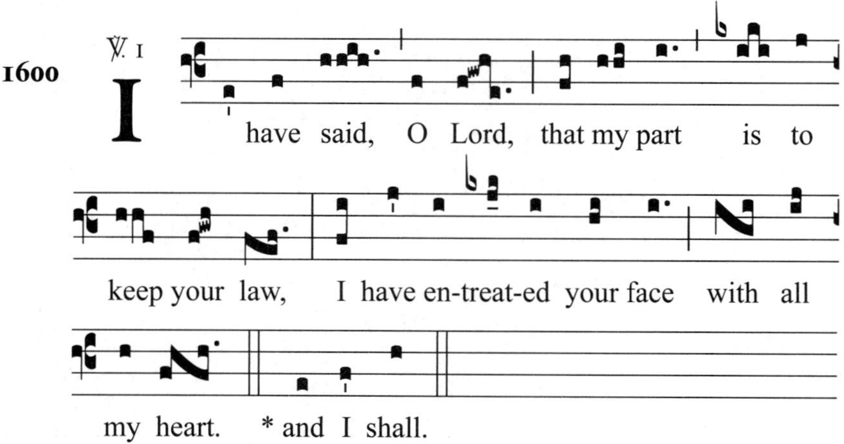
℣. 1
I have said, O Lord, that my part is to
keep your law, I have en-treat-ed your face with all
my heart. * and I shall.

Miserere mei secundum eloquium tuum. Psalm 118:59

1601

℣. 2
HAVE mer-cy on me ac- cord- ing to your word,

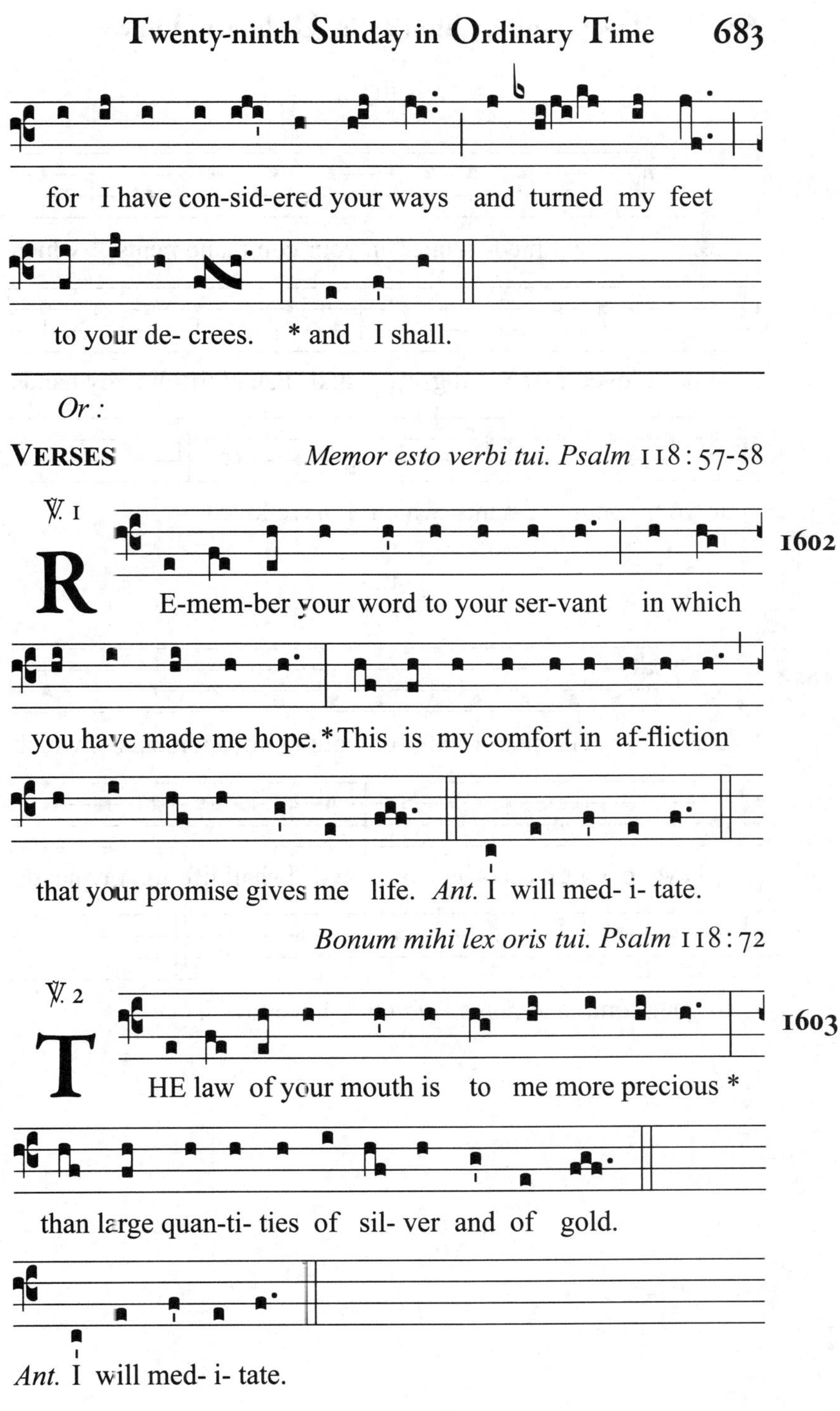
for I have con-sid-ered your ways and turned my feet
to your de- crees. * and I shall.
Or :
VERSES
Memor esto verbi tui. Psalm 118:57-58
℣. 1
R E-mem-ber your word to your ser-vant in which
1602
you have made me hope. * This is my comfort in af-fliction
that your promise gives me life. Ant. I will med- i- tate.
Bonum mihi lex oris tui. Psalm 118:72
℣. 2
T HE law of your mouth is to me more precious *
1603
than large quan-ti- ties of sil- ver and of gold.
Ant. I will med- i- tate.

- iii -

1604

2.
I will med- i- tate on your commandments, * which
I have loved ex-ceed-ing- ly, and I shall lift up my hands
to your commandments, which I have loved.

- iv -

1605

2.
I will med- i- tate on your commandments, * which
I have loved ex-ceed-ing- ly, and I shall lift up my hands
to your commandments, which I have loved.

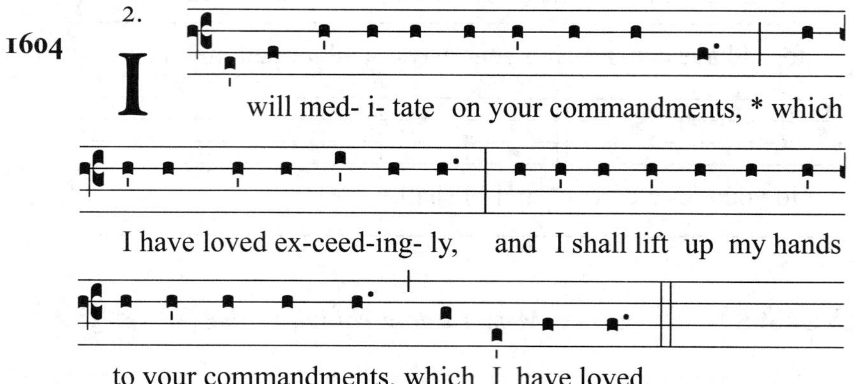

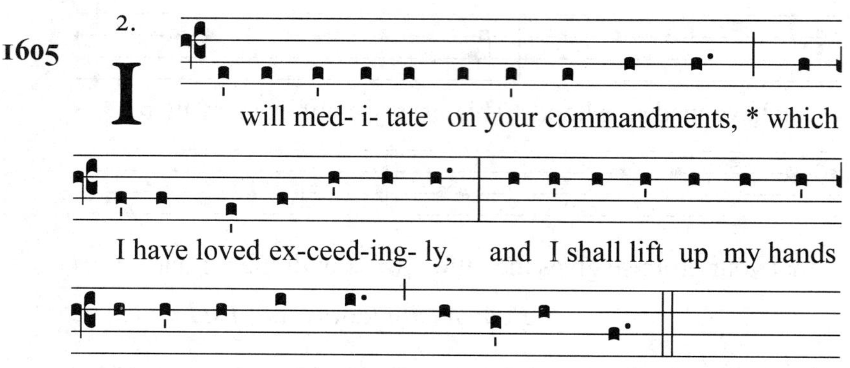

Communion Antiphon *Ecce oculi Domini.*
Ps 32:18-19

- i -

7.
B
E- hold, * the eyes of the Lord are on those
who fear him, who hope in his mer-ci-ful love, to res-cue
their souls from death, to keep them a- live in fam- ine.

1606

- ii -

7.
B
E- hold, the eyes of the Lord * are on those who
fear him, who hope in his mer- ci-ful love, to res-cue their
souls from death, to keep them a- live in fam- ine.

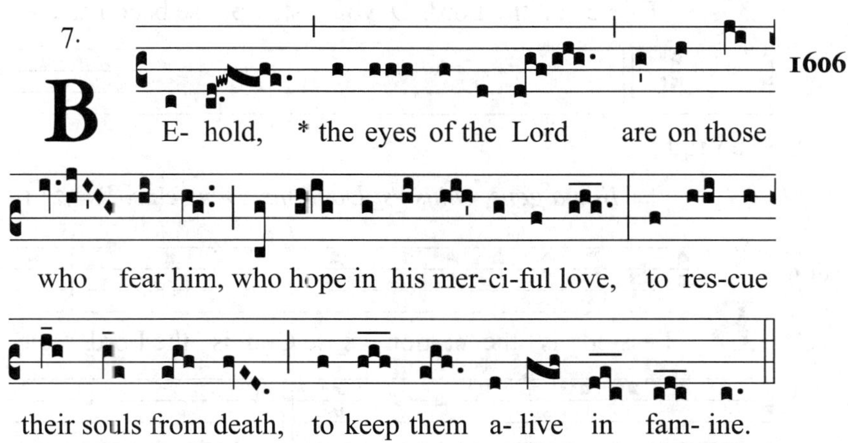

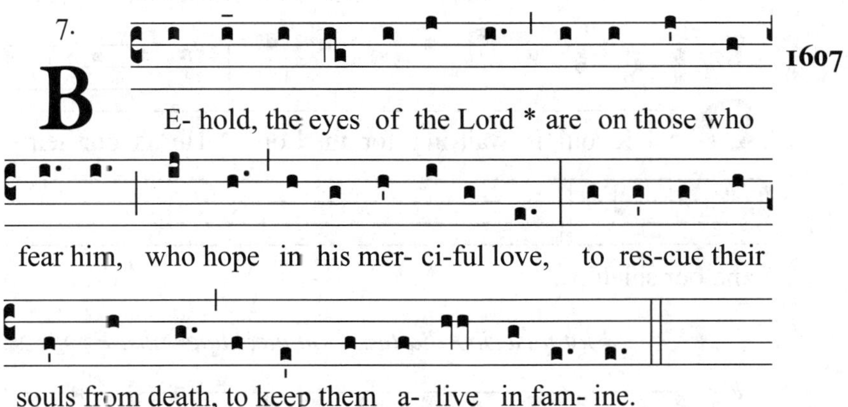

1607

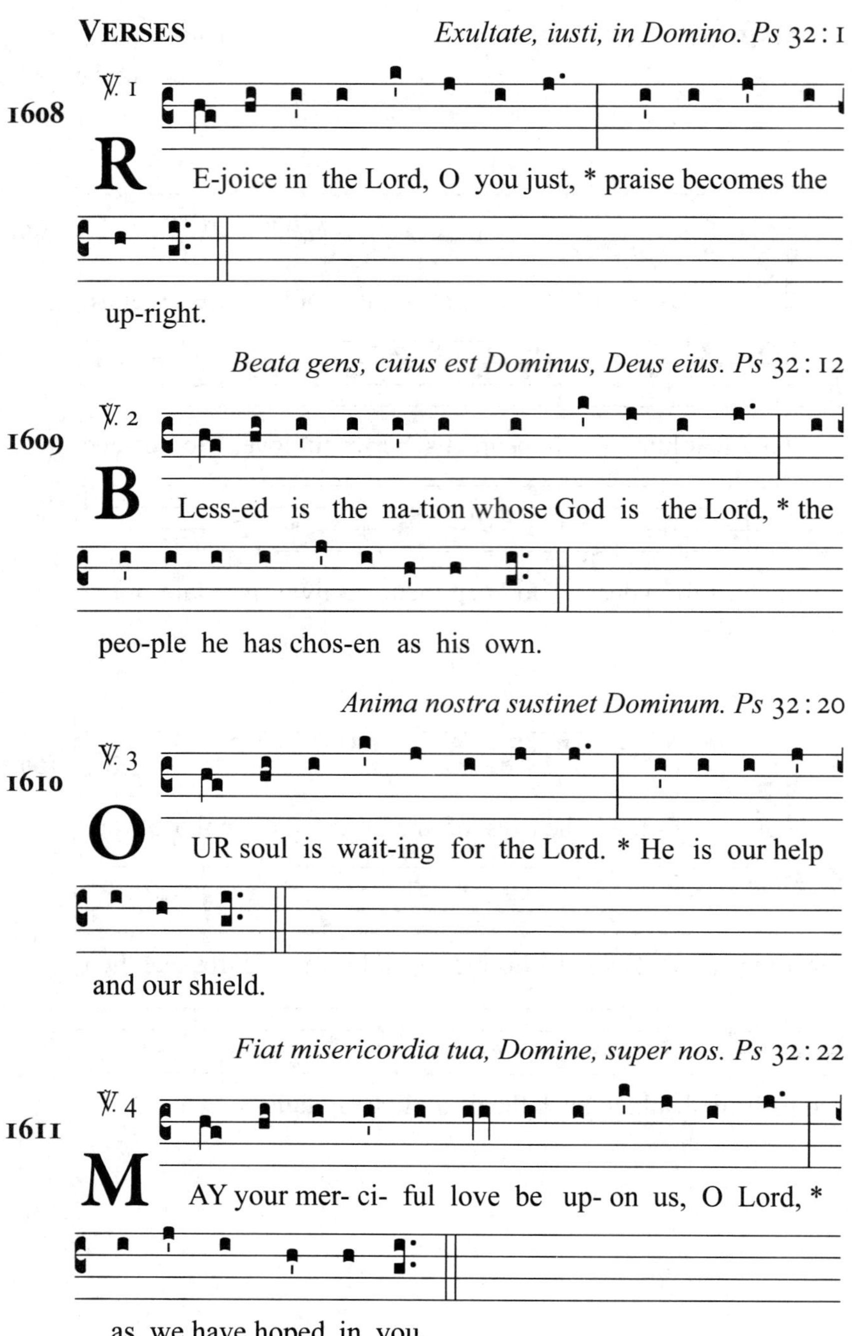
VERSES
Exultate, iusti, in Domino. Ps 32 : 1
℣. 1
1608
REjoice in the Lord, O you just, * praise becomes the up-right.
Beata gens, cuius est Dominus, Deus eius. Ps 32 : 12
℣. 2
1609
BLess-ed is the na-tion whose God is the Lord, * the peo-ple he has chos-en as his own.
Anima nostra sustinet Dominum. Ps 32 : 20
℣. 3
1610
OUR soul is wait-ing for the Lord. * He is our help and our shield.
Fiat misericordia tua, Domine, super nos. Ps 32 : 22
℣. 4
1611
MAY your mer- ci- ful love be up- on us, O Lord, * as we have hoped in you.

- iii -

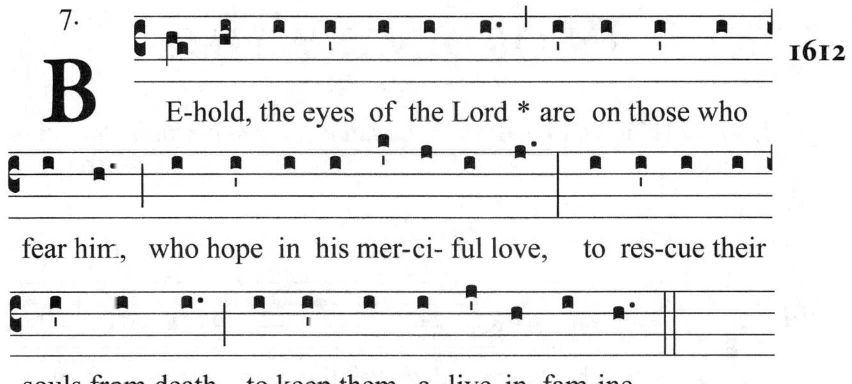
7.
1612
BEHOLD, the eyes of the Lord * are on those who
fear him, who hope in his mer-ci- ful love, to res-cue their
souls from death, to keep them a- live in fam-ine.

- iv -

7. 1613

B E-hold, the eyes of the Lord * are on those who
fear him, who hope in his mer-ci- ful love, to res-cue their
souls from death, to keep them a- live in fam-ine.

THIRTIETH SUNDAY IN ORDINARY TIME

ENTRANCE ANTIPHON *Lætetur cor quærentium Dominum.*
Ps 104:3. 4

- i -

1614

2.
LET the hearts * that seek the Lord re-joice; turn
to the Lord and his strength; constant-ly seek his face.

- ii -

1615

2.
LET the hearts * that seek the Lord re- joice; turn
to the Lord and his strength; constant-ly seek his face.

VERSES *Confitemini Domino. Ps* 104:1

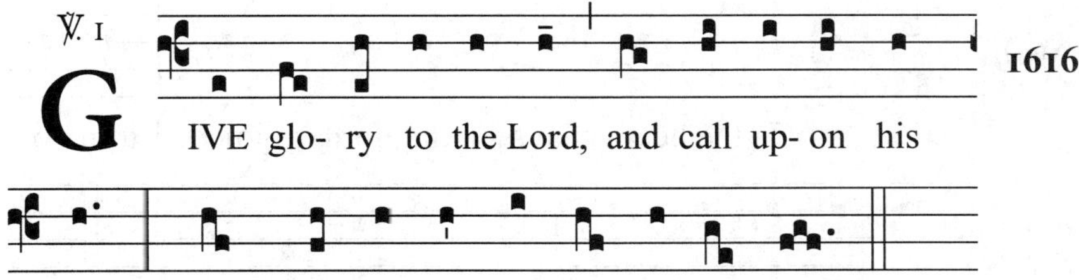
℣. 1
1616
GIVE glo- ry to the Lord, and call up- on his
name ; * make known a-mong the na-tions his deeds.

Quærite Dominum, et confirmamini. Ps 104:4-5

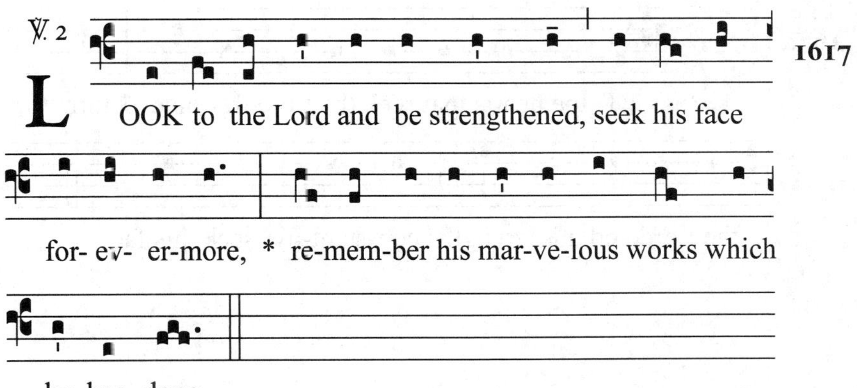
℣. 2
1617
LOOK to the Lord and be strengthened, seek his face
for- ev- er-more, * re-mem-ber his mar-ve-lous works which
he has done.

Semen Abraham, servi eius. Ps 104:6

℣. 3
1618
O child- ren of A- bra- ham, his ser-vant, * O
de-scend-ants of the Ja- cob he chose.

- iii -

1619

2.
LET the hearts that seek the Lord re-joice; * turn to
the Lord and his strength; con-stant- ly seek his face.

- iv -

1620

2.
LET the hearts that seek the Lord re-joice; * turn to
the Lord and his strength; con-stant- ly seek his face.

OFFERTORY ANTIPHON *Domine, vivifica me.*
Ps 118:107. 125

- i -

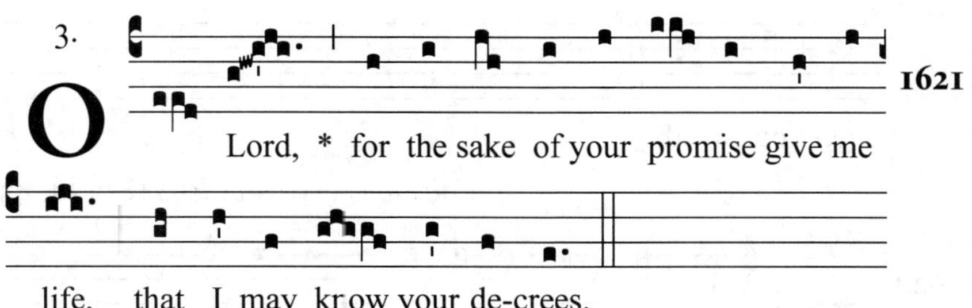
3.
O Lord, * for the sake of your promise give me
life, that I may know your de-crees.

1621

- ii -

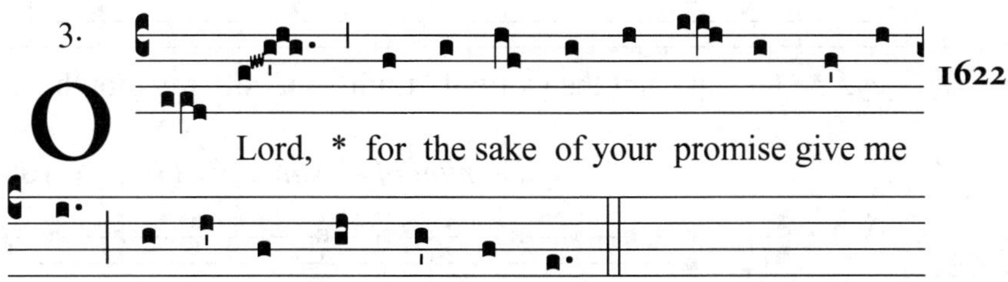
3.
O Lord, * for the sake of your promise give me
life, that I may know your de-crees.

1622

VERSES *In via testimonium tuorum. Ps* 118:16

1623
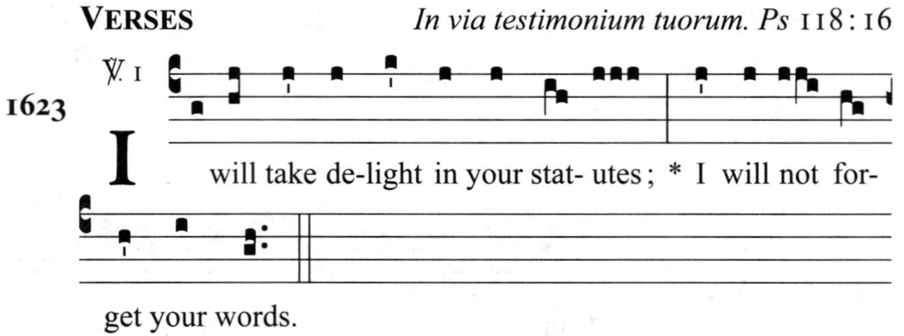
℣. 1
I will take de-light in your stat- utes; * I will not for-
get your words.

Fac cum servo tuo. Ps 118:124. 43

1624
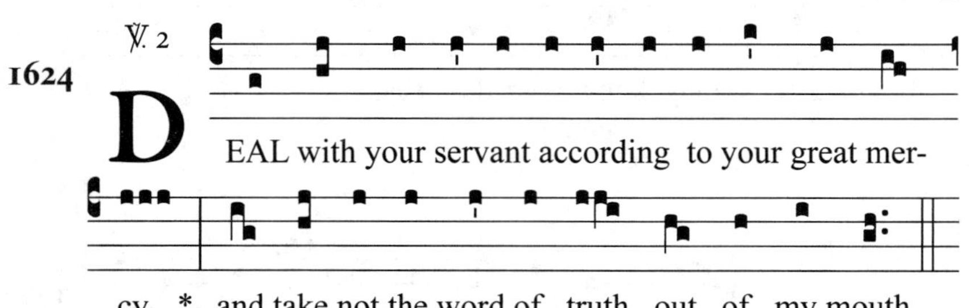
℣. 2
DEAL with your servant according to your great mer-
cy, * and take not the word of truth out of my mouth.

Da mihi intellectum. Ps 118 : 73. 108

1625
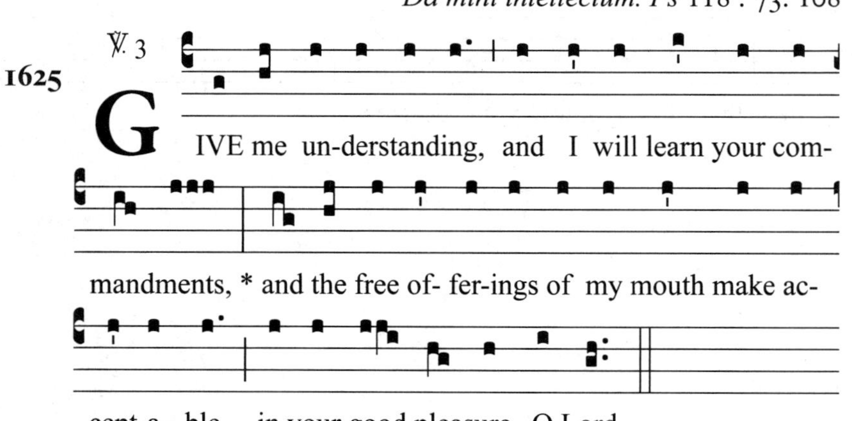
℣. 3
GIVE me un-derstanding, and I will learn your commandments, * and the free of- fer-ings of my mouth make ac-
cept-a- ble, in your good pleasure, O Lord.

- iii -

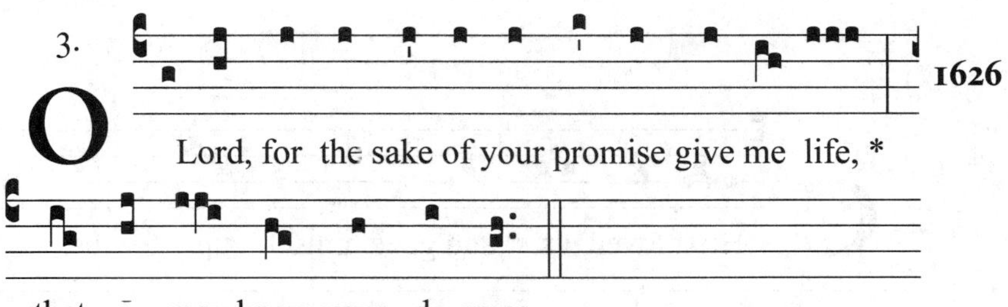
3.
O Lord, for the sake of your promise give me life, *
1626
that I may know your de-crees.

Or:

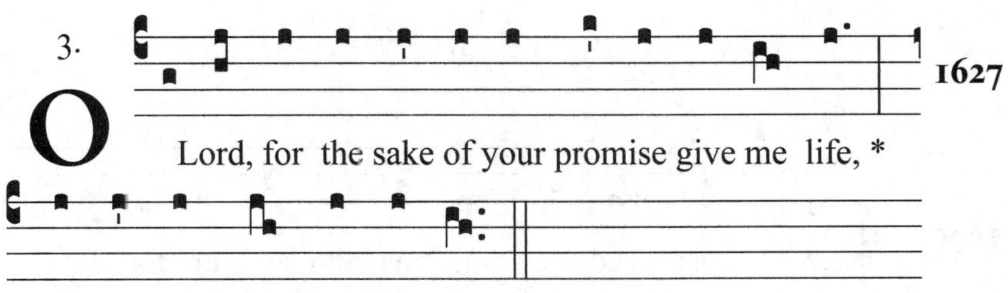
3.
O Lord, for the sake of your promise give me life, *
1627
that I may know your de-crees.

- iv -

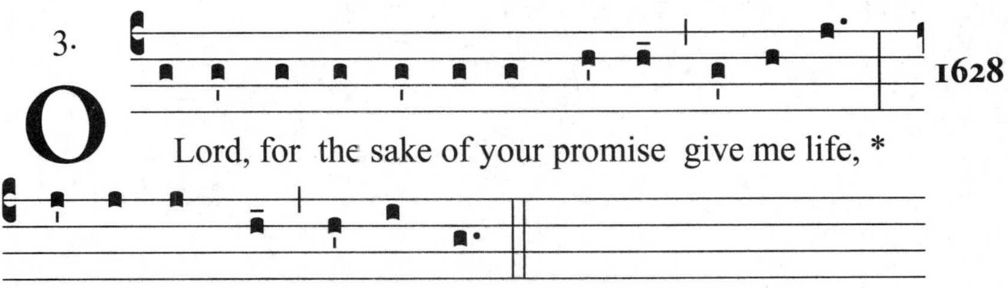
3.
O Lord, for the sake of your promise give me life, *
1628
that I may know your de-crees.

COMMUNION ANTIPHON *Christus dilexit nos.*
Eph 5:2

- i -

1629 6. CHrist loved us, * and gave himself up for us,
as a fra-grant of- fer-ing to God.

- ii -

1630
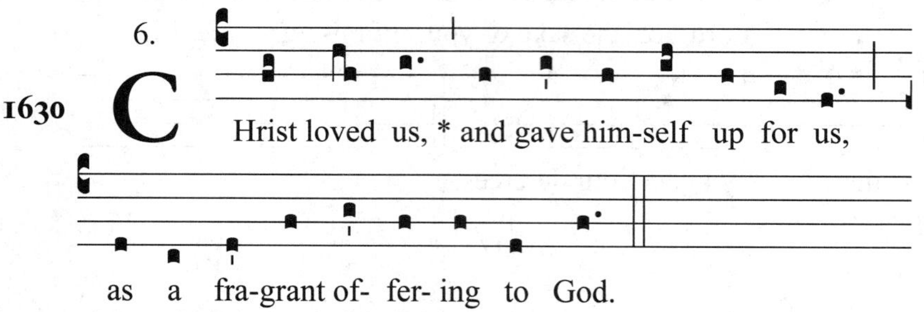
6.
C
Hrist loved us, * and gave him-self up for us,
as a fra-grant of- fer- ing to God.

VERSES *Exultate, iusti, in Domino.* Ps 32:1

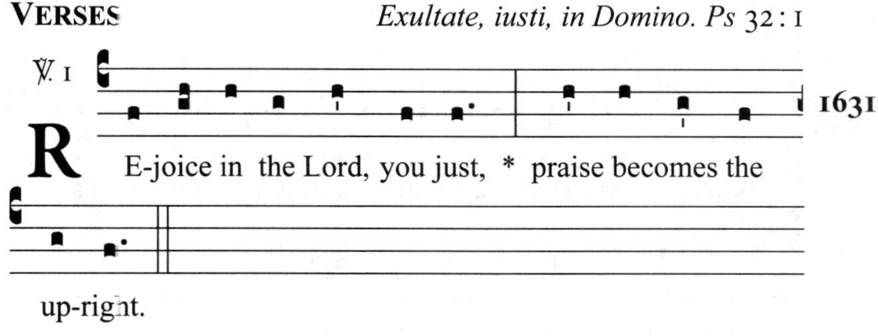
℣. 1
REJOICE in the Lord, you just, * praise becomes the
1631
up-right.

Beata gens, cuius est Dominus, Deus eius. Ps 32:12

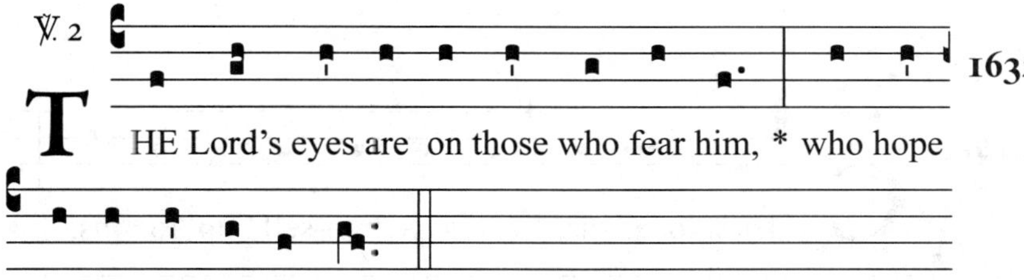
℣. 2
THE Lord's eyes are on those who fear him, * who hope
1632
in his mer- ci- ful love.

Anima nostra sustinet Dominum. Ps 32:20

℣. 3
OUR soul is wait-ing for the Lord. * He is our help
1633
and our shield.

Fiat misericordia tua, Domine, super nos. Ps 32:22

℣. 4
MAY your mer- ci- ful love be up- on us, * as we have
1634

hoped in you.

- iii -

1635 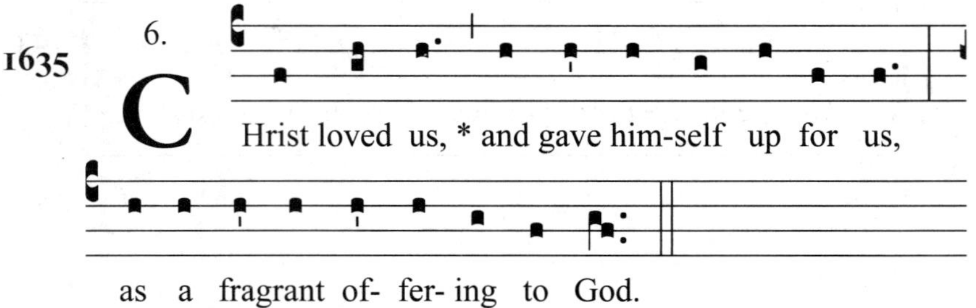
6.
CHrist loved us, * and gave him-self up for us,
as a fragrant of- fer- ing to God.

- iv -

1636 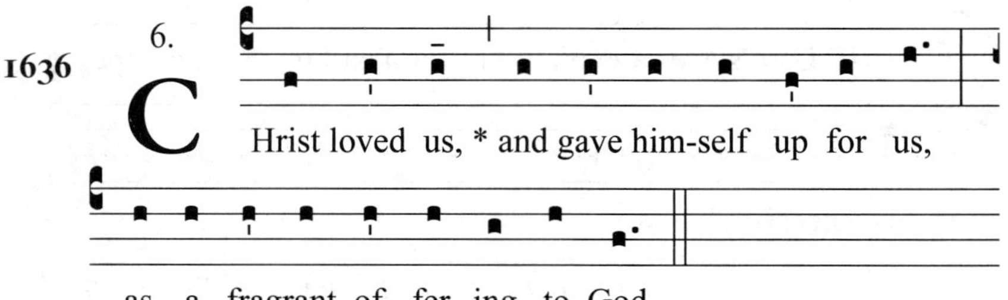
6.
CHrist loved us, * and gave him-self up for us,
as a fragrant of- fer- ing to God.

THIRTY-FIRST SUNDAY IN ORDINARY TIME

ENTRANCE ANTIPHON *Ne derelinquas me.*
Ps 37:22. 23

- i -

7.
F
Orsake me not, * O Lord, my God; be not far
1637
from me! Make haste and come to my help, O Lord,
my strong sal- va- tion.

- ii -

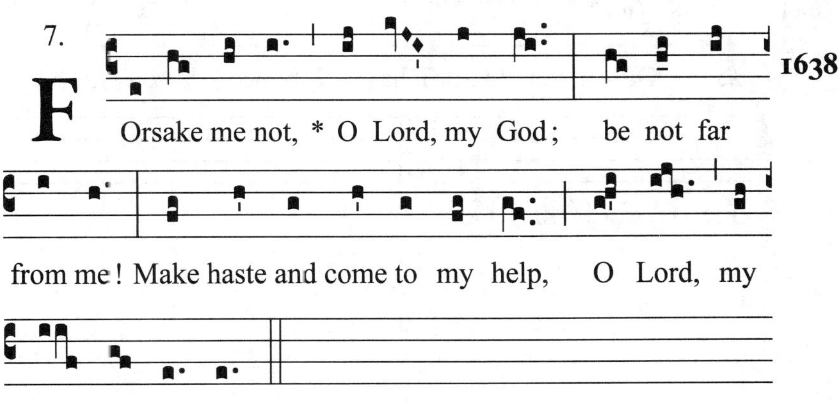
7.
F
Orsake me not, * O Lord, my God; be not far
1638
from me! Make haste and come to my help, O Lord, my
strong sal- va- tion.

VERSES *Domine, ne in furore. Ps* 37 : 2

1639
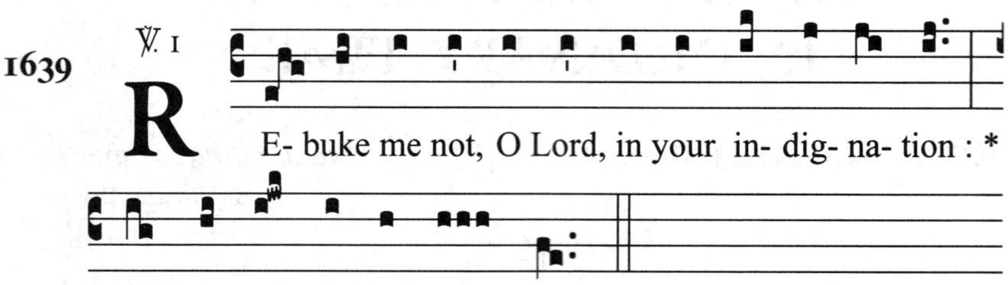
℣. 1
R
E- buke me not, O Lord, in your in- dig- na- tion : *

nor chas-tise me in your wrath.

Cor meum conturbatum est. Ps 37 : 11

1640

℣. 2
M
Y heart is troubled, my strength has left me, * and

the light of my eyes it- self is not with me.

Quoniam in te, Domine, speravi. Psalm 37 : 16

1641

℣. 3
F
OR in you, O Lord, have I hoped : * you will hear
me, O Lord my God.

- iii -

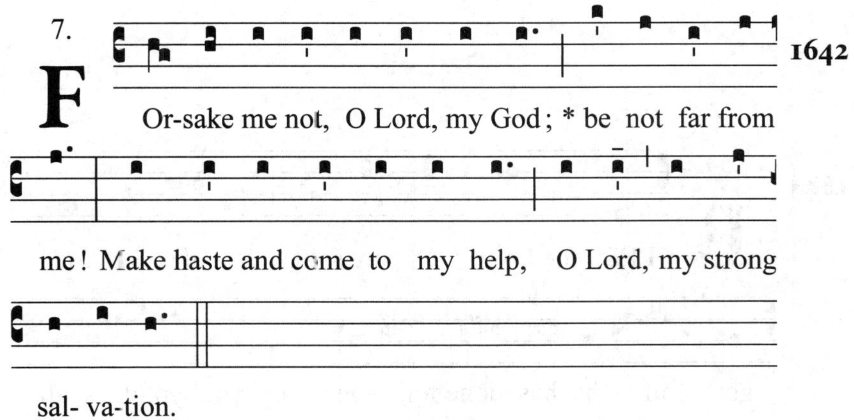
7.
FOr-sake me not, O Lord, my God; * be not far from
me! Make haste and come to my help, O Lord, my strong
sal- va-tion.

1642

- iv -

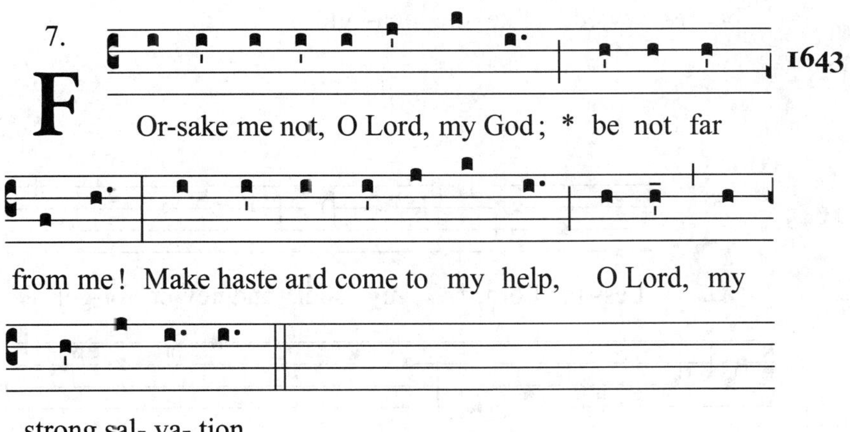
7.
FOr-sake me not, O Lord, my God; * be not far
from me! Make haste and come to my help, O Lord, my
strong sal- va- tion.

1643

OFFERTORY ANTIPHON *Benedic, anima mea, Dominum.*
Ps 102 : 2. 5

- i -

1644

5.
BLESS the Lord, * O my soul, and nev- er for-
get all he has done for you ; and your youth shall
be re- newed like the ea- gle's.

- ii -

1645

5.
BLess the Lord, * O my soul, and nev-er for-get
all he has done for you : and your youth shall be renewed
like the ea- gle's.

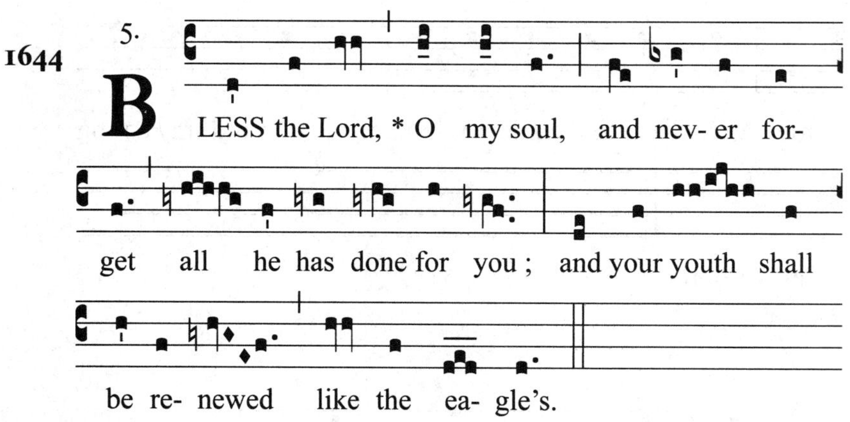

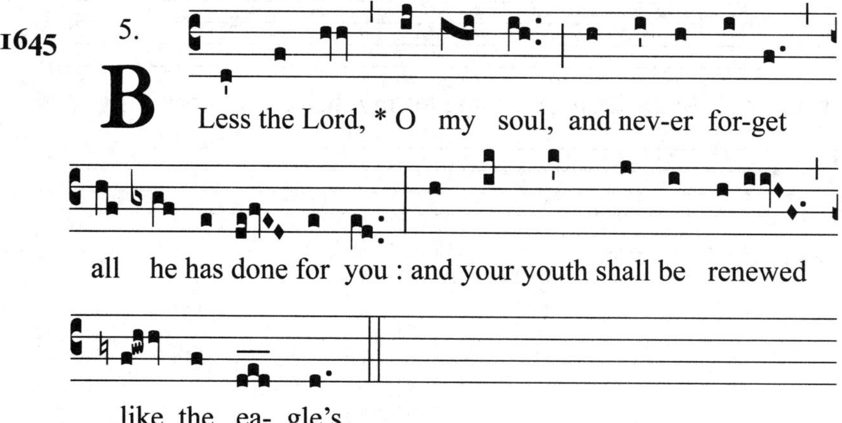

VERSES *Miserator et misericors Dominus. Ps* 102:8

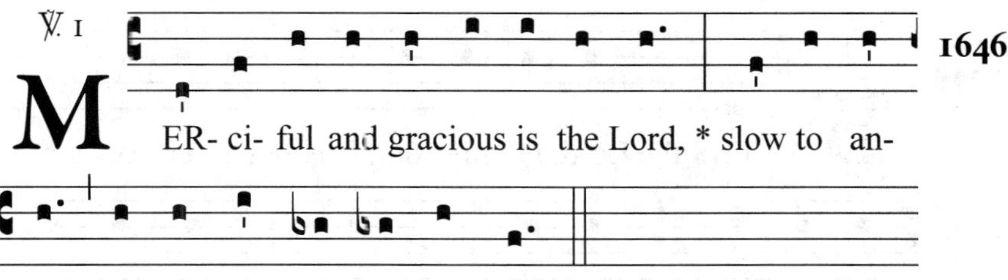
℣. 1
MERCIFUL and gracious is the Lord, * slow to an-
1646

ger and a-bound-ing in kind-ness.

Non in perpetuum irascetur. Ps 102:9

℣. 2
HE will not al-ways be an- gry, * nor will he threat-
1647
en for ev- er.

Quomodo miseretur pater filiorum. Ps 102:13

℣. 3
AS a fa-ther has compassion on his child-ren, *
1648

so the Lord has com-pas-sion on those who fear him.

- iii -

1649

5.
BLESS the Lord, O my soul, * and nev-er for- get
all he has done for you ; and your youth shall be renewed like the ea- gle's.

- iv -

1650

5.
BLESS the Lord, O my soul, * and nev-er for- get
all he has done for you ; and your youth shall be renewed like the ea- gle's.

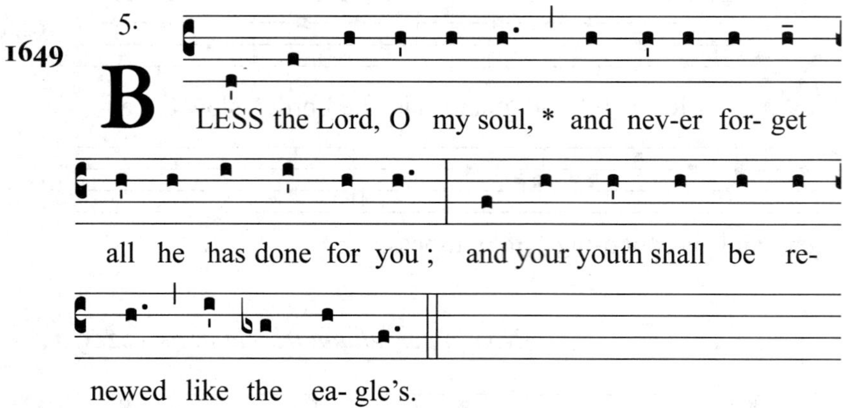

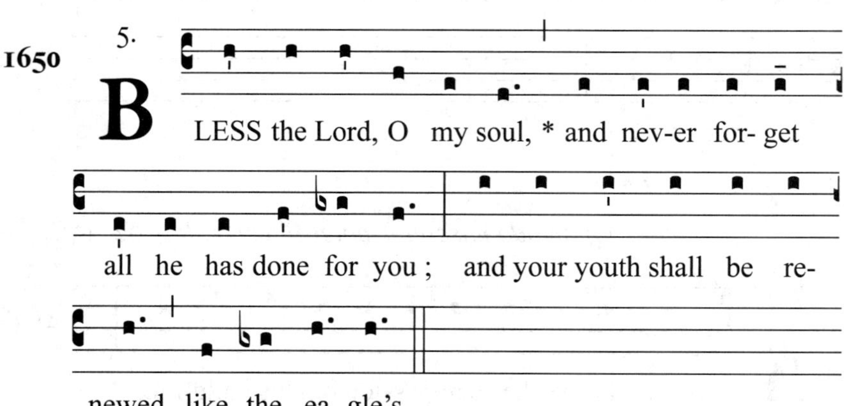

COMMUNION ANTIPHON *Notas mihi fecisti.*
Ps 15:11

- i -

7.
Y
OU will show me* the path of life, the full-
1651

ness of joy in your presence, O Lord.

- ii -

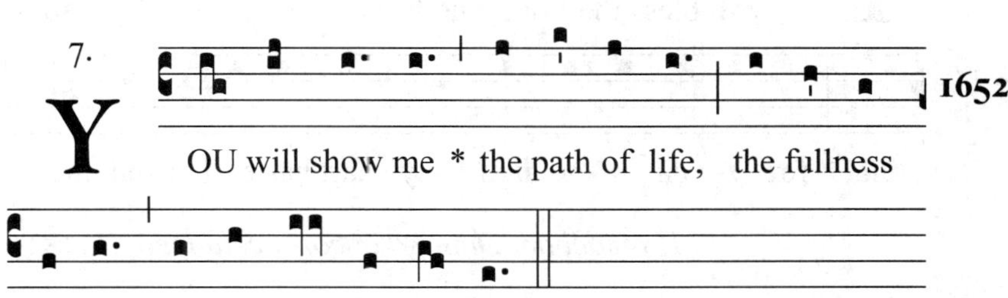
7.
Y
OU will show me * the path of life, the fullness
1652

of joy in your presence, O Lord.

VERSES

Conserva me, Domine. *Ps* 15:1

1653

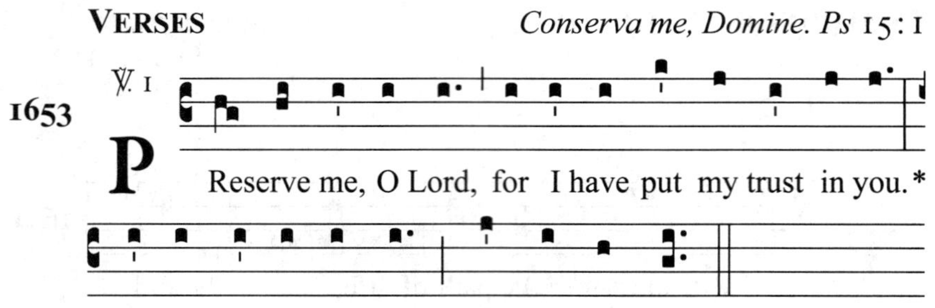
℣. 1
PReserve me, O Lord, for I have put my trust in you. *
I have said to the Lord : You are my God.

Benedicam Dominum, qui tribuit mihi intellectum. *Ps* 15:7

1654

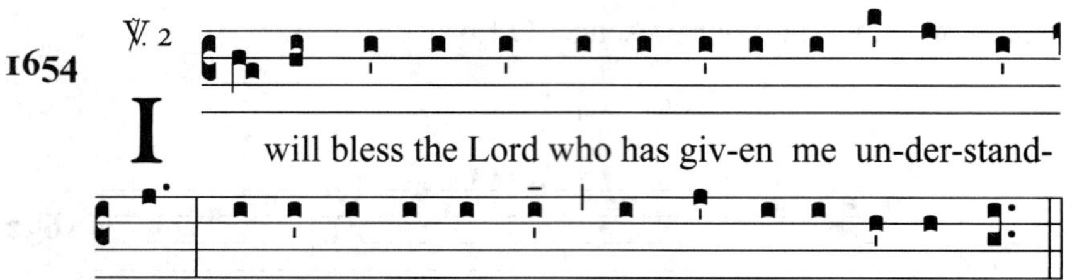
℣. 2
I will bless the Lord who has giv-en me un-der-stand-
ing, * for e- ven in the night my heart has ex-hort-ed me.

Providebam Domino in conspectu meo. *Ps* 15:8

1655

℣. 3
I set the Lord al-ways in my sight. * For he is at
my right hand, that I be not moved.

- iii -

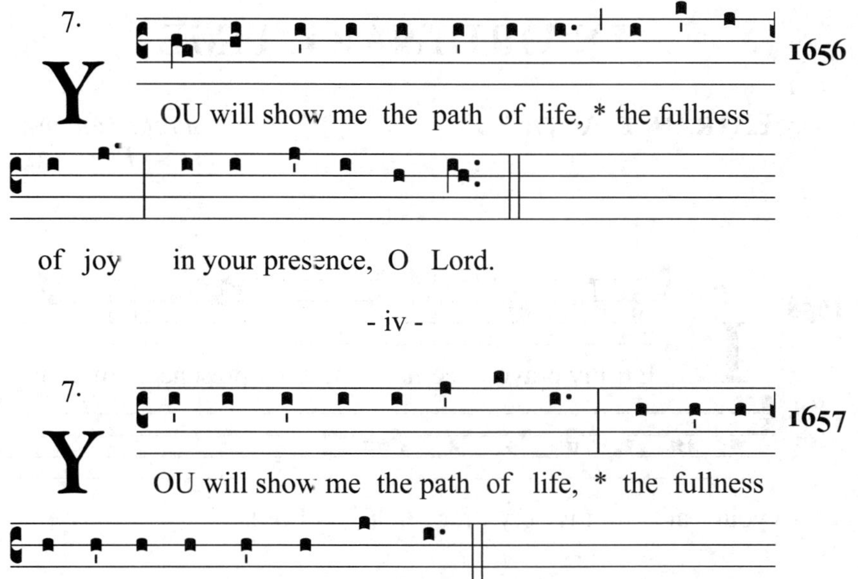
7.
1656
YOU will show me the path of life, * the fullness
of joy in your presence, O Lord.
- iv -
7.
1657
YOU will show me the path of life, * the fullness

of joy in your pres-ence, O Lord.

THIRTY-SECOND SUNDAY IN ORDINARY TIME

ENTRANCE ANTIPHON *Intret oratio mea.*

Ps 87:3. 2

\- i -

1658 3.

LET my prayer * come in- to your presence. In-cline your ear to my cry for help, O Lord.

\- ii -

1659

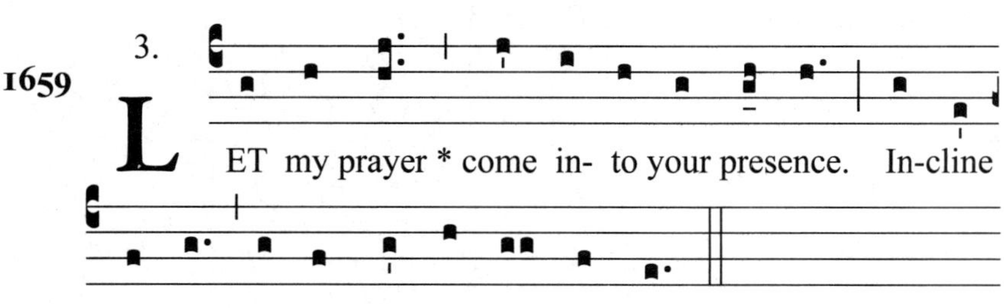
3.
LET my prayer * come in- to your presence. In-cline

your ear to my cry for help, O Lord.

VERSES *Domine Deus salutis meæ. Ps* 87 : 2

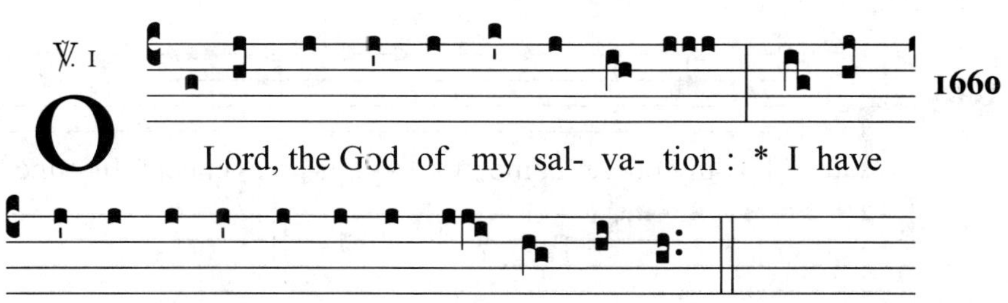
℣. 1
1660
O Lord, the God of my sal- va- tion : * I have
cried in the day and in the night, be- fore you.

Et vita mea inferno appropinquavit. Ps 87 : 4

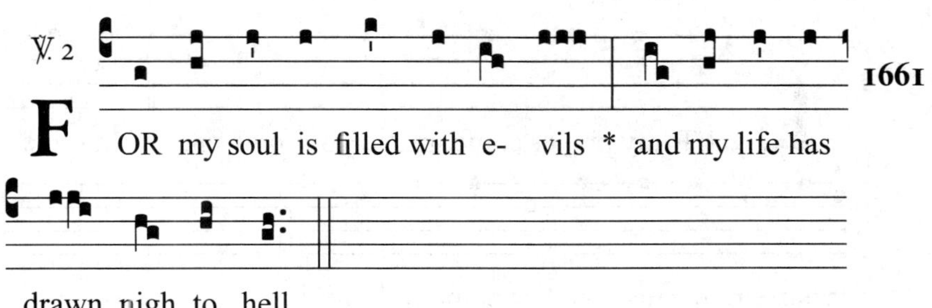
℣. 2
1661
FOR my soul is filled with e- vils * and my life has
drawn nigh to hell.

Et ego ad te, Domine, clamavi. Ps 87 : 14

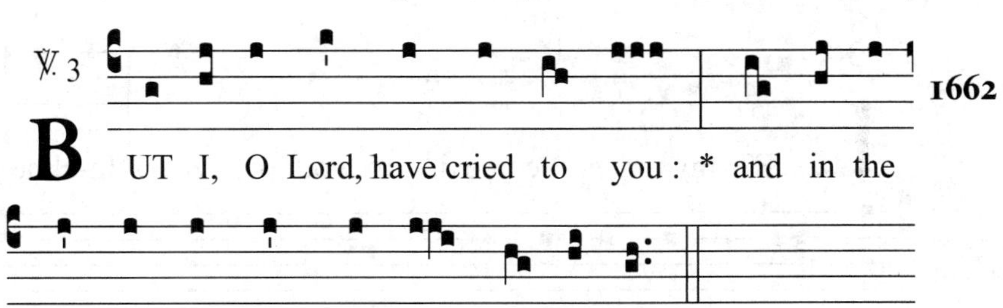
℣. 3
1662
BUT I, O Lord, have cried to you : * and in the
morn-ing my prayer shall come be-fore you.

- iii -

1663

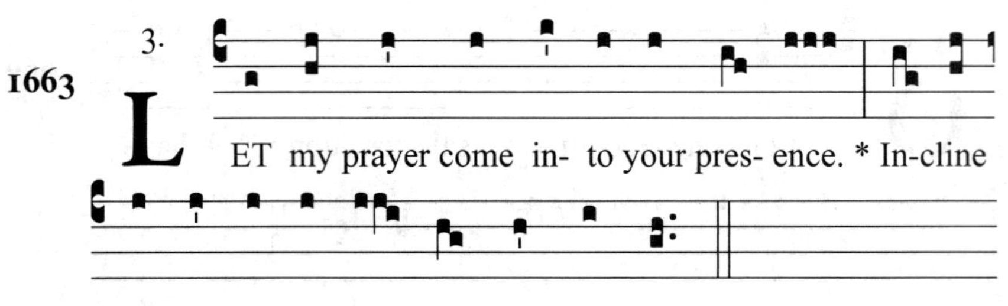

LET my prayer come in- to your pres- ence. * In-cline your ear to my cry for help, O Lord.

Or:

1664

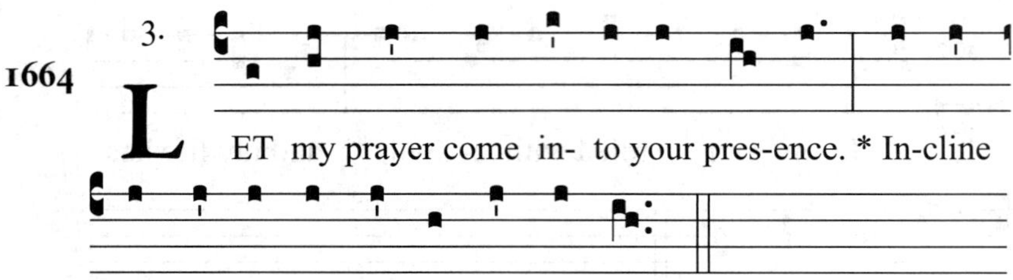

LET my prayer come in- to your pres-ence. * In-cline your ear to my cry for help, O Lord.

- iv -

1665

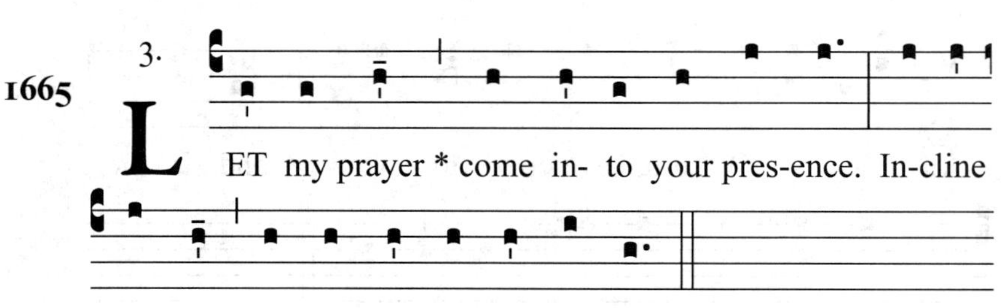

LET my prayer * come in- to your pres-ence. In-cline your ear to my cry for help, O Lord.

Offertory Antiphon *Gressus meos dirige.* *Ps* 118:133

- i -

8.
D
I- rect my steps, O Lord, * ac- cord- ing to your
word, and let no in- i- qui- ty have do- min- ion
o- ver me, O Lord my God.

1666

- ii -

8.
D
I- rect my steps, O Lord, * ac-cord-ing to your word,
and let no in- i- qui- ty have do- min-ion o- ver me,
O Lord my God.

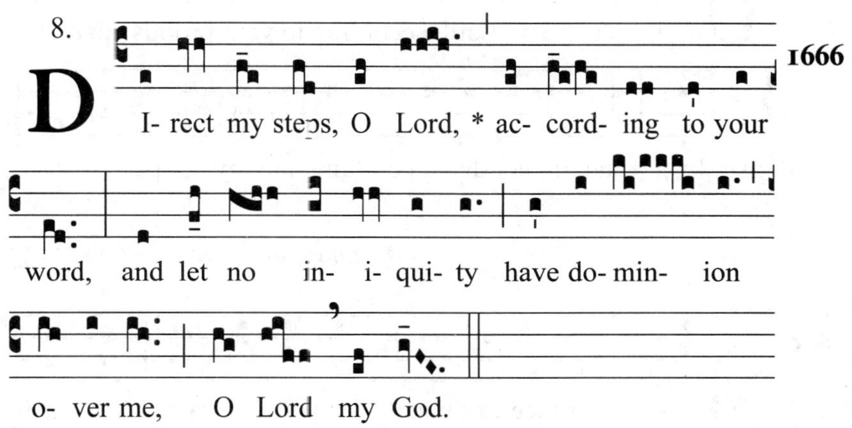

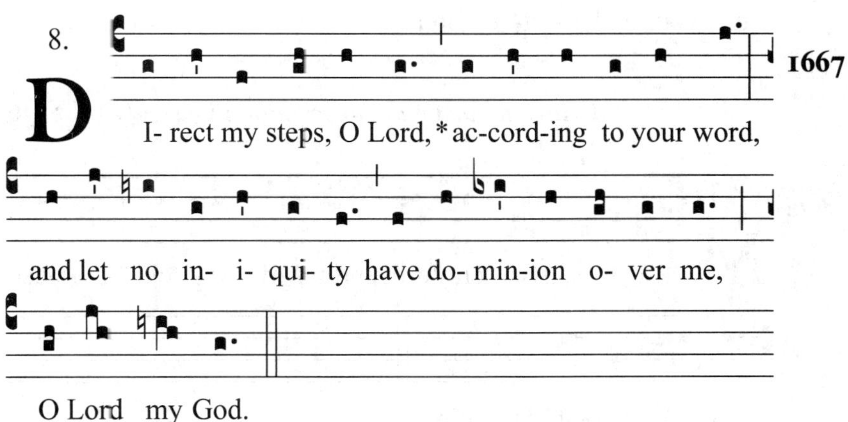

1667

VERSES *Suscipe me, Domine. Ps* 118:116

1668
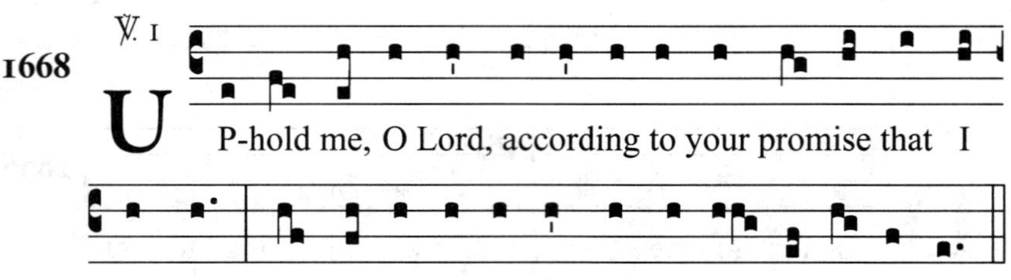
℣. 1
U P-hold me, O Lord, according to your promise that I
may live, * and do not dis-appoint me in my ex-pec-ta-tion.

Faciem tuam illumina. Ps 118:135

1669
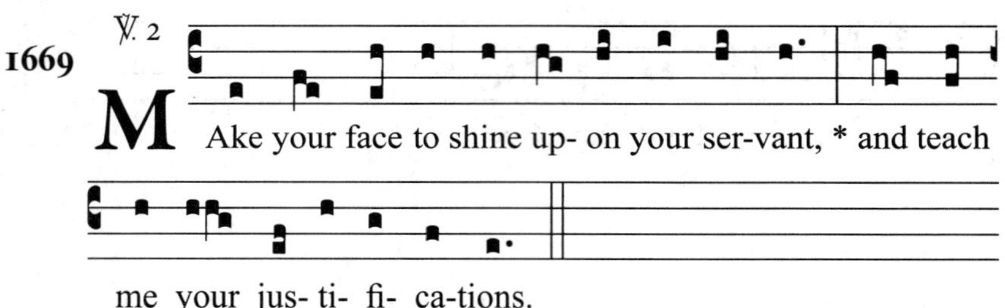
℣. 2
M Ake your face to shine up- on your ser-vant, * and teach
me your jus- ti- fi- ca-tions.

Exitus aquarum deduxerunt oculi mei. Ps 118:136

1670

℣. 3
M Y eyes have sent forth springs of wa- ter, * because
they have not kept your law.

- iii -

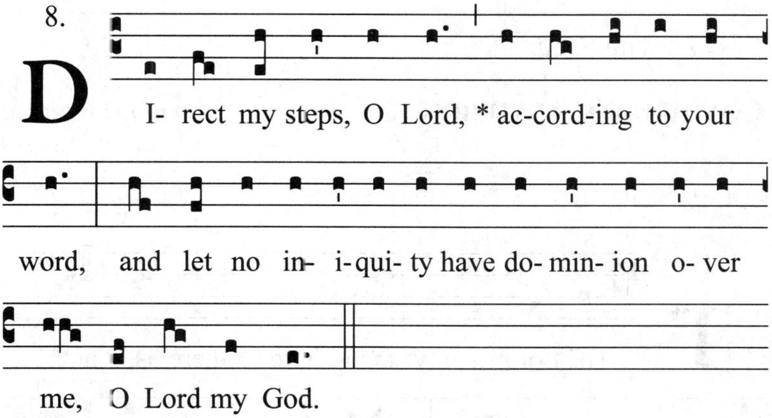

8. 1671

DI- rect my steps, O Lord, * ac-cord-ing to your word, and let no in- i-qui- ty have do- min- ion o- ver me, O Lord my God.

Or:

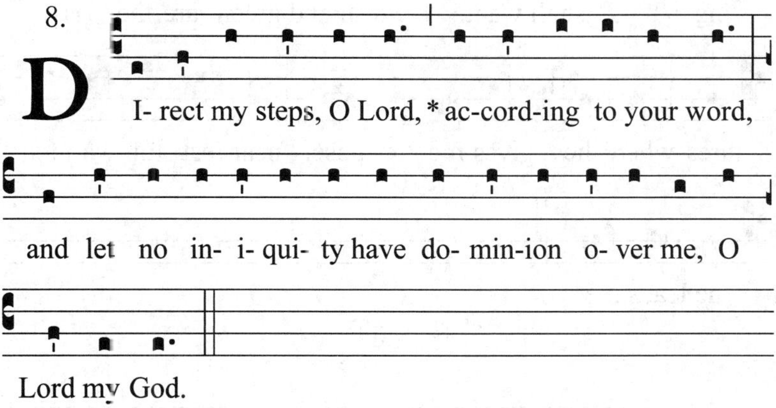

8. 1672

DI- rect my steps, O Lord, * ac-cord-ing to your word, and let no in- i- qui- ty have do- min-ion o- ver me, O Lord my God.

- iv -

8. 1673

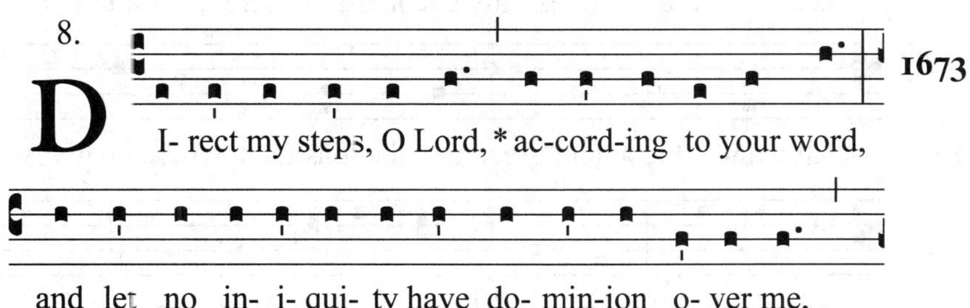
DI- rect my steps, O Lord, * ac-cord-ing to your word,
and let no in- i- qui- ty have do- min-ion o- ver me,

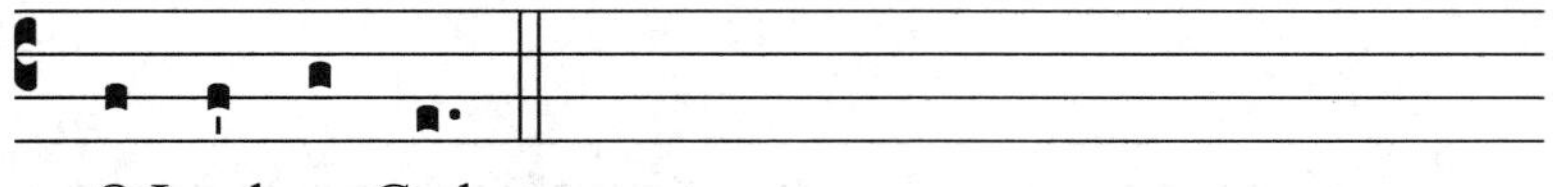
O Lord my God.

Communion Antiphon *Dominus regit me.*
Ps 22:1-2

- i -

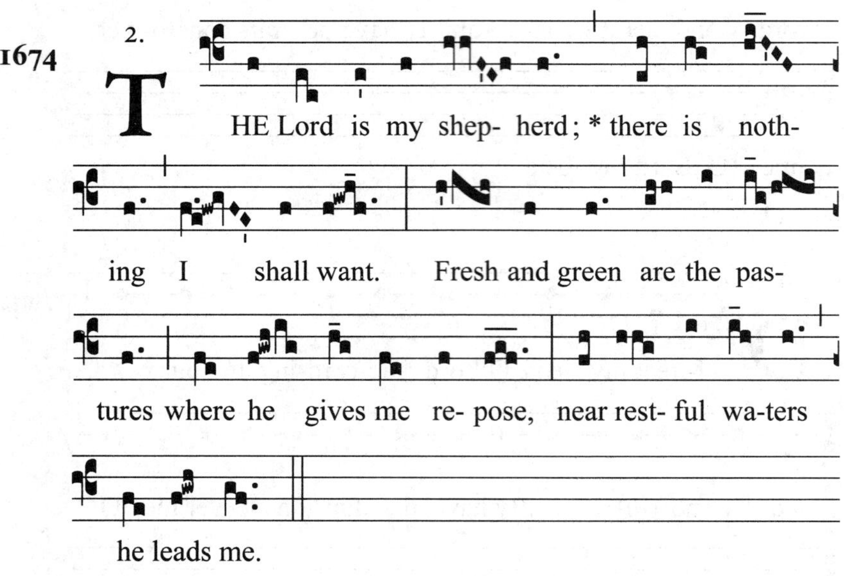
1674
2.
THE Lord is my shep- herd; * there is noth-
ing I shall want. Fresh and green are the pastures where he gives me re- pose, near rest- ful wa-ters
he leads me.

- ii -

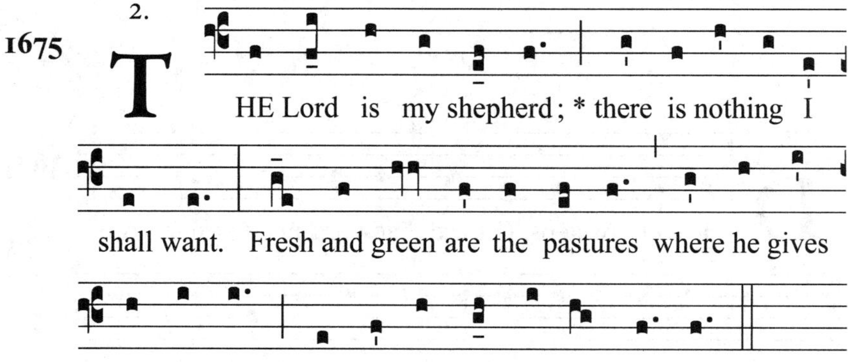
1675
2.
THE Lord is my shepherd; * there is nothing I
shall want. Fresh and green are the pastures where he gives
me re-pose, near rest-ful wa- ters he leads me.

VERSES *Nam et si ambulavero. Ps* 22:4

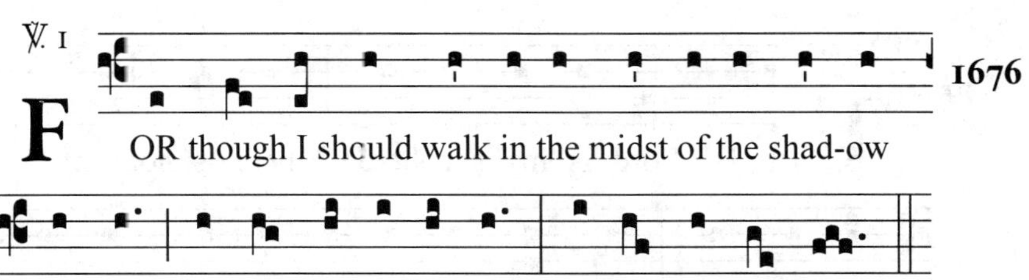
℣. 1
1676
FOR though I should walk in the midst of the shad-ow

of death, I will fear no e- vils, * for you are with me.

Parasti in conspectu meo mensam. Ps 22:5

℣. 2
1677
YOU have prepared a ta- ble be-fore me; * and my

chal-ice which in- e- bri-ates me, how good- ly it is.

Et misericordia tua subsequetur me. Ps 22:6

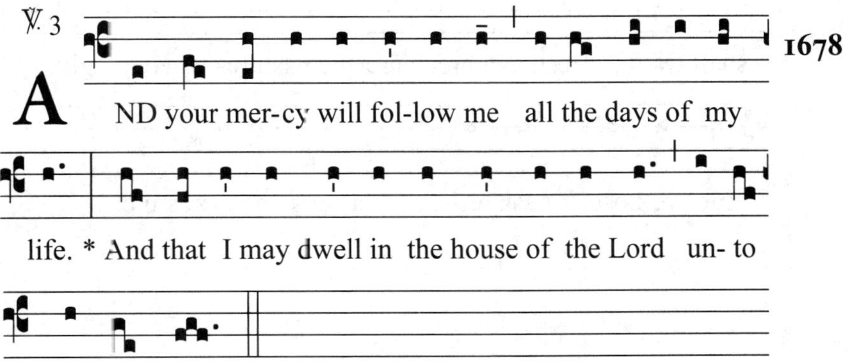
℣. 3
1678
AND your mer-cy will fol-low me all the days of my
life. * And that I may dwell in the house of the Lord un- to

length of days.

- iii -

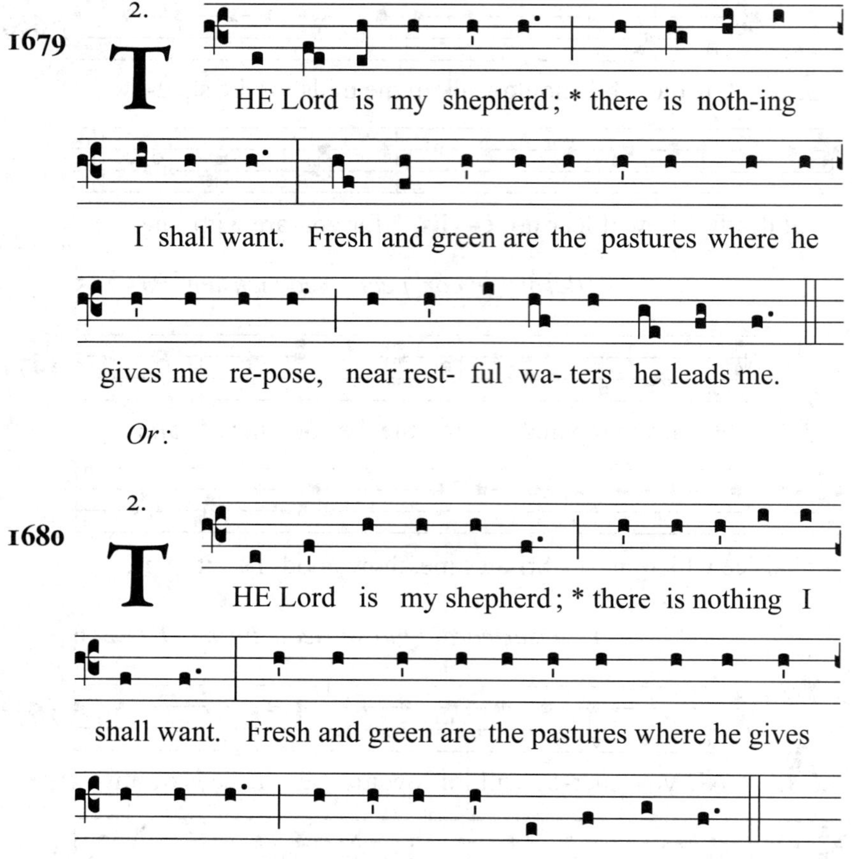
2.
1679
THE Lord is my shepherd; * there is noth-ing
I shall want. Fresh and green are the pastures where he
gives me re-pose, near rest- ful wa- ters he leads me.
Or:
2.
1680
THE Lord is my shepherd; * there is nothing I
shall want. Fresh and green are the pastures where he gives
me re-pose, near rest-ful wa- ters he leads me.

- iv -

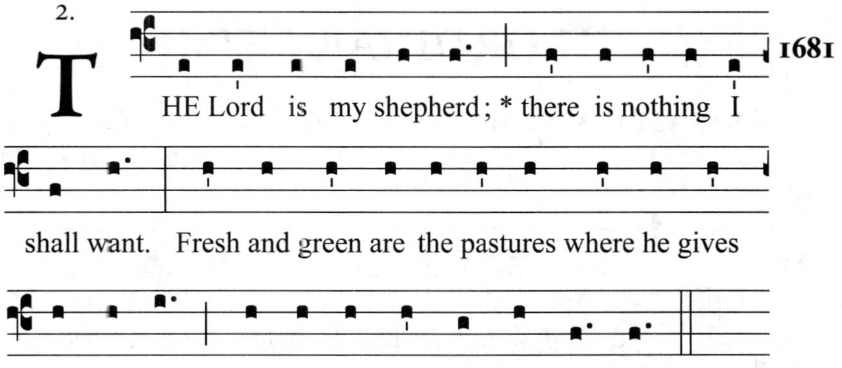
2.
1681
THE Lord is my shepherd; * there is nothing I
shall want. Fresh and green are the pastures where he gives
me re-pose, near rest-ful wa- ters he leads me.

THIRTY-THIRD SUNDAY IN ORDINARY TIME

Entrance Antiphon *Dicit Dominus : Ego cogito.*
Jer 29 : 11. 12. 14

- i -

1682 6.

THE Lord said : * I think thoughts of peace and not of af- flic-tion. You will call up- on me, and I will an- swer you, and I will lead back your cap-tives from ev'- ry place.

- ii -

1683 6.

THE Lord said : * I think thoughts of peace and not of af- flic- tion. You will call up- on me, and I will an-swer you, and I will lead back your cap-tives

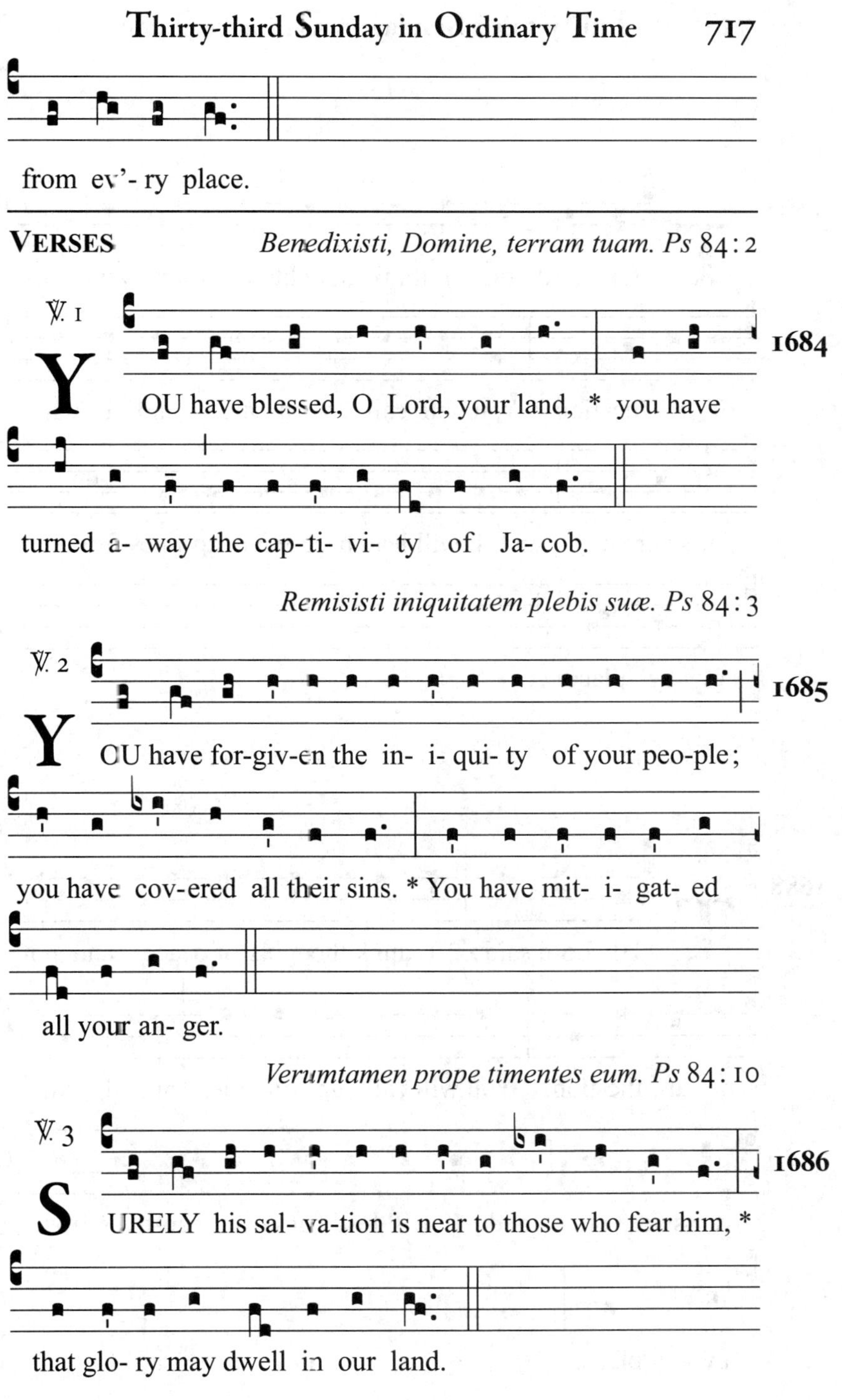
from ev'- ry place.
VERSES
Benedixisti, Domine, terram tuam. Ps 84:2
℣. 1
YOU have blessed, O Lord, your land, * you have
1684
turned a- way the cap- ti- vi- ty of Ja- cob.
Remisisti iniquitatem plebis suæ. Ps 84:3
℣. 2
YOU have for-giv-en the in- i- qui- ty of your peo-ple;
1685
you have cov-ered all their sins. * You have mit- i- gat- ed
all your an- ger.
Verumtamen prope timentes eum. Ps 84:10
℣. 3
SURELY his sal- va-tion is near to those who fear him, *
1686
that glo- ry may dwell in our land.

- iii -

1687
6.
THE Lord said: I think thoughts of peace and not
of af- flic- tion. * You will call up- on me, and I will
an-swer you, and I will lead back your cap-tives from
ev'- ry place.

Or:

1688
6.
THE Lord said: * I think thoughts of peace and not
of af- flic-tion. You will call up- on me, and I will
an-swer you, and I will lead back your cap-tives from
ev'- ry place.

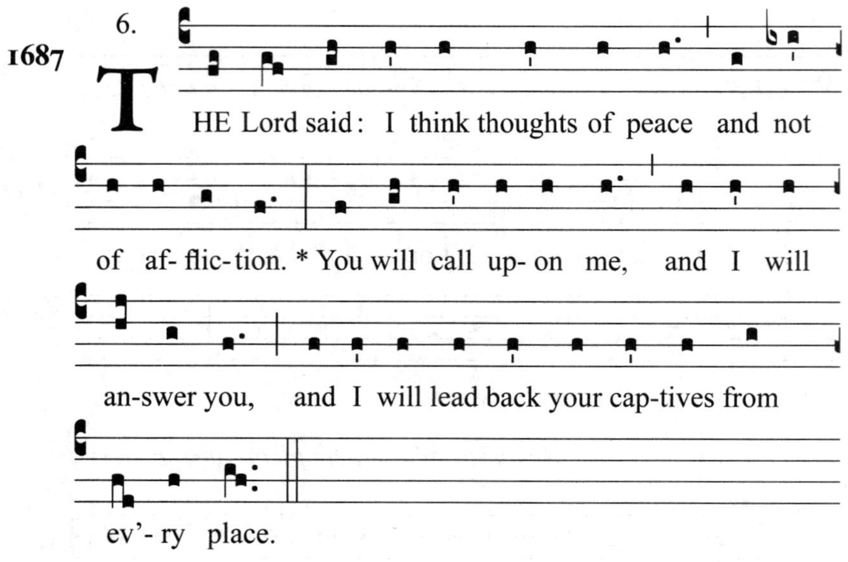

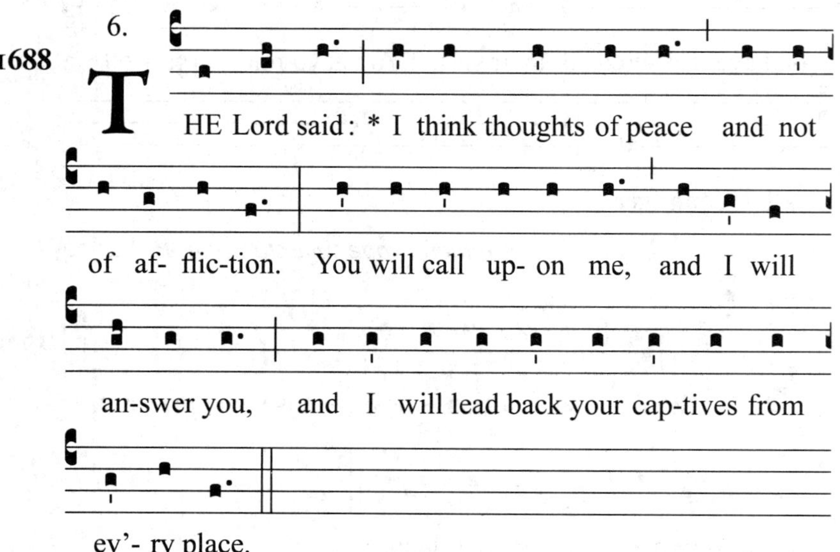

- iv -

6. 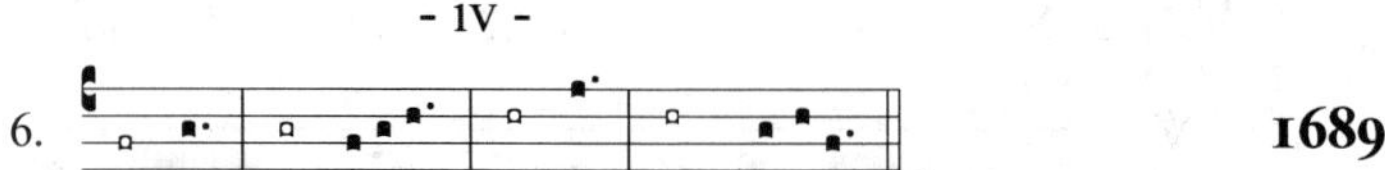 1689

The Lord said : * / I think thoughts of | **peace**
and not | *of af*-**flic**-tion.
You will call upon me, and I will | **an**-swer you,
and I will lead back your captives from | *ev'-ry* **place**.

Offertory Antiphon *De profundis clamavi ad te.*
Ps 129 : 1-2

- i -

2. 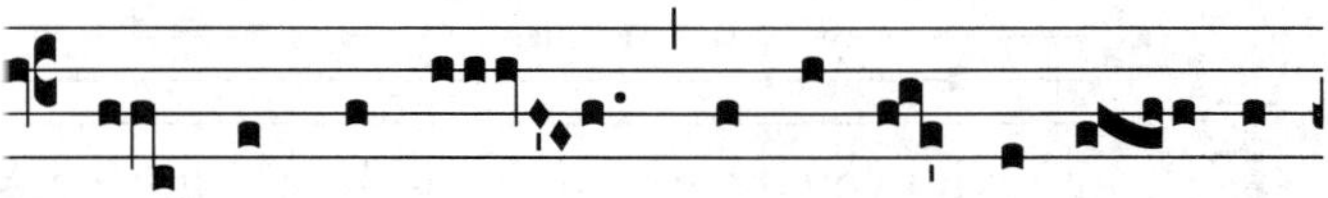 1690

OUT of the depths * have I cried to you, O Lord; Lord, hear my voice. Out of the depths have 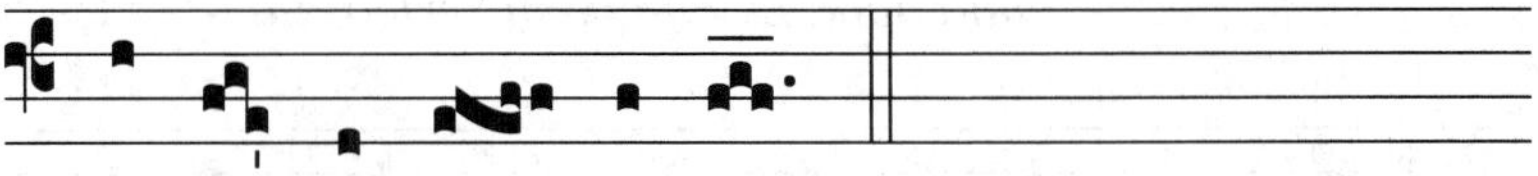 I cried to you, O Lord.

- ii -

2. 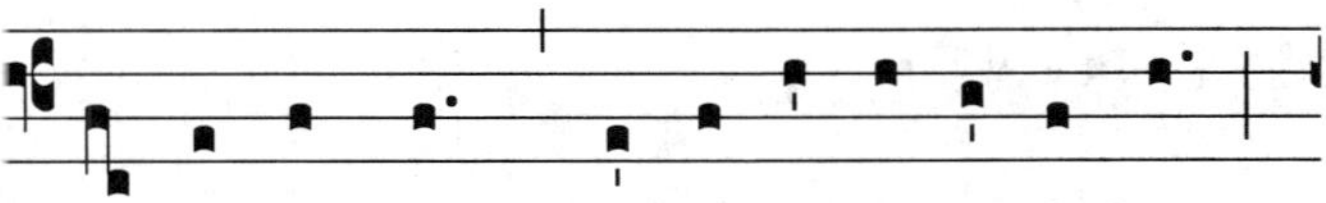 1691

OUT of the depths * have I cried to you, O Lord; Lord, hear my voice. Out of the depths have I cried to you 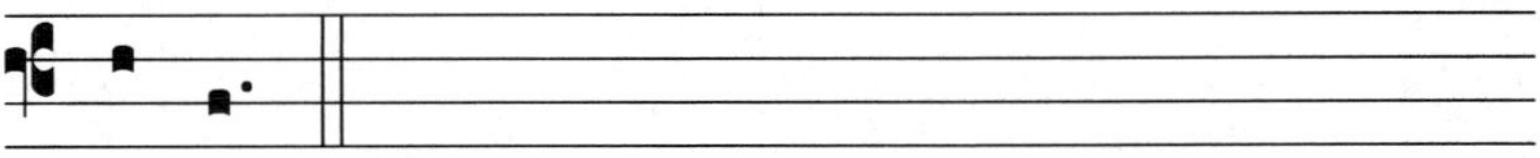 O Lord.

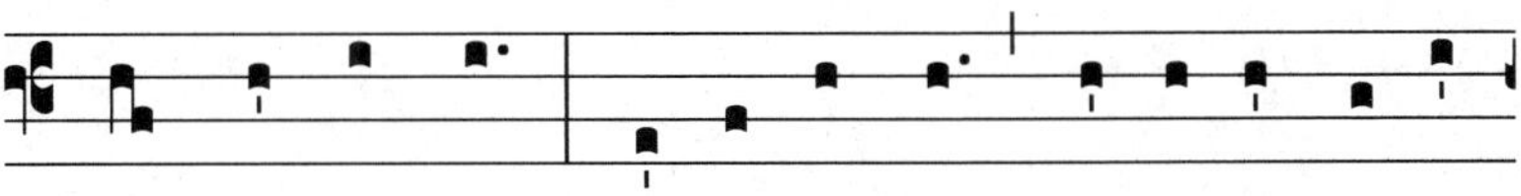

VERSES *Fiant aures tuæ intendentes. Ps* 129:2

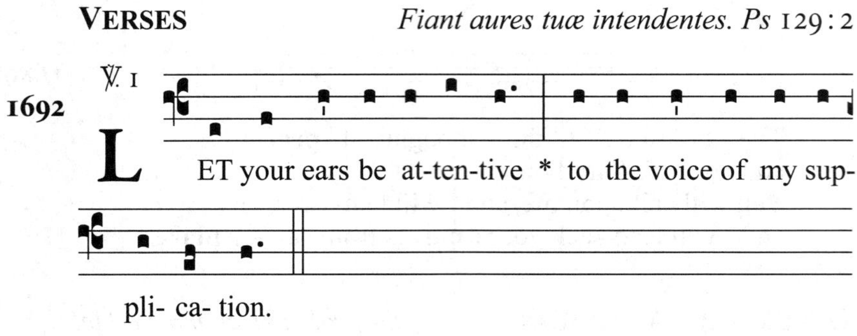
1692
℣. 1
LET your ears be at-ten-tive * to the voice of my sup-
pli- ca- tion.

Quia apud te propitiatio est. Ps 129:4

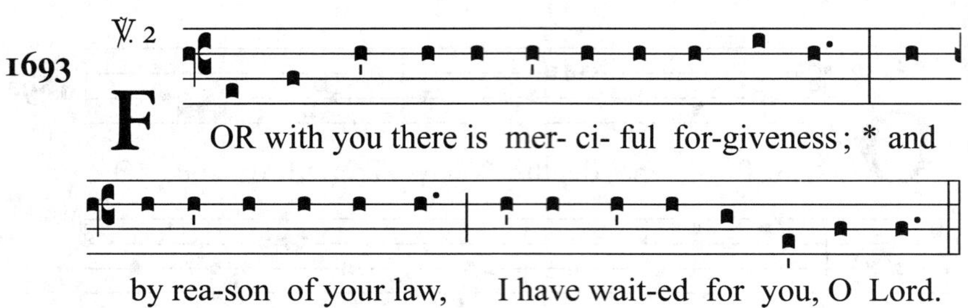
1693
℣. 2
FOR with you there is mer- ci- ful for-giveness; * and
by rea-son of your law, I have wait-ed for you, O Lord.

Quia apud Dominum misericordia. Ps 129:7

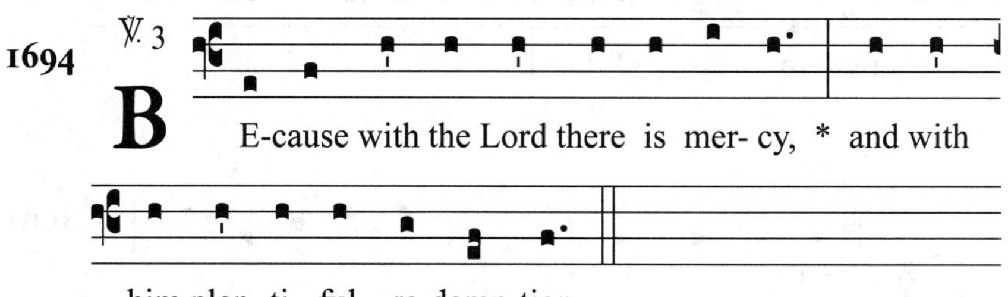
1694
℣. 3
BE-cause with the Lord there is mer- cy, * and with
him plen- ti- ful re-demp-tion.

- iii -

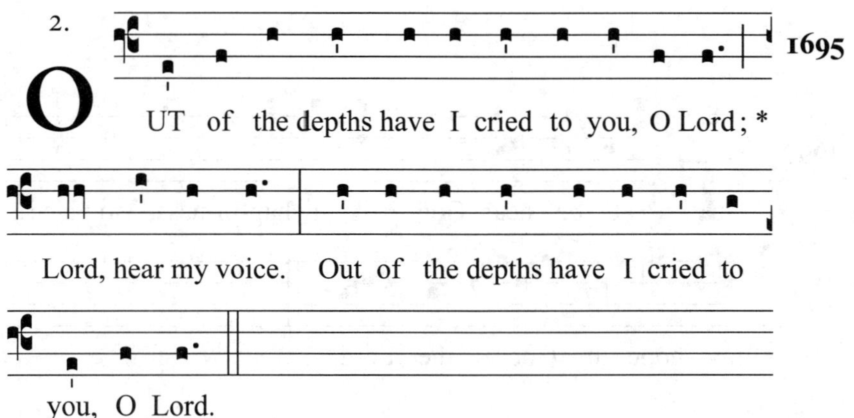
2.
1695
OUT of the depths have I cried to you, O Lord; *
Lord, hear my voice. Out of the depths have I cried to
you, O Lord.

- iv -

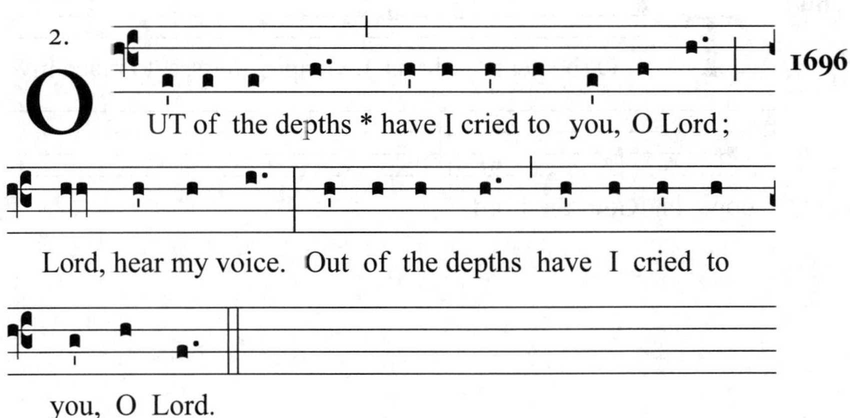
2.
1696
OUT of the depths * have I cried to you, O Lord;
Lord, hear my voice. Out of the depths have I cried to
you, O Lord.

COMMUNION ANTIPHON *Mihi autem adhærere Deo.*
Ps 72:28

- i -

1697

8.
TO be near God * is my hap-pi-ness, to place
my hope in God the Lord.

- ii -

1698

8.
TO be near God * is my hap-pi-ness, to place my
hope in God the Lord.

VERSES *Et ego semper tecum. Ps* 72:23-24

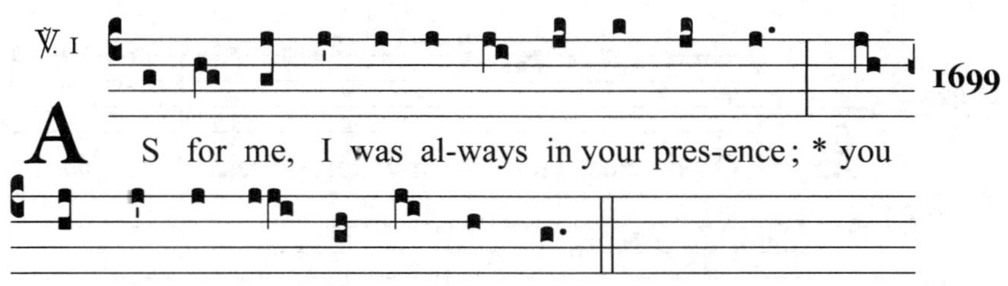
℣. 1
1699
AS for me, I was al-ways in your pres-ence; * you
were hold-ing me by my right hand.

Et in voluntate tua deduxisti me. Ps 72:24

℣. 2
1700
BY your coun-sel you will guide me, * and then you
will lead me to glo- ry.

Et a te quid volui super terram. Ps 72:25

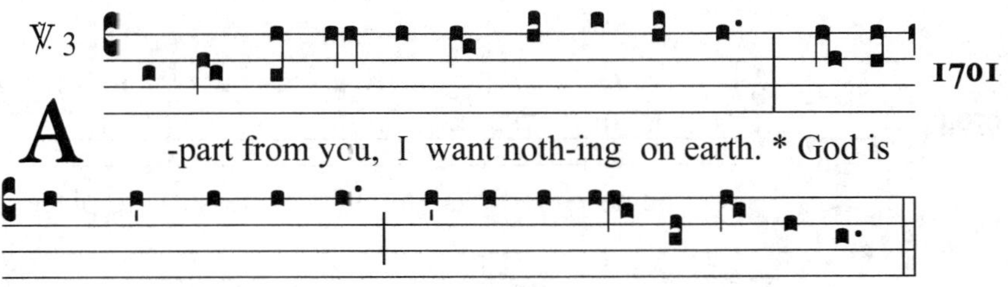
℣. 3
1701
A-part from you, I want noth-ing on earth. * God is
the strength of my heart; God is my por-tion for- ev- er.

- iii -

1702

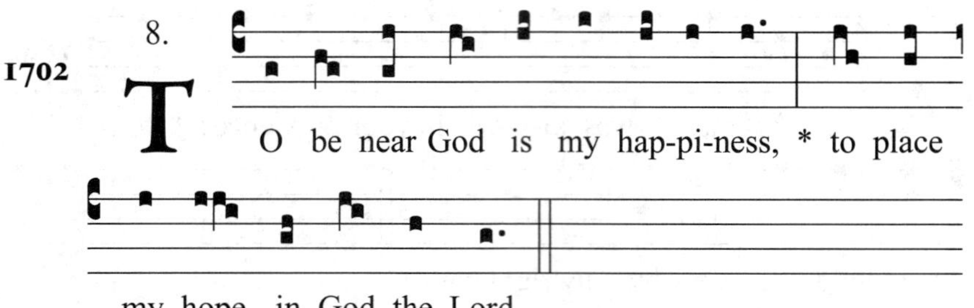
8.
TO be near God is my hap-pi-ness, * to place
my hope in God the Lord.

Or:

1703

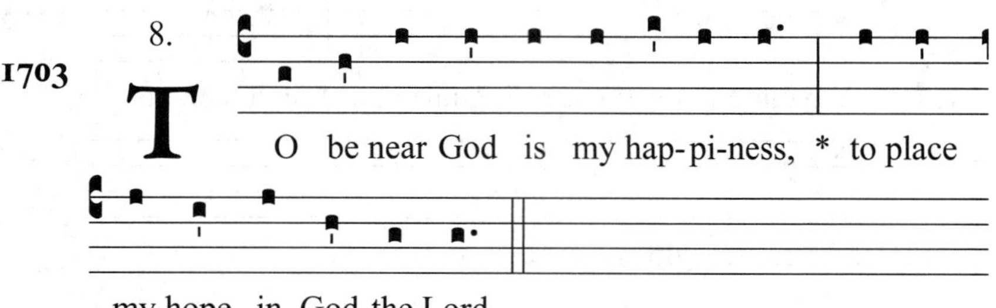
8.
TO be near God is my hap-pi-ness, * to place
my hope in God the Lord.

- iv -

1704

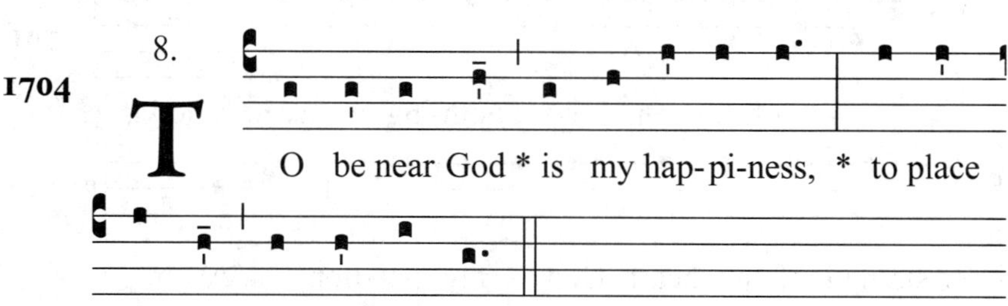
8.
TO be near God * is my hap-pi-ness, * to place
my hope in God the Lord.

THIRTY-FOURTH SUNDAY IN ORDINARY TIME

ENTRANCE ANTIPHON *Loquetur Dominus pacem.*
Ps 84:9

- i -

3.
THE Lord speaks * of peace to his peo- ple and his
ho- ly ones and to those who turn to him.

1705

- ii -

3.
THE Lord speaks * of peace to his peo- ple and his
ho- ly ones and to those who turn to him.

1706

VERSES *Benedixisti, Domine, terram tuam. Ps* 84:2

1707
℣. 1
YOU have blessed, O Lord, your land, * you have
turned a- way the cap- tiv- i- ty of Ja- cob.
Remisisti iniquitatem plebis suæ. Ps 84:3
1708
℣. 2
YOU have for-giv-en the in- iq-ui- ty of your peo-ple;
you have covered all their sins. * You have a- vert- ed all
your rage.
Verumtamen prope timentes eum. Ps 84:10
1709
℣. 3
SURELY his sal- va-tion is near to those who fear

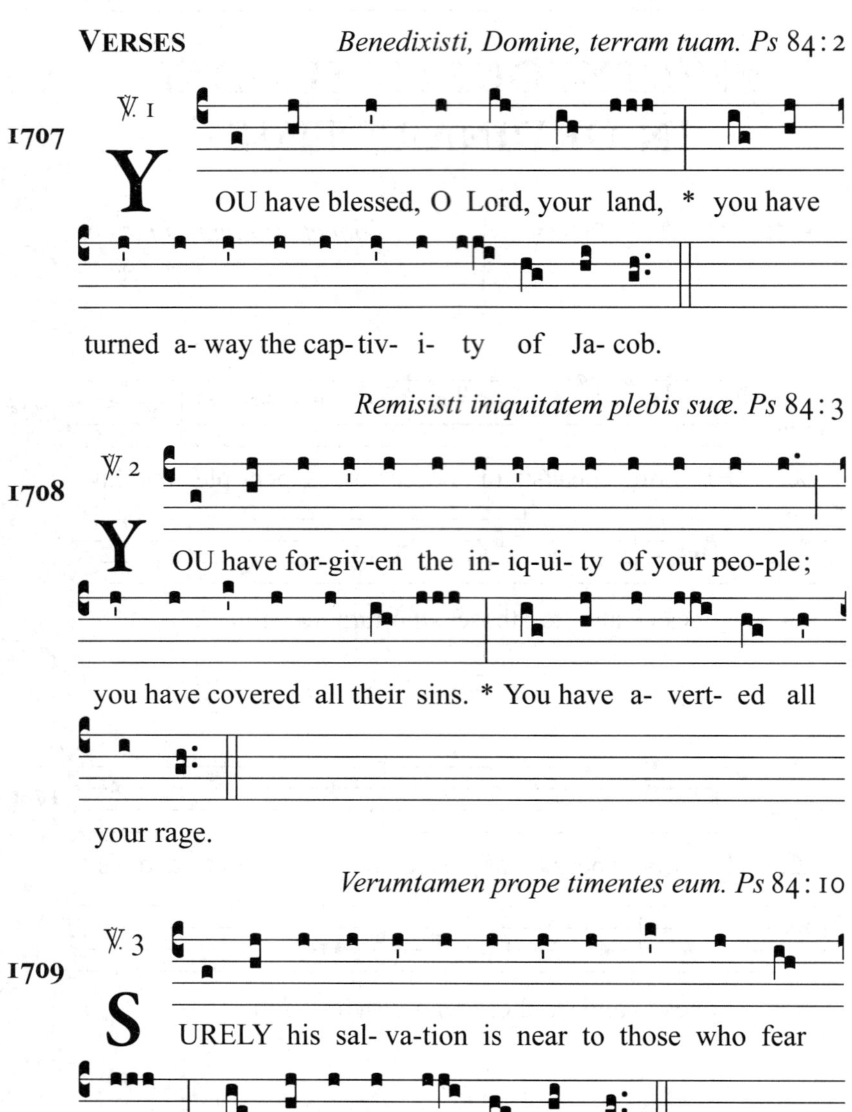

him, * that glo-ry may dwell in our land.

- iii -

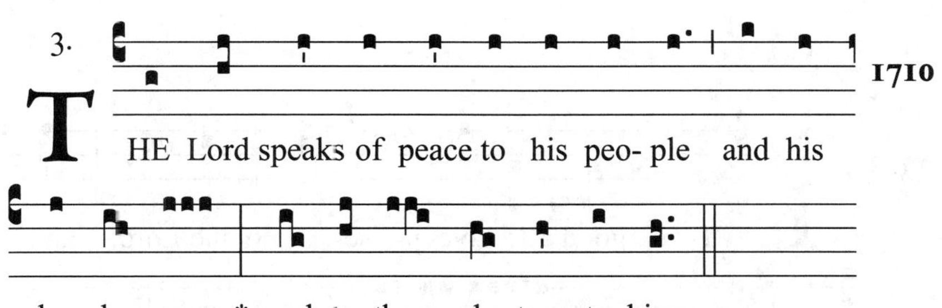
3.
1710
THE Lord speaks of peace to his peo- ple and his
ho- ly ones * and to those who turn to him.

Or:

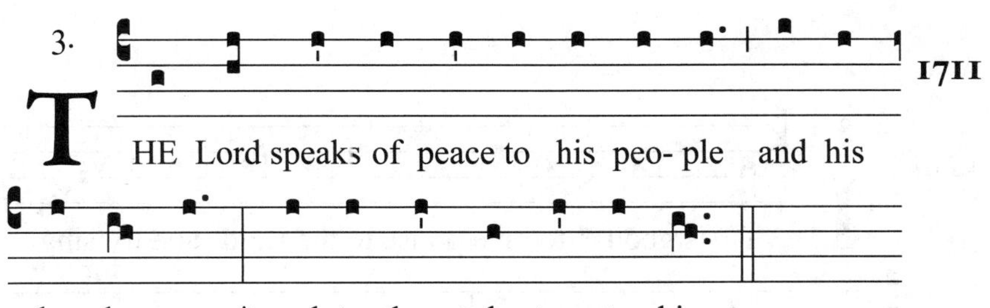
3.
1711
THE Lord speaks of peace to his peo- ple and his
ho- ly ones * and to those who turn to him.

- iv -

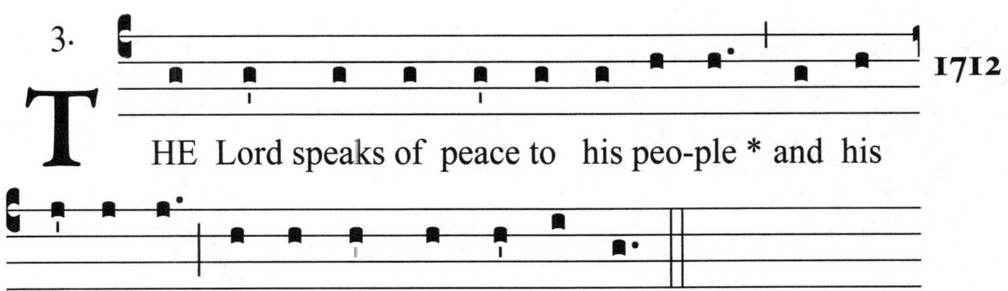
3.
1712
THE Lord speaks of peace to his peo-ple * and his
ho- ly ones and to those who turn to him.

Offertory Antiphon *Bonum est confiteri Domino.*

Ps 91 : 2

- i -

1713

8.
I
T is good * to give praise to the Lord, and
to sing to your name, O Most High.

- ii -

1714
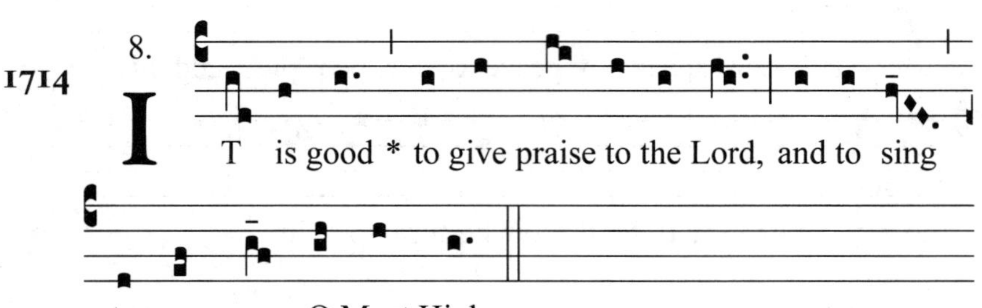
8.
I
T is good * to give praise to the Lord, and to sing
to your name, O Most High.

VERSES *Ad annuntiandum mane. Ps* 91 : 3

℣. 1
1715
TO show forth your mer-cy in the morning, * and your
truth in the night.

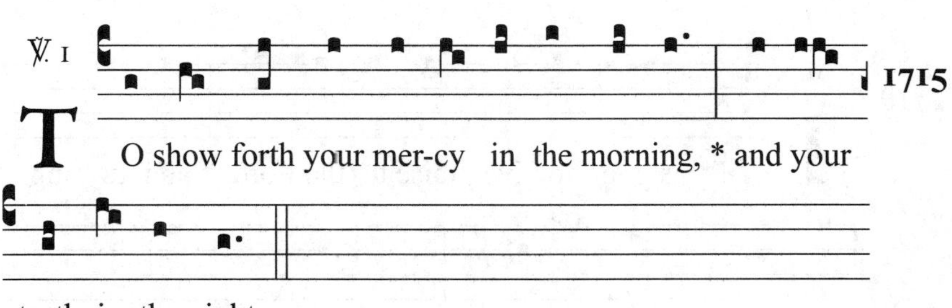

Quia delectasti me, Domine. Ps 91 : 5

℣. 2
1716
FOR you have made me glad, O Lord, by your deeds, *
and at the work of your hands shall I re-joice.

Iustus ut palma florebit. Ps 91:13

℣. 3
1717
THE just man shall flour-ish like the palm tree, * like a
ce- dar of Leb- a- non shall he grow.

- iii -

1718

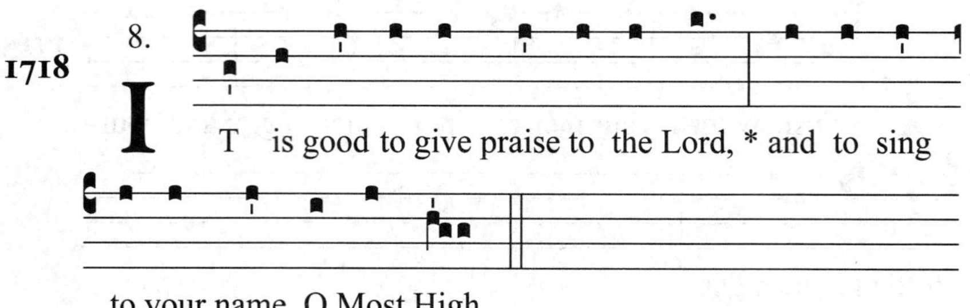
8.
IT is good to give praise to the Lord, * and to sing
to your name, O Most High.

- iv -

1719

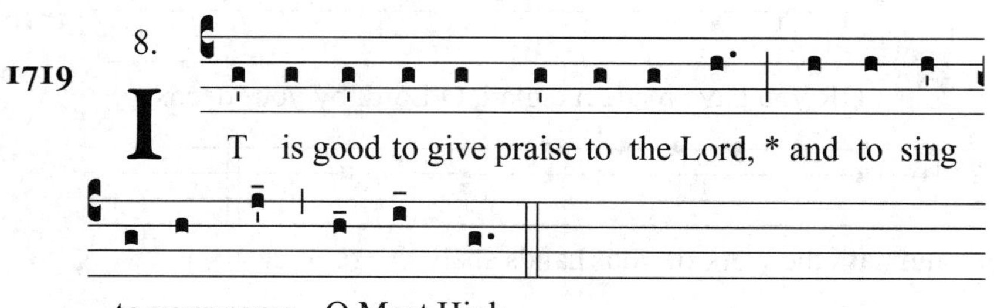
8.
IT is good to give praise to the Lord, * and to sing
to your name, O Most High.

COMMUNION ANTIPHON *Laudate Dominum, omnes gentes.*
Ps 116:1. 2

- i -

8. 1720

O praise the Lord, * all you na-tions, for his mer-

ci- ful love toward us is great.

- ii -

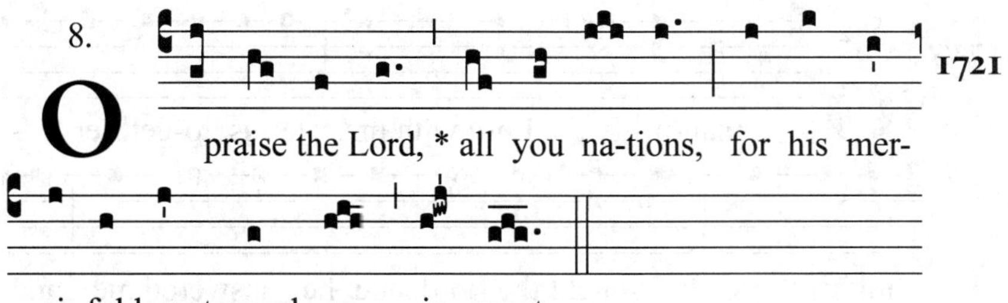
8.
O praise the Lord, * all you na-tions, for his mer-
1721

ci- ful love toward us is great.

VERSES *Benedicam Dominum. Ps* 33: 1-2

1722

℣. 1
I will bless the Lord at all times; his praise shall be
ev- er in my mouth. * Let my soul glo-ry in the Lord; the
low-ly will hear me and be glad.

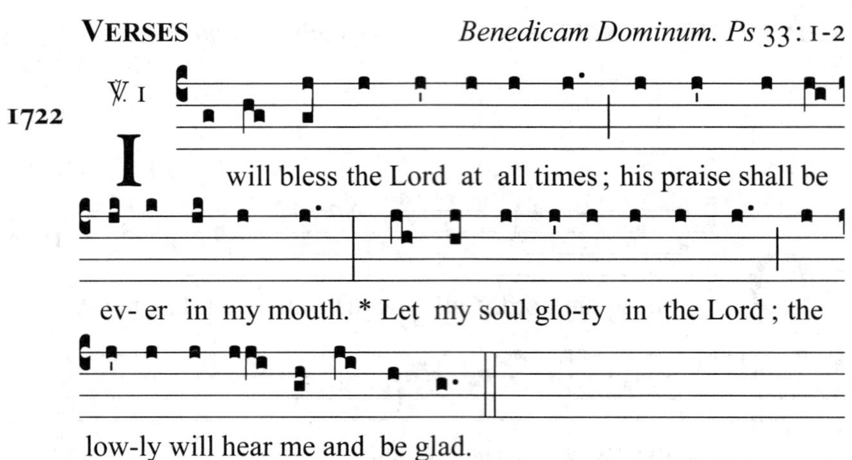

Glorificate Dominum mecum. Ps 33: 4

1723

℣. 2
O mag-ni- fy the Lord with me, let us to-geth-er ex-
tol his name. * I sought the Lord, and he answered me and
de-liv-ered me from all my fears.

Gustate et videte. Ps 33: 9

1724

℣. 3
O taste and see how gracious the Lord is; * bless-ed
the man who hopes in him.

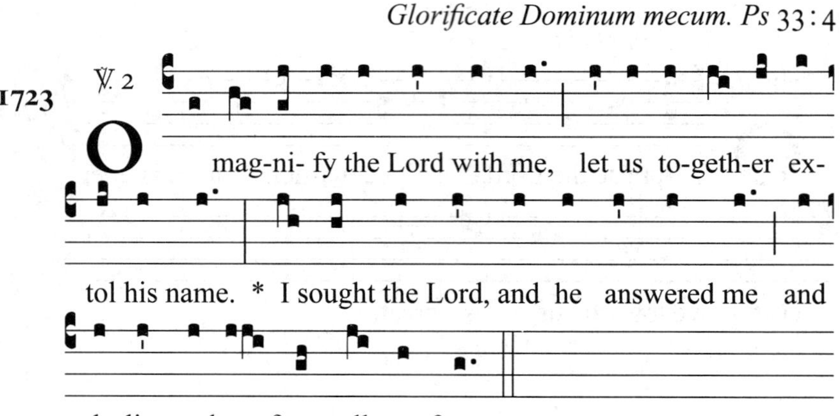

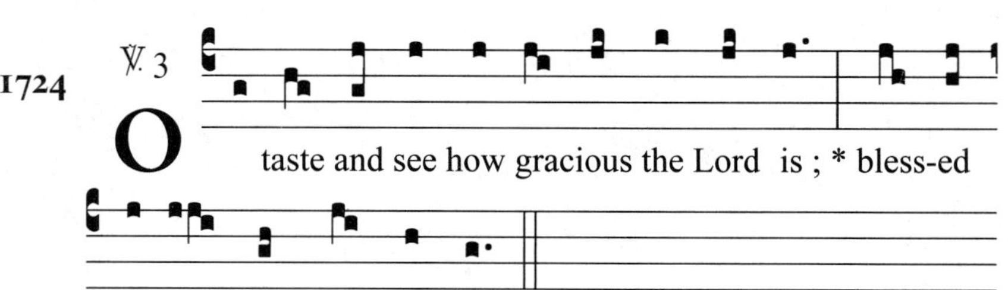

- iii -

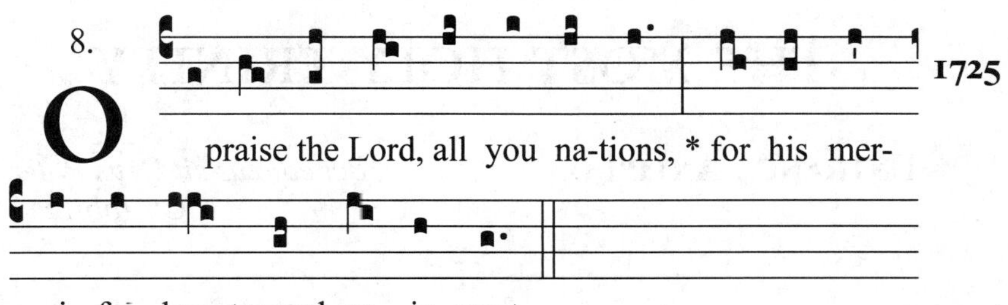
8.
1725
O praise the Lord, all you na-tions, * for his mer-
ci- ful love toward us is great.

Or:

8.
1726
O praise the Lord, all you na-tions, * for his mer-
ci- ful love toward us is great.

- iv -

8.
1727
O praise the Lord, all you na-tions, * for his mer-
ci- ful love toward us is great.

First Sunday after Pentecost

THE MOST HOLY TRINITY

Entrance Antiphon *Benedictus sit Deus Pater.*
Cf. Tob 12:6

- i -

1728

8.
BLess-ed be * God the Fa-ther, and the On- ly-
Be-gotten Son of God, and al- so the Ho- ly Spir- it,
for he has shown us his mer- ci- ful love.

- ii -

1729

8.
BLessed be God the Fa- ther, * and the On- ly- Be-
got-ten Son of God, and al- so the Ho-ly Spir- it, for he
has shown us his mer-ci- ful love.

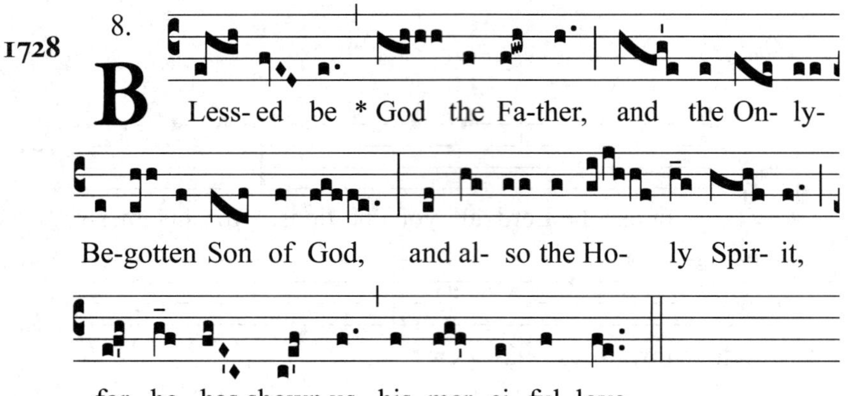

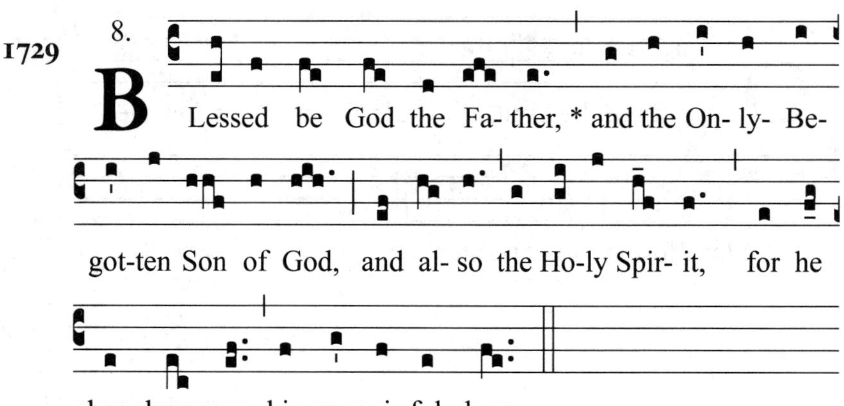

VERSES *Domine, Dominus noster. Ps* 8:2

℣. 1
O Lord, our Lord, how ma-jes-tic * is your Name in
all the earth.
1730

Quid est homo, quod memor es eius? Ps 8:5

℣. 2
WHAT is man that you should be mind-ful of him, *
or the son of man, that you should care for him?
1731

Minuitsi eum paulo minus ab angelis. Ps 8:6

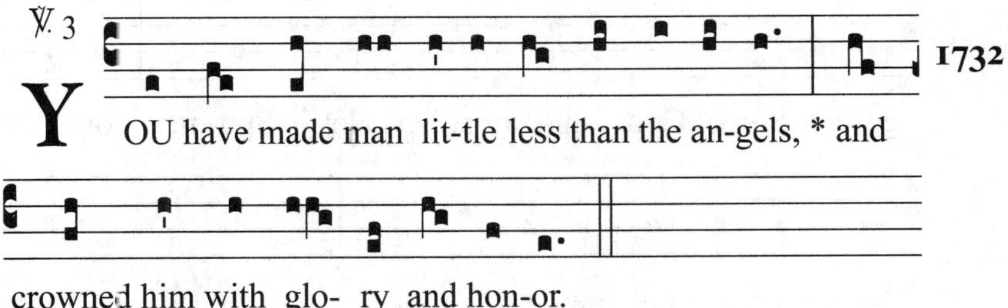
℣. 3
YOU have made man lit-tle less than the an-gels, * and
crowned him with glo- ry and hon-or.
1732

- iii -

1733

8.
BLess- ed be God the Fa-ther, * and the On- ly- Be-
got-ten Son of God, and al- so the Ho- ly Spir-it, for he
has shown us his mer-ci- ful love.

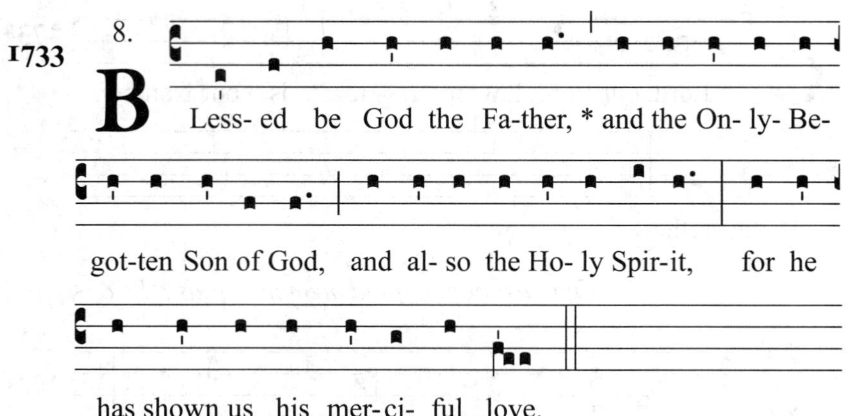

- iv -

1734

8.

BLess- ed be God the Fa-ther, * and the On- ly- Be-

got-ten Son of God, and al- so the Ho- ly Spir- it, for he

has shown us his mer- ci- ful love.

OFFERTORY ANTIPHON *Benedictus sit Deus Pater.*
Cf. Tob 12:6

- i -

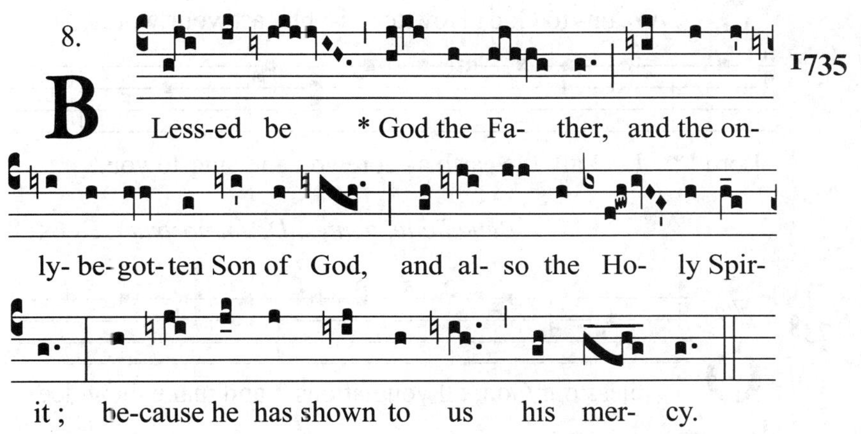
8.
B Less-ed be * God the Fa- ther, and the on-
ly- be- got- ten Son of God, and al- so the Ho- ly Spir-
it ; be-cause he has shown to us his mer- cy.
1735

- ii -

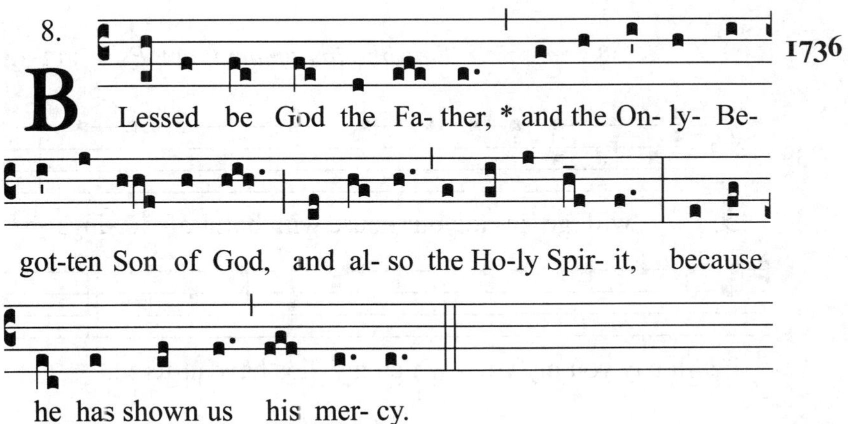
8.
B Lessed be God the Fa- ther, * and the On- ly- Be-
got-ten Son of God, and al- so the Ho-ly Spir- it, because
he has shown us his mer- cy.
1736

VERSES *Dicite Deo : quam terribila sunt. Ps* 65 : 3-4

1737 ℣. 1

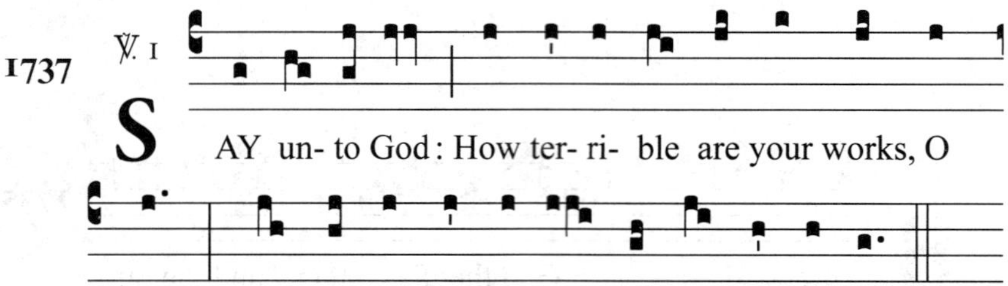

SAY un- to God : How ter- ri- ble are your works, O Lord ! * Let all the earth a- dore you and sing to you.

Benedicite, gentes, Deum nostrum. Ps 65 : 8

1738 ℣. 2

O bless our God, all you nations * and make the voice of his praise to be heard.

Introibo in domum tuam. Ps 65 : 13-14

1739 ℣. 3

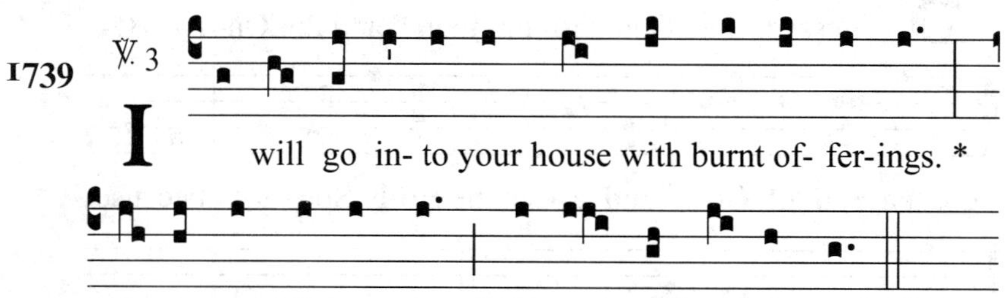

I will go in- to your house with burnt of- fer-ings. * I will pay you my vows which my lips have ut-tered.

- iii -

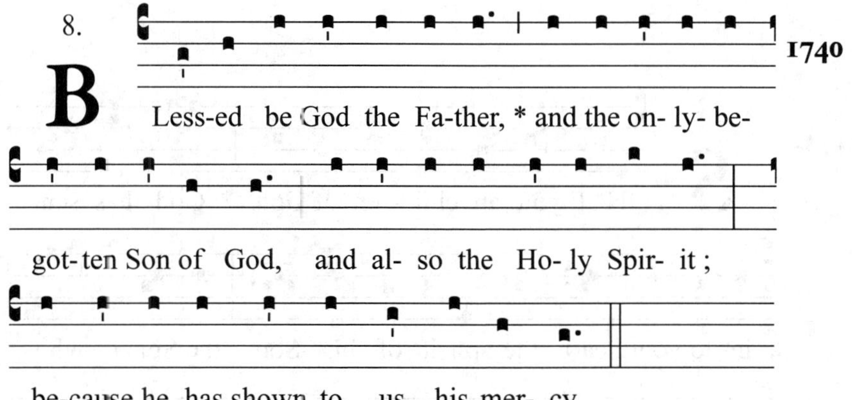
8.
1740
BLess-ed be God the Fa-ther, * and the on- ly- be-
got- ten Son of God, and al- so the Ho- ly Spir- it ;
be-cause he has shown to us his mer- cy.

- iv -

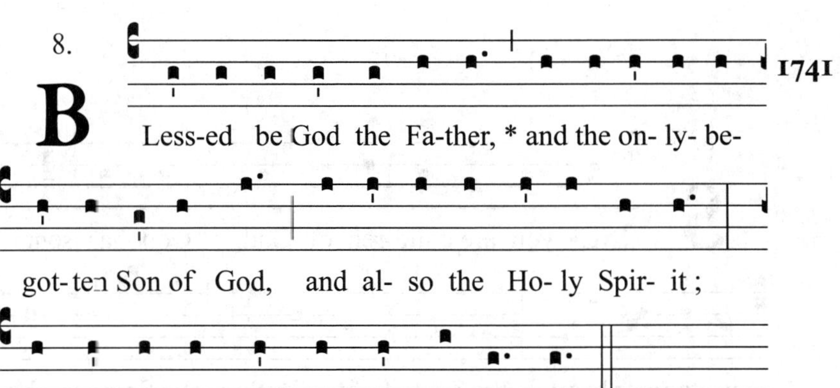
8.
1741
BLess-ed be God the Fa-ther, * and the on- ly- be-
got- ten Son of God, and al- so the Ho- ly Spir- it ;
be-cause he has shown to us his mer- cy.

Communion Antiphon *Quoniam autem estis filii.*
Gal 4:6

- i -

1742
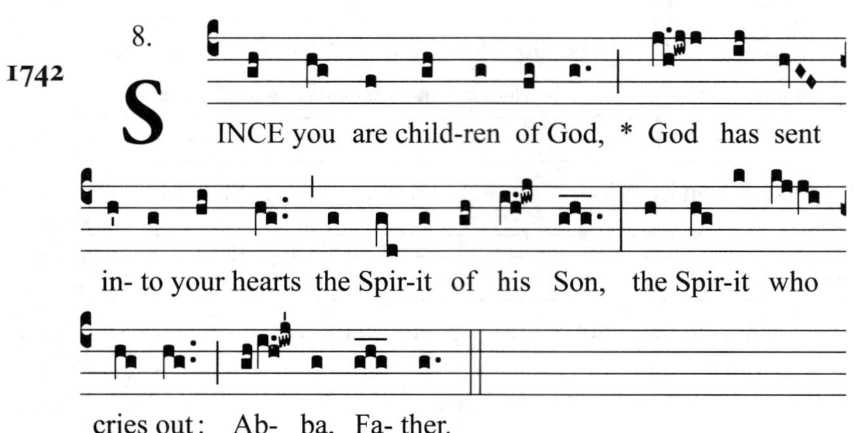
8.
SINCE you are child-ren of God, * God has sent
in- to your hearts the Spir-it of his Son, the Spir-it who
cries out: Ab- ba, Fa- ther.

- ii -

1743
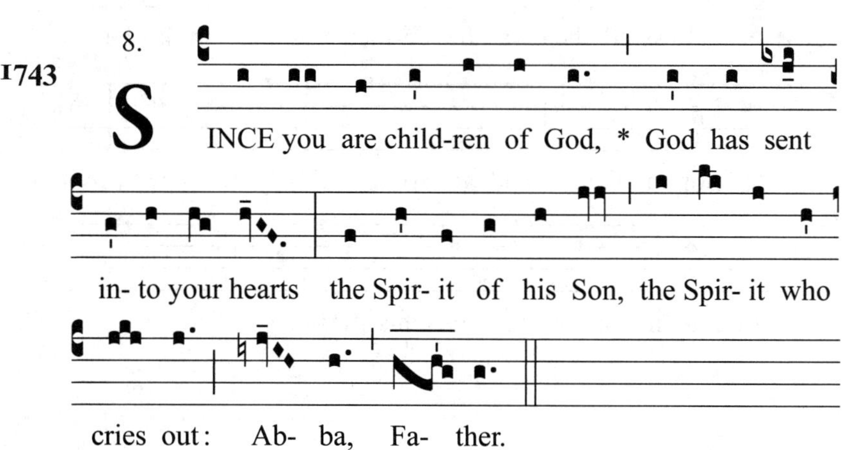
8.
SINCE you are child-ren of God, * God has sent
in- to your hearts the Spir- it of his Son, the Spir- it who
cries out: Ab- ba, Fa- ther.

VERSES *Benedicam Dominum. Ps* 33

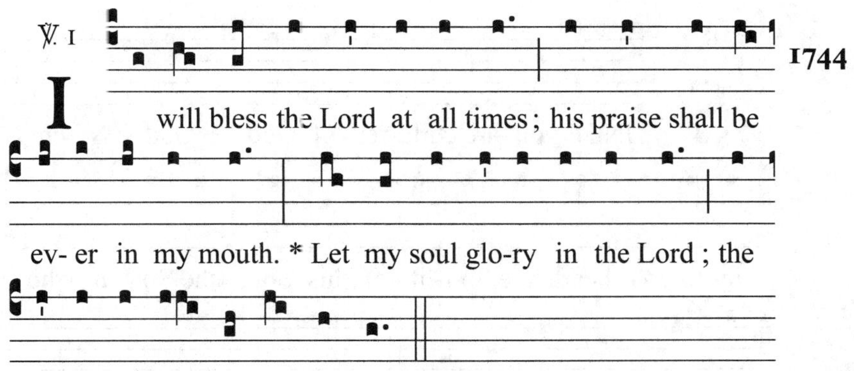
℣. 1
1744
I will bless the Lord at all times; his praise shall be
ev- er in my mouth. * Let my soul glo-ry in the Lord ; the

low-ly will hear me and be glad.

Diverte a malo, et fac bonum. Ps 33 : 15

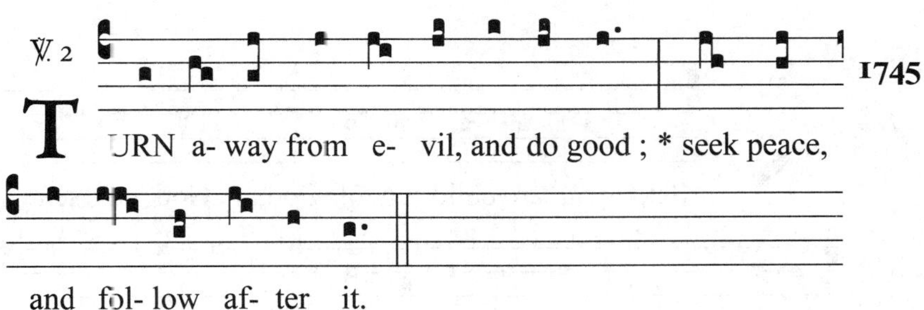
℣. 2
1745
TURN a- way from e- vil, and do good ; * seek peace,
and fol- low af- ter it.

Oculi Domini super iustos. Ps 33 : 16

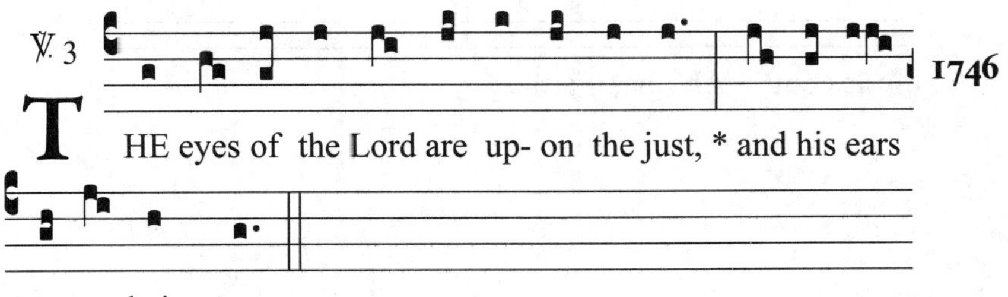
℣. 3
1746
THE eyes of the Lord are up- on the just, * and his ears
un- to their prayers.

- iii -

1747

8.
SINCE you are child-ren of God, * God has sent
in- to your hearts the Spir- it of his Son, the Spir- it who
cries out: Ab- ba, Fa-ther.

- iv -

1748

8.
SINCE you are child-ren of God, * God has sent
in- to your hearts the Spir- it of his Son, the Spir- it who
cries out: Ab- ba, Fa-ther.

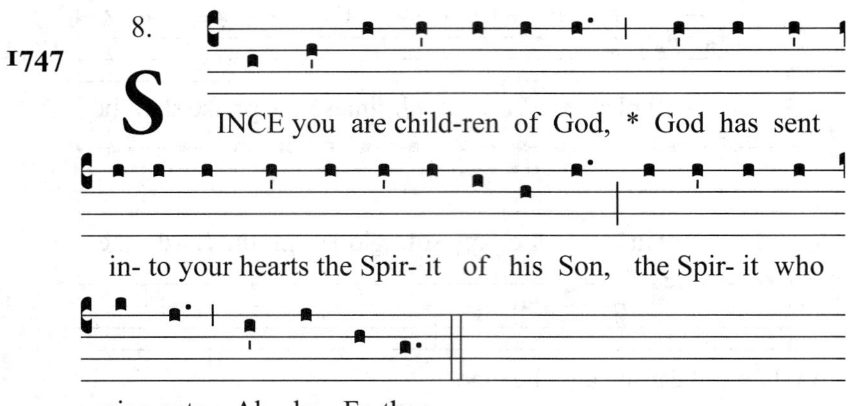

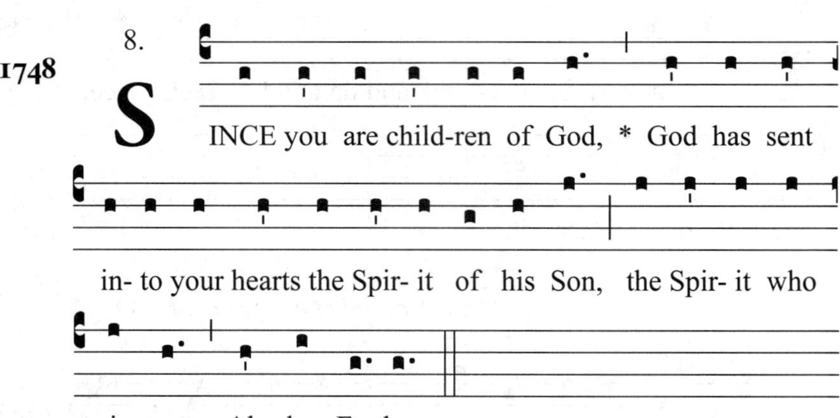

THE MOST HOLY BODY AND BLOOD OF CHRIST (CORPUS CHRISTI)

Entrance Antiphon *Cibavit eos ex adipe frumenti.*
Ps 80 : 17

- i -

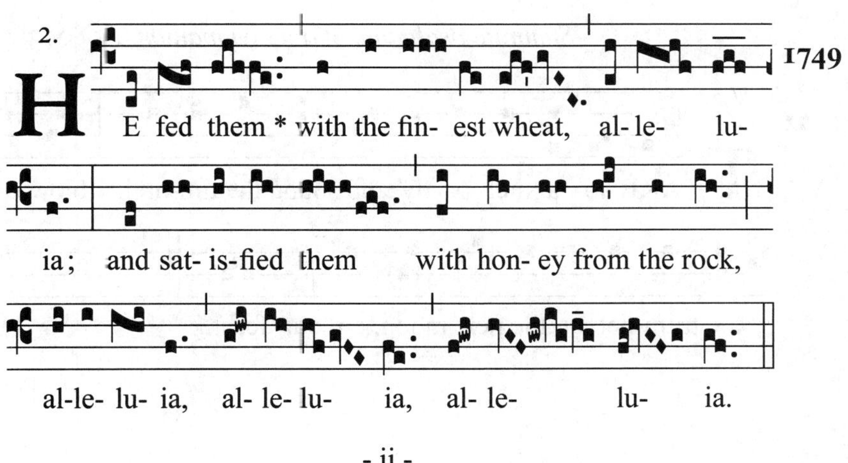
2.
1749
HE fed them * with the fin- est wheat, al- le- lu-
ia; and sat- is-fied them with hon- ey from the rock,
al-le- lu- ia, al- le- lu- ia, al- le- lu- ia.

- ii -

2.
1750
HE fed them * with the fin- est wheat, and sat-is-fied
them with hon- ey from the rock, al- le- lu- ia.

VERSES *Exsultate Deo, adiutori nostro.* Ps 80 : 1

1751

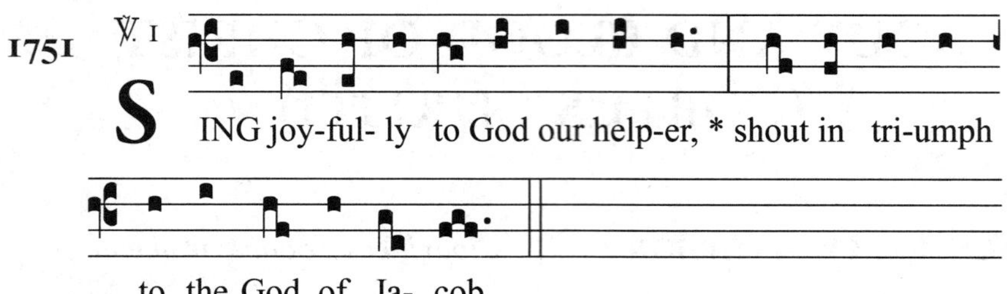
℣. 1
SING joy-ful- ly to God our help-er, * shout in tri-umph
to the God of Ja- cob.

Summite psalmum, et date tympanum. Ps 80 : 3-4

1752

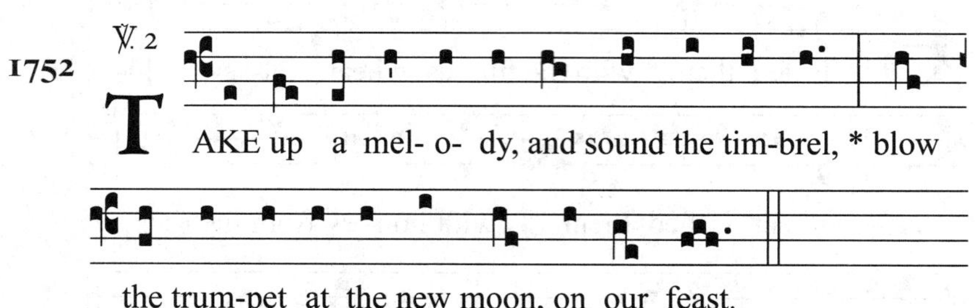
℣. 2
TAKE up a mel- o- dy, and sound the tim-brel, * blow
the trum-pet at the new moon, on our feast.

Quia præceptum in Israel est. Ps 80 : 5

1753

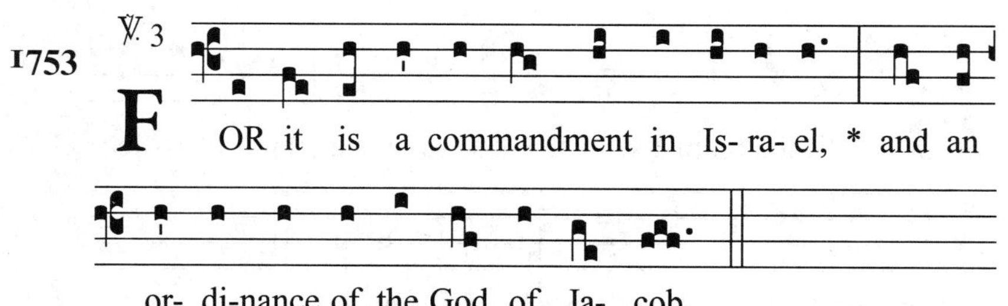
℣. 3
FOR it is a commandment in Is- ra- el, * and an
or- di-nance of the God of Ja- cob.

- iii -

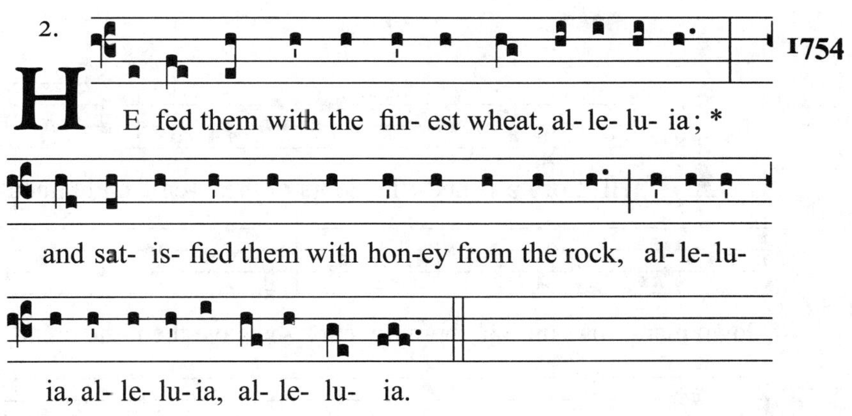
2.
1754
HE fed them with the fin- est wheat, al- le- lu- ia; *
and sat- is- fied them with hon-ey from the rock, al- le- lu-
ia, al- le- lu- ia, al- le- lu- ia.

Or:

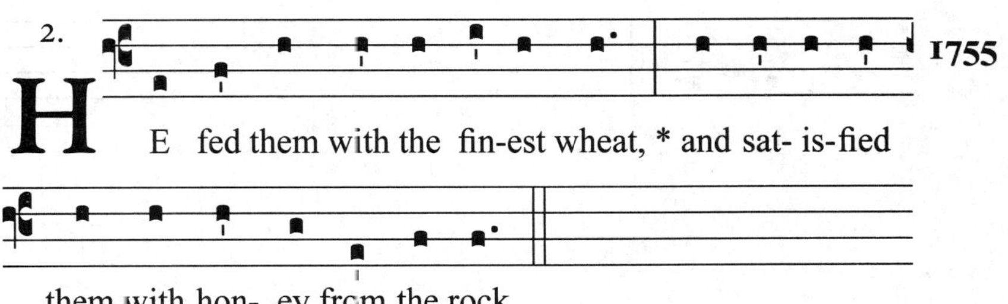
2.
1755
HE fed them with the fin-est wheat, * and sat- is-fied
them with hon- ey from the rock,

- iv -

2.
1756
HE fed them with the fin-est wheat, * and sat- is-fied
them with hon- ey from the rock,

OFFERTORY ANTIPHON *Portas cæli aperuit Dominus.*
Lev 21 : 6

- i -

1757

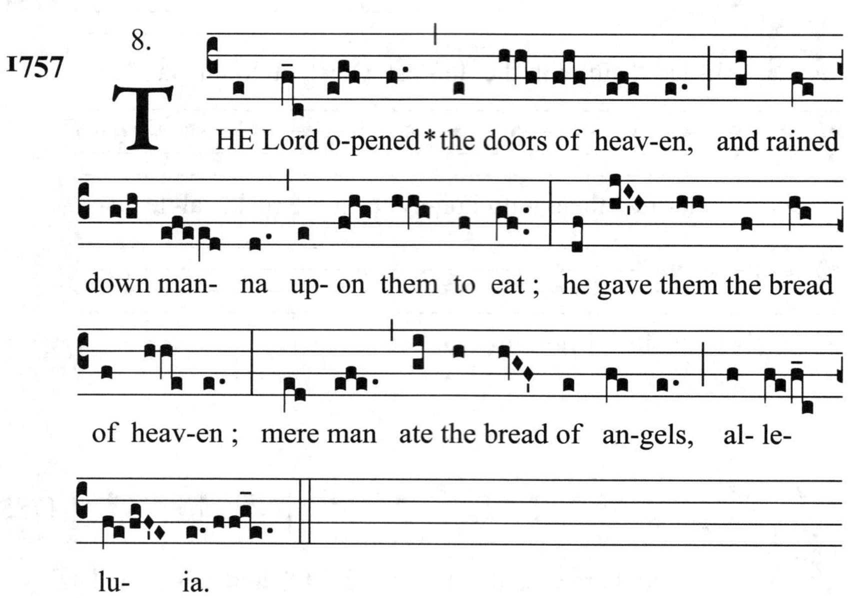
8.
THE Lord o-pened * the doors of heav-en, and rained
down man- na up- on them to eat ; he gave them the bread
of heav-en ; mere man ate the bread of an-gels, al- le-
lu- ia.

- ii -

1758

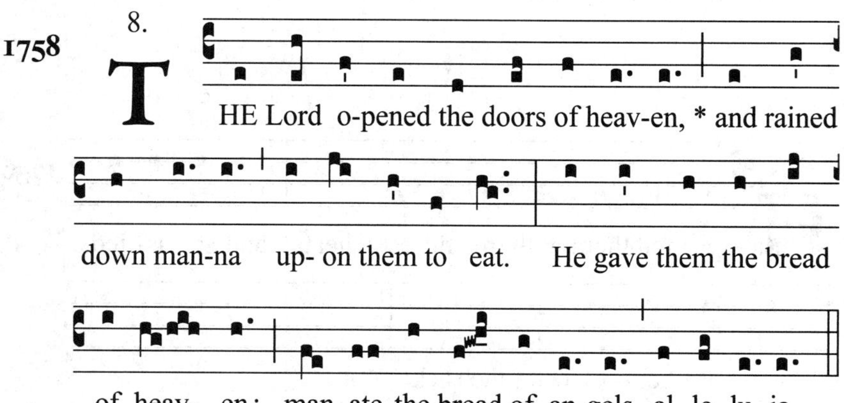
8.
THE Lord o-pened the doors of heav-en, * and rained
down man-na up- on them to eat. He gave them the bread
of heav- en ; man ate the bread of an-gels, al- le- lu- ia.

VERSES *Attendite, populę meus, legem meam. Ps* 77 : 1-2

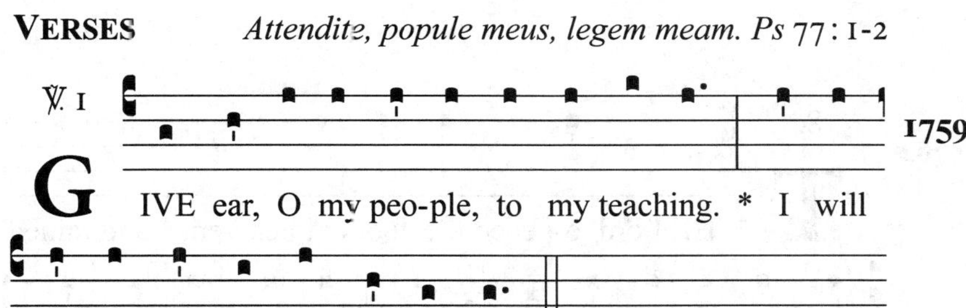
℣. 1
G IVE ear, O my peo-ple, to my teaching. * I will
ut- ter mys- ter- ies from of old.
1759

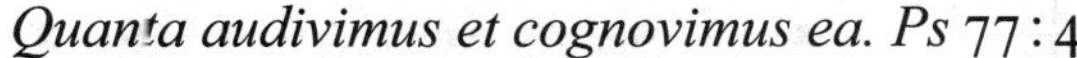
Quanta audivimus et cognovimus ea. Ps 77 : 4

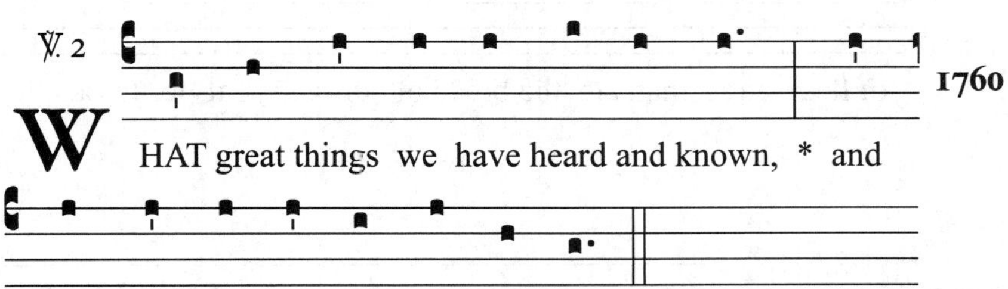
℣. 2
W HAT great things we have heard and known, * and
what things our fa- thers have told us.
1760

Narrantes laudes Domini. Ps 77 : 4

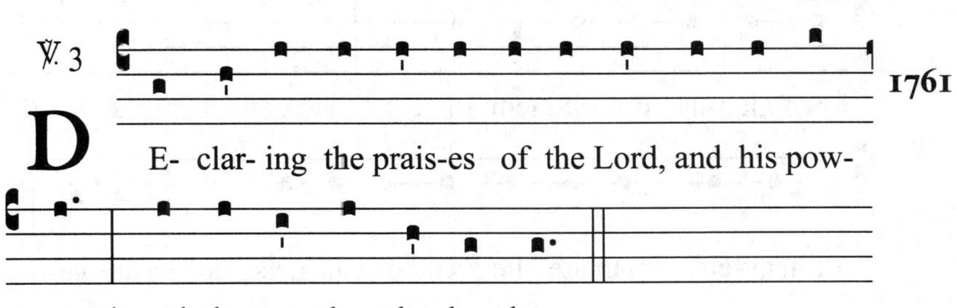
℣. 3
D E- clar- ing the prais-es of the Lord, and his pow-
ers, * and the won-ders he has done.
1761

- iii -

1762

8.
THE Lord o-pened the doors of heav-en, * and rained
down man-na up- on them to eat. He gave them the bread
of heav-en; man ate the bread of an-gels, al- le- lu- ia.

- iv -

1763

8.
THE Lord o-pened the doors of heav-en, * and rained
down man-na up- on them to eat. He gave them the bread
of heav-en; man ate the bread of an-gels, al- le- lu- ia.

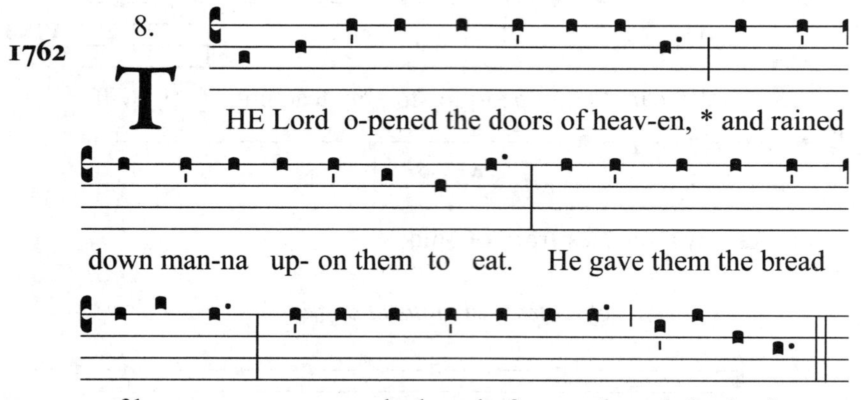

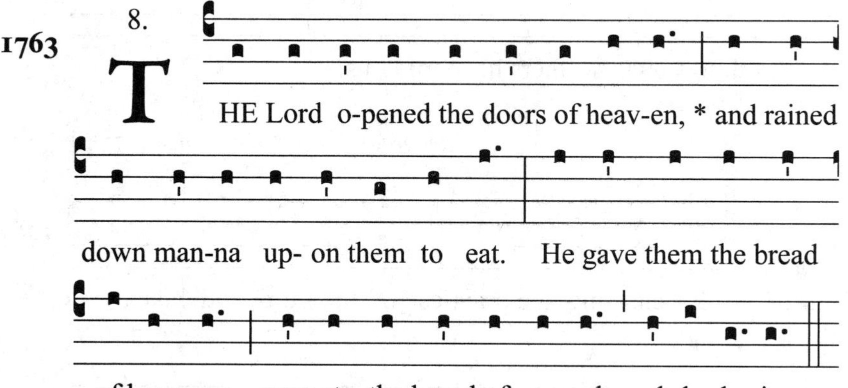

COMMUNION ANTIPHON *Qui manducat carnem meam.*
Jn 6:57

- i -

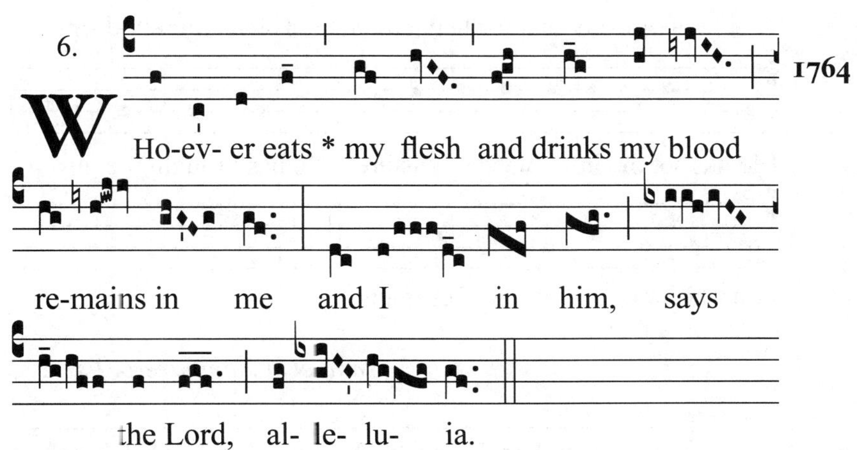
6.
1764
W Ho-ev- er eats * my flesh and drinks my blood
re-mains in me and I in him, says
the Lord, al- le- lu- ia.

- ii -

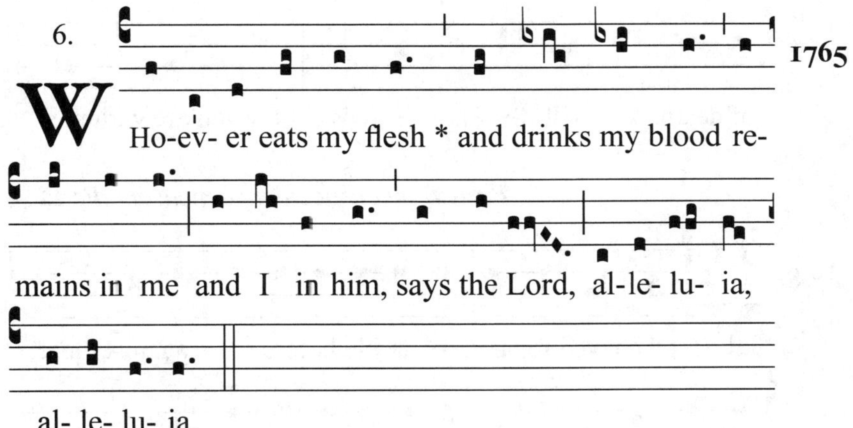
6.
1765
W Ho-ev- er eats my flesh * and drinks my blood re-
mains in me and I in him, says the Lord, al-le- lu- ia,
al- le- lu- ia.

VERSES *Dominus regit me. Ps 22 : 1*

1766

℣. 1
THE Lord is my shepherd, and I shall want noth-ing. *
He has set me in a place of pasture. He has brought me up
on the wa- ter of re-freshment.

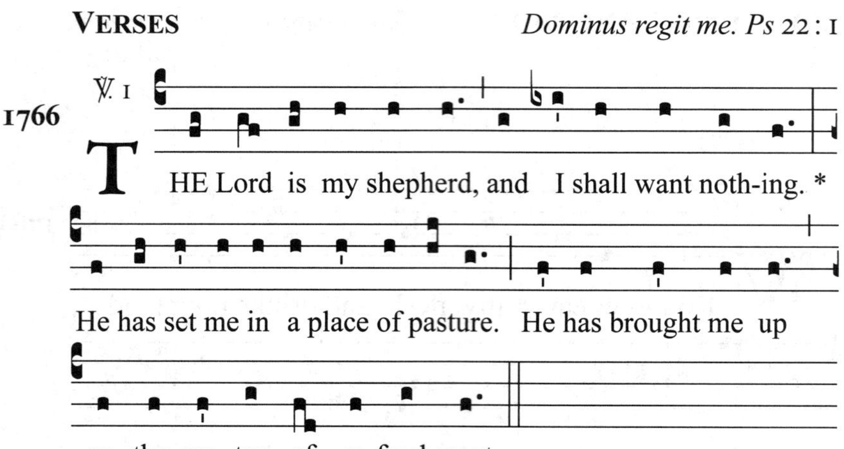

Nam, et si ambulavero. Ps 22 : 4

1767

℣. 2
FOR though I should walk in the midst of the shad-ow
of death, I will fear no e- vils, * for you are with me.

Parasti inconspectu meo mensam. Ps 22 : 5

1768

℣. 3
YOU have prepared a ta-ble before me against those
who af- flict me. * You have anointed my head with oil; and
my chal-ice how good- ly it is !

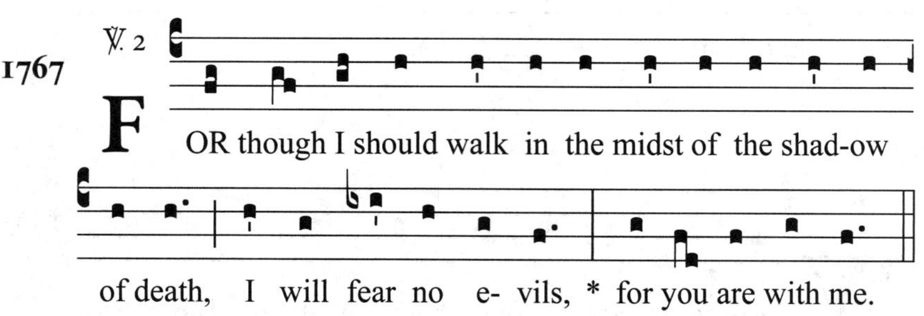

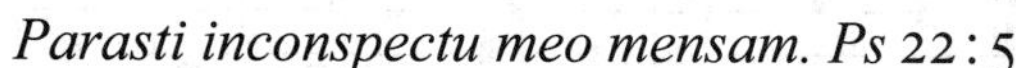

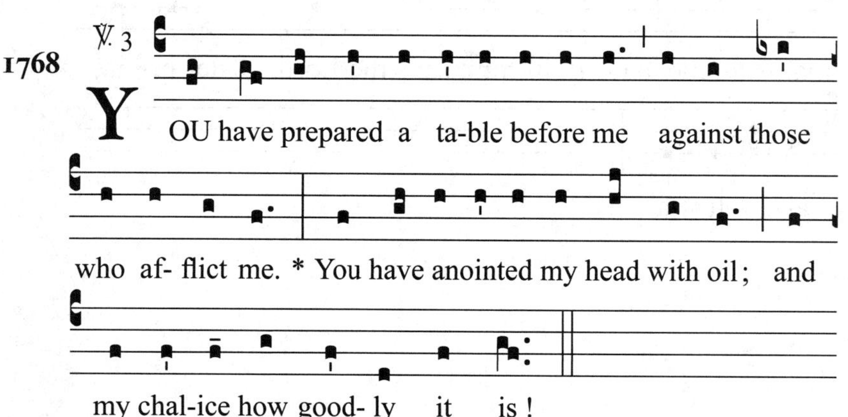

- iii -

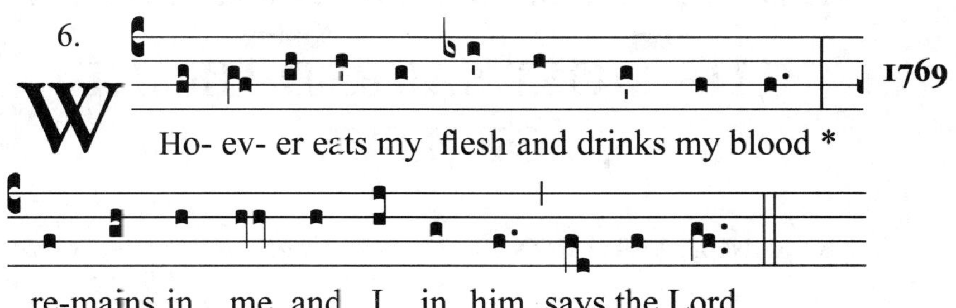
6.
W
Ho- ev- er eats my flesh and drinks my blood *
re-mains in me and I in him, says the Lord.

1769

Or:

6.
W
Ho- ev- er eats my flesh and drinks my blood *
re-mains in me and I in him, says the Lord.

1770

- iv -

6.
W
Ho- ev- er eats my flesh * and drinks my blood
re-mains in me and I in him, says the Lord.

1771

Friday after the Second Sunday after Pentecost

THE MOST SACRED HEART OF JESUS

ENTRANCE ANTIPHON *Cogitationes Cordis eius.*
Ps 32:11. 9

- i -

1772 5. THE de- signs of his Heart * are from age to age, to res- cue their souls from death, and to keep them a- live in fam- ine.

- ii -

1773
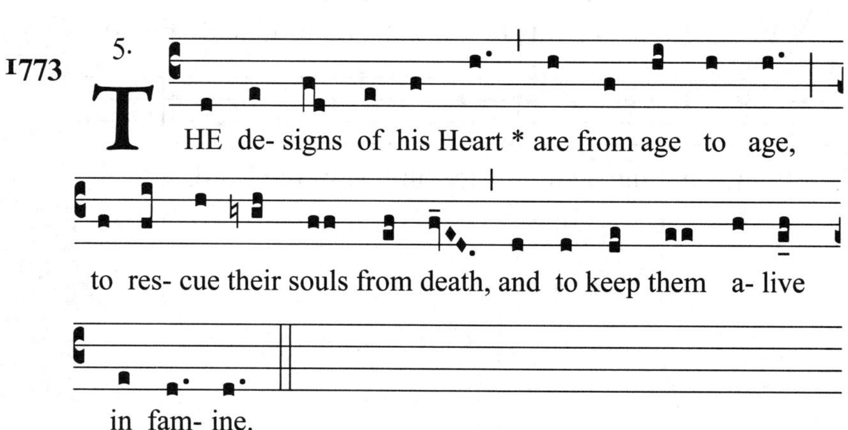
5.
THE de- signs of his Heart * are from age to age,
to res- cue their souls from death, and to keep them a- live
in fam- ine.

VERSES

Exultate, iusti, in Domino. *Ps* 32:1

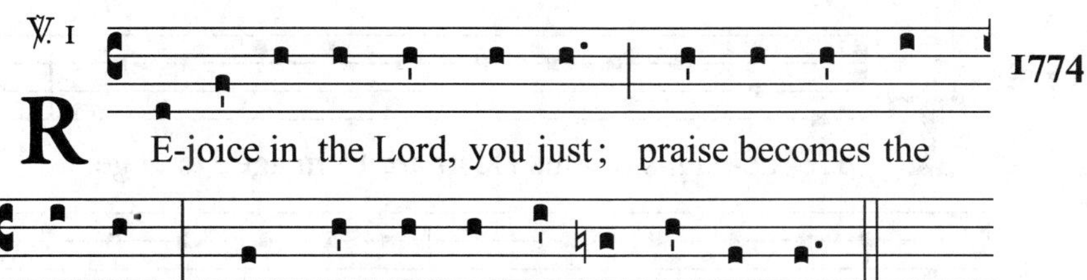
℣. 1
1774
R E-joice in the Lord, you just; praise becomes the

up-right. * Give thanks to the Lord up- on the harp.

Quia rectum est verbum Domini. *Ps* 32:4

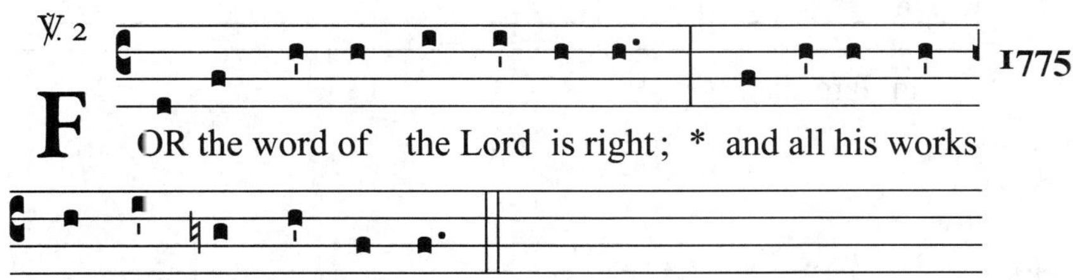
℣. 2
1775
F OR the word of the Lord is right; * and all his works

are done with faith-ful-ness.

Anima nostra sustinet Dominum. *Ps* 32:20

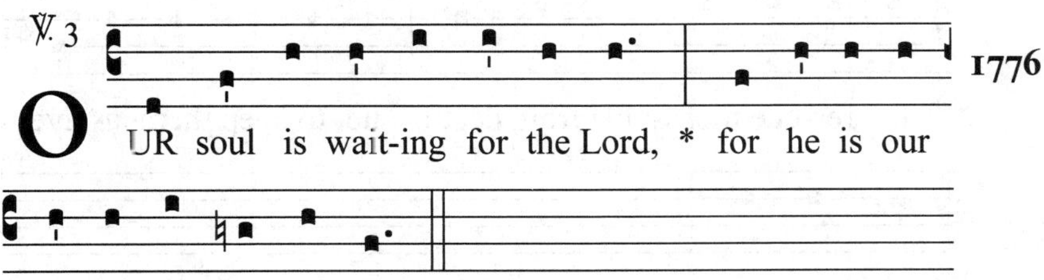
℣. 3
1776
O UR soul is wait-ing for the Lord, * for he is our

help-er and pro- tec- tor.

Fiat misericordia tua, Domine, super nos. *Ps* 32:22

℣. 4
1777
M AY your mer- ci- ful love be up- on us, * as we have

placed all our hope in you.

- iii -

1778

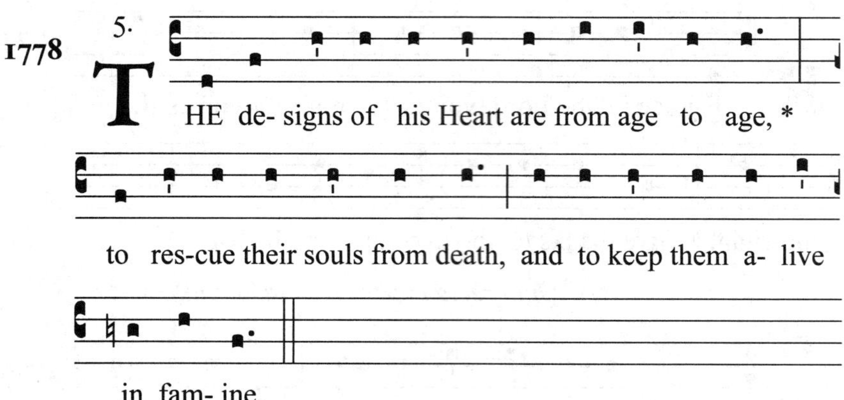
5.
THE de- signs of his Heart are from age to age, *
to res-cue their souls from death, and to keep them a- live
in fam- ine.

- iv -

1779

5.
THE de- signs of his Heart * are from age to age,
to res-cue their souls from death, and to keep them a- live

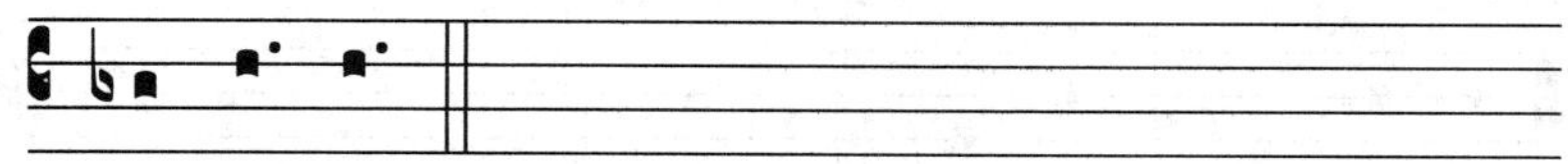
in fam- ine.

OFFERTORY ANTIPHON *Improperium expectavit cor meum.* *Ps* 68:21

Note: *Except were marked with the flat,* "Ti" *is always natural in the antiphons below.*

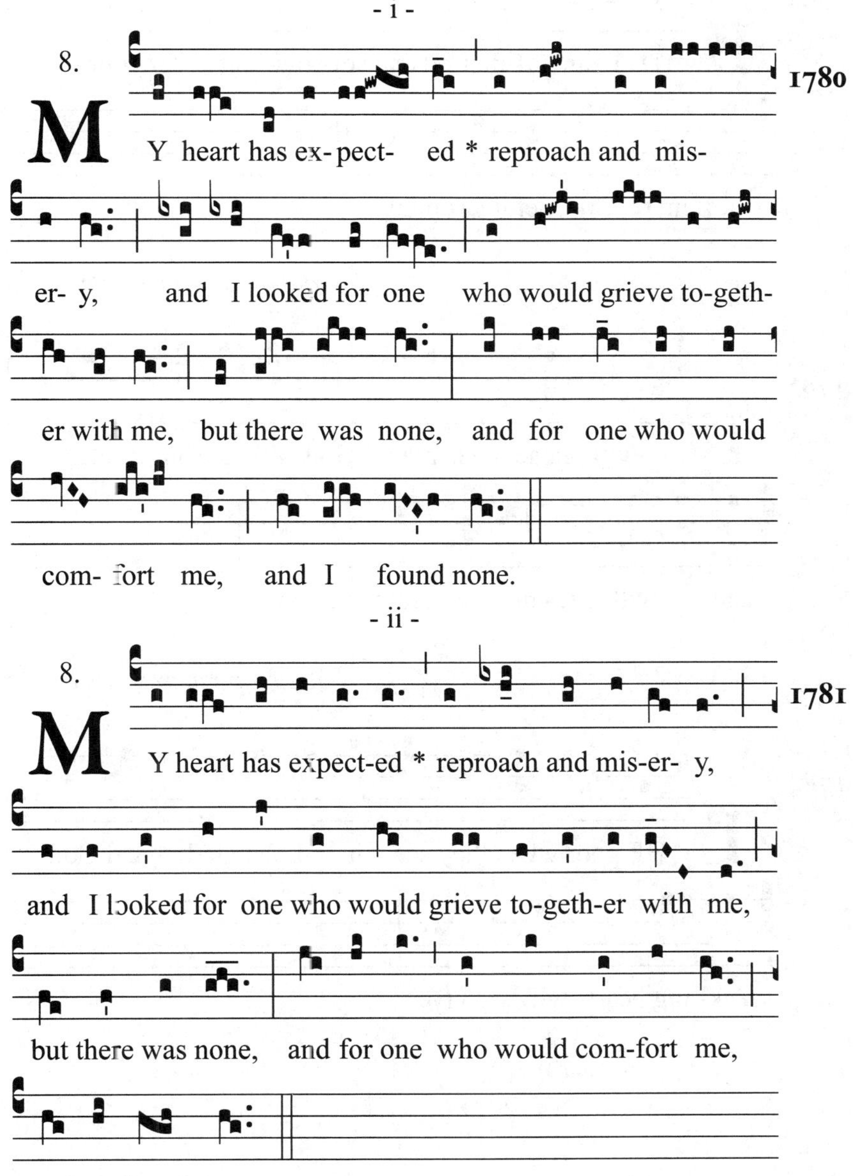
- i -
8.
1780
MY heart has ex-pect- ed * reproach and mis-
er- y, and I looked for one who would grieve to-geth-
er with me, but there was none, and for one who would
com- fort me, and I found none.
- ii -
8.
1781
MY heart has expect-ed * reproach and mis-er- y,
and I looked for one who would grieve to-geth-er with me,
but there was none, and for one who would com-fort me,
and I found none.

VERSES *Ego sum pauper et dolens. Ps* 68 : 30

1782
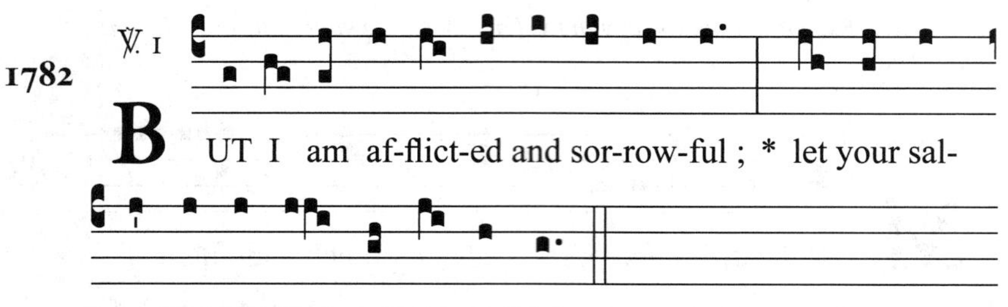
℣. 1
BUT I am af-flict-ed and sor-row-ful ; * let your sal-
va-tion, O God, set me on high.

Laudabo nomen Dei. Ps 68 : 31

1783
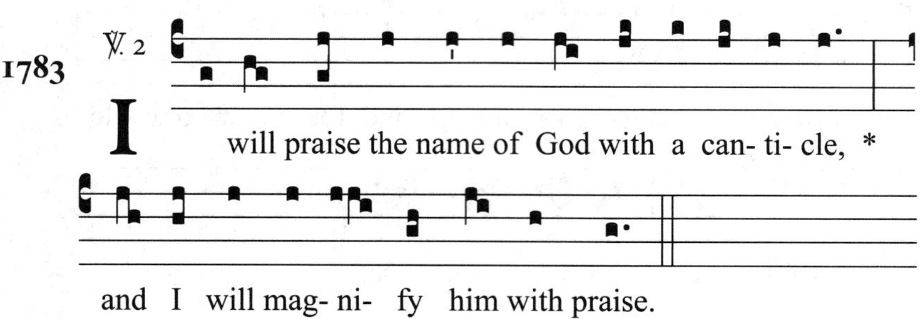
℣. 2
I will praise the name of God with a can- ti- cle, *
and I will mag- ni- fy him with praise.

Videant pauperes. Ps 68 : 33

1784
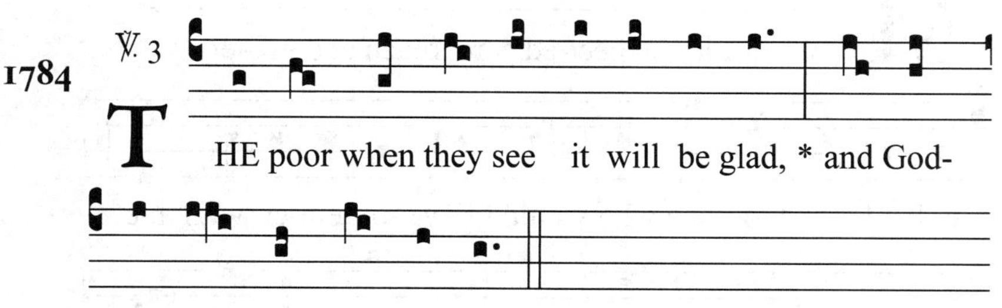
℣. 3
THE poor when they see it will be glad, * and God-
seek- ing hearts will re-vive.

- iii -

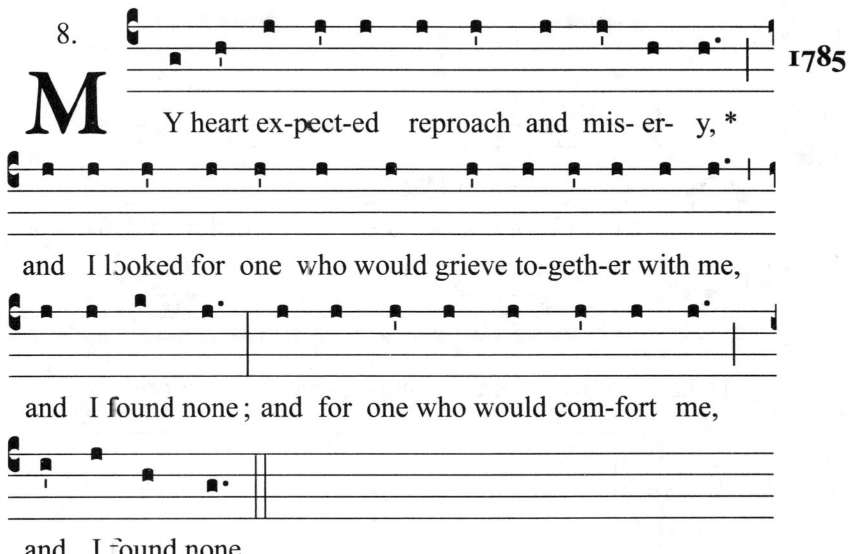
8.
1785
MY heart ex-pect-ed reproach and mis- er- y, *
and I looked for one who would grieve to-geth-er with me,
and I found none; and for one who would com-fort me,
and I found none.

- iv -

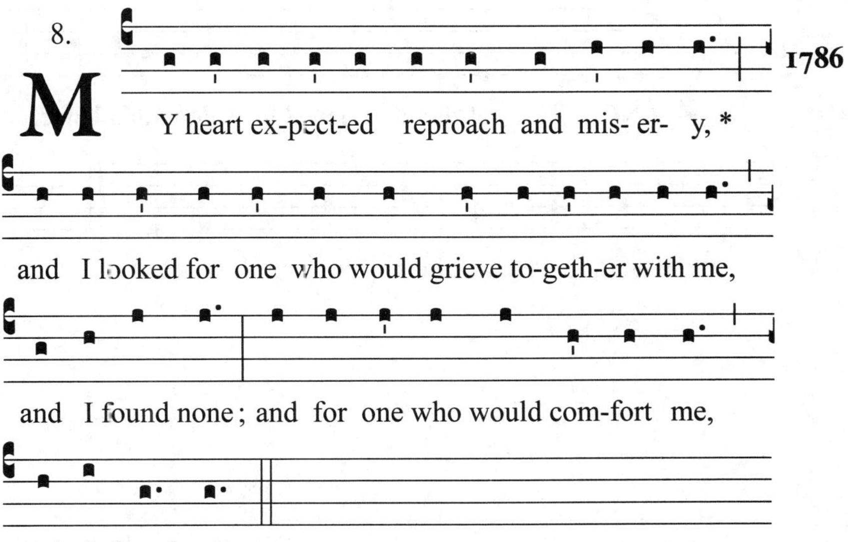
8.
1786
MY heart ex-pect-ed reproach and mis- er- y, *
and I looked for one who would grieve to-geth-er with me,
and I found none; and for one who would com-fort me,
and I found none.

Communion Antiphon *Unus militum lancea.*
Jn 19:34

- i -

1787
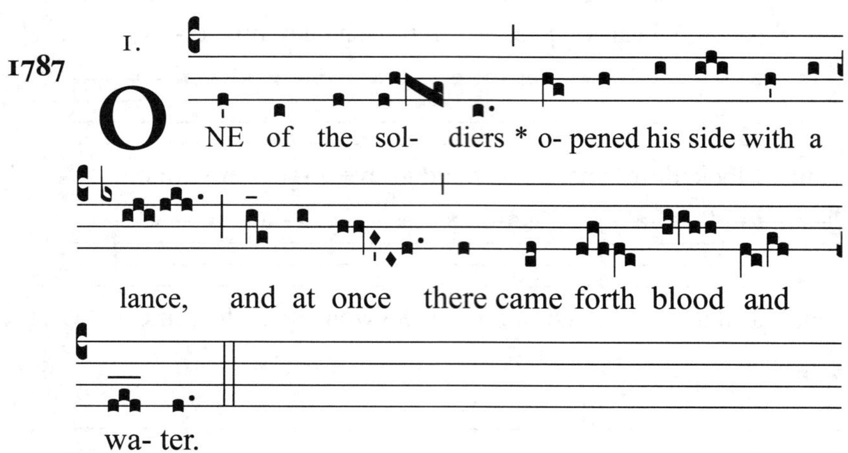
I.
ONE of the sol- diers * o- pened his side with a
lance, and at once there came forth blood and
wa- ter.

- ii -

1788
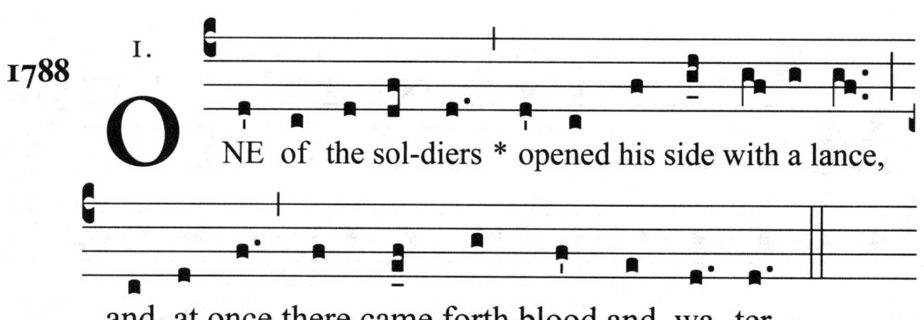
I.
ONE of the sol-diers * opened his side with a lance,
and at once there came forth blood and wa- ter.

VERSES *Misericordias Domini in æternum cantabo. Ps* 88 : 2

℣. 1

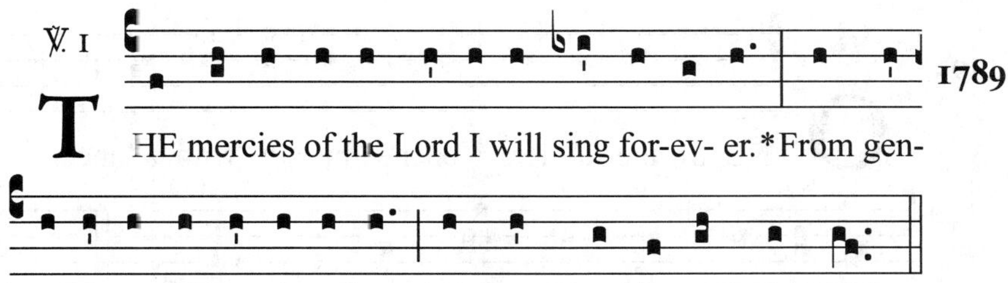
1789
THE mercies of the Lord I will sing for-ev- er. * From gen-

er- a-tion to gen-er- a-tion my mouth will declare your truth.

Inveni David, servum meum. Ps 88 : 21

℣. 2

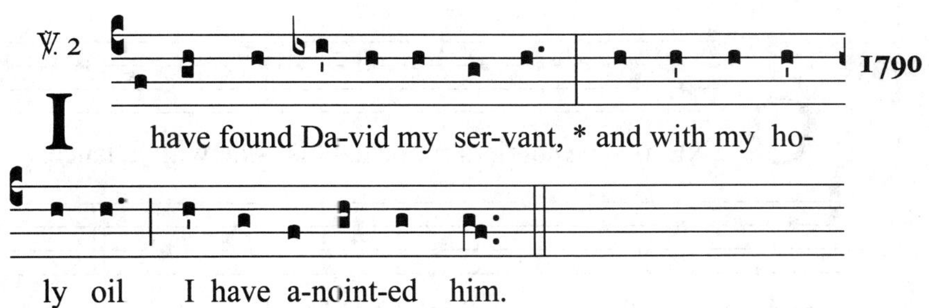
1790
I have found Da-vid my ser-vant, * and with my ho-
ly oil I have a-noint-ed him.

Misericordiam autem meam. Ps 88 : 34

℣. 3

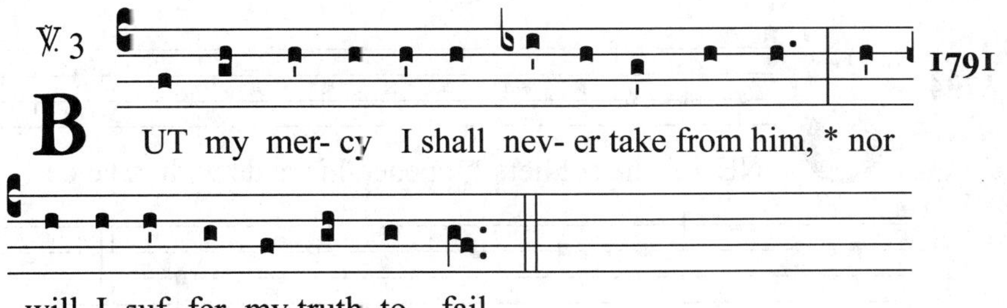
1791
BUT my mer- cy I shall nev- er take from him, * nor
will I suf- fer my truth to fail.

- iii -

1792 I.

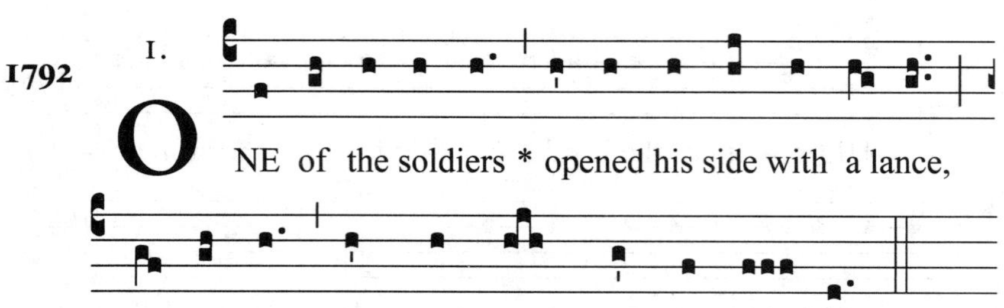

ONE of the soldiers * opened his side with a lance,

and at once there came forth blood and wa- ter.

Or:

1793 I.

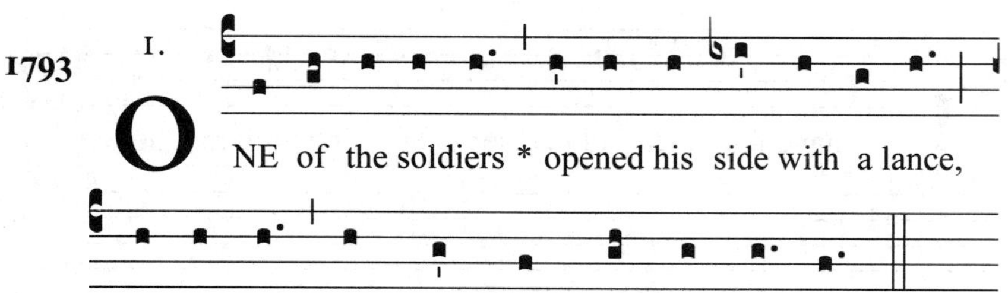

ONE of the soldiers * opened his side with a lance,

and at once there came forth blood and wa- ter.

- iv -

1794 I.

ONE of the soldiers * opened his side with a lance,

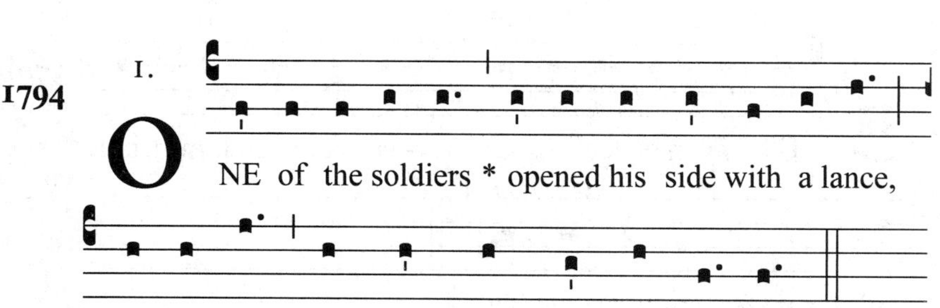

and at once there came forth blood and wa- ter.

Or:

COMMUNION ANTIPHON *Hæc dicit Dominus.*
Cf. Jn 7:37-38

- i -

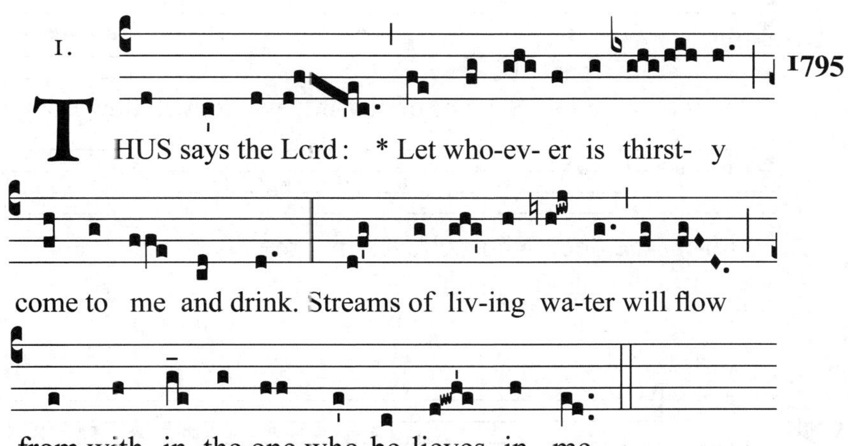
1.
1795
THUS says the Lord: * Let who-ev- er is thirst- y
come to me and drink. Streams of liv-ing wa-ter will flow
from with- in the one who be-lieves in me.

- ii -

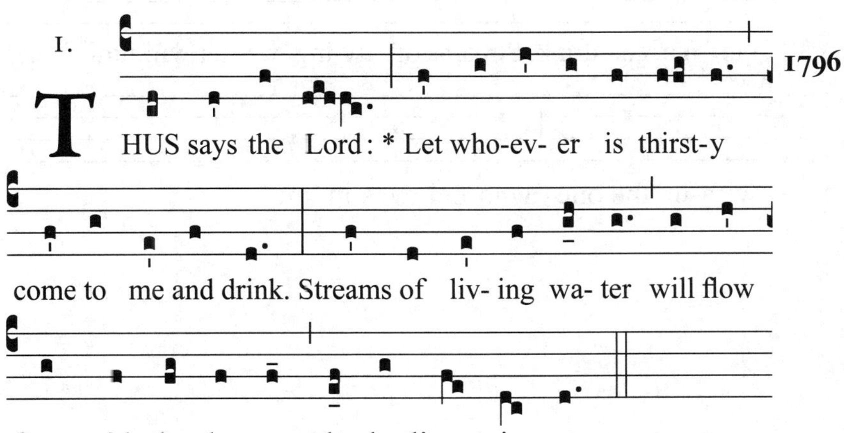
1.
1796
THUS says the Lord: * Let who-ev- er is thirst-y
come to me and drink. Streams of liv- ing wa- ter will flow
from with- in the one who be-lieves in me.

- iii -

1797

I.
THUS says the Lord: * Let who-ev- er is thirst-y come
to me and drink. Streams of liv-ing wa- ter will flow from
with-in the one who believes in me.

- iv -

1798

I.
THUS says the Lord: * Let who-ev- er is thirst-y come
to me and drink. Streams of liv-ing wa- ter will flow from
with-in the one who believes in me.

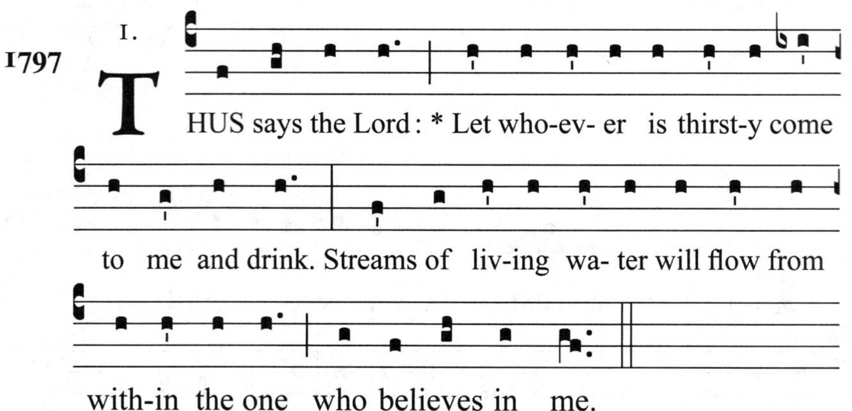

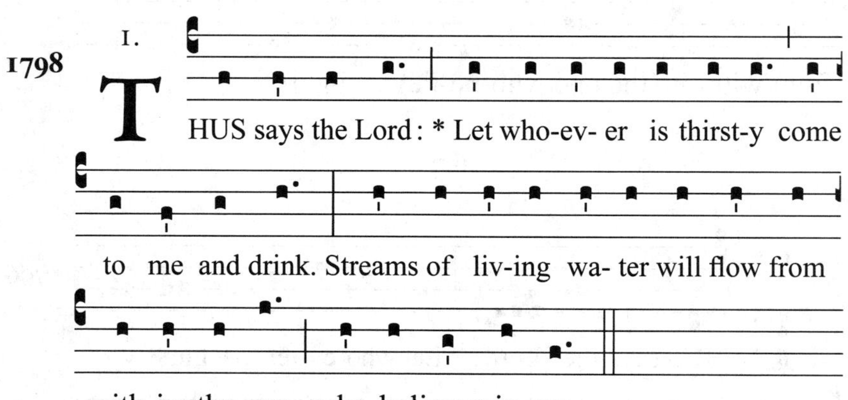

Last Sunday in Ordinary Time

OUR LORD JESUS CHRIST, KING OF THE UNIVERSE

ENTRANCE ANTIPHON *Dignus est Agnus.*
Rev 5:12; 1:6

- i -

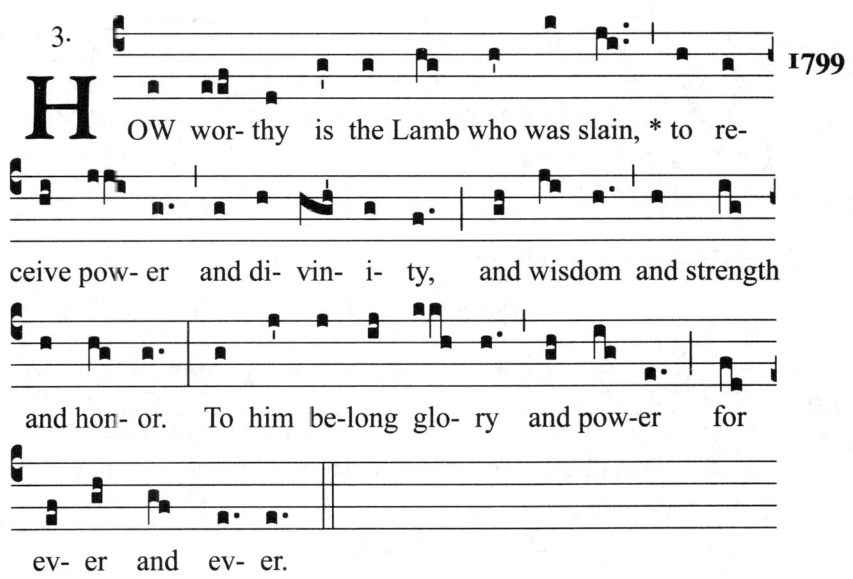
3.
H OW wor- thy is the Lamb who was slain, * to re-
1799
ceive pow- er and di- vin- i- ty, and wisdom and strength
and hon- or. To him be-long glo- ry and pow-er for
ev- er and ev- er.

- ii -

3.
H OW wor- thy * is the Lamb who was slain, to re-
1800
ceive pow- er and di- vin- i- ty, and wis-dom and strength

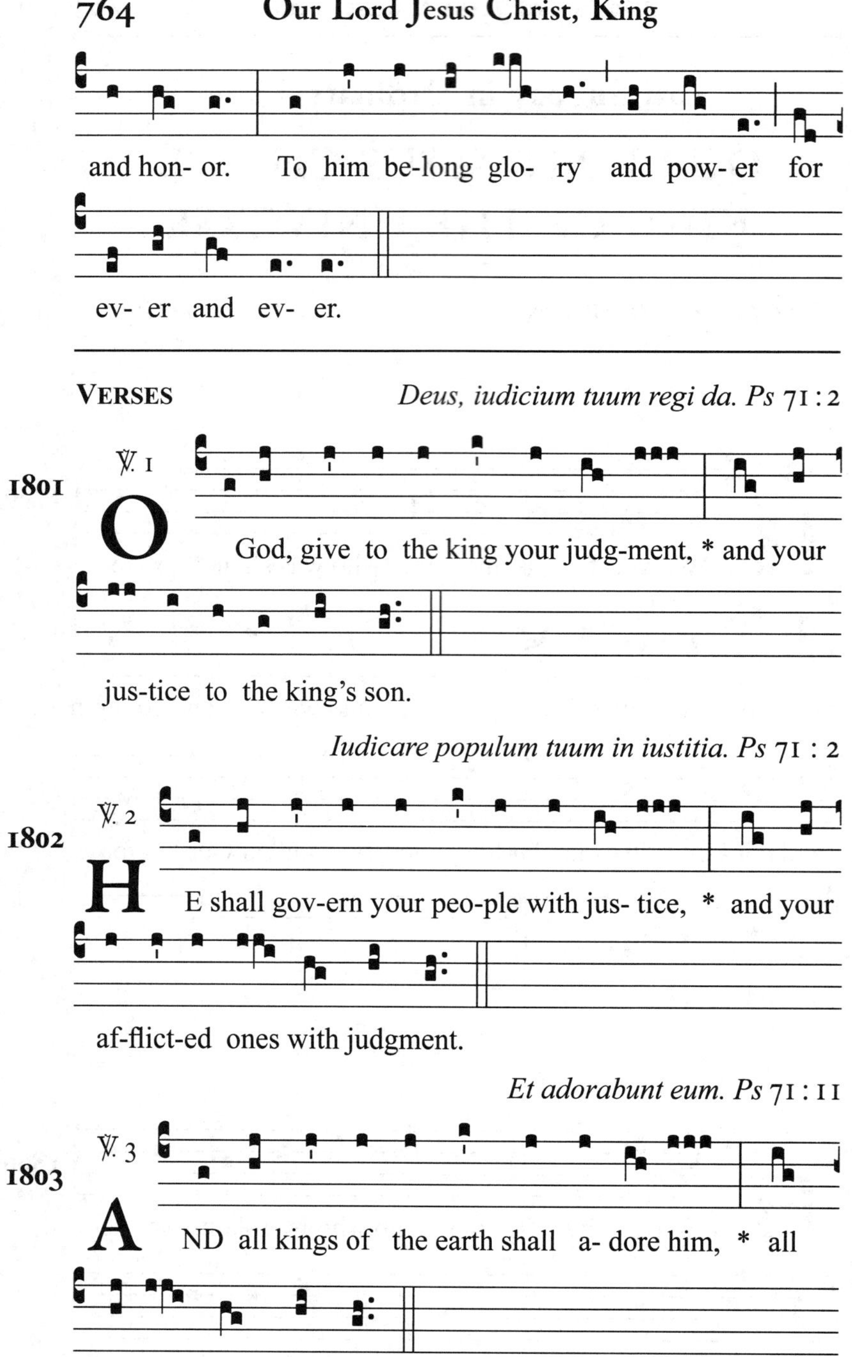

and hon- or. To him be-long glo- ry and pow- er for
ev- er and ev- er.
VERSES
Deus, iudicium tuum regi da. Ps 71 : 2
℣. 1
1801
O God, give to the king your judg-ment, * and your
jus-tice to the king's son.
Iudicare populum tuum in iustitia. Ps 71 : 2
℣. 2
1802
HE shall gov-ern your peo-ple with jus- tice, * and your
af-flict-ed ones with judgment.
Et adorabunt eum. Ps 71 : 11
℣. 3
1803
AND all kings of the earth shall a- dore him, * all
na-tions shall serve him.

- iii -

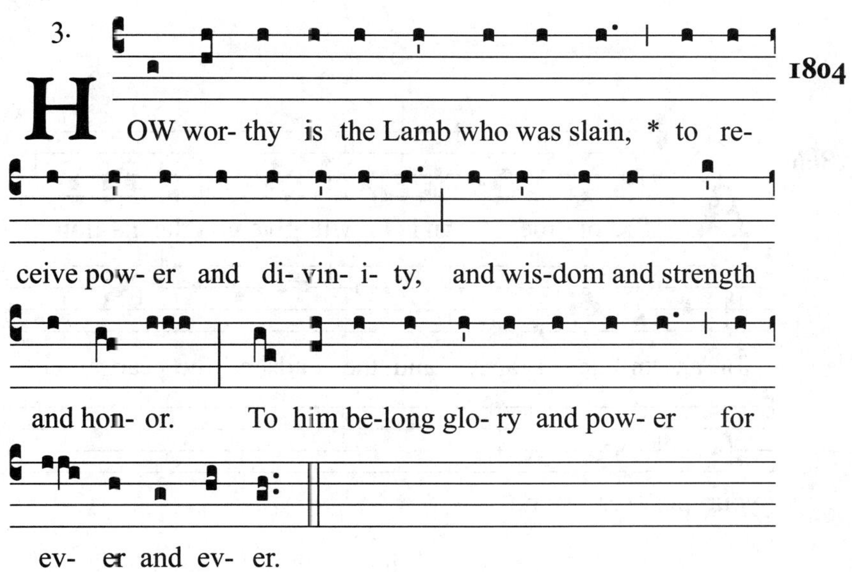
3.
1804
HOW wor- thy is the Lamb who was slain, * to receive pow- er and di- vin- i- ty, and wis-dom and strength
and hon- or. To him be-long glo- ry and pow- er for
ev- er and ev- er.

- iv -

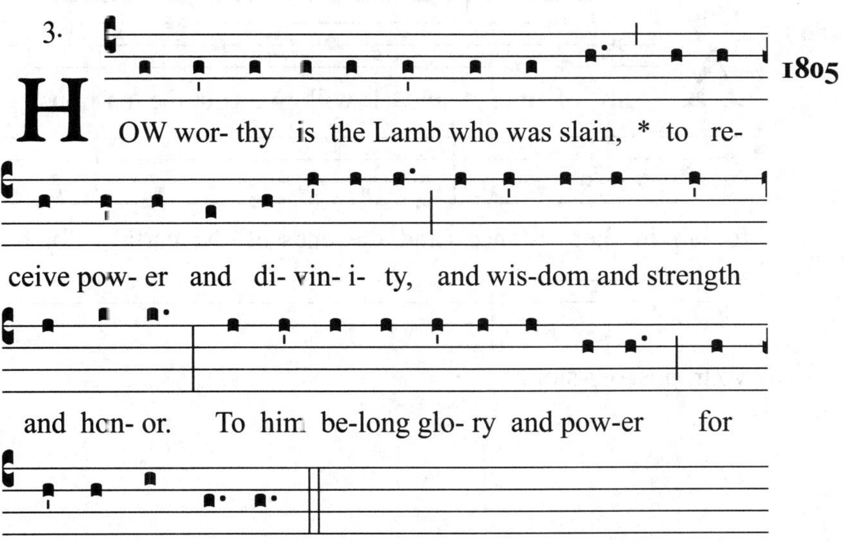
3.
1805
HOW wor- thy is the Lamb who was slain, * to receive pow- er and di- vin- i- ty, and wis-dom and strength
and hon- or. To him be-long glo- ry and pow-er for
ev- er and ev- er.

Offertory Antiphon *Postula a me, et tibi dabo.* *Ps* 2:8

- i -

1806

4.
ASK of me, * and I will give you the na-tions
for an in- her- i-tance and the ends of the earth for
your pos- ses- sion.

- ii -

1807

4.
ASK of me, * and I will give you the na-tions
for an in- her- i-tance and the ends of the earth for
your pos-ses-sion.

VERSES *Ego autem constitutus sum Rex. Ps* 2 : 6

℣. 1
I am ap-point-ed king by him o- ver Si- on his
1808

ho- ly mountain, * preaching his commandment.

Cum exarserit in breve ira eius. Ps 2 : 13

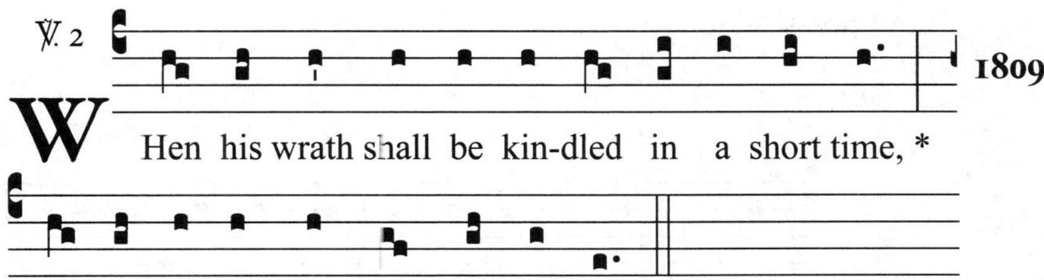
℣. 2
WHen his wrath shall be kin-dled in a short time, *
1809

bless-ed are all those who trust in him.

Iubilate in conspectu regis Domini. Ps 97 : 6. 8

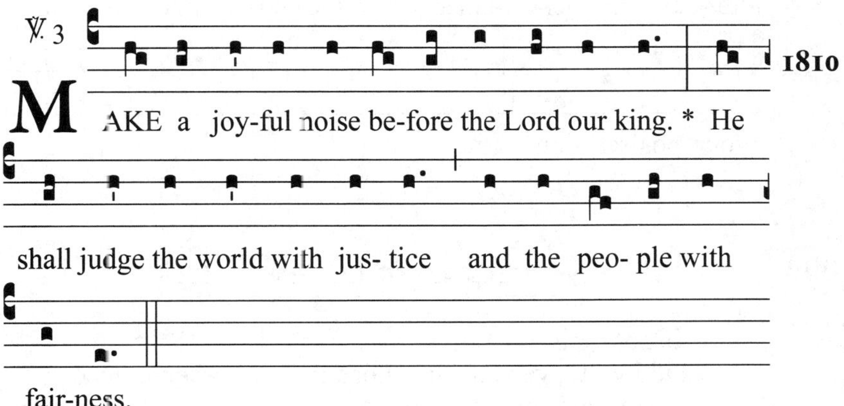
℣. 3
MAKE a joy-ful noise be-fore the Lord our king. * He
1810
shall judge the world with jus- tice and the peo- ple with

fair-ness.

- iii -

1811

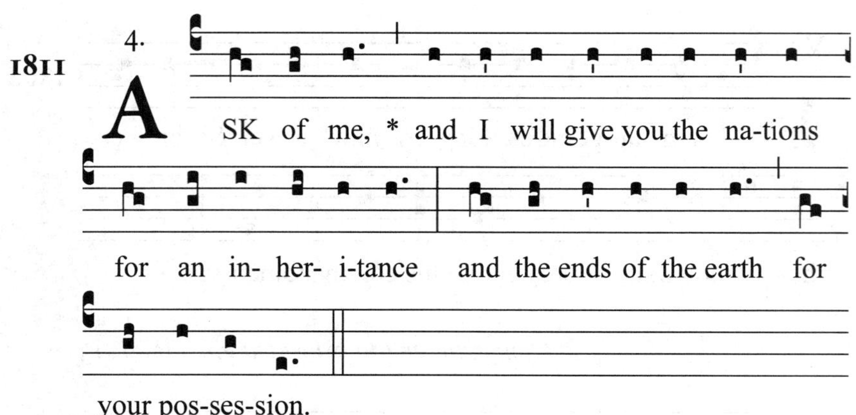
4.
ASK of me, * and I will give you the na-tions
for an in- her- i-tance and the ends of the earth for
your pos-ses-sion.

Or:

1812

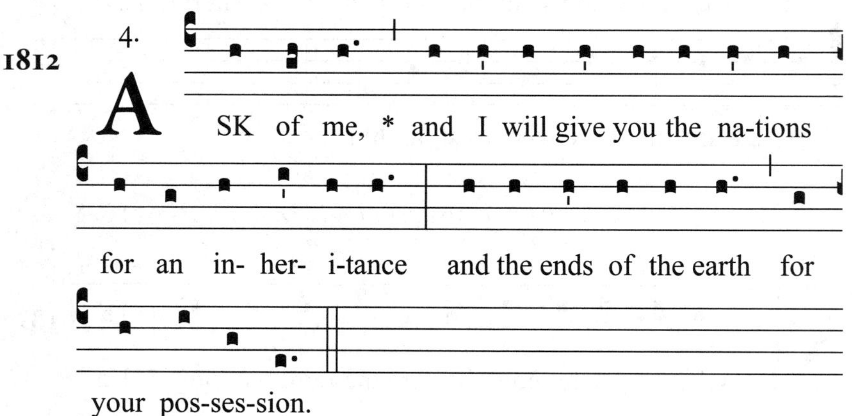
4.
ASK of me, * and I will give you the na-tions
for an in- her- i-tance and the ends of the earth for
your pos-ses-sion.

- iv -

1813

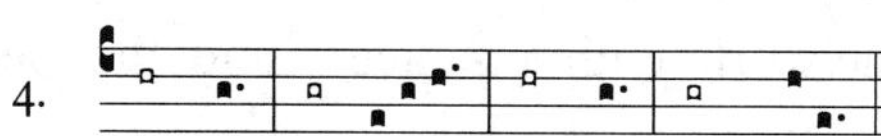
4.

Ask of | **me,**
and I will give you the nations for | *an in*-**her**-it-ance
and the ends of the | **earth**
for your | *pos*-**ses**-sion.

COMMUNION ANTIPHON *Sedebit Dominus Rex.*
Ps 28: 10-11

- i -

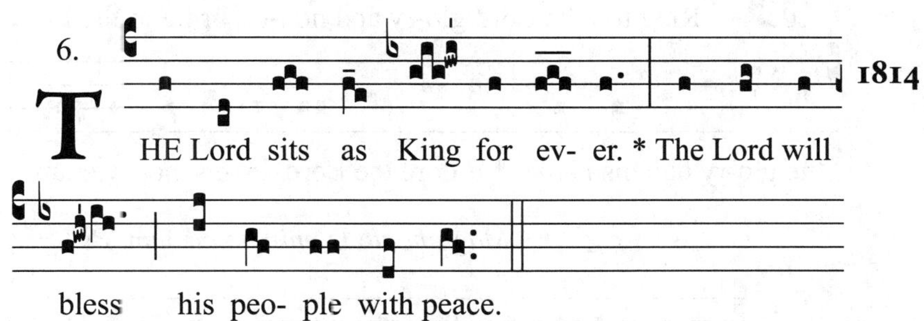
6.
THE Lord sits as King for ev- er. * The Lord will
bless his peo- ple with peace.

1814

- ii -

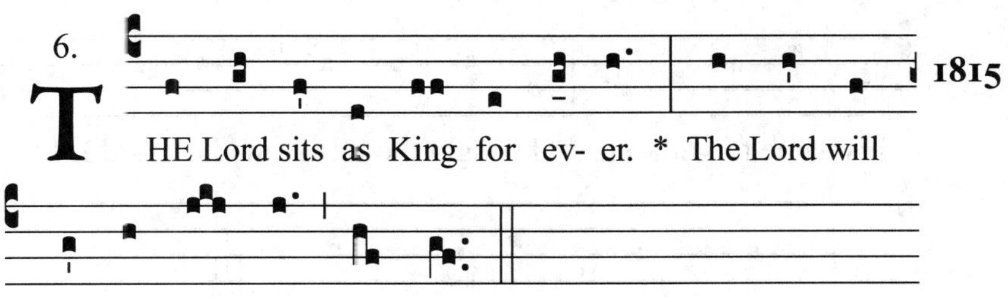
6.
THE Lord sits as King for ev- er. * The Lord will
bless his peo- ple with peace.

1815

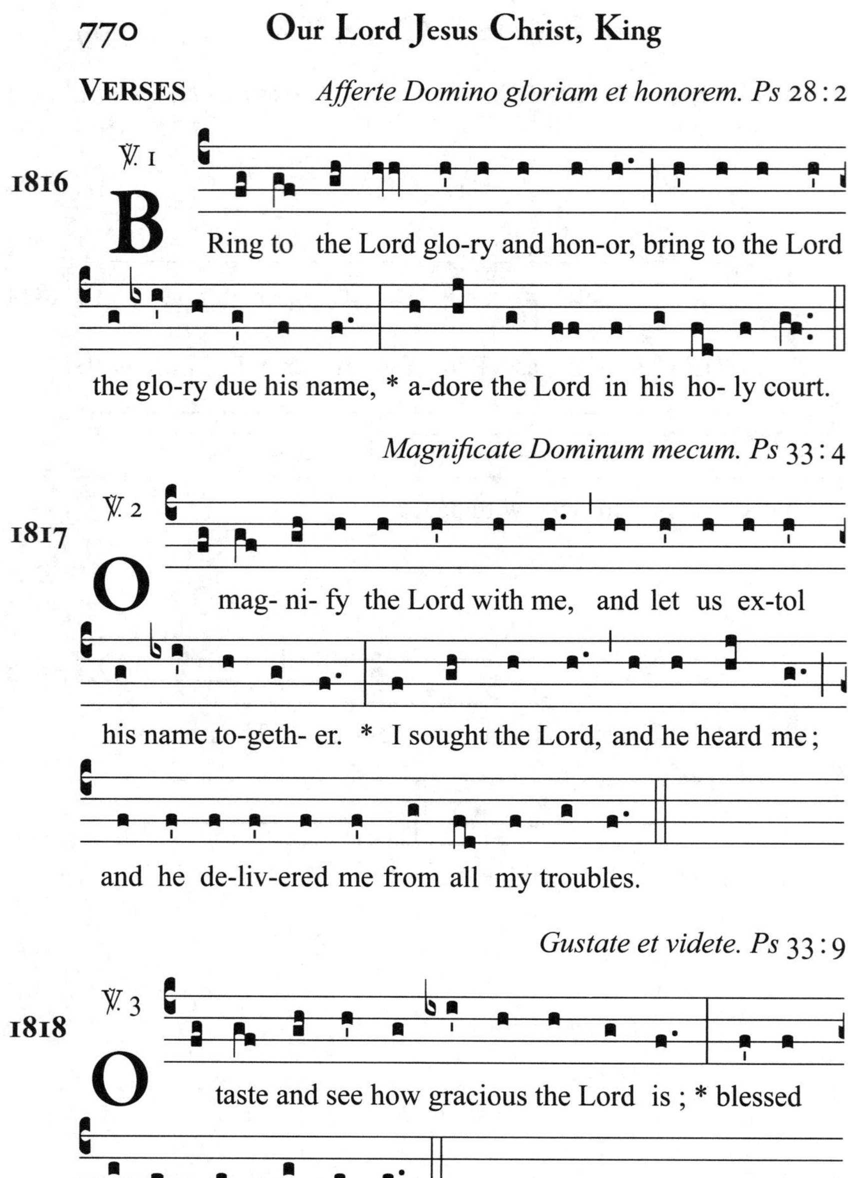
VERSES
Afferte Domino gloriam et honorem. Ps 28 : 2
℣. 1
1816
BRing to the Lord glo-ry and hon-or, bring to the Lord
the glo-ry due his name, * a-dore the Lord in his ho- ly court.
Magnificate Dominum mecum. Ps 33 : 4
℣. 2
1817
O mag- ni- fy the Lord with me, and let us ex-tol
his name to-geth- er. * I sought the Lord, and he heard me;
and he de-liv-ered me from all my troubles.
Gustate et videte. Ps 33 : 9
℣. 3
1818
O taste and see how gracious the Lord is ; * blessed
the man who hopes in him.

- iii -

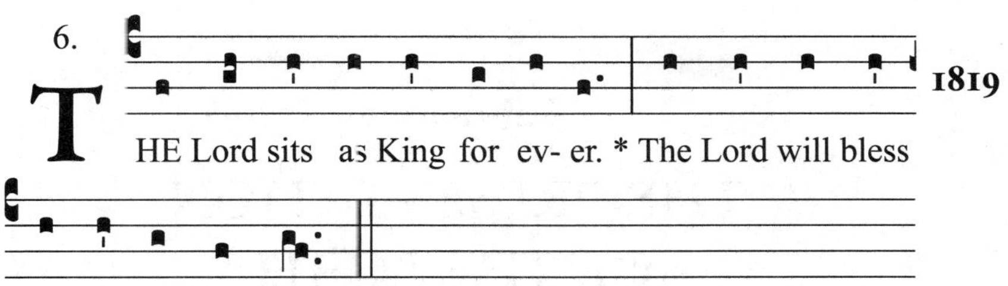
6.
1819
T
HE Lord sits as King for ev- er. * The Lord will bless

his peo-ple with peace.

Or:

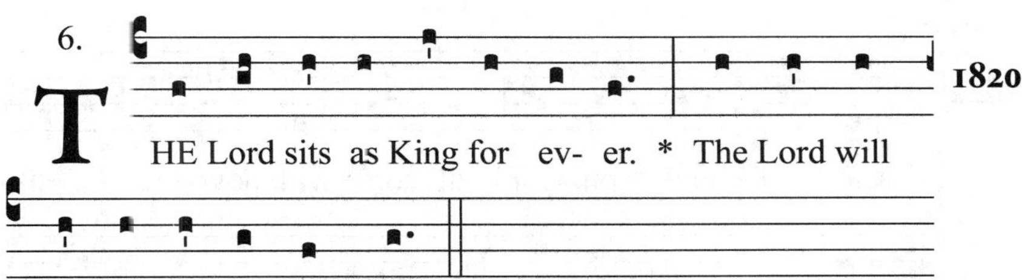
6.
1820
T
HE Lord sits as King for ev- er. * The Lord will

bless his peo-ple with peace.

- iv -

6.
1821
T
HE Lord sits as King for ev- er. * The Lord will

bless his peo-ple with peace.

PROPER OF SAINTS

February 2

THE PRESENTATION OF THE LORD

Antiphon at the Procession *Ecce Dominus noster.*

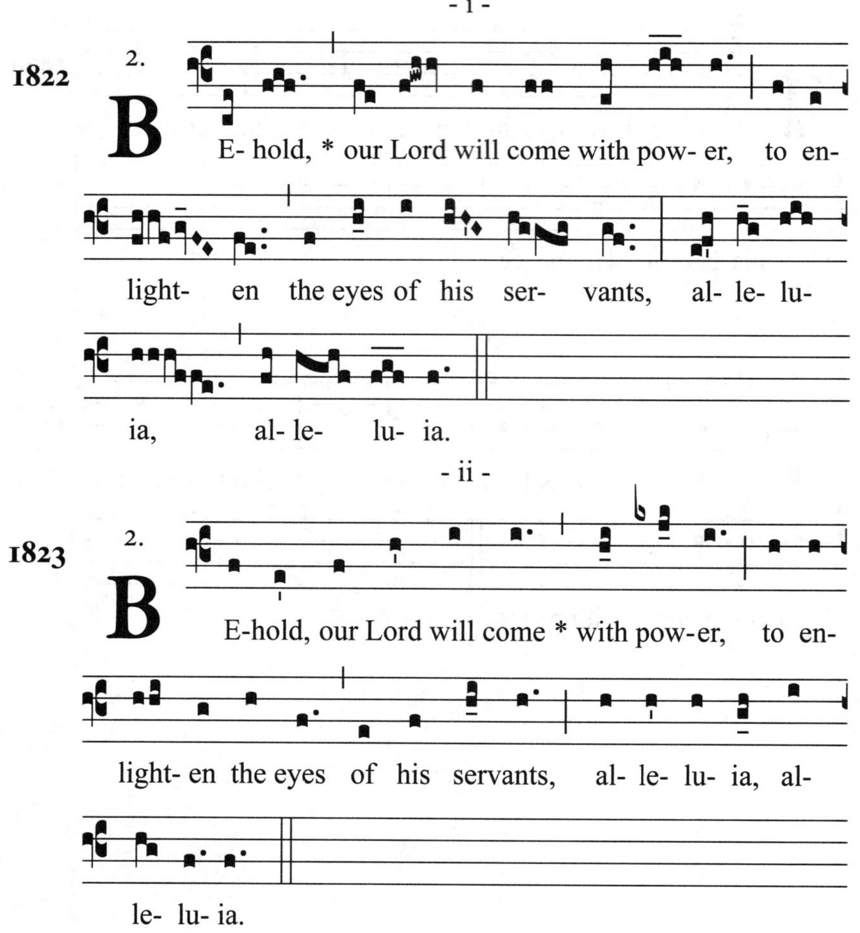

- i -
1822
2.
BEhold, * our Lord will come with pow- er, to en-
light- en the eyes of his ser- vants, al- le- lu-
ia, al- le- lu- ia.
- ii -
1823
2.
BEhold, our Lord will come * with pow-er, to en-
light- en the eyes of his servants, al- le- lu- ia, al-
le- lu- ia.

VERSES *Deus, iudicium tuum regi da. Ps* 71:2

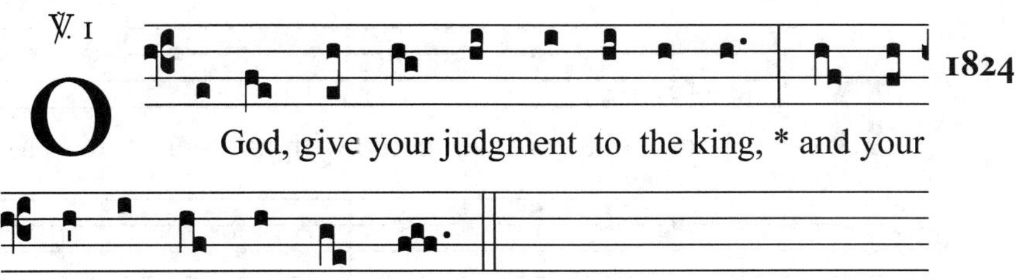
℣. 1
O God, give your judgment to the king, * and your
1824

jus-tice to the king's son.

Iudicare populum tuum in iustitia. Ps 71 : 2

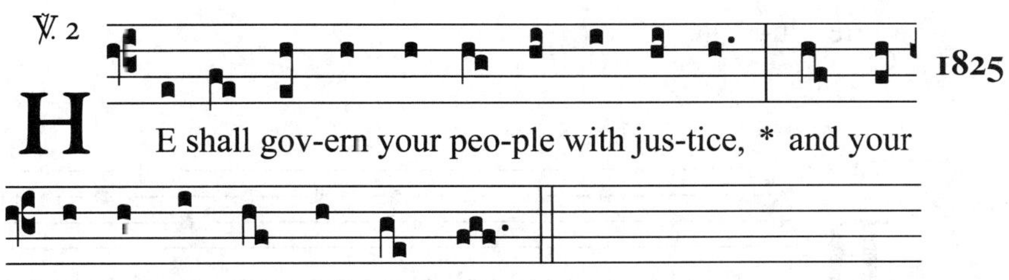
℣. 2
HE shall gov-ern your peo-ple with jus-tice, * and your
1825

af-flict- ed ones with judg- ment.

Et adorabunt eum. Ps 71:11

℣. 3
AND all kings of the earth shall a- dore him, * all
1826

na-tions shall serve him.

- iii -

2.

1827 BE-hold, our Lord will come with pow- er, * to en-

light-en the eyes of his servants, al- le- lu- ia, al-

le- lu- ia.

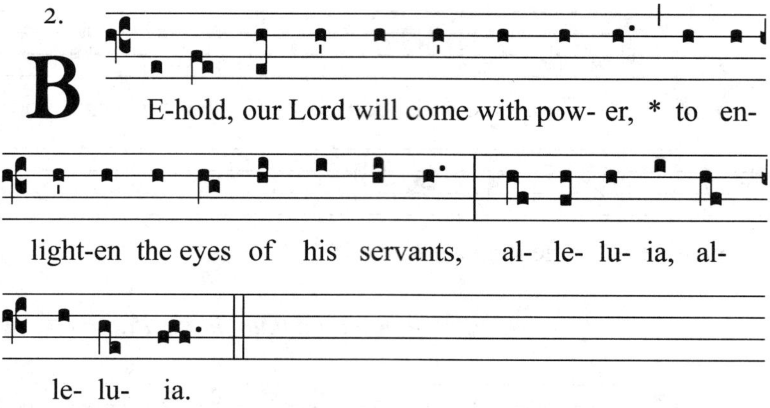

Or:

2.

1828 BE-hold, our Lord will come with pow- er, * to en-

light-en the eyes of his servants, al- le- lu- ia, al-

le- lu- ia.

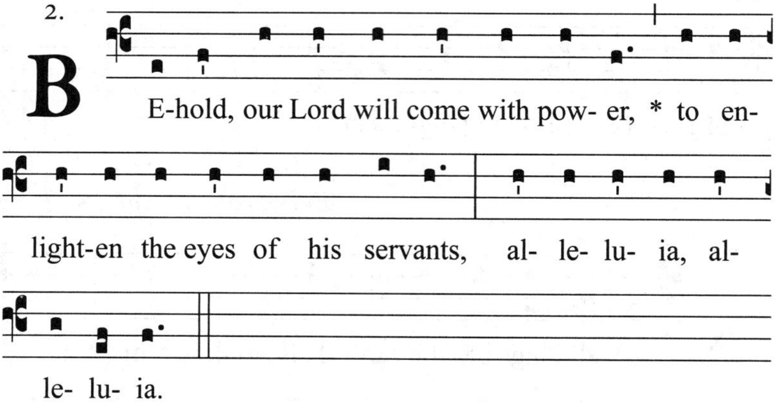

- iv -

1829 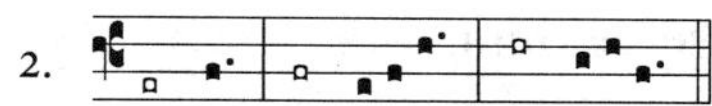

Behold, our Lord will come with | **pow**-er,
to enlighten the eyes | *of his* **ser**-vants,
alleluia, | *al-le*-**lu**-ia.

Antiphon at the Procession. I

Lumen ad revelationem gentium. *Lk* 2:29-32

- i -

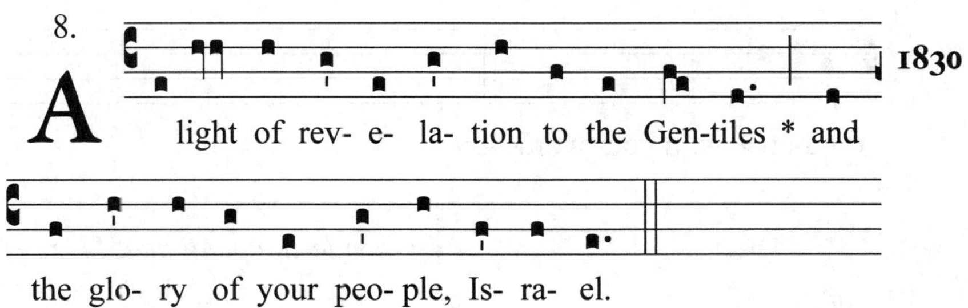
8.
A light of rev- e- la- tion to the Gen-tiles * and
the glo- ry of your peo- ple, Is- ra- el.

1830

- ii -

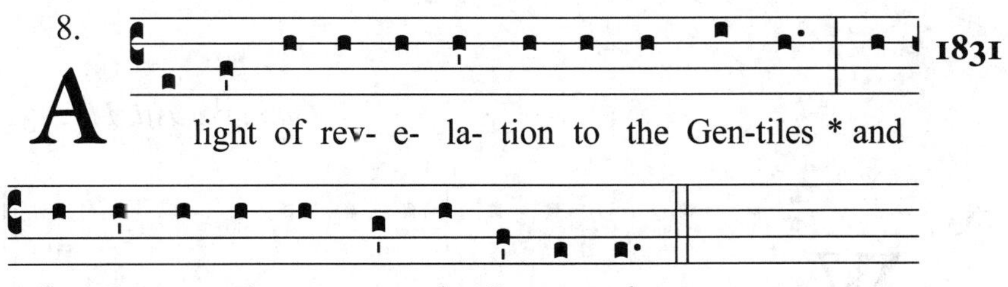
8.
A light of rev- e- la- tion to the Gen-tiles * and
the glo- ry of your peo- ple, Is- ra- el.

1831

VERSES *Nunc dimittis servum tuum, Domine. Lk* 2:29

℣. 1

1832
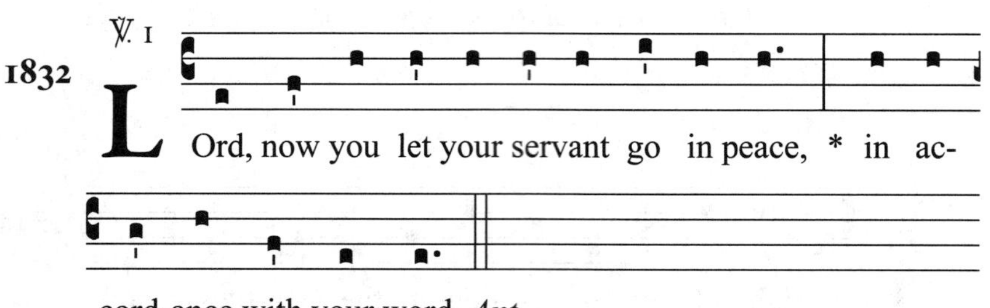

LOrd, now you let your servant go in peace, * in ac-cord-ance with your word. *Ant.*

Quia viderunt oculi mei. Lk 2:31

℣. 2

1833
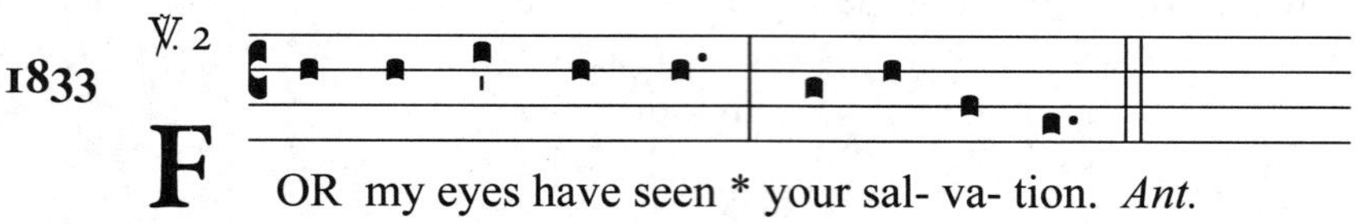

FOR my eyes have seen * your sal- va- tion. *Ant.*

Quod parasti. Lk 2:32

℣. 3

1834
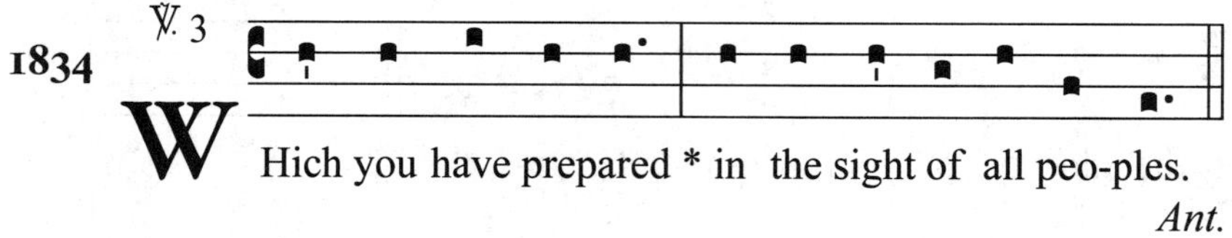

WHich you have prepared * in the sight of all peo-ples. *Ant.*

Antiphon at the Procession. II

Adorna thalamum tuum, Sion.

\- i -

6. 1835

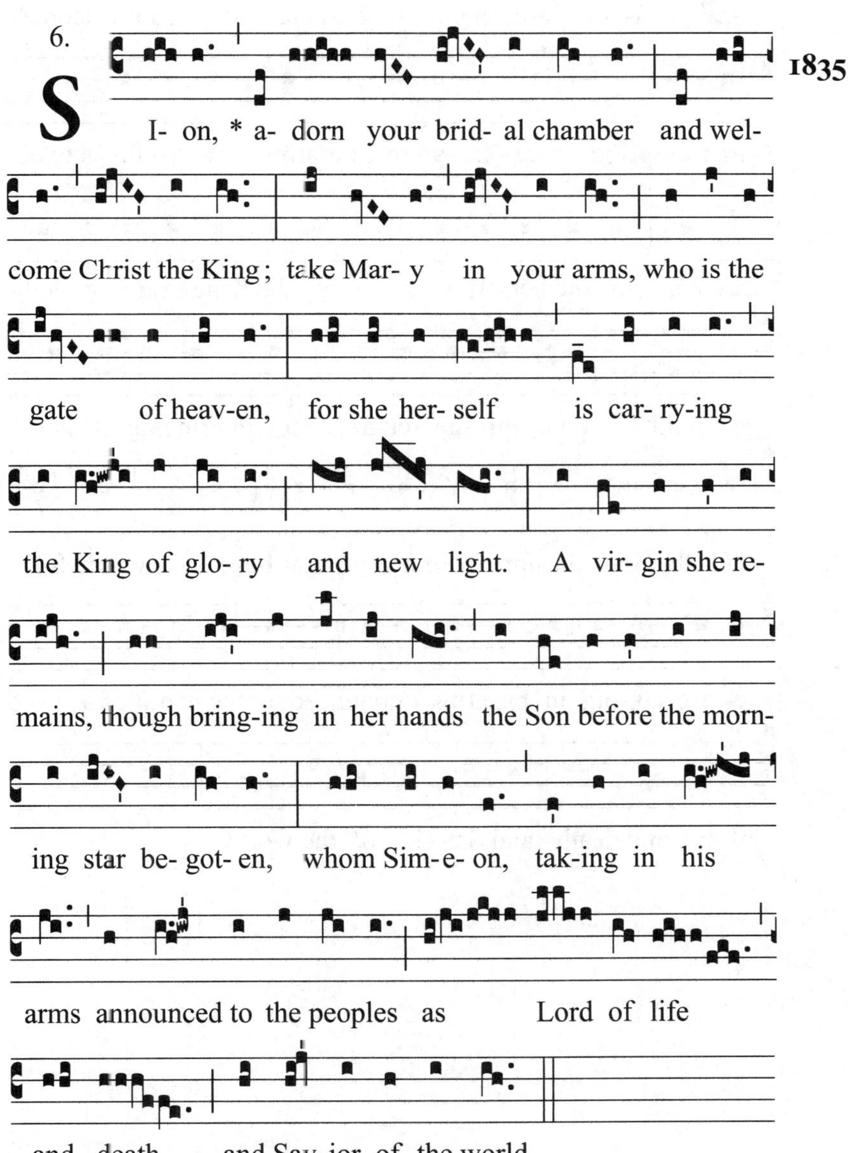
S
I- on, * a- dorn your brid- al chamber and welcome Christ the King; take Mar- y in your arms, who is the
gate of heav-en, for she her- self is car- ry-ing
the King of glo- ry and new light. A vir- gin she re-
mains, though bring-ing in her hands the Son before the morn-
ing star be- got- en, whom Sim-e- on, tak-ing in his
arms announced to the peoples as Lord of life
and death and Sav-ior of the world.

- ii -

1836

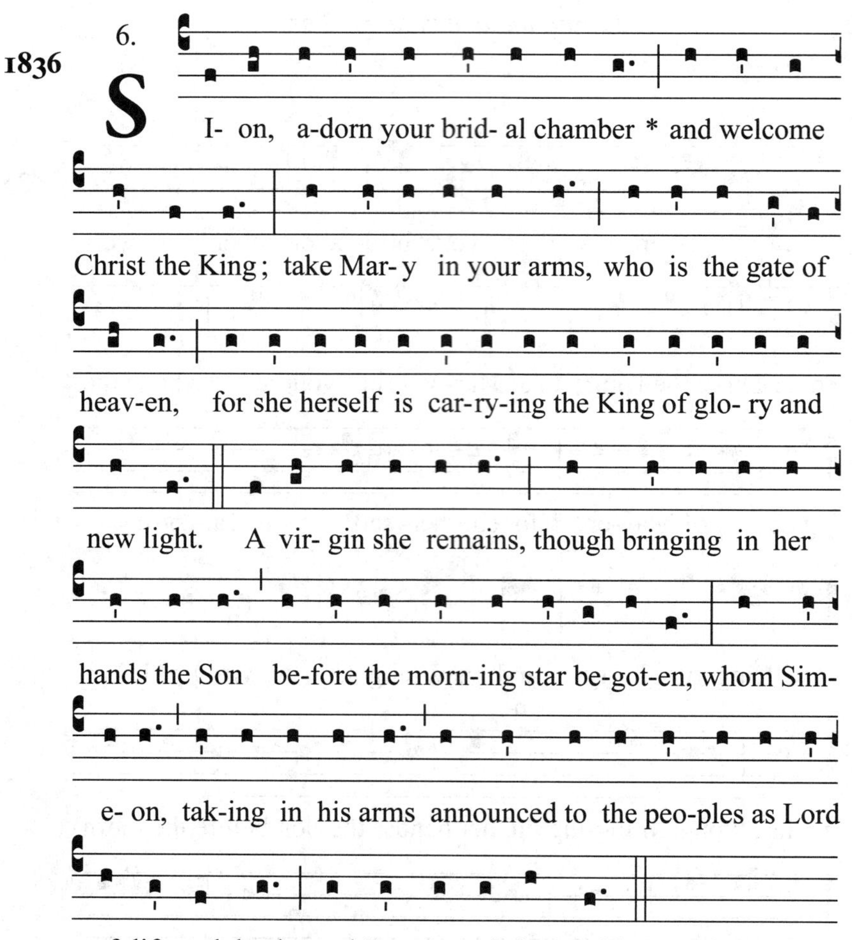
6.
S
I- on, a-dorn your brid- al chamber * and welcome
Christ the King; take Mar- y in your arms, who is the gate of
heav-en, for she herself is car-ry-ing the King of glo- ry and
new light. A vir- gin she remains, though bringing in her
hands the Son be-fore the morn-ing star be-got-en, whom Sim-
e- on, tak-ing in his arms announced to the peo-ples as Lord
of life and death and Sav- ior of the world.

Entrance Antiphon *Suscepimus, Deus.*
Ps 47:10-11

- i -
1.
1837
Your mer-ci-ful love, * O God, we have re-ceived in the midst of your tem-ple. Your praise, O God, like your name, reach-es the ends of the earth; your right hand is filled with sav-ing jus- tice.
- ii -
1.
1838
Your mer-ci- ful love, O God, * we have re- ceived in the midst of your tem-ple. Your praise, O God, like your name, reach-es the ends of the earth; your right hand is filled with sav-ing jus- tice.

VERSES *Magnus Dominus, et laudabilis nimis.* Ps 47:2

1839 ℣. 1 GReat is the Lord and high-ly to be praised, * in the cit- y of our God, up- on his ho- ly moun-tain.

Ipsi videntes, sic admirati sunt. Ps 47:9

1840

℣. 2
AS we have heard, so have we seen, in the cit- y of the
Lord of hosts, * in the cit- y of our God, in the midst of
your tem- ple.

Ut enarretis in progenie altera. Ps 47:14-15

1841

℣. 3
THAT you may tell a fu-ture gen-er- a-tion that such
is our God, * our God for- ev- er and ev- er, it is he
who will lead us.

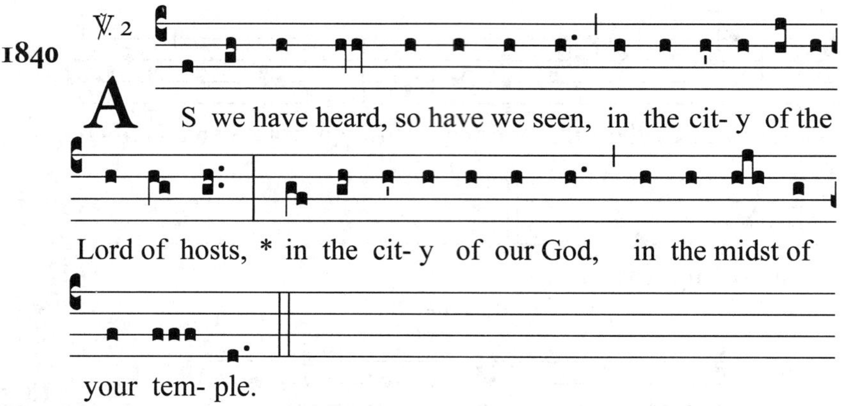

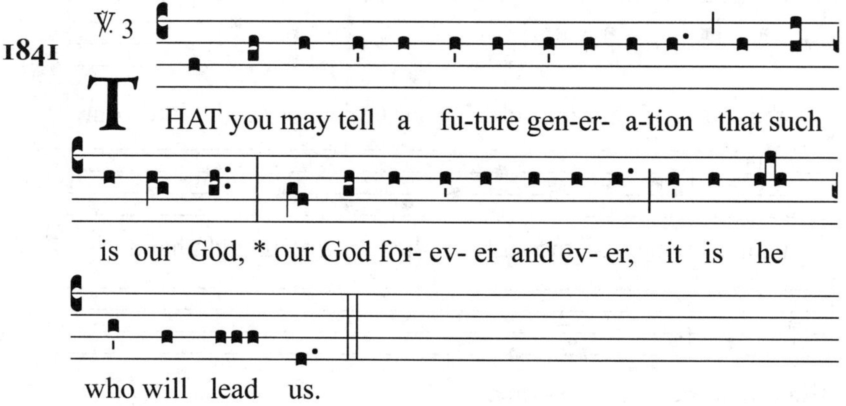

- iii -

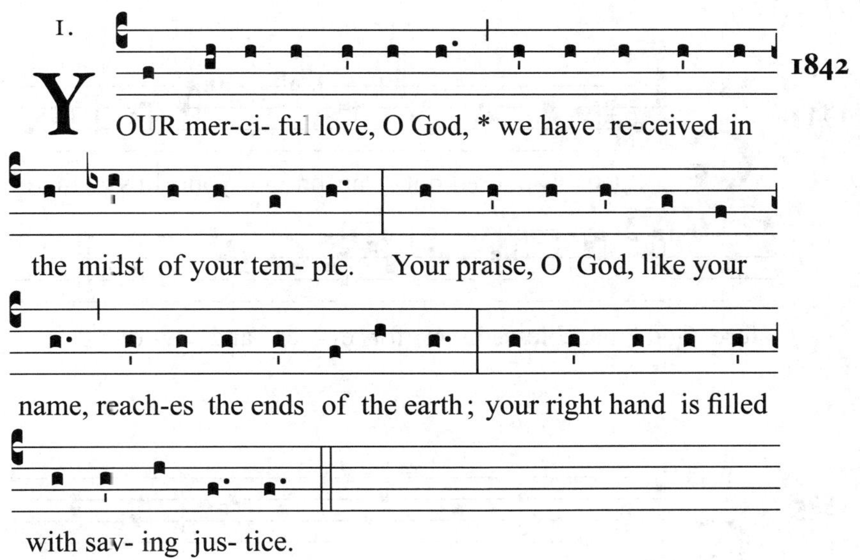
I.
1842
YOUR mer-ci- ful love, O God, * we have re-ceived in
the midst of your tem- ple. Your praise, O God, like your
name, reach-es the ends of the earth; your right hand is filled
with sav- ing jus- tice.

- iv -

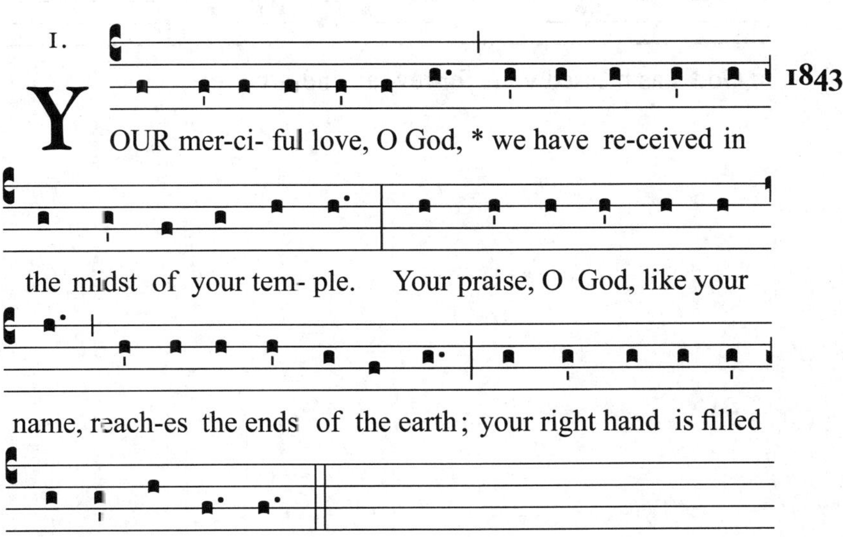
I.
1843
YOUR mer-ci- ful love, O God, * we have re-ceived in
the midst of your tem- ple. Your praise, O God, like your
name, reach-es the ends of the earth; your right hand is filled
with sav- ing jus- tice.

Offertory Antiphon *Diffusa est gratia in labiis tuis.*
Ps 44:3

- i -

1844
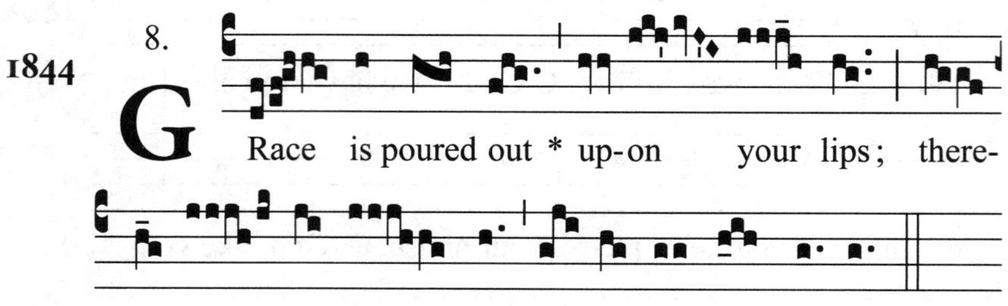
8.
G Race is poured out * up-on your lips; there-

fore God has blessed you for- ev- er and ev- er.

- ii -

1845

8.
G Race is poured out * up- on your lips; there-fore

God has blessed you for- ev- er and ev- er.

Eructavit cor meum verbum bonum. Ps 44:2

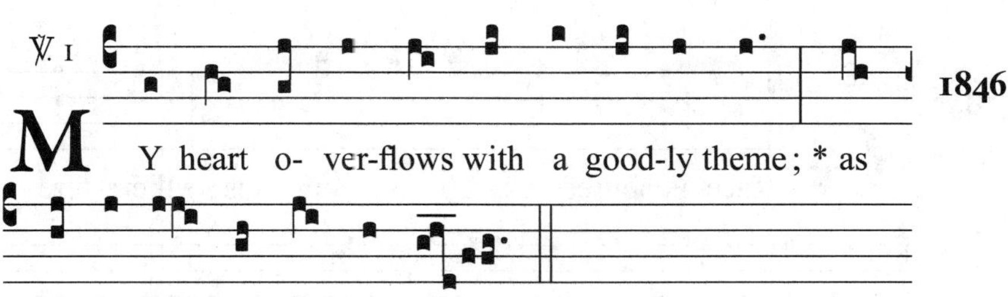
℣. 1
1846
MY heart o- ver-flows with a good-ly theme; * as
I sing my ode to the king.

Speciosus forma præ filiis hominum. Ps 44:3

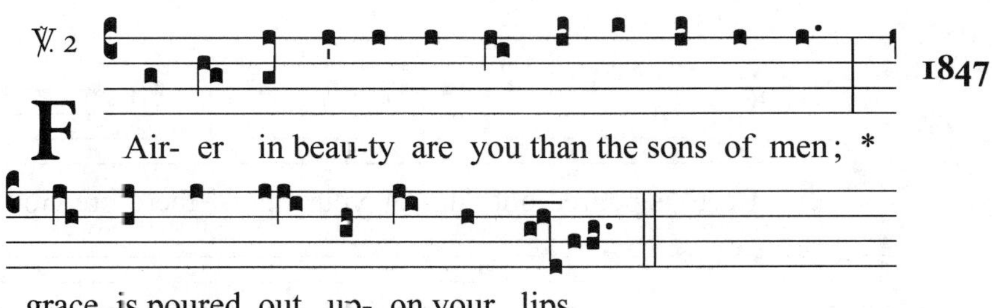
℣. 2
1847
FAir- er in beau-ty are you than the sons of men; *
grace is poured out up- on your lips.

Accingere gladio tuo. Ps 44:4

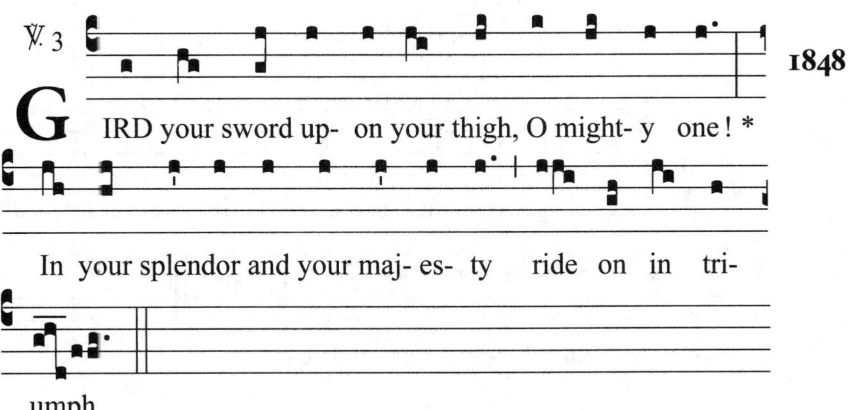
℣. 3
1848
GIRD your sword up- on your thigh, O might- y one! *
In your splendor and your maj- es- ty ride on in tri-
umph

- iii -

1849

8.
GRace is poured out up- on your lips; * there-fore

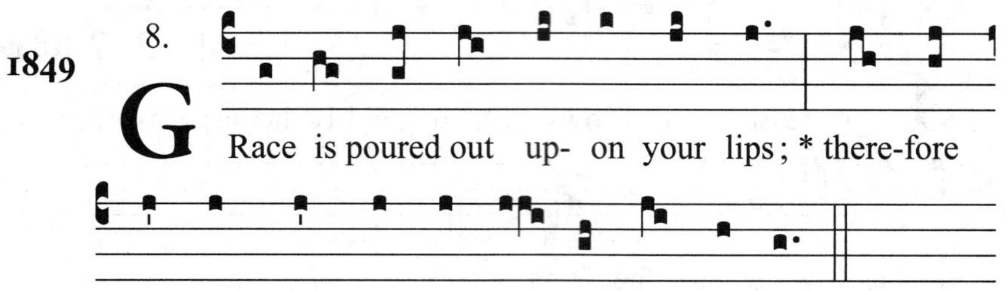

God has blessed you for- ev- er and ev- er.

Or:

1850

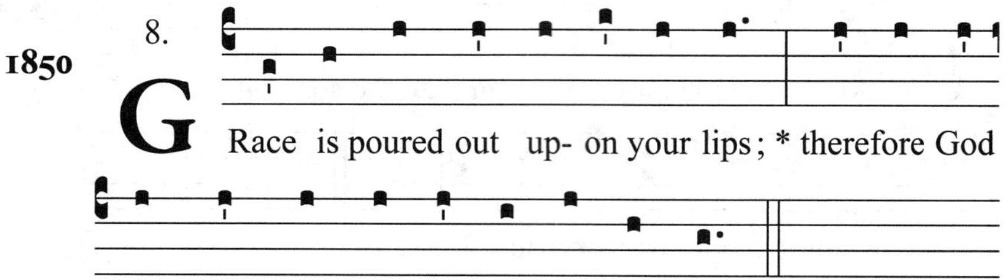

8.
GRace is poured out up- on your lips; * therefore God

has blessed you for- ev- er and ev- er.

- iv -

1851

8.
GRace is poured out * up- on your lips; therefore God

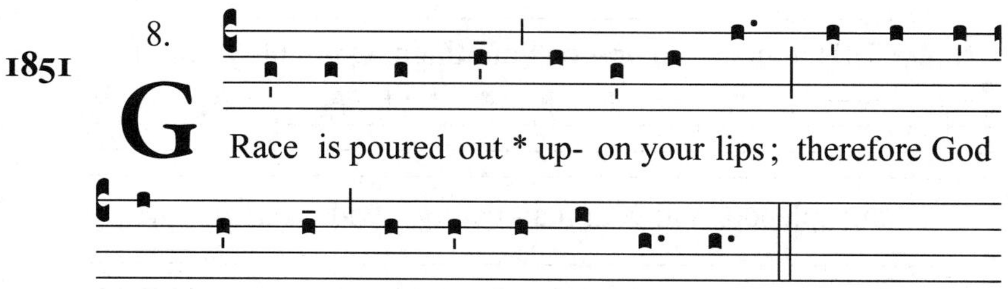

has blessed you for- ev- er and ev- er.

COMMUNION ANTIPHON *Viderunt oculi mei.*
Lk 2:30-31

- i -

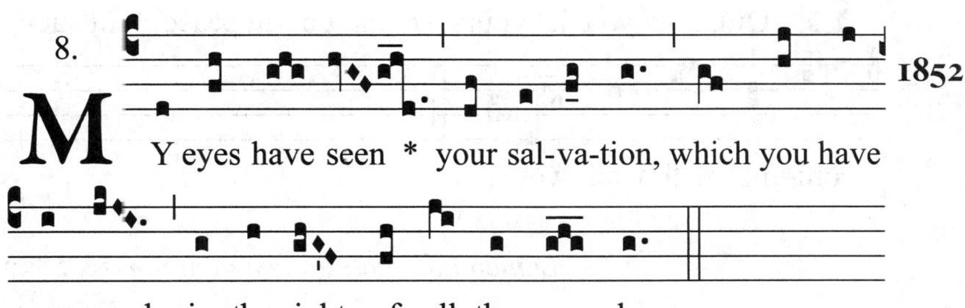
8.
M
Y eyes have seen * your sal-va-tion, which you have
pre-pared in the sight of all the peo-ples.
1852

- ii -

8.
M
Y eyes have seen * your sal-va-tion, which you have
pre-pared in the sight of all the peo-ples.
1853

VERSES *Nunc dimittis servum tuum, Domine. Lk* 2:29

1854
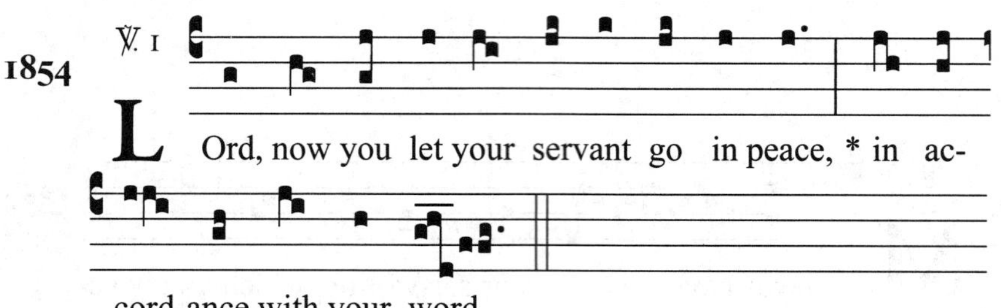
℣. 1
L Ord, now you let your servant go in peace, * in ac-
cord-ance with your word.

Lumen ad revelationem gentium. Lk 2:32

1855
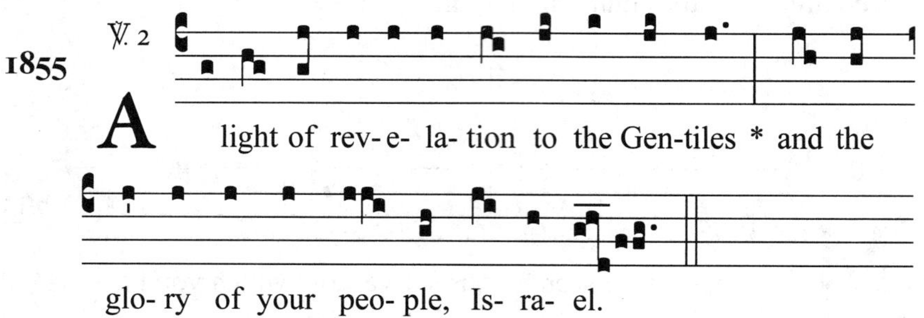
℣. 2
A light of rev-e- la- tion to the Gen-tiles * and the
glo- ry of your peo- ple, Is- ra- el.

- iii -

1856

8.
MY eyes have seen your sal- va-tion, * which you have
prepared in the sight of all the peo-ples.

Or:

1857

8.
MY eyes have seen your sal- va-tion, * which you have
prepared in the sight of all the peo-ples.

- iv -

1858

8.
MY eyes have seen your sal- va-tion, * which you have
prepared in the sight of all the peo-ples.

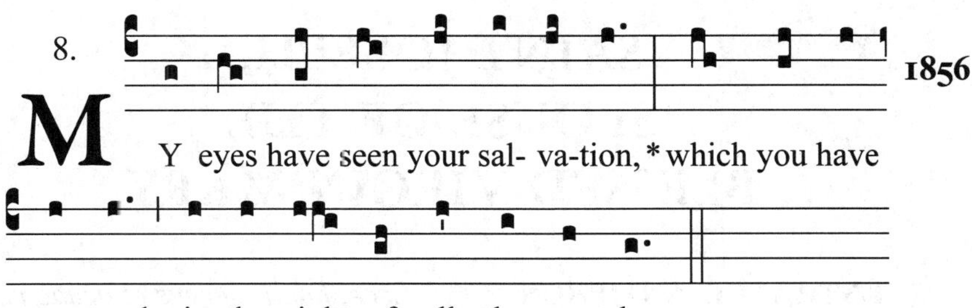

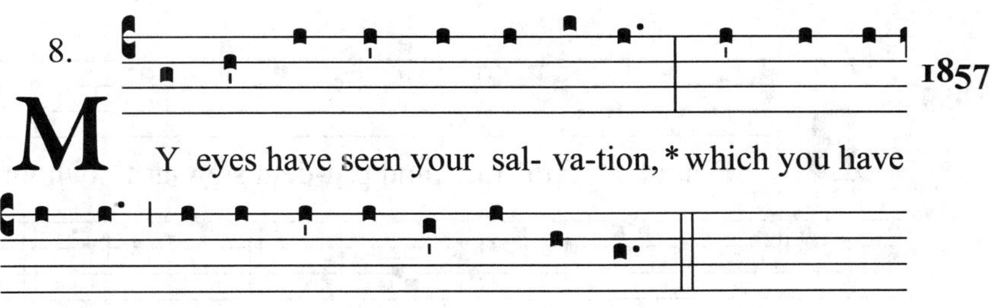

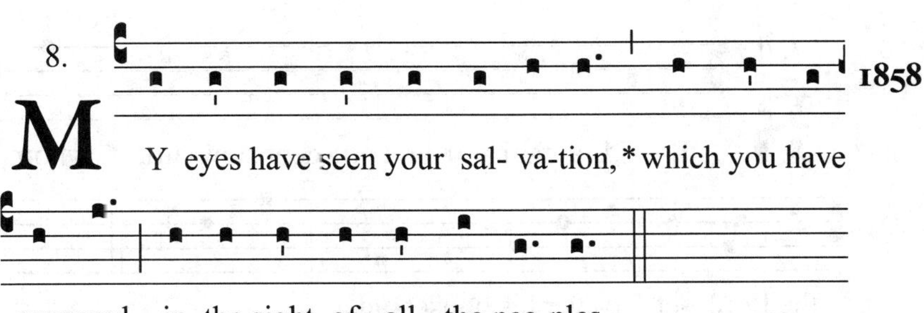

March 19

SAINT JOSEPH, SPOUSE OF THE BLESSED VIRGIN MARY

ENTRANCE ANTIPHON *Ecce, fidelis servus et prudens.*
Lk 12:42

- i -

1859 7. c

BEhold, a faithful * and prudent steward, whom the Lord set over his household.

- ii -

1860 7. d

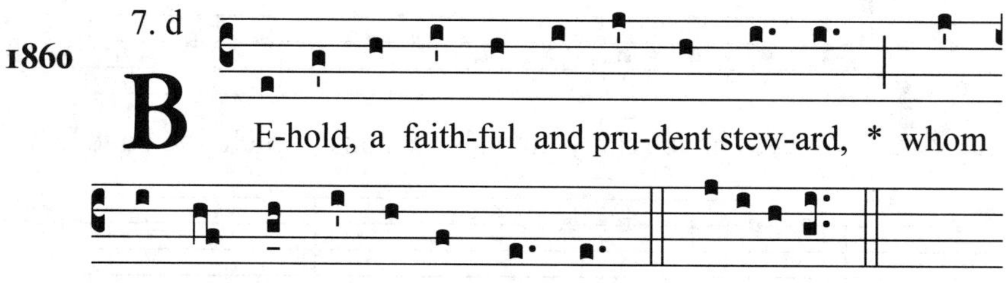
BEhold, a faith-ful and pru-dent stew-ard, * whom
the Lord set o- ver his household.

VERSES *Bonum est confiteri Domino. Ps* 91 : 2-3

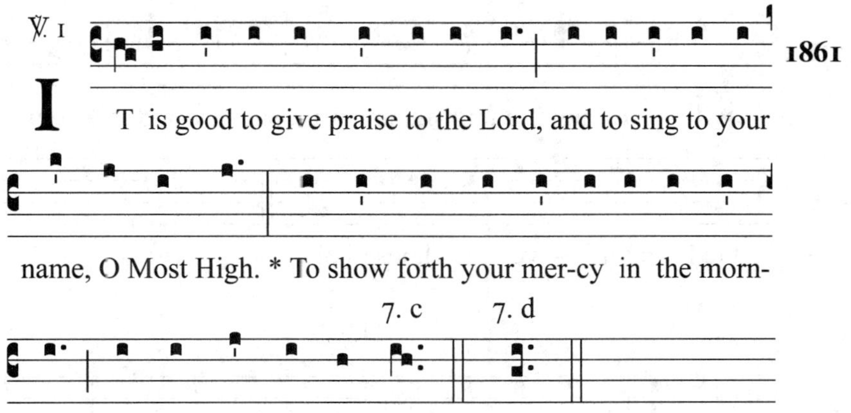
℣. 1
IT is good to give praise to the Lord, and to sing to your
name, O Most High. * To show forth your mer-cy in the morn-
7. c 7. d
ing, and your truth in the night. night.

1861

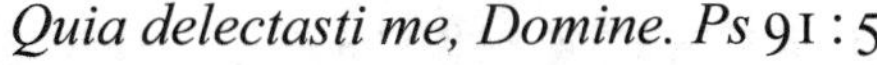
Quia delectasti me, Domine. Ps 91 : 5

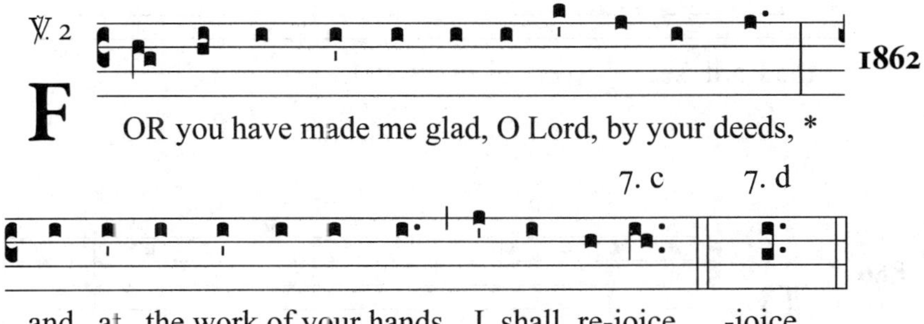
℣. 2
FOR you have made me glad, O Lord, by your deeds, *
7. c 7. d
and at the work of your hands I shall re-joice. -joice.

1862

Iustus ut palma florebit. Ps 91:13

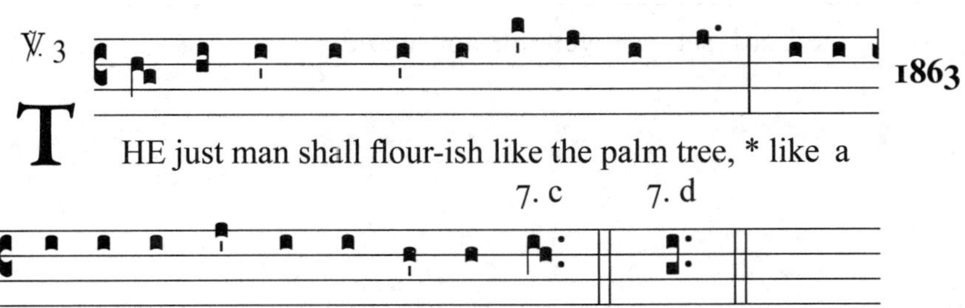
℣. 3
THE just man shall flour-ish like the palm tree, * like a
7. c 7. d
ce- dar of Leb- a- non shall he grow. grow.

1863

- iii -

1864

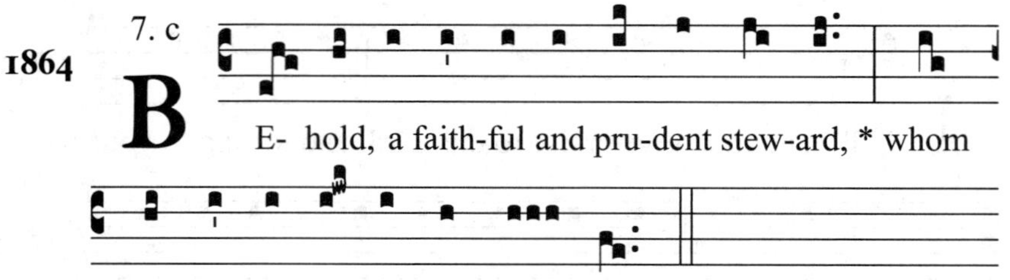
7. c
BEhold, a faith-ful and pru-dent stew-ard, * whom
the Lord set o- ver his house-hold.

Or:

1865

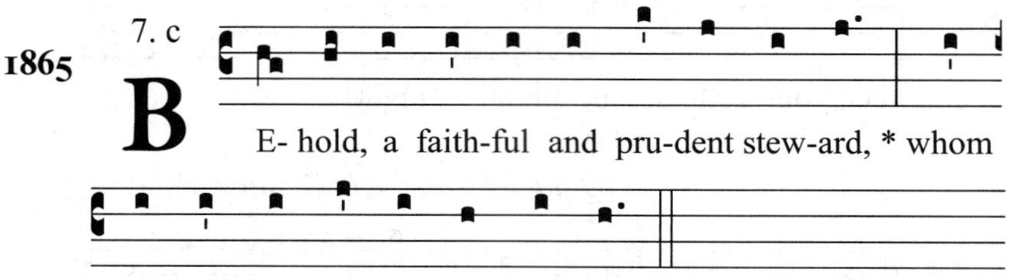
7. c
BEhold, a faith-ful and pru-dent stew-ard, * whom
the Lord set o- ver his household.

- iv -

1866

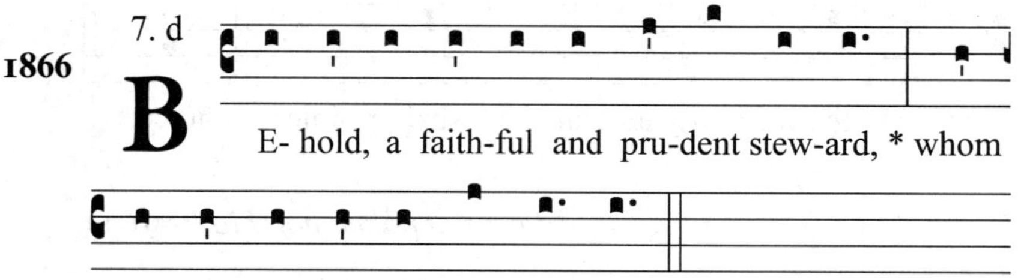
7. d
BEhold, a faith-ful and pru-dent stew-ard, * whom
the Lord set o- ver his household.

OFFERTORY ANTIPHON *Veritas mea.*
Ps 88:25

- i -

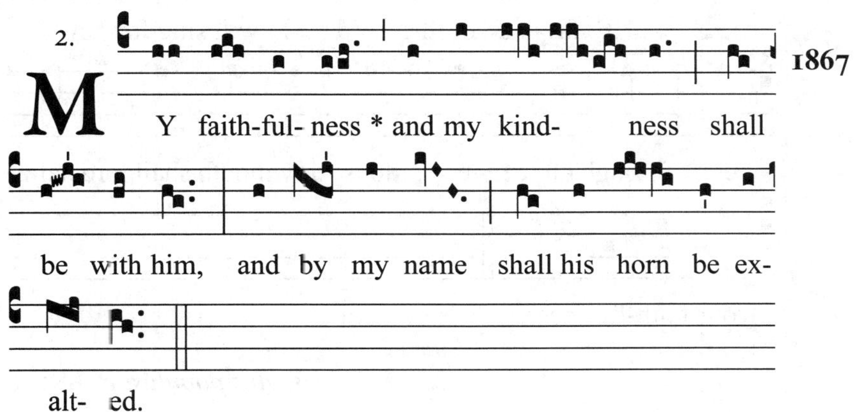
2.
MY faith-ful- ness * and my kind- ness shall
be with him, and by my name shall his horn be ex-
alt- ed.
1867

- ii -

2.
MY faith-ful-ness * and my kindness shall be with
him, and by my name shall his horn be ex- alt- ed.
1868

VERSES *Misericordias Domini. Ps* 88 : 2

1869
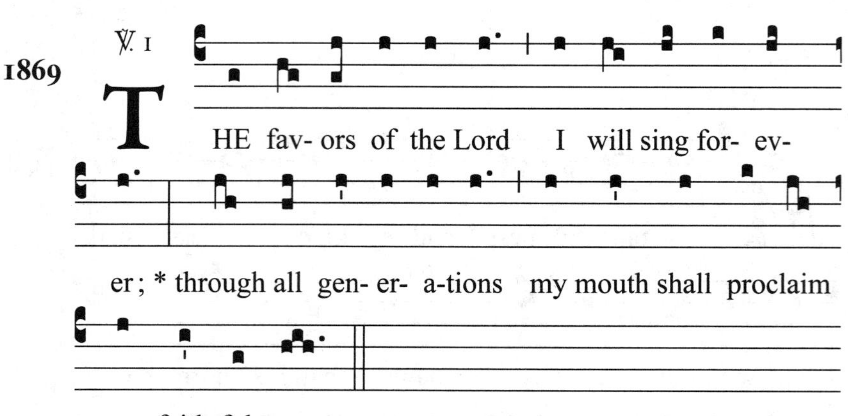
℣. 1
THE favors of the Lord I will sing for- ev-
er; * through all gen- er- a-tions my mouth shall proclaim
your faith-ful- ness.

Beatus populus. Ps 88 : 16

1870
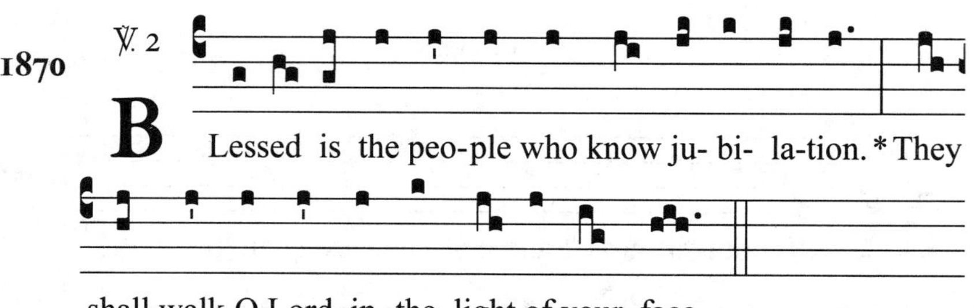
℣. 2
BLessed is the peo-ple who know ju- bi- la-tion. * They
shall walk O Lord, in the light of your face.

Manus autem mea. Ps 88 : 22

1871

℣. 3
THAT my hand may be al-ways with him, * and
that my arm may make him strong.

- iii -

2.
1872
MY faith-ful-ness and my kind-ness shall be with

him, * and by my name shall his horn be ex- alt- ed.

Or:

2.
1873
MY faith-ful-ness and my kind-ness shall be with

him, * and by my name shall his horn be ex- alt- ed.

- iv -

2.
1874
MY faith-ful-ness and my kind-ness * shall be with

him, and by my name shall his horn be ex- alt- ed.

COMMUNION ANTIPHON *Euge, serve bone.*
Mt 25:21

- i -

1875 
7. d
WELL done, * good and faith-ful ser-vant. Come
and share your mas- ter's joy.

- ii -

1876 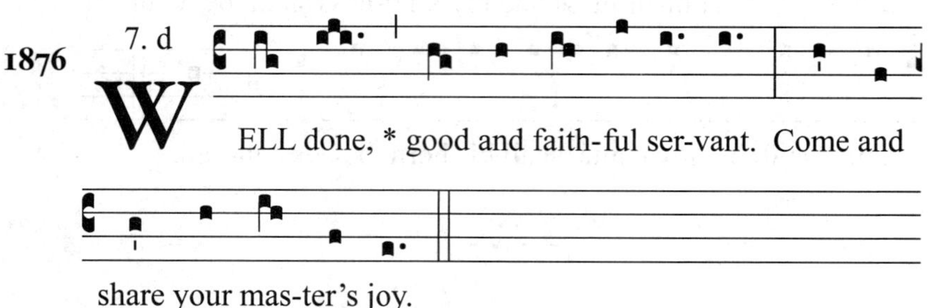
7. d
WELL done, * good and faith-ful ser-vant. Come and
share your mas-ter's joy.

VERSES *Beatus vir qui timet Dominum. Ps* 111:1

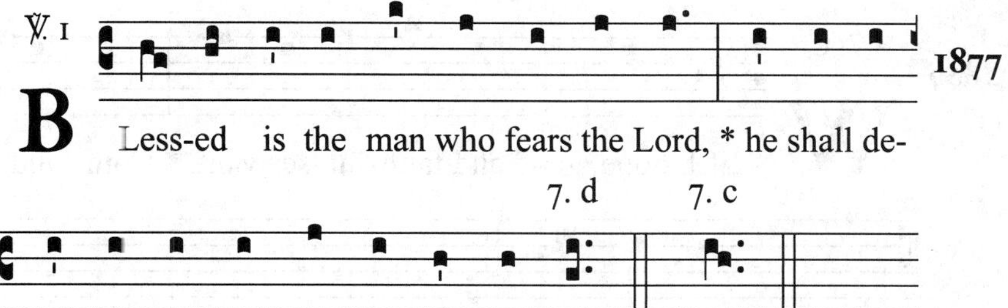
℣. 1
1877
B Less-ed is the man who fears the Lord, * he shall de-
7. d 7. c
light ex-ceed-ing- ly in his commands. -mands.

Exortum est in tenebris. Ps 111:4

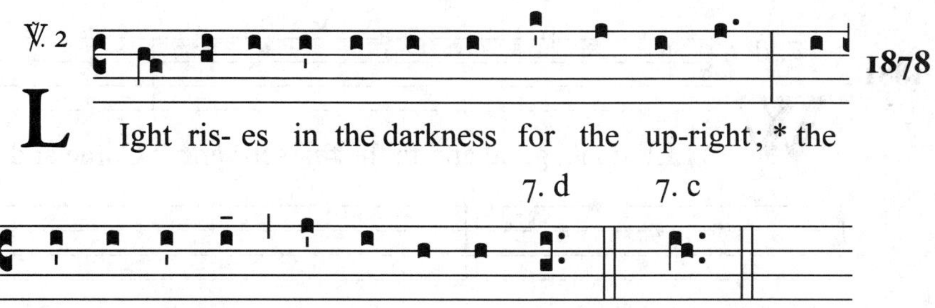
℣. 2
1878
L Ight ris- es in the darkness for the up-right; * the
7. d 7. c
Lord is gracious, mer- ci- ful and just.

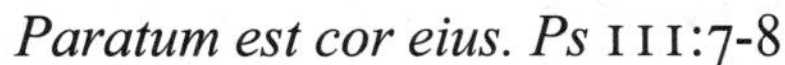

Paratum est cor eius. Ps 111:7-8

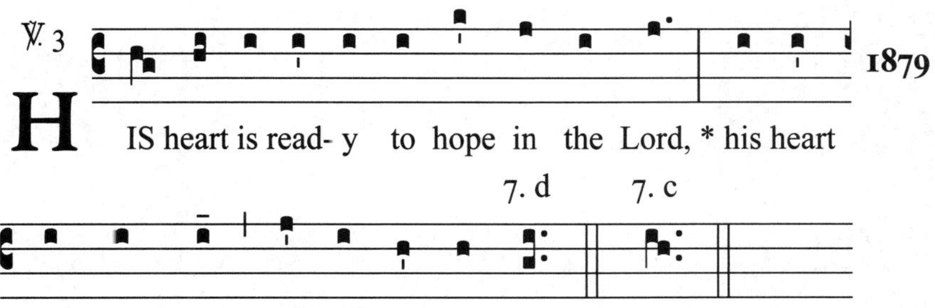
℣. 3
1879
H IS heart is read- y to hope in the Lord, * his heart
7. d 7. c
is strengthened, he shall not be moved. moved

- iii -

1880 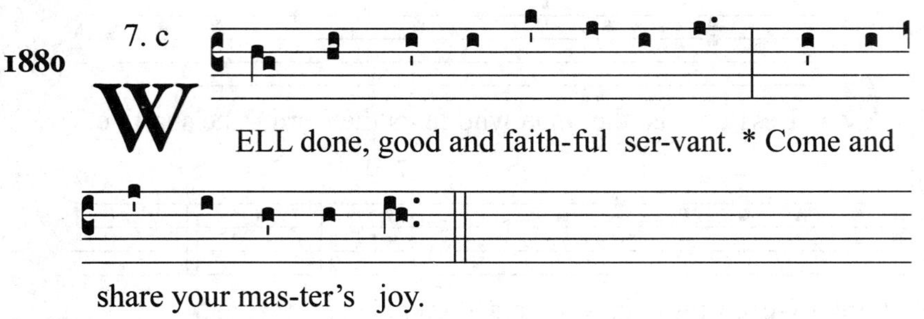
7. c
W ELL done, good and faith-ful ser-vant. * Come and
share your mas-ter's joy.

- iv -

1881 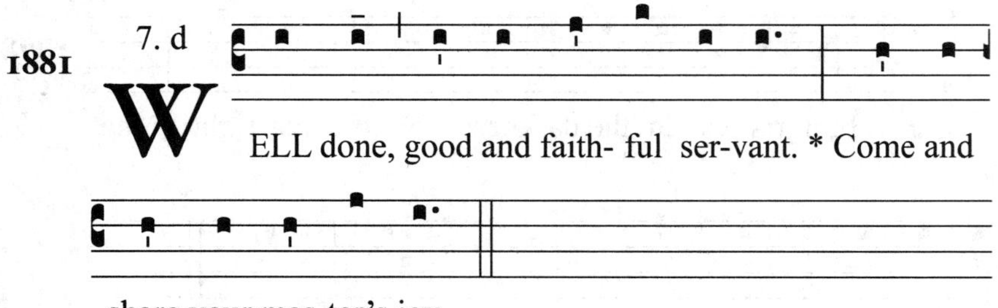
7. d
W ELL done, good and faith- ful ser-vant. * Come and
share your mas-ter's joy.

March 25

THE ANNUNCIATION OF THE LORD

ENTRANCE ANTIPHON *Dominus ingrediens mundum.* *Heb* 10:5. 7

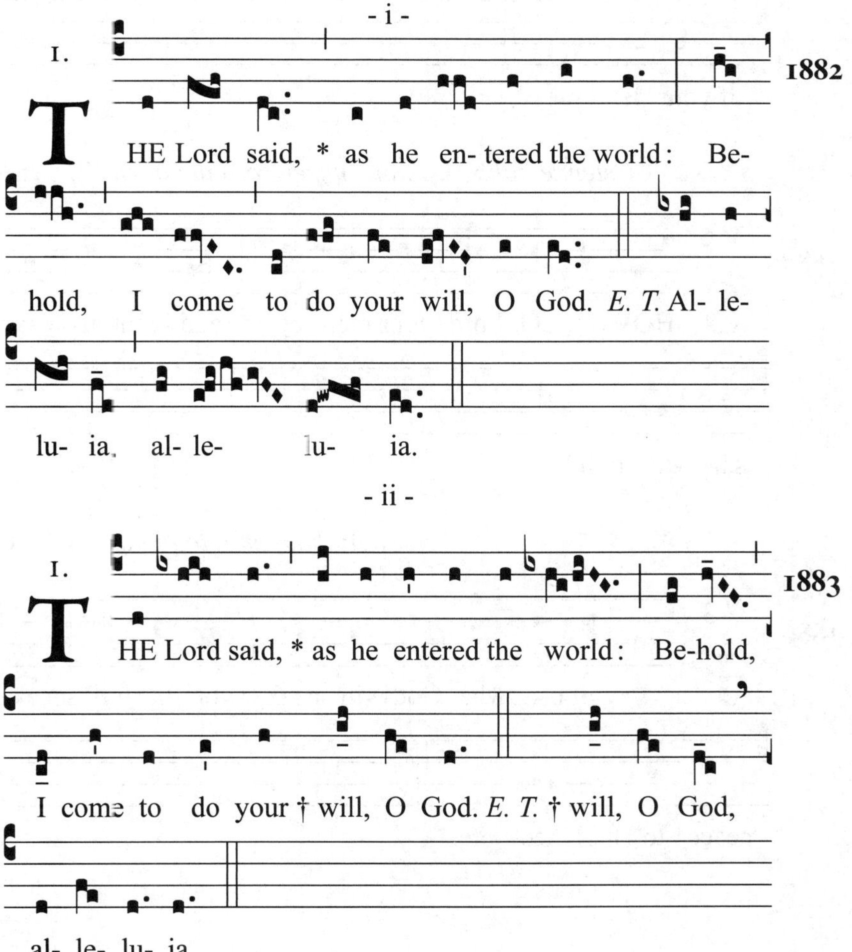

- i -
1.
1882
THE Lord said, * as he en- tered the world: Be-
hold, I come to do your will, O God. E. T. Al- le-
lu- ia, al- le- lu- ia.
- ii -
1.
1883
THE Lord said, * as he entered the world: Be-hold,
I come to do your † will, O God. E. T. † will, O God,
al- le- lu- ia.

VERSES *Benedixisti, Domine, terram tuam. Ps* 84:2. 3

1884

℣. 1
YOU have blessed, O Lord, your land; you have brought
back the captives of Ja- cob. * You have for-giv-en the guilt
of your peo- ple.

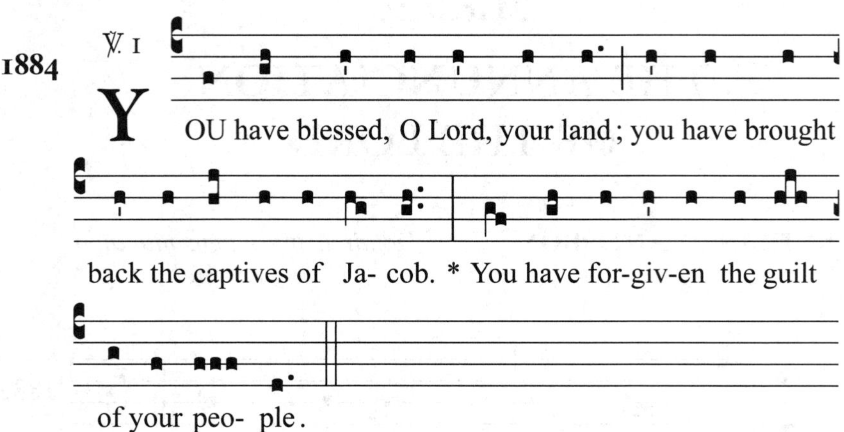

Ostende nobis, Domine, misericordiam tuam. Ps 84:8

1885

℣. 2
SHOW us, O Lord, your mer- cy, * and grant us your
sal- va- tion.

Audiam quid loquatur. Ps 84:9

1886

℣. 3
I will hear what God will speak, * for he will speak
peace to his peo- ple.

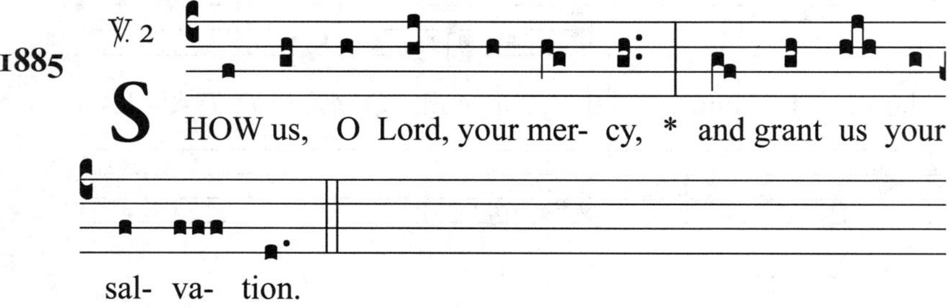

- iii -

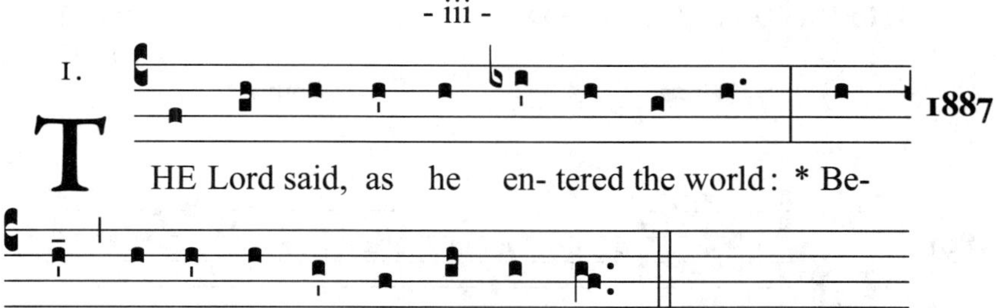
1.
THE Lord said, as he en- tered the world: * Be-
1887

hold, I come to do your will, O God.

Eastertime :

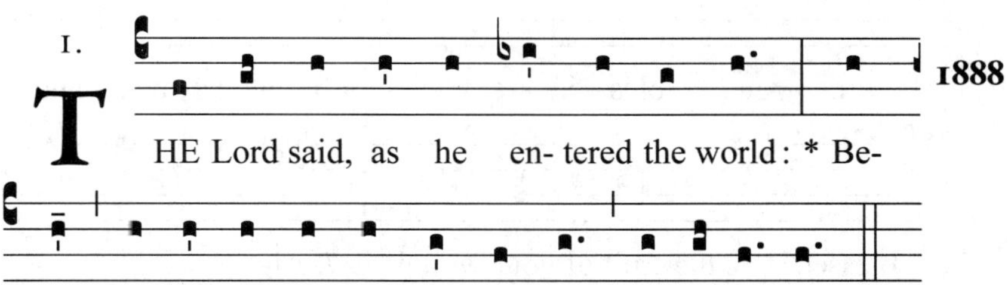
1.
THE Lord said, as he en- tered the world: * Be-
1888

hold, I come to do your will, O God, al- le- lu- ia.

- iv -

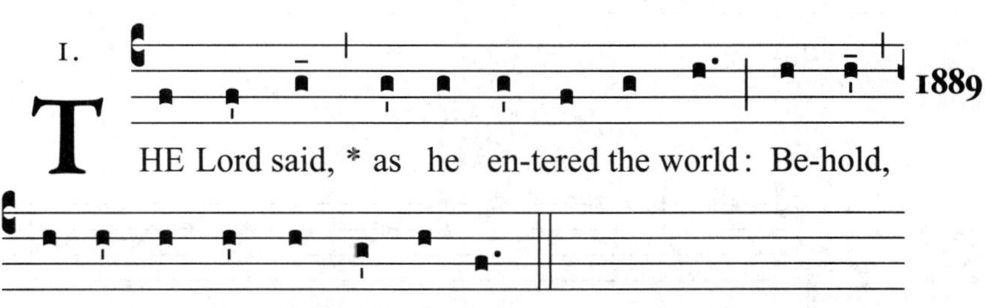
1.
THE Lord said, * as he en-tered the world: Be-hold,
1889

I come to do your will, O God.

Eastertime :

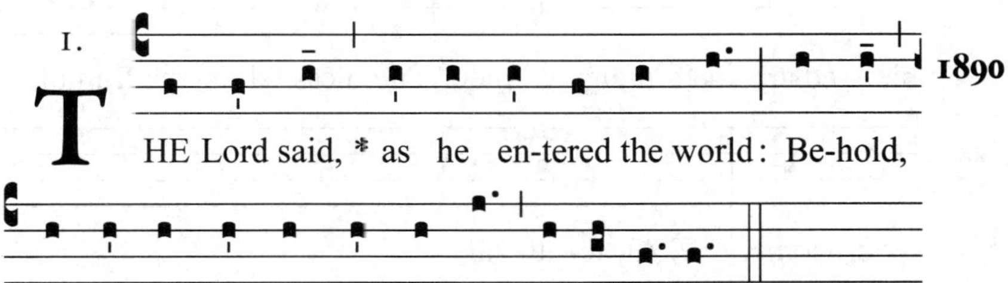
1.
THE Lord said, * as he en-tered the world: Be-hold,
1890

I come to do your will, O God, al- le- lu- ia.

OFFERTORY ANTIPHON *Ave Maria.* *Lk* 1:28. 42

- i -

1891
8.
HAIL, Mar- y, * full of grace ; the Lord is
with you ; bless-ed are you a-mong wo-men, and
blessed is the fruit of your womb. *E. T.* Al- le-
lu- ia.

- ii -

1892
8.
HAIL, Mar- y, * full of grace ; the Lord is with you ;
bless-ed are you a-mong wo-men, and bless-ed is the fruit of
your womb. *E. T.* Al- le- lu- ia.

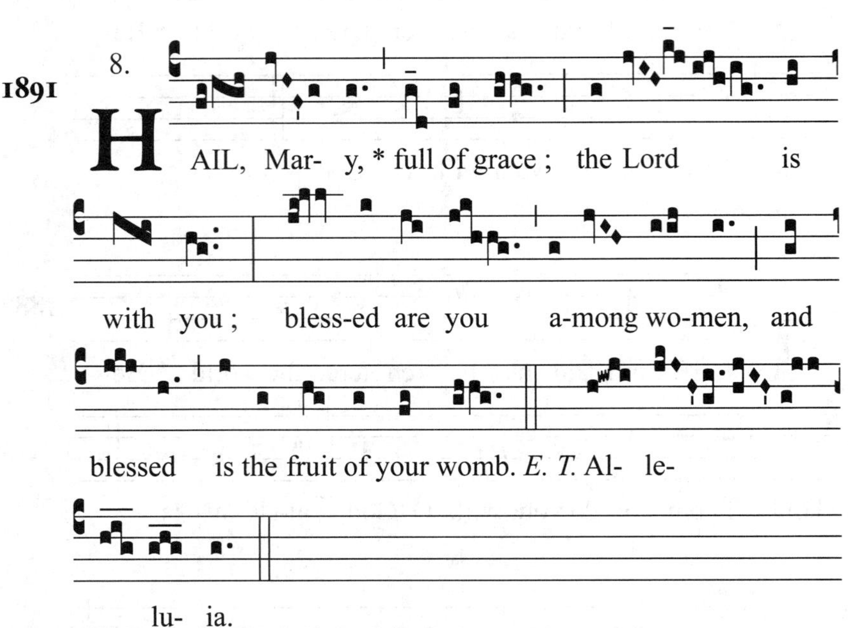

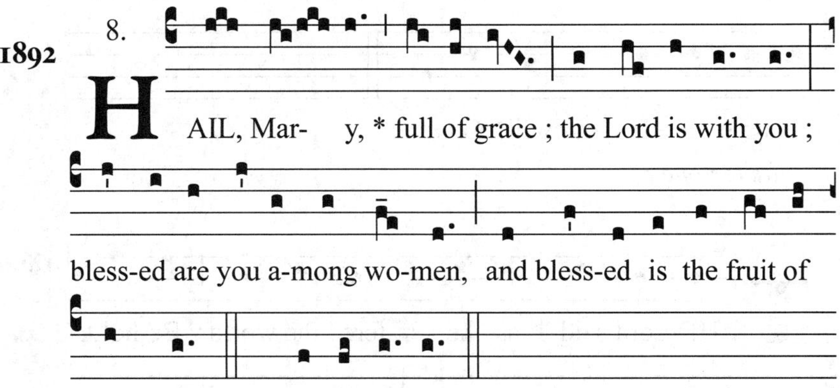

VERSES *Benedixisti, Domine, terram tuam. Ps* 84:2. 3

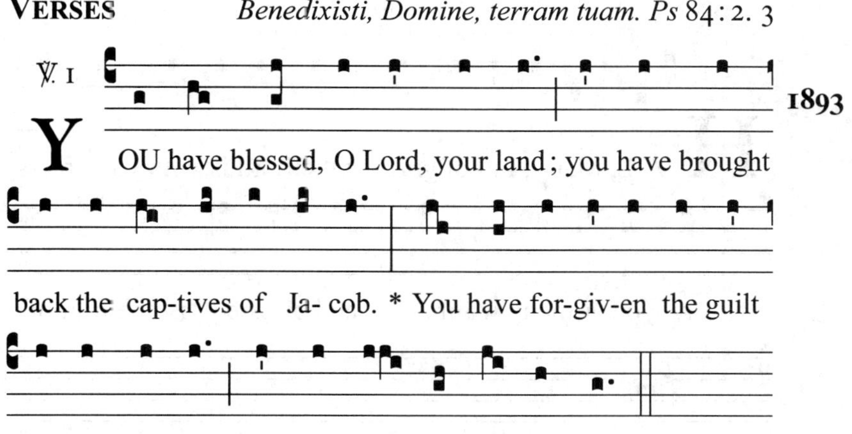

℣. 1
YOU have blessed, O Lord, your land; you have brought
back the cap-tives of Ja- cob. * You have for-giv-en the guilt
of your peo-ple; you have cov-ered all their sins.
1893

Audiam quid loquatur. Ps 84:9

℣. 2
I will hear what God will speak, for he will speak peace
to his people, * and to those who are con-vert-ed to the heart.
1894

Misericordia et veritas. Ps 84:11-12

℣. 3
MEr- cy and truth have met each oth- er ; jus-tice and
peace have kissed. * Truth has sprung out of the earth, and
jus-tice has looked down from heav-en.
1895

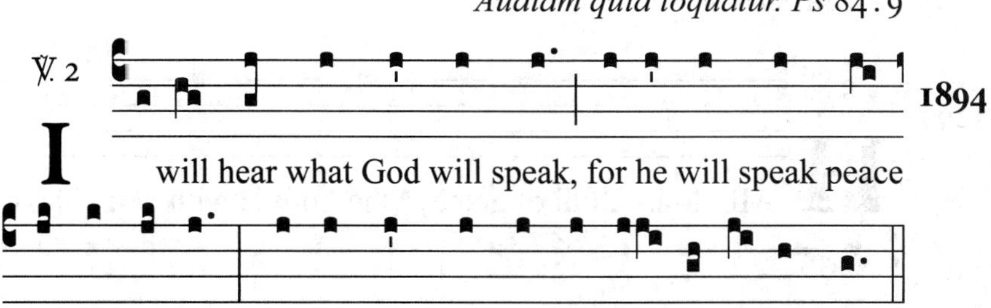

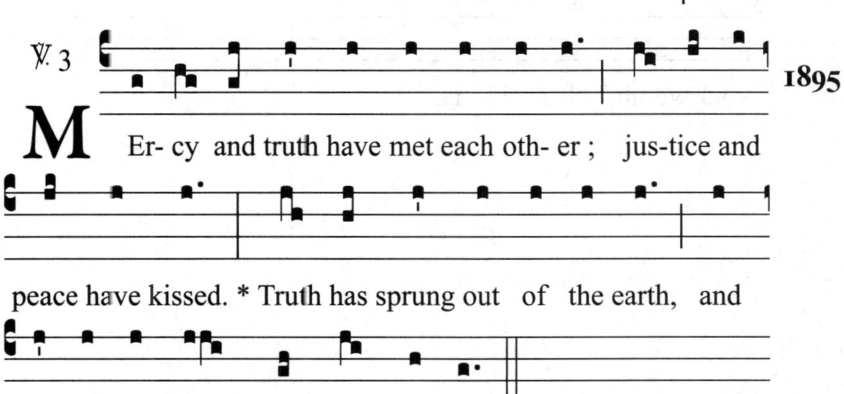

- iii -

1896

8.
HAIL, Mar-y, full of grace ; * the Lord is with you ; bless-
ed are you a-mong wo-men, and bless-ed is the fruit of
your womb.

Eastertime :

1897

8.
HAIL, Mar-y, full of grace ; * the Lord is with you ; bless-
ed are you a-mong wo-men, and bless-ed is the fruit of
your womb, al- le- lu- ia.

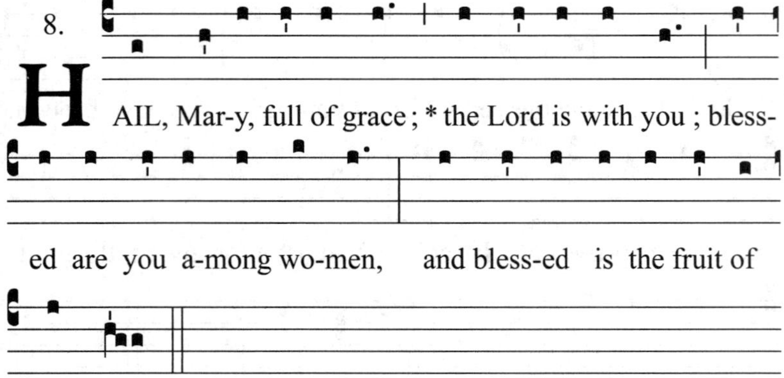

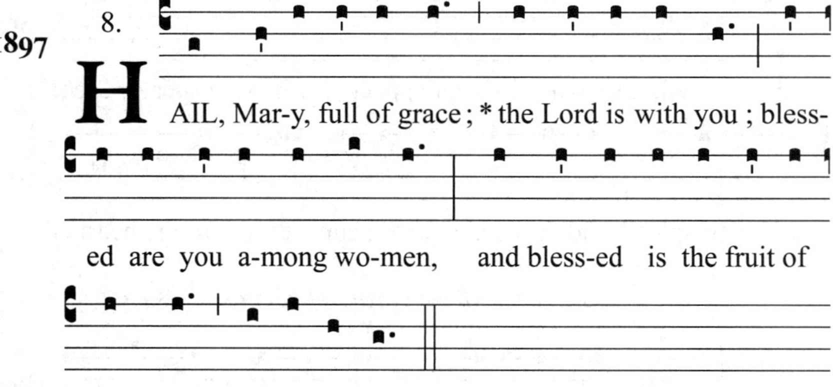

- iv -

8. 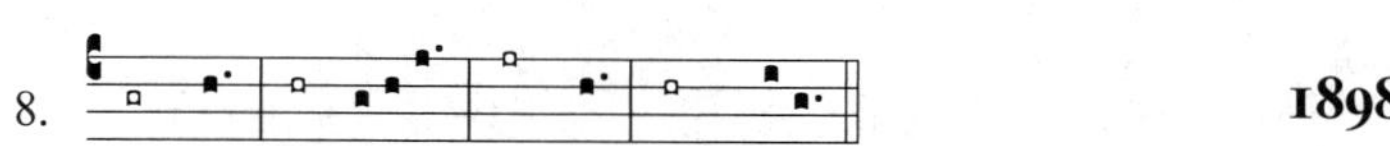 1898

Hail Mary, full of | **grace**, *
the | *Lord is* **with** you;
blessed are you among | **wom**-en,
† and blessed is the fruit of | *your* **womb**.

E. T.: † and blessed is the fruit of your womb, / al- | *le*-**lu**-ia.

COMMUNION ANTIPHON *Ecce, virgo concipiet. Is 7: 14*

- i -

1899

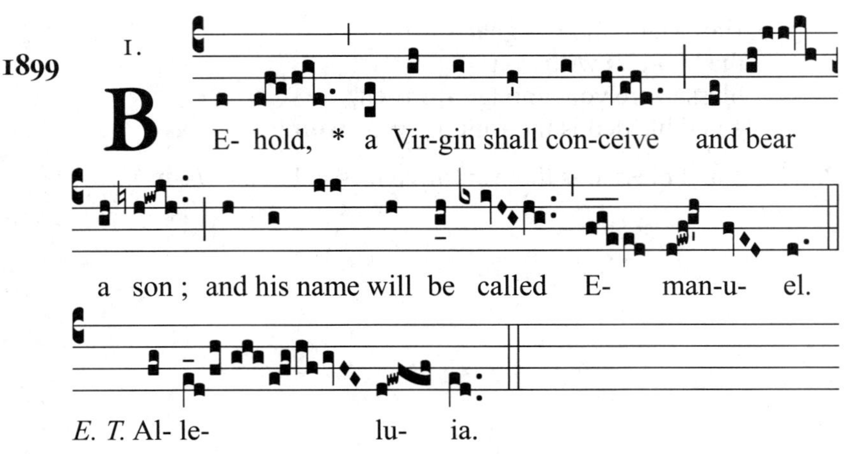
I.
BE- hold, * a Vir-gin shall con-ceive and bear
a son ; and his name will be called E- man-u- el.
E. T. Al- le- lu- ia.

- ii -

1900

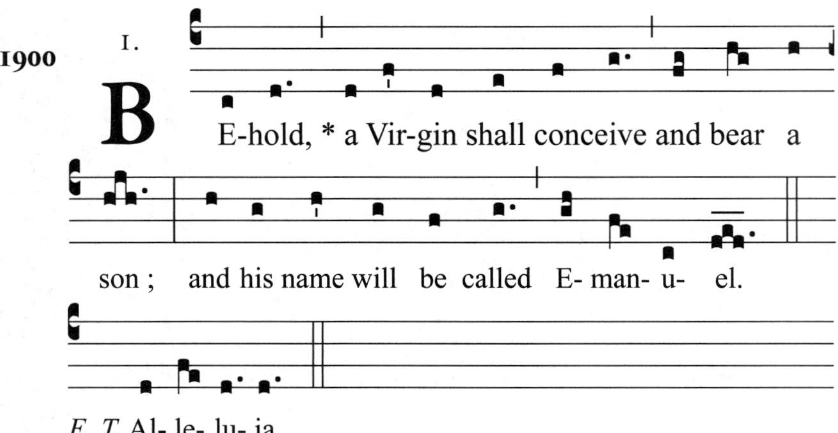
I.
BE-hold, * a Vir-gin shall conceive and bear a
son ; and his name will be called E- man- u- el.
E. T. Al- le- lu- ia.

VERSES

Cæli enarrant gloriam Dei. Ps 18:2

℣. 1
THE heavens show forth the glo- ry of God, * and
the fir-ma-ment de-clares the work of his hands.

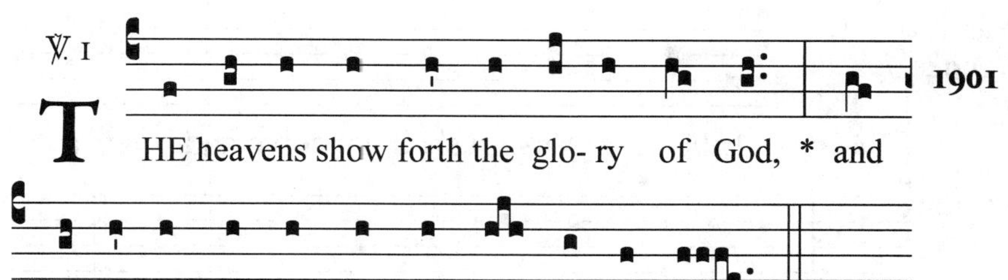

1901

Dies diei eructat verbum. Ps 18:3

℣. 2
DAY un- to day con-veys the mes-sage, * and night
un- to night im-parts know-ledge.

1902

In sole posuit. Ps 18:6

℣. 3
HE has set his tab-er- na-cle in the sun, * and, he
as a bridegroom com-ing out of his brid-al cham-ber.

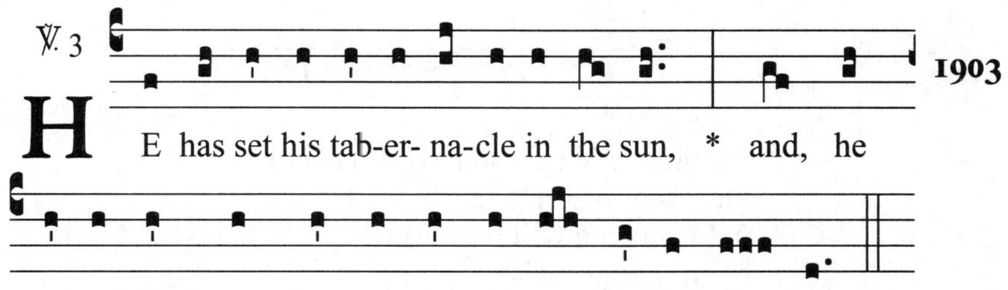

1903

- iii -

1904

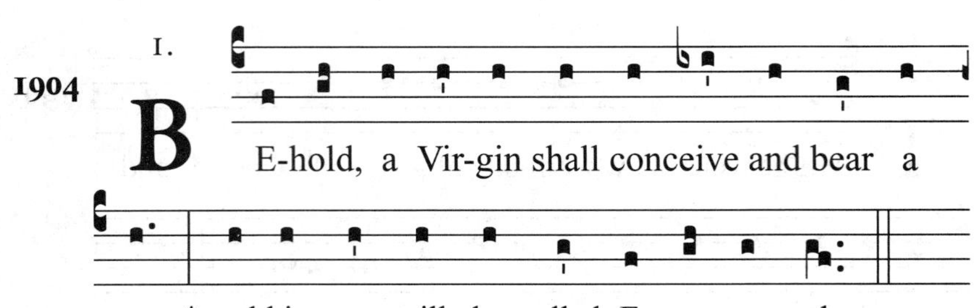
1.
B
E-hold, a Vir-gin shall conceive and bear a

son ; * and his name will be called E- man- u- el.

Eastertime :

1905

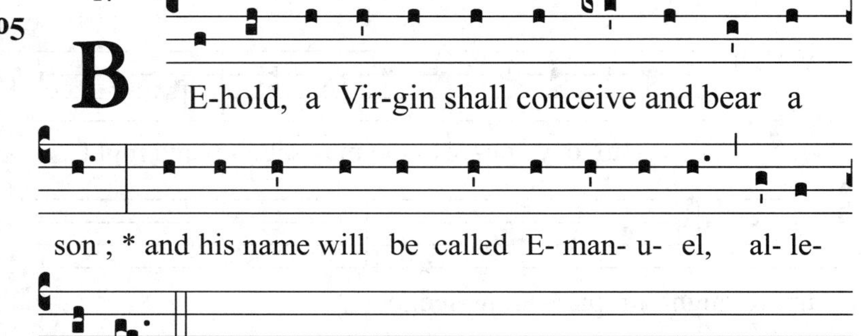
1.
B
E-hold, a Vir-gin shall conceive and bear a
son ; * and his name will be called E- man- u- el, al- le-

lu- ia.

- iv -

1906

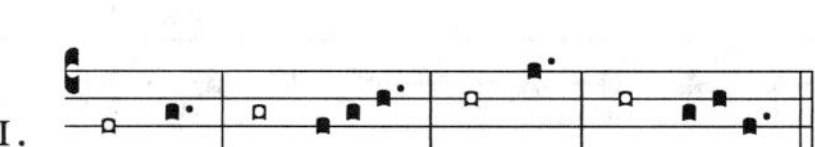
1.

Behold, / a Virgin shall con- | **ceive**
and | *bear a* **son** ;
and his name will be | **called**
† Em- | *man-u*-**el**.

E. T. : † Emmanuel / | *al-le*-**lu**-ia.

June 24

THE NATIVITY OF SAINT JOHN THE BAPTIST

At the Vigil Mass

ENTRANCE ANTIPHON *Hic erat magnus coram Domino.*
Lk 1 : 15. 14

- i -

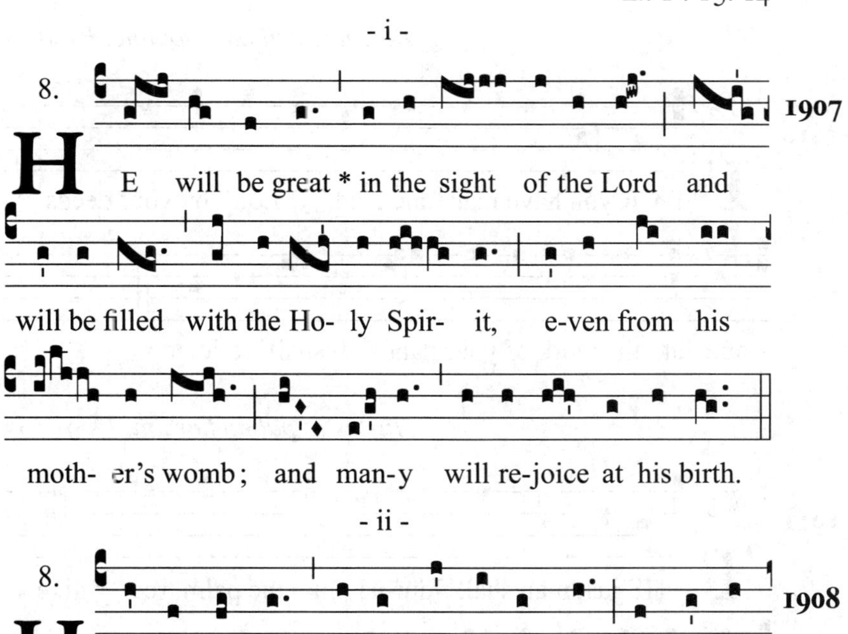
8.
HE will be great * in the sight of the Lord and
will be filled with the Ho- ly Spir- it, e-ven from his
moth- er's womb; and man-y will re-joice at his birth.

1907

- ii -

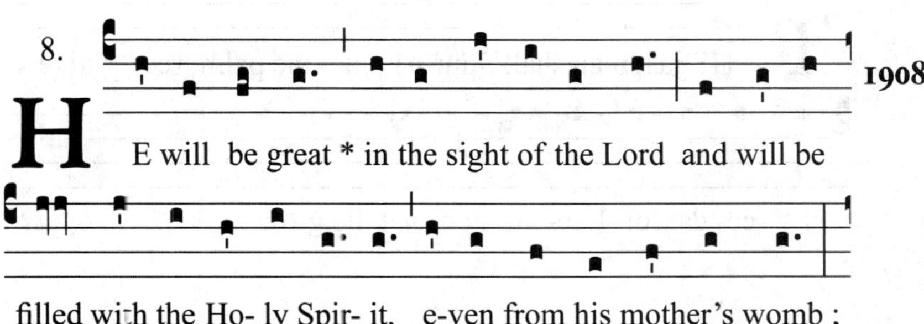
8.
HE will be great * in the sight of the Lord and will be
filled with the Ho- ly Spir- it, e-ven from his mother's womb ;

1908

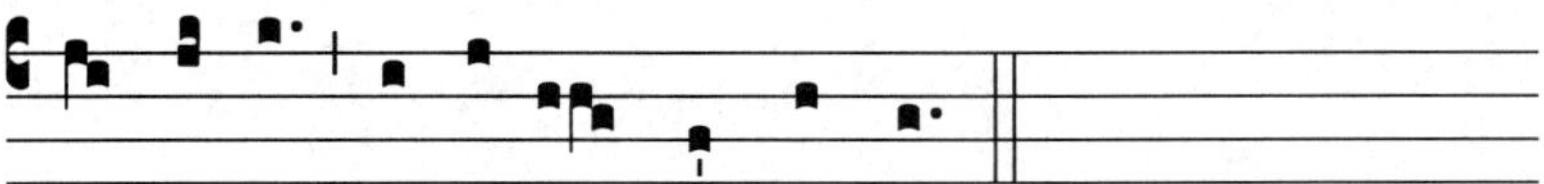
and man-y will re-joice at his birth.

Verses *Bonum est confiteri Domino. Ps* 91 : 2

1909 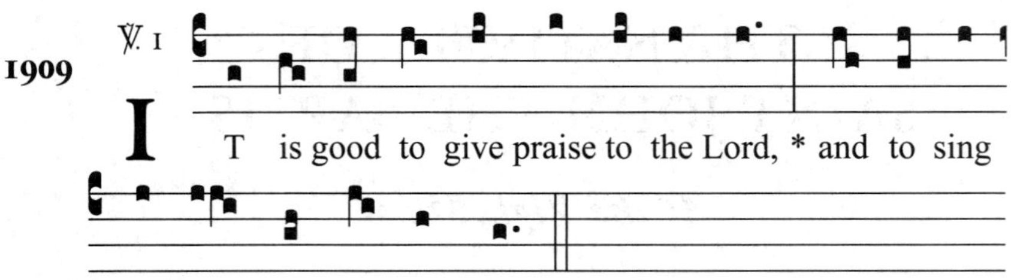
℣. 1
IT is good to give praise to the Lord, * and to sing

to your name, O Most High.

Quia delectasti me, Domine. Ps 91 : 5

1910 
℣. 2
FOR you have made me glad, O Lord, by your deeds, *

and at the work of your hands I shall re-joice.

Iustus ut palma florebit. Ps 91 : 13

1911 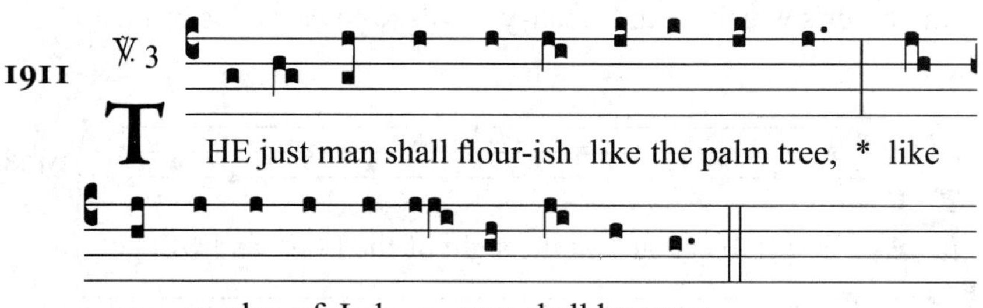
℣. 3
THE just man shall flour-ish like the palm tree, * like

a ce- dar of Leb- a- non shall he grow

- iii -

8.
HE will be great in the sight of the Lord * and will be
filled with the Ho- ly Spir- it, e-ven from his mother's womb ;
and man-y will rejoice at his birth.

1912

- iv -

8.
HE will be great in the sight of the Lord * and will be
filled with the Ho- ly Spir- it, e-ven from his mother's womb;
and man-y will rejoice at his birth.

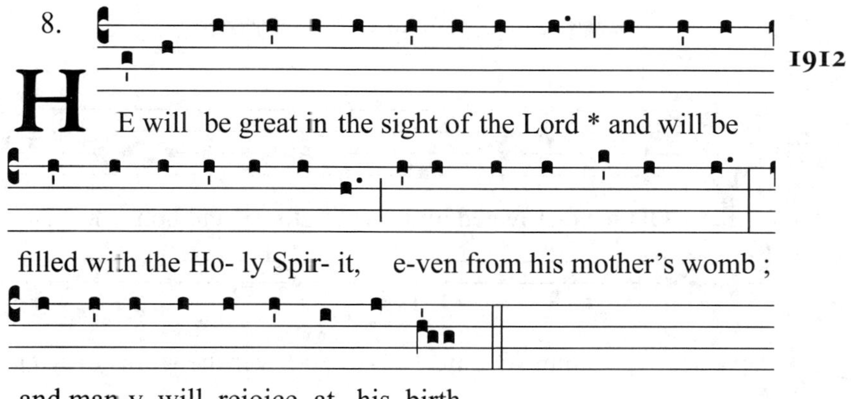

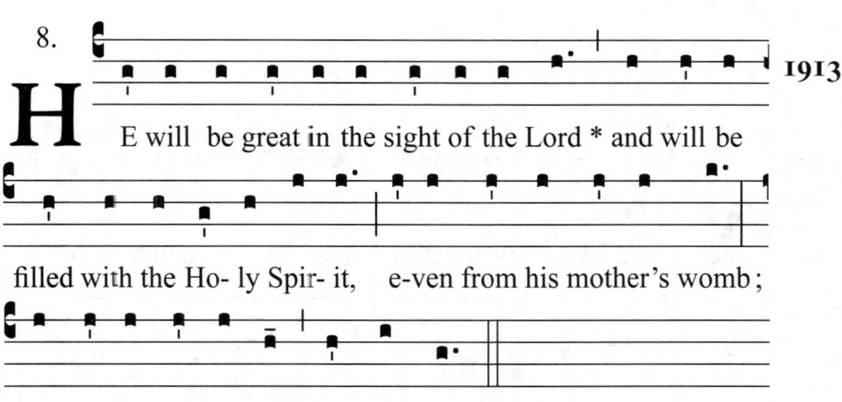

1913

OFFERTORY ANTIPHON *Gloria et honore coronasti eum.*
Ps 8 : 6-7

- i -

1914

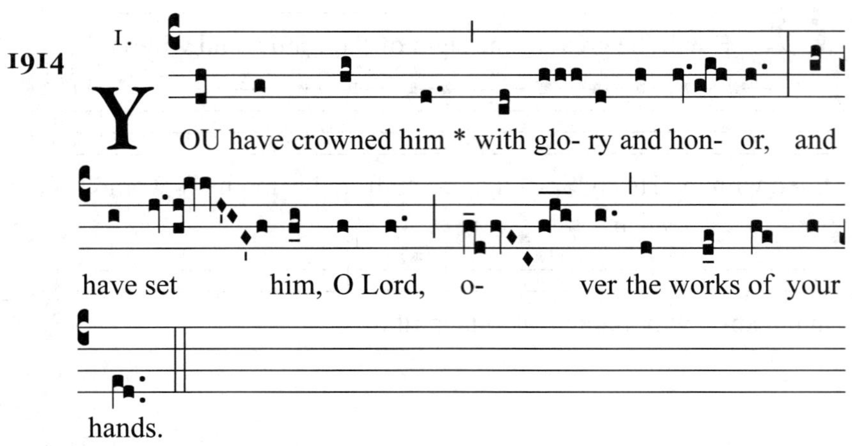
I.
YOU have crowned him * with glo- ry and hon- or, and
have set him, O Lord, o- ver the works of your
hands.

- ii -

1915

I.
YOU have crowned him * with glo- ry and hon- or,
and have set him, O Lord, o- ver the works of your hands.

VERSES *Domine, Dominus noster. Ps* 8:2

℣. 1

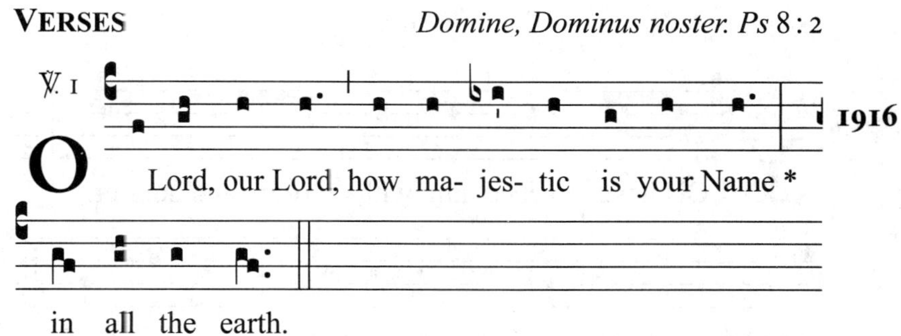

O Lord, our Lord, how ma- jes- tic is your Name * 1916

in all the earth.

Quia est homo, quod memor es eius? Ps 8:5

℣. 2

WHAT is man that you should be mind-ful of him, * 1917

or the son of man, that you should care for him?

Minuisti eum paulo minus ab angelis. Ps 8:6

℣. 3

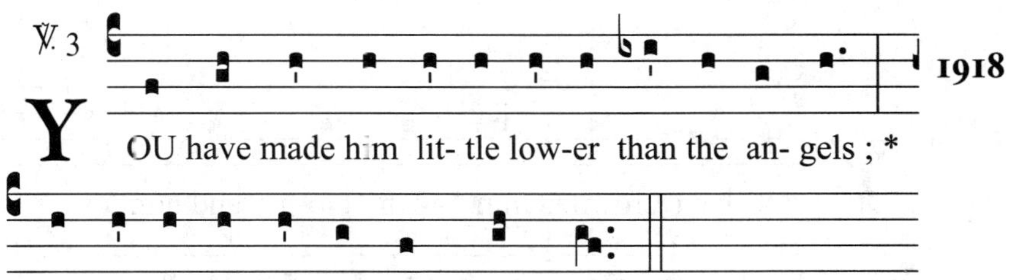

YOU have made him lit- tle low-er than the an- gels; * 1918

with glo- ry and hon- or you crowned him.

- iii -

1919

I.
YOU have crowned him with glo- ry and hon- or, *
and have set him, O Lord, o- ver the works of your hands.

Or:

1920

I.
YOU have crowned him with glo- ry and hon- or, *
and have set him, O Lord, o- ver the works of your hands.

- iv -

1921

I.
YOU have crowned him * with glo- ry and hon- or,
and have set him, O Lord, o- ver the works of your hands.

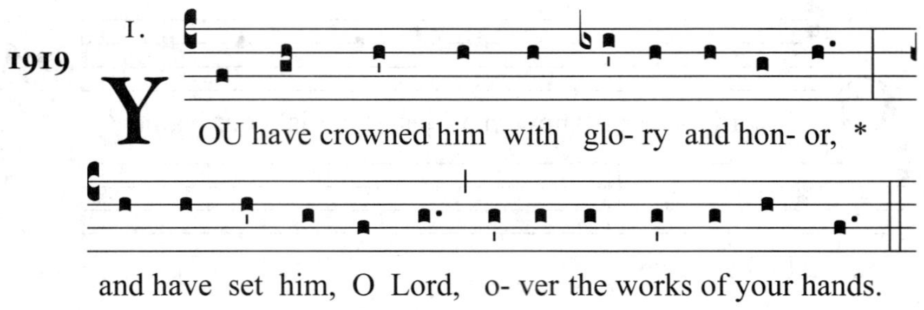

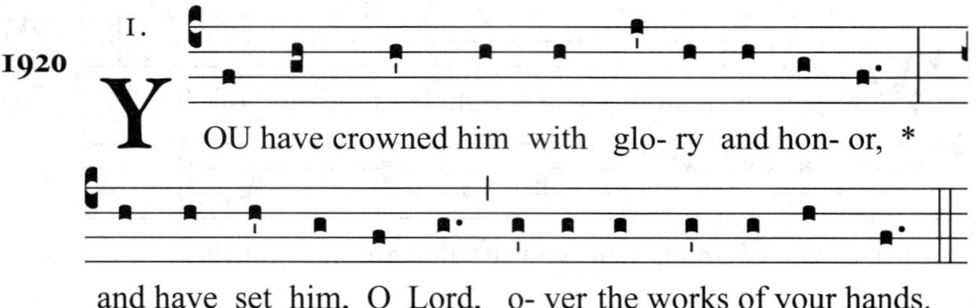

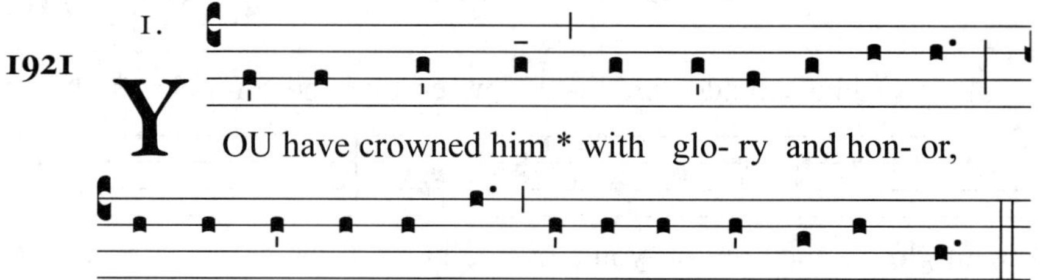

COMMUNION ANTIPHON *Benedictus Dominus Deus Israel.* *Lk* 1 : 68

- i -

6.
1922
BLESS-ed be * the Lord, the God of Is- ra- el !
He has vis- it- ed his peo- ple and redeemed them.

- ii -

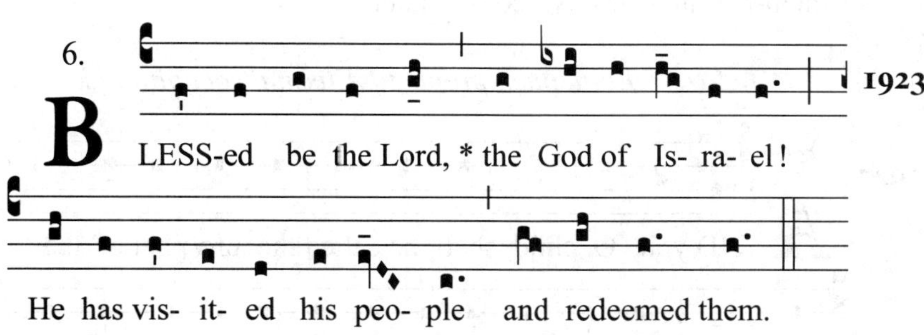
6.
1923
BLESS-ed be the Lord, * the God of Is- ra- el !
He has vis- it- ed his peo- ple and redeemed them.

VERSES *Et erexit cornu salutis nobis. Lk* 1 : 69

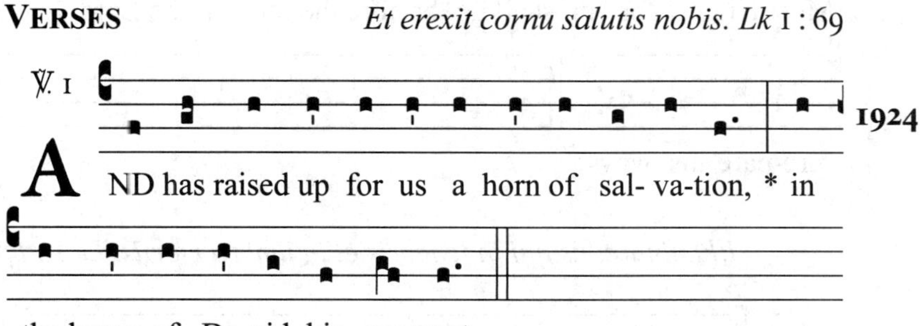
℣. 1
1924
AND has raised up for us a horn of sal- va-tion, * in
the house of Da-vid his ser-vant.

Sicut locutus est per os sanctorum. Lk 1 : 70

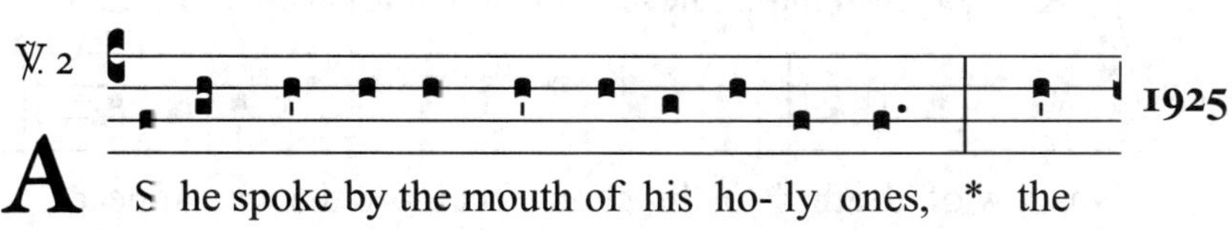
℣. 2
1925
AS he spoke by the mouth of his ho- ly ones, * the

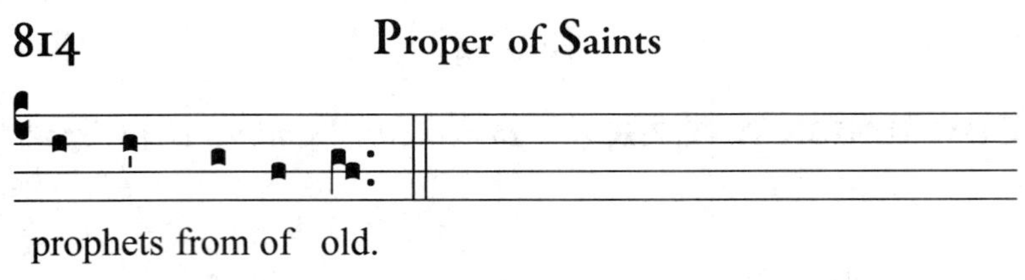
prophets from of old.

Ad faciendam misericordiam cum patribus nostris. Lk 1 : 72

1926
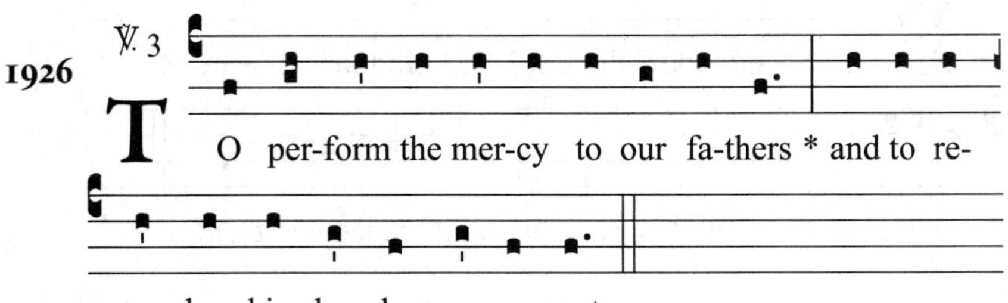
℣. 3
TO per-form the mer-cy to our fa-thers * and to re-
mem-ber his ho- ly cov- e- nant,

Et tu, puer, propheta Altissimi vocabitur. Lk 1 : 76

1927
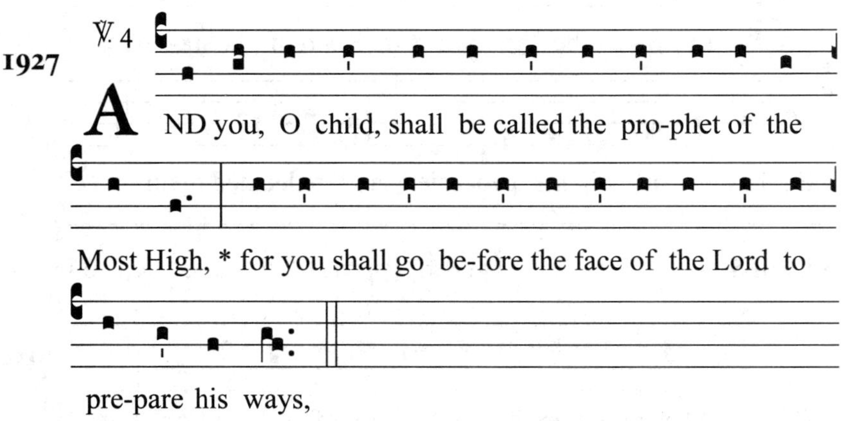
℣. 4
AND you, O child, shall be called the pro-phet of the
Most High, * for you shall go be-fore the face of the Lord to
pre-pare his ways,

Illuminare his qui in tenebris et in umbra mortis. Lk 1 : 79

1928
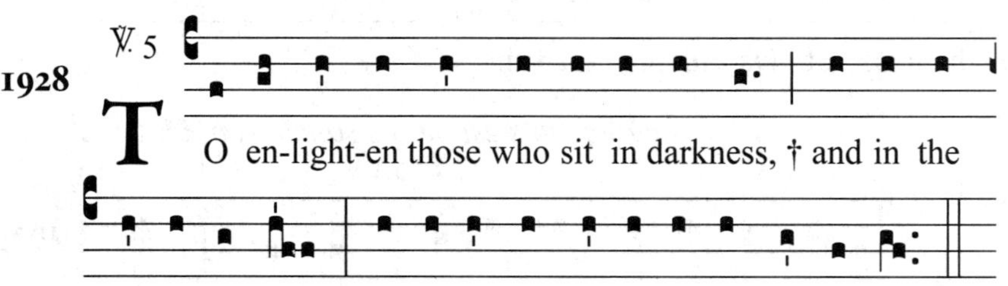
℣. 5
TO en-light-en those who sit in darkness, † and in the
shadow of death, * to direct our feet in- to the way of peace.

- iii -

6.
BLESS-ed be the Lord, the God of Is- ra- el ! *
1929

He has vis- it- ed his peo- ple and redeemed them.

Or:

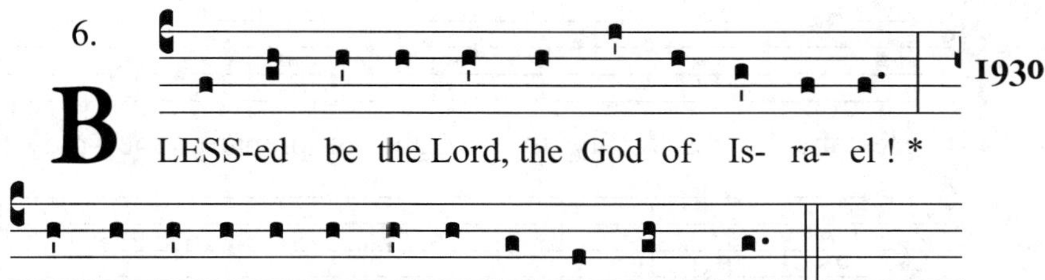
6.
BLESS-ed be the Lord, the God of Is- ra- el ! *
1930

He has vis- it- ed his peo- ple and redeemed them.

- iv -

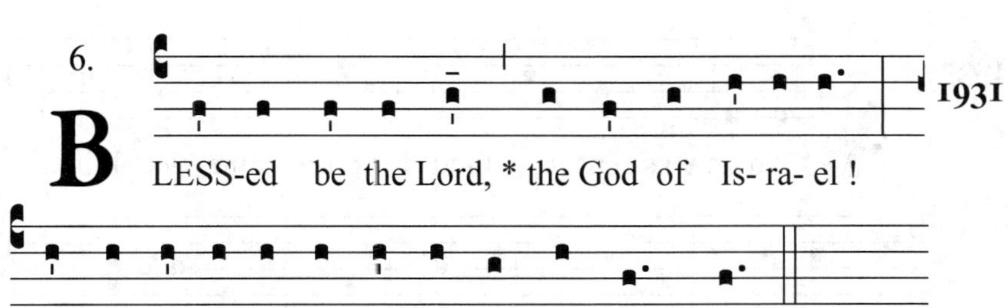
6.
BLESS-ed be the Lord, * the God of Is- ra- el !
1931

He has vis- it- ed his peo- ple and redeemed them.

At the Mass during the Day

Entrance Antiphon *Fuit homo missus a Deo.*
Jn 1:6-7; *Lk* 1:17

- i -

1932
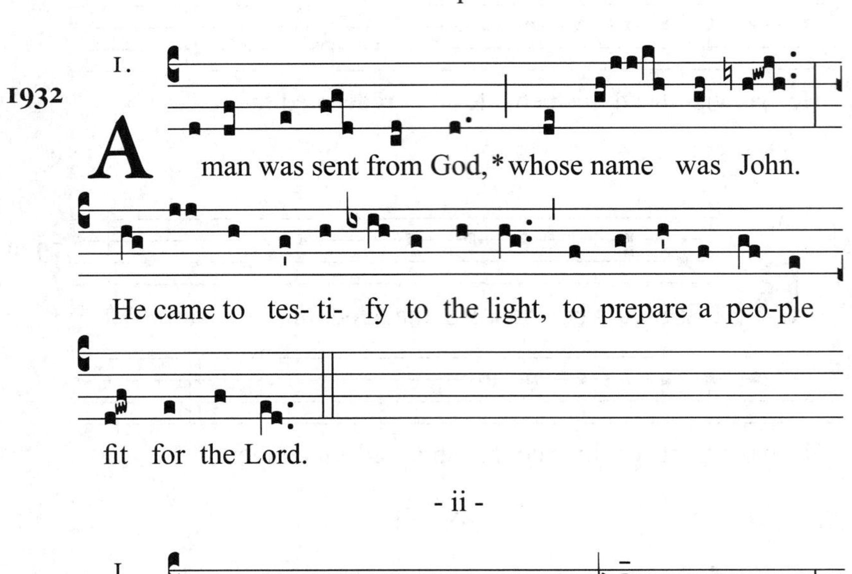
I.
A man was sent from God, * whose name was John.
He came to tes- ti- fy to the light, to prepare a peo-ple
fit for the Lord.

- ii -

1933
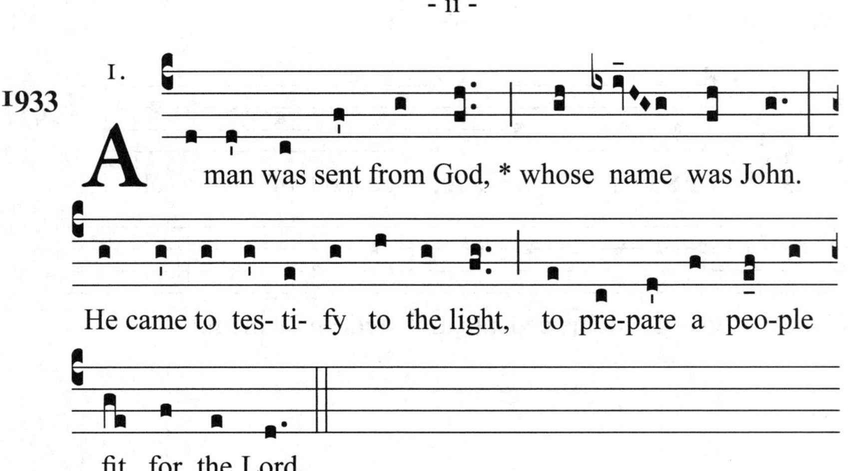
I.
A man was sent from God, * whose name was John.
He came to tes- ti- fy to the light, to pre-pare a peo-ple
fit for the Lord.

VERSES *Bonum est confiteri Domino. Ps* 91 : 2

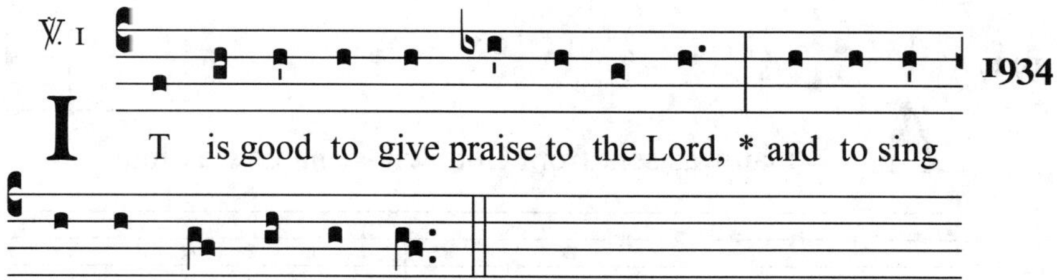
℣. 1
IT is good to give praise to the Lord, * and to sing
to your name, O Most High.
1934

Quia delectasti me, Domine. Ps 91 : 5

℣. 2
FOR by your deeds, O Lord, you have made me glad, *
and at the work of your hands I shall re- joice.
1935

Iustus ut palma florebit. Ps 91 : 13

℣. 3
THE just man shall flour-ish like the palm tree, * like
a ce- dar of Leb- a- non shall he grow
1936

- iii -

1937

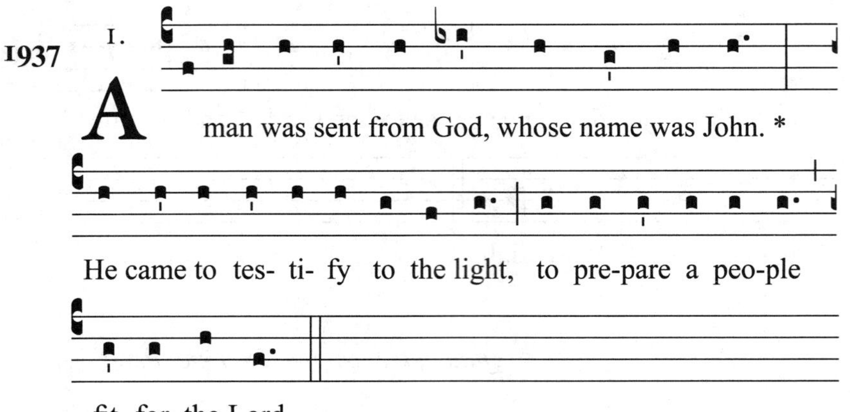
I.
A man was sent from God, whose name was John. *
He came to tes- ti- fy to the light, to pre-pare a peo-ple
fit for the Lord.

- iv -

1938

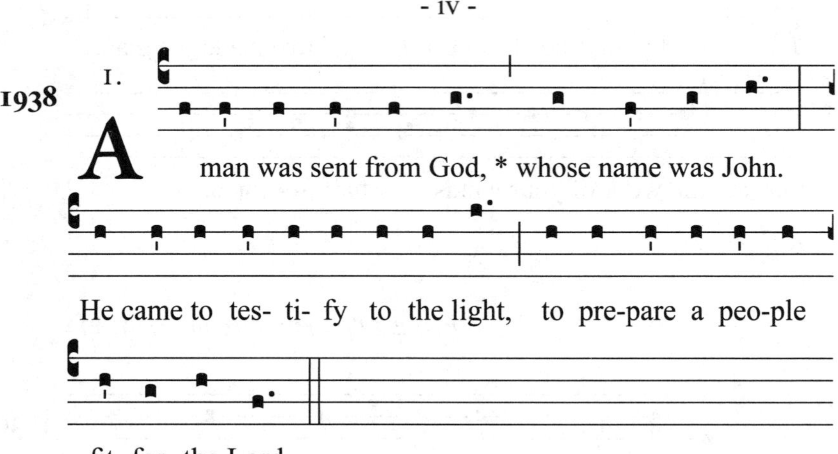
I.
A man was sent from God, * whose name was John.
He came to tes- ti- fy to the light, to pre-pare a peo-ple
fit for the Lord.

OFFERTORY ANTIPHON *Iustus ut palma florebit.*
Ps 91:13

- i -

1.
1939
THE just man shall flourish * like the palm tree, like a

ce-dar of Leb-a- non shall he grow.

- ii -

1.
1940
THE just man shall flourish like the palm tree, * like a
ce- dar of Leb- a- non shall he grow.

VERSES *Bonum est confiteri Domino. Ps* 91 : 2

1941

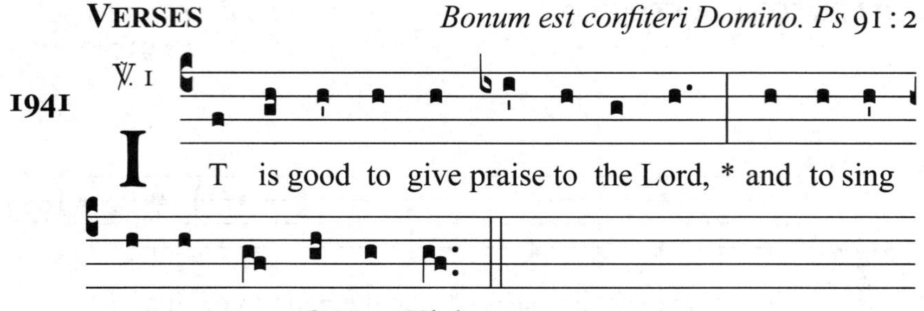
℣. 1
IT is good to give praise to the Lord, * and to sing
to your name, O Most High.

Quia delectasti me, Domine. Ps 91 : 5

1942

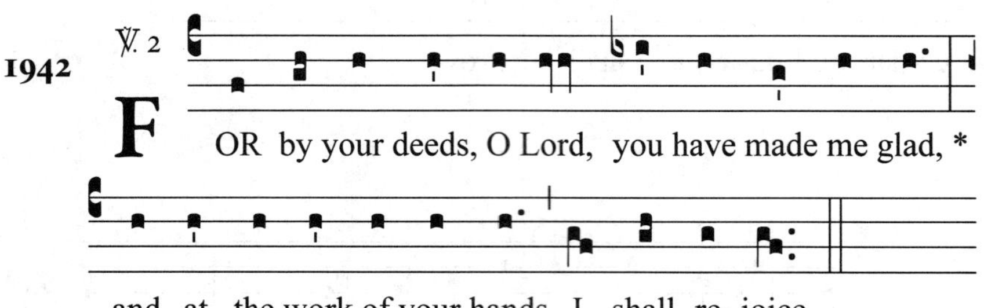
℣. 2
FOR by your deeds, O Lord, you have made me glad, *
and at the work of your hands I shall re- joice.

Plantati in domo Domini. Ps 91 : 14

1943

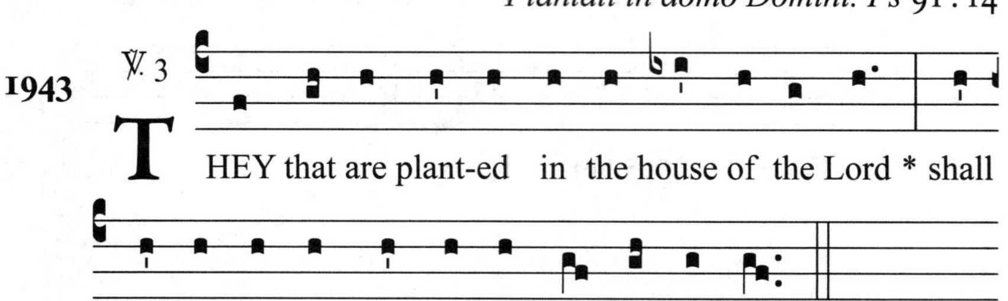
℣. 3
THEY that are plant-ed in the house of the Lord * shall
flour-ish in the courts of the house of our God.

- iii -

I.
THE just man shall flour-ish like the palm tree, * like a
1944

ce-dar of Leb- a- non shall he grow.

Or:

I.
THE just man shall flour-ish like the palm tree, * like a
1945

ce-dar of Leb- a- non shall he grow.

- iv -

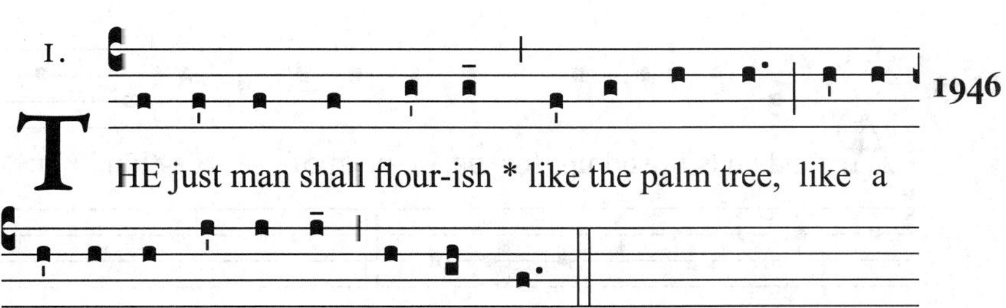
I.
THE just man shall flour-ish * like the palm tree, like a
1946

ce-dar of Leb- a- non shall he grow.

COMMUNION ANTIPHON *Per viscera misericordiæ Dei nostri. Lk* 1:78

- i -

1947
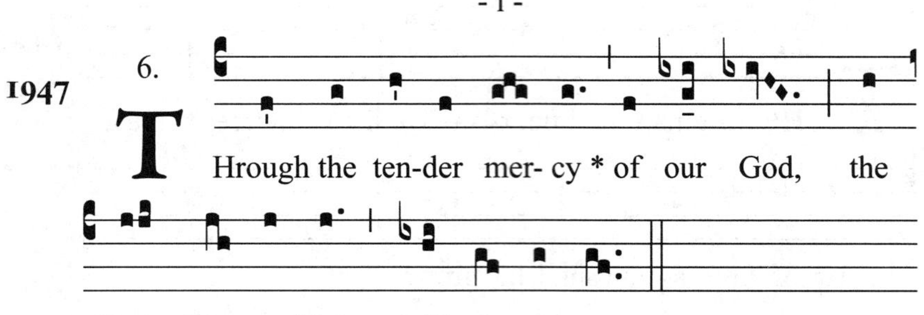
6.
THrough the ten-der mer- cy * of our God, the
Dawn from on high will vis- it us.

- ii -

1948
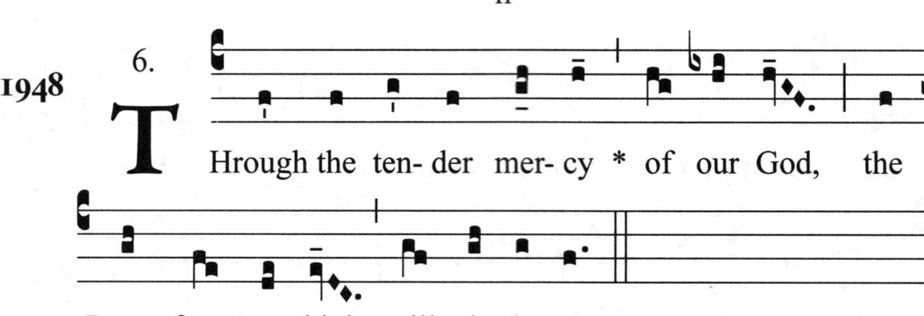
6.
THrough the ten- der mer- cy * of our God, the
Dawn from on high will vis- it us.

VERSES *Et erexit cornu salutis nobis. Lk* 1:69

1949
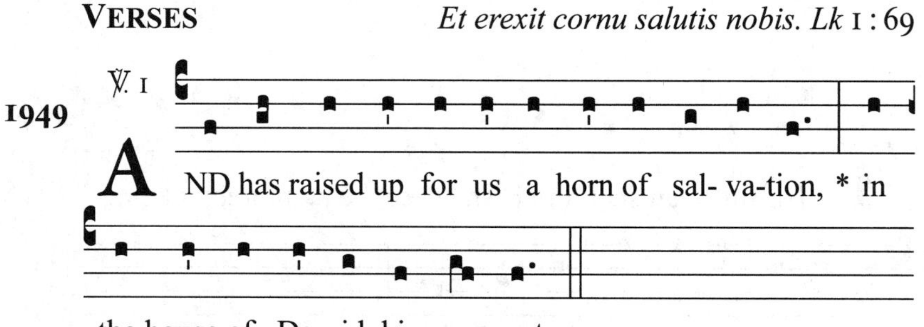
℣. 1
AND has raised up for us a horn of sal- va-tion, * in
the house of Da-vid his ser-vant.

Sicut locutus est per os sanctorum. Lk 1:70

1950
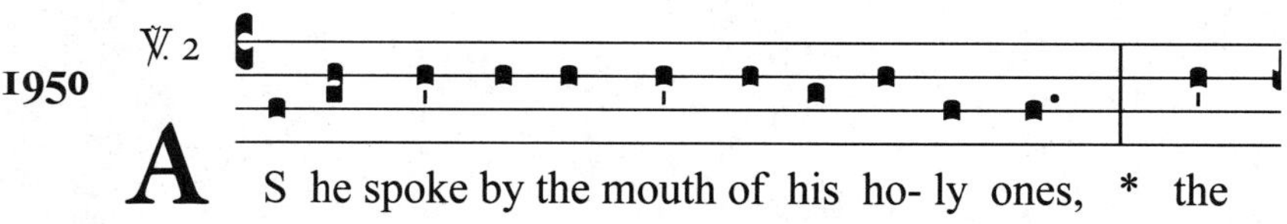
℣. 2
AS he spoke by the mouth of his ho- ly ones, * the

prophets from of old.

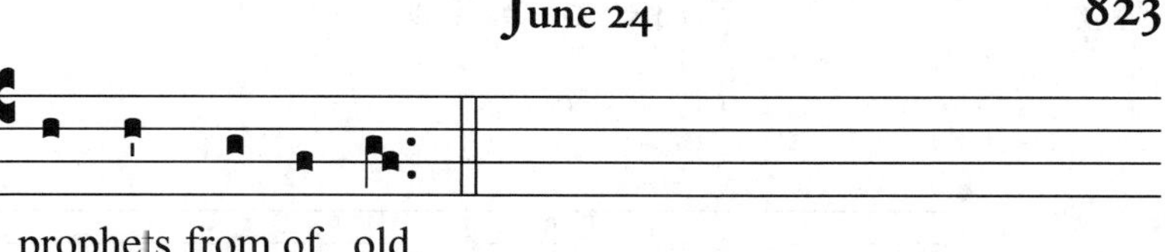

Ad faciendam misericordiam cum patribus nostris. Lk 1 : 72

℣. 3
TO per-form the mer-cy to our fa-thers * and to re- 1951
mem-ber his ho- ly cov- e- nant,

Et tu, puer, propheta Altissimi vocabitur. Lk 1 : 76

℣. 4
AND you, O child, shall be called the proph-et of the 1952
Most High, * for you shall go be-fore the face of the Lord to
pre-pare his ways,

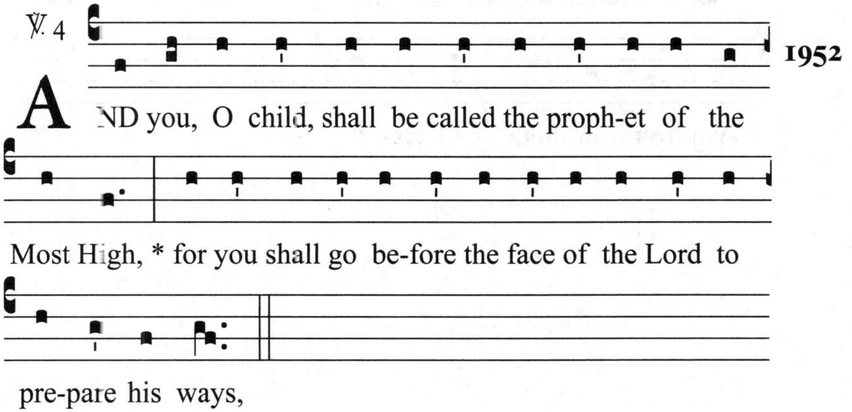

Illuminare his qui in tenebris et in umbra mortis. Lk 1 : 79

℣. 5
TO en-light-en those who sit in darkness, † and in the 1953
shadow of death, * to direct our feet in- to the way of peace.

- iii -

1954

6.
THrough the ten- der mer- cy of our God, * the
Dawn from on high will vis- it us.

- iv -

1955

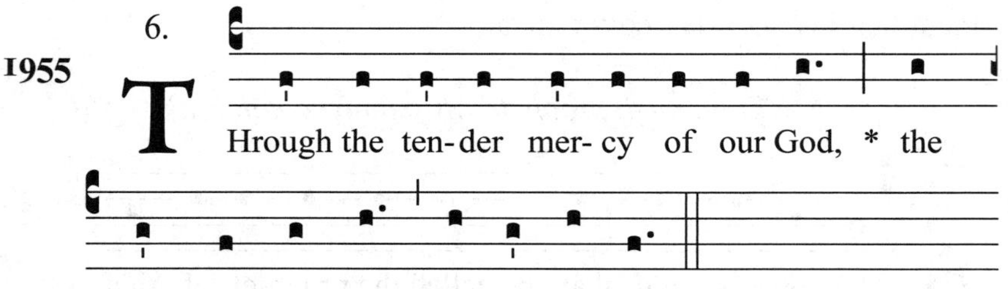
6.
THrough the ten- der mer- cy of our God, * the
Dawn from on high will vis- it us.

June 29

SAINTS PETER AND PAUL, APOSTLES

At the Vigil Mass

Entrance Antiphon *Petrus apostolus et Paulus doctor.*

- i -

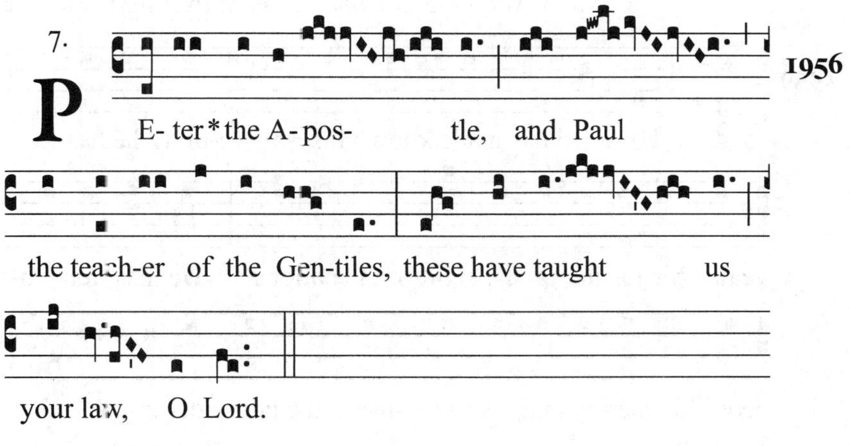
7.
1956
PE- ter * the A- pos- tle, and Paul
the teach-er of the Gen-tiles, these have taught us
your law, O Lord.

- ii -

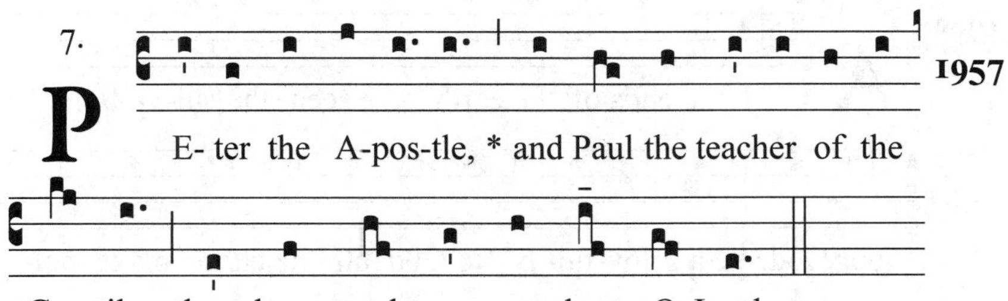
7.
1957
PE- ter the A-pos-tle, * and Paul the teacher of the
Gen-tiles, these have taught us your law, O Lord.

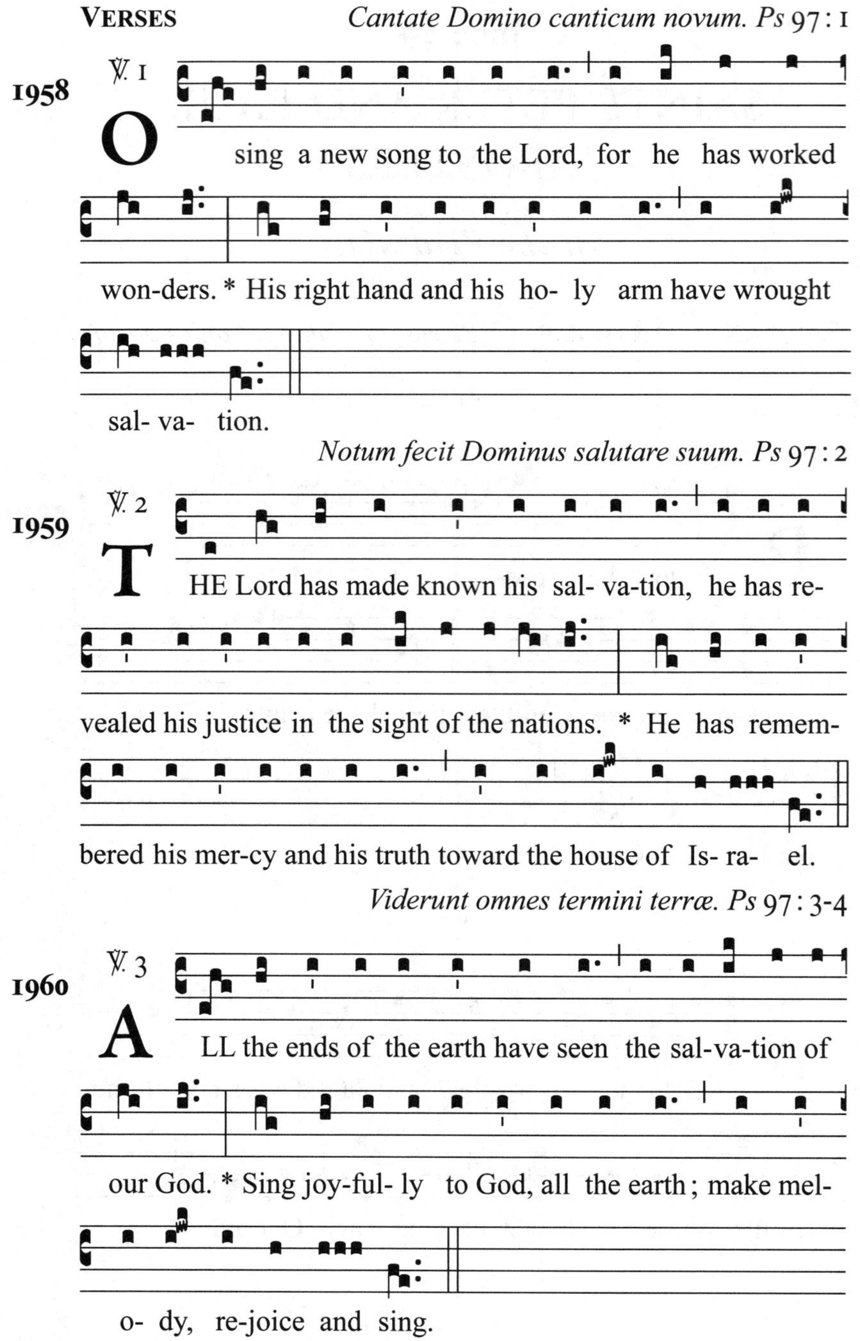
VERSES
Cantate Domino canticum novum. Ps 97 : 1
1958
℣. 1
O sing a new song to the Lord, for he has worked
won-ders. * His right hand and his ho- ly arm have wrought
sal- va- tion.
Notum fecit Dominus salutare suum. Ps 97 : 2
1959
℣. 2
THE Lord has made known his sal- va-tion, he has revealed his justice in the sight of the nations. * He has remembered his mer-cy and his truth toward the house of Is- ra- el.
Viderunt omnes termini terræ. Ps 97 : 3-4
1960
℣. 3
ALL the ends of the earth have seen the sal-va-tion of
our God. * Sing joy-ful- ly to God, all the earth; make mel-
o- dy, re-joice and sing.

- iii -

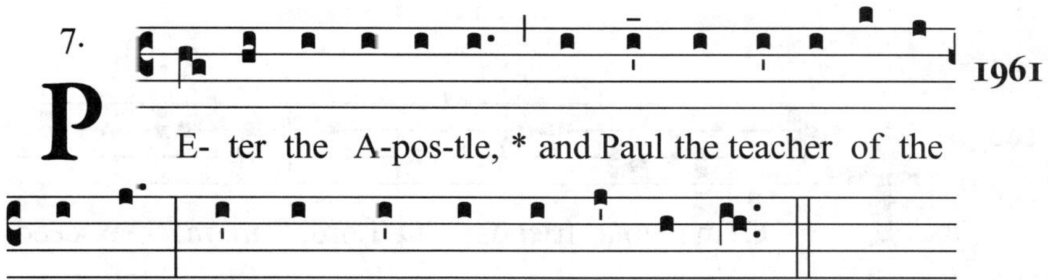
7.
1961
PE- ter the A-pos-tle, * and Paul the teacher of the

Gen-tiles, these have taught us your law, O Lord.

- iv -

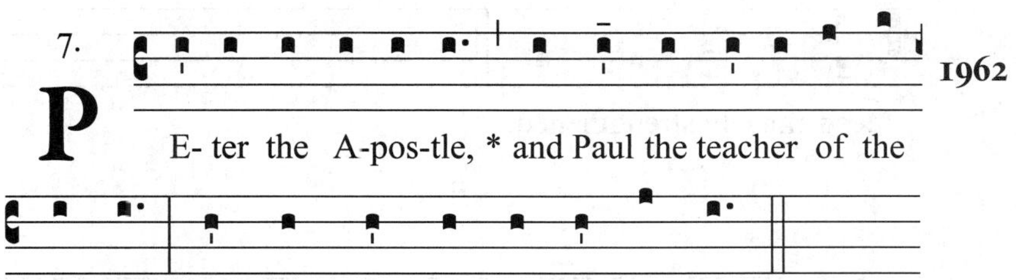
7.
1962
PE- ter the A-pos-tle, * and Paul the teacher of the

Gen-tiles, these have taught us your law, O Lord.

Offertory Antiphon *Mihi autem nimis. Ps* 138:17

- i -

1963

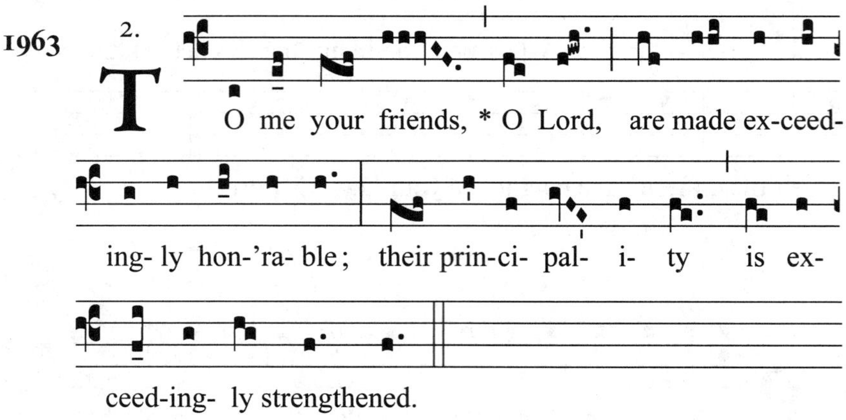
2.
TO me your friends, * O Lord, are made ex-ceed-
ing- ly hon-'ra- ble; their prin-ci- pal- i- ty is ex-
ceed-ing- ly strengthened.

- ii -

1964

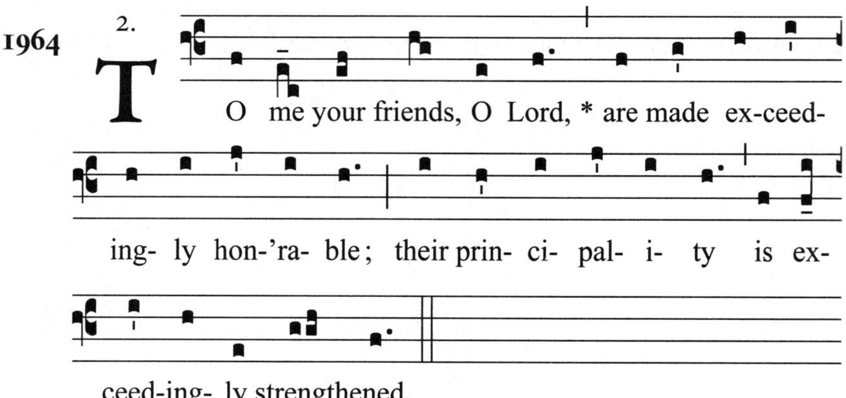
2.
TO me your friends, O Lord, * are made ex-ceed-
ing- ly hon-'ra- ble; their prin- ci- pal- i- ty is ex-
ceed-ing- ly strengthened.

VERSES *Domine, probasti me. Ps* 138 : 1-2

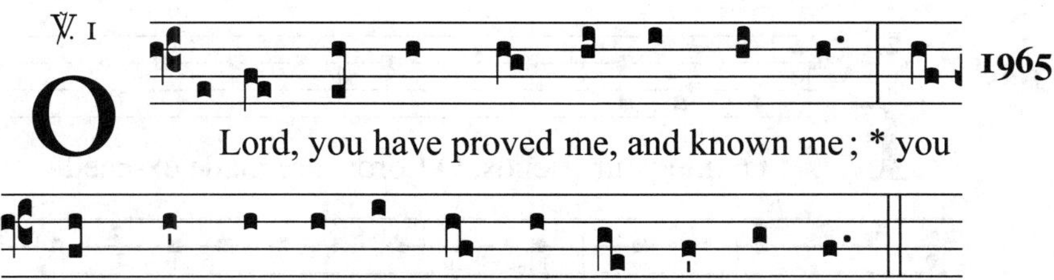
℣. 1
O Lord, you have proved me, and known me; * you 1965
have known my sit-ting down, and my ris- ing up.

Intellexisti cogitatones meas de longe. Ps 138 : 3

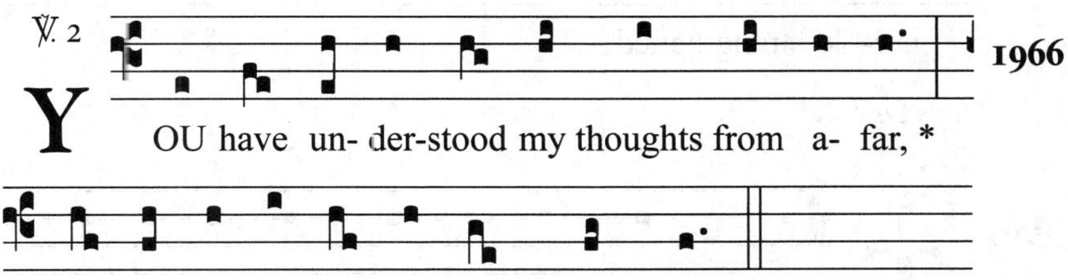
℣. 2
YOU have un- der-stood my thoughts from a- far, * 1966
my path and my way you have searched out.

Quia tu possedisti renes meos. Ps 138 : 13

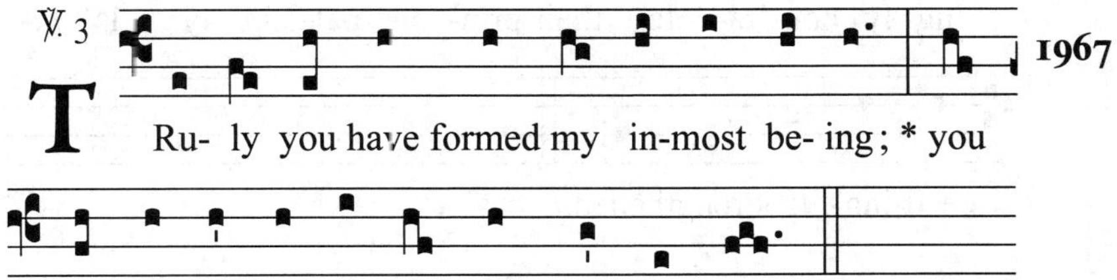
℣. 3
TRu- ly you have formed my in-most be- ing; * you 1967
have pro-tect- ed me from my moth-er's womb.

- iii -

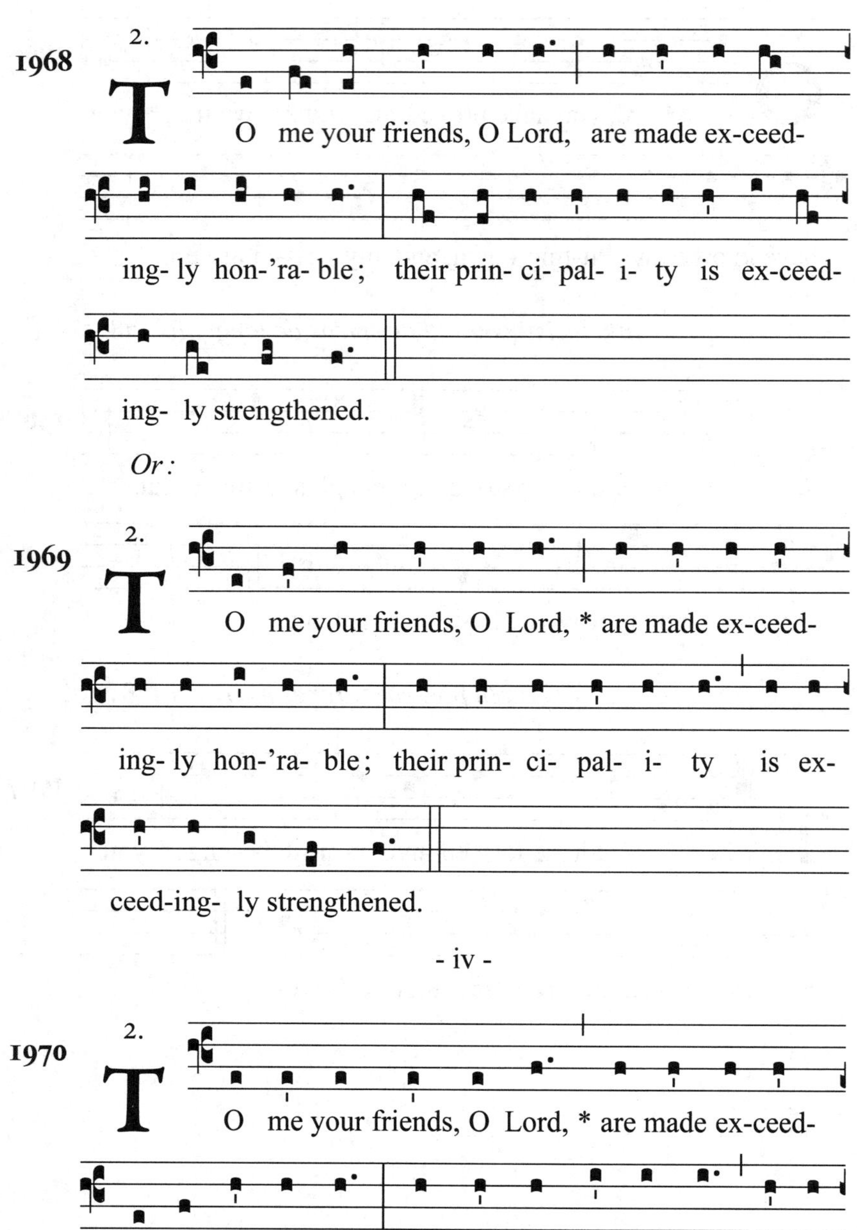
1968
2.
TO me your friends, O Lord, are made ex-ceed-
ing- ly hon-'ra- ble; their prin- ci- pal- i- ty is ex-ceed-
ing- ly strengthened.
Or:
1969
2.
TO me your friends, O Lord, * are made ex-ceed-
ing- ly hon-'ra- ble; their prin- ci- pal- i- ty is ex-
ceed-ing- ly strengthened.
- iv -
1970
2.
TO me your friends, O Lord, * are made ex-ceed-
ing- ly hon-'ra- ble; their prin- ci- pal- i- ty is ex-

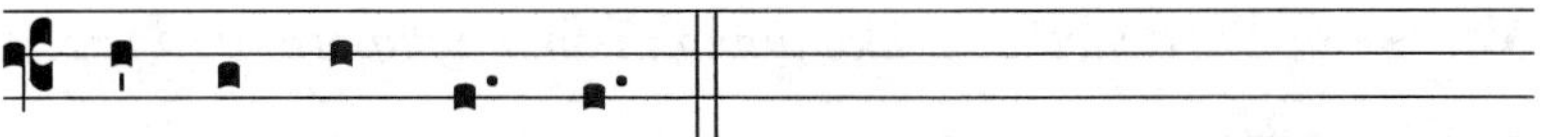

ceed-ing- ly strengthened.

Communion Antiphon *Simon Ioannis, diligis me?*
Jn 21:15. 17

- i -

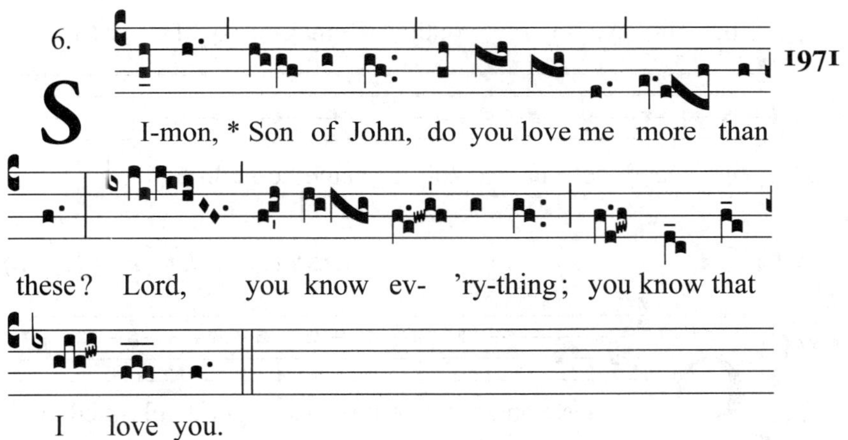
6.
S I-mon, * Son of John, do you love me more than 1971
these? Lord, you know ev- 'ry-thing; you know that
I love you.

- ii -

6.
S I- mon, Son of John, * do you love me more than 1972
these? Lord, you know ev-'ry-thing; you know that I
love you.

VERSES *Benedicam Dominum in omni tempore. Ps* 33:2. 4

1973 ℣. 1

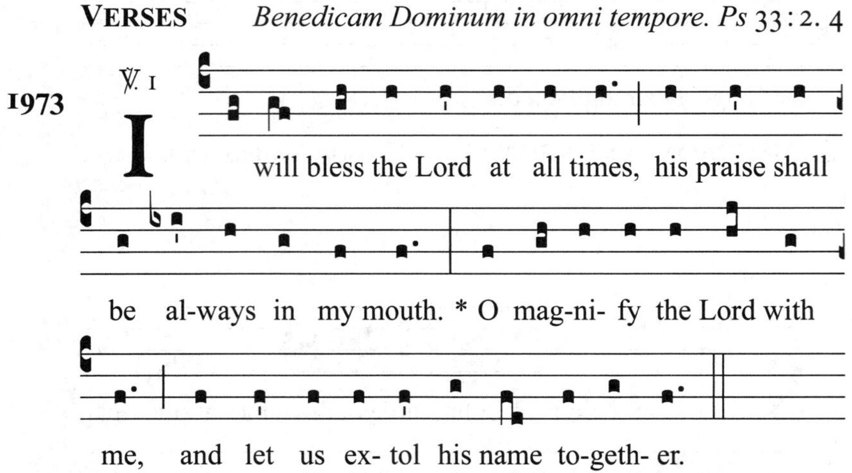
I will bless the Lord at all times, his praise shall
be al-ways in my mouth. * O mag-ni- fy the Lord with
me, and let us ex- tol his name to-geth- er.

Gustate et videte. Ps 33:9. 19

1974 ℣. 2

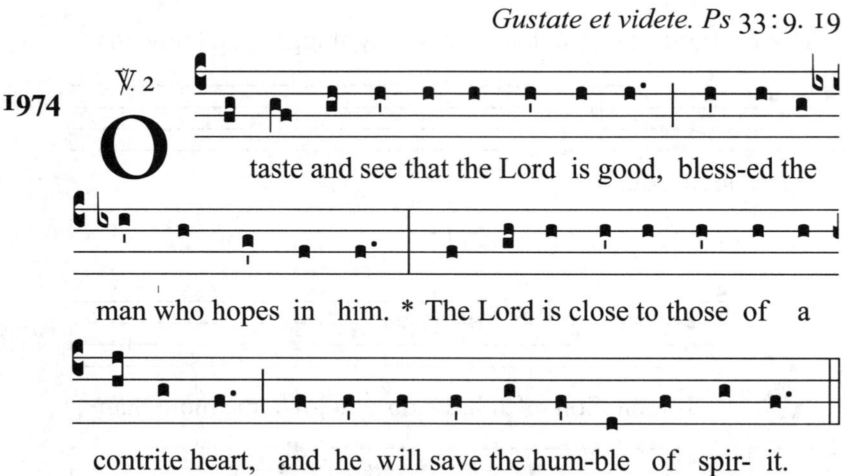
O taste and see that the Lord is good, bless-ed the
man who hopes in him. * The Lord is close to those of a
contrite heart, and he will save the hum-ble of spir- it.

Or Ps 33 *simple tone, pp.* 338-39.

- iii -

1975 6.

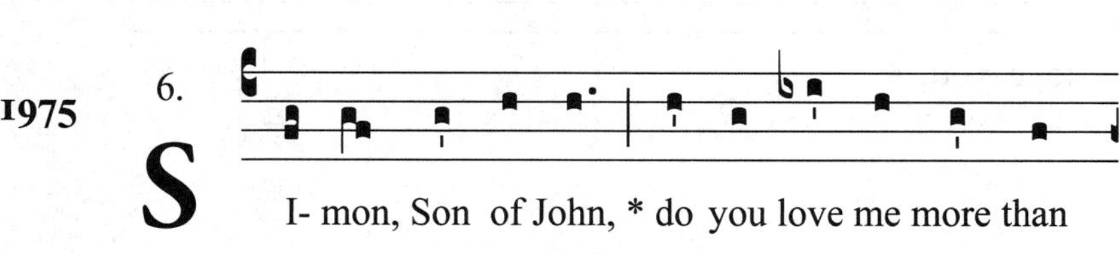
S I- mon, Son of John, * do you love me more than

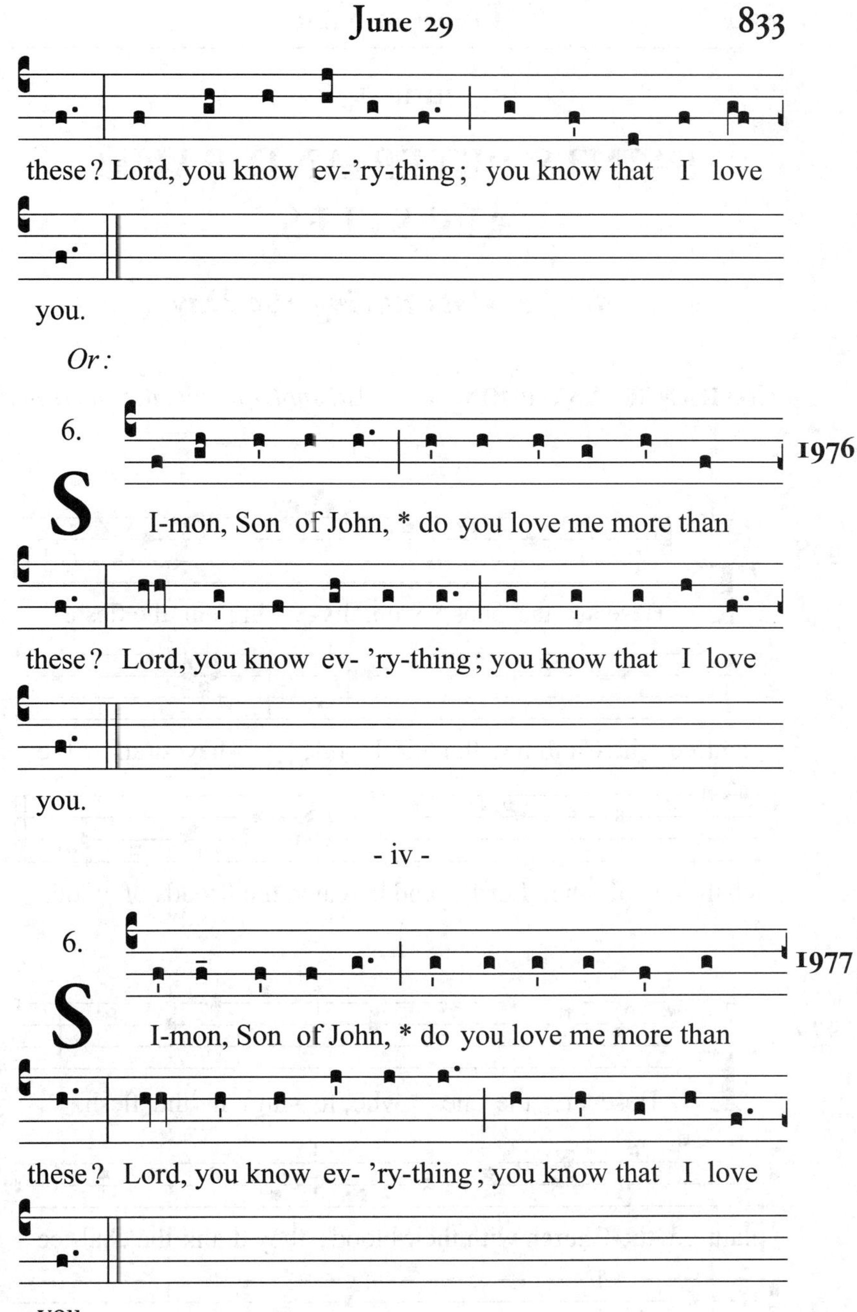
these? Lord, you know ev-'ry-thing; you know that I love
you.
Or:
6.
1976
S I-mon, Son of John, * do you love me more than
these? Lord, you know ev- 'ry-thing; you know that I love
you.
- iv -
6.
1977
S I-mon, Son of John, * do you love me more than
these? Lord, you know ev- 'ry-thing; you know that I love
you.

June 29

SAINTS PETER AND PAUL, APOSTLES

At the Mass during the Day

Entrance Antiphon *Isti sunt, qui viventes in carne.*

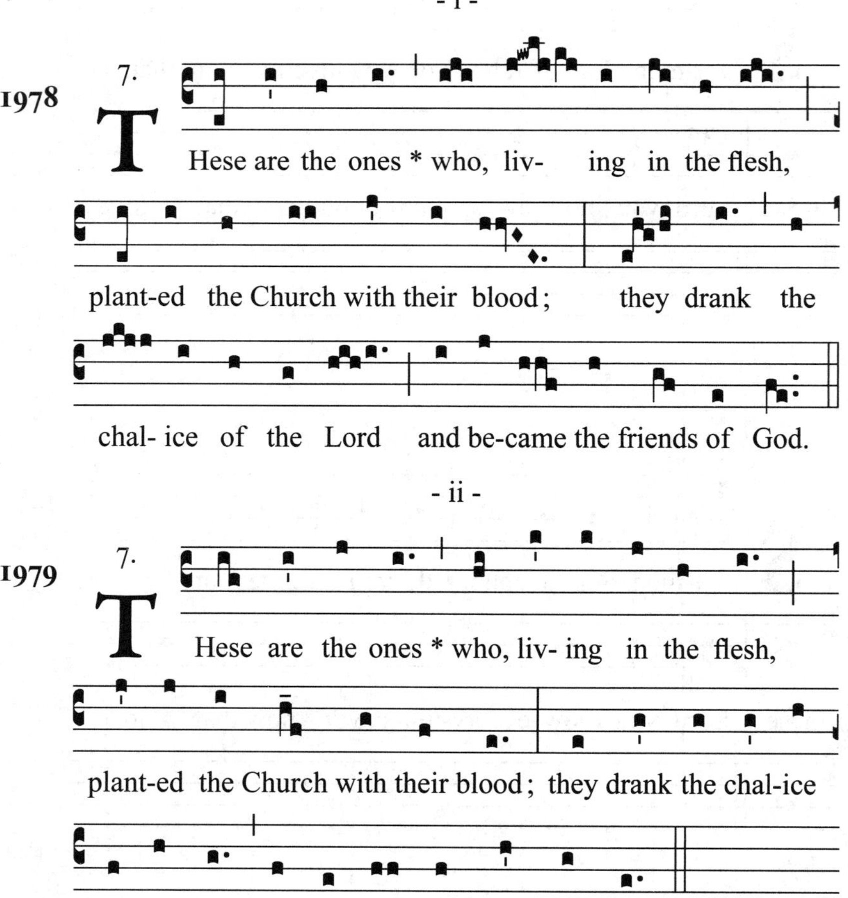
- i -
1978 7.
THese are the ones * who, liv- ing in the flesh,
plant-ed the Church with their blood; they drank the
chal- ice of the Lord and be-came the friends of God.
- ii -
1979 7.
THese are the ones * who, liv- ing in the flesh,
plant-ed the Church with their blood; they drank the chal-ice
of the Lord and be-came the friends of God.

VERSES *Domine, probasti me. Ps* 138 : 1-2

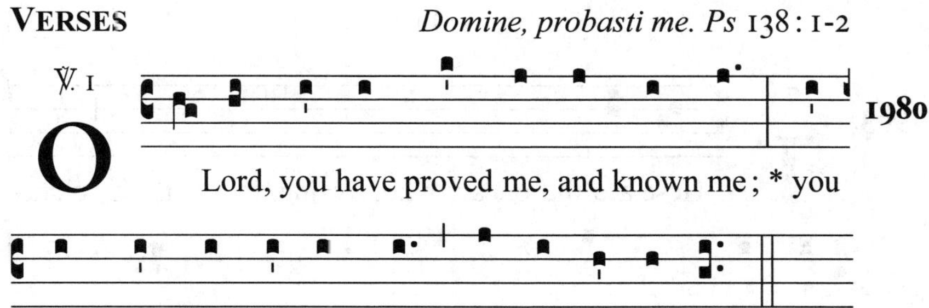
℣. 1
1980
O Lord, you have proved me, and known me; * you

have known my sit-ting down, and my ris-ing up.

Intellexisti cogitatones meas de longe. Ps 138 : 3

℣. 2
1981
YOU have un-der-stood my thoughts from a-far, *

my path and my way you have searched out.

Quia tu possedisti renes meos. Ps 138 : 13

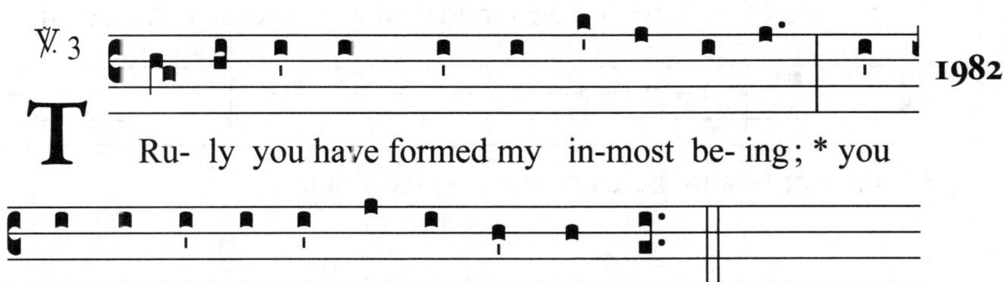
℣. 3
1982
TRu-ly you have formed my in-most be-ing; * you

have pro-tect-ed me from my moth-er's womb.

Or Ps 97 *solemn tone, p.* 826.

- iii -

1983

7.
THese are the ones * who, liv-ing in the flesh, plant-
ed the Church with their blood; they drank the chal-ice of
the Lord and be-came the friends of God.

- iv -

1984

7.
THese are the ones * who, liv-ing in the flesh, plant-
ed the Church with their blood; they drank the chal-ice of
the Lord and be-came the friends of God.

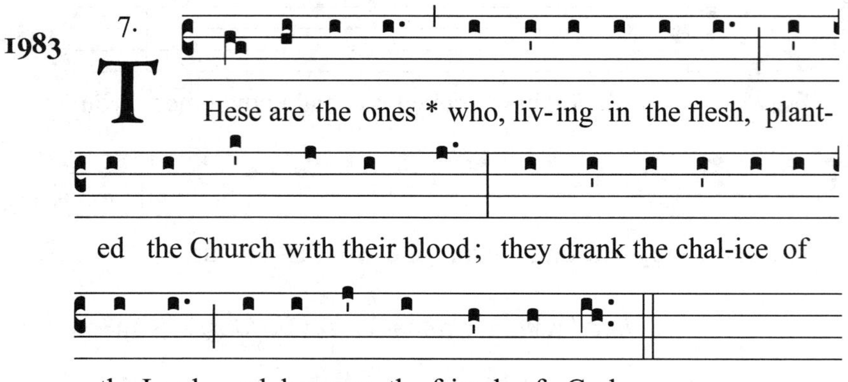

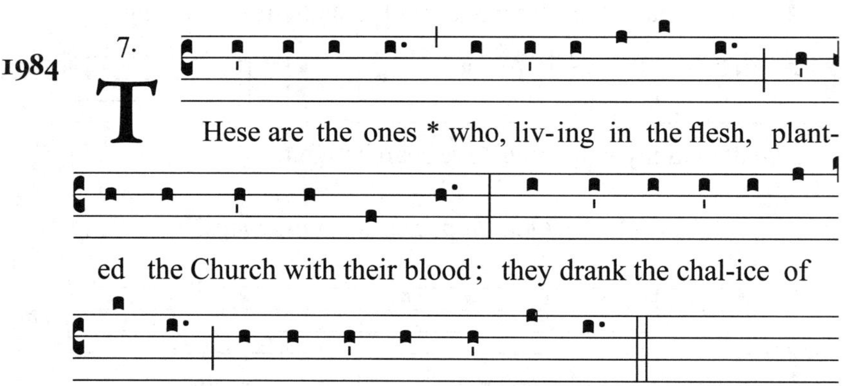

OFFERTORY ANTIPHON *Constitues eos principes.*
Ps 44:17. 18

- i -

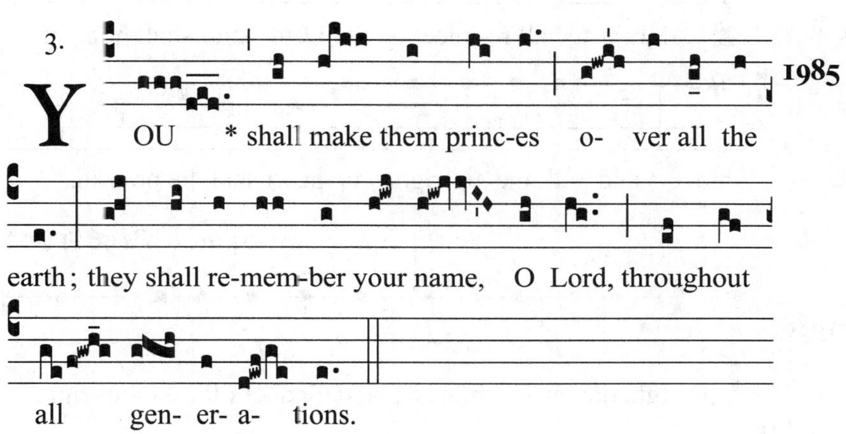
3.
1985
YOU * shall make them princ-es o- ver all the
earth; they shall re-mem-ber your name, O Lord, throughout
all gen- er- a- tions.

- ii -

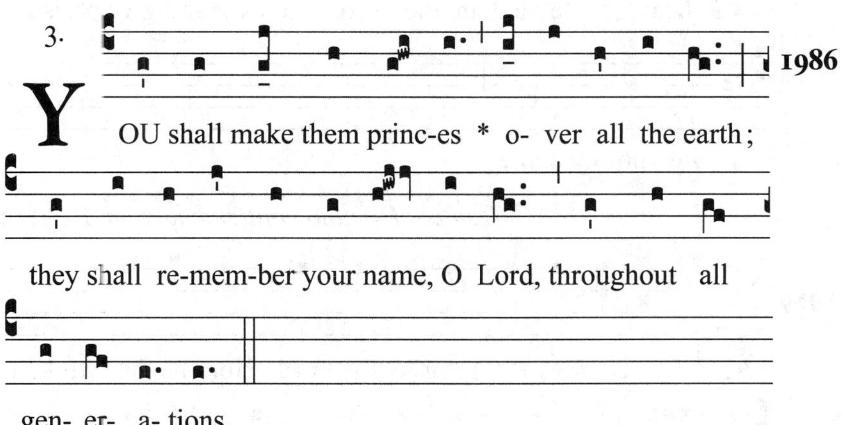
3.
1986
YOU shall make them princ-es * o- ver all the earth;
they shall re-mem-ber your name, O Lord, throughout all
gen- er- a- tions.

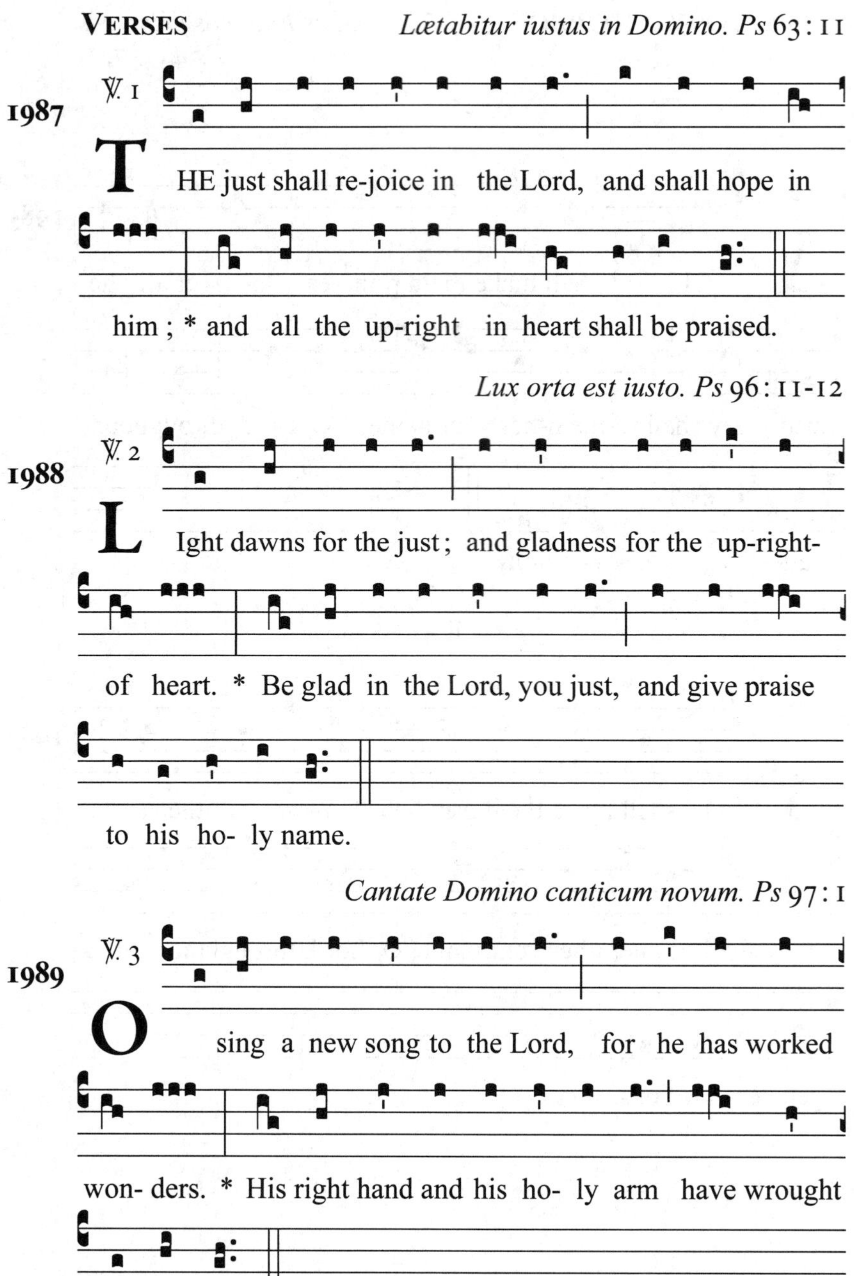
VERSES
Lætabitur iustus in Domino. Ps 63 : 11
℣. 1
1987
THE just shall re-joice in the Lord, and shall hope in
him ; * and all the up-right in heart shall be praised.
Lux orta est iusto. Ps 96 : 11-12
℣. 2
1988
LIght dawns for the just ; and gladness for the up-right-
of heart. * Be glad in the Lord, you just, and give praise
to his ho- ly name.
Cantate Domino canticum novum. Ps 97 : 1
℣. 3
1989
O sing a new song to the Lord, for he has worked
won- ders. * His right hand and his ho- ly arm have wrought
sal- va- tion.

- iii -

1990

8.
YOU shall make them princ-es o- ver all the earth; *
they shall re-mem-ber your name, O Lord, throughout all
gen- er- a- tions.

- iv -

1991

8.
YOU shall make them princ-es * o- ver all the earth;
they shall re-mem-ber your name, O Lord, throughout all gen-
er- a- tions.

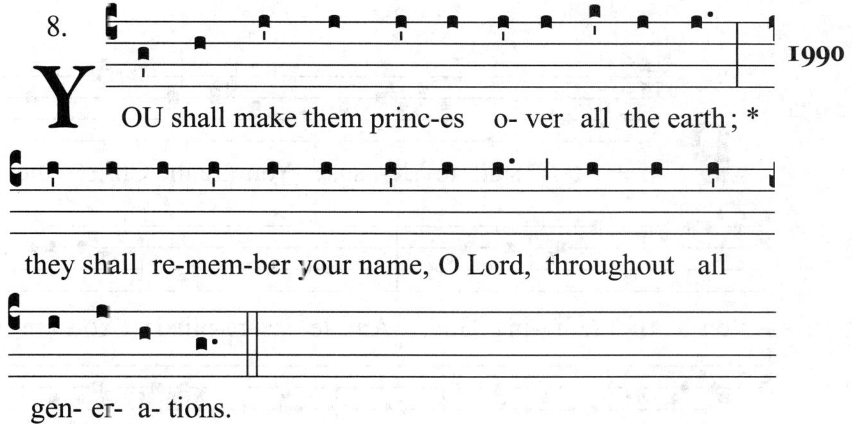

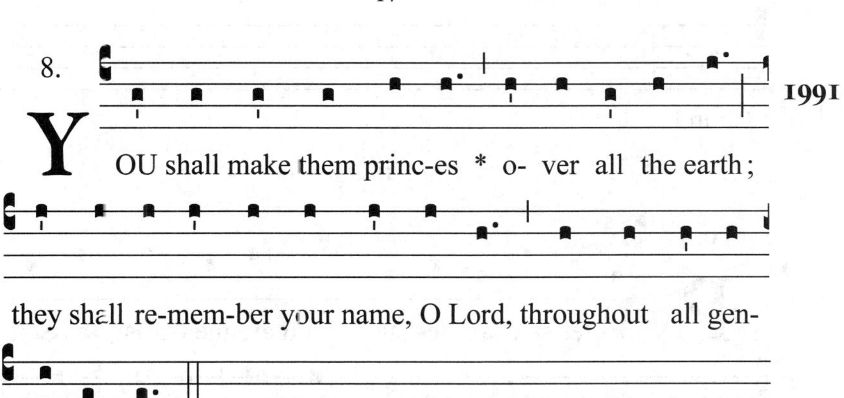

Communion Antiphon *Dixit Petrus. Mt* 16 : 16. 18

- i -

1992
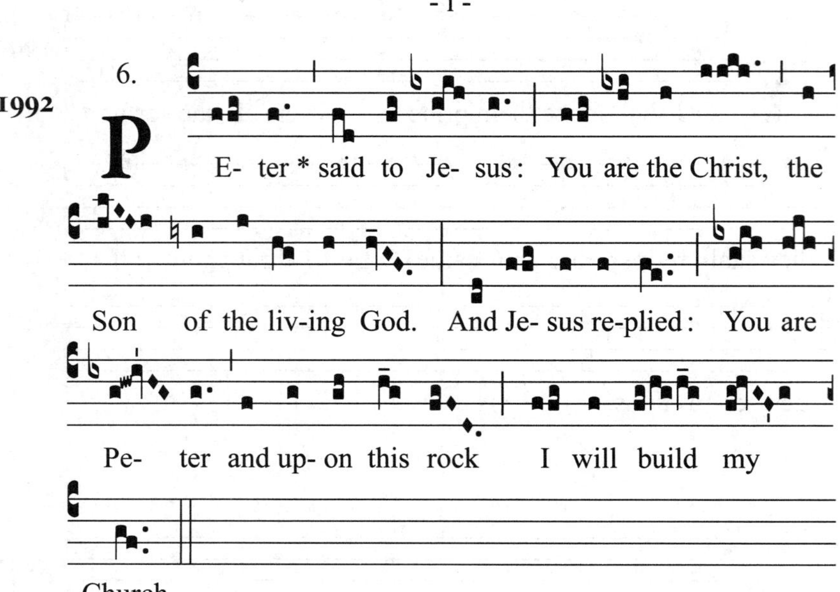
6.
P
E- ter * said to Je- sus : You are the Christ, the
Son of the liv-ing God. And Je- sus re-plied : You are
Pe- ter and up- on this rock I will build my
Church.

- ii -

1993
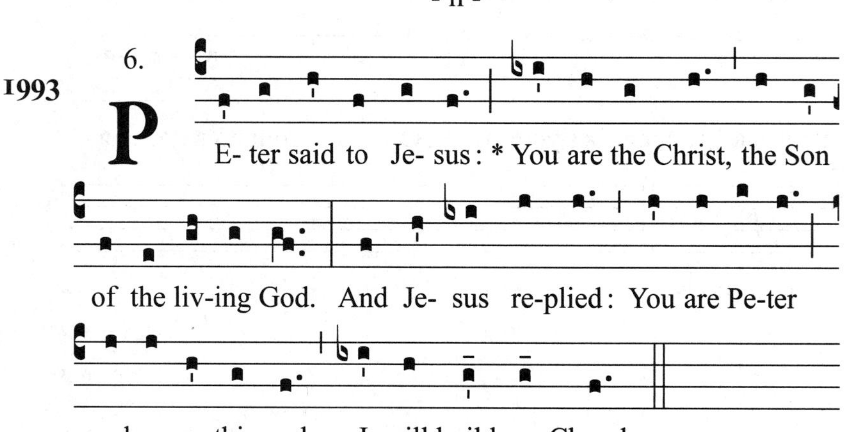
6.
P
E- ter said to Je- sus : * You are the Christ, the Son
of the liv-ing God. And Je- sus re-plied : You are Pe-ter
and up-on this rock I will build my Church.

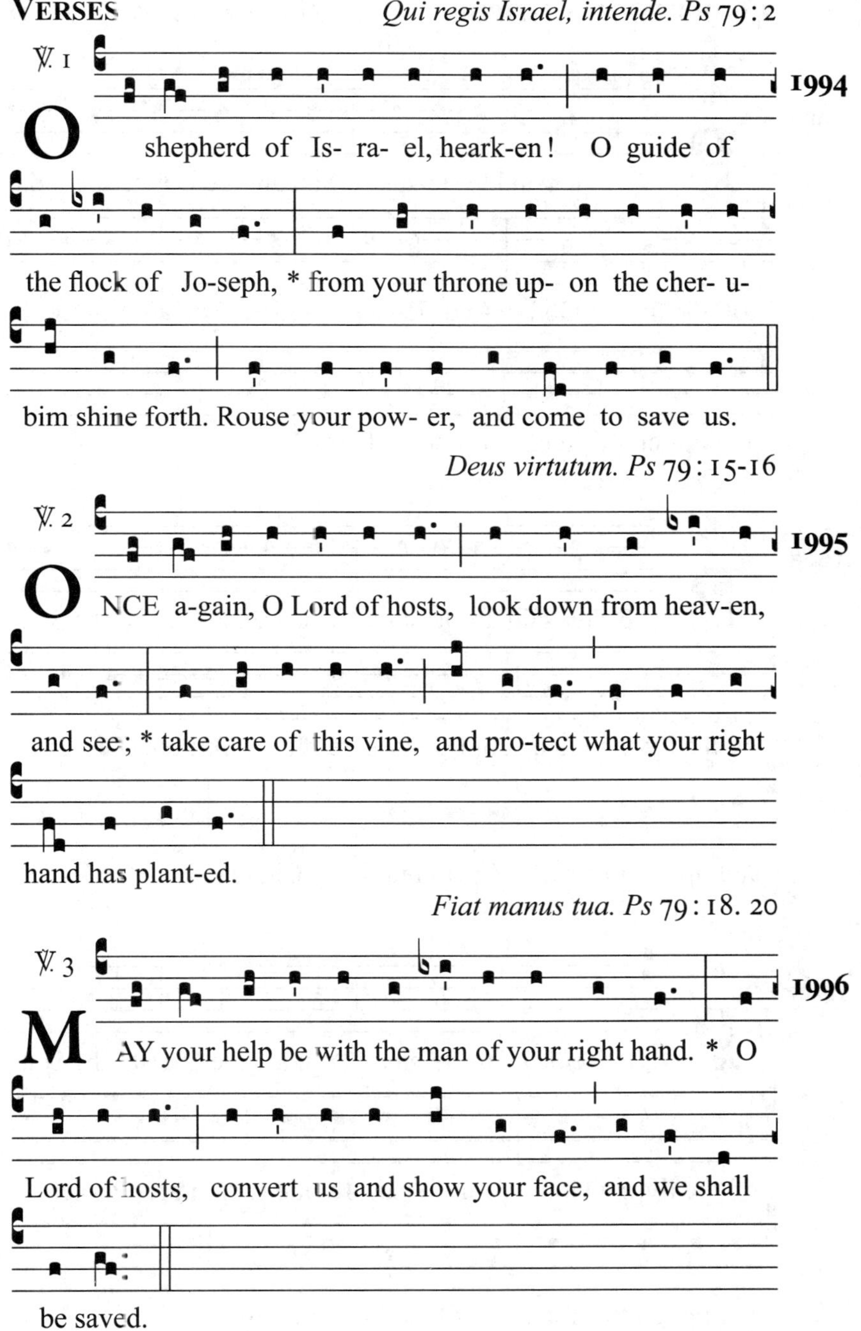
VERSES
Qui regis Israel, intende. Ps 79:2
℣. 1
1994
O shepherd of Is- ra- el, heark-en! O guide of
the flock of Jo-seph, * from your throne up- on the cher- u-
bim shine forth. Rouse your pow- er, and come to save us.
Deus virtutum. Ps 79:15-16
℣. 2
1995
ONCE a-gain, O Lord of hosts, look down from heav-en,
and see; * take care of this vine, and pro-tect what your right
hand has plant-ed.
Fiat manus tua. Ps 79:18. 20
℣. 3
1996
MAY your help be with the man of your right hand. * O
Lord of hosts, convert us and show your face, and we shall
be saved.

COMMUNION ANTIPHON *Dixit Petrus. Mt* 16 : 16. 18

- iii -
1997
6.
P
E- ter said to Je-sus : * You are the Christ, the Son
of the liv-ing God. And Je- sus re-plied : You are Pe- ter
and up- on this rock I will build my Church.
Or :
1998
6.
P
E- ter said to Je-sus : * You are the Christ, the Son
of the liv-ing God. And Je- sus re-plied : You are Pe- ter
and up- on this rock I will build my Church.
- iv -
1999
6.
P
E- ter said to Je-sus : * You are the Christ, the Son
of the liv-ing God. And Je- sus re-plied : You are Pe- ter
and up- on this rock I will build my Church.

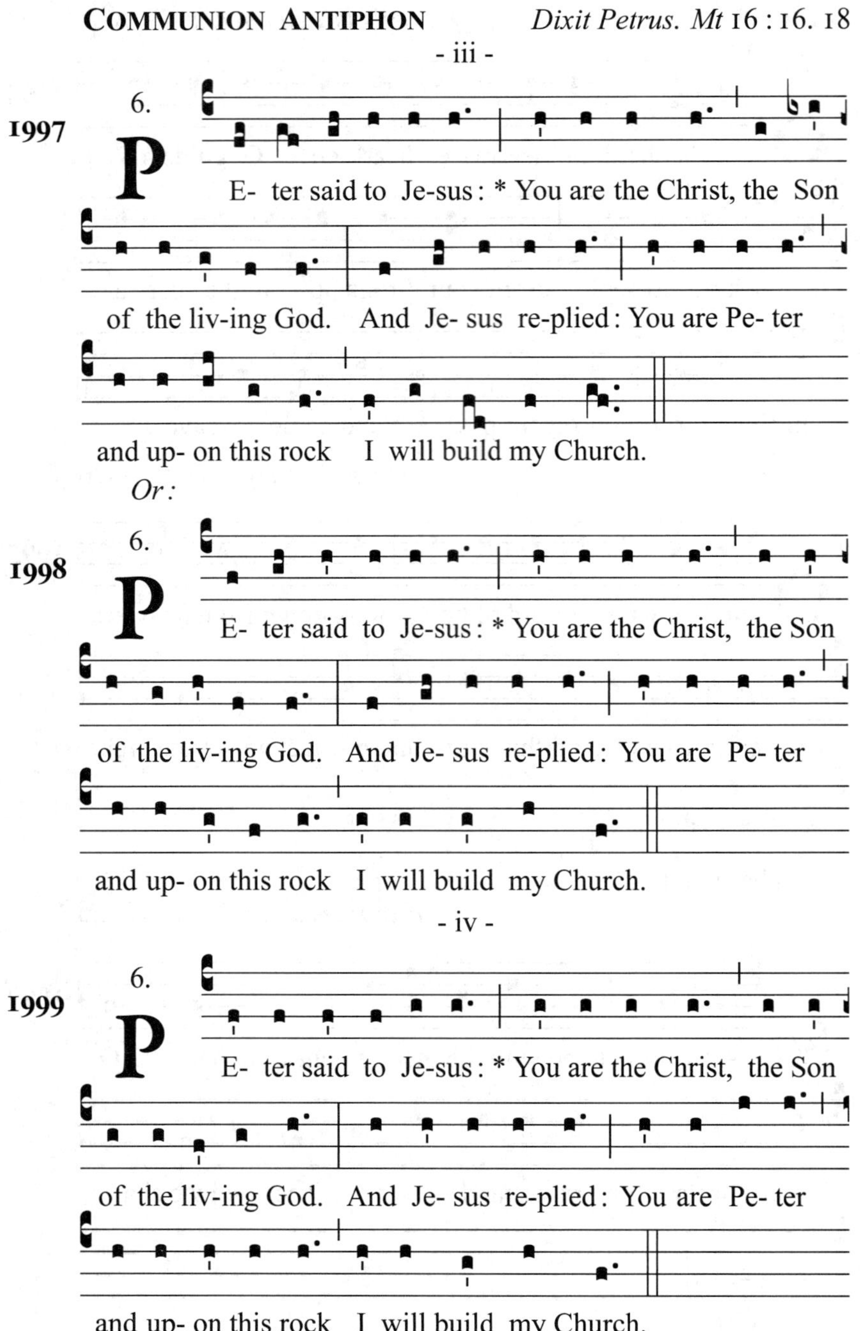

August 6

THE TRANSFIGURATION OF THE LORD

Entrance Antiphon *In splendenti nube.*

- i -

7. 2000

IN a re-splen-dent cloud * the Ho-ly Spir-it ap-peared. The Fa-ther's voice was heard: This is my be-lov-ed Son, with whom I am well pleased. Lis- ten to him.

- ii -

7.
2001
IN a re-splen-dent cloud * the Ho-ly Spir-it appeared. The Fa-ther's voice was heard: This is my be-lov-
ed Son, with whom I am well pleased. Lis- ten to him.

VERSES *Quam dilecta tabernacula tua. Ps* 83:1. 5

2002
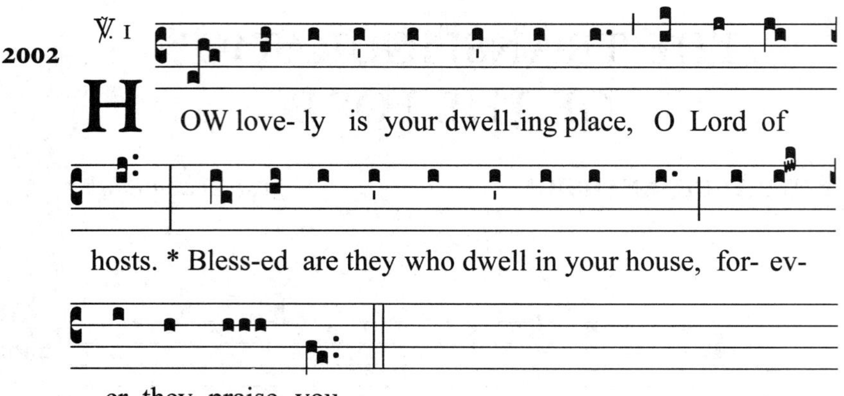
℣. 1
HOW love- ly is your dwell-ing place, O Lord of
hosts. * Bless-ed are they who dwell in your house, for- ev-
er they praise you.

Protector noster, aspice, Deus. Ps 83:10-11

2003
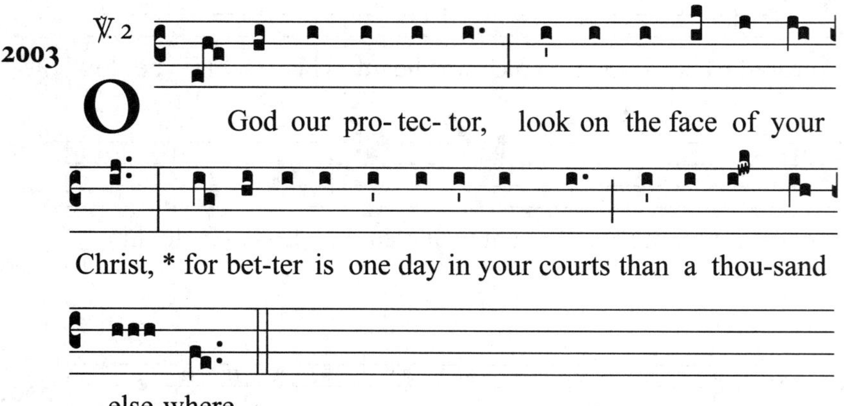
℣. 2
O God our pro- tec- tor, look on the face of your
Christ, * for bet-ter is one day in your courts than a thou-sand
else-where.

- iii -

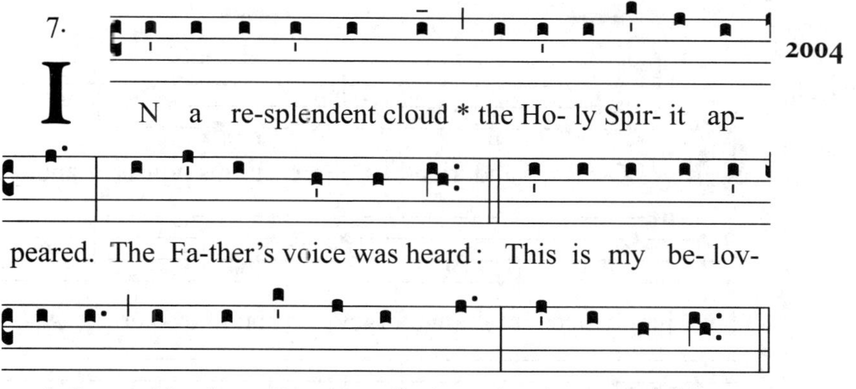
7.
2004
IN a re-splendent cloud * the Ho- ly Spir- it appeared. The Fa-ther's voice was heard: This is my be- loved Son, with whom I am well pleased. Lis-ten to him.

- iv -

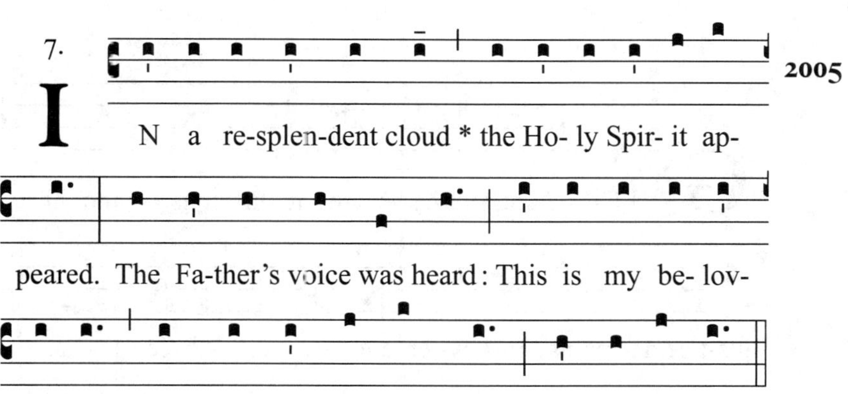
7.
2005
IN a re-splen-dent cloud * the Ho- ly Spir- it appeared. The Fa-ther's voice was heard: This is my be- loved Son, with whom I am well pleased. Lis- ten to him.

OFFERTORY ANTIPHON *Gloria et honore. Ps* 111:3

- i -

2006

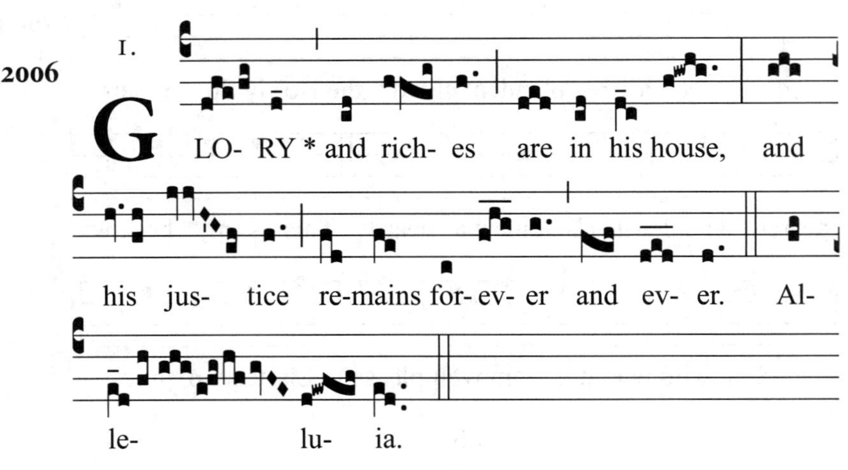
I.
GLO- RY * and rich- es are in his house, and
his jus- tice re-mains for- ev- er and ev- er. Al-
le- lu- ia.

- ii -

2007

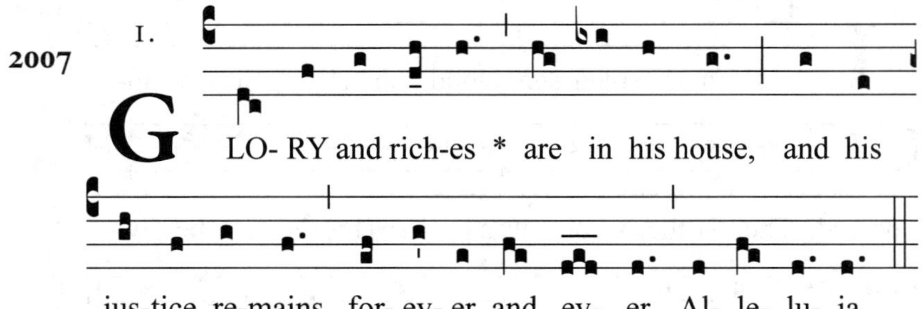
I.
GLO- RY and rich-es * are in his house, and his
jus-tice re-mains for- ev- er and ev- er. Al- le- lu- ia.

VERSES *Beatus vir qui timet Dominum. Ps* 111

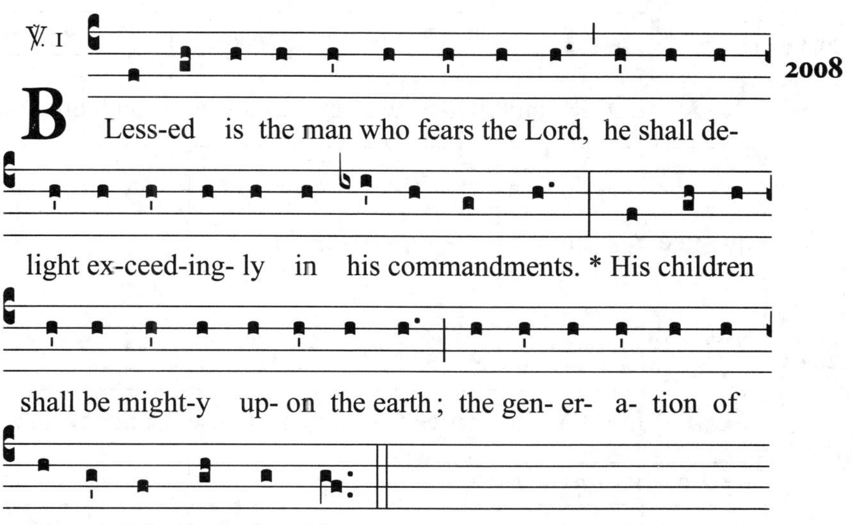
℣. 1
2008
BLess-ed is the man who fears the Lord, he shall de-
light ex-ceed-ing- ly in his commandments. * His children
shall be might-y up- on the earth; the gen- er- a- tion of
the up-right shall be blest.

Exortum est in tenebris. Ps 111:4

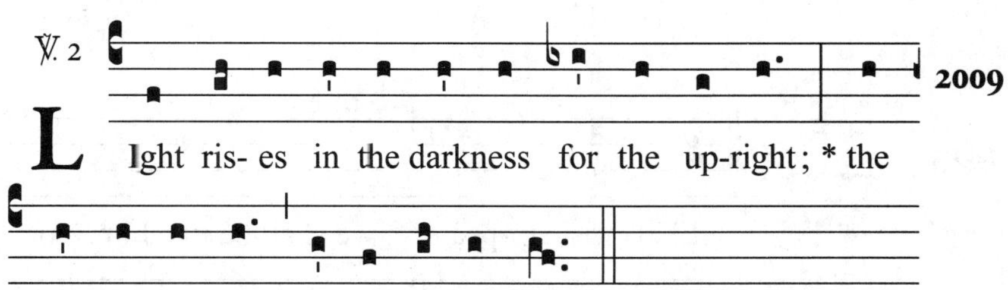
℣. 2
2009
LIght ris- es in the darkness for the up-right; * the
Lord is gracious, mer-ci- ful and just.

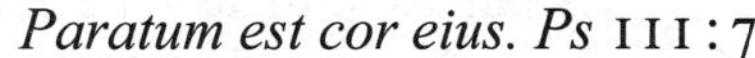
Paratum est cor eius. Ps 111:7

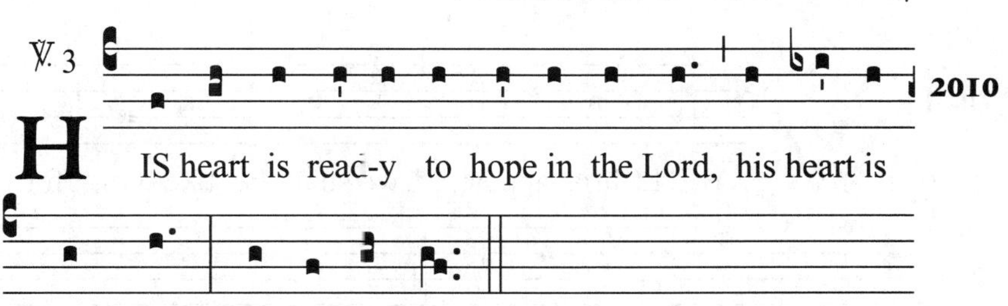
℣. 3
2010
HIS heart is read-y to hope in the Lord, his heart is
strengthened. * He will not fear.

- iii -

2011

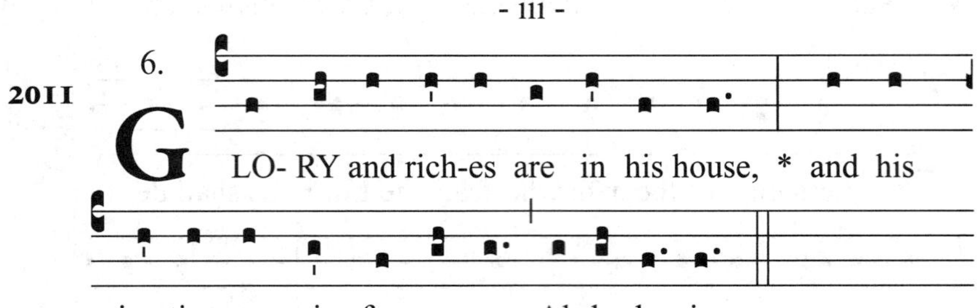
6.
GLO- RY and rich-es are in his house, * and his

jus-tice re-mains for- ev- er. Al- le- lu- ia.

- iv -

2012

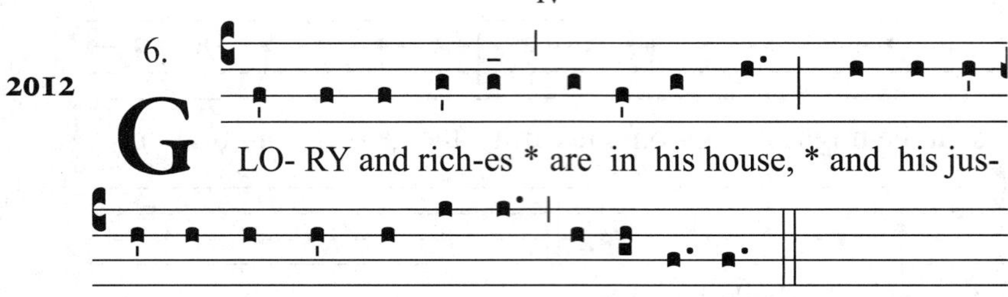
6.
GLO- RY and rich-es * are in his house, * and his jus-

jus-tice re-mains for- ev- er. Al- le- lu- ia.

Communion Antiphon *Cum Christus apparuerit.*

1 *Jn* 3:2

2013

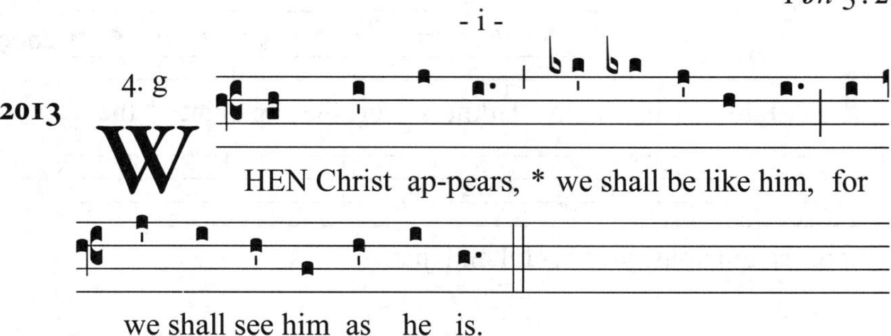
- i -
4. g
WHEN Christ ap-pears, * we shall be like him, for
we shall see him as he is.

- ii -

2014

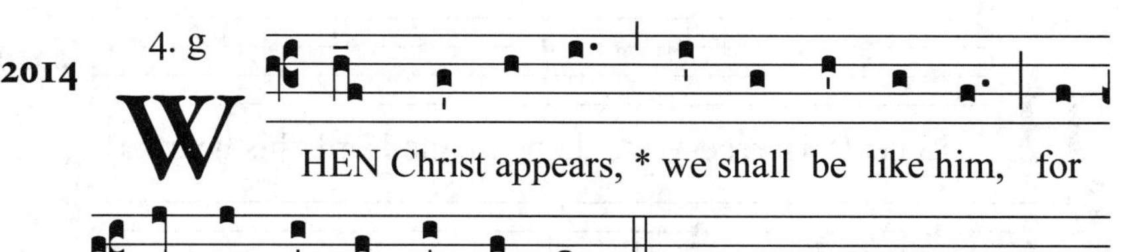
4. g
WHEN Christ appears, * we shall be like him, for

we shall see him as he is.

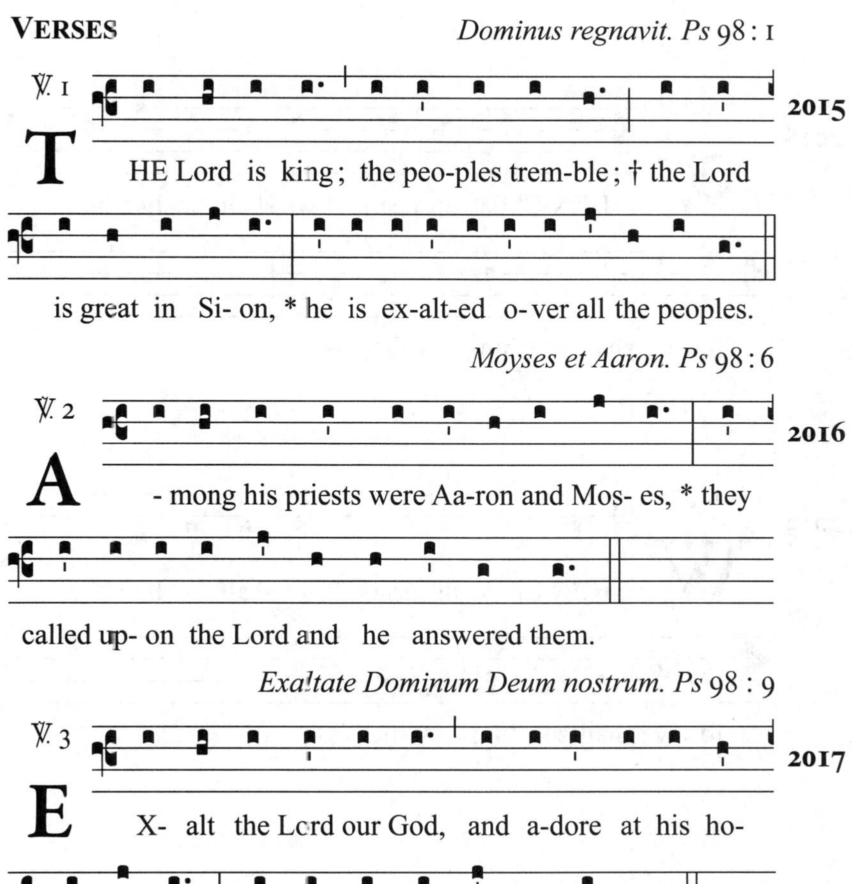
VERSES
Dominus regnavit. Ps 98 : 1
℣. 1 2015
THE Lord is king; the peo-ples trem-ble; † the Lord
is great in Si- on, * he is ex-alt-ed o-ver all the peoples.
Moyses et Aaron. Ps 98 : 6
℣. 2 2016
A - mong his priests were Aa-ron and Mos- es, * they
called up- on the Lord and he answered them.
Exaltate Dominum Deum nostrum. Ps 98 : 9
℣. 3 2017
EX- alt the Lord our God, and a-dore at his ho-
ly mountain, * for the Lord, our God, is ho- ly.

- iii -

2018

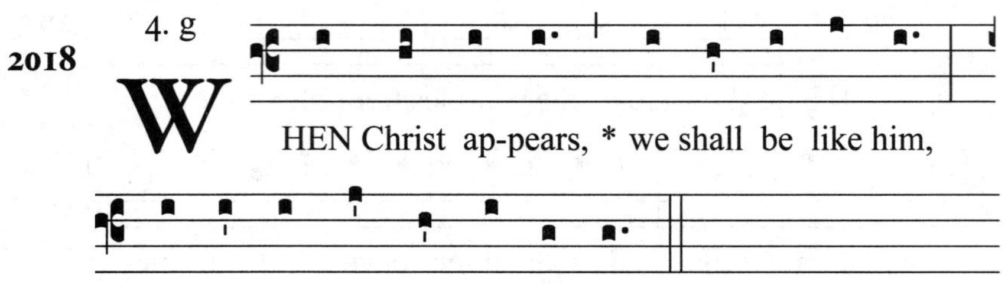
4. g
WHEN Christ ap-pears, * we shall be like him,
for we shall see him as he is.

- iv -

2019

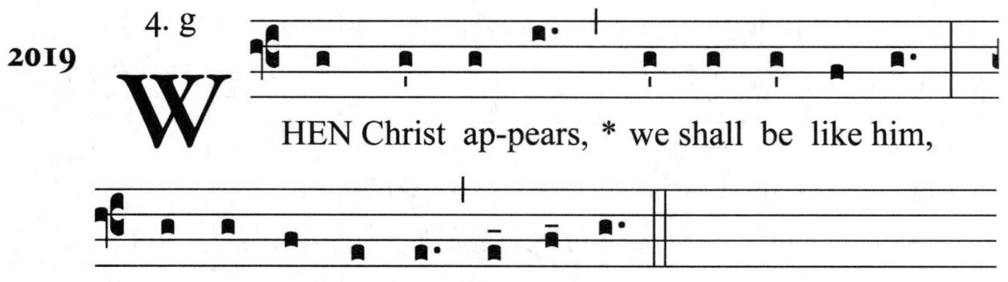
4. g
WHEN Christ ap-pears, * we shall be like him,
for we shall see him as he is.

August 15

THE ASSUMPTION OF THE BLESSED VIRGIN MARY

At the Vigil Mass

Entrance Antiphon *Gloriosa dicta sunt de te.*

- i -

8.

GLo- ri-ous things * are spok-en of you, O Mar- y, * 2020

who to- day were ex- alt- ed a-bove the choirs of An-gels

in- to e- ter- nal tri- umph with Christ.

- ii -

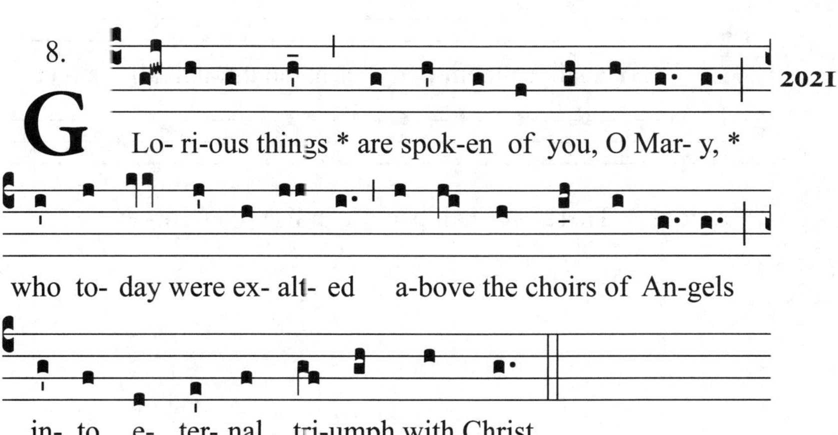
8.
GLo- ri-ous things * are spok-en of you, O Mar- y, *
2021
who to- day were ex- alt- ed a-bove the choirs of An-gels
in- to e- ter- nal tri-umph with Christ.

VERSES *Eructavit cor meum verbum bonum.* Ps 44:2

2022
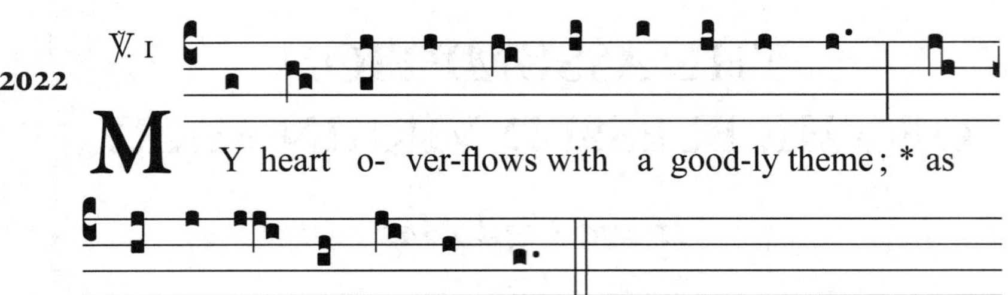
℣. 1
MY heart o- ver-flows with a good-ly theme; * as
I sing my ode to the king.

Audi, filia, et vide. Ps 44:11

2023
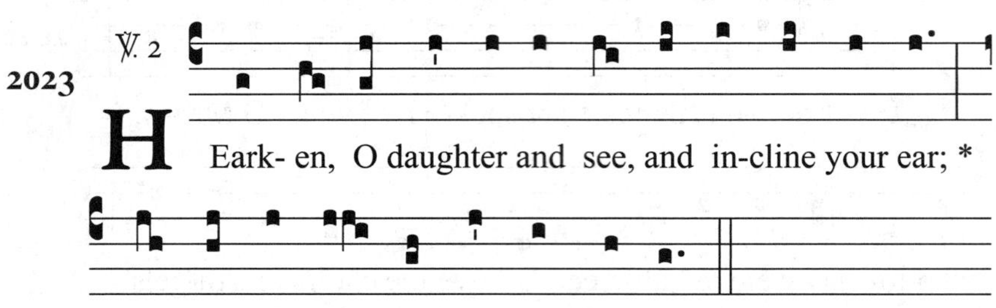
℣. 2
HEark- en, O daughter and see, and in-cline your ear; *
so shall the king de- sire your beau-ty.

Propterea populi confitebuntur tibi. Ps 44:18

2024
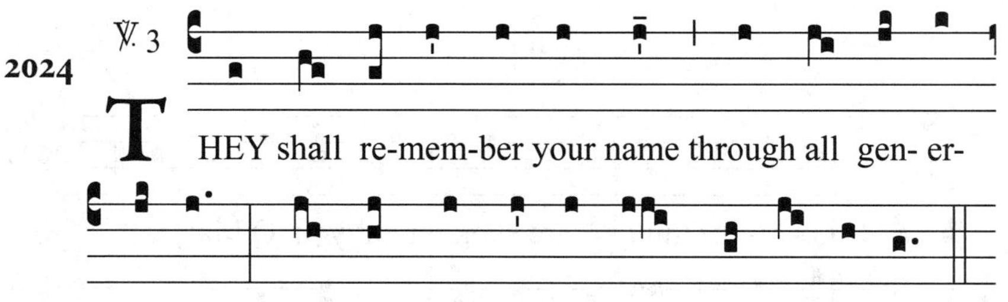
℣. 3
THEY shall re-mem-ber your name through all gen- er-
a-tions. * Therefore shall peo-ple praise you for- ev- er.

- iii -

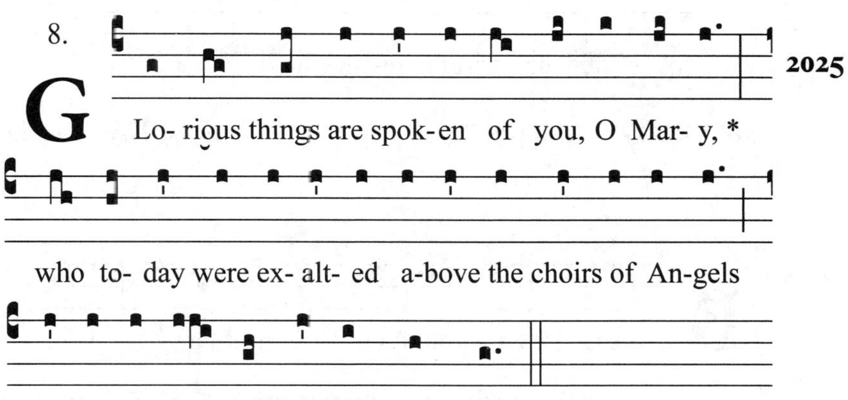
8.
2025
GLo- rious things are spok-en of you, O Mar- y, *
who to- day were ex- alt- ed a-bove the choirs of An-gels
in- to e- ter- nal triumph with Christ.

Or:

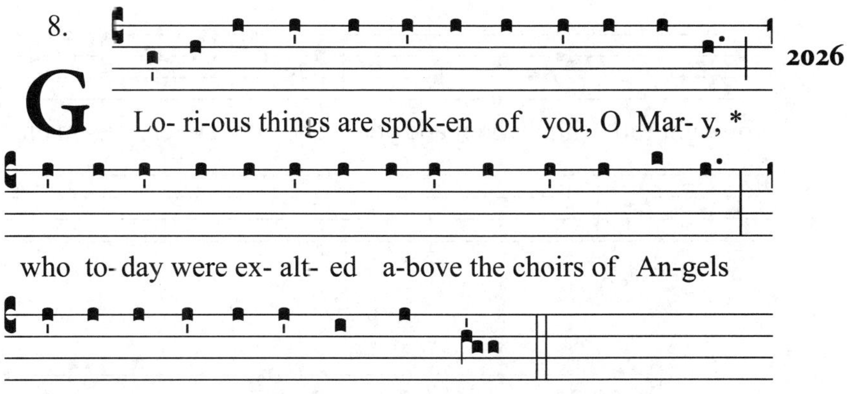
8.
2026
GLo- ri-ous things are spok-en of you, O Mar- y, *
who to- day were ex- alt- ed a-bove the choirs of An-gels
in- to e- ter- nal tri-umph with Christ.

- iv -

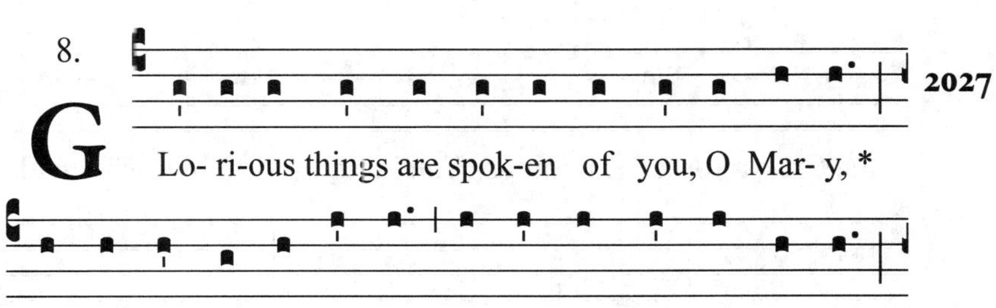
8.
2027
GLo- ri-ous things are spok-en of you, O Mar- y, *
who to-day were ex- alt- ed a-bove the choirs of An-gels

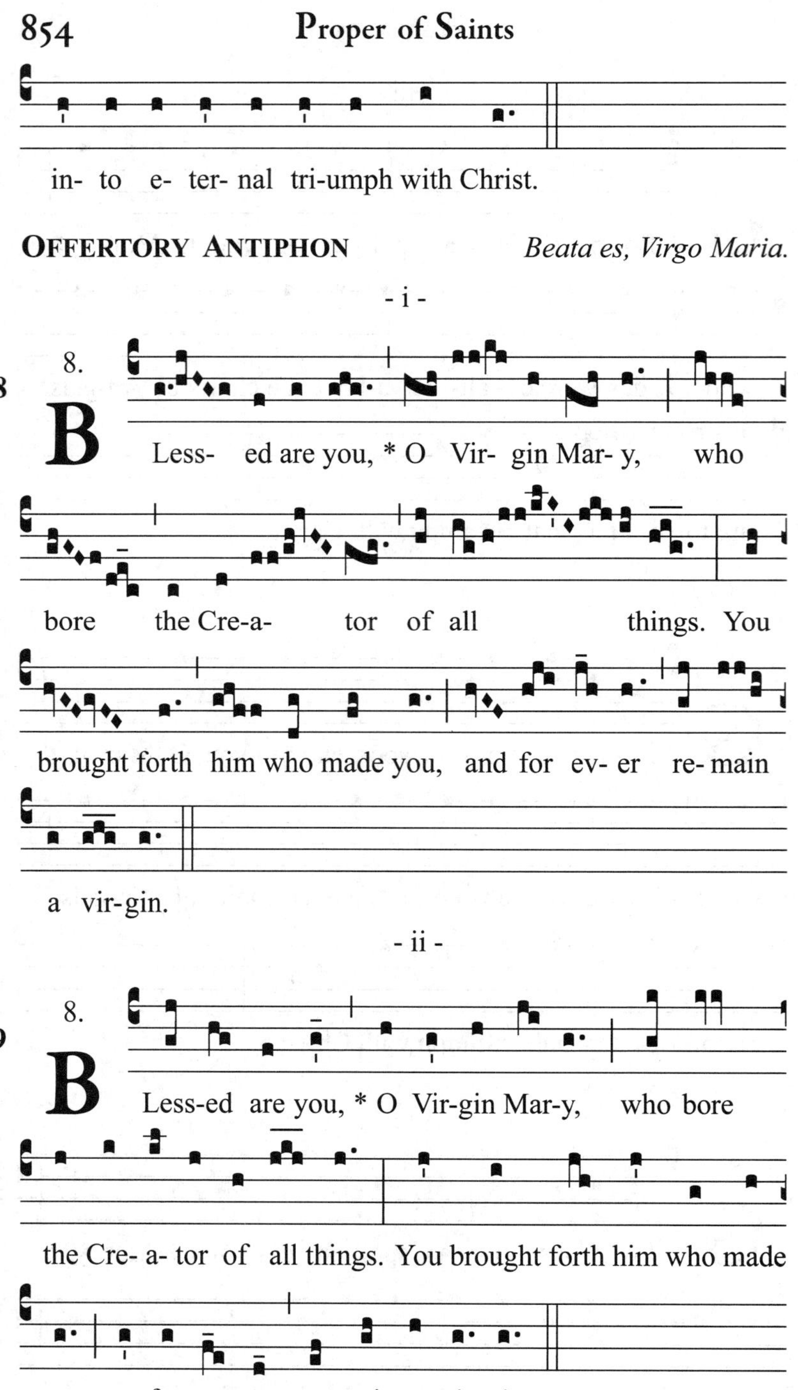
in- to e- ter- nal tri-umph with Christ.
8.
B Less- ed are you, * O Vir- gin Mar- y, who
bore the Cre-a- tor of all things. You
brought forth him who made you, and for ev- er re- main
a vir-gin.
8.
B Less-ed are you, * O Vir-gin Mar-y, who bore
the Cre- a- tor of all things. You brought forth him who made
you, yet for ev- er re-main a vir- gin.

Offertory Antiphon *Beata es, Virgo Maria.*

- i -

2028

- ii -

2029

VERSES *Eructavit cor meum verbum bonum. Ps* 44 : 2

℣. 1
MY heart o- ver-flows with a good-ly theme ; * as

2030

I sing my ode to the king.

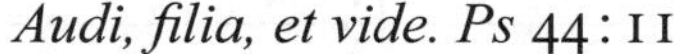
Audi, filia, et vide. Ps 44 : 11

℣. 2
HEark- en, O daughter and see, and in-cline your ear; *

2031

so shall the king de- sire your beau-ty.

Memores erunt nominis tui. Ps 44 : 18

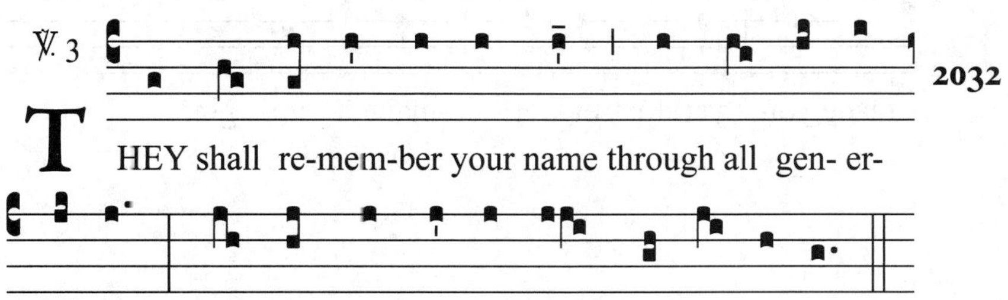
℣. 3
THEY shall re-mem-ber your name through all gen- er-

2032

a-tions. * Therefore shall peo-ple praise you for- ev- er.

- iii -

2033
8.
Blessed are you, O Virgin Mary, * who bore the Creator of all things. You brought forth him who made you, yet for ever remain a virgin.

- iv -

2034
8.
Blessed are you, O Virgin Mary, * who bore the Creator of all things. You brought forth him who made you, yet for ever remain a virgin.

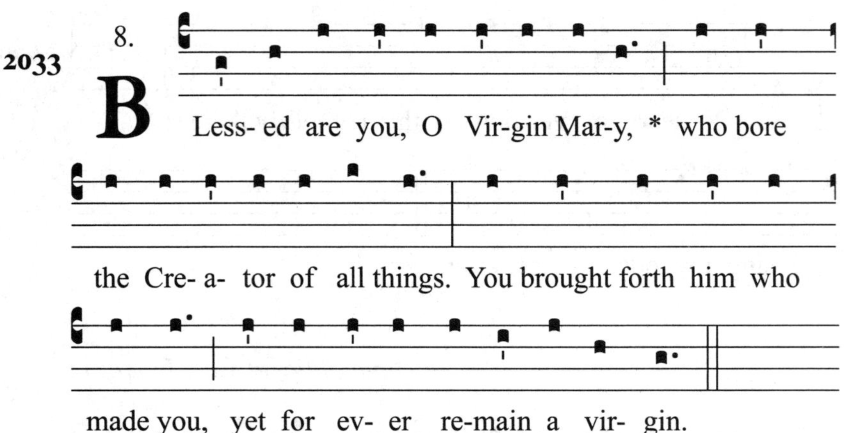

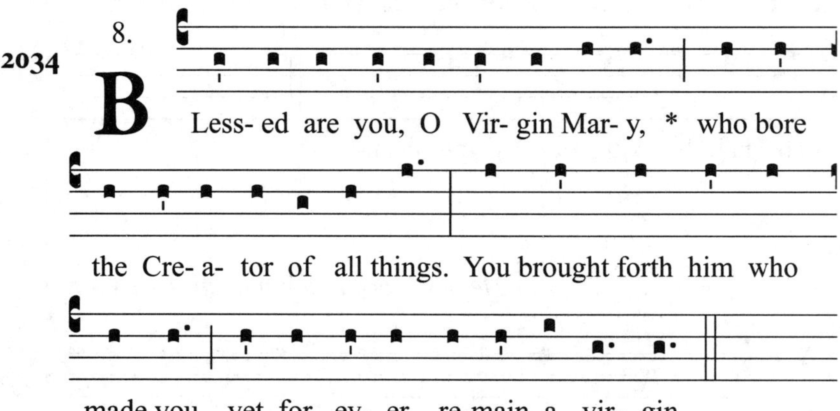

COMMUNION ANTIPHON *Beata viscera Mariæ Virginis.*
Cf. Lk 11:27

- i -

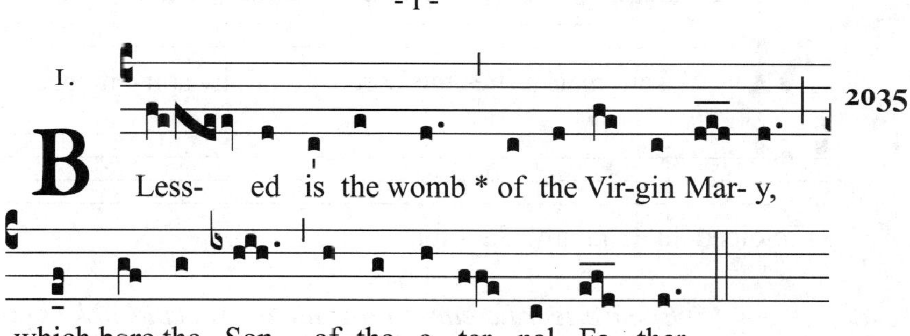
1.
2035
BLess-ed is the womb * of the Vir-gin Mar-y,
which bore the Son of the e- ter- nal Fa- ther.

- ii -

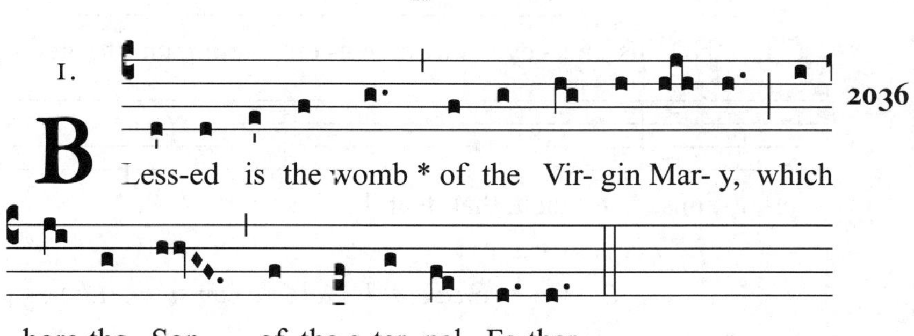
1.
2036
BLess-ed is the womb * of the Vir- gin Mar- y, which
bore the Son of the e-ter- nal Fa-ther.

Magnificat anima mea Dominum. Lk 1 : 47

2037

℣. 1
MY soul mag-ni-fies the Lord, * and my spir- it has
rejoiced in God my Sav- ior.

Et misericordia eius a progenie in progenies. Lk 1 : 50

2038
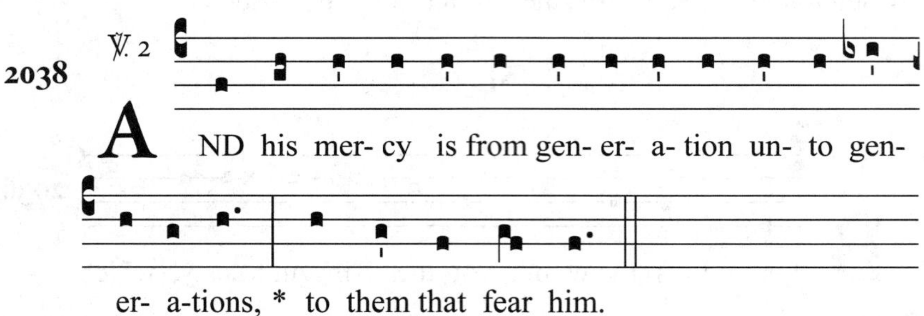
℣. 2
AND his mer- cy is from gen- er- a- tion un- to gen-
er- a-tions, * to them that fear him.

Suscepit Israel puerum suum. Lk 1 : 54

2039
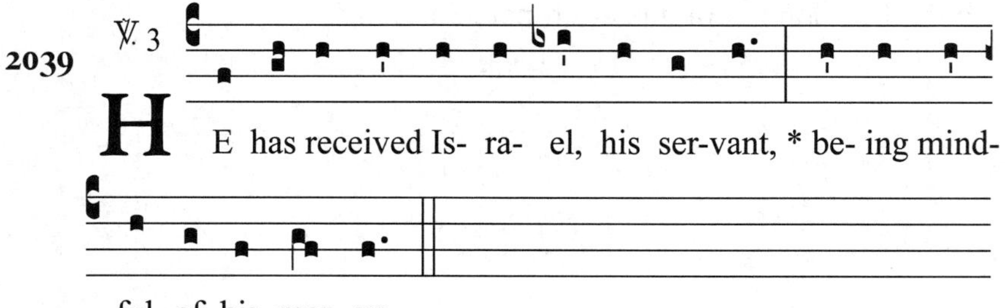
℣. 3
HE has received Is- ra- el, his ser-vant, * be- ing mind-
ful of his mer- cy.

- iii -

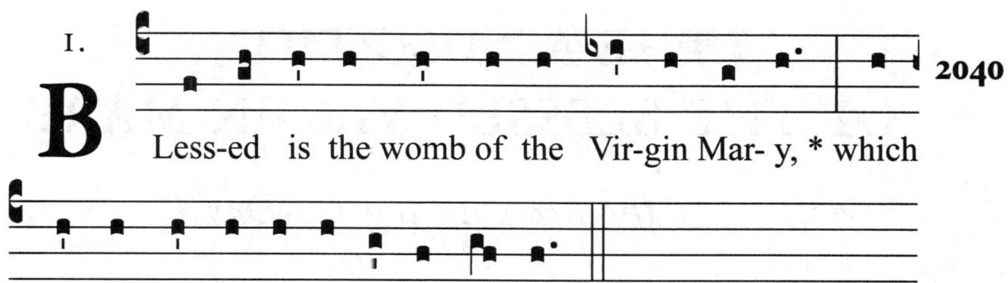
1.
B
Less-ed is the womb of the Vir-gin Mar- y, * which
2040

bore the Son of the e- ter-nal Fa-ther.

- iv -

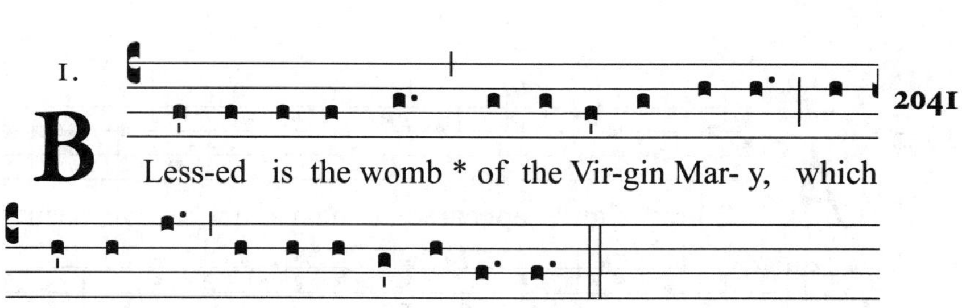
1.
B
Less-ed is the womb * of the Vir-gin Mar- y, which
2041

bore the Son of the e- ter-nal Fa-ther.

August 15

THE ASSUMPTION OF THE BLESSED VIRGIN MARY

At the Mass during the Day

ENTRANCE ANTIPHON *Signum magnum apparuit in cælo.*
Rev. 12:1

- i -

2042

7.
A great sign * appeared in heav- en: a wo- man
clothed with the sun, and the moon be-neath her feet, and
on her head a crown of twelve stars.

- ii -

2043

7.
A great sign * appeared in heav- en: a wo- man
clothed with the sun, and the moon beneath her feet, and

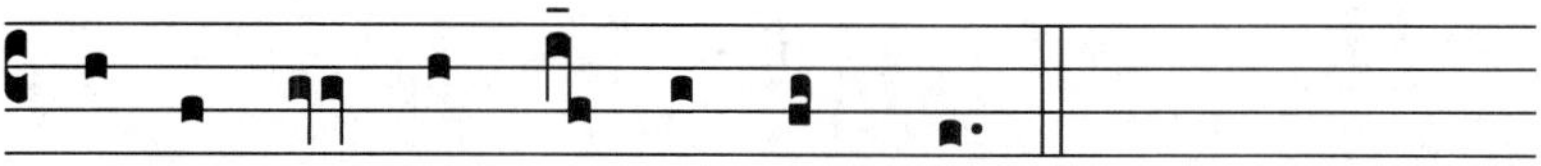

on her head a crown of twelve stars.

Ps 97, *solemn tone, p.* 67.

VERSES *Cantate Domino canticum novum. Ps* 97:1

℣. 1

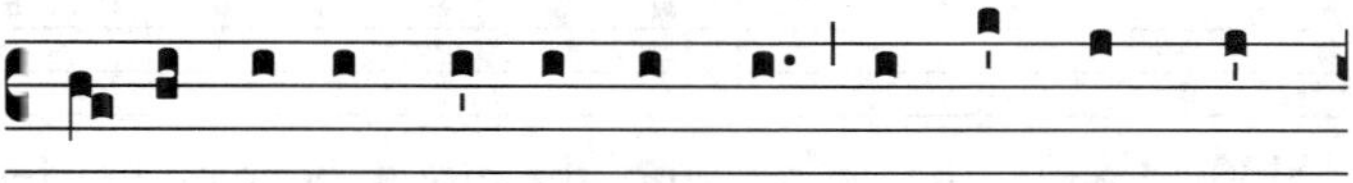

O sing a new song to the Lord, for he has worked 2044

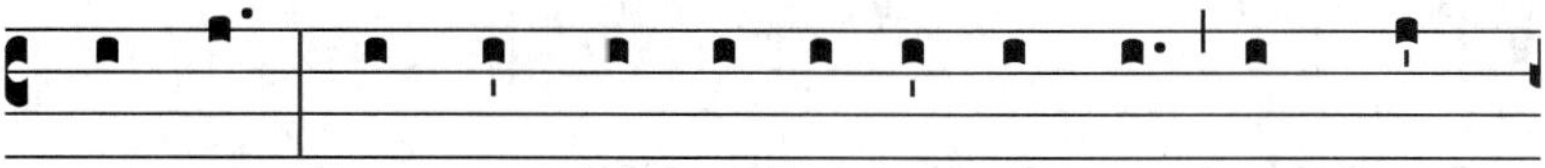

won-ders. * His right hand and his ho- ly arm have wrought

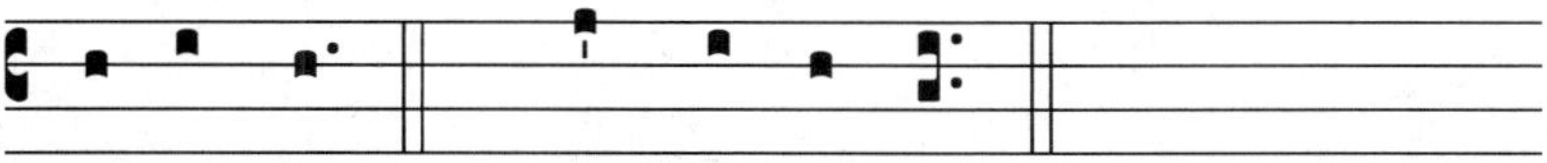

sal- va- tion. *Or:* wrought sal- va- tion.

Recordatus est misericordiæ suæ. Ps 97:3

℣. 2

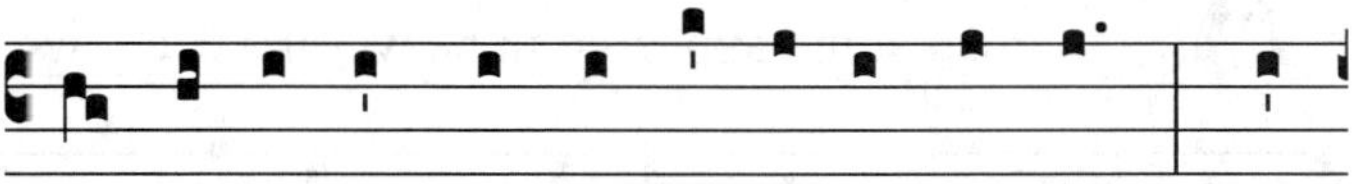

HE has remembered his mer-cy and his truth * toward 2045

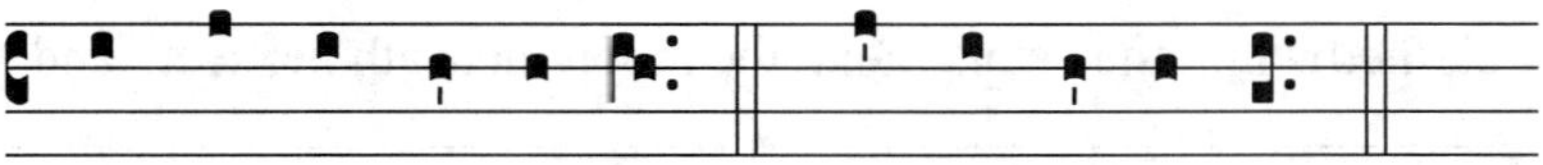

the house of Is- ra- el. *Or:* house of Is- ra- el.

Iubilate Deo, omnis terra. Ps 97:4

℣. 3 2046

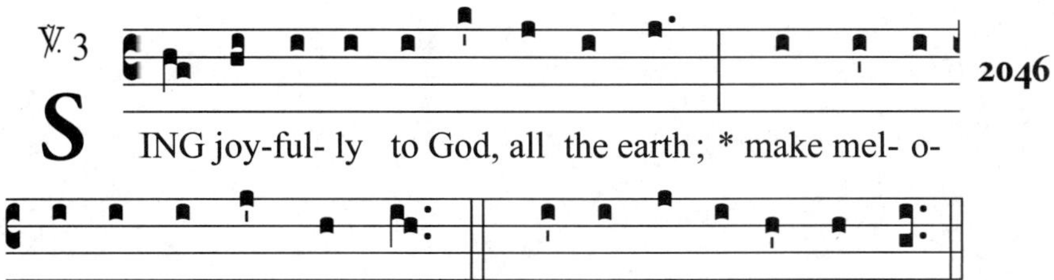
S
ING joy-ful- ly to God, all the earth; * make mel- o-

o- dy, re-joice and sing. *Or:* mel- o- dy, rejoice and sing.

- iii -

2047

7.
A great sign appeared in heav- en : * a wo- man
clothed with the sun, and the moon beneath her feet, and
on her head a crown of twelve stars.

- iv -

2048

7.
A great sign appeared in heav- en : * a wo- man
clothed with the sun, and the moon beneath her feet, and
on her head a crown of twelve stars.

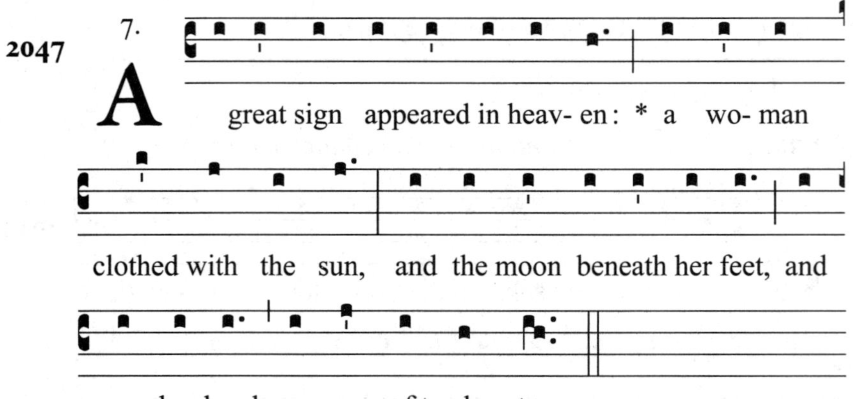

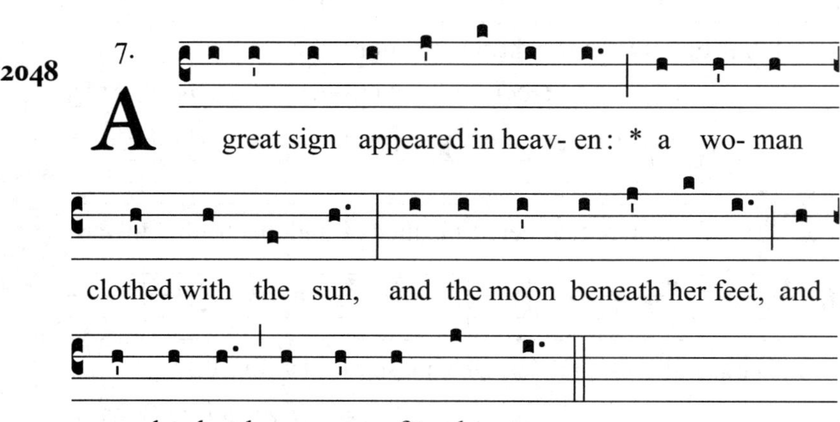

OFFERTORY ANTIPHON *Assumpta est Maria in cælo.*

- i -

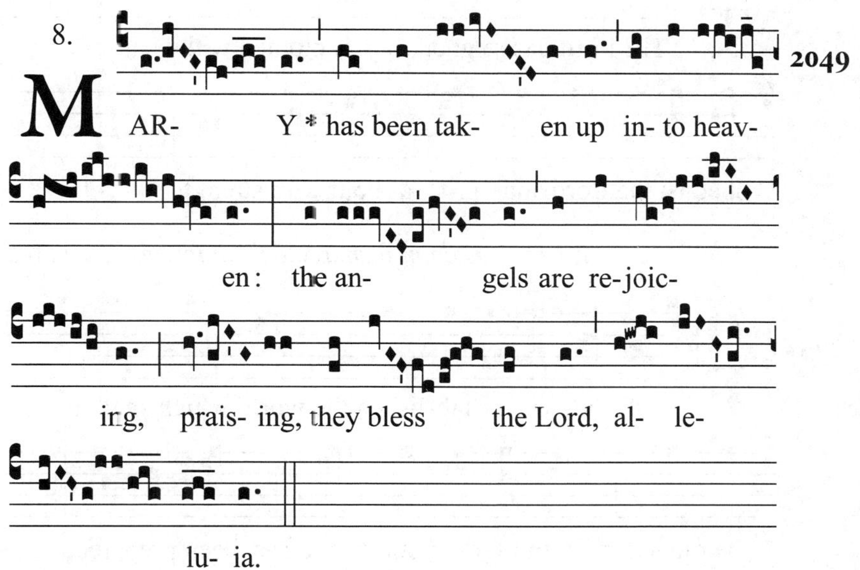
8.
2049
MARY * has been taken up into heaven: the angels are rejoicing, praising, they bless the Lord, alleluia.

- ii -

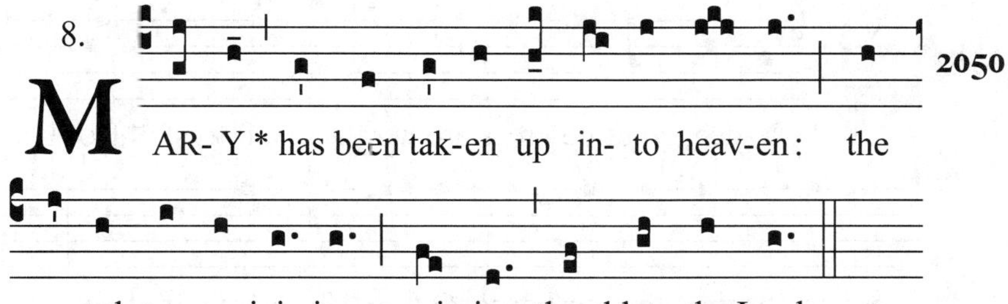
8.
2050
MARY * has been taken up into heaven: the angels are rejoicing, praising, they bless the Lord.

VERSES *Dominus regnavit. Ps* 92 : 1

2051 ℣. 1

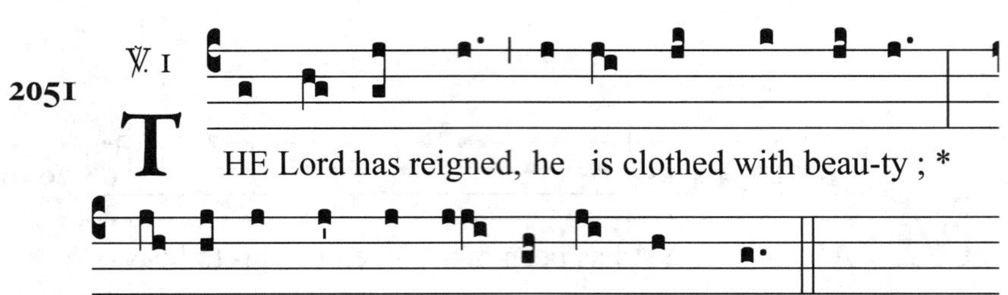

THE Lord has reigned, he is clothed with beau-ty ; * robed is the Lord and girt a- bout with strength.

Etenim formavit orbem terræ. Ps 92 : 1-2

2052 ℣. 2

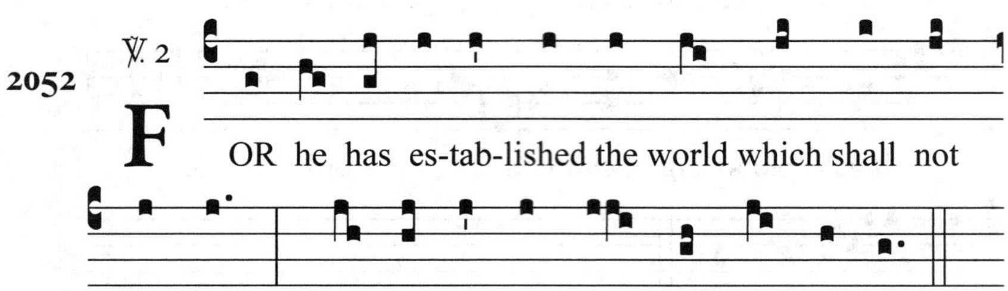

FOR he has es-tab-lished the world which shall not be moved. * From of old your throne has been prepared.

Testimonia tua credibilia facta sunt nimis. Ps 92 : 5

2053 ℣. 3

IN-deed your de-crees are worth-y of trust. * Ho- li-ness is fit-ting to your house, O Lord, for length of days.

- iii -

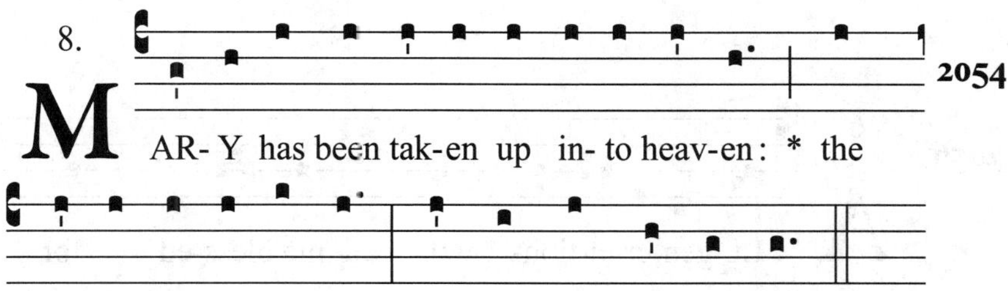
8.
2054
MARY has been tak-en up in- to heav-en: * the
an-gels are re-joic-ing, prais- ing, they bless the Lord.

- iv -

8.
2055
MARY has been tak-en up in- to heav-en: * the
an-gels are re-joic-ing, prais- ing, they bless the Lord.

COMMUNION ANTIPHON *Beatam me dicent.*
Lk 1:48-49

- i -

2056
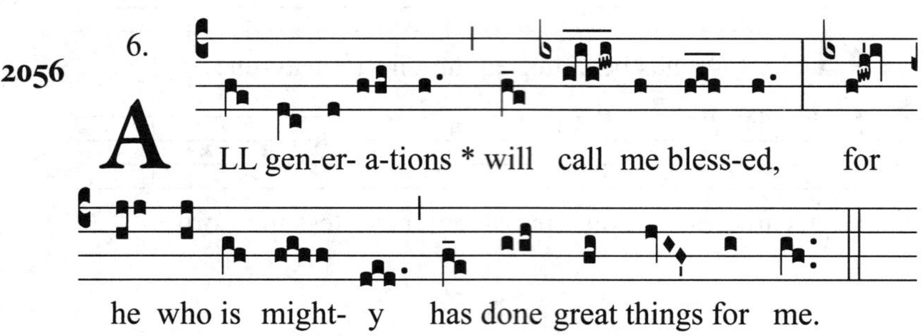
6.
ALL gen-er- a-tions * will call me bless-ed, for
he who is might- y has done great things for me.

- ii -

2057
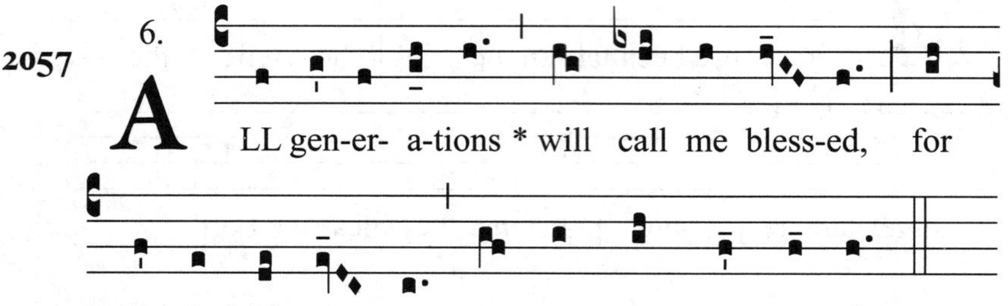
6.
ALL gen-er- a-tions * will call me bless-ed, for
he who is might- y has done great things for me.

Magnificat anima mea Dominum. Lk 1 : 47

℣. 1
2058
MY soul mag-ni-fies the Lord, * and my spir- it has
rejoiced in God my Sav- ior.

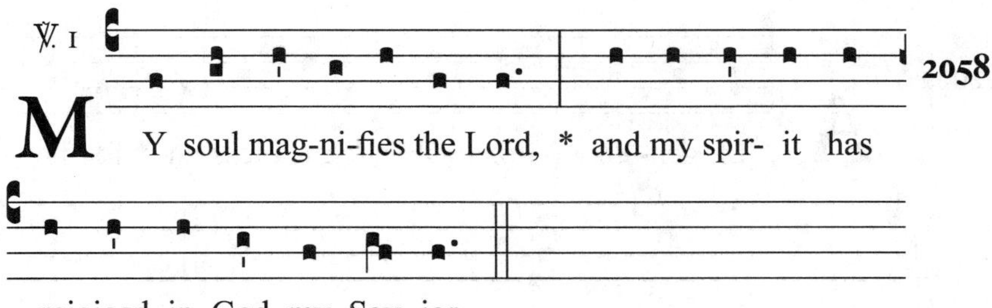

Et misericordia eius a progenie in progenies. Lk 1 : 50

℣. 2
2059
AND his mer- cy is from gen- er- a- tion un- to gen-
er- a- tions, * to them that fear him.

Suscepit Israel puerum suum. Lk 1 : 54

℣. 3
2060
HE has received Is- ra- el, his ser-vant, * be- ing mind-
ful of his mer- cy.

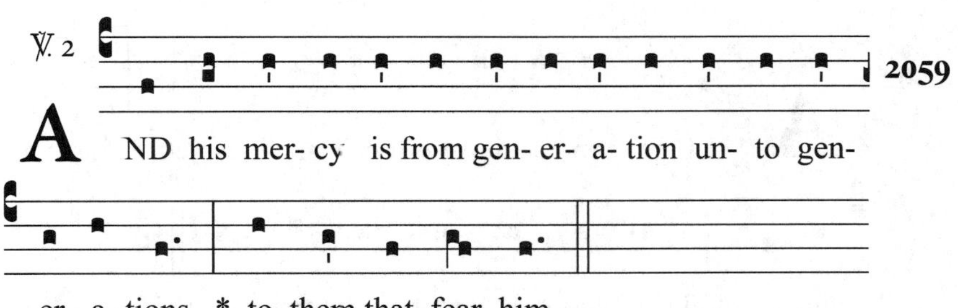

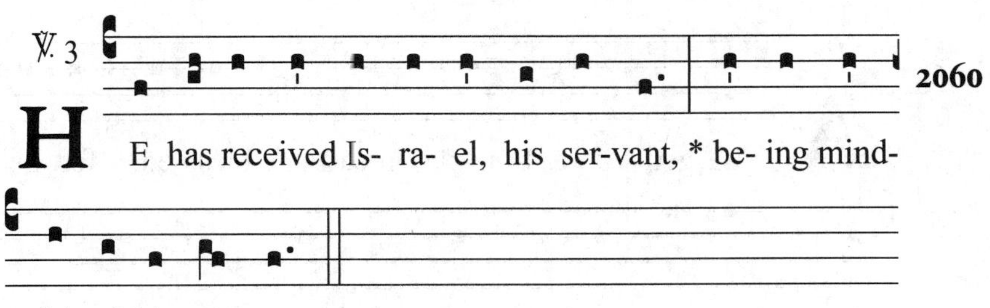

- iii -

2061

6.
ALL gen- er- a- tions will call me bless-ed, * for he
who is might-y has done great things for me.

Or:

2062

6.
ALL gen- er- a- tions will call me bless-ed, * for he
who is might-y has done great things for me.

- iv -

2063

6.
ALL gen- er- a- tions * will call me bless-ed, for he
who is might-y has done great things for me.

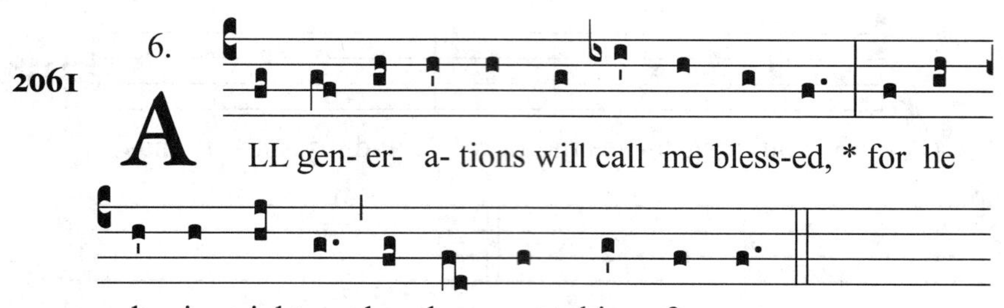

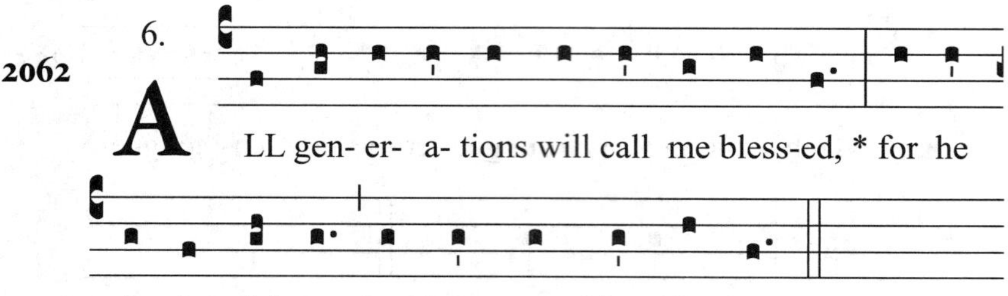

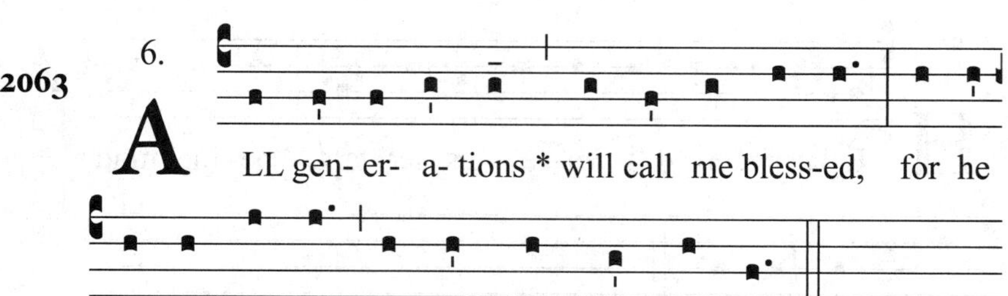

September 14

THE EXALTATION OF THE HOLY CROSS

ENTRANCE ANTIPHON *Nos autem gloriari. Cf. Gal* 6 : 14

- i -

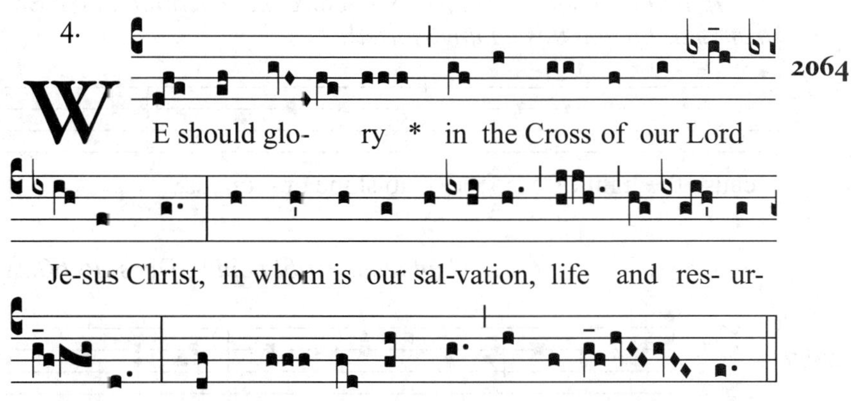
4.
W
E should glo- ry * in the Cross of our Lord
2064
Je-sus Christ, in whom is our sal-vation, life and res- ur-
rec- tion, through whom we are saved and de- liv- ered.

- ii -

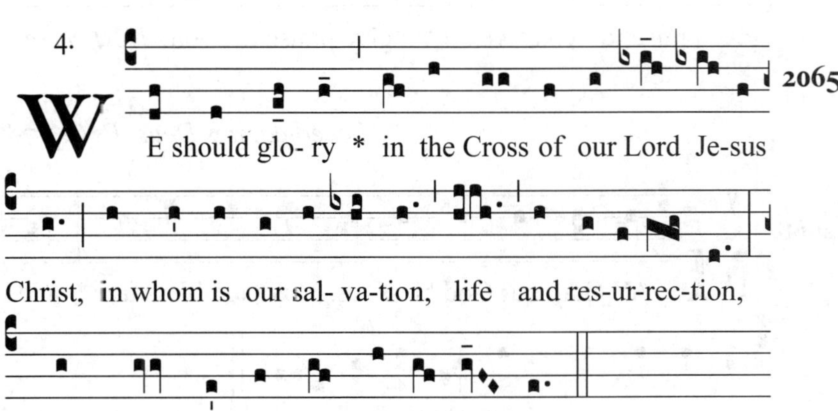
4.
W
E should glo- ry * in the Cross of our Lord Je-sus
2065
Christ, in whom is our sal- va-tion, life and res-ur-rec-tion,
through whom we are saved and de- liv- ered.

VERSES *Deus misereatur nostri. Ps* 66 : 2

2066
℣. 1
MAY God have mer-cy up- on us, and bless us ; * may
he cause the light of his face to shine up- on us. Ant.

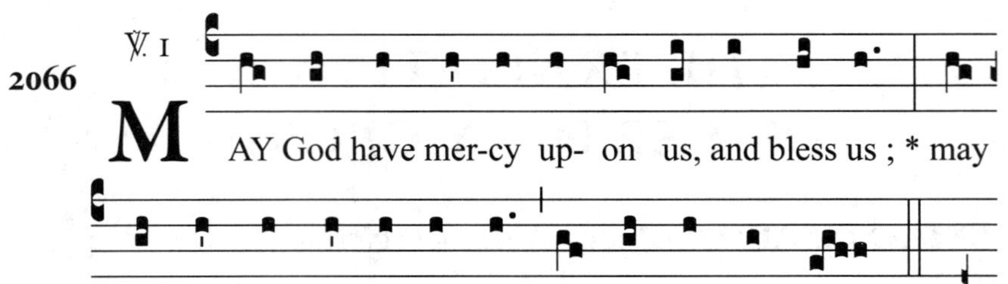

If another Psalm verse follows before the repetition of the Entrance Antiphon, this ending is used:

cause the light of his face to shine up- on us.

Confiteantur tibi populi, Deus. Ps 66 : 4

2067
℣. 2
LET peo-ple confess to you, O God ; * let all peo-ple
give praise to you. Ant. Or : give praise to you. Next verse.

Benedicat nos Deus. Ps 66 : 7-8

2068
℣. 3
MAY God, our God bless us. May God bless us, * and
may all the ends of the earth re-vere him. Ant.

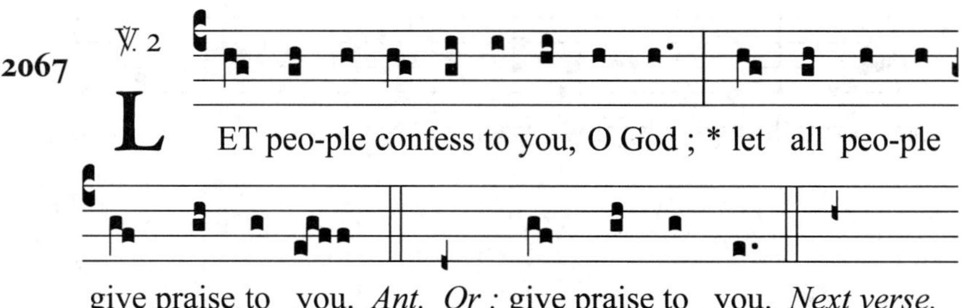

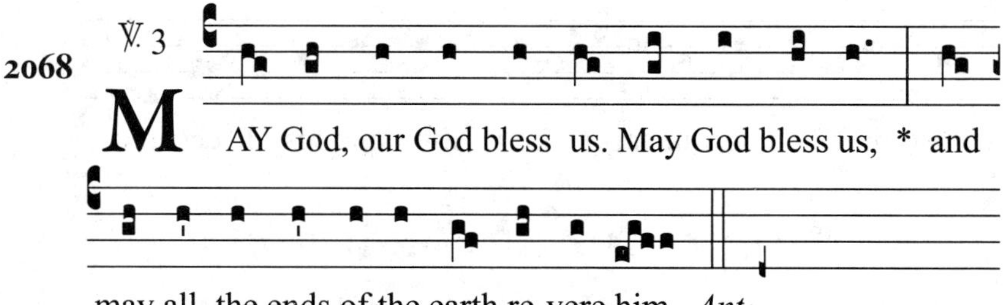

- iii -

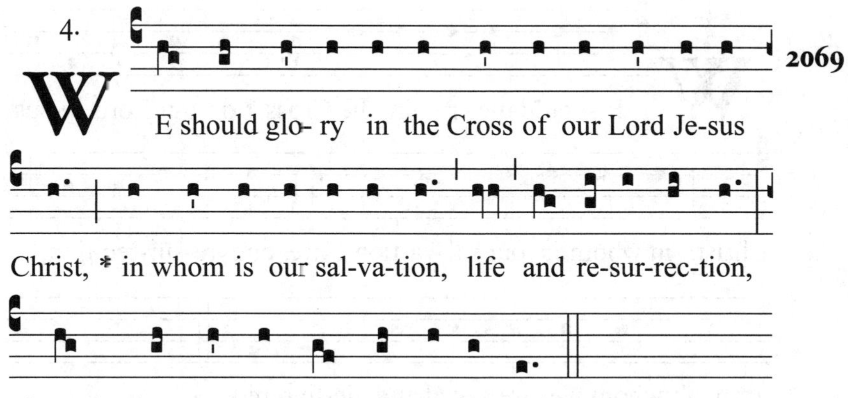
4.
2069
WE should glo- ry in the Cross of our Lord Je-sus
Christ, * in whom is our sal-va-tion, life and re-sur-rec-tion,
through whom we are saved and de-liv-ered.

Or:

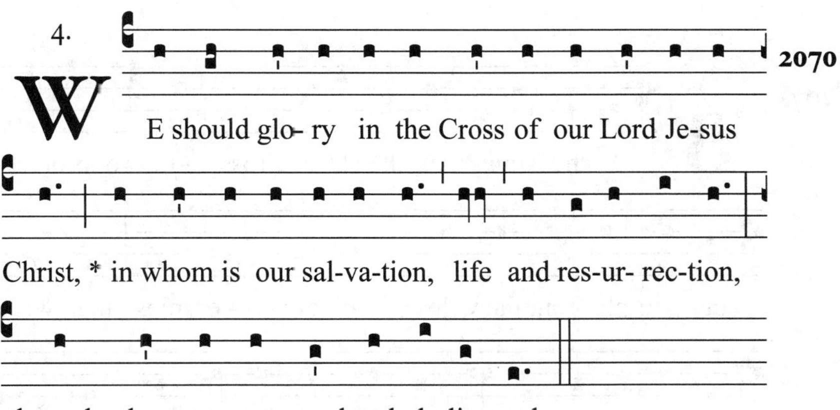
4.
2070
WE should glo- ry in the Cross of our Lord Je-sus
Christ, * in whom is our sal-va-tion, life and res-ur- rec-tion,
through whom we are saved and de-liv-ered.

- iv -

2071 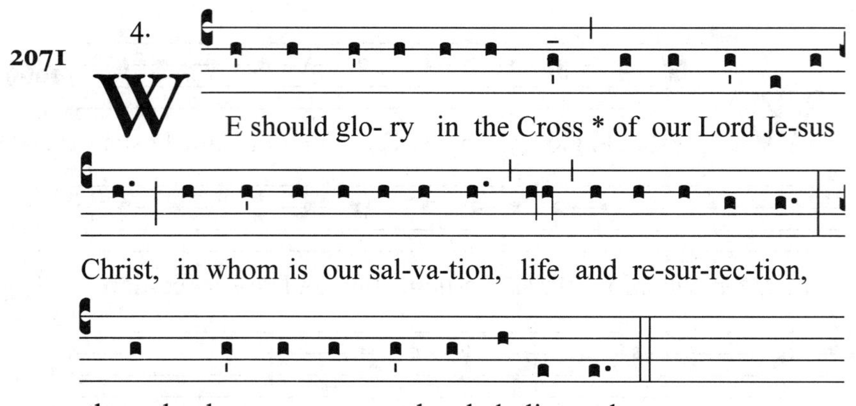
4.
WE should glo- ry in the Cross * of our Lord Je-sus
Christ, in whom is our sal-va-tion, life and re-sur-rec-tion,
through whom we are saved and de-liv-ered.

OFFERTORY ANTIPHON *Protege, Domine plebem tuam.*

- i -

2072 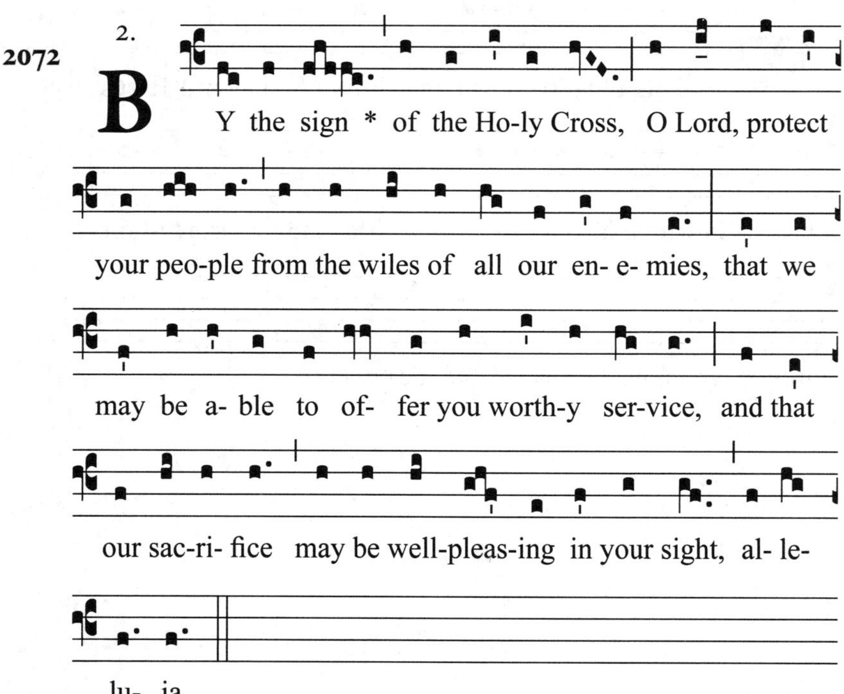
2.
BY the sign * of the Ho-ly Cross, O Lord, protect
your peo-ple from the wiles of all our en- e- mies, that we
may be a- ble to of- fer you worth-y ser-vice, and that
our sac-ri- fice may be well-pleas-ing in your sight, al- le-
lu- ia.

Verses. *Annuntiate inter gentes. Ps* 95:3

℣. 1
2073
DEclare his glo-ry a-mong the na-tions ; * his wonders
a-mong all the peo-ples.

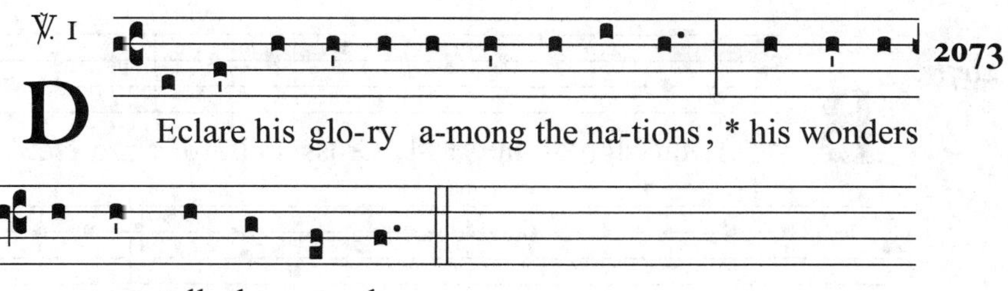

Confessio et pulchritudo. Ps 95:6

℣. 2
2074
IN his presence are praise and beau-ty, * ho- li-ness
and maj- es- ty are in his sanc-tu- ar- y.

Afferte Domino. Ps 95:7

℣. 3
2075
BRing to the Lord, you fam- i- lies of the na-tions, *
bring to the Lord glo- ry and hon-or.

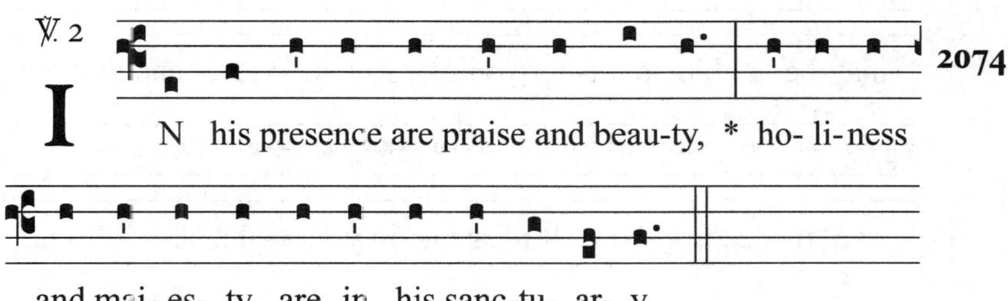

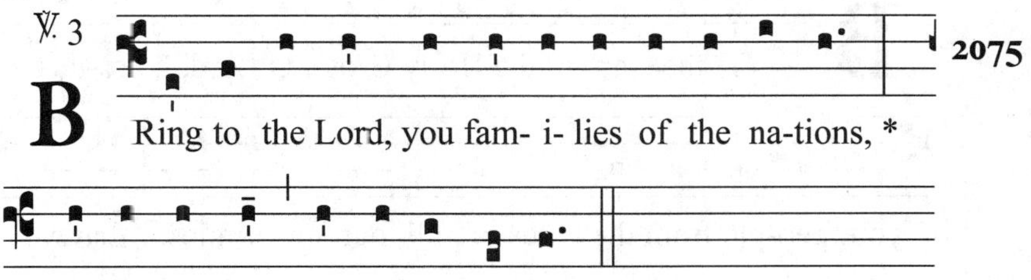

- iii -

2076

2.
BY the sign of the Ho-ly Cross, O Lord, * pro-tect
your peo-ple from the wiles of all our en- e-mies, that we
may be a- ble to of- fer you worth-y ser-vice, and that our
sac- ri- fice may be well-pleasing in your sight, al- le- lu- ia.

- iv -

2077

2.
BY the sign of the Ho-ly Cross, O Lord, * pro-tect
your peo-ple from the wiles of all our en- e-mies, that we
may be a- ble to of- fer you worth-y ser-vice, and that our
sac- ri-fice may be well-pleasing in your sight, al- le- lu- ia.

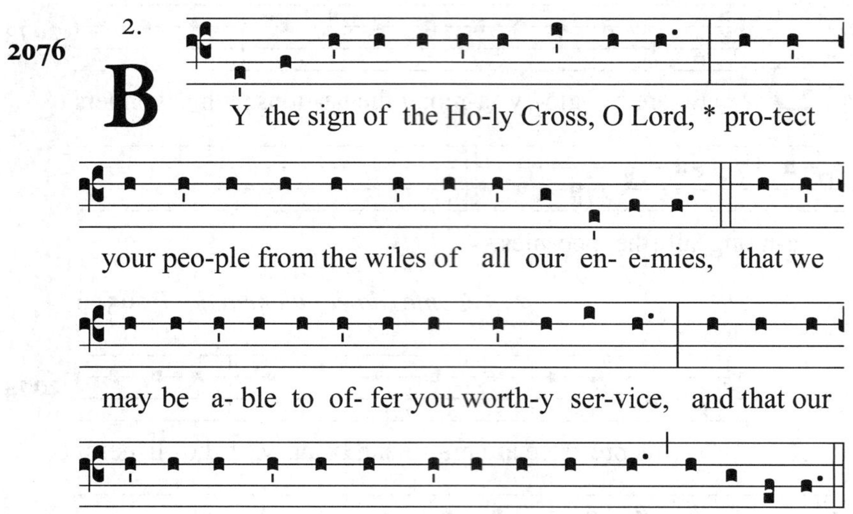

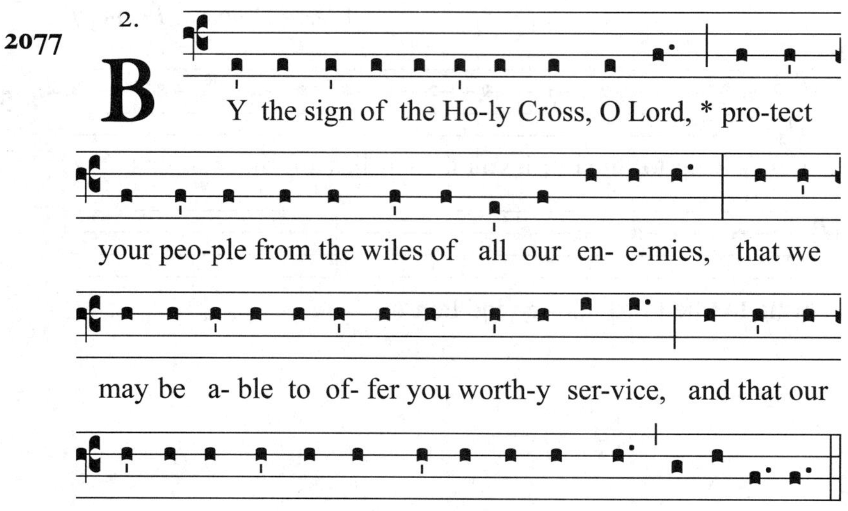

COMMUNION ANTIPHON *Ego si exaltatus fuero.* *Jn* 12:32

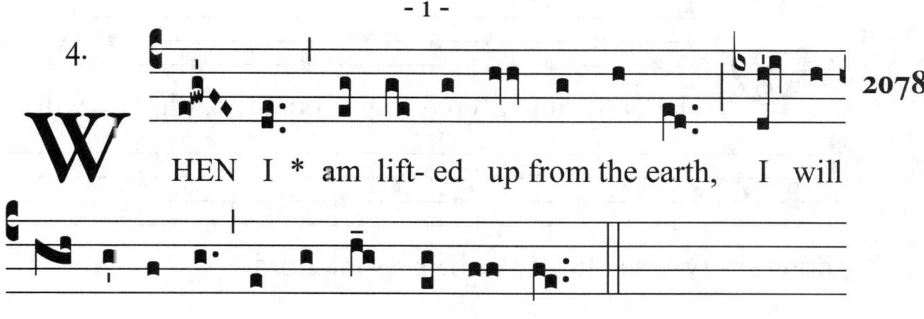
-i-
4.
WHEN I * am lift- ed up from the earth, I will
2078
draw ev- ry-one to my-self, says the Lord.

VERSES *Diligam te, Domine. Ps* 17:2

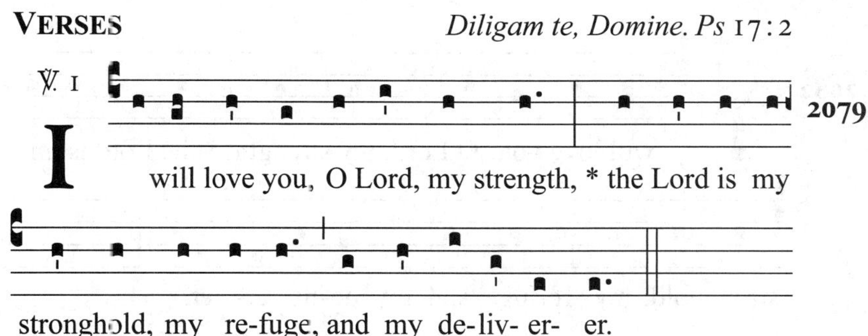
℣. 1
I will love you, O Lord, my strength, * the Lord is my
2079
stronghold, my re-fuge, and my de-liv- er- er.

Deus meus adiutor meus. Ps 17:3

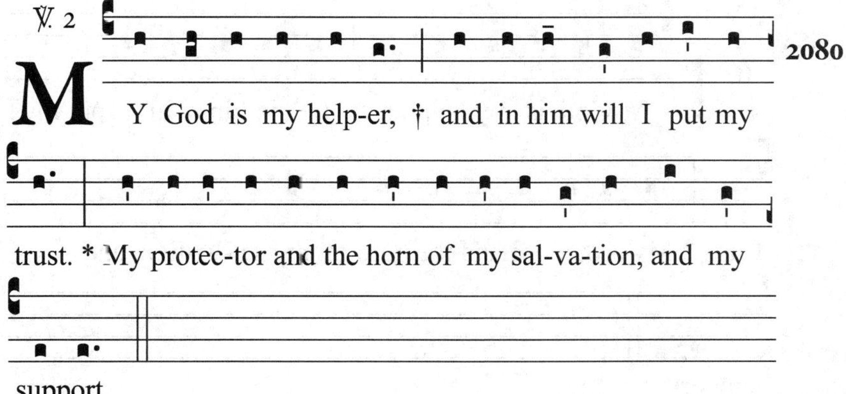
℣. 2
MY God is my help-er, † and in him will I put my
2080
trust. * My protec-tor and the horn of my sal-va-tion, and my
support

- ii -

2081

4. g
W HEN I am lift- ed up from the earth, * I will
draw ev- ry- one to my- self, says the Lord.

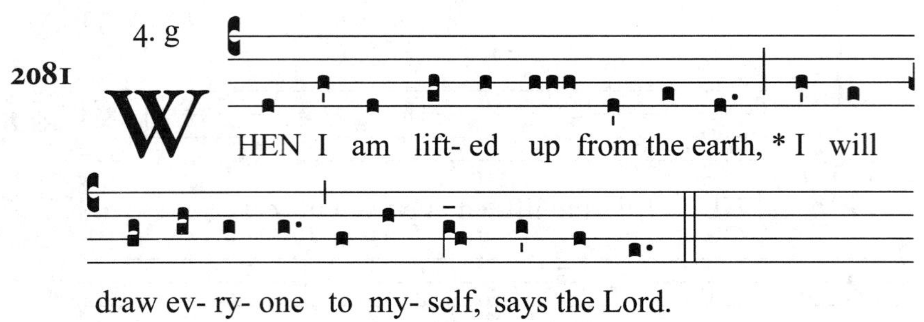

VERSES *Diligam te, Domine. Ps* 17:2

2082

℣. 1
I will love you, O Lord, my strength, * the Lord is my
stronghold, my re-fuge, and my de-liv- er- er.

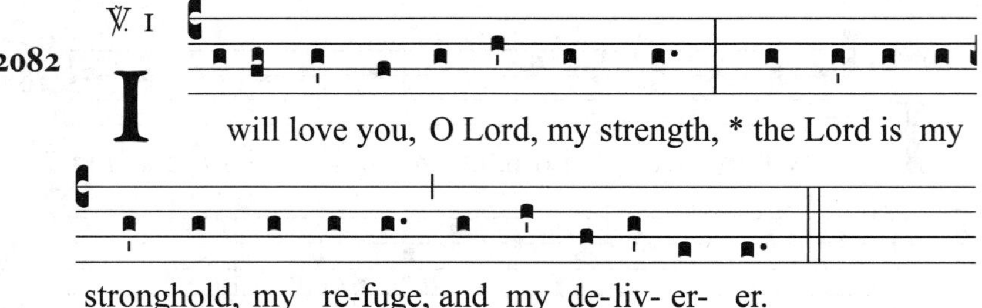

Deus meus adiutor meus. Ps 17:3

2083

℣. 2
M Y God is my help-er, † and in him will I put my
trust. * My protec-tor and the horn of my sal-va-tion, and my
support.

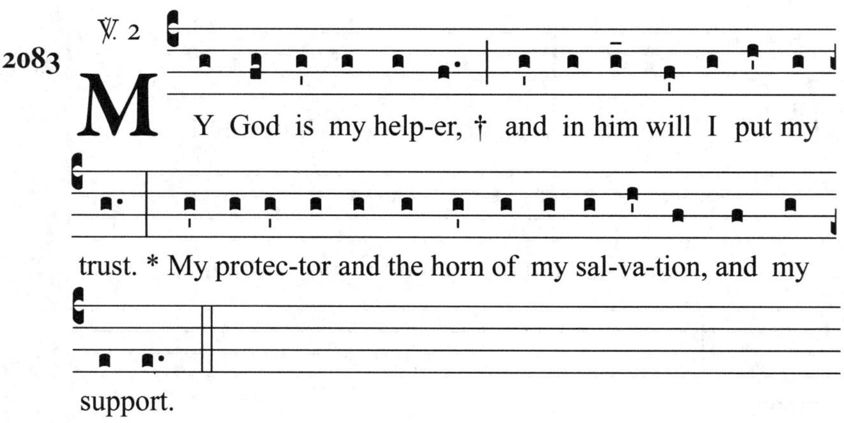

2084 ℣. 3. Prais-ing, | I will | *call up*-**on** the Lord. *
and I shall be | **saved** *from my* **en**-e-mies.

- iii -

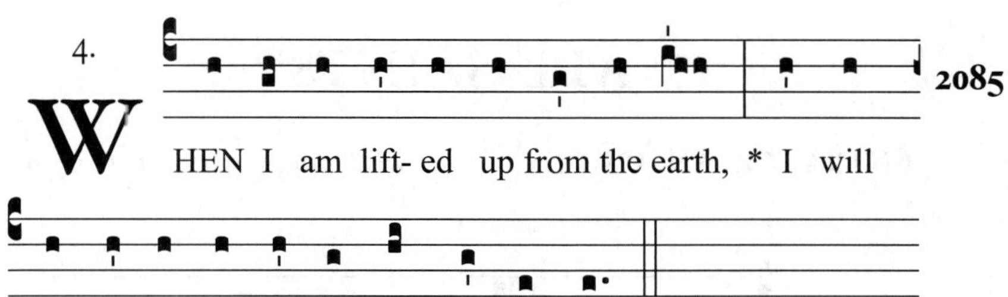
4.
WHEN I am lift- ed up from the earth, * I will
2085

draw ev- ry- one to my-self, says the Lord.

Or:

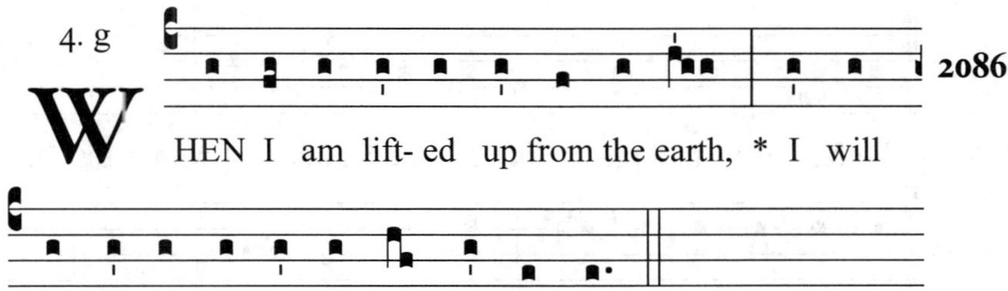
4. g
WHEN I am lift- ed up from the earth, * I will
2086

draw ev- ry- one to my-self, says the Lord.

- iv -

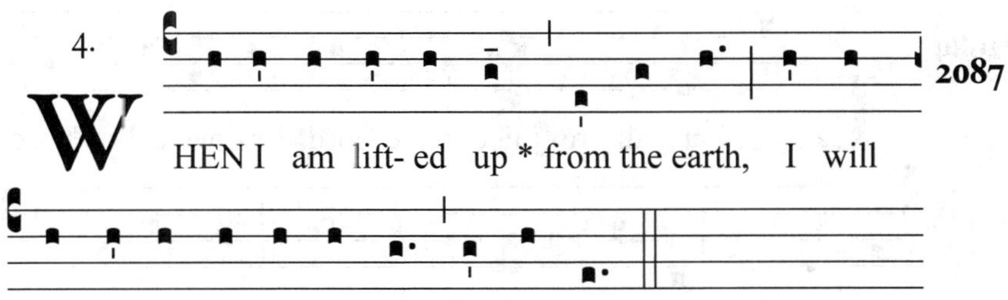
4.
WHEN I am lift- ed up * from the earth, I will
2087

draw ev- ry- one to my-self, says the Lord.

November 1

ALL SAINTS

ENTRANCE ANTIPHON *Gaudeamus omnes in Domino.*

- i -

2088

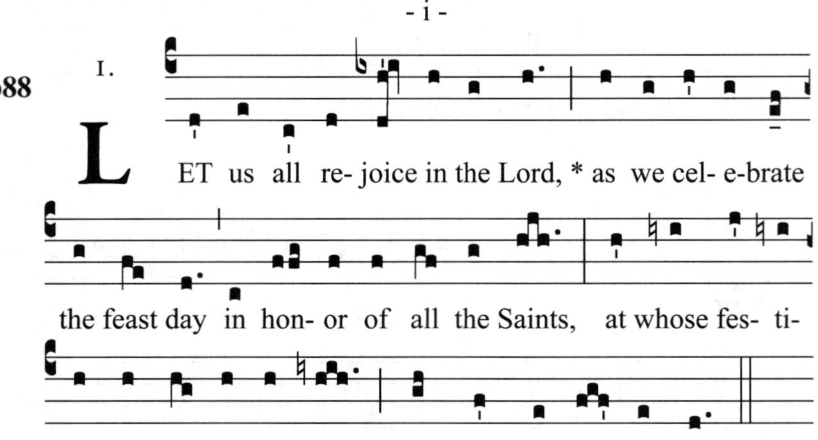
I.
LET us all re- joice in the Lord, * as we cel- e-brate
the feast day in hon- or of all the Saints, at whose fes- ti-
val the An-gels re- joice and praise the Son of God.

- ii -

2089

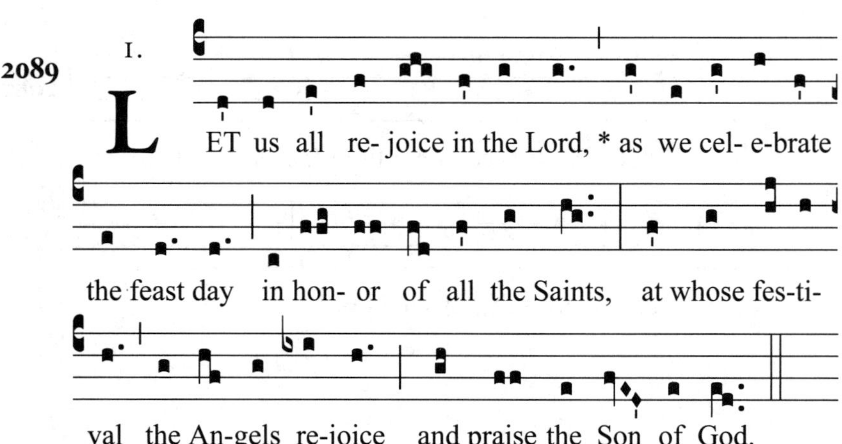
I.
LET us all re- joice in the Lord, * as we cel- e-brate
the feast day in hon- or of all the Saints, at whose fes-ti-
val the An-gels re-joice and praise the Son of God.

VERSES *Exsultate, iusti, in Domino. Ps* 32: 1

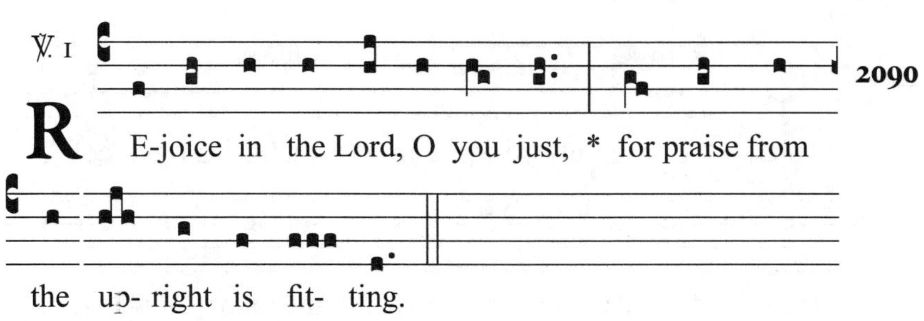
℣. 1
2090
R E-joice in the Lord, O you just, * for praise from
the up- right is fit- ting.

Ecce, oculi Domini. Ps 32: 18

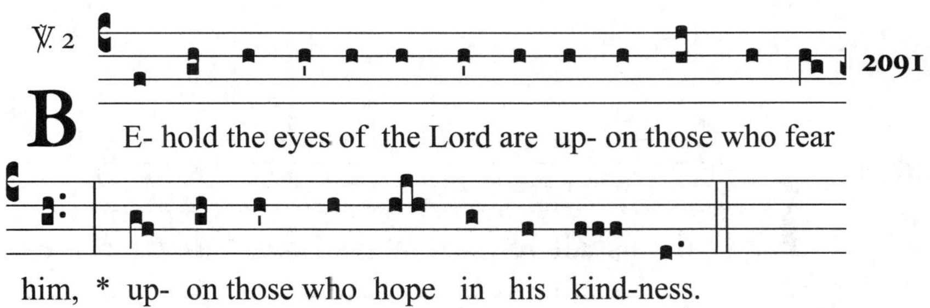
℣. 2
2091
B E- hold the eyes of the Lord are up- on those who fear
him, * up- on those who hope in his kind-ness.

Iuxta est Dominus. Ps 33: 19

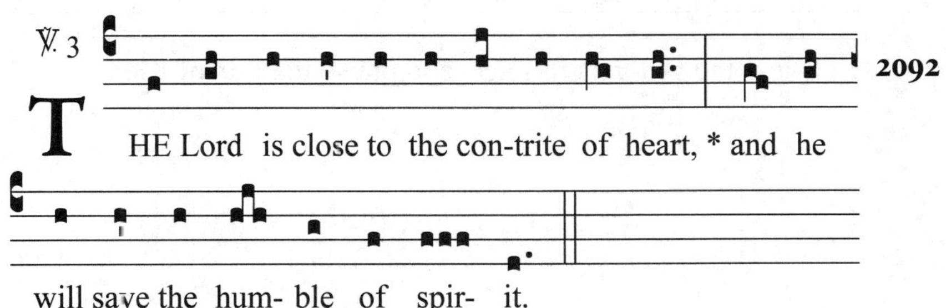
℣. 3
2092
T HE Lord is close to the con-trite of heart, * and he
will save the hum- ble of spir- it.

- iii -

2093

I.
LET us all re-joice in the Lord, * as we cel- e-
brate the feast day in hon-or of all the Saints, at whose fes-
ti- val the An-gels re-joice and praise the Son of God.

- iv -

2094

I.
LET us all re-joice in the Lord, * as we cel- e-
brate the feast day in hon-or of all the Saints, at whose fes-
ti- val the An-gels re-joice and praise the Son of God.

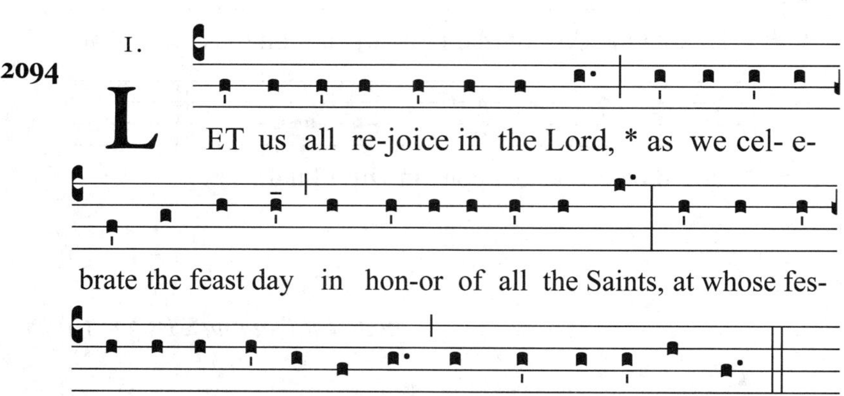

OFFERTORY ANTIPHON *Iustorum animæ. Wis* 3:1-2. 3

- i -

1\.

THE souls of the just * are in the hand of God, and 2095

no tor-ment shall touch them. They seemed, in view of the

fool-ish, to be dead; but they are in peace, al- le- lu- ia.

- ii -

1\.

THE souls of the just * are in the hand of God, and 2096

no tor-ment shall touch them. They seemed, in view of the

fool-ish, to be dead; but they are in peace, al- le- lu- ia.

VERSES *Exsultate, iusti, in Domino. Ps* 32: 1

2097

℣. 1
REJOICE in the Lord, O you just, * for praise from the up-right is fit-ting.

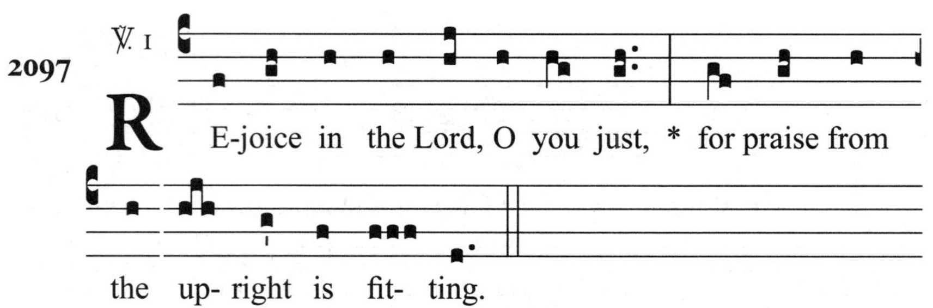

Ecce, oculi Domini. Ps 32 : 18

2098

℣. 2
BEHOLD the eyes of the Lord are up-on those who fear him, * up-on those who hope in his kind-ness.

Iuxta est Dominus. Ps 33 : 19

2099

℣. 3
THE Lord is close to the con-trite of heart, * and he will save the hum-ble of spir-it.

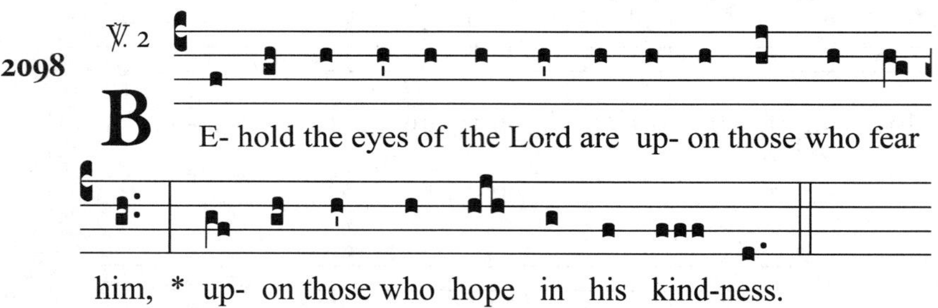

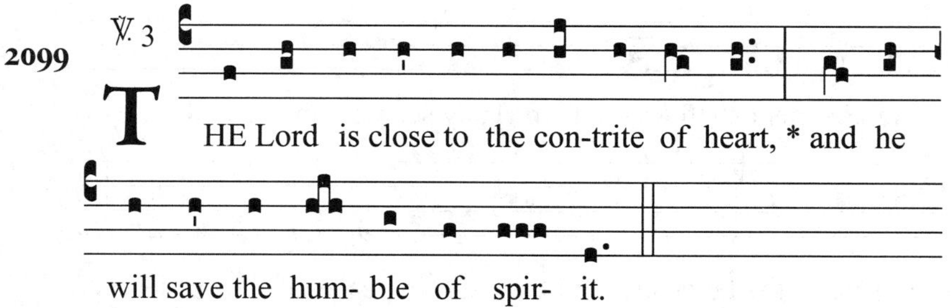

- iii -

I. 2100

THE souls of the just are in the hand of God, * and
no tor-ment shall touch them. They seemed, in view of the
fool-ish, to be dead; but they are in peace, al- le- lu- ia.

- iv -

I. 2101

THE souls of the just are in the hand of God, * and
no tor-ment shall touch them. They seemed, in view of the
fool-ish, to be dead; but they are in peace, al- le- lu- ia.

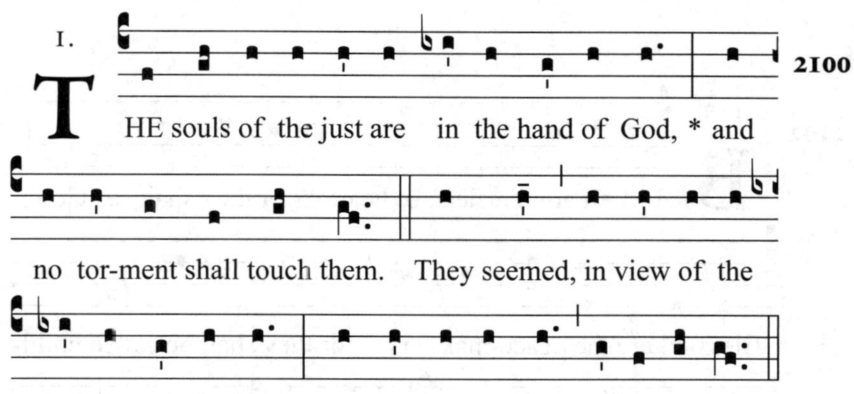

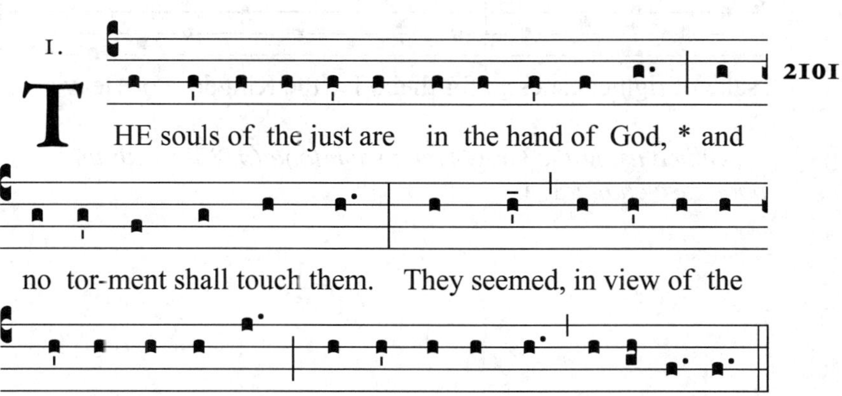

COMMUNION ANTIPHON *Beati mundo corde. Mt* 5:8-10

- ii -

2102

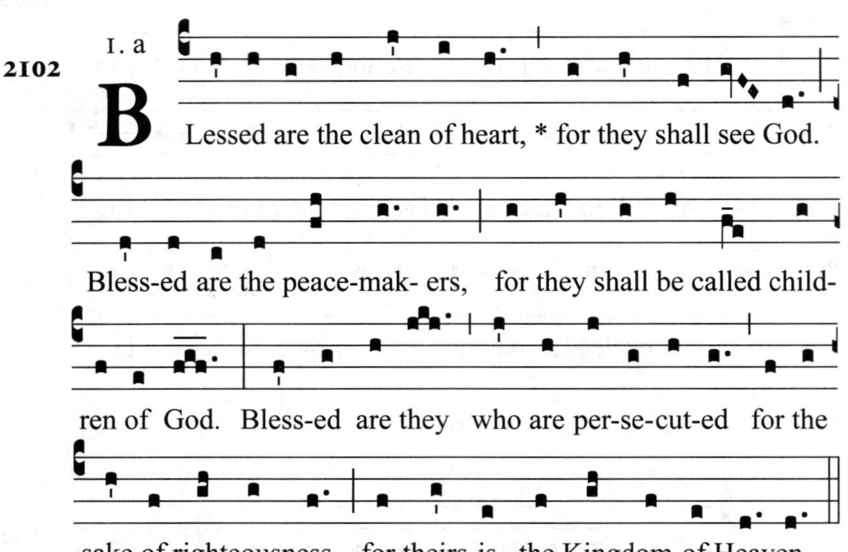
I. a
BLessed are the clean of heart, * for they shall see God.
Bless-ed are the peace-mak- ers, for they shall be called child-
ren of God. Bless-ed are they who are per-se-cut-ed for the
sake of righteousness, for theirs is the Kingdom of Heaven.

When using the Gregorian psalm tone (p. 885) with this antiphon, use ending I. a.

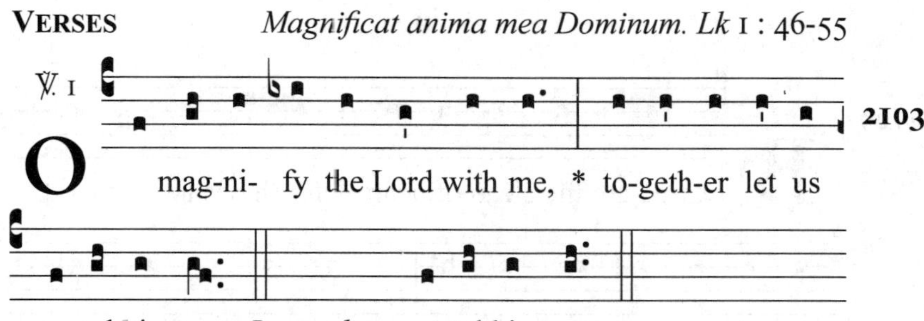
VERSES Magnificat anima mea Dominum. Lk 1 : 46-55
℣. 1
2103
O mag-ni- fy the Lord with me, * to-geth-er let us
ex-tol his name. I. a ending : ex-tol his name.

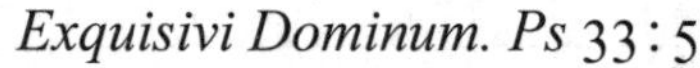
Exquisivi Dominum. Ps 33 : 5

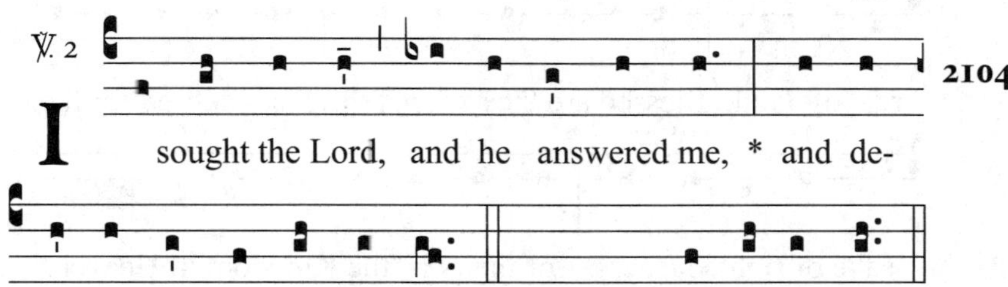
℣. 2
2104
I sought the Lord, and he answered me, * and de-
liv-ered me from all my fears. I. a ending : from all my fears.

Immittet angelus Domini. Ps 33 : 8

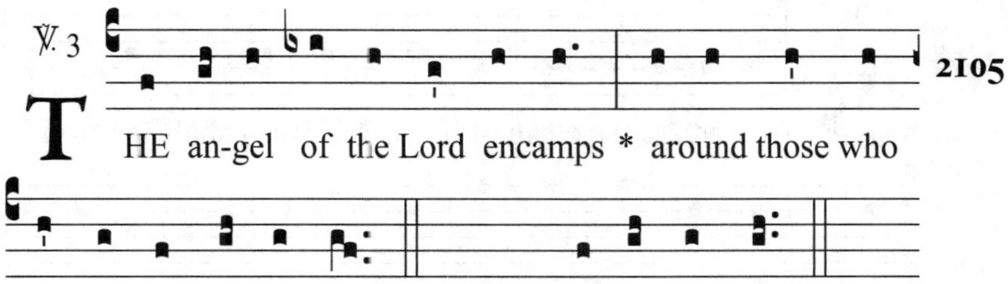
℣. 3
2105
THE an-gel of the Lord encamps * around those who
fear him, to res-cue them. I. a ending : to res-cue them.

Gustate et videte. Ps 33 : 9

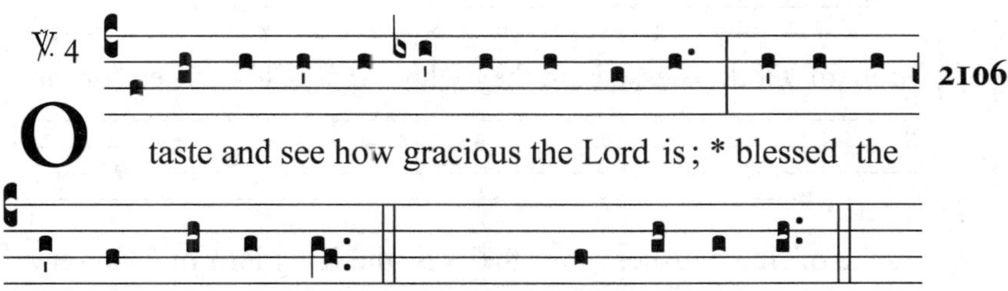
℣. 4
2106
O taste and see how gracious the Lord is ; * blessed the
man who hopes in him. I. a ending : who hopes in him.

- iii -

2107

I.
BLessed are the clean of heart, * for they shall see God.
Blessed are the peace-mak-ers, for they shall be called child-
ren of God. Blessed are they who are per- se- cut- ed for the
sake of righteousness, for theirs is the Kingdom of Heaven.

- iv -

2108

I.
BLessed are the clean of heart, * for they shall see God.
Blessed are the peace-mak-ers, for they shall be called child-
ren of God. Blessed are they who are per- se- cut- ed for the
sake of righteousness, for theirs is the Kingdom of Heav-en.

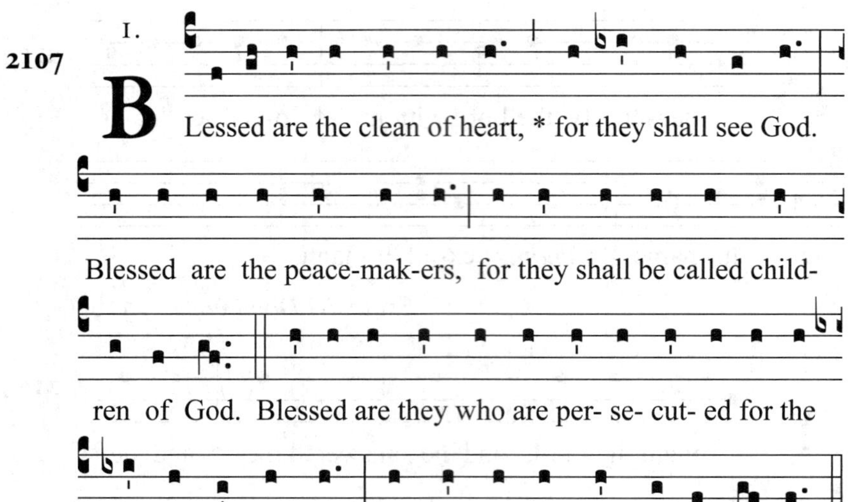

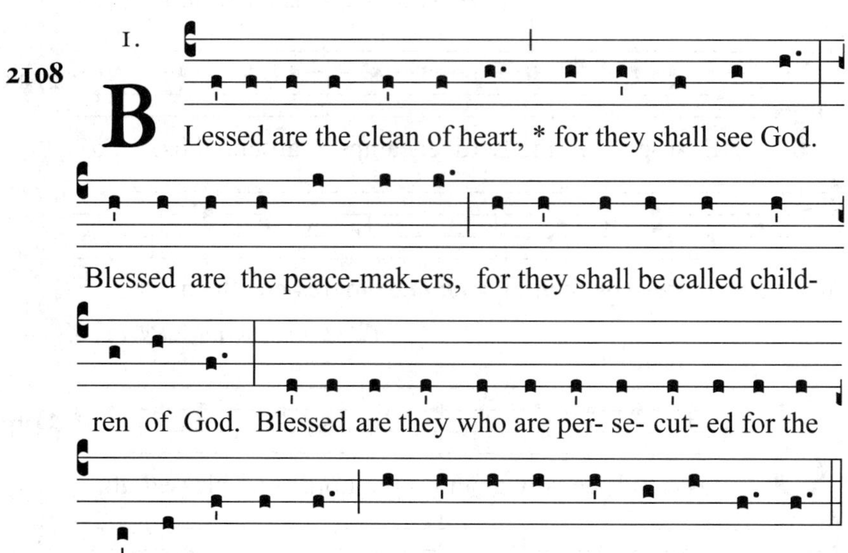

November 2

THE COMMEMORATION OF ALL THE FAITHFUL DEPARTED (ALL SOULS' DAY)

ENTRANCE ANTIPHON *Cf.* 6 *Esdr* 2:34-35

6.
2109
E - ter-nal rest * grant un- to them, O Lord, and let per-
pe- tu- al light shine up- on them.

Or:

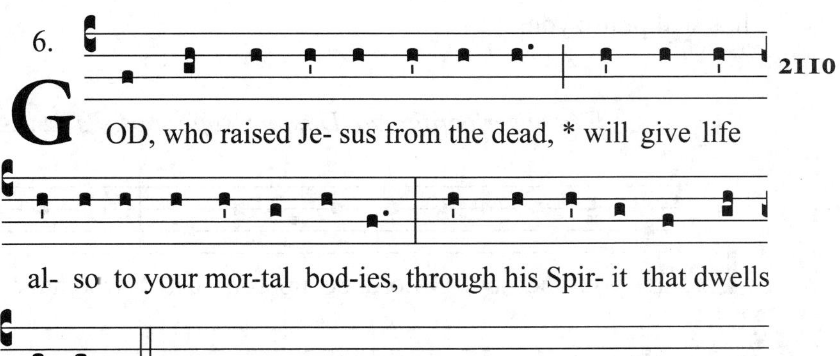
6.
2110
GOD, who raised Je- sus from the dead, * will give life
al- so to your mor-tal bod-ies, through his Spir- it that dwells
in you.

VERSES *Te decet hymnus, Deus, in Sion. Ps* 64:2-3

2111
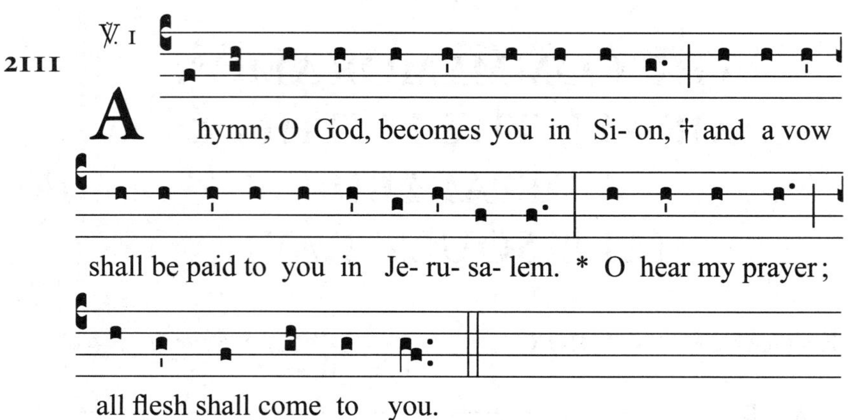
℣. 1
A hymn, O God, becomes you in Si- on, † and a vow
shall be paid to you in Je- ru- sa- lem. * O hear my prayer;
all flesh shall come to you.

Quoniam melior est misericordia tua. Ps 62:4

2112
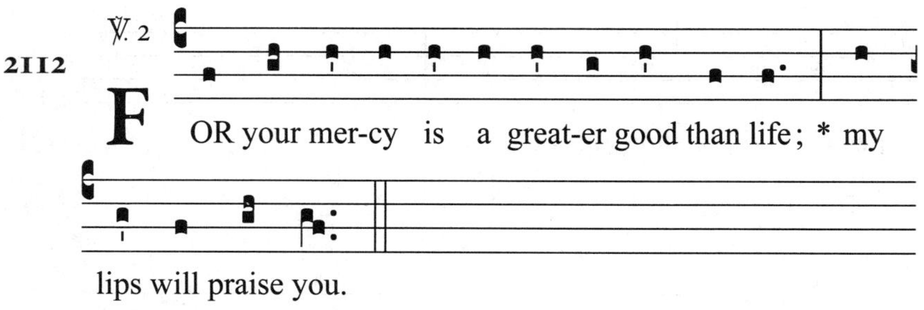
℣. 2
FOR your mer-cy is a great-er good than life; * my
lips will praise you.

Fiat misericordia tua, Domine, super nos. Ps 32:22

2113

℣. 3
LET your mer- cy, O Lord, be up- on us, * who have
placed all our hope in you.

OFFERTORY ANTIPHON

Out of the depths, p. 719 or The Lord is my shepherd, p. 712.

COMMUNION ANTIPHON *4 Esdr 2:35*

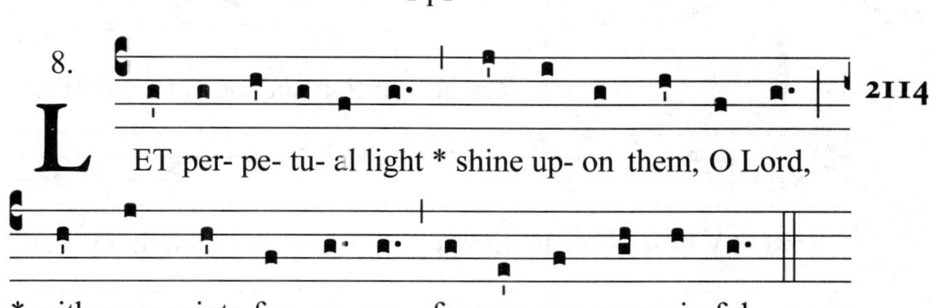
- i -
8.
LET per- pe- tu- al light * shine up- on them, O Lord,
2114
* with your saints for ev- er, for you are mer- ci- ful.

VERSE

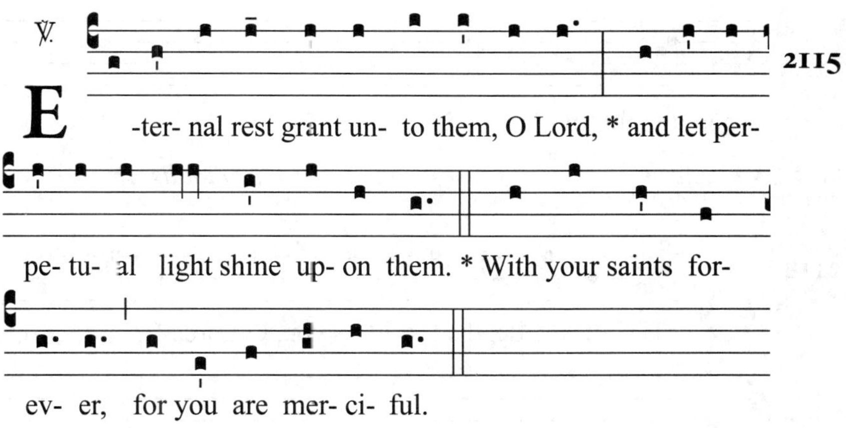
℣.
E -ter- nal rest grant un- to them, O Lord, * and let per-
2115
pe- tu- al light shine up- on them. * With your saints for-
ev- er, for you are mer- ci- ful.

- iii -

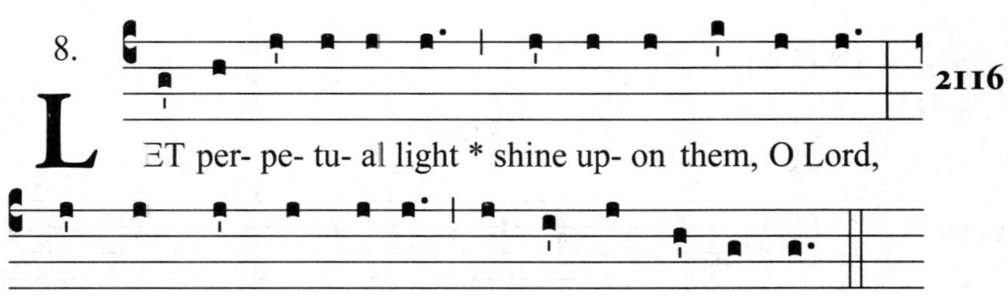
8.
LET per- pe- tu- al light * shine up- on them, O Lord,
2116
with your saints for ev- er, for you are mer- ci- ful.

Or:

- i -

Ego sum resurrectio et vita. Jn 11:26

2117 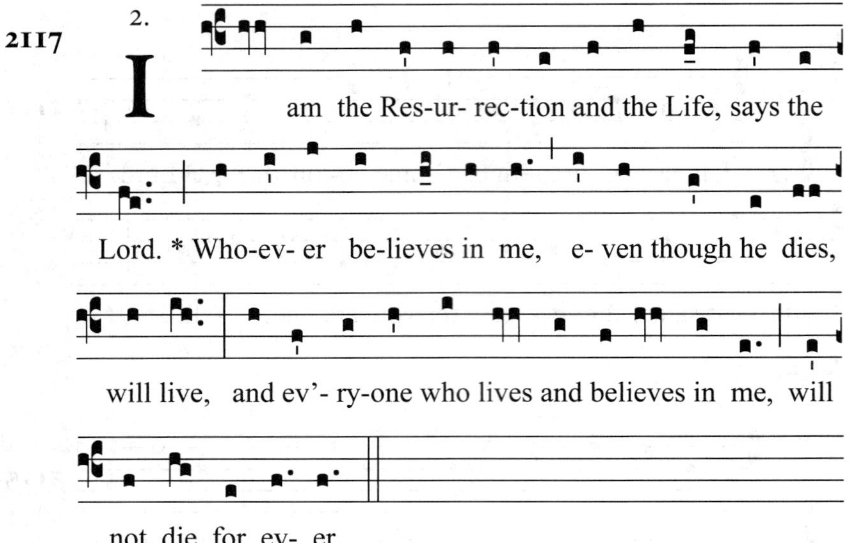
2.
I am the Res-ur- rec-tion and the Life, says the
Lord. * Who-ev- er be-lieves in me, e- ven though he dies,
will live, and ev'- ry-one who lives and believes in me, will
not die for ev- er.

VERSE *De profundis. Ps* 129:1-2

2118 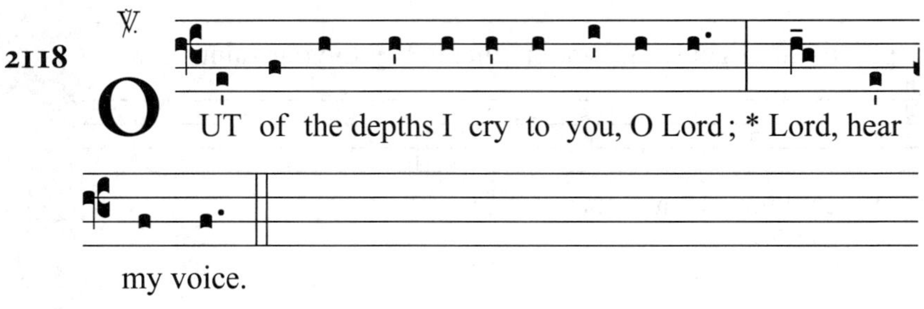
℣.
OUT of the depths I cry to you, O Lord; * Lord, hear
my voice.

Ps 129, *p.* 720.

- iii -

2119 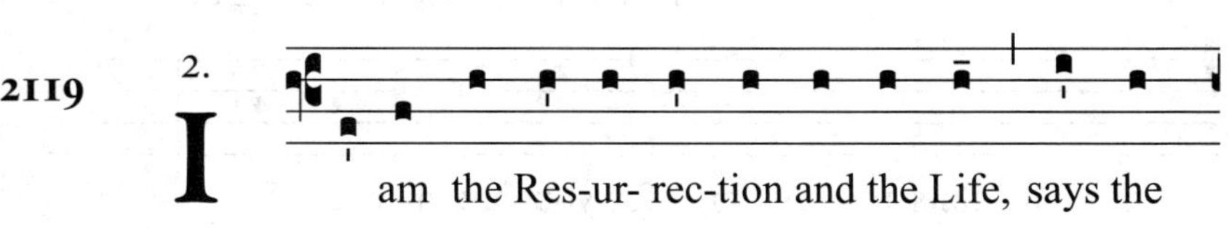
2.
I am the Res-ur- rec-tion and the Life, says the

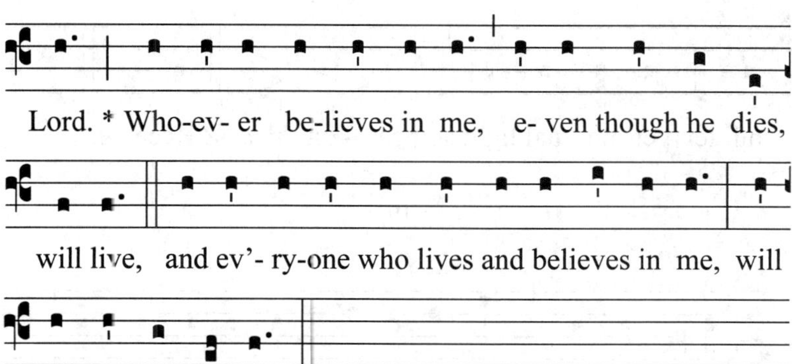
Lord. * Who-ev- er be-lieves in me, e- ven though he dies,
will live, and ev'- ry-one who lives and believes in me, will

not die for ev- er.

Taken from the Roman Missal, *Ritual Masses, Masses for the Dead:*

AT THE FINAL COMMENDATION

RESPONSORY *Subvenite, sancti Dei.*

- i -
4.
2120
SAints of God, * come to *his* aid! Has-ten to meet *him*,
an-gels of the Lord! ℟. Receive *his* soul and pre-sent *him*
to God the Most High. ℣. May Christ, who called you, take you
to himself; may an-gels lead you to the bos-om of A- bra-
ham. ℟. Receive. ℣. E-ter-nal rest grant un- to *him*, O Lord,

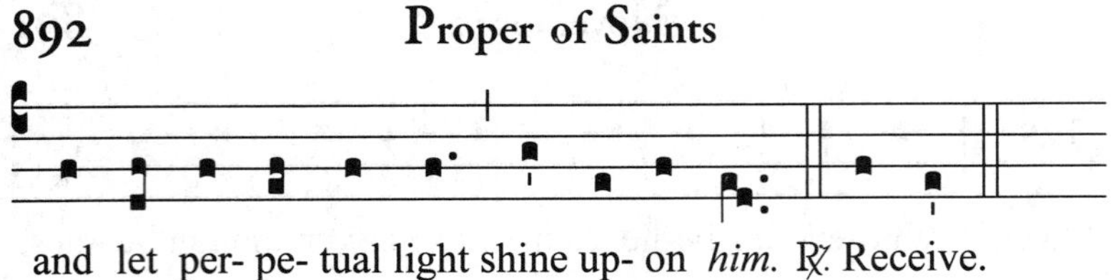
and let per- pe- tual light shine up- on *him.* ℟. Receive.

- iii -

2121 7.

SAints of God, * come to *his* aid! Has-ten to meet *him,* an-

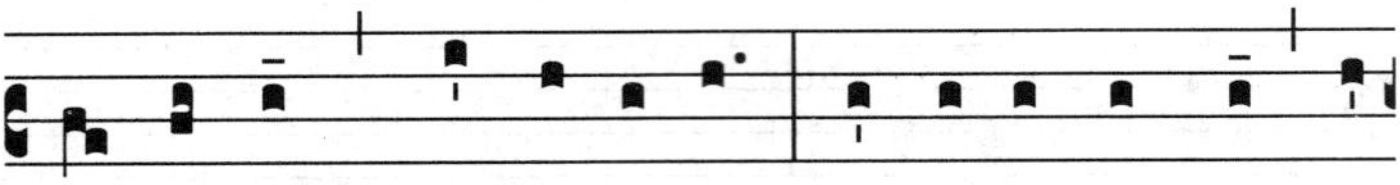

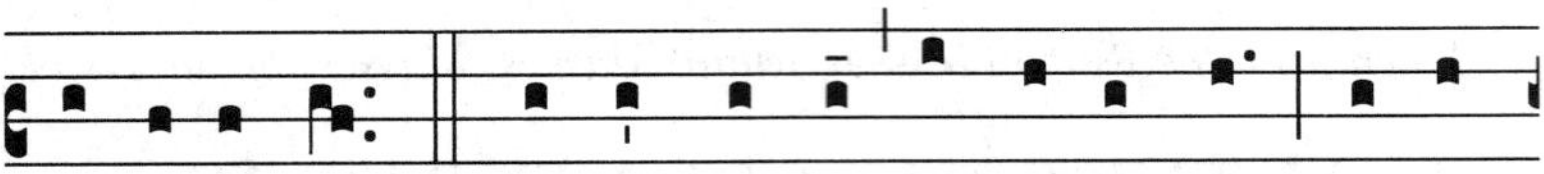

gels of the Lord! ℟. Receive *his* soul and present *him* to God

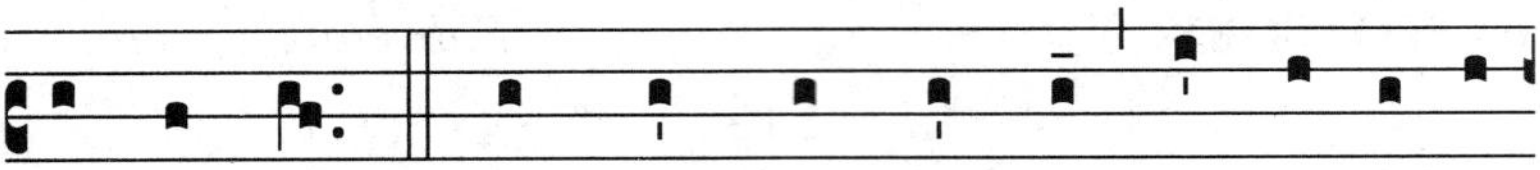

the Most High. ℣. May Christ, who called you, take you to him-

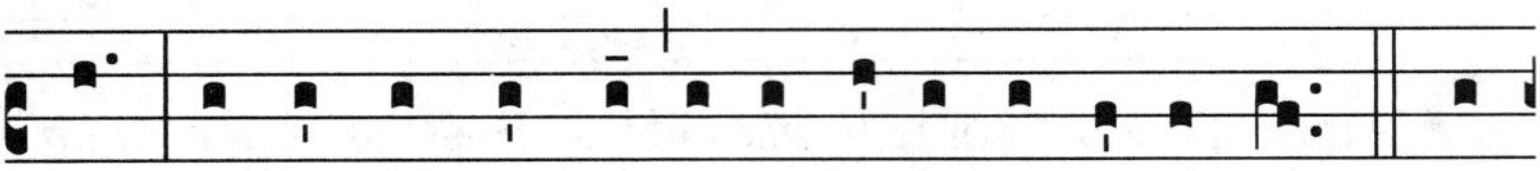

self; may an-gels lead you to the bosom of A-bra-ham. ℟. Re-

ceive. ℣. E-ter-nal rest grant un- to *him,* O Lord, and let per-

pe- tu- al light shine up- on *him.* ℟. Receive.

- iv -

2122 6.

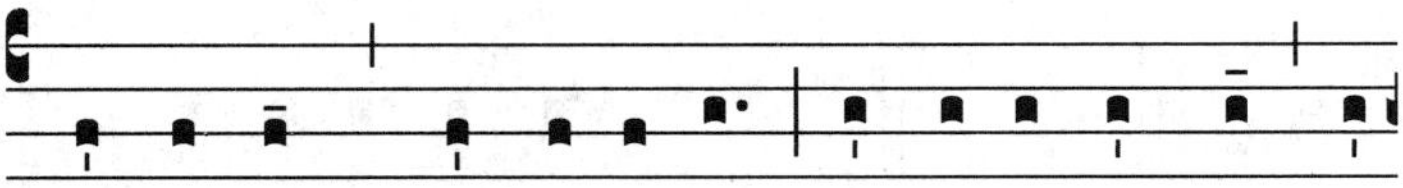

SAints of God, * come to *his* aid! Has-ten to meet *him,* an-

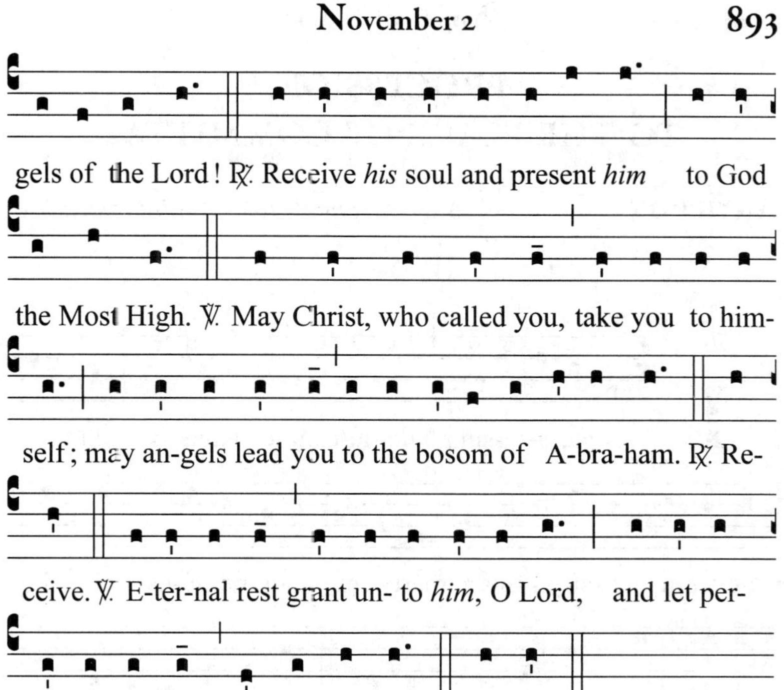
gels of the Lord! ℟. Receive *his* soul and present *him* to God
the Most High. ℣. May Christ, who called you, take you to himself; may an-gels lead you to the bosom of A-bra-ham. ℟. Receive. ℣. E-ter-nal rest grant un- to *him*, O Lord, and let per-
pe- tu- al light shine up- on *him*. ℟. Receive.

PROCESSION TO THE PLACE OF COMMITTAL

Antiphon *May the angels take you into paradise.*

- i -

2123 7.

IN par-a-dí-sum * de-dú-cant te ánge- li : in tu-o advéntu suscí-pi- ant te márty-res, et perdú-cant te in ci-vi- tá-tem sanctam Ie- rú-sa- lem. Chor-us ange- ló-rum te sus- cí- pi- at, et cum Lá-za-ro quondam páupe- re æ- tér- nam há-be- as réqui- em.

- iii -

8.
2124
MAY the an-gels take you in- to par- a-dise; * may
the mar-tyrs come to welcome you on your way, and lead
you in- to the ho- ly cit- y, Je- ru- sa-lem. May the choir
of an-gels, welcome you, and with Laz- a- rus who once
was poor, may you have ev- er- last- ing life.

- iv -

2125 8.

MAY the an-gels take you in- to par- a-dise; * may
the mar-tyrs come to welcome you on your way, and lead
you in- to the ho- ly cit- y, Je- ru- sa-lem. May the choir
of an-gels, welcome you, and with Laz- a- rus who once
was poor, may you have ev- er- last- ing life.

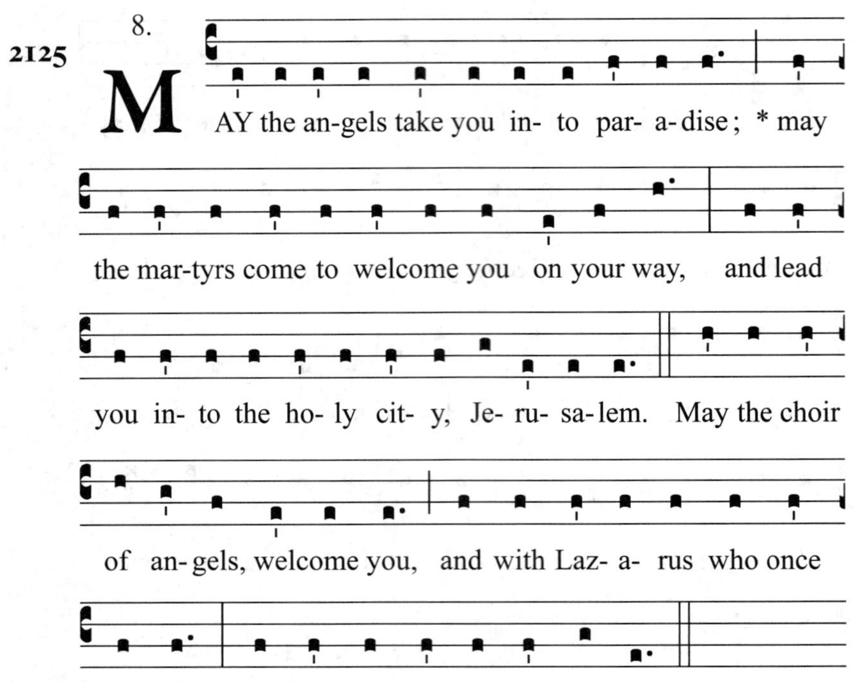

ANTIPHONS

ad libitum

8.
MY Re-deem-er lives, * and on the last day he will
re- new me.
2126

℣ 1 *The Lord* | is gracious and | **mer**-ci-ful, *
slow to anger, / abound- | *ing in* **kind**-ness. (℟)

℣ 2 *The love* | of the Lord is from eternity to e- | **ter**-ni-ty *
toward | *those who* **fear** him. (℟) *Ps* 102:8. 17

4. g
HE shall dwell in your tab- er- na- cle * and rest up- on
your ho- ly mountain.
2127

℣ 1 He who walks without blemish, | *and works* **jus**-tice. *
He who speaks truth | *in his* **heart**. (℟)

℣ 2 Who harms not his | *fel-low* **man**, *
nor takes up a reproach a- | *gainst his* **neigh**-bor. (℟)
Ps 14:2. 3

7.
HE shall dwell * in your tab- er- na- cle and rest
2128

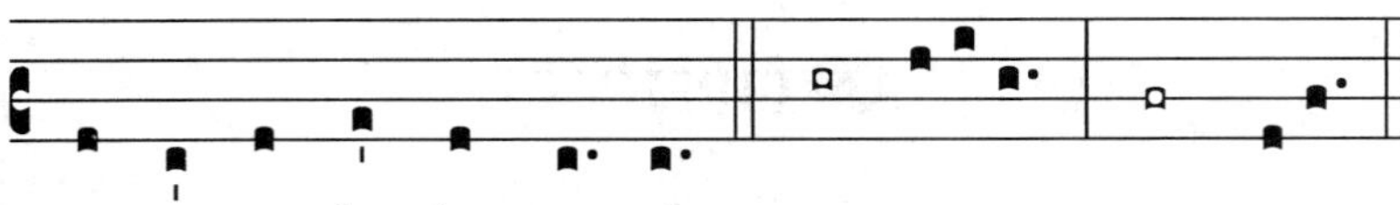
up- on your ho- ly mountain.

℣. 1 He who walks without blemish, | *and works* **jus**-tice. *
He who speaks truth in | *his* **heart**. (℟.)

℣. 2 Who harms not his | *fel-low* **man**, *
nor takes up a reproach against | *his* **neigh**-bor. (℟.) *Ps* 14:2. 3

2129

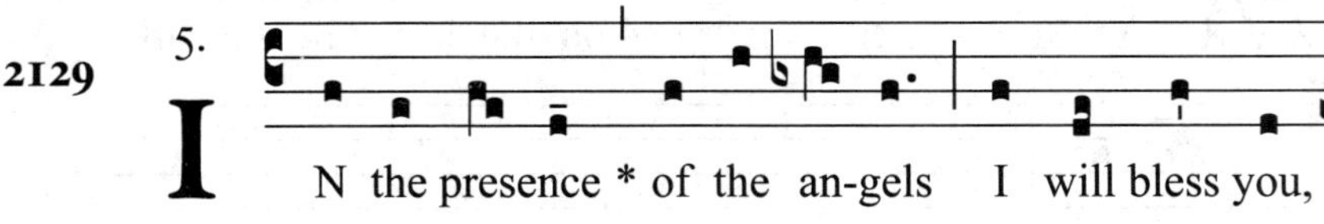
5.
I N the presence * of the an-gels I will bless you,

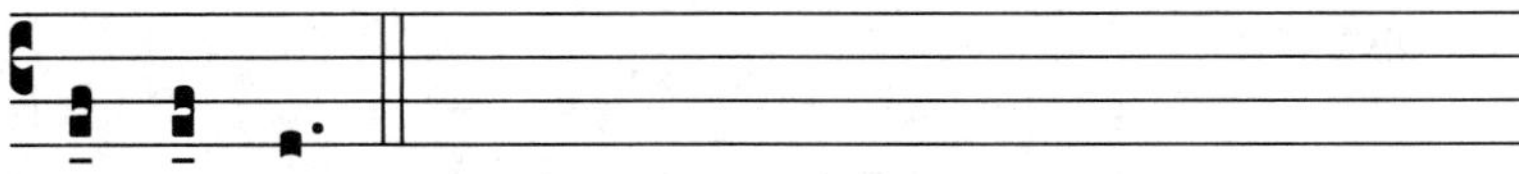
O my God. *Ps* 137:1

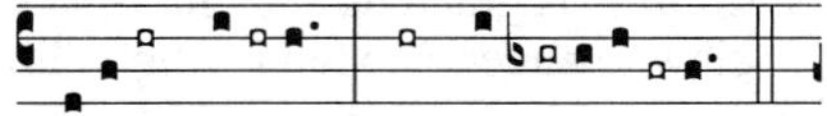

℣. 1 *Though I* | walk in the midst of af- | **flic**-tion *
you give me life and | **frus**-trate my **en**-e-mies. (℟.)

℣. 2 *You stretch* | out your hand and | **save** me, *
your hand will | **do** all **things** for me. (℟.) *Ps* 137:7

2130

2.
I heard a voice * from heav-en say-ing : Bless-ed
are the dead who die in the Lord. *Rev* 14:13

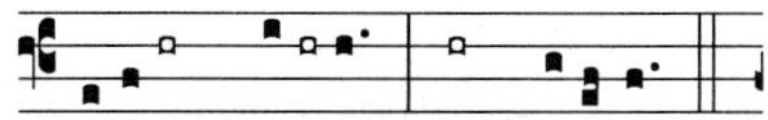

℣. 1 *The Lord* | keeps you from all | **e**-vil : *
may the Lord | *keep* **your** soul. (℟.)

℣. 2 *May the* | Lord keep your coming in and your | **go**-ing out : *
from henceforth now and | *for* **ev**-er. (℟.) *Ps* 120:7.8

November 9

THE DEDICATION OF THE LATERAN BASILICA

Entrance Antiphon *Vidi civitatem sanctam. Rev* 25:2

- i -

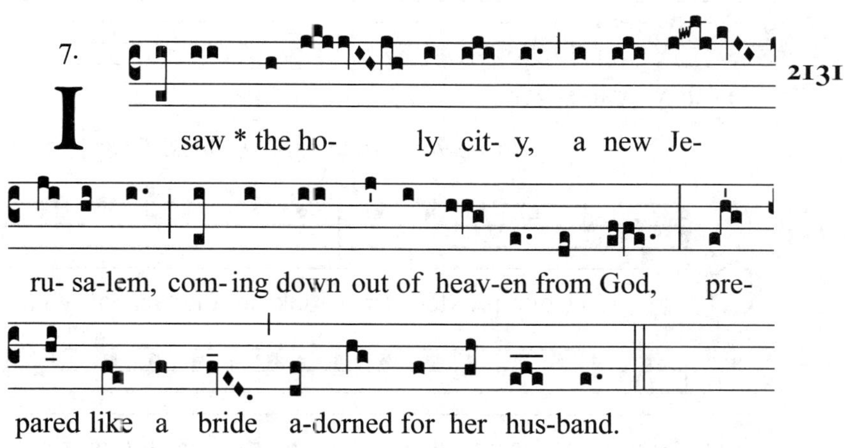
7.
I saw * the ho- ly cit- y, a new Je-
ru- sa-lem, com- ing down out of heav-en from God, prepared like a bride a-dorned for her hus-band.

2131

- ii -

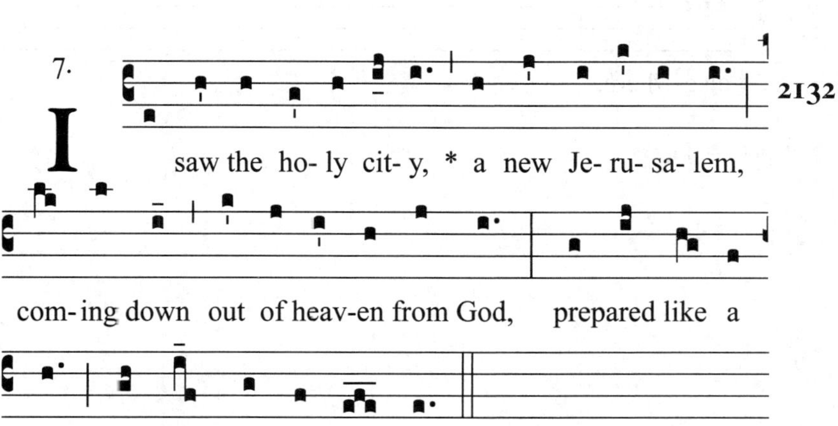
7.
I saw the ho- ly cit- y, * a new Je- ru- sa- lem,
com- ing down out of heav-en from God, prepared like a
bride a-dorned for her hus-band.

2132

VERSES *Quam dilecta tabernacula tua. Ps* 83:1. 5

2133
℣. 1
HOW love- ly is your dwell-ing place, O Lord of
hosts. * Bless-ed are they who dwell in your house, for- ev-
er they praise you.

Protector noster, aspice, Deus. Ps 83:10-11

2134
℣. 2
O God our pro- tec- tor, look on the face of your
Christ, * for bet-ter is one day in your courts than a thou-sand
else-where.

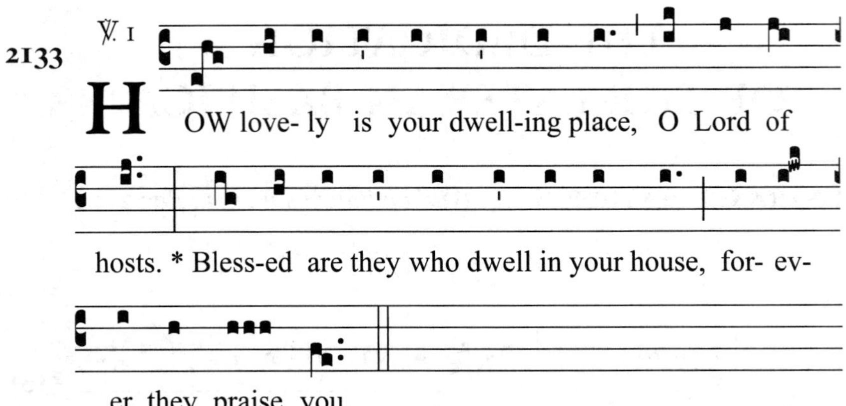

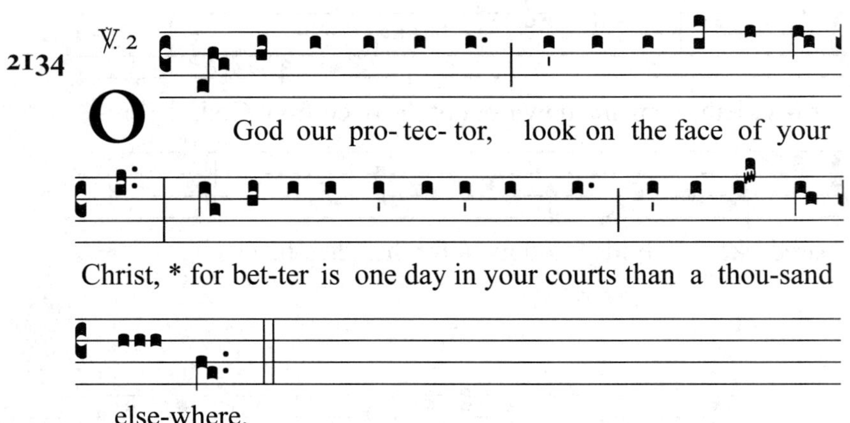

- iii -

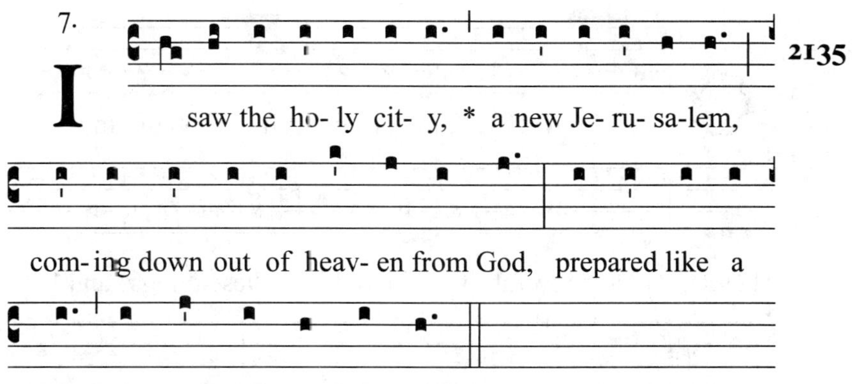
7.
2135
I saw the ho- ly cit- y, * a new Je- ru- sa-lem,
com- ing down out of heav- en from God, prepared like a
bride a-dorned for her hus-band.

- iv -

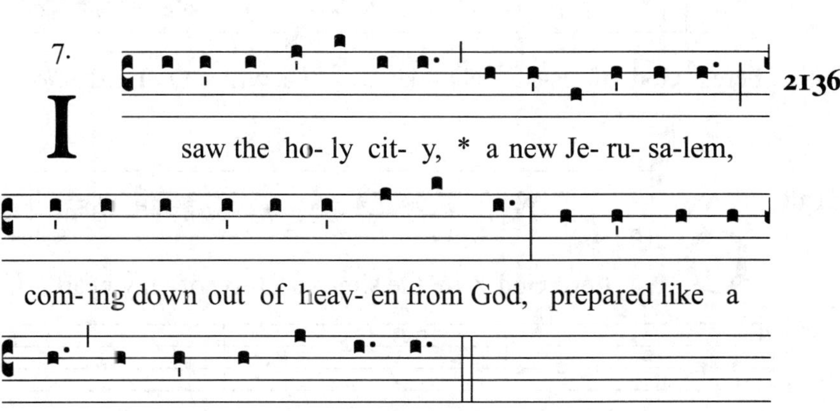
7.
2136
I saw the ho- ly cit- y, * a new Je- ru- sa-lem,
com- ing down out of heav- en from God, prepared like a
bride a-dorned for her hus-band.

OFFERTORY ANTIPHON *Domine Deus.* 1 *Chron* 29:17. 18

- i -
2137
6.
O Lord God, * in the sim- pli- ci- ty of my
heart I have joy-ful- ly of-fered all these things; and I
have seen with great joy your peo- ple who are pres- ent
here. God of Is- ra- el, keep this will, O Lord God.
- ii -
2138
6.
O Lord God, * in the sim-pli- ci- ty of my heart
I have joy-ful- ly of- fered all these things; and I have seen
with great joy your peo-ple who are pres-ent here. O God
of Is- ra- el, keep this will, Lord God.

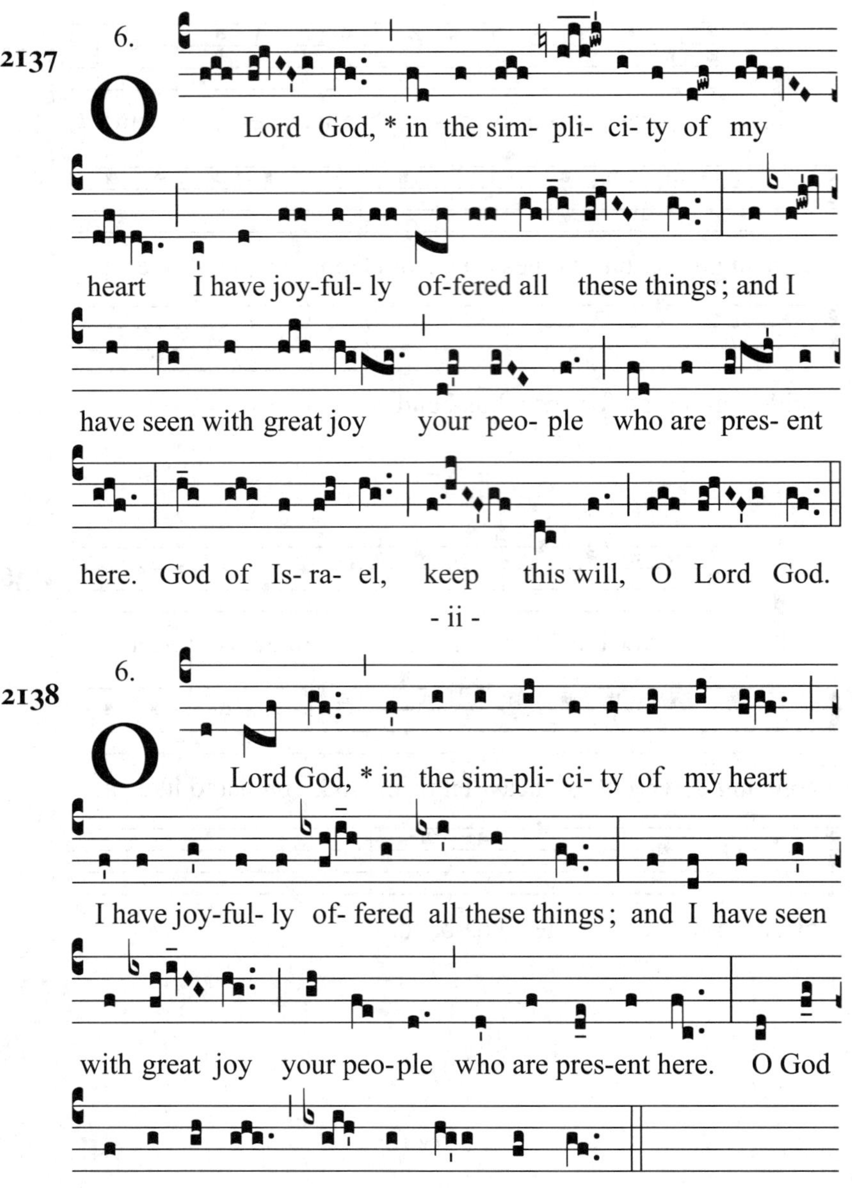

Cf. also I, Daniel, *p.* 624 *and* Moses consecrated, *p.* 634.

VERSES

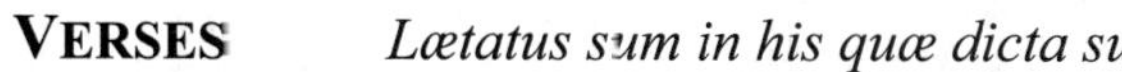

Lætatus sum in his quæ dicta sunt mihi. Ps 121 : 1

℣. 1
2139
I rejoiced at the things that were said to me : * We
will go in- to the house of the Lord.

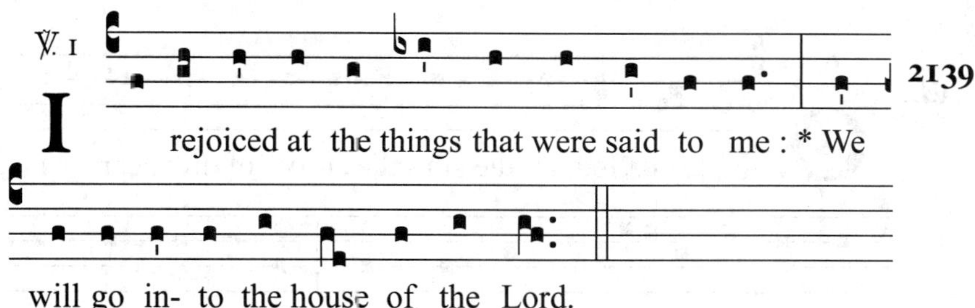

Stantes erant pedes nostri. Ps 121 : 2-3

℣. 2
2140
OUR feet were stand-ing in your courts, O Je- ru- sa-
lem, * Je- ru- sa- lem, which is built as a cit- y, which is
com-pact to- geth- er.

Rogate quæ ad pacem sunt Ierusalem. Ps 121 : 6-7

℣. 3
2141
PRAY for the things that are for the peace of Je- ru- sa-
lem, and a- bundance for those who love you. * Let peace be
in your strength, and a- bundance with- in your tow- ers.

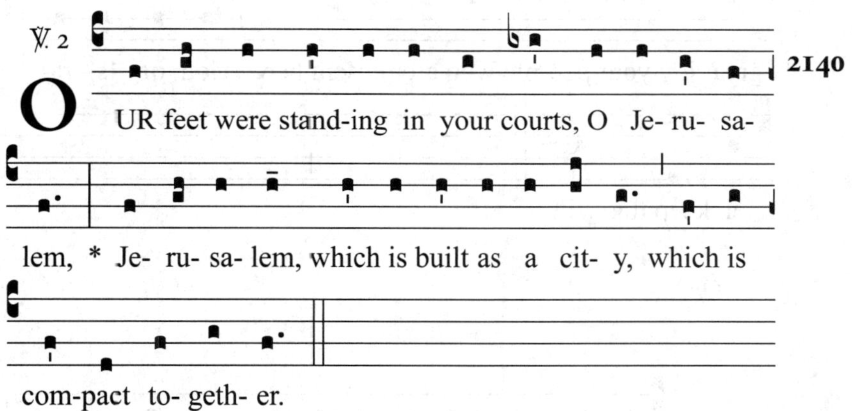

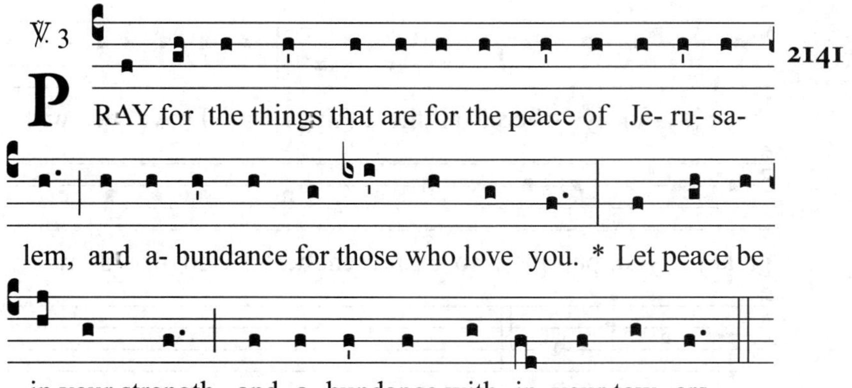

- iii -

2142
6.
O Lord God, in the sim-pli- ci- ty of my heart * I
have joy-ful- ly of-fered all these things; and I have seen with
great joy your peo-ple who are present here. God of Is- ra-
el, keep this will.

Or:

2143
6.
O Lord God, * in the sim-pli- ci- ty of my heart I
have joy-ful- ly offered all these things; and I have seen with
great joy your peo-ple who are present here. God of Is- ra-
el, keep this will.

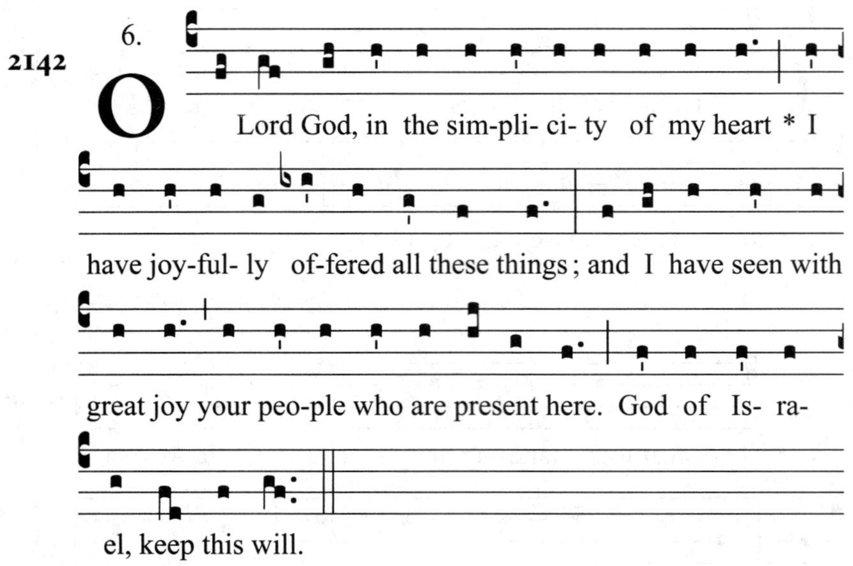

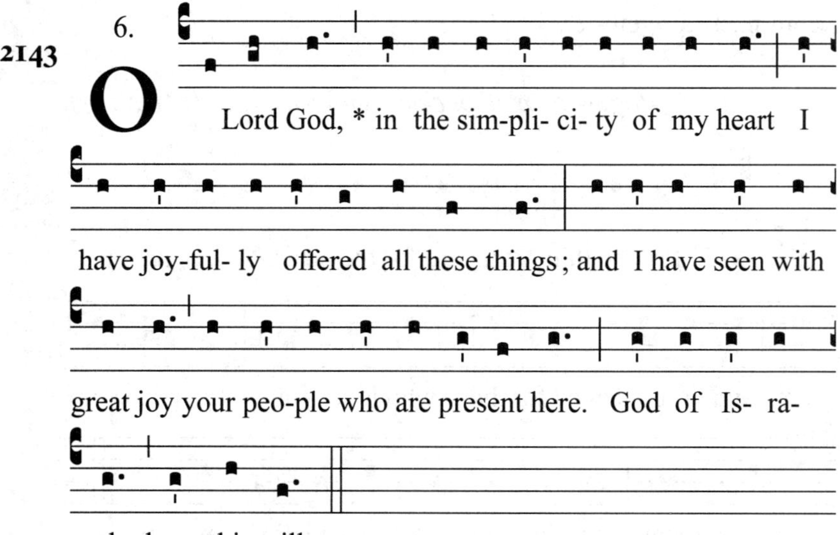

- iv -

6. 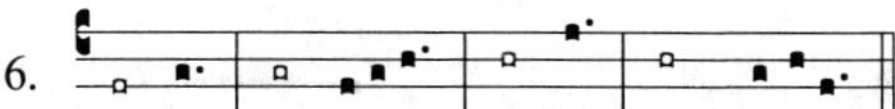 2144

O Lord God, / in the simplicity of my | **heart** *
I have joyfully offered | *all these* **things**;
and I have seen with great joy /
your people who are present | **here**.
God of Israel, / | *keep this* **will**.

COMMUNION ANTIPHON *Tamquam lapidi vivi. Cf.* 1 *Pet* 2:5

- i -

2145

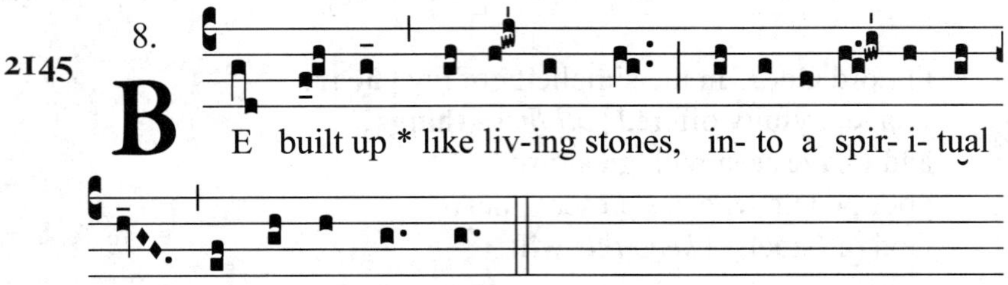
8.
BE built up * like liv-ing stones, in- to a spir- i- tual
house, a ho- ly priesthood.

- ii -

2146 8.

BE built up * like liv-ing stones, in- to a spir- i- tual

house, a ho- ly priesthood.

VERSES *Benedicam Dominum. Ps* 33 : 1-2

℣. 1
2147
I will bless the Lord at all times; his praise shall be
ev- er in my mouth. * Let my soul glo-ry in the Lord ; the
low-ly will hear me and be glad.

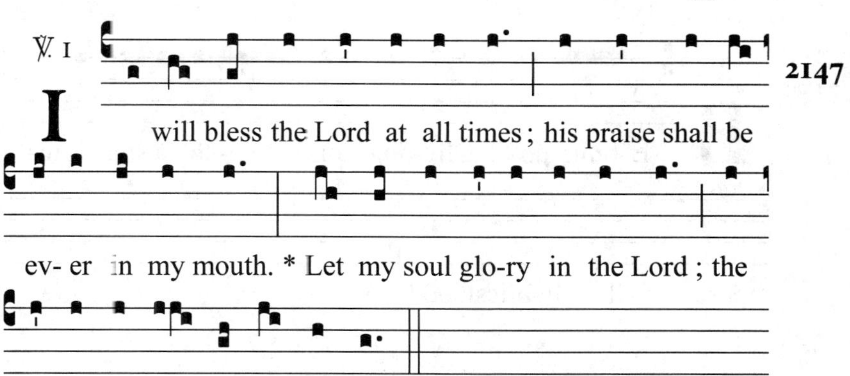

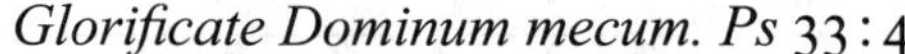

Glorificate Dominum mecum. Ps 33 : 4

℣. 2
2148
O mag-ni- fy the Lord with me, let us to-geth-er ex-
tol his name. * I sought the Lord, and he answered me and
de-liv-ered me from all my fears.

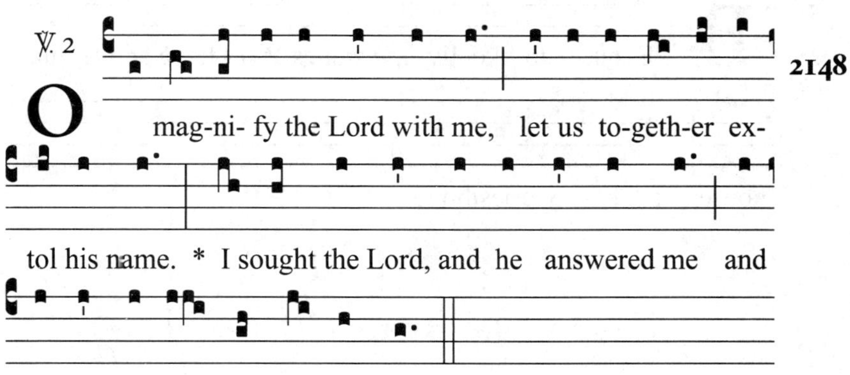

Gustate et videte. Ps 33 : 9

℣. 3
2149
O taste and see how gracious the Lord is ; * bless-ed
the man who hopes in him.

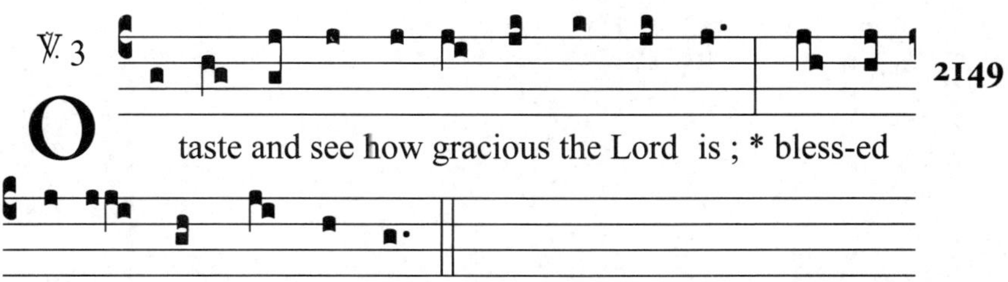

Cf. also Ps 33, *simple tone, p.* 372.

- iii -

2150 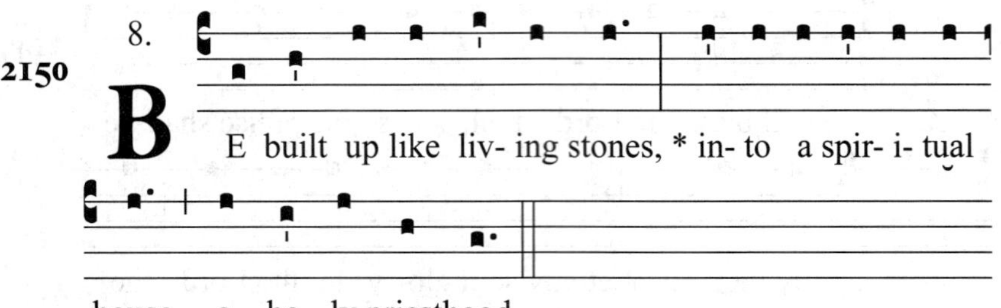
8.
BE built up like liv- ing stones, * in- to a spir- i- tual
house, a ho- ly priesthood.

- iv -

2151 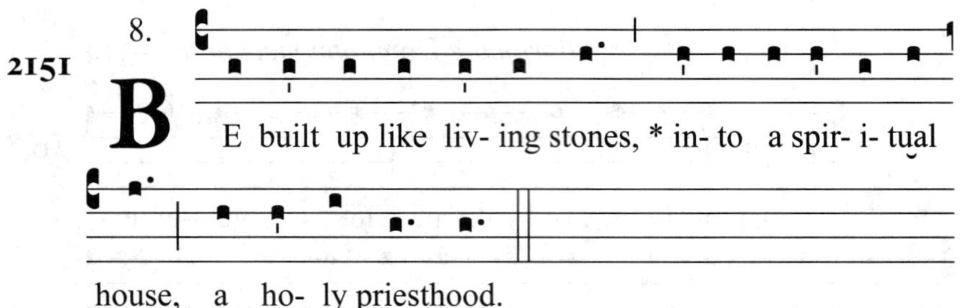
8.
BE built up like liv- ing stones, * in- to a spir- i- tual
house, a ho- ly priesthood.

December 8

THE IMMACULATE CONCEPTION OF THE BLESSED VIRGIN MARY

ENTRANCE ANTIPHON *Gaudens gaudebo. Is* 61 : 10

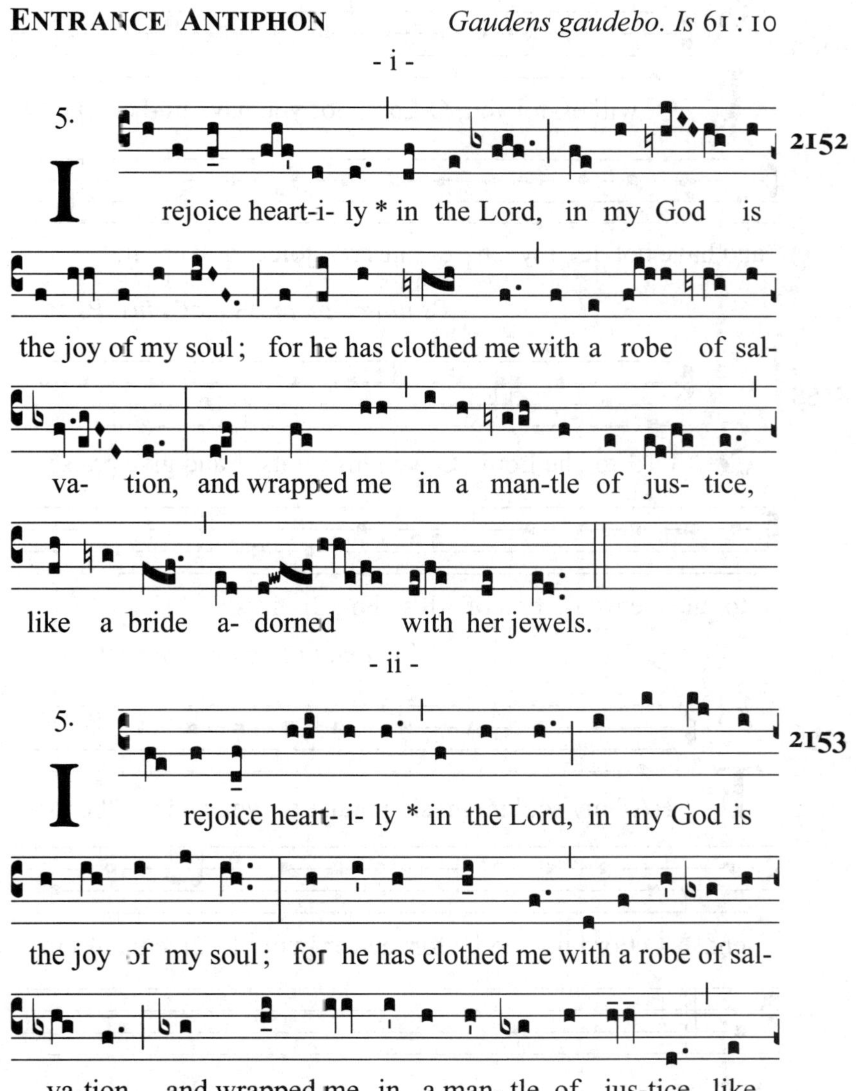
- i -
5.
I rejoice heart-i- ly * in the Lord, in my God is 2152
the joy of my soul; for he has clothed me with a robe of sal-
va- tion, and wrapped me in a man-tle of jus- tice,
like a bride a- dorned with her jewels.
- ii -
5.
I rejoice heart- i- ly * in the Lord, in my God is 2153
the joy of my soul; for he has clothed me with a robe of sal-
va-tion, and wrapped me in a man- tle of jus-tice, like

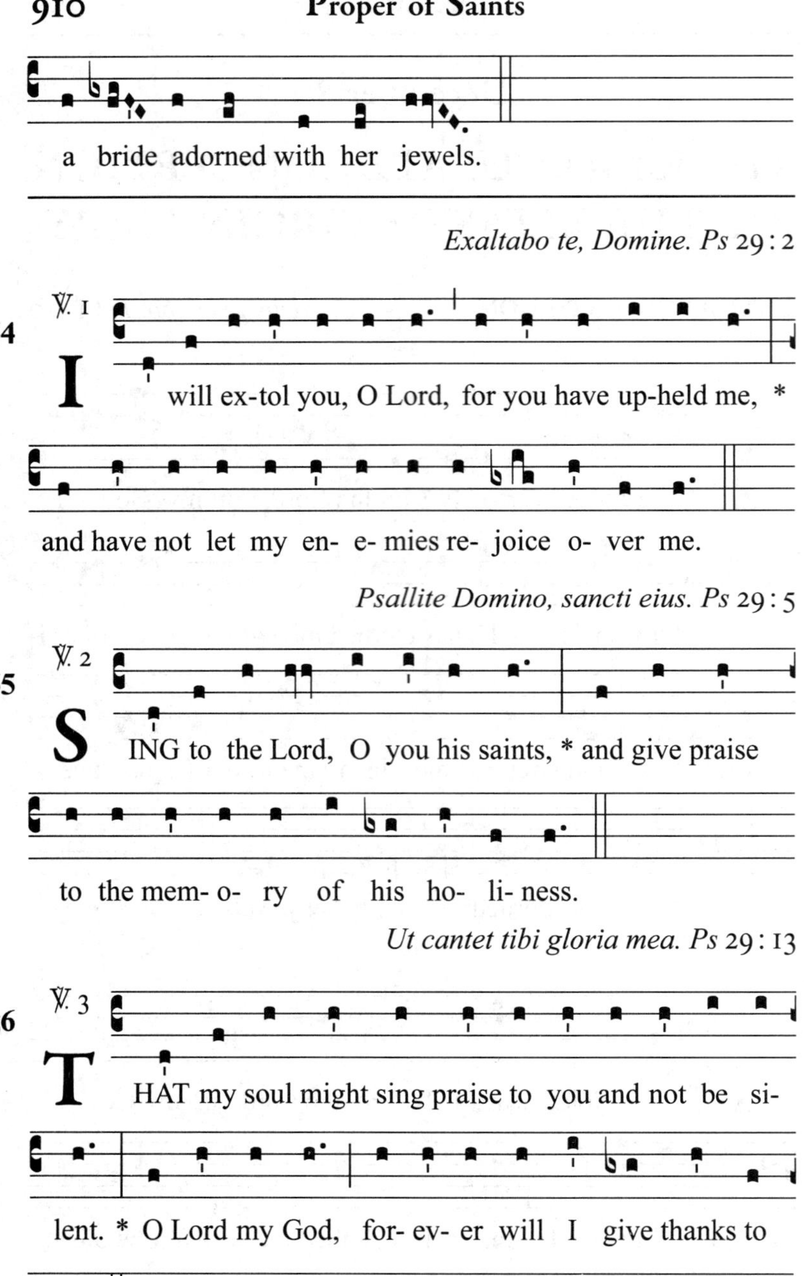
a bride adorned with her jewels.
Exaltabo te, Domine. Ps 29:2
℣. 1
2154
I will ex-tol you, O Lord, for you have up-held me, *
and have not let my en- e- mies re- joice o- ver me.
Psallite Domino, sancti eius. Ps 29:5
℣. 2
2155
SING to the Lord, O you his saints, * and give praise
to the mem- o- ry of his ho- li- ness.
Ut cantet tibi gloria mea. Ps 29:13
℣. 3
2156
THAT my soul might sing praise to you and not be si-
lent. * O Lord my God, for- ev- er will I give thanks to
you.

- iii -

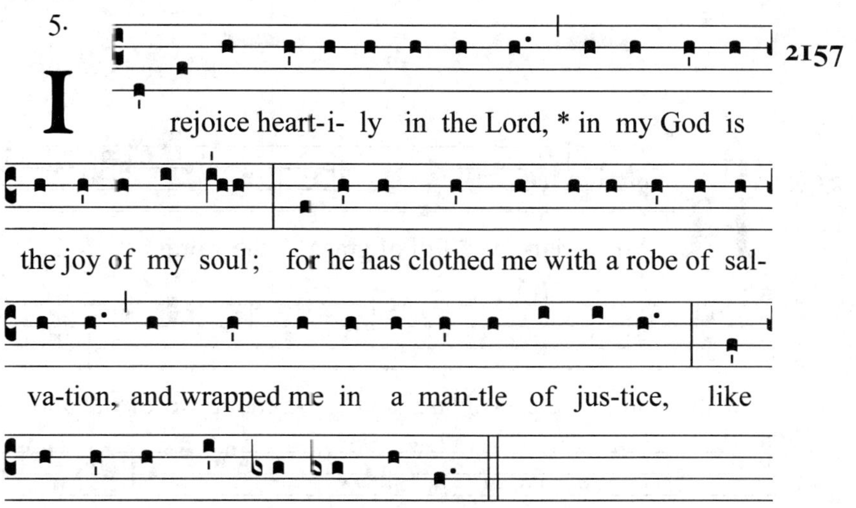
5.
2157
I rejoice heart-i- ly in the Lord, * in my God is
the joy of my soul; for he has clothed me with a robe of sal-
va-tion, and wrapped me in a man-tle of jus-tice, like
a bride a-dorned with her jew-els.

- iv -

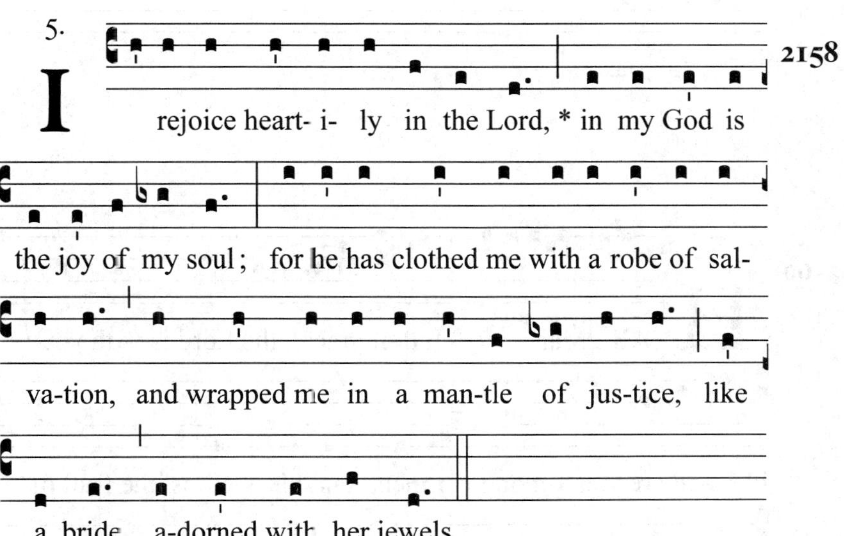
5.
2158
I rejoice heart- i- ly in the Lord, * in my God is
the joy of my soul; for he has clothed me with a robe of sal-
va-tion, and wrapped me in a man-tle of jus-tice, like
a bride a-dorned with her jewels.

OFFERTORY ANTIPHON *Ave Maria.*
Luke 1:28. 42

- i -

2159

8.
HAIL, Mar- y, * full of grace; the Lord is
with you; bless-ed are you a-mong wo-men, and
blessed is the fruit of your womb. *E. T.* Al- le-
lu- ia.

- ii -

2160

8.
HAIL, Mar- y, * full of grace; the Lord is with you;
bless-ed are you a-mong wo-men, and bless-ed is the fruit of
your womb. *E. T.* Al- le- lu- ia.

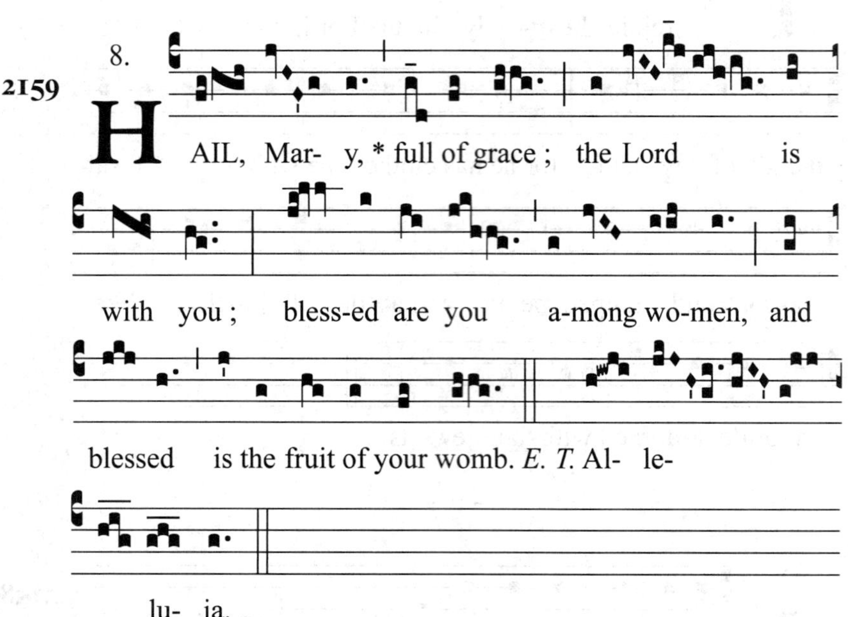

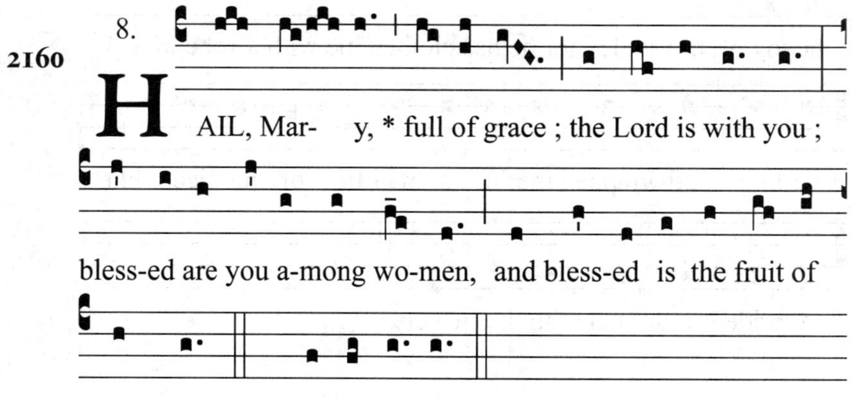

VERSES
Benedixisti, Domine, terram tuam. Ps 84:2. 3
℣. 1
2161
YOU have blessed, O Lord, your land; you have brought
back the captives of Ja- cob. * You have for-giv-en the guilt
of your peo- ple.
Audiam quid loquatur. Ps 84:9
℣. 2
2162
I will hear what God will speak, for he will speak peace
to his peo-ple, * and to those who are con-vert-ed to the heart.
Misericordia et veritas obviaverunt sibi. Ps 84:11
℣. 3
2163
MEr- cy and truth have met each oth- er; jus-tice and
peace have kissed. * Truth has sprung out of the earth, and

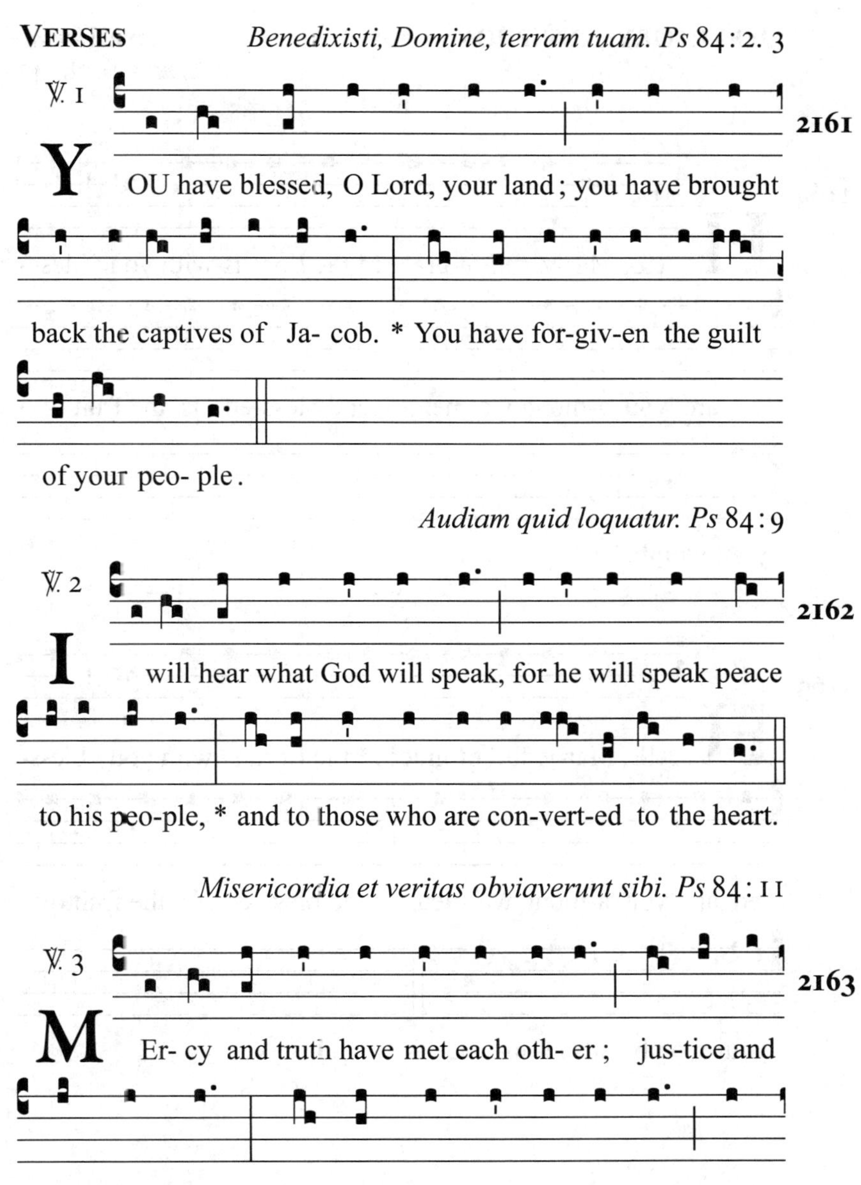

jus-tice has looked down from heav-en.

Offertory Antiphon *Ave Maria.*
Luke 1 : 28. 42

- iii -

2164 8.

HAIL, Mar-y, full of grace ; * the Lord is with you ; bless-ed are you a-mong wo-men, and bless-ed is the fruit of your womb.

- iv -

2165 8.

HAIL, Mar-y, full of grace ; * the Lord is with you ; bless-ed are you a-mong wo-men, and bless-ed is the fruit of your womb, al- le- lu- ia.

COMMUNION ANTIPHON *Gloriosa dicta sunt de te.*

- i -

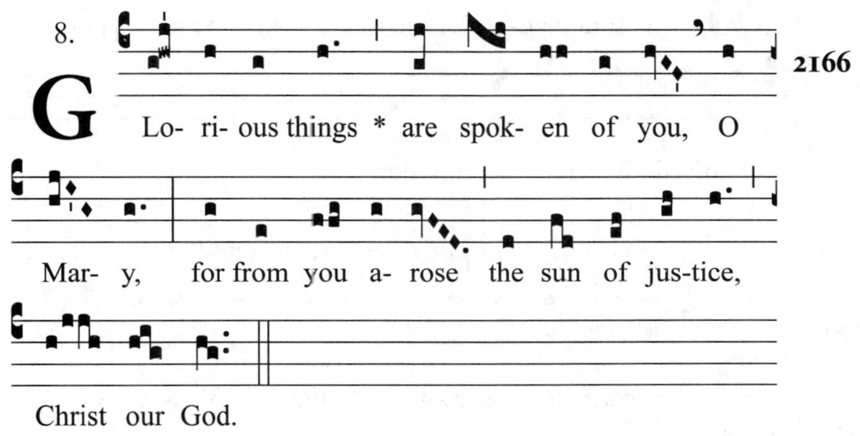
8.
2166
GLo- ri- ous things * are spok- en of you, O
Mar- y, for from you a- rose the sun of jus-tice,
Christ our God.

- ii -

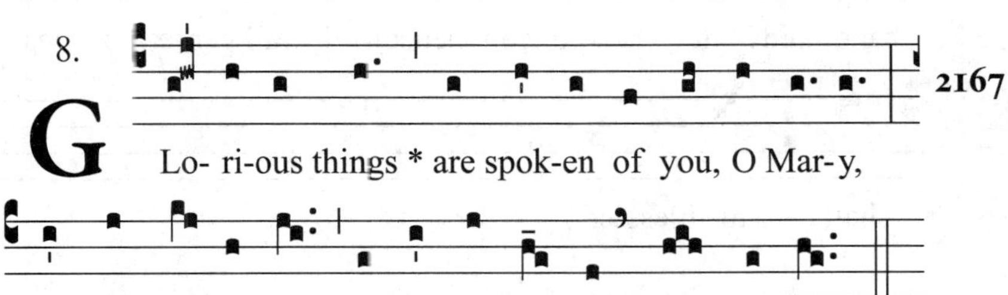
8.
2167
GLo- ri-ous things * are spok-en of you, O Mar-y,
for from you a- rose the sun of jus-tice, Christ our God.

Magnificat anima mea Dominum. Lk 1 : 47

2168

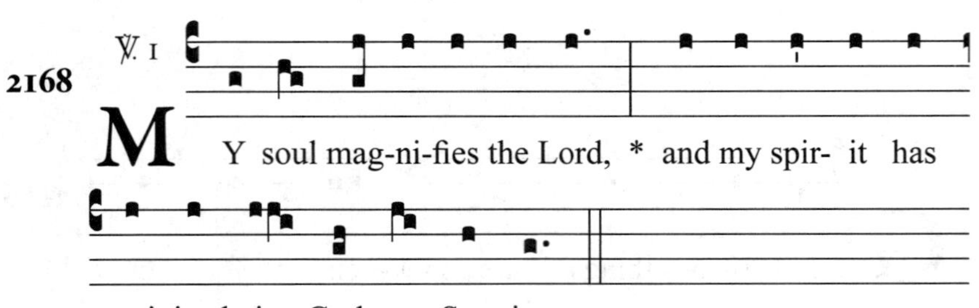
℣. 1
MY soul mag-ni-fies the Lord, * and my spir- it has
rejoiced in God my Sav- ior.

Quia respexit humilitatem ancillæ suæ. Lk 1 : 48

2169

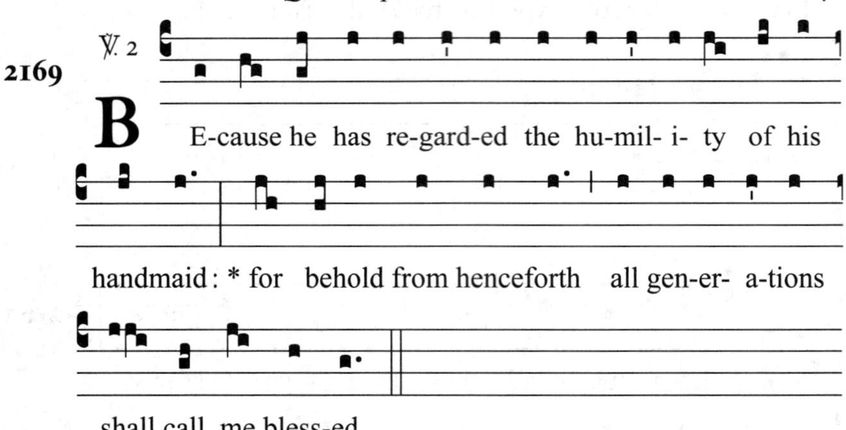
℣. 2
BE-cause he has re-gard-ed the hu-mil- i- ty of his
handmaid : * for behold from henceforth all gen-er- a-tions
shall call me bless-ed.

Quia fecit mihi magna qui potens est. Lk 1 : 49

2170

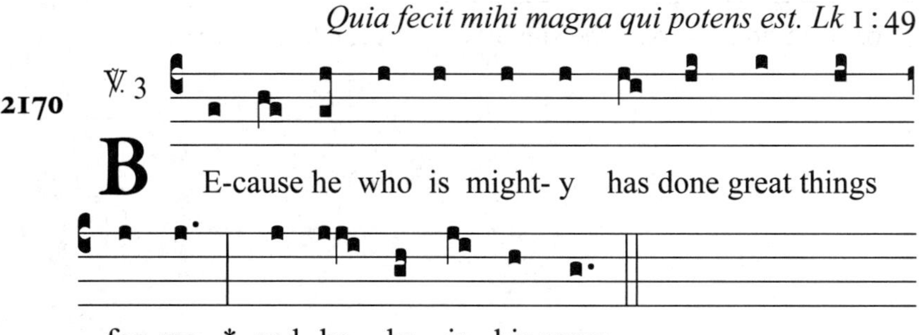
℣. 3
BE-cause he who is might- y has done great things
for me, * and ho- ly is his name.

- iii -

8. 2171

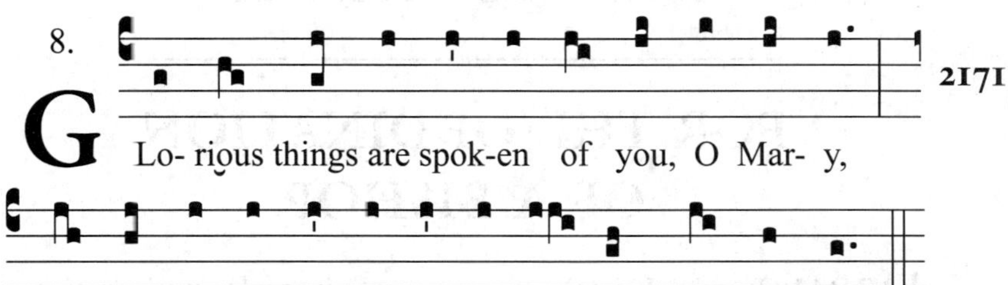

G Lo- rious things are spok-en of you, O Mar- y,

for from you a- rose the sun of jus- tice, Christ our God.

Or:

8. 2172

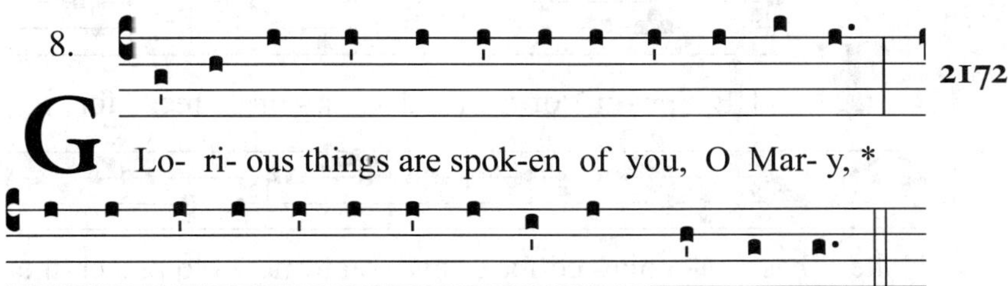

G Lo- ri- ous things are spok-en of you, O Mar- y, *

for from you a- rose the sun of jus-tice, Christ our God.

- iv -

8. 2173

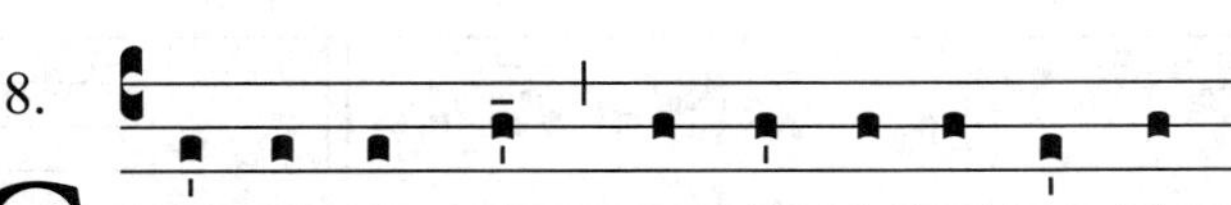

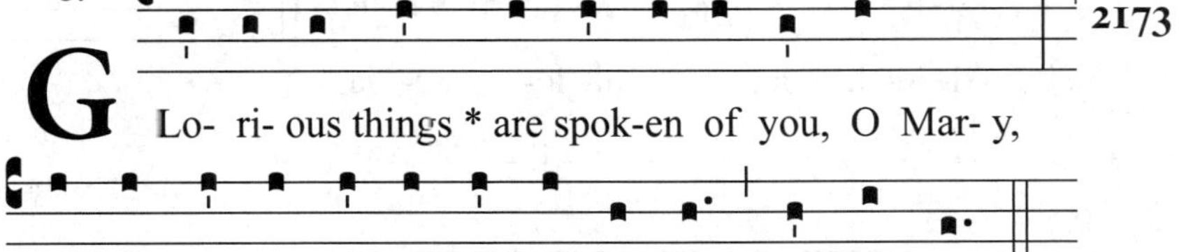

G Lo- ri- ous things * are spok-en of you, O Mar- y,

for from you a- rose the sun of jus-tice, Christ our God.

RITUAL MASSES

FOR THE ORDINATION OF A BISHOP

Entrance Antiphon *Spiritus Domini super me.*
Cf. Lk 4:18

- i -

2174 2.

THE Spir- it * of the Lord is up- on me, for

he has a- noint- ed me and sent me to preach the

good news to the poor, to heal the broken-heart- ed.

E. T. Al- le- lu- ia, al- le- lu- ia.

- ii -

2175 2.

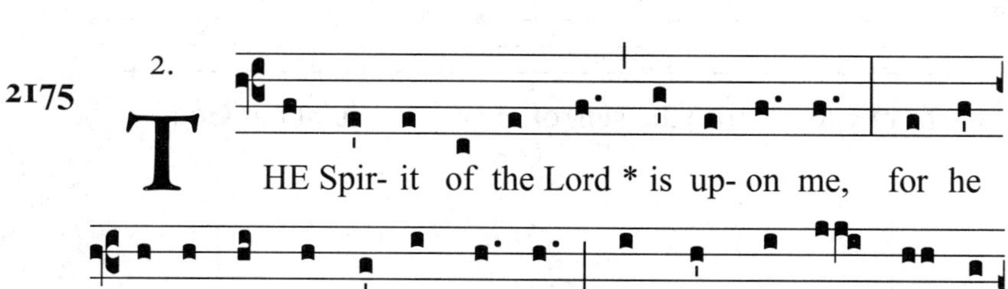
THE Spir- it of the Lord * is up- on me, for he
has a-noint-ed me and sent me to preach the good news to

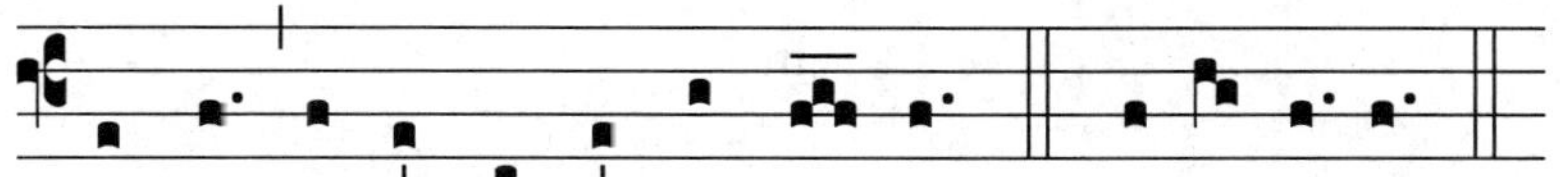

the poor, to heal the bro-ken-heart-ed. *E. T.* Al- le- lu- ia.

VERSES *Deus, Deus meus, ad te de luce vigilo. Ps* 62:2-3

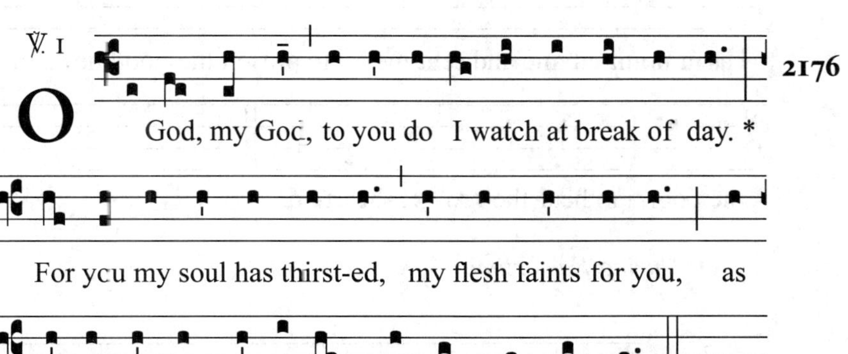

℣. 1
O God, my God, to you do I watch at break of day. *
2176
For you my soul has thirst-ed, my flesh faints for you, as
in a dry and wear-y land where no wa- ter is.

Sic benedicam te in vita mea. Ps 62:5

℣. 2
THUS will I bless you all my life long, * and in your
2177
name I will lift up my hands.

Verse 3: *For you are my help, p.* 351.

- iii -

2178

2.
THE Spir- it of the Lord is up- on me, * for he
has a-noint-ed me and sent me to preach the good news to
the poor, to heal the bro-ken-heart-ed.

Or, during Eastertime:

2179

2.
THE Spir- it of the Lord is up- on me, * for he
has a-nointed me and sent me to preach the good news to
the poor, to heal the bro-ken-heart-ed, al- le- lu- ia.

2. 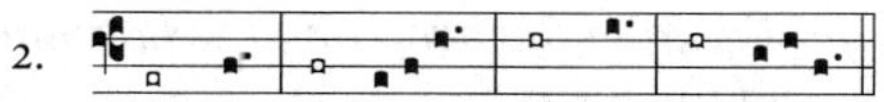

- iv -

The Spirit of the Lord is up- | **on** me, 2180
for he has anointed | *me and* **sent** me
to preach the good news to the | **poor**,
to heal the | *bro-ken*-**heart**-ed.

Or, during Eastertime:

The Spirit of the Lord is up- | **on** me, 2181
for he has anointed | *me and* **sent** me
to preach the good news to the | **poor**,
to heal the broken-hearted, / | *al-le*-**lu**-ia.

After the anointing of the head and the handing on of the book of the Gospels and the insignia:

ANTIPHON *Euntes in mundum.*
Cf. Mk 16:15

2182
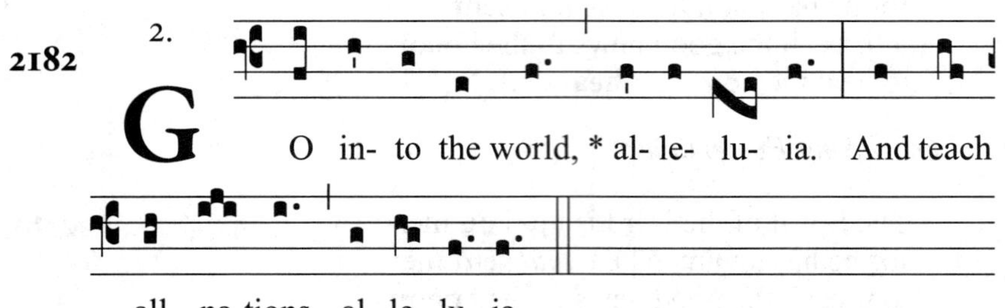
2.
GO in- to the world, * al- le- lu- ia. And teach
all na-tions, al- le- lu- ia.

Or:

2183

2.
GO in- to the world, * al- le- lu- ia. And teach all
na-tions, al- le- lu- ia.

Or in Lent:

2184

2.
GO in- to the world. * And teach all na-tions.

VERSES. *Annuntiate inter gentes. Ps* 95:3

℣. 1
DEclare his glo-ry a-mong the na-tions; * his wonders
a-mong all the peo-ples.

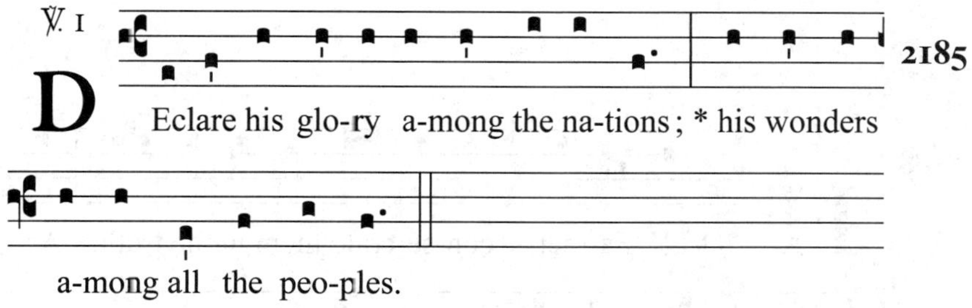

2185

Confessio et pulchritudo. Ps 95:6

℣. 2
IN his presence are praise and beau- ty, * ho- li-ness
and maj- es- ty are in his ho- ly place.

2186

Afferte Domino. Ps 95:7

℣. 3
BRing to the Lord, you fam- i- lies of the na-tions, *
bring to the Lord glo- ry and hon- or.

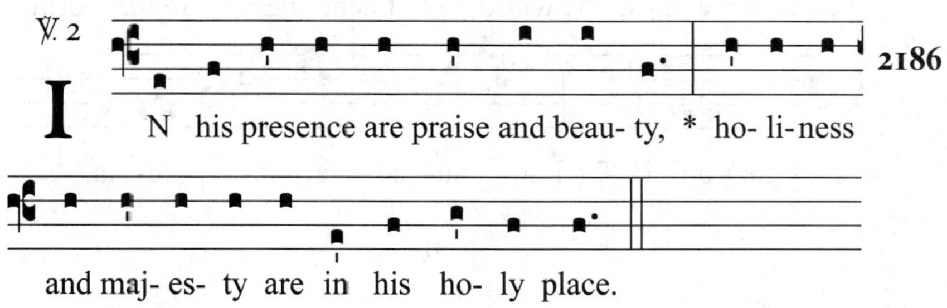

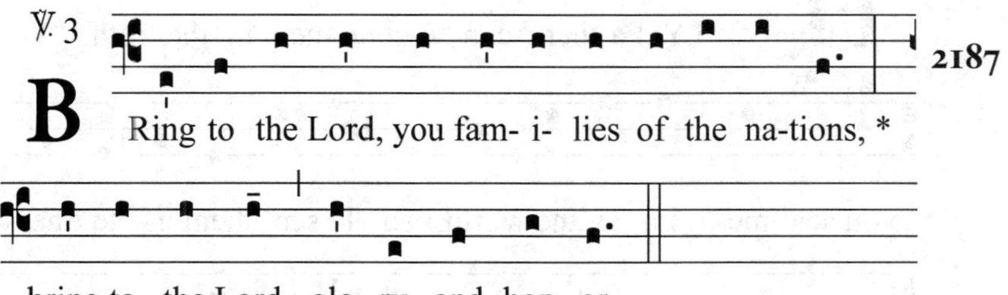

2187

COMMUNION ANTIPHON *Pater sancte, sanctifica eos.*
Jn 17:17-18

- i -

2188

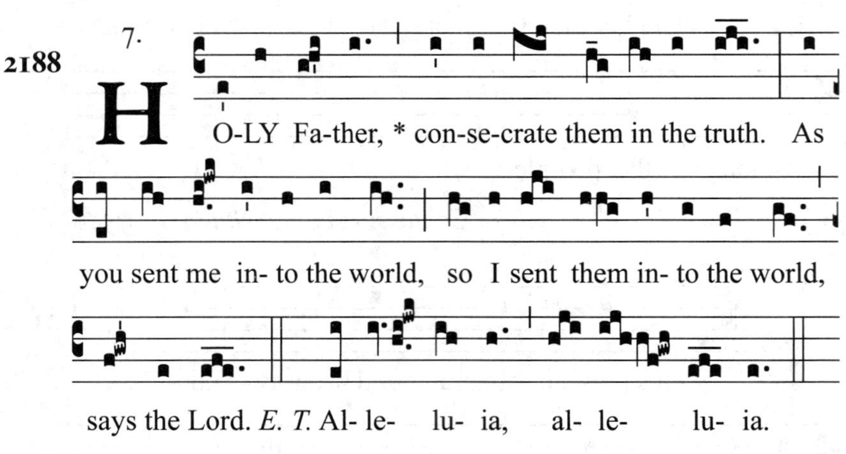
7.
H O-LY Fa-ther, * con-se-crate them in the truth. As
you sent me in- to the world, so I sent them in- to the world,
says the Lord. E. T. Al- le- lu- ia, al- le- lu- ia.

- ii -

2189

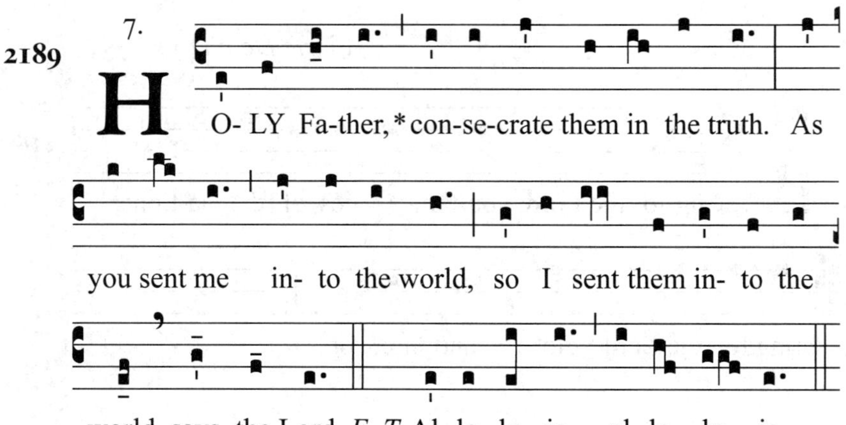
7.
H O- LY Fa-ther, * con-se-crate them in the truth. As
you sent me in- to the world, so I sent them in- to the
world, says the Lord. E. T. Al- le- lu- ia, al- le- lu- ia.

VERSES *Ad te levavi animam meam. Ps* 24:1

℣. 1

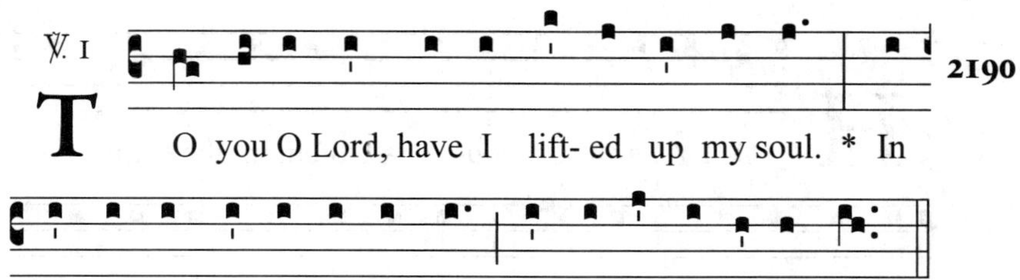
TO you O Lord, have I lift- ed up my soul. * In

2190

you, O my God, I put my trust; let me not be put to shame.

Vias tuas, Domine, demonstra mihi. Ps 24:4

℣. 2

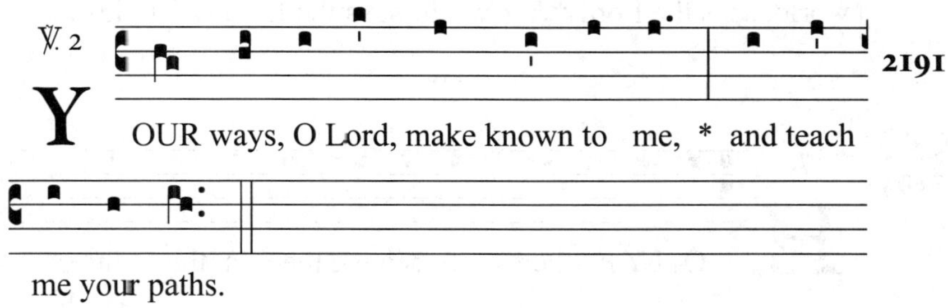
YOUR ways, O Lord, make known to me, * and teach
me your paths.

2191

Custodi animam meam. Ps 24:20

℣. 3

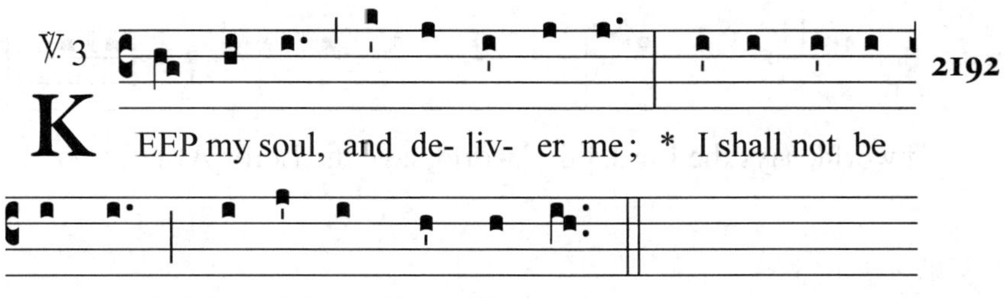
KEEP my soul, and de- liv- er me; * I shall not be

2192

ashamed, for I have hoped in you.

- iii -

2193
7.
HOLY Fa-ther, * con-secrate them in the truth. As
you sent me in- to the world, so I sent them in- to the
† world, says the Lord. † E. T. world, says the Lord. Al-le-lu- ia.

- iv -

2194
7.
HOLY Fa-ther, * con-secrate them in the truth. As
you sent me in- to the world, so I sent them in- to the
† world, says the Lord. † E. T. world, says the Lord. Al-le-lu- ia.

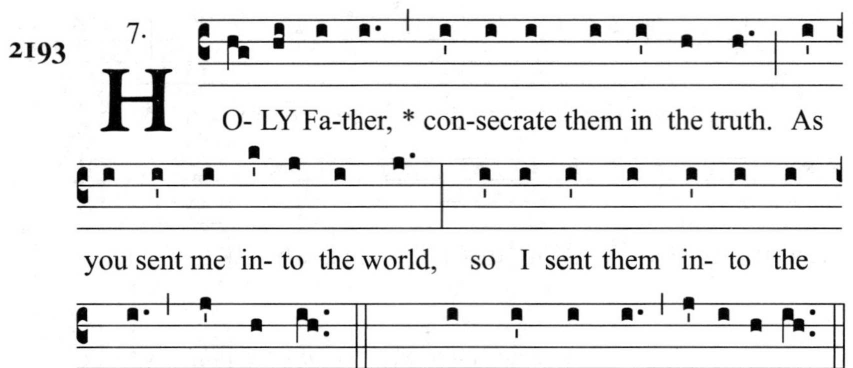

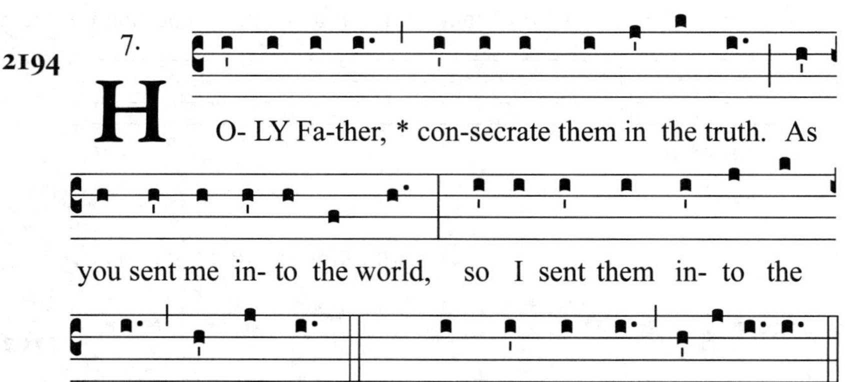

FOR THE ORDINATION OF PRIESTS

ENTRANCE ANTIPHON *Pastores dabo vobis.*
Jer 3:15

- i -

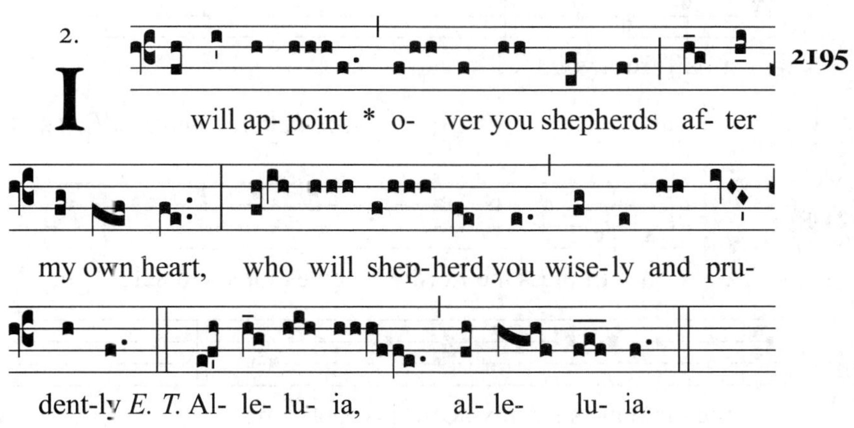
2.
I will ap- point * o- ver you shepherds af- ter
2195
my own heart, who will shep-herd you wise-ly and prudent-ly E. T. Al- le- lu- ia, al- le- lu- ia.

- ii -

Ti *natural on "own" in the phrase "after my own heart."*

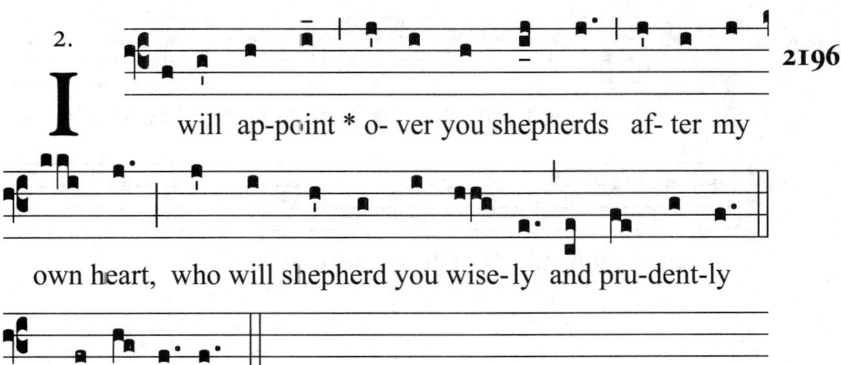
2.
I will ap-point * o- ver you shepherds af- ter my
2196
own heart, who will shepherd you wise-ly and pru-dent-ly
E. T. Al- le- lu- ia.

VERSES *Conserva me, Domine. Ps* 15:1-2

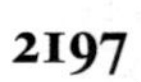
2197
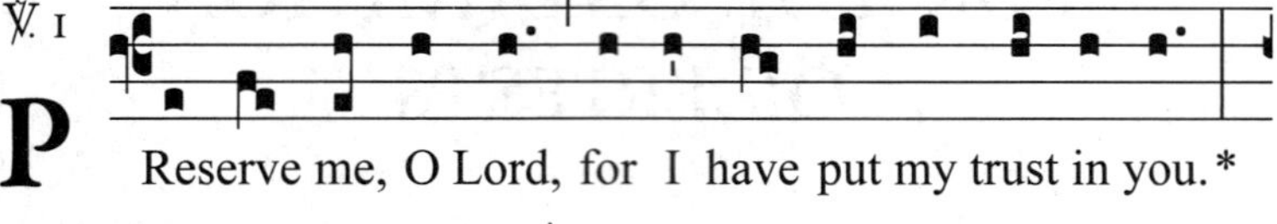
℣. 1
PReserve me, O Lord, for I have put my trust in you.*
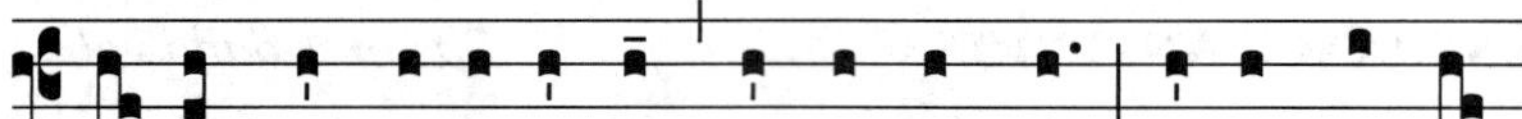
I have said to the Lord, You are my Lord; I have no good
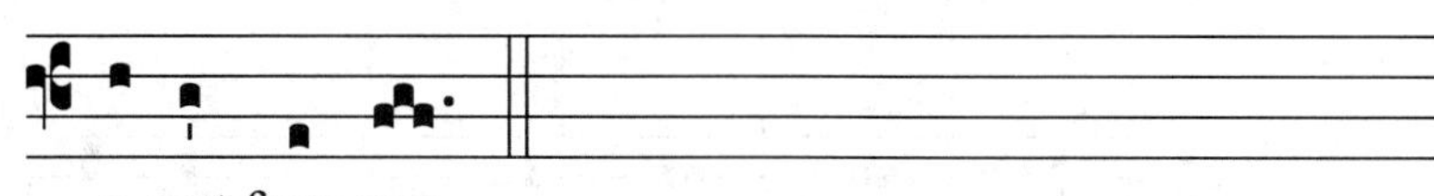
a-part from you.

Benedicam Dominum. Ps 15:7

2198

℣. 2
I will bless the Lord who gives me coun-sel; * in
the night al- so my heart instructs me.

Providebam Dominum. Ps 15:8

2199
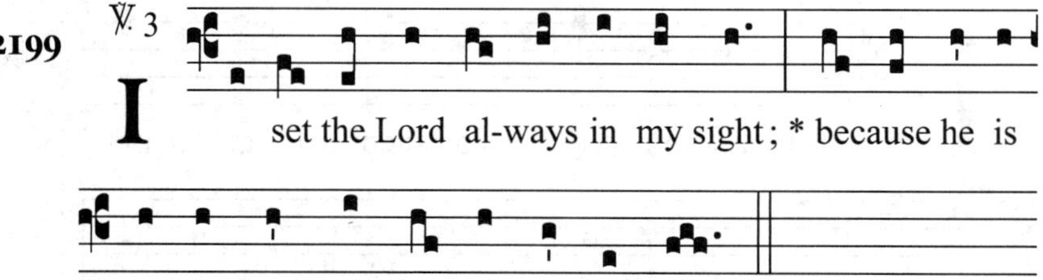
℣. 3
I set the Lord al-ways in my sight; * because he is
at my right hand, I shall not be moved.

- iii -

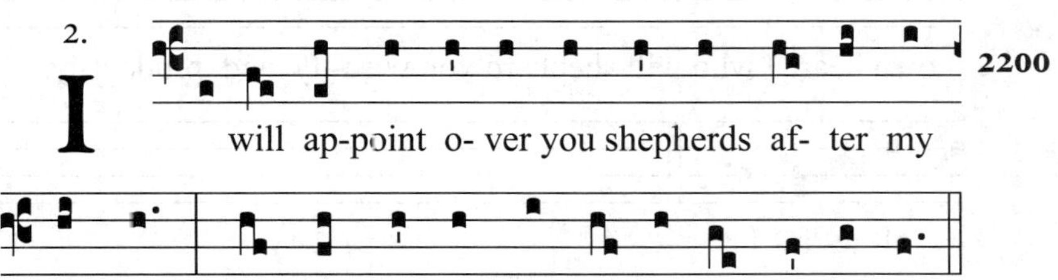
2. 2200

I will ap-point o- ver you shepherds af- ter my own heart, * who will shepherd you wise-ly and prudent-ly

During Easter Time:

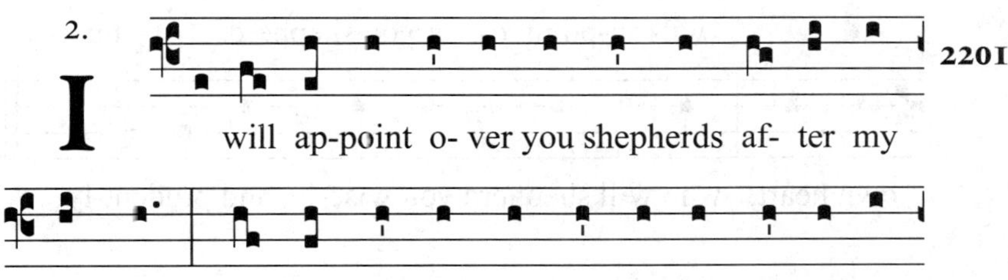
2. 2201

I will ap-point o- ver you shepherds af- ter my own heart, * who will shepherd you wise- ly and prudent-ly,

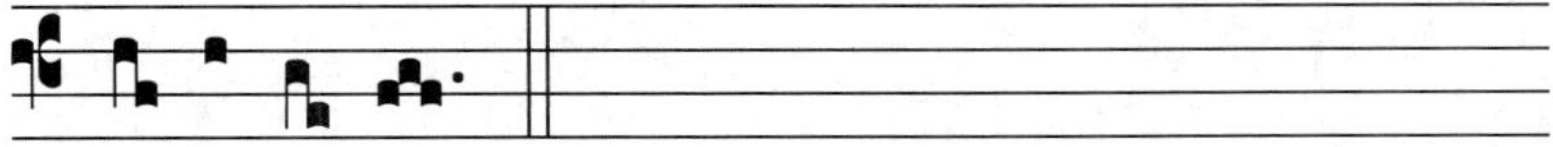
al- le- lu- ia.

Or:

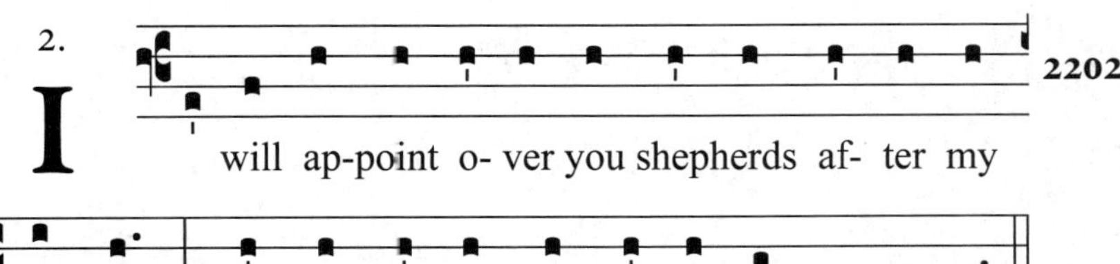
2. 2202

I will ap-point o- ver you shepherds af- ter my own heart, * who will shepherd you wise-ly and prudent-ly

During Easter Time:

2. 2203

I will ap-point o- ver you shepherds af- ter my

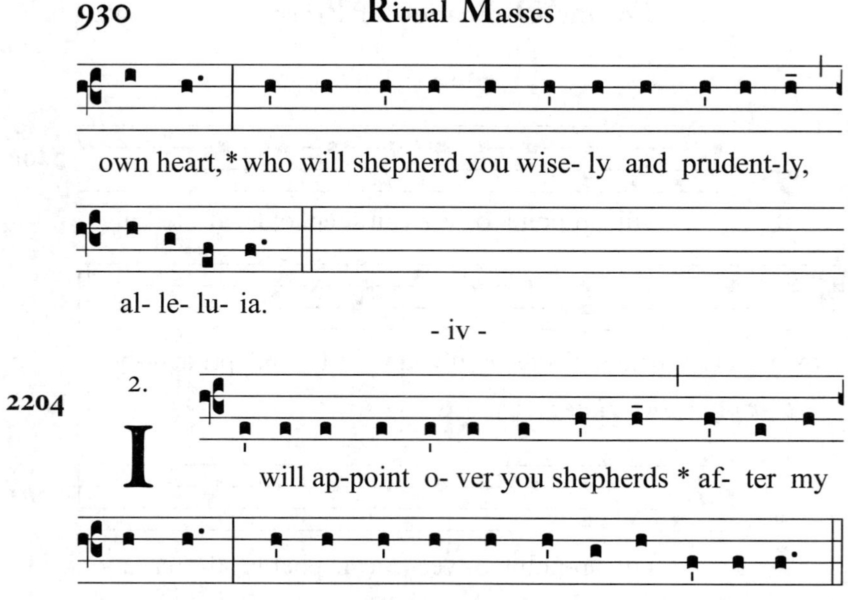
own heart, * who will shepherd you wise- ly and prudent-ly,
al- le- lu- ia.
- iv -
2204
2.
I will ap-point o- ver you shepherds * af- ter my
own heart, who will shepherd you wise-ly and prudent-ly

During the investiture with stole and chasuable and the anointing of the hands, the following antiphon is sung:

ANTIPHON *Sacerdos in æternum.*

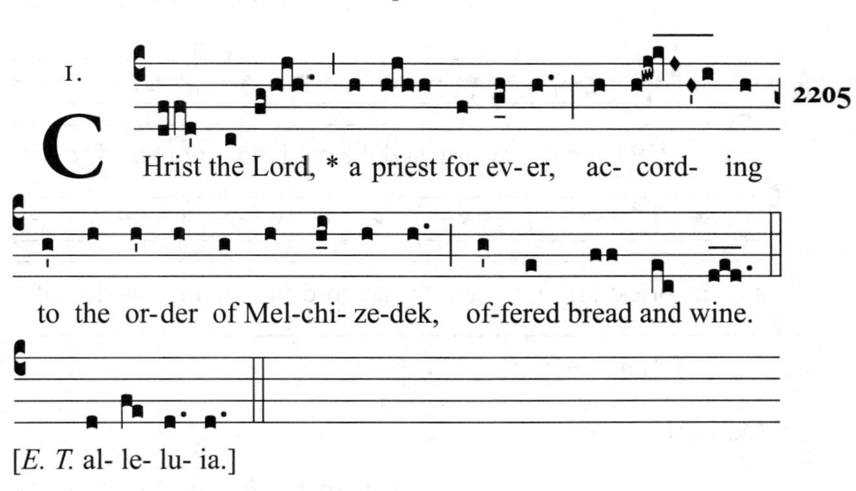
- i -
1.
C Hrist the Lord, * a priest for ev- er, ac- cord- ing
2205
to the or-der of Mel-chi- ze-dek, of-fered bread and wine.
[*E. T.* al- le- lu- ia.]

VERSES *Dixit Dominus Domino meo. Ps* 109 : 1

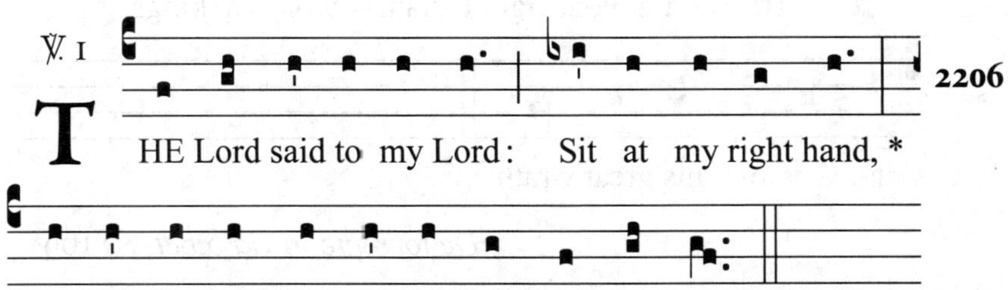
℣. 1
T HE Lord said to my Lord: Sit at my right hand, *
2206
un- til I make your en- e- mies your foot-stool.

Virgam virtutis tuæ. Ps 109 : 2

℣. 2
T HE Lord will send forth from Si- on † the scep-ter of
2207

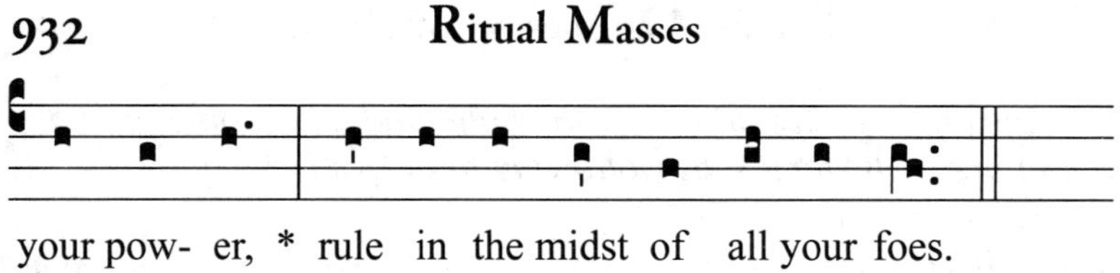
your pow- er, * rule in the midst of all your foes.

Iuravit Dominus. Ps 109:4

2208
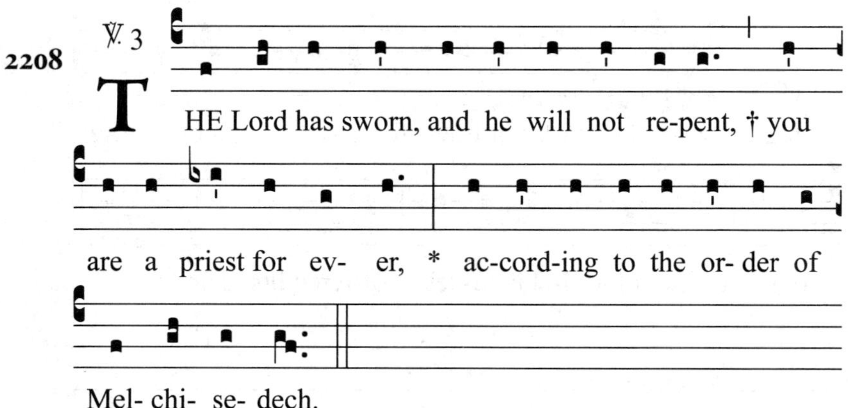
℣. 3
THE Lord has sworn, and he will not re-pent, † you
are a priest for ev- er, * ac-cord-ing to the or- der of
Mel- chi- se- dech.

Dominus a dextris tuis. Ps 109:5

2209

℣. 4
THE Lord at your right hand has brok- en kings * in
the day of his great wrath.

De torrente in via bibet. Ps 109:7

2210
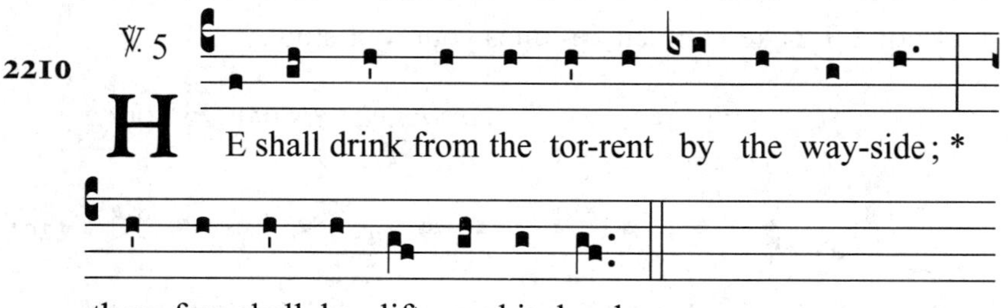
℣. 5
HE shall drink from the tor-rent by the way-side; *
there-fore shall he lift up his head.

- iii -

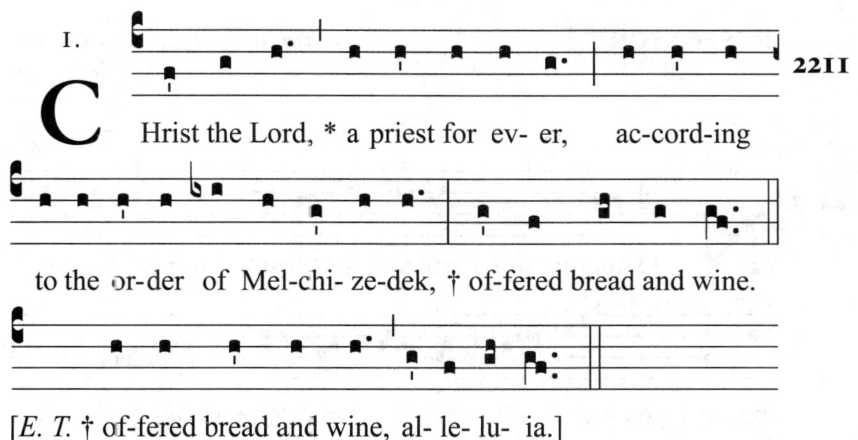
I.
2211
CHrist the Lord, * a priest for ev- er, ac-cord-ing
to the or-der of Mel-chi- ze-dek, † of-fered bread and wine.
[E. T. † of-fered bread and wine, al- le- lu- ia.]

- iv -

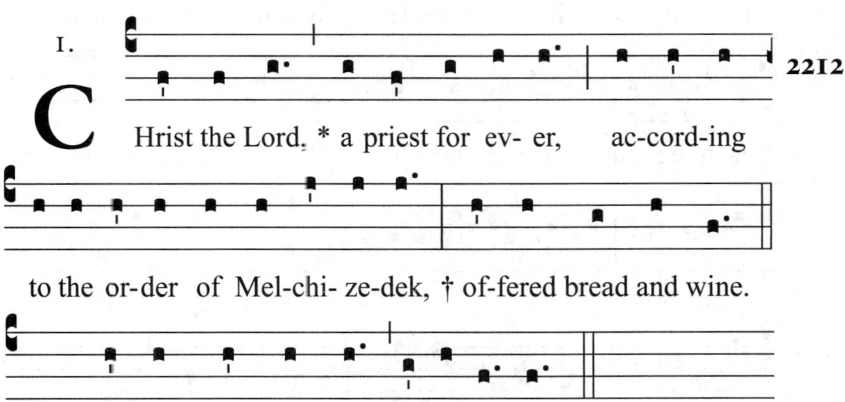
I.
2212
CHrist the Lord, * a priest for ev- er, ac-cord-ing
to the or-der of Mel-chi- ze-dek, † of-fered bread and wine.
[E. T. † of-fered bread and wine, al- le- lu- ia.]

During the fraternal kiss, the following Responsory may be sung. The alleluia is sung except during Lent.

RESPONSORY *Iam non dicam vos servos.*
Cf. Jn 15-17

- i -

2213 8. NO long-er * do I call you ser- vants, but my friends,

because you know all that I have done a- mong you, al-

le- lu- ia. * Re-ceive the Ho- ly Spir-it as an Ad-vocate

a-mong you: † He is the Spir- it whom the Fa- ther will

send you, al- le- lu- ia. ℣. You are my friends

if you do what I command you. * Re-ceive. ℣. Glo-ry

be to the Fa-ther, and to the Son, and to the

Ho- ly Spir- it. † He is

- ii -

8. 2214

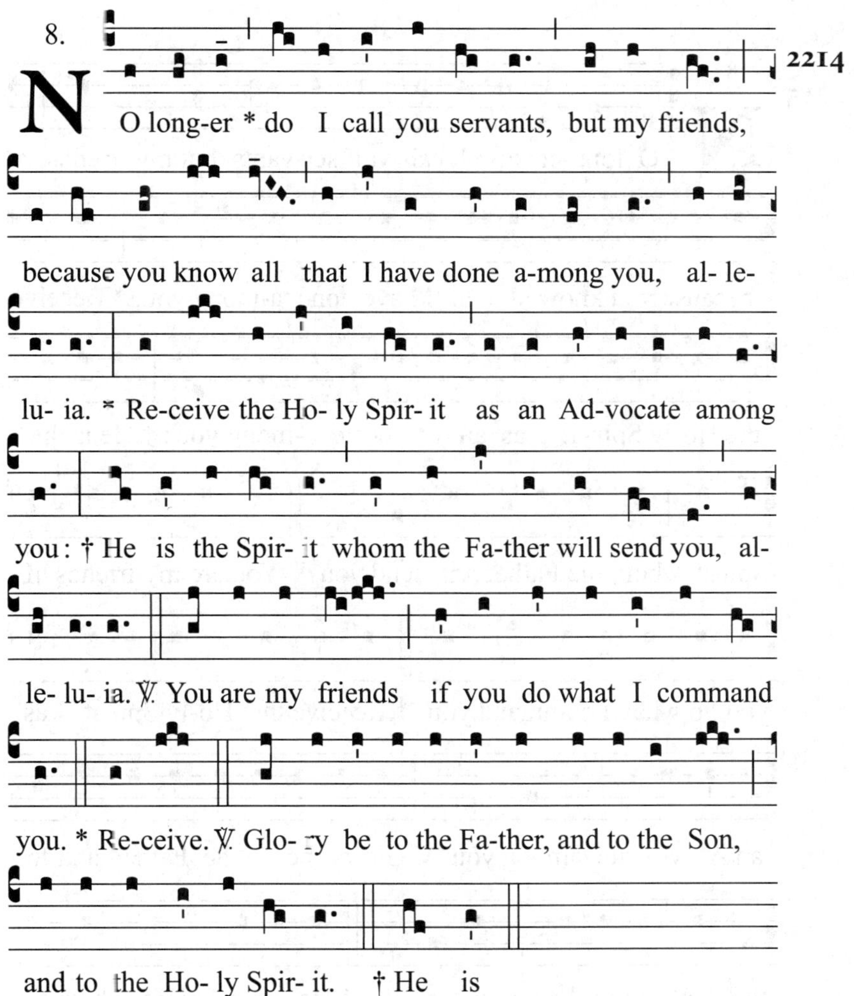
NO long-er * do I call you servants, but my friends,
because you know all that I have done a-mong you, al- le-
lu- ia. * Re-ceive the Ho- ly Spir- it as an Ad-vocate among
you : † He is the Spir- it whom the Fa-ther will send you, al-
le- lu- ia. ℣. You are my friends if you do what I command
you. * Re-ceive. ℣. Glo- ry be to the Fa-ther, and to the Son,
and to the Ho- ly Spir- it. † He is

- iii -

During Lent:

2215

8.
NO long-er do I call you ser-vants, but my friends, *
because you know all that I have done a-mong you. * Receive
the Ho-ly Spir- it as an Ad-vocate a-mong you: † He is the
Spir-it whom the Father will send you. ℣. You are my friends if
you do what I command you. * Receive the Ho-ly Spir-it as
an Ad-vo-cate among you. ℣. Glo-ry be to the Father, and to
the Son, and to the Ho- ly Spir-it. † He is the Spir-it whom the
Fa-ther will send you.

- iv -

The alleluia is sung except during Lent.

8.
2216
NO long-er do I call you servants, but my friends, *
because you know all that I have done a-mong you, al- le-
lu- ia. * Re-ceive the Ho- ly Spir- it as an Ad-vo-cate among
you: † He is the Spir- it whom the Fa-ther will send you, al-
le- lu- ia. ℣. You are my friends if you do what I command
you. * Re-ceive. ℣. Glo- ry be to the Fa-ther, and to the Son,
and to the Ho- ly Spir- it. † He is

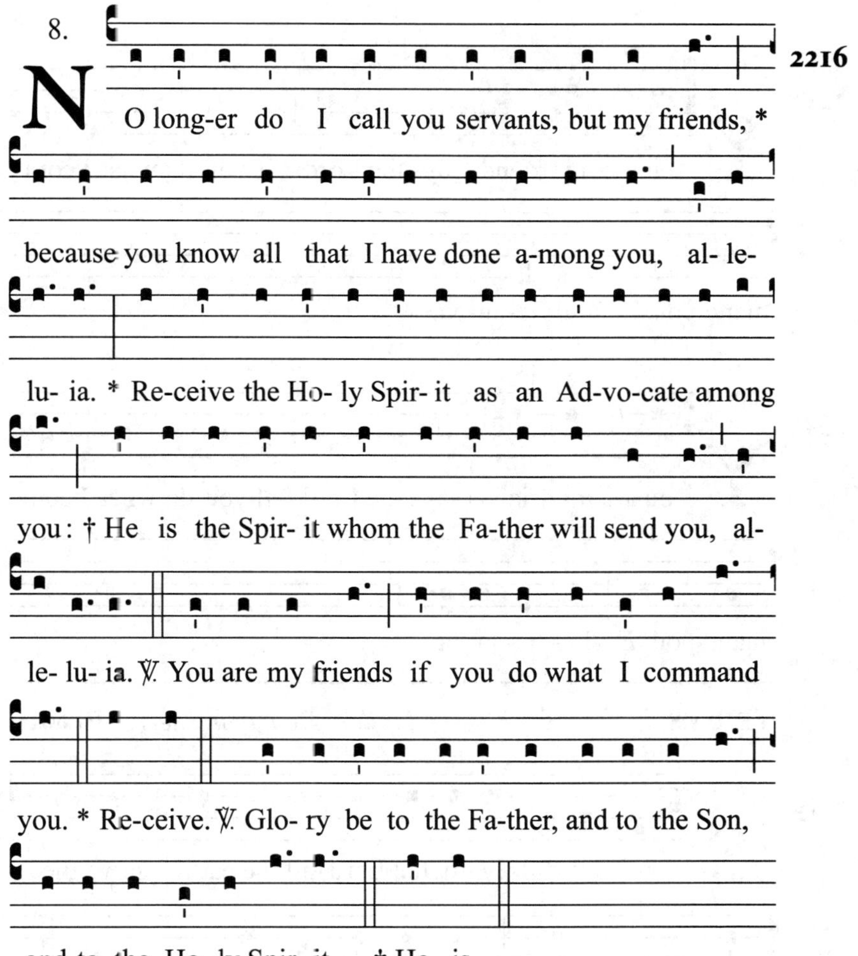

Or the following antiphon may be sung:

ANTIPHON *Vos amici mei estis.*
Cf. Jn 14-17

- i -

2217 8.

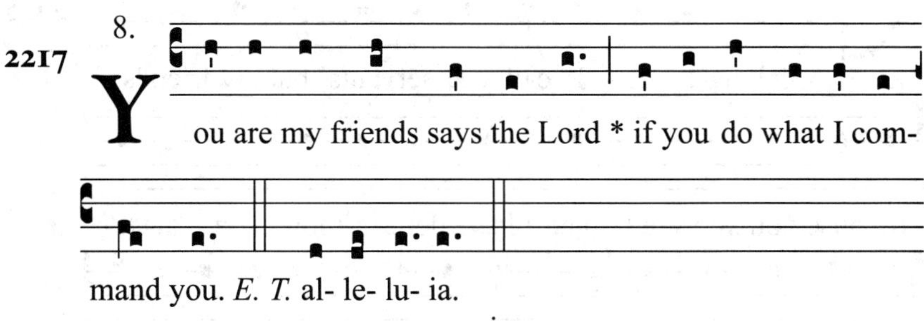

Y ou are my friends says the Lord * if you do what I com-

mand you. *E. T.* al- le- lu- ia.

- iv -

2218 8.

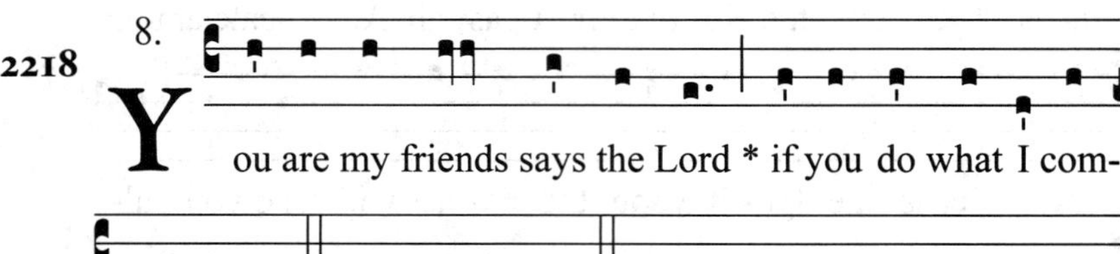

Y ou are my friends says the Lord * if you do what I com-

mand you. *E. T.* al- le- lu- ia.

VERSES *Iubilate Deo, omnis terra. Ps* 99 : 2

2219 ℣. 1

S ING joy-ful- ly to the Lord, all the earth; serve the

Lord with glad-ness; * come be-fore him with joy-ful song.

Scitote, quoniam Dominus. Ps 99 : 3

2220 ℣. 2

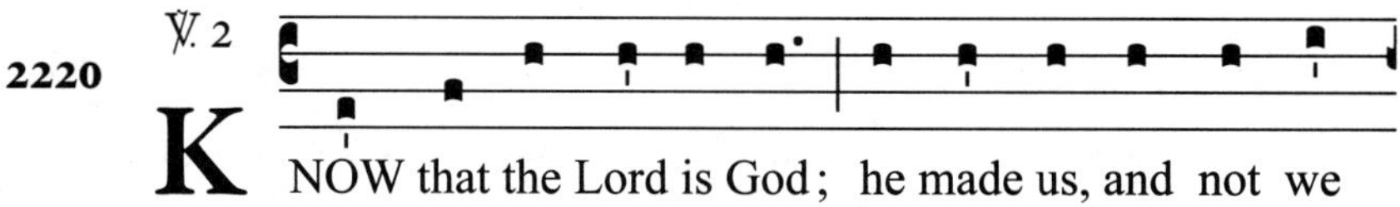

K NOW that the Lord is God; he made us, and not we

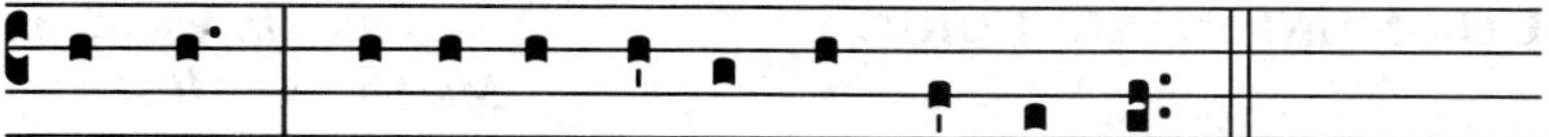

ourselves. * We are his peo-ple, the flock he tends.

Introite portas eius. Ps 99 : 4

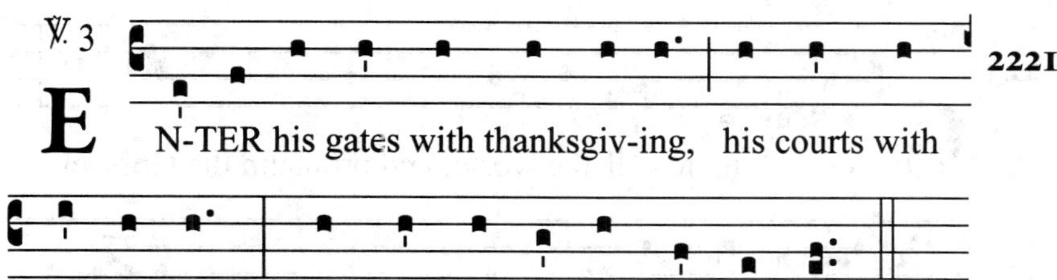

℣. 3 E N-TER his gates with thanksgiv-ing, his courts with 2221

songs of praise ; * give thanks to him and bless his name.

Quoniam suavis est Dominus. Ps 99 : 5

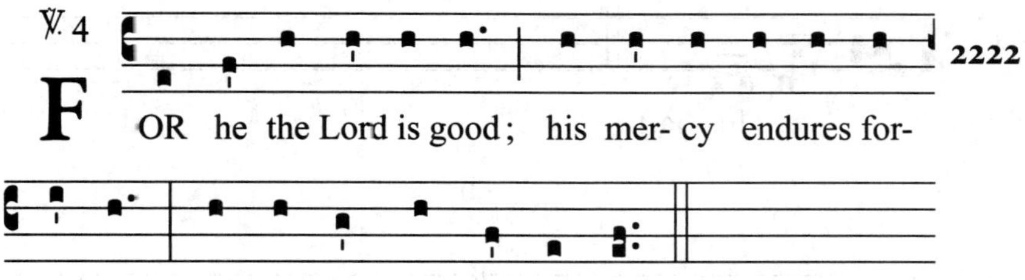

℣. 4 F OR he the Lord is good ; his mer- cy endures for- 2222

ev- er, * and his truth from age to age.

Communion Antiphon *Euntes in mundum.*
Mk 16:15; *Mt* 28:20

- i -

2223

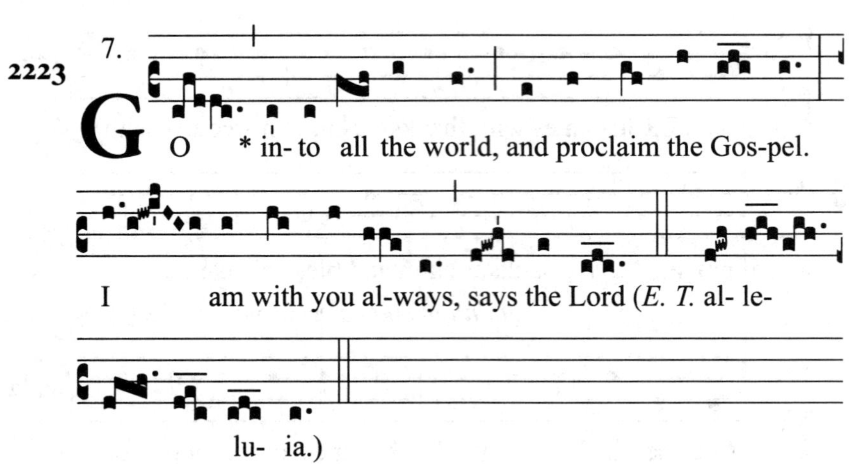
7.
GO * in-to all the world, and proclaim the Gos-pel.
I am with you al-ways, says the Lord (*E. T.* al- le-
lu- ia.)

- ii -

2224

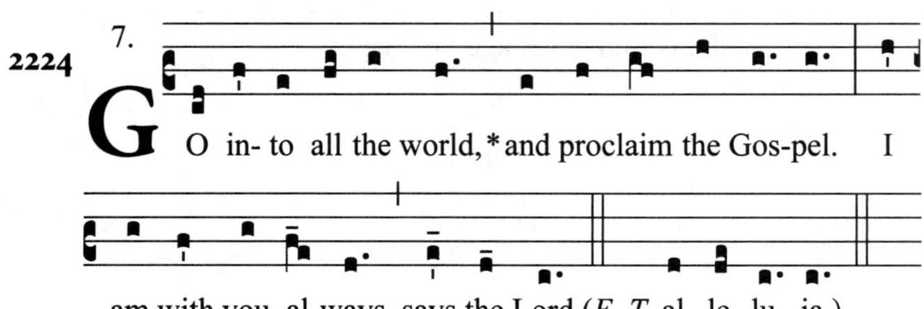
7.
GO in- to all the world, * and proclaim the Gos-pel. I
am with you al-ways, says the Lord (*E. T.* al- le- lu- ia.)

VERSES

Benedicam Dominum in omni tempore. Ps 33:2

℣. 1
2225
I will bless the Lord at all times, * his praise shall be

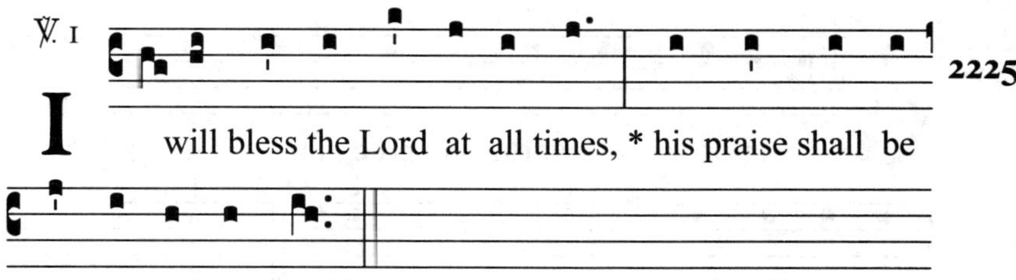

al-ways in my mouth.

Magnificate Dominum mecum. Ps 33:4

℣. 2
2226
O mag-ni- fy the Lord with me, * to-geth-er let us

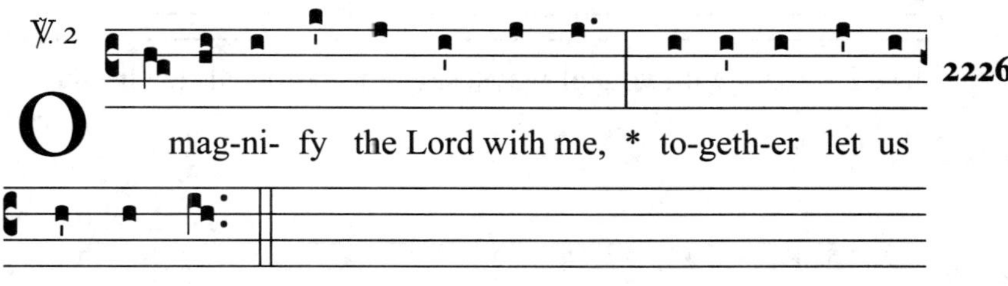

praise his Name.

Accedite ad eum et illuminamini. Ps 33:6

℣. 3
2227
COME to him and be en-lightened, * that your fac- es

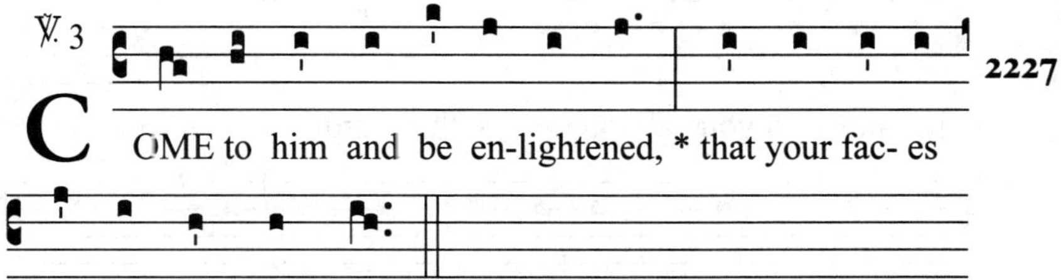

may not blush with shame.

Gustate et videte. Ps 33:9

℣. 4
2228
O taste and see how good the Lord is, * bless-ed is

the man who hopes in him.

- iii -

2229

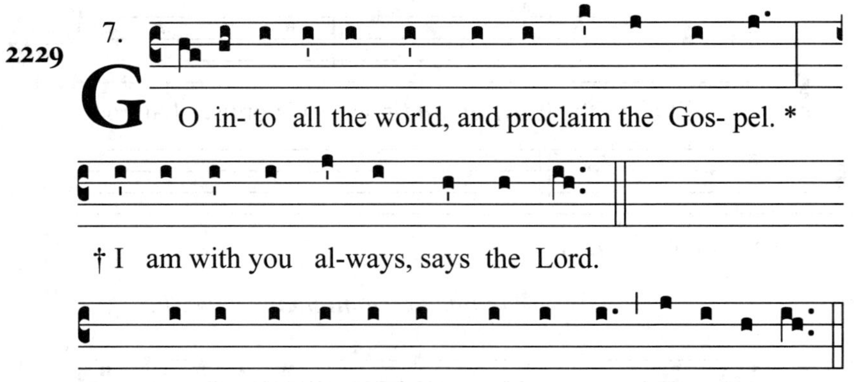
7.
GO in- to all the world, and proclaim the Gos- pel. *
† I am with you al-ways, says the Lord.
† *E. T.* I am with you al-ways, says the Lord, al- le- lu- ia.

- iv -

2230 7.

GO in- to all the world, and proclaim the Gos- pel. *

† I am with you al-ways, says the Lord.

† *E. T.* I am with you al-ways, says the Lord, al- le- lu- ia.

FOR THE ORDINATION OF DEACONS

ENTRANCE ANTIPHON *Si quis mihi ministrat.* *John* 12:26

- ii -
4. A
W HO- ev- er serves me * must fol-low me, and
where I am, there al- so will my ser-vant be.
2231

VERSES *Conserva me, Domine. Ps* 15:1-2

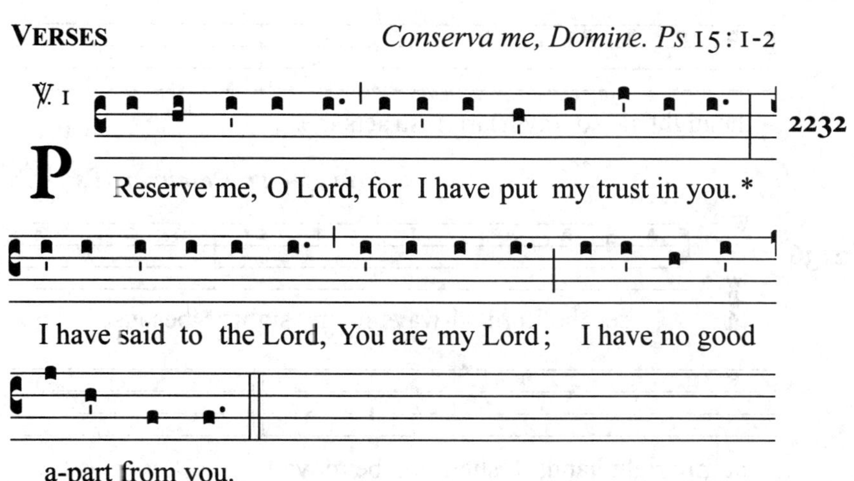
℣. 1
P Reserve me, O Lord, for I have put my trust in you.*
I have said to the Lord, You are my Lord; I have no good
a-part from you.
2232

Dominus pars hereditatis meæ. Ps 15:5

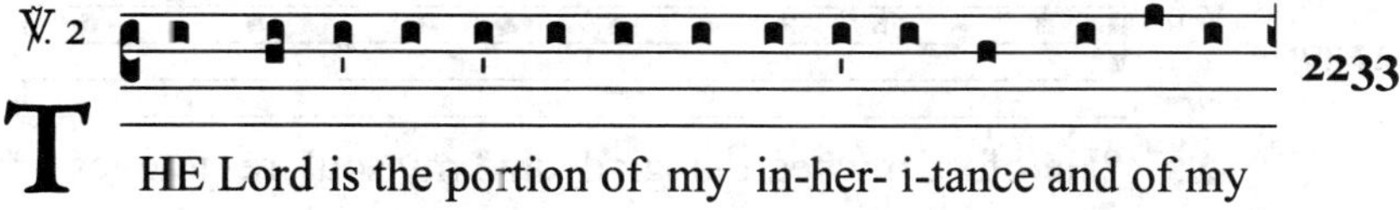
℣. 2
T HE Lord is the portion of my in-her- i-tance and of my
2233

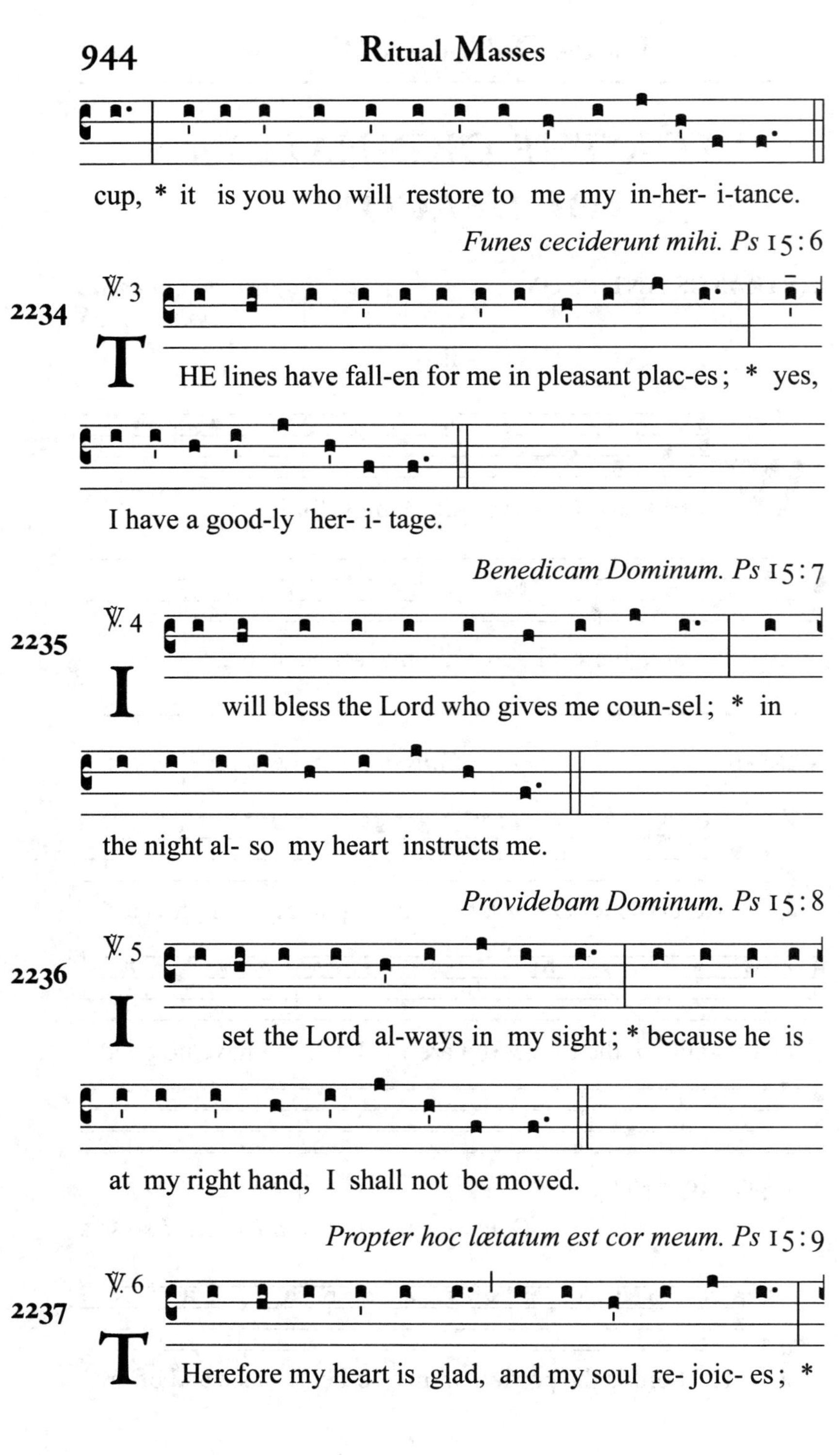
cup, * it is you who will restore to me my in-her- i-tance.
Funes ceciderunt mihi. Ps 15:6
2234
℣. 3
THE lines have fall-en for me in pleasant plac-es; * yes,
I have a good-ly her- i- tage.
Benedicam Dominum. Ps 15:7
2235
℣. 4
I will bless the Lord who gives me coun-sel; * in
the night al- so my heart instructs me.
Providebam Dominum. Ps 15:8
2236
℣. 5
I set the Lord al-ways in my sight; * because he is
at my right hand, I shall not be moved.
Propter hoc lætatum est cor meum. Ps 15:9
2237
℣. 6
THerefore my heart is glad, and my soul re- joic- es; *

my flesh al- so shall rest in hope.

Notas mihi fecisti. Ps 15:11

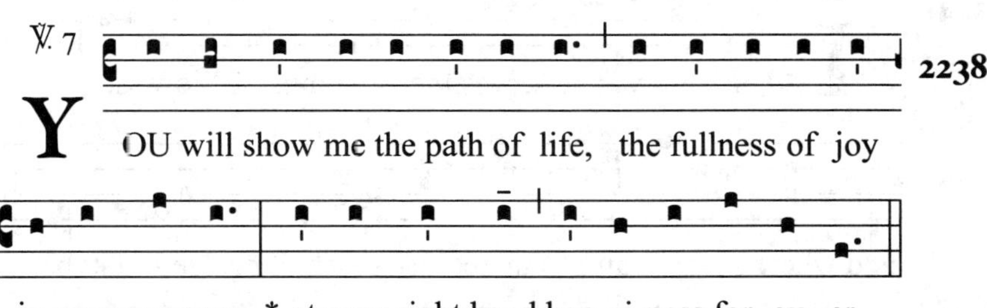
℣. 7
Y OU will show me the path of life, the fullness of joy
in your presence, * at your right hand hap-pi-ness for ev- er.

2238

- iii -

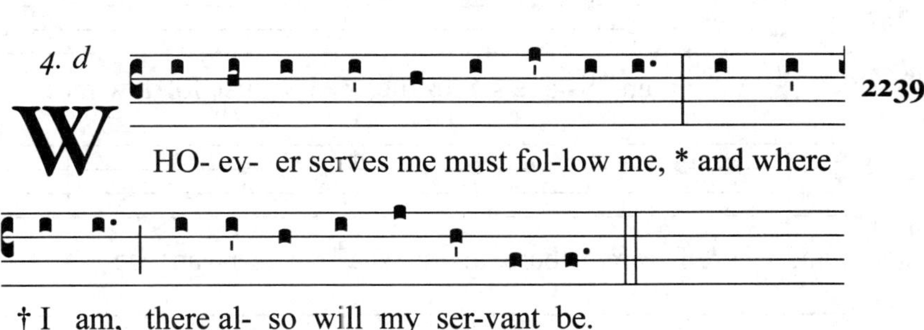
4. d
W HO- ev- er serves me must fol-low me, * and where
† I am, there al- so will my ser-vant be.

2239

† *E. T.* I am, there al- so will my servant be, al- le- lu- ia.

- iv -

4. d
W HO- ev- er serves me must fol-low me, * and where

2240

I am, there al- so will my ser-vant be. *E. T.* Al- le- lu- ia.

Another setting:

- i -

2241

5.
IF an- y- one serves me, * he must fol-low me;
and where I am, there al- so shall my ser-vant be.

- iii -

2242

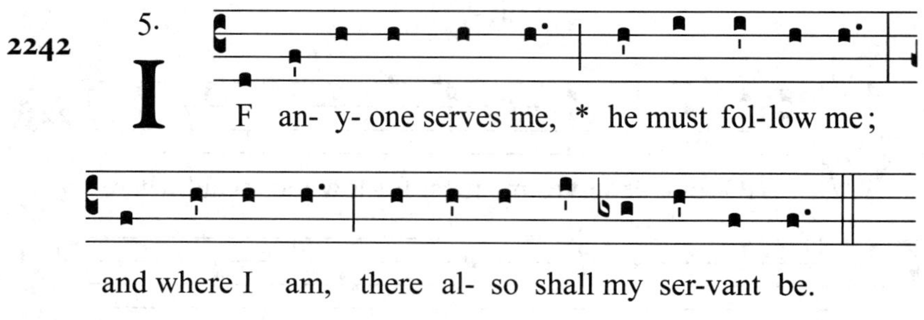
5.
IF an- y- one serves me, * he must fol-low me;
and where I am, there al- so shall my ser-vant be.

Verses *Conserva me, Domine. Ps* 15:1-2

2243 ℣. 1 PReserve me, O Lord, for I have put my trust in you.* I have said to the Lord, You are my Lord; I have no good a- part from you.

Dominus pars hereditatis meæ. Ps 15:5

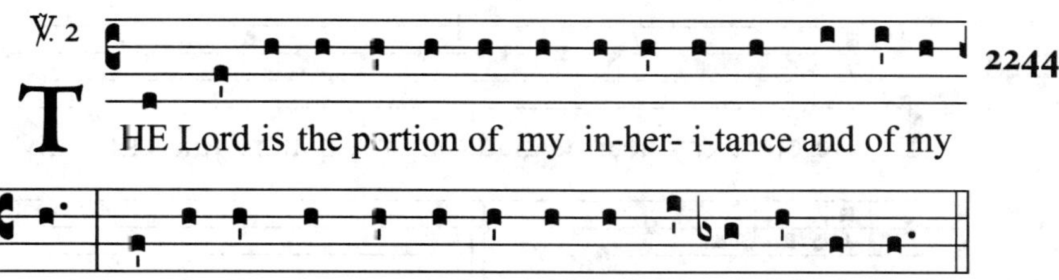
℣. 2
2244
THE Lord is the portion of my in-her- i-tance and of my

cup, * it is you who will restore to me my in-her- i-tance.

Funes ceciderunt mihi. Ps 15:6

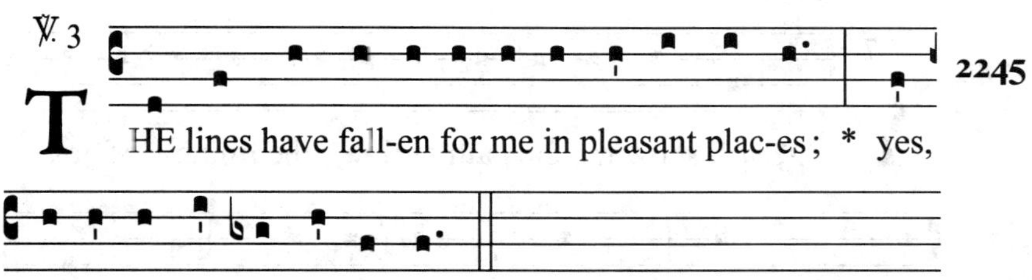
℣. 3
2245
THE lines have fall-en for me in pleasant plac-es; * yes,

I have a good-ly her- i- tage.

Benedicam Dominum. Ps 15:7

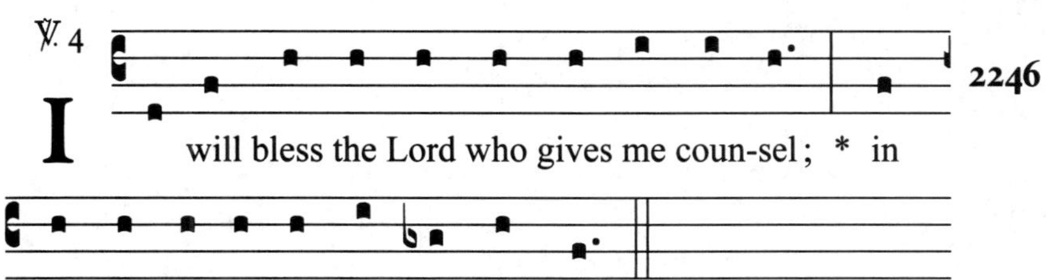
℣. 4
2246
I will bless the Lord who gives me coun-sel; * in

the night al- so my heart instructs me.

Providebam Dominum. Ps 15:8

℣. 5
2247
I set the Lord al-ways in my sight; * because he is

at my right hand, I shall not be moved.

Propter hoc laetatum est cor meum. Ps 15:9

2248
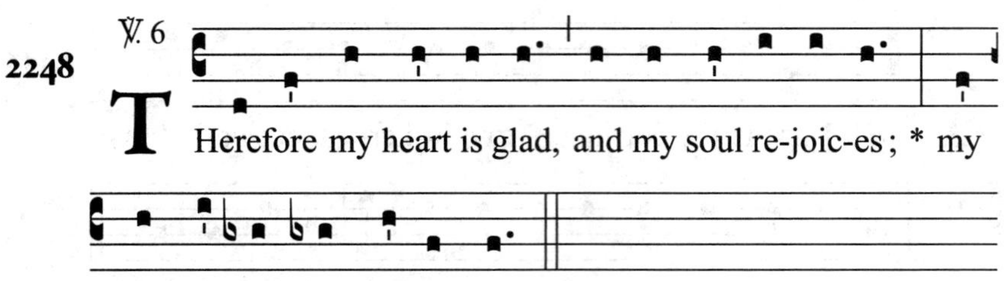
℣. 6
THerefore my heart is glad, and my soul re-joic-es; * my
flesh al- so shall rest in hope.

Notas mihi fecisti. Ps 15:11

2249
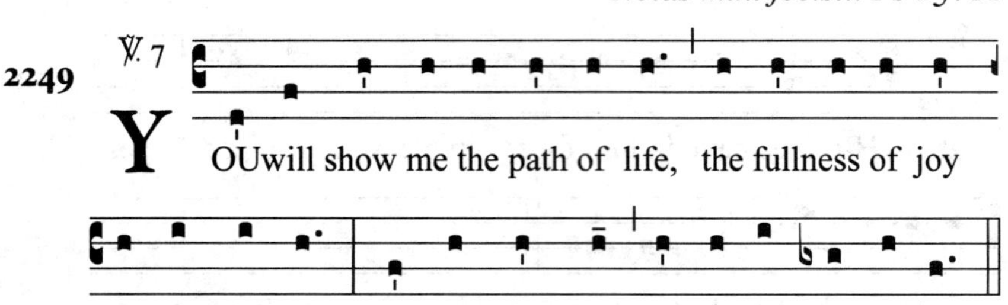
℣. 7
YOU will show me the path of life, the fullness of joy
in your presence, * at your right hand hap-pi-ness for ev- er.

During the investiture with the diaconal stole and dalmatic the following antiphon may be sung:

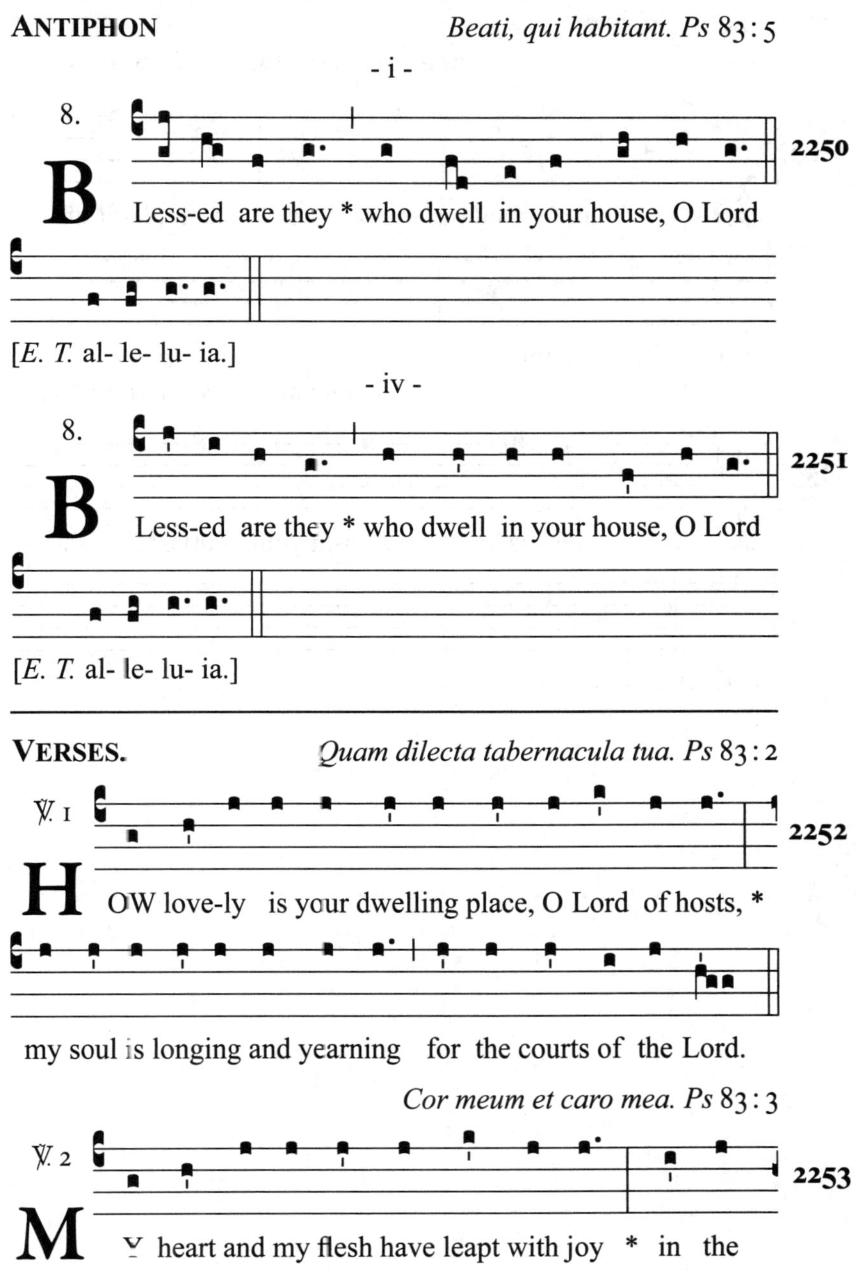
ANTIPHON
Beati, qui habitant. Ps 83:5
- i -
8.
BLess-ed are they * who dwell in your house, O Lord
2250
[E. T. al- le- lu- ia.]
- iv -
8.
BLess-ed are they * who dwell in your house, O Lord
2251
[E. T. al- le- lu- ia.]
VERSES.
Quam dilecta tabernacula tua. Ps 83:2
℣. 1
HOW love-ly is your dwelling place, O Lord of hosts, *
2252
my soul is longing and yearning for the courts of the Lord.
Cor meum et caro mea. Ps 83:3
℣. 2
MY heart and my flesh have leapt with joy * in the
2253

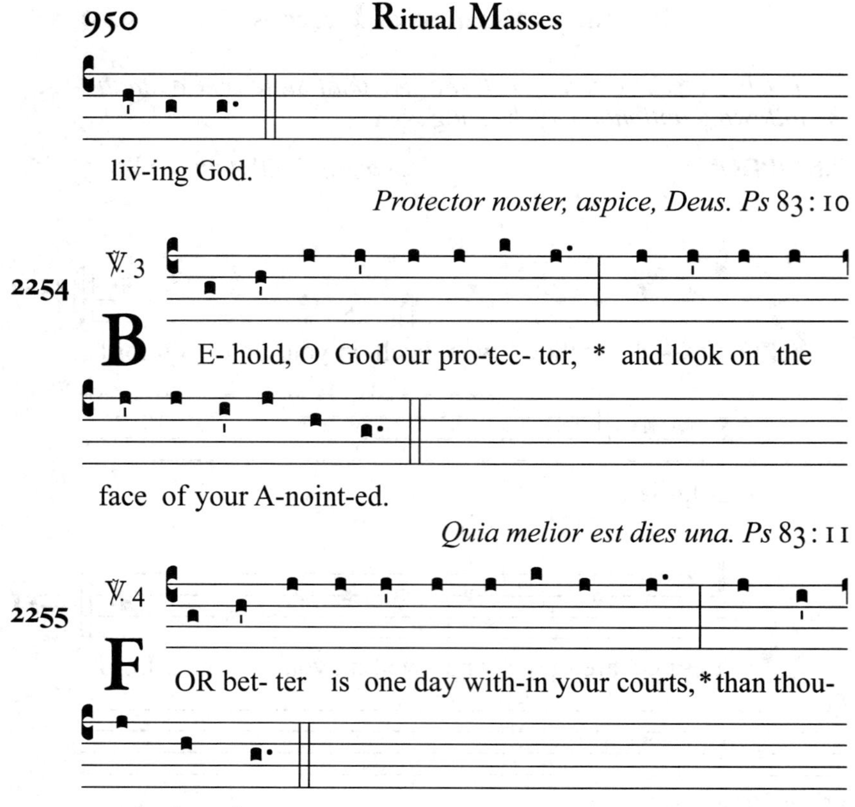
liv-ing God.
Protector noster, aspice, Deus. Ps 83 : 10
2254
℣. 3
BEHOLD, O God our pro-tec-tor, * and look on the
face of your A-noint-ed.
Quia melior est dies una. Ps 83 : 11
2255
℣. 4
FOR bet-ter is one day with-in your courts, * than thousands else-where.

During the fraternal kiss the following antiphon may be sung:

ANTIPHON *Qui mihi ministrat. Jn* 12:26

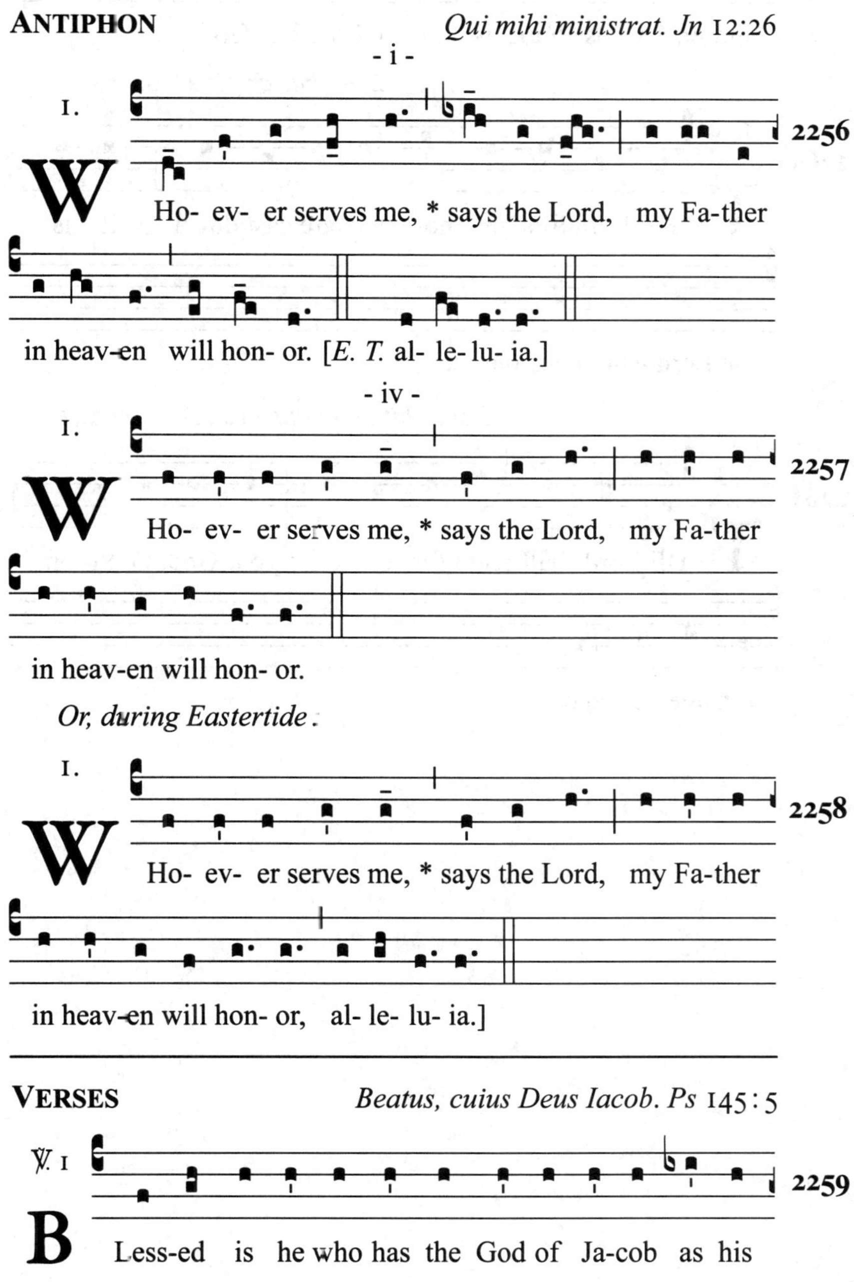
- i -
1.
2256
WHo- ev- er serves me, * says the Lord, my Fa-ther
in heav-en will hon- or. [*E. T.* al- le- lu- ia.]
- iv -
1.
2257
WHo- ev- er serves me, * says the Lord, my Fa-ther
in heav-en will hon- or.
Or, during Eastertide.
1.
2258
WHo- ev- er serves me, * says the Lord, my Fa-ther
in heav-en will hon- or, al- le- lu- ia.]

VERSES *Beatus, cuius Deus Iacob. Ps* 145:5

℣. 1 2259

BLess-ed is he who has the God of Ja-cob as his

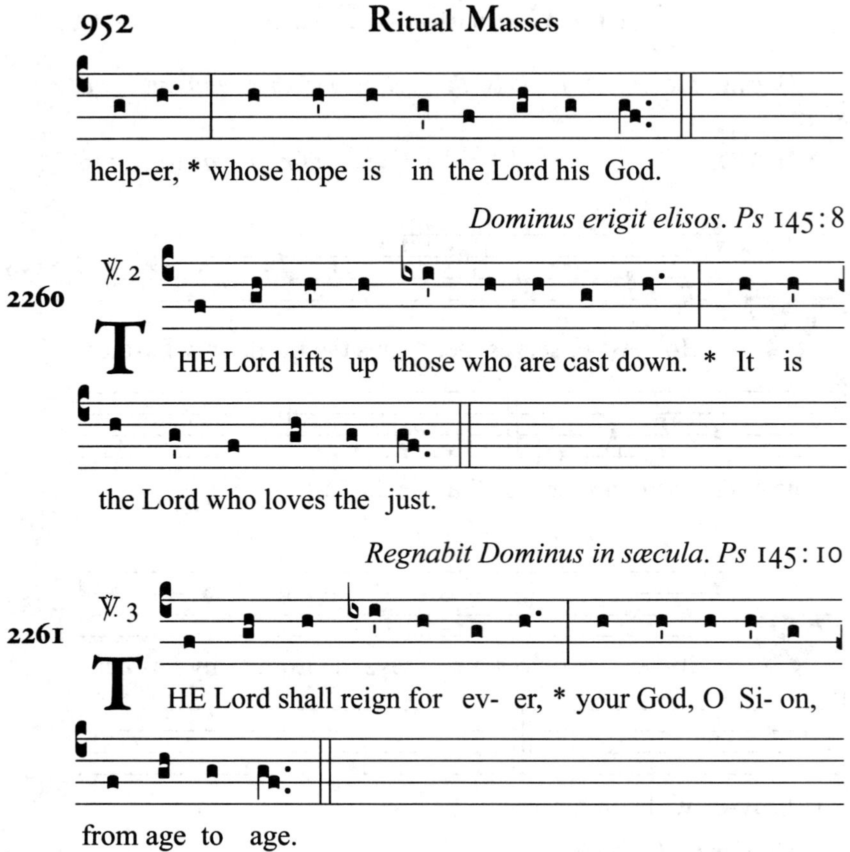
help-er, * whose hope is in the Lord his God.
Dominus erigit elisos. Ps 145:8
℣. 2
2260
THE Lord lifts up those who are cast down. * It is
the Lord who loves the just.
Regnabit Dominus in sæcula. Ps 145:10
℣. 3
2261
THE Lord shall reign for ev- er, * your God, O Si- on,
from age to age.

COMMUNION ANTIPHON *Filius hominis.* *Mt* 20:28

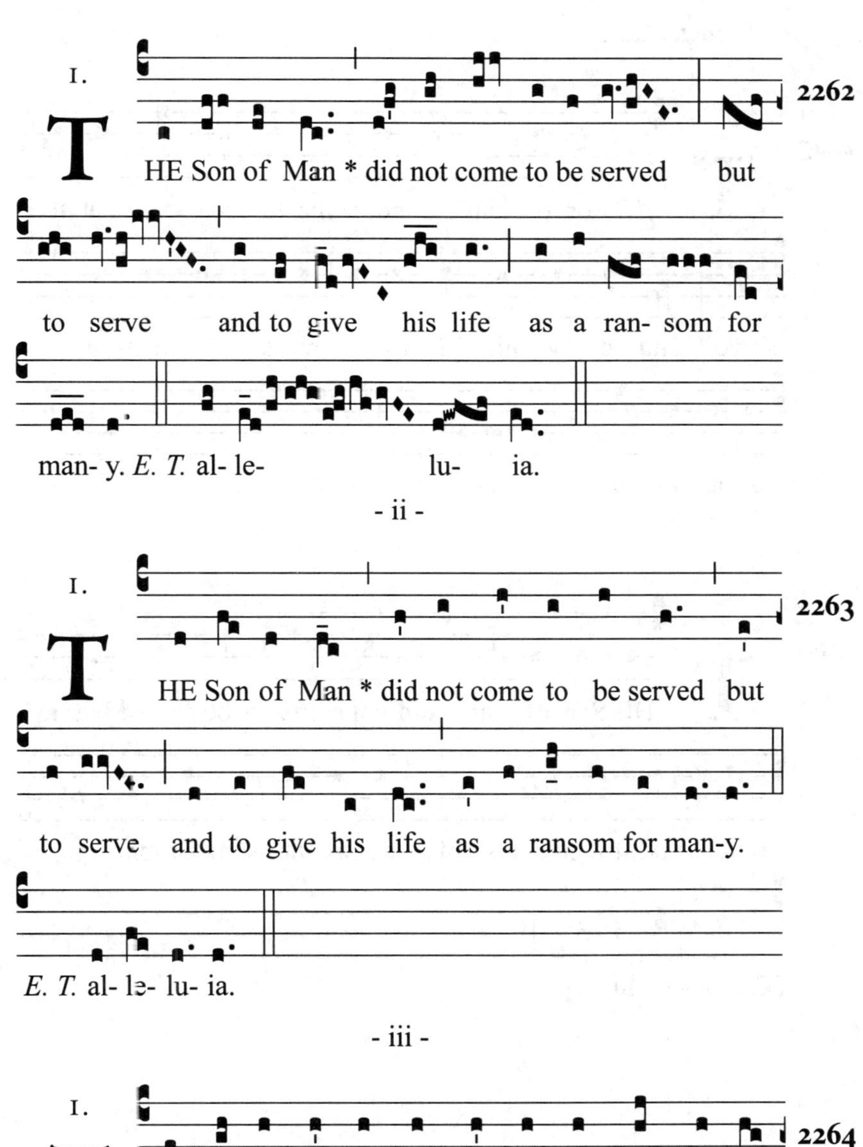
- i -
1.
THE Son of Man * did not come to be served but 2262
to serve and to give his life as a ran- som for
man- y. E. T. al- le- lu- ia.
- ii -
1.
THE Son of Man * did not come to be served but 2263
to serve and to give his life as a ransom for man-y.
E. T. al- le- lu- ia.
- iii -
1.
THE Son of Man did not come to be served but to 2264

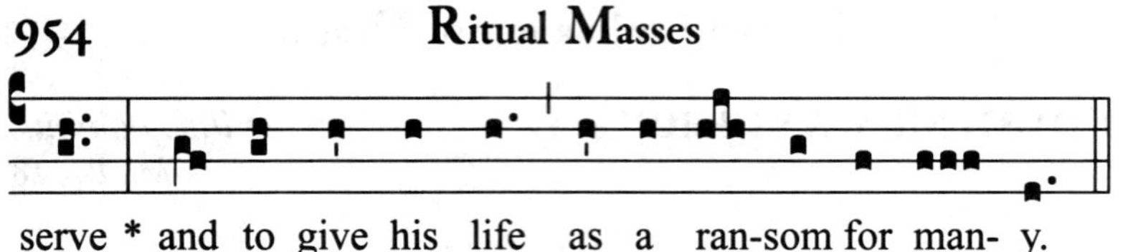
serve * and to give his life as a ran-som for man- y.

Eastertide:

2265

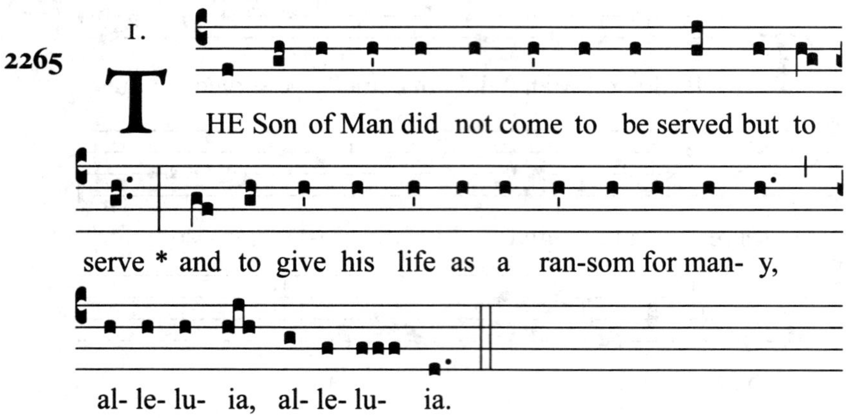
I.
THE Son of Man did not come to be served but to
serve * and to give his life as a ran-som for man- y,
al- le- lu- ia, al- le- lu- ia.

- iv -

2266

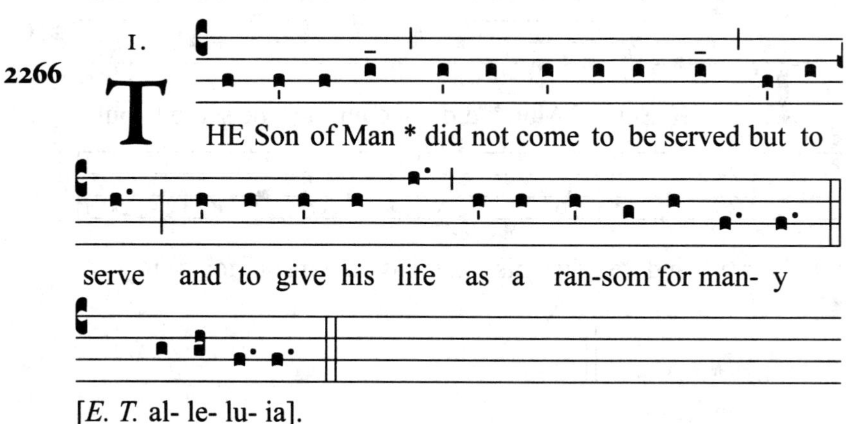
I.
THE Son of Man * did not come to be served but to
serve and to give his life as a ran-som for man- y
[E. T. al- le- lu- ia].

FOR THE CELEBRATION OF MARRIAGE

ENTRANCE ANTIPHON *Mittat vos Dominus auxilium de Sion.*
Ps 19:3. 5

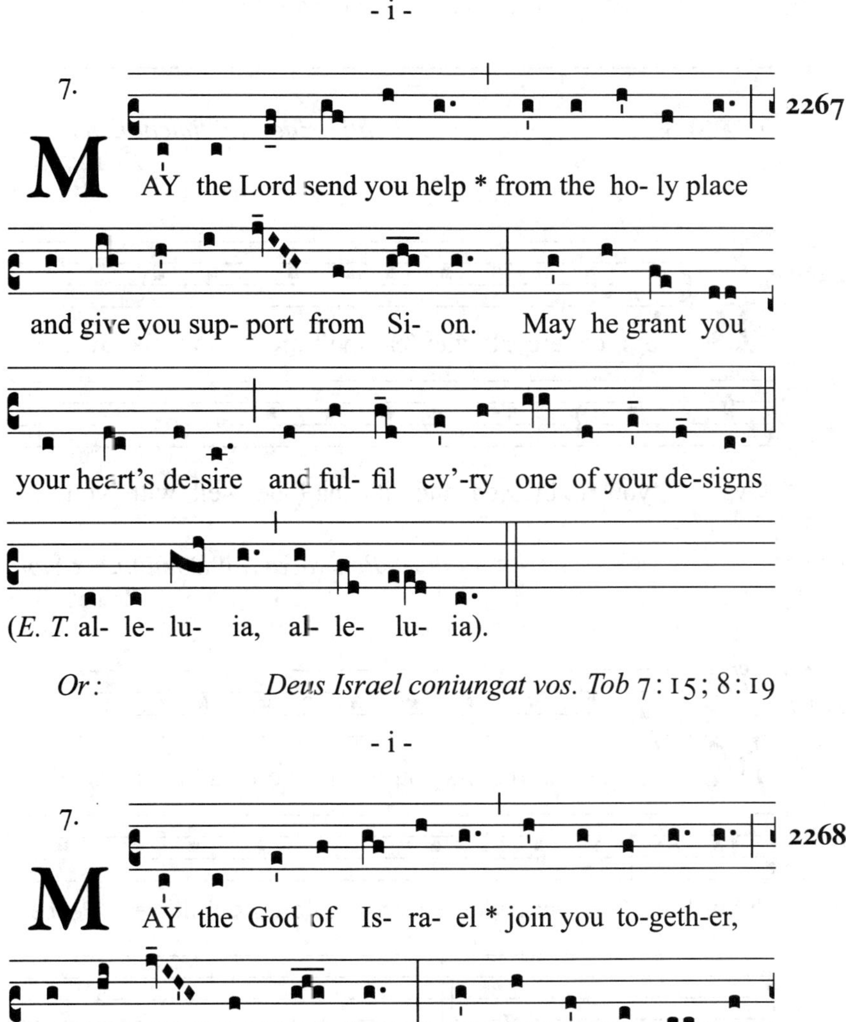
- i -
7.
2267
MAY the Lord send you help * from the ho- ly place
and give you sup- port from Si- on. May he grant you
your heart's de-sire and ful- fil ev'-ry one of your de-signs
(*E. T.* al- le- lu- ia, al- le- lu- ia).
Or: *Deus Israel coniungat vos. Tob* 7:15; 8:19
- i -
7.
2268
MAY the God of Is- ra- el * join you to-geth-er,
and may he be with you, who was mer- ci- ful to

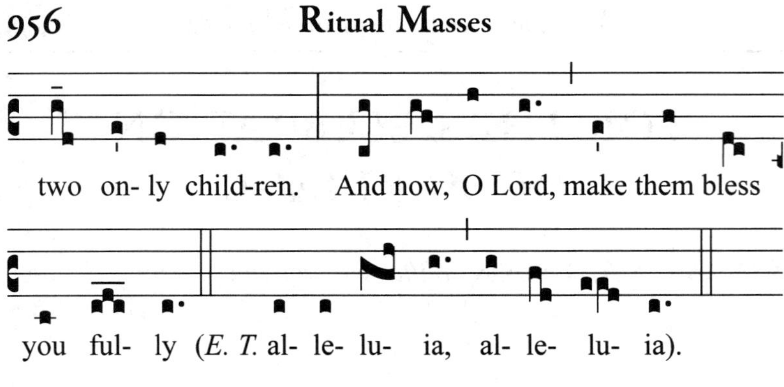
two on- ly child-ren. And now, O Lord, make them bless
you ful- ly (*E. T.* al- le- lu- ia, al- le- lu- ia).

VERSES

Beati omnes qui timent Dominum.
Ps 127:1-2

2269
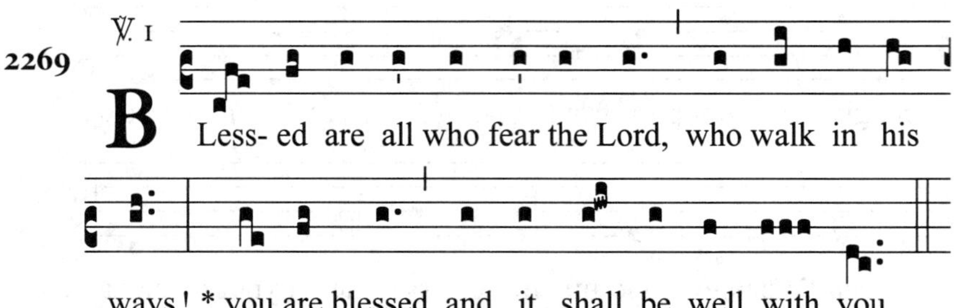
℣. 1
BLess- ed are all who fear the Lord, who walk in his
ways! * you are blessed and it shall be well with you.

Benedicat tibi Dominus ex Sion.
Ps 127:5-6

2270
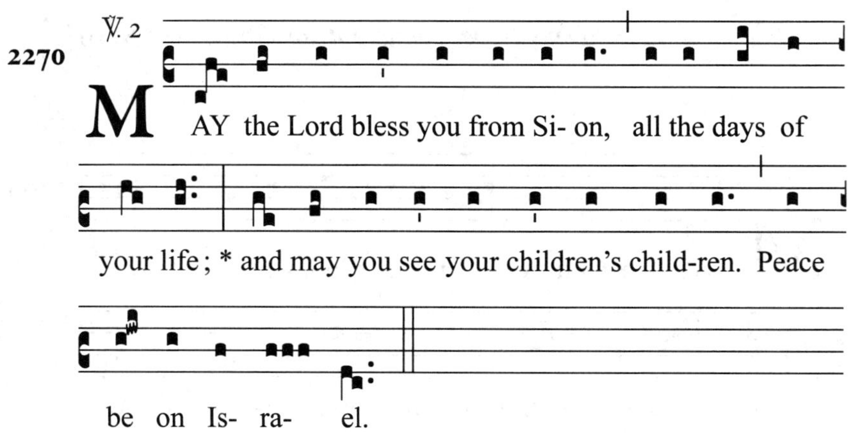
℣. 2
MAY the Lord bless you from Si- on, all the days of
your life; * and may you see your children's child-ren. Peace
be on Is- ra- el.

Or: *Mittat vos Dominus auxilium de Sion. Ps* 19:3.5

- i -
3.
2271
MAY the Lord send you help * from the ho- ly place
and give you sup- port from Si- on. May he grant you
your heart's de- sire and ful- fil ev'- ry one of your
de- signs (*E. T.* al- le- lu- ia, al- le- lu- ia).
Or:
- ii -
3.
2272
MAY the Lord send you help * from the ho- ly place
and give you sup- port from Si- on. May he grant you your
heart's de- sire and ful- fil ev'- ry one of your de-signs (*E. T.*
al- le- lu- ia).

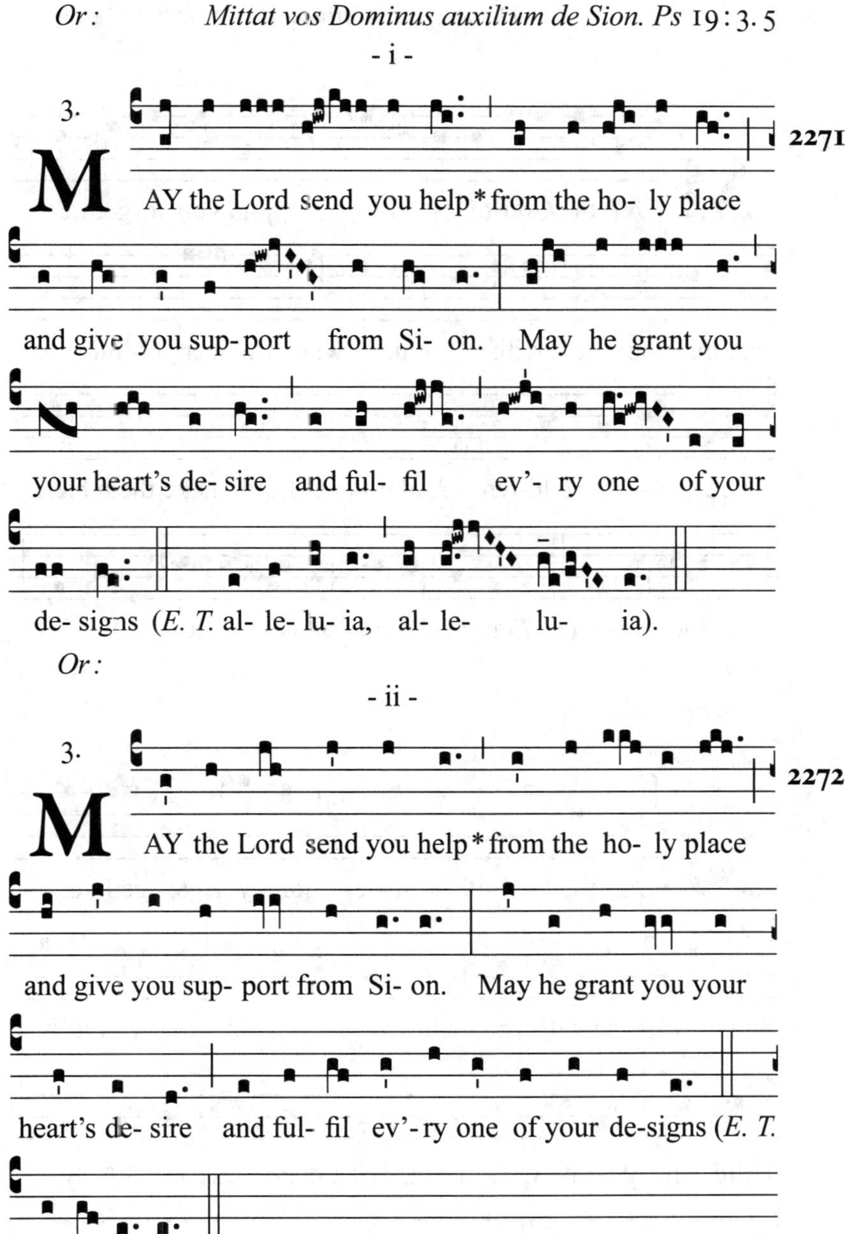

Or: *Deus Israel coniungat vos. Tob* 7:15; 8:19

\- i -

2275 3.

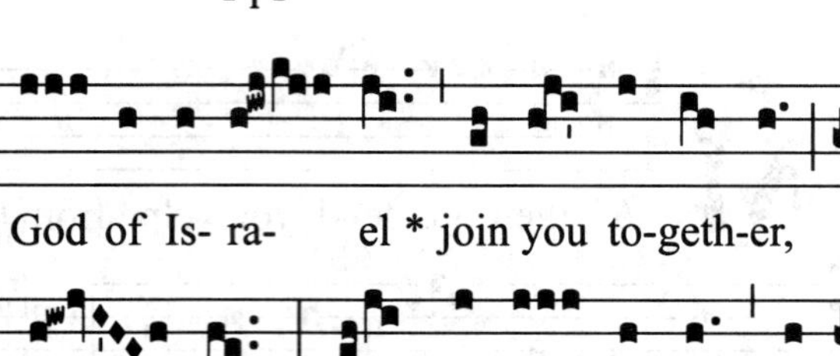

MAY the God of Is- ra- el * join you to-geth-er,

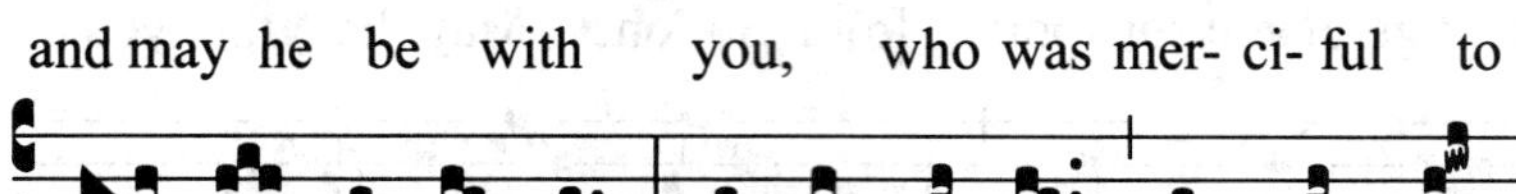

and may he be with you, who was mer- ci- ful to

two on- ly child-ren. And now, O Lord, make them bless

you ful- ly (*E. T.* al- le- lu- ia, al- le- lu- ia).

Or:

\- ii -

2276 3.

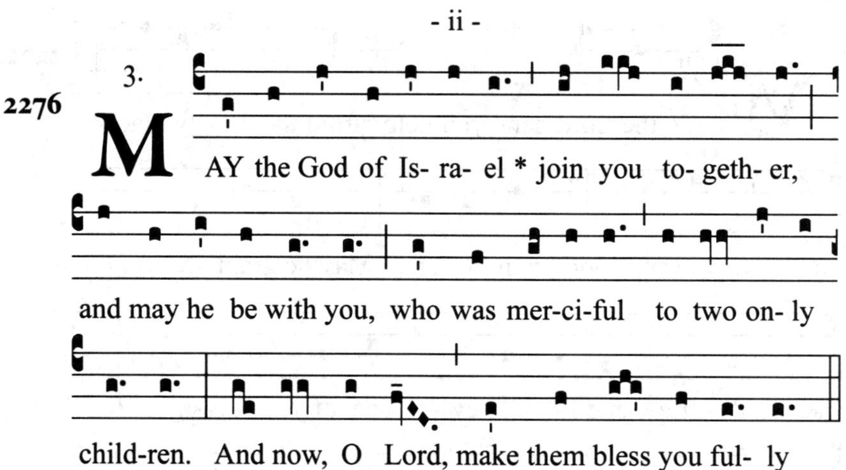
MAY the God of Is- ra- el * join you to- geth- er,
and may he be with you, who was mer-ci-ful to two on- ly
child-ren. And now, O Lord, make them bless you ful- ly

(*E. T.* al- le- lu- ia).

Or: *Mittat vos Dominus auxilium de Sion. Ps* 19:3.5

- iii -

8.
2277
MAY the Lord send you help from the ho- ly place *
and give you sup-port from Si- on. May he grant you your
heart's de- sire and ful- fil ev'- ry one of your de-signs.

During Eastertide:

8.
2278
MAY the Lord send you help from the ho- ly place *
and give you sup-port from Si- on. May he grant you your
heart's de- sire and ful- fil ev'- ry one of your de-signs,
al- le- lu- ia, al- le- lu- ia.

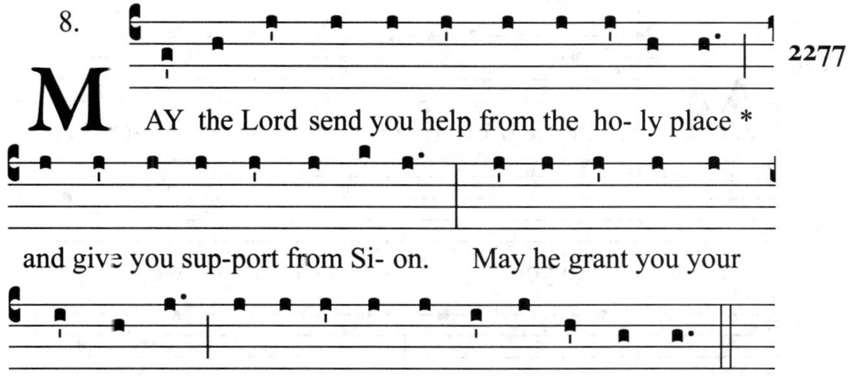

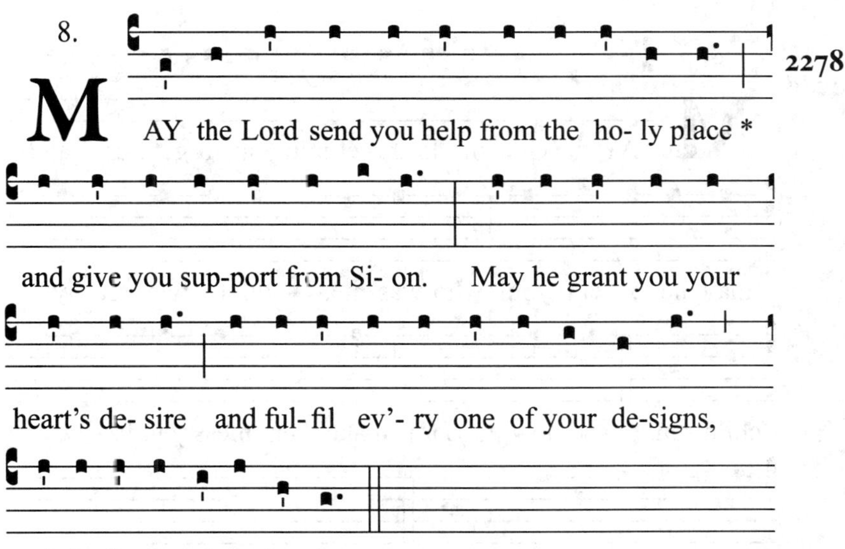

Or: *Deus Israel coniungat vos. Tob* 7:15; 8:19

- iii -

2279

8.
MAY the God of Is- ra- el join you to-geth-er, * and
may he be with you, who was mer-ci- ful to two on- ly
child-ren. And now, O Lord, make them bless you ful- ly.

During Eastertide:

2280

8.
MAY the God of Is- ra- el join you to-geth-er, * and
may he be with you, who was mer-ci- ful to two on- ly
child-ren. And now, O Lord, make them bless you ful- ly.
al- le- lu- ia, al- le- lu- ia.

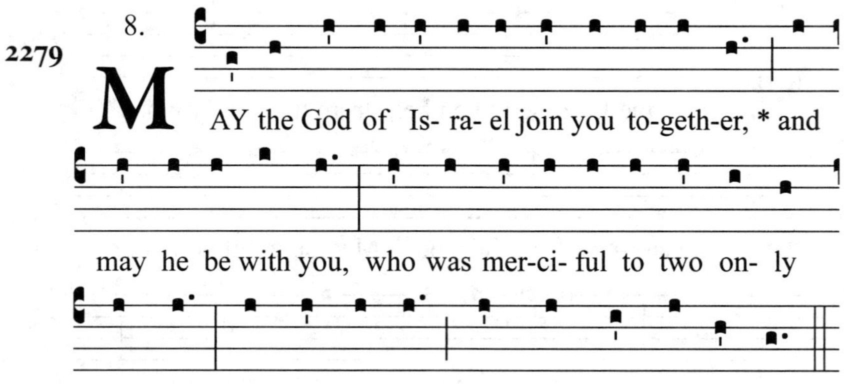

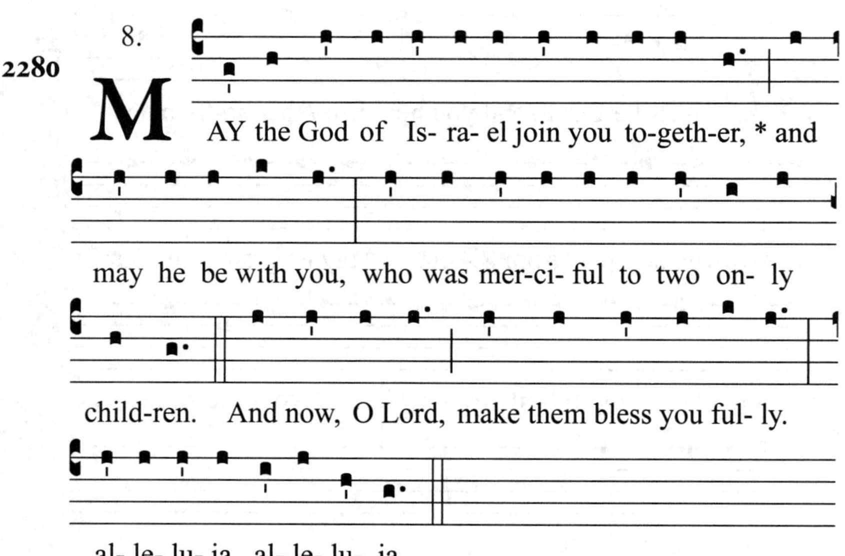

Mittat vos Dominus auxilium de Sion. Ps 19:3. 5

- iv -

May the Lord send you help from the holy | **place** * 2281
and give you sup- | *port from* **Si**-on.
May he grant you your heart's de- | **sire**
and fulfil every one of your | *de*-**signs**.

During Eastertide:

May the Lord send you help from the holy | **place** * 2282
and give you sup- | *port from* **Si**-on.
May he grant you your heart's de- | **sire**
and fulfil every one of your designs, / al- | *le*-**lu**- ia.

Offertory Antiphon *In te speravi, Domine.*
Ps 30:15-16

\- i -

2283

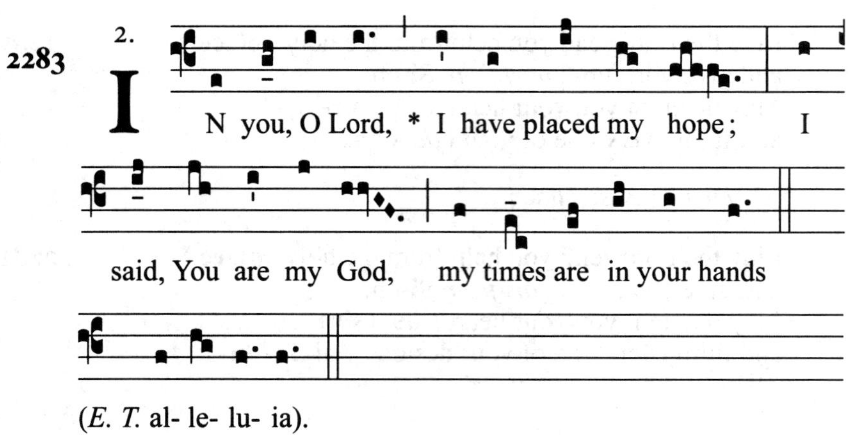
2.
I
N you, O Lord, * I have placed my hope; I
said, You are my God, my times are in your hands
(*E. T.* al- le- lu- ia).

\- ii -

2284

2.
I
N you, O Lord, have I hoped. * I said, You are my
God. My times are in your hands (*E. T.* al- le- lu- ia).

VERSES *In manus tuas, Domine. Ps* 30 : 2

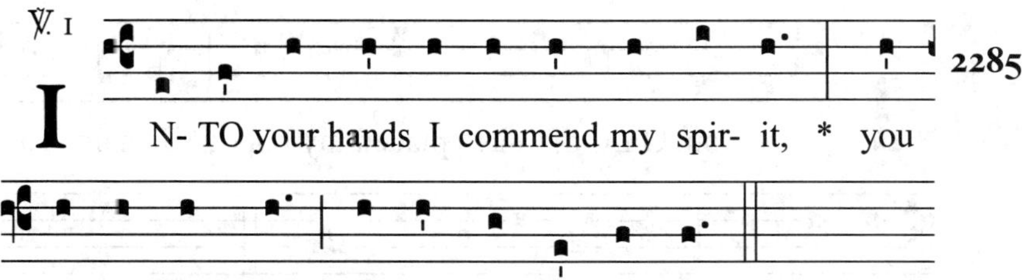
℣. 1
2285
INTO your hands I commend my spir- it, * you
have redeemed me, O Lord, the God of truth.

Illustra faciem tuam super servum tuum. Ps 30 : 17

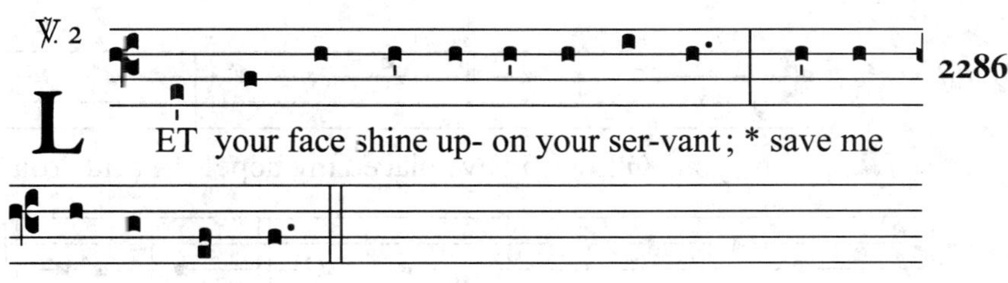
℣. 2
2286
LET your face shine up- on your ser-vant; * save me
in your kind-ness.

Quam magna multitudo dulcedinis tuæ. Ps 30 : 20

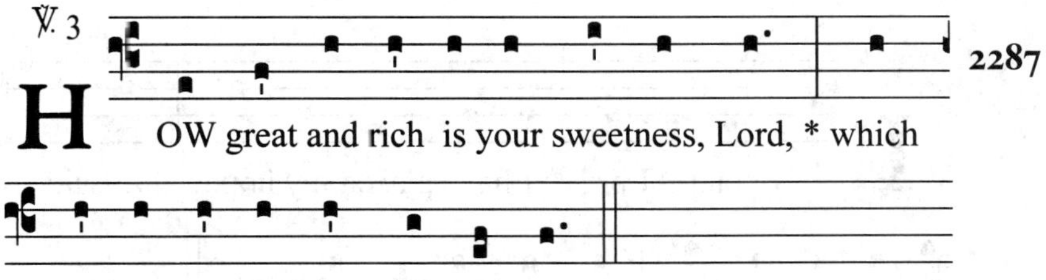
℣. 3
2287
HOW great and rich is your sweetness, Lord, * which
you laid up for those who fear you.

Diligite Dominum, omnes. Ps 30 : 29

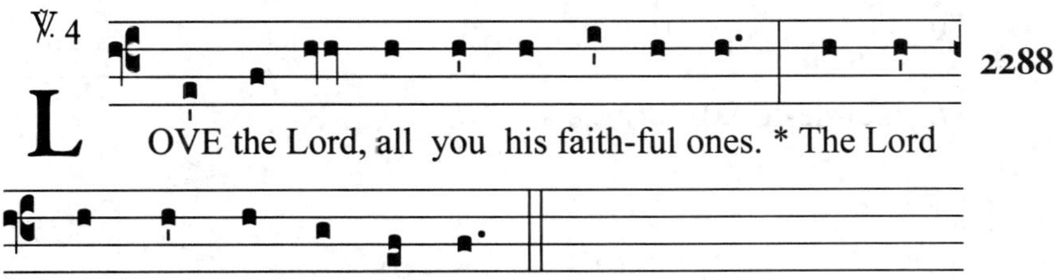
℣. 4
2288
LOVE the Lord, all you his faith-ful ones. * The Lord
keeps those who are con-stant.

- iii -

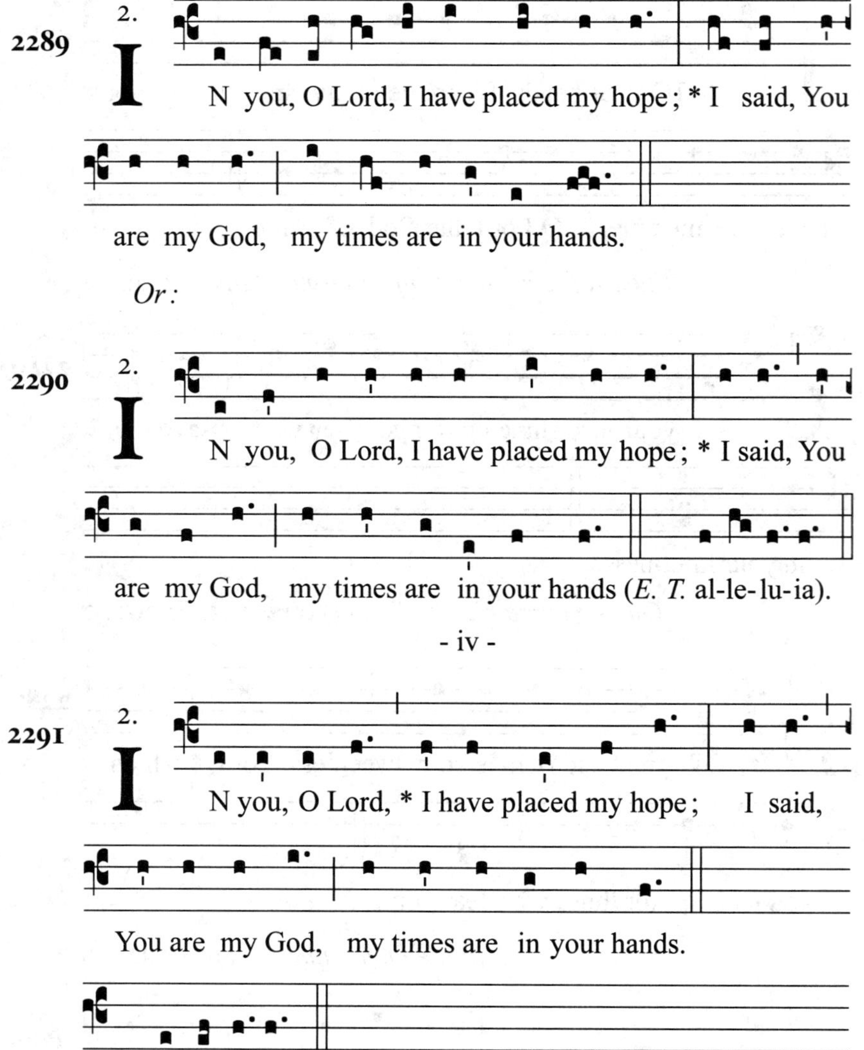
2289
2.
IN you, O Lord, I have placed my hope; * I said, You
are my God, my times are in your hands.
Or:
2290
2.
IN you, O Lord, I have placed my hope; * I said, You
are my God, my times are in your hands (*E. T.* al-le-lu-ia).
- iv -
2291
2.
IN you, O Lord, * I have placed my hope; I said,
You are my God, my times are in your hands.
(*E. T.* al- le-lu-ia).

COMMUNION ANTIPHON *Ecce sic benedicetur.* *Ps* 127:4. 6

- i -

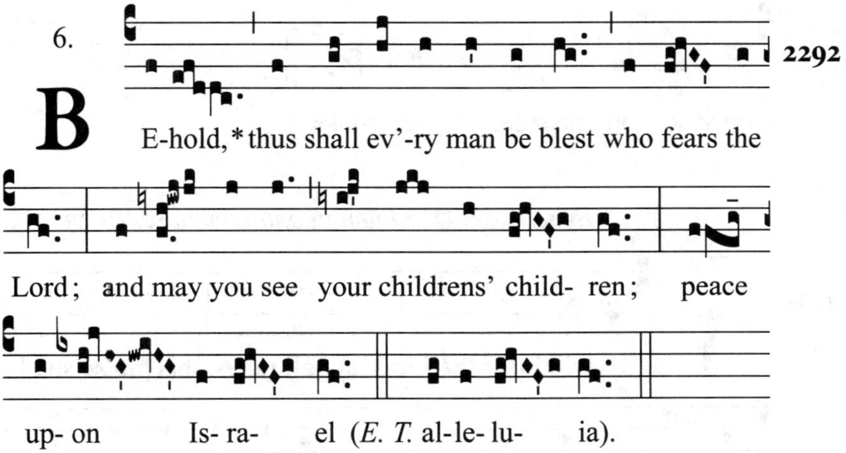

6. 2292

B E-hold, * thus shall ev'-ry man be blest who fears the Lord; and may you see your childrens' child- ren; peace up- on Is- ra- el (*E. T.* al-le- lu- ia).

- ii -

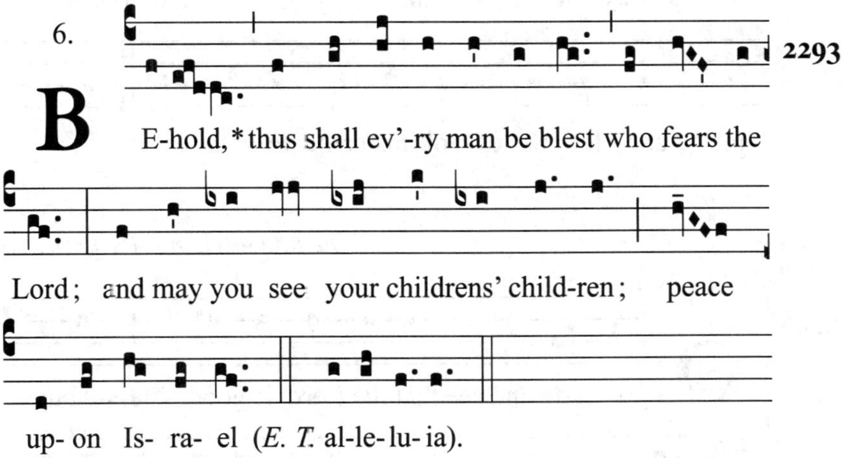

6. 2293

B E-hold, * thus shall ev'-ry man be blest who fears the Lord; and may you see your childrens' child-ren; peace up- on Is- ra- el (*E. T.* al-le-lu- ia).

VERSES *Labores manuum tuarum.* *Ps* 127:2-3

2294

F OR you shall eat the labors of your hands: blessed

are you and it shall be well with you. * Your wife as a fruitful vine on the sides of your house.

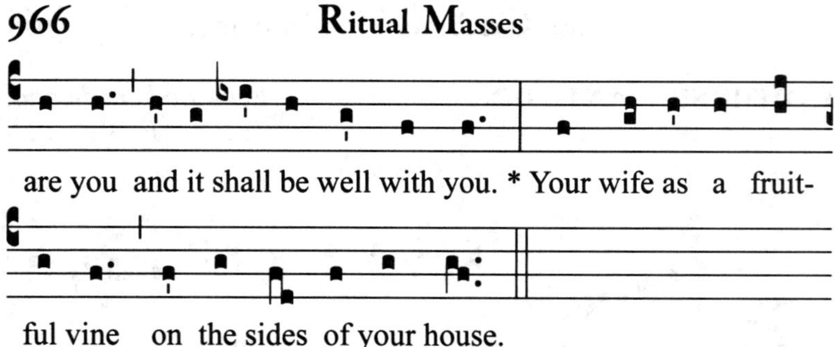

Benedicam Dominum in omni tempore. Ps 33:2. 4

2295

℣. 2
I will bless the Lord at all times, his praise shall
be al-ways in my mouth. * O mag-ni- fy the Lord with
me, and let us ex- tol his name to-geth- er.

Gustate et videte. Ps 33:9. 19

2296

℣. 3
O taste and see that the Lord is good, bless-ed the
man who hopes in him. * The Lord is close to those of a
contrite heart, and he will save the hum-ble of spir- it.

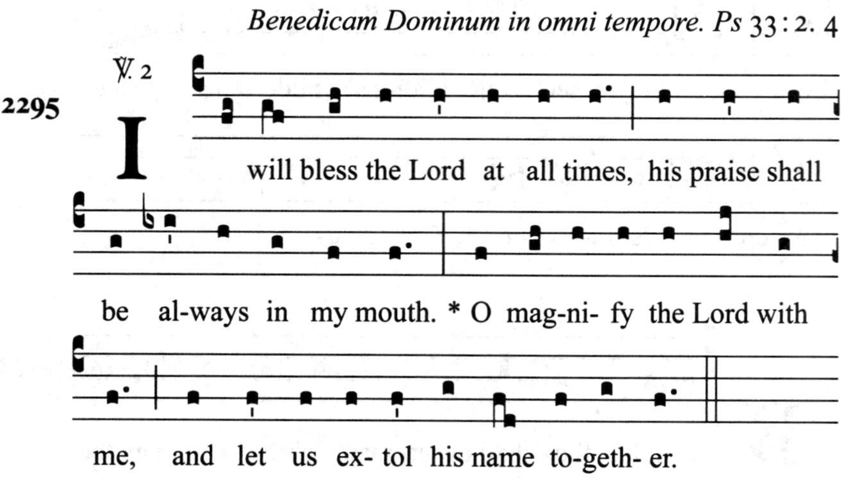

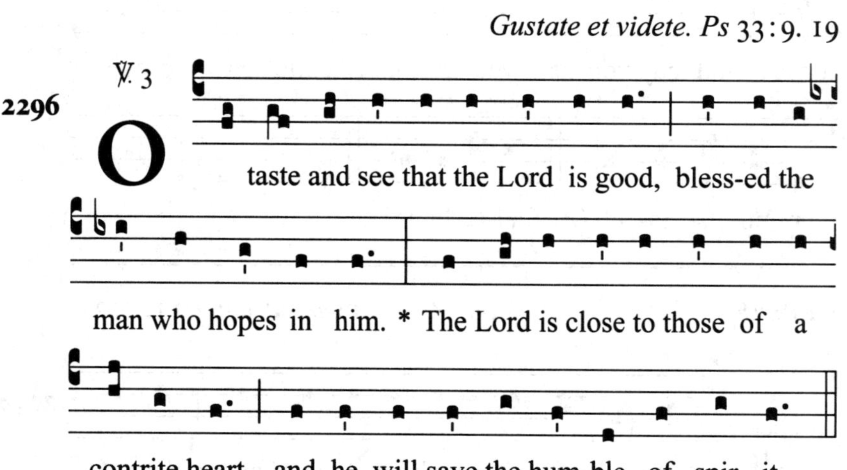

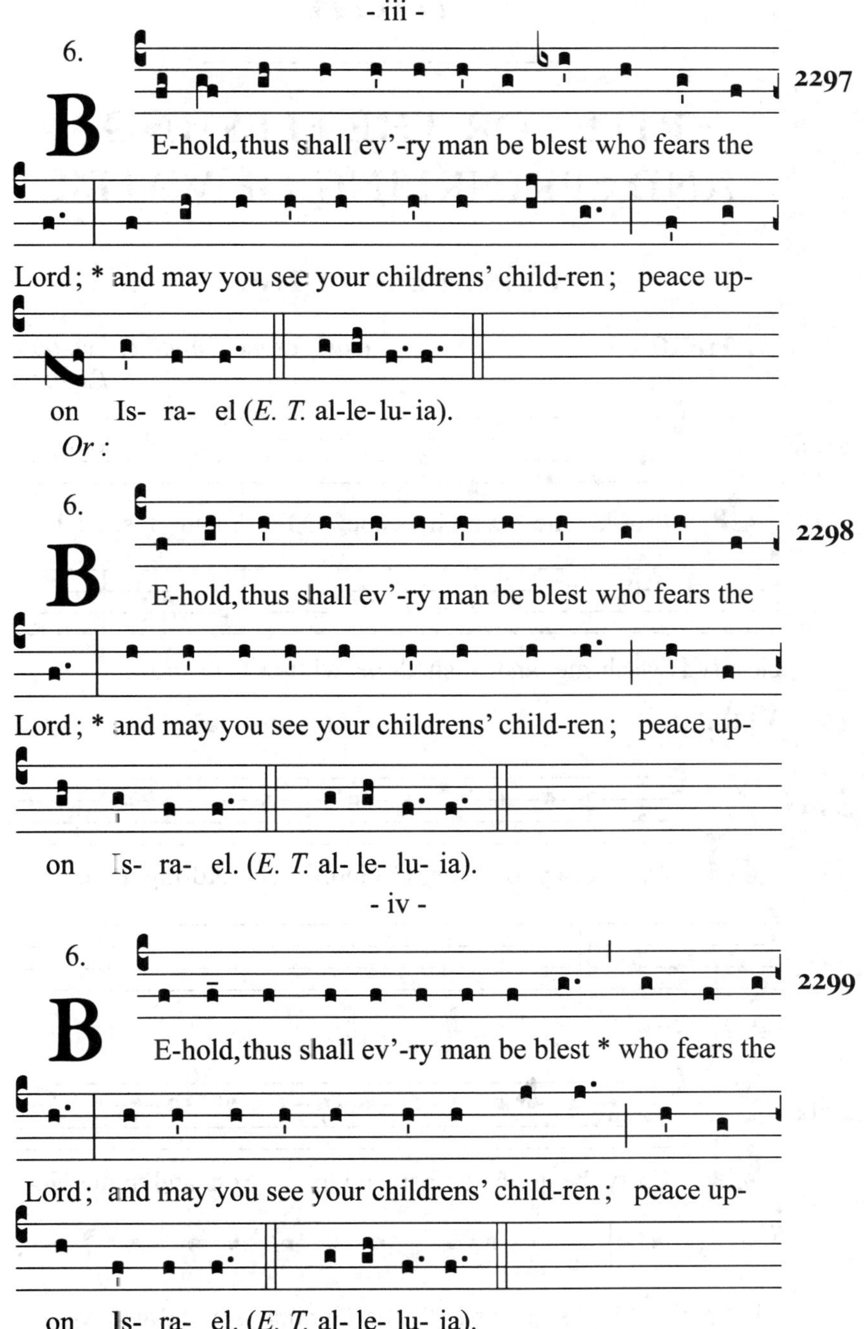
- iii -
6.
2297
BE-hold, thus shall ev'-ry man be blest who fears the
Lord; * and may you see your childrens' child-ren; peace up-
on Is- ra- el (*E. T.* al-le-lu-ia).
Or :
6.
2298
BE-hold, thus shall ev'-ry man be blest who fears the
Lord; * and may you see your childrens' child-ren; peace up-
on Is- ra- el. (*E. T.* al- le- lu- ia).
- iv -
6.
2299
BE-hold, thus shall ev'-ry man be blest * who fears the
Lord; and may you see your childrens' child-ren; peace up-
on Is- ra- el. (*E. T.* al- le- lu- ia).

VARIA

RITE FOR THE BLESSING AND SPRINKLING OF WATER

OUTSIDE EASTER TIME

ANTIPHON 1 *Asperges me, Domine, hyssopo.* *Ps* 50:9

2300

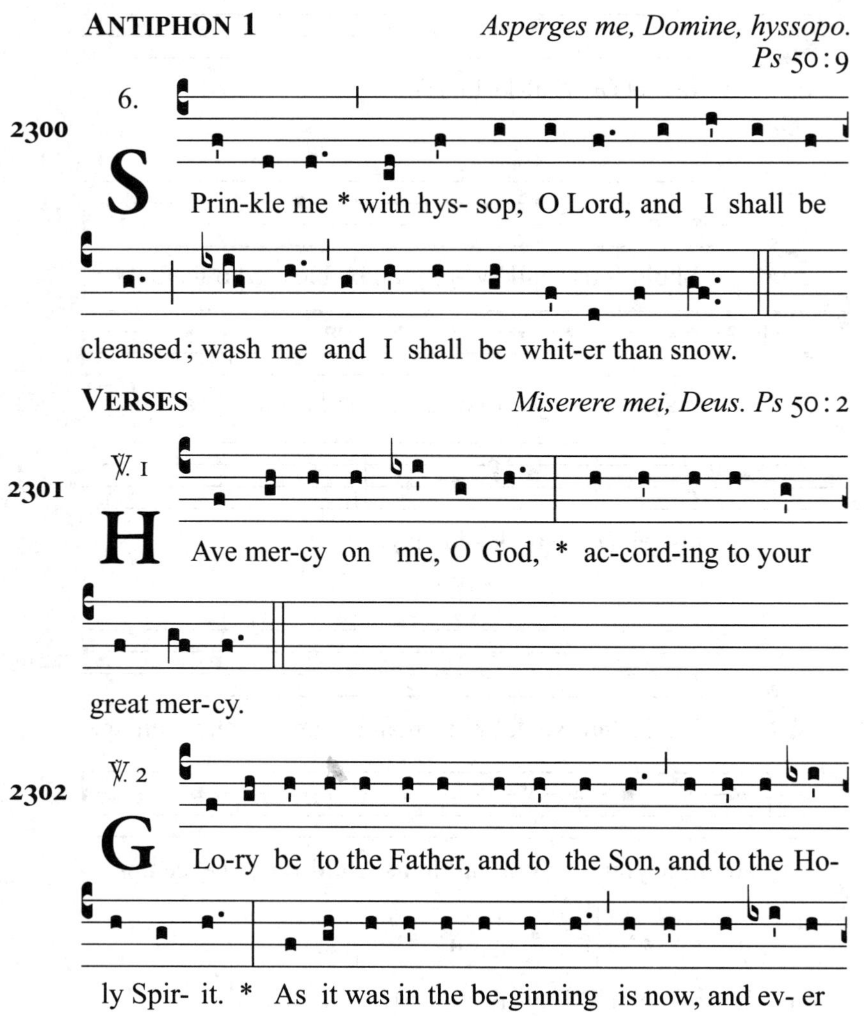
6.
SPrin-kle me * with hys- sop, O Lord, and I shall be
cleansed; wash me and I shall be whit-er than snow.
VERSES
Miserere mei, Deus. Ps 50:2
℣. 1
HAve mer-cy on me, O God, * ac-cord-ing to your
great mer-cy.
℣. 2
GLo-ry be to the Father, and to the Son, and to the Ho-
ly Spir- it. * As it was in the be-ginning is now, and ev- er

2301

2302

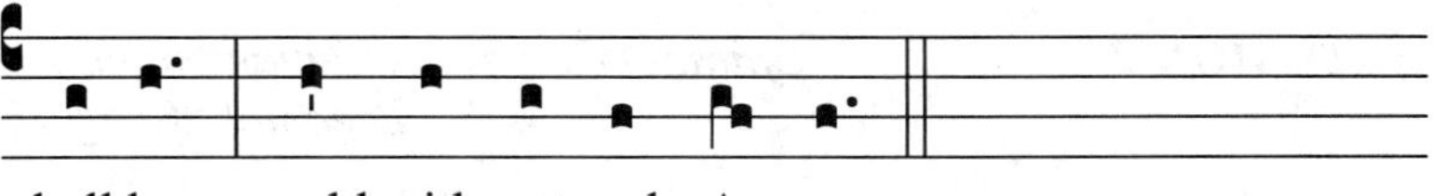
shall be, world with-out end. A- men.

Or:

7.

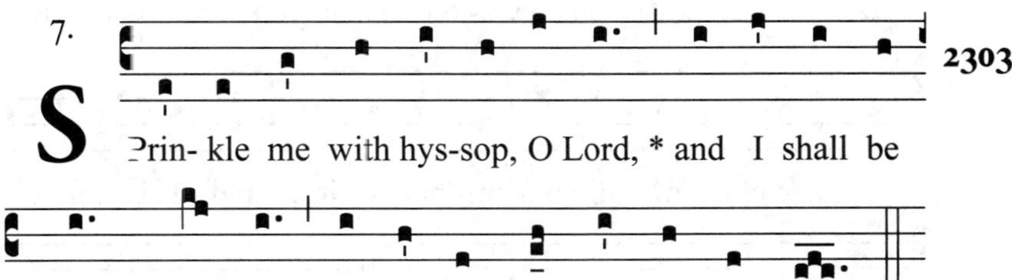
SPrin- kle me with hys-sop, O Lord, * and I shall be
cleansed; wash me and I shall be whit- er than snow.

2303

VERSES *Miserere mei, Deus. Ps* 50 : 2

℣. 1

HAve mer-cy on me, O God, * ac-cord-ing to your
great mer- cy.

2304

℣. 2

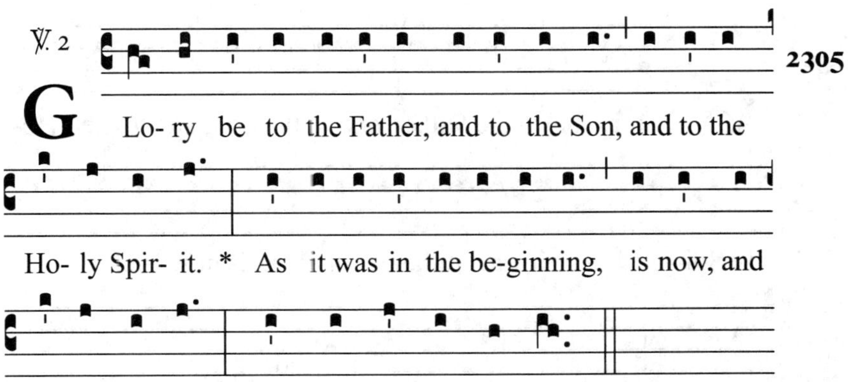
GLo- ry be to the Father, and to the Son, and to the
Ho- ly Spir- it. * As it was in the be-ginning, is now, and
ev- er shall be, world with-out end. A- men.

2305

ANTIPHON 2 *Effundam super vos aquam mundam.*
Ezechiel 36:25-26

2306 6.

I will pour * clean wa- ter up- on you, and you will be made clean of all your im- pur- i- ties, and I shall give you a new spir- it, says the Lord.

VERSES *Miserere mei, Deus. Ps* 50:2

2307 ℣. 1

HAve mer- cy on me, O God, * ac-cord-ing to your great mer- cy.

2308 ℣. 2

GLo-ry be to the Father, and to the Son, and to the Ho- ly Spir- it. * As it was in the be-ginning, is now, and ev- er shall be, world with-out end. A- men.

Or:

7.
2309
I will pour clean wa- ter up- on you, * and you will
be made clean of all your im- pur- i- ties, and I shall give
you a new spir- it, says the Lord.

VERSES *Miserere mei, Deus. Ps* 50:2

℣. 1
2310
HAve mer-cy on me, O God, * ac-cord-ing to your
great mer- cy.

℣. 2
2311
GLo- ry be to the Father, and to the Son, and to the
Ho- ly Spir- it. * As it was in the be-ginning, is now, and
ev- er shall be, world with-out end. A- men.

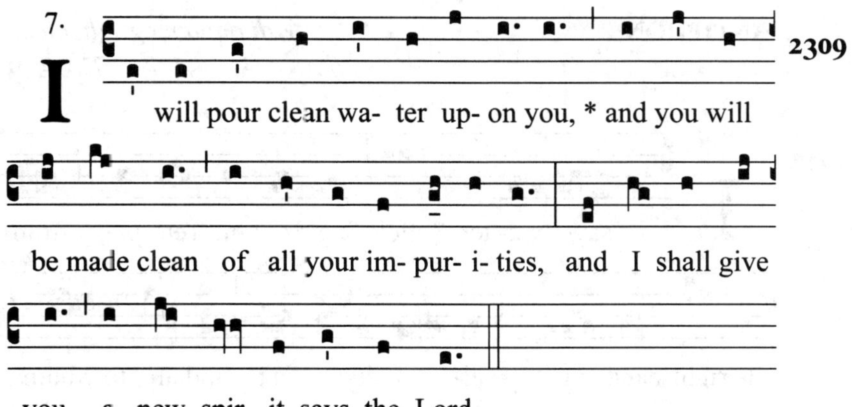

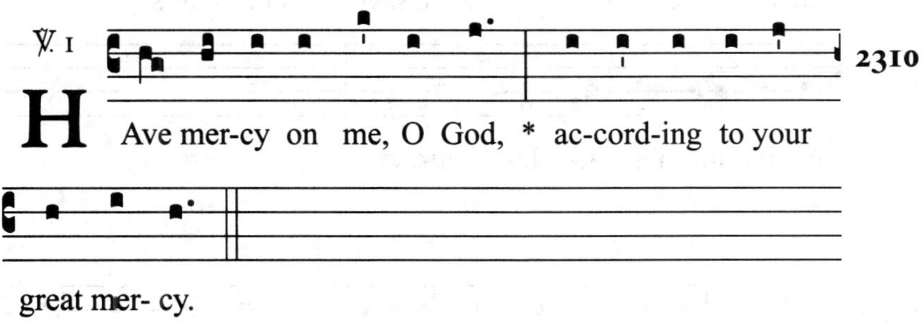

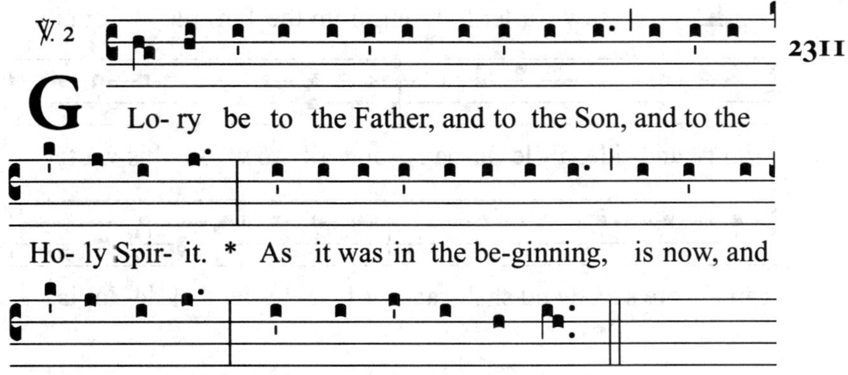

DURING EASTER TIME

ANTIPHON *Vidi aquam egredientem.*
Cf. Ez 47: 1-2. 9

2312
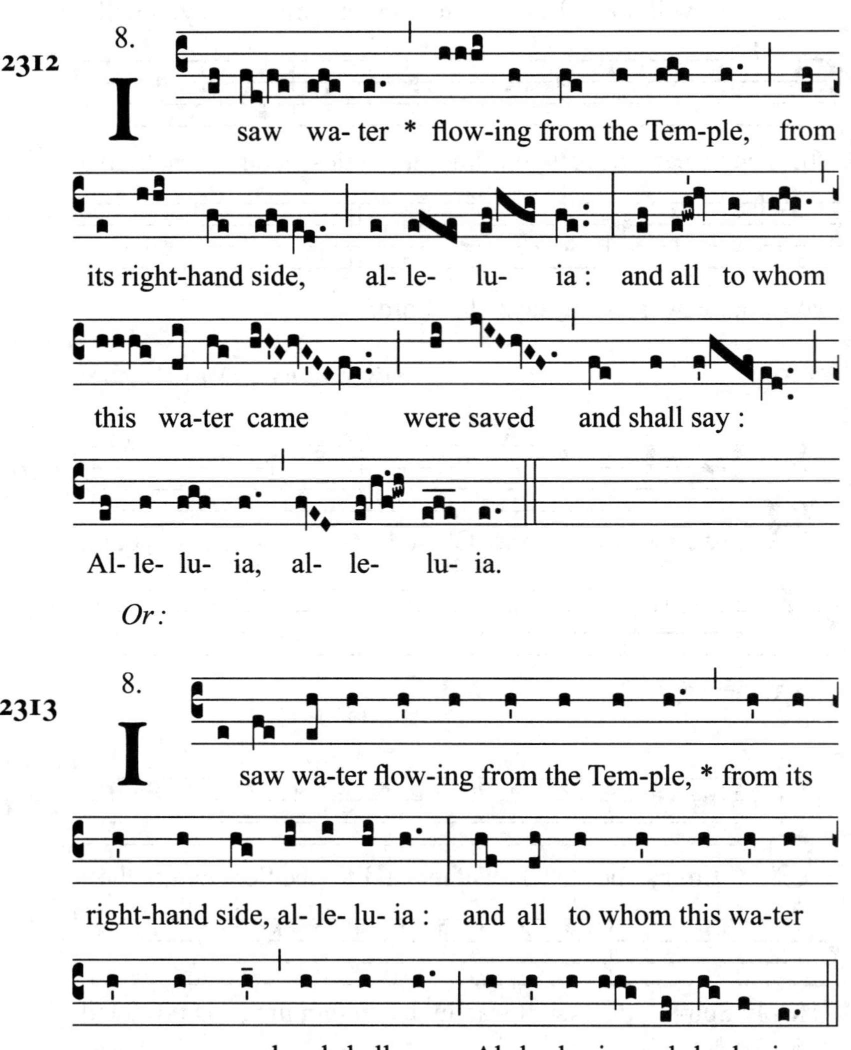
8.
I saw wa- ter * flow-ing from the Tem-ple, from
its right-hand side, al- le- lu- ia : and all to whom
this wa-ter came were saved and shall say :
Al- le- lu- ia, al- le- lu- ia.
Or :
2313
8.
I saw wa-ter flow-ing from the Tem-ple, * from its
right-hand side, al- le- lu- ia : and all to whom this wa-ter
came were saved and shall say : Al- le- lu- ia, al- le- lu- ia.

VERSES *Confitemini Domino, quoniam bonus. Ps* 117:1

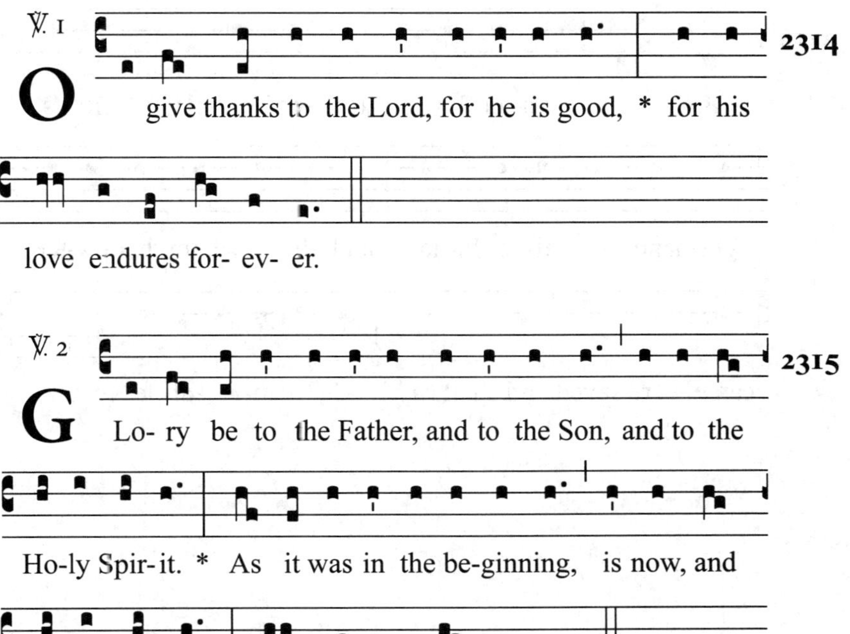
℣. 1
O give thanks to the Lord, for he is good, * for his 2314
love endures for- ev- er.
℣. 2
GLo- ry be to the Father, and to the Son, and to the 2315
Ho-ly Spir-it. * As it was in the be-ginning, is now, and

ev- er shall be, world with-out end. A- men.

Or:

2316 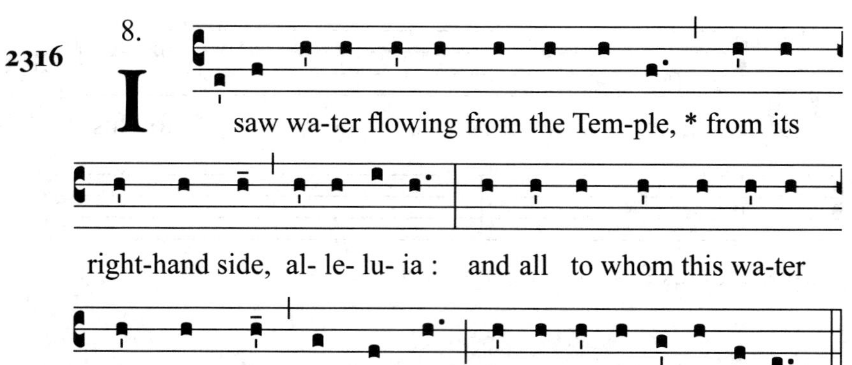
8.
I saw wa-ter flowing from the Tem-ple, * from its
right-hand side, al- le- lu- ia : and all to whom this wa-ter
came were saved and shall say : Al- le- lu- ia, al- le- lu- ia.

VERSES *Confitemini Domino, quoniam bonus. Ps* 117:1

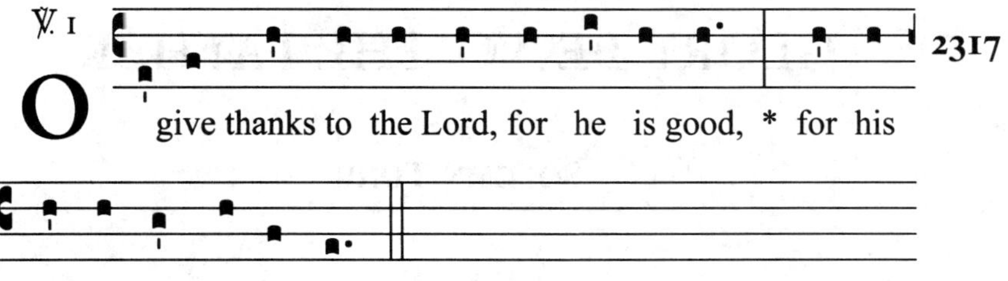
℣. 1
2317
O give thanks to the Lord, for he is good, * for his
love endures for-ev- er.

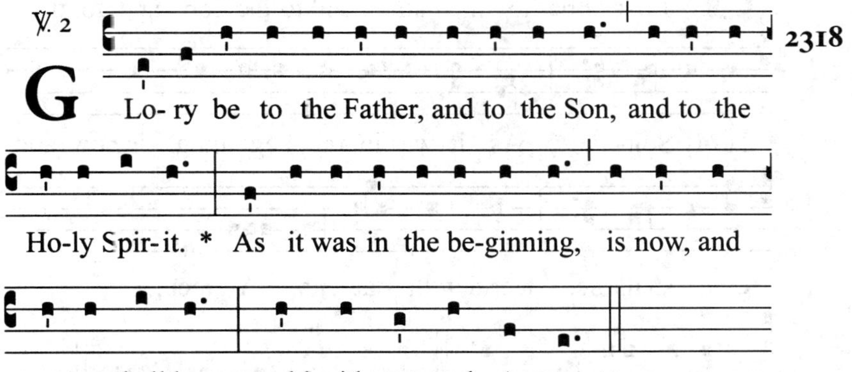
℣. 2
2318
GLo-ry be to the Father, and to the Son, and to the
Ho-ly Spir-it. * As it was in the be-ginning, is now, and
ev- er shall be, world with-out end. A- men.

TONES FOR THE GLORY BE TO THE FATHER

SOLEMN TONE

2319 1.

G Lo-ry be to the Father, and to the Son, and to the
Ho-ly Spir- it. * As it was in the beginning, is now, and
ev- er shall be, world with- out end. A- men.
Or: O i o e a e. Or: O i o e a e.

2320 2.

G Lo- ry be to the Father, and to the Son, and to the
Ho- ly Spir- it. * As it was in the beginning, is now, and
ev- er shall be, world with-out end. A- men.

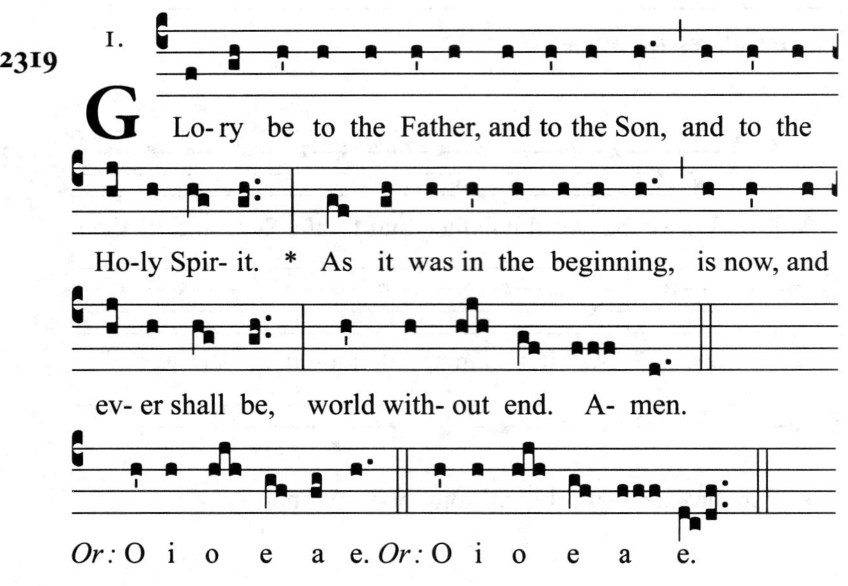

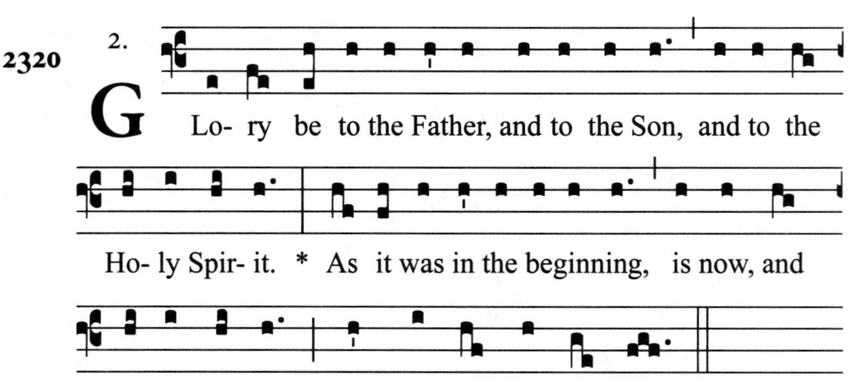

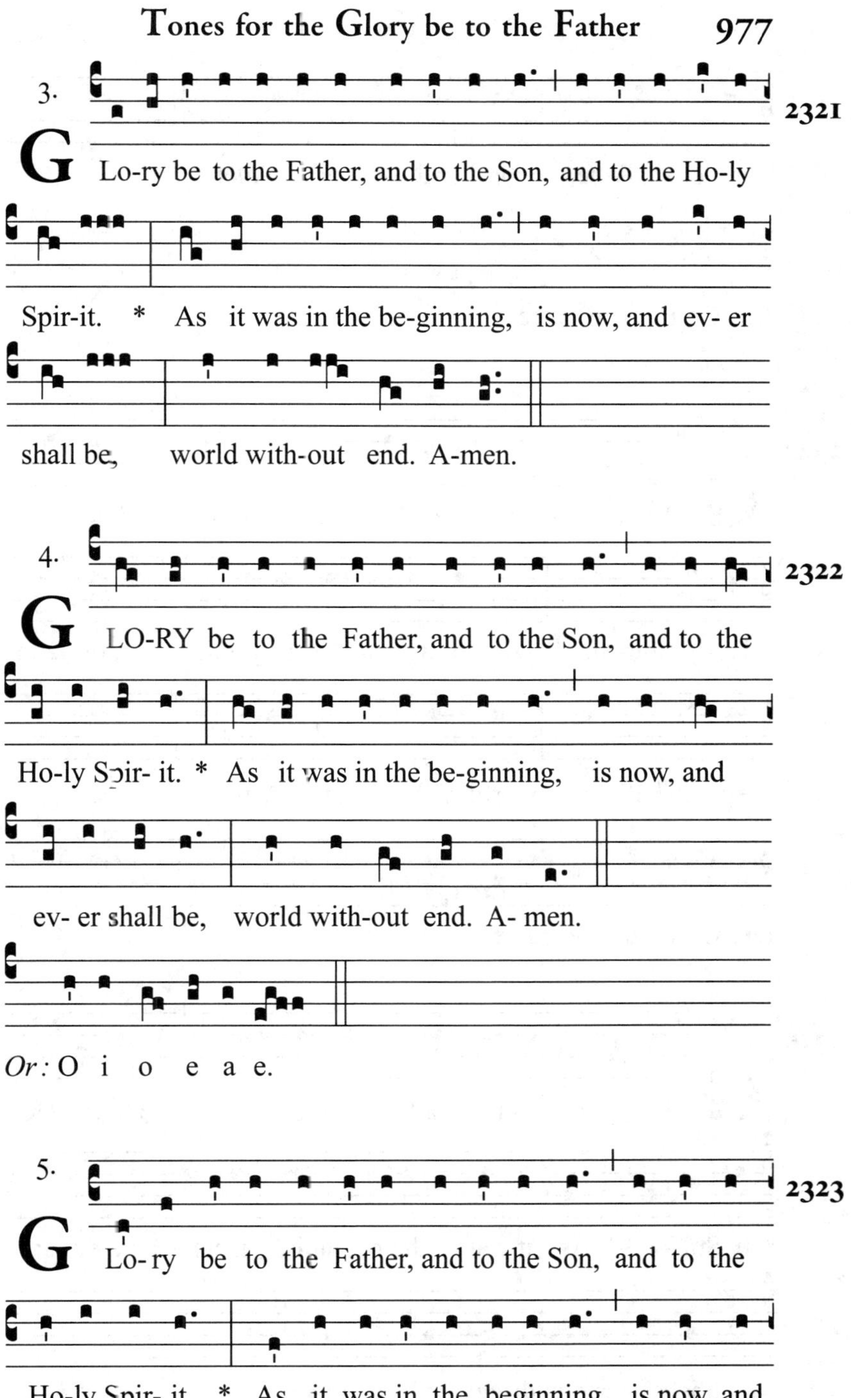
3.
2321
GLo-ry be to the Father, and to the Son, and to the Ho-ly
Spir-it. * As it was in the be-ginning, is now, and ev- er
shall be, world with-out end. A-men.
4.
2322
GLO-RY be to the Father, and to the Son, and to the
Ho-ly Spir- it. * As it was in the be-ginning, is now, and
ev- er shall be, world with-out end. A- men.
Or: O i o e a e.
5.
2323
GLo- ry be to the Father, and to the Son, and to the
Ho-ly Spir- it. * As it was in the beginning, is now, and

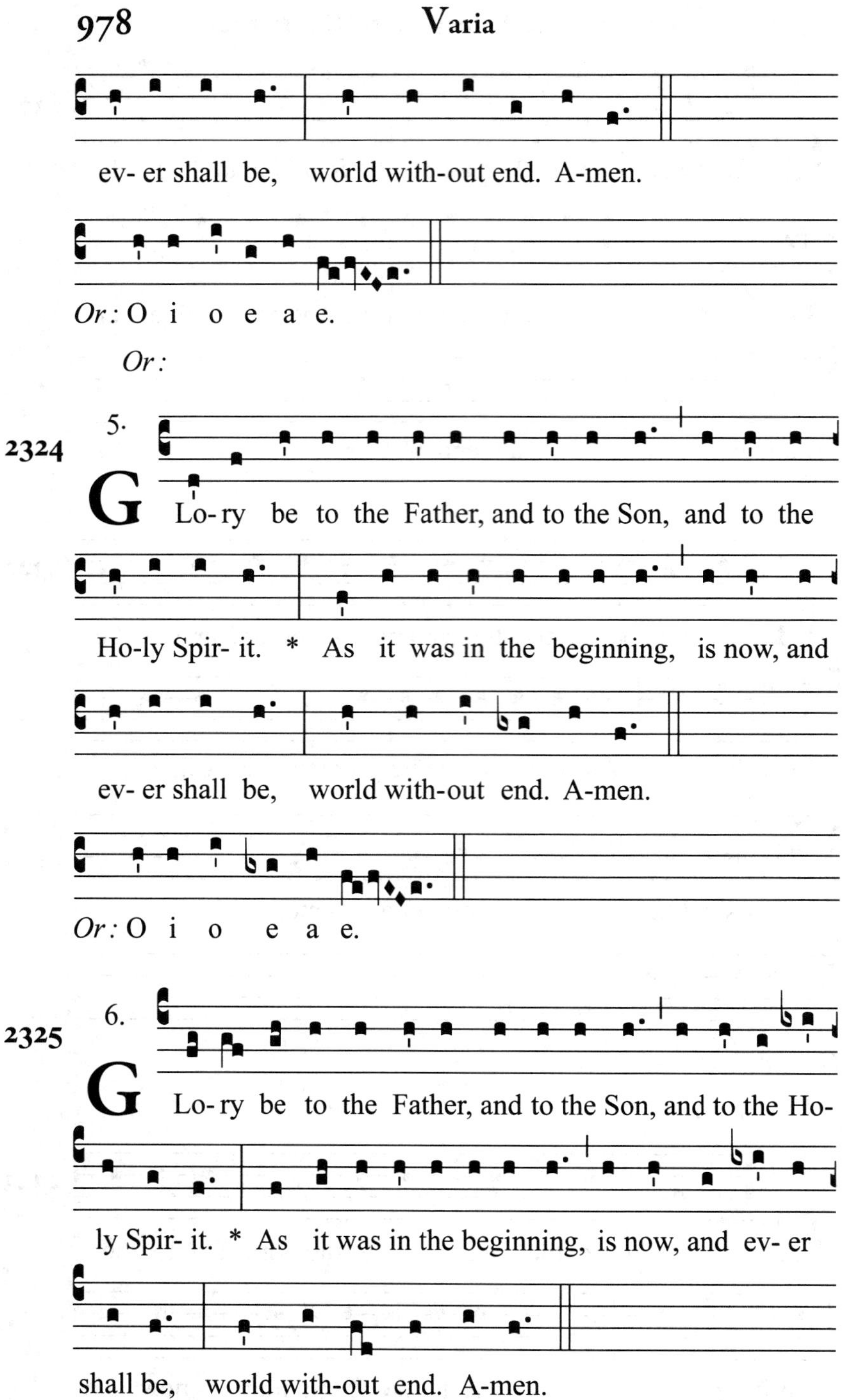
ev- er shall be, world with-out end. A-men.
Or: O i o e a e.
Or:
2324 5.
GLo-ry be to the Father, and to the Son, and to the
Ho-ly Spir- it. * As it was in the beginning, is now, and
ev- er shall be, world with-out end. A-men.
Or: O i o e a e.
2325 6.
GLo-ry be to the Father, and to the Son, and to the Ho-
ly Spir- it. * As it was in the beginning, is now, and ev- er
shall be, world with-out end. A-men.

Or: O i o e a e.
7.
2326
GLo- ry be to the Fa-ther, and to the Son, and to the
Ho-ly Spir- it. * As it was in the beginning, is now, and
ev- er shall be, world with- out end. A- men.
8.
2327
GLO-RY be to the Father, and to the Son, and to the
Ho- ly Spir-it. * As it was in the be-ginning, is now, and
ev- er shall be, world with-out end. A-men.
Or: O i o e a e.

SIMPLE TONE

2328 1.

G Lo-ry be to the Father, and to the Son, * and to the
Ho- ly Spir- it. * As it was in the be-ginning, is now,
and ev- er shall be, world with-out end. A- men.

Or: O i o e a e. Or: O i o e a e.

2329 2.

G Lo-ry be to the Father, and to the Son, and to the
Ho- ly Spir- it. * As it was in the be-ginning, is now,
and ev- er shall be, world with-out end. A-men.

Or:

2330 2.

G Lo-ry be to the Father, and to the Son, and to the

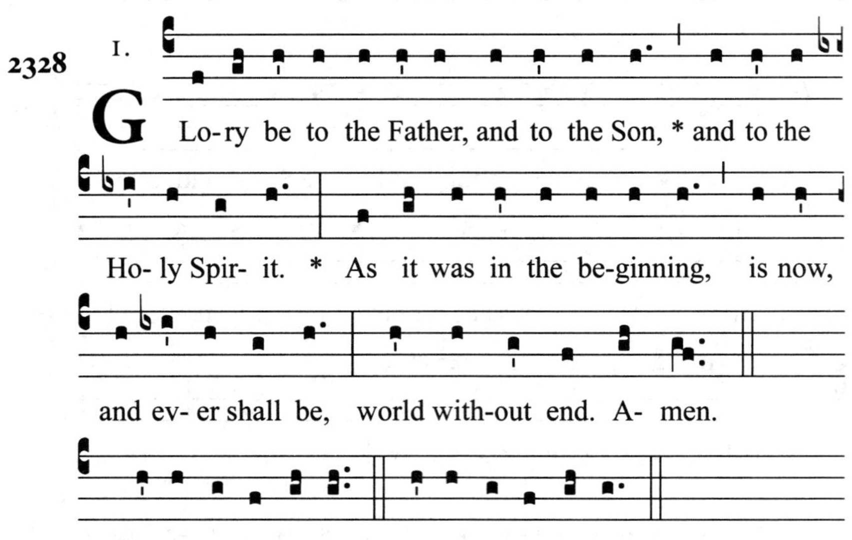

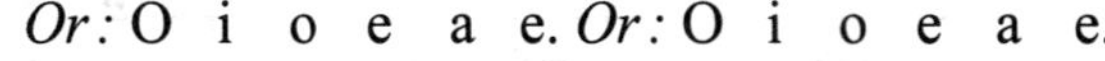

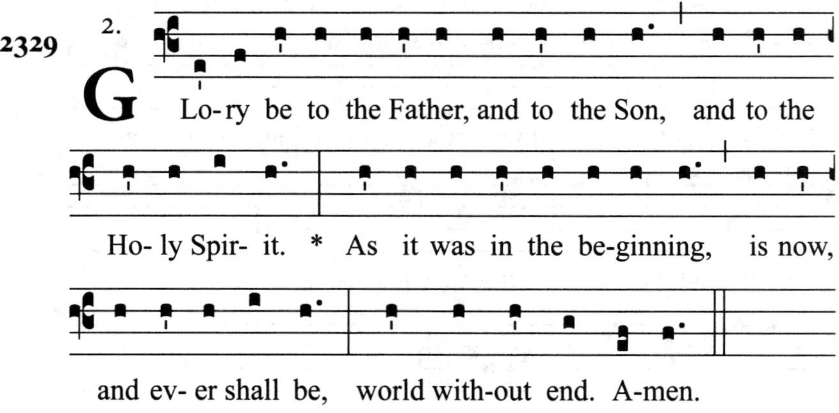

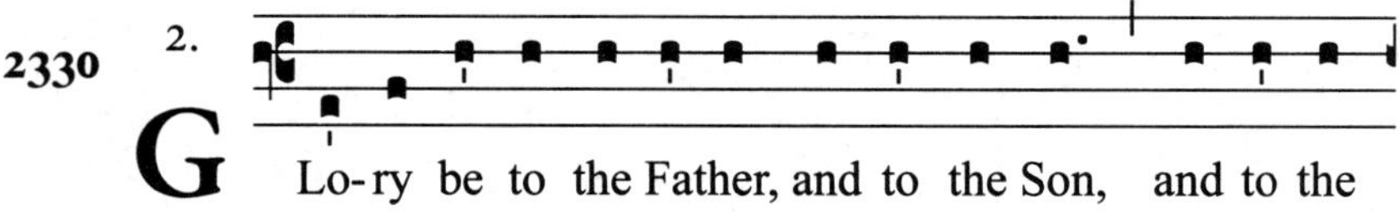

Ho- ly Spir- it. * As it was in the be-ginning, is now,

and ev- er shall be, world with-out end. A-men.

3. 2331

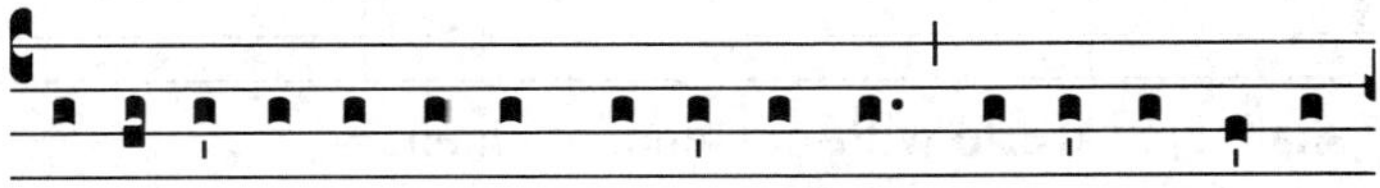

GLo-ry be to the Father, and to the Son, and to the Ho-ly

Spir- it. * As it was in the be-ginning, is now, and ev- er

shall be, world with-out end. A- men.

4. g 2332

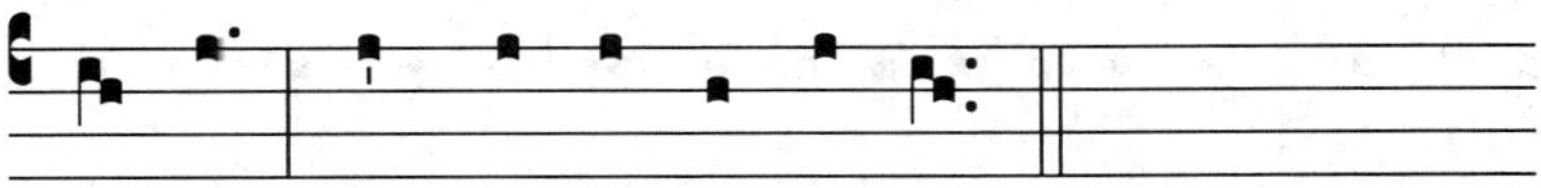

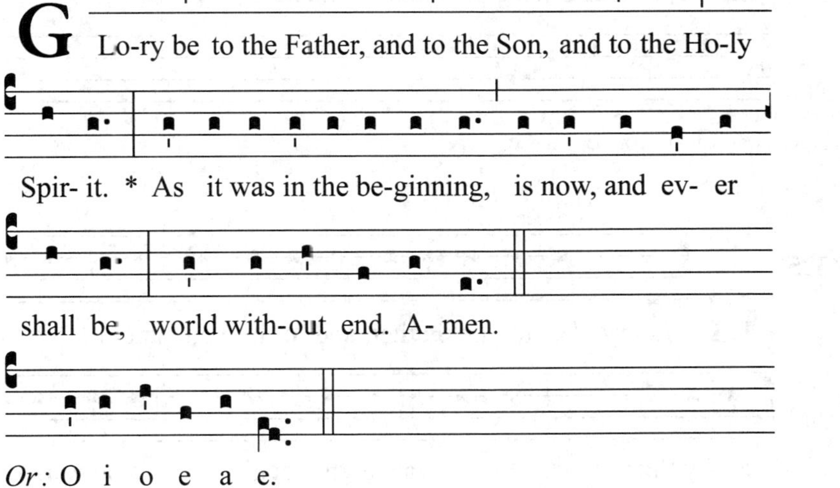
GLo-ry be to the Father, and to the Son, and to the Ho-ly
Spir- it. * As it was in the be-ginning, is now, and ev- er
shall be, world with-out end. A- men.
Or: O i o e a e.

2333

4. a
GLo-ry be to the Father, and to the Son, and to the Ho-ly
Spir- it. * As it was in the be-ginning, is now, and ev- er
shall be, world with-out end. A- men.
4. A
GLo-ry be to the Father, and to the Son, and to the Ho-ly
Spir- it. * As it was in the be-ginning, is now, and ev- er
shall be, world with-out end. A- men.
Or: O i o e a e.
5.
GLo- ry be to the Father, and to the Son, and to the
Ho-ly Spir- it. * As it was in the beginning, is now, and

2334

2335

ev- er shall be, world with-out end. A-men.
Or: O i o e a e.
5.
2336
GLo-ry be to the Father, and to the Son, and to the
Ho-ly Spir- it. * As it was in the beginning, is now, and
ev- er shall be, world with-out end. A-men.
Or: O i o e a e.
6.
2337
GLo-ry be to the Father, and to the Son, and to the
Ho- ly Spir-it. * As it was in the be-ginning, is now,
and ev- er shall be, world with-out end. A-men.

2338

2339

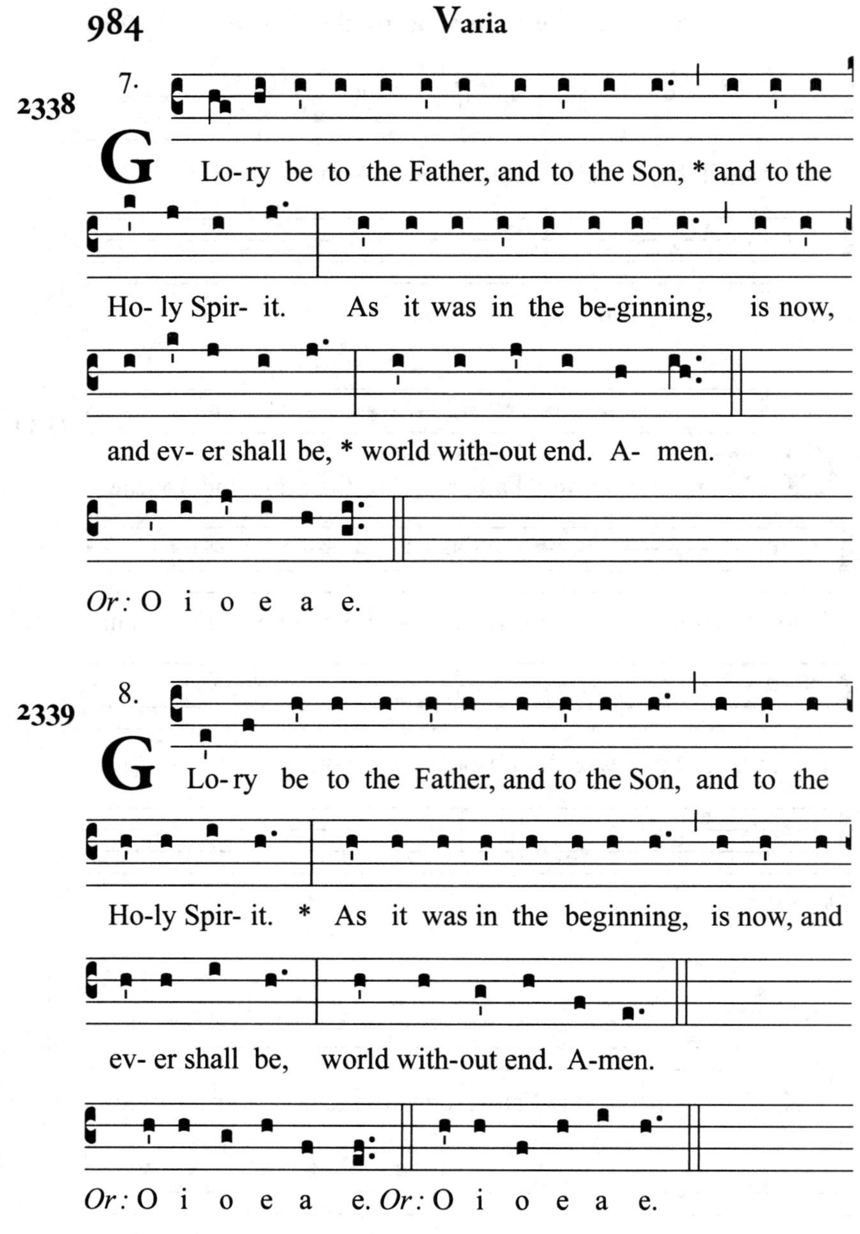
7.
GLo-ry be to the Father, and to the Son, * and to the
Ho- ly Spir- it. As it was in the be-ginning, is now,
and ev- er shall be, * world with-out end. A- men.
Or: O i o e a e.
8.
GLo-ry be to the Father, and to the Son, and to the
Ho-ly Spir- it. * As it was in the beginning, is now, and
ev- er shall be, world with-out end. A-men.
Or: O i o e a e. Or: O i o e a e.

INDICES

ALPHABETICAL INDEX OF CHANTS

Entrances

Offertories

Communions

Hymns

Gospel Canticles

Antiphons

Refrains

Responsories

Varia

GENERAL INDEX

PROPER OF TIME

Advent

Christmas Time

Lent

Holy Week

The Sacred Paschal Triduum

Easter Time

PROPER OF SAINTS

RITUAL MASSES

VARIA

ACKNOWLEDGEMENTS

The editor wishes to express grateful appreciation to the following whose generous assistance has made this volume possible:

His Eminence Raymond Leo Cardinal Burke

His Excellency Archbishop Salvatore J. Cordileone

His Excellency Bishop Robert F. Vasa

Fr. Kurt Belsole, O.S.B.

Dr. Horst Buchholz

Fr. Zachary Edgar

Fr. Daniel C. Gill

Fr. J. Patrick Hough, S.J.

Dr. Peter Kwasniewski

Fr. Herbert Palmer, O.S.B.

Fr. Edward Richard, M.S.

Fr. Dylan Schrader

Fr. Joseph Stobba, O.S.A.

Fr. David Voss

Deacon Paul Spalla

Sister Jane Fleishner, O.S.B.
and the Benedictine Sisters
of Saint Mary Priory, Nauvoo, IL

Carmelite Sisters of the Divine Heart of Jesus,
Saint Agnes Home, St. Louis, MO

Mrs. Rachel Alvelais

The Henry Bokuniewicz Family

The William Hallberg Family

The George Martin Weber Family